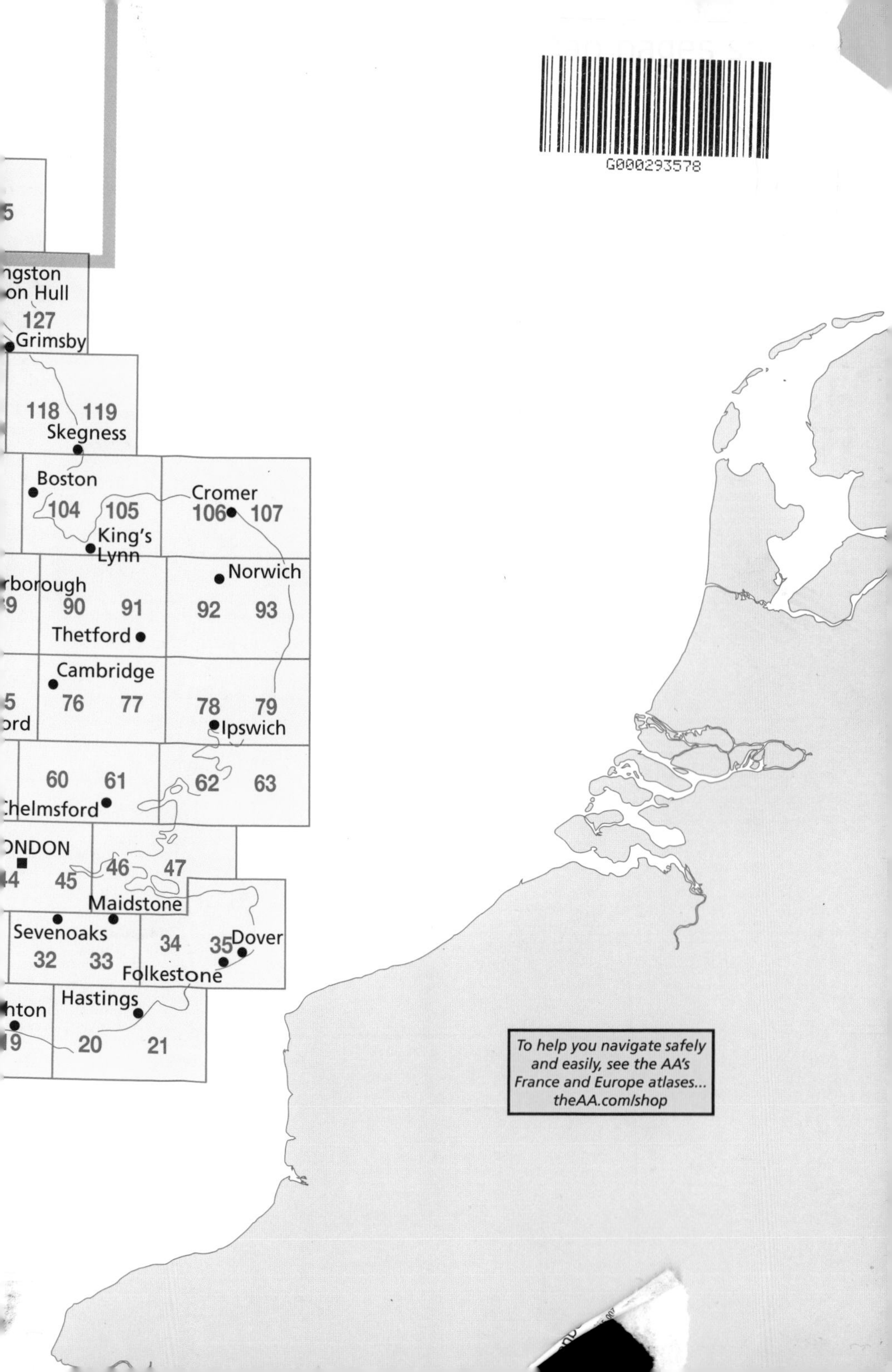

5
gston
on Hull
127
Grimsby
118
119
Skegness
Boston
Cromer
104
105
106
107
King's
Lynn
Norwich
rborough
9
90
91
92
93
Thetford
Cambridge
5
ord
76
77
78
79
Ipswich
60
61
62
63
helmsford
NDON
4
45
46
47
Maidstone
Sevenoaks
32
33
34
35
Dover
Folkestone
Hastings
hton
9
20
21

Mileage chart

The mileage chart shows distances in miles between two towns along AA-recommended routes. Using motorways and other main roads this is normally the fastest route, though not necessarily the shortest.

The journey times, shown in hours and minutes, are average off-peak driving times along AA-recommended routes. These times should be used as a guide only and do not allow for unforeseen traffic delays, rest breaks or fuel stops.

For example, the 378 miles (608 km) journey between Glasgow and Norwich should take approximately 7 hours 28 minutes.

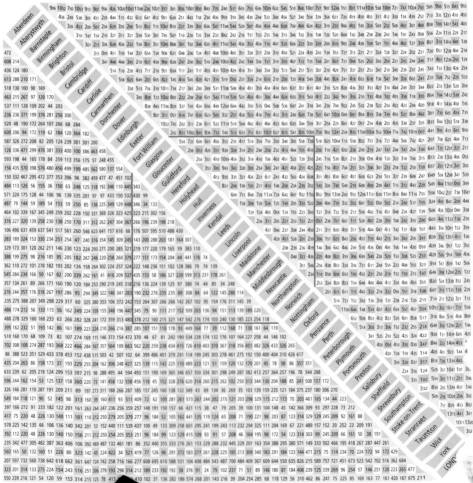

Journey times

	Aberystwyth	Barnstaple	Birmingham	Brighton	Bristol	Cambridge	Cardiff	Carlisle	Carmarthen	Dorchester	Dover	Edinburgh	Exeter	Fort William	Glasgow	Gloucester	Guildford	Hereford	Holyhead	Hull	Inverness	Kendal	Leeds	Lincoln	Liverpool	Maidstone	Manchester	Middlesbrough	Newcastle	Northampton	Norwich	Nottingham	Oxford	Penzance	Perth	Peterborough	Plymouth	Portsmouth	Preston	Salisbury	Sheffield	Shrewsbury	Southampton	Stoke-on-Trent	Stranraer	Taunton	Wick	York	LONDON
Aberdeen	906	1052	750	1051	913	907	936	426	1020	1047	1108	236	1027	357	301	836	1007	850	843	735	240	517	655	753	636	1029	632	545	510	840	1007	757	907	1246	151	837	1114	1039	558	1009	721	747	1024	703	505	950	513	643	955
Aberystwyth		436	249	538	301	431	229	444	115	432	612	647	412	901	624	251	443	158	234	436	959	359	345	430	244	533	304	456	527	340	554	339	354	631	720	419	459	455	317	412	350	154	439	252	713	335	1231	410	455
Barnstaple			326	423	200	501	234	629	335	206	513	832	115	1047	810	227	339	303	636	547	1144	544	529	507	456	434	448	628	700	409	624	422	319	233	906	452	145	324	503	232	500	403	307	400	858	109	1417	543	403
Birmingham				310	147	154	210	327	311	321	334	530	301	745	507	110	226	125	334	233	842	242	216	157	153	255	146	315	346	102	316	108	126	520	604	142	348	258	200	243	146	101	243	058	556	224	1115	229	217
Brighton					301	213	336	628	436	232	154	831	351	1045	808	301	102	348	635	451	1143	543	436	353	454	116	447	535	606	223	320	329	200	610	905	248	438	109	501	151	406	402	127	359	857	319	1416	449	128
Bristol						315	059	451	159	144	337	654	134	908	631	048	206	124	457	408	1005	405	351	328	317	258	310	450	521	224	439	243	134	353	727	313	221	217	324	128	321	224	202	221	720	057	1238	404	218
Cambridge							347	448	448	345	210	637	438	906	628	247	200	302	516	248	1003	422	242	149	336	131	319	335	407	112	135	144	201	657	721	044	525	252	342	254	221	243	244	240	717	401	1236	250	129
Cardiff								514	116	230	413	717	210	931	654	117	241	117	455	431	1029	429	414	351	340	334	333	513	544	257	511	307	210	429	751	337	257	253	347	210	345	239	237	245	743	133	1302	428	254
Carlisle									558	625	649	207	605	422	145	414	545	429	421	316	519	056	237	334	214	610	210	200	125	418	549	338	445	824	241	418	652	618	136	547	300	326	602	241	233	528	752	225	533
Carmarthen										330	513	756	310	1011	734	217	341	200	349	531	1108	508	454	451	359	434	414	605	637	357	611	407	310	529	830	436	357	353	427	310	444	249	337	344	822	233	1341	520	354
Dorchester											345	828	123	1042	805	222	208	258	631	542	1139	539	525	454	451	306	444	624	655	315	503	417	222	342	901	356	210	135	458	102	455	358	118	355	854	104	1412	538	242
Dover												838	445	1106	829	337	145	424	656	449	1204	604	442	350	515	046	508	536	607	241	318	345	236	704	922	245	532	238	522	254	422	423	244	420	918	411	1436	450	145
Edinburgh													807	311	057	616	747	630	623	505	332	257	426	523	416	759	412	315	240	620	738	527	647	1026	049	607	854	819	338	749	455	527	804	442	301	730	605	414	735
Exeter														1022	745	202	311	238	611	522	1119	519	504	442	431	406	423	603	635	344	559	357	254	225	841	427	057	254	438	203	435	338	237	335	833	044	1352	518	338
Fort William															242	831	1002	845	838	733	140	512	653	751	631	1027	627	615	541	835	1005	754	902	1241	234	835	1109	1034	552	1004	716	742	1019	657	441	945	413	641	950
Glasgow																554	725	609	601	456	353	235	417	514	354	750	350	340	305	558	728	518	625	1004	115	558	832	757	316	727	440	506	742	421	207	708	625	404	713
Gloucester																	208	053	420	331	928	328	314	251	240	258	232	413	444	155	410	206	110	421	650	236	249	219	247	147	244	147	204	144	643	125	1201	327	217
Guildford																		254	551	410	1059	459	352	314	410	106	403	451	523	139	310	245	116	530	821	210	358	058	418	120	323	318	106	315	813	238	1332	406	052
Hereford																			353	345	943	343	328	305	254	345	247	427	458	211	425	221	156	457	704	251	325	306	301	233	258	122	250	159	657	201	1215	341	303
Holyhead																				412	935	335	321	426	221	617	241	432	503	424	638	351	451	830	657	457	658	623	254	553	327	239	608	247	649	534	1208	347	539
Hull																					831	249	109	105	217	410	148	200	234	239	332	143	326	740	549	219	608	458	209	447	115	312	443	229	545	444	1103	058	349
Inverness																						609	751	848	728	1124	724	642	607	932	1102	852	959	1338	243	932	1206	1131	650	1101	814	840	1116	755	556	1042	237	738	1047
Kendal																							158	308	129	526	125	149	205	333	522	300	400	739	332	352	607	532	050	502	214	240	517	155	324	443	843	209	448
Leeds																								129	124	405	054	124	155	223	343	127	310	722	510	213	550	442	116	431	048	224	427	139	506	426	1024	040	338
Lincoln																									236	311	205	221	253	151	227	057	238	701	607	117	529	407	228	359	108	242	355	200	603	405	1122	136	250
Liverpool																										437	046	237	308	244	450	211	311	650	450	317	518	444	047	413	142	137	428	107	443	354	1001	152	359
Maidstone																											429	457	528	201	239	306	157	625	843	206	453	159	443	215	343	343	205	341	839	332	1357	411	106
Manchester																												208	239	236	419	146	304	642	446	249	510	436	045	405	106	144	420	059	439	346	957	122	352
Middlesbrough																													048	321	436	225	408	822	359	306	650	540	226	529	153	338	525	253	429	526	914	109	436
Newcastle																														351	506	256	438	853	324	336	721	611	244	559	223	408	555	323	354	557	839	142	506
Northampton																															234	114	058	604	653	100	432	231	250	219	152	150	215	147	646	308	1204	235	123
Norwich																																253	324	820	823	154	648	400	444	413	324	406	403	355	820	524	1338	352	245
Nottingham																																	201	615	611	115	443	333	218	322	056	151	318	108	607	319	1125	139	229
Oxford																																		514	721	152	342	136	318	125	238	218	120	215	714	217	1232	321	115
Penzance																																			1100	646	148	514	657	423	654	557	457	554	1053	303	1611	737	558
Perth																																				652	928	853	412	823	535	601	838	517	318	804	516	458	809
Peterborough																																					514	303	313	306	152	232	255	214	648	350	1206	221	146
Plymouth																																						341	525	250	522	425	324	422	920	131	1439	605	425
Portsmouth																																							450	054	410	350	030	347	846	222	1404	453	[illegible]
Preston																																								420	134	159	435	114	405	401	923	144	[illegible]
Salisbury																																									359	320	037	317	816	130	1334	442	[illegible]
Sheffield																																										224	356	124	529	357	1047	107	[illegible]
Shrewsbury																																											335	102	554	301	1112	251	306
Southampton																																												332	830	205	1349	437	140
Stoke-on-Trent																																													509	258	1028	206	302
Stranraer																																														757	829	453	802
Taunton																																															1315	441	301
Wick																																																1011	1320
York																																																	352

Distances

	Aberdeen	Aberystwyth	Barnstaple	Birmingham	Brighton	Bristol	Cambridge	Cardiff	Carlisle	Carmarthen	Dorchester	Dover	Edinburgh	Exeter	Fort William	Glasgow	Gloucester	Guildford	Hereford	Holyhead	Hull	Inverness	Kendal	Leeds	Lincoln	Liverpool	Maidstone	Manchester	Middlesbrough	Newcastle	Northampton	Norwich	Nottingham	Oxford	Penzance	Perth	Peterborough	Plymouth	Portsmouth	Preston	Salisbury	Sheffield	Shrewsbury	Southampton	Stoke-on-Trent	Stranraer	Taunton	Wick	York
Aberystwyth	472																																																
Barnstaple	608	214																																															
Birmingham	436	124	180																																														
Brighton	613	288	210	171																																													
Bristol	518	130	100	90	169																																												
Cambridge	463	215	267	97	120	170																																											
Cardiff	537	111	128	109	202	44	203																																										
Carlisle	236	236	371	199	376	281	256	300																																									
Carmarthen	520	48	190	172	264	107	266	68	284																																								
Dorchester	600	206	94	172	119	62	184	120	364	182																																							
Dover	587	326	272	208	82	205	124	239	381	301	200																																						
Edinburgh	126	336	471	299	476	381	333	400	100	386	463	458																																					
Exeter	593	198	44	165	178	84	259	113	356	175	57	248	455																																				
Fort William	156	435	570	398	576	480	456	499	199	485	562	580	137	554																																			
Glasgow	150	332	467	295	472	377	353	396	96	382	459	477	47	451	102																																		
Gloucester	484	113	126	56	155	36	150	63	248	125	118	192	346	110	445	343																																	
Guildford	571	224	175	128	44	106	96	139	335	201	97	97	433	150	532	430	99																																
Hereford	487	79	144	59	189	54	153	59	250	85	136	225	349	129	448	346	34	133																															
Holyhead	464	102	339	167	345	249	259	202	228	150	331	369	326	323	425	323	215	302	156																														
Hull	376	227	320	139	258	230	138	250	170	311	312	262	247	304	367	266	196	239	198	218																													
Inverness	106	496	631	459	637	541	517	561	260	546	623	641	157	616	66	176	507	595	510	488	430																												
Kendal	283	189	324	153	330	234	251	254	47	240	316	354	145	309	245	143	200	288	203	181	164	307																											
Leeds	329	173	301	120	262	211	146	230	123	224	293	271	200	285	321	219	177	220	179	165	59	383	110																										
Lincoln	388	199	275	98	216	185	95	205	182	267	246	220	258	260	379	277	151	173	154	204	44	441	176	74																									
Liverpool	362	110	272	101	278	182	193	202	126	158	264	302	224	257	324	222	148	236	151	102	128	386	79	74	139																								
Maidstone	545	284	234	166	50	167	82	200	339	262	161	41	416	209	537	435	153	58	186	327	220	599	313	231	178	261																							
Manchester	357	134	261	89	266	171	160	190	120	184	253	290	219	245	318	216	136	224	139	125	97	380	74	44	85	34	248																						
Middlesbrough	276	244	357	176	318	267	197	286	95	294	349	322	146	341	283	190	232	276	235	235	89	308	84	64	122	145	280	114																					
Newcastle	235	275	388	207	349	298	229	317	60	325	380	353	106	372	242	153	264	307	266	266	142	267	102	95	154	176	311	145	39																				
Northampton	486	174	212	56	133	115	56	162	249	224	159	155	348	196	447	345	79	90	111	217	152	509	203	136	94	151	113	139	189	220																			
Norwich	488	278	329	160	168	233	63	266	282	328	241	172	359	313	480	378	212	160	215	321	147	542	276	174	103	240	130	185	223	254	118																		
Nottingham	395	162	232	51	193	142	86	161	189	223	224	210	266	216	387	285	107	151	110	178	93	449	164	77	39	112	168	71	130	161	64	119																	
Oxford	510	160	170	68	109	73	82	107	274	169	115	146	373	154	472	370	48	67	81	242	190	534	228	174	132	176	107	164	227	258	44	146	102																
Penzance	702	308	108	274	287	193	368	222	466	284	167	357	564	109	663	562	220	259	238	434	415	726	419	403	370	367	318	356	451	482	326	433	326	265															
Perth	86	388	523	351	529	433	378	453	152	438	515	503	42	507	102	64	399	486	401	379	291	114	199	245	303	278	461	275	192	150	400	404	310	426	617														
Peterborough	435	204	263	86	158	173	37	193	229	255	204	162	306	248	427	325	139	115	142	225	110	489	223	121	51	159	120	132	170	201	45	78	58	86	357	351													
Plymouth	633	239	62	205	218	124	299	153	397	215	98	288	495	44	594	493	151	190	169	365	346	657	350	334	301	298	249	287	382	413	257	364	257	196	78	544	288												
Portsmouth	596	244	162	154	53	125	137	158	360	220	73	141	458	132	558	456	118	45	152	328	276	620	314	260	215	262	102	250	313	344	130	204	188	85	241	508	157	172											
Preston	326	146	281	110	287	191	209	211	89	197	273	311	188	266	287	185	157	245	160	138	122	349	43	69	134	36	269	35	103	139	159	235	121	184	375	237	180	306	270										
Salisbury	549	184	118	121	90	52	145	98	313	160	39	160	411	93	511	409	72	62	105	281	261	573	267	244	202	215	121	203	298	329	115	212	173	70	203	461	165	134	44	223									
Sheffield	397	166	272	91	233	182	122	201	161	263	264	247	236	256	359	257	148	191	150	157	66	421	115	38	47	79	205	39	100	131	104	148	45	142	366	309	93	297	228	73	212								
Shrewsbury	417	75	220	48	226	130	140	111	181	110	212	250	279	205	379	277	96	184	52	105	162	441	135	119	124	65	208	71	190	221	98	203	87	123	314	329	129	245	209	92	161	88							
Southampton	578	225	142	135	66	106	136	140	342	201	53	152	440	111	539	437	100	49	133	309	258	601	295	241	199	243	113	232	294	325	111	204	169	67	221	489	157	152	20	252	23	209	191						
Stoke-on-Trent	392	112	220	48	226	130	140	150	156	211	212	250	254	205	353	251	96	184	99	123	129	415	109	93	91	57	208	46	164	195	98	172	54	123	314	303	99	245	209	66	161	50	38	191					
Stranraer	235	342	477	305	482	387	363	406	106	392	469	487	132	461	181	86	352	440	355	333	276	261	153	229	288	232	445	229	201	163	354	388	295	380	571	149	333	502	466	195	418	267	287	447	261				
Taunton	560	165	50	132	160	51	226	80	323	142	45	224	422	34	521	419	77	126	96	291	272	583	277	261	228	225	185	213	309	340	183	291	184	123	144	471	215	75	114	234	70	224	172	94	172	429			
Wick	207	597	732	560	738	642	618	662	361	647	724	742	258	716	166	277	608	695	610	588	531	104	408	484	543	487	700	484	409	367	609	644	550	635	826	215	589	757	721	451	673	523	542	702	516	362	684		
York	323	201	314	133	275	224	154	243	116	251	306	279	193	298	314	212	189	233	192	192	38	376	91	24	79	102	237	71	51	89	146	180	87	184	408	239	125	339	269	96	254	57	146	251	120	223	265	477	
LONDON	550	239	216	121	54	120	59	153	314	215	125	78	413	[illegible]	[illegible]	410	102	31	136	282	186	574	268	201	143	216	39	204	254	285	68	118	129	56	310	462	86	241	75	225	85	169	163	77	161	420	167	675	211

Distances in miles (on[illegible]ls 1.6093 km)

DRIVER'S ATLAS
BRITAIN

Atlas contents

Map pages south	inside front cover
Mileage chart and journey times	endpaper
Route planner	II–VII
Motorways	VIII–X
Restricted junctions	VIII–IX
Smart motorways	X
Atlas symbols	1
Road maps 1:250,000 scale	2–237
Western Isles 1:700,000 scale	232–233
Orkney Islands 1:636,000 scale	234
Shetland Islands 1:636,000 scale	235
Channel Islands 1:150,000 scale	236
Isle of Man 1:317,000 scale	237
Index to place names	238–318
County, administrative area map	238–239
Place name index	240–318
Ireland	endpaper
Map pages north	inside back cover

16th edition June 2017

© AA Media Limited 2017

Cartography: All cartography in this atlas edited, designed and produced by the Mapping Services Department of AA Publishing (A05505).

This atlas contains Ordnance Survey data © Crown copyright and database right 2017.

 This atlas is based upon Crown Copyright and is reproduced with the permission of Land & Property Services under delegated authority from the Controller of Her Majesty's Stationery Office, © Crown copyright and database right 2017, PMLPA No. 100497

 © Ordnance Survey Ireland/ Government of Ireland. Copyright Permit No. MP000717

Publisher's notes: Published by AA Publishing (a trading name of AA Media Limited, whose registered office is Fanum House, Basing View, Basingstoke, Hampshire RG21 4EA, UK. Registered number 06112600).

ISBN: 978 0 7495 7856 5 (flexibound)

A CIP catalogue record for this book is available from The British Library.

Disclaimer: The contents of this atlas are believed to be correct at the time of the latest revision, it will not contain any subsequent amended, new or temporary information including diversions and traffic control or enforcement systems. The publishers cannot be held responsible or liable for any loss or damage occasioned to any person acting or refraining from action as a result of any use or reliance on material in this atlas, nor for any errors, omissions or changes in such material. This does not affect your statutory rights.

The publishers would welcome information to correct any errors or omissions and to keep this atlas up to date. Please write to the Atlas Editor, AA Publishing, The Automobile Association, Fanum House, Basing View, Basingstoke, Hampshire RG21 4EA, UK.
E-mail: roadatlasfeedback@theaa.com

Acknowledgements: AA Publishing would like to thank the following for their assistance in producing this atlas: Crematoria database provided by Cremation Society of Great Britain. Cadw, English Heritage, Forestry Commission, Historic Scotland, Johnsons, National Trust and National Trust for Scotland, RSPB, The Wildlife Trust, Scottish Natural Heritage, Natural England, The Countryside Council for Wales. Award winning beaches from 'Blue Flag' and 'Keep Scotland Beautiful' (summer 2016 data): for latest information visit www.blueflag.org and www.keepscotlandbeautiful.org

Printer: 1010 Printing International Ltd.

Scale 1:250,000
or 3.95 miles to 1 inch

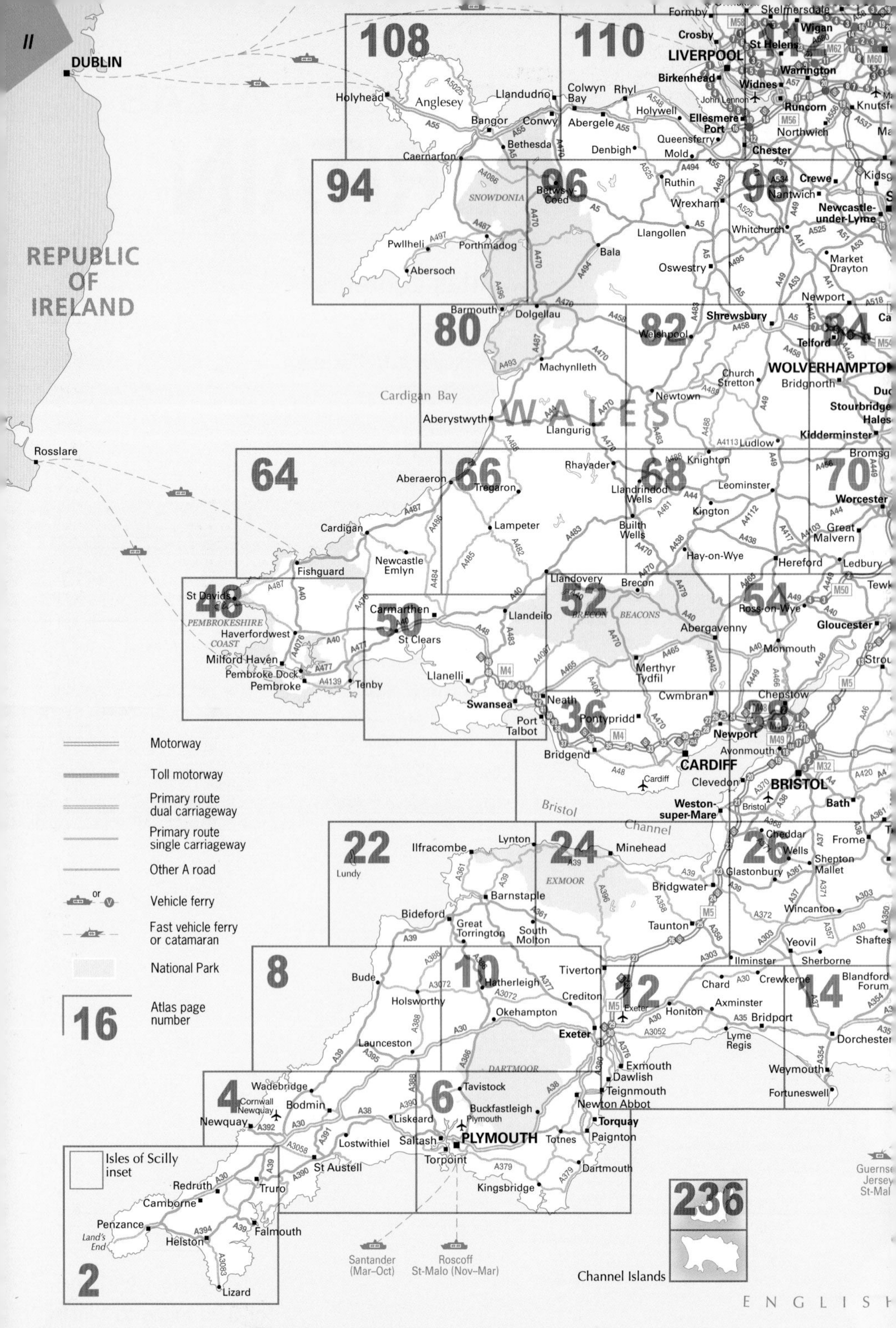
DUBLIN
REPUBLIC OF IRELAND
Rosslare
108
110
94
96
98
80
82
84
64
66
68
70
46
50
52
54
36
38
22
24
26
8
10
12
14
4
6
2
236
Formby
Skelmersdale
Crosby
Wigan
St Helens
LIVERPOOL
Birkenhead
Warrington
Widnes
John Lennon
Runcorn
Knutsford
Ellesmere Port
Northwich
Queensferry
Chester
Mold
Holyhead
Anglesey
Llandudno
Colwyn Bay
Rhyl
Holywell
Bangor
Conwy
Abergele
Bethesda
Denbigh
Caernarfon
Ruthin
Crewe
Kidsgrove
SNOWDONIA
Betws-y-Coed
Wrexham
Nantwich
Newcastle-under-Lyme
Pwllheli
Porthmadog
Llangollen
Whitchurch
Abersoch
Bala
Oswestry
Market Drayton
Newport
Barmouth
Dolgellau
Shrewsbury
Telford
Welshpool
Machynlleth
WOLVERHAMPTON
Church Stretton
Bridgnorth
Cardigan Bay
Newtown
Stourbridge
Halesowen
Aberystwyth
WALES
Llangurig
Kidderminster
Ludlow
Rhayader
Knighton
Bromsgrove
Aberaeron
Tregaron
Llandrindod Wells
Leominster
Worcester
Kington
Cardigan
Lampeter
Builth Wells
Great Malvern
Newcastle Emlyn
Hay-on-Wye
Hereford
Ledbury
Fishguard
Llandovery
Brecon
Tewkesbury
St Davids
Carmarthen
Llandeilo
BRECON BEACONS
Ross-on-Wye
PEMBROKESHIRE COAST
Abergavenny
Gloucester
Haverfordwest
St Clears
Milford Haven
Merthyr Tydfil
Monmouth
Pembroke Dock
Llanelli
Stroud
Pembroke
Tenby
Swansea
Neath
Cwmbran
Chepstow
Port Talbot
Pontypridd
Newport
Bridgend
Avonmouth
CARDIFF
Cardiff
BRISTOL
Clevedon
Bristol
Bath
Weston-super-Mare
Bristol Channel
Lundy
Ilfracombe
Lynton
Minehead
Cheddar
Wells
Frome
Shepton Mallet
EXMOOR
Glastonbury
Bridgwater
Barnstaple
Wincanton
Bideford
Great Torrington
South Molton
Taunton
Yeovil
Shaftesbury
Ilminster
Sherborne
Bude
Hatherleigh
Tiverton
Chard
Crewkerne
Blandford Forum
Holsworthy
Crediton
Axminster
Okehampton
Exeter
Honiton
Bridport
Lyme Regis
Dorchester
Launceston
DARTMOOR
Exmouth
Weymouth
Dawlish
Wadebridge
Tavistock
Teignmouth
Fortuneswell
Cornwall Newquay
Bodmin
Buckfastleigh
Newton Abbot
Newquay
Liskeard
Plymouth
Torquay
Lostwithiel
Saltash
PLYMOUTH
Totnes
Paignton
Torpoint
St Austell
Dartmouth
Kingsbridge
Isles of Scilly inset
Redruth
Truro
Camborne
Penzance
Land's End
Helston
Falmouth
Lizard
Santander (Mar–Oct)
Roscoff St-Malo (Nov–Mar)
Channel Islands
Guernsey Jersey St-Malo
ENGLISH
Motorway
Toll motorway
Primary route dual carriageway
Primary route single carriageway
Other A road
or
Vehicle ferry
Fast vehicle ferry or catamaran
National Park
16
Atlas page number

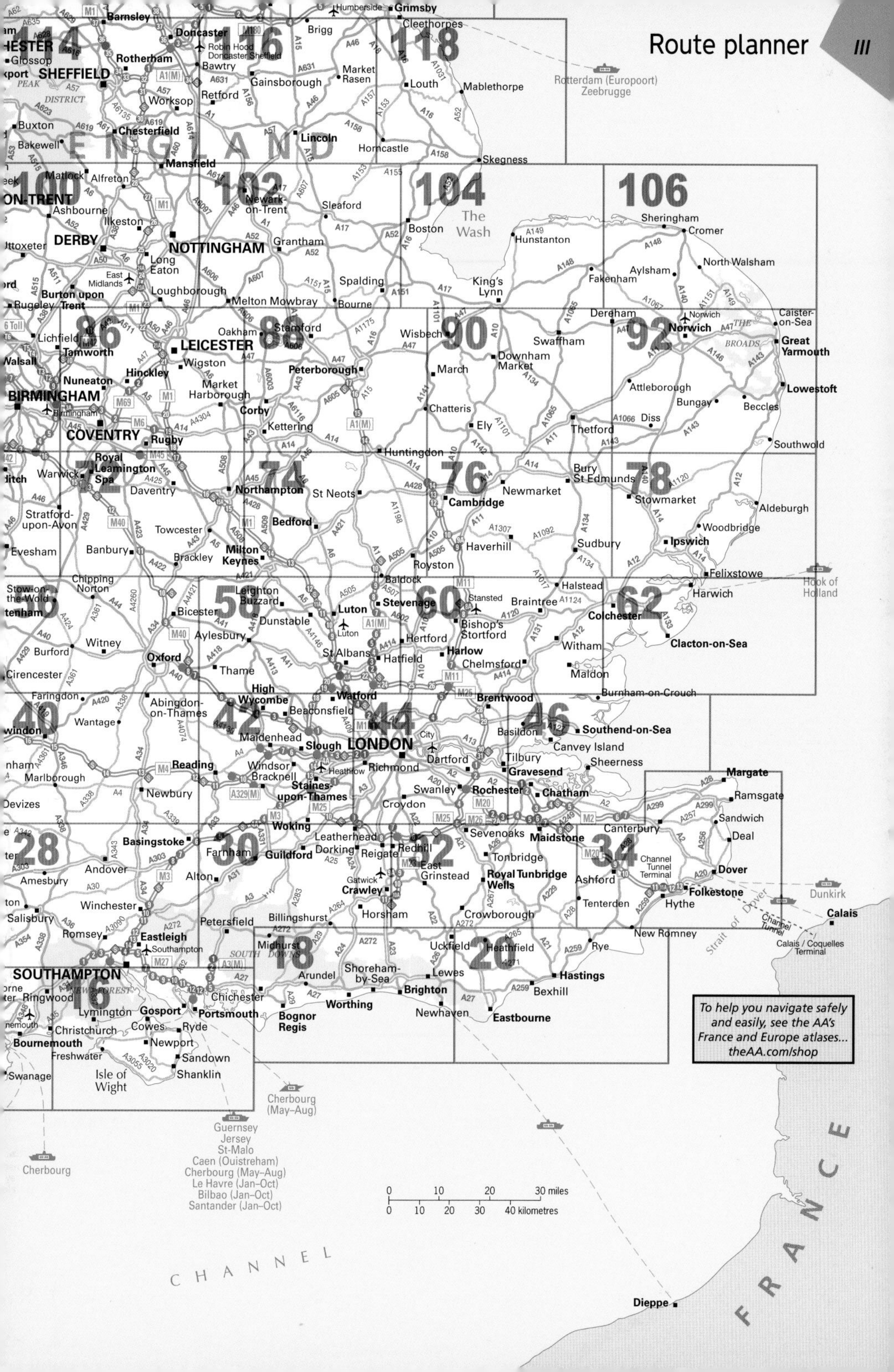

To help you navigate safely and easily, see the AA's France and Europe atlases... theAA.com/shop

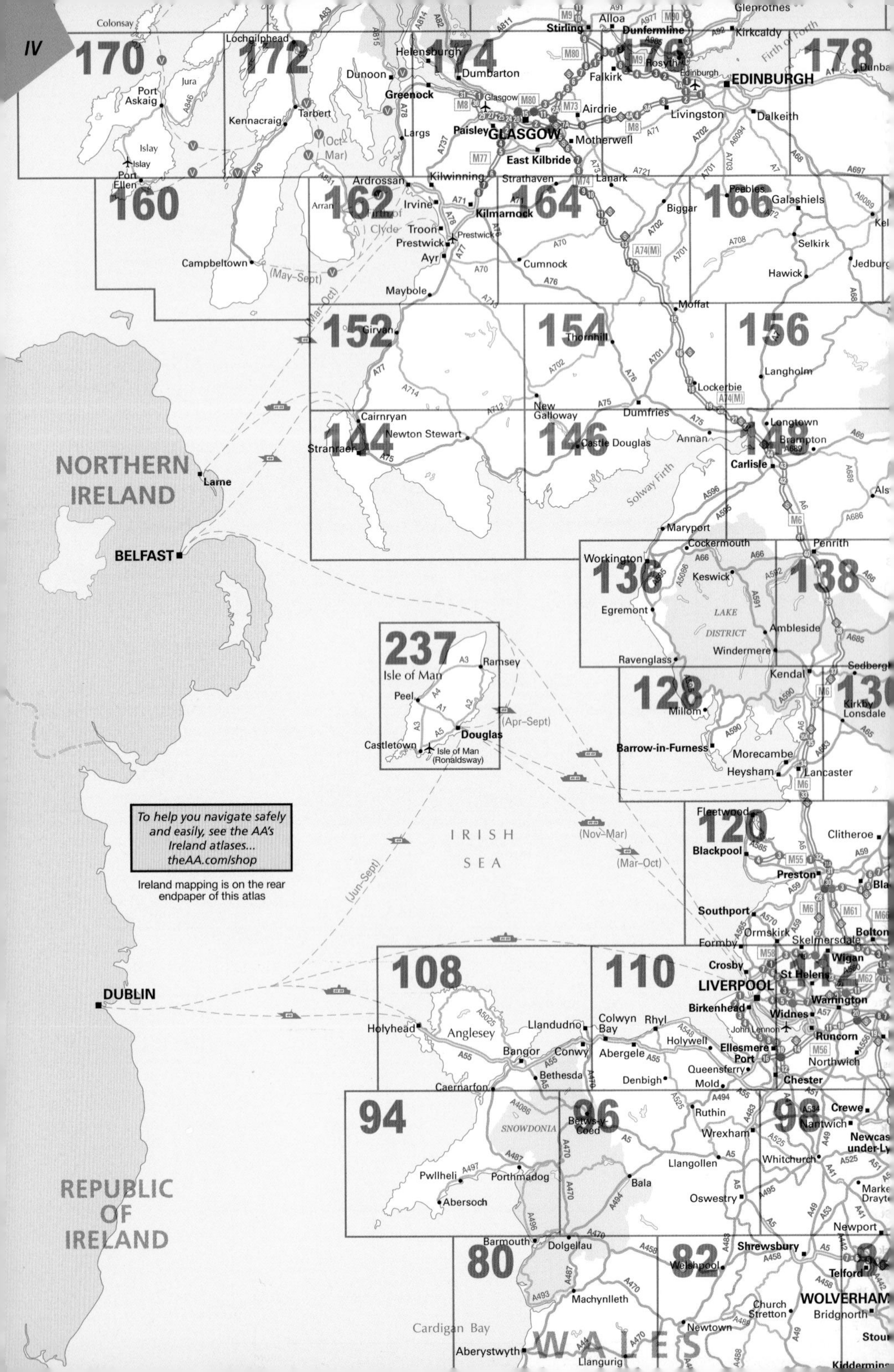
170
172
174
176
178
160
162
164
166
152
154
156
144
146
148
136
138
128
130
237
Isle of Man
120
108
110
112
94
96
98
80
82
84
Colonsay
Lochgilphead
Jura
Port Askaig
Islay
Port Ellen
Kennacraig
Tarbert
(Oct–Mar)
Helensburgh
Dunoon
Dumbarton
Greenock
Largs
Glasgow
Paisley
GLASGOW
East Kilbride
Motherwell
Airdrie
Stirling
Alloa
Dunfermline
Kirkcaldy
Glenrothes
Rosyth
Falkirk
Firth of Forth
Edinburgh
EDINBURGH
Livingston
Dalkeith
Dunbar
Ardrossan
Arran
Firth of Clyde
Irvine
Kilwinning
Kilmarnock
Troon
Prestwick
Ayr
Strathaven
Lanark
Biggar
Peebles
Galashiels
Kelso
Selkirk
Hawick
Jedburgh
Campbeltown
(May–Sept)
Cumnock
Maybole
(Mar–Oct)
Girvan
Moffat
Thornhill
Langholm
Lockerbie
Cairnryan
Newton Stewart
Stranraer
New Galloway
Castle Douglas
Dumfries
Annan
Longtown
Brampton
Carlisle
Solway Firth
NORTHERN IRELAND
Larne
BELFAST
Maryport
Cockermouth
Workington
Keswick
Penrith
Egremont
LAKE DISTRICT
Ambleside
Windermere
Ravenglass
Kendal
Sedbergh
Millom
Kirkby Lonsdale
Barrow-in-Furness
Morecambe
Heysham
Lancaster
Ramsey
Peel
Douglas
Castletown
Isle of Man (Ronaldsway)
(Apr–Sept)
(Nov–Mar)
(Mar–Oct)
(Jun–Sept)
IRISH SEA
To help you navigate safely and easily, see the AA's Ireland atlases... theAA.com/shop
Ireland mapping is on the rear endpaper of this atlas
Fleetwood
Blackpool
Clitheroe
Preston
Southport
Ormskirk
Formby
Bolton
Skelmersdale
Wigan
Crosby
St Helens
LIVERPOOL
Birkenhead
Warrington
Widnes
John Lennon
Runcorn
Ellesmere Port
Northwich
Chester
DUBLIN
Holyhead
Anglesey
Llandudno
Colwyn Bay
Rhyl
Holywell
Bangor
Conwy
Abergele
Bethesda
Denbigh
Queensferry
Mold
Caernarfon
SNOWDONIA
Betws-y-Coed
Ruthin
Wrexham
Crewe
Nantwich
Newcastle-under-Lyme
Whitchurch
Llangollen
Pwllheli
Porthmadog
Bala
Oswestry
Market Drayton
Abersoch
Newport
REPUBLIC OF IRELAND
Barmouth
Dolgellau
Shrewsbury
Welshpool
Telford
Machynlleth
Church Stretton
WOLVERHAMPTON
Bridgnorth
Cardigan Bay
Newtown
Aberystwyth
WALES
Llangurig
Kidderminster

EMERGENCY DIVERSION ROUTES

In an emergency it may be necessary to close a section of motorway or other main road to traffic, so a temporary sign may advise drivers to follow a diversion route. To help drivers navigate the route, black symbols on yellow patches may be permanently displayed on existing direction signs, including motorway signs. Symbols may also be used on separate signs with yellow backgrounds.

For further information see *theaa.com/motoring_advice/ general-advice/emergency-diversion-routes.html*

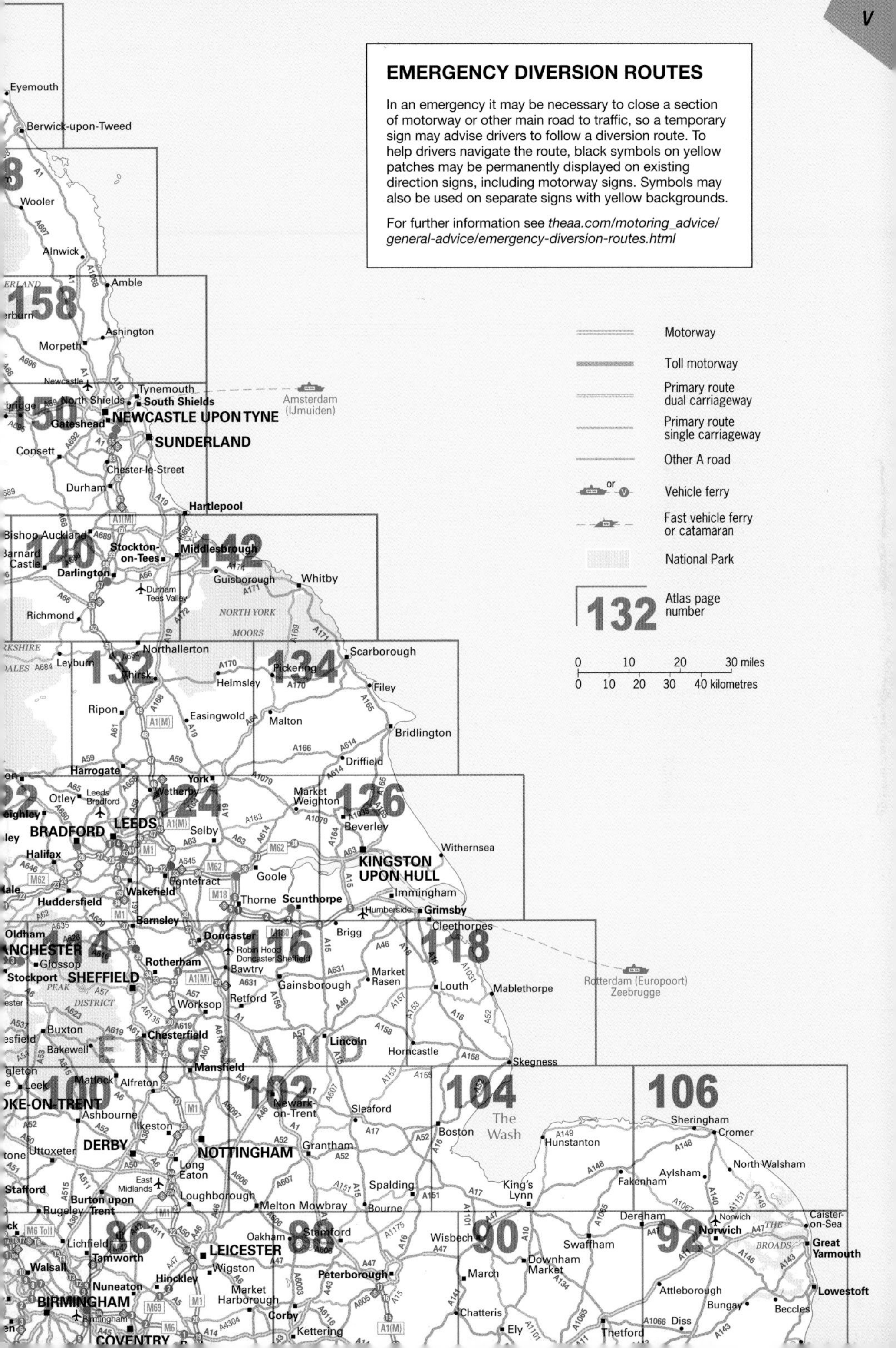

FERRY OPERATORS

Hebrides and west coast Scotland
calmac.co.uk
skyeferry.co.uk
western-ferries.co.uk

Orkney and Shetland
northlinkferries.co.uk
pentlandferries.co.uk
orkneyferries.co.uk
shetland.gov.uk/ferries

Isle of Man
steam-packet.com

Ireland
irishferries.com
poferries.com
stenaline.co.uk

North Sea (Scandinavia and Benelux)
dfdsseaways.co.uk
poferries.com

Isle of Wight
wightlink.co.uk
redfunnel.co.uk

Channel Islands
condorferries.co.uk

France and Belgium
brittany-ferries.co.uk
condorferries.co.uk
eurotunnel.com
dfdsseaways.co.uk
poferries.com

Northern Spain
brittany-ferries.co.uk

Motorway
Toll motorway
Primary route dual carriageway
Primary route single carriageway
Other A road
or V Vehicle ferry
Fast vehicle ferry or catamaran
National Park
192 Atlas page number

0 10 20 30 miles
0 10 20 30 40 kilometres

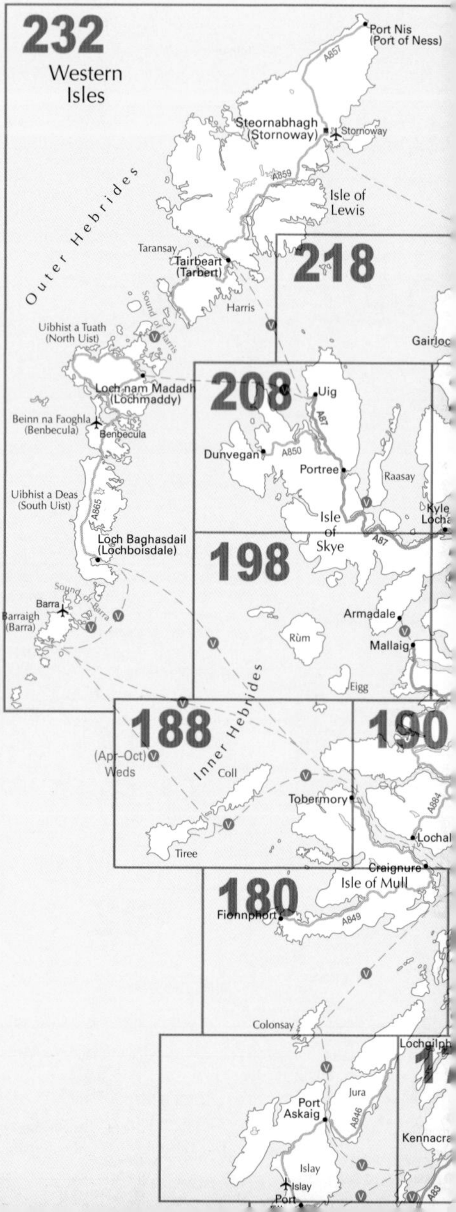

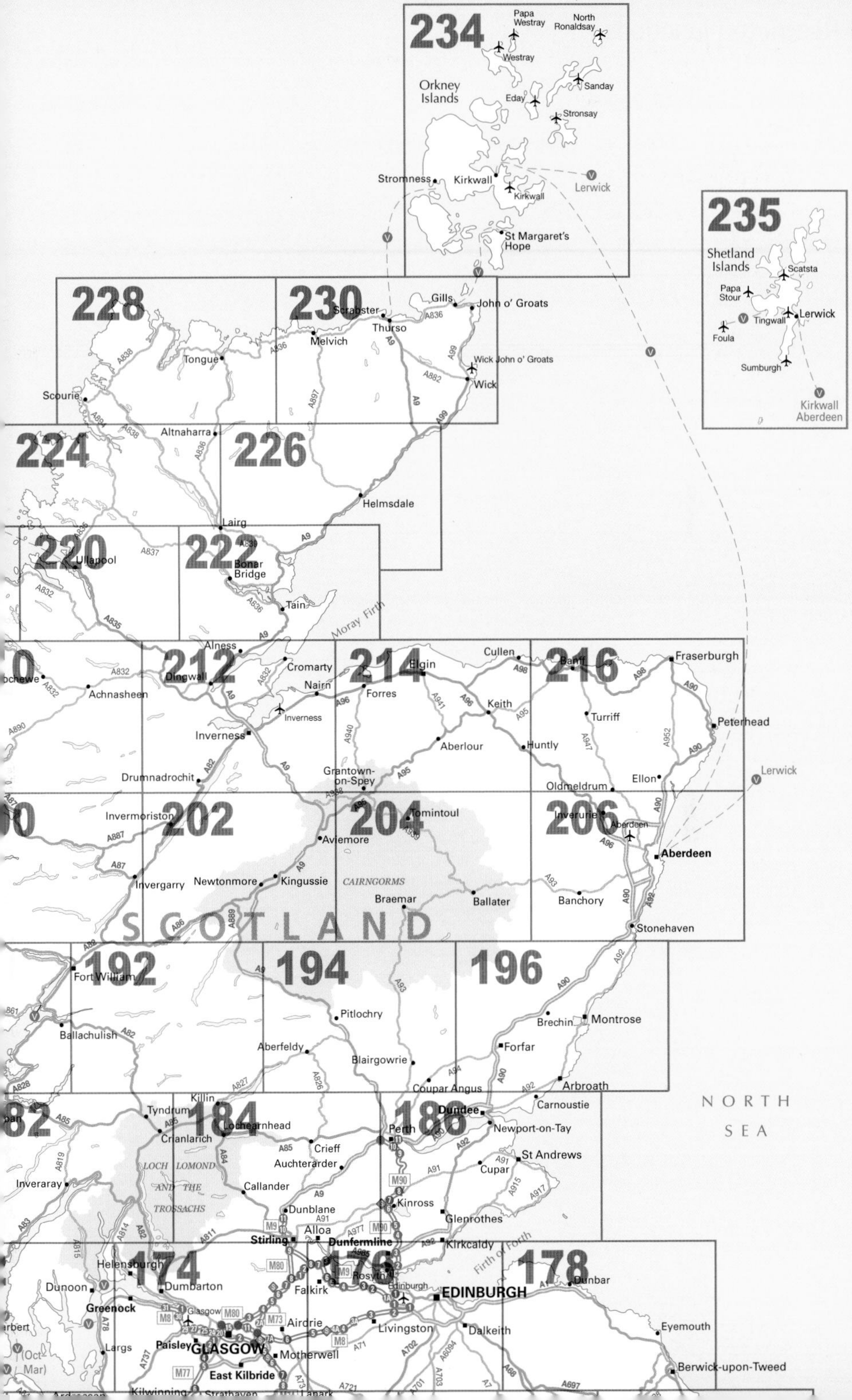
234
Papa Westray
North Ronaldsay
Westray
Orkney Islands
Sanday
Eday
Stronsay
Stromness
Kirkwall
Kirkwall
Lerwick
St Margaret's Hope
235
Shetland Islands
Scatsta
Papa Stour
Lerwick
Tingwall
Foula
Sumburgh
Kirkwall Aberdeen
228
230
Scrabster
Thurso
Gills
John o' Groats
Melvich
Tongue
Scourie
Wick John o' Groats
Wick
224
226
Altnaharra
Helmsdale
Lairg
220
222
Ullapool
Bonar Bridge
Tain
Moray Firth
Alness
212
214
216
Cullen
Banff
Fraserburgh
Dingwall
Cromarty
Nairn
Elgin
Forres
Keith
Achnasheen
Inverness
Inverness
Turriff
Peterhead
Aberlour
Huntly
Drumnadrochit
Grantown-on-Spey
Oldmeldrum
Ellon
Lerwick
Invermoriston
202
204
206
Tomintoul
Inverurie
Aberdeen
Aviemore
Aberdeen
Invergarry
Newtonmore
Kingussie
CAIRNGORMS
Braemar
Ballater
Banchory
SCOTLAND
Stonehaven
192
194
196
Fort William
Pitlochry
Brechin
Montrose
Ballachulish
Aberfeldy
Forfar
Blairgowrie
Coupar Angus
Arbroath
NORTH SEA
Killin
Tyndrum
184
186
Dundee
Carnoustie
Crianlarich
Lochearnhead
Perth
Newport-on-Tay
Crieff
St Andrews
LOCH LOMOND AND THE TROSSACHS
Auchterarder
Cupar
Inveraray
Callander
Kinross
Dunblane
Glenrothes
Alloa
Stirling
Dunfermline
Kirkcaldy
Firth of Forth
Helensburgh
174
176
178
Rosyth
Dunbar
Dunoon
Dumbarton
Falkirk
Edinburgh
EDINBURGH
Greenock
Glasgow
Airdrie
Livingston
Dalkeith
Eyemouth
Paisley
GLASGOW
Motherwell
Largs
East Kilbride
Berwick-upon-Tweed
Kilwinning
Lanark

Restricted junctions

Motorway and Primary Route junctions which have access or exit restrictions are shown on the map pages thus:

M1 London - Leeds

Junction	Northbound	Southbound
2	Access only from A1 *(northbound)*	Exit only to A1 *(southbound)*
4	Access only from A41 *(northbound)*	Exit only to A41 *(southbound)*
6A	Access only from M25 (no link from A405)	Exit only to M25 (no link from A405)
7	Access only from A414	Exit only to A414
17	Exit only to M45	Access only from M45
19	Exit only to M6 *(northbound)*	Exit only to A14 *(southbound)*
21A	Exit only, no access	Access only, no exit
23A	Access only from A42	No restriction
24A	Access only, no exit	Exit only, no access
35A	Exit only, no access	Access only, no exit
43	Exit only to M621	Access only from M621
48	Exit only to A1(M) *(northbound)*	Access only from A1(M) *(southbound)*

M2 Rochester - Faversham

Junction	Westbound	Eastbound
1	No exit to A2 *(eastbound)*	No access from A2 *(westbound)*

M3 Sunbury - Southampton

Junction	Northeastbound	Southwestbound
8	Access only from A303, no exit	Exit only to A303, no access
10	Exit only, no access	Access only, no exit
14	Access from M27 only, no exit	No access to M27 *(westbound)*

M4 London - South Wales

Junction	Westbound	Eastbound
1	Access only from A4 *(westbound)*	Exit only to A4 *(eastbound)*
2	Access only from A4 *(westbound)*	Access only from A4 *(eastbound)*
21	Exit only to M48	Access only from M48
23	Access only from M48	Exit only to M48
25	Exit only, no access	Access only, no exit
25A	Exit only, no access	Access only, no exit
29	Exit only to A48(M)	Access only from A48(M)
38	Exit only, no access	No restriction
39	Access only, no exit	No access or exit
42	Exit only to A483	Access only from A483

M5 Birmingham - Exeter

Junction	Northeastbound	Southwestbound
10	Access only, no exit	Exit only, no access
11A	Access only from A417 *(westbound)*	Exit only to A417 *(eastbound)*
18A	Exit only to M49	Access only from M49
18	Exit only, no access	Access only, no exit

M6 Toll Motorway

Junction	Northwestbound	Southeastbound
T1	Access only, no exit	No access or exit
T2	No access or exit	Exit only, no access
T5	Access only, no exit	Exit only to A5148 *(northbound)*, no access
T7	Exit only, no access	Access only, no exit
T8	Exit only, no access	Access only, no exit

M6 Rugby - Carlisle

Junction	Northbound	Southbound
3A	Exit only to M6 Toll	Access only from M6 Toll
4	Exit only to M42 *(southbound)* & A446	Exit only to A446
4A	Access only from M42 *(southbound)*	Exit only to M42
5	Exit only, no access	Access only, no exit
10A	Exit only to M54	Access only from M54
11A	Access only from M6 Toll	Exit only to M6 Toll
with M56 (jct 20A)	No restriction	Access only from M56 *(eastbound)*
20	Exit only to M56 *(westbound)*	Access only from M56 *(eastbound)*
24	Access only, no exit	Exit only, no access
25	Exit only, no access	Access only, no exit
30	Access only from M61	Exit only to M61

Junction	Northbound	Southbound
31A	Exit only, no access	Access only, no exit
45	Exit only, no access	Access only, no exit

M8 Edinburgh - Bishopton

Junction	Westbound	Eastbound
6	Exit only, no access	Access only, no exit
6A	Access only, no exit	Exit only, no access
7	Access only, no exit	Exit only, no access
7A	Exit only, no access	Access only from A725 *(northbound)*, no exit
8	No access from M73 *(southbound)* or from A8 *(eastbound)* & A89	No exit to M73 *(northbound)* or to A8 *(westbound)* & A89
9	Access only, no exit	Exit only, no access
13	Access only from M80 *(southbound)*	Exit only to M80 *(northbound)*
14	Access only, no exit	Exit only, no access
16	Exit only to A804	Access only from A879
17	Exit only to A82	No restriction
18	Access only from A82 *(eastbound)*	Exit only to A814
19	No access from A814 *(westbound)*	Exit only to A814 *(westbound)*
20	Exit only, no access	Access only, no exit
21	Access only, no exit	Exit only to A8
22	Exit only to M77 *(southbound)*	Access only from M77 *(northbound)*
23	Exit only to B768	Access only from B768
25	No access or exit from or to A8	No access or exit from or to A8
25A	Exit only, no access	Access only, no exit
28	Exit only, no access	Access only, no exit
28A	Exit only to A737	Access only from A737

M9 Edinburgh - Dunblane

Junction	Northwestbound	Southeastbound
2	Access only, no exit	Exit only, no access
3	Exit only, no access	Access only, no exit
6	Access only, no exit	Exit only to A905
8	Exit only to M876 *(southwestbound)*	Access only from M876 *(northeastbound)*

M11 London - Cambridge

Junction	Northbound	Southbound
4	Access only from A406 *(eastbound)*	Exit only to A406
5	Exit only, no access	Access only, no exit
8A	Exit only, no access	No direct access, use jct 8
9	Exit only to A11	Access only from A11
13	Exit only, no access	Access only, no exit
14	Exit only, no access	Access only, no exit

M20 Swanley - Folkestone

Junction	Northwestbound	Southeastbound
2	Staggered junction; follow signs - access only	Staggered junction; follow signs - exit only
3	Exit only to M26 *(westbound)*	Access only from M26 *(eastbound)*
5	Access only from A20	For access follow signs - exit only to A20
6	No restriction	For exit follow signs
11A	Access only, no exit	Exit only, no access

M23 Hooley - Crawley

Junction	Northbound	Southbound
7	Exit only to A23 *(northbound)*	Access only from A23 *(southbound)*
10A	Access only, no exit	Exit only, no access

M25 London Orbital Motorway

Junction	Clockwise	Anticlockwise
1B	No direct access, use slip road to jct 2 Exit only	Access only, no exit
5	No exit to M26 *(eastbound)*	No access from M26
19	Exit only, no access	Access only, no exit
21	Access only from M1 *(southbound)* Exit only to M1 *(northbound)*	Access only from M1 *(southbound)* Exit only to M1 *(northbound)*
31	No exit (use slip road via jct 30), access only	No access (use slip road via jct 30), exit only

M26 Sevenoaks - Wrotham

Junction	Westbound	Eastbound
with M25 (jct 5)	Exit only to clockwise M25 *(westbound)*	Access only from anticlockwise M25 *(eastbound)*
with M20 (jct 3)	Access only from M20 *(northwestbound)*	Exit only to M20 *(southeastbound)*

M27 Cadnam - Portsmouth

Junction	Westbound	Eastbound
4	Staggered junction; follow signs - access only from M3 *(southbound)*. Exit only to M3 *(northbound)*	Staggered junction; follow signs - access only from M3 *(southbound)*. Exit only to M3 *(northbound)*
10	Exit only, no access	Access only, no exit
12	Staggered junction; follow signs - exit only to M275 *(southbound)*	Staggered junction; follow signs - access only from M275 *(northbound)*

M40 London - Birmingham

Junction	Northwestbound	Southeastbound
3	Exit only, no access	Access only, no exit
7	Exit only, no access	Access only, no exit
8	Exit only to M40/A40	Access only from M40/A40
13	Exit only, no access	Access only, no exit
14	Access only, no exit	Exit only, no access
16	Access only, no exit	Exit only, no access

M42 Bromsgrove - Measham

Junction	Northeastbound	Southwestbound
1	Access only, no exit	Exit only, no access
7	Exit only to M6 *(northwestbound)*	Access only from M6 *(northwestbound)*
7A	Exit only to M6 *(southeastbound)*	No access or exit
8	Access only from M6 *(southeastbound)*	Exit only to M6 *(northwestbound)*

M45 Coventry - M1

Junction	Westbound	Eastbound
Dunchurch (unnumbered)	Access only from A45	Exit only, no access
with M1 (jct 17)	Access only from M1 *(northbound)*	Exit only to M1 *(southbound)*

M48 Chepstow

Junction	Westbound	Eastbound
21	Access only from M4 *(westbound)*	Exit only to M4 *(eastbound)*
23	No exit to M4 *(eastbound)*	No Access from M4 *(westbound)*

M53 Mersey Tunnel - Chester

Junction	Northbound	Southbound
11	Access only from M56 *(westbound)* Exit only to M56 *(eastbound)*	Access only from M56 *(westbound)* Exit only to M56 *(eastbound)*

M54 Telford - Birmingham

Junction	Westbound	Eastbound
with M6 (jct 10A)	Access only from M6 *(northbound)*	Exit only to M6 *(southbound)*

M56 Chester - Manchester

Junction	Westbound	Eastbound
1	Access only from M60 *(westbound)*	Exit only to M60 *(eastbound)* & A34 *(northbound)*
2	Exit only, no access	Access only, no exit
3	Access only, no exit	Exit only, no access
4	Exit only, no access	Access only, no exit
7	Exit only, no access	No restriction
8	Access only, no exit	No access or exit
9	No exit to M6 *(southbound)*	No access from M6 *(northbound)*
15	Exit only to M53	Access only from M53
16	No access or exit	No restriction

M57 Liverpool Outer Ring Road

Junction	Northwestbound	Southeastbound
3	Access only, no exit	Exit only, no access
5	Access only from A580 *(westbound)*	Exit only, no access

M58 Liverpool - Wigan

Junction	Westbound	Eastbound
1	Exit only, no access	Access only, no exit

M60 Manchester Orbital

Junction	Clockwise	Anticlockwise
2	Access only, no exit	Exit only, no access
3	No access from M56	Access only from A34 *(northbound)*
4	Access only from A34 *(northbound)*. Exit only to M56	Access only from M56 *(eastbound)*. Exit only to A34 *(southbound)*
5	Access and exit only from and to A5103 *(northbound)*	Access and exit only from and to A5103 *(southbound)*
7	No direct access, use slip road to jct 8. Exit only to A56	Access only from A56. No exit, use jct 8
14	Access from A580 *(eastbound)*	Exit only to A580 *(westbound)*
16	Access only, no exit	Exit only, no access
20	Exit only, no access	Access only, no exit
22	No restriction	Exit only, no access
25	Exit only, no access	No restriction
26	No restriction	Exit only, no access
27	Access only, no exit	Exit only, no access

M61 Manchester - Preston

Junction	Northwestbound	Southeastbound
3	No access or exit	Exit only, no access
with M6 (jct 30)	Exit only to M6 *(northbound)*	Access only from M6 *(southbound)*

M62 Liverpool - Kingston upon Hull

Junction	Westbound	Eastbound
23	Access only, no exit	Exit only, no access
32A	No access to A1(M) *(southbound)*	No restriction

M65 Preston - Colne

Junction	Northeastbound	Southwestbound
9	Exit only, no access	Access only, no exit
11	Access only, no exit	Exit only, no access

M66 Bury

Junction	Northbound	Southbound
with A56	Exit only to A56 *(northbound)*	Access only from A56 *(southbound)*
1	Exit only, no access	Access only, no exit

M67 Hyde Bypass

Junction	Westbound	Eastbound
1	Access only, no exit	Exit only, no access
2	Exit only, no access	Access only, no exit
3	Exit only, no access	No restriction

M69 Coventry - Leicester

Junction	Northbound	Southbound
2	Access only, no exit	Exit only, no access

M73 East of Glasgow

Junction	Northbound	Southbound
1	No exit to A74 & A721	No exit to A74 & A721
2	No access from or exit to A89. No access from *(eastbound)*	No access from or exit to A89. No exit to M8 *(westbound)*

M74 and A74(M) Glasgow - Gretna

Junction	Northbound	Southbound
3	Exit only, no access	Access only, no exit
3A	Access only, no exit	Exit only, no access
4	No access from A74 & A721	Access only, no exit to A74 & A721
7	Access only, no exit	Exit only, no access
9	No access or exit	Exit only, no access
10	No restriction	Access only, no exit
11	Access only, no exit	Exit only, no access
12	Exit only, no access	Access only, no exit
18	Exit only, no access	Access only, no exit

M77 Glasgow - Kilmarnock

Junction	Northbound	Southbound
with M8 (jct 22)	No exit to M8 *(westbound)*	No access from M8 *(eastbound)*
4	Access only, no exit	Exit only, no access
6	Access only, no exit	Exit only, no access
7	Access only, no exit	No restriction
8	Exit only, no access	Exit only, no access

M80 Glasgow - Stirling

Junction	Northbound	Southbound
4A	Exit only, no access	Access only, no exit
6A	Access only, no exit	Exit only, no access
8	Exit only to M876 *(northeastbound)*	Access only from M876 *(southwestbound)*

M90 Edinburgh - Perth

Junction	Northbound	Southbound
1	No exit, access only	Exit only to A90 *(eastbound)*
2A	Exit only to A92 *(eastbound)*	Access only from A92 *(westbound)*
7	Access only, no exit	Exit only, no access
8	Exit only, no access	Access only, no exit
10	No access from A912. No exit to A912 *(southbound)*	No access from A912 *(northbound)* No exit to A912

M180 Doncaster - Grimsby

Junction	Westbound	Eastbound
1	Access only, no exit	Exit only, no access

M606 Bradford Spur

Junction	Northbound	Southbound
2	Exit only, no access	No restriction

M621 Leeds - M1

Junction	Clockwise	Anticlockwise
2A	Access only, no exit	Exit only, no access
4	No exit or access	No restriction
5	Access only, no exit	Exit only, no access
6	Exit only, no access	Access only, no exit
with M1 (jct 43)	Exit only to M1 *(southbound)*	Access only from M1 *(northbound)*

M876 Bonnybridge - Kincardine Bridge

Junction	Northeastbound	Southwestbound
with M80 (jct 5)	Access only from M80 *(northeastbound)*	Exit only to M80 *(southwestbound)*
with M9 (jct 8)	Exit only to M9 *(eastbound)*	Access only from M9 *(westbound)*

A1(M) South Mimms - Baldock

Junction	Northbound	Southbound
2	Exit only, no access	Access only, no exit
3	No restriction	Exit only, no access
5	Access only, no exit	No access or exit

A1(M) Pontefract - Bedale

Junction	Northbound	Southbound
41	No access to M62 *(eastbound)*	No restriction
43	Access only from M1 *(northbound)*	Exit only to M1 *(southbound)*

A1(M) Scotch Corner - Newcastle upon Tyne

Junction	Northbound	Southbound
57	Exit only to A66(M) *(eastbound)*	Access only from A66(M) *(westbound)*
65	No access Exit only to A194(M) & A1 *(northbound)*	No exit Access only from A194(M) & A1 *(southbound)*

A3(M) Horndean - Havant

Junction	Northbound	Southbound
1	Access only from A3	Exit only to A3
4	Exit only, no access	Access only, no exit

A38(M) Birmingham, Victoria Road (Park Circus)

Junction	Northbound	Southbound
with B4132	No exit	No access

A48(M) Cardiff Spur

Junction	Westbound	Eastbound
29	Access only from M4 *(westbound)*	Exit only to M4 *(eastbound)*
29A	Exit only to A48 *(westbound)*	Access only from A48 *(eastbound)*

A57(M) Manchester, Brook Street (A34)

Junction	Westbound	Eastbound
with A34	No exit	No access

A58(M) Leeds, Park Lane and Westgate

Junction	Northbound	Southbound
with A58	No restriction	No access

A64(M) Leeds, Clay Pit Lane (A58)

Junction	Westbound	Eastbound
with A58	No exit (to Clay Pit Lane)	No access (from Clay Pit Lane)

A66(M) Darlington Spur

Junction	Westbound	Eastbound
with A1(M) (jct 57)	Exit only to A1(M) *(southbound)*	Access only from A1(M) *(northbound)*

A74(M) Gretna - Abington

Junction	Northbound	Southbound
18	Exit only, no access	No exit

A194(M) Newcastle upon Tyne

Junction	Northbound	Southbound
with A1(M) (jct 65)	Access only from A1(M) *(northbound)*	Exit only to A1(M) *(southbound)*

A12 M25 - Ipswich

Junction	Northeastbound	Southwestbound
13	Access only, no exit	No restriction
14	Exit only, no access	Access only, no exit
20A	Exit only, no access	Access only, no exit
20B	Access only, no exit	Exit only, no access
21	No restriction	Access only, no exit
23	Exit only, no access	Access only, no exit
24	Access only, no exit	Exit only, no access
27	Exit only, no access	Access only, no exit
Dedham & Stratford St Mary (unnumbered)	Exit only	Access only

A14 M1 - Felixstowe

Junction	Westbound	Eastbound
with M1/M6 (jct19)	Exit only to M6 and M1 *(northbound)*	Access only from M6 and M1 *(southbound)*
4	Exit only, no access	Access only, no exit
31	Exit only to M11 *(for London)*	Access only, no exit
31A	Exit only to A14 *(northbound)*	Access only, no exit
34	Access only, no exit	Exit only, no access
36	Exit only to A11, access only from A1303	Access only from A11
38	Access only from A11	Exit only to A11
39	Exit only, no access	Access only, no exit
61	Access only, no exit	Exit only, no access

A55 Holyhead - Chester

Junction	Westbound	Eastbound
8A	Exit only, no access	Access only, no exit
23A	Access only, no exit	Exit only, no access
24A	Exit only, no access	No access or exit
27A	No restriction	No access or exit
33A	Exit only, no access	No access or exit
33B	Exit only, no access	Access only, no exit
36A	Exit only to A5104	Access only from A5104

Smart motorways

Since Britain's first motorway (the Preston Bypass) opened in 1958, motorways have changed significantly. A vast increase in car journeys over the last 60 years has meant that motorways quickly filled to capacity. To combat this, the recent development of **smart motorways** uses technology to monitor and actively manage traffic flow and congestion.

Various active traffic management methods are used:

- Traffic flow is monitored using CCTV
- Speed limits are changed to smooth traffic flow and reduce stop-start driving
- Capacity of the motorway can be increased by either temporarily or permanently opening the hard shoulder to traffic
- Warning signs and messages alert drivers to hazards and traffic jams ahead
- Lanes can be closed in the case of an accident or emergency by displaying a red X sign
- Emergency refuge areas are located regularly along the motorway where there is no hard shoulder available

Smart motorways can be classified into three different types as shown below. The table lists smart motorways operating by 2018 and the colour-coded text indicates the type of smart motorway.

CONTROLLED MOTORWAY	Variable speed limits without hard shoulder (the hard shoulder is used in emergencies only)
HARD SHOULDER RUNNING	Variable speed limits with part-time hard shoulder (the hard shoulder is open to traffic at busy times when signs permit)
ALL LANE RUNNING	Variable speed limits with hard shoulder as permanent running lane (there is no hard shoulder); this is standard for all new smart motorway schemes since 2013

SMART MOTORWAY SECTIONS	
M1	J6A–10, J10–13, J25–28, J28–31, J31–32, J32–35A, J39–42
M3	J2–4A
M4	J19–20, J24–28
M5	J4A–6, J15–17
M6	J4–10A, J10A–13
M9	J1–1A
M20	J4–7
M25	J2–3, J5–6, J6–23, J23–27, J27–30
M42	J3A–7, J7–9
M60	J8–18
M62	J18–20, J25–26, J26–28, J28–29, J29–30
M90	M9 J1A–M90 J3

Quick tips

- Never drive in a lane closed by a red X

- Keep to the speed limit shown on the gantries
- A solid white line indicates the hard shoulder – do not drive in it unless directed
- A broken white line indicates a normal running lane
- Exit the smart motorway where possible if your vehicle is in difficulty. In an emergency, move onto the hard shoulder where there is one, or the nearest emergency refuge area
- Put on your hazard lights if you break down

M4	Motorway with number
T4 Toll Toll	Toll motorway with toll station
3	Restricted motorway junctions
S Fleet	Motorway service area
	Motorway and junction under construction
A3	Primary route single/dual carriageway
1	Primary route junction with and without number
3	Restricted primary route junctions
S	Primary route service area
BATH	Primary route destination
A1123	Other A road single/dual carriageway
B2070	B road single/dual carriageway
	Minor road, more than 4 metres wide, less than 4 metres wide
	Roundabout
	Interchange/junction
	Narrow primary/other A/B road with passing places (Scotland)
	Road under construction/ approved
	Road tunnel
Toll	Road toll, steep gradient (arrows point downhill)
5	Distance in miles between symbols
	Railway line, in tunnel
	Railway station and level crossing
	Tourist railway
628 637 Lecht Summit	Height in metres, mountain pass
or V	Vehicle ferry
	Fast vehicle ferry or catamaran
	Airport, heliport,
F	International freight terminal
H	24-hour Accident & Emergency hospital
C	Crematorium
P+R	Park and Ride (at least 6 days per week)
	City, town, village or other built-up area
	National boundary, county or administrative boundary
	Scenic route
	Tourist Information Centre (all year/seasonal)
	Visitor or heritage centre
	Caravan site (AA inspected)
	Camping site (AA inspected)
	Caravan & camping site (AA inspected)
	Abbey, cathedral or priory
	Ruined abbey, cathedral or priory
	Castle, historic house or building
M	Museum or art gallery
	Industrial interest
	Aqueduct or viaduct
	Garden, arboretum
	Vineyard, Brewery or distillery
	Country park, theme park
	Agricultural showground
	Farm or animal centre
	Zoological or wildlife collection
	Bird collection, aquarium
RSPB	RSPB site
	National Nature Reserve (England, Scotland, Wales)
	Local nature reserve
	Wildlife Trust reserve
	Forest drive
	National trail
	Picnic site
	Waterfall
	Viewpoint
	Hill-fort
	Prehistoric monument, Roman antiquity
1066	Battle site with year
	Steam railway centre
	Cave
	Windmill, monument
	Beach (award winning)
	Lighthouse
	Golf course (AA listed)
	Football stadium
	County cricket ground
	Rugby Union national stadium
	International athletics stadium
	Horse racing, show jumping
	Air show venue, motor-racing circuit
	Ski slope (natural, artificial)
	National Trust property (England & Wales, Scotland)
	English Heritage site
	Historic Scotland site
	Cadw (Welsh heritage) site
	Major shopping centre, other place of interest
	Attraction within urban area
	World Heritage Site (UNESCO)
	National Park and National Scenic Area (Scotland)
	Forest Park
	Heritage coast

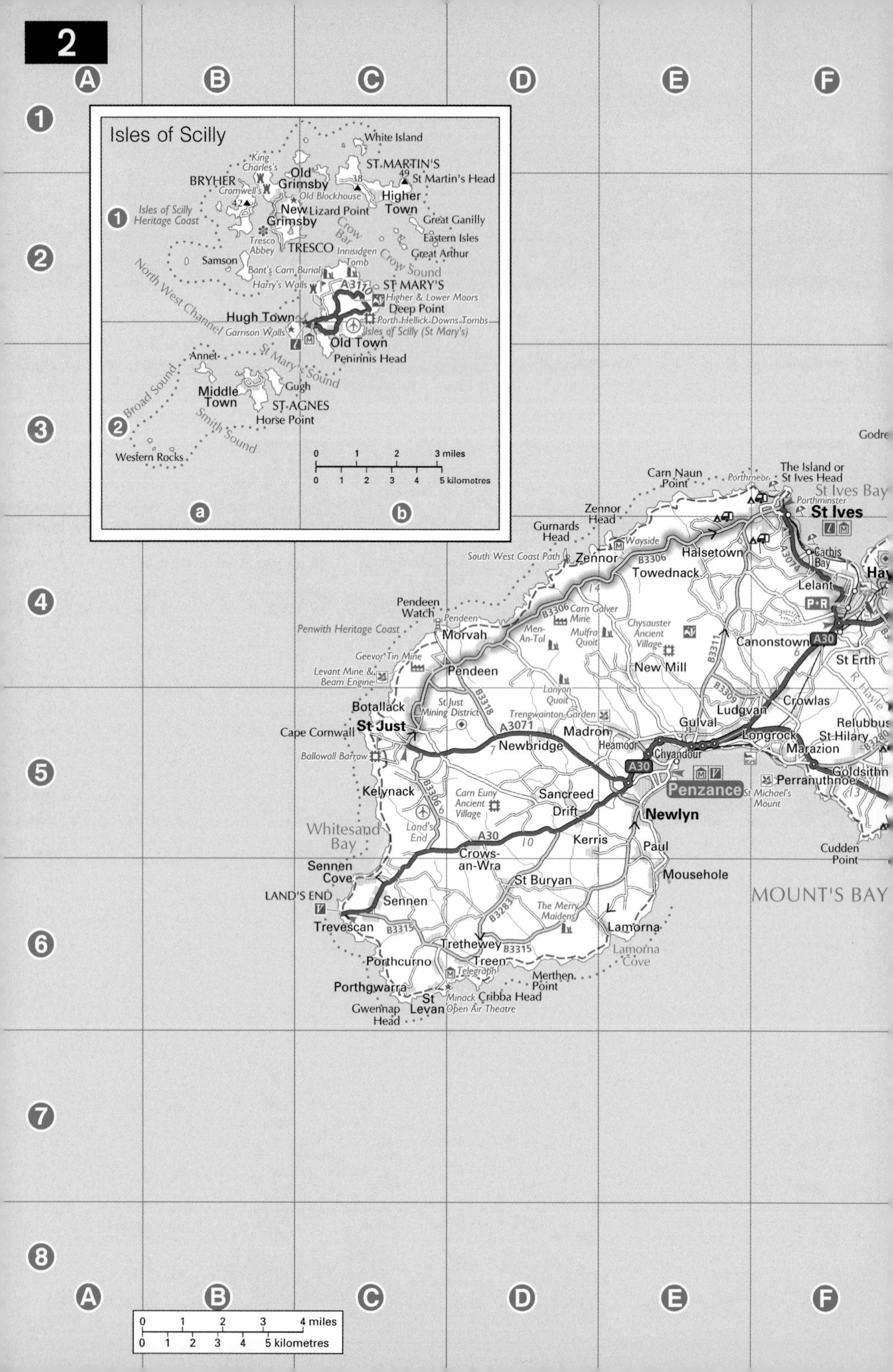
Isles of Scilly
White Island
ST MARTIN'S
St Martin's Head
King Charles's
BRYHER
Cromwell's
Old Grimsby
Old Blockhouse
Higher Town
New Grimsby
Lizard Point
Isles of Scilly Heritage Coast
Great Ganilly
Eastern Isles
Tresco Abbey
TRESCO
Crow Bar
Innisidgen Tomb
Great Arthur
Samson
Bant's Carn Burial
Crow Sound
Harry's Walls
A3110
ST MARY'S
Higher & Lower Moors
North West Channel
Deep Point
Hugh Town
Porth Hellick Downs Tombs
Garrison Walls
Isles of Scilly (St Mary's)
Old Town
Peninnis Head
Annet
St Mary's Sound
Broad Sound
Gugh
Middle Town
ST AGNES
Horse Point
Smith Sound
Western Rocks
0 1 2 3 miles
0 1 2 3 4 5 kilometres
Godre
Carn Naun Point
Porthmeor
The Island or St Ives Head
St Ives Bay
Porthminster
St Ives
Zennor Head
Gurnards Head
Wayside
Halsetown
Carbis Bay
South West Coast Path
Zennor
B3306
Towednack
A3074
Hay
Lelant
P+R
Pendeen Watch
Carn Galver Mine
Pendeen
Penwith Heritage Coast
Men-An-Tol
Mulfra Quoit
Chysauster Ancient Village
Morvah
B3311
Canonstown
A30
St Erth
Geevor Tin Mine
New Mill
Levant Mine & Beam Engine
Pendeen
R Hayle
B3309
Lanyon Quoit
B3318
Crowlas
Botallack
St Just Mining District
Trengwainton Garden
Ludgvan
Gulval
Relubbus
St Just
A3071
Madron
Longrock
St Hilary
Cape Cornwall
Newbridge
Heamoor
Chyandour
Marazion
B3280
Ballowall Barrow
Goldsithney
Penzance
Perranuthnoe
St Michael's Mount
Kelynack
Carn Euny Ancient Village
Sancreed
B3306
Drift
Newlyn
Land's End
Whitesand Bay
A30
Kerris
Paul
Cudden Point
Crows-an-Wra
Sennen Cove
Mousehole
St Buryan
MOUNT'S BAY
LAND'S END
Sennen
B3283
The Merry Maidens
Trevescan
B3315
Lamorna
Trethewey
B3315
Lamorna Cove
Porthcurno
Treen
Telegraph
Merthen Point
Porthgwarra
St Levan
Minack Open Air Theatre
Cribba Head
Gwennap Head
0 1 2 3 4 miles
0 1 2 3 4 5 kilometres

Ligger or Perran Bay
Rose
Perranporth
Cligga Point
Bolingey
Goonhavern
St Newlyn East
Lappa Valley
Enodoc
Summercourt
Scarcewater
Fiddlers Green
Mitchell
St Agnes Heritage Coast
Trevellas Downs
ST AGNES HEAD
St Agnes
Perranzabuloe
Penhallow
Zelah
St Allen
Ladock
Mithian
Callestick
Barkla Shop
Trispen
Wheal Coates
Goonvrea
Goonbell
St Erme
St Agnes Mining District
Mount Hawke
Porthtowan
Shortlanesend
Idless
Probus
Tresillian
South West Coast Path
Mawla
Cambrose
Wheal Peevor
Portreath
Godrevy-Portreath Heritage Coast
Blackwater
Threemilestone
Kenwyn
Truro
Illogan
Chacewater
Navax Point
Scorrier
Higher Town
St Clement
Tehidy
South Tehidy
Mount Ambrose
Gwennap Mining District
Malpas
Kea
St Michael Penkevil
Ruan Lanihorne
St Day
Reskadinnick
East Pool Mine
Redruth
Twelveheads
Playing Place
Lamorran
Pool
Tuckingmill
Carn Brea
Carharrack
Bissoe
Carnon Downs
Kehelland
Trelissick Garden
Carn Brea
Carnkie
Philleigh
Camborne
Devoran
Lanner
Gwennap
Perranwell
Connor Downs
Penponds
Perranarworthal
Angarrack
Barripper
Troon
Four Lanes
Penhalvean
Kennall Vale
Devoran & Perran
Feock
Carnhell Green
Gwinear
Trewithian
Realwa
Ponsanooth
Mylor Bridge
Gerrans Bay
St Erth Praze
Stithians
St Just-in-Roseland
Praze-an-Beeble
Portscatho
Carrick Roads
Mylor
Gerrans
Carnkie
Longdowns
Mabe Burnthouse
Penryn
Flushing
Leedstown
Crowan
Porkellis
Rame
Greeb Point
Godolphin House
Pendennis Castle
Castle
St Mawes
Budock Water
Argal & College Water Park
Pendennis Point
Wendron Mining District
Bohortha
Godolphin Cross
Trenear
Poldark Mine
Treverva
Falmouth
Prospidnick
Wendron
Trescowe
Seworgan
South West Coast Path
ZONE POINT
Carleen
Crowntown
Helston Heritage Railway
Penjerrick
Gyllyngvase
Coverack Bridges
Brill
Falmouth Bay
Sithney
Ashton
Breage
Constantine
Mawnan Smith
Trebah
Carwinion
ROSEMULLION HEAD
Porth Navas
Helston
Gweek
Glendurgan Garden
Helford Passage
Durgan
Mawnan
Trewavas Mining District
Trewavas Head
Seal Sanctuary
Helford River
Flambards
Helford
Porthleven
St Anthony
Mawgan
Manaccan
Nare Point
Garras
St Martin
Halliggye Fogou
Gunwalloe
Porthallow
White Cross
Porthoustock
Manacle Point
Cury
St Keverne
The Lizard
Poldhu Point
Marconi Memorial
GOONHILLY DOWNS
Lowland Point
Mullion Cove
Mullion
Mullion Island
Coverack
Ruan Major
Kuggar
Predannack Head
Black Head
South West Coast Path
Vellan Head
Ruan Minor
The Lizard
Cadgwith
The Lizard Heritage Coast
Devil's Frying Pan
Lizard Head
Kynance Cove
Church Cove
Lizard
Bass Point
LIZARD POINT
Lizard Lighthouse & Heritage Centre
A30
A39
A390
A393
A394
A3083
A3075
A3076
A3078
A3047
B3284
B3285
B3277
B3300
B3301
B3297
B3298
B3303
B3280
B3302
B3304
B3293
B3296
B3294
B3289
B3275
G
H
J
K
L
M
1
2
3
4
5
6
7
8

A
B
C
8
D
E
F
1
2
3
4
5
6
7
8
Rumps Point
Port Quin Bay
Kelland Head
Varley Head
Pentire Point
Padstow Bay
Port Quin
Port Isaac
Bee Centre
Hayle Bay
Polzeath
Trelights
Stepper Point
Trebetherick
B3314
St Endellion
St Minver
Trevose Head Heritage Coast
Gunver Head
TREVOSE HEAD
Mother Ivey's Bay
Harlyn Bay
Dinas Head
Prideaux Place
Rock
Constantine Bay
Harlyn
Trevone
Padstow
Windmill
Chapel Amble
St Merryn
A389
B3276
Porthcothan
St Issey
Wadebridge
St Breock
Little Petherick
Royal Cornwall
Park Head
Penrose
Rumford
Trenance
St Ervan
St Jidgey
Burlawn
Bedruthan Steps
St Eval
Crealy Great Adventure Park
St Breock Downs Monolith
Trenance
Nine Maidens
B3274
Berryls Point
Mawgan Porth
A39
Ruthernbridge
Griffins Point
Trevarrian
Vale of Mawgan
St Mawgan
Talskiddy
Rosenannon
Watergate Bay
St Wenn
Withiel
Cornwall Newquay
Towan Head
Newquay Bay
St Columb Minor
A3059
St Columb Major
Tregonetha
Newquay
Porth
Castle-an-Dinas
Fistral Bay
Victoria
A3058
West Pentire
Colan
Kelsey Head
Pentire
Mountjoy
A30
Ruthvoes
Holywell Bay
Crantock
Lane
Quintrell Downs
A392
Goss Moor
Roche
St Columb Road
Indian Queens
Penhale Point
Tresean
Kestle Mill
B3279
Holywell
Treveal
Dairyland Farm World
Fraddon
Bugle
Ligger Point
Trerice
Cubert
A3058
Whitemoor
St Newlyn East
St Dennis
Ligger or Perran Bay
Lappa Valley
St Enoder
A30
Stenalees
Carthew
Summercourt
Nanpean
Treviscoe
Wheal Martyn
A3076
Rose
Fiddlers Green
A3075
Scarcewater
Foxhole
Perranporth
Mitchell
B3285
Cligga Point
Goonhavern
A3058
High Street
St Austell
Bolingey
St Stephen
Trewoon
St Agnes Heritage Coast
Trevellas Downs
B3285
ST AGNES HEAD
Perranzabuloe
Zelah
A39
Penhallow
St Allen
Coombe
St Agnes
Mithian
Callestick
Trispen
Ladock
Polgooth
Wheal Coates
Barkla Shop
Grampound Road
Goonvrea
Goonbell
St Erme
B3275
Sticker
St Agnes Mining District
Hewas Water
B3277
Porthtowan
Mount Hawke
B3284
Probus
A390
Idless
Shortlanesend
Trewithen
Grampound
Creed
Lost Gardens of Heligan
Mawla
P+R
Tresillian
Cambrose
River Fal
B3287
St Ewe
Wheal Peevor
Blackwater
A390
Threemilestone
Kestle
B3300
Kenwyn
Truro
Polmassick
Chacewater
A30
Higher Town
Tregony
Scorrier
St Clement
Gwennap Mining District
Mount Ambrose
Kea
Malpas
East Pool Mine
St Day
3
St Michael Penkevil
Ruan Lanihorne
A3078
St Michael Caerhays
Caerhays Castle
Redruth
Twelveheads
Lamorran
Carn Brea
Carharrack
B3298
Playing Place
Bissoe
Carnon Downs
Boswinger
Gwennap
Trelissick Garden
Carnkie
Devoran
Philleigh
Camborne
Lanner
A393
Perranwell
Veryan Bay
B3297
Perranarworthal
A39
Veryan
Portloe
Kennall Vale
Devoran & Perran
Feock
B3289
DODMAN POINT
Four Lanes
Penhalvean
The Roseland Heritage Coast
Ponsanooth
Trewithian
Stithians
Mylor Bridge
Gerrans Bay
Nare Head
St Just-in-Roseland
Carrick Roads
Percuil
Portscatho
B3280
B3297
Carnkie
Longdowns
Mylor
Gerrans
Mabe Burnthouse
Penryn
P+R
St Mawes
Rame
A39
Flushing
Greeb Point
Pendennis Castle
Castle
Budock
Wendron Mining District
Poldark Mine
A394
Pendennis Point
Trenear
Bohortha
Falmouth
South West Coast Path
Seworgan
Penjerrick
ZONE
0 1 2 3 4 miles
0 1 2 3 4 5 kilometres

BODMIN MOOR
Trewalder
Helstone
Altarnun
Wesley Cottage
Trewint
Polyphant
St Teath
Treveighan
8
BROWN WILLY
419
346
347
Michaelstow
Churchtown
St Breward
De Lank River
Jamaica Inn
Bolventor
Illand
Trebullett
Lezant
St Tudy
St Kew Highway
North Hill
Coad's Green
Treburley
Middlewood
Bathpool
Bray Shop
Kingston
SMALLACOMBE DOWNS
River Fowey
Caradon Mining District
Henwood
Upton
Rilla Mill
Linkinhorne
Stoke Climsland
South Hill
St Mabyn
Blisland
Colliford Lake
Temple
Colliford Lake Park
BROWNGELLY DOWNS
Cheesewring
The Hurlers Stone Circles
Minions
Sterts Open-Air Theatre
Sibleyback Lake
Pencarrow House
Washaway
Helland
Golberdon
Pensilva
Callington
Frogwell
Common Moor
Darite
Warleggan
Cardinham
Mount
St Neot
Golitha Falls
King Doniert's Stone
Trethevy Quoit
Tremar
St Cleer
St Ive
Merrymeet
Cadson Bury
Bodmin
Lanivet
Bodmin & Wenford Railway
Carnglaze Caverns
Dobwalls
Liskeard
Moorswater
Trevelmond
West Taphouse
East Taphouse
St Pinnock
Quethiock
Pillaton
Menheniot
R Tiddy
9
Lanhydrock
Sweetshouse
Restormel Castle
Lockengate
Helman Tor
Bodwen
1643
Herodsfoot
St Keyne
Tideford
Lostwithiel
Lanlivery
Porfell Wildlife Park
Duloe
Widegates
Budge's Shop
St Erney
Luxulyan
Luxulyan Valley
Trerulefoot
Lerryn
Muchlarnick
Sandplace
Hessenford
Polbathic
Penwithick
Trethurgy
Lanreath
R Fowey
St Blazey
Eden Project
Tywardreath
Golant
St Veep
Penpoll
Pelynt
St Martin
Monkey Sanctuary
Seaton Valley
Sheviock
Par
Lanteglos Highway
Seaton
Downderry
Portwrinkle
Bodinnick
Looe
Looe Bay
Polkerris
Fowey
Crumplehorn
Model Village
Porthallow
Charlestown
Porthpean
Lansallos
St Catherine's Castle
Polruan
Polperro
Talland Bay
Looe or St George's Island
St Austell Bay
Lantic Bay
Pencarrow Head
Lantivet Bay
South West Coast Path
Gribbin Head - Polperro Heritage Coast
Apprentice
GRIBBIN HEAD
Black Head
Chapel Point
A30
A39
A388
A389
A38
A390
A391
A387
A3082
B3314
B3267
B3266
B3268
B3269
B3257
B3254
B3251
B3252
B3253
B3359
B3247
B3249
G
H
J
K
L
M
1
2
3
4
5
6
7
8

Lawhitton
Meadwell
Kelly
Chillaton
North Brentor
Bradstone
Milton Abbot
DARTMOOR
FOREST
517
501 COCKS HILL
539 GREAT MIS TOR
442 COXTOR
9
10
Lezant
Trekenner
Dunterton
Chaddlehanger
Mary Tavy
Cudliptown
Treburley
Rezare
Bealsmill
Lamerton
Peter Tavy
Wistman's Wood
A388
Kingston
Sydenham Damerel
Bray Shop
Horsebridge
B3357
B3362
Tavistock
Stoke Climsland
Oldmill
Latchley
Merrivale Prehistoric Settlement
Princetown
West Dart River
406 ROYAL HILL
Hexworthy
South Hill
Luckett
Downgate
Chilsworthy
A390
Gulworthy
Sampford Spiney
Whitchurch
B3212
347
Kit Hill
B3267
St Ann's Chapel
Gunnislake
River Tavy
R Meavy
Golberdon
Harrowbarrow
Dupath Well
Albaston
Morwellham Quay
Horrabridge
Walkhampton
Callington
Metherell
Cotehele House
Calstock
Calstock Viaduct
The Garden House
Burrator Reservoir
Frogwell
St Dominick
B3257
Buckland Monachorum
Dousland
Yelverton
Sheepstor
DARTMOOR
Cadson Bury
Buckland Abbey
Meavy
R Plym
St Mellion
TamarValley Mining District
Bere Alston
Milton Combe
Upper Plym Valley
480
Sowton
Clearbrook
NATIONAL
Quethiock
St Mellion
Cotts
Weir Quay
Pillaton
A388
Maristow
Dewerstone
471 SHELL TOP
5
Bere Ferrers
Cargreen
A386
Shaugh Prior
Hatt
River Tamar
PARK
R Tiddy
Landulph
Tamerton Foliot
Roborough
Bickleigh
R Erme
Botusfleming
Carkeel
Plymouth
P+R
Saltash
B3373
B3432
Boringdon
Tideford
A38
Landrake
Dartmoor Zoological Park
Lutton
Harford
Trematon
Toll
Crownhill
Cornwood
BUTTERDON HILL
St Erney
Saltash
South Pill
PLYMOUTH
B3417
Hemerdon
Sparkwell
Trerulefoot
B3249
Trehan
St Stephens
St Budeaux
Eggbuckland
Bittaford
St Germans
Churchtown Farm Community
Antony House
A3064
B3396
Venton
Ivybridge
Woodland
Polbathic
Plympton
B3214
Saltram House
A379
A38
Lee Mill
Sheviock
A374
Antony
Torpoint
Devonport
A374
Crafthole
B3247
St John
St John's Lake
Stonehouse
Cremyll
Smeaton's Tower
Mountbatten Centre
Elburton
Westlake
Ermington
Portwrinkle
Plymstock
Brixton
Worston
River Yealm
Modbury
Whitsand Bay
Freathy
Millbrook
South West Coast Path
B3247
Mount Edgcumbe
The Sound
Hooe
Spriddlestone
Yealmpton
12
Dunstone
River Erme
Kingsand
Staddiscombe
Cawsand
Cawsand Bay
Down Thomas
West Wembury
B3186
Holbeton
Rame
Heybrook Bay
Wembury
Newton Ferrers
Penlee Point
RAME HEAD
Bridgend
Rame Head Heritage Coast
Wembury Bay
Gara Point
Noss Mayo
Mothecombe
Kingston
Erme Mouth
Ringmore
Stoke Point
Beacon Point
Bigbury-on-Sea
Burgh Island
Santander (Apr-Oct)
Roscoff St-Malo (Nov-Mar)
Bigbury Bay
A
B
C
D
E
F
1
2
3
4
5
6
7
8
0 1 2 3 4 miles
0 1 2 3 4 5 kilometres

G
H
J
K
L
M
1
2
3
4
5
6
7
8
11
12
Grimspound
Manaton
Water
Becky Falls
Lustleigh
Hennock
Canonteign Falls
Trusham
Harcombe
Chudleigh
Southcott
Hound Tor Medieval Village
Bovey Tracey
HAYTOR 454
Haytor Vale
Widecombe in the Moor
Dunstone
The Church House
477 RIPPON TOR
Ilsington
Liverton
Chudleigh Knighton
Brimley
Coldeast
Halford
Ugbrooke Park
Ideford
Luton
Ashcombe
Cockwood
Model Railway
Dawlish Warren
Dawlish
Stover
Sandygate
Preston
Teigngrace
Kingsteignton
Bishopsteignton
Coombe
Holcombe
Teignmouth
Ponsworthy
Buckland in the Moor
Lower Town
Poundsgate
Bickington
Highweek
Newton Abbot
Bradley Manor
Netherton
Coombe Cellars
Ringmore
Shaldon
Combeinteignhead
Stokeinteignhead
Middle Rocombe
Lower Gabwell
Higher Gabwell
Maidencombe
Holne
River Dart
Hembury Castle
Ashburton
Woodland
West Ogwell
East Ogwell
Denbury
Wildlife Hospital
Abbotskerswell
Decoy
Kingskerswell
Coffinswell
Daccombe
Barton
Coombe Pafford
Model Village
Babbacombe Bay
Oddicombe
St Marychurch
Babbacombe
Ellacombe
TORQUAY
Buckfast
Buckfastleigh
Forder Green
Devon Distillery
Torbryan
Ipplepen
Woolston Green
Broadhempston
Staverton
Combe Fishacre
Compton Castle
Compton
Shiphay
Cockington
Butterfly Farm & Otter Sanctuary
South Devon Railway
Deancombe
Dean
Dean Prior
Pennywell Farm
Dartington
Littlehempston
Marldon
Hollicombe
Preston
Rockend
Meadfoot
Hopes Nose
Harbourneford
Rattery
Cott
Berry Pomeroy
Berry Pomeroy Castle
Westerland
Lutton
Totnes Castle
Tigley
Blagdon
Paignton
Tor Bay
Totnes
Longcombe
Collaton St Mary
Belsford
Harberton
Aish
Yalberton
Goodrington
Brixham
Breakwater
Sharpham
Avonwick
Diptford
Luscombe
Ashprington
Stoke Gabriel
Waddeton
Galmpton
Harbour
BERRY HEAD
North Huish
Harbertonford
Tuckenhay
Cornworthy
Dittisham
Churston Ferrers
St Mary Bay
Ugborough
Washbourne
East Cornworthy
Greenway
Higher Brixham
Sharkham Point
Curtisknowle
Allaleigh
Halwell
Capton
Paignton & Dartmouth Railway
Moreleigh
Woodlands
Dartmouth
Coleton Fishacre
Scabbacombe Head
Blackawton
Kingswear
Bayard's Cove Fort
Dartmouth Castle
Warfleet
Woodleigh
Loddiswell
Stoke Fleming
Aveton Gifford
East Allington
Blackpool
Blackpool Sands
Churchstow
Goveton
Strete
South Devon Heritage Coast
Buckland-Tout-Saints
Harleston
Slapton
Kingsbridge
Sherford
Frittiscombe
Start Bay
Upton
East Charleton
Chillington
South Milton
West Alvington
West Charleton
Stokenham
Frogmore
Torcross
Sutton
Kingsbridge Estuary
South Pool
Beeson
Beesands
Malborough
Salcombe
Chivelstone
Kellaton
Collaton
East Portlemouth
South Allington
South West Coast Path
Overbeck's House
Rickham
Start Point
Bolt Head
East Prawle
Prawle Point
A38
A380
A381
A383
A384
A385
A379
A3022
A3122
B3387
B3344
B3193
B3192
B3196
B3205
B3060

A
B
C
D
E
F
1
2
3
4
5
6
7
8
Higher Sha
Lower Sha
Bude
Bay
Dizzard Point
St
Gennys
Crackington Haven
Cambeak
Co
Sweets
Wai
Co
B3263
15
Marsh
Witchcraft
Pentire Point - Widemouth
Heritage Coast
Boscastle
Tresparrett
Lesnewth
Otte
Trevalga
B3263
Castle
TINTAGEL HEAD
Tintagel
Trethevey
B3266
Bossiney
B3262
Old Post Office
Davidstow
Penhallic Point
Treknow
Trewarmett
Tremail
B3314
B3266
South West Coast Path
Delabole
Pengelly
Westdowns
Camelford
Crowdy
Reservoir
Port Isaac
Bay
Rumps
Point
Kelland
Head
Varley
Head
Lanteglos
Trewalder
Port Quin
Bay
Helstone
B3314
Pentire Point
Port
Quin
Port
Isaac
Port Gaverne
B3267
St Teath
Padstow Bay
Long
Cross
B3267
419
BROWN
WILLY
Bee Centre
Hayle Bay
Trelights
Pendoggett
Treveighan
Polzeath
Michaelstow
Trevose
Heritage Coast
4
B3314
St Minver
St Endellion
A39
Churchtown
TREVOSE HEAD
Mother Ivey's Bay
Trequite
St
Tudy
De Lank River
Jamaica
Dinas
Head
St Kew
St Kew
Highway
St Breward
0 1 2 3 4 miles
0 1 2 3 4 5 kilometres

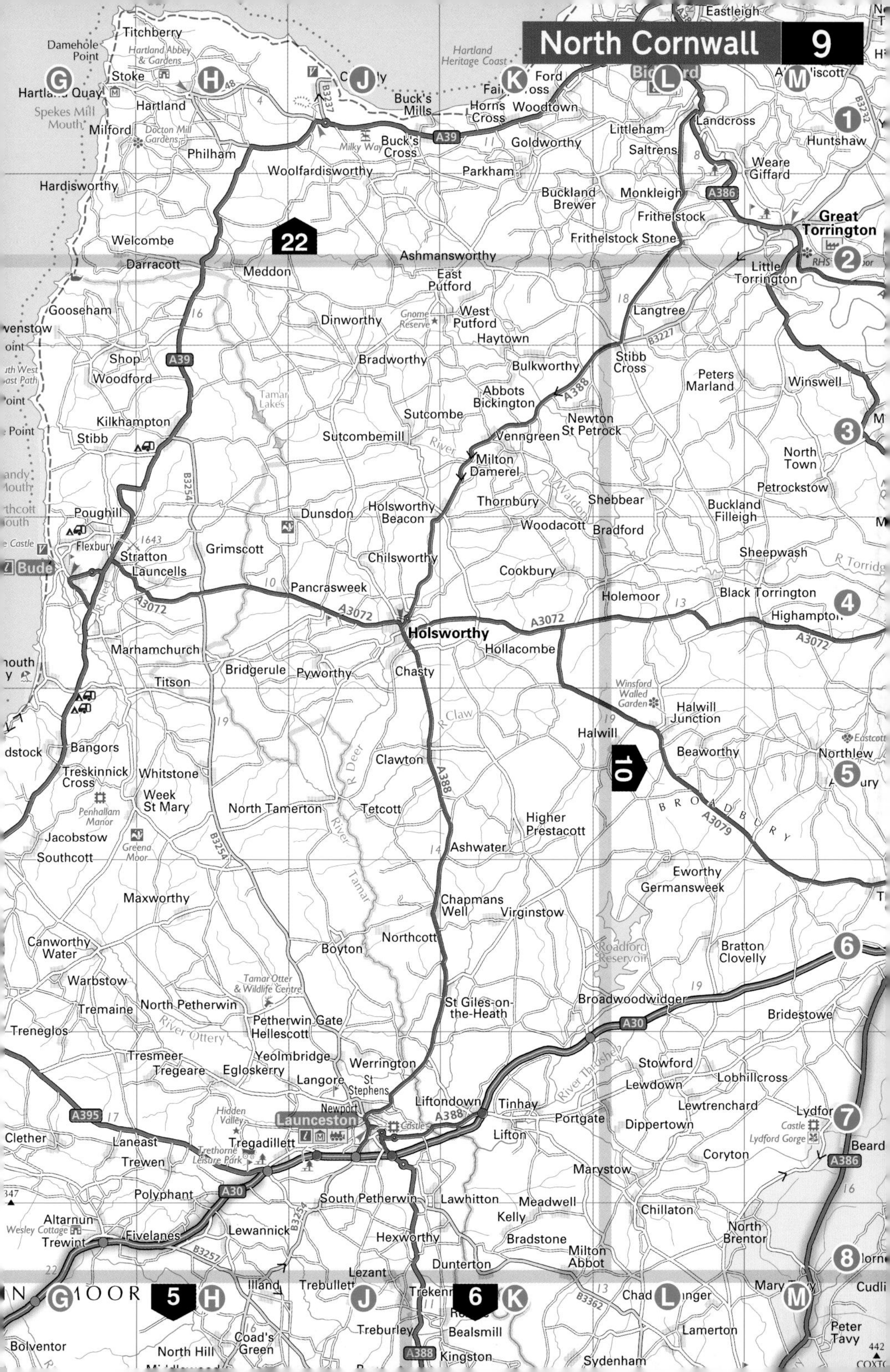
Eastleigh
Titchberry
Damehole Point
Hartland Abbey & Gardens
Stoke
Hartland Quay
Hartland
Spekes Mill Mouth
Milford
Docton Mill Gardens
Philham
Hartland Heritage Coast
Buck's Mills
Horns Cross
Woodtown
Ford
Buck's Cross
Milky Way
A39
Goldworthy
Littleham
Landcross
Huntshaw
Saltrens
Weare Giffard
Woolfardisworthy
Parkham
Hardisworthy
Buckland Brewer
Monkleigh
A386
Frithelstock
Great Torrington
Welcombe
Frithelstock Stone
22
Ashmansworthy
Darracott
Meddon
East Putford
Little Torrington
Gooseham
Dinworthy
Gnome Reserve
West Putford
Langtree
Haytown
B3227
Shop
A39
Bradworthy
Bulkworthy
Stibb Cross
Peters Marland
Woodford
Tamar Lakes
Abbots Bickington
A388
Winswell
Kilkhampton
Sutcombe
Newton St Petrock
Stibb
Sutcombemill
Venngreen
River
Milton Damerel
North Town
B3254
Thornbury
Shebbear
Petrockstow
Poughill
Holsworthy Beacon
Dunsdon
Buckland Filleigh
Flexbury
Woodacott
Bradford
Stratton
Grimscott
Chilsworthy
Sheepwash
Bude
Launcells
Cookbury
Pancrasweek
Holemoor
Black Torrington
A3072
Highampton
Holsworthy
Hollacombe
Marhamchurch
Bridgerule
Pyworthy
Chasty
Titson
Winsford Walled Garden
Halwill Junction
R Claw
Halwill
Bangors
R Deer
Beaworthy
Northlew
Treskinnick Cross
Whitstone
Clawton
10
Week St Mary
Penhallam Manor
North Tamerton
Tetcott
Higher Prestacott
BROADBURY
A3079
Jacobstow
Greena Moor
River
Southcott
Ashwater
Eworthy
Germansweek
Maxworthy
Tamar
Chapmans Well
Virginstow
Canworthy Water
Northcott
Boyton
Roadford Reservoir
Bratton Clovelly
Warbstow
Tamar Otter & Wildlife Centre
Broadwoodwidger
North Petherwin
St Giles-on-the-Heath
Bridestowe
Tremaine
Treneglos
Petherwin Gate
Hellescott
River Ottery
A30
Tresmeer
Yeolmbridge
Werrington
Stowford
River Thrushel
Tregeare
Egloskerry
Langore
St Stephens
Lobhillcross
Lewdown
Liftondown
Tinhay
Lewtrenchard
A395
Hidden Valley
Newport
Launceston
Castle
A388
Portgate
Dippertown
Castle
Lydford Gorge
Clether
Laneast
Tregadillett
Trethorne Leisure Park
Lifton
Beard
Trewen
Coryton
A386
Marystow
Polyphant
A30
South Petherwin
Lawhitton
Meadwell
Kelly
Chillaton
Altarnun
Wesley Cottage
Trewint
Fivelanes
Lewannick
B3254
Hexworthy
Bradstone
North Brentor
B3257
Milton Abbot
Lezant
Dunterton
Illand
Trebullett
Trekenner
Chaddlehanger
Mary Tavy
Cudli
B3362
5
6
Treburley
Bealsmill
Lamerton
Peter Tavy
Coad's Green
Bolventor
North Hill
A388
Kingston
Sydenham

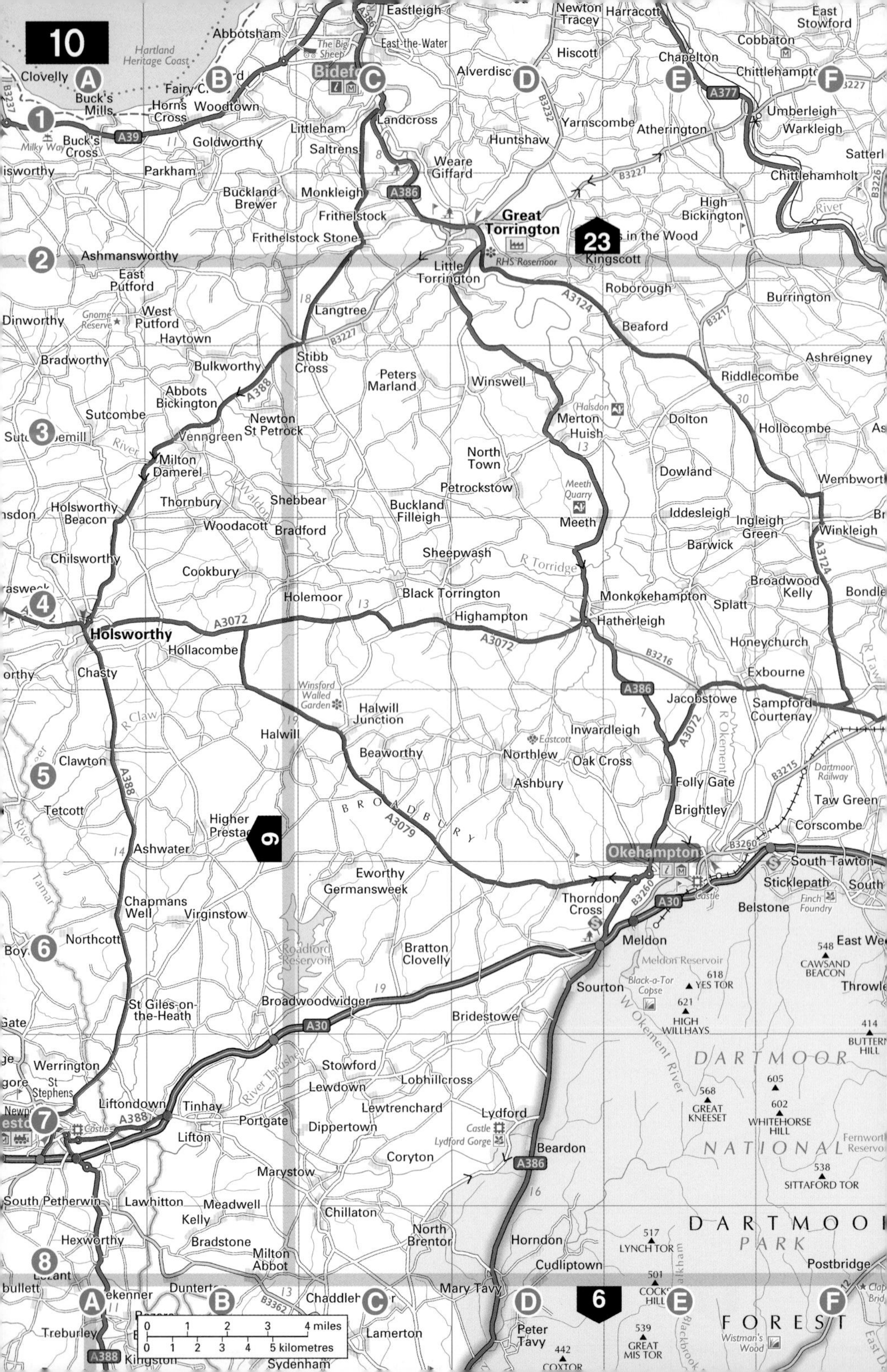
Hartland Heritage Coast
Clovelly
Buck's Mills
Abbotsham
Fairy Cross
Horns Cross
Woodtown
Milky Way
Buck's Cross
A39
B3237
Goldworthy
Parkham
Eastleigh
The Big Sheep
East-the-Water
Bideford
Landcross
Littleham
Saltrens
Monkleigh
Buckland Brewer
Frithelstock
Frithelstock Stone
Newton Tracey
Harracott
Hiscott
Alverdiscott
B3232
Yarnscombe
Huntshaw
Weare Giffard
A386
Great Torrington
RHS Rosemoor
Little Torrington
East Stowford
Cobbaton
Chapelton
Chittlehampton
A377
B3227
Umberleigh
Warkleigh
Atherington
Satterleigh
Chittlehamholt
B3226
High Bickington
River Taw
23
Kingscott
Roborough
Burrington
Ashmansworthy
East Putford
West Putford
Gnome Reserve
Dinworthy
Haytown
Langtree
Stibb Cross
B3227
Bradworthy
Bulkworthy
Abbots Bickington
A388
Peters Marland
Winswell
A3124
Beaford
B3217
Ashreigney
Riddlecombe
Sutcombe
Sutcombemill
Newton St Petrock
Venngreen
River Waldon
Milton Damerel
Thornbury
Shebbear
Halsdon
Merton
Huish
North Town
Petrockstow
Meeth Quarry
Meeth
Dolton
Hollocombe
Dowland
Wembworthy
Holsworthy Beacon
Woodacott
Bradford
Buckland Filleigh
Iddesleigh
Ingleigh Green
Winkleigh
Barwick
Chilsworthy
Sheepwash
R Torridge
Cookbury
Broadwood Kelly
Holemoor
Black Torrington
Monkokehampton
Splatt
Bondleigh
Holsworthy
A3072
Highampton
Hatherleigh
Hollacombe
Honeychurch
B3216
Chasty
Exbourne
A386
Winsford Walled Garden
Halwill Junction
Jacobstowe
Sampford Courtenay
R Claw
Halwill
Beaworthy
Eastcott
Inwardleigh
R Okement
Clawton
Northlew
Oak Cross
Ashbury
Folly Gate
B3215
Dartmoor Railway
Tetcott
BROADBURY
A3079
Brightley
Taw Green
Higher Prestacott
6
Corscombe
Ashwater
B3260
Okehampton
South Tawton
Eworthy
Germansweek
Castle
Sticklepath
Thorndon Cross
A30
Finch Foundry
Belstone
Chapmans Well
Virginstow
River Tamar
Northcott
Roadford Reservoir
Bratton Clovelly
Meldon
Meldon Reservoir
548
CAWSAND BEACON
East Week
Sourton
Black-a-Tor Copse
618
YES TOR
621
HIGH WILLHAYS
Throwleigh
St Giles-on-the-Heath
Broadwoodwidger
Bridestowe
W Okement River
414
BUTTERN HILL
Werrington
St Stephens
River Thrushel
Stowford
Lobhillcross
DARTMOOR
Lewdown
Liftondown
Tinhay
605
Lewtrenchard
568
GREAT KNEESET
602
WHITEHORSE HILL
Newport
Lifton
Portgate
Dippertown
Lydford
Castle
Lydford Gorge
Beardon
NATIONAL
Fernworthy Reservoir
Coryton
538
SITTAFORD TOR
Marystow
South Petherwin
Lawhitton
Meadwell
Kelly
Chillaton
North Brentor
DARTMOOR
Hexworthy
Bradstone
Horndon
517
LYNCH TOR
PARK
Lezant
Milton Abbot
Cudliptown
Postbridge
Trebullett
Rezare
Dunterton
Chaddlehanger
Mary Tavy
501
COCKS HILL
Clapper Bridge
Treburley
B3362
Lamerton
Peter Tavy
539
GREAT MIS TOR
Blackbrook
FOREST
Wistman's Wood
East Dart
442
COXTOR
Kingston
Sydenham
A388
0 1 2 3 4 miles
0 1 2 3 4 5 kilometres
1 2 3 4 5 6 7 8
A B C D E F

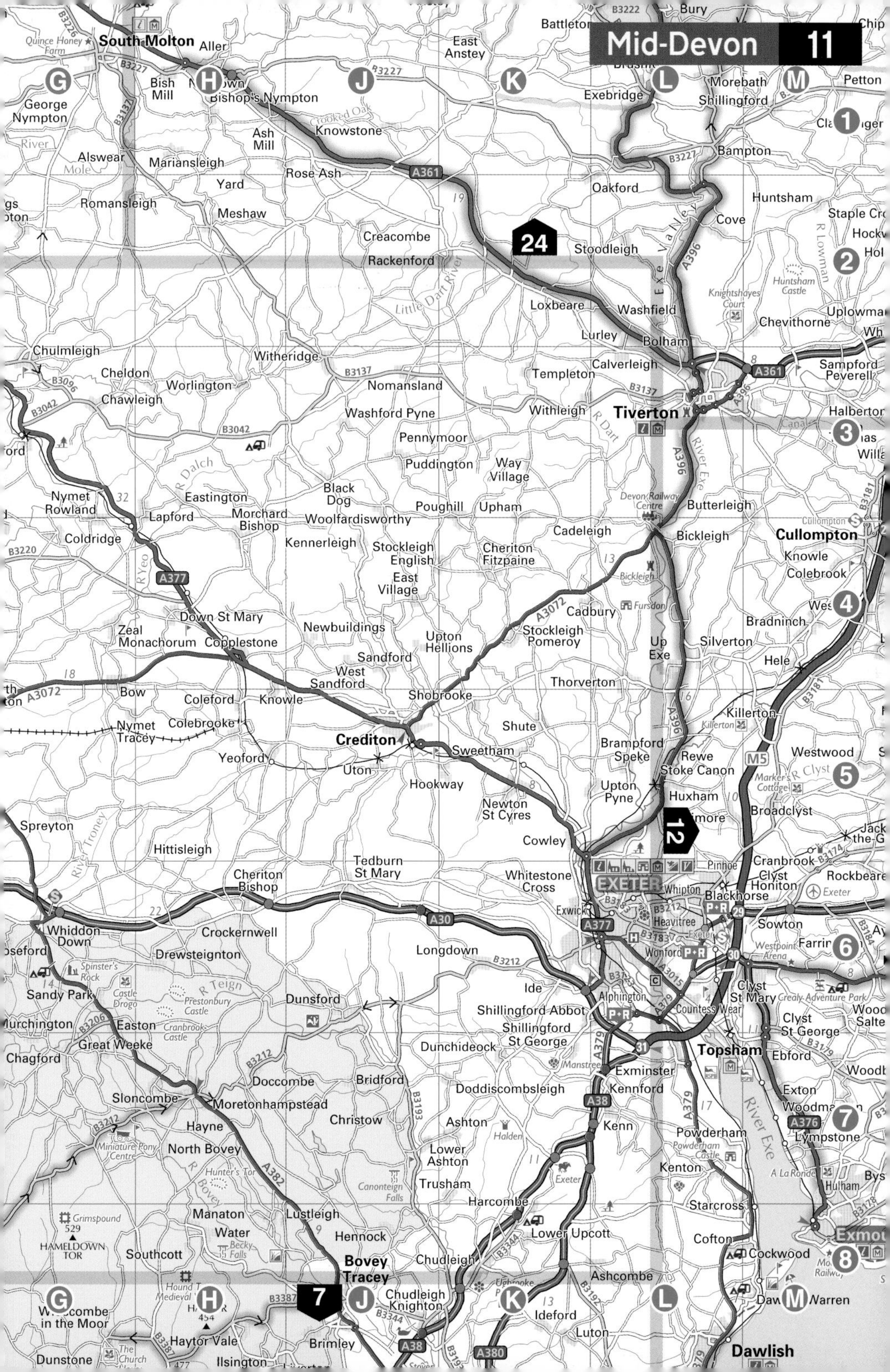
South Molton
Quince Honey Farm
Aller
East Anstey
Battleton
Bury
Bish Mill
Bishop's Nympton
Knowstone
Crooked Oak
Exebridge
Morebath
Shillingford
Petton
George Nympton
Ash Mill
Bampton
Alswear
Mariansleigh
River Mole
Rose Ash
A361
Oakford
Huntsham
Romansleigh
Yard
Meshaw
Cove
Staple Cross
Creacombe
24
Stoodleigh
Hockworthy
Rackenford
Exe Valley
A396
R Lowman
Huntsham Castle
Little Dart River
Loxbeare
Washfield
Knightshayes Court
Chevithorne
Uplowman
Lurley
Bolham
Chulmleigh
Witheridge
Calverleigh
Sampford Peverell
Cheldon
Worlington
B3137
Nomansland
Templeton
Chawleigh
B3096
B3042
Washford Pyne
Withleigh
Tiverton
Halberton
Canal
Pennymoor
R Dart
River Exe
Puddington
Way Village
R Dalch
Nymet Rowland
Eastington
Black Dog
Devon Railway Centre
Butterleigh
Lapford
Morchard Bishop
Poughill
Upham
Woolfardisworthy
Cullompton
Coldridge
Kennerleigh
Stockleigh English
Cheriton Fitzpaine
Cadeleigh
Bickleigh
Knowle
Colebrook
B3220
R Yeo
A377
East Village
A3072
Fursdon
Cadbury
Down St Mary
Bradninch
Zeal Monachorum
Copplestone
Newbuildings
Upton Hellions
Stockleigh Pomeroy
Up Exe
Silverton
Sandford
Hele
West Sandford
Thorverton
Bow
Coleford
Knowle
Shobrooke
Killerton
Nymet Tracey
Colebrooke
Crediton
Shute
Brampford Speke
Rewe
Westwood
Yeoford
Uton
Sweetham
M5
Stoke Canon
Marker's Cottage
R Clyst
Hookway
Upton Pyne
Huxham
Newton St Cyres
Broadclyst
Spreyton
River Troney
12
Cowley
Hittisleigh
Tedburn St Mary
Whitestone Cross
Cranbrook
Pinhoe
Cheriton Bishop
EXETER
Whipton
Clyst Honiton
Rockbeare
Blackhorse
Exeter
Exwick
Heavitree
A30
Whiddon Down
Crockernwell
A377
Sowton
Longdown
Wonford
Westpoint Arena
Farringdon
Drewsteignton
B3212
Spinster's Rock
R Teign
Castle Drogo
Prestonbury Castle
Ide
Clyst St Mary
Sandy Park
Dunsford
Alphington
Crealy Adventure Park
Shillingford Abbot
Countess Wear
Clyst St George
Easton
Cranbrook Castle
Shillingford St George
Great Weeke
Dunchideock
Topsham
Ebford
Chagford
A379
Manstree
Exminster
Doccombe
Bridford
Doddiscombsleigh
Kennford
Exton
Sloncombe
Moretonhampstead
A38
Woodmanton
Christow
A376
Hayne
Ashton
Kenn
Powderham
Lympstone
Miniature Pony Centre
North Bovey
Halden
Powderham Castle
River Exe
Lower Ashton
Hunter's Tor
A382
Kenton
A La Ronde
R Bovey
Canonteign Falls
Trusham
Hulham
Grimspound
Manaton
Lustleigh
Harcombe
Starcross
Exmouth
529
HAMELDOWN TOR
Water
Hennock
Lower Upcott
Cofton
Becky Falls
Southcott
Bovey Tracey
Chudleigh
Cockwood
Hound Tor Medieval Village
Ashcombe
Widecombe in the Moor
7
Chudleigh Knighton
Ugbrooke Park
Dawlish Warren
HAYTOR
454
B3387
B3344
Ideford
Haytor Vale
Brimley
Luton
Dunstone
The Church
Ilsington
A380
Dawlish

Lurley
Bolham
Whitnage
Appledore
Woodgate
Rosemary Lane
Clayhidon
Templeton
Calverleigh
A361
Sampford Peverell
Prescott
Culmstock
Hemyock
Stapley
A
B
C
D
E
F
25
Withleigh
R Dart
Tiverton
Halberton
Holme
Craddock
Bolham Water
Churchi
Bolham R
A396
River Exe
Ash Thomas
Willand
Coldharbour Mill
Ashill
1
dington
Way Village
River Culm
Diggerland
Blackborough
Smeatharpe
Devon Railway Centre
Bradfield
Madford River
ughill
Upham
Butterleigh
B3181
Kentisbeare
Sheldon
Cadeleigh
Cullompton
Upotter
Cheriton Fitzpaine
Bickleigh
Cullompton
28
Dunkeswell
Luppitt
Knowle
Rawridge
2
Colebrook
Dulford
Kerswell
Bickleigh
Wolford Chapel
Fursdon
Westcott
A373
Beacon
A3072
Cadbury
Broadhembury
Stockleigh Pomeroy
Bradninch
Norman's Green
Colliton
Hembury Castle
Upton Hellions
Up Exe
Silverton
Langford
Upton
Dumpdon Hill
Combe Raleigh
A30
brooke
Hele
Plymtree
Luton
Thorverton
Payhembury
Awliscombe
Killerton
Clyst Hydon
Buckerell
Weston
Shute
Killerton
Talaton
Offwell
Brampford Speke
Clyst St Lawrence
Feniton
Honiton
3
etham
Rewe
Westwood
Newtown
M5
Stoke Canon
R Clyst
Escot
Fenny Bridges
Gittisham
okway
Marker's Cottage
Alfington
Upton Pyne
Huxham
Whimple
Newton St Cyres
Broadclyst
Fairmile
Church Green
11
Poltimore
A30
Taleford
Ottery St Mary
Cowley
Jack-in-the-Green
Hand and Pen
Cadhay House
B3174
Pinhoe
Cranbrook
Allercombe
Whitestone Cross
EXETER
Clyst Honiton
Rockbeare
A375
Whipton
Exeter
West Hill
Blackhorse
Sand
Southleigh
Exwick
Marsh Green
Fluxton
A30
P+R
Heavitree
Wiggaton
Blackbury Camp
4
A377
29
Sowton
Aylesbeare
B3183
Tipton St John
Coombe
ngdown
Wonford
Exeter
Farringdon
Westpoint Arena
B3180
B3184
Sidbury
A305
B3212
30
Perkins Village
Venn Ottery
Harcombe
A3015
Ide
Clyst St Mary
A3052
Southerton
Harpford
Bowd
Sidford
Alphington
Crealy Adventure Park
Shillingford Abbot
Countess Wear
Woodbury Salterton
B3178
Newton Poppleford
The Donkey Sanctuary
Street
Shillingford St George
P+R
Clyst St George
B3176
Woolbrook
Salcombe Regis
Weston
Bran
unchideock
31
Topsham
B3179
B3180
Colaton Raleigh
South West Coast Path
A379
Ebford
Sidmouth
Exminster
Woodbury
Mamhead
Dunchideock
5
A38
Kennford
Exton
Pinn
River Exe
Yettington
Bicton Park
Ashton
Woodmanton
B3180
Otterton
Jurassic Coast (Dorset & East Devon Coast)
Halden
A376
East Budleigh
Kenn
Powderham
Lympstone
Bystock
Otterton Mill
Lower Ashton
Powderham Castle
B3179
Dalditch
River Otter
Ladram Bay
Exeter
B3178
Kenton
A La Ronde
Bystock
Knowle
Kersbrook
rusham
Hulham
Harcombe
Starcross
B3178
Littleham
Lower Upcott
Budleigh Salterton
B3344
Cofton
Exmouth
6
Cockwood
Model Railway
World of Country Life
Ugbrooke Park
Ashcombe
Sandy Bay
B3192
Ideford
Dawlish Warren
Luton
A380
Dawlish
B3193
7
A379
andygate
Holcombe
Bishopsteignton
Coombe
A381
Teignmouth
eignm
7
Coombe Cellars
R Teign
Ringmore
Shaldon
Netherton
Combeinteignhead
Stokeinteignhead
Decoy
Middle Rocombe
Lower Gabwell
Higher Gabwell
otskerswell
Coffinswell
Maidencombe
Kingskerswell
Daccombe
8
Barton
Coombe Pafford
Model
Babbacombe Bay
St Marychurch
Babbacombe
Ellacombe
TORQUAY
Compton Castle
Compton
A380
Cockington
A379
Marldon
0 1 2 3 4 miles
0 1 2 3 4 5 kilometres

25
26
14
G
H
J
K
L
M
1
2
3
4
5
6
7
8
Broadway
Horton
Buckland St Mary
Birch Wood
Donyatt
Ilminster
Seavington
Wigborough
Norton
Epswood
Combe St Nicholas
Beetham
Dowlish Wake
Ludney
St George
Merriott
Hardington Mandeville
Hardington Moor
East Coker
Northay
Wadeford
Chardleigh Green
Knowle St Giles
Cudworth
Chillington
Higher Chillington
Crewkerne
Haselbury Plucknett
Pendomer
Closworth
Whitestaunton
Higher Wambrook
Howley
Chaffcombe
Purtington
Roundham
North Perrott
Hardington Marsh
BIRTS HILL
Halstock
A303
A30
Yarcombe
Chard
Cricket St Thomas
Woolminstone
Hewish
Misterton
South Perrott
Wambrook
Forton
Whatley
Wayford
Clapton
Stockland Hill
Burridge
Tatworth
Winsham
Seaborough
Mosterton
Corscombe
East Chelborough
Stockland
Furley
Chard Junction
Forde Abbey
Laymore
Netherhay
Drimpton
Chedington
River Axe
Chardstock
Membury
Alston
Tytherleigh
Hewood
Thorncombe
Blackdown
Burstock
Broadwindsor
Benville
Holditch
Churchill
Ham
Dalwood
Loughwood Meeting House
Smallridge
Birdsmoorgate
Pilsdon Pen
Stoke Abbott
Beaminster
Higher Wraxhall
Hooke
Hawkchurch
Bettiscombe
Mapperton
Wilmington
A35
Axminster
Weycroft
Marshwood
Pilsdon
Netherbury
North Poorton
South Poorton
Lambert's Castle
Melplash
Waytown
Shute
Kilmington
Shute Barton
Monkton Wyld
Coney's Castle
Marshwood Vale
Broadoak
Salway Ash
West Milton
Powerstock Common
Powerstock
Nettlecombe
Wootton Fitzpaine
Whitchurch Canonicorum
Whitford
Musbury
Maidenhayne
Harcombe Bottom
Catherston Leweston
Ryall
North Chideock
Pymore
Bradpole
Loders
Colyton
Uplyme
Morcombelake
Symondsbury
Allington
St Andrews Well
Uploders
Musbury Castle
Charmouth
Chideock
Bridport
Walditch
Colyford
Axmouth
Rousdon
Lyme Regis
Golden Cap
Seatown
Eype
Watton
Bothenhampton
Seaton
Seaton Tramway
Shipton Gorge
Chilcombe
Litton Cheney
West Bay
Beer
Pecorama
Jurassic Coast (Dorset & East Devon Coast)
Burton Bradstock
Puncknowle
Abbotsbury Castle
Swyre
West Bexington
Coast Path
LYME BAY
A358
A3066
A356
B3162
B3165
B3167
B3164
B3163
B3261
B3172
B3174
A3052
B3157

26
13
Sturminster Newton
Stourton Caundle
Allweston
North Wootton
Bradford Abbas
Barwick
East Coker
Stof
Thornford
Yetminster
Folke
Caundle Marsh
Bishop's Caundle
Lydlinch
Bagber
Hammoon
Fontmell Parva
Fiddleford
Okeford
Sturminster Common
Fifehead Neville
Okeford Fitzpaine
Shillingstone
Holwell
Crouch Hill
King's Stag
Kingston
Hazelbury Bryan
Fifehead St Quintin
Belchalwell
Harding Moor
Hardington Marsh
Pendomer
Closworth
Beer Hackett
Ryme Intrinseca
Knighton
Hamlet
Leigh
Glanvilles Wootton
Pulham
BIRTS HILL
Halstock
Melbury Osmond
Chetnole
Stockwood
Hermitage
Middlemarsh
Duntish
Wonston
Droop
Ibberton
Turnworth
Woolland
Bulbarrow Hill
East Chelborough
Melbury Bubb
Lyon's Gate
Buckland Newton
Mappowder
Winterborne Houghton
Evershot
Holywell
Batcombe
Minterne Magna
Minterne House
Henley
Higher Ansty
Lower Ansty
Melcombe Bingham
Hilton
Winterborne Clenston
Benville
Uphall
Rampisham
Frome St Quintin
Alton Pancras
Cerne Giant
Plush
Milton Abbey
Milton Abbas
Lower Wraxhall
Higher Wraxhall
Hooke
Mapperton
Cerne Abbas
Cerne Abbey
Cattistock
Sydling St Nicholas
Piddletrenthide
Cheselbourne
Bingham
Chilfrome
North Poorton
South Poorton
Toller Porcorum
Maiden Newton
Nether Cerne
White Lackington
PUDDLETON DOWN
Dewlish
Powerstock
Powerstock Common
Toller Fratrum
Godmanstone
Piddlehinton
Milborne St Andrew
Hog Cliff
Nettlecombe
West Compton Abbas
Wynford Eagle
Frampton
Higher Waterston
EGGARDON HILL
Charlton Down
Athelhampton
Tolpuddle
Loders
Uploders
Southover
Grimstone
Stratton
Puddletown
Burleston
Affpuddle
Compton Valence
Spyway
Askerswell
Charminster
YELLOWHAM HILL
Hardy's Cottage
Briantspuddle
Bradford Peverell
Higher Bockhampton
Tincleton
Pallington
Kingston Russell
Winterbourne Abbas
Dorchester
Stinsford
Woodsford
Chilcombe
Barrows
The Nine Stones
Kingston Maurward
West Stafford
Clouds Hill
Litton Cheney
Long Bredy
Poundbury
Martinstown
Winterborne Came
River Frome
R Bride
Winterbourne Steepleton
Maiden Castle
Whitcombe
Moreton
Puncknowle
Littlebredy
Valley of Stones
Kingston Russell
Hardy Monument
Winterborne Monkton
West Knighton
Crossways
Winfrith
Tank
Swyre
West Bexington
Abbotsbury Castle
WHITE HILL
Portesham
Tadnoll
Broadmayne
Warmwell
Abbotsbury
Owermoigne
Wool
South West Coast Path
Bincombe
White Horse
Poxwell
East Knighton
Jurassic Coast (Dorset & East Devon Coast)
Abbey Remains
Rodden
St Catherine's Chapel
Swannery
Osmington
Winfrith Newburgh
Langton Herring
Buckland Ripers
Overcombe
Preston
Jordan Hill
Upton
West Chaldon
East Chaldon (Chaldon Herring)
Osmington Mills
CHALDON DOWN
Chesil Beach
The Fleet
Chickerell
Fleet
Water Gardens
Weymouth Bay
Ringstead Bay
West Lulworth
Lulworth Cove
BINDON HILL
Chesil Bank & The Fleet
Westham
Weymouth
Sea Life Tower
Durdle Door
Wyke Regis
Nothe Fort
Sandsfoot
Portland Harbour
Chesil Beach
Portland Castle
Fortuneswell
West Bay
PORTLAND
Easton
Portland
Portland Bill
PORTLAND BILL
A30
A37
A352
A3030
A357
A356
B3163
B3146
B3143
A354
B3142
A35
B3150
B3147
B3159
B3157
B3390
A353
A352
B3071
B3155
B3156
B3070
A B C D E F
1 2 3 4 5 6 7 8
0 1 2 3 4 miles
0 1 2 3 4 5 kilometres

Waldron
Iwerne Minster
Shroton
Iwerne Courtney
New Town
Farnham
Chettle
Tarrant Gunville
Gussage St Andrew
Boveridge
Cranborne
Bellows Cross
Alderholt
27
28
16
G
H
J
K
L
M
1
2
3
4
5
6
7
8
Gussage St Michael
Tarrant Hinton
A354
Long Crichel
Gussage All Saints
Church & Earthworks
Edmondsham
Dorset Heavy Horse Farm Park
North Gorley
South Gorley
Ibsley Common
Ibsley
Stourpaine
Pimperne
Tarrant Launceston
Tarrant Monkton
Moor Crichel
Romford
Verwood
Rockford Common
Royal Signals
Manswood
Woodlands
Horton
Tarrant Rawston
Witchampton
Mannington
Three Legged Cross
Moors Valley
Ringwood
Poulner
A31
A338
A350
A351
A35
A341
A349
A348
A347
A3060
A3049
A3040
A3068
B3078
B3081
B3072
B3082
B3075
B3074
B3073
B3061
B3065
B3369
B3068
B3070
B3351
B3069
B3347
B3059
St Mary
Charlton Marshall
Charlton on the Hill
Tarrant Rushton
Tarrant Keyneston
Hinton Martell
St Leonards
Liberty's Owl, Raptor & Reptile Centre
Kingston Great Common
Thornicombe
Tarrant Crawford
Badbury Rings
Honeybrook
Holt
Holt Heath
West Moors
Avon Heath
Spetisbury
Shapwick
Kingston Lacy
Abbott Street
Hillbutts
Colehill
Ferndown
FOXBURY HILL
Bisterne
Sandford
Sturminster Marshall
Pamphill
Wimborne Minster
Leigh Park
Hampreston
Knoll
R. Avon
Avon
Ripley
Bransgore
Longham
Dudsbury
Bournemouth Aviation
Hurn
Sopley
Winterborne Zelston
Merley
West Parley
Kinson
Cudnell
Bearwood
West Howe
Ensbury
Red Hill
Adventure Wonderland
West Morden
Morden
Broadstone
East Howe
Throop
Burton
East Morden
Lytchett Matravers
Upton Heath
Canford Heath
Wallisdown
Moordown
Winton
Iford
Somerford
Christchurch
Mudeford
Upton
Newtown
Branksome
Pokesdown
Tuckton
Castle
Wick
Christchurch Bay
Morden Bog
Organford
Lytchett Minster
Hamworthy
Lower Hamworthy
Parkstone
Westbourne
Branksome Park
Boscombe
Southbourne
Hengistbury Head
HENGISTBURY
BOURNEMOUTH
Lilliput
POOLE
Canford Cliffs
Sandford
Northport
Arne
Poole Harbour
Brownsea Island
Sandbanks
Binnegar
Wareham
Ridge
POOLE BAY
East Stoke
Stoborough
West Holme
East Holme
Stoborough Heath
Toll
Purbeck Heritage Coast
Hartland Moor
The Blue Pool
ISLE OF PURBECK
Studland Beach
Studland Bay
P+R
East Lulworth
Corfe Castle
Studland
THE FORELAND
Cherbourg
Purbeck Hills
Church Knowle
Swanage Railway
Harman's Cross
Ulwell
Ballard Point
Swanage Bay
Purbeck Marine
Kingston
Swanage
Guernsey
Jersey
St-Malo
Kimmeridge
Kimmeridge Bay
South West Coast Path
Langton Matravers
Durlston
DURLSTON HEAD
Jurassic Coast (Dorset & East Devon Coast)
Chapman's Pool
Worth Matravers
Anvil Point
ST ALDHELM'S OR ST ALBAN'S HEAD
Piddle or River Trent

28
15
A
B
C
D
E
F
1
2
3
4
5
6
7
8
Brook Hill
Fritham
Brook
Rufus Stone
Copythorne
Cadnam
Calmore
Winsor
Testwood
M271
Shirley
Portswood
West End
Bitterne
Millbrook
Totton
Netley Marsh
Bartley
Woodlands
Furzey
Minstead
Eling
Toll
Northam
Sholing
SOUTHAMPTON
Toll
Woolston
Isle of Wight Ferry Terminal
Ashurst
Longdown Activity Farm
Marchwood
Netley Abbey
Bursledon
North Gorley
South Gorley
Ibsley Common
Rockford Common
NEW FOREST
NATIONAL PARK
Emery Down
Lyndhurst
New Forest Wildlife Park
Dibden
Netley
Southampton Water
Sarisbury
Bank
Beaulieu River
Langdown
Royal Victoria
Dibden Purlieu
Hythe
Hamble-le-Rice
Warsash
A31
A35
A337
A336
A326
A3025
B3056
Liberty's Owl, Raptor & Reptile Centre
Burley Street
Rhinefield Ornamental Drive
Hardley
Holbury
Fawley
Kingston Great Common
MARKWAY HILL
Burley
National Motor Museum
Calshot Castle
Calshot
Blackfield
B3054
B3053
Brockenhurst
Beaulieu
B3055
Sandford
Bisterne
Thorney Hill
Bucklers Hard
North Solent
Langley
Stanswood Bay
East Boldre
Exbury
Ripley
Sway
Boldre
Pilley
Bransgore
B3058
Norleywood
Needs Ore Point
Spinners
South Baddesley
Cowes
East End
THE SOLENT
Sammy Miller Motorcycle
Burton
New Milton
Hordle
Lymington
Gurnard Bay
Gurnard
Walkford
Ashley
Everton
Rew Street
Somerford
Highcliffe
Braxton
Hamstead Heritage Coast
Thorness Bay
Northwood
Christchurch
Highcliffe Castle
Barton-on-Sea
Newtown Bay
Mudeford
Wick
Keyhaven
Porchfield
Newtown
Southbourne
Christchurch Bay
Milford on Sea
Hengistbury Head
HENGISTBURY HEAD
Hurst Castle
Sconce Point
Yarmouth
Old Town Hall
Colemans
Yarmouth Castle
Colwell Bay
Ningwood
Shalfleet
A3054
Carisbrooke
Totland
Norton Green
Thorley Street
B3401
Newbridge
Carisbrooke Castle
Totland Bay
Freshwater
Wellow
Tapnell
Afton
Chessell Pottery Barns
Water Mill
Calbourne
Bowcombe
Blackwater
ISLE OF WIGHT
Needles Park
Dimbola
B3399
BRIGHSTONE DOWN
Alum Bay
B3322
THE NEEDLES
Compton Bay & Downs
Gatcombe
Needles Old Battery & New Battery
Compton Bay
Brook
Hulverstone
Manor Garden
Chillerton
Hanover Point
Mottistone
Limerstone
Shorwell
Tennyson Heritage Coast
Brighstone
Chilton Chine
Kingston
Brighstone Bay
A3055
Chale Green
Atherfield Point
St Catherine's Down
Chale
Whale Chine
Blackgang Chine
Niton
Rocken End
ST CATHERINE'S POINT
A3020
B3323
B3325
0 1 2 3 4 miles
0 1 2 3 4 5 kilometres

Waltham Chase
Shirrell Heath
Soberton Heath
Hambledon
Catherington
Blendworth
Curdridge
Shedfield
Newtown
29
30
Wickham
Forestside
Stoughton
Bow Hill
Walderton
Curbridge
Worlds End
North Boarhunt
Anmore
Soake
Cowplain
Rowland's Castle
Burridge
Whiteley
Swanwick
WATERLOOVILLE
Southwick
Stakes
Leigh Park
Westbourne
Funtington
Woodend
West Stoke
Mid Lavant
East Ashling
Boarhunt
Ports Down
Purbrook
HAVANT
Woodmancote
West Ashling
Royal Armouries Fort Nelson
Titchfield Abbey
Catisfield
Wallington
Bedhampton
Hambrook
Southbourne
Broadbridge
Cosham
Drayton
Farlington
Brockhampton
Langstone
Emsworth
Nutbourne
Walton
Fishbourne
Titchfield
FAREHAM
Portchester
Castle
Portsmouth Harbour
Whale Island
Hilsea
Northney
Chidham
Bosham
Dell Quay
Apuldram
Stubbington
Titchfield Haven
Hill Head
Bridgemary
Fort Brockhurst
Elson
Continental Ferry Terminal
North End
North Hayling
Stoke
THORNEY ISLAND
West Thorney
HAYLING ISLAND
Donnington
Rowner
Hardway
Portsmouth Dockyard
Langstone Harbour
West Itchenor
Birdham
GOSPORT
Portsea
Fratton
Chichester Harbour
Lee-on-the-Solent
Spinnaker Tower
Shipton Green
Isle of Wight Ferry Terminal
Southsea
West Town
South Hayling
East Head
West Wittering
Somerley
Stokes Bay
Alverstoke
Eastney
Fort Cumberland
Hayling Bay
PORTSMOUTH
Gilkicker Point
East Wittering
Earnley
Bracklesham
18
Osborne
East Cowes
Osborne House
Osborne Bay
Spitbank Fort
SPITHEAD
Bracklesham Bay
Whippingham
Wootton Bridge
Fishbourne
Ryde
Selsey
Binstead
Puckpool Point
Brickfields Horse Country
Nettlestone Point
Seaview
Rosemary
Havenstreet
Nettlestone
Little Whitefield
Isle of Wight Steam Railway
St Helens
Robin Hill
East Ashey
The Duver
Bembridge
Newport
Nunwell
Brading
Bembridge Windmill
Lifeboat Station
FORELAND
Shipwreck Centre
Guernsey
Jersey
St-Malo
Caen (Ouistreham)
Cherbourg (May-Aug)
Le Havre (Jan-Oct)
Bilbao (Jan-Oct)
Santander (Jan-Oct)
Cherbourg (May-Aug)
ISLE OF WIGHT
Arreton
Newchurch
Alverstone
Bembridge Down
Whitecliff Bay
Bembridge & Culver Downs
Dinosaur Isle
Merstone
Queen's Bower
Yaverland
Culver Cliff
Winford
Lake
Sandown
Branstone
Sandown Bay
Apse Heath
Sandford
Whiteley Bank
Shanklin
Shanklin Chine
Old Smithy & Gardens
Luccombe Village
Luccombe Chine
Appuldurcombe House
Wroxall
Ventnor Downs
DUNNOSE
Whitwell
IOW Glass
Ventnor
Botanic Garden
St Lawrence
The Undercliffe
Binnel Bay
G
H
J
K
L
M
1
2
3
4
5
6
7
8

Liphook
Linchmere
Kingsley Green
Hollycombe Steam
Fernhurst
Black Down 280
BLACKDOWN HILL
Northchapel
Plaistow
Ifold
Loxwood
B2133
A29
A264
Five Oaks
Barns Green
Billingshurst
B2070
Milland
Woodmansgreen
A286
Lurgashall
Ebernoe Common
Kirdford
Redford
Henley
Lickfold
Lurgashall
Balls Cross
Wisborough Green
A272
Fishers
SOUTH DOWNS NATIONAL PARK
Fyning
Chithurst
Iping
Woolbeding
Lodsworth
River
Upperton
A283
Coneyhurst Common
R Rother
Trotton
Stedham
Easebourne
Petworth House
Adversane
Iping & Stedham Common
Midhurst
Tillington
Petworth
Byworth
River Arun
Broadford Bridge
Coolham
Nyewood
Harting
30
Minsted
Selham
Little Bognor
Codmore Hill
B2139
Elsted
Cocking Causeway
West Lavington
South Ambersham
Stopham
Nutbourne
East Harting
Didling
Fittleworth
Pulborough
Marehill
West Chiltington
Harting Beacon
Treyford
249 Bepton
LINCH DOWN
Cocking
Upper Norwood
Duncton
Coates
Thakeham
Heyshott
Graffham
Burton & Chingford Ponds
Hardham
B2138
South Downs Way
Duncton Hill
Barlavington
Coldwaltham
Greatham
Abingworth
Ashington
East Lavington
Roman Villa
Watersfield
Chilgrove
B2141
LEVIN DOWN 170
255 DUNCTON HILL
Sutton
East Marden
Singleton
Bignor
Rackham
Parham
Storrington
West Dean
225 BIGNOR HILL
Upwaltham
Bury
Amberley
212 KITHURST HILL
Washington
Stoughton
Charlton
East Dean
Weald & Downland Open Air
Goodwood
Houghton
Amberley Museum
Bow Hill
The Trundle
206 THE TRUNDLE
Halnaker Hill
North Stoke
Kingley Vale
Walderton
West Stoke
144 NORE HILL
South Stoke
167 HARROW HILL
East Lavant
Eartham
Offham
Burpham
Mid Lavant
Denmans Garden
Slindon
A284
Wepham
Findon
Waterbeach
Arundel Wetland Centre
Strettington
Halnaker
West Ashling
East Ashling
Priory
Fontwell
Arundel
Warningcamp
A280
A24
Summersdale
Boxgrove
A27
Clapham
Poling Corner
Patching
High Salvington
Fontwell Park
Binsted
Broadbridge
Tangmere
Norton
Westhampnett
Nyton
Walberton
Fishbourne
Walton
Roman Palace
Aldingbourne
Eastergate
Poling
Durrington
Salvington
Westergate
North End
Lyminster
Angmering
HIGHDOWN HILL
A2032
Chichester
Oving
Woodgate
Barnham
B2233
Wick
A259
Bosham
Dell Quay
Apuldram
Colworth
Yapton
Ford
B2187
West Tarring
Merston
Shripney
Bilsham
Climping
Rustington
Ferring
Goring-by-Sea
West Worthing
Donnington
Runcton
Flansham
East Preston
B2140
Littlehampton
Hunston
North Mundham
B2201
B2166
Birdham
South Mundham
Bersted
B2259
B2132
Middleton-on-Sea
B2179
Street End
Sidlesham
Rose Green
Felpham
Highleigh
Nyetimber
Aldwick
BOGNOR REGIS
17
B2198
Earnley
B2145
Pagham Harbour
Pagham
Church Norton
Bracklesham Bay
Selsey
SELSEY BILL
0 1 2 3 4 miles
0 1 2 3 4 5 kilometres

Horsham
St Leonards Forest
Handcross
Nymans House
Balcombe
Wakehurst Place
South of England
Ardingly Reservoir
Ouse Valley
Hoathly
Highbrook
Ardingly
Bluebell Railway
Horsted Keynes
Nutley
Sweethaws
Fairwarp
High Hurstwood
Five Ash Down
Maresfield
Splayne's Green
Buxted
Mannings Heath
Monk's Gate
Southwater
Nuthurst
Copsale
Maplehurst
Slaugham
Lower Beeding
Warninglid
Crabtree
Staplefield
Borde Hill
Cuckfield
Lindfield
Danehill
Haywards Heath
Bolnore
Sheffield Park
Fletching
Piltdown
Scayne's Hill
Newick
Uckfield
Framfield
New Town
Ridgewood
Bolney
Bolney Wine Estate
Ansty
West Grinstead
Cowfold
Partridge Green
Twineham
Hickstead
Sayers Common
Worlds End
Wivelsfield
North Chailey
Wivelsfield Green
Burgess Hill
Chailey
South Chailey
Town Littleworth
East Sussex National
Lavender Line
Little Horsted
Isfield
Henfield
Blackstone
Albourne
Hurstpierpoint
Plumpton Green
Keymer
Hassocks
Ditchling
East Chiltington
Barcombe
Barcombe Cross
Halland
Bentley Wildfowl & Motor Museum
Shortgate
Woodmancote
Clayton
Wolstonbury
Streat
Westmeston
Plumpton
Upper Wellingham
Whitesmith
Woods Mill
Small Dole
Pyecombe
Ditchling Beacon
Hamsey
Laughton
Poynings
Edburton
Upper Beeding
Farm & Newtimber Hill
Pangdean
Mount Harry
Offham
Ringmer
Truleigh Hill
Fulking
Devil's Dyke
Saddlescombe
South Downs National Park
Lewes
Wallands Park
South Malling
Mount Caburn
Glynde Place
Glynde
Bramber
St Mary's House
Stanmer
Botolphs
Coombes
Lancing College Chapel
Patcham
Coldean
Withdean
Hollingbury
Falmer
Moulsecoomb
Castle Hill
South Downs Way
Kingston near Lewes
Iford
Beddingham
Firle
Firle Place
Charleston
Mile Oak
Hangleton
West Blatchington
Portslade
Preston
Newmarket Hill
Rodmell
Monk's House
Breaky Bottom
Firle Beacon
Berwick
Old Shoreham
Shoreham
Southwick
Woodingdean
Southease
Tarring Neville
Kemp Town
Lancing
Shoreham-by-Sea
Portslade-by-Sea
HOVE
BRIGHTON
i360
Ovingdean
Telscombe
South Heighton
Denton
Alfriston
WORTHING
Piddinghoe
Paradise Park
Saltdean
Rottingdean
Newhaven
Norton
Bishopstone
East Blatchington
Peacehaven
Newhaven Fort
Seaford Bay
Sutton
Seaford
Seaford Head
Dieppe
A22 A23 A26 A27 A259 A270 A272 A273 A275 A281 A283 A2037 A2300
B2026 B2028 B2036 B2066 B2110 B2111 B2112 B2113 B2114 B2115 B2116 B2117 B2123 B2124 B2135 B2192 B2195
31 32 20
G H J K L M
1 2 3 4 5 6 7 8

Tidebrook
Rotherfield
Ticehurst
Hawkhurst
Highgate
Pashley Manor
River Limden
The Moor
Kent Ditch
Merriments
Sweethaws
Fairwarp
Stonegate
Witherenden Hill
Hurst Green
Mayfield
Etchingham
High Hurstwood
River Rother
Bodiam
Five Ash Down
Pound Green
32
Five Ashes
33
Burwash
Bateman's
Salehurst
Buxted
Hadlow Down
Wilderness Wood
Burwash Common
Burwash Weald
Robertsbridge
Broad Oak
Staplecross
Cross in Hand
Heathfield
Cade St
R Dudwell
Darwell Reservoir
Uckfield
Blackboys
Framfield
Brightling
Punnett's Town
Mountfield
New Town
Ridgewood
Three Cups Corner
Wood's Corner
East Sussex National
Lavender Line
Waldron
Little London
Maynard's Green
Dallington
Netherfield
Whatlington
Little Horsted
Rushlake Green
Warbleton
Vines Cross
Horam
Battle
Halland
East Hoathly
Wildfowl Motor Museum
Gun Hill
Bodle Street Green
1066 Hastings
Shortgate
Chiddingly
Cowbeech
Whitesmith
Catsfield
Muddles Green
Crowhurst
Laughton
Hellingly
Herstmonceux
Ringmer
19
Windmill Hill
Ninfield
Henley's Down
The Truggery
Magham Down
Boreham Street
Lower Dicker
Horsebridge
Lunsford's Cross
Knockhatch
Ripe
Upper Dicker
Leap Cross
Hailsham
Herstmonceux Castle Gardens
Observatory Science Centre
Hooe
Glynde Place
Chalvington
Michelham Priory
Wartling
Little Common
Sidley
Leon
Pevensey Levels
Firle
Selmeston
Arlington
Cooden
Firle Place 219
Charleston
Bexhill
FIRLE BEACON
Alciston
Polegate
Tarring Neville
Berwick
Drusillas
Wilmington
Westham
Pevensey
Castle
Wannock
Lower Willingdon
South Heighton
Alfriston
Folkington
The Long Man of Wilmington
Langney
Pevensey Bay
Willingdon
Hampden Park
Clergy House
Ratton Village
Sovereign Harbour
Litlington
Jevington
Norton
Bishopstone
St Anthony's Hill
Lullington Heath
Miniature
Roselands
East Blatchington
Langney Point
South Downs Way
Westdean
Seaford Bay
Sutton
Old Town
Friston
EASTBOURNE
Seaford
Seven Sisters
Seaford Head
East Dean
Beachy Head Countryside Centre
BEACHY HEAD
Sussex Heritage Coast
Dieppe
A26
A27
A22
A267
A265
A21
A272
A271
A269
A259
A2100
A2690
A2036
A2270
A2280
A2290
A295
B2100
B2101
B2102
B2192
B2124
B2203
B2096
B2095
B2204
B2244
B2104
B2103
B2182
B2092
0 1 2 3 4 miles
0 1 2 3 4 5 kilometres

Rolvenden
Reading Street
A2070
Newchurch
Burmarsh
A259
Small Hythe
Chapel Down Winery
Smallhythe Place
Horne's Place Chapel
Rolvenden Layne
34
B2080
Appledore
Snargate
Kenzett Green
St Mary in the Marsh
Martello
hurst
Kent & East Sussex Railway
ISLE OF OXNEY
Aeronautical
Brenzett
Ivychurch
St Mary's Bay
Newenden
B2082
Stone in Oxney
Romney Marsh
Wittersham
The Stocks
Royal Military Canal
A259
Old Romney
Romney Warren
Rother Levels
River Rother
Brookland
Northiam
B2071
Littlestone-on-Sea
B2088
Iden
New Romney
Beckley
A268
Rye Foreign
A259
Greatstone-on-Sea
B2165
Clayhill
Houghton Green
WALLAND MARSH
Peasmarsh
Playden
B2075
Lydd
Rye
East Guldeford
Lydd
Broad Oak
R Tillingham
B2089
Cock Marling
Camber
Broadland Row
Udimore
Camber Castle
Brede
River Brede
Rye Harbour
Dungeness
Broad Street
Winchelsea
Rye Bay
A28
Icklesham
The Old Lighthouse
DUNGENESS
Guestling Thorn
Three Oaks
A259
Pett
Guestling Green
Cliff End
Fairlight
Ore
Hastings
HASTINGS
G
H
J
K
L
M
1
2
3
4
5
6
7
8

A
B
C
D
E
F
1
2
3
4
5
6
7
8
North West Point
Lundy Heritage Coast
LUNDY
142
Marine Reserve
Marisco
Shutter Point
Surf Point
Baggy Point
Croyde
BARNSTAPLE
OR
BIDEFORD BAY
Westward
HARTLAND POINT
Shipload Bay
Titchberry
Damehole Point
Hartland Abbey & Gardens
Stoke
Hartland Quay
Spekes Mill Mouth
Hartland
B3248
Milford
Docton Mill Gardens
Philham
Clovelly
B3237
Buck's Mills
Milky Way
Buck's Cross
A39
Woolfardisworthy
Hartland Heritage Coast
Abbotsham
Ford
Fairy Cross
Horns Cross
Woodtown
Goldworthy
Parkham
Hardisworthy
Welcombe
Darracott
Ashmansworthy
East Putford
9
Gooseham
Morwenstow
Higher Sharpnose Point
South West Coast Path
Lower Sharpnose Point
Steeple Point
Shop
Woodford
Kilkhampton
Dinworthy
Gnome Reserve
West Putford
Haytown
Bradworthy
Bulkworthy
Tamar Lakes
Abbots Bickington
Sutcombe
A388
River
Milton Damerel
Thornbury
Holsworthy
B3254
Northcott
0 1 2 3 4 miles
0 1 2 3 4 5 kilometres

G
H
J
K
L
M
1
2
3
4
5
6
7
8
Foreland Point
Lynmouth Bay
Lynton
Lynmouth
Countisbury
Brendon
Rockford
Watersmeet
Woody Bay
Elwill Bay
Martinhoe
Trentishoe
Toll
Dean
Barbrook
Lynton & Barnstaple Railway
Parracombe
Combe Martin Bay
Watermouth Castle
Water Mouth
Hele Bay
Ilfracombe
Hele
Bull Point
Lee Bay
Lee
Slade
Chambercombe Manor
Hele Corn Mill
Rockham Bay
Mortehoe
Combe Martin
Berrynarbor
A399
Wildlife & Dinosaur Park
Kentisbury
B3343
A3123
B3229
Trimstone
West Down
A361
Chapel Wood
North Buckland
Bittadon
Clifton
A39
Wistlandpound Reservoir
HOAROAK HILL 474
EXMOOR FOREST
Arlington
Arlington Court
Exmoor Zoo
Challacombe
Barton Town
Shoulsbury Castle
B3358
River Barle
Georgeham
Croyde
Darracott
B3230
Milltown
Loxhore
Higher Muddiford
Muddiford
Knowle
Boode
Marwood
Marwood Hill
Guineaford
B3231
Saunton
Lower Loxhore
Bratton Fleming
R Bray
24
SPAN HEAD
Kinsford Water
Braunton
Heanton Punchardon
Shirwell
Prixford
A399
Braunton Burrows
Wrafton
Ashford
Bradiford
Stoke Rivers
Brayford
Chivenor
Pilton
Goodleigh
High Bray
River Taw
Derby
Gunn
Charles
Bentwichen
Isley Marsh
Fremington
Bickington
A3125
Barnstaple
Stoodleigh
B3233
Crow Point
Roundswell
Landkey
Swimbridge Newland
West Buckland
Heasley Mill
P+R
East Buckland
North Molton
Appledore
Instow
Tawstock
Northam
A39
Tapeley Park
St John's Chapel
Bishop's Tawton
Hannaford
Swimbridge
A361
Upcott
B3236
Westleigh
Castle Hill
Horwood
Eastleigh
Newton Tracey
Harracott
East Stowford
Filleigh
B3226
A386
The Big Sheep
East-the-Water
Hiscott
Cobbaton
Quince Honey Farm
South Molton
Aller
Chapelton
Bideford
Alverdiscott
Chittlehampton
B3227
Bish Mill
B3227
B3232
A377
Umberleigh
George Nympton
B3137
Landcross
Yarnscombe
Atherington
Warkleigh
Huntshaw
River Mole
Alswear
Ash Mill
Weare Giffard
Satterleigh
Mariansleigh
B3227
Chittlehamholt
Yard
A386
Great Torrington
High Bickington
River Taw
Kings Nympton
Romansleigh
Meshaw
Frithelstock
St Giles in the Wood
RHS Rosemoor
Kingscott
Little Torrington
10
Roborough
Burrington
A3124
Langtree
B3217
Beaford
B3227
Chulmleigh
Ashreigney
Peters Marland
Winswell
Riddlecombe
Cheldon
B3096
Worlington
Chawleigh
Halsdon
B3042
B3042
Merton
Huish
Dolton
Hollocombe
Ashley
North Town
Eggesford
Dowland
Wembworthy
Petrockstow
Meeth Quarry
Buckland
Nymet Rowland
R Dalch
Eastington

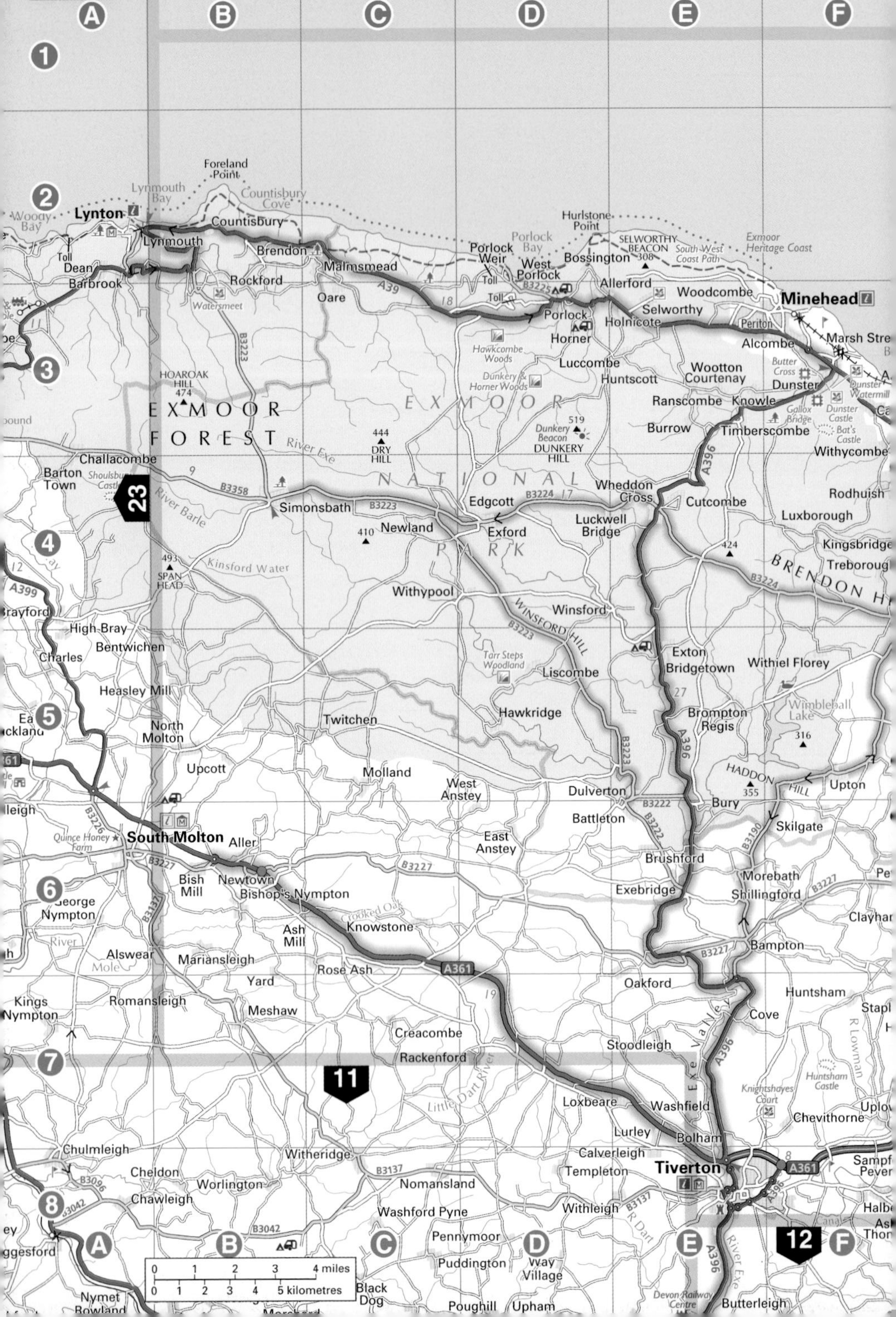
A
B
C
D
E
F
1
2
3
4
5
6
7
8
Foreland Point
Lynmouth Bay
Countisbury Cove
Woody Bay
Lynton
Lynmouth
Countisbury
Brendon
Malmsmead
Toll
Dean
Barbrook
Rockford
Watersmeet
Oare
A39
18
Hurlstone Point
Porlock Bay
Porlock Weir
West Porlock
B3225
Bossington
SELWORTHY BEACON 308
South West Coast Path
Exmoor Heritage Coast
Allerford
Woodcombe
Minehead
Selworthy
Porlock
Horner
Holnicote
Periton
Alcombe
Marsh Street
Hawkcombe Woods
Luccombe
Wootton Courtenay
Butter Cross
Dunster
Dunster Watermill
Dunkery & Horner Woods
Huntscott
Ranscombe
Knowle
Gallox Bridge
Dunster Castle
Bat's Castle
Burrow
Timberscombe
Withycombe
519
Dunkery Beacon
DUNKERY HILL
B3223
HOAROAK HILL 474
EXMOOR FOREST
EXMOOR
444 DRY HILL
River Exe
NATIONAL
PARK
Challacombe
Barton Town
Shoulsbury Castle
23
River Barle
B3358
9
Simonsbath
B3223
Newland
410
Edgcott
B3224
17
Exford
Wheddon Cross
Cutcombe
Rodhuish
Luxborough
Luckwell Bridge
424
Kingsbridge
Treborough
BRENDON HILLS
B3224
A396
493 SPAN HEAD
Kinsford Water
A399
Brayford
High Bray
Bentwichen
Charles
Heasley Mill
North Molton
Withypool
WINSFORD HILL
Winsford
B3223
Tarr Steps Woodland
Liscombe
Exton
Bridgetown
Withiel Florey
Hawkridge
27
Brompton Regis
Wimbleball Lake
316
Twitchen
HADDON HILL
355
Upton
A361
Upcott
Molland
West Anstey
B3223
Dulverton
Bury
Battleton
B3222
Skilgate
B3190
B3226
Quince Honey Farm
South Molton
Aller
East Anstey
Brushford
B3227
Bish Mill
Newtown
Bishop's Nympton
Exebridge
Morebath
Shillingford
B3227
George Nympton
B3137
Crooked Oak
Knowstone
Ash Mill
Clayhanger
River Mole
Alswear
Mariansleigh
Rose Ash
A361
B3227
Bampton
Yard
Oakford
Kings Nympton
Romansleigh
19
Meshaw
Huntsham
Cove
Creacombe
Exe Valley
R Lowman
Stoodleigh
Rackenford
11
Little Dart River
Huntsham Castle
Knightshayes Court
Loxbeare
Washfield
Chevithorne
Lurley
Bolham
Chulmleigh
Witheridge
Calverleigh
Tiverton
A361
Sampford Peverell
8
B3096
Cheldon
Worlington
B3137
Nomansland
Templeton
Chawleigh
B3042
Washford Pyne
Withleigh
B3137
R. Dart
Canal
B3042
Pennymoor
Puddington
Way Village
River Exe
A396
12
Eggesford
0 1 2 3 4 miles
0 1 2 3 4 5 kilometres
Black Dog
Devon Railway Centre
Butterleigh
Nymet Rowland
Poughill
Upham

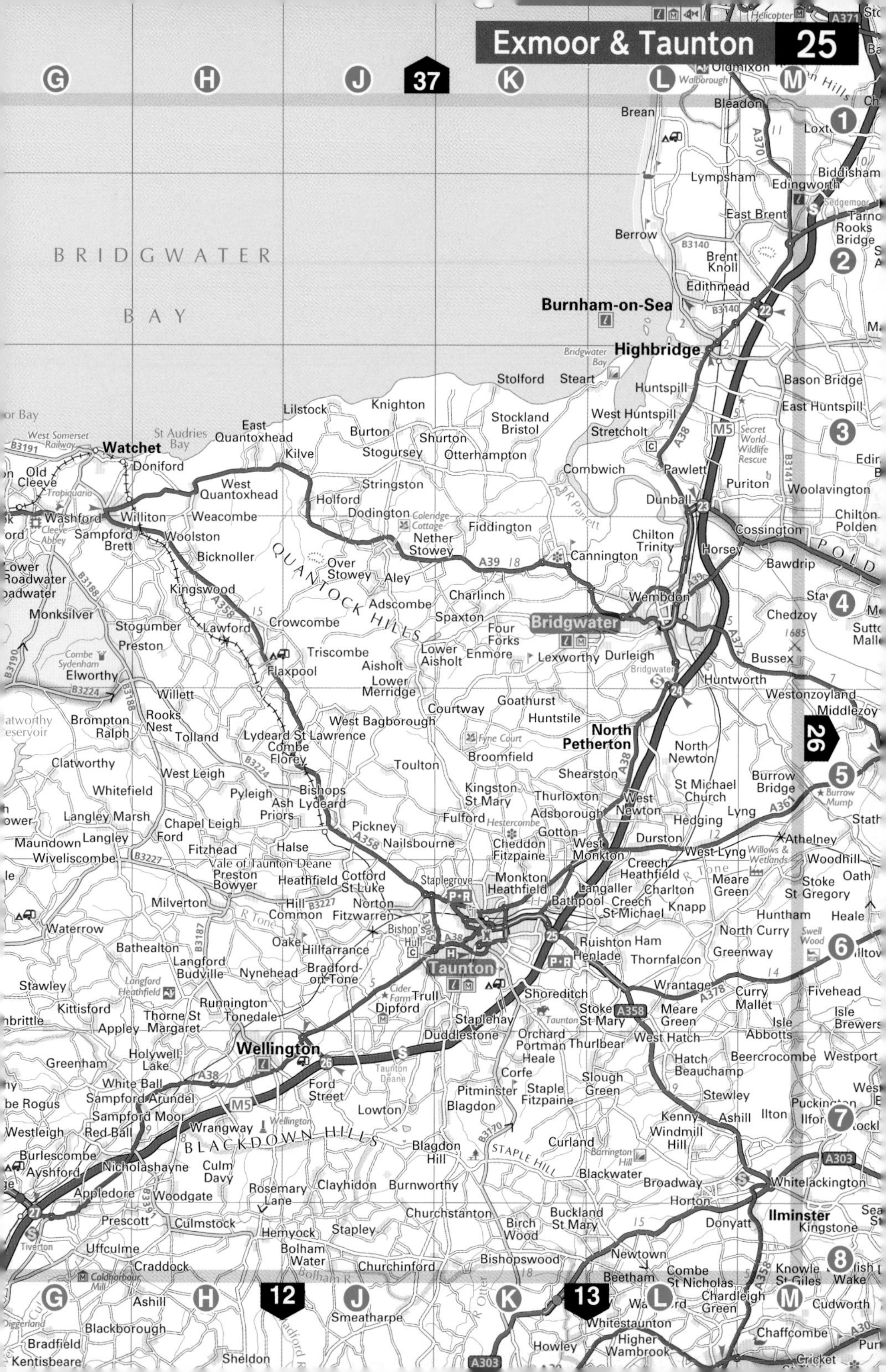

BRIDGWATER BAY
Burnham-on-Sea
Highbridge
Watchet
Bridgwater
North Petherton
Taunton
Wellington
Ilminster
QUANTOCK HILLS
BLACKDOWN HILLS
STAPLE HILL
Vale of Taunton Deane
Brean
Bleadon
Lympsham
Edingworth
Biddisham
East Brent
Berrow
Brent Knoll
Edithmead
Bason Bridge
East Huntspill
Huntspill
Stolford
Steart
West Huntspill
Stretcholt
Pawlett
Puriton
Woolavington
Dunball
Cossington
Chilton Polden
Chilton Trinity
Horsey
Bawdrip
Cannington
Wembdon
Chedzoy
Combwich
Lilstock
Knighton
Burton
Shurton
Stogursey
Otterhampton
Stockland Bristol
Kilve
East Quantoxhead
West Quantoxhead
St Audries Bay
Doniford
Williton
Washford
Old Cleeve
Sampford Brett
Woolston
Bicknoller
Weacombe
Holford
Stringston
Dodington
Nether Stowey
Over Stowey
Aley
Fiddington
Charlinch
Spaxton
Adscombe
Four Forks
Enmore
Lower Aisholt
Aisholt
Lexworthy
Durleigh
Triscombe
Crowcombe
Kingswood
Lawford
Stogumber
Preston
Monksilver
Elworthy
Flaxpool
Lower Merridge
Courtway
Goathurst
Huntstile
Huntworth
Bussex
Westonzoyland
Middlezoy
Willett
Brompton Ralph
Rooks Nest
Tolland
Lydeard St Lawrence
Combe Florey
West Bagborough
Broomfield
Toulton
Clatworthy
West Leigh
Whitefield
Pyleigh
Ash Priors
Bishops Lydeard
Kingston St Mary
Thurloxton
Shearston
North Newton
St Michael Church
Burrow Bridge
Lyng
Langley Marsh
Chapel Leigh
Ford
Maundown
Langley
Wiveliscombe
Fitzhead
Halse
Pickney
Nailsbourne
Fulford
Adsborough
Gotton
Cheddon Fitzpaine
West Monkton
Durston
West Lyng
Athelney
Hedging
West Newton
Preston Bowyer
Heathfield
Cotford St Luke
Norton Fitzwarren
Staplegrove
Monkton Heathfield
Creech Heathfield
Langaller
Bathpool
Charlton
Creech St Michael
Knapp
Meare Green
Stoke St Gregory
Woodhill
Oath
Huntham
Heale
North Curry
Milverton
Hill Common
Oake
Hillfarrance
Bishop's Hull
Waterrow
Bathealton
Langford Budville
Nynehead
Bradford-on-Tone
Ruishton
Ham
Henlade
Thornfalcon
Greenway
Stawley
Kittisford
Runnington
Tonedale
Thorne St Margaret
Appley
Trull
Dipford
Shoreditch
Stoke St Mary
Meare Green
Wrantage
Curry Mallet
Fivehead
Isle Brewers
Isle Abbotts
Staplehay
Duddlestone
Orchard Portman
Thurlbear
West Hatch
Hatch Beauchamp
Beercrocombe
Westport
Holywell Lake
Greenham
White Ball
Sampford Arundel
Sampford Moor
Westleigh
Red Ball
Wrangway
Ford Street
Lowton
Corfe
Pitminster
Blagdon
Staple Fitzpaine
Slough Green
Stewley
Ashill
Ilton
Kenny
Windmill Hill
Curland
Blagdon Hill
Burlescombe
Ayshford
Nicholashayne
Culm Davy
Appledore
Woodgate
Rosemary Lane
Clayhidon
Burnworthy
Blackwater
Broadway
Horton
Whitelackington
Prescott
Culmstock
Hemyock
Stapley
Churchstanton
Birch Wood
Buckland St Mary
Donyatt
Kingstone
Uffculme
Bolham Water
Craddock
Churchinford
Bishopswood
Newtown
Beetham
Combe St Nicholas
Chardleigh Green
Knowle St Giles
Cudworth
Ashill
Smeatharpe
Whitestaunton
Higher Wambrook
Howley
Chaffcombe
Blackborough
Bradfield
Kentisbeare
Sheldon
Cricket

37
26
12
13

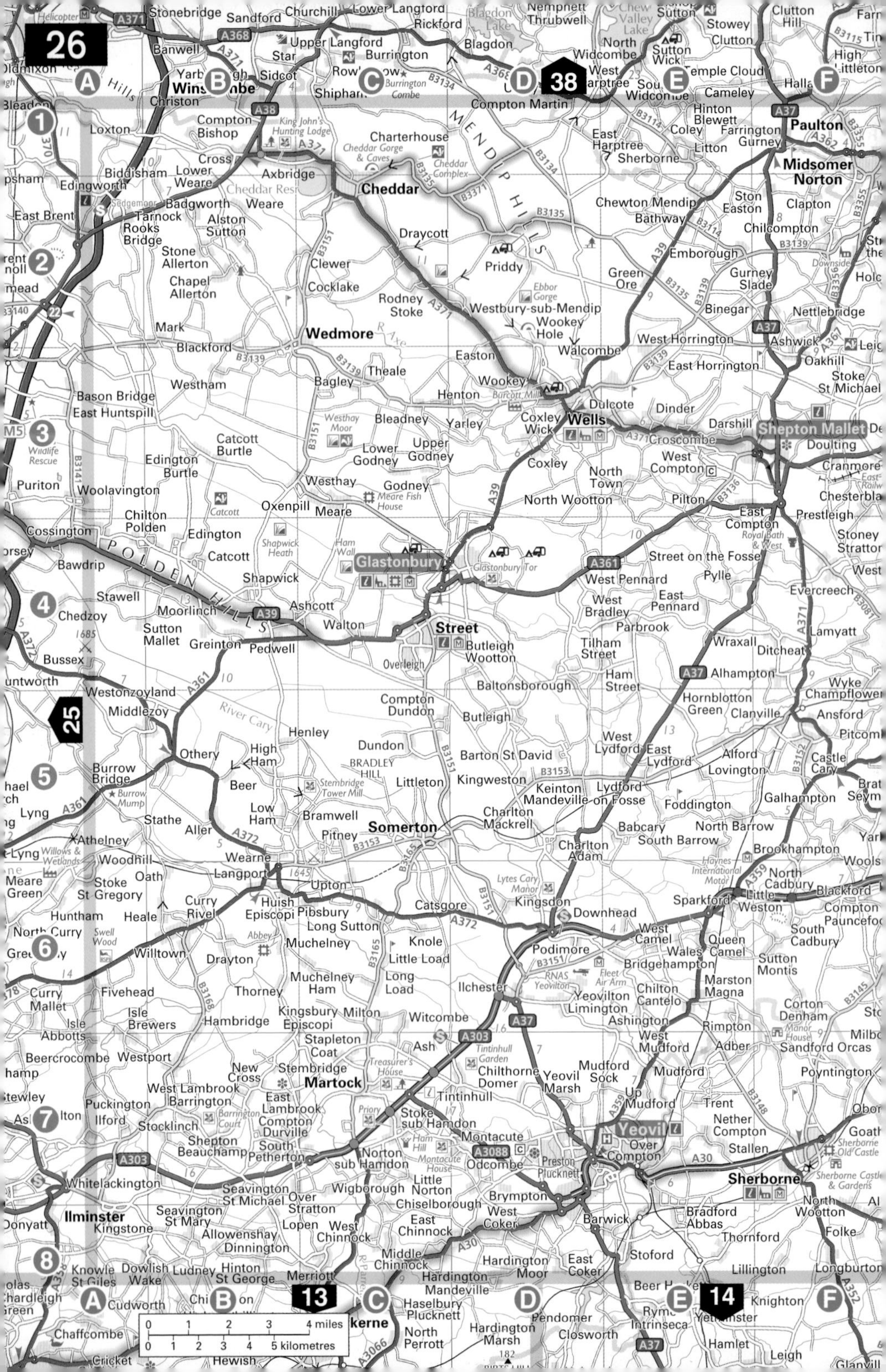
Stonebridge
Sandford
Churchill
Lower Langford
Rickford
Blagdon Lake
Nempnett Thrubwell
Chew Valley Lake
Sutton
Stowey
Clutton Hill
Clutton
Banwell
Upper Langford
Burrington
Blagdon
North Widcombe
Sutton Wick
Temple Cloud
High Littleton
Oldmixon
Yarborough
Winscombe
Sidcot
Star
Rowberrow
Burrington Combe
Shipham
West Harptree
Widcombe
Cameley
Hallatrow
Bleadon
Christon
Compton Martin
Hinton Blewett
Coley
Farrington Gurney
Paulton
Loxton
Compton Bishop
King John's Hunting Lodge
Charterhouse
Cheddar Gorge & Caves
MENDIP HILLS
East Harptree
Sherborne
Litton
Midsomer Norton
Cross
Biddisham
Lower Weare
Axbridge
Cheddar Res
Cheddar
Cheddar Complex
Edingworth
Sedgemoor
Badgworth
Weare
Tarnock
East Brent
Rooks Bridge
Alston Sutton
Chewton Mendip
Ston Easton
Clapton
Bathway
Chilcompton
Draycott
Stone Allerton
Clewer
Emborough
Priddy
Green Ore
Gurney Slade
Downside
Chapel Allerton
Cocklake
Ebbor Gorge
Rodney Stoke
Westbury-sub-Mendip
Binegar
Nettlebridge
Mark
Wookey Hole
Wedmore
R Axe
Blackford
West Horrington
Ashwick
Walcombe
Easton
East Horrington
Oakhill
Theale
Stoke St Michael
Westham
Bagley
Wookey
Bason Bridge
Henton
Burcott Mill
Dulcote
Dinder
East Huntspill
Westhay Moor
Bleadney
Coxley Wick
Wells
Darshill
Shepton Mallet
Yarley
Croscombe
Doulting
Wildlife Rescue
Catcott Burtle
Lower Godney
Upper Godney
Coxley
Edington Burtle
West Compton
Cranmore
Puriton
Woolavington
Westhay
Godney
North Town
Meare Fish House
Chesterblade
Oxenpill
Meare
North Wootton
Pilton
Catcott
Chilton Polden
East Compton
Prestleigh
Royal Bath & West
Cossington
Edington
Shapwick Heath
Ham Wall
Stoney Stratton
Catcott
Glastonbury
Street on the Fosse
Bawdrip
Glastonbury Tor
West Pennard
Pylle
POLDEN HILLS
Shapwick
East Pennard
Evercreech
Stawell
West Bradley
Ashcott
Chedzoy
Moorlinch
Parbrook
Lamyatt
Sutton Mallet
Walton
Street
Bussex
Greinton
Pedwell
Butleigh Wootton
Tilham Street
Wraxall
Ditcheat
Overleigh
Ham Street
Alhampton
Westonzoyland
Baltonsborough
Wyke Champflower
Compton Dundon
Hornblotton Green
Middlezoy
River Cary
Butleigh
Clanville
Ansford
Henley
Pitcombe
West Lydford
Othery
High Ham
Dundon
Barton St David
East Lydford
Alford
Castle Cary
BRADLEY HILL
Burrow Bridge
Lovington
Beer
Stembridge Tower Mill
Littleton
Kingweston
Keinton Mandeville
Lydford on Fosse
Burrow Mump
Foddington
Galhampton
Lyng
Stathe
Low Ham
Bramwell
Charlton Mackrell
Aller
Somerton
Babcary
North Barrow
Athelney
Pitney
South Barrow
Willows & Wetlands
Woodhill
Wearne
Charlton Adam
Brookhampton
Langport
Haynes International Motor
Meare Green
Stoke St Gregory
Oath
Upton
Lytes Cary Manor
North Cadbury
Blackford
Curry Rivel
Huish Episcopi
Kingsdon
Sparkford
Little Weston
Compton Pauncefoot
Hunthan
Heale
Pibsbury
Catsgore
Downhead
North Curry
Swell Wood
Long Sutton
West Camel
South Cadbury
Abbey
Muchelney
Knole
Podimore
Queen Camel
Willtown
Drayton
Little Load
Wales
Bridgehampton
Sutton Montis
Curry Mallet
Fivehead
Muchelney Ham
Long Load
Ilchester
RNAS Yeovilton
Fleet Air Arm
Yeovilton
Chilton Cantelo
Marston Magna
Thorney
Limington
Corton Denham
Isle Brewers
Hambridge
Kingsbury Episcopi
Milton
Witcombe
Ashington
Isle Abbotts
Rimpton
Manor House
Stapleton
Coat
Ash
Tintinhull Garden
West Mudford
Adber
Sandford Orcas
Beercrocombe
Westport
Chilthorne Domer
Mudford Sock
Treasurer's House
New Cross
Stembridge
Yeovil Marsh
Mudford
Poyntington
Stewley
West Lambrook
Martock
Tintinhull
Up Mudford
Puckington
Barrington
East Lambrook
Priory
Stoke sub Hamdon
Trent
Ilton
Ilford
Stocklinch
Barrington Court
Compton Durville
Ham Hill
Montacute
Yeovil
Nether Compton
Shepton Beauchamp
South Petherton
Norton sub Hamdon
Montacute House
Odcombe
Preston Plucknett
Over Compton
Stallen
Sherborne Old Castle
Whitelackington
Seavington St Michael
Over Stratton
Wigborough
Little Norton
Brympton
Sherborne
Sherborne Castle & Gardens
Ilminster
Seavington St Mary
Chiselborough
West Coker
Barwick
Bradford Abbas
North Wootton
Kingstone
Allowenshay
Lopen
West Chinnock
East Chinnock
Thornford
Folke
Donyatt
Dinnington
Middle Chinnock
Hardington Moor
Stoford
Knowle St Giles
Dowlish Wake
Ludney
Hinton St George
Merriott
Hardington Mandeville
East Coker
Lillington
Longburton
Chardleigh Green
Cudworth
Chillington
Haselbury Plucknett
Beer Hackett
Knighton
Crewkerne
Pendomer
Ryme Intrinseca
Yetminster
Chaffcombe
North Perrott
Hardington Marsh
Closworth
Hamlet
Leigh
Cricket
Hewish
Glanvilles
0 1 2 3 4 miles
0 1 2 3 4 5 kilometres
A B C D E F
1 2 3 4 5 6 7 8
38
25
13
14
A371 A368 A38 A39 A37 A361 A372 A303 A3088 A30 A359 A352 A3066 M5
B3134 B3135 B3114 B3371 B3139 B3151 B3136 B3153 B3165 B3168 B3151 B3148 B3145 B3152 B3081 B3355 B3356

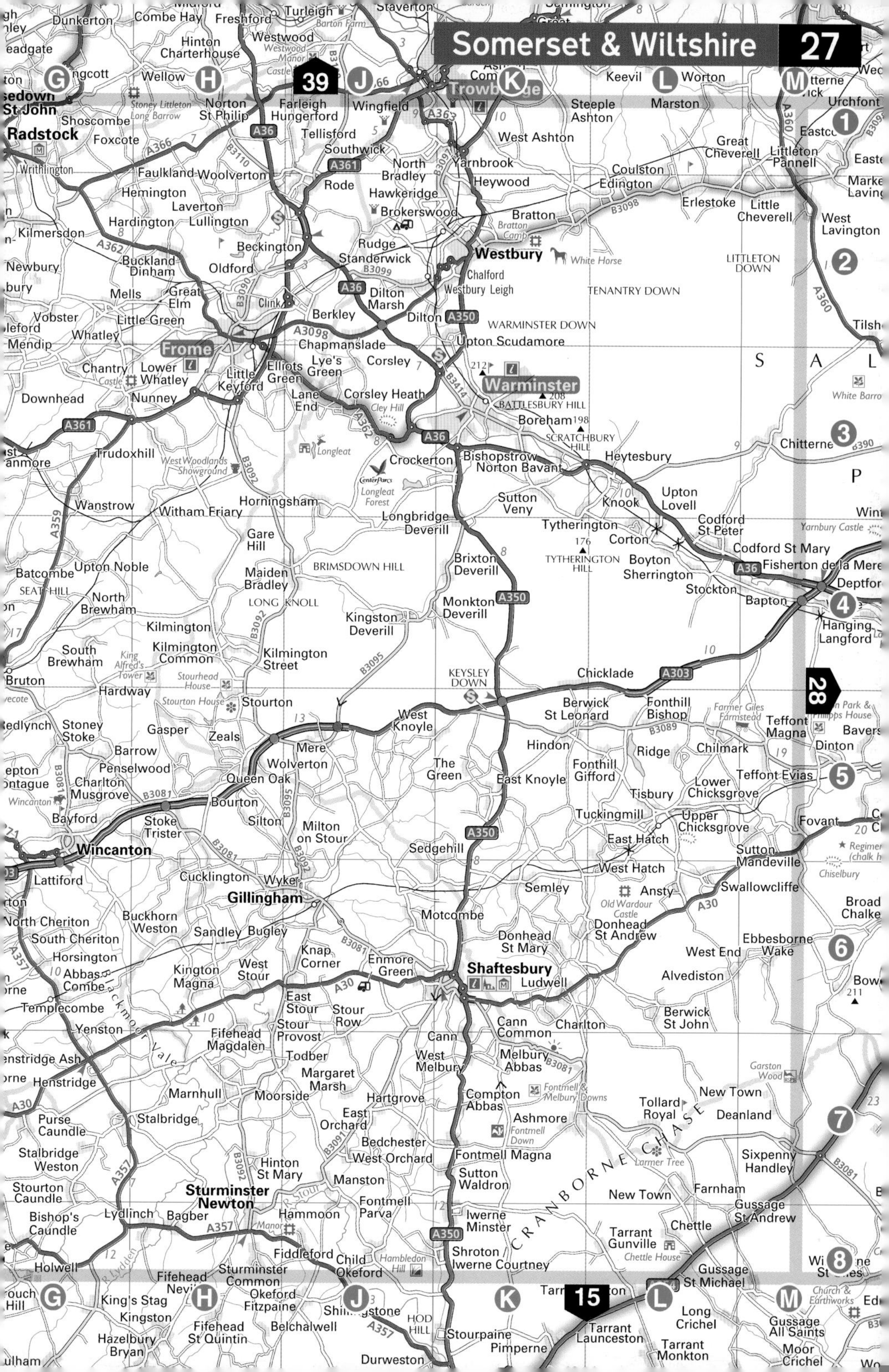

Dunkerton
Combe Hay
Freshford
Turleigh
Staverton
Barton Farm
Hinton Charterhouse
Westwood
Westwood Manor
Castle
Wellow
Farleigh Hungerford
Wingfield
Trowbridge
Keevil
Worton
Steeple Ashton
Marston
Urchfont
Norton St Philip
Stoney Littleton Long Barrow
Radstock
Shoscombe
Foxcote
Tellisford
Southwick
West Ashton
Great Cheverell
Littleton Pannell
Writhlington
Faulkland
Woolverton
North Bradley
Yarnbrook
Coulston
Edington
Rode
Heywood
Hemington
Hawkeridge
Laverton
Brokerswood
Erlestoke
Little Cheverell
West Lavington
Hardington
Lullington
Bratton
Bratton Camp
Kilmersdon
Beckington
Rudge
Westbury
White Horse
Buckland Dinham
Standerwick
Newbury
Oldford
Chalford
Westbury Leigh
LITTLETON DOWN
Mells
Great Elm
Clink
Dilton Marsh
TENANTRY DOWN
Vobster
Little Green
Berkley
Dilton
Whatley
WARMINSTER DOWN
Chapmanslade
Upton Scudamore
Frome
Lye's Green
Corsley
Chantry
Lower Whatley
Elliots Green
Little Keyford
Warminster
Downhead
Nunney
Lane End
Corsley Heath
Cley Hill
BATTLESBURY HILL
White Barrow
Boreham
SCRATCHBURY HILL
Trudoxhill
Longleat
Crockerton
Bishopstrow
Norton Bavant
Heytesbury
Chitterne
West Woodlands Showground
Center Parcs Longleat Forest
Horningsham
Sutton Veny
Knook
Upton Lovell
Wanstrow
Witham Friary
Longbridge Deverill
Tytherington
Codford St Peter
Yarnbury Castle
Gare Hill
Corton
Codford St Mary
Brixton Deverill
TYTHERINGTON HILL
Boyton
Fisherton de la Mere
Batcombe
Upton Noble
BRIMSDOWN HILL
Sherrington
Deptford
SEAT HILL
Maiden Bradley
North Brewham
LONG KNOLL
Stockton
Bapton
Monkton Deverill
Kingston Deverill
Kilmington
Hanging Langford
South Brewham
King Alfred's Tower
Kilmington Common
Kilmington Street
Bruton
Stourhead House
KEYSLEY DOWN
Chicklade
Hardway
Stourton House
Stourton
West Knoyle
Berwick St Leonard
Fonthill Bishop
Farmer Giles Farmstead
Teffont Magna
Stoney Stoke
Gasper
Zeals
Dinton
Barrow
Mere
Hindon
Ridge
Chilmark
Penselwood
Wolverton
The Green
Fonthill Gifford
Teffont Evias
Charlton Musgrove
Queen Oak
East Knoyle
Lower Chicksgrove
Tisbury
Wincanton
Bourton
Stoke Trister
Silton
Milton on Stour
Tuckingmill
Upper Chicksgrove
Fovant
Bayford
East Hatch
Sedgehill
Sutton Mandeville
Wincanton
West Hatch
Lattiford
Cucklington
Wyke
Semley
Ansty
Swallowcliffe
Chiselbury
Gillingham
Old Wardour Castle
Broad Chalke
North Cheriton
Buckhorn Weston
Motcombe
Donhead St Andrew
South Cheriton
Sandley
Bugley
Donhead St Mary
Ebbesborne Wake
Horsington
Knap Corner
Enmore Green
West End
Kington Magna
West Stour
Shaftesbury
Abbas Combe
Ludwell
Alvediston
East Stour
Stour Row
Templecombe
Cann Common
Yenston
Stour Provost
Cann
Charlton
Berwick St John
Fifehead Magdalen
Blackmore Vale
Todber
West Melbury
Melbury Abbas
Henstridge Ash
Margaret Marsh
Henstridge
Marnhull
Moorside
Hartgrove
Compton Abbas
Fontmell & Melbury Downs
Garston Wood
Tollard Royal
New Town
Deanland
Purse Caundle
Stalbridge
East Orchard
Ashmore
Fontmell Down
CRANBORNE CHASE
Bedchester
Stalbridge Weston
West Orchard
Fontmell Magna
Larmer Tree
Sixpenny Handley
Hinton St Mary
Sutton Waldron
Stourton Caundle
Sturminster Newton
Manston
New Town
Farnham
Gussage St Andrew
Lydlinch
Bagber
Hammoon
Fontmell Parva
Iwerne Minster
Bishop's Caundle
Manor
Tarrant Gunville
Chettle
Chettle House
Holwell
Fiddleford
Child Okeford
Hambledon Hill
Shroton
Iwerne Courtney
Fifehead Neville
Sturminster Common
Gussage St Michael
Wimborne St Giles
Okeford Fitzpaine
Church & Earthworks
King's Stag
Shillingstone
HOD HILL
Long Crichel
Kingston
Fifehead St Quintin
Belchalwell
Stourpaine
Tarrant Launceston
Gussage All Saints
Hazelbury Bryan
Pimperne
Tarrant Monkton
Moor Crichel
Durweston
S A L
P

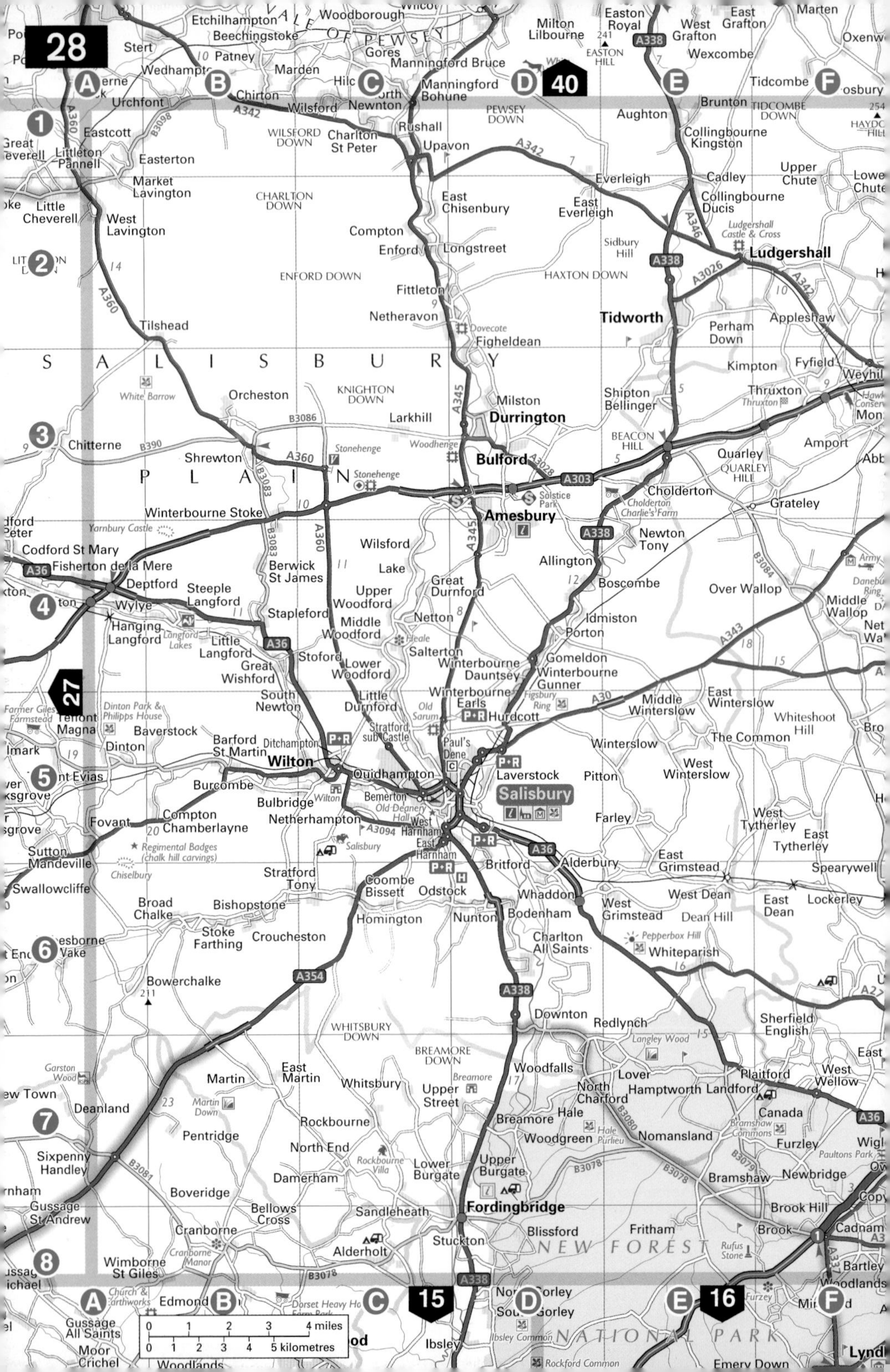
VALE OF PEWSEY
Etchilhampton
Woodborough
Beechingstoke
Milton Lilbourne
Easton Royal
East Grafton
West Grafton
Marten
Stert
Patney
Gores
Manningford Bruce
Wexcombe
Wedhampton
Marden
Easton Hill
Chirton
Manningford Bohune
Tidcombe
Urchfont
Wilsford
Newnton
Brunton
Tidcombe Down
Pewsey Down
Aughton
Eastcott
Rushall
Wilsford Down
Charlton St Peter
Collingbourne Kingston
Littleton Pannell
Upavon
Easterton
Everleigh
Cadley
Upper Chute
Market Lavington
Charlton Down
East Chisenbury
East Everleigh
Collingbourne Ducis
Little Cheverell
West Lavington
Compton
Ludgershall Castle & Cross
Ludgershall
Enford
Longstreet
Sidbury Hill
Enford Down
Haxton Down
Fittleton
Tidworth
Netheravon
Dovecote
Figheldean
Perham Down
Appleshaw
Tilshead
SALISBURY PLAIN
Kimpton
Fyfield
Weyhill
White Barrow
Orcheston
Knighton Down
Milton
Durrington
Shipton Bellinger
Thruxton
Larkhill
Chitterne
Shrewton
Stonehenge
Woodhenge
Bulford
Beacon Hill
Quarley
Quarley Hill
Amport
Solstice Park
Cholderton
Cholderton Charlie's Farm
Grateley
Amesbury
Winterbourne Stoke
Yarnbury Castle
Newton Tony
Codford St Mary
Fisherton de la Mere
Wilsford
Allington
Berwick St James
Lake
Boscombe
Deptford
Steeple Langford
Great Durnford
Over Wallop
Middle Wallop
Wylye
Upper Woodford
Stapleford
Netton
Idmiston
Hanging Langford
Langford Lakes
Little Langford
Middle Woodford
Heale
Porton
Great Wishford
Stoford
Lower Woodford
Salterton
Winterbourne Dauntsey
Gomeldon
Winterbourne Gunner
South Newton
Little Durnford
Winterbourne Earls
Figsbury Ring
Middle Winterslow
East Winterslow
Whiteshoot Hill
Teffont Magna
Dinton Park & Philipps House
Farmer Giles Farmstead
Baverstock
Barford St Martin
Ditchampton
Old Sarum
Stratford sub Castle
Hurdcott
Dinton
Wilton
Paul's Dene
Winterslow
The Common
Quidhampton
Laverstock
Pitton
West Winterslow
Burcombe
Bulbridge
Bemerton
Salisbury
Netherhampton
Old Deanery Hall
West Harnham
Farley
West Tytherley
East Tytherley
Fovant
Compton Chamberlayne
East Harnham
Sutton Mandeville
Regimental Badges (chalk hill carvings)
Chiselbury
Britford
Alderbury
East Grimstead
Spearywell
Swallowcliffe
Stratford Tony
Coombe Bissett
Odstock
Whaddon
West Dean
East Dean
Lockerley
Broad Chalke
Bishopstone
Homington
Nunton
Bodenham
West Grimstead
Dean Hill
Stoke Farthing
Croucheston
Charlton All Saints
Pepperbox Hill
Whiteparish
Bowerchalke
Downton
Redlynch
Sherfield English
Whitsbury Down
Langley Wood
Breamore Down
East Martin
Woodfalls
Lover
Plaitford
West Wellow
Garston Wood
Martin
Whitsbury
Upper Street
Breamore
North Charford
Hamptworth
Landford
Deanland
Martin Down
Canada
Rockbourne
Breamore
Hale
Hale Purlieu
Nomansland
Bramshaw Commons
Furzley
Pentridge
Woodgreen
North End
Paultons Park
Sixpenny Handley
Rockbourne Villa
Lower Burgate
Upper Burgate
Bramshaw
Newbridge
Damerham
Boveridge
Gussage St Andrew
Bellows Cross
Sandleheath
Fordingbridge
Brook Hill
Cranborne
Cranborne Manor
Blissford
Fritham
Brook
Cadnam
Alderholt
Stuckton
NEW FOREST
Rufus Stone
Wimborne St Giles
Bartley
Woodlands
Church & Earthworks
Edmondsham
Dorset Heavy Horse Farm Park
North Gorley
South Gorley
Furzey
Minstead
Gussage All Saints
Ibsley
Ibsley Common
NATIONAL PARK
Moor Crichel
Woodlands
Rockford Common
Emery Down
Lyndhurst
A360
A342
A338
A346
A3026
A345
A303
A3028
A36
A343
A30
A3094
A354
A337
B3098
B3086
B390
B3083
B3084
B3081
B3078
B3080
B3079
40
15
16
27
0 1 2 3 4 miles
0 1 2 3 4 5 kilometres

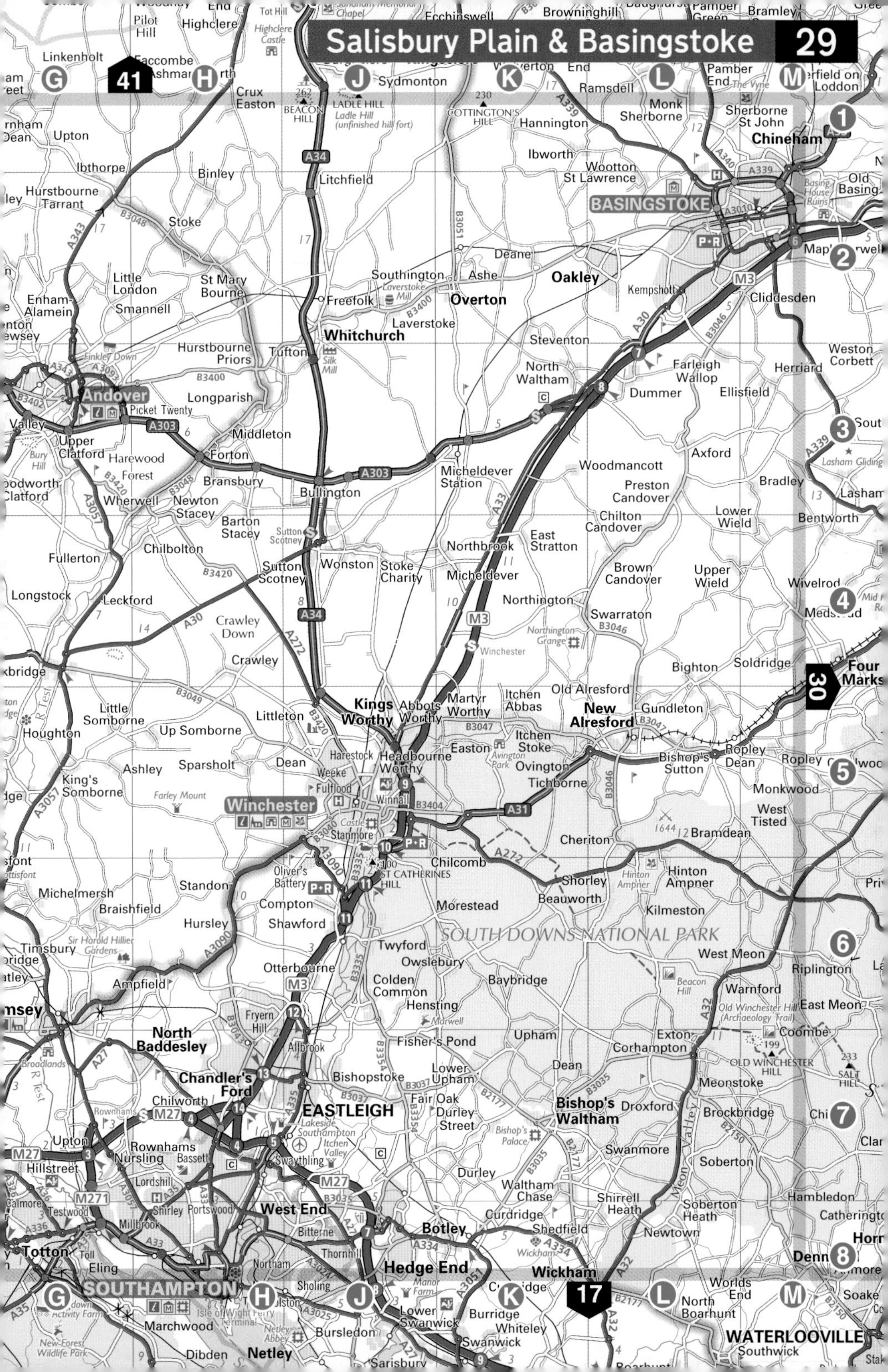
41
30
17
G
H
J
K
L
M
1
2
3
4
5
6
7
8
Pilot Hill
Highclere
Highclere Castle
Linkenholt
Faccombe
Crux Easton
Sydmonton
262
BEACON HILL
LADLE HILL
Ladle Hill (unfinished hill fort)
230
COTTINGTON'S HILL
Browninghill
Ramsdell
Monk Sherborne
Pamber End
The Vyne
Sherborne St John
Chineham
Hannington
Ibworth
Wootton St Lawrence
BASINGSTOKE
Basing House (Ruins)
Old Basing
Upton
Ibthorpe
Binley
Litchfield
Hurstbourne Tarrant
Stoke
Deane
Southington
Laverstoke Mill
Ashe
Oakley
Kempshott
Cliddesden
Little London
St Mary Bourne
Enham-Alamein
Smannell
Freefolk
Overton
Laverstoke
Whitchurch
Finkley Down
Hurstbourne Priors
Tufton
Silk Mill
Steventon
North Waltham
Farleigh Wallop
Dummer
Herriard
Ellisfield
Weston Corbett
Andover
Picket Twenty
Longparish
Middleton
Valley
Upper Clatford
Bury Hill
Harewood Forest
Forton
Bransbury
Bullington
Micheldever Station
Woodmancott
Axford
Preston Candover
Bradley
Lasham Gliding
Lasham
Chilton Candover
Lower Wield
Bentworth
Wherwell
Newton Stacey
Barton Stacey
Sutton Scotney
Northbrook
East Stratton
Fullerton
Chilbolton
Wonston
Stoke Charity
Micheldever
Brown Candover
Upper Wield
Wivelrod
Longstock
Leckford
Crawley Down
Northington
Swarraton
Northington Grange
Winchester
Crawley
Bighton
Soldridge
Four Marks
Little Somborne
Houghton
Up Somborne
Littleton
Kings Worthy
Abbots Worthy
Martyr Worthy
Itchen Abbas
Old Alresford
New Alresford
Gundleton
Itchen Stoke
Easton
Avington Park
Harestock
Headbourne Worthy
Weeke
Fulflood
Winnall
Ovington
Tichborne
Bishop's Sutton
Ropley Dean
Ropley
Monkwood
West Tisted
King's Somborne
Ashley
Sparsholt
Dean
Farley Mount
Winchester
Castle
Stanmore
Cheriton
Bramdean
1644
Chilcomb
ST CATHERINES HILL
Oliver's Battery
Shorley
Hinton Ampner
Beauworth
Kilmeston
Michelmersh
Braishfield
Standon
Compton
Hursley
Shawford
Morestead
SOUTH DOWNS NATIONAL PARK
Sir Harold Hillier Gardens
Timsbury
Twyford
Owslebury
West Meon
Ripplington
Ampfield
Otterbourne
Colden Common
Baybridge
Beacon Hill
Warnford
East Meon
Hensting
Marwell
Old Winchester Hill (Archaeology Trail)
Coombe
North Baddesley
Fryern Hill
Allbrook
Fisher's Pond
Upham
Exton
Corhampton
199
OLD WINCHESTER HILL
233
SALT HILL
Broadlands
Chandler's Ford
Bishopstoke
Lower Upham
Dean
Meonstoke
Chilworth
EASTLEIGH
Fair Oak
Durley Street
Bishop's Waltham
Droxford
Brockbridge
Rownhams
Lakeside
Southampton
Itchen Valley
Bishop's Palace
Upton
Nursling
Bassett
Swaythling
Swanmore
Hillstreet
Lordshill
Durley
Soberton
Meon Valley
Testwood
Shirley
Portswood
West End
Waltham Chase
Shirrell Heath
Hambledon
Millbrook
Bitterne
Curdridge
Soberton Heath
Catherington
Totton
Eling
Thornhill
Botley
Shedfield
Newtown
Wickham
Northam
Hedge End
Manor Farm
Wickham
Sholing
Denmead
Worlds End
North Boarhunt
Soake
SOUTHAMPTON
Isle of Wight Ferry Terminal
Lower Swanwick
Burridge
Whiteley
Marchwood
Netley Abbey
Bursledon
Swanwick
WATERLOOVILLE
Southwick
New Forest Wildlife Park
Dibden
Netley
Sarisbury
A34
A339
A340
A3010
M3
A343
B3048
B3051
B3400
A3093
B3402
A303
B3420
A3057
A30
B3046
A33
B3049
A272
B3047
B3404
A31
A3090
B3335
B3040
B3354
A32
M27
A27
B3043
A335
B3037
B3035
B2177
A36
M271
A3024
A3025
A334
B2150
A35
P+R

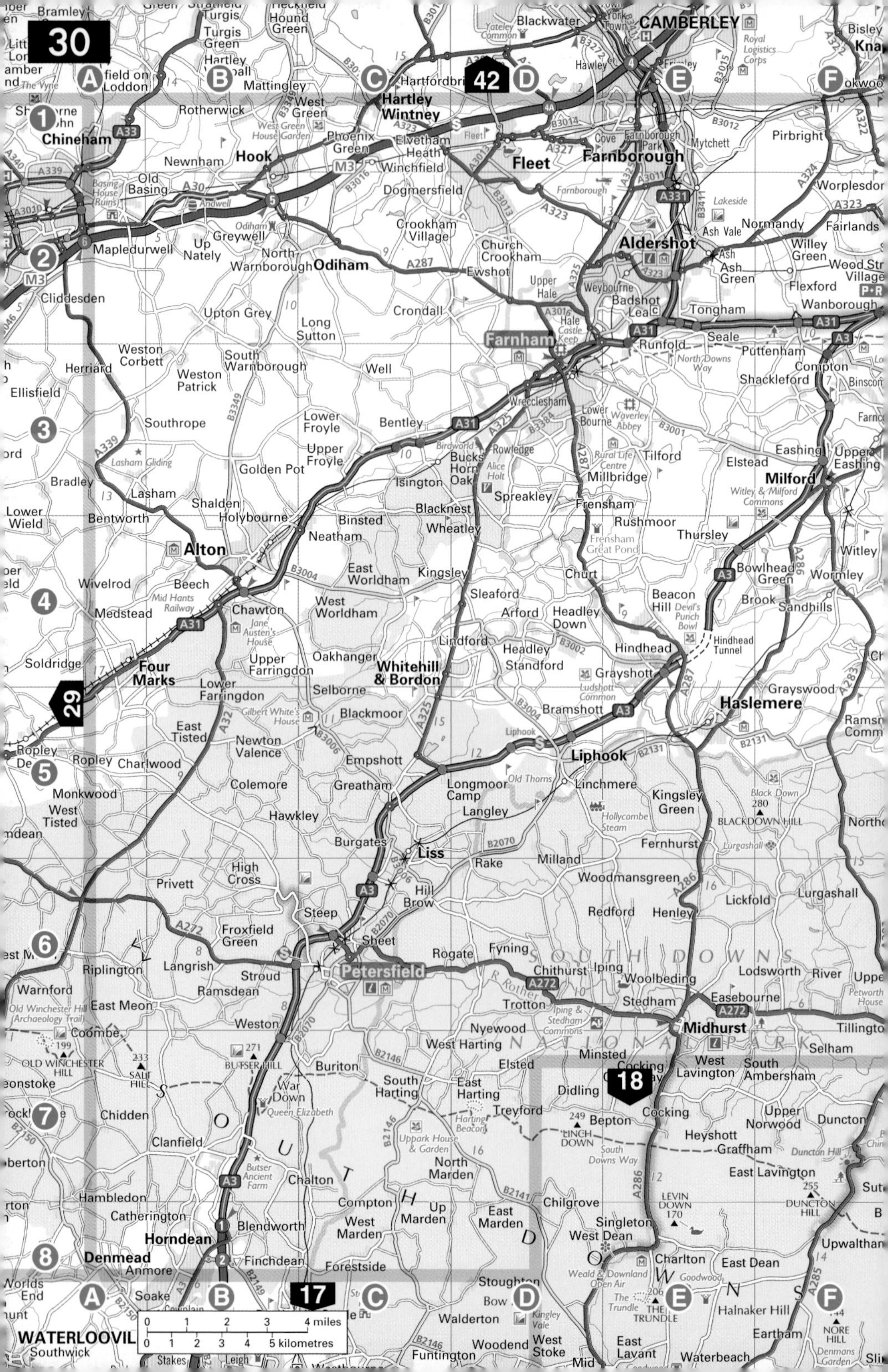
42
29
18
17
A
B
C
D
E
F
1
2
3
4
5
6
7
8
Bramley
Turgis
Turgis Green
Hound Green
Hartley Wespall
Stratfield on Loddon
The Vyne
Sherborne St John
Chineham
A33
Rotherwick
Mattingley
West Green
West Green House Garden
Hartley Wintney
Hartfordbridge
Blackwater
Yateley Common
CAMBERLEY
Royal Logistics Corps
Hawley
Frimley
Bisley
Knaphill
Pokwood
Newnham
Hook
Phoenix Green
Elvetham Heath
Winchfield
Fleet
Cove
Farnborough Park
Farnborough
Mytchett
Pirbright
Worplesdon
Old Basing
Basing House (Ruins)
A339
A340
A30
Andwell
M3
Dogmersfield
Crookham Village
Farnborough
A331
Lakeside
Normandy
Fairlands
A323
Mapledurwell
Up Nately
Greywell
Odiham
North Warnborough
Church Crookham
Aldershot
Ash Vale
Ash
Ash Green
Willey Green
Wood Street Village
Flexford
Cliddesden
Upton Grey
Long Sutton
Crondall
Ewshot
A287
Upper Hale
Hale
Weybourne
Badshot Lea
Tongham
Wanborough
A31
Farnham
Castle Keep
Runfold
Seale
Puttenham
North Downs Way
A3
Compton
Shackleford
Binscombe
Weston Corbett
Herriard
South Warnborough
Weston Patrick
Well
Ellisfield
B3349
Southrope
Lower Froyle
Bentley
Wrecclesham
A325
B3384
Lower Bourne
Waverley Abbey
B3001
Eashing
Upper Eashing
Lasham Gliding
A339
Upper Froyle
Golden Pot
Birdworld
Rowledge
Alice Holt
Bucks Horn Oak
Isington
Rural Life Centre
Tilford
Millbridge
Elstead
Milford
Bradley
Lasham
Shalden
Holybourne
Blacknest
Binsted
Wheatley
Spreakley
Frensham
Witley & Milford Commons
Lower Wield
Bentworth
Alton
Neatham
Rushmoor
Thursley
Frensham Great Pond
Witley
East Worldham
B3004
Kingsley
Churt
Bowlhead Green
A286
Wormley
Wivelrod
Beech
Mid Hants Railway
Medstead
Chawton
Jane Austen's House
West Worldham
Sleaford
Arford
Headley Down
Beacon Hill
Devil's Punch Bowl
Brook
Sandhills
Lindford
Headley
B3002
Hindhead
Hindhead Tunnel
Soldridge
Four Marks
Upper Farringdon
Oakhanger
Whitehill & Bordon
Standford
Grayshott
Ludshott Common
Grayswood
A283
Lower Farringdon
Selborne
Gilbert White's House
Blackmoor
Bramshott
Haslemere
Ramsnest Common
East Tisted
A32
Newton Valence
B3006
Empshott
Liphook
B2131
Ropley
Ropley Dean
Charlwood
Colemore
Greatham
Longmoor Camp
Old Thorns
Linchmere
Kingsley Green
Black Down
280
BLACKDOWN HILL
Monkwood
West Tisted
Hawkley
Langley
Hollycombe Steam
Northchapel
Burgates
Liss
B2070
Rake
Milland
Fernhurst
Lurgashall
High Cross
Privett
A272
Hill Brow
Woodmansgreen
Redford
Henley
Lickfold
Lurgashall
Steep
Froxfield Green
Sheet
Rogate
Fyning
SOUTH DOWNS
Riplington
Langrish
Stroud
Petersfield
Chithurst
Iping
Woolbeding
Lodsworth
River
Upperton
Warnford
Ramsdean
R Rother
Trotton
Stedham
Easebourne
Petworth House
Old Winchester Hill (Archaeology Trail)
East Meon
Coombe
Weston
Iping & Stedham Commons
Midhurst
Tillington
199
OLD WINCHESTER HILL
233
SALT HILL
271
BUTSER HILL
Nyewood
West Harting
NATIONAL PARK
Selham
Buriton
B2146
Elsted
Minsted
Cocking Causeway
West Lavington
South Ambersham
Exton
Meonstoke
War Down
Queen Elizabeth
South Harting
East Harting
Didling
Droxford
Chidden
Harting Beacon
Treyford
249
Bepton
Cocking
Upper Norwood
Duncton
Clanfield
Uppark House & Garden
LINCH DOWN
Heyshott
South Downs Way
Graffham
Duncton Hill
Hambledon
Butser Ancient Farm
Chalton
North Marden
East Lavington
Catherington
Compton
Up Marden
B2141
Chilgrove
LEVIN DOWN
170
255
DUNCTON HILL
Horndean
Blendworth
West Marden
East Marden
Singleton
West Dean
Upwaltham
Denmead
Anmore
Finchdean
B2149
Forestside
Charlton
East Dean
Worlds End
Soake
Stoughton
Weald & Downland Open Air
Goodwood
A285
Waterlooville
Cowplain
B2150
Bow Hill
The Trundle
206
THE TRUNDLE
Halnaker Hill
144
NORE HILL
Walderton
Kingley Vale
Eartham
Denmans Garden
WATERLOOVILLE
Southwick
B2146
Woodend
West Stoke
East Lavant
Waterbeach
Funtington
Stakes
Leigh
0 1 2 3 4 miles
0 1 2 3 4 5 kilometres

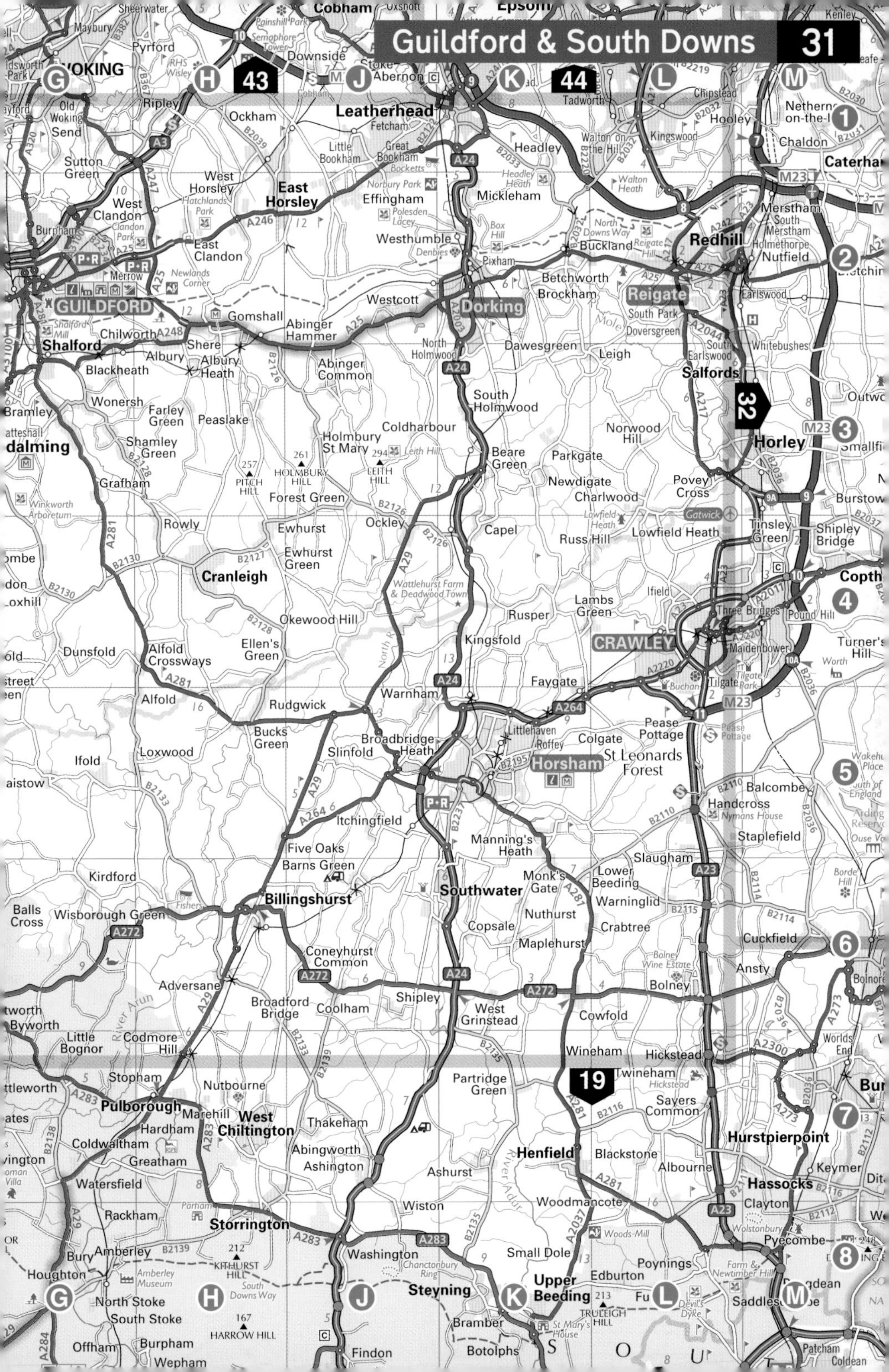

G
H
J
K
L
M
43
44
32
19
1
2
3
4
5
6
7
8
Sheerwater
Maybury
Pyrford
WOKING
RHS Wisley
Painshill Park
Semaphore Tower
Cobham
Oxshott
Downside
Stoke d'Abernon
Epsom
Kenley
Tadworth
Chipstead
Netherne-on-the-Hill
Hooley
Chaldon
Caterham
Old Woking
Send
Ripley
Ockham
Leatherhead
Fetcham
Little Bookham
Great Bookham
Bocketts
Headley
Headley Heath
Walton on the Hill
Kingswood
Walton Heath
Sutton Green
West Horsley
Hatchlands Park
East Horsley
Norbury Park
Effingham
Polesden Lacey
Mickleham
Box Hill
West Clandon
Clandon Park
Burpham
East Clandon
Westhumble
Denbies
Pixham
North Downs Way
Buckland
Reigate Hill
Redhill
Merstham
South Merstham
Holmethorpe
Nutfield
Bletchingley
Merrow
Newlands Corner
GUILDFORD
Shalford Mill
Gomshall
Abinger Hammer
Westcott
Dorking
Betchworth
Brockham
Reigate
South Park
Earlswood
Doversgreen
Shalford
Chilworth
Albury
Shere
Albury Heath
Blackheath
Abinger Common
North Holmwood
Dawesgreen
Leigh
South Earlswood
Whitebushes
Salfords
Bramley
Wonersh
Farley Green
Peaslake
South Holmwood
Outwood
Godalming
Shamley Green
Holmbury St Mary
Coldharbour
Leith Hill
Beare Green
Parkgate
Norwood Hill
Horley
Smallfield
Grafham
Pitch Hill
Holmbury Hill
Forest Green
Newdigate
Charlwood
Povey Cross
Burstow
Winkworth Arboretum
Gatwick
Lowfield Heath
Rowly
Ewhurst
Ockley
Capel
Russ Hill
Tinsley Green
Shipley Bridge
Ewhurst Green
Cranleigh
Wattlehurst Farm & Deadwood Town
Ifield
Copthorne
Dunsfold
Okewood Hill
Rusper
Lambs Green
Three Bridges
Pound Hill
Alfold Crossways
Ellen's Green
Kingsfold
CRAWLEY
Maidenbower
Turner's Hill
Worth
Alfold
Rudgwick
Warnham
Faygate
Buchan
Tilgate
Tilgate Park
Bucks Green
Broadbridge Heath
Littlehaven
Roffey
Colgate
Pease Pottage
Ifold
Loxwood
Slinfold
Horsham
St Leonards Forest
Wakehurst Place
Balcombe
Handcross
Nymans House
South of England
Ardingly Reservoir
Itchingfield
Staplefield
Ouse Valley
Five Oaks
Barns Green
Manning's Heath
Slaugham
Kirdford
Monk's Gate
Lower Beeding
Borde Hill
Balls Cross
Wisborough Green
Fishers
Billingshurst
Southwater
Warninglid
Nuthurst
Copsale
Crabtree
Cuckfield
Maplehurst
Coneyhurst Common
Bolney Wine Estate
Ansty
Bolnore
Adversane
Shipley
Bolney
Broadford Bridge
Coolham
West Grinstead
Cowfold
River Arun
Byworth
Little Bognor
Codmore Hill
Wineham
Hickstead
Worlds End
Stopham
Partridge Green
Twineham
Pulborough
Marehill
Nutbourne
West Chiltington
Sayers Common
Hardham
Thakeham
Hurstpierpoint
Coldwaltham
Greatham
Abingworth
Ashington
Henfield
Blackstone
Albourne
Keymer
Watersfield
Ashurst
River Adur
Hassocks
Rackham
Parham
Wiston
Woodmancote
Clayton
Storrington
Wolstonbury
Woods-Mill
Pycombe
Bury
Amberley
Kithurst Hill
Washington
Chanctonbury Ring
Small Dole
Poynings
Houghton
Amberley Museum
South Downs Way
Steyning
Upper Beeding
Edburton
Farm & Newtimber Hill
North Stoke
Truleigh Hill
Devil's Dyke
South Stoke
Harrow Hill
Bramber
St Mary's House
Saddlescombe
Offham
Burpham
Wepham
Findon
Botolphs
Patcham
Coldean
SOUTH

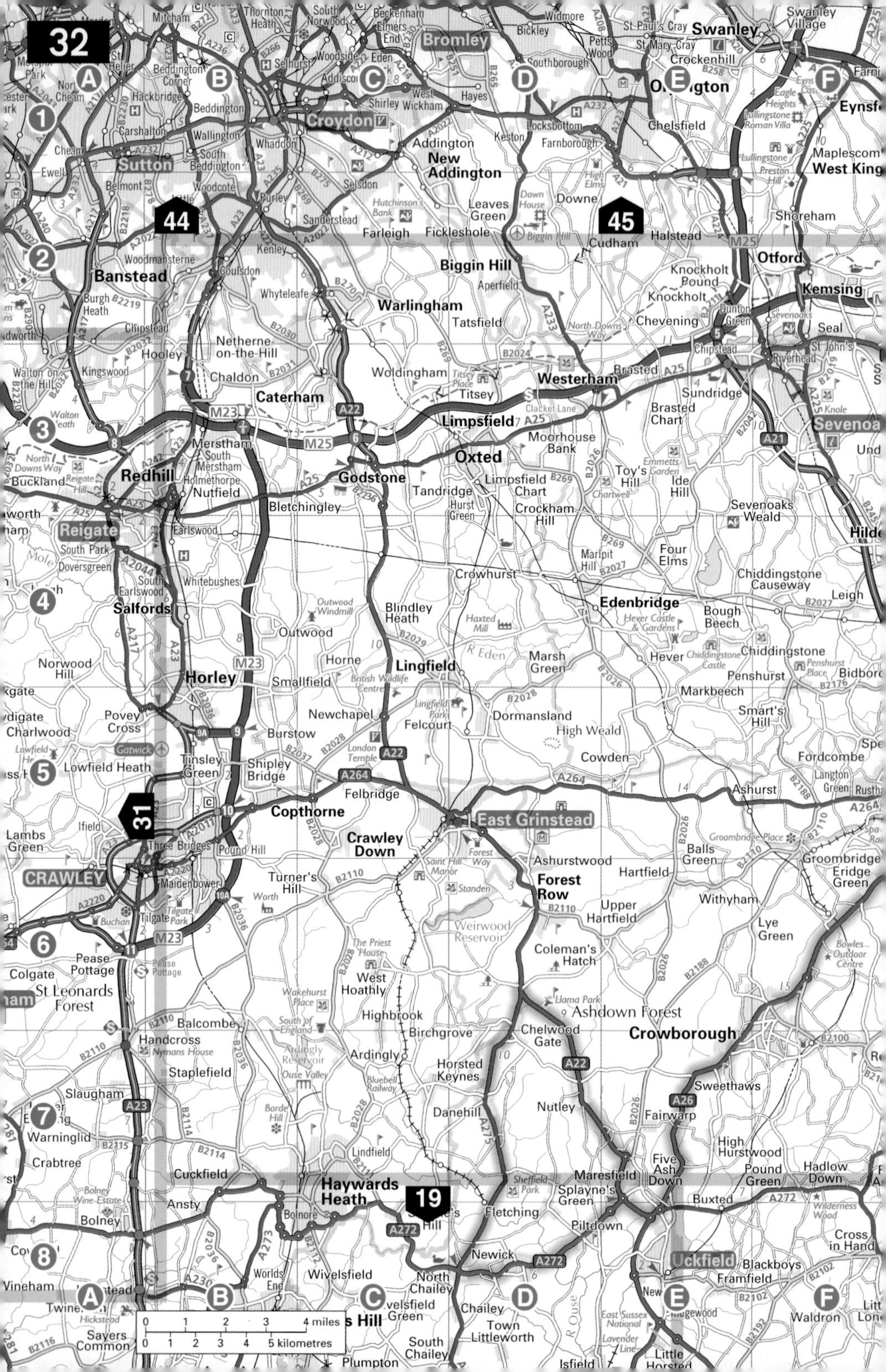

Mitcham
Thornton Heath
South Norwood
Beckenham
Elmers End
Bromley
Widmore
Bickley
St Paul's Cray
Swanley
Swanley Village
St Mary Cray
Petts Wood
Crockenhill
Southborough
St Helier
Beddington Corner
Selhurst
Woodside
Eden Park
Addiscombe
Hayes
West Wickham
Shirley
Orpington
Eynsford
Lullingstone Roman Villa
Hackbridge
Beddington
Carshalton
Wallington
Croydon
Whaddon
Cheam
North Cheam
Ewell
Sutton
South Beddington
Addington
New Addington
Keston
Locksbottom
Farnborough
Chelsfield
West Kingsdown
Maplescombe
Belmont
Woodcote
Purley
Selsdon
Sanderstead
Hutchinson's Bank
Leaves Green
Downe
High Elms
Down House
Lullingstone
Preston Hill
Shoreham
Farleigh
Fickleshole
Biggin Hill
Cudham
Halstead
M25
Otford
Kenley
Woodmansterne
Banstead
Coulsdon
Whyteleafe
Aperfield
Knockholt Pound
Knockholt
Kemsing
Burgh Heath
Chipstead
Warlingham
Tatsfield
North Downs Way
Chevening
Dunton Green
Sevenoaks
Seal
St John's
Riverhead
Netherne-on-the-Hill
Hooley
Kingswood
Walton on the Hill
Chaldon
Woldingham
Titsey Place
Titsey
Westerham
Brasted
Chipstead
Sundridge
Caterham
Clacket Lane
Limpsfield
Brasted Chart
Knole
Walton Heath
M23
A22
Merstham
South Merstham
M25
Moorhouse Bank
Oxted
Godstone
Buckland
Reigate Hill
Redhill
Holmethorpe
Nutfield
Tandridge
Limpsfield Chart
Toy's Hill
Emmetts Garden
Ide Hill
Chartwell
Bletchingley
Hurst Green
Crockham Hill
Sevenoaks Weald
Reigate
Earlswood
South Park
Doversgreen
Whitebushes
South Earlswood
Salfords
Four Elms
Marlpit Hill
Crowhurst
Chiddingstone Causeway
Leigh
Edenbridge
Outwood Windmill
Blindley Heath
Haxted Mill
Outwood
Hever Castle & Gardens
Bough Beech
Hever
Chiddingstone Castle
Chiddingstone
Norwood Hill
R Eden
Marsh Green
Horne
Lingfield
Horley
Smallfield
British Wildlife Centre
Penshurst
Penshurst Place
Bidborough
Markbeech
Lingfield Park
Dormansland
Smart's Hill
Povey Cross
Charlwood
Newchapel
Felcourt
High Weald
Burstow
Gatwick
Lowfield Heath
Tinsley Green
London Temple
Cowden
Fordcombe
Shipley Bridge
Langton Green
A264
Ashurst
Rusthall
Ifield
Lambs Green
Copthorne
Felbridge
East Grinstead
Three Bridges
Pound Hill
Crawley Down
CRAWLEY
Maidenbower
Ashurstwood
Groombridge Place
Balls Green
Groombridge
Eridge Green
Hartfield
Forest Way
Saint Hill Manor
Standen
Turner's Hill
Worth
Forest Row
Upper Hartfield
Withyham
Buchan
Tilgate Park
Weirwood Reservoir
Lye Green
Pease Pottage
Colgate
The Priest House
Coleman's Hatch
Bowles Outdoor Centre
St Leonards Forest
West Hoathly
Wakehurst Place
Llama Park
Ashdown Forest
Highbrook
Balcombe
South of England
Birchgrove
Chelwood Gate
Crowborough
Handcross
Nymans House
Ardingly Reservoir
Ardingly
Horsted Keynes
Staplefield
Ouse Valley
Bluebell Railway
Slaugham
Sweethaws
Danehill
Nutley
Fairwarp
Warninglid
Borde Hill
Crabtree
Lindfield
High Hurstwood
Five Ash Down
Cuckfield
Haywards Heath
Sheffield Park
Maresfield
Splayne's Green
Pound Green
Hadlow Down
Bolney Wine Estate
Ansty
Fletching
Buxted
Wilderness Wood
Bolney
Bolnore
Piltdown
Cross in Hand
Newick
Uckfield
Blackboys
Framfield
Vineham
Worlds End
Wivelsfield
North Chailey
Chailey
Hickstead
Sayers Common
Wivelsfield Green
Town Littleworth
East Sussex National
Ridgewood
Waldron
South Chailey
Lavender Line
R Ouse
Plumpton
Isfield
Little Horsted
0 1 2 3 4 miles
0 1 2 3 4 5 kilometres
44
45
31
19

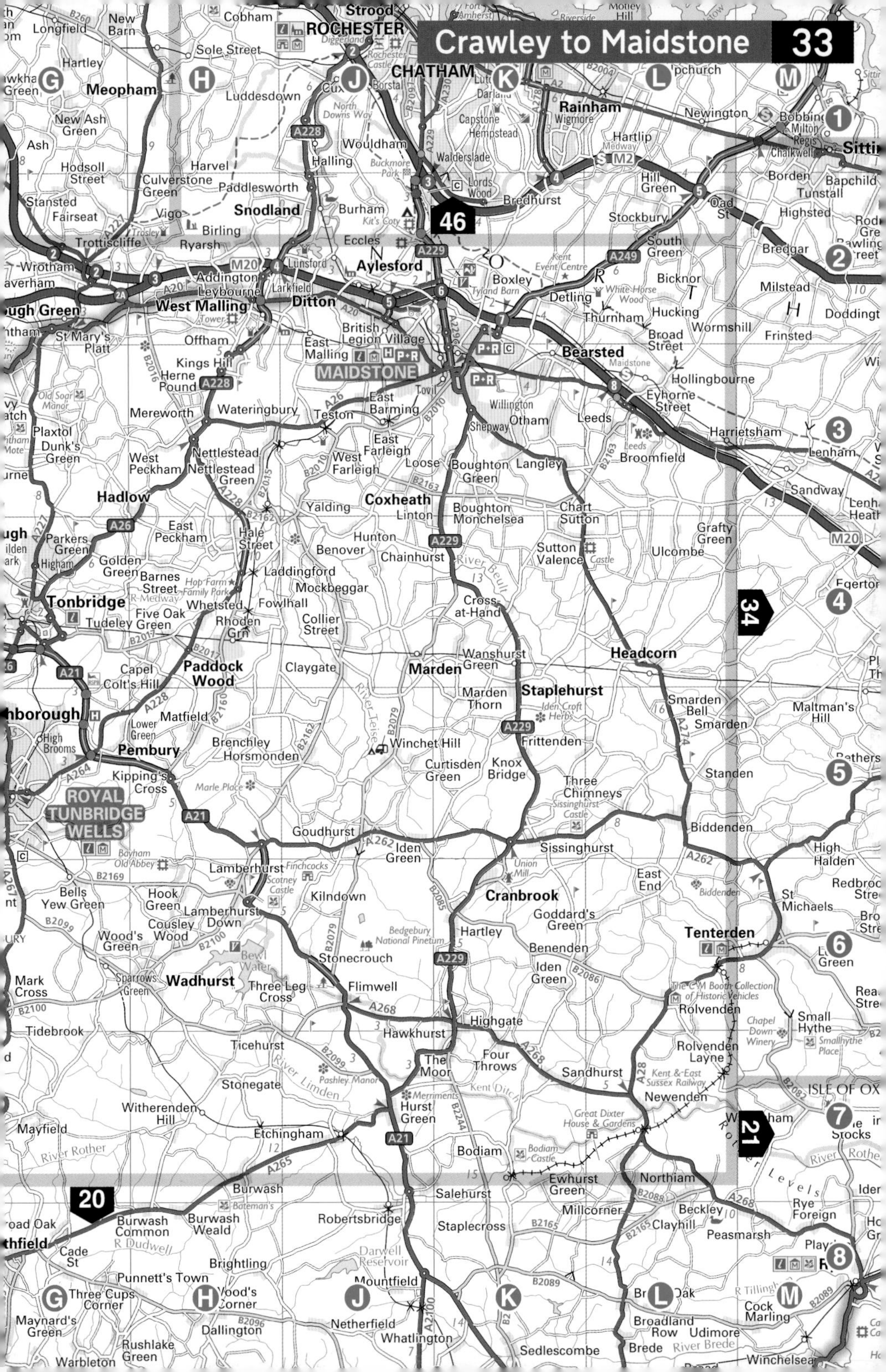
Strood
Cobham
ROCHESTER
CHATHAM
Longfield
New Barn
Sole Street
Hartley
Meopham
Luddesdown
New Ash Green
Ash
Hodsoll Street
Harvel
Culverstone Green
Paddlesworth
Stansted
Fairseat
Vigo
Snodland
Birling
Trottiscliffe
Ryarsh
Wrotham
Addington
Leybourne
West Malling
Larkfield
Lunsford
Ditton
Aylesford
Eccles
Burham
Wouldham
Halling
Cuxton
Borstal
Walderslade
Lords Wood
Bredhurst
Capstone
Hempstead
Darland
Rainham
Wigmore
Hartlip
Newington
Upchurch
Bobbing
Milton Regis
Chalkwell
Sittingbourne
Borden
Bapchild
Tunstall
Highsted
Rodmersham Green
Bredgar
Milstead
Doddington
Frinsted
Stockbury
South Green
Hill Green
Oad Street
Bicknor
Hucking
Wormshill
Detling
Thurnham
Broad Street
Boxley
Bearsted
Hollingbourne
Eyhorne Street
Harrietsham
Lenham
Sandway
Lenham Heath
MAIDSTONE
British Legion Village
East Malling
Offham
Kings Hill
Herne Pound
St Mary's Platt
Borough Green
Mereworth
Wateringbury
Teston
East Barming
Tovil
Willington
Otham
Shepway
Leeds
Broomfield
Langley
Boughton Green
Loose
East Farleigh
West Farleigh
Coxheath
Linton
Yalding
Nettlestead
Nettlestead Green
West Peckham
Plaxtol
Dunk's Green
Hadlow
East Peckham
Hale Street
Boughton Monchelsea
Chart Sutton
Sutton Valence
Ulcombe
Grafty Green
Hunton
Benover
Chainhurst
Laddingford
Mockbeggar
Fowlhall
Whetsted
Rhoden Green
Five Oak
Tudeley Green
Tonbridge
Parkers Green
Golden Green
Barnes Street
Higham
Collier Street
Cross-at-Hand
Wanshurst Green
Headcorn
Egerton
Marden
Claygate
Paddock Wood
Capel
Colt's Hill
Marden Thorn
Staplehurst
Smarden Bell
Smarden
Maltman's Hill
Matfield
Lower Green
Brenchley
Horsmonden
Pembury
Southborough
High Brooms
Kipping's Cross
Winchet Hill
Curtisden Green
Knox Bridge
Frittenden
Three Chimneys
Standen
Biddenden
ROYAL TUNBRIDGE WELLS
Goudhurst
Iden Green
Sissinghurst
High Halden
Lamberhurst
Bells Yew Green
Hook Green
Lamberhurst Down
Kilndown
Cranbrook
East End
St Michaels
Goddard's Green
Tenterden
Cousley Wood
Wood's Green
Hartley
Benenden
Iden Green
Bedgebury National Pinetum
Stonecrouch
Bewl Water
Wadhurst
Three Leg Cross
Flimwell
Mark Cross
Sparrows Green
Rolvenden
Small Hythe
Highgate
Hawkhurst
Tidebrook
Ticehurst
The Moor
Four Throws
Rolvenden Layne
Sandhurst
Newenden
Stonegate
Hurst Green
Witherenden Hill
Mayfield
Etchingham
Bodiam
Northiam
Wittersham
Isle of Oxney
River Rother
Burwash
Salehurst
Ewhurst Green
Burwash Common
Burwash Weald
Robertsbridge
Millcorner
Staplecross
Beckley
Clayhill
Peasmarsh
Rye Foreign
Playden
Rye
Heathfield
Cade Street
Brightling
Punnett's Town
Three Cups Corner
Wood's Corner
Mountfield
Broad Oak
Cock Marling
Maynard's Green
Dallington
Netherfield
Broadland Row
Udimore
Whatlington
Brede
Sedlescombe
Rushlake Green
Warbleton
Winchelsea
46
34
21
20

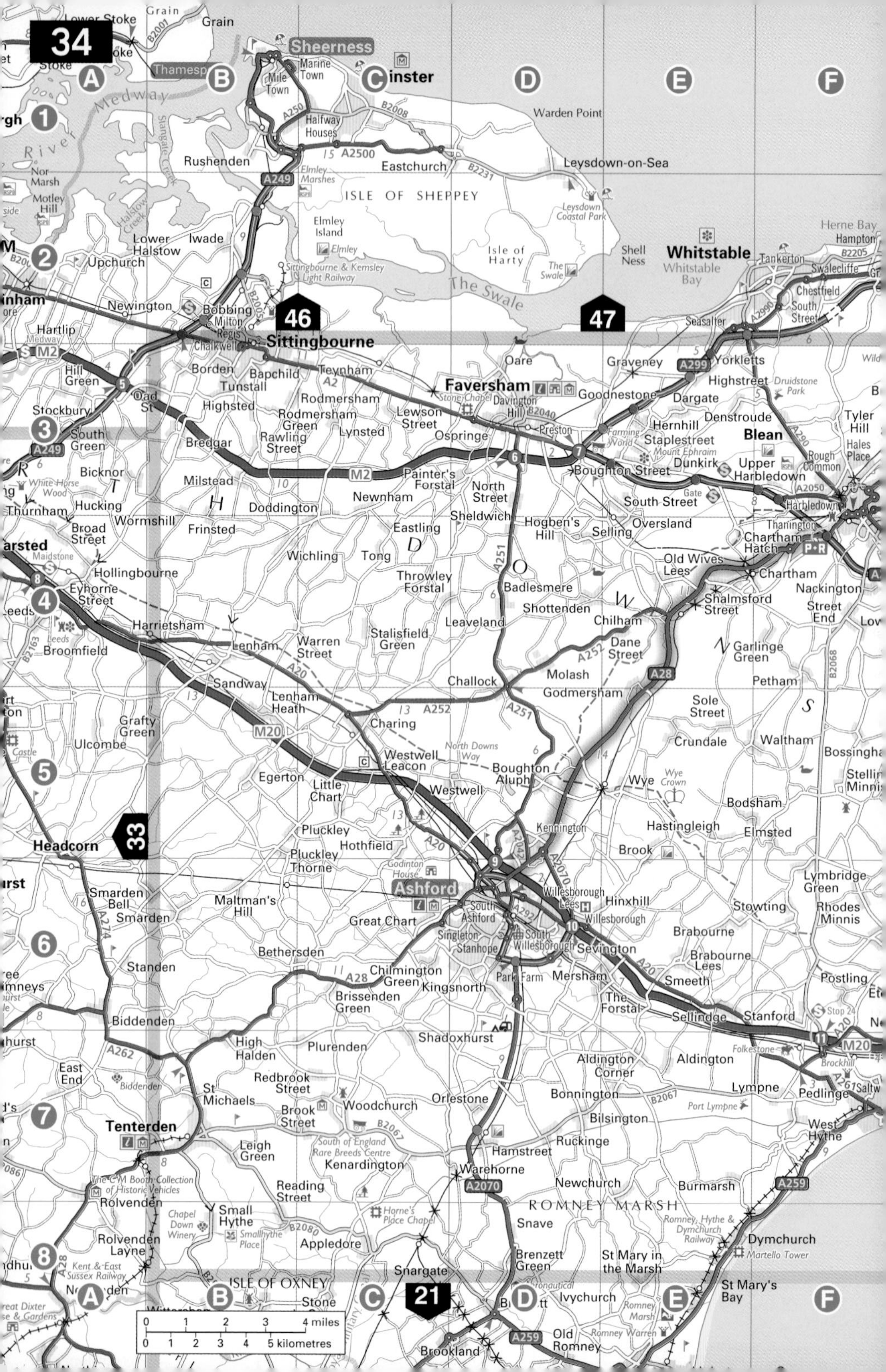
A
B
C
D
E
F
1
2
3
4
5
6
7
8
Lower Stoke
Grain
Stoke
Thamesport
River Medway
Stangate Creek
Sheerness
Marine Town
Mile Town
Minster
Halfway Houses
Warden Point
Rushenden
A2500
Eastchurch
B2231
Leysdown-on-Sea
A249
Elmley Marshes
ISLE OF SHEPPEY
Nor Marsh
Motley Hill
Halstow Creek
Elmley Island
Elmley
Leysdown Coastal Park
Herne Bay
Hampton
Lower Halstow
Iwade
Isle of Harty
Shell Ness
Whitstable
Tankerton
B2205
Upchurch
Sittingbourne & Kemsley Light Railway
The Swale
Whitstable Bay
Swalecliffe
Chestfield
South Street
Newington
Bobbing
Milton Regis
46
47
Seasalter
Hartlip
Chalkwell
Sittingbourne
M2
Yorkletts
Hill Green
Borden
Bapchild
Teynham
Oare
Graveney
A299
A2
Highstreet
Druidstone Park
Tunstall
Rodmersham
Faversham
Goodnestone
Dargate
Stockbury
Oad St
Highsted
Rodmersham Green
Lewson Street
Stone Chapel
Davington Hill
B2040
Denstroude
Tyler Hill
South Green
A249
Bredgar
Rawling Street
Lynsted
Ospringe
Preston
Farming World
Hernhill
Staplestreet
Blean
Mount Ephraim
Dunkirk
Hales Place
Upper Harbledown
Rough Common
Bicknor
White Horse Wood
Milstead
Painter's Forstal
Boughton Street
Thurnham
Hucking
Newnham
North Street
South Street
Harbledown
Broad Street
Wormshill
Doddington
Frinsted
Sheldwich
Hogben's Hill
Selling
Oversland
Thanington
Chartham Hatch
Eastling
Maidstone
Wichling
Tong
Old Wives Lees
Chartham
Hollingbourne
Throwley Forstal
A251
Badlesmere
Nackington
Eyhorne Street
Shottenden
Shalmsford Street
Street End
Leeds
Harrietsham
Leaveland
Chilham
Broomfield
Lenham
Warren Street
Stalisfield Green
Dane Street
A252
Garlinge Green
A20
Challock
Molash
Sandway
Godmersham
A28
Petham
Lenham Heath
A252
A251
Sole Street
Grafty Green
Charing
Castle
Ulcombe
M20
Westwell Leacon
North Downs Way
Crundale
Waltham
Bossingham
Boughton Aluph
Egerton
Little Chart
Westwell
Wye
Wye Crown
Bodsham
Hastingleigh
Kennington
Pluckley
Hothfield
Brook
Elmsted
Headcorn
33
Pluckley Thorne
Godinton House
Lymbridge Green
Ashford
Smarden Bell
Maltman's Hill
South Ashford
Willesborough Lees
Hinxhill
Willesborough
Stowting
Rhodes Minnis
Smarden
A274
Great Chart
Singleton
Stanhope
South Willesborough
Sevington
Brabourne
Bethersden
Brabourne Lees
Standen
Chilmington Green
A28
Park Farm
Mersham
Smeeth
Postling
Kingsnorth
Brissenden Green
The Forstal
Sellindge
Stanford
Stop 24
Biddenden
Shadoxhurst
M20
High Halden
Plurenden
Aldington Corner
Aldington
Folkestone
Brockhill
A262
East End
Biddenden
Redbrook Street
St Michaels
Orlestone
Bonnington
Lympne
Pedlinge
Saltwood
Brook Street
Woodchurch
B2067
Port Lympne
Tenterden
Bilsington
West Hythe
South of England Rare Breeds Centre
Ruckinge
Leigh Green
Hamstreet
Kenardington
Warehorne
The C M Booth Collection of Historic Vehicles
Reading Street
A2070
Newchurch
Burmarsh
A259
Rolvenden
ROMNEY MARSH
Chapel Down Winery
Small Hythe
Smallhythe Place
Horne's Place Chapel
Snave
Romney, Hythe & Dymchurch Railway
Dymchurch
Rolvenden Layne
B2080
Appledore
Brenzett Green
St Mary in the Marsh
Martello Tower
Kent & East Sussex Railway
Snargate
Newenden
ISLE OF OXNEY
21
St Mary's Bay
Great Dixter House & Gardens
Stone
Ivychurch
Romney Marsh
A259
Old Romney
Romney Warren
Brookland
0 1 2 3 4 miles
0 1 2 3 4 5 kilometres

G H J K L M
1 2 3 4 5 6 7 8
MARGATE
Foreness Point
Botany Bay
Cliftonville
Kingsgate
NORTH FORELAND
Joss Bay
North Foreland
St Mildred's Bay
Westgate-on-Sea
Westbrook
Northdown
Minnis Bay
Reculver Towers & Roman Fort
Herne Bay
Bishopstone
Reculver
Birchington
Garlinge
Reading Street
St Peter's
Broadstairs
Beltinge
ISLE OF THANET
Lydden
Hornby
Westwood
Broomfield
St Nicholas-at-Wade
Acol
RAF Manston
Dumpton
Herne
Boyden Gate
Sarre
Monkton
Manston
Hereson
St Lawrence
Ramsgate
East Blean
Chislet
Durlock
Hoath
Upstreet
West Stourmouth
Minster
St Augustine's Cross
Viking Ship 'Hugin'
Pegwell
Pegwell Bay
R Stour
East Stourmouth
Westmarsh
Hersden
Westbere
Richborough Roman Fort
Stodmarsh
Preston
Elmstone
Cop Street
Sandwich Bay
Town Hall
Wickhambreaux
Hoaden
Littlebourne
Wingham
Seaton
Ash
Sandwich
Royal St Georges
Ickham
Durlock
Wingham
Marshborough
Stone Cross
Toll
Bramling
Staple
Woodnesborough
Bekesbourne
Statenborough
Worth
Goodnestone
Eastry
Patrixbourne
Ham
Hacklinge
Adisham
Ratling
Chillenden
Finglesham
Aylesham
Nonington
Fowlmead
Sholden
The Downs
North Downs Way
Betteshanger
Northbourne
Deal
Tilmanstone
Great Mongeham
Upper Deal
Womenswold
Elvington
Plant Centre
Barham
Lower Eythorne
Ripple
Walmer
Castle
Eythorne
Barfrestone
Sutton
Woolage Green
East Studdal
Ringwould
East Kent Railway
Shepherdswell
Ashley
Sutton Downs
Kingsdown
North Downs Way
West Langdon
Martin
Denton
Lydden Hill
Coldred
Wootton
Lydden
Whitfield
East Langdon
St John's Commandery
Lydden Temple Ewell
Guston
St Margaret's at Cliffe
St Margaret's Bay
Selsted
Ewell Minnis
Kearsney
West Cliffe
The Pines
SOUTH FORELAND
Swingfield Minnis
Swingfield Street
River
Lighthouse
South Foreland Heritage Coast
World of Butterflies
Buckland
Castle
The White Cliffs of Dover
Densole
Alkham
St Radigunds
South Alkham
Maxton
Upper Standen
Drellingore
West Hougham
DOVER
Dunkirk Calais
Hawkinge
Lower Standen
Capel-le-Ferne
Battle of Britain
Channel Tunnel Terminal
Cheriton
Samphire Hoe
Dover - Folkestone Heritage Coast
Channel Tunnel (Rail)
Morehall
East Wear Bay
Sandgate
FOLKESTONE
STRAIT OF DOVER
A299 A28 A253 A256 A257 A258 A2 A20 A260 A259 A255 A254 B2051 B2052 B2050 B2190 B2046 B2011

Craig Llangiwg
Cilybebyll
Gellinudd
Crynant
Mynydd March Hywel
River Dulais
Alltwen
Vale of Neath
A465
Blaengwrach
Rhigos
Hirwaun
Penywaun
Cwmdare
Llwydcoed
Trecynon
Aberdare
(Aberdâr)
Aberaman
Cwmaman
Abercwmboi
River Neath
383
RESOLVEN MOUNTAIN
Resolven
Melin Cwrt
600
CRAIG-Y-LLYN
A4061
Mynydd Ystradffernol
Blaenrhondda
A4233
Fforchneol
Faerdre
Ynysmeudwy
B4464
B4291
A4067
Glais
Bryn-côch
Cilfrew
Cadoxton Juxta-Neath
A474
B4434
Clyne
493
MOEL-YR HYRDDAD
Aberdulais
Tin Works & Waterfall
52
Birchgrove
Tonna
Cefn Mawr
Glyncorrwg
Treherbert
Maerdy
478
Llansamlet
Neath
(Castell-nedd)
Cefn Morfydd
Afan Forest Park
Blaengwynfi
Rhondda Valley
Treorchy
Ferndale
Ystrad
Winshwen
A48
A465
Abercregan
Duffryn
Cymer
A4107
Abergwynfi
Cwmparc
Pentre
A4217
Cimla
Tonmawr
Cynonville
Croeserw
571
WERFA
19
A4061
B4223
B4287
Efail-fach
Pont-rhyd-y-fen
Afan Forest Park
Caerau
556
MYNYDD CAERAU
Pentre-chwyth
Crymlyn Bog
Briton Ferry
FOEL MYNYDDAU
371
MOEL TRAWSNANT
Mynydd Llangeinwyr
Nant-y-moel
Clydach Vale
Llwynypia
Trealaw
B4290
P+R
A483
371
Pwll-y-glaw
Blaengarw
National Waterfront
Baglan
B4286
B4282
Bryn
A4061
Tonypandy
Penygraig
Cwmafan
Maesteg
Pontycymer
Cricklepit Mill
Glanllynfi
Ogmore Vale
Gilfach Goch
Aberavon
Port Talbot
Swansea Bay
Mynydd Margam
Cwmfelin
A4064
B4564
B4278
Taibach
Llangynwyd
Llangeinor
Lewistown
Margam
51
Stones Museum
321
MOEL TON-MAWR
Betws
A4093
A4093
A4241
A4063
Bryngarw
Blackmill
Margam
Coytrahen
Brynmenyn
A4061
Mynydd Maendy
B4283
M4
Tondu
Heol-y-Cyw
Brynna Woods
Afon Kenfig
Cefn Cribwr
Aberkenfig
Sarn Park
Pant-ffrwyth
Brynna
Llanharan
B4280
Pyle
(Y Pîl)
B4281
Mawdlam
North Cornelly
Bridgend
(Pen-y-Bont-ar-Ogwr)
Castle
Coity
Pencoed
A473
Llanilid
Llanharry
Brynsadler
Kenfig
South Cornelly
Laleston
B4181
A4229
NEWTON DOWN
A473
Coychurch
A4106
Rest Bay
Nottage
Tythegston
A48
A473
Merthyr Mawr
Treoes
Llangan
Ystradowen
Newton
Candleston
Ogmore Castle
Corntown
Trerhyngyll
Porthcawl
Porthcawl Point
Trecco Bay
Ogmore
Ewenny
Penllyn
Maendy
B4265
St Bride's Major
Colwinston
Pentre Meyrick
B4268
St Quentin's Castle
Ogmore-by-Sea
B4524
Llysworney
Cowbridge
Southerndown
Llandow
B4270
Llanblethian
Llandough
St Hilary
Wick
Sigingstone
Llandow
B4270
St Mary Church
Broughton
Flemingston
Monknash
B4265
Llanmaes
Marcross
St Donats
Nash Point
Nash Point & Visitor Centre
Llantwit Major
(Llanilltud Fawr)
St Athan
Cwm Colhuw
B4265
Gileston
Glamorgan Heritage Coast
Limpert Bay
A B C D E F
1 2 3 4 5 6 7 8
0 1 2 3 4 miles
0 1 2 3 4 5 kilometres

Merthyr Tudful
Pentrebach
Tirphil
New Tredegar
Troedyrhiw
Bedlinog
Brithdir
Manmoel
Markham
Bedwellty
Argoed
Abertillery
(Abertyleri)
Llanhilleth
Pontypool
(Pont-y-Pŵl)
Monkswood
Usk
(Brynbuga)
Llandegfedd Reservoir
Llanbadoc
Llanllowel
Coed-y-paen
Llangybi
Llantrisant
Aberfan
Cwmfelin
Merthyr Vale
Bargoed
(Bargod)
Gilfach
Oakdale
Crumlin
Griffithstown
New Inn
Treharris
Trelewis
Llancaiach Fawr
Gelligaer
Pengam
Penmaen
Blackwood
Pontllanfraith
Newbridge
Mynydd Maen
Greenmeadow Community Farm
Pontnewydd
Croesyceiliog
Llandegveth
Forge Hammer
Cwmbran
(Cwmbrân)
Tredunnock
Ynysboeth
Nelson
Hengoed
Pentwynmawr
Maesycwmmer
Abercarn
Cwmcarn
Cwmcarn Forest Drive
Llantarnam
Llanfrechfa
Abercynon
Ynysybwl
Ystrad Mynach
Ynysddu
Mynydd Lan
Pontywaun
Ponthir
Llanhennock
Rhondda Heritage Park
Cilfynydd
Mynydd Eglwysilan
Senghenydd
Cwmfelinfach
Wattsville
Crosskeys
Risca
Henllys
Caerleon
Celtic Manor
Barry Sidings
Pontypridd
Abertridwr
Llanbradach
Bedwas
Machen
Bettws
Malpas
Lower Machen
Cefn
Maindee
Christchurch
Trefforest
Groes-Wen
R. Rhymney
Rogerstone
Bassaleg
Rhiwderyn
Pen-y-coedcae
Llantwit Fardre
Caerphilly
(Caerffili)
Rudry
Draethen
Liswerry
Llanwern
Newport
(Casnewydd-ar-Wysg)
Church Village
Beddau
Tyn-y-nant
Efail Isaf
Parc Cefn Onn
Michaelstone-y-Fedw
Tredegar House
Castell Coch
Llantrisant
Taff's Well
Tongwynlais
Lisvane
Cardiff Gate
Castleton
Nash
Goldcliff
Newport Wetlands
Creigiau
Pentyrch
Rhiwbina
Llanishen
Llanedeyrn
St Mellons
Marshfield
St Brides Wentlooge
Groes-faen
Miskin
Llanrumney
Cardiff West
Radyr
Whitchurch
Birchgrove
Rumney
Peterstone Wentlooge
Clawdd-coch
St Fagans
Llandaff
Roath
Pengam
Pendoylan
St Brides-super-Ely
National History Museum
Fairwater
River Ely
Canton
Splottlands
Peterston-super-Ely
St George's
Ely
Caerau
Principality
Cardiff
(Caerdydd)
St Nicholas
Wales Millennium Centre
Severn Estuary
Bonvilston
Tinkinswood
St Lythans
Dyffryn Gardens
Burial Chamber
Michaelston-le-Pit
Llandough
Penarth Head
Llantrithyd
Wenvoe
St Andrew's Major
Cogan
Penarth
Dinas Powys
Lower Penarth
Cosmeston Lakes & Medieval Village
Moulton
Penmark
Welsh Hawking Centre
Cadoxton
Lavernock
Lavernock Point
Sully
Barry
(Y Barri)
Barry Island
Sully Island
Porthkerry
Rhoose
Cold Knap Point
Whitmore Bay
Flat Holm
Steep Holm
Woodspring Bay
Sand Point
Wick St Lawrence
Sand Bay
Kewstoke
St Georges
Toll
Milton
Worle
Ashcombe
Weston-super-Mare
Helicopter
Locking
Hutton
Brean Down
Tropical Bird Garden
Uphill
Oldmixon
Walborough
Bleadon
Brean
Loxton
Lympsham
Edingworth
Biddisham
Clevedon
38
53
25

Usk
(Brynbuga)
Lydney
Chepstow
(Cas-gwent)
Caerleon
NEWPORT
(CASNEWYDD-AR-WYSG)
Caldicot
(Cil-y-coed)
Thornbury
SEVERN ESTUARY
River Severn
Avonmouth
Portishead
BRISTOL
Clevedon
Nailsea
Long Ashton
Keynsham
Yatton
Congresbury
Winscombe
Cheddar
Midsomer Norton
Tintern Parva
St Briavels
Llandogo
Shirenewton
Magor
Undy
Redwick
Goldcliff
Whitson
Nash
Severn Beach
Pilning
Almondsbury
Aust
Tockington
Olveston
Portbury
Easton-in-Gordano
Clapton-in-Gordano
Weston-in-Gordano
Walton-in-Gordano
Tickenham
Wraxall
Backwell
Brockley
Claverham
Cleeve
Wrington
Blagdon
Churchill
Sandford
Banwell
Felton
Winford
Chew Magna
Whitchurch
Pensford
Second Severn Crossing
Toll westbound only
Woodspring Bay
Kewstoke
St Georges
Worle
Bleadon
Bleadon Hills
Locking
Hutton
Chew Valley Lake
Blagdon Lake
0 1 2 3 4 miles
0 1 2 3 4 5 kilometres
54
37
26

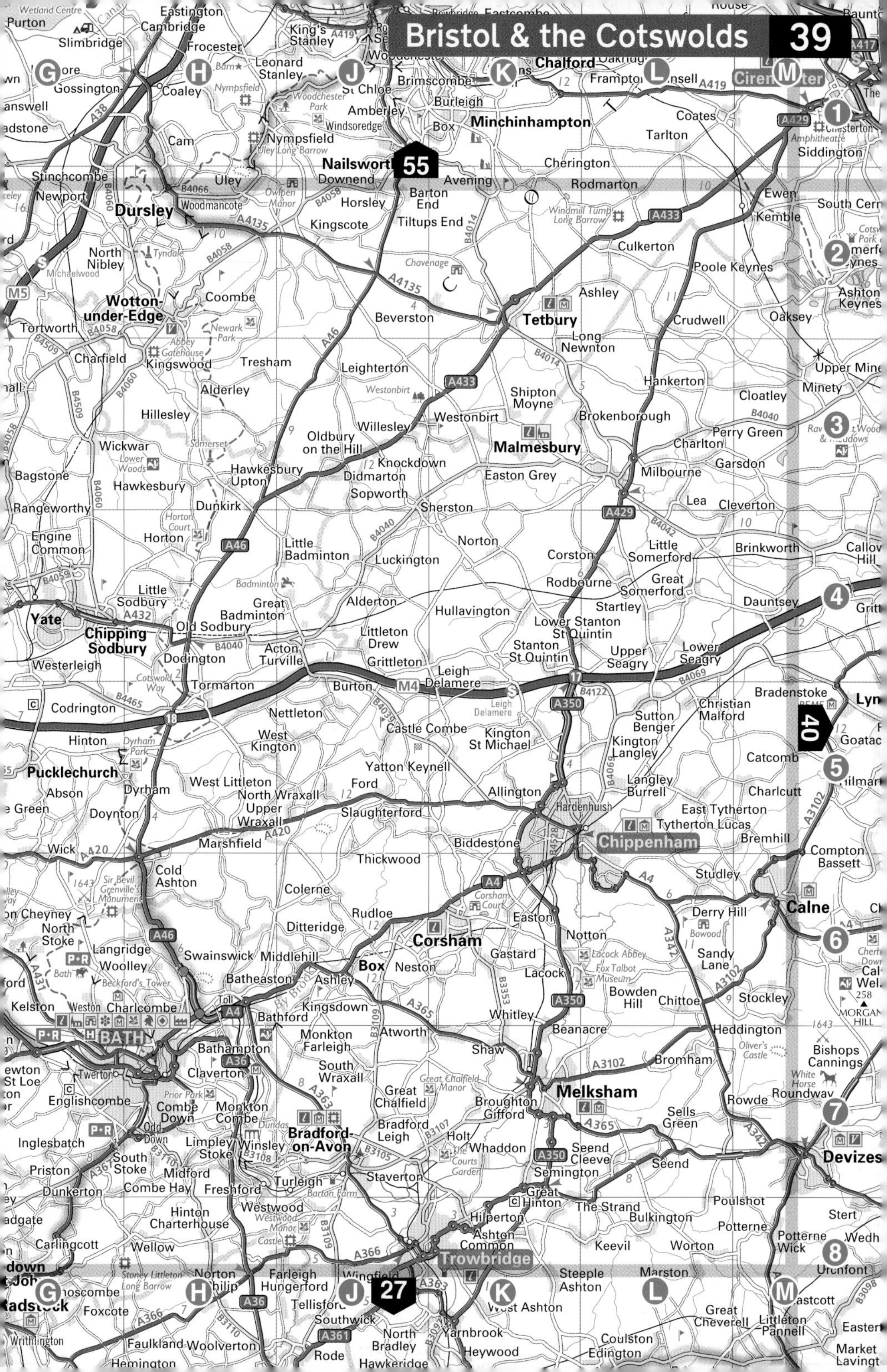

Eastington
Cambridge
Slimbridge
Frocester
King's Stanley
Leonard Stanley
Chalford
Frampton
Cirencester
Gossington
Coaley
Nympsfield
St Chloe
Brimscombe
Amberley
Burleigh
Minchinhampton
Coates
Tarlton
Siddington
Cam
Woodchester Park
Windsoredge
Box
Nailsworth
Downend
Avening
Cherington
Rodmarton
Stinchcombe
Uley
Uley Long Barrow
Newport
Dursley
Woodmancote
Owlpen Manor
Horsley
Barton End
Tiltups End
Kingscote
Windmill Tump Long Barrow
Ewen
Kemble
South Cerney
North Nibley
Tyndale
Michaelwood
Chavenage
Culkerton
Poole Keynes
Ashton Keynes
Wotton-under-Edge
Coombe
Beverston
Tetbury
Ashley
Crudwell
Oaksey
Tortworth
Newark Park
Long Newnton
Charfield
Kingswood
Tresham
Leighterton
Upper Minety
Minety
Hankerton
Cloatley
Alderley
Westonbirt
Shipton Moyne
Hillesley
Willesley
Brokenborough
Perry Green
Wickwar
Lower Woods
Oldbury on the Hill
Malmesbury
Charlton
Ravensroost Wood & Meadows
Knockdown
Hawkesbury Upton
Hawkesbury
Didmarton
Easton Grey
Garsdon
Milbourne
Bagstone
Sopworth
Sherston
Lea
Cleverton
Rangeworthy
Dunkirk
Horton Court
Engine Common
Horton
Little Badminton
Norton
Luckington
Little Somerford
Brinkworth
Corston
Great Somerford
Rodbourne
Badminton
Little Sodbury
Great Badminton
Alderton
Hullavington
Startley
Dauntsey
Yate
Chipping Sodbury
Old Sodbury
Littleton Drew
Lower Stanton St Quintin
Stanton St Quintin
Acton Turville
Grittleton
Upper Seagry
Lower Seagry
Westerleigh
Dodington
Tormarton
Cotswold Way
Burton
Leigh Delamere
Bradenstoke
Lyneham
Codrington
Nettleton
Castle Combe
Christian Malford
Sutton Benger
Kington St Michael
Kington Langley
Goatacre
Hinton
Dyrham Park
West Kington
Catcomb
Pucklechurch
Dyrham
West Littleton
Yatton Keynell
Langley Burrell
Hilmarton
Abson
North Wraxall
Ford
Allington
Charlcutt
Doynton
Upper Wraxall
Slaughterford
Hardenhuish
East Tytherton
Tytherton Lucas
Chippenham
Wick
Marshfield
Biddestone
Bremhill
Compton Bassett
Cold Ashton
Thickwood
Studley
Sir Bevil Grenville's Monument
Colerne
Corsham Court
Calne
North Stoke
Rudloe
Easton
Derry Hill
Bowood
Ditteridge
Notton
Corsham
Gastard
Sandy Lane
Langridge
Woolley
Swainswick
Middlehill
Box
Neston
Lacock
Lacock Abbey
Fox Talbot Museum
Cherhill Down
Beckford's Tower
Batheaston
Ashley
Bowden Hill
Chittoe
Stockley
Kelston
Weston
Charlcombe
Kingsdown
Whitley
Morgan Hill
Bath
Bathford
Monkton Farleigh
Atworth
Beanacre
Heddington
Bathampton
Shaw
Bishops Cannings
Claverton
South Wraxall
Oliver's Castle
Bromham
Twerton
Great Chalfield Manor
Great Chalfield
White Horse
Englishcombe
Prior Park
Melksham
Roundway
Combe Down
Monkton Combe
Broughton Gifford
Rowde
Sells Green
Bradford-on-Avon
Bradford Leigh
Holt
Inglesbatch
Odd Down
Limpley Stoke
Winsley
Whaddon
Seend Cleeve
Seend
Devizes
South Stoke
The Courts Garden
Semington
Priston
Midford
Staverton
Combe Hay
Freshford
Turleigh
Barton Farm
Great Hinton
Dunkerton
The Strand
Poulshot
Westwood
Westwood Manor
Hilperton
Bulkington
Stert
Hinton Charterhouse
Potterne
Carlingcott
Wellow
Ashton Common
Keevil
Worton
Potterne Wick
Trowbridge
Stoney Littleton Long Barrow
Norton St Philip
Farleigh Hungerford
Wingfield
Steeple Ashton
Marston
Urchfont
Radstock
Foxcote
Tellisford
West Ashton
Eastcott
Southwick
Great Cheverell
Littleton Pannell
North Bradley
Yarnbrook
Writhlington
Faulkland
Woolverton
Rode
Heywood
Coulston
Edington
Hemington
Hawkeridge
Market Lavington
M4
M5
A46
A433
A429
A4135
A420
A4
A36
A363
A365
A350
A3102
A342
A366
A361
A432
A417
A419
B4058
B4060
B4066
B4509
B4014
B4040
B4042
B4069
B4122
B4465
B4528
B3109
B3107
B3105
B3108
B3110
B3353
B3098
55
40
27

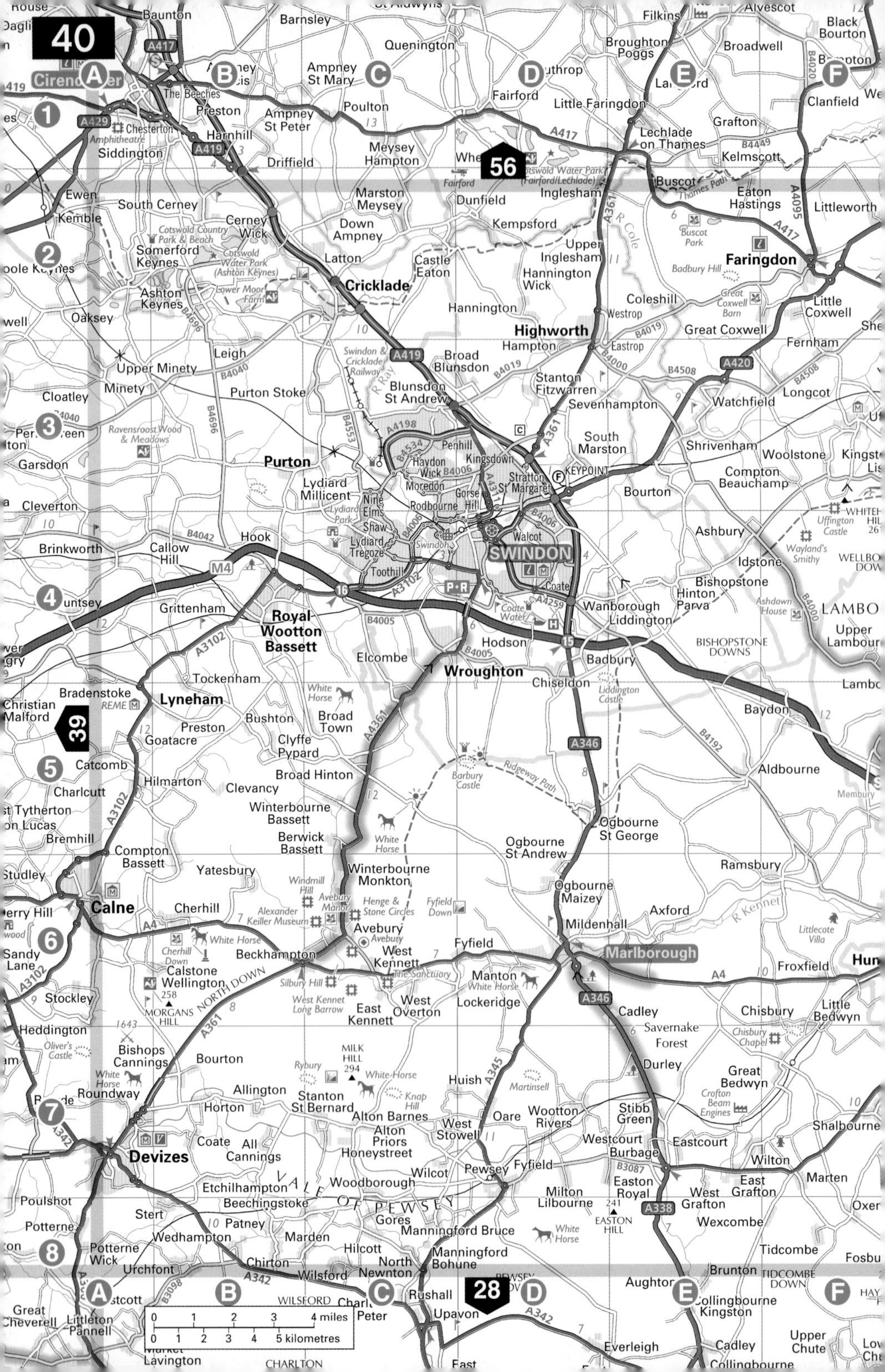

Baunton
Barnsley
Quenington
Filkins
Alvescot
Black Bourton
Broughton Poggs
Broadwell
Cirencester
Ampney St Mary
Fairford
Little Faringdon
Clanfield
The Beeches
Preston
Ampney St Peter
Poulton
Chesterton
Amphitheatre
Siddington
Harnhill
Driffield
Meysey Hampton
Lechlade on Thames
Grafton
Kelmscott
Buscot
Cotswold Water Park (Fairford/Lechlade)
Inglesham
Eaton Hastings
Littleworth
Ewen
Kemble
South Cerney
Cerney Wick
Marston Meysey
Dunfield
Kempsford
Down Ampney
Cotswold Country Park & Beach
Somerford Keynes
Cotswold Water Park (Ashton Keynes)
Poole Keynes
Latton
Castle Eaton
Upper Inglesham
Hannington Wick
Buscot Park
Badbury Hill
Faringdon
Ashton Keynes
Lower Moor Farm
Cricklade
Coleshill
Great Coxwell Barn
Little Coxwell
Oaksey
Hannington
Westrop
Highworth
Eastrop
Great Coxwell
Fernham
Swindon & Cricklade Railway
Broad Blunsdon
Hampton
Upper Minety
Leigh
Minety
Blunsdon St Andrew
Stanton Fitzwarren
Watchfield
Longcot
Cloatley
Purton Stoke
Sevenhampton
Ravensroost Wood & Meadows
Penhill
South Marston
Shrivenham
Garsdon
Purton
Haydon Wick
Kingsdown
Woolstone
Lydiard Millicent
Moredon
Stratton St Margaret
KEYPOINT
Compton Beauchamp
Cleverton
Nine Elms
Rodbourne
Gorse Hill
Bourton
Lydiard Park
Shaw
Lydiard Tregoze
Walcot
SWINDON
Ashbury
Uffington Castle
Brinkworth
Callow Hill
Hook
Toothill
Wayland's Smithy
Idstone
Coate
Bishopstone
Hinton Parva
Ashdown House
Grittenham
Royal Wootton Bassett
Coate Water
Wanborough
Liddington
Elcombe
Hodson
BISHOPSTONE DOWNS
Upper Lambourn
Tockenham
Wroughton
Chiseldon
Badbury
Bradenstoke
Christian Malford
REME
Lyneham
White Horse
Broad Town
Liddington Castle
Baydon
Preston
Goatacre
Bushton
Clyffe Pypard
Catcomb
Hilmarton
Broad Hinton
Barbury Castle
Ridgeway Path
Aldbourne
Charlcutt
Clevancy
Winterbourne Bassett
Membury
Bremhill
Berwick Bassett
Ogbourne St George
Ogbourne St Andrew
Compton Bassett
Yatesbury
Ramsbury
Winterbourne Monkton
Windmill Hill
Avebury Manor
Ogbourne Maizey
Calne
Cherhill
Alexander Keiller Museum
Henge & Stone Circles
Fyfield Down
Axford
R Kennet
Littlecote Villa
Avebury
Mildenhall
Fyfield
Marlborough
Cherhill Down
Beckhampton
West Kennett
Sandy Lane
Calstone Wellington
Silbury Hill
The Sanctuary
Manton
Froxfield
MORGANS HILL
NORTH DOWN
West Kennet Long Barrow
East Kennett
West Overton
Lockeridge
Stockley
Cadley
Chisbury
Little Bedwyn
Savernake Forest
Chisbury Chapel
Heddington
Oliver's Castle
Bishops Cannings
MILK HILL
Durley
Bourton
Rybury
Great Bedwyn
Huish
Martinsell
Roundway
Allington
Stanton St Bernard
Knap Hill
Crofton Beam Engines
Horton
Alton Barnes
Oare
Wootton Rivers
Stibb Green
West Stowell
Alton Priors
Shalbourne
Devizes
Coate
All Cannings
Honeystreet
Westcourt
Burbage
Eastcourt
Wilcot
Pewsey
Fyfield
Wilton
Etchilhampton
VALE OF PEWSEY
Woodborough
Easton Royal
Milton Lilbourne
Marten
Poulshot
Beechingstoke
EASTON HILL
West Grafton
East Grafton
Stert
Gores
Wexcombe
Potterne
Patney
Marden
Manningford Bruce
Wedhampton
Potterne Wick
Hilcot
Manningford Bohune
Tidcombe
Urchfont
Chirton
North Newnton
Brunton
Wilsford
TIDCOMBE DOWN
Aughton
Rushall
Collingbourne Kingston
Great Cheverell
Littleton Pannell
Charlton
Upavon
Everleigh
Market Lavington
CHARLTON
Upper Chute
Cadley
Collingbourne
0 1 2 3 4 miles
0 1 2 3 4 5 kilometres

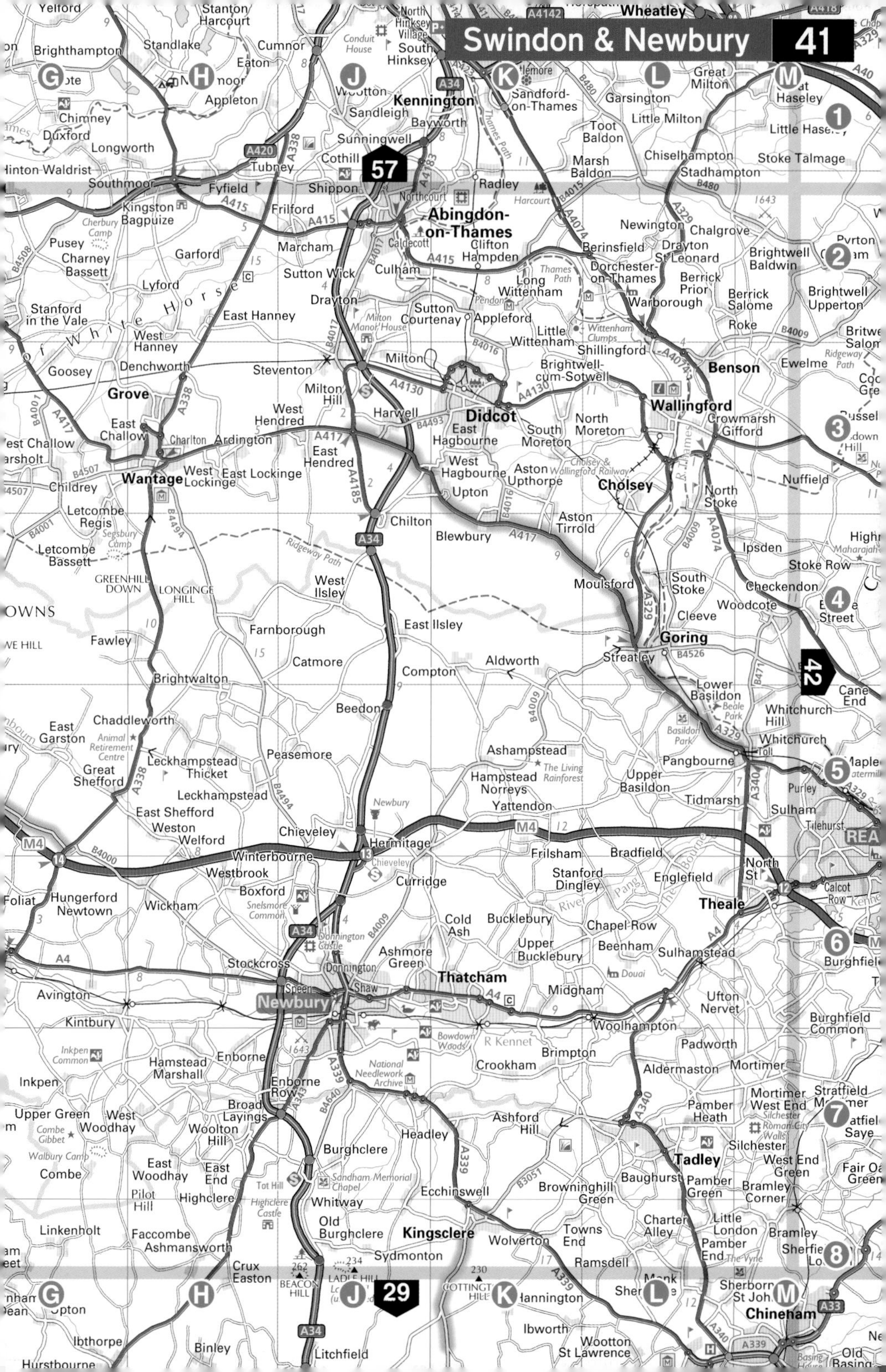
Yelford
Stanton Harcourt
North Hinksey Village
A4142
Wheatley
Brighthampton
Standlake
Cumnor
Conduit House
South Hinksey
Eaton
Appleton
Wootton
Kennington
Sandford-on-Thames
Garsington
Great Milton
Great Haseley
Chimney
Duxford
Sandleigh
Bayworth
Little Milton
Little Haseley
Longworth
A338
Sunningwell
Toot Baldon
A420
Cothill
A4183
Thames Path
Chiselhampton
Stoke Talmage
Hinton Waldrist
Tubney
57
Marsh Baldon
Stadhampton
Southmoor
Fyfield
Shippon
Radley
B480
Kingston Bagpuize
A415
Frilford
Northcourt
Harcourt
B4015
Cherbury Camp
Abingdon-on-Thames
Newington
A329
Chalgrove
Pusey
Caldecott
Clifton Hampden
Berinsfield
Drayton St Leonard
Pyrton
Charney Bassett
Garford
Marcham
A415
A4074
Brightwell Baldwin
Culham
Dorchester-on-Thames
Sutton Wick
Long Wittenham
Berrick Prior
Berrick Salome
Brightwell Upperton
Lyford
Warborough
Stanford in the Vale
Drayton
Sutton Courtenay
Pendon
East Hanney
Appleford
Little Wittenham
Wittenham Clumps
Roke
B4009
West Hanney
Milton Manor House
Shillingford
Ridgeway Path
Goosey
Denchworth
Steventon
Milton
B4016
Benson
Ewelme
Brightwell-cum-Sotwell
Grove
Milton Hill
A4130
Didcot
Wallingford
West Hendred
Harwell
North Moreton
Crowmarsh Gifford
East Challow
B4493
East Hagbourne
South Moreton
Charlton
Ardington
A417
West Challow
East Hendred
Childrey
Wantage
West Lockinge
East Lockinge
West Hagbourne
Aston Upthorpe
Cholsey & Wallingford Railway
Cholsey
Nuffield
B4507
B4494
A4185
Upton
North Stoke
Letcombe Regis
Chilton
B4016
Aston Tirrold
B4001
Segsbury Camp
A34
Blewbury
A417
A4074
Ipsden
Letcombe Bassett
Ridgeway Path
Maharajah's
Stoke Row
GREENHILL DOWN
LONGINGE HILL
West Ilsley
Moulsford
South Stoke
Checkendon
Woodcote
Cleeve
A329
East Ilsley
Fawley
Farnborough
Goring
Streatley
B4526
Catmore
Aldworth
42
Compton
Brightwalton
Lower Basildon
Beale Park
B471
Cane End
Beedon
B4009
Whitchurch Hill
East Garston
Chaddleworth
Basildon Park
A329
Animal Retirement Centre
Whitchurch
Toll
Peasemore
Ashampstead
Leckhampstead Thicket
Great Shefford
The Living Rainforest
Pangbourne
Hampstead Norreys
Upper Basildon
Purley
A340
Leckhampstead
Newbury
Tidmarsh
Yattendon
Sulham
East Shefford
Weston
A338
B4494
Tilehurst
Chieveley
M4
Welford
Hermitage
Frilsham
Bradfield
M4
14
B4000
Winterbourne
13
Chieveley
Westbrook
Stanford Dingley
Englefield
North St
Calcot Row
Foliat
Hungerford Newtown
Wickham
Boxford
Curridge
River Pang
The Bourne
Snelsmore Common
Theale
Cold Ash
Bucklebury
Chapel Row
A34
Donnington Castle
B4009
Ashmore Green
Upper Bucklebury
Beenham
Sulhamstead
A4
Burghfield
A4
Stockcross
Donnington
Douai
Avington
Speen
Shaw
Thatcham
A4
Midgham
Ufton Nervet
Newbury
Kintbury
Bowdown Woods
R Kennet
Woolhampton
Burghfield Common
Inkpen Common
Padworth
Hamstead Marshall
Enborne
Brimpton
1643
National Needlework Archive
Crookham
A339
Aldermaston
Mortimer
Inkpen
Enborne Row
A340
Mortimer West End
Stratfield Mortimer
B4640
Pamber Heath
Upper Green
West Woodhay
Broad Layings
A343
Silchester Roman City Walls
Ashford Hill
Headley
Combe Gibbet
Woolton Hill
Tadley
Silchester
Walbury Camp
Burghclere
A339
West End Green
East Woodhay
East End
B3051
Baughurst
Pamber Green
Bramley Corner
Combe
Sandham Memorial Chapel
Browninghill Green
Tot Hill
Pilot Hill
Highclere
Highclere Castle
Whitway
Ecchinswell
Charter Alley
Little London
Linkenholt
Old Burghclere
Kingsclere
Bramley
Faccombe
Ashmansworth
Wolverton
Towns End
Pamber End
Sydmonton
The Vyne
Sherfield on Loddon
Crux Easton
234
262
BEACON HILL
LADLE HILL
230
COTTINGTON HILL
Ramsdell
A339
Sherborne St John
29
Hannington
Upton
Chineham
A33
A34
Ibthorpe
Ibworth
Wootton St Lawrence
A340
A339
Binley
Litchfield
Hurstbourne
Old Basing

Rycote Chapel
Towersey
Longwick
Monks Risborough
Dunsmore
Lee
The Lee Clump
Bellingdon
Asheridge
Chartridge
Moreton
Pitch Green
Whiteleaf
Cross (hill carving)
Princes Risborough
Great Hampden
Ballinger Common
South Heath
Haseley
Tetsw
Sydenham
Emmington
Hent
Bledlow
Saunderton
Loosley Row
Lacey Green
Prestwood
Great Missenden
Hyde Heath
Little Haseley
Postcombe
Chinnor & Princes Risborough Railway
Chinnor
Crowell
LODGE HILL
Roald Dahl
Stoke Talmage
Kingston Blount
Aston Rowant
58
Little Kingshill
Little Missenden
Amersham
Great Kingshill
Amersham Old Town
Hughenden Valley
Cryers Hill
Holmer Green
South Weston
Lewknor
Radnage
Bledlow Ridge
Bradenham
Naphill
Hughenden Manor
Widmer End
Hazlemere
Penn Street
Pyrton
Cuxham
Shirburn
Stokenchurch
The City
Beacon's Bottom
Hell-Fire Caves
Downley
Winchmore Hill
Brightwell Baldwin
Berrick Salome
Brightwell Upperton
Watlington
Roke
Ibstone
West Wycombe Park
HIGH WYCOMBE
Britwell Salome
Ridgeway Path
Cadmore End
Cressex
Wycombe Marsh
Bekonscot Model Village
Benson
Ewelme
Turville
Lane End
Booker
Cookley Green
Fingest
Loudwater
Beaconsfield
Russell's Water
Skirmett
Frieth
Flackwell Heath
Pishill
Stonor House & Gardens
Gansdown Hill
Park Corner
Stonor
Rockwell End
Marlow Bottom
Wooburn Green
Bourne End
Nuffield Place
Warburg
Nettlebed
Marlow
Little Marlow
Wooburn
Hedgerley
Nuffield
Crocker End
Fawley
Hambleden
Odds Farm Park
Egypt
North Stoke
Hedsor
Cookham
Highmoor
Bix
Lower Assendon
Mill End
Bisham
Burnham Beeches
Cliveden
Ipsden
Maharajah's Well
Highmoor Cross
Remenham
Aston
Medmenham
Cookham Rise
Stoke Row
Greys Court
River & Rowing
Remenham Hill
Hurley
Cookham Dean
Maidenhead
Taplow
Farnham Royal
Checkendon
Exlade Street
Greys Green
Rotherfield Greys
Henley-on-Thames
Cockpole Green
Burchett's Green
North Town
Burnham
Rotherfield Peppard
Warren Row
Fishery Estate
Cippenham
Sonning Common
The Herb Farm
Lower Shiplake
Wargrave
Knowl Hill
Littlewick Green
Bray
Braywick
Dorney
Dorney Court
Eton Wick
Whitchurch
Beale Park
Cane End
Kidmore End
Woodlands Park
White Waltham
Holyport
Eton
Tokers Green
Dunsden Green
Binfield Heath
Shiplake
Thames Path
Hare Hatch
Waltham St Lawrence
Ruscombe
Fifield
Mapledurham
Watermill
Play Hatch
Charvil
Dedworth
Purley
Caversham
Sonning
Twyford
Paley Street
Sulham
Tilehurst
READING
Whistley Green
Shurlock Row
Legoland
Windsor
Woodley
Maiden's Green
Cranbourne
North St
Calcot Row
Kennet & Avon
Ure
Dinton Pastures
Hurst
Warfield
Winkfield
Theale
Whitley
Earley
Winnersh
Binfield
Newell Green
Winkfield Row
Woodside
Guards Polo Club
Virginia Water
Reading
Sindlesham
Bullbrook
North Ascot
Ascot
Burghfield
Three Mile Cross
Shinfield
Wokingham
Sunninghill
Sunningdale
Ufton Nervet
Arborfield
Great Hollands
BRACKNELL
Burghfield Common
Spencers Wood
Arborfield Cross
Barkham
Gardeners Green
TOWER HILL
Farley Hill
Swallowfield
California
Wellingtonia Avenue
Look Out Discovery Centre
Swinley Forest
Windlesham
Sunningdale Chobham Common
Mortimer
Mortimer West End
Stratfield Mortimer
Beech Hill
Riseley
Wellington
Finchampstead
Crowthorne
Wildmoor Heath
Bagshot
Lightwater
Silchester Roman City Walls
Stratfield Saye
Owlsmoor
Sandhurst
Silchester
Eversley
Eversley Cross
West End
West End Green
Fair Oak Green
Stratfield Turgis
Heckfield
Hound Green
Yateley
College Town
Bramley Corner
Turgis Green
Blackwater
York Town
CAMBERLEY
Bisley
Little London
Bramley
Hartley Wespall
Yateley Common
Hawley
Frimley
Royal Logistics Corps
Sherfield on Loddon
Mattingley
Hartfordbridge
Brookwood
Sherborne St John
West Green
Hartley Wintney
30
Chineham
Elvetham Heath
Cove
Farnborough Park
Mytchett
Pirbright
Fleet
Farnborough
Winchfield
Dogmersfield
Worplesdon
0 1 2 3 4 miles
0 1 2 3 4 5 kilometres
41
M40
M4
M3
A404(M)
A329(M)

Bovingdon
Kings Langley
Radlett
Potters Bar
Chorleywood
WATFORD
Rickmansworth
Bushey
Borehamwood
Barnet
Chalfont St Peter
Harefield
Gerrards Cross
Harrow
Wembley
Uxbridge
Camden Town
Ealing
Hammersmith
Hounslow
Richmond
Kingston upon Thames
Wimbledon
Staines-upon-Thames
Sunbury-on-Thames
Walton-on-Thames
Chertsey
Addlestone
Weybridge
Esher
Byfleet
Cobham
Epsom
Sutton
Banstead
WOKING
Leatherhead
59
44
31

Kings Langley
Colney
Park
Cuffley
Chipperfield
Abbots Langley
Bricket Wood
How Wood
De Havilland Aircraft Heritage Centre
South Mimms
Potters Bar
Northaw
Belsize
Sarratt
Radlett
Shenley
Ridge
Botany
Latimer
Chenies
Amersham on the Hill
Amersham Common
Little Chalfont
Chorleywood
Chorleywood West
Rickmansworth
WATFORD
Chandler's Cross
Studio Tour
Aldenham
Letchmore Heath
Green Street
Borehamwood
Bushey
Croxley Green
Elstree
Barnet
Arkley
Monken Hadley
Hadley Wood
Cockfosters
New Barnet
East Barnet
Trent
Chiltern Open Air
Batchworth
Oxhey
Merry Hill
Bushey Heath
London Gateway
Totteridge
Totteridge Fields
Highwood Hill
Mill Hill
Southgate
Friern Barnet
Chalfont St Giles
Seer Green
Chalfont Common
Chalfont St Peter
Eastbury
Stanmore
Edgware
Northwood
Hatch End
Harrow Weald
Wealdstone
Harefield
Ruislip Woods
Pinner Green
Pinner
Eastcote
Ruislip
Harrow
Harrow on the Hill
Kenton
Kingsbury
RAF Hendon
Hendon
Church End
Finchley
Muswell Hill
Hornsey
Crouch End
Highgate
Golders Green
Brent Cross
Brent Resr
Fryent
Neasden
Kenwood House
Hampstead
Holloway
Fenton House
Denham Green
Denham
Gerrards Cross
Bayhurst Wood
Grand Union Canal
R Colne
Ickenham
Sudbury
Wembley
Wembley Complex
Cricklewood
Willesden
Harlesden
Kilburn
St John's Wood
Lord's
Camden Town
Kentish Town
Farnham Common
Fulmer
Black Park
Uxbridge
New Denham
North Hillingdon
Gutteridge Wood
Stoke Poges
Iver Heath
Cowley
Hayes End
Yeading
Northolt
Perivale
Alperton
Park Royal
Greenford
Wood End
Hayes
Ealing
Acton
Shepherd's Bush
Marylebone
Paddington
George Green
Iver
Yiewsley
West Drayton
Lake Farm
Stockley Park
Minet
Southall
Norwood Green
Hanwell
Hammersmith
Olympia
Kensington
Kensington Palace
Westminster
Chelsea
Upton
Langley
Datchet
Colnbrook
Poyle
Harlington
Cranford
Heston
Brentford
Chiswick
Kew
Kew Palace
Syon
Osterley
Chiswick House
London Wetland Centre
Carlyle's House
Battersea
Fulham
Brixton
Clapham
Frogmore House
Old Windsor
Horton
Heathrow
Stanwell
West Bedfont
Hatton
Hounslow
Isleworth
Twickenham
Mortlake
Barnes
East Sheen
Richmond
Putney
Roehampton
Wandsworth
Wraysbury
Hythe End
Runnymede
East Bedfont
Bedfont Lakes
Feltham
Marble Hill
Petersham
Ham House
Richmond Park
All England Tennis
Earlsfield
Balham
Tooting Bec
Streatham
Egham
Savill Garden
Englefield Green
Valley Gardens
Thorpe Lea
Thorpe
Staines-upon-Thames
Queen Mary Resr
Ashford
Lower Feltham
Felthamhill
Hanworth
Kempton Park
Teddington
Ham
Kingston upon Thames
Wimbledon
Tooting
Merton
Sunbury-on-Thames
Hampton
Hampton Wick
Norbiton
New Malden
Raynes Park
Morden
Mitcham
Norbury
Virginia Water
Thorpe Park
Littleton
Upper Halliford
Lower Halliford
West Molesey
East Molesey
Hampton Court Palace
Surbiton
Thames Ditton
Motspur Park
St Helier
Beddington Corner
Lyne
Chertsey
Shepperton
Walton-on-Thames
Long Ditton
Tolworth
Worcester Park
North Cheam
Hackbridge
Beddington
Great Cockcrow
Thames Path
Oatlands Park
Sandown Park
Hinchley Wood
Carshalton
Wallington
Addlestone
Weybridge
Esher
Hersham
West End
Hook
Chessington
Cheam
Ewell
Sutton
South Beddington
Ottershaw
Burrowhill
Chobham
Woodham
New Haw
Claremont Landscape Garden
Claygate
Chessington World of Adventures
Belmont
Little Woodcote
Woodcote
West Byfleet
Byfleet
Sheerwater
Fairmile
Cobham
Oxshott
Epsom
Ashtead Common
Horsell
Maybury
Pyrford
Painshill Park
Semaphore Tower
Downside
Epsom Downs
Banstead
Woodmansterne
Coulsdon
WOKING
Goldsworth Park
RHS Wisley
Stoke D'Abernon
Leatherhead
Ashtead
Burgh Heath
Tadworth
Chipstead
St Johns
Mayford
Old Woking
Send
Ripley
Ockham
Fetcham
Headley
Walton on the Hill
Kingswood
Hooley
Netherne-on-the-Hill
Chaldon
Sutton Green
West
Little Bookham
Great Bookham
Bocketts
Norbury Park
Effingham
Polesden Lacey
Mickleham
Headley Heath
Box Hill
Merstham
South Merstham
M25
M1
M40
M4
M3
A1(M)
A40
A41
A406
A3
A30
59
43
31
A B C D E F
1 2 3 4 5 6 7 8
0 1 2 3 4 miles
0 1 2 3 4 5 kilometres

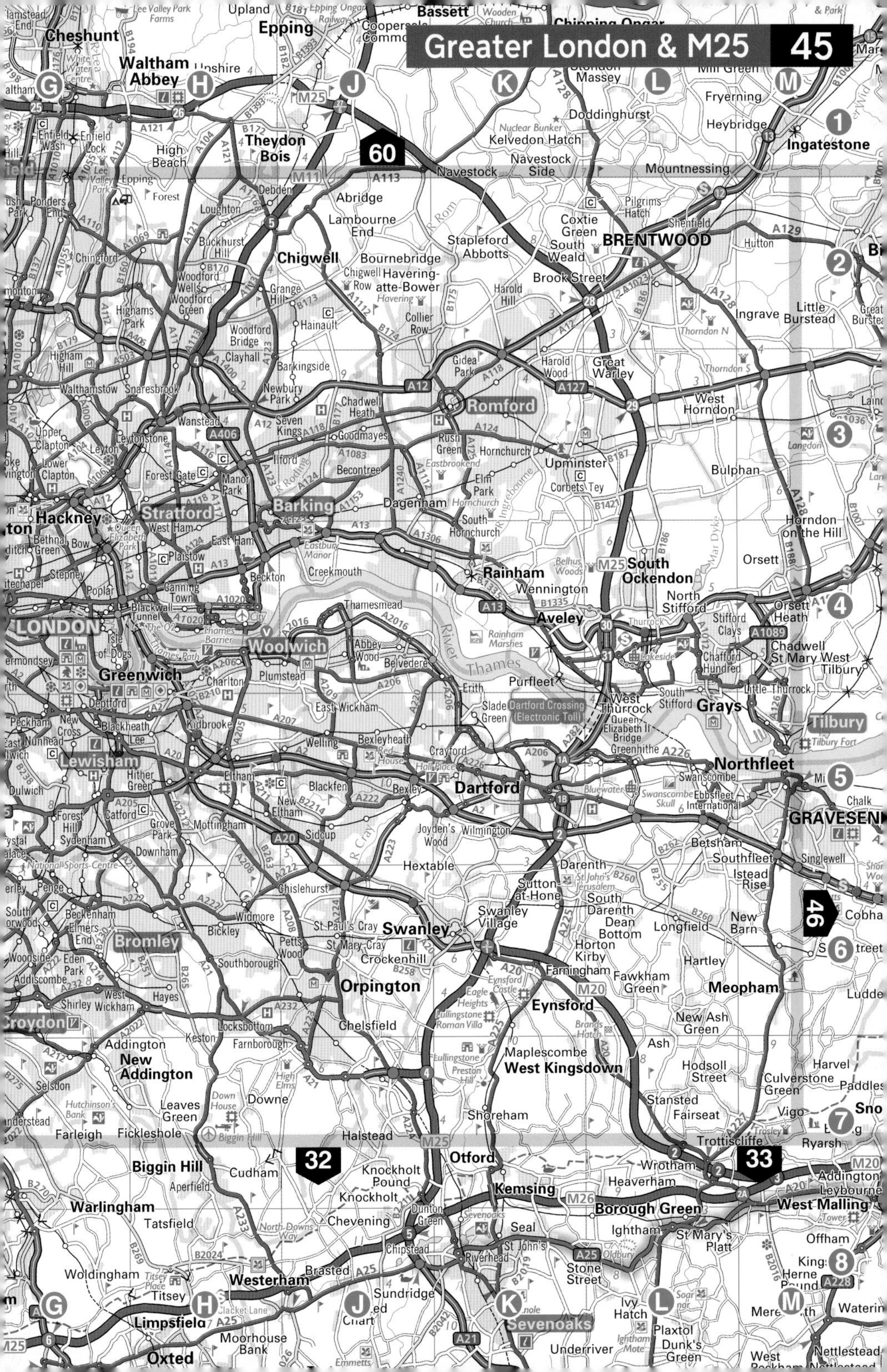
Cheshunt
Waltham Abbey
Upshire
Epping
Upland
Bassett
Coopersale Common
Chipping Ongar
Stondon Massey
Mill Green
Fryerning
Heybridge
Ingatestone
Doddinghurst
Kelvedon Hatch
Nuclear Bunker
Navestock Side
Navestock
Mountnessing
Theydon Bois
High Beach
Enfield Wash
Enfield Lock
Lee Valley Park
Epping Forest
Ponders End
Debden
Loughton
Abridge
Lambourne End
Chigwell
Chigwell Row
Buckhurst Hill
Chingford
Woodford Wells
Woodford Green
Woodford Bridge
Grange Hill
Hainault
Bournebridge
Havering-atte-Bower
Collier Row
Stapleford Abbotts
Harold Hill
Harold Wood
Coxtie Green
South Weald
Pilgrims Hatch
Shenfield
BRENTWOOD
Hutton
Brook Street
Ingrave
Little Burstead
Thorndon N
Thorndon S
Great Warley
West Horndon
Langdon
Bulphan
Horndon on the Hill
Orsett
Orsett Heath
Higham Hill
Highams Park
Walthamstow
Snaresbrook
Clayhall
Barkingside
Newbury Park
Seven Kings
Goodmayes
Chadwell Heath
Gidea Park
Romford
Rush Green
Hornchurch
Upminster
Corbets Tey
Eastbrookend
Elm Park
Dagenham
Becontree
Ilford
Barking
Wanstead
Leytonstone
Leyton
Upper Clapton
Lower Clapton
Forest Gate
Manor Park
Hackney
Stratford
West Ham
East Ham
Plaistow
Bethnal Green
Bow
Stepney
Poplar
Canning Town
Beckton
Creekmouth
Eastbury Manor
South Hornchurch
Rainham
Wennington
Belhus Woods
South Ockendon
North Stifford
Stifford Clays
Aveley
Thurrock
Lakeside
Chafford Hundred
Chadwell St Mary
West Tilbury
Little Thurrock
Tilbury
Tilbury Fort
Grays
South Stifford
West Thurrock
Purfleet
Rainham Marshes
River Thames
Dartford Crossing (Electronic Toll)
Queen Elizabeth II Bridge
Greenhithe
Northfleet
Swanscombe
Swanscombe Skull
Ebbsfleet International
Bluewater
GRAVESEND
Chalk
LONDON
Blackwall Tunnel
The O2
Isle of Dogs
Thames Barrier
Thames Path
Woolwich
Thamesmead
Abbey Wood
Belvedere
Plumstead
Greenwich
Charlton
Deptford
East Wickham
Erith
Slade Green
Peckham
New Cross
Blackheath
Lee
Nunhead
Kidbrooke
Welling
Bexleyheath
Red House
Crayford
Hall Place
Dartford
Bexley
Lewisham
Hither Green
Eltham
Blackfen
New Eltham
Sidcup
Joyden's Wood
Wilmington
Dulwich
Forest Hill
Catford
Grove Park
Mottingham
Sydenham
Downham
National Sports Centre
Hextable
Darenth
Sutton-at-Hone
St John's Jerusalem
South Darenth
Betsham
Southfleet
Istead Rise
Singlewell
Penge
Beckenham
Elmers End
Chislehurst
Widmore
Bickley
Bromley
St Paul's Cray
St Mary Cray
Swanley
Swanley Village
Dean Bottom
Horton Kirby
Longfield
New Barn
Hartley
Woodside
Eden Park
Addiscombe
Shirley
West Wickham
Hayes
Southborough
Petts Wood
Crockenhill
Orpington
Farningham
Eynsford Castle
Eynsford
Eagle Heights
Lullingstone Roman Villa
Fawkham Green
Meopham
New Ash Green
Croydon
Addington
New Addington
Keston
Locksbottom
Farnborough
Chelsfield
Brands Hatch
Ash
Hodsoll Street
Culverstone Green
Harvel
Paddlesworth
Maplescombe
West Kingsdown
Lullingstone
Preston Hill
High Elms
Downe
Down House
Selsdon
Hutchinson's Bank
Leaves Green
Shoreham
Stansted
Fairseat
Vigo
Trosley
Ryarsh
Farleigh
Fickleshole
Biggin Hill
Halstead
Trottiscliffe
Cudham
Aperfield
Knockholt Pound
Knockholt
Otford
Kemsing
Wrotham
Heaverham
Addington
Leybourne
West Malling
Warlingham
Tatsfield
Chevening
Dunton Green
Sevenoaks
Seal
Borough Green
Ightham
St Mary's Platt
Offham
North Downs Way
Woldingham
Titsey Place
Titsey
Westerham
Brasted
Chipstead
Riverhead
St John's
Stone Street
Oldbury
Kings Hill
Herne Pound
Sundridge
Ide Hill
Ivy Hatch
Mereworth
Clacket Lane
Limpsfield
Moorhouse Bank
Oxted
Chart
Knole
Sevenoaks
Underriver
Plaxtol
Dunk's Green
Ightham Mote
Emmetts
West Peckham
Nettlestead
Wateringbury
60
32
33
46

A
B
C
D
E
F
1
2
3
4
5
6
7
8
61
45
33
Margaretting
Galleywood
Margaretting Tye
Fryerning
Ingatestone
Stock
West Hanningfield
Hanningfield Reservoir
Coalhill
East Hanningfield
Bicknacre
Cock Clarks
Rudley Green
Purleigh
Mundon Hill
Maylandsea
Steeple
Mayland
Latchingdon
Howegreen
Woodham Ferrers
Stow Maries
Cold Norton
Althorne
RHS Hyde Hall
Tropical Wings
South Woodham Ferrers
North Fambridge
Bridgemarsh Island
River Crouch
South Hanningfield
Downham
Ramsden Bellhouse
Hutton
Billericay
South Green
Wickford
Runwell
Battlesbridge
Hullbridge
South Fambridge
Canewdon
Paglesham
Rawreth
Shotgate
Barleylands
Little Burstead
Great Burstead
Ingrave
Crays Hill
Hockley
Ashingdon
Hawkwell
Rayleigh
Rochford
Great Stambridge
Eastend
Potton Is
Barling
R Roach
North Benfleet
BASILDON
Bowers Gifford
New Thundersley
Thundersley
Southend
Eastwood
Laindon
Lee Chapel
Vange
Pitsea
Belfairs Woodland
Hadleigh
Prittlewell
Little Wakering
Great Wakering
Bournes Green
Langdon
Wat Tyler
South Essex
South Benfleet
Hadleigh Castle
Leigh-on-Sea
Westcliff-on-Sea
Southchurch
Thorpe Bay
North Shoeburyness
Shoeburyness
East Beach
Shoebury Ness
Bulphan
Langdon Hills
One Tree Hill
Fobbing
Horndon on the Hill
Corringham
Canvey Heights
Leigh Beck
Canvey Point
Canvey Island
SOUTHEND-ON-SEA
Orsett
Coryton
Stanford le Hope
LONDON GATEWAY TERMINAL
THAMES ESTUARY
Orsett Heath
Stifford Clays
Thurrock Thameside
Chadwell St Mary
West Tilbury
Little Thurrock
Grays
East Tilbury
Tilbury
Coalhouse Fort
Tilbury Fort
HOO PENINSULA
Cliffe Pools
Cliffe
Cooling
St Mary's Hoo
Allhallows
Isle of Grain
Lower Stoke
Grain
Northward Hill
High Halstow
Fenn Street
Middle Stoke
Stoke
Thamesport
Sheerness
Marine Town
Mile Town
Northfleet
Milton
Church Street
Chalk
GRAVESEND
Cliffe Woods
Chattenden
Hoo St Werburgh
River Medway
Halfway Houses
Higham
Southfleet
Singlewell
Istead Rise
Shorne Woods
Shorne
Wainscott
Upnor Castle
Frindsbury
The Historic Dockyard, Chatham
Nor Marsh
Motley Hill
Rushenden
Elmley Marshes
ISLE
Owletts
Cobham
Strood
ROCHESTER
Fort Amherst
Brompton
Riverside
New Barn
Sole Street
Diggerland
Rochester Castle
Grange
GILLINGHAM
Lower Halstow
Iwade
Elmley Island
Meopham
Luddesdown
Cuxton
Borstal
CHATHAM
Luton
Darland
Upchurch
Sittingbourne & Kemsley Light Railway
North Downs Way
Capstone
Hempstead
Rainham
Wigmore
Newington
Bobbing
Milton Regis
Chalkwell
Sittingbourne
Harvel
Wouldham
Halling
Walderslade
Hartlip
Medway
Culverstone Green
Paddlesworth
Buckmore Park
Lords Wood
Bredhurst
Hill Green
Borden
Bapchild
Tunstall
Teynham
Vigo
Snodland
Burham
Kit's Coty
Blue Bell Hill
Stockbury
Oad St
Highsted
Rodmersham
Rodmersham Green
Lynsted
Birling
Ryarsh
Eccles
Aylesford
South Green
Bredgar
Rawling Street
Kent Event Centre
Addington
Lunsford
Boxley
Bicknor
Leybourne
Larkfield
Tyland Barn
White Horse Wood
Milstead
West Malling
Ditton
Detling
Thurnham
Hucking
Wormshill
Doddington
Tower
British Legion Village
Broad Street
Frinsted
Offham
East Malling
Bearsted
Kings Hill
Maidstone
MAIDSTONE
Wichling
Herne Pound
Tovil
Hollingbourne
Wateringbury
East Barming
Willington
Otham
Leeds
Eyhorne Street
Harrietsham
Lenham
Warren Street
Shepway
Leeds
Broomfield
West Peckham
Boughton
Langley
NORTH DOWNS
0 1 2 3 4 miles
0 1 2 3 4 5 kilometres
A12
A130
A129
A132
A1245
A127
A176
A1235
A1321
A13
A1015
A1159
B1013
A1014
A1013
A1089
A126
A228
B2000
B2001
A2
A226
A289
A230
A278
B2004
A229
A249
A250
A2500
M2
M20
A20
A26
B1002
B1007
B1418
B1010
B1012
B1018
B1021
B148
B1036
B1006
B1014
A130
B1016
B1017
B1420
B188
B2016
B2163

G
H
J
K
L
M
1
2
3
4
5
6
7
8
62
34
35
35
Dengie
dham
insier
n-Crouch
Holliwell Point
Foulness Point
Courtsend
Churchend
FOULNESS ISLAND
Warden Point
Leysdown-on-Sea
B2231
EPPEY
Leysdown Coastal Park
Isle of Harty
The Swale
The Swale
Shell Ness
Whitstable
Whitstable Bay
Herne Bay
Herne Bay
Hampton
Bishopstone
Reculver Towers & Roman Fort
Reculver
Minnis Bay
St Mildred's Bay
Westgate-on-Sea
Birchington
Beltinge
Tankerton
B2205
Swalecliffe
Greenhill
A299
Broomfield
St Nicholas-at-Wade
A28
Acol
B2190
Monkton
Durlock
Minster
R Stour
Chestfield
South Street
Herne
Boyden Gate
Sarre
A253
Chislet
East Blean
Seasalter
A2990
Hoath
Upstreet
West Stourmouth
East Stourmouth
Westmarsh
Oare
Yorkletts
A299
Wildwood
A291
Hersden
Faversham
Goodnestone
Highstreet
Druidstone Park
Broad Oak
Stone Chapel
Davington Hill
B2040
Dargate
Denstroude
Tyler Hill
Westbere
Preston
Elmstone
Cop Street
Ospringe
Preston
Hernhill
Blean
Sturry
Stodmarsh
Farming World
Staplestreet
A290
Hales Place
Hoaden
Mount Ephraim
Dunkirk
Upper Harbledown
Rough Common
Fordwich
Town Hall
Wickhambreaux
Boughton Street
Littlebourne
Wingham
Seaton
Ash
North Street
Gate
A2050
Canterbury
Ickham
Durlock
A257
South Street
Harbledown
Thanington
Wingham
Marshborough
Stone Cross
Sheldwich
Hogben's Hill
Selling
Oversland
Chartham Hatch
Howletts
A2050
Bramling
Woodnesborough
Staple
Statenborough
A251
Old Wives Lees
Chartham
Bekesbourne
A2
Badlesmere
Patrixbourne
B2046
Goodnestone
Eastry
Petham
Shalmsford Street
Street End
Bridge
Adisham
Chillenden
Shottenden
Rattling
Leaveland
Chilham
Lower Hardres
Bishopsbourne
Aylesham
Nonington
Betteshanger
A252
Dane Street
Garlinge Green
North Downs Way

A
B
C
D
E
F
1
2
3
4
5
6
7
8
Pen Brush
Garn Fawr
Trefasser
Pembrokeshire Coast Path
Manorowen
St Nicholas
Ynys Daullyn
Granston
Carreg Sampson
64
Porthgain
Trefin
Mathry
Llangloffan Fen
A487
B4331
Letterston
Abereiddy
Llanrhian
Berea
Croes-goch
Treglemais
ST DAVID'S HEAD
Treleddyd-fawr
Whitesands Bay
Rhodiad-y-brenin
B4583
Bishop's Palace
Caer Farchell
River Solva
B4330
Llandeloy
St Davids
(Tyddewi)
Whitchurch
Treffgarne Owen
Hayscastle
Hayscastle Cross
RAMSEY ISLAND
Ramsey Sound
RSPB
Solva
Penycwn
178
DUDWELL MT
Newgale
St David's Peninsula Heritage Coast
PEMBROKESHIRE COAST NATIONAL PARK
Roch
Wolfsdale
Simpson Cross
Rickets Head
Nolton Haven
Nolton
Keeston
St Brides Bay
St Brides Bay Heritage Coast
Druidston
Haroldston West
Portfield Gate
B4341
Broad Haven
Broadway
B4327
Dreen Hill
A4076
Little Haven
Walton West
Pembrokeshire Coast Path
Talbenny
Tiers Cross
Walwyn's Castle
A477
SKOMER ISLAND
Wooltack Point
Marloes
St Ishmael's
Herbrandston
Steynton
Broad Sound
Marloes & Dale Heritage Coast
Hubberston
Hakin
Waterston
Dale
Westdale Bay
Great Castle Head
Dale Point
Llanstadwell
SKOKHOLM ISLAND
Milford Haven
Milford Haven
(Aberdaugleddau)
Angle
Angle Bay
St Ann's Head
Rhoscrowther
B4320
Rosslare
Castlemartin Brook
Freshwater West
B4319
Castlemartin
Warren
Merrion
Linney Head
Pembrokeshire Coast Path
0 1 2 3 4 miles
0 1 2 3 4 5 kilometres

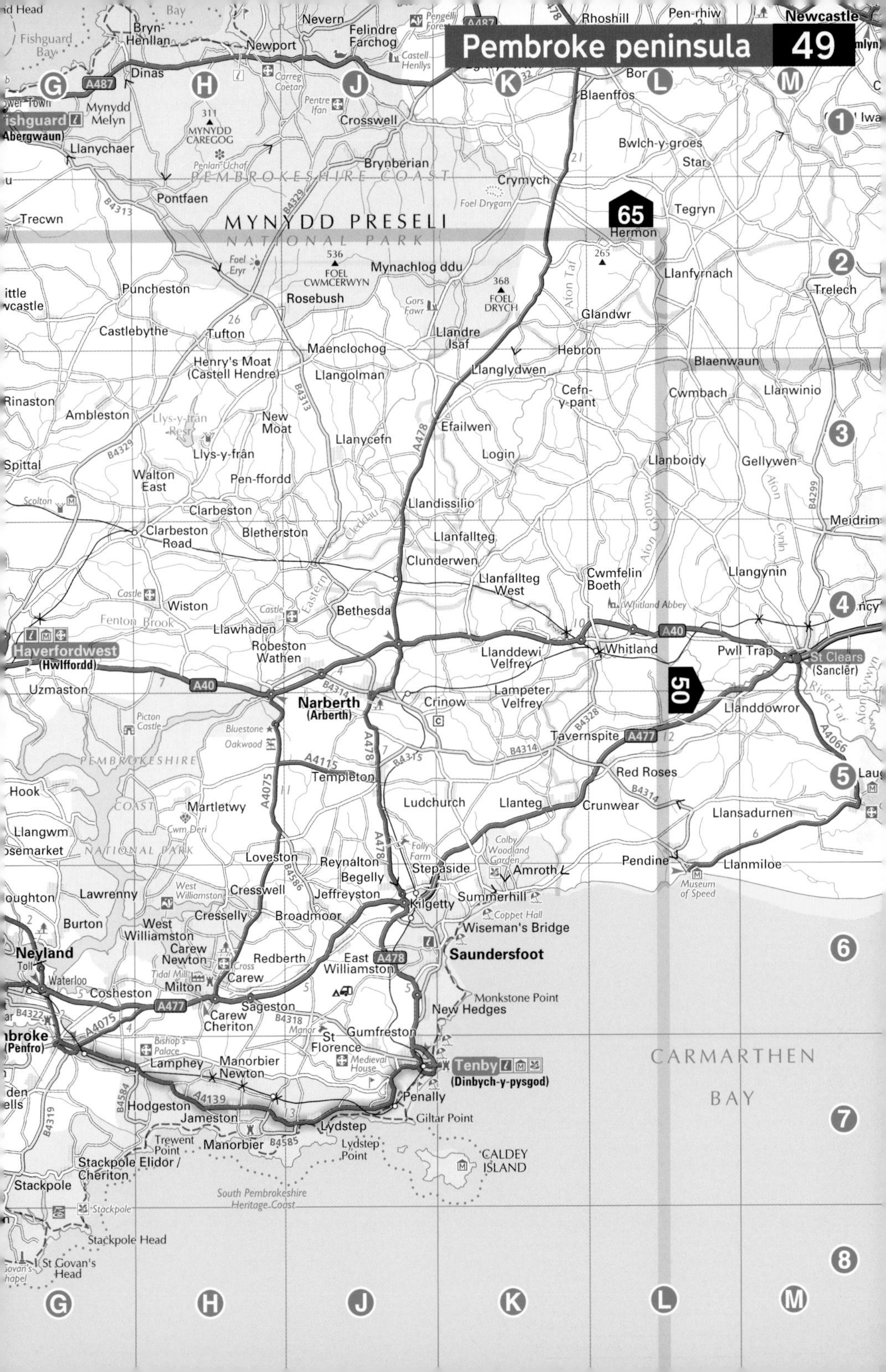
Newcastle
Nevern
Felindre Farchog
Pengelli Forest
Castell Henllys
Rhoshill
Pen-rhiw
Bryn-Henllan
Newport
Dinas
Fishguard Bay
Fishguard (Abergwaun)
Lower Town
Mynydd Melyn
Carreg Coetan
Pentre Ifan
Crosswell
311 MYNYDD CAREGOG
Penlan-Uchaf
Llanychaer
Brynberian
Blaenffos
Bwlch-y-groes
Star
Crymych
Foel Drygarn
PEMBROKESHIRE COAST
Pontfaen
Trecwn
MYNYDD PRESELI
NATIONAL PARK
65
Hermon
Tegryn
265
Llanfyrnach
Trelech
Foel Eryr
536 FOEL CWMCERWYN
Mynachlog ddu
368 FOEL DRYCH
Gors Fawr
Puncheston
Rosebush
Little Newcastle
Castlebythe
Tufton
Glandwr
Afon Taf
Llandre Isaf
Maenclochog
Hebron
Henry's Moat (Castell Hendre)
Llangolman
Llanglydwen
Blaenwaun
Cwmbach
Llanwinio
Cefn-y-pant
Rinaston
Ambleston
Llys-y-frân Resr
New Moat
Llanycefn
Efailwen
Llys-y-frân
Login
Llanboidy
Gellywen
Spittal
Walton East
Pen-ffordd
Scolton
Clarbeston
Llandissilio
Meidrim
Clarbeston Road
Bletherston
Llanfallteg
Afon Gronw
Afon Cynin
Clunderwen
Llanfallteg West
Cwmfelin Boeth
Llangynin
Castle
Wiston
Eastern Cleddau
Whitland Abbey
Fenton Brook
Castle
Bethesda
Llawhaden
Haverfordwest (Hwlffordd)
Robeston Wathen
Llanddewi Velfrey
Whitland
Pwll Trap
St Clears (Sanclêr)
Uzmaston
Narberth (Arberth)
Crinow
Lampeter Velfrey
50
Llanddowror
River Taf
Afon Cywyn
Picton Castle
Bluestone
Oakwood
Tavernspite
PEMBROKESHIRE
Templeton
Red Roses
Laugharne
Hook
COAST
Martletwy
Ludchurch
Llanteg
Crunwear
Llansadurnen
Llangwm
Cwm Deri
Rosemarket
NATIONAL PARK
Loveston
Reynalton
Folly Farm
Colby Woodland Garden
Pendine
Llanmiloe
Stepaside
Amroth
Museum of Speed
Begelly
Houghton
Lawrenny
West Williamston
Cresswell
Jeffreyston
Summerhill
Kilgetty
Burton
Cresselly
Broadmoor
Coppet Hall
Wiseman's Bridge
West Williamston
Neyland
Toll
Carew Newton
Redberth
East Williamston
Saundersfoot
Cross
Tidal Mill
Carew
Waterloo
Cosheston
Milton
Monkstone Point
Carew Cheriton
Sageston
New Hedges
Manor
Gumfreston
Pembroke (Penfro)
St Florence
Bishop's Palace
Medieval House
Lamphey
Manorbier Newton
Tenby (Dinbych-y-pysgod)
CARMARTHEN BAY
Penally
Hodgeston
Jameston
Lydstep
Giltar Point
Trewent Point
Manorbier
Lydstep Point
CALDEY ISLAND
Stackpole Elidor / Cheriton
Stackpole
South Pembrokeshire Heritage Coast
Stackpole
Stackpole Head
St Govan's Head
St Govan's Chapel
A487
A478
A40
A477
A4075
A4139
A4066
B4313
B4329
B4314
B4315
B4316
B4318
B4322
B4328
B4299
B4584
B4585
B4586
B4319
A4115
G
H
J
K
L
M
1
2
3
4
5
6
7
8

Llanfyrnach
Trelech
Llanpumsaint
Glandwr
Hebron
Pontar
65
Blaenwaun
Cynwyl Elfed
River Gwili
Blaen-y-Coed
Rhydargaeau
Cefn-y-pant
Cwmbach
Llanwinio
Talog
Gwili Railway
B4301
Efailwen
Login
Llanboidy
Gellywen
Abernant
Bronwydd
A484
Afon Gronw
Afon Cynin
B4299
Meidrim
Carmarthen
(Caerfyrddin)
Abergwili
Llangunnor
B4300
Tre-gynwr
Cwmfelin Boeth
Llanfallteg West
Llangynin
B4298
A40
Johnstown
United Counties
Llanllwch
Whitland Abbey
Bancyfelin
A48
Llanddewi Velfrey
Whitland
Pwll Trap
St Clears
(Sanclêr)
Cwmffrwd
Croesyceiliog
Lampeter Velfrey
49
Afon Cywyn
River Taf
Llangynog
Idole
Bancycapel
Llangendeirne
B4328
Llanddowror
Tavernspite
A477
B4314
A4066
B4312
Llanybri
Pontantwn
Red Roses
Laugharne
Bancffosfelen
Llanteg
Crunwear
Llansteffan
Llandyfaelog
Llansadurnen
Castle
River Towy
Ferryside
Four Roads
Colby Woodland Garden
Amroth
Pendine
Llanmiloe
Wharley Point
Ginst Point
Museum of Speed
Llansaint
Pontyates
Mynyddgarreg
Summerhill
Coppet Hall
Wiseman's Bridge
R Gwendraeth
Kidwelly
(Cydweli)
B4317
Ffos Las
Carway
Five Roads
Saundersfoot
Trimsaran
Pen-y-Mynydd
Monkstone Point
Pembrey
Pembrey Forest
B4308
Ffrwd Farm Mire
Cefn Sidan
Tenby
(Dinbych-y-pysgod)
CARMARTHEN
BAY
Archddu
Burry Port
(Porth Tywyn)
B4311
Pwll
CALDEY ISLAND
Burry Inlet
Whiteford Burrows
Broughton Bay
Llanmadoc
Landimore
Burry Holms
Cheriton
Llangennith
Burry Green
Oldwalls
Rhossili Bay
Rhossili Downs
Reynoldston
Llanddewi
Rhossili
Knelston
Visitor Centre
WORMS HEAD
Middleton
A4118
B4247
Gower Coast
Paviland
Port Eynon
Overton
Culver Hole
Port Eynon Point
A
B
C
D
E
F
1
2
3
4
5
6
7
8
0 1 2 3 4 miles
0 1 2 3 4 5 kilometres

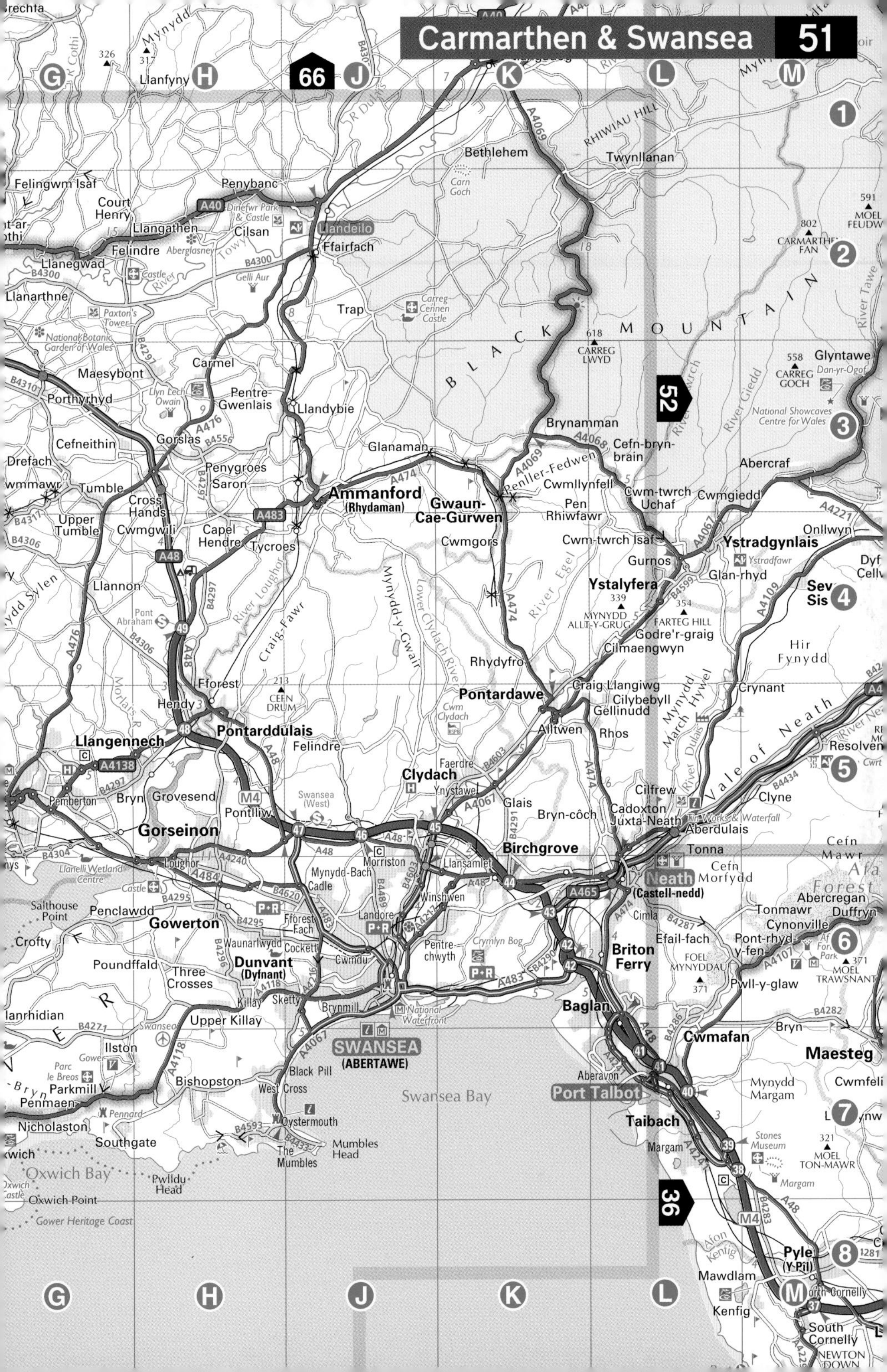
66
52
36
G
H
J
K
L
M
1
2
3
4
5
6
7
8
Llanfyny
Mynydd
326
317
R Cothi
A40
B4300
A4069
RHIWIAU HILL
Twynllanan
Bethlehem
Carn Goch
591
MOEL FEUDW
802
CARMARTHEN FAN
Felingwm Isaf
Penybanc
Court Henry
Dinefwr Park & Castle
Llangathen
Cilsan
Llandeilo
Aberglasney
Felindre
Ffairfach
Llanegwad
B4300
Castle
Gelli Aur
Llanarthne
Trap
Carreg Cennen Castle
Paxton's Tower
National Botanic Garden of Wales
B L A C K   M O U N T A I N
618
CARREG LWYD
558
CARREG GOCH
Glyntawe
Dan-yr-Ogof
River Tawe
Carmel
Maesybont
B4310
Porthyrhyd
Llyn Llech Owain
Pentre-Gwenlais
Llandybie
National Showcaves Centre for Wales
River Giedd
Brynamman
A4068
Cefn-bryn-brain
Abercraf
Cefneithin
Gorslas
A476
B4556
Glanaman
A474
Drefach
Penygroes
Saron
Penller-Fedwen
Cwmllynfell
Tumble
Cross Hands
B4297
Ammanford
(Rhydaman)
Gwaun-Cae-Gurwen
Pen Rhiwfawr
Cwm-twrch Uchaf
Cwmgiedd
A4221
Upper Tumble
Cwmgwili
A483
Capel Hendre
Tycroes
Cwmgors
Cwm-twrch Isaf
A4067
Ystradgynlais
Onllwyn
Ystradfawr
B4317
B4306
Llannon
River Loughor
Mynydd-y-Gwair
Lower Clydach River
River Egel
Gurnos
Glan-rhyd
Ystalyfera
A48
A4109
Pont Abraham
49
Craig-Fawr
339
MYNYDD ALLT-Y-GRUG
B4599
354
FARTEG HILL
Godre'r-graig
Cilmaengwyn
Hir Fynydd
B4306
A476
A474
Rhydyfro
Morlais R
Fforest
213
CEFN DRUM
Pontardawe
Craig Llangiwg
Cilybebyll
Gellinudd
Mynydd March Hywel
Crynant
Hendy
Cwm Clydach
Vale of Neath
River Neath
Llangennech
48
Pontarddulais
Felindre
Alltwen
Rhos
River Dulais
Resolven
A4138
B4297
Faerdre
B4603
Clydach
Ynystawe
A474
Cilfrew
B4434
Clyne
Pemberton
Bryn
Grovesend
M4
Pontlliw
Swansea (West)
A4067
Glais
Bryn-côch
Cadoxton Juxta-Neath
Tin Works & Waterfall
Aberdulais
Gorseinon
47
46
45
A48
B4291
Cefn Mawr
B4304
Llanelli Wetland Centre
Loughor
A4240
A484
A48
Mynydd-Bach
Morriston
Llansamlet
Birchgrove
Tonna
Cefn Morfydd
Neath
(Castell-nedd)
Forest
Castle
B4295
Salthouse Point
Penclawdd
B4620
Cadle
B4489
B4603
44
Winshwen
A465
43
Abercregan
Tonmawr
Duffryn
Gowerton
B4295
Fforest Fach
A483
Landore
A4217
Cimla
B4287
Cynonville
Crofty
B4296
Waunarlwydd
Cockett
Pentre-chwyth
Crymlyn Bog
42
Efail-fach
Briton Ferry
Pont-rhyd-y-fen
Afan Forest Park
Poundffald
Dunvant
(Dyfnant)
Cwmdu
B4290
FOEL MYNYDDAU
371
MOEL TRAWSNANT
Three Crosses
A4118
A4216
A483
Pwll-y-glaw
A4107
Llanrhidian
Killay
Sketty
Brynmill
National Waterfront
Baglan
B4286
B4282
Bryn
Upper Killay
Swansea
B4271
Ilston
A4118
A4067
SWANSEA
(ABERTAWE)
A48
Cwmafan
Maesteg
Gower
Parc le Breos
Black Pill
41
Aberavon
Mynydd Margam
Cwmfelin
Parkmill
Bishopston
West Cross
Swansea Bay
Port Talbot
40
Penmaen
Pennard
Oystermouth
Taibach
B4593
B4433
Mumbles Head
The Mumbles
Stones Museum
Nicholaston
Southgate
39
Margam
A4241
321
MOEL TON-MAWR
Oxwich Bay
Pwlldu Head
38
Margam
Oxwich Castle
Oxwich Point
Gower Heritage Coast
B4283
Afon Kenfig
Pyle
(Y Pîl)
Mawdlam
North Cornelly
Kenfig
37
South Cornelly
NEWTON DOWN

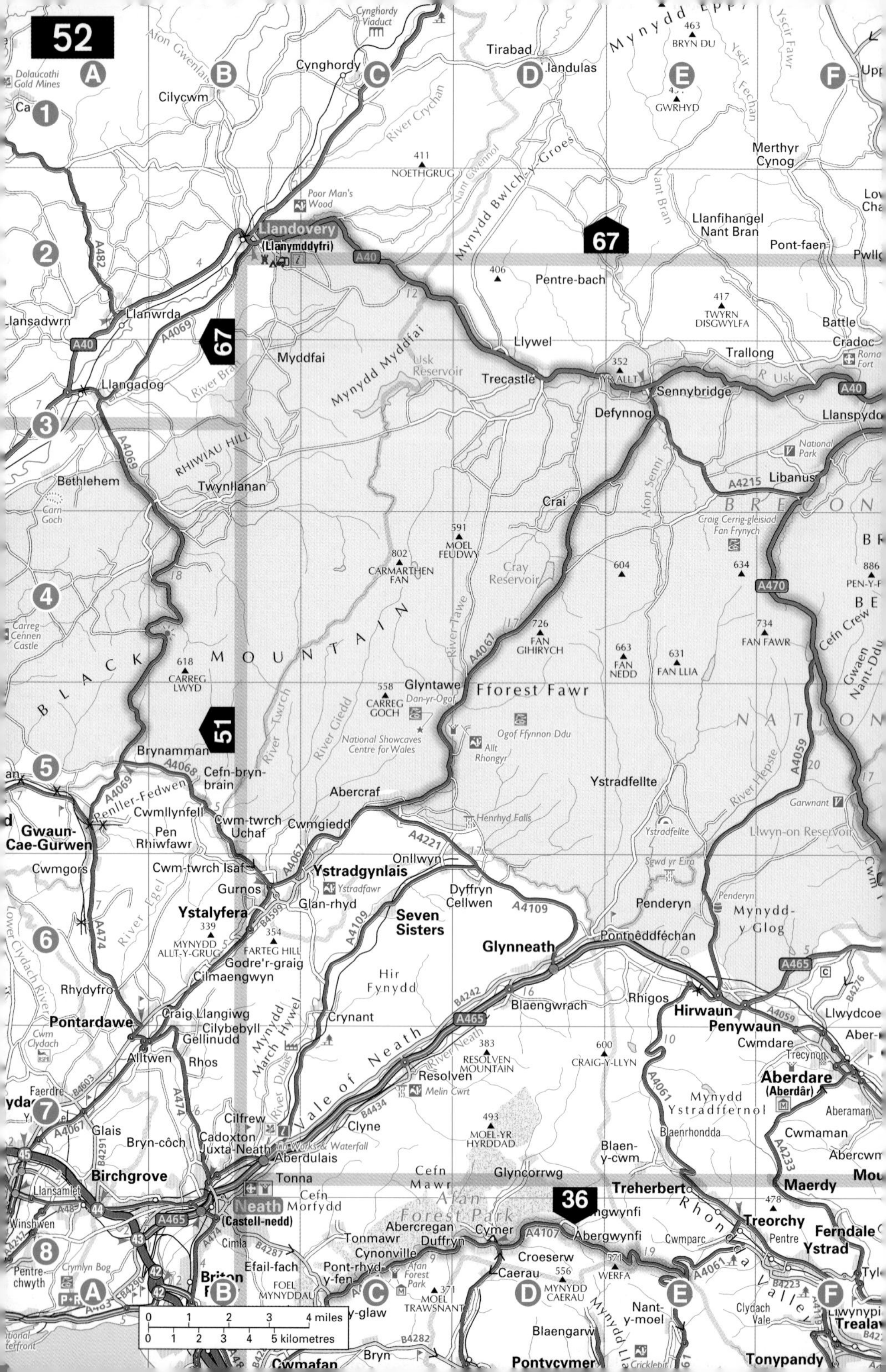

Dolaucothi Gold Mines
Afon Gwenlais
Cynghordy Viaduct
Cynghordy
Cilycwm
Tirabad
Llandulas
Mynydd Epynt
463 BRYN DU
GWRHYD
Yscir Fawr
Yscir Fechan
River Crychan
411 NOETHGRUG
Nant Gwennol
Mynydd Bwlch-y-Groes
Merthyr Cynog
Poor Man's Wood
Nant Bran
Llanfihangel Nant Bran
Pont-faen
Llandovery
(Llanymddyfri)
67
A40
A482
406
Pentre-bach
417 TWYRN DISGWYLFA
Battle
Llanwrda
Llansadwrn
A4069
Myddfai
Mynydd Myddfai
Usk Reservoir
Llywel
Trecastle
352 YR ALLT
Trallong
Sennybridge
Cradoc
Roman Fort
Llangadog
River Bran
Defynnog
R Usk
Llanspyddid
RHIWIAU HILL
National Park
Bethlehem
Carn Goch
Twynllanan
A4215
Libanus
Crai
BRECON
Craig Cerrig-gleisiad Fan Frynych
591 MOEL FEUDWY
802 CARMARTHEN FAN
Cray Reservoir
604
634
886 PEN-Y-F
Afon Senni
A470
Carreg Cennen Castle
726 FAN GIHIRYCH
734 FAN FAWR
Cefn Crew
618 CARREG LWYD
BLACK MOUNTAIN
River Tawe
A4067
663 FAN NEDD
631 FAN LLIA
Gwaen Nant-Ddu
558 CARREG GOCH
Glyntawe
Dan-yr-Ogof
Fforest Fawr
River Twrch
River Giedd
National Showcaves Centre for Wales
Ogof Ffynnon Ddu
Allt Rhongyr
NATIONAL
51
Brynamman
A4068
Cefn-bryn-brain
Ystradfellte
River Hepste
A4059
Abercraf
Penller-Fedwen
Cwmllynfell
Garwnant
Gwaun-Cae-Gurwen
Pen Rhiwfawr
Cwm-twrch Uchaf
Cwmgiedd
Henrhyd Falls
Ystradfellte
Llwyn-on Reservoir
A4221
Onllwyn
Cwmgors
Cwm-twrch Isaf
Gurnos
Ystradgynlais
Ystradfawr
Sgwd yr Eira
Dyffryn Cellwen
Glan-rhyd
Seven Sisters
A4109
Penderyn
Mynydd-y-Glog
Lower Clydach River
River Egel
Ystalyfera
339 MYNYDD ALLT-Y-GRUG
354 FARTEG HILL
B4599
Godre'r-graig
Glynneath
Pontnêddféchan
Cilmaengwyn
A474
Hir Fynydd
A465
Rhydyfro
B4242
Blaengwrach
Rhigos
Hirwaun
Penywaun
Llwydcoed
Pontardawe
Craig Llangiwg
Cilybebyll
Gellinudd
Crynant
Mynydd March Hywel
Cwm Clydach RSPB
Alltwen
Rhos
Vale of Neath
River Neath
383 RESOLVEN MOUNTAIN
600 CRAIG-Y-LLYN
Cwmdare
Trecynon
Aberdare
(Aberdâr)
Faerdre
B4603
River Dulais
Resolven
Melin Cwrt
A4061
Mynydd Ystradffernol
Aberaman
Glais
A4067
Cilfrew
B4434
Clyne
493 MOEL-YR HYRDDAD
Blaenrhondda
Cwmaman
Bryn-côch
B4291
Cadoxton Juxta-Neath
Tin Works & Waterfall
Aberdulais
Blaen-y-cwm
A4233
Abercwmboi
Birchgrove
Tonna
Cefn Mawr
Glyncorrwg
Treherbert
Maerdy
Llansamlet
Neath
(Castell-nedd)
Cefn Morfydd
Afan Forest Park
36
Blaengwynfi
478
Treorchy
Ferndale
Winsh-wen
Abercregan
Cymer
A4107
Abergwynfi
Cwmparc
Pentre
Ystrad
Tonmawr
Cimla
B4287
Cynonville
Duffryn
Croeserw
Rhondda Valley
Pentre-chwyth
Crymlyn Bog
Efail-fach
Pont-rhyd-y-fen
Afan Forest Park
Caerau
556 MYNYDD CAERAU
571 WERFA
B4223
Briton Ferry
FOEL MYNYDDAU
371 MOEL TRAWSNANT
Nant-y-moel
Clydach Vale
Llwynypia
Trealaw
Mynydd Llangeinwyr
Blaengarw
B4282
Bryn
Cwmafan
Pontycymer
Cricklebit
Tonypandy
0 1 2 3 4 miles
0 1 2 3 4 5 kilometres

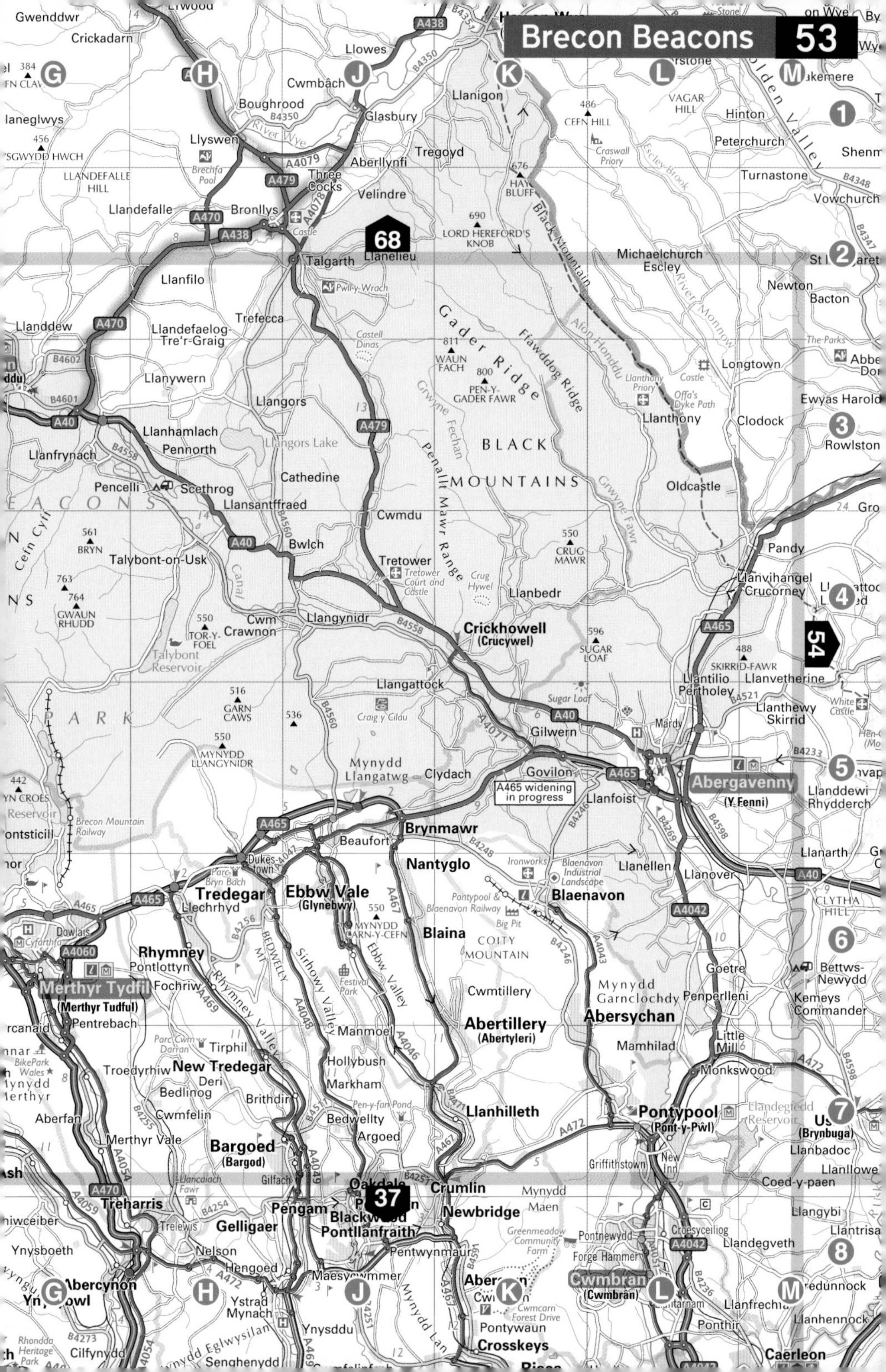
Gwenddwr
Crickadarn
Llowes
Cwmbâch
Boughrood
Glasbury
Llanigon
VAGAR HILL
Hinton
CEFN HILL
Peterchurch
Craswall Priory
Escley Brook
Golden Valley
Llyswen
Brechfa Pool
Aberllynfi
Tregoyd
Three Cocks
Velindre
HAY BLUFF
Turnastone
Vowchurch
LLANDEFALLE HILL
Llandefalle
Bronllys
Castle
LORD HEREFORD'S KNOB
Black Mountain
Talgarth
Llanelieu
Michaelchurch Escley
River Monnow
Newton
Bacton
Llanfilo
Pwll-y-Wrach
Gader Ridge
Ffawddog Ridge
Afon Honddu
Llanddew
Llandefaelog-Tre'r-Graig
Trefecca
Castell Dinas
WAUN FACH
PEN-Y-GADER FAWR
Llanthony Priory
Offa's Dyke Path
Longtown
The Parks
Llanywern
Llangors
Grwyne Fechan
Llanthony
Clodock
Ewyas Harold
Rowlston
Llanhamlach
Pennorth
Llangors Lake
Penallt Mawr Range
BLACK MOUNTAINS
Llanfrynach
Cathedine
Oldcastle
Pencelli
Scethrog
Grwyne Fawr
Llansantffraed
Cwmdu
Cefn Cyff
BRYN
Bwlch
CRUG MAWR
Pandy
Talybont-on-Usk
Canal
Tretower
Tretower Court and Castle
Crug Hywel
Llanvihangel Crucorney
GWAUN RHUDD
Llanbedr
TOR-Y-FOEL
Cwm Crawnon
Llangynidr
Crickhowell (Crucywel)
SUGAR LOAF
Talybont Reservoir
SKIRRID-FAWR
Llantilio Pertholey
Llanvetherine
Llangattock
Sugar Loaf
GARN CAWS
Craig y Cilau
Gilwern
Llanthewy Skirrid
White Castle
PARK
MYNYDD LLANGYNIDR
Mardy
Mynydd Llangatwg
Clydach
Govilon
A465 widening in progress
Abergavenny (Y Fenni)
Llanfoist
Llanddewi Rhydderch
Brecon Mountain Railway
Brynmawr
Beaufort
Nantyglo
Ironworks
Blaenavon Industrial Landscape
Llanellen
Llanover
Llanarth
Dukestown
Parc Bryn Bach
Tredegar
Ebbw Vale (Glynebwy)
Pontypool & Blaenavon Railway
Blaenavon
Llechrhyd
MYNYDD CARN-Y-CEFN
Big Pit
CLYTHA HILL
Dowlais
Cyfarthfa
Blaina
COITY MOUNTAIN
Rhymney
Pontlottyn
Festival Park
Sirhowy Valley
Ebbw Valley
Rhymney Valley
Mynydd Garnclochdy
Goetre
Penperlleni
Bettws-Newydd
Kemeys Commander
Merthyr Tydfil (Merthyr Tudful)
Fochriw
Cwmtillery
Pentrebach
Abertillery (Abertyleri)
Abersychan
Manmoel
Parc Cwm Darran
Tirphil
Mamhilad
Little Mill
BikePark Wales
Troedyrhiw
New Tredegar
Hollybush
Monkswood
Deri
Bedlinog
Markham
Brithdir
Pen-y-fan Pond
Llanhilleth
Pontypool (Pont-y-Pŵl)
Llandegfedd Reservoir
Usk (Brynbuga)
Aberfan
Cwmfelin
Bedwellty
Merthyr Vale
Argoed
Bargoed (Bargod)
Llanbadoc
Griffithstown
New Inn
Llanllowell
Llancaiach Fawr
Gilfach
Oakdale
Crumlin
Mynydd Maen
Coed-y-paen
Treharris
Pengam
Blackwood
Newbridge
Gelligaer
Pontllanfraith
Greenmeadow Community Farm
Pontnewydd
Croesyceiliog
Llangybi
Llantrisant
Trelewis
Nelson
Pentwynmawr
Forge Hammer
Llandegveth
Ynysboeth
Hengoed
Maesycwmmer
Cwmbran (Cwmbrân)
Abercynon
Ystrad Mynach
Cwmcarn Forest Drive
Llanfrechfa
Llanhennock
Rhondda Heritage Park
Ynysddu
Pontywaun
Ponthir
Cilfynydd
Senghenydd
Crosskeys
Caerleon
68
54
37

54
Golden Valley
Peterchurch
Turnastone
Vowchurch
Kingstone
St Margarets
Newton
Bacton
Longtown
Abbey Dore
Ewyas Harold
Pontrilas
Rowlstone
Kentchurch
Grosmont
Pandy
Llanvihangel Crucorney
Llangattock Lingoed
Craig Serrethin
Cross Ash
Skirrid-Fawr
Llanvetherine
White Castle
Tal-y-coed
Hen-Gwrt (Moat)
Llantilio-Crossenny
Llanvapley
Abergavenny
(Y Fenni)
Llanddewi Rhydderch
Penrhos
Llanarth
Great Oak
Tregare
Dingestow
Bryngwyn
Raglan Castle
Clytha Hill
Raglan
Bettws-Newydd
Kemeys Commander
Llandenny
Kingcoed
Usk
(Brynbuga)
Usk Rural Life
Llanbadoc
Llanllowell
Coed-y-paen
Llangybi
Llantrisant
Llangwm
Springdale Farm
Gwernesney
Pentre
Wolvesnewton
Llansoy
Llanishen
Kilgwrrwg Common
Newchurch
Gaerllwyd
Itton Common
St Arvans
Itton
Mynydd-bach
Shirenewton
Mounton
Pwllmeyric
Newton Green
Llanvaches
Llanmelin
Runston Chapel
Caerleon
Llanhennock
Llanfrechfa
Little Mill
Devauden
Chapel Hill
Tintern Parva
Tintern Abbey
Trellech
Harold's Stones
Newmills
Pen-y-clawdd
Cwmcarvan
Mitchel Troy
Monmouth
(Trefynwy)
The Kymin
Monmouthshire
Penallt
Redbrook
Pen-twyn
Whitebrook
Llandogo
Brockweir
St Briavels
St Briavels Castle
Offa's Dyke Path
Hewelsfield
Woolaston Common
Aylburton
Alvington
Netherend
Woolaston
Stroat
Tidenham
National Diving Centre
Woodcroft
Lancaut
Tutshill
Sedbury
Chepstow
(Cas-gwent)
Bulwarks Camp
River Severn
Oldbury-on-Severn
Rockhampton
Lower Morton
Cowhill
Lydney
Allaston
Bream
Dean Forest Railway
Yorkley
Parkend
Ellwood
Clearwell
Clearwell Caves
Newland
Highbury Wood
Perrygrove Railway
Puzzlewood
Whitecliffe
Coleford
Milkwall
Broadwell
Upper Soudley
Beechenhurst Lodge
Forest of Dean
Cinderford
Ruspidge
Upper Lydbrook
Brierley
English Bicknor
Symonds Yat (West)
Symonds Yat
Doward
Staunton
Ruardean Woodside
Ruardean Hill
Ruardean
Drybrook
Mitcheldean
Hope Mansell
East Dean
Walford
Goodrich
Goodrich Castle
Old Forge
Wye Valley
Marstow
Whitchurch
Welsh Newton
Llangrove
Pencraig
Llangarron
Llancloudy
Glewstone
Wilton
Ross-on-Wye
Weston under Penyard
Peterstow
St Owens Cross
Tretire
St Weonards
Michaelchurch
Bridstow
Upper Grove Common
Sellack
Baysham
Strangford
Brampton Abbotts
Harewood End
Hoarwithy
King's Caple
Foy
How Caple
Pen-allt
Carey
Brockhampton
Stocking
Much Birch
Little Birch
Ballingham
Sollers Hope
Westons Cider
Little Dewchurch
Kingsthorne
Kivernoll
Callow
Aconbury
Fownhope
Holme Lacy
Woolhope
Rushall
Mordiford
Dinedor
Dinedor Hill
Rotherwas Chapel
Lower Bullingham
Hampton Bishop
Hereford
Blackmarstone
Belmont
Clehonger
Ruckhall
Breinton
Madley
Cublington
Shenmore
Tyberton
Coldwell
Allensmore
Hungerstone
Thruxton
Wormbridge
Kilpeck
Much Dewchurch
Wormelow Tump
Bagwy Llydiart
Orcop Hill
Orcop
Garway
Skenfrith Castle
Skenfrith
Broad Oak
Newcastle
St Maughans Green
Rockfield
Buckholt
Dixton
Bridge Sollers
Cannon Bridge
Sugwas Pool
Kenchester
The Weir
Stretton Sugwas
Holmer
Lyde
Shelwick
Lugwardine
Bartestree
Hagley
Dormington
Weston Beggard
Perton
Stoke Edith
Shucknall
Yarkhill
Ashperton
Tarrington
Canon Frome
Putley Green
Putley
Aylton
Kempley
Crow Hill
Linton
Linton Hill
69
53
38
A40
A49
A465
A466
A4137
A449
A48
A4136
A438
A4103
B4348
B4352
B4349
B4347
B4399
B4224
B4521
B4233
B4234
B4228
B4293
B4235
B4598
B4231
B4226
B4028
B4061
A472
0 1 2 3 4 miles
0 1 2 3 4 5 kilometres

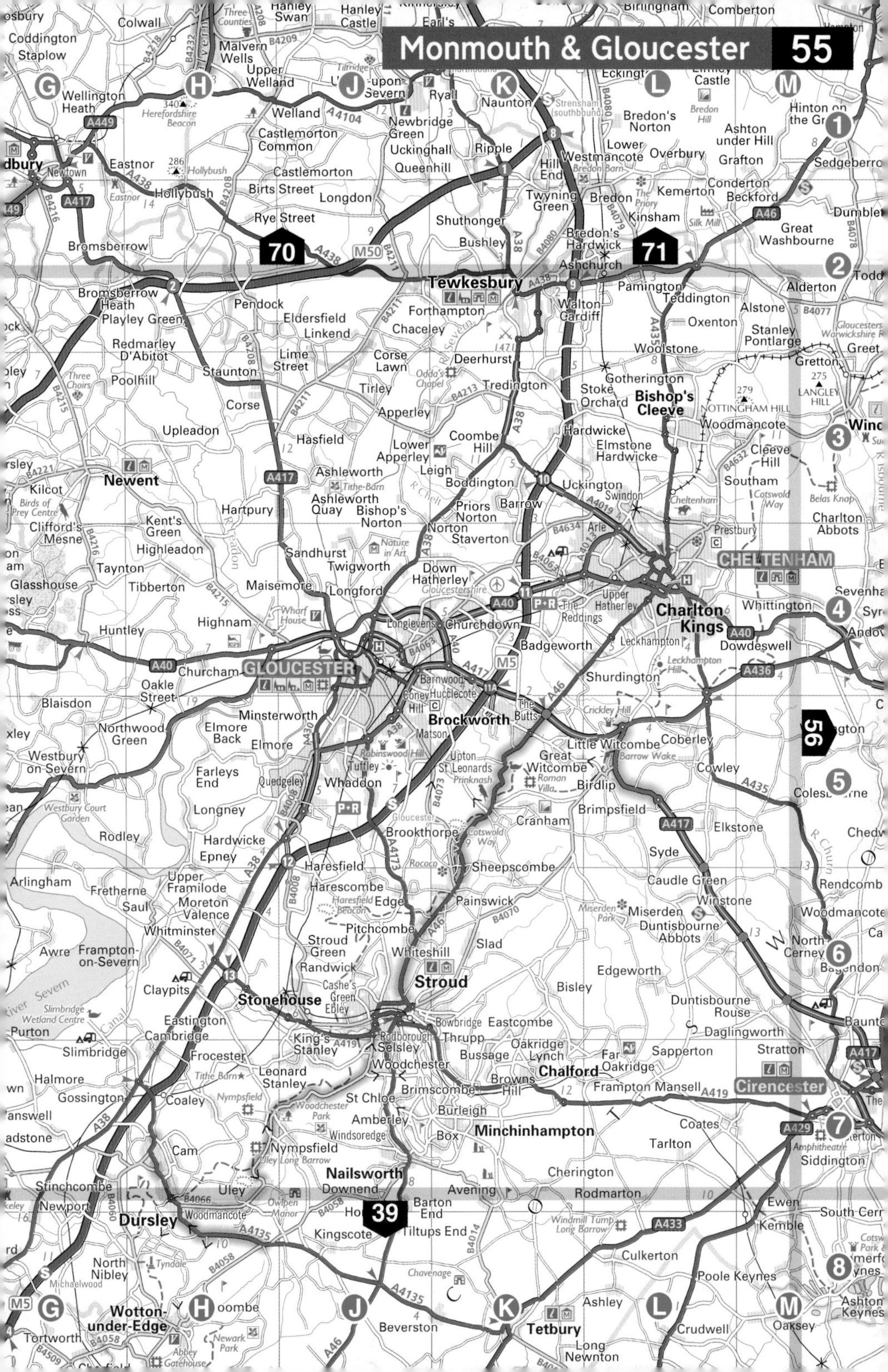
Colwall
Coddington
Staplow
Malvern Wells
Upper Welland
Hanley Swan
Hanley Castle
Wellington Heath
Herefordshire Beacon
Welland
Newbridge Green
Ryall
Naunton
Castlemorton Common
Uckinghall
Ripple
Eastnor
Hollybush
Castlemorton
Queenhill
Newtown
Birts Street
Longdon
Rye Street
Bromsberrow
Shuthonger
Bushley
Tewkesbury
Bromsberrow Heath
Playley Green
Pendock
Eldersfield
Linkend
Forthampton
Chaceley
Redmarley D'Abitot
Staunton
Lime Street
Corse Lawn
Deerhurst
Poolhill
Corse
Tirley
Odda's Chapel
Tredington
Upleadon
Apperley
Hasfield
Lower Apperley
Coombe Hill
Leigh
Ashleworth
Tithe Barn
Boddington
Newent
Kilcot
Birds of Prey Centre
Clifford's Mesne
Hartpury
Kent's Green
Highleadon
Ashleworth Quay
Bishop's Norton
Norton
Priors Norton
Barrow
Staverton
Taynton
Glasshouse
Tibberton
Sandhurst
Twigworth
Nature in Art
Down Hatherley
Maisemore
Longford
Gloucestershire
Highnam
Wharf House
Longlevens
Churchdown
Huntley
Churcham
GLOUCESTER
Oakle Street
Blaisdon
Barnwood
Hucclecote
Coney Hill
Brockworth
Matson
Minsterworth
Northwood Green
Elmore Back
Elmore
Westbury on Severn
Robinswood Hill
Tuffley
Upton St Leonards
Prinknash
Farleys End
Quedgeley
Whaddon
Westbury Court Garden
Longney
Rodley
Gloucester
Brookthorpe
Hardwicke
Epney
Arlingham
Haresfield
Upper Framilode
Fretherne
Saul
Moreton Valence
Harescombe
Haresfield Beacon
Edge
Rococo
Whitminster
Pitchcombe
Stroud Green
Randwick
Whiteshill
Stroud
Awre
Frampton-on-Severn
Claypits
Stonehouse
Cashe's Green
Ebley
Slimbridge Wetland Centre
River Severn
Eastington
Cambridge
Slimbridge
King's Stanley
Selsley
Rodborough
Frocester
Tithe Barn
Leonard Stanley
Woodchester
Halmore
Gossington
Coaley
Nympsfield
Woodchester Park
St Chloe
Amberley
Windsoredge
Cam
Nympsfield
Uley Long Barrow
Stinchcombe
Uley
Newport
Dursley
Woodmancote
Owlpen Manor
North Nibley
Tyndale
Michaelwood
Wotton-under-Edge
Tortworth
Newark Park
Abbey Gatehouse
Kingscote
Nailsworth
Downend
Horsley
Barton End
Tiltups End
Chavenage
Beverston
Tetbury
Strensham (southbound)
Eckington
Bredon's Norton
Bredon Hill
Elmley Castle
Hinton on the Green
Ashton under Hill
Grafton
Sedgeberrow
Lower Westmancote
Overbury
Hill End
Bredon Barn
Twyning Green
Bredon
The Priory
Kemerton
Conderton
Beckford
Kinsham
Silk Mill
Bredon's Hardwick
Great Washbourne
Dumbleton
Ashchurch
Pamington
Alderton
Teddington
Walton Cardiff
Oxenton
Alstone
Stanley Pontlarge
Gloucestershire Warwickshire Railway
Woolstone
Gretton
Gotherington
Stoke Orchard
Bishop's Cleeve
Nottingham Hill
Langley Hill
Woodmancote
Hardwicke
Elmstone Hardwicke
Cleeve Hill
Southam
Cotswold Way
Belas Knap
Uckington
Swindon
Cheltenham
Charlton Abbots
Arle
Prestbury
CHELTENHAM
Upper Hatherley
The Reddings
Charlton Kings
Whittington
Sevenhampton
Badgeworth
Leckhampton
Leckhampton Hill
Dowdeswell
Andoversford
Shurdington
The Butts
Crickley Hill
Little Witcombe
Coberley
Great Witcombe
Roman Villa
Barrow Wake
Birdlip
Cowley
Colesbourne
Cranham
Brimpsfield
Elkstone
Sheepscombe
Syde
Caudle Green
Rendcomb
Painswick
Winstone
Miserden Park
Miserden
Duntisbourne Abbots
Woodmancote
North Cerney
Bagendon
Slad
Bisley
Edgeworth
Duntisbourne Rouse
Daglingworth
Bowbridge
Eastcombe
Thrupp
Bussage
Oakridge Lynch
Chalford
Far Oakridge
Sapperton
Stratton
Cirencester
Brimscombe
Browns Hill
Frampton Mansell
Burleigh
Box
Minchinhampton
Coates
Tarlton
Amphitheatre
Siddington
Cherington
Avening
Rodmarton
Ewen
Kemble
South Cerney
Windmill Tump Long Barrow
Culkerton
Poole Keynes
Ashley
Crudwell
Long Newton
Oaksey
Ashton Keynes
M50
M5
A40
A38
A46
A417
A419
A429
A433
A435
A436
A438
A449
A4104
A4019
A4013
A4135
A4173
A430
A4063
B4008
B4058
B4060
B4066
B4070
B4071
B4073
B4077
B4078
B4079
B4080
B4208
B4209
B4211
B4213
B4215
B4216
B4218
B4221
B4232
B4632
B4634
B4014
B4509
70
71
56
39

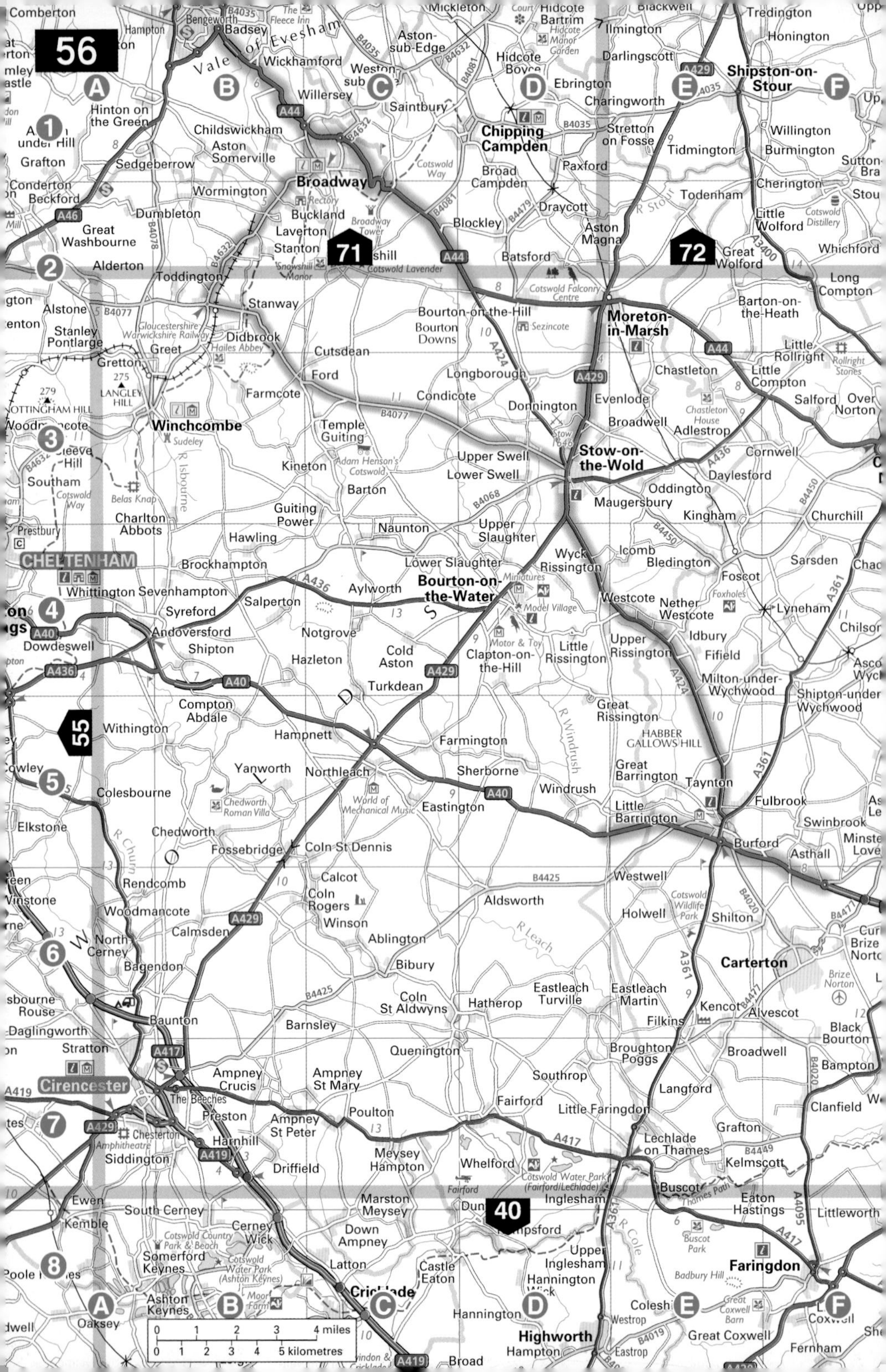

A B C D E F
1 2 3 4 5 6 7 8
71
72
55
40
Comberton
Hampton
Bengeworth
Badsey
Vale of Evesham
The Fleece Inn
Mickleton
Hidcote Bartrim
Hidcote Manor Garden
Blackwell
Tredington
Ilmington
Honington
Aston-sub-Edge
Weston-sub-Edge
Wickhamford
Hidcote Boyce
Darlingscott
Shipston-on-Stour
Ebrington
Willersey
Saintbury
Charingworth
Hinton on the Green
Childswickham
Chipping Campden
Stretton on Fosse
Willington
Aston under Hill
Aston Somerville
Tidmington
Burmington
Sutton-under-Brailes
Grafton
Sedgeberrow
Cotswold Way
Paxford
Broad Campden
Conderton
Beckford
Wormington
Broadway
Cherington
Todenham
Rectory
R Stour
Dumbleton
Buckland
Draycott
Little Wolford
Cotswold Distillery
Great Washbourne
Laverton
Broadway Tower
Blockley
Aston Magna
Stanton
Snowshill
Snowshill Manor
Cotswold Lavender
Batsford
Great Wolford
Whichford
Alderton
Toddington
Cotswold Falconry Centre
Long Compton
Alstone
Stanway
Bourton-on-the-Hill
Barton-on-the-Heath
Gloucestershire Warwickshire Railway
Bourton Downs
Sezincote
Moreton-in-Marsh
Stanley Pontlarge
Didbrook
Hailes Abbey
Greet
Cutsdean
Gretton
Ford
Longborough
Chastleton
Little Rollright
Rollright Stones
Little Compton
Langley Hill
Nottingham Hill
Farmcote
Condicote
Evenlode
Donnington
Chastleton House
Salford
Over Norton
Woodmancote
Winchcombe
Sudeley
Temple Guiting
Broadwell
Adlestrop
Cleeve Hill
Kineton
Adam Henson's Cotswold
Upper Swell
Lower Swell
Stow-on-the-Wold
Cornwell
Southam
Belas Knap
R Isbourne
Barton
Daylesford
Oddington
Maugersbury
Guiting Power
Prestbury
Charlton Abbots
Naunton
Upper Slaughter
Kingham
Churchill
Hawling
Icomb
Bledington
Wyck Rissington
Sarsden
Cheltenham
Brockhampton
Lower Slaughter
Foscot
Whittington
Sevenhampton
Salperton
Aylworth
Bourton-on-the-Water
Miniatures
Foxholes
Syreford
Model Village
Westcote
Nether Westcote
Lyneham
Dowdeswell
Andoversford
Notgrove
Motor & Toy
Idbury
Shipton
Hazleton
Cold Aston
Clapton-on-the-Hill
Little Rissington
Upper Rissington
Fifield
Turkdean
Milton-under-Wychwood
Shipton-under-Wychwood
Compton Abdale
Great Rissington
Withington
Hampnett
Farmington
HABBER GALLOWS HILL
R Windrush
Cowley
Yanworth
Northleach
Sherborne
Great Barrington
Taynton
Colesbourne
Chedworth Roman Villa
World of Mechanical Music
Eastington
Windrush
Fulbrook
Little Barrington
Swinbrook
Elkstone
Chedworth
Fossebridge
Coln St Dennis
Burford
Asthall
Calcot
Westwell
Rendcomb
Coln Rogers
Aldsworth
Winstone
Woodmancote
Winson
Cotswold Wildlife Park
Holwell
Shilton
Calmsden
North Cerney
Ablington
R Leach
Carterton
Bagendon
Bibury
Eastleach Turville
Eastleach Martin
Coln St Aldwyns
Hatherop
Kencot
Alvescot
Brize Norton
Baunton
Barnsley
Filkins
Black Bourton
Daglingworth
Stratton
Quenington
Broughton Poggs
Broadwell
Bampton
Cirencester
Ampney Crucis
Ampney St Mary
Southrop
Langford
The Beeches
Preston
Poulton
Fairford
Little Faringdon
Clanfield
Ampney St Peter
Chesterton
Amphitheatre
Harnhill
Grafton
Lechlade on Thames
Siddington
Meysey Hampton
Whelford
Cotswold Water Park (Fairford/Lechlade)
Kelmscott
Driffield
Buscot
Thames Path
Ewen
Marston Meysey
Inglesham
Eaton Hastings
Littleworth
Kemble
South Cerney
Cerney Wick
Kempsford
Cotswold Country Park & Beach
Down Ampney
Buscot Park
R Cole
Somerford Keynes
Cotswold Water Park (Ashton Keynes)
Upper Inglesham
Latton
Castle Eaton
Hannington Wick
Faringdon
Badbury Hill
Ashton Keynes
Cricklade
Great Coxwell Barn
Oaksey
Hannington
Coleshill
Westrop
Coxwell
Highworth
Great Coxwell
Hampton
Eastrop
Broad
Fernham
0 1 2 3 4 miles
0 1 2 3 4 5 kilometres

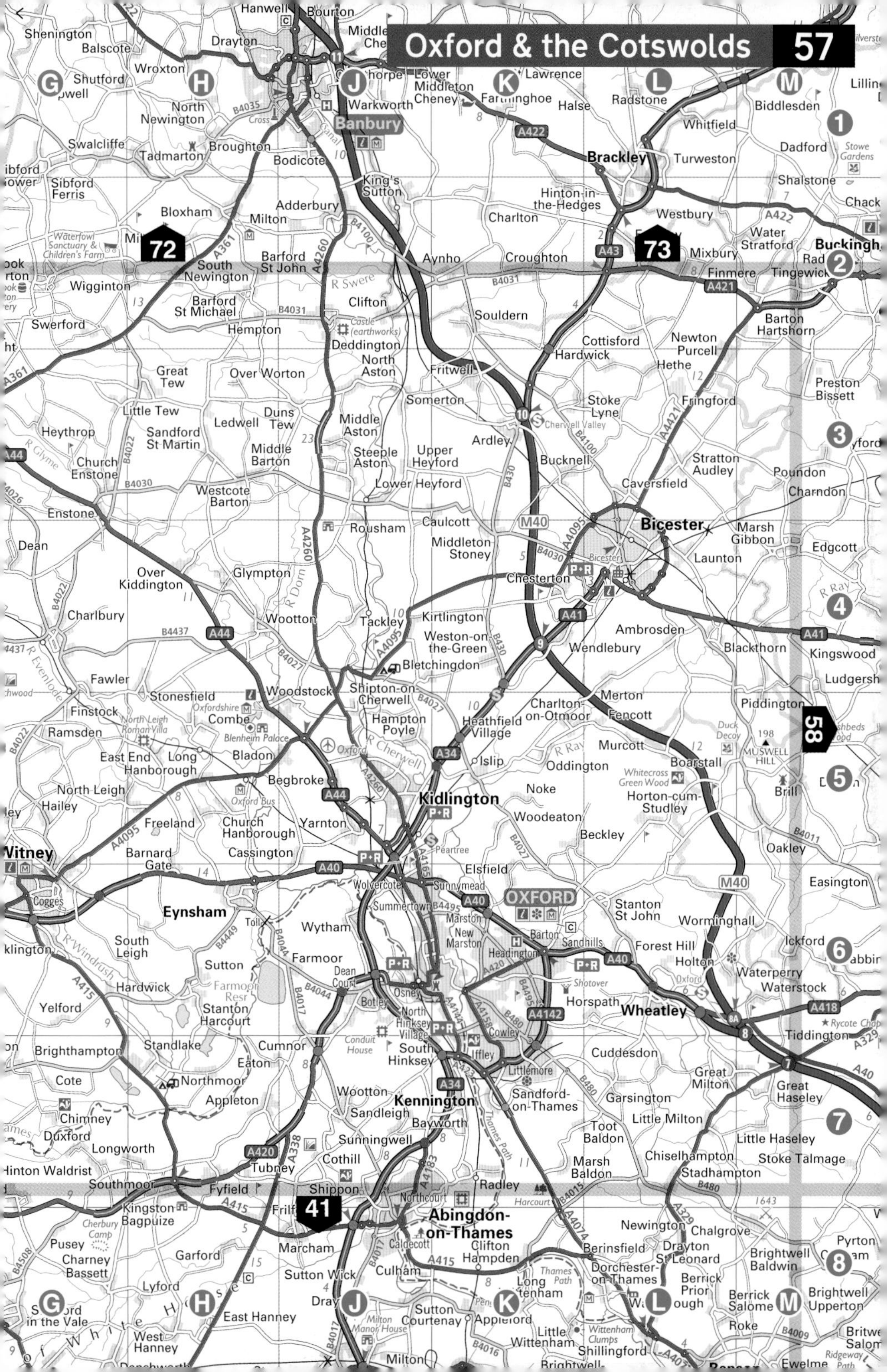
Hanwell
Bourton
Shenington
Balscote
Drayton
Middleton Cheney
Wroxton
Shutford
North Newington
Warkworth
Banbury
Lower Middleton Cheney
Lawrence
Farthinghoe
Halse
Radstone
Biddlesden
Whitfield
Dadford
Stowe Gardens
Swalcliffe
Tadmarton
Broughton
Bodicote
Brackley
Turweston
Shalstone
Sibford Ferris
Bloxham
Adderbury
Milton
King's Sutton
Hinton-in-the-Hedges
Charlton
Westbury
Water Stratford
Buckingham
Waterfowl Sanctuary & Children's Farm
South Newington
Barford St John
Aynho
Croughton
Mixbury
Finmere
Tingewick
Wigginton
Barford St Michael
R Swere
Clifton
Souldern
Swerford
Hempton
Castle (earthworks)
Deddington
North Aston
Cottisford
Hardwick
Newton Purcell
Hethe
Barton Hartshorn
Great Tew
Over Worton
Fritwell
Somerton
Stoke Lyne
Fringford
Preston Bissett
Little Tew
Duns Tew
Ledwell
Middle Aston
Cherwell Valley
Heythrop
Sandford St Martin
Middle Barton
Steeple Aston
Upper Heyford
Ardley
Bucknell
Stratton Audley
Church Enstone
Westcote Barton
Lower Heyford
Caversfield
Poundon
Charndon
Enstone
Rousham
Caulcott
Middleton Stoney
Bicester
Marsh Gibbon
Edgcott
Dean
Launton
Over Kiddington
Glympton
Chesterton
Charlbury
Wootton
Tackley
Kirtlington
Weston-on-the-Green
Ambrosden
Blackthorn
Kingswood
Fawler
Bletchingdon
Wendlebury
Ludgershall
Stonesfield
Woodstock
Shipton-on-Cherwell
Merton
Piddington
Finstock
Oxfordshire Museum
Combe
North Leigh Roman Villa
Hampton Poyle
Charlton-on-Otmoor
Fencott
Ramsden
Blenheim Palace
Heathfield Village
Duck Decoy
Muswell Hill
East End
Long Hanborough
Bladon
Oxford
R Cherwell
Islip
Murcott
Oddington
Boarstall
Brill
North Leigh
Hailey
Begbroke
Kidlington
Noke
Whitecross Green Wood
Horton-cum-Studley
Oxford Bus
Freeland
Church Hanborough
Yarnton
Woodeaton
Beckley
Witney
Barnard Gate
Cassington
Peartree
Elsfield
Oakley
Wolvercote
Sunnymead
OXFORD
Easington
Cogges
Eynsham
Summertown
Marston
Stanton St John
Worminghall
Toll
Wytham
New Marston
Barton
Sandhills
Forest Hill
Ickford
South Leigh
Headington
Holton
Sutton
Farmoor
Dean Court
Shotover
Oxford
Waterperry
Hardwick
Farmoor Resr
Osney
Horspath
Waterstock
Botley
Wheatley
Yelford
Stanton Harcourt
North Hinksey Village
Cowley
Rycote Chapel
Tiddington
Standlake
Cumnor
Conduit House
South Hinksey
Iffley
Brighthampton
Eaton
Littlemore
Cuddesdon
Great Milton
Great Haseley
Cote
Northmoor
Sandford-on-Thames
Appleton
Wootton
Kennington
Garsington
Chimney
Sandleigh
Bayworth
Little Milton
Duxford
Thames Path
Toot Baldon
Longworth
Sunningwell
Little Haseley
Cothill
Chiselhampton
Stoke Talmage
Hinton Waldrist
Tubney
Marsh Baldon
Stadhampton
Southmoor
Fyfield
Shippon
Radley
Kingston Bagpuize
Frilford
Northcourt
Abingdon-on-Thames
Harcourt
Cherbury Camp
Newington
Chalgrove
Pusey
Charney Bassett
Marcham
Caldecott
Clifton Hampden
Berinsfield
Drayton St Leonard
Brightwell Baldwin
Pyrton
Garford
Sutton Wick
Culham
Dorchester-on-Thames
Long Wittenham
Berrick Prior
Berrick Salome
Brightwell Upperton
Lyford
Drayton
Sutton Courtenay
Appleford
Warborough
Stanford in the Vale
East Hanney
Milton Manor House
Little Wittenham
Wittenham Clumps
Roke
West Hanney
Shillingford
Britwell Salome
Milton
Ewelme
Ridgeway Path
Vale of White Horse

Whittlebury
Haversham
Newport Pagnell
Wharley End
Potterspury
Silverstone
Cosgrove
Great Linford
Puxley
New Bradwell
A509
Willen
Cranfield
Moulsoe
Lillingstone Lovell
Lillingston Dayrell
Old Stratford
Stony Stratford
Wolverton
Bradwell
P+R
Broughton
Biddlesden
Deanshanger
Passenham
Salford
Wicken
MILTON KEYNES
Gulliver's Land
Woolstone
A4146
Dadford
Stowe Gardens
Calverton
Xscape
Woughton on the Green
Lower End
A421
Shalstone
Akeley
Leckhampstead
Loughton
Wavendon
Aspley Guise
Chackmore
Maids Moreton
Beachampton
Shenley Church End
Walton
Simpson
Woburn Sands
A422
Water Stratford
Buckingham
Thornton
Shenley Brook End
Aspley Heath
Radclive
73
Nash
Whaddon
74
Bow Brickhill
Tingewick
Fenny Stratford
Bletchley
Woburn
A5
Thornborough
A421
B4034
Bletchley
Little Brickhill
Barton Hartshorn
Gawcott
Great Horwood
Newton Longville
Great Brickhill
Padbury
Little Horwood
A4146
Adstock
B4033
Stockgrove
King's Wood
Preston Bissett
Hillesden
Drayton Parslow
Stoke Hammond
A413
Addington
Mursley
Heath and Reach
Winslow
Steeple Claydon
Hollingdon
Twyford
Middle Claydon
Swanbourne
Soulbury
B4032
Hockliffe
Clipstone
Poundon
Claydon House
East Claydon
Stewkley
A4012
Charndon
Hoggeston
Linslade
Granborough
Dunton
Leighton Buzzard
Marsh Gibbon
Botolph Claydon
Burcott
Stanbridge
Edgcott
North Marston
Cublington
Wing
Ascott
Billington
Finemere Wood
Little Billington
Eaton Green
186
QUAINTON HILL
Oving
Ledburn
R Ray
Grendon Underwood
Whitchurch
Slapton
Pitchcott
Aston Abbotts
Mentmore
Northall
A41
Quainton
Blackthorn
Kingswood
Buckinghamshire Railway Centre
Hardwick
Horton
Woodham
A418
Wingrave
Ludgershall
Weedon
Rowsham
Grand Union Canal
Westcott
Waddesdon
Cheddington
B488
Piddington
Hulcott
Wotton Underwood
Waddesdon Manor
Bierton
Ivinghoe
Duck Decoy
57
Rushbeds Wood
Long Marston
Berryfields
Watermead
Windmill
Pitstone
Muswell Hill
Upper Winchendon
Wilstone
Marsworth
Aylesbury
Brill
Dorton
Ashendon
R Thame
Buckland
Nether Winchendon
Lower Hartwell
Stone
Southcourt
Aston Clinton
Drayton Beauchamp
Tring
B4011
Chilton
Cuddington
Upton
Oakley
Dinton
Sedrup
Weston Turville
B4635
Stoke Mandeville
Chearsley
Westlington
Bucks Goat Centre
Halton
Wigginton
M40
Easington
A418
Long Crendon Courthouse
Haddenham
Bishopstone
A413
Dancersend
Long Crendon
Ford
Wendover Woods
Hastoe
Tiggywinkles Wildlife Hospital
North Lee
B4009
Ridgeway Path
Wendover
Ickford
Little Kimble
Berkhamsted
Shabbington
Thame
A4129
St Leonards
Cholesbury
Waterperry
Owlswick
Meadle
Ellesborough
Buckland Common
Waterstock
Kingsey
Great Kimble
Ilmer
Askett
Pulpit Hill
Lee Clump
Bellingdon
A418
Longwick
Monks Risborough
Dunsmore
Rycote Chapel
Towersey
The Lee
Asheridge
Tiddington
A329
Moreton
Whiteleaf
Cross (hill carving)
Chartridge
Pitch Green
B4012
Princes Risborough
Great Hampden
Ballinger Common
Emmington
Henton
A413
Great Haseley
A40
Tetsworth
Sydenham
B4445
B4009
Bledlow
Saunderton
Loosley Row
Prestwood
South Heath
Chinnor & Princes Risborough Railway
Lacey Green
Great Missenden
Hyde Heath
Little Haseley
Postcombe
Chinnor
209
LODGE HILL
Roald Dahl
B485
Crowell
Stoke Talmage
Kingston Blount
Speen
A4010
Aston Rowant
Little Kingshill
Little Missenden
Amersham
Walter's Ash
Radnage
Great Kingshill
Amersham Old Town
South Weston
42
Hughenden Valley
Lewknor
Bledlow Ridge
Bradenham
Cryers Hill
Holmer Green
Pyrton
Naphill
The City
A4128
Penn Street
Cuxham
Hughenden Manor
Widmer End
Hazlemere
Brightwell Baldwin
Shirburn
B4009
Stokenchurch
Beacon's Bottom
Hell-Fire Caves
Downley
A404
Winchmore Hill
Berrick Salome
Watlington
Brightwell Upperton
A40
Coleshill
Wycombe Park
HIGH WYCOMBE
Roke
B4009
M40
Cadmore End
Cressex
B474
A355
Bekonscot Model Village
Ewelme
Ridgeway Path
Wycombe
0 1 2 3 4 miles
0 1 2 3 4 5 kilometres

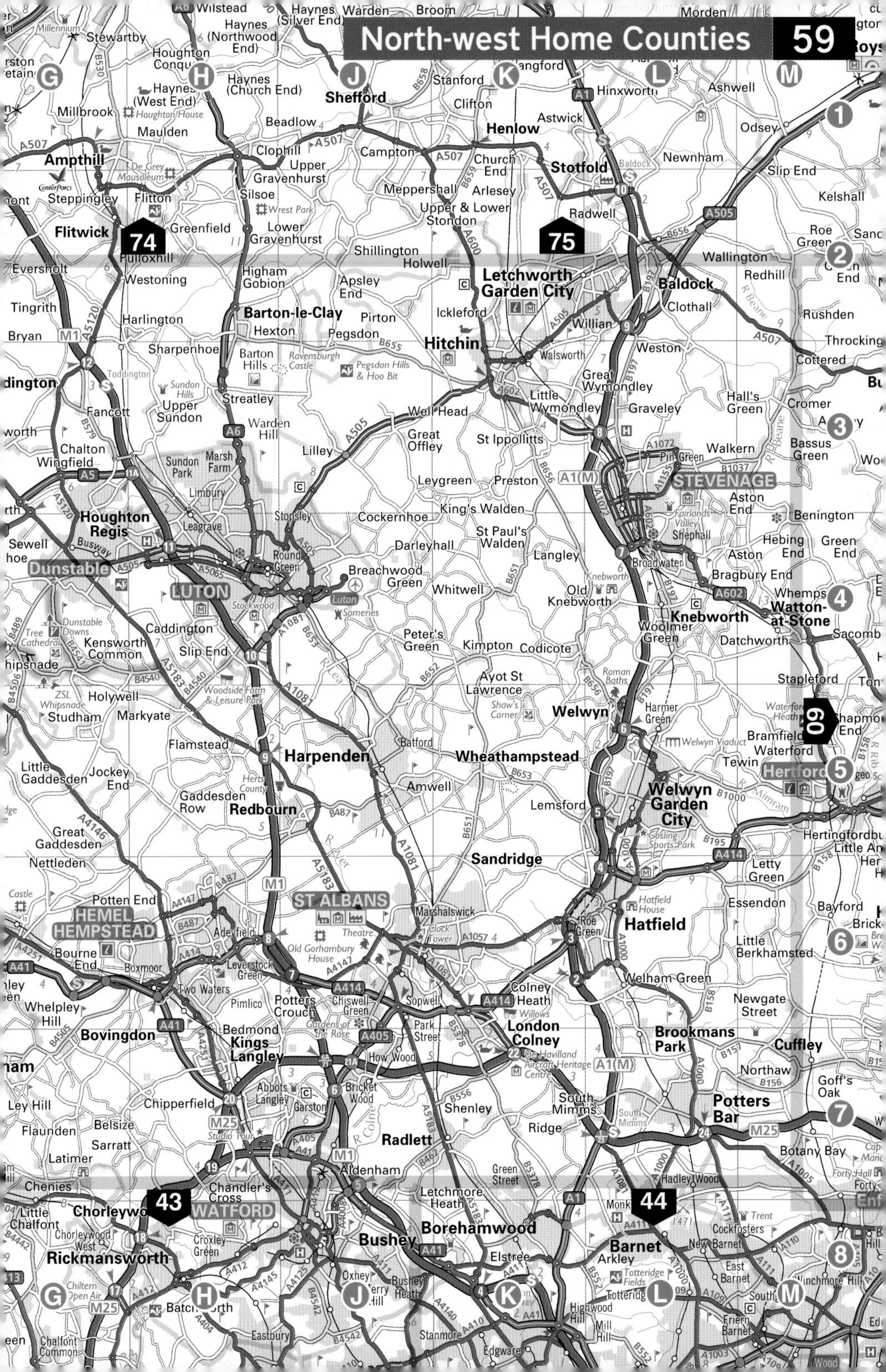
Wilstead
Haynes (Silver End)
Warden
Broom
Morden
Haynes (Northwood End)
Houghton Conquest
Stewartby
Millennium
Haynes (Church End)
Haynes (West End)
Houghton House
Shefford
Stanford
Langford
Hinxworth
Ashwell
Millbrook
Maulden
Beadlow
Clifton
Henlow
Astwick
Odsey
Ampthill
Clophill
Campton
Church End
Stotfold
Newnham
De Grey Mausoleum
Upper Gravenhurst
Meppershall
Arlesey
Baldock
Slip End
Kelshall
CenterParcs
Steppingley
Flitton
Silsoe
Wrest Park
Upper & Lower Stondon
Radwell
Flitwick
Greenfield
Lower Gravenhurst
Roe Green
Pulloxhill
Shillington
Holwell
Wallington
Redhill
Eversholt
Westoning
Higham Gobion
Apsley End
Letchworth Garden City
Baldock
Clothall
Tingrith
Harlington
Barton-le-Clay
Pirton
Ickleford
Willian
Rushden
Bryan
Hexton
Pegsdon
Hitchin
Weston
Throcking
Sharpenhoe
Barton Hills
Ravensburgh Castle
Pegsdon Hills & Hoo Bit
Walsworth
Cottered
Toddington
Sundon Hills
Great Wymondley
dington
Upper Sundon
Streatley
Little Wymondley
Hall's Green
Cromer
Fancott
Warden Hill
Well Head
Graveley
Great Offley
St Ippollitts
Walkern
Bassus Green
Chalton
Lilley
Wingfield
Sundon Park
Marsh Farm
Limbury
Leygreen
Preston
STEVENAGE
Aston End
Houghton Regis
Leagrave
Stopsley
Cockernhoe
King's Walden
Fairlands Valley
Benington
Shephall
Sewell
Busway
Round Green
Darleyhall
St Paul's Walden
Langley
Hebing End
Green End
Aston
Broadwater
Dunstable
LUTON
Breachwood Green
Bragbury End
Knebworth
Whitwell
Old Knebworth
Whempstead
Watton-at-Stone
Stockwood
Luton
Someries
Knebworth
Tree Cathedral
Dunstable Downs
Caddington
Woolmer Green
Datchworth
Kensworth Common
Peter's Green
Kimpton
Codicote
Sacombe
Whipsnade
Slip End
Ayot St Lawrence
Stapleford
Woodside Farm & Leisure Park
Roman Baths
ZSL Whipsnade
Holywell
Shaw's Corner
Harmer Green
Studham
Markyate
Welwyn
Waterford Heath
Chapmore End
Welwyn Viaduct
Bramfield
Batford
Waterford
Flamstead
Harpenden
Wheathampstead
Tewin
Little Gaddesden
Jockey End
Hertford
Herts County
Amwell
Gaddesden Row
Redbourn
Lemsford
Welwyn Garden City
Hertingfordbury
Great Gaddesden
Gosling Sports Park
Little Amwell
Nettleden
Sandridge
Letty Green
Castle
Potten End
ST ALBANS
Hatfield House
Essendon
Bayford
HEMEL HEMPSTEAD
Adeyfield
Marshalswick
Roe Green
Hatfield
Brickendon
Theatre
Clock Tower
Old Gorhambury House
Little Berkhamsted
Bourne End
Boxmoor
Leverstock Green
Welham Green
Two Waters
Colney Heath
Willows
Whelpley Hill
Pimlico
Potters Crouch
Chiswell Green
Sopwell
Newgate Street
Gardens of the Rose
London Colney
Brookmans Park
Bovingdon
Bedmond
Park Street
Cuffley
Kings Langley
How Wood
De Havilland Aircraft Heritage Centre
Northaw
Goff's Oak
Abbots Langley
Bricket Wood
Garston
Ley Hill
Chipperfield
Shenley
South Mimms
Potters Bar
Belsize
Flaunden
Studio Tour
Radlett
Ridge
Sarratt
Botany Bay
Latimer
Aldenham
Green Street
Chenies
Chandler's Cross
Hadley Wood
Letchmore Heath
Monken
Trent
Forty Hall
Chorleywood
WATFORD
Little Chalfont
Chorleywood West
Croxley Green
Bushey
Borehamwood
Barnet
Cockfosters
New Barnet
Rickmansworth
Elstree
Arkley
Totteridge Fields
East Barnet
Chiltern Open Air
Oxhey
Bushey Heath
Totteridge
Southgate
Winchmore Hill
Batchworth
Highwood Hill
Mill Hill
Friern Barnet
Chalfont Common
Eastbury
Stanmore
Edgware

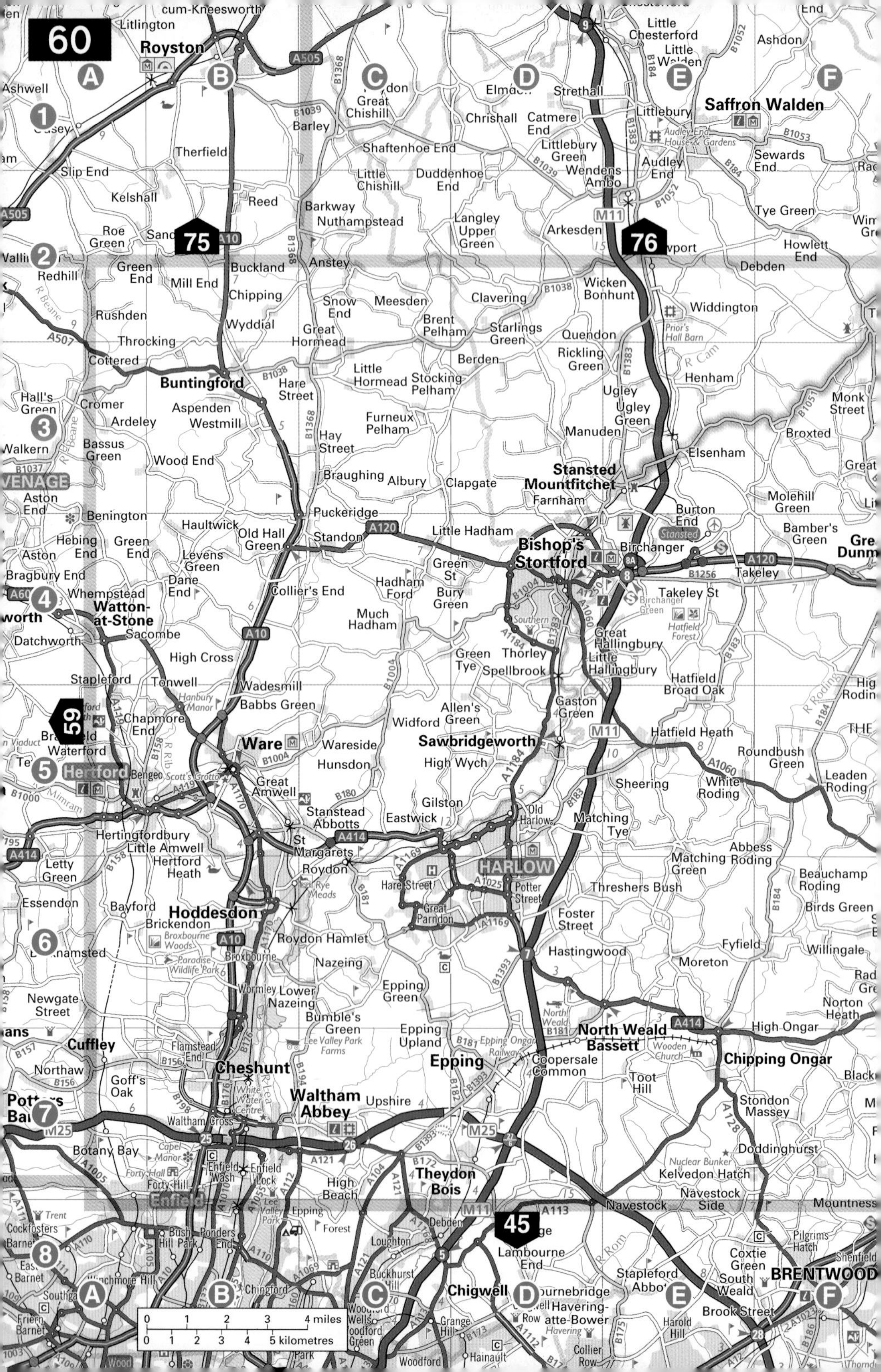

Litlington
Royston
A505
B1368
Little Chesterford
Little Walden
B184
B1052
Ashdon
Ashwell
Great Chishill
Elmdon
Strethall
Saffron Walden
Barley
B1039
Chrishall
Catmere End
Littlebury
Audley End House & Gardens
B1053
Therfield
Shaftenhoe End
Littlebury Green
Wendens Ambo
Audley End
Sewards End
Slip End
Little Chishill
Duddenhoe End
B1383
Kelshall
Reed
Barkway
Nuthampstead
M11
Tye Green
Roe Green
A10
Langley Upper Green
Arkesden
Howlett End
Redhill
Buckland
Anstey
Debden
Green End
Mill End
Chipping
Wicken Bonhunt
B1038
Clavering
Snow End
Meesden
Widdington
Rushden
R Beane
Wyddial
Brent Pelham
Great Hormead
Starlings Green
Quendon
Prior's Hall Barn
A507
Throcking
Rickling Green
R Cam
Cottered
Berden
Buntingford
Little Hormead
Stocking Pelham
Hare Street
Henham
Hall's Green
Cromer
Aspenden
Ugley
Monk Street
Ardeley
Westmill
B1051
Ugley Green
Furneux Pelham
Manuden
Walkern
Bassus Green
Hay Street
Broxted
Elsenham
B1037
Wood End
Stansted Mountfitchet
Braughing
Albury
Clapgate
Aston End
Farnham
Molehill Green
Benington
Puckeridge
Burton End
Stansted
Haultwick
Old Hall Green
Standon
A120
Little Hadham
Bamber's Green
Hebing End
Green End
Bishop's Stortford
Birchanger
Aston
Levens Green
Green St
Bragbury End
Dane End
Hadham Ford
B1256
Takeley
Whempstead
Collier's End
Bury Green
B1004
A1250
Takeley St
Watton-at-Stone
Much Hadham
Southern
Birchanger Green
Hatfield Forest
Sacombe
A10
A1184
Great Hallingbury
B183
Datchworth
Green Tye
Thorley
High Cross
A1060
Little Hallingbury
Spellbrook
Hatfield Broad Oak
Stapleford
Tonwell
Wadesmill
Hanbury Manor
Babbs Green
R Roding
59
Chapmore End
Gaston Green
B184
A119
Allen's Green
Widford
Hatfield Heath
Waterford
B158
R Rib
Ware
Wareside
Sawbridgeworth
M11
Roundbush Green
Hertford
Bengeo
Scott's Grotto
Hunsdon
High Wych
Sheering
White Roding
Leaden Roding
B1000
Mimram
A1170
Great Amwell
B180
Gilston
Stanstead Abbotts
Old Harlow
Eastwick
Matching Tye
Hertingfordbury
A414
St Margarets
Little Amwell
Abbess Roding
A414
Letty Green
Hertford Heath
Roydon
A1169
HARLOW
Matching Green
Beauchamp Roding
Rye Meads
Hare Street
A1025
Threshers Bush
Essendon
Potter Street
Bayford
Hoddesdon
B181
Great Parndon
Foster Street
Birds Green
Brickendon
A1169
Broxbourne Woods
A10
Roydon Hamlet
Fyfield
Paradise Wildlife Park
Broxbourne
Hastingwood
Willingale
Nazeing
B1393
Moreton
Wormley
Lower Nazeing
Epping Green
Newgate Street
Bumble's Green
North Weald
Norton Heath
A414
High Ongar
Lee Valley Park Farms
Epping Upland
North Weald Bassett
B181
Cuffley
Flamstead End
Epping Ongar Railway
Wooden Church
Chipping Ongar
B157
B156
Epping
Coopersale Common
Northaw
Cheshunt
B156
Goff's Oak
Toot Hill
White Water Centre
R Lea
Waltham Abbey
Upshire
Stondon Massey
A128
B198
Potters Bar
M25
Waltham Cross
M25
B1393
Doddinghurst
Botany Bay
Capel Manor
A121
Nuclear Bunker
Kelvedon Hatch
A1005
Forty Hall
Enfield Wash
Enfield Lock
Theydon Bois
Forty Hill
High Beach
A104
Navestock Side
Enfield
Lee Valley Park
Epping Forest
A113
Navestock
Mountnessing
Trent
M11
45
Cockfosters
Bush Hill Park
Ponders End
Debden
Lambourne End
Pilgrims Hatch
Barnet
A110
A105
A110
Loughton
R Rom
Coxtie Green
Shenfield
East Barnet
Winchmore Hill
Chingford
A1069
Buckhurst Hill
Chigwell
Stapleford Abbotts
South Weald
BRENTWOOD
Southgate
Woodford Wells
Woodford Green
Grange Hill
Havering-atte-Bower
Havering
Harold Hill
Brook Street
Friern Barnet
B173
Chigwell Row
Hainault
Collier Row
A1112
Woodford
B175
A1023
B186
Wood
0 1 2 3 4 miles
0 1 2 3 4 5 kilometres

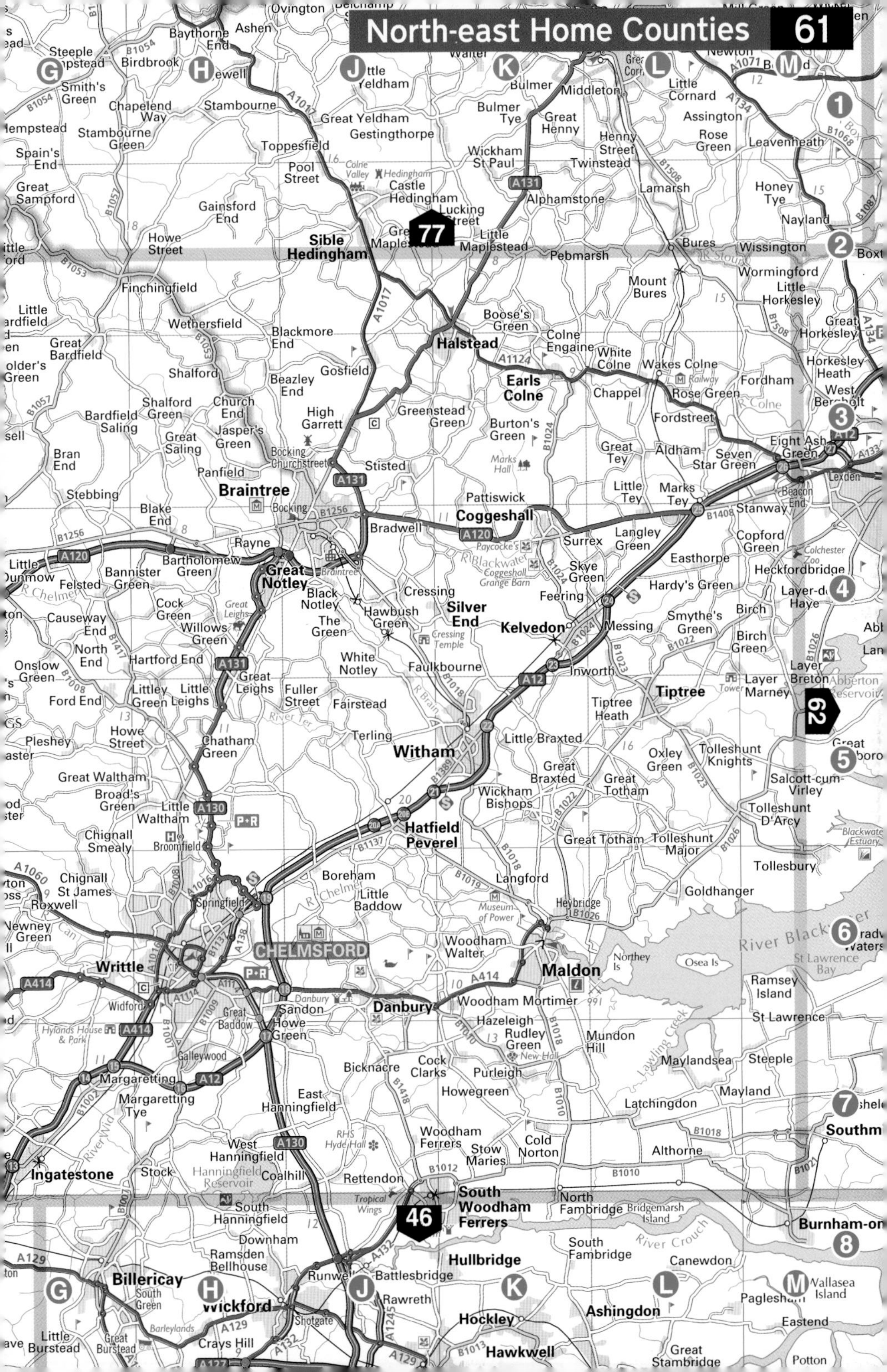
Ovington
Baythorne End
Ashen
Steeple Bumpstead
Birdbrook
Hewell
Little Yeldham
Bulmer
Middleton
Little Cornard
Assington
Leavenheath
Smith's Green
Chapelend Way
Stambourne
Great Yeldham
Gestingthorpe
Bulmer Tye
Great Henny
Henny Street
Rose Green
Hempstead
Stambourne Green
Toppesfield
Wickham St Paul
Twinstead
Spain's End
Pool Street
Colne Valley
Hedingham
Castle Hedingham
Lamarsh
Honey Tye
Great Sampford
Gainsford End
Lucking Street
Alphamstone
Nayland
Howe Street
Sible Hedingham
Great Maplestead
Little Maplestead
Pebmarsh
Bures
Wissington
Wormingford
Little Horkesley
Finchingfield
Mount Bures
Little Bardfield
Wethersfield
Boose's Green
Great Horkesley
Great Bardfield
Blackmore End
Halstead
Colne Engaine
White Colne
Horkesley Heath
Holder's Green
Shalford
Gosfield
Wakes Colne
Fordham
Beazley End
Earls Colne
Chappel
Rose Green
West Bergholt
Shalford Green
Church End
Railway
R Colne
Bardfield Saling
High Garrett
Greenstead Green
Burton's Green
Fordstreet
Jasper's Green
Great Saling
Great Tey
Aldham
Seven Star Green
Eight Ash Green
Bran End
Bocking Churchstreet
Stisted
Marks Hall
Panfield
Little Tey
Marks Tey
Lexden
Beacon End
Stebbing
Braintree
Pattiswick
Coggeshall
Stanway
Blake End
Bocking
Bradwell
Langley Green
Copford Green
Rayne
Paycocke's
Surrex
Little Dunmow
Bartholomew Green
Great Notley
R Blackwater
Coggeshall Grange Barn
Skye Green
Easthorpe
Colchester Zoo
Heckfordbridge
Felsted
Bannister Green
Braintree
Feering
Hardy's Green
Layer-de-la-Haye
R Chelmer
Cock Green
Great Leighs
Black Notley
Cressing
Silver End
Causeway End
Hawbush Green
Kelvedon
Messing
Smythe's Green
Birch
Willows Green
The Green
Cressing Temple
Birch Green
North End
White Notley
Faulkbourne
Inworth
Onslow Green
Hartford End
Great Leighs
Layer Breton
Layer Marney
Abberton Reservoir
Tower
Tiptree
Ford End
Littley Green
Little Leighs
Fuller Street
Fairstead
Tiptree Heath
R Brain
River Ter
Pleshey
Howe Street
Terling
Little Braxted
Great Wigborough
Chatham Green
Witham
Oxley Green
Tolleshunt Knights
Great Braxted
Great Waltham
Great Totham
Salcott-cum-Virley
Broad's Green
Wickham Bishops
Little Waltham
P+R
Tolleshunt D'Arcy
Chignall Smealy
Broomfield
Hatfield Peverel
Great Totham
Tolleshunt Major
Blackwater Estuary
Tollesbury
Chignall St James
Boreham
Langford
Roxwell
Springfield
Little Baddow
Museum of Power
Heybridge
Goldhanger
R Chelmer
Newney Green
CHELMSFORD
Woodham Walter
River Blackwater
Bradwell Waters
Northey Is
Osea Is
St Lawrence Bay
Writtle
Maldon
Ramsey Island
Widford
Danbury
Sandon
Woodham Mortimer
Great Baddow
Howe Green
Hazeleigh
Hylands House & Park
Rudley Green
Mundon Hill
St Lawrence
Galleywood
New Hall
Lawling Creek
Maylandsea
Steeple
Bicknacre
Cock Clarks
Purleigh
Margaretting
Howegreen
Mayland
East Hanningfield
Latchingdon
Margaretting Tye
Tillingham
River Wid
Woodham Ferrers
RHS Hyde Hall
Cold Norton
Stow Maries
Southminster
Althorne
West Hanningfield
Hanningfield Reservoir
Ingatestone
Stock
Coalhill
Rettendon
South Woodham Ferrers
North Fambridge
Bridgemarsh Island
Tropical Wings
South Hanningfield
Burnham-on-Crouch
Downham
River Crouch
South Fambridge
Ramsden Bellhouse
Hullbridge
Canewdon
Billericay
South Green
Runwell
Battlesbridge
Wallasea Island
Wickford
Rawreth
Paglesham
Shotgate
Ashingdon
Barleylands
Hockley
Eastend
Little Burstead
Great Burstead
Crays Hill
Hawkwell
Great Stambridge
Potton
77
62
46

Hadleigh
Washbrook
Chattisham
Copdock
Layham
Great Wenham
Raydon
Wherstead
Nacton
Bucklesham
Freston
Levington
Woolverstone
Tattingstone White Horse
Tattingstone
Holbrook
Alton Water
Chelmondiston
River Orwell
Trimley St Martin
Shotley
Erwarton
Harkstead
Shotley Street
Shotley Gate
Stutton
Bentley
Capel St Mary
Lower Raydon
Holton St Mary
Shelley
Polstead
Stoke-by-Nayland
Leavenheath
Honey Tye
Nayland
Thorington Street
Higham
Stratford St Mary
East Bergholt
Flatford Mill & Bridge Cottage
Cattawade
Holbrook Bay
River Stour
International Ferry Terminal
Boxted
Carter's
Wissington
Wormingford
Little Horkesley
Boxted Cross
Dedham
Langham
Mistley Towers
Mistley
Manningtree
New Mistley
Wrabness
Stour Estuary
Bradfield
Ramsey
Upper Dovercourt
Dovercourt
Harwich
Great Horkesley
Boxted
Lawford
Ardleigh Heath
Ardleigh
Little Bromley
Horsleycross Street
Bradfield Heath
Wix
Little Oakley
Fordham
Horkesley Heath
West Bergholt
High Woods
Parson's Heath
Great Bromley
Tendring Heath
Stones Green
Great Oakley
Pennyhole Bay
Eight Ash Green
Seven Green
COLCHESTER
Lexden
Hythe
Elmstead Market
Little Bentley
Tendring Green
Goose Green
Hare Green
Beaumont
Horsey Island
Stanway
Beacon End
Frating Green
Beth Chatto
Tendring
Thorpe Green
Thorpe-le-Soken
Kirby-le-Soken
Naze Tower
Copford Green
Colchester Zoo
Wivenhoe
Frating
Great Bentley
Weeley
Heckfordbridge
Rowhedge
Fingringhoe
Alresford
High Park Corner
Weeley Heath
Kirby Cross
Frinton
Layer-de-la-Haye
Birch
Aingers Green
Thorrington
Cook's Green
Fingringhoe Wick
Abberton
Langenhoe
Birch Green
Colne Estuary
R Colne
Little Clacton
Great Holland
Layer Breton
Abberton Reservoir
Peldon
Brightlingsea
Hurst Green
Great Clacton
Holland-on-Sea
Layer Marney
Tower
St Osyth
MERSEA ISLAND
Cudmore Grove
East Mersea
Rush Green
CLACTON-ON-SEA
Great Wigborough
Salcott-cum-Virley
Colne Point
Jaywick
West Mersea
Tolleshunt D'Arcy
Blackwater Estuary
Colne Point
Shinglehead Point
Tollesbury
River Blackwater
Sales Point
St Peter's Chapel
Bradwell Waterside
Bradwell-on-Sea
St Lawrence Bay
Ramsey Island
St Lawrence
Tillingham
Steeple
Dengie
Asheldham
Southminster
Holliwell Point
Burnham-on-Crouch
Foulness Point
Wallasea Island
Paglesham
Courtsend
Eastend
FOULNESS ISLAND
Potton
A B C D E F
1 2 3 4 5 6 7 8
77
78
61
47
A12
A14
A137
A120
A133
A134
A1232
B1068
B1070
B1029
B1352
B1414
B1035
B1033
B1034
B1027
B1441
B1442
B1032
B1025
B1026
B1021
B1080
B1456
0 1 2 3 4 miles
0 1 2 3 4 5 kilometres

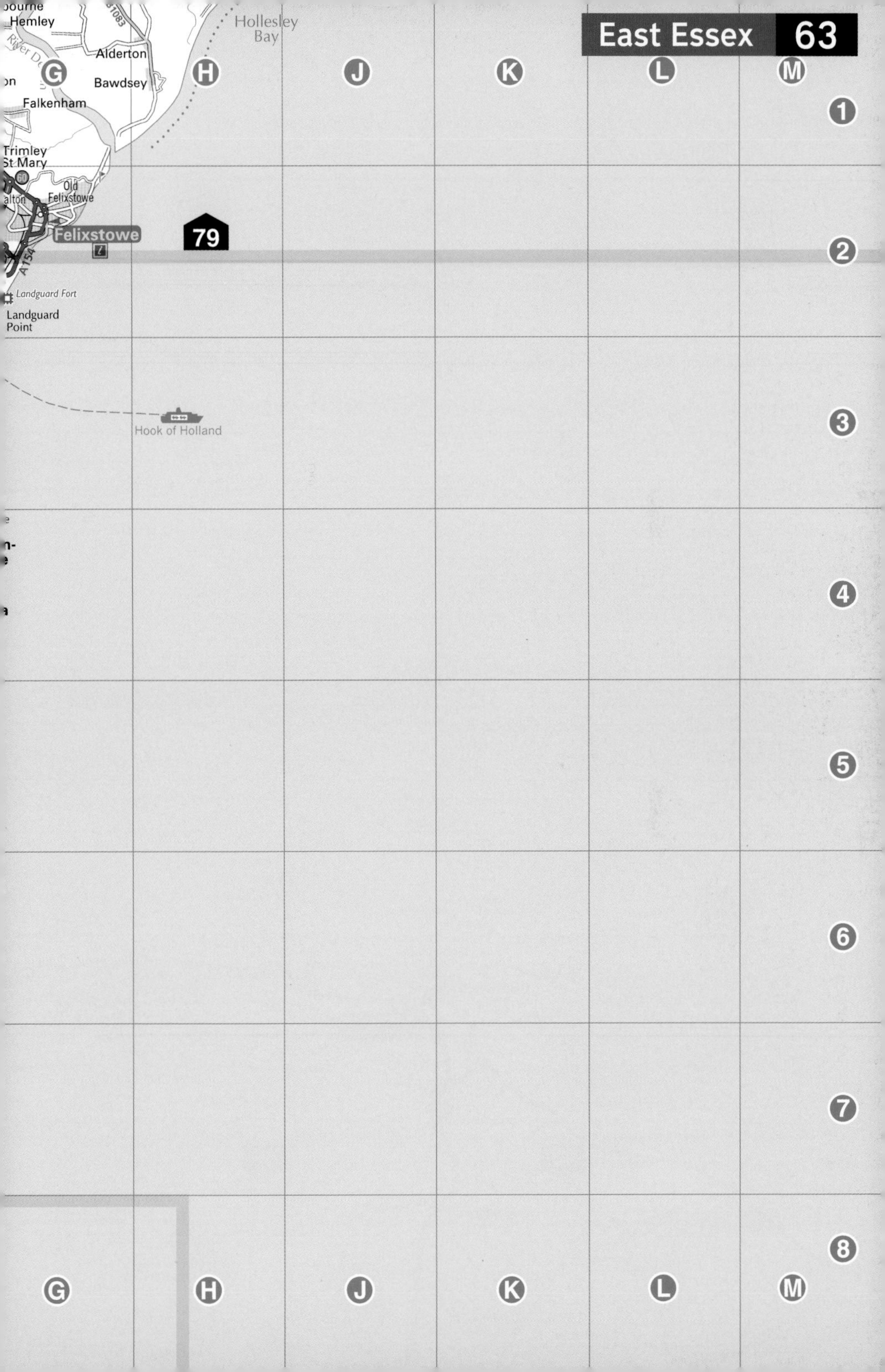
Hemley
B1083
Hollesley
Bay
Alderton
Bawdsey
River Deben
Falkenham
Trimley
St Mary
Old
Felixstowe
Felixstowe
79
A154
Landguard Fort
Landguard
Point
Hook of Holland
G
H
J
K
L
M
1
2
3
4
5
6
7
8

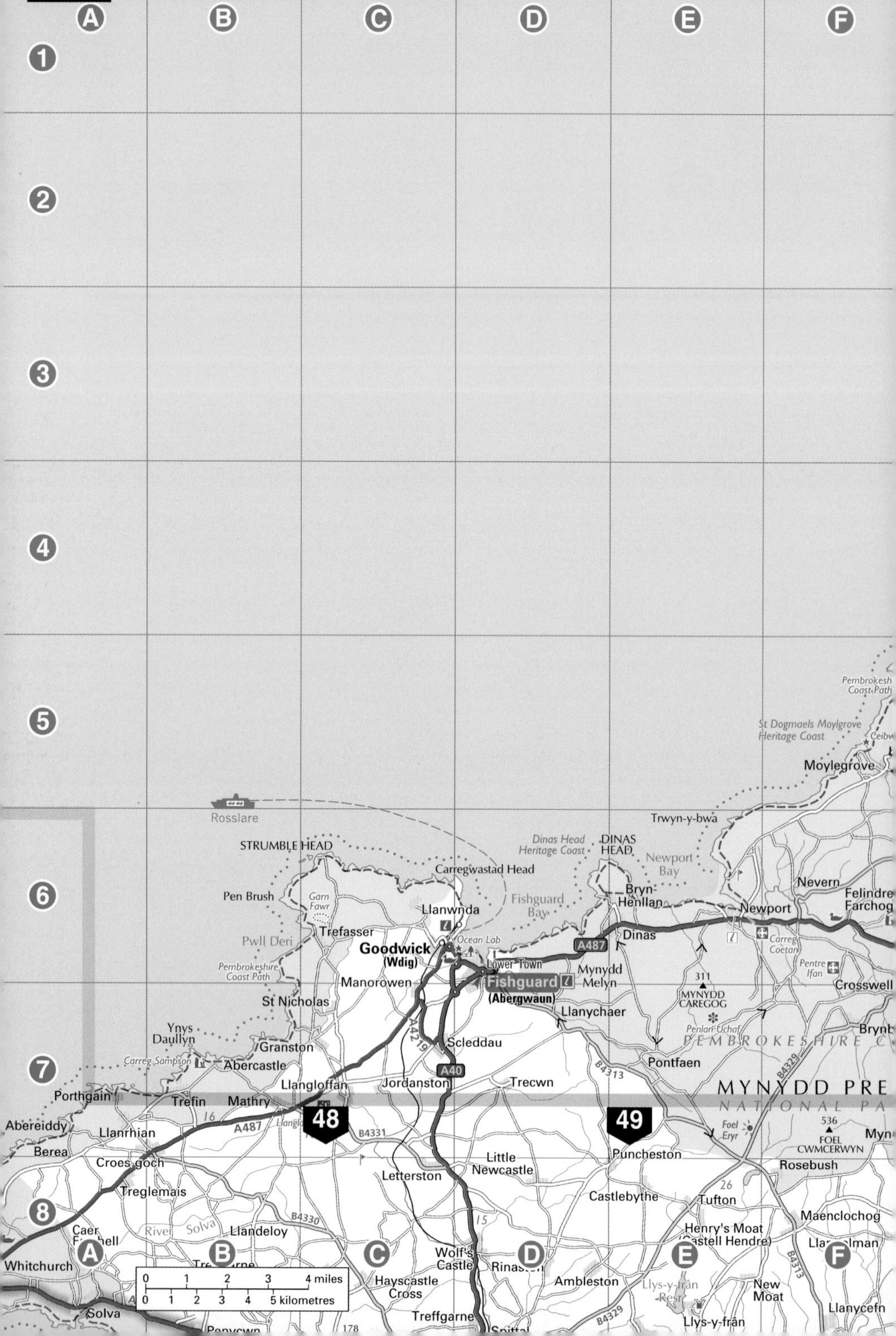
Rosslare
STRUMBLE HEAD
Pen Brush
Garn Fawr
Trefasser
Pwll Deri
Pembrokeshire Coast Path
St Nicholas
Ynys Daullyn
Granston
Carreg Sampson
Abercastle
Porthgain
Abereiddy
Llangloffan
Trefin
Mathry
Llanrhian
Berea
Croes-goch
Treglemais
Caer Farchell
River Solva
Llandeloy
Whitchurch
Solva
Penycwm
Carregwastad Head
Llanwnda
Ocean Lab
Goodwick
(Wdig)
Manorowen
Fishguard Bay
Lower Town
Fishguard
(Abergwaun)
A4219
Scleddau
A40
Jordanston
48
B4331
Letterston
B4330
Wolf's Castle
Hayscastle Cross
Treffgarne
178
Spittal
Trecwn
Little Newcastle
15
Rinaston
Dinas Head Heritage Coast
DINAS HEAD
Bryn-Henllan
Newport Bay
Dinas
A487
Mynydd Melyn
Llanychaer
B4313
Pontfaen
49
Puncheston
Castlebythe
Ambleston
Llys-y-frân Resr
Llys-y-frân
B4329
Henry's Moat
(Castell Hendre)
Tufton
26
New Moat
Trwyn-y-bwa
Newport
Carreg Coetan
311
MYNYDD CAREGOG
Penlan-Uchaf
PEMBROKESHIRE C
MYNYDD PRE
NATIONAL PA
Foel Eryr
536
FOEL CWMCERWYN
Rosebush
Maenclochog
Llanycefn
Nevern
Felindre Farchog
Pentre Ifan
Crosswell
Brynb
Myn
Moylegrove
St Dogmaels Moylgrove Heritage Coast
Pembrokesh Coast Path
Ceibw
16
0 1 2 3 4 miles
0 1 2 3 4 5 kilometres

Aberarth
Aberaeron
New Quay
(Ceinewydd)
Ceredigion Heritage Coast
Llanina
Llwyncelyn
Maen-y-groes
Gilfachrheda
Llanarth
Cross Inn
Oakford
Cwmtydu
Nanternis
Caerwedros
Dihewyd
Ynys-Lochtyn
Pendinas Lochtyn
Llwyndafydd
Mydroilyn
Llangrannog
Pontgarreg
Plwmp
Penbryn
Pentregat
Cardigan Island
Mwnt Beach
Cardigan Island Coastal Farm Park
Felinwynt Rainforest & Butterfly Centre
Tresaith
Aberporth
Sarnau
Brynhoffnant
Talgarreg
Y Ferwig
Tremain
Blaenannerch
Tan-y-groes
Glynarthen
Poppit Sands
Penparc
Blaenporth
Rhydlewis
Ffostrasol
Cwrt-newydd
Abbey & Coach House
Cardigan
(Aberteifi)
Bettws Evan
Hawen
Pontshaen
Dogmaels
Beulah
Troedyraur
Penrhiw-pal
Tre-groes
Llanwen
Ponthirwaun
Brongest
Maesllyn
Pren-gwyn
Rhydowen
Pen-y-bryn
Welsh Wildlife Centre
Llechryd
Llandygwydd
Croes-lan
Teifi Marshes
Castle
Afon Teifi
TIVY SIDE
Capel Dewi
Cilgerran
Cwm-cou
Rock Mill Woollen & Water Mill
Abercych
Cenarth
National Coracle Centre
Adpar
Llandyfriog
Teifi Valley Railway
Penrhiwllan
Llandysul
Llanfihangel-ar-arth
Rhoshill
Pen-rhiw
Newcastle Emlyn
(Castell Newydd Emlyn)
Henllan
Llangeler
Pontwelly
Newchapel
Drefach
National Wool
Felindre
Glynteg
Pentre-cwrt
Eglwyswrw
Boncath
Cwmhiraeth
Blaenffos
Capel-Iwan
Pencader
Bwlch-y-groes
Cwmpengraig
Rhos
Star
Gwyddgr
Crymych
Foel Drygarn
Tegryn
Alltwalis
Cwmduad
Hermon
Llanfyrnach
Trelech
FOEL DRYCH
Glandwr
Llanpumsaint
Llandre Isaf
Hebron
River Gwili
Pontarsai
Blaenwaun
Blaen-y-Coed
Cynwyl Elfed
Llanglydwen
Gwili Railway
Cefn-y-pant
Cwmbach
Talog
Felingw
Efailwen
Login
Abernant
A487
A486
A484
A478
A475
A485
B4342
B4338
B4321
B4334
B4333
B4571
B4570
B4546
B4548
B4332
B4459
B4476
B4336
B4299
B4301
A484
66
49
50

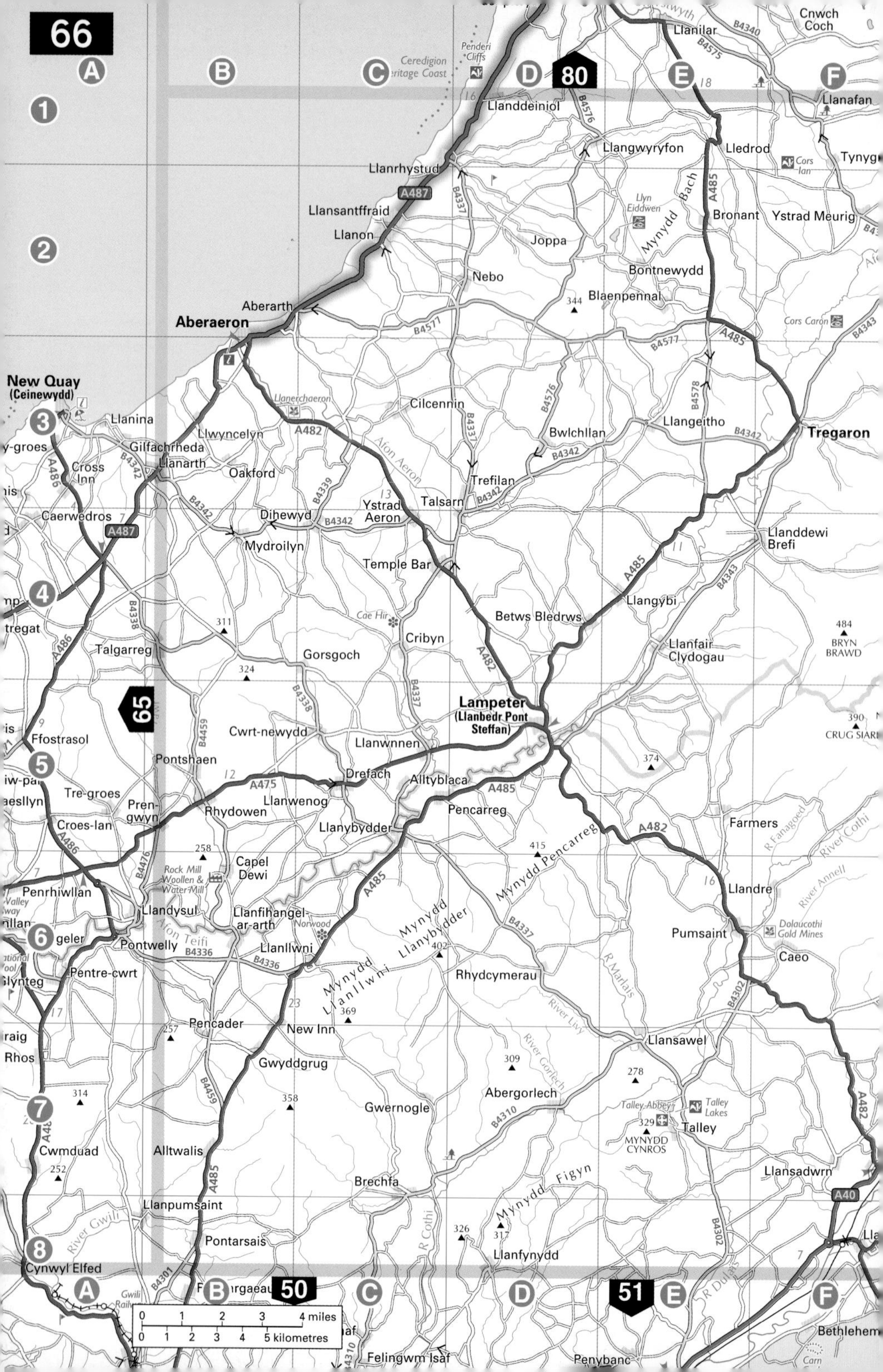
A
B
C
D
E
F
1
2
3
4
5
6
7
8
80
65
50
51
Ceredigion Heritage Coast
Penderi Cliffs
Llanilar
Cnwch Coch
B4340
B4575
Llanafan
Llanddeiniol
B4576
Llangwyryfon
Lledrod
Tynygr
Cors Ian
Llanrhystud
A487
B4337
Llansantffraid
Llanon
Llyn Eiddwen
Mynydd Bach
A485
Bronant
Ystrad Meurig
Joppa
Nebo
Bontnewydd
344
Blaenpennal
Aberarth
Aberaeron
B4571
B4577
Cors Caron
B4343
New Quay (Ceinewydd)
Llanerchaeron
Cilcennin
B4576
B4578
Llanina
Llangeitho
B4342
Tregaron
Llwyncelyn
A482
Bwlchllan
Gilfachrheda
Llanarth
Cross Inn
A486
Oakford
Afon Aeron
Trefilan
B4339
Talsarn
Caerwedros
Dihewyd
Ystrad Aeron
Mydroilyn
Llanddewi Brefi
Temple Bar
Betws Bledrws
Llangybi
Cae Hir
311
Cribyn
Talgarreg
B4338
Gorsgoch
Llanfair Clydogau
484
BRYN BRAWD
324
Lampeter (Llanbedr Pont Steffan)
390
CRUG SIARI
B4459
Cwrt-newydd
Ffostrasol
Llanwnnen
374
Pontshaen
Drefach
Alltyblaca
A475
Tre-groes
Llanwenog
Pencarreg
Prengwyn
Rhydowen
Llanybydder
Croes-lan
Farmers
R Fanagoed
River Cothi
415
Mynydd Pencarreg
258
Capel Dewi
Rock Mill Woollen & Water Mill
B4476
Penrhiwllan
Llandre
River Annell
Llandysul
Afon Teifi
Llanfihangel-ar-arth
Norwood
Mynydd Llanybydder
B4337
Pumsaint
Dolaucothi Gold Mines
Pontwelly
B4336
Llanllwni
402
Caeo
Pentre-cwrt
Mynydd Llanllwni
Rhydcymerau
R Marlais
B4302
369
River Livy
Pencader
New Inn
257
Llansawel
309
River Gorlech
Gwyddgrug
278
Abergorlech
314
358
Talley Abbey
Talley Lakes
B4459
Gwernogle
B4310
329
Talley
MYNYDD CYNROS
Cwmduad
Alltwalis
252
Llansadwrn
Mynydd Figyn
A40
Brechfa
Llanpumsaint
326
317
River Gwili
R Cothi
Pontarsais
Llanfynydd
Cynwyl Elfed
B4301
Gwili Railway
R Dulais
0 1 2 3 4 miles
0 1 2 3 4 5 kilometres
Felingwm Isaf
Penybanc
Bethlehem
Carn

81
52
89
Cwmystwyth
Pontrhydygroes
Ysbyty Ystwyth
GEIFAS
St Harmon
Gilfach
Craig-Goch Resr
Pen-y-Garreg Resr
Rhayader
(Rhaeadr Gwy)
Llansantffraed-Cwmdeuddwr
Nantmel
Ffair Rhos
Pontrhydfendigaid
Abbey
DIBYN DU
Claerwen Reservoir
Garreg-Ddu Resr
Elan Village
Elan Valley
Caban Coch Resr
Llanwrthwl
Llanyre
Llandrindod
Howey
PEN-MAEN-WERN
CEFN CNWC
DRYGARN FAWR
River Towy
Newbridge-on-Wye
Esgair Cerrig
Abergwesyn Common
Afon Irfon
Llanafan-Fawr
PEN CARREG-DÂN
CEFN COCH
Cwmbach Llechrhyd
CARNEDDAU
Vicarage Meadows
Abergwesyn
CEFN CRUG
Royal Welsh
Llanelwedd
PEN-Y-GURNOS
CEFN FANNOG
Beulah
Cilmery
Prince Llewelyn
Builth Wells
(Llanfair-ym-Muallt)
River Doethie
Garth
CARCWM
Llyn Brianne
MYNYDD TRAWSNANT
Gwenffrwd-Dinas
River Brun
Llanwrtyd Wells
Garth Hill
BANC-Y-CELYN
Llangammarch Wells
Cefngorwydd
DRUM DDU
Rhandirmwyn
Sugar Loaf
Cynghordy Viaduct
Mynydd Eppynt
BRYN DU
Yscir Fawr
Gwenddwr
Tirabad
Llandulas
Cynghordy
Upper Chapel
CEFN CLAWDD
GWRHYD
Yscir Fechan
River Crychan
Llaneglwys
YSGWYDD HWCH
Merthyr Cynog
NOETHGRUG
Nant Gwennol
Mynydd Bwlch-y-Groes
Nant Bran
Lower Chapel
Poor Man's Wood
Llanfihangel Nant Bran
Llandovery
(Llanymddyfri)
Pont-faen
Pwllgloyw
TWYRN DISGWYLFA
Battle
Llanddew
Llywel
Cradoc
Roman Fort
Myddfai
Trallong
Brecon
(Aberhonddu)
Usk Reservoir
Mynydd Myddfai
River Bran
Trecastle
YR ALLT
Sennybridge
R Usk
Defynnog
Llanspyddid
Llanfrynach
Twynllanan
Libanus
Crai
BRECON BEACO

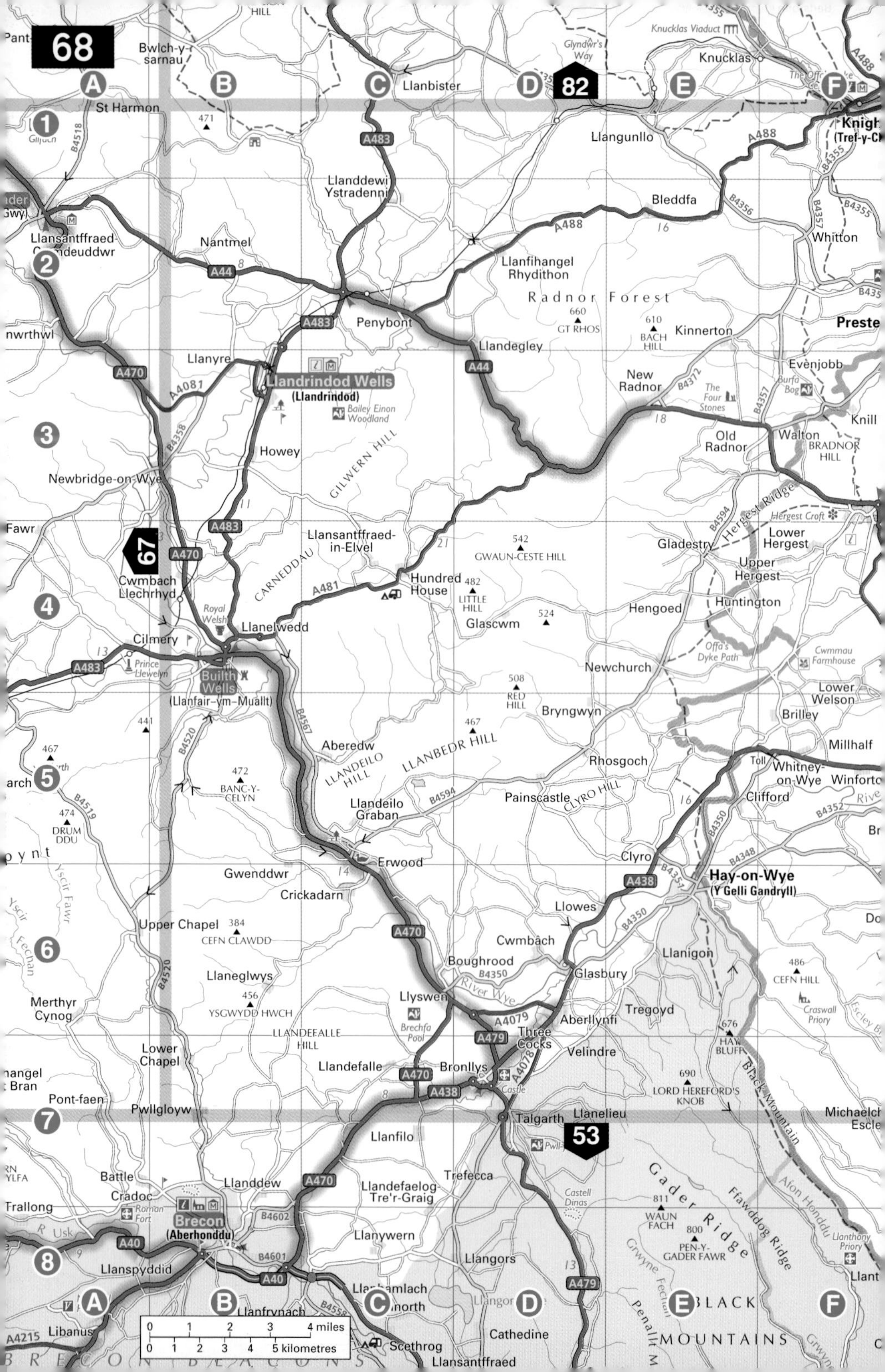

St Harmon
Bwlch-y-sarnau
Llanbister
Knucklas Viaduct
Glyndwr's Way
Knucklas
82
Llangunllo
Knighton (Tref-y-Clawdd)
Llanddewi Ystradenni
Bleddfa
Whitton
Llansantffraed-Cwmdeuddwr
Nantmel
Llanfihangel Rhydithon
Radnor Forest
Penybont
660 GT RHOS
610 BACH HILL
Kinnerton
Presteigne
Llanyre
Llandrindod Wells (Llandrindod)
Llandegley
Evenjobb
New Radnor
The Four Stones
Burfa Bog
Bailey Einon Woodland
Howey
Old Radnor
Walton
Knill
BRADNOR HILL
Newbridge-on-Wye
GILWERN HILL
Hergest Ridge
Hergest Croft
Llansantffraed-in-Elvel
542 GWAUN-CESTE HILL
Gladestry
Lower Hergest
Upper Hergest
67
Cwmbach Llechrhyd
CARNEDDAU
Hundred House
482 LITTLE HILL
Huntington
Hengoed
Royal Welsh
Llanelwedd
Glascwm
524
Cilmery
Prince Llewelyn
Builth Wells (Llanfair-ym-Muallt)
Offa's Dyke Path
Newchurch
Cwmmau Farmhouse
508 RED HILL
Lower Welson
441
467
Bryngwyn
Brilley
Aberedw
LLANBEDR HILL
Millhalf
472 BANC-Y-CELYN
LLANDEILO HILL
Rhosgoch
Toll
Whitney-on-Wye
Winforton
Painscastle
CLYRO HILL
Clifford
474 DRUM DDU
Llandeilo Graban
Clyro
Hay-on-Wye (Y Gelli Gandryll)
Erwood
Gwenddwr
Crickadarn
Llowes
Upper Chapel
384 CEFN CLAWDD
Cwmbâch
Llanigon
Boughrood
Glasbury
486 CEFN HILL
Llaneglwys
River Wye
Merthyr Cynog
456 YSGWYDD HWCH
Llyswen
Brechfa Pool
Tregoyd
Craswall Priory
LLANDEFALLE HILL
Three Cocks
Aberllynfi
676 HAY BLUFF
Lower Chapel
Velindre
Llandefalle
Bronllys
Castle
690 LORD HEREFORD'S KNOB
Black Mountain
Pont-faen
Pwllgloyw
Talgarth
Llanelieu
53
Michaelchurch Escley
Llanfilo
Battle
Llanddew
Trefecca
Gader Ridge
Ffawddog Ridge
Cradoc
Roman Fort
Llandefaelog-Tre'r-Graig
Castell Dinas
811 WAUN FACH
Trallong
Brecon (Aberhonddu)
R Usk
800 PEN-Y-GADER FAWR
Afon Honddu
Llanthony Priory
Llanywern
Llanspyddid
Llangors
Llanhamlach
Llanfrynach
Cathedine
BLACK MOUNTAINS
Libanus
Scethrog
Llansantffraed
BRECON BEACONS
0 1 2 3 4 miles
0 1 2 3 4 5 kilometres
A470 A483 A44 A488 A4081 A481 A438 A479 A4079 A40 A4215 B4518 B4358 B4520 B4519 B4567 B4594 B4350 B4351 B4348 B4352 B4372 B4357 B4356 B4355 B4602 B4601 B4558

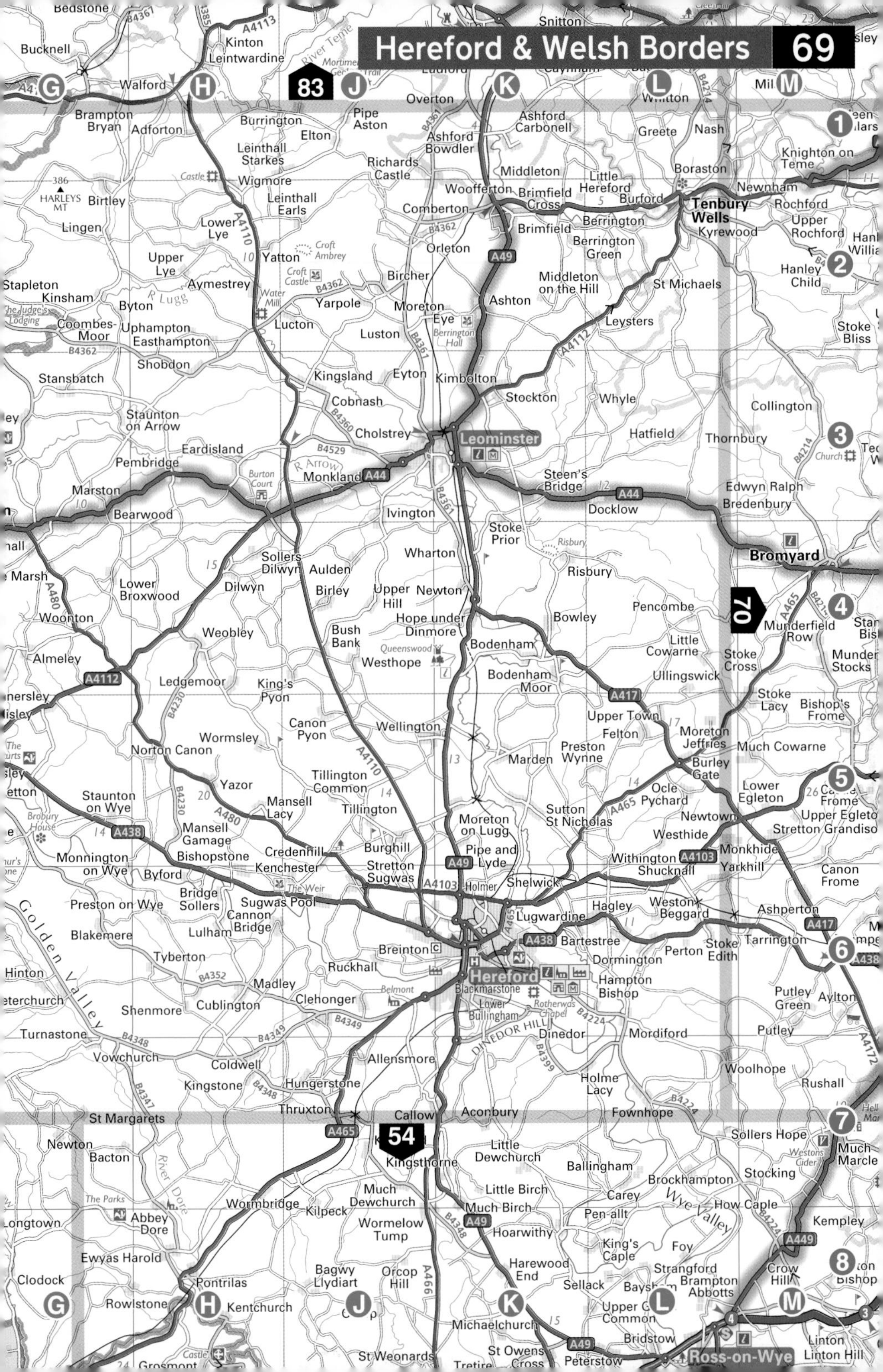
Bedstone
Bucknell
Kinton
Leintwardine
A4113
B4361
River Teme
Mortimer Trail
Snitton
Walford
Brampton Bryan
Adforton
83
Overton
Pipe Aston
Burrington
Elton
Ashford Bowdler
Ashford Carbonell
Greete
Nash
Whitton
Mill
Knighton on Teme
Leinthall Starkes
Richards Castle
Middleton
Little Hereford
Boraston
Newnham
386 HARLEYS MT
Birtley
Castle
Wigmore
Leinthall Earls
Wooferton
Brimfield Cross
Burford
Tenbury Wells
Rochford
Lingen
Lower Lye
Comberton
B4362
Brimfield
Berrington
Kyrewood
Upper Rochford
Hanley William
A4110
Croft Ambrey
Orleton
A49
Berrington Green
Upper Lye
Yatton
Bircher
Middleton on the Hill
Hanley Child
Stapleton
Kinsham
Aymestrey
Croft Castle
St Michaels
R Lugg
Water Mill
Yarpole
Moreton
Eye
Ashton
Byton
The Judge's Lodging
Coombes-Moor
Uphampton
Easthampton
Lucton
Luston
Berrington Hall
Leysters
A4112
Stoke Bliss
B4362
Shobdon
B4361
Stansbatch
Kingsland
Eyton
Kimbolton
Cobnash
Stockton
Whyle
Collington
B4360
Staunton on Arrow
Cholstrey
Leominster
Hatfield
Thornbury
B4529
Eardisland
R Arrow
Pembridge
Burton Court
Monkland
A44
Steen's Bridge
Church
B4214
Marston
Edwyn Ralph
Bredenbury
Bearwood
Docklow
Ivington
Stoke Prior
Risbury
Wharton
Bromyard
Sollers Dilwyn
Aulden
Risbury
Lower Broxwood
Dilwyn
Birley
Upper Hill
Newton
70
Pencombe
A480
Woonton
Hope under Dinmore
Bowley
A465
Munderfield Row
Weobley
Bush Bank
Bodenham
Little Cowarne
Almeley
Queenswood
Westhope
Stoke Cross
Munderfield Stocks
A4112
Ledgemoor
King's Pyon
Bodenham Moor
Ullingswick
B4230
A417
Upper Town
Stoke Lacy
Bishop's Frome
Canon Pyon
Wellington
Felton
Moreton Jeffries
Wormsley
Much Cowarne
Norton Canon
Marden
Preston Wynne
Burley Gate
Tillington Common
A4110
Ocle Pychard
Lower Eggleton
Yazor
Staunton on Wye
Mansell Lacy
Tillington
Sutton St Nicholas
Newtown
Upper Eggleton
Brobury House
A438
Mansell Gamage
Moreton on Lugg
Westhide
Stretton Grandison
Bishopstone
Credenhill
Burghill
Pipe and Lyde
Monkhide
Monnington on Wye
Byford
Kenchester
Stretton Sugwas
Withington
A4103
Shucknall
Yarkhill
Canon Frome
Bridge Sollers
The Weir
Holmer
Shelwick
Preston on Wye
Sugwas Pool
Cannon Bridge
Lugwardine
Hagley
Weston Beggard
Ashperton
Golden Valley
Blakemere
Lulham
Bartestree
A417
Tarrington
Tyberton
Breinton
Dormington
Perton
Stoke Edith
Hinton
Ruckhall
Hereford
Hampton Bishop
B4352
Madley
Blackmarstone
Belmont
Putley Green
Aylton
Clehonger
Shenmore
Cublington
Lower Bullingham
Rotherwas Chapel
B4224
B4349
Dinedor Hill
Dinedor
Mordiford
Putley
Turnastone
B4348
Vowchurch
Coldwell
Allensmore
B4399
A4172
Woolhope
Kingstone
Hungerstone
Holme Lacy
Rushall
B4347
Thruxton
Callow
Aconbury
Fownhope
St Margarets
A465
54
Little Dewchurch
Sollers Hope
Newton
Bacton
Kingsthorne
Ballingham
Westons Cider
Much Marcle
River Dore
Much Dewchurch
Little Birch
Brockhampton
Stocking
The Parks
Wormbridge
Kilpeck
Much Birch
Carey
Wye Valley
How Caple
Abbey Dore
Longtown
Wormelow Tump
A49
Hoarwithy
Pen-allt
Kempley
B4348
King's Caple
Foy
A449
Ewyas Harold
A466
Harewood End
Strangford
Crow Hill
Clodock
Pontrilas
Bagwy Llydiart
Orcop Hill
Sellack
Brampton Abbotts
Rowlstone
Kentchurch
Upper Common
Michaelchurch
Bridstow
Castle
Grosmont
St Weonards
Tretire
St Owens Cross
Peterstow
Ross-on-Wye
Linton
Linton Hill
Snitton
Kempley

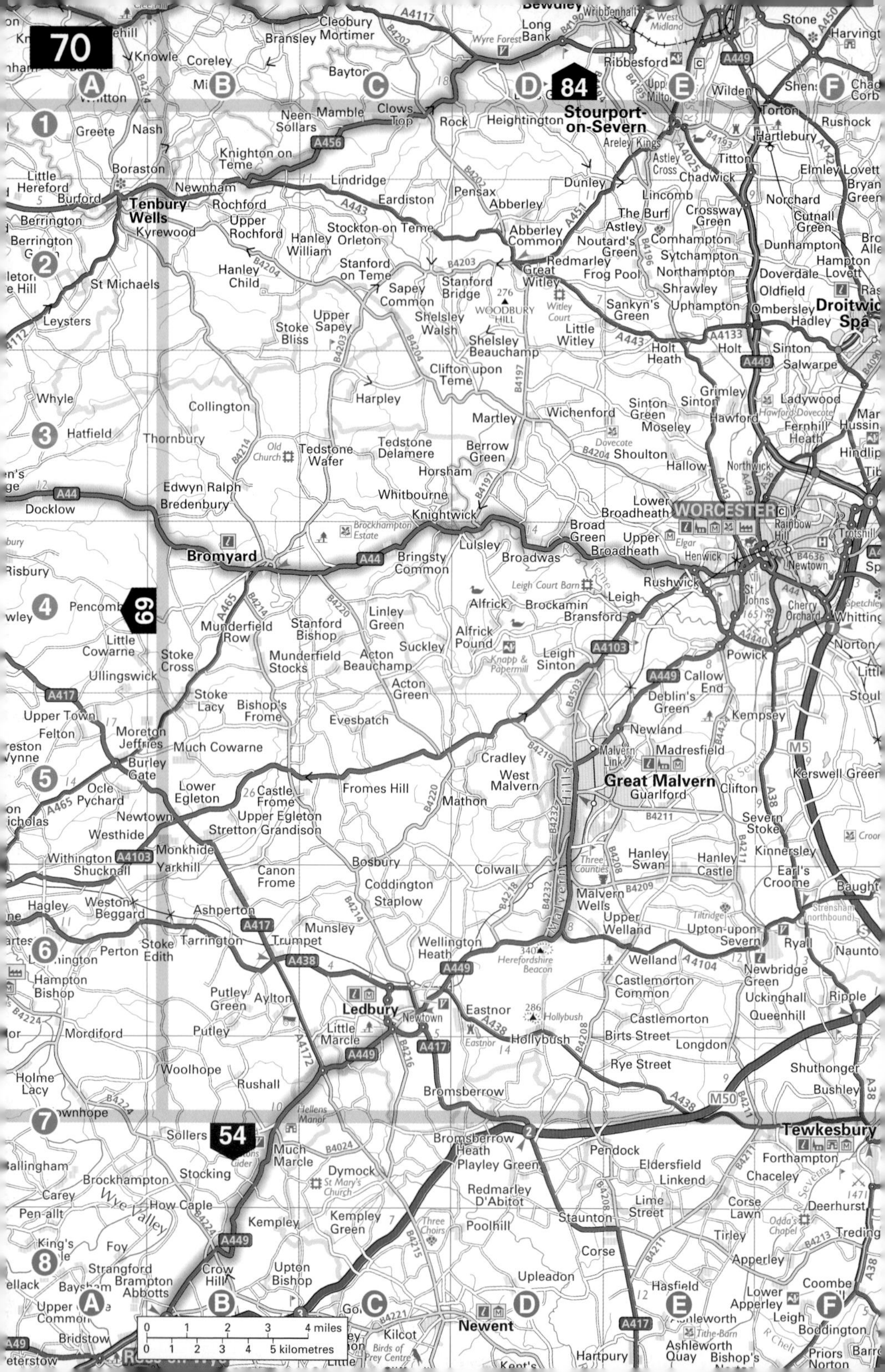
70
84
69
54
A
B
C
D
E
F
1
2
3
4
5
6
7
8
Bewdley
Wribbenhall
West Midland
Stone
Harvington
Cleobury Mortimer
Bransley
Long Bank
Wyre Forest
Knowle
Coreley
Baytor
Ribbesford
Upper Milton
Wilden
Chaddesley Corbett
Whitton
Neen Sollars
Mamble
Clows Top
Rock
Heightington
Stourport-on-Severn
Areley Kings
Torton
Rushock
Greete
Nash
Hartlebury
Astley Cross
Titton
Elmley Lovett
Knighton on Teme
Boraston
Lindridge
Pensax
Dunley
Chadwick
Bryan's Green
Little Hereford
Burford
Newnham
Tenbury Wells
Rochford
Eardiston
Abberley
Lincomb
Norchard
Berrington
Kyrewood
Upper Rochford
Hanley William
Stockton-on-Teme
Orleton
Abberley Common
The Burf
Astley
Noutard's Green
Crossway Green
Comhampton
Cutnall Green
Berrington Green
Hanley Child
Stanford on Teme
Stanford Bridge
Great Witley
Redmarley
Frog Pool
Sytchampton
Northampton
Dunhampton
Hampton Lovett
St Michaels
Sapey Common
Woodbury Hill
Witley Court
Shrawley
Doverdale
Oldfield
Leysters
Upper Sapey
Stoke Bliss
Shelsley Walsh
Shelsley Beauchamp
Little Witley
Sankyn's Green
Uphampton
Ombersley
Hadley
Droitwich Spa
Holt Heath
Holt
Sinton
Salwarpe
Clifton upon Teme
Whyle
Collington
Harpley
Grimley
Sinton Green
Sinton
Ladywood
Hawford Dovecote
Hatfield
Thornbury
Old Church
Tedstone Wafer
Tedstone Delamere
Martley
Wichenford
Moseley
Hawford
Fernhill Heath
Berrow Green
Dovecote
Shoulton
Hallow
Horsham
Northwick
Hindlip
Edwyn Ralph
Bredenbury
Whitbourne
Lower Broadheath
Docklow
Knightwick
WORCESTER
Rainbow Hill
Brockhampton Estate
Lulsley
Broad Green
Upper Broadheath
Elgar
Henwick
Bromyard
Bringsty Common
Broadwas
Leigh Court Barn
Rushwick
Newtown
Risbury
Alfrick
Brockamin
Leigh
St Johns
Cherry Orchard
Pencombe
Linley Green
Stanford Bishop
Bransford
Whittington
Munderfield Row
Alfrick Pound
Little Cowarne
Suckley
Knapp & Papermill
Leigh Sinton
Powick
Norton
Stoke Cross
Munderfield Stocks
Acton Beauchamp
Callow End
Ullingswick
Acton Green
Stoke Lacy
Bishop's Frome
Deblin's Green
Upper Town
Evesbatch
Kempsey
Felton
Moreton Jeffries
Much Cowarne
Newland
Madresfield
Burley Gate
Cradley
Malvern Link
Ocle Pychard
Lower Egleton
West Malvern
Great Malvern
Kerswell Green
Castle Frome
Fromes Hill
Mathon
Guarlford
Clifton
Newtown
Upper Egleton
Stretton Grandison
Severn Stoke
Westhide
Monkhide
Withington
Yarkhill
Shucknall
Canon Frome
Bosbury
Colwall
Three Counties
Hanley Swan
Hanley Castle
Kinnersley
Earl's Croome
Coddington
Staplow
Malvern Wells
Weston Beggard
Hagley
Ashperton
Upper Welland
Tiltridge
Strensham (northbound)
Baughton
Munsley
Stoke Edith
Perton
Tarrington
Trumpet
Wellington Heath
Upton-upon-Severn
Ryall
Naunton
Hampton Bishop
Herefordshire Beacon
Welland
Newbridge Green
Castlemorton Common
Uckinghall
Ripple
Putley Green
Aylton
Ledbury
Eastnor
Hollybush
Castlemorton
Queenhill
Mordiford
Putley
Little Marcle
Newtown
Birts Street
Longdon
Holme Lacy
Woolhope
Rushall
Rye Street
Shuthonger
Bushley
Bromsberrow
Fownhope
Hellens Manor
Sollers
Much Marcle
Bromsberrow Heath
Tewkesbury
Pendock
Forthampton
Ballingham
Eldersfield
Dymock
Playley Green
Linkend
Chaceley
Brockhampton
Stocking
St Mary's Church
Carey
Redmarley D'Abitot
Lime Street
Corse Lawn
Deerhurst
Wye Valley
Pen-allt
How Caple
Kempley
Kempley Green
Three Choirs
Poolhill
Staunton
Odda's Chapel
Foy
Tirley
Tredington
Corse
Apperley
Strangford
Brampton Abbotts
Crow Hill
Upton Bishop
Upleadon
Hasfield
Lower Apperley
Coombe Hill
Upper Cross
Gorsley
Newent
Ashleworth
Leigh
Boddington
Tithe Barn
Bridstow
Kilcot
Birds of Prey Centre
Ashleworth Quay
Hartpury
Bishop's Norton
Priors Norton
Ross-on-Wye
A4117
B4202
B4190
A449
A450
A456
B4193
A4025
B4202
A451
B4196
A443
B4204
B4203
A4133
B4203
B4204
B4197
A44
B4214
A465
B4220
A4103
B4503
B4219
B4232
A417
B4224
A438
A4172
B4208
B4209
B4211
B4424
A38
M5
B4636
A4440
A4104
M50
B4216
B4215
B4024
B4221
B4213
A4096
0 1 2 3 4 miles
0 1 2 3 4 5 kilometres

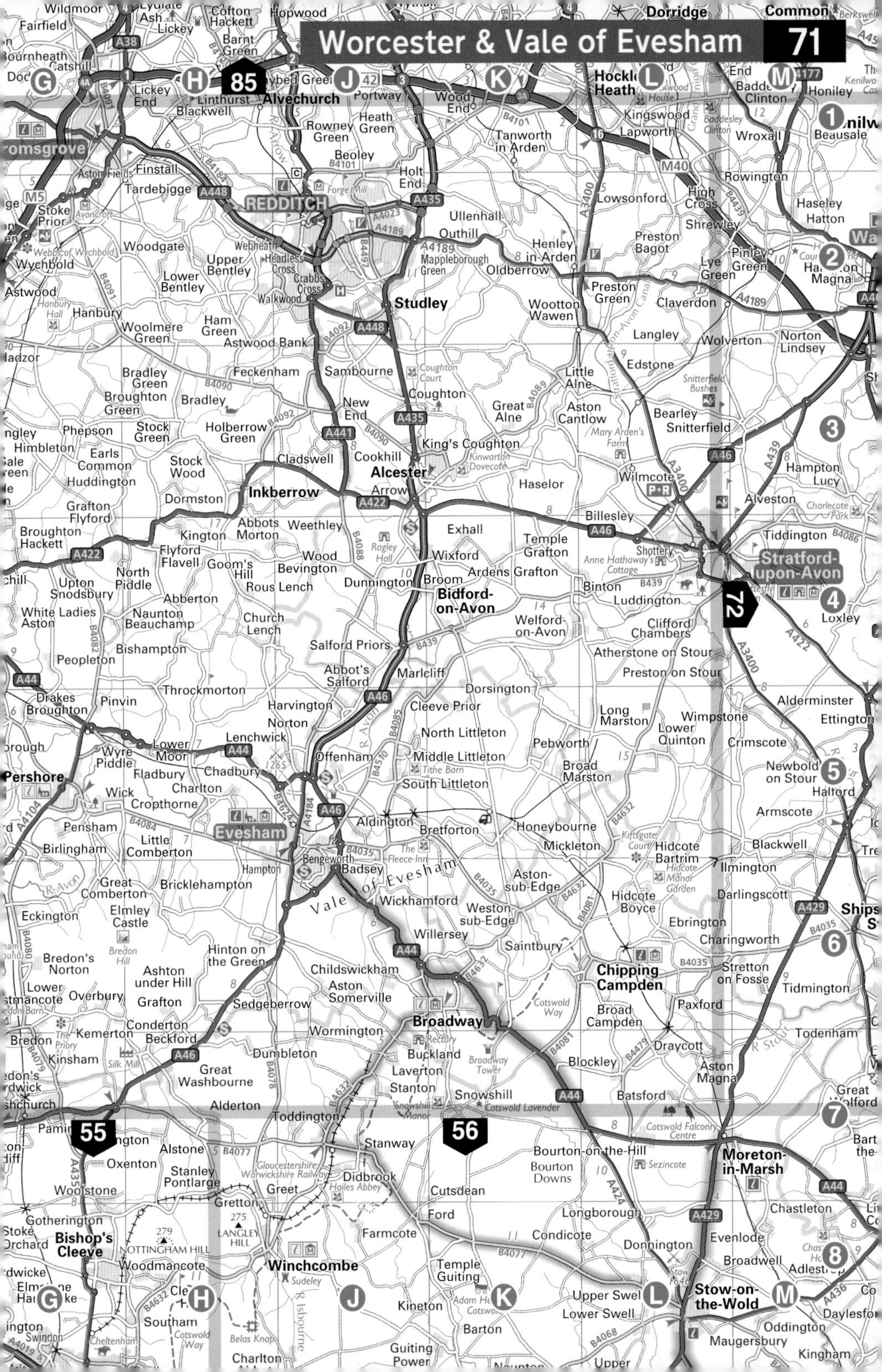
Wildmoor
Fairfield
Bournheath
Catshill
Lydiate Ash
Lickey
Cofton Hackett
Barnt Green
Hopwood
Dorridge
Common
Lickey End
Blackwell
Linthurst
85
Alvechurch
Portway
Wood End
Hockley Heath
Kingswood
Lapworth
Baddesley Clinton
Honiley
Wroxall
Beausale
Bromsgrove
Finstall
Aston Fields
Tardebigge
Stoke Prior
Avoncroft
Webbs of Wychbold
Wychbold
Astwood
Woodgate
Upper Bentley
Lower Bentley
Webheath
Headless Cross
Crabbs Cross
Walkwood
REDDITCH
Rowney Green
Heath Green
Beoley
Holt End
Forge Mill
Tanworth in Arden
Lowsonford
High Cross
Rowington
Haseley
Hatton
Shrewley
Ullenhall
Outhill
Mappleborough Green
Oldberrow
Henley-in-Arden
Preston Bagot
Pinley Green
Lye Green
Hampton Magna
Claverdon
Preston Green
Wootton Wawen
Studley
Hanbury
Hanbury Hall
Woolmere Green
Ham Green
Astwood Bank
Langley
Wolverton
Norton Lindsey
Edstone
Feckenham
Sambourne
Coughton Court
Coughton
Bradley Green
Bradley
Broughton Green
Stock Green
Holberrow Green
Phepson
Himbleton
Earls Common
Huddington
Stock Wood
Cladswell
Cookhill
New End
Great Alne
Little Alne
Aston Cantlow
Mary Arden's Farm
Snitterfield Bushes
Bearley
Snitterfield
King's Coughton
Kinwarton Dovecote
Alcester
Arrow
Haselor
Wilmcote
Hampton Lucy
Alveston
Charlecote Park
Inkberrow
Dormston
Grafton Flyford
Broughton Hackett
Abbots Morton
Kington
Weethley
Ragley Hall
Exhall
Temple Grafton
Billesley
Shottery
Anne Hathaway's Cottage
Tiddington
Stratford-upon-Avon
Flyford Flavell
Goom's Hill
Wood Bevington
Rous Lench
Wixford
Ardens Grafton
Broom
Dunnington
Bidford-on-Avon
Binton
Luddington
Welford-on-Avon
Clifford Chambers
72
Loxley
Upton Snodsbury
North Piddle
Abberton
White Ladies Aston
Naunton Beauchamp
Church Lench
Bishampton
Peopleton
Salford Priors
Atherstone on Stour
Preston on Stour
Abbot's Salford
Marlcliff
Dorsington
Throckmorton
Pinvin
Drakes Broughton
Harvington
Cleeve Prior
Long Marston
Wimpstone
Alderminster
Ettington
Norton
Lenchwick
North Littleton
Lower Quinton
Crimscote
Wyre Piddle
Lower Moor
Pebworth
Offenham
Middle Littleton
Tithe Barn
South Littleton
Broad Marston
Newbold on Stour
Halford
Pershore
Fladbury
Chadbury
Charlton
Wick
Cropthorne
Armscote
Pensham
Evesham
Aldington
Bretforton
Honeybourne
Birlingham
Little Comberton
Bengeworth
Hampton
The Fleece Inn
Mickleton
Kiftsgate Court
Hidcote Bartrim
Ilmington
Blackwell
Badsey
Hidcote Manor Garden
Great Comberton
Bricklehampton
Vale of Evesham
Aston-sub-Edge
Hidcote Boyce
Darlingscott
Eckington
Elmley Castle
Wickhamford
Weston sub-Edge
Ebrington
Shipston
Willersey
Charingworth
Bredon Hill
Bredon's Norton
Hinton on the Green
Saintbury
Ashton under Hill
Childswickham
Chipping Campden
Stretton on Fosse
Tidmington
Lower Westmancote
Overbury
Grafton
Aston Somerville
Sedgeberrow
Cotswold Way
Broad Campden
Paxford
Broadway
Conderton
Kemerton
Beckford
Wormington
Draycott
Todenham
Bredon
The Priory
Kinsham
Silk Mill
Dumbleton
Rectory
Buckland
Broadway Tower
Blockley
Aston Magna
Great Washbourne
Laverton
Stanton
Great Wolford
Alderton
Snowshill
Snowshill Manor
Cotswold Lavender
Batsford
Cotswold Falconry Centre
Toddington
55
56
Stanway
Moreton-in-Marsh
Alstone
Oxenton
Bourton-on-the-Hill
Sezincote
Bourton Downs
Stanley Pontlarge
Gloucestershire Warwickshire Railway
Didbrook
Hailes Abbey
Cutsdean
Woolstone
Greet
Gretton
Chastleton
Gotherington
LANGLEY HILL
NOTTINGHAM HILL
Ford
Longborough
Farmcote
Condicote
Evenlode
Bishop's Cleeve
Donnington
Broadwell
Adlestrop
Woodmancote
Winchcombe
Temple Guiting
Sudeley
Upper Swell
Lower Swell
Stow-on-the-Wold
Kineton
Oddington
Daylesford
Southam
Belas Knap
Barton
Maugersbury
Swindon
Cheltenham
Guiting Power
Charlton
Kingham
R Isbourne
R Avon
R Arrow
R Stour

Dorridge
Common
Berkswell
Lunt Roman Fort
Brandon Marsh
Wolston
Church Lawford
Ryton-on-Dunsmore
Coventry
Baginton
Chadwick End
A4141
A4177
A452
A429
Crackley
The Spring
Kenilworth Castle
Honiley
Baddesley Clinton
Hockley Heath
Kingswood
Lapworth
Baddesley Clinton
Grand Union Canal
Wroxall
Kenilworth
Beausale
B4103
A46
Stoneleigh
Stoneleigh
Stareton
National Agricultural Centre
Ryton Wood
Princethorpe
Stretton-on-Dunsmore
Bourton on Dunsmore
Thurlaston
Draycote
A4071
A45
B4453
B4429
M40
Rowington
High Cross
Lowsonford
A3400
Shrewley
Haseley
Hatton
Leek Wootton
Ashow
Old Milverton
Weston under Wetherley
Wappenbury
Frankton
Eathorpe
Marton
Birdingbury
Hunningham
Draycote Water
Leamington Hastings
Hill
A426
A423
A445
B4113
B4115
A452
ROYAL LEAMINGTON SPA
Warwick
Milverton
Preston Bagot
Pinley Green
Hatton Country World
Hampton Magna
Lye Green
Newbold Comyn
Offchurch
Long Itchington
Broadwell
Preston Green
Claverdon
A4189
A425
A46
A452
B4087
Radford Semele
Whitnash
Grand Union Canal
Warwickshire Exhibition Centre
Bascote
Stockton
Langley
Wolverton
Norton Lindsey
Stratford-upon-Avon Canal
Edstone
Little Alne
Aston Cantlow
Arden's Farm
Snitterfield Bushes
Bearley
Snitterfield
Sherbourne
Barford
Oakley Wood
Wasperton
Bishop's Tachbrook
Ufton
Ufton Fields
Harbury
Southam
NAPTON HILL
Napton on the Hill
Chapel Green
R Itchen
Wilmcote
Billesley
Shottery
Anne Hathaway's Cottage
Hampton Lucy
Alveston
Charlecote Park
Charlecote
Newbold Pacey
Ashorne
Moreton Morrell
Lighthorne
Chesterton
Chesterton Green
Bishop's Itchington
Ladbroke
Priors Marston
Priors Hardwick
Tiddington
Wellesbourne
Lighthorne Heath
British Motor Museum
Knightcote
Wormleighton
Stratford-upon-Avon
Butterfly Farm
Binton
Luddington
Clifford Chambers
Loxley
Compton Verney
Gaydon
Northend
Chadshunt
Burton Dassett
Magpie Hill
Fenny Compton
Wharf
Lower Boddington
Atherstone on Stour
Preston on Stour
Combrook
Kineton
Little Kineton
Avon Dassett
Claydon
Long Marston
Lower Quinton
Wimpstone
Alderminster
Ettington
Butlers Marston
Pillerton Hersey
Edgehill 1642
Radway
Edgehill
Warmington
Farnborough
Farnborough Hall
Crimscote
Pillerton Priors
Ratley
The National Herb Centre
Mollington
Newbold on Stour
Halford
Fullready
Oxhill
Shotteswell
Cropredy
Armscote
Whatcote
Idlicote
Middle Tysoe
Upton House & Gardens
Hornton
Great Bourton
Kiftsgate Court
Hidcote Bartrim
Hidcote Manor Garden
Blackwell
Ilmington
Tredington
Upper Tysoe
Horley
Hanwell
Little Bourton
Honington
Shenington
Drayton
Hidcote Boyce
Darlingscott
Shipston-on-Stour
Balscote
Winderton
Wroxton
Ebrington
Charingworth
Upper Brailes
Lower Brailes
Shutford
Epwell
North Newington
Chipping Campden
Stretton on Fosse
Willington
Tidmington
Burmington
Swalcliffe
Tadmarton
Broughton
Bodicote
Banbury
Broad Campden
Paxford
Sutton-under-Brailes
Sibford Gower
Sibford Ferris
Cherington
Stourton
Todenham
Draycott
Blockley
Aston Magna
Little Wolford
Cotswold Distillery
Bloxham
Adderbury
Milton
Batsford
Great Wolford
Whichford
Milcombe
Waterfowl Sanctuary & Children's Farm
Hook Norton
Barford St John
South Newington
Cotswold Falconry Centre
Long Compton
Hook Norton Brewery
Wigginton
Barford St Michael
Moreton-in-Marsh
Sezincote
Barton-on-the-Heath
Swerford
Hempton
Little Rollright
Rollright Stones
Great Rollright
Chastleton
Little Compton
Great Tew
Over Worton
Deddington
Longborough
Evenlode
Salford
Over Norton
Donnington
Chastleton House
Broadwell
Adlestone
Little Tew
Ledwell
Duns Tew
Middle Aston
Upper Swell
Stow-on-the-Wold
Cornwell
Chipping Norton
Heythrop
Sandford St Martin
Middle Barton
Steeple Aston
Lower Swell
Church Enstone
Westcote Barton
Churchill
Enstone
Kingham
Upper
A44
A424
A429
A436
A361
A4260
B4035
B4450
B4026
B4022
B4030
B4031
B4068
0 1 2 3 4 miles
0 1 2 3 4 5 kilometres

86
71
56

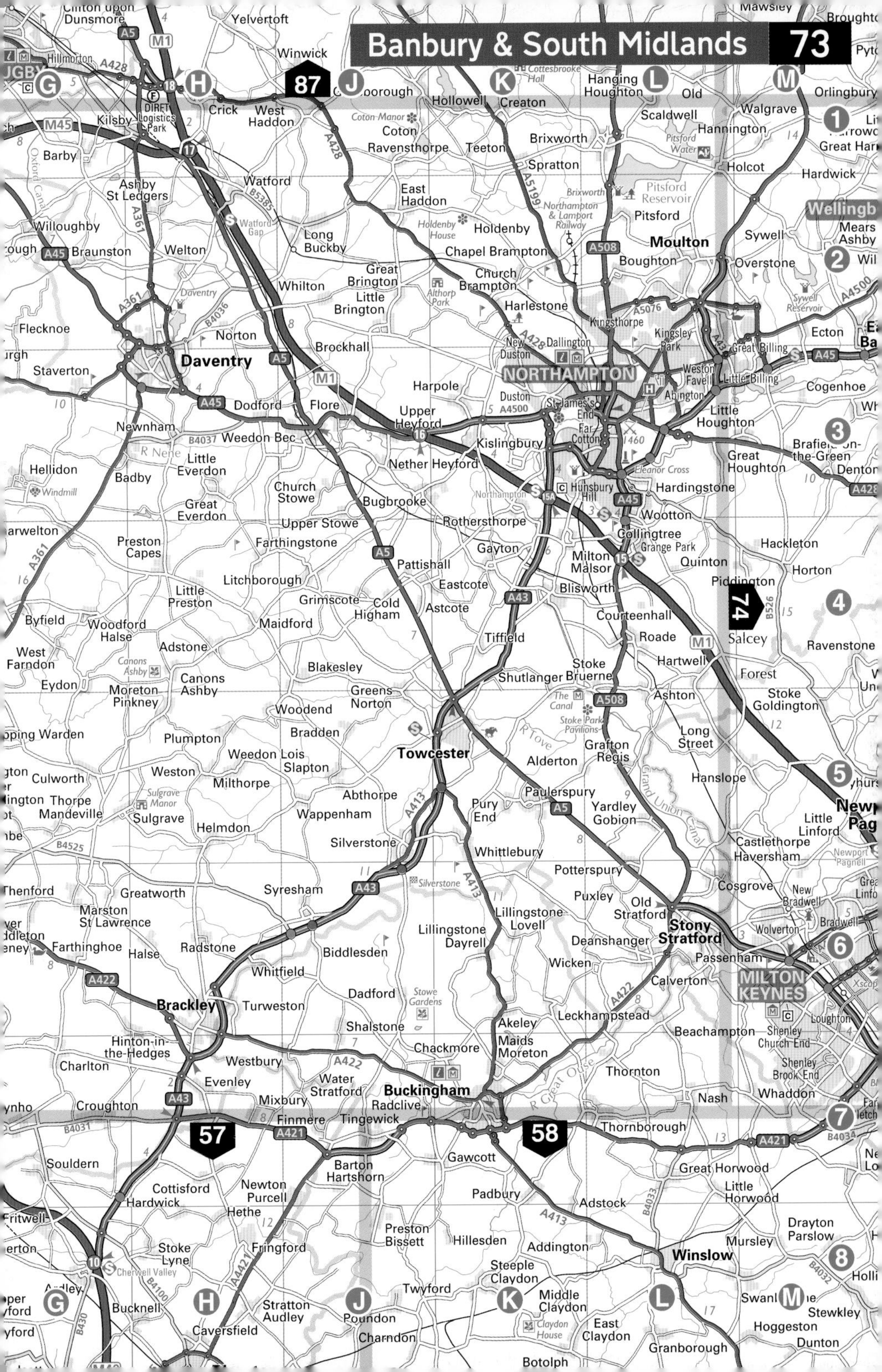
Clifton upon Dunsmore
Yelvertoft
Winwick
Hillmorton
RUGBY
Kilsby
DIRFT Logistics Park
Crick
West Haddon
87
Guilsborough
Hollowell
Creaton
Cottesbrooke Hall
Hanging Houghton
Old
Orlingbury
Walgrave
Scaldwell
Hannington
Coton Manor
Coton
Ravensthorpe
Teeton
Brixworth
Pitsford Water
Great Harrowden
Barby
Oxford Canal
Watford
Spratton
Holcot
Hardwick
Ashby St Ledgers
East Haddon
Brixworth
Pitsford Reservoir
Northampton & Lamport Railway
Wellingborough
Watford Gap
Holdenby House
Holdenby
Pitsford
Willoughby
Long Buckby
Moulton
Sywell
Mears Ashby
Braunston
Welton
Chapel Brampton
Boughton
Overstone
Great Brington
Church Brampton
Whilton
Little Brington
Althorp Park
Daventry
Harlestone
Kingsthorpe
Sywell Reservoir
Flecknoe
Norton
Kingsley Park
Ecton
Earls Barton
Brockhall
New Duston
Dallington
Great Billing
Daventry
Staverton
NORTHAMPTON
Weston Favell
Little Billing
Harpole
Abington
Cogenhoe
Newnham
Dodford
Flore
Upper Heyford
Duston
St James's End
Little Houghton
Far Cotton
Whiston
Weedon Bec
Kislingbury
R Nene
Little Everdon
Brafield-on-the-Green
Hellidon
Badby
Nether Heyford
Great Houghton
Eleanor Cross
Denton
Windmill
Church Stowe
Northampton
Hunsbury Hill
Hardingstone
Great Everdon
Bugbrooke
Wootton
Catesby
Upper Stowe
Rothersthorpe
Collingtree
Grange Park
Hackleton
Charwelton
Preston Capes
Farthingstone
Gayton
Quinton
Horton
Pattishall
Milton Malsor
Piddington
Little Preston
Litchborough
Eastcote
Blisworth
74
Salcey
Grimscote
Cold Higham
Astcote
Courteenhall
Byfield
Woodford Halse
Maidford
Tiffield
Roade
Ravenstone
West Farndon
Adstone
Canons Ashby
Hartwell
Forest
Blakesley
Stoke Bruerne
Shutlanger
Eydon
Moreton Pinkney
Canons Ashby
Greens Norton
The Canal
Ashton
Stoke Goldington
Woodend
Stoke Park Pavilions
Chipping Warden
Plumpton
Bradden
Towcester
R Tove
Long Street
Weedon Lois
Slapton
Grafton Regis
Alderton
Culworth
Weston
Milthorpe
Hanslope
Thorpe Mandeville
Sulgrave Manor
Sulgrave
Abthorpe
Paulerspury
Pury End
Yardley Gobion
Grand Union Canal
Newport Pagnell
Little Linford
Helmdon
Wappenham
Silverstone
Whittlebury
Castlethorpe
Haversham
Thenford
Greatworth
Syresham
Silverstone
Potterspury
Cosgrove
New Bradwell
Marston St Lawrence
Puxley
Old Stratford
Lillingstone Lovell
Stony Stratford
Wolverton
Bradwell
Farthinghoe
Halse
Radstone
Biddlesden
Lillingstone Dayrell
Deanshanger
Passenham
Whitfield
Wicken
Calverton
MILTON KEYNES
Brackley
Turweston
Dadford
Stowe Gardens
Leckhampstead
Akeley
Shalstone
Hinton-in-the-Hedges
Maids Moreton
Beachampton
Shenley Church End
Loughton
Chackmore
Westbury
Charlton
Evenley
Water Stratford
Thornton
Shenley Brook End
Buckingham
Mixbury
Croughton
Radclive
R Great Ouse
Nash
Whaddon
Finmere
Tingewick
57
58
Thornborough
Gawcott
Barton Hartshorn
Souldern
Great Horwood
Cottisford
Newton Purcell
Hardwick
Padbury
Little Horwood
Adstock
Hethe
Fritwell
Preston Bissett
Drayton Parslow
Hillesden
Mursley
Fringford
Addington
Stoke Lyne
Winslow
Steeple Claydon
Cherwell Valley
Middle Claydon
Twyford
Swanbourne
Stewkley
Bucknell
Stratton Audley
Poundon
Claydon House
East Claydon
Hoggeston
Caversfield
Charndon
Dunton
Granborough
Botolph Claydon

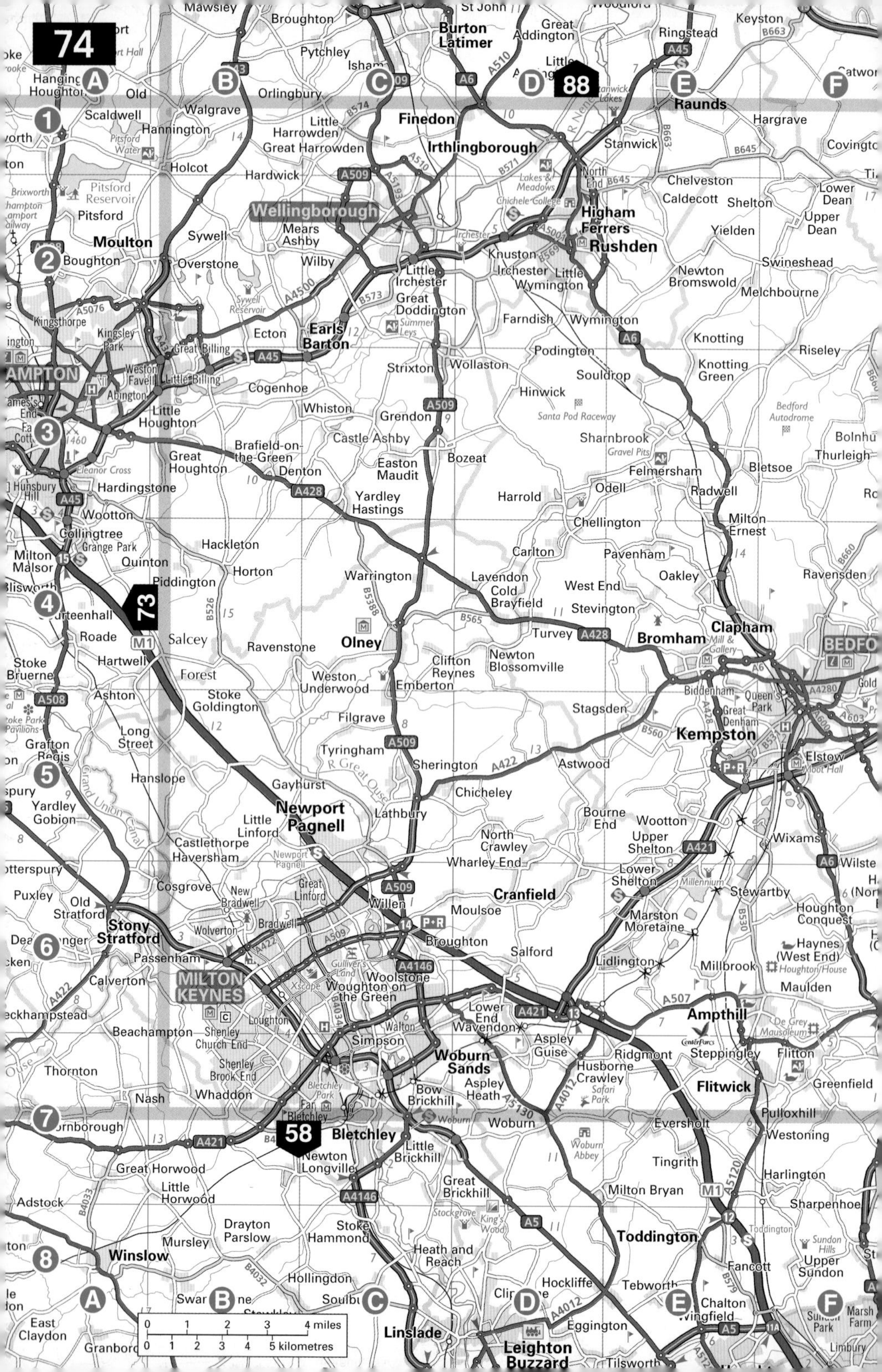
Mawsley
Broughton
Burton Latimer
St John
Great Addington
Woodford
Ringstead
Keyston
Hanging Houghton
Old
Orlingbury
Pytchley
Isham
Little Addington
Raunds
Scaldwell
Walgrave
Hannington
Little Harrowden
Great Harrowden
Finedon
Irthlingborough
Stanwick
Hargrave
Covington
Pitsford Water
Holcot
Hardwick
Chelveston
Caldecott
Shelton
Lower Dean
Upper Dean
Pitsford Reservoir
Brixworth
Pitsford
Wellingborough
Mears Ashby
Sywell
Lakes & Meadows
Chichele College
Higham Ferrers
Rushden
Yielden
Moulton
Boughton
Overstone
Wilby
Little Irchester
Irchester
Knuston
Little Wymington
Newton Bromswold
Swineshead
Melchbourne
Kingsthorpe
Kingsley Park
Sywell Reservoir
Great Doddington
Summer Leys
Farndish
Wymington
Knotting
Riseley
Knotting Green
Ecton
Earls Barton
Great Billing
Weston Favell
Little Billing
Abington
NORTHAMPTON
Strixton
Wollaston
Podington
Souldrop
Cogenhoe
Whiston
Grendon
Hinwick
Santa Pod Raceway
Bedford Autodrome
Little Houghton
Castle Ashby
Sharnbrook
Gravel Pits
Bolnhurst
Thurleigh
Great Houghton
Brafield-on-the-Green
Denton
Easton Maudit
Bozeat
Felmersham
Bletsoe
Eleanor Cross
Hunsbury Hill
Hardingstone
Yardley Hastings
Harrold
Odell
Radwell
Wootton
Collingtree
Grange Park
Chellington
Milton Ernest
Hackleton
Carlton
Pavenham
Milton Malsor
Quinton
Horton
Warrington
Lavendon
Cold Brayfield
West End
Oakley
Ravensden
Blisworth
Piddington
Stevington
Courteenhall
Roade
Salcey
Ravenstone
Olney
Turvey
Bromham
Mill & Gallery
Clapham
BEDFORD
Stoke Bruerne
Hartwell
Forest
Clifton Reynes
Newton Blossomville
Weston Underwood
Emberton
Ashton
Stoke Goldington
Biddenham
Queen's Park
Great Denham
Stagsden
Stoke Park Pavilions
Long Street
Filgrave
Kempston
Grafton Regis
Tyringham
Sherington
Astwood
Elstow
Moot Hall
R Great Ouse
Hanslope
Chicheley
Grand Union Canal
Yardley Gobion
Gayhurst
Little Linford
Newport Pagnell
Lathbury
Bourne End
Wootton
Upper Shelton
Wixams
Castlethorpe
Haversham
North Crawley
Wharley End
Lower Shelton
Wilstead
Potterspury
Cosgrove
New Bradwell
Great Linford
Willen
Cranfield
Stewartby
Millennium
Puxley
Old Stratford
Stony Stratford
Wolverton
Bradwell
Moulsoe
Marston Moretaine
Houghton Conquest
Deanshanger
Passenham
Broughton
Salford
Lidlington
Haynes (West End)
Houghton House
Millbrook
Calverton
MILTON KEYNES
Gulliver's Land
Xscape
Woolstone
Woughton on the Green
Lower End
Wavendon
Maulden
Leckhampstead
Beachampton
Shenley Church End
Loughton
Walton
Simpson
Aspley Guise
Ampthill
De Grey Mausoleum
Center Parcs
Steppingley
Flitton
Ridgmont
Woburn Sands
Husborne Crawley
Safari Park
Thornton
Shenley Brook End
Bletchley Park
Bow Brickhill
Aspley Heath
Flitwick
Greenfield
Nash
Whaddon
Fenny Stratford
Bletchley
Woburn
Eversholt
Pulloxhill
Thornborough
Little Brickhill
Woburn Abbey
Westoning
Newton Longville
Tingrith
Great Horwood
Great Brickhill
Harlington
Little Horwood
Milton Bryan
Adstock
Stockgrove
King's Wood
Sharpenhoe
Drayton Parslow
Stoke Hammond
Toddington
Mursley
Sundon Hills
Upper Sundon
Winslow
Heath and Reach
Fancott
Hollingdon
Hockliffe
Tebworth
Swanbourne
Soulbury
Clipstone
Chalton
Wingfield
Sundon Park
Marsh Farm
East Claydon
Linslade
Eggington
Leighton Buzzard
Granborough
Tilsworth
Limbury
0 1 2 3 4 miles
0 1 2 3 4 5 kilometres
A B C D E F
1 2 3 4 5 6 7 8
88 73 58
M1 A5 A6 A43 A45 A421 A422 A428 A4146 A509 A5193 A510 A508 A4500 A5076 A5130 A4012 A507 A603 A600 A4280 A5120 A5001 A509
B574 B571 B645 B663 B573 B526 B5388 B565 B560 B531 B530 B4034 B4033 B4032 B579 B660

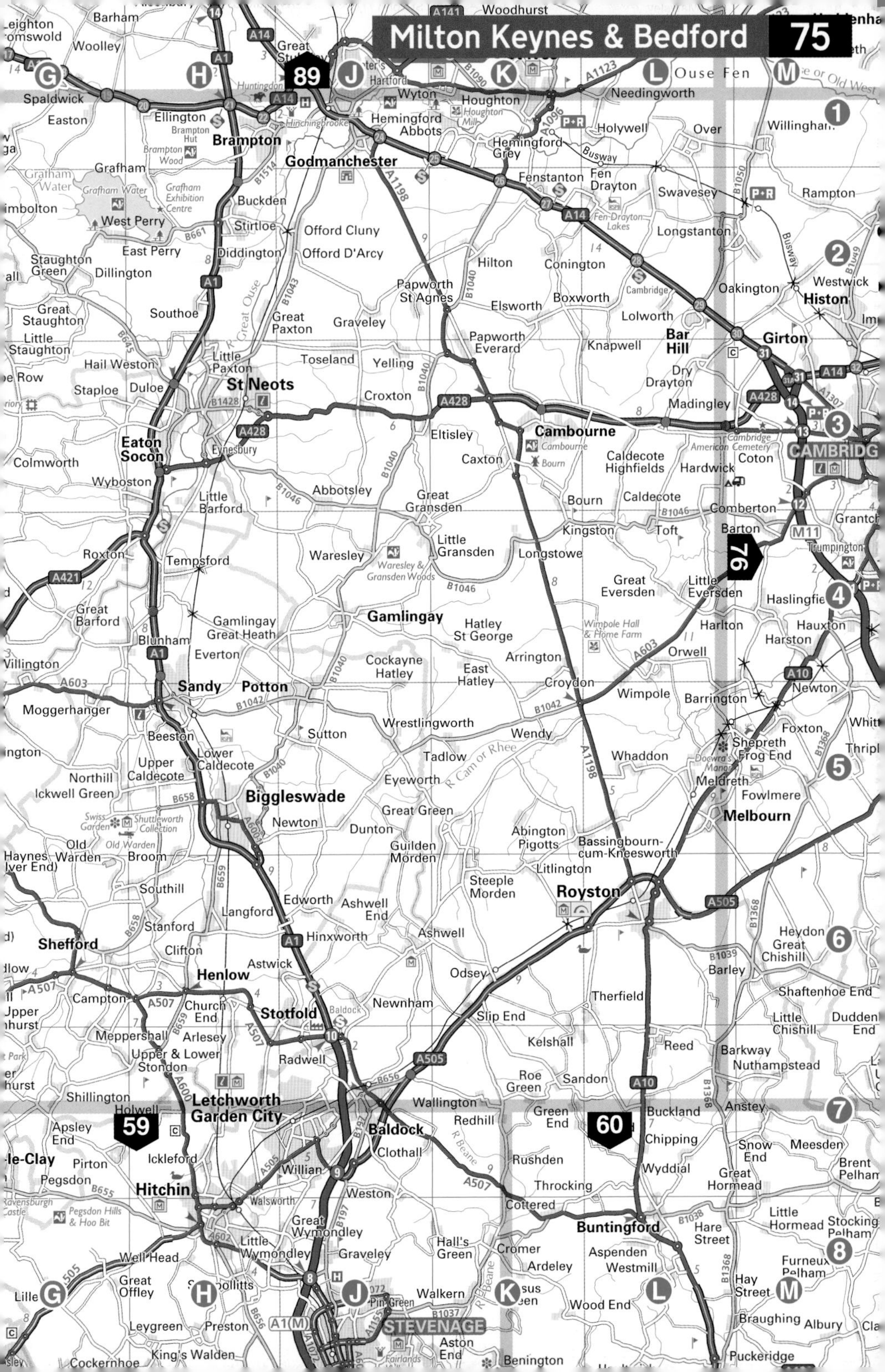
Leighton
Bromswold
Barham
Woolley
Spaldwick
Easton
Ellington
Brampton
Brampton Hut
Brampton Wood
Huntingdon
Hinchingbrooke
Great Stukeley
Hartford
Wyton
Houghton
Houghton Mill
Hemingford Abbots
Hemingford Grey
Godmanchester
Woodhurst
Ouse Fen
Needingworth
Holywell
Over
Willingham
Busway
Fenstanton
Fen Drayton
Fen Drayton Lakes
Swavesey
Rampton
Longstanton
Grafham
Grafham Water
Grafham Exhibition Centre
Kimbolton
West Perry
East Perry
Buckden
Stirtloe
Diddington
Offord Cluny
Offord D'Arcy
Staughton Green
Dillington
Hilton
Conington
Westwick
Histon
Oakington
Cambridge
Papworth St Agnes
Elsworth
Boxworth
Lolworth
Great Staughton
Little Staughton
Southoe
Great Paxton
Graveley
Papworth Everard
Knapwell
Bar Hill
Girton
Dry Drayton
Madingley
Hail Weston
Little Paxton
Toseland
Yelling
Staploe
Duloe
St Neots
Croxton
Eltisley
Cambourne
Eaton Socon
Eynesbury
Colmworth
Wyboston
Caxton
Bourn
Caldecote Highfields
Hardwick
Coton
American Cemetery
CAMBRIDGE
Little Barford
Abbotsley
Great Gransden
Caldecote
Comberton
Barton
Grantchester
Trumpington
Kingston
Toft
Roxton
Tempsford
Waresley
Waresley & Gransden Woods
Little Gransden
Longstowe
Great Eversden
Little Eversden
Haslingfield
Great Barford
Gamlingay Great Heath
Gamlingay
Hatley St George
Wimpole Hall & Home Farm
Harlton
Hauxton
Harston
Blunham
Everton
Cockayne Hatley
East Hatley
Arrington
Orwell
Willington
Sandy
Potton
Croydon
Wimpole
Barrington
Newton
Moggerhanger
Wrestlingworth
Wendy
Foxton
Shepreth
Frog End
Beeston
Sutton
Tadlow
R Cam or Rhee
Whaddon
Docwra's Manor
Lower Caldecote
Upper Caldecote
Northill
Ickwell Green
Eyeworth
Meldreth
Fowlmere
Biggleswade
Melbourn
Swiss Garden
Shuttleworth Collection
Old Warden
Newton
Dunton
Great Green
Abington Pigotts
Bassingbourn-cum-Kneesworth
Haynes
Broom
Guilden Morden
Litlington
Southill
Steeple Morden
Royston
Edworth
Ashwell End
Langford
Stanford
Shefford
Hinxworth
Ashwell
Heydon
Great Chishill
Clifton
Henlow
Astwick
Odsey
Barley
Campton
Church End
Stotfold
Baldock
Newnham
Slip End
Shaftenhoe End
Little Chishill
Therfield
Meppershall
Arlesey
Radwell
Kelshall
Reed
Barkway
Nuthampstead
Upper & Lower Stondon
Roe Green
Sandon
Shillington
Letchworth Garden City
Wallington
Buckland
Anstey
Holwell
Green End
Redhill
Chipping
Meesden
Apsley End
Baldock
Clothall
Snow End
Pirton
Ickleford
Willian
Rushden
Wyddial
Great Hormead
Brent Pelham
Pegsdon
Hitchin
Walsworth
Weston
Throcking
Cottered
Buntingford
Little Hormead
Stocking Pelham
Pegsdon Hills & Hoo Bit
Ravensburgh Castle
Great Wymondley
Little Wymondley
Hall's Green
Cromer
Aspenden
Hare Street
Graveley
Ardeley
Westmill
Furneux Pelham
Well Head
Great Offley
Walkern
Wood End
Hay Street
Lilley
Pin Green
Braughing
Albury
Leygreen
Preston
STEVENAGE
Aston End
Cockernhoe
King's Walden
Fairlands
Benington
Puckeridge
A1
A14
A1(M)
A428
A421
A603
A505
A507
A10
M11
A1198
A600
B1040
B1046
B1042
B1043
B1514
B661
B645
B1428
B658
B659
B656
B1037
B1038
B1039
B1368
B1050
B1049
A1096
A1123
A1307
A1155
A6001
A602
A141
1
2
3
4
5
6
7
8
89
76
59
60
G
H
J
K
L
M

A1123
Earith
Haddenham
Aldreth
Wilburton
Thetford
Stretham
Ouse Fen
Ouse or Old West River
90
Stream Mere
Soham
Isleham
Priory Church
A B C D E F
1 2 3 4 5 6 7 8
Needingworth
P+R
Holywell
Over
Willingham
A1123
Wicken Fen
Wicken
Fordham
Downfield
New River
Chittering
R Cam
Fen Drayton
Swavesey
Busway
B1050
Rampton
Denny Abbey & Farmland Museum
Chippenham
Snailwell
Fen Drayton Lakes
A14
Longstanton
Cottenham
Waterbeach
Burwell
B1102
B1103
Reach
Exning
Oakington
Westwick
Landbeach
Histon
Impington
Boxworth
Cambridge
Lolworth
Bar Hill
Girton
Milton
Anglesey Abbey
Lode
Swaffham Prior
A1304
Newmarket
Knapwell
Dry Drayton
Horningsea
Swaffham Bulbeck
National Stud
Stow-cum-Quy
Bottisham
A1303
Madingley
A428
A1307
A1309
Chesterton
Fen Ditton
Cheveley
Woodditton
B1061
Cambridge American Cemetery
CAMBRIDGE
Coton
Caldecote Highfields
Hardwick
Romsey
Cambridge
Teversham
Little Wilbraham
Stetchworth
A11
Six Mile Bottom
Dullingham
Ditton Green
Bourn
Caldecote
B1046
Comberton
Great Wilbraham
Westley Waterless
Kingston
Toft
Barton
M11
Grantchester
A1134
Cherry Hinton
Fulbourn
Burrough Green
75
Trumpington
Brinkley
Wandlebury
Great Eversden
Little Eversden
Haslingfield
A1301
Great Shelford
Weston Colville
West Wratting
Carlton
Weston Green
Wimpole Hall & Home Farm
Harlton
Hauxton
Harston
B1052
A603
Orwell
Little Shelford
Stapleford
R Granta
Balsham
Carlton Green
Little Thurlow
Fourwentways
A10
Newton
Babraham
Little Abington
West Wickham
Wimpole
Barrington
Sawston
Chilford Hall
A505
Great Abington
Hildersham
Streetly End
Withersfield
Foxton
Whittlesford
Duxford Chapel
Pampisford
Linton
Shepreth
Frog End
B1368
Thriplow
Horseheath
Whaddon
Docwra's Manor
Zoological Gardens
Mill Green
Meldreth
Fowlmere
Duxford
Hinxton
Bartlow
IWM Duxford
Melbourn
Shudy Camps
Hadstock
Ickleton
Great Chesterford
Bassingbourn-cum-Kneesworth
Steventon End
Castle Camps
Little Chesterford
Ashdon
Royston
Helions Bumpstead
Little Walden
B1184
Steeple Bumpstead
Heydon
Great Chishill
Elmdon
Strethall
Saffron Walden
B1039
Barley
Chrishall
Catmere End
Littlebury
B1383
Audley End House & Gardens
B1053
B1054
Therfield
Shaftenhoe End
Littlebury Green
Sewards End
Hempstead
Little Chishill
Duddenhoe End
Wendens Ambo
Audley End
B184
Radwinter
Spain's End
Reed
Barkway
Nuthampstead
Langley Upper Green
Tye Green
Great Sampford
Sandon
Arkesden
Wimbish Green
Howlett End
B1051
Newport
Buckland
Anstey
Debden
Little Sampford
Mill End
60
Chipping
Snow End
Meesden
Clavering
B1038
Wicken Bonhunt
Widdington
Wyddial
Great Hormead
Brent Pelham
Starlings Green
Prior's Hall Barn
Thaxted
Little Bardfield
Quendon
Bardfield End Green
Great Bardfield
Berden
Rickling Green
Buntingford
Little Hormead
Stocking Pelham
Hare Street
Henham
Holder's Green
Ugley
Monk Street
Sibley's Green
Westmill
Ugley Green
Furneux Pelham
Manuden
Broxted
B1057
Hay Street
Lindsell
Wood End
Elsenham
Great Easton
Bran End
Stansted Mountfitchet
Molehill Green
Farnham
Little Easton
Puckeridge
Burton End
0 1 2 3 4 miles
0 1 2 3 4 5 kilometres

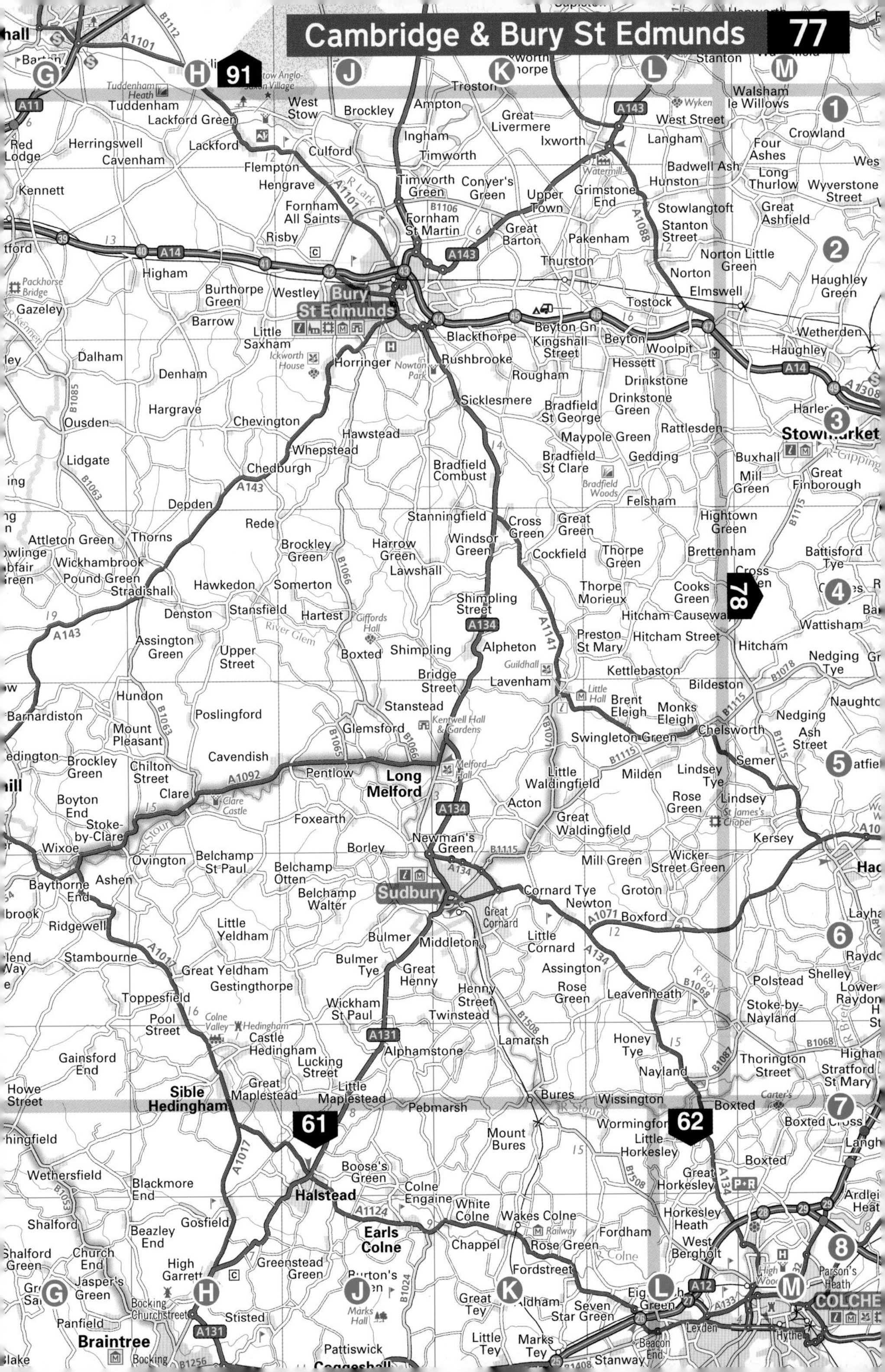
91
78
61
62
G
H
J
K
L
M
1
2
3
4
5
6
7
8
A11
A1101
B1112
A14
A143
A1088
A134
A1141
A1092
A131
A1017
A1071
A1124
A12
A133
B1106
B1085
B1063
B1066
B1065
B1115
B1078
B1071
B1068
B1087
B1508
B1024
B1053
B1256
B1408
A1308
Barton
Tuddenham Heath
West Stow Anglo-Saxon Village
Troston
Ampton
Great Livermere
Ixworth
Stanton
Walsham le Willows
Wyken
Tuddenham
Lackford Green
Lackford
West Stow
Brockley
Ingham
Timworth
Culford
West Street
Langham
Crowland
Four Ashes
Red Lodge
Herringswell
Cavenham
Flempton
Hengrave
Watermill
Badwell Ash
Hunston
Long Thurlow
Wyverstone Street
Kennett
R Lark
Timworth Green
Conyer's Green
Upper Town
Grimstone End
Stowlangtoft
Great Ashfield
Fornham All Saints
Fornham St Martin
Great Barton
Pakenham
Stanton Street
Risby
Norton Little Green
Higham
Packhorse Bridge
Burthorpe Green
Westley
Bury St Edmunds
Thurston
Norton
Haughley Green
Elmswell
Gazeley
Barrow
Tostock
Little Saxham
Blackthorpe
Beyton Gn
Kingshall Street
Beyton
Wetherden
Woolpit
Haughley
Ickworth House
Horringer
Nowton Park
Rushbrooke
Hessett
Dalham
Denham
Rougham
Drinkstone
Ousden
Hargrave
Chevington
Sicklesmere
Bradfield St George
Drinkstone Green
Harleston
Stowmarket
Hawstead
Rattlesden
Maypole Green
Whepstead
Lidgate
Bradfield Combust
Bradfield St Clare
Gedding
Buxhall
Chedburgh
Bradfield Woods
Mill Green
Great Finborough
Felsham
Depden
Stanningfield
Cross Green
Great Green
Hightown Green
Rede
Attleton Green
Thorns
Brockley Green
Harrow Green
Windsor Green
Cockfield
Thorpe Green
Brettenham
Battisford Tye
Wickhambrook
Pound Green
Lawshall
Cross Green
Stradishall
Hawkedon
Somerton
Thorpe Morieux
Cooks Green
Shimpling Street
Denston
Stansfield
Hartest
Giffords Hall
Hitcham Causeway
Wattisham
River Glem
Preston St Mary
Hitcham Street
Assington Green
Alpheton
Upper Street
Boxted
Shimpling
Hitcham
Nedging Tye
Guildhall
Bridge Street
Lavenham
Kettlebaston
Bildeston
Hundon
Little Hall
Brent Eleigh
Monks Eleigh
Naughton
Barnardiston
Poslingford
Stanstead
Nedging
Kentwell Hall & Gardens
Mount Pleasant
Glemsford
Swingleton Green
Chelsworth
Ash Street
Kedington
Cavendish
Semer
Brockley Green
Chilton Street
Pentlow
Long Melford
Melford Hall
Little Waldingfield
Milden
Lindsey Tye
Clare
Boyton End
Clare Castle
Acton
Rose Green
Lindsey
Stoke-by-Clare
Foxearth
Great Waldingfield
St James's Chapel
Wixoe
R Stour
Kersey
Newman's Green
Borley
Ovington
Belchamp St Paul
Mill Green
Wicker Street Green
Baythorne End
Ashen
Belchamp Otten
Sudbury
Cornard Tye
Groton
Belchamp Walter
Newton
Great Cornard
Boxford
Ridgewell
Little Yeldham
Bulmer
Middleton
Little Cornard
Stambourne
Bulmer Tye
Assington
Great Yeldham
Great Henny
Shelley
Gestingthorpe
Henny Street
Rose Green
Leavenheath
Polstead
R Box
Toppesfield
Wickham St Paul
Twinstead
Stoke-by-Nayland
Pool Street
Colne Valley
Hedingham
Castle Hedingham
Lamarsh
Honey Tye
Alphamstone
Gainsford End
Lucking Street
Nayland
Thorington Street
Stratford St Mary
Howe Street
Sible Hedingham
Great Maplestead
Little Maplestead
Pebmarsh
Bures
Wissington
Boxted
Carter's
Boxted Cross
Wormingford
Mount Bures
Little Horkesley
Wethersfield
Boose's Green
Great Horkesley
Boxted
Blackmore End
Halstead
Colne Engaine
White Colne
Wakes Colne
Colne Valley Railway
Horkesley Heath
Fordham
Shalford
Gosfield
Beazley End
Earls Colne
Chappel
Rose Green
West Bergholt
Shalford Green
Church End
Greenstead Green
Fordstreet
R Colne
High Woods
High Garrett
Burton's Green
Parson's Heath
Jasper's Green
Marks Hall
Great Tey
Aldham
Seven Star Green
Eight Ash Green
Bocking Churchstreet
Stisted
Lexden
Panfield
Hythe
Braintree
Little Tey
Marks Tey
Beacon End
Bocking
Pattiswick
Coggeshall
Stanway
Colchester

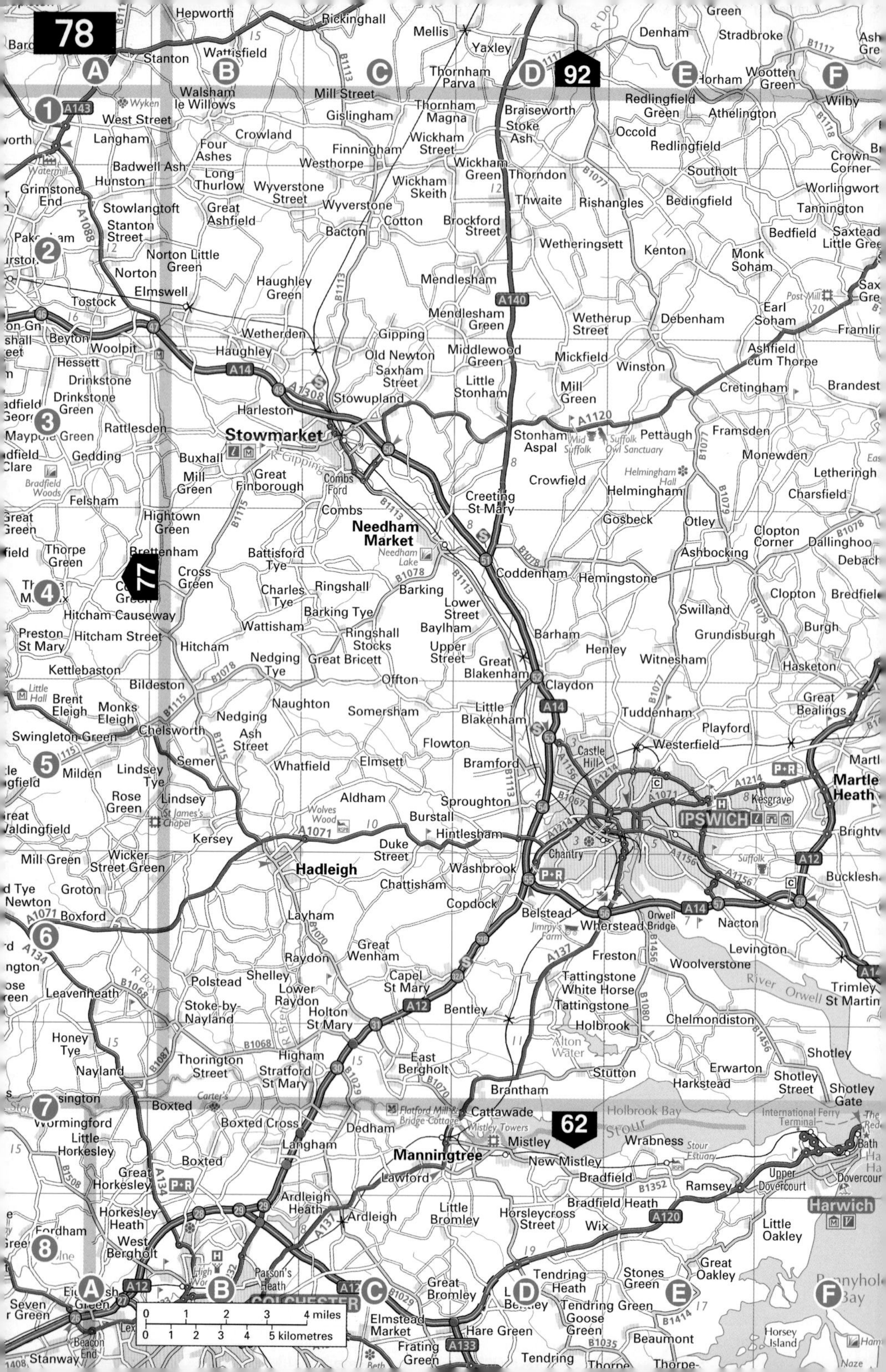
Hepworth
Rickinghall
Mellis
Yaxley
Denham
Stradbroke
Green
Stanton
Wattisfield
Thornham Parva
92
Horham
Wootten Green
Walsham le Willows
Wyken
Mill Street
Thornham Magna
Braiseworth
Redlingfield Green
Athelington
Wilby
West Street
Gislingham
Stoke Ash
Occold
Redlingfield
Langham
Crowland
Four Ashes
Wickham Street
Finningham
Badwell Ash
Westhorpe
Wickham Green
Thorndon
Southolt
Crown Corner
Watermill
Hunston
Long Thurlow
Wyverstone Street
Wickham Skeith
Grimstone End
Stowlangtoft
Great Ashfield
Wyverstone
Thwaite
Rishangles
Bedingfield
Worlingworth
Tannington
Stanton Street
Cotton
Brockford Street
Bacton
Bedfield
Saxtead Little Green
Wetheringsett
Kenton
Monk Soham
Norton Little Green
Norton
Haughley Green
Mendlesham
Elmswell
Post Mill
Saxtead Green
Tostock
Mendlesham Green
Wetherup Street
Debenham
Earl Soham
Beyton
Wetherden
Gipping
Framlingham
Woolpit
Haughley
Old Newton
Middlewood Green
Mickfield
Ashfield cum Thorpe
Hessett
Saxham Street
Winston
Drinkstone
Little Stonham
Mill Green
Cretingham
Brandeston
Drinkstone Green
Stowupland
Harleston
Rattlesden
Stowmarket
Stonham Aspal
Mid Suffolk
Suffolk Owl Sanctuary
Pettaugh
Framsden
Maypole Green
Gedding
Buxhall
R Gipping
Monewden
Bradfield Woods
Mill Green
Great Finborough
Combs Ford
Crowfield
Helmingham Hall
Helmingham
Letheringham
Felsham
Combs
Creeting St Mary
Charsfield
Hightown Green
Needham Market
Needham Lake
Gosbeck
Otley
Clopton Corner
Dallinghoo
Brettenham
Thorpe Green
Battisford Tye
Coddenham
Ashbocking
Debach
77
Cross Green
Charles Tye
Ringshall
Barking
Hemingstone
Clopton
Bredfield
Hitcham Causeway
Lower Street
Swilland
Barking Tye
Baylham
Preston St Mary
Hitcham Street
Wattisham
Ringshall Stocks
Barham
Grundisburgh
Burgh
Hitcham
Nedging Tye
Great Bricett
Upper Street
Great Blakenham
Henley
Witnesham
Kettlebaston
Offton
Claydon
Hasketon
Little Hall
Bildeston
Brent Eleigh
Monks Eleigh
Naughton
Somersham
Little Blakenham
Tuddenham
Great Bealings
Nedging
Chelsworth
Ash Street
Swingleton Green
Flowton
Playford
Westerfield
Semer
Whatfield
Elmsett
Bramford
Castle Hill
Martlesham
Milden
Lindsey Tye
Rose Green
Lindsey
Aldham
Sproughton
Kesgrave
Martlesham Heath
St James's Chapel
Wolves Wood
Burstall
IPSWICH
Waldingfield
Kersey
Hintlesham
Brightwell
Mill Green
Wicker Street Green
Duke Street
Chantry
Hadleigh
Washbrook
Suffolk
Bucklesham
Groton
Chattisham
Newton
Boxford
Copdock
Belstead
Layham
Wherstead
Orwell Bridge
Nacton
Jimmy's Farm
Great Wenham
Freston
Levington
Raydon
Woolverstone
Polstead
Shelley
Capel St Mary
River Orwell
Leavenheath
Lower Raydon
Tattingstone White Horse
Trimley St Martin
Stoke-by-Nayland
Holton St Mary
Bentley
Tattingstone
Chelmondiston
Honey Tye
Holbrook
Alton Water
Thorington Street
Higham
East Bergholt
Shotley
Nayland
Stratford St Mary
Stutton
Erwarton
Harkstead
Shotley Street
Brantham
Shotley Gate
Bures
Boxted
Carter's
Cattawade
Flatford Mill & Bridge Cottage
Holbrook Bay
International Ferry Terminal
Wormingford
Boxted Cross
Mistley Towers
Mistley
62
Stour
Wrabness
Stour Estuary
Little Horkesley
Dedham
Langham
Manningtree
New Mistley
Bath
Boxted
Bradfield
Great Horkesley
Lawford
Ramsey
Upper Dovercourt
Dovercourt
Ardleigh Heath
Harwich
Horkesley Heath
Little Bromley
Horsleycross Street
Bradfield Heath
Wix
Little Oakley
Fordham
Ardleigh
West Bergholt
High Woods
Parson's Heath
COLCHESTER
Great Bromley
Tendring Heath
Stones Green
Great Oakley
Hamford Water
Eight Ash Green
Tendring Green
Seven Star Green
Elmstead Market
Little Bentley
Goose Green
Beacon End
Hare Green
Beaumont
Horsey Island
Stanway
Frating Green
Tendring
Thorpe-le-Soken
A
B
C
D
E
F
1
2
3
4
5
6
7
8
A143
A1088
A14
A1308
A140
A1120
A1071
A1214
A1156
A137
A12
A134
A120
A133
B1113
B1115
B1078
B1077
B1079
B1117
B1118
B1068
B1070
B1087
B1508
B1029
B1456
B1080
B1352
B1414
B1035
B1067
0 1 2 3 4 miles
0 1 2 3 4 5 kilometres

Cratfield
Huntingfield
Walpole
Blackheath
Blythburgh
Walberswick
Thorington
Bramfield
93
Laxfield
Heveningham
Ubbeston Green
Dunwich Forest
Suffolk Coast
Darsham
Westleton Heath
Dunwich
Sibton
Peasenhall
Yoxford
Westleton
Middleton
Minsmere
Dunwich Heath
Badingham
Middleton Moor
Bruisyard
Bruisyard Street
Theberton
Eastbridge
Cransford
Rendham
Kelsale
Leiston Abbey
Shawsgate
Carlton
Saxmundham
Swefling
Knodishall
North Green
Great Glemham
Benhall Street
Benhall Green
Sternfield
Leiston
Aldringham
Thorpe Ness
Stratford St Andrew
Friday Street
Friston
Knodishall Common
Thorpeness
Hacheston
Farnham
Snape
North Warren
Marlesford
Little Glemham
Snape Street
Snape Maltings
Aldeburgh
Blaxhall
Campsea Ash
Tunstall
Aldeburgh Bay
Rendlesham
River Alde
Ufford
Chillesford
Sudbourne
Eyke
Bromeswell
Butley
Castle
Orford
Orford Ness
Capel St Andrew
Sutton
Boyton
Orfordness-Havergate
Suffolk Heritage Coast
Shottisham
Hollesley
River Ore
North Weir Point
Hemley
Hollesley Bay
River Deben
Alderton
Bawdsey
Falkenham
Trimley St Mary
Old Felixstowe
Felixstowe
Landguard Fort
Landguard Point
Hook of Holland
A12
A144
A1120
A1094
A1152
A154
B1117
B1387
B1125
B1122
B1120
B1119
B1121
B1353
B1069
B1078
B1084
B1083
G
H
J
K
L
M
1
2
3
4
5
6
7
8

95
66
A
B
C
D
E
F
1
2
3
4
5
6
7
8
CARDIGAN
BAY
Mawddach Valley
Llanelltyd
Toll
Penmaenpool
A496
Barmouth
Barmouth Bridge
Barmouth Bay
Afon Mawddach
A493
Fairbourne Steam Railway
Fairbourne
SNOWDONIA
NATIONAL
PARK
621
Llwyngwril
Castell y Bere
Afon Dysynni
Llangelynin
Rhoslefain
Abergynolwyn
667
Llanegryn
Talyllyn Railway
633
TAREN HENDRE
Bryncrug
B4405
Dolgoch Falls
Aber Dysynni
Tywyn
Pennal
Dovey
Aberdovey
Aberdyfi
A493
Afon Dyfi (River Dovey)
Ynys-hir
Dyfi
Dyfi Furnace
A487
B4353
Cwm Clettwr
Tre Taliesin
Borth
Tal-y-bont
B4353
Ceredigion Heritage Coast
Llandre
Rhyd-y-pennau
Bont-goch Elerch
B4572
Bow Street
Salem
Clarach Bay
Cliff Railway & Camera Obscura
A4159
Penrhyn-coch
Pen-bont Rhydybeddau
Waunfawr
Capel-Dewi
Aberystwyth
P+R
Llanbadarn Fawr
Capel Bangor
Goginan
Rheidol power station
Capel Seion
Coed Penglanowen
A4120
Llanfarian
Llanfihangel-y-Creuddyn
Blaenplwyf
A485
Afon Ystwyth
Cnwch Coch
Llanilar
B4340
B4575
Penderi Cliffs
Ceredigion Heritage Coast
Llanddeiniol
B4576
Llanafan
Llangwyryfon
Lledrod
Cors Ian
Tynygraig
Llanrhystud
0 1 2 3 4 miles
0 1 2 3 4 5 kilometres

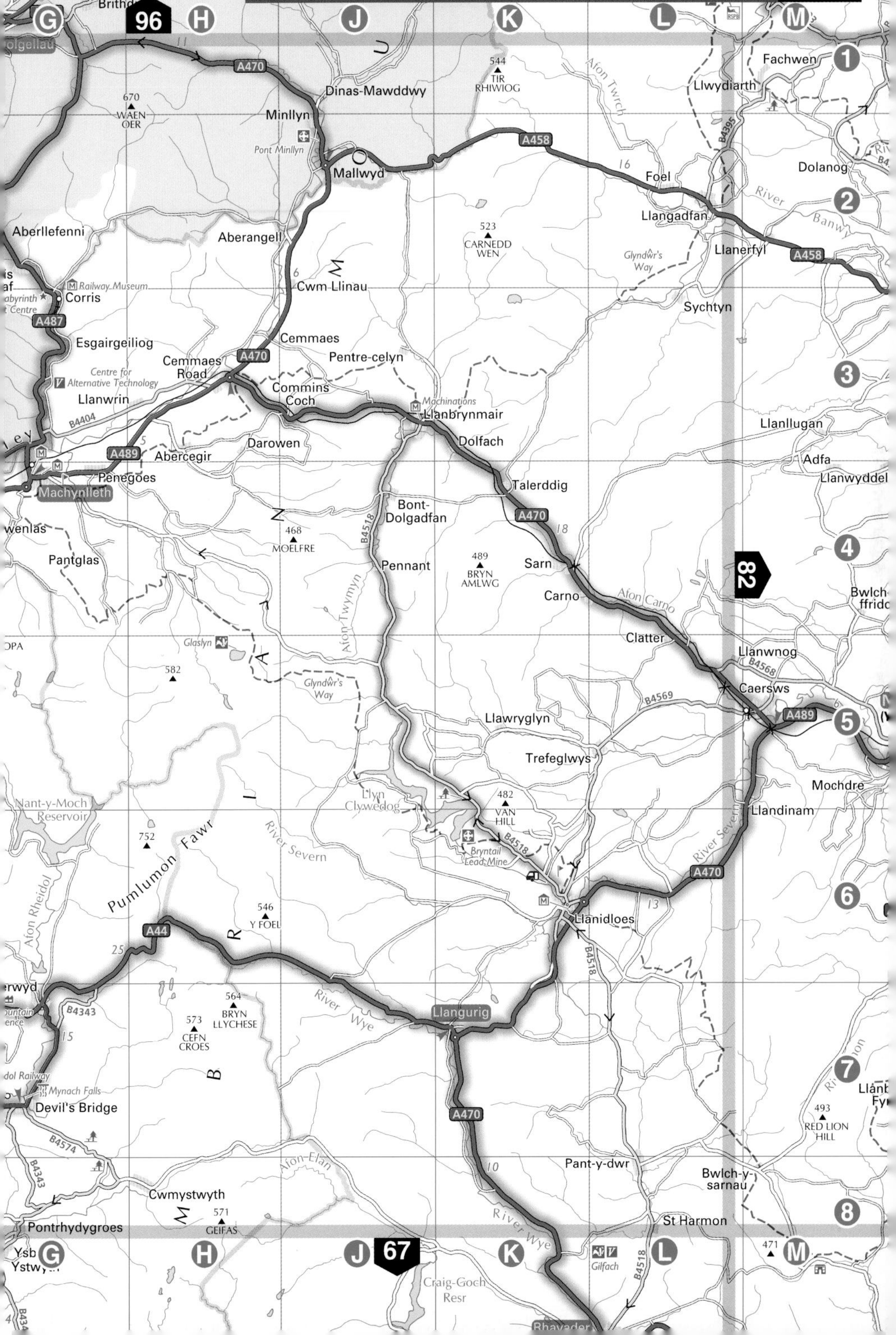
G
H
J
K
L
M
96
82
67
1
2
3
4
5
6
7
8
Brithdir
Dolgellau
A470
B4416
670
WAEN
OER
Dinas-Mawddwy
Minllyn
Pont Minllyn
Mallwyd
544
TIR
RHIWIOG
Afon Twrch
A458
Llwydiarth
Fachwen
Dolanog
Foel
Llangadfan
Llanerfyl
River Banwy
B4395
523
CARNEDD
WEN
Glyndŵr's Way
Sychtyn
Aberllefenni
Aberangell
Railway Museum
Corris
A487
Esgairgeiliog
Cwm Llinau
Cemmaes
Cemmaes Road
Pentre-celyn
Centre for Alternative Technology
Llanwrin
Commins Coch
Machinations
Llanbrynmair
Dolfach
B4404
Darowen
A489
Abercegir
Penegoes
Machynlleth
Talerddig
Bont-Dolgadfan
B4518
468
MOELFRE
Pantglas
Pennant
489
BRYN
AMLWG
Sarn
Carno
Afon Carno
Afon Twymyn
Llanllugan
Adfa
Llanwyddelan
Bwlch-y-ffridd
Glaslyn
582
Clatter
Llanwnog
B4568
Caersws
B4569
Llawryglyn
Trefeglwys
Nant-y-Moch Reservoir
Llyn Clywedog
482
VAN
HILL
Bryntail Lead Mine
752
Pumlumon Fawr
River Severn
Mochdre
Llandinam
Afon Rheidol
546
Y FOEL
Llanidloes
A44
B4343
564
BRYN
LLYCHESE
573
CEFN
CROES
River Wye
Llangurig
Mynach Falls
Devil's Bridge
B4574
Cwmystwyth
571
GEIFAS
Afon Elan
Pant-y-dwr
Bwlch-y-sarnau
493
RED LION
HILL
St Harmon
Pontrhydygroes
Gilfach
471
Craig-Goch Resr
Rhayader

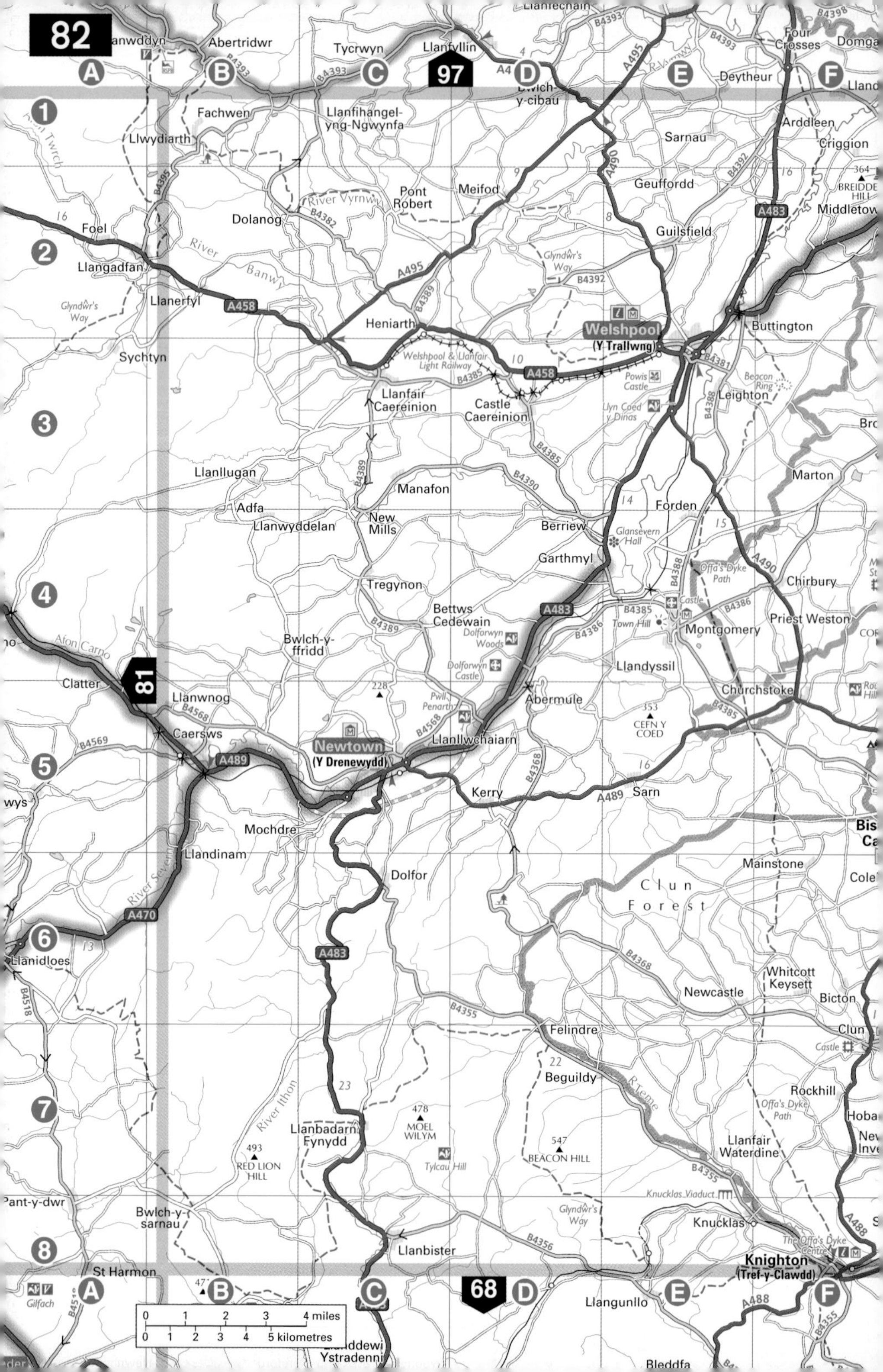
Llanfechain
B4398
Four Crosses
Domga
anwddyn
Abertridwr
Tycrwyn
Llanfyllin
97
B4393
A
B
C
D
E
F
B4393
R. Vyrnwy
Deytheur
Llandr
A495
Bwlch-y-cibau
Fachwen
Llanfihangel-yng-Ngwynfa
Arddleen
Criggion
Afon Twrch
Llwydiarth
Sarnau
B4395
A490
B4392
364
BREIDDEN HILL
Pont Robert
Meifod
Geufordd
Middletown
River Vyrnwy
Dolanog
B4382
A483
16
Foel
Guilsfield
River Banwy
Llangadfan
Glyndŵr's Way
A495
B4392
Llanerfyl
A458
B4389
Heniarth
Welshpool
(Y Trallwng)
Buttington
Sychtyn
Welshpool & Llanfair Light Railway
10
B4385
A458
B4381
Powis Castle
Beacon Ring
Llanfair Caereinion
Castle Caereinion
Llyn Coed y Dinas
Leighton
B4388
Bro
B4385
B4389
Llanllugan
B4390
Marton
Manafon
Adfa
14
Forden
Llanwyddelan
New Mills
Berriew
15
Glansevern Hall
Garthmyl
A490
B4388
Offa's Dyke Path
Tregynon
Chirbury
A483
B4385
Castle
B4386
Bettws Cedewain
Town Hill
Montgomery
Priest Weston
Afon Carno
B4389
Dolforwyn Woods
B4386
COR
Bwlch-y-ffridd
Llandyssil
Dolforwyn Castle
81
Clatter
228
Pwll Penarth
Churchstoke
Llanwnog
Abermule
B4385
B4568
353
CEFN Y COED
B4568
Caersws
Llanllwchaiarn
B4569
Newtown
(Y Drenewydd)
A489
B4368
16
Kerry
A489
Sarn
wys
Mochdre
Bis
Ca
Llandinam
River Severn
Mainstone
Dolfor
Cole
Clun Forest
A470
13
Llanidloes
A483
B4368
Whitcott Keysett
Newcastle
Bicton
B4518
B4355
Felindre
Clun
Castle
22
Beguildy
R. Teme
23
Rockhill
Offa's Dyke Path
River Ithon
478
MOEL WILYM
Hoba
Llanbadarn Fynydd
Llanfair Waterdine
Nev Inve
493
RED LION HILL
Tylcau Hill
547
BEACON HILL
B4355
Knucklas Viaduct
A488
Pant-y-dwr
Glyndŵr's Way
Bwlch-y-sarnau
Knucklas
The Offa's Dyke Centre
Llanbister
B4356
Knighton
(Tref-y-Clawdd)
St Harmon
471
68
Gilfach
Llangunllo
A488
B4518
0 1 2 3 4 miles
0 1 2 3 4 5 kilometres
B4355
Llanddewi Ystradenni
Bleddfa

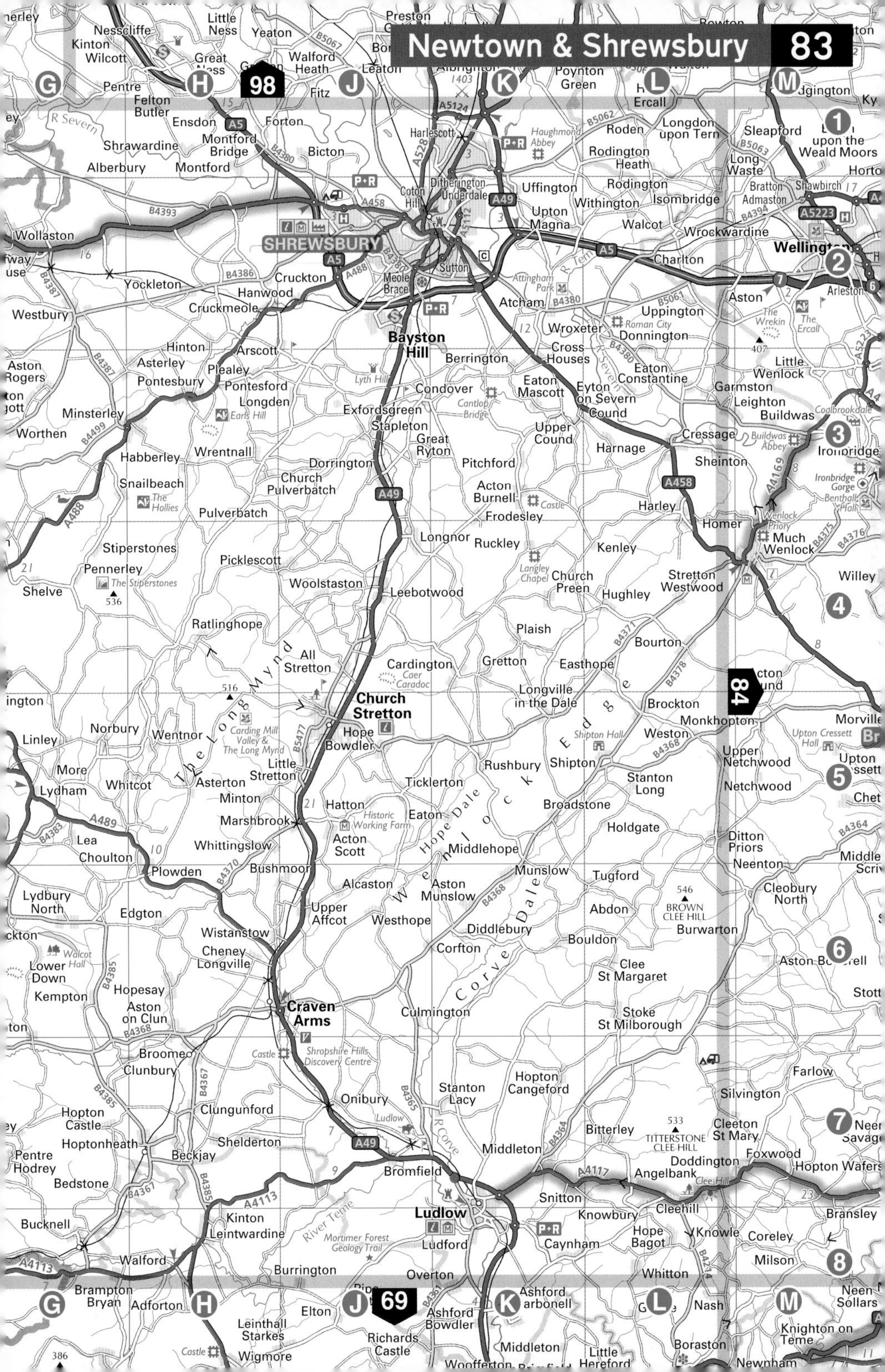

Nesscliffe
Kinton
Wilcott
Little Ness
Yeaton
Great Ness
Preston
Walford Heath
Leaton
Fitz
Albrighton
Poynton Green
Ercall
Rowton
Pentre
Felton Butler
Ensdon
Forton
R Severn
Shrawardine
Montford Bridge
Montford
Bicton
Alberbury
Harlescott
Haughmond Abbey
Roden
Longdon upon Tern
Sleapford
upon the Weald Moors
Rodington Heath
Rodington
Long Waste
Bratton
Admaston
Shawbirch
Coton Hill
Ditherington
Underdale
Uffington
Upton Magna
Withington
Isombridge
Walcot
Wrockwardine
Wollaston
SHREWSBURY
Wellington
Charlton
Yockleton
Cruckton
Hanwood
Cruckmeole
Meole Brace
Sutton
Attingham Park
Atcham
Aston
The Wrekin
The Ercall
Arleston
Westbury
Uppington
Wroxeter
Roman City
Donnington
Bayston Hill
Hinton
Arscott
Asterley
Aston Rogers
Plealey
Pontesbury
Pontesford
Lyth Hill
Berrington
Cross Houses
Eaton Constantine
Little Wenlock
Garmston
Leighton
Buildwas
Coalbrookdale
Longden
Condover
Eaton Mascott
Eyton on Severn
Cound
Minsterley
Earls Hill
Exfordsgreen
Cantlop Bridge
Worthen
Stapleton
Upper Cound
Harnage
Cressage
Buildwas Abbey
Ironbridge
Habberley
Wrentnall
Great Ryton
Dorrington
Pitchford
Sheinton
Ironbridge Gorge
Benthall Hall
Snailbeach
The Hollies
Church Pulverbatch
Acton Burnell
Castle
Pulverbatch
Frodesley
Harley
Homer
Wenlock Priory
Much Wenlock
Stiperstones
Longnor
Ruckley
Kenley
Picklescott
Pennerley
The Stiperstones
Shelve
Woolstaston
Leebotwood
Langley Chapel
Church Preen
Hughley
Stretton Westwood
Willey
Ratlinghope
Plaish
Bourton
All Stretton
The Long Mynd
Cardington
Caer Caradoc
Gretton
Easthope
Acton Round
Longville in the Dale
Brockton
Monkhopton
Morville
Church Stretton
Hope Bowdler
Norbury
Wentnor
Carding Mill Valley & The Long Mynd
Shipton Hall
Weston
Upton Cressett Hall
Linley
Rushbury
Shipton
Upper Netchwood
Netchwood
Little Stretton
More
Lydham
Whitcot
Asterton
Minton
Ticklerton
Stanton Long
Wenlock Edge
Hope Dale
Broadstone
Marshbrook
Hatton
Historic Working Farm
Eaton
Holdgate
Ditton Priors
Lea
Acton Scott
Middlehope
Choulton
Whittingslow
Plowden
Bushmoor
Munslow
Tugford
Neenton
Lydbury North
Alcaston
Aston Munslow
BROWN CLEE HILL
Cleobury North
Edgton
Upper Affcot
Westhope
Abdon
Burwarton
Wistanstow
Diddlebury
Corve Dale
Bouldon
Walcot Hall
Cheney Longville
Corfton
Lower Down
Clee St Margaret
Kempton
Hopesay
Craven Arms
Aston on Clun
Culmington
Stoke St Milborough
Broome
Clunbury
Castle
Shropshire Hills Discovery Centre
Hopton Cangeford
Farlow
Stanton Lacy
Silvington
Hopton Castle
Clungunford
Onibury
Ludlow
R Corve
Bitterley
Cleeton St Mary
TITTERSTONE CLEE HILL
Hoptonheath
Shelderton
Beckjay
Middleton
Doddington
Foxwood
Pentre Hodrey
Bromfield
Angelbank
Hopton Wafers
Bedstone
Clee Hill
Snitton
Cleehill
Kinton
Leintwardine
Ludlow
Knowbury
Bransley
Bucknell
River Teme
Mortimer Forest Geology Trail
Hope Bagot
Knowle
Coreley
Caynham
Ludford
Milson
Walford
Burrington
Whitton
Overton
Brampton Bryan
Adforton
Elton
Ashford Carbonell
Ashford Bowdler
Nash
Neen Sollars
Leinthall Starkes
Richards Castle
Boraston
Knighton on Teme
Castle
Wigmore
Middleton
Little Hereford
Woofferton
Newnham
A5
A49
A458
A488
A5124
A528
A5112
A5223
A4169
A489
A4113
A4117
B5067
B4380
B4393
B4386
B4387
B4499
B5062
B5063
B4394
B5061
B4376
B4375
B4371
B4378
B4368
B5477
B4370
B4383
B4385
B4367
B4365
B4364
B4214
B4361
98
84
69

Rowton
Cherrington
Tibberton
Forton
Newport
Coton
Gnosall Heath
Haughton
Walton
Waters Upton
Edgmond
Outwoods
Poynton Green
98
99
Longford
Chetwynd Aston
Church Aston
Ercall
Kynnersley
Church Eaton
Longdon upon Tern
Sleapford
Eyton upon the Weald Moors
Preston upon the Weald Moors
Lilleshall
Stockton
High Onn
Woodcote
Great Chatwell
Orslow
Rodington Heath
Long Waste
Horton
Heath Hill
Bickford
Rodington
Withington
Isombridge
Bratton
Admaston
Shawbirch
TELFORD
Donnington
Lilleshall Abbey
Brineton
Walcot
Wrockwardine
Trench
Granville
Donnington Wood
Sheriffhales
Weston Heath
Blymhill
Wheaton Aston
Lapley
Wellington
Hadley
Oakengates
Crackleybank
Weston-under-Lizard
Stretton
Charlton
Priorslee
Aston
Arleston
Telford
Weston Park
Bishop's Wood
Uppington
The Wrekin
The Ercall
Wroxeter
Roman City
Donnington
Hollinswood
Tong Norton
Boscobel House
Shifnal
Brewood
Eaton Constantine
Dawley
Horsehay
Stirchley
White Ladies Priory
Tong
Little Wenlock
Chillington
Eyton on Severn
Garmston
Leighton
Buildwas
Cound
Coalbrookdale
Cressage
Buildwas Abbey
Harnage
Madeley
Kemberton
RAF Cosford
Codsall Wood
Codsall
Sheinton
Ironbridge
Albrighton
Kingswood Common
Ironbridge Gorge
Blists Hill
Coalport
Ryton
Oaken
Benthall Hall
Sutton Maddock
Boningale
Harley
Broseley
Beckbury
Homer
Wenlock Priory
Much Wenlock
Norton
Burnhill Green
Kenley
Badger
Stockton
Pattingham
Perton
Tettenhall
Tettenhall Wood
Stretton Westwood
Church Preen
Hughley
Willey
Stableford
Ackleton
Wightwick
Chesterton
Wightwick Manor
Bourton
Nordley
Astley Abbots
Lower Penn
Easthope
Cross Lane Head
Rindleford
Worfield
Wyken
Hilton
Orton
Acton Round
Seisdon
Bromley
Hopstone
Brockton
83
Monkhopton
Morville
Roughton
Aston
Trysull
Shipton Hall
Weston
Upton Cressett Hall
Bridgnorth
Stanmore
Claverley
Ounsdale
Wombourne
Upper Netchwood
Upton Cressett
Heathton
Halfpenny Green
Smestow
Shipton
Oldbury
Stanton Long
Netchwood
Quatford
Swindon
Himley
Chetton
Eardington
Wolverhampton Halfpenny Green
Bobbington
Holdgate
Highgate Common
Six Ashes
Wall Heath
Ditton Priors
Chelmarsh
Kingswinford
Neenton
Middleton Scriven
Dudmaston
Quatt
Tugford
546
BROWN CLEE HILL
Cleobury North
Glazeley
Tuckhill
Wordsley
Sutton
Abdon
Hampton
Enville
Sidbury
Burwarton
Birdsgreen
Compton
Stourton
Billingsley
Alveley
Clee St Margaret
Woodhill
Aston Botterell
Dunsley
Wollaston
Chorley
Severn Valley
Romsley
Stottesdon
Highley
Kinver
STOURBRIDGE
Stoke St Milborough
Fenn Green
Rays Farm
Whittington
Bodenham Arboretum
Upper Arley
Shatterford
Farlow
Kinlet
Cookley
Churchill
Silvington
Severn Valley Railway
Wolverley
Cleeton St Mary
533
TITTERSTONE CLEE HILL
Neen Savage
Buttonoak
Franche
Blakedown
Broadwaters
Foxwood
Doddington
Wyre Forest
Habberley
Angelbank
Hopton Wafers
Blakebrook
KIDDERMINSTER
Bewdley
Cleehill
Cleobury Mortimer
Wribbenhall
Long Bank
West Midland
Stone
Knowbury
Bransley
Wyre Forest
Harvington
Hope Bagot
Knowle
Coreley
Ribbesford
Bayton
Upper Milton
Wilden
Shenstone
Milson
Bliss Gate
Whitton
Clows Top
Torton
Neen Sollars
Mamble
Rock
70
Stourport-on-Severn
Hartlebury
Nash
Areley Kings
Astley Cross
Titton
Chadwick
Elmley Lovett
Little Hereford
Newnham
Dunley
0 1 2 3 4 miles
0 1 2 3 4 5 kilometres
M54
A5
A41
A442
A458
A4169
A464
A454
A449
A456
A4117
A518
A5223
B5062
B4394
B4373
B4375
B4376
B4176
B4364
B4363
B4555
B4194
B4190
B4202
B4371
B4378
B4368
B4214

Walton-on-the-Hill
Milford
Brocton
Bishton
Colton
Blithbury
Hamstall Ridware
Hadley End
Dunstall
Branston
Acton Trussell
Bednall
CANNOCK CHASE
Wolseley Bridge
Etchinghill
Rugeley
Hill Ridware
Nethertown
Yoxall
Penkridge
Slitting Mill
Mavesyn Ridware
King's Bromley
Wychnor
Rosliston
Castle Gresley
Coton in the Elms
Brereton
Birches Valley Forest Centre
Armitage
Upper Longdon
Longdon
Longdon Green
Castle Ring
Alrewas
National Memorial
Fradley
Lullington
Huntington
Hednesford
Green Heath
Cannock Chase
Elmhurst
Edingale
Gentleshaw
Farewell
Lichfield
Heath Hayes & Wimblebury
Hatherton
Chase Terrace
Boney Hay
Burntwood Green
Streethay
Elford
Clifton Campville
Haunton
Harlaston
CANNOCK
Norton Canes
Burntwood
Chasewater Railway
Chasetown
Hammerwich
Thorpe Constantine
Shareshill
Cheslyn Hay
Great Wyrley
Little Wyrley
Brownhills
Letocetum Baths
Wall
Whittington
Staffordshire Regiment
Comberford
Seckington
Wigginton
Featherstone
Upper Landywood
Pelsall
Stonnall
Shenstone
Hopwas
Shuttington
Amington
TAMWORTH
Kettlebrook
Glascote
Moseley Old Hall
Essington
Wood Hayes
Bloxwich
Blakenall Heath
Weeford
Hints
Little Hay
M6 Toll
Rushall
Stubbers Green
Leighswood
Wood End
Wednesfield
Short Heath
Harden
Daw End
Aldridge
Drayton Manor
Fazeley
Two Gates
Dordon
WOLVERHAMPTON
Heath Town
Portobello
Lane Head
Willenhall
Coal Pool
Little Aston
Mere Green
Drayton Bassett
Whateley
Baddesley Ensor
Moseley
Monmore Green
Ettingshall
Darlaston Green
Darlaston
WALSALL
Caldmore
Palfrey
Hardwick
Four Oaks
Doe Bank
Middleton
Middleton Hall
Ash End House
Barr Beacon
Sutton Park
Whitehouse Common
Allen End
Hurley Common
Bilston
King's Hill
Wednesbury
Yew Tree
ROYAL SUTTON COLDFIELD
Kingsbury
Hurley
Great Barr
Maney
The Belfry
Foul End
Bradley
Coseley
Friar Park
Charlemont
Hill Top
Queslett
Kingstanding
New Oscott
Boldmere
Wylde Green
Wishaw
Nether Whitacre
Cinder Hill
Ocker Hill
Tipton
Golds Green
Newton
Hamstead
Perry
Short Heath
Walmley
Walmley Ash
Curdworth
Lea Marston
Whitacre Heath
Hurst Hill
Tipton Green
Wrens Nest
Churchfield
Alexander Stadium
Sandwell Valley
Perry Barr
Erdington
Water Orton
Hoggrill's End
HAMS HALL
Dudley Port
Swan Village
WEST BROMWICH
Brown's Green
Birchfield
Witton
Gravelly Hill
Tyburn
Over Whitacre
DUDLEY
Handsworth
Washwood Heath
Castle Bromwich
Shustoke
Rounds Green
Oldbury
Smethwick
Aston
Ward End
Shard End
Kingshurst
Coleshill
Netherton
Rowley Regis
Portway
Saltley
Stechford
Kitt's Green
Maxstoke
Primrose Hill
BIRMINGHAM
Ladywood
Small Heath
Tile Cross
Chelmsley Wood
Marston Green
Blackheath
Cradley Heath
Coombeswood
Bearwood
Yardley
Lyndon Green
Forest of Arden
Quarry Bank
Cradley
Lye
Woodgate Valley
Harborne
Edgbaston
Tyseley
Sheldon
Birmingham
Little Packington
HALESOWEN
Wollescote
Moor Street
Woodgate
Balsall Heath
Sparkhill
Acock's Green
NEC
Stonebridge
Hasbury
Hayley Green
Halesowen Abbey
Bartley Green
Bournbrook
Selly Oak
Moseley
Wake Green
Sarehole Mill
Olton
Ulverley Green
Elmdon
Bickenhill
Meriden
National Motorcycle
Hagley Hall
Illey
Frankley
Cadbury World
Bournville
King's Heath
Hall Green
Lode Heath
Hampton-in-Arden
Clent Hills
Clent
Romsley
Cotteridge
Lifford
Alcester Lane End
Sharman's Cross
Four Oaks
Yardley Wood
SOLIHULL
Eastcote
Berkswell
Northfield
King's Norton
Highter's Heath
Shirley
West Heath
Maypole
Walker's Heath
Major's Green
Barston
Bell End
Windmill Hill
Rubery
Longbridge
Knowle
Carol Green
Wildmoor
Lydiate Ash
Cofton Hackett
Hopwood
Wythall
Dorridge
Balsall Common
Fairfield
Lickey
Darley Green
Bournheath
Catshill
Barnt Green
Hopwood Park
Tanner's Green
Earlswood
Chessetts Wood
Chadwick End
Dodford
Lickey End
Withybed Green
Hockley Heath
Packwood House
Baddesley Clinton
Honiley
Linthurst
Alvechurch
Portway
Wood End
Blackwell
Kingswood
Bromsgrove
Rowney Green
Tanworth in Arden
Lapworth
Wroxall
Kenilworth
Beausale
Beoley
Finstall
Aston Fields
Holt End
Rowington
Grand Union Canal
Birmingham & Fazeley Canal
Trent & Mersey Canal
R Trent
R Tame
R Arrow

Dunstall
Branston
Branston Water Park
Barton-under-Needwood
Yoxall
Wychnor
Alrewas
Fradley
Streethay
Elford
Whittington
Staffordshire Regiment
Hopwas
Hints
Swadlincote
Blackfordby
Smisby
Lount
Worthington
Belton
Shepshed
Osgathorpe
Staunton Harold Church
Walton-on-Trent
Castle Gresley
Cauldwell
Rosliston
Linton
Coton in the Elms
Overseal
Lullington
Netherseal
Edingale
Clifton Campville
Chilcote
Harlaston
Haunton
Thorpe Constantine
No Man's Heath
Comberford
Seckington
Newton Regis
Wigginton
Shuttington
Amington
Alvecote
TAMWORTH
Kettlebrook
Glascote
Fazeley
Drayton Manor
Two Gates
Drayton Bassett
Whateley
Middleton
Middleton Hall
Ash End House
Allen End
Kingsbury
Wishaw
Curdworth
Water Orton
Tyburn
Castle Bromwich
Shard End
Kingshurst
Kitt's Green
Chelmsley Wood
Tile Cross
Marston Green
Lyndon Green
Sheldon
Birmingham
NEC
Elmdon
Bickenhill
Lode Heath
SOLIHULL
Knowle
Dorridge
Darley Green
Chessetts Wood
Lockley Heath
Packwood House
Lapworth
Kingswood
Norris Hill
Ashby-de-la-Zouch
Moira
Donisthorpe
Oakthorpe
Measham
Appleby Magna
Appleby Parva
Norton-Juxta-Twycross
Austrey
Twycross
Orton-on-the-Hill
Warton
Polesworth
Pooley
Dordon
Grendon
Baddesley Ensor
Whittington
Atherstone
Hurley Common
Hurley
Baxterley
Bentley
Mancetter
Ridge Lane
Hartshill Hayes
Oldbury
Hartshill
Birchley Heath
Foul End
Nether Whitacre
Lea Marston
Whiteacre Heath
Hoggrill's End
HAMS HALL
Shustoke
Over Whitacre
Coleshill
Maxstoke
Fillongley
Forest of Arden
Little Packington
Stonebridge
Meriden
National Motorcycle
Hampton-in-Arden
Eastcote
Barston
Balsall Common
Berkswell
Chadwick End
Baddesley Clinton
Honiley
Kenilworth
Kenilworth Castle
The Spring
Crackley
Four Oaks
Berkswell
Reeves Green
Carol Green
Tile Hill
Eastern Green
Allesley
Pickford
Jaguar Daimler
Corley
Keresley
Ash Green
Holbrooks
Radford
Earlsdon
Canley
COVENTRY
Stivichall
Lunt Roman Fort
Coventry
Baginton
Stoneleigh
Bubbenhall
Ashow
Agricultural Centre
Leek Wootton
Weston under Wetherley
Wappenbury
Princethorpe
Ryton Wood
Stretton-on-Dunsmore
Ryton-on-Dunsmore
Frankton
Bourton on Dunsmore
Thurlaston
Draycote
Swannington
Whitwick
Mount St Bernard
Charnwood Forest
Packington
Ravenstone
Coalville
Bardon
Normanton le Heath
Sence Valley Forest Park
Donington le Heath
Heather
Leicester (Markfield)
Swepstone
Ellistown
Ibstock
Stanton under Bardon
Snarestone
Newton Burgoland
Bagworth
Thornton
Ashby Canal
Odstone
Barton in the Beans
Shackerstone
Nailstone
Bilstone
Congerstone
Barlestone
Carlton
Osbaston
Tropical Birdland
The Battlefield Line
Market Bosworth
Newbold Verdon
Desford
Cadeby
Sheepy Magna
Sheepy Parva
Sibson
Sutton Cheney
Peckleton
Kirkby Mallory
Mallory Park
Ratcliffe Culey
Upton
Shenton
1485 Bosworth Battlefield
Stapleton
Atterton
Dadlington
Earl Shilton
Witherley
Fenny Drayton
Higham on the Hill
Stoke Golding
Barwell
Elmesthorpe
Hinckley
Burbage Common & Woods
Weddington
NUNEATON
Sketchley
Burbage
Stoney Stanton
Sapcote
Aston Flamville
Ansley
Stockingford
Attleborough
Arley
Astley
Arbury Hall
Griff
Burton Hastings
Bramcote
Wolvey
Wolvey Heath
Copston Magna
Wigston Parva
Frolesworth
Bedworth
Bulkington
Exhall
Aldermans Green
Longford
Foleshill
Potters Green
Henley Green
Wyken
Walsgrave on Sowe
Coombe Abbey
Shilton
Ansty
Withybrook
Monks Kirby
Stretton under Fosse
Street Ashton
Easenhall
Harborough Magna
Brinklow
Bretford
Stoke
Binley
Binley Woods
Willenhall
Brandon
Brandon Marsh
Wolston
Church Lawford
Long Lawford
Newton
R Trent
R Tame
R Mease
R Anker
R Sence
R Leam
Coventry Canal
Birmingham & Fazeley Canal
Grand Union Canal
A444
B5353
A514
A511
B587
A512
A38
A51
A5
A513
B5404
B5493
M42
A42
A453
A4091
A446
A4097
A452
B4114
M6
A47
B4666
B4668
B5000
B4116
B4098
B4111
B4102
B4112
B4113
B4109
B4029
B4065
M69
B4455
B4027
A4600
A4082
A428
A46
A45
A4071
A4177
A4141
A3400
B4101
B4104
A4114
A429
B4115
B4113
B4453
B582
B585
A447
B590
B4669
B578
A4114
B4642
A4429
M40
B4438
B4102
86
100
85
72
A
B
C
D
E
F
1
2
3
4
5
6
7
8
0 1 2 3 4 miles
0 1 2 3 4 5 kilometres

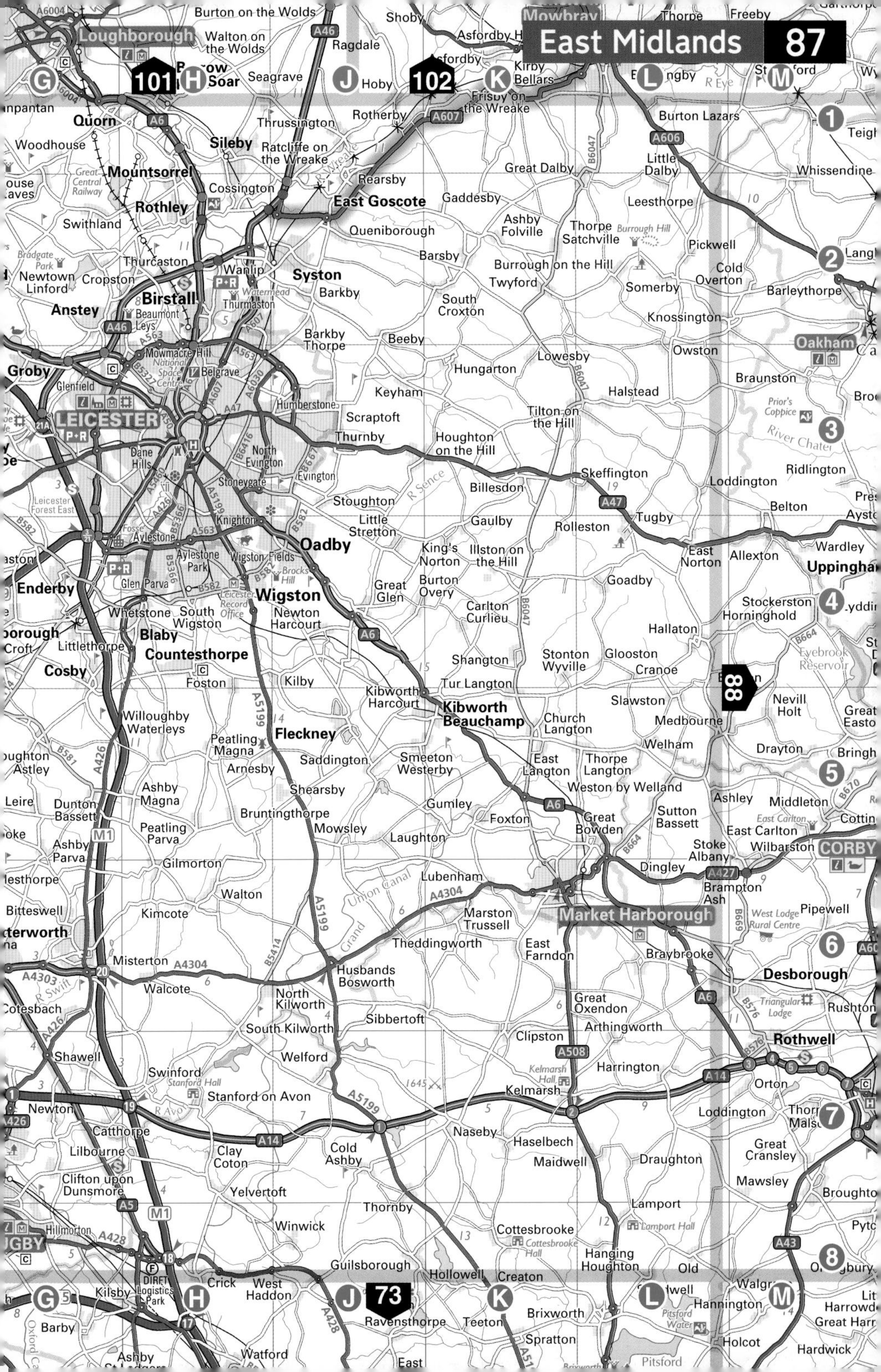
Loughborough
Burton on the Wolds
Walton on the Wolds
Shoby
Ragdale
Asfordby
Kirby Bellars
Thorpe
Freeby
Seagrave
Hoby
Frisby on the Wreake
Quorn
Thrussington
Rotherby
Burton Lazars
Woodhouse
Sileby
Ratcliffe on the Wreake
Great Dalby
Little Dalby
Whissendine
Mountsorrel
Great Central Railway
Cossington
Rearsby
East Goscote
Gaddesby
Leesthorpe
Rothley
Swithland
Queniborough
Ashby Folville
Thorpe Satchville
Burrough Hill
Pickwell
Bradgate Park
Thurcaston
Barsby
Burrough on the Hill
Cold Overton
Newtown Linford
Cropston
Wanlip
Syston
Twyford
Somerby
Barleythorpe
Birstall
Watermead
Thurmaston
Barkby
South Croxton
Knossington
Anstey
Beaumont Leys
Barkby Thorpe
Beeby
Owston
Oakham
Groby
Mowmacre Hill
National Space Centre
Belgrave
Hungarton
Lowesby
Braunston
Glenfield
Keyham
Halstead
Humberstone
Prior's Coppice
LEICESTER
Scraptoft
Tilton on the Hill
River Chater
Thurnby
Houghton on the Hill
Dane Hills
North Evington
Evington
Skeffington
Ridlington
Loddington
Stoneygate
Billesdon
Leicester Forest East
Stoughton
R Sence
Belton
Little Stretton
Gaulby
Rolleston
Tugby
Aylestone
Knighton
Oadby
King's Norton
Illston on the Hill
East Norton
Allexton
Wardley
Aylestone Park
Wigston Fields
Brocks Hill
Uppingham
Enderby
Glen Parva
Great Glen
Burton Overy
Goadby
Leicester Record Office
Wigston
Whetstone
South Wigston
Newton Harcourt
Carlton Curlieu
Stockerston
Horninghold
Blaby
Hallaton
Littlethorpe
Countesthorpe
Shangton
Stonton Wyville
Glooston
Eyebrook Reservoir
Cosby
Foston
Kilby
Cranoe
Tur Langton
Kibworth Harcourt
Slawston
Nevill Holt
Kibworth Beauchamp
Church Langton
Medbourne
Willoughby Waterleys
Fleckney
Peatling Magna
Welham
Drayton
Saddington
Smeeton Westerby
East Langton
Thorpe Langton
Arnesby
Weston by Welland
Shearsby
Ashley
Middleton
Dunton Bassett
Ashby Magna
Bruntingthorpe
Gumley
Foxton
Great Bowden
Sutton Bassett
East Carlton
Mowsley
Peatling Parva
Laughton
Stoke Albany
Wilbarston
CORBY
Ashby Parva
Gilmorton
Dingley
Lubenham
Brampton Ash
Union Canal
Walton
Bitteswell
Kimcote
Marston Trussell
Pipewell
West Lodge Rural Centre
Market Harborough
Grand
Theddingworth
East Farndon
Braybrooke
Misterton
Husbands Bosworth
Desborough
R Swift
Walcote
North Kilworth
Great Oxendon
Triangular Lodge
Cotesbach
Sibbertoft
Arthingworth
Rushton
South Kilworth
Clipston
Rothwell
Shawell
Welford
Kelmarsh Hall
Harrington
Swinford
Stanford Hall
Stanford on Avon
Kelmarsh
Orton
Newton
R Avon
Loddington
Catthorpe
Naseby
Haselbech
Lilbourne
Clay Coton
Cold Ashby
Maidwell
Draughton
Great Cransley
Clifton upon Dunsmore
Mawsley
Yelvertoft
Broughton
Thornby
Lamport
Hillmorton
Lamport Hall
Winwick
Cottesbrooke
Cottesbrooke Hall
RUGBY
DIRFT Logistics Park
Guilsborough
Hanging Houghton
Crick
West Haddon
Hollowell
Creaton
Old
Kilsby
Ravensthorpe
Teeton
Brixworth
Hannington
Harrowden
Great Harrowden
Barby
Pitsford Water
Holcot
Spratton
Hardwick
Ashby St Ledgers
Watford
East
Pitsford
Oxford Canal
A6004
A46
A6
A607
A606
B6047
A563
A5327
A6030
A47
A50
A426
B5366
A5199
B582
B581
B664
B669
B670
A4304
A427
A508
B5414
A4303
A14
A5
A428
A43
B576
M1
101
102
88
73
G
H
J
K
L
M
1
2
3
4
5
6
7
8
1645

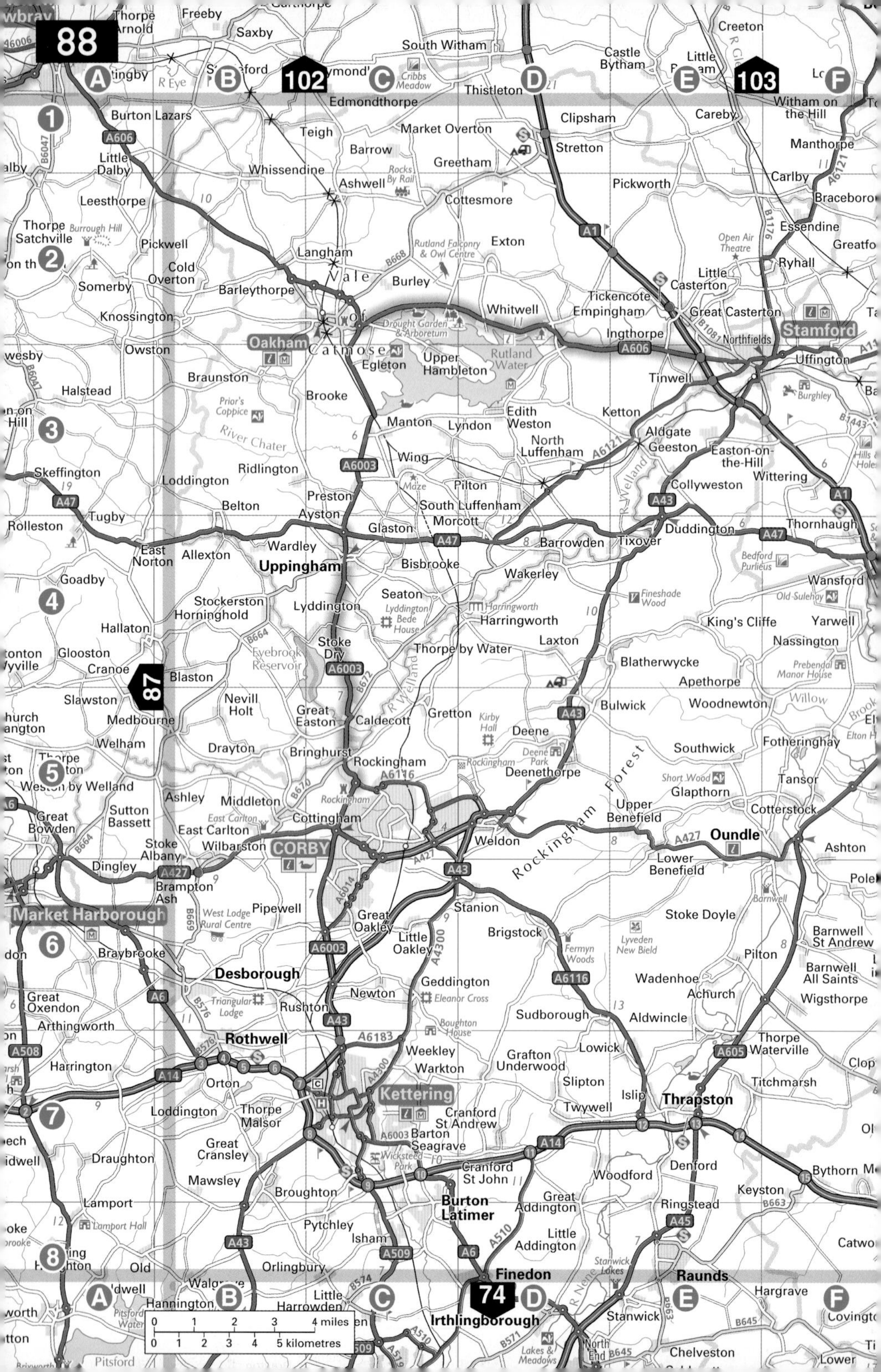
102
103
87
74
A
B
C
D
E
F
1
2
3
4
5
6
7
8
Thorpe Arnold
Freeby
Saxby
South Witham
Castle Bytham
Little Bytham
Creeton
Cribbs Meadow
Thistleton
Edmondthorpe
Witham on the Hill
Burton Lazars
Teigh
Market Overton
Clipsham
Stretton
Careby
Manthorpe
A606
B6047
Little Dalby
Barrow
Greetham
Whissendine
Rocks By Rail
Ashwell
Pickworth
Carlby
Cottesmore
Braceborough
Leesthorpe
Thorpe Satchville
Burrough Hill
Pickwell
Rutland Falconry & Owl Centre
Exton
A1
Open Air Theatre
Essendine
Langham
Ryhall
Cold Overton
Somerby
Barleythorpe
Vale
B668
Burley
Little Casterton
Knossington
Whitwell
Tickencote
Empingham
Great Casterton
Stamford
Drought Garden & Arboretum
Oakham
Catmose
Egleton
Upper Hambleton
Rutland Water
Ingthorpe
Northfields
B1081
Uffington
Owston
Braunston
Tinwell
Burghley
Halstead
Prior's Coppice
Brooke
Edith Weston
Ketton
River Chater
Manton
Lyndon
North Luffenham
Aldgate
Geeston
Easton-on-the-Hill
Wittering
Skeffington
Ridlington
Loddington
A6003
Wing
A6121
R Welland
Collyweston
Maze
Pilton
Preston
A47
Tugby
Belton
South Luffenham
A43
Rolleston
Ayston
Morcott
Duddington
Thornhaugh
Glaston
Barrowden
Tixover
Wardley
East Norton
Allexton
Uppingham
Bisbrooke
Wakerley
Bedford Purlieus
Goadby
Wansford
Seaton
Fineshade Wood
Old Sulehay
Stockerston
Horninghold
Lyddington
Lyddington Bede House
Harringworth
King's Cliffe
Yarwell
Hallaton
B664
Laxton
Nassington
Glooston
Stoke Dry
Thorpe by Water
Cranoe
Eyebrook Reservoir
Blatherwycke
Prebendal Manor House
Blaston
Apethorpe
B672
Slawston
Nevill Holt
Woodnewton
Medbourne
Great Easton
Caldecott
Gretton
Kirby Hall
Bulwick
Willow Brook
Welham
Deene
Southwick
Fotheringhay
Elton Hall
Drayton
Bringhurst
Rockingham
Deene Park
Thorpe Langton
Weston by Welland
Short Wood
Tansor
Deenethorpe
Rockingham Forest
A6116
B670
Glapthorn
Ashley
Middleton
Upper Benefield
Cotterstock
Great Bowden
Sutton Bassett
East Carlton
Cottingham
Oundle
East Carlton
A427
Weldon
Ashton
Stoke Albany
Wilbarston
CORBY
Lower Benefield
Dingley
Brampton Ash
Stanion
Barnwell
Market Harborough
B669
West Lodge Rural Centre
Pipewell
A6014
Stoke Doyle
Brigstock
Barnwell St Andrew
Great Oakley
Little Oakley
A4300
Lyveden New Bield
Fermyn Woods
Pilton
Braybrooke
Barnwell All Saints
Desborough
Wadenhoe
A6
Geddington
Achurch
Wigsthorpe
Great Oxendon
Triangular Lodge
Rushton
Newton
Eleanor Cross
B576
Sudborough
Aldwincle
Arthingworth
Boughton House
Rothwell
A6183
Thorpe Waterville
A508
Weekley
Lowick
A605
Harrington
Grafton Underwood
Warkton
Titchmarsh
A14
Orton
Slipton
Kettering
Islip
Thrapston
Loddington
Thorpe Malsor
Twywell
Cranford St Andrew
Barton Seagrave
Great Cransley
Draughton
Wicksteed Park
Cranford St John
Woodford
Denford
Bythorn
Mawsley
Broughton
Great Addington
Keyston
Burton Latimer
Ringstead
Lamport
Lamport Hall
B663
Pytchley
A45
Isham
Little Addington
A510
A509
Hanging Houghton
Old
Orlingbury
Stanwick Lakes
Finedon
Raunds
Walgrave
Little Harrowden
B574
Hargrave
Hannington
Pitsford Water
R Nene
Stanwick
Irthlingborough
B645
Covington
North End
Chelveston
Lakes & Meadows
B571
Pitsford
Lower
0 1 2 3 4 miles
0 1 2 3 4 5 kilometres

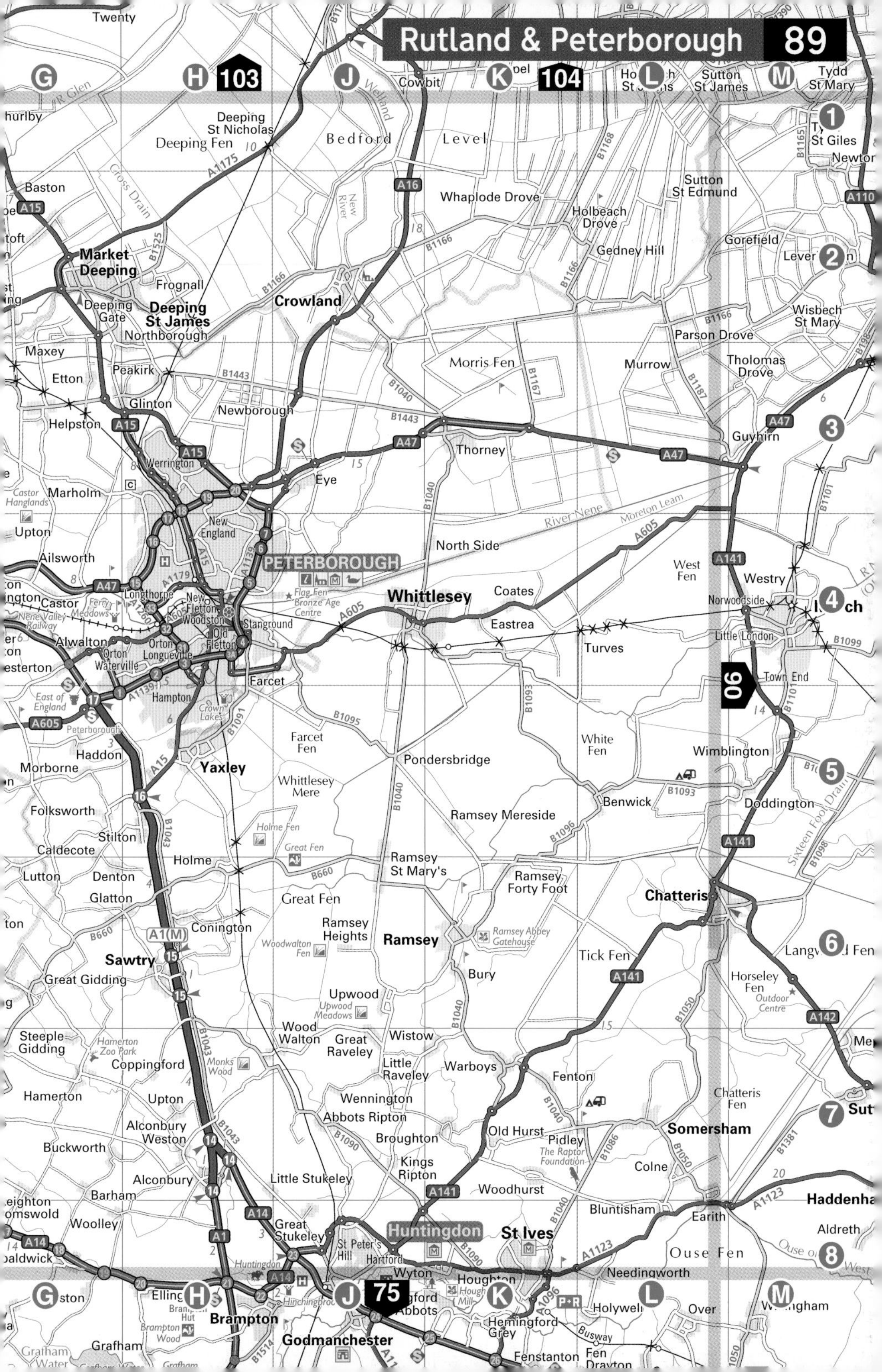
Twenty
G
H
103
J
K
104
L
M
Cowbit
Sutton St James
Tydd St Mary
Deeping St Nicholas
Deeping Fen
Bedford Level
Welland
A1175
Cross Drain
New River
Baston
A15
A16
Whaplode Drove
Holbeach Drove
Sutton St Edmund
Tydd St Giles
Newton
A1101
B1165
B1168
Market Deeping
Deeping Gate
Deeping St James
Northborough
Frognall
B1525
B1166
Crowland
Gedney Hill
Gorefield
Leverington
Wisbech St Mary
Parson Drove
Murrow
Tholomas Drove
Maxey
Etton
Peakirk
Glinton
Helpston
B1443
Newborough
Morris Fen
B1040
B1167
B1187
Thorney
A47
Guyhirn
B1198
Werrington
Eye
Marholm
Castor Hanglands
Upton
Ailsworth
New England
PETERBOROUGH
Flag Fen Bronze Age Centre
River Nene
Moreton Leam
North Side
A605
Whittlesey
Coates
Eastrea
Turves
West Fen
Westry
Norwoodside
Little London
B1099
B1101
Castor
Ferry Meadows
Nene Valley Railway
Longthorpe
New Fletton
Woodston
Old Fletton
Stanground
Alwalton
Orton Waterville
Orton Longueville
A1260
A1139
A1179
Hampton
Farcet
East of England
Peterborough
Crown Lakes
B1091
B1095
B1093
Town End
90
Haddon
Morborne
Yaxley
Farcet Fen
Whittlesey Mere
Pondersbridge
White Fen
Wimblington
Benwick
Doddington
Sixteen Foot Drain
Folksworth
Stilton
B1043
Holme Fen
Ramsey Mereside
B1096
Caldecote
Great Fen
Ramsey St Mary's
B660
Holme
Lutton
Denton
Glatton
Ramsey Forty Foot
Chatteris
A141
B1098
Conington
Ramsey Heights
Ramsey
Ramsey Abbey Gatehouse
Woodwalton Fen
A1(M)
Sawtry
Great Gidding
Bury
Tick Fen
Horseley Fen
Outdoor Centre
A142
Upwood
Upwood Meadows
Wood Walton
Great Raveley
Wistow
Steeple Gidding
Hamerton Zoo Park
Coppingford
Monks Wood
Little Raveley
Warboys
Fenton
B1050
Hamerton
Upton
Wennington
Abbots Ripton
Chatteris Fen
Alconbury Weston
Old Hurst
Pidley
Somersham
The Raptor Foundation
B1086
Buckworth
B1090
Broughton
Kings Ripton
Colne
B1381
Alconbury
Little Stukeley
Woodhurst
Bluntisham
Earith
A1123
Haddenham
Barham
Woolley
A14
A1
Great Stukeley
Huntingdon
St Ives
Aldreth
Ouse Fen
St Peter's Hill
Hartford
Wyton
Houghton
Needingworth
Hough Mill
Brampton Hut
Brampton
Brampton Wood
Hinchingbrooke
Godmanchester
75
Hemingford Abbots
Hemingford Grey
A1096
Holywell
Over
Busway
Fenstanton
Fen Drayton
Grafham
Grafham Water
B1514
Langwood Fen
Sutton
Willingham

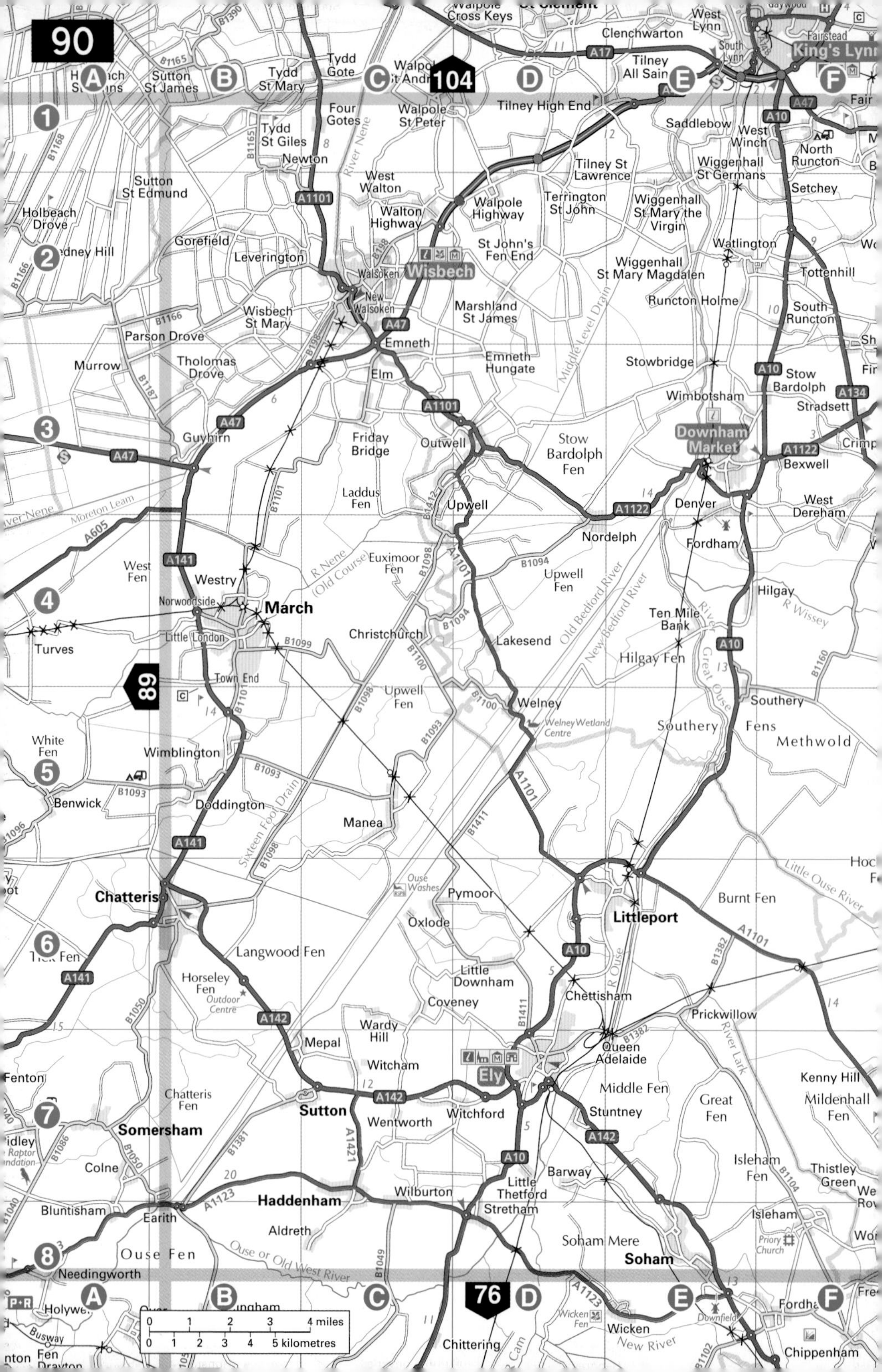
Walpole Cross Keys
St Clement
West Lynn
Clenchwarton
Fairstead
King's Lynn
South Lynn
A17
Tilney All Saints
Holbeach St Johns
Sutton St James
B1165
B1390
Tydd St Mary
Tydd Gote
Walpole St Andrew
104
Tilney High End
Fair
A47
A10
Four Gotes
Walpole St Peter
Tydd St Giles
Newton
Saddlebow
West Winch
North Runcton
B1168
B1165
River Nene
Tilney St Lawrence
Wiggenhall St Germans
Sutton St Edmund
West Walton
Setchey
A1101
Walpole Highway
Terrington St John
Wiggenhall St Mary the Virgin
Holbeach Drove
Walton Highway
Gorefield
St John's Fen End
Watlington
Gedney Hill
Leverington
Wisbech
Walsoken
Wiggenhall St Mary Magdalen
Tottenhill
B1166
New Walsoken
Runcton Holme
Marshland St James
South Runcton
Parson Drove
Wisbech St Mary
B198
Middle Level Drain
Emneth
Murrow
Tholomas Drove
Emneth Hungate
Stowbridge
Stow Bardolph
Elm
A1101
Wimbotsham
B1187
Stradsett
A134
Guyhirn
Friday Bridge
Outwell
Stow Bardolph Fen
Downham Market
A1122
Bexwell
Crimplesham
A47
Laddus Fen
Upwell
Denver
West Dereham
Moreton Leam
River Nene
B1101
A605
A1122
Nordelph
Fordham
West Fen
A141
Euximoor Fen
R Nene (Old Course)
B1098
A1101
B1094
Upwell Fen
Old Bedford River
New Bedford River
Westry
Hilgay
R Wissey
Norwoodside
March
Ten Mile Bank
Turves
Little London
B1099
Christchurch
B1094
Lakesend
River Great Ouse
A10
Hilgay Fen
B1160
89
Town End
B1100
Welney
Welney Wetland Centre
Southery
White Fen
Wimblington
Upwell Fen
Southery Fens
Methwold
B1093
B1098
B1093
Benwick
Doddington
Manea
Sixteen Foot Drain
A1101
B1096
A141
B1411
Chatteris
Ouse Washes
Pymoor
Littleport
Burnt Fen
Little Ouse River
Oxlode
A1101
Langwood Fen
B1382
A10
Tick Fen
A141
Horseley Fen
Outdoor Centre
Little Downham
Chettisham
R Ouse
Coveney
Prickwillow
A142
Wardy Hill
B1411
River Lark
B1050
Mepal
Queen Adelaide
B1382
Witcham
Ely
Kenny Hill
Fenton
Chatteris Fen
Middle Fen
Mildenhall Fen
Sutton
A142
Witchford
Great Fen
Stuntney
Somersham
Wentworth
A1421
A142
Colne
B1086
B1050
B1381
A10
Isleham Fen
Thistley Green
Barway
Little Thetford
B1104
A1123
Haddenham
Wilburton
Stretham
Bluntisham
Earth
Isleham
Aldreth
Priory Church
Ouse Fen
Ouse or Old West River
Soham Mere
B1049
Needingworth
Soham
P+R
76
Holywell
A1123
Fordham
Wicken Fen
Downfield
Busway
Fen Drayton
Chittering
Wicken
New River
Chippenham
R Cam
B1102
0 1 2 3 4 miles
0 1 2 3 4 5 kilometres

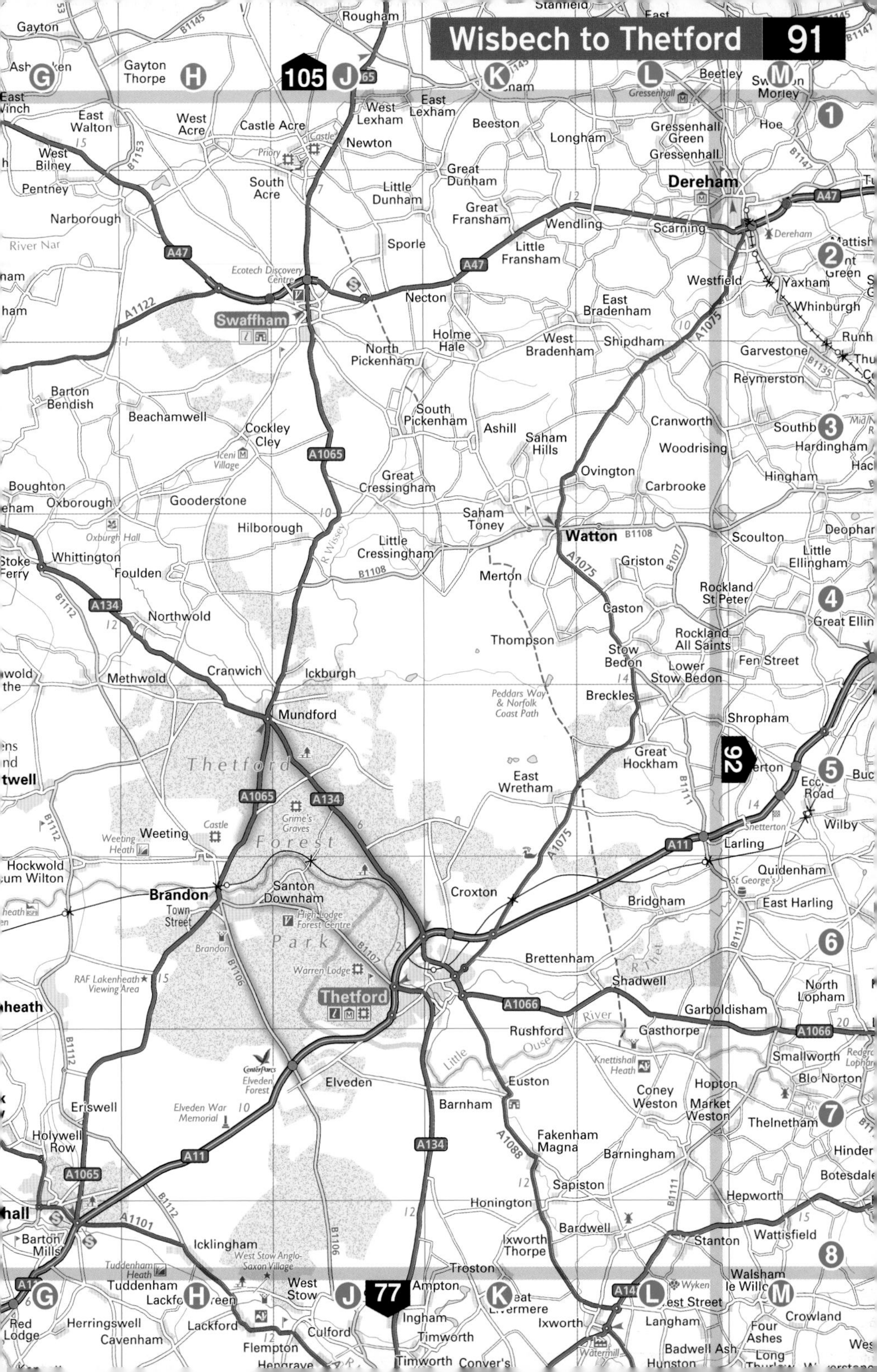

105
77
92
G
H
J
K
L
M
1
2
3
4
5
6
7
8
Gayton
Gayton Thorpe
Rougham
Stanfield
East
Beetley
Swanton Morley
Gressenhall
East Winch
East Walton
West Acre
Castle Acre
Castle
Priory
West Lexham
East Lexham
Newton
Beeston
Longham
Gressenhall Green
Gressenhall
Hoe
West Bilney
Pentney
Narborough
River Nar
South Acre
Little Dunham
Great Dunham
Great Fransham
Dereham
Wendling
Scarning
Little Fransham
Sporle
Mattishall
Yaxham
Whinburgh
Westfield
Ecotech Discovery Centre
Swaffham
Necton
East Bradenham
West Bradenham
Shipdham
Holme Hale
North Pickenham
Garvestone
Reymerston
Barton Bendish
Beachamwell
Cockley Cley
Iceni Village
South Pickenham
Ashill
Saham Hills
Cranworth
Woodrising
Southburgh
Hardingham
Hingham
Ovington
Carbrooke
Boughton
Oxborough
Gooderstone
Great Cressingham
Hilborough
Saham Toney
Watton
Scoulton
Deopham
Oxburgh Hall
Stoke Ferry
Whittington
Foulden
Little Cressingham
R Wissey
Merton
Griston
Little Ellingham
Rockland St Peter
Northwold
Caston
Great Ellingham
Thompson
Rockland All Saints
Stow Bedon
Lower Stow Bedon
Fen Street
Methwold
Cranwich
Ickburgh
Peddars Way & Norfolk Coast Path
Breckles
Mundford
Shropham
Thetford Forest Park
Great Hockham
Snetterton
Eccles Road
East Wretham
Grime's Graves
Castle
Weeting
Weeting Heath
Wilby
Larling
Quidenham
Hockwold cum Wilton
Brandon
Town Street
Santon Downham
High Lodge Forest Centre
Croxton
St George's
Bridgham
East Harling
Brettenham
Warren Lodge
RAF Lakenheath Viewing Area
Thetford
Shadwell
R Thet
Garboldisham
North Lopham
Rushford
River Little Ouse
Gasthorpe
Smallworth
Knettishall Heath
Blo Norton
Elveden
Euston
Center Parcs Elveden Forest
Coney Weston
Hopton
Market Weston
Thelnetham
Eriswell
Elveden War Memorial
Barnham
Fakenham Magna
Holywell Row
Barningham
Hinderclay
Botesdale
Sapiston
Honington
Hepworth
Bardwell
Wattisfield
Barton Mills
Icklingham
Ixworth Thorpe
Stanton
Tuddenham Heath
West Stow Anglo-Saxon Village
Troston
Walsham le Willows
Tuddenham
Lackford Green
West Stow
Ampton
Great Livermere
Wyken
West Street
Red Lodge
Herringswell
Cavenham
Lackford
Ingham
Ixworth
Langham
Crowland
Four Ashes
Flempton
Culford
Timworth
Watermill
Badwell Ash
Hengrave
Timworth Conyer's
Hunston
Long Thurlow
A47
A1122
A1065
A134
A1075
A11
A1066
A1088
A1101
B1145
B1153
B1147
B1135
B1108
B1077
B1112
B1111
B1106
B1107

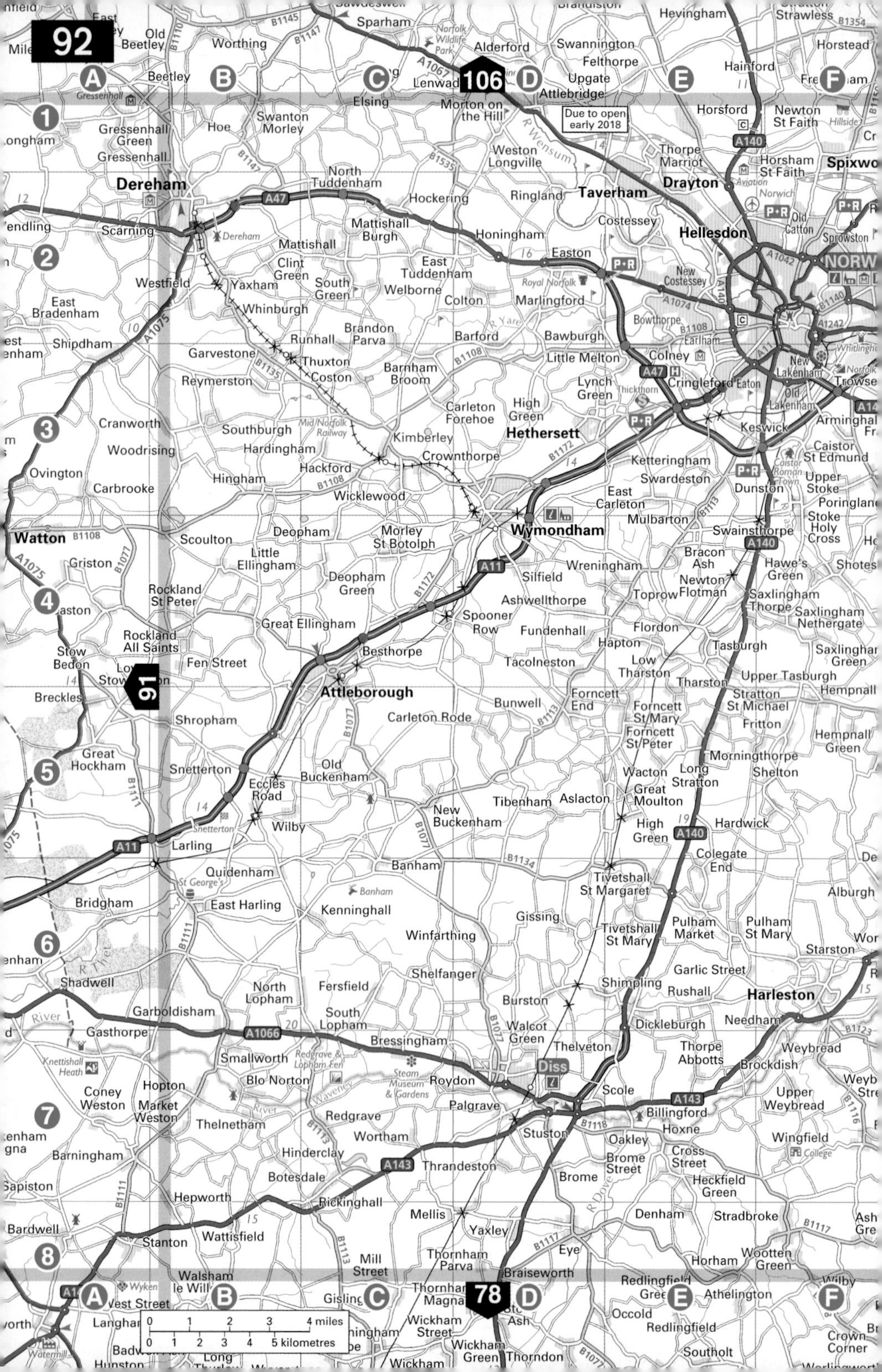
A
B
C
D
E
F
1
2
3
4
5
6
7
8
106
91
78
Sparham
Norfolk Wildlife Park
Alderford
Swannington
Hevingham
Strawless
Horstead
Old Beetley
Worthing
Felthorpe
Hainford
Beetley
Lenwade
Upgate
Attlebridge
Gressenhall
Elsing
Morton on the Hill
Due to open early 2018
Horsford
Newton St Faith
Hillside
Longham
Gressenhall Green
Hoe
Swanton Morley
Weston Longville
Thorpe Marriot
Horsham St Faith
Spixworth
Dereham
North Tuddenham
Ringland
Taverham
Drayton
Aviation
Norwich
Hockering
Costessey
Old Catton
Sprowston
Scarning
Mattishall Burgh
Honingham
Hellesdon
Mattishall
Easton
Clint Green
East Tuddenham
Yaxham
South Green
Welborne
Royal Norfolk
New Costessey
Westfield
Colton
Marlingford
East Bradenham
Whinburgh
Bowthorpe
Brandon Parva
Barford
Bawburgh
Earlham
Shipdham
Runhall
Garvestone
Thuxton
Barnham Broom
Little Melton
Colney
New Lakenham
Coston
Lynch Green
Reymerston
Thickthorn
Cringleford
Eaton
Trowse
Cranworth
Carleton Forehoe
High Green
Old Lakenham
Southburgh
Mid Norfolk Railway
Hethersett
Keswick
Arminghall
Woodrising
Hardingham
Kimberley
Caistor St Edmund
Crownthorpe
Ketteringham
Ovington
Hackford
Hingham
Swardeston
Caistor Roman Town
Upper Stoke
Carbrooke
Wicklewood
East Carleton
Dunston
Poringland
Watton
Mulbarton
Stoke Holy Cross
Scoulton
Deopham
Morley St Botolph
Wymondham
Swainsthorpe
Griston
Little Ellingham
Wreningham
Bracon Ash
Hawe's Green
Shotesham
Deopham Green
Silfield
Newton Flotman
Saxlingham Thorpe
Rockland St Peter
Toprow
Ashwellthorpe
Saxlingham Nethergate
Caston
Spooner Row
Great Ellingham
Fundenhall
Flordon
Rockland All Saints
Hapton
Tasburgh
Saxlingham Green
Stow Bedon
Besthorpe
Fen Street
Tacolneston
Low Tharston
Upper Tasburgh
Low Stow
Attleborough
Tharston
Hempnall
Breckles
Bunwell
Forncett End
Stratton St Michael
Forncett St Mary
Carleton Rode
Shropham
Forncett St Peter
Fritton
Hempnall Green
Great Hockham
Morningthorpe
Old Buckenham
Wacton
Long Stratton
Snetterton
Shelton
Eccles Road
Great Moulton
Tibenham
Aslacton
New Buckenham
High Green
Wilby
Hardwick
Larling
Colegate End
Banham
Quidenham
Tivetshall St Margaret
St George's
Alburgh
Bridgham
East Harling
Kenninghall
Gissing
Winfarthing
Pulham Market
Pulham St Mary
Tivetshall St Mary
Starston
Shadwell
Shelfanger
Garlic Street
Fersfield
North Lopham
Shimpling
Rushall
Harleston
Burston
Garboldisham
South Lopham
Dickleburgh
Needham
Gasthorpe
Walcot Green
Bressingham
River
Thelveton
Thorpe Abbotts
Weybread
Knettishall Heath
Smallworth
Redgrave & Lopham Fen
Diss
Brockdish
Blo Norton
Steam Museum & Gardens
Roydon
Scole
Upper Weybread
Coney Weston
Hopton
Market Weston
Palgrave
Billingford
Thelnetham
Redgrave
Stuston
Hoxne
Wingfield
College
Oakley
Wortham
Brome Street
Cross Street
Barningham
Hinderclay
Thrandeston
Brome
Heckfield Green
Sapiston
Botesdale
Hepworth
Rickinghall
Mellis
Denham
Stradbroke
Bardwell
Wattisfield
Yaxley
Eye
Stanton
Thornham Parva
Horham
Wootten Green
Mill Street
Braiseworth
Walsham le Willows
Redlingfield
Wyken
West Street
Gislingham
Thornham Magna
Athelington
Wilby
Langham
Occold
Redlingfield
Wickham Street
Badwell Ash
Wickham Green
Thorndon
Southolt
Crown Corner
Watermill
Long Thurlow
Wickham
R Wensum
R Yare
R Thet
Waveney
R Dove
A47
A140
A11
A1067
A1075
A1074
A1066
A143
A1042
A1242
B1145
B1147
B1110
B1354
B1535
B1135
B1108
B1172
B1113
B1077
B1111
B1134
B1118
B1116
B1117
B1123
B1140
0 1 2 3 4 miles
0 1 2 3 4 5 kilometres

G
H
107
J
K
L
M
1
2
3
4
5
6
7
8
Wroxham Barns
Irstead
Potter Heigham
Ludham
Martham
Hoveton
BeWILDerwood
RAF Air Defence Radar
Upper Street
Horning
Upper Street
Repps
Rollesby
Ormesby Broad
Hemsby
Hemsby Hole
Scratby
Bure Marshes
Woodbastwick
Broads Wildlife Centre
Ranworth Broad
Thurne
Fleggburgh/ Burgh St Margaret
Ormesby St Michael
California
Salhouse
Ranworth
Fairhaven
Pilson Green
Clippesby
Cargate Green
Billockby
Ormesby St Margaret
Caister-on-Sea
Little Plumstead
Panxworth
South Walsham
Filby
Thrigby
Mautby
Caister
Upton
Thrigby Hall
West End
West Caister
Blofield Heath
Great Plumstead
North Burlingham
Acle
Stokesby
Witton
Stracey Arms Windpump
Runham
Blofield
Lingwood
Damgate
Beighton
Tunstall
THE BROADS
Brundall
Strumpshaw
Postwick
South Burlingham
Moulton St Mary
Halvergate
River Yare
Elizabethan House
GREAT YARMOUTH
Southtown
Buckenham
Surlingham
Freethorpe
Berney Marshes
Burgh Castle
Bramerton
Hassingham
Wickhampton
Gorleston on Sea
East Port
Rockland St Mary
Cantley
Freethorpe Common
Berney Arms Windmill
Burgh Castle
Bradwell
Claxton
Limpenhoe
Belton
Carleton St Peter
Langley Street
Ashby St Mary
Pettitts Animal Adventure Park
Reedham
Hardley Street
Bergh Apton
Thurton
Fritton
Fritton Lake
St Olave's Priory
Chedgrave
Hopton on Sea
Lound
Brooke
R Chet
Loddon
Norton Subcourse
Thurlton
St Olaves
Herringfleet
Somerleyton Hall & Gardens
Mundham
Hales
Blundeston
Corton
Seething
Haddiscoe
Somerleyton
Kirstead Green
Raveningham
Pleasurewood Hills
Thwaite St Mary
Maypole Green
Toft Monks
Stockton
Oulton
Woodton
Kirby Cane
Wheatacre
Burgh St Peter
Lowestoft Ness
Hedenham
Aldeby
Oulton Broad
Ellingham
LOWESTOFT
Kirkley
Street
Gillingham
Ditchingham
Broome
Geldeston
River Waveney
Bungay
Shipmeadow
Worlingham
Pakefield
Barnby
Earsham
Mettingham
Barsham
Beccles
North Cove
Carlton Colville
Ringsfield
Gisleham
Ilketshall St Andrew
Mutford
Aviation
Rushmere
Hulver Street
Kessingland
Flixton
Ringsfield Corner
Winter Flora
Black Street
Africa Alive!
Ilketshall St Margaret
Homersfield
Henstead
Sotterley
St Margaret South Elmham
Redisham
Benacre
Benacre Ness
Shadingfield
Wrentham
St Cross South Elmham
Stone Street
Stoven
Covehithe
Rumburgh
Brampton
South Cove
Suffolk Heritage Coast
St James South Elmham
Westhall
Spexhall
Uggeshall
Wissett
Wangford
Oasis Camel Park
Sole Bay
Linstead Parva
Chediston
Holton
Halesworth
Blyford
Hen Reedbeds
Southwold
Cookley
Wenhaston
Cratfield
Blythburgh
Huntingfield
Walpole
Walberswick
Thorington
Bramfield
Dunwich Forest
Suffolk Coast
Laxfield
Heveningham
Ubbeston Green
R Yox
79
Darsham
Westleton Heath
Dunwich
Sibton
Peasenhall
Yoxford
Westleton
A47
A1062
A149
A1064
B1152
B1140
A146
A143
B1136
B1074
B1375
B1385
A1117
A1145
B1062
B1332
A144
A145
A12
B1127
B1126
A1095
B1123
B1124
B1117
B1387
B1534
A1120
B1135

Aberffraw Bay Heritage Coast
Llanddy
CAERNARFON
BAY
Lleyn Heritage Coast
Trwyn y Grolech
Carreg Ddu
Porth Nefyn
Morfa Nefyn
Nefyn
Pistyll
B4417
Edern
Bodfuan
A497
Porth Ysgaden
Tudweiliog
LLEYN
Dinas
371
Carn Fadrun
B4415
Porth Colman
Bryn-mawr
Llaniestyn
Rhyd-y-clafdy
A499
Penrhos
Pen-y-graig
Llangwnnadl
Meyllteyrn
Llanbedrog
Sarn
Botwnnog
B4413
Bryncroes
Trwyn Llanbed
Porthoer
Rhoshirwaun
Plas yn Rhiw
St Tudwal's Road
Llangian
Abersoch
Y Rhiw
Llanengan
Aberdaron
Llanfaelrhys
Porth Neigwl or Hell's Mouth
Bwlchtocyn
Marchros
St Tudwal's Island East
St Tudwal's Island West
Porth Ysgo
Aberdaron Bay
Porth Ceiriad
Bardsey Sound
St Mary's
Ynys Enlli
BARDSEY ISLAND
Lleyn Heritage Coast
0 1 2 3 4 miles
0 1 2 3 4 5 kilometres

Newborough
Anglesey Sea Zoo
Foel Farm Park
Saron
Rhiwlas
Llanrug
Caernarfon
Caernarfon Castle
Segontium
Caeathro
Cwm-y-glo
Brynrefail
Deiniolen
Ceunant
Llyn Padarn
Llanberis Lake Railway
Padarn
National Slate
Dinorwic
923
ELIDIR FAWR
1044
CARNEDD DAFYDD
Llyn Cowlyd
Llyn Ogwen
Llyn Crafnant
Llanddwyn Bay
Abermenai Point
Welsh Highland Railway
Gypsy Wood
Foryd Bay
Bontnewydd
442
Llanberis
Electric Mountain
Dolbadarn Castle
Llyn Peris
946
Y GARN
917
Y TRYFAN
National Mountain Centre (Plas y Brenin)
Airworld Aviation
Waunfawr
Llanwnda
Rhostryfan
726
MOEL EILIO
Snowdon Mountain Railway
Nant Peris
Pass of Llanberis
1001
GLYDER FAWR
994
GLYDER-FACH
Llandwrog
Groeslon
Parc Glynllifon
Carmel
Slateworks
Llyn Cwellyn
698
MYNYDD MAWR
1085
SNOWDON
Yr Wyddfa
Llyn Llydaw
872
MOEL-SIABOD
Penygroes
Talysarn
Rhyd-Ddu
Llyn Gwynant
Dolwyddelan Castle
Pontlyfni
Llanllyfni
Nebo
Nasareth
655
SNOWDONIA
747
YR ARAN
Beddgelert Forest
Craflwyn & Beddgelert
Welsh Highland Railway
Beddgelert
Sygun Copper Mine
Llechwedd Slate Caverns
Blaenau Ffestiniog
Caeau Tan y Bwlch
Pant Glas
NATIONAL PARK
782
MOEL HEBOG
Nantmor
522
Y-GYRN-DDU
Llanaelhaearn
Bryncir
Garn-Dolbenmaen
Dolbenmaen
552
MOEL DDU
Croesor
770
MOELWYN MAWR
711
MOELWYN BACH
Tan-y-Grisiau Reservoir
658
Ffestiniog
PENINSULA
Golan
Prenteg
Rhyd
Ffestiniog Railway
St Cybi's Well
Llangybi
Afon Glaslyn
Afon Dwyfawr
Garreg
Plas Tan y Bwlch
Maentwrog
Y Ffor
Pentrefelin
Tremadog
Penrhyndeudraeth
Gellilydan
Llanystumdwy
Chwilog
Porthmadog
Gwaith Powdwr
Amphitheatre
Criccieth
Castle
Minffordd
Portmeirion
Ffestiniog Railway
Penarth Fawr Medieval House
Borth-y-Gest
Traeth Bach
Llyn Trawsfynydd
Trawsfynydd
Talsarnau
Harlech Point
Llanfihangel-y-traethau
Pen-ychain
Morfa Harlech
624
MOEL YSGYFARNOGOD
Tremadog Bay
Harlech
Harlech Castle
Llanfair
720
RHINOG FAWR
Rhinog
Afon Eden
Afon Gain
Llandanwg
Llanbedr
Shell Island
Morfa Dyffryn
Coed y Brenin
754
Y LLETHR
589
MOELFRE
Afon Gamlan
Coed Ganllwyd
Afon Ysgethin
Llanenddwyn
750
DIFFWYS
Dyffryn Ardudwy
Burial Chamber
Llanddwywe
Tal-y-bont
Mawddach Valley
Llanelltyd
Cymer Abbey
Toll
Penmaenpool
Barmouth
Barmouth Bridge
Afon Mawddach
Barmouth Bay
Fairbourne
CADER IDRIS
A487
A4086
A4244
B4366
A4085
A499
A498
A470
B4418
B4411
B4410
A497
B4354
A496
B4573
A493
G
H
J
K
L
M
1
2
3
4
5
6
7
8
108
109
96
80

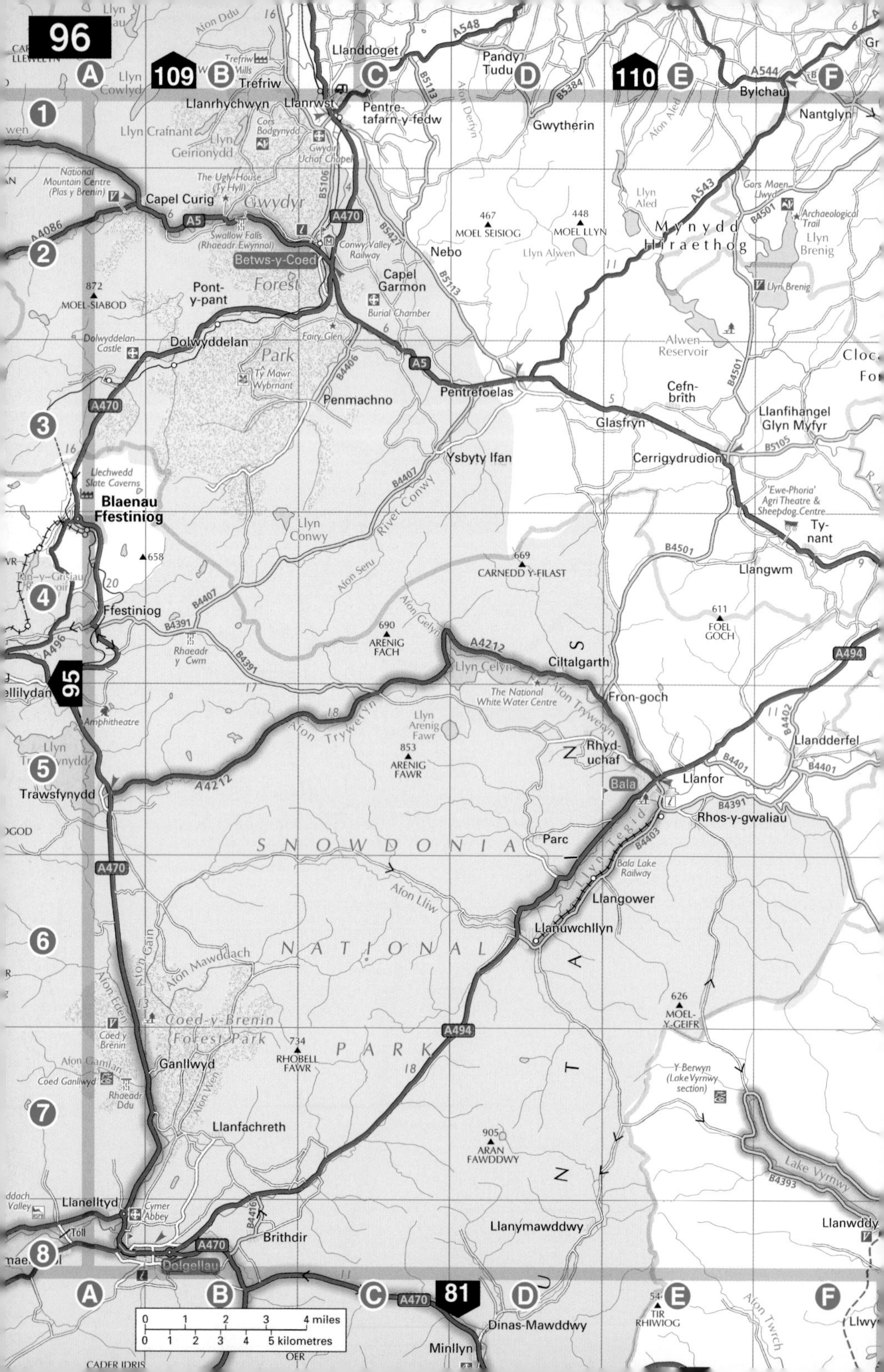
109
110
95
81
A
B
C
D
E
F
1
2
3
4
5
6
7
8
Llyn Cowlyd
Trefriw Mills
Trefriw
Llanddoget
Pandy Tudu
Bylchau
Nantglyn
Llanrhychwyn
Llanrwst
Pentre-tafarn-y-fedw
Gwytherin
Afon Ddu
Afon Derfyn
Afon Aled
A548
A544
B5113
B5384
Llyn Crafnant
Cors Bodgynydd
Llyn Geirionydd
Gwydir Uchaf Chapel
National Mountain Centre (Plas y Brenin)
The Ugly House (Ty Hyll)
Capel Curig
Gwydyr
A5
A4086
B5106
A470
Swallow Falls (Rhaeadr Ewynnol)
Conwy Valley Railway
B5427
Betws-y-Coed
Forest
Capel Garmon
Burial Chamber
Nebo
467
MOEL SEISIOG
448
MOEL LLYN
Llyn Alwen
Llyn Aled
A543
Mynydd Hiraethog
Gors Maen Llwyd
B4501
Archaeological Trail
Llyn Brenig
872
MOEL-SIABOD
Pont-y-pant
Dolwyddelan Castle
Dolwyddelan
Fairy Glen
Park
Ty Mawr Wybrnant
B4406
Penmachno
Pentrefoelas
Alwen Reservoir
Cefn-brith
Glasfryn
Llanfihangel Glyn Myfyr
B5105
Cerrigydrudion
Ysbyty Ifan
B4407
River Conwy
Llechwedd Slate Caverns
Blaenau Ffestiniog
658
Llyn Conwy
'Ewe-Phoria' Agri Theatre & Sheepdog Centre
Ty-nant
Tan-y-Grisiau
669
CARNEDD Y-FILAST
Afon Serw
Afon Gelyn
Llangwm
Ffestiniog
B4391
A496
Rhaeadr y Cwm
690
ARENIG FACH
A4212
Llyn Celyn
Ciltalgarth
611
FOEL GOCH
A494
The National White Water Centre
Afon Tryweryn
Fron-goch
Llyn Arenig Fawr
853
ARENIG FAWR
Amphitheatre
Llyn Trawsfynydd
Trawsfynydd
Rhyd-uchaf
Bala
B4402
Llandderfel
Llanfor
B4401
Rhos-y-gwaliau
Llyn Tegid
B4403
Parc
SNOWDONIA
NATIONAL
PARK
Bala Lake Railway
Afon Lliw
Llangower
Llanuwchllyn
Afon Gain
Afon Mawddach
Afon Eden
626
MOEL-Y-GEIFR
Coed-y-Brenin Forest Park
Coed y Brenin
734
RHOBELL FAWR
Afon Gamlan
Coed Ganllwyd
Rhaeadr Ddu
Ganllwyd
Afon Wen
Y Berwyn (Lake Vyrnwy section)
Llanfachreth
905
ARAN FAWDDWY
Lake Vyrnwy
B4393
Llanelltyd
Cymer Abbey
B4416
Brithdir
Llanymawddwy
Llanwddyn
Toll
Dolgellau
A470
0 1 2 3 4 miles
0 1 2 3 4 5 kilometres
Dinas-Mawddwy
Minllyn
544
TIR RHIWIOG
Afon Twrch
CADER IDRIS
Trawsfynydd

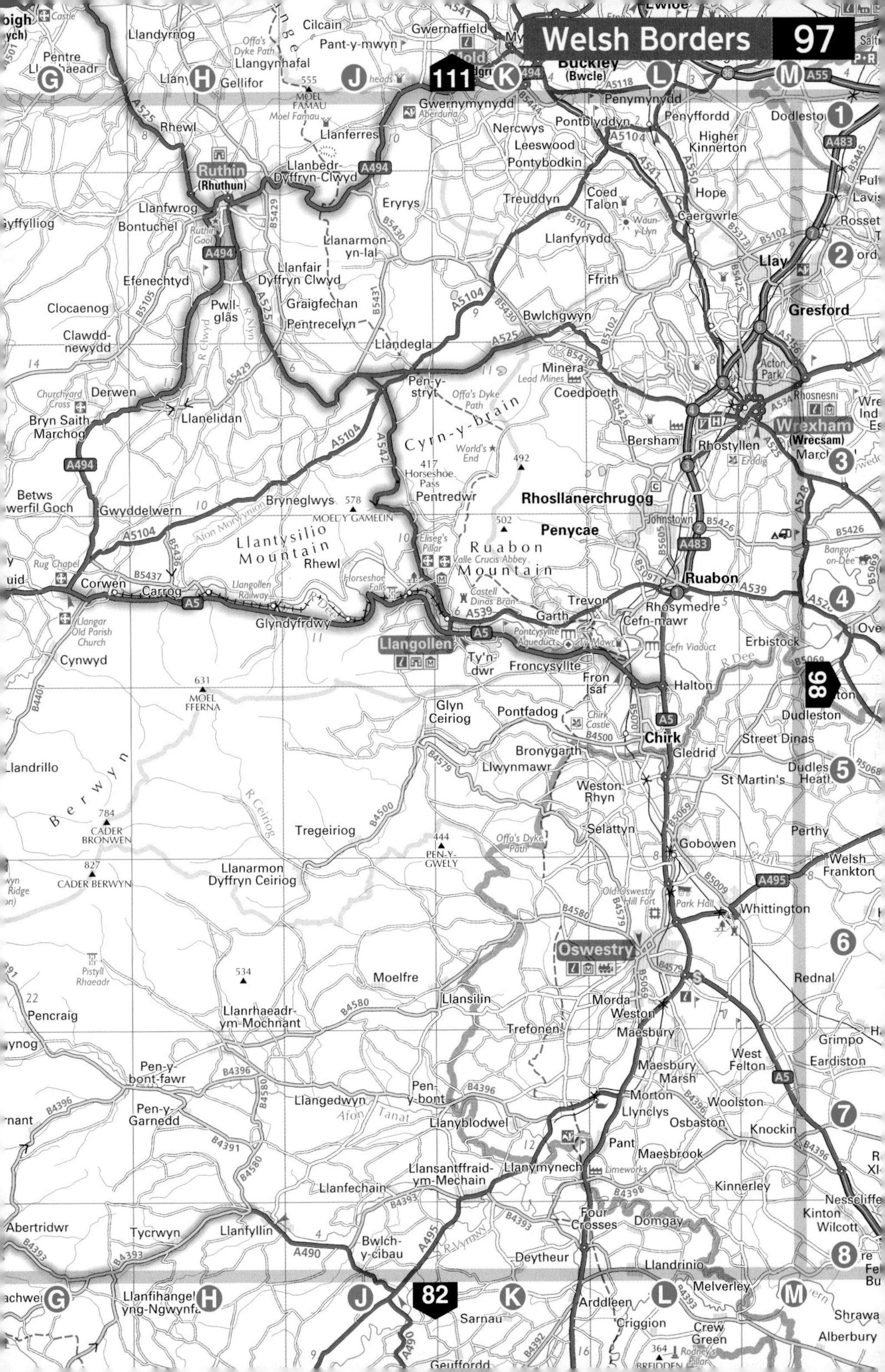

Llandyrnog
Cilcain
Gwernaffield
Pant-y-mwyn
Offa's Dyke Path
Llangynhafal
Pentre
Gellifor
Mold
Buckley
(Bwcle)
111
555
MOEL FAMAU
Moel Famau
Gwernymynydd
Aberduna
Penymynydd
Penyffordd
Dodleston
Rhewl
Llanferres
Nercwys
Pontblyddyn
Leeswood
Higher Kinnerton
Ruthin
(Rhuthun)
Llanbedr-Dyffryn-Clwyd
Pontybodkin
Llanfwrog
Eryrys
Treuddyn
Coed Talon
Hope
Bontuchel
Ruthin Gaol
Llanarmon-yn-Ial
Waun-y-Llyn
Caergwrle
Llanfynydd
Rossett
Llay
Llanfair Dyffryn Clwyd
Efenechtyd
Ffrith
Graigfechan
Clocaenog
Pwll-glâs
R Alyn
Pentrecelyn
Bwlchgwyn
Gresford
Clawdd-newydd
R Clwyd
Llandegla
Minera
Lead Mines
Acton Park
Churchyard Cross
Derwen
Pen-y-stryt
Offa's Dyke Path
Coedpoeth
Rhosnesni
Bryn Saith Marchog
Llanelidan
Cyrn-y-brain
Wrexham
(Wrecsam)
World's End
Bersham
Rhostyllen
Erddig
492
417
Horseshoe Pass
Betws Gwerfil Goch
Pentredwr
Rhosllanerchrugog
Gwyddelwern
Bryneglwys
578
MOEL Y GAMELIN
Afon Morwynion
502
Johnstown
Penycae
Llantysilio Mountain
Eliseg's Pillar
Ruabon Mountain
Valle Crucis Abbey
Bangor-on-Dee
Rug Chapel
Rhewl
Corwen
Carrog
Llangollen Railway
Horseshoe Falls
Castell Dinas Bran
Ruabon
Trevor
Rhosymedre
Glyndyfrdwy
R Dee
Garth
Cefn-mawr
Llangar Old Parish Church
Llangollen
Pontcysyllte Aqueduct
Ty Mawr
Cefn Viaduct
Erbistock
Cynwyd
Ty'n-dwr
Froncysyllte
Fron Isaf
Halton
631
MOEL FFERNA
Glyn Ceiriog
Pontfadog
Chirk Castle
Dudleston
Chirk
Gledrid
Street Dinas
Llandrillo
Bronygarth
Llwynmawr
Dudleston Heath
Berwyn
St Martin's
R Ceiriog
Weston Rhyn
784
CADER BRONWEN
Tregeiriog
Selattyn
Perthy
444
PEN-Y-GWELY
Offa's Dyke Path
Gobowen
827
CADER BERWYN
Llanarmon Dyffryn Ceiriog
Welsh Frankton
Old Oswestry Hill Fort
Park Hall
Whittington
Oswestry
Pistyll Rhaeadr
534
Moelfre
Rednal
Llansilin
Morda
Pencraig
Weston
Llanrhaeadr-ym-Mochnant
Trefonen
Maesbury
Grimpo
West Felton
Eardiston
Pen-y-bont-fawr
Maesbury Marsh
Pen-y-bont
Morton
Llangedwyn
Woolston
Llynclys
Pen-y-Garnedd
Afon Tanat
Llanyblodwel
Osbaston
Knockin
Pant
Maesbrook
Llansantffraid-ym-Mechain
Llanymynech
Limeworks
Llanfechain
Kinnerley
Nesscliffe
Four Crosses
Domgay
Kinton
Abertridwr
Tycrwyn
Llanfyllin
Wilcott
Bwlch-y-cibau
R Vyrnwy
Deytheur
Llandrinio
Melverley
Llanfihangel yng-Ngwynfa
82
Arddleen
Sarnau
Criggion
Shrawardine
Crew Green
Alberbury
364
Rodney's Pillar
BREIDDEN
Geufford

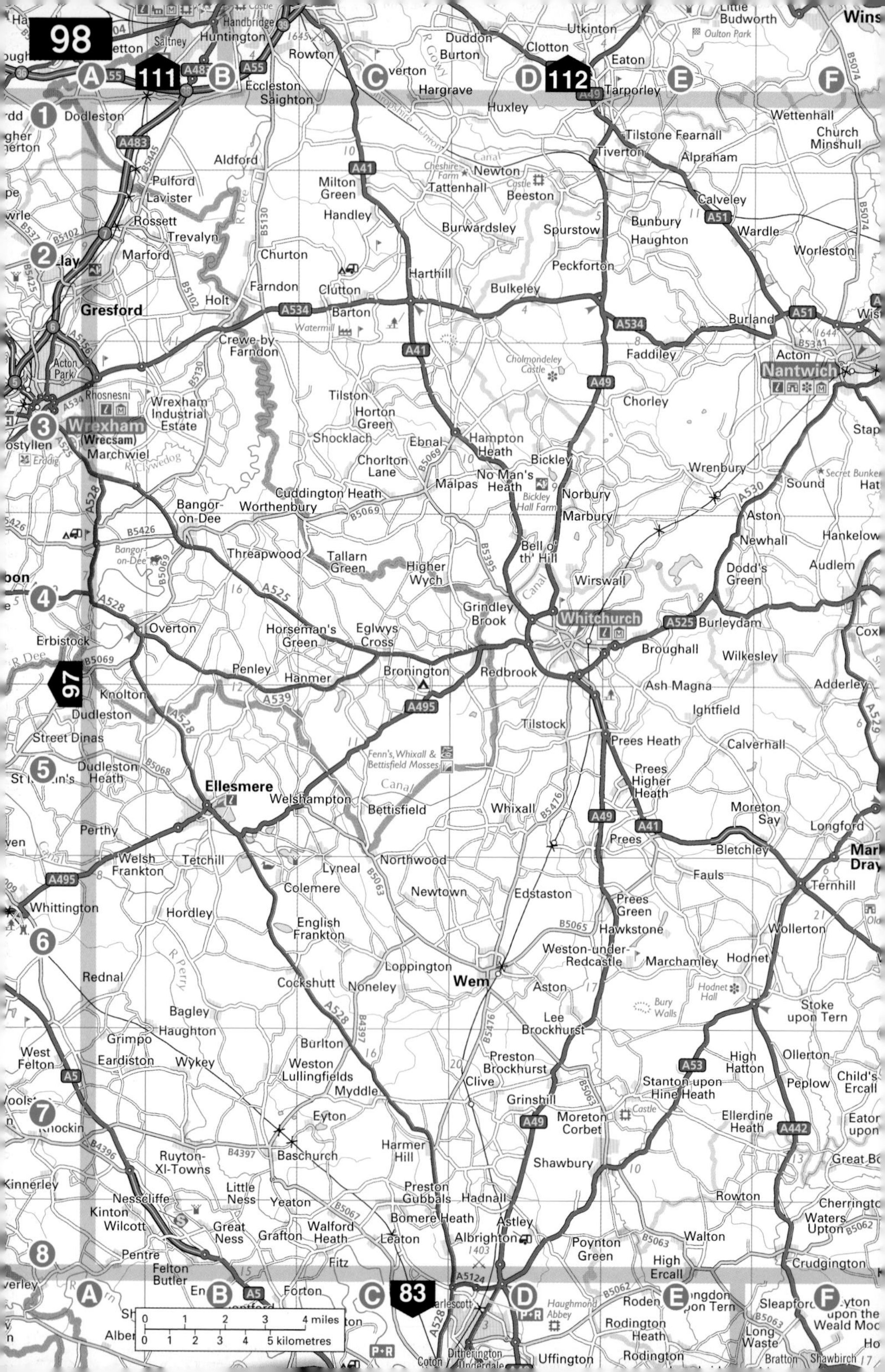
111
112
97
83
A B C D E F
1 2 3 4 5 6 7 8
Handbridge
Saltney
Huntington
Rowton
Duddon
Burton
Utkinton
Clotton
Eaton
Little Budworth
Oulton Park
Wins
Eccleston
Saighton
Hargrave
Huxley
Tarporley
Dodleston
Wettenhall
Church Minshull
Tilstone Fearnall
Tiverton
Alpraham
Aldford
Pulford
Lavister
Rossett
Trevalyn
Marford
Gresford
Holt
Milton Green
Handley
Cheshire Farm
Newton
Tattenhall
Castle
Beeston
Burwardsley
Spurstow
Bunbury
Haughton
Calveley
Wardle
Worleston
Churton
Farndon
Clutton
Barton
Harthill
Bulkeley
Peckforton
Watermill
Burland
Acton
Nantwich
Faddiley
Crewe-by-Farndon
Cholmondeley Castle
Acton Park
Rhosnesni
Wrexham Industrial Estate
Wrexham (Wrecsam)
Erddig
Marchwiel
R Clywedog
Tilston
Horton Green
Shocklach
Ebnal
Hampton Heath
Chorlton Lane
Malpas
No Man's Heath
Bickley
Bickley Hall Farm
Chorley
Wrenbury
Sound
Secret Bunker
Cuddington Heath
Worthenbury
Bangor-on-Dee
Norbury
Marbury
Aston
Newhall
Hankelow
Threapwood
Tallarn Green
Higher Wych
Bell o' th' Hill
Wirswall
Dodd's Green
Audlem
Grindley Brook
Whitchurch
Burleydam
Overton
Erbistock
R Dee
Horseman's Green
Eglwys Cross
Broughall
Wilkesley
Penley
Hanmer
Bronington
Redbrook
Ash Magna
Adderley
Knolton
Dudleston
Tilstock
Ightfield
Street Dinas
Prees Heath
Calverhall
Fenn's, Whixall & Bettisfield Mosses
Dudleston Heath
Prees Higher Heath
Canal
Ellesmere
Welshampton
Bettisfield
Whixall
Moreton Say
Longford
Perthy
Prees
Bletchley
Welsh Frankton
Tetchill
Lyneal
Northwood
Fauls
Ternhill
Colemere
Newtown
Edstaston
Whittington
Hordley
Prees Green
English Frankton
Hawkstone
Wollerton
Weston-under-Redcastle
Marchamley
Hodnet
Rednal
R Perry
Loppington
Cockshutt
Noneley
Wem
Aston
Hodnet Hall
Bury Walls
Stoke upon Tern
Bagley
Lee Brockhurst
Grimpo
Haughton
West Felton
Eardiston
Wykey
Burlton
Weston Lullingfields
Preston Brockhurst
High Hatton
Ollerton
Clive
Stanton upon Hine Heath
Peplow
Child's Ercall
Myddle
Grinshill
Eyton
Moreton Corbet
Ellerdine Heath
Knockin
Harmer Hill
Baschurch
Ruyton-XI-Towns
Shawbury
Great Bo
Kinnerley
Little Ness
Preston Gubbals
Hadnall
Rowton
Nesscliffe
Yeaton
Bomere Heath
Astley
Cherrington
Kinton
Wilcott
Great Ness
Grafton
Walford Heath
Leaton
Albrighton
Waters Upton
Pentre
Poynton Green
Walton
Fitz
High Ercall
Crudgington
Felton Butler
Forton
Haughmond Abbey
Roden
Sleapford
Rodington Heath
Long Waste
Uffington
Rodington
Bratton
Shawbirch
Coton
Ditherington
Underdale
P+R
0 1 2 3 4 miles
0 1 2 3 4 5 kilometres
A55 A483 A41 A49 A51 A534 A525 A528 A495 A539 A5 A53 A442 A5124
B5445 B5102 B5130 B5425 B5069 B5426 B5395 B5068 B5476 B5063 B5065 B4397 B4396 B5067 B5062 B5074 B5341

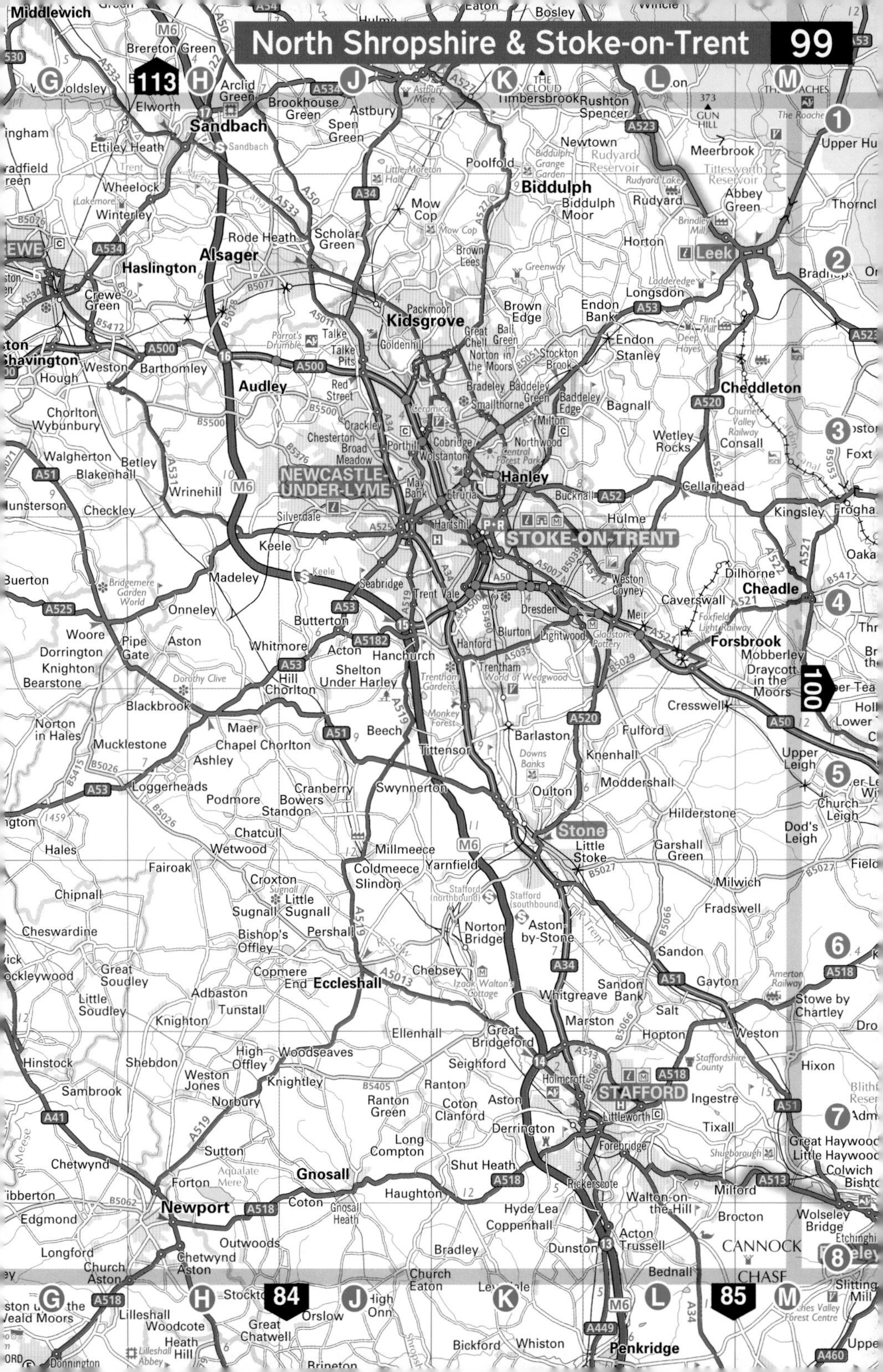
Middlewich
113
Brereton Green
Arclid Green
Sandbach
Brookhouse Green
Astbury
Spen Green
Timbersbrook
Rushton Spencer
Elworth
Ettiley Heath
Wheelock
Winterley
Rode Heath
Alsager
Haslington
Crewe Green
Scholar Green
Mow Cop
Biddulph
Biddulph Moor
Rudyard
Meerbrook
Abbey Green
Leek
Horton
Longsdon
Endon Bank
Endon
Stanley
Brown Edge
Kidsgrove
Talke
Talke Pits
Goldenhill
Packmoor
Weston
Barthomley
Shavington
Hough
Audley
Red Street
Chorlton
Wybunbury
Walgherton
Betley
Blakenhall
Wrinehill
Checkley
NEWCASTLE-UNDER-LYME
Chesterton
Crackley
Porthill
Wolstanton
Cobridge
Hanley
Smallthorne
Milton
Baddeley Edge
Bagnall
Northwood
Cheddleton
Wetley Rocks
Consall
Cellarhead
Bucknall
Hulme
STOKE-ON-TRENT
Keele
Silverdale
Madeley
Onneley
Buerton
Woore
Pipe Gate
Aston
Dorrington
Knighton
Bearstone
Whitmore
Acton
Butterton
Seabridge
Trent Vale
Hanford
Blurton
Lightwood
Dresden
Weston Coyney
Meir
Caverswall
Dilhorne
Cheadle
Forsbrook
Kingsley
Froghall
Oakamoor
Mobberley
Draycott in the Moors
Cresswell
Hanchurch
Shelton Under Harley
Hill Chorlton
Trentham
Barlaston
Blackbrook
Maer
Chapel Chorlton
Ashley
Beech
Tittensor
Fulford
Knenhall
Moddershall
Norton in Hales
Mucklestone
Loggerheads
Podmore
Cranberry
Bowers
Standon
Swynnerton
Oulton
Upper Leigh
Church Leigh
Dod's Leigh
Hilderstone
Stone
Little Stoke
Garshall Green
Hales
Chatcull
Wetwood
Fairoak
Millmeece
Coldmeece
Yarnfield
Slindon
Croxton
Little Sugnall
Sugnall
Chipnall
Cheswardine
Bishop's Offley
Pershall
Milwich
Fradswell
Norton Bridge
Aston-by-Stone
Sandon
Great Soudley
Little Soudley
Copmere End
Eccleshall
Chebsey
Adbaston
Tunstall
Knighton
Whitgreave
Sandon Bank
Gayton
Salt
Stowe by Chartley
Marston
Hopton
Weston
Ellenhall
Great Bridgeford
Hinstock
Shebdon
High Offley
Woodseaves
Seighford
Weston Jones
Knightley
Sambrook
Norbury
Ranton
Ranton Green
Coton Clanford
Aston
Holmcroft
STAFFORD
Ingestre
Littleworth
Hixon
Derrington
Tixall
Great Haywood
Little Haywood
Colwich
Chetwynd
Sutton
Long Compton
Forebridge
Forton
Gnosall
Shut Heath
Rickerscote
Milford
Newport
Coton
Haughton
Walton-on-the-Hill
Edgmond
Hyde Lea
Coppenhall
Brocton
Wolseley Bridge
Longford
Outwoods
Bradley
Dunston
Acton Trussell
CANNOCK CHASE
Church Aston
Chetwynd Aston
Church Eaton
Bednall
Lilleshall
Woodcote
Great Chatwell
Orslow
High Onn
Heath Hill
Bickford
Whiston
Penkridge
Donnington
Brineton
84
85
100

A
B
C
D
E
F
1
2
3
4
5
6
7
8
114
99
85
86
PEAK DISTRICT
NATIONAL PARK
Longnor
Crowdecote
Pilsbury
Arbor Low Stone Circle
Youlgreave
Haddon Hall
Alport
Stanton in Peak
Middleton
Birchover
Churchtown
Darley Bridge
Wensley
Darley Dale
Oker Side
Forest
The Roaches
Hartington
Brund
Sheen
Heathcote
Upper Hulme
Upper Elkstone
Hartington
Hulme End
River Dove
Biggin
Elton
Winster
Market House
Cable Car
Heights of Abraham
Bonsall
Gulliver's Kingdom
Masson Mills
Matlock
Cromford
Thorncliff
R Hamps
Warslow
Grangemill
Aldwark
Ible
Middleton
National Stone Centre
Middleton Top
Bolehill
Abbey Green
Bradnop
Onecote
Butterton
Alstonefield
Alsop en le Dale
Longcliffe
Brassington
Wirksworth
Wetton
Grindon
Hope
Ford
Milldale
Parwich
Ballidon
Hopton
Carsington
R Manifold
Dove Dale
Tissington
Bradbourne
Carsington Water
Cheddleton
Winkhill
Waterfall
Ilam
Ilam Park
Calton
Fenny Bentley
Hognaston
Kirk Ireton
Kniveton
Churnet Valley
Ipstones
Waterhouses
Cauldon
Caldon Canal
Thorpe
Blackwall
Idridgehay
Ecclesbourne Valley Railway
Foxt
Blore
Atlow
Mapleton
Ashbourne
Hulland Ward
Hillcliff Lane
Shottle
Whiston
Kingsley
Froghall
Near Cotton
Stanton
Mayfield
Hulland
Turnditch
Cowers Lane
Bradley
Cross o' th' hands
Hazelwood
Cotton Dell
Ramshorn
Middle Mayfield
Clifton
Oakamoor
Wootton
Farley
Upper Ellastone
Church Mayfield
Osmaston
Dilhorne
Cheadle
Alton Towers
Ellastone
Snelston
Darley Moor
Mugginton
Forsbrook
Threapwood
Alton
Wyaston
Weston Underwood
Mobberley
Bradley in the Moors
Denstone
Norbury
Shirley
Brailsford
Kedleston
Greatgate
Roston
Rodsley
Kedleston Hall
Upper Tean
Croxden
Abbey
Rocester
Yeaveley
Hollington
Kirk Langley
Hollington
Lower Tean
Marston Montgomery
Great Cubley
Alkmonton
Thurvaston
Longlane
Checkley
Longford
Upper Leigh
Fole
Little Cubley
Lees Green
Lees
Mackworth
Lower Leigh
Withington
Stramshall
Somersal Herbert
Boylestone
Sutton Brook
Radbourne
Church Leigh
Upper Nobut
Harehill
Trusley
Dod's Leigh
Doveridge
Lane Ends
Mickleover
Field
Uttoxeter
Church Broughton
Sutton on the Hill
Bramshall
Milwich
R Dove
Sudbury Hall
Foston
Burnaston
Fradswell
Birch Cross
Sudbury
Marchington
Scropton
Hatton
Etwall
Hilton
Kingstone
Gorsty Hill
Marston on Dove
Egginton
Amerton Railway
Draycott in the Clay
Tutbury
Rolleston on Dove
Stowe by Chartley
Willington
Hanbury
Repton
Drointon
Weston
Newborough
Stretton
Milton
Hixon
Newton
Abbots Bromley
Anslow
Anslow Gate
Newton Solney
Horninglow
Blithfield Reservoir
FA National Football Centre
BURTON UPON TRENT
Admaston
Great Haywood
Hoar Cross
Newchurch
Rangemore
Winshill
Bretby
Shugborough
Little Haywood
Tatenhill
Colwich
Stapenhill
Milford
Bishton
Colton
Hadley End
Dunstall
Branston
Branston Water Park
Swadlincote
Brocton
Wolseley Bridge
Blithbury
Hamstall Ridware
Olive Green
Woodhouses
Barton-under-Needwood
Etchinghill
Hill Ridware
Walton-on-Trent
CANNOCK CHASE
Rugeley
Morrey
Yoxall
Trent Valley
Castle Gresley
Cauldwell
Slitting Mill
Mavesyn Ridware
Nethertown
King's Bromley
Wychnor
Rosliston
Cannock Chase Valley Forest Centre
Coton in the Elms
Overseal
Alrewas
National Memorial
Fradley
Longdon
Donisthorpe
R Trent
R Derwent
Tixall
Dove Valley
0 1 2 3 4 miles
0 1 2 3 4 5 kilometres
A53
A523
A52
A515
A517
A50
A522
A521
A518
A51
A513
A511
A38
A5121
A444
A514
A516
A5012
A460
B5053
B5054
B5056
B5035
B5023
B5032
B5417
B5033
B5030
B5027
B5017
B5013
B5014
B5234
B5016
B5008
B5353
B5020

MANSFIELD
NOTTINGHAM
DERBY
Loughborough
Sutton-in-Ashfield
Kirkby-in-Ashfield
Alfreton
South Normanton
Pinxton
Selston
Somercotes
Swanwick
Ripley
Codnor
Heanor
Eastwood
Hucknall
Ravenshead
Blidworth
Rainworth
Bilsthorpe
Farnsfield
Calverton
Arnold
Burton Joyce
Radcliffe on Trent
West Bridgford
Beeston
Stapleford
Ilkeston
Long Eaton
Clifton
Ruddington
Cotgrave
Keyworth
Kegworth
Castle Donington
Melbourne
Shepshed
Whitwick
Barrow upon Soar
Sileby
Mountsorrel
East Leake
Borrowash
Ockbrook
Belper
Clay Cross
North Wingfield
Sherwood Forest
SHERWOOD FOREST
M1
A38
A52
A60
A453
A6
A46
A606
A6097
A617
A614
A610
A42
A511
A512
115
102
87

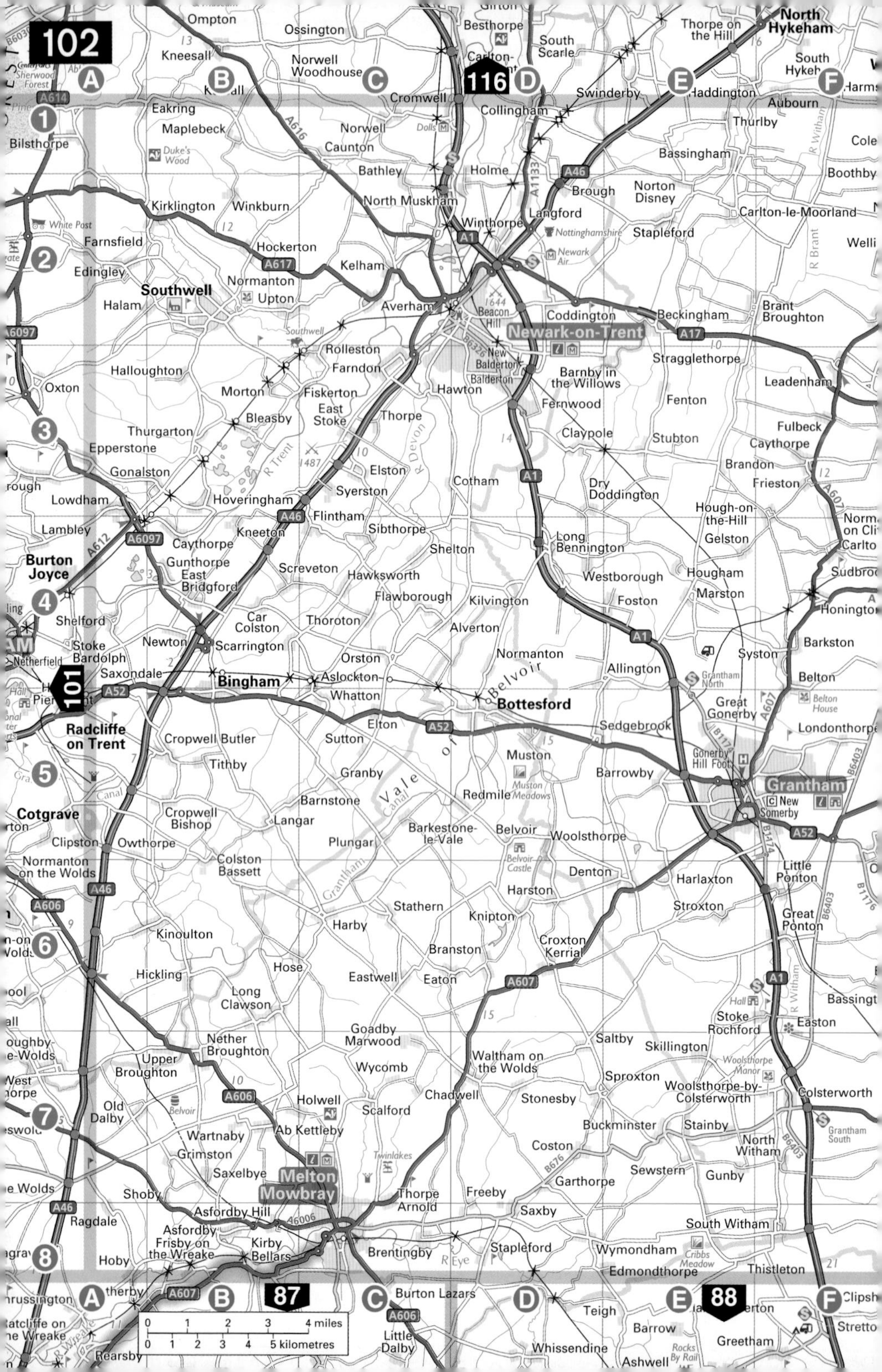

Ompton
Ossington
Besthorpe
South Scarle
Thorpe on the Hill
North Hykeham
Kneesall
Norwell Woodhouse
Carlton-on-Trent
South Hykeham
Sherwood Forest
A614
Cromwell
116
Swinderby
Haddington
Harmston
Eakring
Collingham
Aubourn
Maplebeck
Norwell
Dolls
Thurlby
Bilsthorpe
Duke's Wood
Caunton
A616
Bassingham
R Witham
Bathley
Holme
A46
A1133
Brough
Norton Disney
Boothby
Kirklington
Winkburn
North Muskham
Langford
Carlton-le-Moorland
White Post
Winthorpe
A1
Nottinghamshire
Stapleford
Farnsfield
Hockerton
Newark Air
R Brant
Edingley
A617
Kelham
Normanton
Upton
Southwell
Halam
Averham
1644
Beacon Hill
Coddington
Beckingham
Brant Broughton
A6097
Southwell
Newark-on-Trent
A17
Rolleston
B6326
Farndon
New Balderton
Barnby in the Willows
Stragglethorpe
Halloughton
Balderton
Leadenham
Oxton
Morton
Fiskerton
Hawton
Fenton
East Stoke
Thorpe
Fernwood
Bleasby
R Devon
Claypole
Stubton
Fulbeck
Thurgarton
Caythorpe
Epperstone
R Trent
1487
Elston
Brandon
Gonalston
Cotham
A1
Frieston
Syerston
Dry Doddington
A607
Lowdham
Hoveringham
Flintham
Hough-on-the-Hill
A46
Sibthorpe
Lambley
A612
Kneeton
Long Bennington
Gelston
A6097
Caythorpe
Shelton
Carlton
Burton Joyce
Gunthorpe
East Bridgford
Screveton
Hawksworth
Westborough
Hougham
Sudbrook
Flawborough
Kilvington
Foston
Marston
Shelford
Car Colston
Thoroton
Honington
Alverton
A1
Newton
Barkston
Stoke Bardolph
Scarrington
Normanton
Syston
Netherfield
Orston
Allington
Grantham North
Saxondale
Belvoir
Belton
Bingham
Aslockton
101
A52
Whatton
Bottesford
Great Gonerby
Belton House
Elton
A52
Sedgebrook
Radcliffe on Trent
Cropwell Butler
Sutton
Londonthorpe
B1174
Muston
Gonerby Hill Foot
Tithby
B6403
Granby
Barrowby
Vale of Belvoir
Muston Meadows
Grantham
Barnstone
Redmile
New Somerby
Cotgrave
Canal
Cropwell Bishop
Langar
Barkestone-le-Vale
Belvoir
Woolsthorpe
Clipston
Owthorpe
Plungar
A52
Belvoir Castle
B1174
Normanton on the Wolds
Colston Bassett
Denton
Harlaxton
Little Ponton
Grantham Canal
Harston
A46
A606
B1176
Stroxton
B6403
Stathern
Knipton
Great Ponton
Harby
Kinoulton
Croxton Kerrial
Branston
Hose
Hickling
Eastwell
Eaton
A607
A1
Long Clawson
Hall
R Witham
Bassingthorpe
Stoke Rochford
Goadby Marwood
Easton
Nether Broughton
Saltby
Skillington
Upper Broughton
Waltham on the Wolds
Woolsthorpe Manor
Wycomb
Sproxton
Woolsthorpe-by-Colsterworth
Colsterworth
A606
Chadwell
Old Dalby
Holwell
Scalford
Stonesby
Buckminster
Stainby
Grantham South
Ab Kettleby
Wartnaby
Coston
North Witham
B6403
Grimston
B676
Twinlakes
Saxelbye
Melton Mowbray
Sewstern
Garthorpe
Gunby
Shoby
Thorpe Arnold
Freeby
A46
Asfordby Hill
Ragdale
A6006
Saxby
South Witham
Asfordby
Frisby on the Wreake
Kirby Bellars
Stapleford
Wymondham
Cribbs Meadow
Brentingby
R Eye
Hoby
Edmondthorpe
Thistleton
Thrussington
Atherby
A607
87
Burton Lazars
88
Clipsham
A606
Teigh
Barrow
Stretton
Ratcliffe on the Wreake
R Wreake
Greetham
Little Dalby
Rocks By Rail
Rearsby
Whissendine
Ashwell
0 1 2 3 4 miles
0 1 2 3 4 5 kilometres

Nocton
Metheringham
Blankney
Scopwick
Kirkby Green
Martin
Timberland
Woodhall Spa
Kirkby on Bain
Kirkstead
Tattershall Thorpe
Tattershall
Tattershall Castle
Tattershall College
Coningsby
Battle of Britain Memorial Flight
Tumby
Tumby Woodside
Revesby
Mareham le Fen
East Kirkby
New Bolingbroke
Ashby de la Launde
Rowston
Thorpe Tilney
Walcott
Billinghay
Digby
Dorrington
Bloxholm
Ruskington
Cranwell
Anwick
North Kyme
South Kyme
Dogdyke
Chapel Hill
Hawthorn Hill
New York
Scrub Hill
West Fen
Holland Fen
Gipsey Bridge
Frithville
Sibsey Trader Windmill
Fishtoft Drove
Langrick
Anton's Gowt
Leasingham
North Rauceby
Holdingham
Sleaford
South Rauceby
Quarrington
Evedon
Ewerby
Kirkby la Thorpe
Howell
Asgarby
Heckington
The Pearoom
Great Hale
Little Hale
East Heckington
Boston
Witham Way
Silk Willoughby
Burton Pedwardine
Scredington
Helpringham
Swarby
Aswarby
Culverthorpe
Heydour
Aisby
Aunsby
Osbournby
Spanby
Swaton
Swineshead
Bicker
Kirton
Dembleby
Newton
Haceby
Braceby
Walcot
Threekingham
Horbling
Billingborough
Northorpe
Donington
Wigtoft
Sutterton
Algarkirk
Burtoft
Quadring Eaudike
Quadring
Sapperton
Pickworth
Folkingham
Humby
Laughton
Pointon
Westhorpe
Gosberton
Fosdyke
Skeldyke
Aslackby
Lenton
Ingoldsby
Risegate
Dowsby
Rippingale
Surfleet
Moulton Seas End
Irnham
Kirkby Underwood
Dunsby
Pinchbeck
Corby Glen
Hacconby
Hanthorpe
Morton
Elsthorpe
Grimsthorpe
Grimsthorpe Castle
Swinstead
Edenham
Dyke
Springfields
Mill Green
Spalding
Fulney
Weston
Moulton
Bourne
Twenty
Creeton
Little Bytham
Lound
Witham on the Hill
Toft
Thurlby
Manthorpe
Carlby
Baston
Deeping Fen
Bedford
Level
Cowbit
Moulton Chapel
R Witham
R Slea
R Welland
R Glen
South Forty Foot Drain
Timberland Delph
117
118
104
89

Old Bolingbroke
Bolingbroke Castle
Toynton All Saints
Halton Holegate
Great Steeping
Monksthorpe
Burgh le Marsh
A158
Natureland Seal Sanctuary
Northcote
B1195
Bratoft
118
119
in the Marsh
East Kirkby
Lincolnshire Aviation
Little Steeping
Firsby
Skegness
Revesby
Mareham le Fen
Stickford
Keal Cotes
Croft
Fendike Corner
Thorpe St Peter
Wainfleet Haven
Wainfleet All Saints
Tumby Woodside
New Bolingbroke
Stickney
New Leake
Wainfleet St Mary
A52
Gibraltar Point
Eastville
East Fen
Friskney
A16
West Fen
B1183
Northlands
Leake Common Side
Sibsey Trader Windmill
Sibsey
Frithville
B1184
Fishtoft Drove
Wrangle
Old Leake
Hilldyke
Leverton
Anton's Gowt
Benington
Witham Way
Butterwick
Boston
A1121
Freiston
Fishtoft
Scrane End
Wyberton East
B1391
B1397
Havenside
103
Kirton
Frampton
The Haven
Frampton Marsh
THE WASH
Skeldyke
Sutterton
Algarkirk
Fosdyke
Holbeach St Matthew
R Welland
Holbeach St Mark's
Holbeach Marsh
Gedney Drove End
B1359
B1357
A17
Moulton Seas End
Saracen's Head
Holbeach Bank
Holbeach Hurn
Gedney Dyke
Holbeach Clough
Lutton
Fleet Hargate
The Wash
Weston
A151
B1515
Holbeach
Moulton
Whaplode
Fleet
Gedney
Butterfly & Falconry Park
Great Ouse
Long Sutton
Gedney Broadgate
Sutton Bridge
B1165
Terrington St Clement
B1168
Walpole Cross Keys
West Lynn
B1390
Clenchwarton
Moulton Chapel
Tydd Gote
Tilney All Saints
Holbeach St Johns
Sutton St James
Tydd St Mary
Walpole St Andrew
Tilney High End
A47
Four Gotes
Walpole St Peter
89
90
Level
Tydd St Giles
River Nene
0 1 2 3 4 miles
0 1 2 3 4 5 kilometres
Newton
West Walton
Tilney St Lawrence
Sutton

G
H
J
K
L
M
1
2
3
4
5
6
7
8
North Norfolk Heritage Coast
Holkham Bay
Blakeney Poir
Scolt Head Island
Brancaster Bay
Peddars Way & Norfolk Coast Path
Holme Dunes
Holme next the Sea
Brancaster
Brancaster Staithe
Burnham Norton
Burnham Overy Staithe
Holkham
Wells-next-the-Sea
A149
Stiff
Old Hunstanton
Thornham
Titchwell
Branodunum Roman Fort
Burnham Deepdale
B1155
Holkham Hall
Burnham Market
Burnham Overy
Burnham Thorpe
Warham
unstanton
Ringstead
B1355
B1105
Wighton
B1153
B1155
Summerfield
North Creake
Creake Abbey
Wells & Walsingham Light Railway
ham Priory
arket Cross
106
Heacham
Norfolk Lavender
Peddars Way & Norfolk Coast Path
The Shrine of Our Lady
Docking
Stanhoe
Little Walsingham
Great Walsingham
Sedgeford
B1454
B1155
South Creake
North Barsham
Hindringham
Houghton St Giles
Thursfo
Fring
Bircham Newton
West Barsham
East Barsham
Great Snoring
Snettisham
Park
Thursford
Snettisham
Syderstone
R Stiffkey
A148
Ingoldisthorpe
Shernborne
Great Bircham
Bircham Tofts
Wicken Green Village
Little Snoring
Croxto
B1440
B1454
Sculthorpe
Dersingham
Kettlestone
Anmer
Dunton
Shereford
Pensthorpe Waterfowl Park
Dersingham Bog
Tattersett
Coxford
Fakenham
ferton
Houghton Hall
West Rudham
Hempton
Sandringham
West Newton
New Houghton
B1146
Little Ryburgh
Babingley River
Tatterford
East Rudham
Toftrees
A149
A148
Flitcham
Great Ryburgh
B1440
B1439
Helhoughton
East Raynham
Colkirk
A1067
R Wensum
Harpley
astle Rising
Hillington
West Raynham
Little Massingham
Gateley
Castle
South Raynham
Horningtoft
Congham
A148
Great Massingham
Roydon
Grimston
Weasenham St Peter
Whissonsett
Wootton
Roydon Common
B1110
A148
A149
Weasenham All Saints
Wellingham
Brisley
North Elmham
B1153
Tittleshall
Stanfield
Rougham
East Bilney
B1145
Gayton
B1145
Fairstead
Bawsey
Old Beetley
King's Lynn
Mileham
Ashwicken
Gayton Thorpe
B1146
B1145
A1065
Beetl
Litcham
Fair Green
East Winch
Gressenhall
East Lexham
West Lexham
East Walton
91
Bee
Gressenhall Green
North Runcton
Middleton
West Bilney
Castle
Newton
Priory
Longham
Blackborough End
Great Dunham
Gressenhall
B1153
South
Derehan
etchey

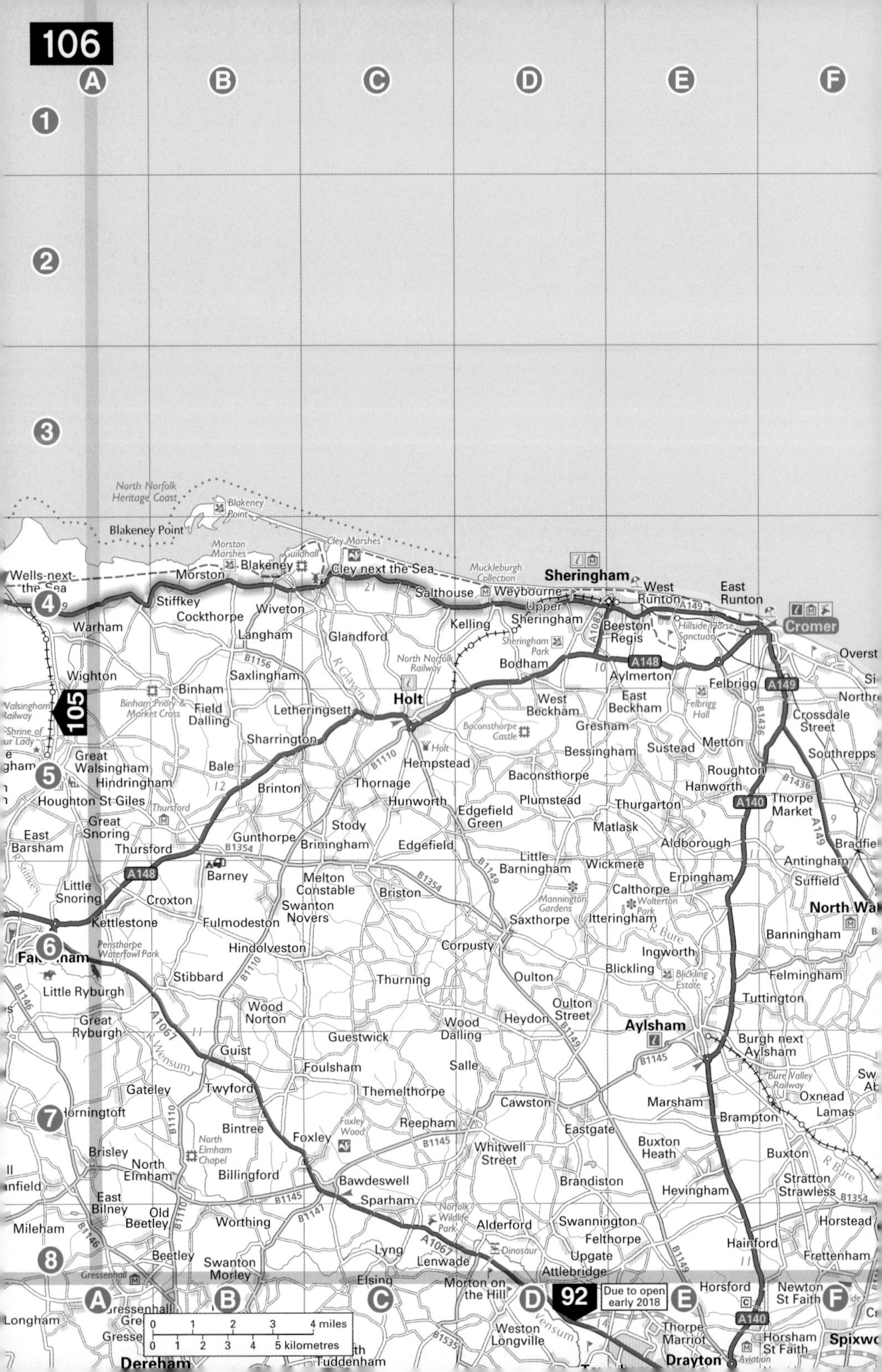

A
B
C
D
E
F
1
2
3
4
5
6
7
8
North Norfolk Heritage Coast
Blakeney Point
Morston Marshes
Guildhall
Cley Marshes
Wells-next-the Sea
Morston
Blakeney
Cley next the Sea
Muckleburgh Collection
Sheringham
Salthouse
Weybourne
Upper Sheringham
West Runton
East Runton
Cromer
Overst
Stiffkey
Warham
Cockthorpe
Wiveton
Langham
Glandford
Kelling
Sheringham Park
Beeston Regis
Hillside Horse Sanctuary
North Norfolk Railway
Bodham
Aylmerton
A148
A149
A1082
B1156
R Glaven
Wighton
Binham
Binham Priory & Market Cross
Walsingham Railway
Shrine of Our Lady
105
Field Dalling
Saxlingham
Letheringsett
Holt
West Beckham
East Beckham
Felbrigg
Felbrigg Hall
Northr
Crossdale Street
Gresham
Baconsthorpe Castle
Sharrington
Great Walsingham
Bale
Hempstead
Bessingham
Sustead
Metton
Southrepps
Hindringham
Houghton St Giles
Brinton
Thornage
Baconsthorpe
Roughton
Hanworth
B1436
A140
Thorpe Market
Thursford
Hunworth
Plumstead
Thurgarton
East Barsham
Great Snoring
Gunthorpe
Stody
Edgefield Green
Matlask
Aldborough
Bradfie
Briningham
Edgefield
B1354
Barney
Little Barningham
Wickmere
Antingham
Little Snoring
Melton Constable
Briston
Erpingham
Calthorpe
Suffield
Croxton
Swanton Novers
Mannington Gardens
Wolterton Park
North Wa
Kettlestone
Fulmodeston
Saxthorpe
Itteringham
Banningham
Fakenham
Pensthorpe Waterfowl Park
Hindolveston
Corpusty
R Bure
Ingworth
Blickling
Blickling Estate
Felmingham
Little Ryburgh
Stibbard
B1110
Thurning
Oulton
Tuttington
B1146
Wood Norton
Oulton Street
Great Ryburgh
A1067
Heydon
Wood Dalling
B1149
Aylsham
Burgh next Aylsham
Guestwick
R Wensum
Guist
Salle
B1145
Foulsham
Gateley
Twyford
Themelthorpe
Cawston
Marsham
Bure Valley Railway
Oxnead
Lamas
Horningtoft
Reepham
Brampton
Bintree
Foxley Wood
North Elmham Chapel
Foxley
Eastgate
Buxton Heath
Brisley
Whitwell Street
Buxton
North Elmham
Billingford
Bawdeswell
Brandiston
Stratton Strawless
East Bilney
Sparham
B1147
Hevingham
Old Beetley
Norfolk Wildlife Park
Alderford
Swannington
Horstead
Mileham
Worthing
Felthorpe
Hainford
Beetley
Lyng
Dinosaur
Upgate
Frettenham
Swanton Morley
Lenwade
Attlebridge
Gressenhall
Elsing
Morton on the Hill
92
Due to open early 2018
Horsford
Newton St Faith
Longham
Weston Longville
Thorpe Marriot
Horsham St Faith
Spixwo
Dereham
Tuddenham
Drayton
Aviation
B1535
Vensum
0 1 2 3 4 miles
0 1 2 3 4 5 kilometres

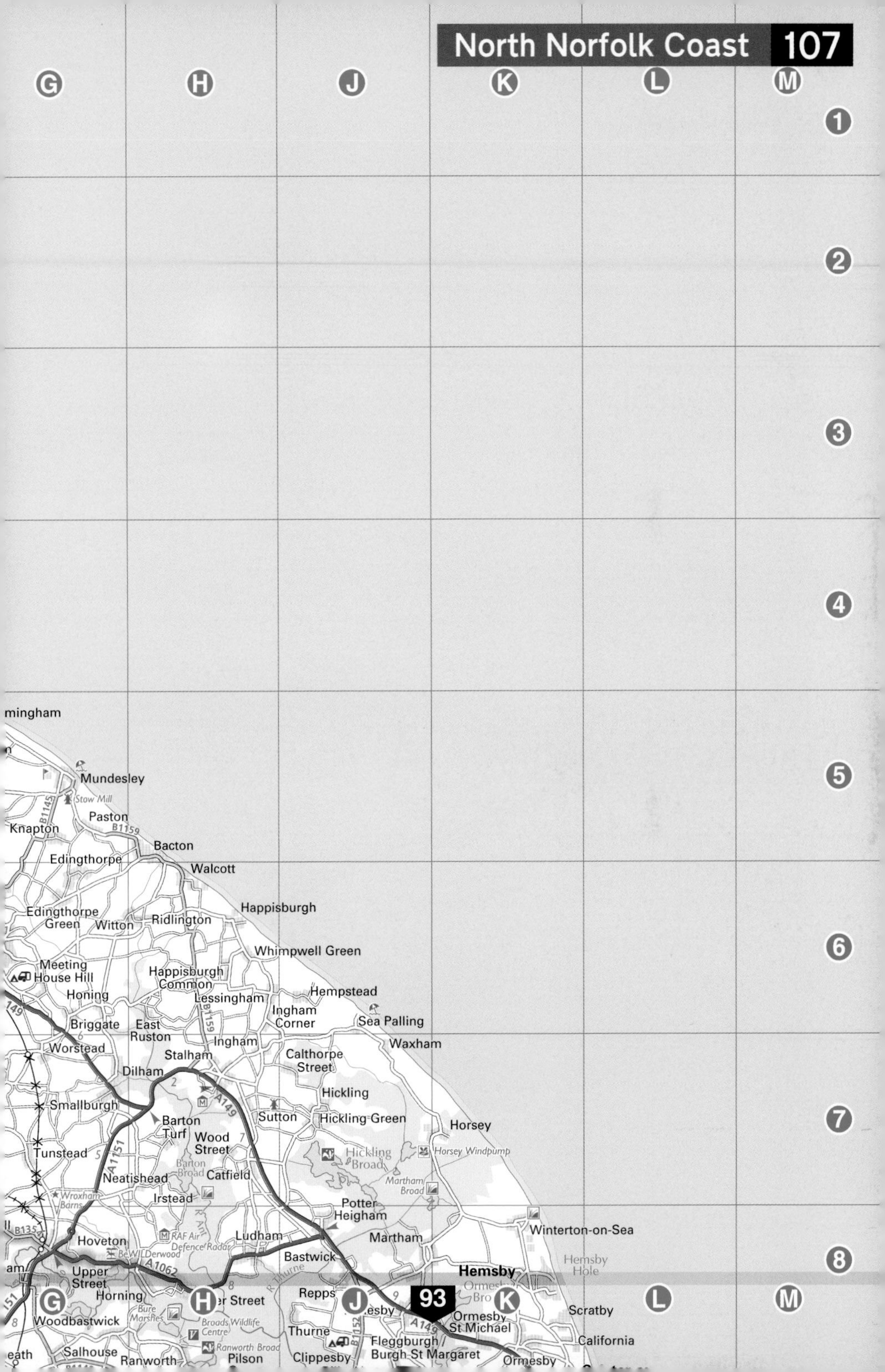
G
H
J
K
L
M
1
2
3
4
5
6
7
8
mingham
Mundesley
Stow Mill
B1145
Paston
B1159
Knapton
Bacton
Edingthorpe
Walcott
Edingthorpe Green
Witton
Ridlington
Happisburgh
Whimpwell Green
Meeting House Hill
Happisburgh Common
Honing
Lessingham
Hempstead
B1159
Ingham Corner
Sea Palling
Briggate
East Ruston
Worstead
Ingham
Waxham
Stalham
Calthorpe Street
Dilham
A149
Hickling
Smallburgh
Barton Turf
Sutton
Hickling Green
Horsey
Wood Street
Tunstead
A1151
Hickling Broad
Horsey Windpump
Barton Broad
Catfield
Neatishead
Martham Broad
Wroxham Barns
Irstead
Potter Heigham
B1354
Hoveton
RAF Air Defence Radar
Ludham
Winterton-on-Sea
Martham
BeWILDerwood
A1062
Bastwick
Hemsby
Hemsby Hole
Upper Street
R. Thurne
Horning
Repps
Ormesby Broad
Scratby
Woodbastwick
Bure Marshes
Broads Wildlife Centre
Thurne
Ormesby St Michael
B1152
A149
Fleggburgh / Burgh St Margaret
California
Ranworth Broad
Salhouse
Ranworth
Pilson
Clippesby
Ormesby
93

A
B
C
D
E
F
1
2
3
4
5
6
7
8
The Skerries
CARMEL HEAD
Hen Borth
Cemlyn Bay
Wylfa Head
Cemaes Bay
North Anglesey Heritage Coast
Porth Wen
Bull Bay
Amlwch
Llaneili
Cemaes
A5025
Burwen
Tregele
Llanfechell
Bodewryd
Penysarn
Llanfairynghornwy
Swtan Folk
Holyhead Bay
Church Bay
Llanrhyddlad
Carreglefn
Rhosybol
Dublin
Dublin
Llanfaethlu
Capel Parc
Llyn Alaw
B5111
Porth Tywynmawr
Llanddeusant
Llynnon Mill
Afon Alaw
Elim
North Stack
Llanfwrog
Gogarth Bay
Breakwater
Holyhead
(Caergybi)
Llanerchymedd
Holyhead Mountain Hut Circles
B5112
Capel Coch
South Stack
Ellins Tower
Penrhos Feliw
Llanfachraeth
Llyn Llywenan
Holyhead Mountain Heritage Coast
Kingsland
Llanynghenedl
ANGLESEY
Penrhyn Mawr
A5
Presaddfed
B5109
Valley
A5025
Bodedern
Trefignath
A55
Trearddur Bay
B5111
B4545
Caergeiliog
B5112
HOLY ISLAND
Four Mile Bridge
Llanfihangel yn Nhowyn
Bryngwran
Llynfaes
B5109
Cefni Reservoir
Oriel Ynys Môn
Llanfair-yn-Neubwll
Bodffordd
Gwalchmai
Valley
Rhoscolyn
Rhoscolyn Head
Anglesey
A5
A4080
Ty Newydd
Cymyran Bay
A55
A5114
Pencarnisiog
Llanfaelog
Llangristiolus
Rhosneigr
Din Dryfol
A4080
Henblas
Pentre Berw
B4422
Barclodiad y Gawres
Bethel
Afon Cefni
B4419
Porth Trecastell
Aberffraw
Llangadwaladr
Malltraeth
Anglesey Circuit
Bodowyr Burial Chamber
A4080
Llangaffo
B4421
B4419
Aberffraw Bay
Dwyran
Newborough
B4419
Aberffraw Bay Heritage Coast
Malltraeth Bay
Foel Farm Park
Newborough Warren
Caernarfon
Llanddwyn Island
Caernarfon Castle
Welsh Highland Railway
Foryd Bay
Airworld Aviation
0 1 2 3 4 miles
0 1 2 3 4 5 kilometres

95

G
H
J
K
L
M
1
2
3
4
5
6
7
8
Dulas Bay
Seawatch Centre
Moelfre
Llanallgo
Benllech
Cors Goch
Red Wharf Bay
Red Wharf Bay
Llanddona
Pentraeth
A5025
B5109
Hafoty Medieval House
Gaol
Beaumaris Castle
Beaumaris
Courthouse
Llansadwrn
Llandegfan
A545
Menai Bridge (Porthaethwy)
Llanfairpwllgwyngyll
Anglesey Column
Britannia Bridge
Bryn Celli Ddu
Plas Newydd
Bangor
Penrhyn Castle
Spinnies Abergowen
Llandygai
A4087
A55
Y Felinheli
GreenWood Forest Park
B4547
Pentir
Rhyd-y-groes
Seion
Bethel
Llanddeiniolen
Saron
Rhiwlas
A4244
B4366
Llanrug
Deiniolen
Segontium
Caeathro
Cwm-y-glo
Brynrefail
Llyn Padarn
Llanberis Lake Railway
Llanberis
Electric Mountain
Dolbadarn Castle
National Slate
Llyn Peris
Waunfawr
A4085
95
Puffin Island
Penmon Priory
Toll
Black Point
Llangoed
B5109
Llanfairfechan
Penmaenmawr
Dwygyfylchi
Abergwyngregyn
Coedydd Aber
Aber Falls
Afon Anafon
Tal-y-bont
Llanllechid
Rachub
Tregarth
Bethesda
Glasinfryn
B4409
ZipWorld
580 MOEL WINION
757 Y DROSGL
942 FOEL-FRAS
Afon Caseg
A5
1062 CARNEDD LLEWELYN
1044 CARNEDD DAFYDD
923 ELIDIR FAWR
946 Y GARN
917 Y TRYFAN
Llyn Ogwen
National Mountain Centre
SNOWDONIA NATIONAL PARK
610 TAL-Y-FAN
Afon Dulyn
Llyn Eigiau
Llyn Cowlyd
Llyn Crafnant
Llyn Geirionydd
The Ugly House
Conwy Bay
Great Orme Heritage Coast
GREAT ORMES HEAD
Great Orme Tramway
Toll
Llandudno
Deganwy
A546
B5115
A470
Conwy
Conwy Castle
Capelulo
Henryd
Rowen
B5106
Ty'n-y-Groes
Llanbedr-y-Cennin
Tal-y-Bont
Dolgarrog
Surf Snowdonia
Afon Ddu
Trefriw Woollen Mills
Trefriw
Vale of Conwy
Llanrwst
Gwydir Uchaf Chapel
96
Little Ormes
Penrhyn Bay
B5115
Llandrillo-yn-Rhos
Llandudno Junction
Llansanffraid Glan Conwy
Bodnant
Graig
Tal-y-Cafn
Eglwysbach
Llanddoget
Pentre-afarn-y-fedw
B5113
110

A
B
C
D
E
F
1
2
3
4
5
6
7
8
Little Ormes Head
Penrhyn Bay
Rhôs-on-Sea
Colwyn Bay
(Bae Colwyn)
Llandrillo-yn-Rhos
Llandudno Junction
Conwy Castle
Old Colwyn
Llanelian-yn-Rhôs
Bryn-y-Maen
Llansanffraid Glan Conwy
Llanddulas
Llysfaen
Rhyd-y-foel
Abergele
Abergele Roads
Pensarn
Towyn
Kinmel Bay
Rhyl
Miniature Railway
Prestatyn
Gronant
Llanasa
Gwaenysgor
Meliden
Trelawnyd
Dyserth
Cwm
Rhuddlan
Castle
Offa's Dyke
Rhuallt
Bodelwyddan
St George
Bodelwyddan Castle
St Asaph
Tremeirchion
Caerwys
Dolwen
Betws-yn-Rhos
Bodnant
Graig
Tal-y-Cafn
Eglwysbach
Vale of Conwy
Llanfair Talhaiarn
River Elwy
Llannefydd
Trefnant
Vale of Clwyd
Bodfari
River Clwyd
Llangernyw
Llansannan
Henllan
Denbigh Friary
Denbigh
(Dinbych)
Castle
Groes
Pentre Llanrhaeadr
Llandyrnog
Llanynys
Llanddoget
Pandy Tudur
Llanrwst
Bylchau
Gwytherin
Gwydir Uchaf Chapel
A55
A470
A547
A548
A544
A543
A525
A541
A5151
B5115
B5113
B5383
B5381
B5382
B5384
B5428
B5429
B5119
B5118
B5435
B4501
0 1 2 3 4 miles
0 1 2 3 4 5 kilometres

109
96
97

120
112
97
98
LIVERPOOL
BAY
Dublin
Douglas
(Mar-Oct)
Belfast
(Nov-Mar)
Ainsdale Sand Dunes
Halsall
Formby
Formby Point
Little Altcar
Great Altcar
Hightown
Ince Blundell
Homer Green
Maghull
Lydiate
Lunt
Ormskirk
Aughton
Aughton Park
Skelmersdale
Bickerstaffe
Rainford
Little Crosby
Sefton
Kennessee Green
Melling
KIRKBY
Netherton
Blundellsands
Brighton le Sands
CROSBY
Waterloo
Seaforth
EURO RAIL TERMINAL
Litherland
Orrell
Aintree
Fazakerley
Croxteth
Knowsley
Eccleston
Knowsley Safari Park
BOOTLE
Norris Green
Croxteth Hall
West Derby
Knotty Ash
Kirkdale
Anfield
LIVERPOOL
Everton
Prescot
Whiston
Roby
Huyton
WALLASEY
New Brighton
Egremont
Liscard
Poulton
Seacombe
Mersey Tunnels
Albert Dock
Toxteth
Moreton
Hoylake
Royal Liverpool
Hilbre Island
Red Rocks Marsh
Middle Eye
Little Eye
West Kirby
Greasby
Upton
Claughton
BIRKENHEAD
Oxton
Tranmere
Rock Ferry
New Ferry
Port Sunlight River
Frankby
Roydon
Arrowe
WIRRAL
Thingwall
Thurstaston
Irby
Wirral
Heswall
Barnston
Port Sunlight
Bebington
Brimstage
Spital
Bromborough
Eastham
Thornton Hough
Childwall
National Wildflower Centre
Sefton
Allerton
Dingle
Aigburth
Grassendale
Garston
Woolton
Halewood
Speke
Speke Hall
Oglet
Hale
River Mersey
River Dee
Ffynnongroyw
Mostyn
Glan-y-don
Whitford
Greenfield Valley
Basingwerk Abbey
Greenfield
Gorsedd
Carmel
Parkgate
Neston
Willaston
Childer Thornton
Overpool
ELLESMERE PORT
Ince
Elton
Holywell (Treffynnon)
St Winefride's Well
Bagillt
Calcot
Brynford
Dolphin
Ness Botanic Gardens
Burton
Cheshire Oaks
Blue Planet
Little Stanney
Thornton-le-Moors
Stoak
Flint (Y Fflint)
Castle
Dee Estuary
Puddington
Capenhurst
Shotwick
Backford
Wervin
Picton
Lixwm
Rhes-y-cae
Halkyn
Ysceifiog
Connah's Quay
Great Saughall
Mollington
Mickle Trafford
Bridge Trafford
Dunham-on-the-Hill
Nannerch
Little Saughall
Upton
Guilden Sutton
Little Barrow
Northop
Northop Hall
Wepre Park
Shotton
Queensferry
Sealand
Blacon
Newton
Coed y Felin
Rhosesmor
Aston
Ewloe Castle
Soughton
Mancot
CHESTER
Stamford Bridge
Barrow
Littleton
Ewloe
Hawarden
Castle
Handbridge
Cilcain
Gwernaffield
Mynydd Isa
Bretton
Saltney
Huntington
Pant-y-mwyn
Mold (Yr Wyddgrug)
Buckley (Bwcle)
Broughton
Rowton
Loggerheads
Gwernymynydd
Penymynydd
Eccleston
Saighton
Moel Famau
Aberduna
Pontblyddyn
Penyffordd
Kinnerton
Higher Kinnerton
Dodleston
Llanferres
Leeswood
Pontybodkin
Aldford
Llanbedr-Dyffryn-Clwyd
Pulford
Milton
M58
M57
M62
M53
M56
A565
A5147
B5195
A59
A577
A506
A570
A580
A58
A57
A5080
A5300
A562
A561
A554
A551
A553
A5027
A552
A551
B5139
B5140
A540
A5137
B5136
B5137
A41
B5133
A548
A5026
A5119
A55
A550
A494
A5117
A5104
A483
A549
A5118
A541
A51
A56
B5463
B5132
B5129
B5125
B5126
B5123
B5121
B5445

120
121
111
98
Burscough
Newburgh
Appley Bridge
Blackrod
Standish
Ormskirk
Haskayne
Shevington
Aspull
Ashurst
Elmer's Green
Beacon
WIGAN
Westhoughton
Skelmersdale
Up Holland
Digmoor
Scholes
Newtown
Aughton Park
Aughton
Ince Blundell
Lydiate
Maghull
Homer Green
Bickerstaffe
Far Moor
Orrell
Pemberton
Ince-in-Makerfield
Hindley
Lunt
Kennessee Green
Sefton
Melling
Rainford
Bryn Gates
Three Sisters
Abram
Netherton
Billinge
KIRKBY
Crank
Moss Bank
Ashton-in-Makerfield
Pennington Flash
Haydock Park
Litherland
Aintree
Golborne
Seaforth
Orrell
Fazakerley
Croxteth
Knowsley
Haydock
Blackbrook
ST HELENS
Eccleston
BOOTLE
Norris Green
Croxteth Hall
Knowsley Safari Park
Broad Oak
Earlestown
Newton-le-Willows
Peasley Cross
Collins Green
Croft
Kirkdale
Anfield
West Derby
Knotty Ash
Prescot
Whiston
Burtonwood
Winwick
Risley
Everton
LIVERPOOL
Roby
Huyton
Rainhill
Rainhill Stoops
Clock Face
Locking Stumps
Hulme
Birchwood
Mersey Tunnels
Sankey Valley
Orford
Woolston
Albert Dock
Childwall
WARRINGTON
Toxteth
National Wildflower Centre
Cronton
Upton
Farnworth
Latchford
Thelwall
Sefton
Dingle
Allerton
Woolton
Rock Ferry
Aigburth
Hough Green
Appleton
Halewood
Higher Walton
Stockton Heath
New Ferry
Grassendale
WIDNES
Port Sunlight River
Appleton Thorn
Port Sunlight
Garston
Ditton
Catalyst
West Bank
Moore
Walton Hall
Mersey Crossing (Electronic Toll)
Appleton
Bebington
Speke
Hatton
Stretton
Speke Hall
Norton
Daresbury
Spital
Bromborough
Eastham
John Lennon
Hale
RUNCORN
Halton
Oglet
Preston on the Hill
Preston Brook
River Mersey
Dutton
Higher Whitley
Lower Whitley
Antrobus
Sutton Weaver
Aston
ELLESMERE PORT
Willaston
Childer Thornton
Overpool
Frodsham
Comberbach
Little Leigh
Marbury
Manchester Ship Canal
Ince
Warburtons & Hunters Wood
Mersey View
Elton
Acton Bridge
Anderton Boat Lift
Capenhurst
Cheshire Oaks
Kingsley
Helsby
Crowton
Barnton
Blue Planet
Little Stanney
Thornton-le-Moors
Hapsford
Alvanley
Onston
Winnington
Northwich
Stoak
Weaverham
Shotwick
Backford
Hatch Mere
Norley
Rudheath
Leftwich
Wervin
Picton
Dunham-on-the-Hill
Hatchmere
Manley
Hartford
Great Saughall
Bridge Trafford
Mouldsworth
Blakemere
Cuddington
Davenham
Mollington
Mickle Trafford
Plemstall
Long Green
Delamere
Mount Pleasant
Linmere
Little Saughall
Upton
Little Barrow
Ashton
Forest Park
Blakemere Village
Moulton
Whitegate
Sealand
Guilden Sutton
Hollowmoor Heath
Blacon
Newton
Delamere
Stamford Bridge
Great Barrow
Kelsall
CHESTER
Littleton
Castle
Tarvin
Oscroft
Cotebrook
Little Budworth
Hawarden
Handbridge
Huntington
Utkinton
Oulton Park
Bretton
Saltney
Rowton
Duddon
Burton
Clotton
Eaton
Waverton
Eccleston
Hargrave
Tarporley
Saighton
Huxley
Dodleston
Wettenhall
Tilstone Fearnall
Church Minshull
Tiverton
Alpraham
Pulford
Milton
Newton
Cheshire Farm
Tattenhall
River Weaver
R Gowy
Shropshire Union Canal
0 1 2 3 4 miles
0 1 2 3 4 5 kilometres

BOLTON
Farnworth
Little Lever
Radcliffe
Whitefield
Royton
Diggle
Dobcross
Uppermill
Greenfield
Chadderton
MIDDLETON
OLDHAM
Kearsley
Walkden
Prestwich
Pendlebury
Swinton
Failsworth
Mossley
Worsley
MANCHESTER
Ashton-under-Lyne
Stalybridge
Eccles
SALFORD
Droylsden
Audenshaw
Dukinfield
Urmston
Stretford
Denton
Hyde
Irlam
Romiley
Carrington
Partington
Sale
STOCKPORT
Marple
Cheadle
Gatley
Hazel Grove
Altrincham
Bowdon
Hale
New Mills
Disley
High Lane
Bramhall
Poynton
Whaley Bridge
Wilmslow
Knutsford
Alderley Edge
Bollington
Prestbury
Macclesfield
Holmes Chapel
Middlewich
Congleton
Biddulph
Sandbach
122
114
99
Manchester

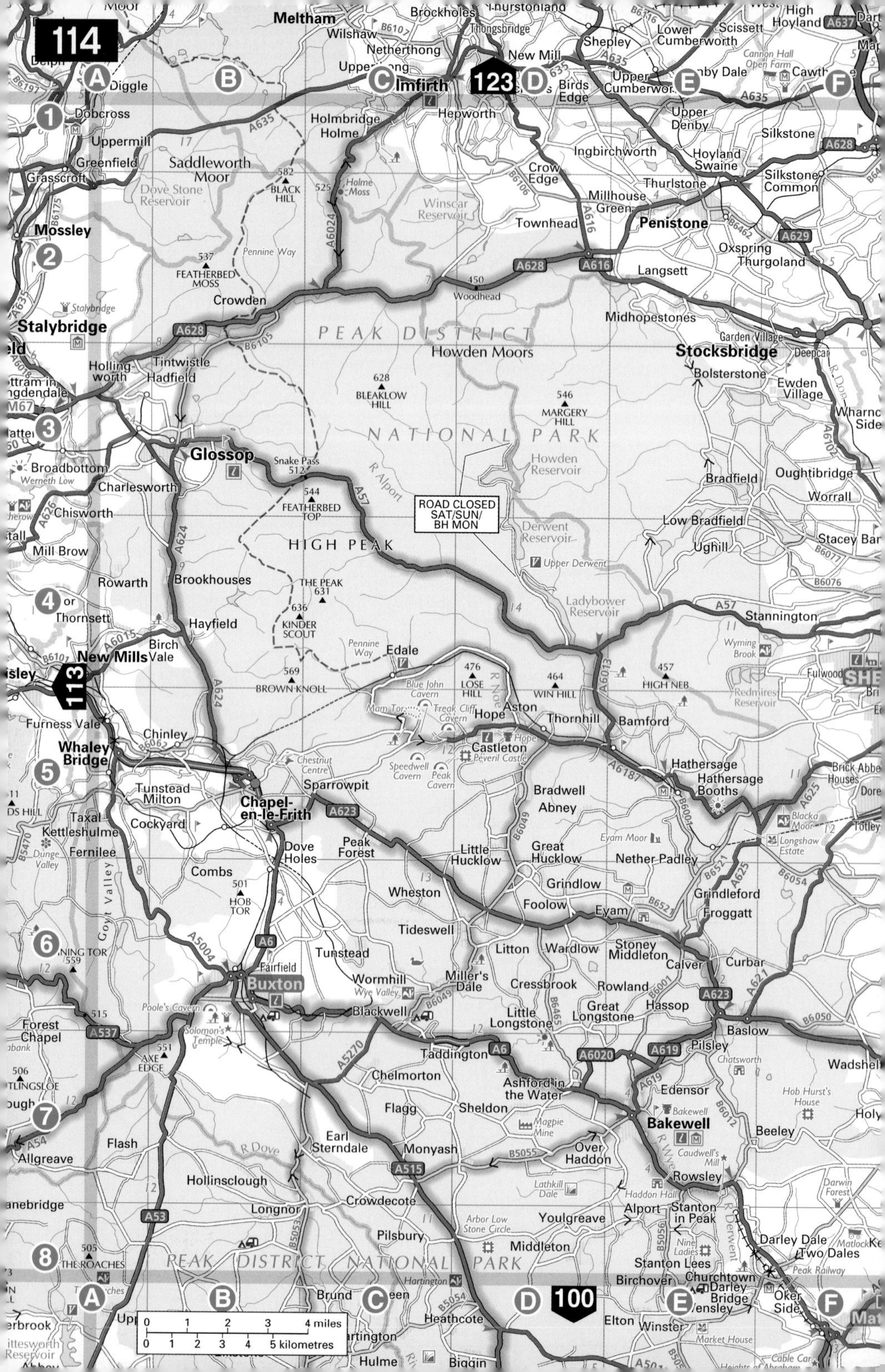
Meltham
Brockholes
Thurstonland
Wilshaw
Netherthong
Thongsbridge
Upperthong
Holmfirth
New Mill
123
Shepley
Lower Cumberworth
Scissett
High Hoyland
Upper Cumberworth
Denby Dale
Cawthorne
Birds Edge
Diggle
Dobcross
Uppermill
Greenfield
Grasscroft
Saddleworth Moor
Dove Stone Reservoir
Holmbridge
Holme
Hepworth
Holme Moss
BLACK HILL
582
525
Upper Denby
Silkstone
Ingbirchworth
Hoyland Swaine
Crow Edge
Silkstone Common
Thurlstone
Millhouse Green
Winscar Reservoir
Townhead
Penistone
Mossley
Pennine Way
FEATHERBED MOSS
537
Oxspring
Thurgoland
Langsett
Crowden
450
Woodhead
Stalybridge
Midhopestones
PEAK DISTRICT
Howden Moors
Garden Village
Stockbridge
Deepcar
Hollingworth
Tintwistle
Hadfield
Bolsterstone
Ewden Village
628
BLEAKLOW HILL
546
MARGERY HILL
NATIONAL PARK
Howden Reservoir
Broadbottom
Werneth Low
Glossop
Snake Pass
512
544
FEATHERBED TOP
R Alport
Bradfield
Oughtibridge
Charlesworth
Worrall
Chisworth
ROAD CLOSED SAT/SUN/ BH MON
Derwent Reservoir
Low Bradfield
Stacey Bank
Mill Brow
HIGH PEAK
Ughill
Upper Derwent
Rowarth
Brookhouses
THE PEAK
631
Ladybower Reservoir
Stannington
Thornsett
636
KINDER SCOUT
Hayfield
Birch Vale
New Mills
Pennine Way
Edale
Wyming Brook
Fulwood
569
BROWN KNOLL
476
LOSE HILL
464
WIN HILL
457
HIGH NEB
Redmires Reservoir
113
Blue John Cavern
Mam Tor
Treak Cliff Cavern
Hope
Aston
Thornhill
Bamford
Furness Vale
Chinley
Whaley Bridge
Castleton
Peveril Castle
Chestnut Centre
Speedwell Cavern
Peak Cavern
Hathersage
Hathersage Booths
Brick Abbey Houses
Dore
Tunstead Milton
Sparrowpit
Chapel-en-le-Frith
Bradwell
Abney
Taxal
Kettleshulme
Cockyard
Dunge Valley
Fernilee
Dove Holes
Peak Forest
Little Hucklow
Great Hucklow
Eyam Moor
Nether Padley
Blacka Moor
Totley
Longshaw Estate
Goyt Valley
Combs
501
HOB TOR
Wheston
Grindlow
Grindleford
Foolow
Eyam
Froggatt
Tideswell
Litton
Wardlow
Stoney Middleton
Calver
Curbar
Tunstead
Fairfield
Buxton
Wormhill
Wye Valley
Miller's Dale
Cressbrook
Rowland
Hassop
Poole's Cavern
Blackwell
Little Longstone
Great Longstone
Forest Chapel
515
Solomon's Temple
551
AXE EDGE
Taddington
Baslow
Pilsley
Chatsworth
Wadshelf
506
Chelmorton
Ashford in the Water
Edensor
Hob Hurst's House
Flagg
Sheldon
Magpie Mine
Bakewell
Beeley
Allgreave
Flash
Earl Sterndale
R Dove
Monyash
Over Haddon
Caudwell's Mill
Hollinsclough
Lathkill Dale
Rowsley
Haddon Hall
Darwin Forest
Longnor
Crowdecote
Alport
Stanton in Peak
Youlgreave
Arbor Low Stone Circle
Pilsbury
Nine Ladies
Darley Dale
Two Dales
Middleton
505
THE ROACHES
PEAK DISTRICT NATIONAL PARK
Stanton Lees
Peak Railway
Hartington
Birchover
Churchtown
Darley Bridge
Oker Side
Brund
Heathcote
100
Elton
Winster
Wensley
Market House
Hartington
Hulme
Biggin
Cable Car
0 1 2 3 4 miles
0 1 2 3 4 5 kilometres
A628
A635
A6024
A616
A629
A57
A624
A626
A6015
A6013
A6187
A623
A625
A6187
B6001
B6521
B6054
A621
A6
A5004
A537
A54
A53
A515
A5270
A6020
A619
B6049
B6465
B5055
B5053
B5054
B5056
B6012
B6050
B6105
B6106
B6462
B6077
B6076
B6062
B6175
A6102

124
116
101
G
H
J
K
L
M
1
2
3
4
5
6
7
8
Carlton
South Kirkby
Hampole
Skellow
Thorpe
Bramwith
Grimethorpe
New Lodge
Cudworth
BARNSLEY
Monk Bretton Priory
Little Houghton
Great Houghton
Thurnscoe
Brodsworth
Hall & Gardens
Hickleton
Hooton Pagnell
Pickburn
Toll Bar
Scawthorpe
Arksey
Bentley
Dunsville
Edenthorpe
Armthorpe
Wheatley Hills
Billingley
Darfield
Worsbrough Dale
Worsbrough Bridge
Wombwell
Worsbrough
Blacker Hill
Bolton upon Dearne
Broom Hill
Goldthorpe
Barnburgh
Harlington
High Melton
Marr
Scawsby
Cusworth
Cusworth Hall
DONCASTER
Old Cantley
Hexthorpe
Lakeside Village
Branton
Adwick upon Dearne
Sprotbrough
Mexborough
Warmsworth
DONCASTER RAILPORT
Balby
Bessacarr
Auckley
Yorkshire
Blax
Brampton
Hoyland Nether
Wath upon Dearne
Tankersley
Elsecar Workshops
Cadeby
Castle
Denaby
Conisbrough
New Edlington
Loversall
iPORT
iPort Logistics Park
Finningley
Robin Hood Doncaster Sheffield
Rossington
New Rossington
Harley
Wentworth
Swinton
Old Edlington
Clifton
Hooton Roberts
Nether Haugh
Thorpe Hesley
Scholes
Rawmarsh
Thrybergh
Greasbrough
Ravenfield
Wadworth
apeltown
Micklebring
Braithwell
Stainton
Austerfield
Bawtry
Ecclesfield
Kimberworth
ROTHERHAM
Bramley
Tickhill
Spital Hill
Shiregreen
Herringthorpe
Magna
Maltby
Bircotes
Wincobank
Meadowhall
Broom
Hooton Levitt
Scaftworth
Scrooby
Tinsley
Wickersley
Styrrup
Harworth
Grimesthorpe
Brinsworth
Whiston
Morthen
Slade Hooton
Stone
Carbrook
Greenland
Thurcroft
Roche Abbey
Oldcotes
Blyth
Mattersey
Attercliffe
Catcliffe
Treeton
Ulley
Brookhouse
Laughton-en-le-Morthen
Firbeck
Langold
Torworth
Handsworth
Aughton
Brampton-en-le-Morthen
Letwell
Arbourthorne
Heeley
Richmond
Woodhouse
Fence
Aston
Dinnington
North Anston
Gildingwells
North Carlton
Hodsock
Sutton cum Lound
Intake
Hollins End
Hackenthorpe
Beighton
Todwick
Kiveton Park
South Anston
Woodsetts
South Carlton
Carlton in Lindrick
Wigthorpe
Highlane
Rother Valley
Wales
R Ryton
Ridgeway
Mosborough
Ford
Killamarsh
Woodall
Harthill
Thorpe Salvin
Shireoaks
Scofton
Ranby
Troway
Eckington
Worksop
Spinkhill
Renishaw
Marsh Lane
Renishall Hall
Apperknowle
Dronfield
West Handley
Middle Handley
Unstone
Sitwell
Barlborough
Whitwell
Hodthorpe
Revolution House
Harlesthorpe
Mastin Moor
Clowne
Clumber Park
Whittington
Barlow
Staveley
Stanfree
Creswell
Creswell Crags
Welbeck Abbey
R Poulter
Bothamsall
Shuttlewood
Elmton
Brimington
Holbeck
Linacres Reservoirs
Newbold
CHESTERFIELD
Long Duckmanton
Whaley Thorns
Norton
New Brampton
Arkwright Town
Bolsover
Whaley
Upper Langwith
Cuckney
Nether Langwith
Meden Vale
R Meden
Perlethorpe
Sutton Scarsdale Hall
Hills Town
Scarcliffe
Langwith
Church Warsop
Budby
Sherwood Forest
Walton
Temple Normanton
Palterton
Langwith Junction
Market Warsop
Ollerton
New Ollerton
Wingerworth
Heath
Grassmoor
Shirebrook
Edwinstowe
Glapwell
Stony Houghton
New Houghton
Wellow
Holmewood
North Wingfield
Stainsby Mill
Ault Hucknall
Hardwick Hall
Sherwood Forest Miniature Railway
R Maun
Kings Clipstone
Rufford
Alton
Pleasley
Mansfield Woodhouse
Clipstone
Sherwood Pines
Center Parcs Sherwood Forest
Rufford Abbey
Ashover
Clay Cross
Hardstoft
Eakri
Handley
Teversal
Pilsley
Stretton
Dunsill
Tibshelf
MANSFIELD
Bilsthorpe
Morton
Higham
Stonebroom
Newton
Sutton-in-Ashfield
Huthwaite
Highoredish
FOREST

M180
A18
A1146
Hatfield Woodhouse
Sandtoft
Dunsville
125
Burringham
Althorpe
M181
Brumby
B1450
Ashby
A1029
Broughton
Wressle
Yaddlethorpe
Bottesford
M180
Westgate
Belton
Beltoft
East Butterwick
West Butterwick
Carrhouse
A630
A614
M18
Old Cantley
Branton
Auckley
Blaxton
Wroot
A161
Epworth
Old Rectory
Low Burnham
Owston Ferry
Susworth
Scotterthorpe
Messingham
Manton
Scawby
Sturton
B1398
B1400
Scotter
Gainsthorpe Medieval Village
Westwoodside
B1396
Haxey
East Lound
East Ferry
A159
Scotton
Kirton in Lindsey
B1206
Finningley
Rossington
Robin Hood Doncaster Sheffield
A638
Graiselound
Wildsworth
Laughton
Northorpe
R Idle
Gunthorpe
West Stockwith
Grayingham
Misson
Misterton
East Stockwith
Blyton
B1205
Blyborough
Austerfield
B6463
Bawtry
A631
B1403
Walkerith
Pilham
Aisby
Willoughton
Walkeringham
R Trent
Morton
Corringham
R Eau
Harwell
Chesterfield Canal
Gringley on the Hill
Gainsborough
Hemswell
Hemswell Cliff
Scaftworth
Everton
Scrooby
Drakeholes
Wiseton
Beckingham
A631
Springthorpe
Harpswell
Mattersey
Mattersey Abbey
Saundby
Heapham
Glentworth
A614
B6045
Ranskill
Clayworth
Torworth
Lound
Wetlands Animal Park
R Idle
Bole
North Wheatley
Lea
Upton
R Till
A620
B1241
Kexby
Fillingham
115
Sutton cum Lound
Hayton
South Wheatley
Knaith
Sturton le Steeple
Willingham by Stow
Barnby Moor
Idle Valley
Clarborough
A156
Coates
Ingham
North Leverton with Habblesthorpe
Fenton
Gate Burton
R Ryton
Retford
Welham
Littleborough
Marton
Stow
Cammeringham
Brattleby
Babworth
Scofton
Ranby
South Leverton
A1500
A1
B6079
Ordsall
Grove
Cottam
Brampton
Sturton by Stow
Scampton
Aisthorpe
B6420
Treswell
Sundown Adventureland
Torksey
Bransby
Eaton
Nether Headon
Rampton
A57
A638
Stokeham
Fenton
North Carlton
South Carlton
A1
Headon
Laneham
Clumber Park
A614
Gamston
Upton
East Drayton
A156
Saxilby
Fossdyke Navigation
Elkesley
Rockley
Askham
Laughterton
Kettlethorpe
Burton
West Drayton
Dunham-on-Trent
Toll
Markham Moor
Bothamsall
Milton
Ragnall
Newton on Trent
Burton Waters
A57
Sibthorpe
Darlton
North Clifton
Thorney
East Markham
Skellingthorpe
Bevercotes
West Markham
Fledborough
B1190
Walesby
Tuxford
High Marnham
South Clifton
Harby
LINCOLN
Perlethorpe
A6075
Wigsley
B6387
Skegby
Spalford
Doddington
A46
Birchwood
Hartsholme
Swanpool
Kirton
Normanton on Trent
Low Marnham
Ollerton
Boughton
Egmanton
A1133
New Ollerton
Laxton
Weston
Grassthorpe
Whisby
Eagle
Swallow Beck
Sutton on Trent
Road Transport
Wellow
Holocaust Centre & Museum
B1164
Moorhouse
North Scarle
Bracebridge Low Fields
A1434
Girton
Ompton
North Hykeham
Ossington
B6030
Rufford
Rufford Abbey
Besthorpe
Thorpe on the Hill
Kneesall
Norwell Woodhouse
South Scarle
Carlton-on-Trent
South Hykeham
Eakring
Kersall
Haddington
Harmston
Swinderby
A614
Cromwell
Aubourn
Mapleb
102
Thurlby
Bilsthorpe
Dolls
Coleby
Bassingham
Bathley
Holme
A46
Brough
Norton
Boothby
A1133
0 1 2 3 4 miles
0 1 2 3 4 5 kilometres

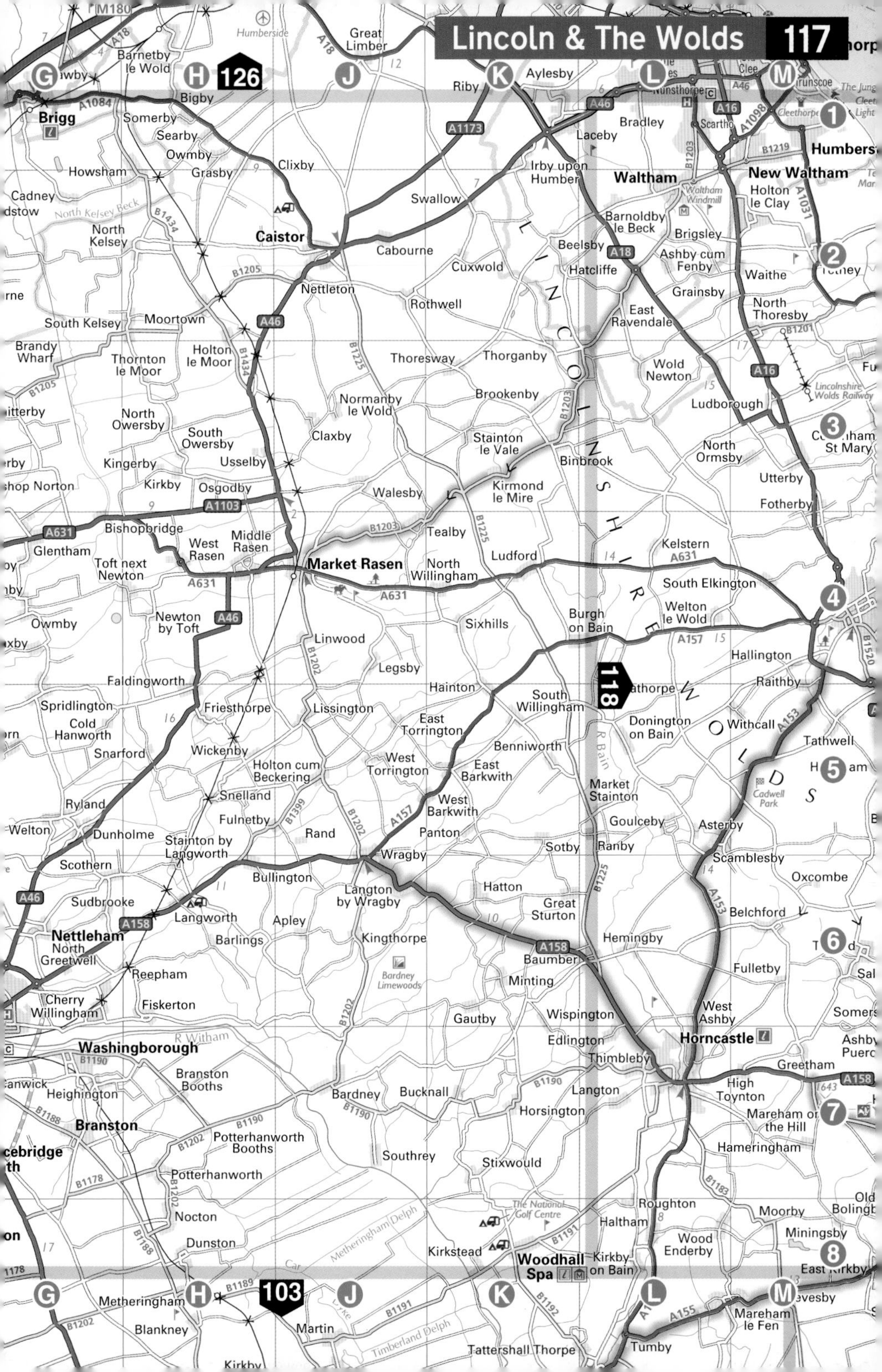
M180
Humberside
Great Limber
A18
Barnetby le Wold
126
Aylesby
Riby
Bigby
Brigg
A1084
Somerby
Searby
Owmby
Grasby
Clixby
Howsham
Cadney
North Kelsey Beck
B1434
North Kelsey
Caistor
A1173
Swallow
A46
Laceby
Bradley
Irby upon Humber
Waltham
Waltham Windmill
New Waltham
Holton le Clay
Humberston
A1031
A16
A1098
B1219
B1203
Scartho
Cleethorpes
Barnoldby le Beck
Brigsley
Beelsby
A18
Hatcliffe
Ashby cum Fenby
Tetney
Waithe
Grainsby
North Thoresby
B1201
Cabourne
Cuxwold
B1205
Nettleton
Rothwell
East Ravendale
Moortown
South Kelsey
Holton le Moor
Thornton le Moor
Brandy Wharf
B1225
Thoresway
Thorganby
Wold Newton
Lincolnshire Wolds Railway
Ludborough
Normanby le Wold
Brookenby
North Owersby
South Owersby
Claxby
Stainton le Vale
Binbrook
North Ormsby
Covenham St Mary
Kingerby
Usselby
Utterby
Kirkby
Osgodby
Kirmond le Mire
Walesby
Fotherby
A1103
A631
Bishopbridge
West Rasen
Middle Rasen
B1203
Tealby
Glentham
Toft next Newton
Market Rasen
North Willingham
Ludford
Kelstern
South Elkington
Newton by Toft
Owmby
Sixhills
Burgh on Bain
Welton le Wold
A157
Linwood
B1202
Legsby
Hallington
Faldingworth
Hainton
Raithby
118
Spridlington
Friesthorpe
Lissington
South Willingham
Donington on Bain
Withcall
A153
Cold Hanworth
Snarford
East Torrington
Tathwell
Wickenby
West Torrington
Benniworth
Holton cum Beckering
East Barkwith
R Bain
Market Stainton
Cadwell Park
Ryland
Snelland
West Barkwith
B1399
Fulnetby
Goulceby
Asterby
Welton
Dunholme
Rand
Panton
Stainton by Langworth
Sotby
Ranby
Wragby
Scamblesby
Scothern
Bullington
Oxcombe
Langton by Wragby
Hatton
Sudbrooke
Great Sturton
Belchford
A158
Langworth
Apley
Nettleham
Barlings
Kingthorpe
Hemingby
North Greetwell
Baumber
Fulletby
Reepham
Bardney Limewoods
Minting
Cherry Willingham
Fiskerton
Gautby
Wispington
West Ashby
R Witham
Washingborough
Edlington
Horncastle
Thimbleby
Greetham
B1190
Branston Booths
Langton
High Toynton
Heighington
Bardney
Bucknall
Horsington
Mareham on the Hill
Branston
B1188
Potterhanworth Booths
Hamerningham
Southrey
Stixwould
B1178
Potterhanworth
B1183
Roughton
Moorby
The National Golf Centre
Nocton
Haltham
Miningsby
Metheringham Delph
Dunston
Wood Enderby
Kirkstead
B1191
Woodhall Spa
Kirkby on Bain
East Kirkby
103
Metheringham
B1189
B1202
Blankney
Martin
B1192
A155
Mareham le Fen
Timberland Delph
Tattershall Thorpe
Tumby
Revesby
LINCOLNSHIRE WOLDS
G
H
J
K
L
M
1
2
3
4
5
6
7
8

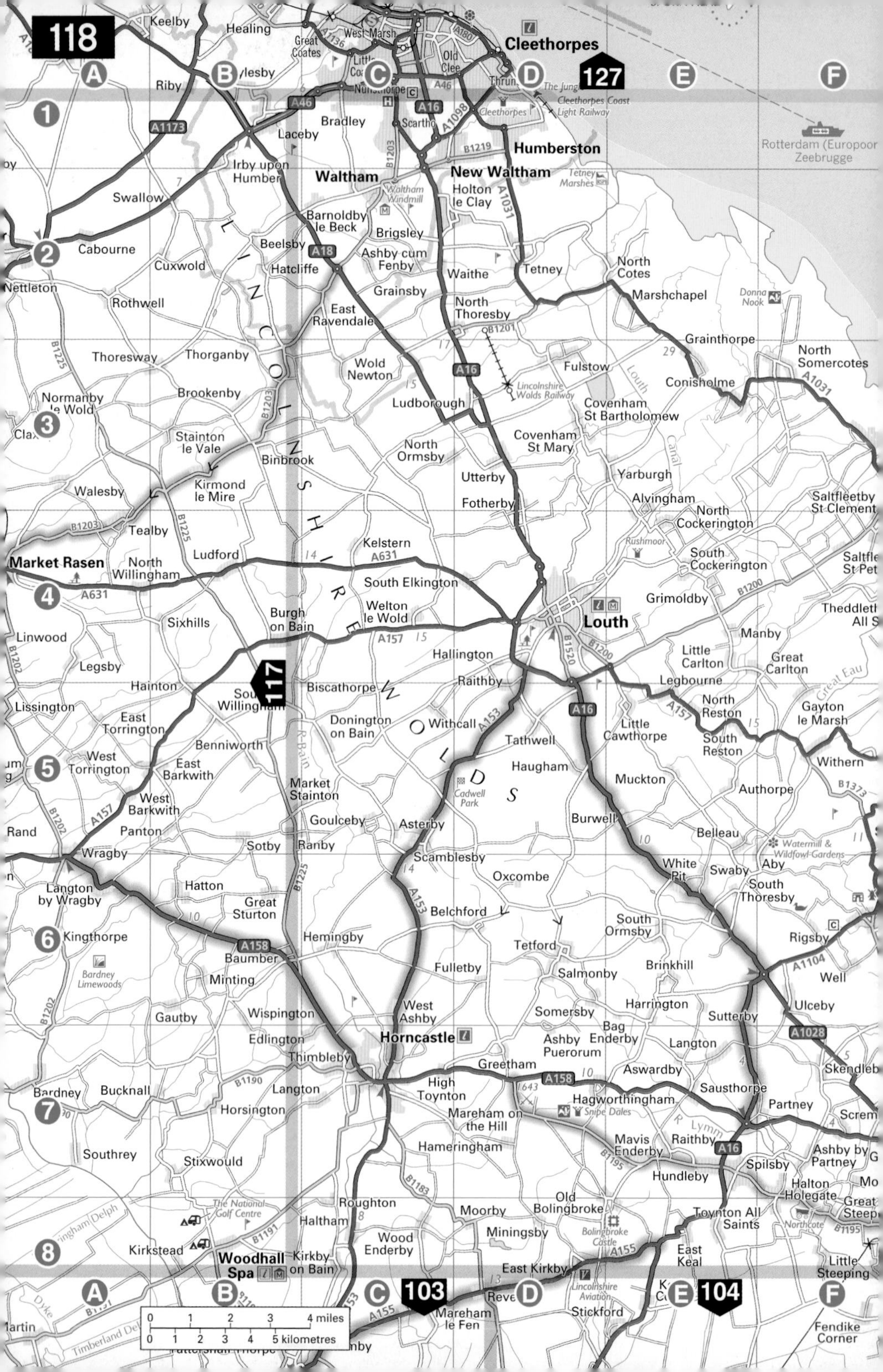
Keelby
Healing
Great Coates
West Marsh
Little Coates
Old Clee
Cleethorpes
127
A
B
C
D
E
F
Riby
Aylesby
Nunsthorpe
The Jungle
Cleethorpes Coast Light Railway
Cleethorpes
A46
A16
A1098
A1173
A46
Bradley
Scartho
Laceby
B1219
Humberston
Rotterdam (Europoort)
Zeebrugge
Irby upon Humber
B1203
Waltham
New Waltham
Tetney Marshes
Swallow
Waltham Windmill
Holton le Clay
A1031
Barnoldby le Beck
Brigsley
Cabourne
Beelsby
A18
Ashby cum Fenby
Cuxwold
Hatcliffe
Waithe
Tetney
North Cotes
Nettleton
Rothwell
Grainsby
Marshchapel
Donna Nook
East Ravendale
North Thoresby
B1201
Grainthorpe
B1225
Thoresway
Thorganby
Wold Newton
Fulstow
North Somercotes
Conisholme
A1031
A16
Louth Canal
Normanby le Wold
Brookenby
Ludborough
Lincolnshire Wolds Railway
Covenham St Bartholomew
B1203
Claxby
Stainton le Vale
North Ormsby
Covenham St Mary
LINCOLNSHIRE WOLDS
Binbrook
Utterby
Yarburgh
Walesby
Kirmond le Mire
Fotherby
Alvingham
Saltfleetby St Clement
North Cockerington
B1203
Tealby
B1225
Kelstern
Rushmoor
South Cockerington
Saltfleetby St Peter
Market Rasen
North Willingham
Ludford
A631
South Elkington
Grimoldby
B1200
A631
Welton le Wold
Louth
Theddlethorpe All Saints
Linwood
Sixhills
Burgh on Bain
A157
Manby
B1520
B1200
Hallington
Little Carlton
Great Carlton
Legsby
117
Hainton
Biscathorpe
Raithby
Legbourne
Great Eau
Lissington
South Willingham
A16
North Reston
Gayton le Marsh
East Torrington
Donington on Bain
Withcall
A153
Little Cawthorpe
A157
South Reston
West Torrington
Benniworth
R. Bain
Tathwell
Withern
East Barkwith
Haugham
Muckton
Market Stainton
Cadwell Park
B1373
West Barkwith
Authorpe
B1202
A157
Panton
Goulceby
Asterby
Burwell
Rand
Sotby
Ranby
Belleau
Wragby
Scamblesby
Watermill & Wildfowl Gardens
White Pit
Swaby
Aby
Langton by Wragby
Hatton
B1225
Oxcombe
South Thoresby
Great Sturton
A153
Belchford
South Ormsby
Kingthorpe
A158
Hemingby
Tetford
Rigsby
Baumber
Bardney Limewoods
Fulletby
Salmonby
Brinkhill
A1104
Well
Minting
Gautby
Wispington
West Ashby
Somersby
Harrington
Sutterby
Ulceby
B1202
Edlington
Horncastle
Ashby Puerorum
Bag Enderby
Langton
A1028
Thimbleby
Greetham
Aswardby
Skendleby
A158
Bardney
Bucknall
B1190
Langton
High Toynton
Sausthorpe
Horsington
Hagworthingham
Partney
Snipe Dales
Scremby
Mareham on the Hill
R. Lymn
Mavis Enderby
Raithby
A16
Southrey
Hameringham
B1195
Ashby by Partney
Stixwould
Spilsby
Hundleby
B1183
Halton Holegate
Roughton
Old Bolingbroke
Great Steeping
The National Golf Centre
Moorby
Toynton All Saints
Billinghay Delph
Haltham
Northcote
B1191
Miningsby
Bolingbroke Castle
B1195
Kirkstead
Wood Enderby
A155
East Keal
Woodhall Spa
Kirkby on Bain
Little Steeping
East Kirkby
Dyke
Revesby
Lincolnshire Aviation
103
104
Mareham le Fen
Stickford
Timberland Delph
A155
Fendike Corner
0 1 2 3 4 miles
0 1 2 3 4 5 kilometres

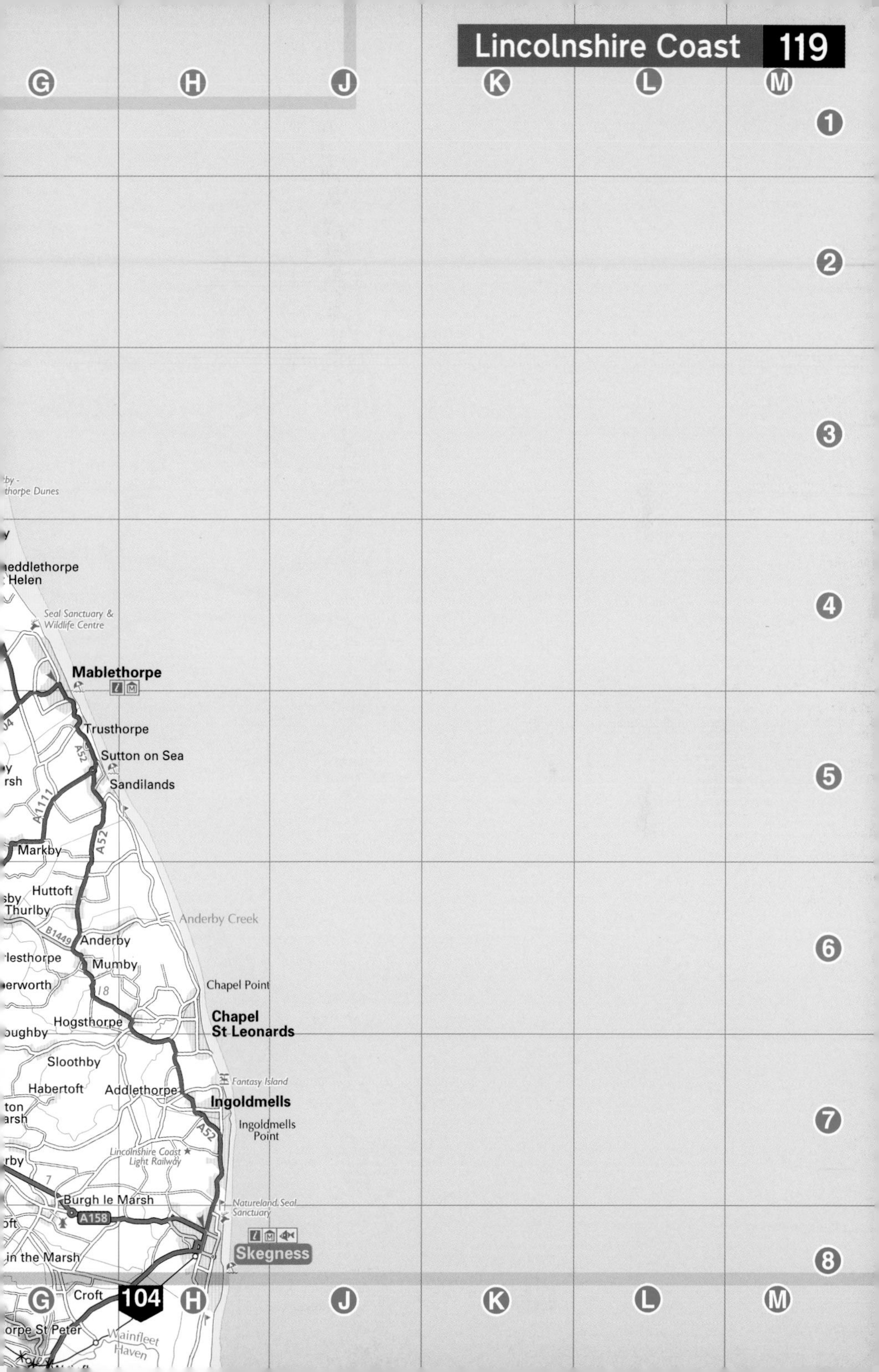
Seal Sanctuary & Wildlife Centre
Mablethorpe
Trusthorpe
A52
Sutton on Sea
Sandilands
A1111
Markby
Huttoft
Thurlby
Anderby Creek
B1449
Anderby
Mumby
Chapel Point
Hogsthorpe
Chapel St Leonards
Sloothby
Fantasy Island
Habertoft
Addlethorpe
Ingoldmells
Ingoldmells Point
Lincolnshire Coast Light Railway
Burgh le Marsh
A158
Natureland Seal Sanctuary
Skegness
Croft
104
Wainfleet Haven
G
H
J
K
L
M
1
2
3
4
5
6
7
8

129
111
A B C D E F
1 2 3 4 5 6 7 8
Glasson
Cockersand
Cockerha
Knott End-on-Sea
Pilling
Preesall
COCKERHAM
Winmarle
Fleetwood
Rossall Point
A588
B5377
A587
River Wyre
Stalmine
Eagland Hill
B5268
A585
Staynall
Cleveleys
Moss Edge
Thornton
Hambleton
Out Rawcliffe
B5412
Little Singleton
Great Eccleston
Toll
A586
Copp
A584
B5124
Warbreck
Poulton-le-Fylde
Singleton
North Shore
Hoohill
Elswick
B5269
B5266
Thistleton
A585
BLACKPOOL
Esprick
Wharles
Staining
Model Village
B5260
Great Marton
Weeton
M55
A583
Great Plumpton
Wesham
Treales
South Shore
Kirkham
B5261
A5230
Westby
Blackpool
Wrea Green
Newton with Scales
Clift
B5259
St Anne's
Kellamergh
A584
Freckleton
Lytham Hall
Ansdell
Royal Lytham & St Annes
Warton
Fairhaven
River Ribble
Lytham St Anne's
Discovery Centre
A584
Lytham
Hesketh Bank
Becconsall
Banks
Tarleton
A565
SOUTHPORT
Mere Brow
A59
Pleasureland
P+R
Leisure Lakes
B5246
Holmeswood
Rufford
Windmill Animal Farm
A5267
Birkdale
The Royal Birkdale
B5243
Martin Mere Wetland Centre
Scarisbrick
Shirdley Hill
Burscough Bridge
A570
Bescar
Ainsdale
A565
Heaton's Bridge
B5242
Halsall
Burscough
Ainsdale Sand-Dunes
Leeds & Liverpool Canal
B5240
Barton
Haskayne
Ormskirk
A577
Cabin Hill
Freshfield
Formby
Little Altcar
Great Altcar
B5195
A5147
Aughton
Aughton Park
A59
Skelmersda
A506
Hightown
A565
0 1 2 3 4 miles
0 1 2 3 4 5 kilometres

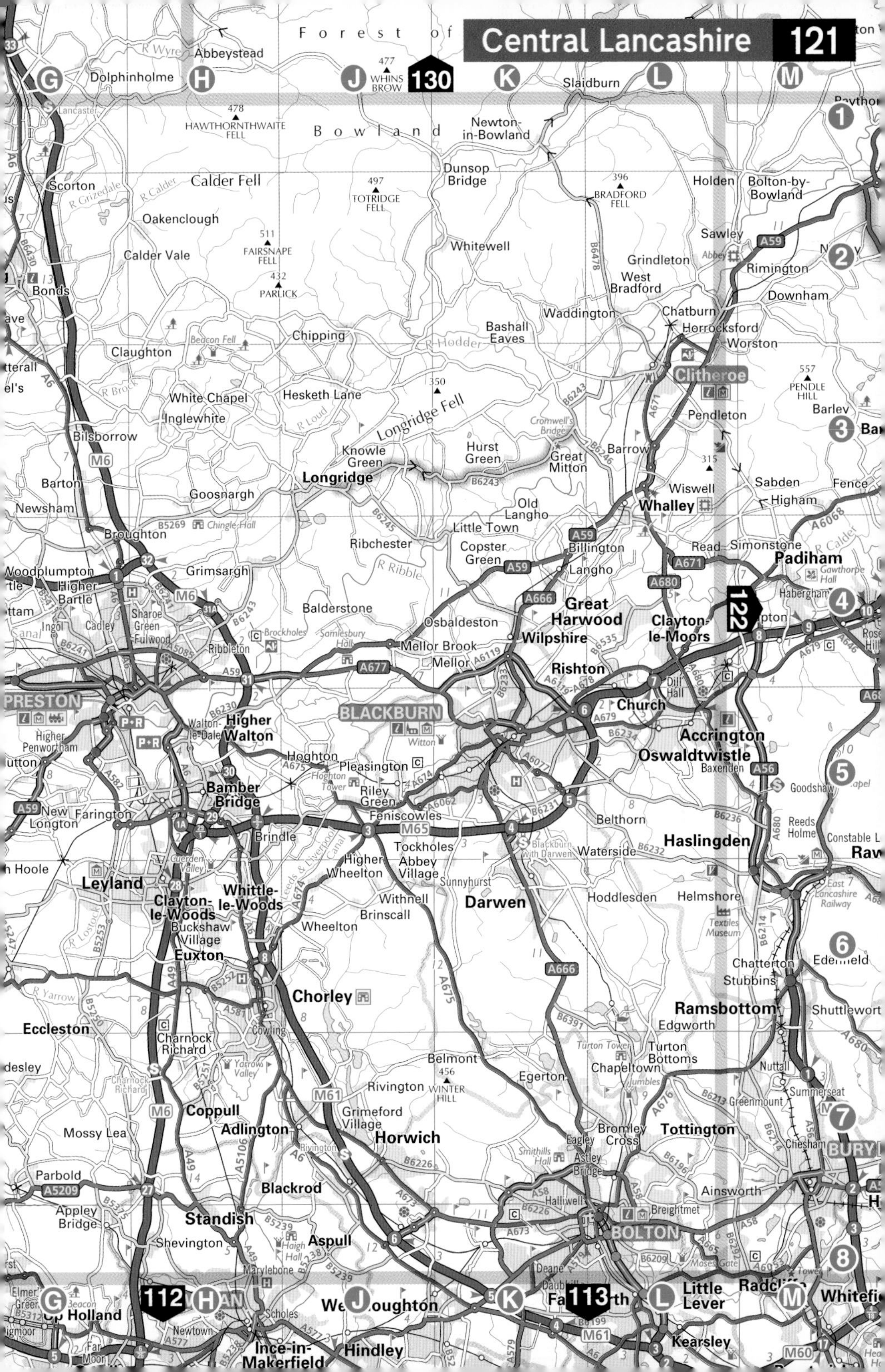
Forest of
Bowland
Abbeystead
Dolphinholme
477
WHINS BROW
130
Slaidburn
478
HAWTHORNTHWAITE FELL
Newton-in-Bowland
Dunsop Bridge
Scorton
Calder Fell
497
TOTRIDGE FELL
396
BRADFORD FELL
Holden
Bolton-by-Bowland
Oakenclough
511
FAIRSNAPE FELL
Whitewell
Sawley
Calder Vale
432
PARLICK
Grindleton
West Bradford
Rimington
Downham
Bonds
Waddington
Chatburn
Horrocksford
Worston
Bashall Eaves
Chipping
Beacon Fell
R Hodder
Claughton
Clitheroe
557
PENDLE HILL
350
White Chapel
Hesketh Lane
Longridge Fell
Pendleton
Barley
Inglewhite
Cromwell's Bridge
Bilsborrow
Knowle Green
Hurst Green
Great Mitton
Barrow
M6
Longridge
315
Barton
Goosnargh
Wiswell
Sabden
Fence
Newsham
Whalley
Higham
Old Langho
B5269
Chingle Hall
Little Town
Broughton
Ribchester
Copster Green
Billington
Read
Simonstone
Padiham
R Ribble
Woodplumpton
Grimsargh
A59
Langho
Gawthorpe Hall
Higher Bartle
Great Harwood
Habergham
Balderstone
Clayton-le-Moors
122
Sharoe Green
Fulwood
Cadley
Ingol
Osbaldeston
Brockholes
Samlesbury Hall
Wilpshire
Mellor Brook
Ribbleton
Mellor
Rishton
A677
PRESTON
Dill Hall
Church
BLACKBURN
Walton-le-Dale
Higher Walton
Witton
Accrington
Higher Penwortham
Hoghton
Pleasington
Oswaldtwistle
Baxenden
Hoghton Tower
Riley Green
Goodshaw
Bamber Bridge
New Longton
Farington
Feniscowles
Belthorn
Reeds Holme
Constable Lee
Brindle
M65
Tockholes
Haslingden
Hoole
Higher Wheelton
Abbey Village
Blackburn with Darwen
Waterside
Cuerden Valley
Leyland
Sunnyhurst
Clayton-le-Woods
Whittle-le-Woods
Withnell
Darwen
Hoddlesden
Helmshore
East Lancashire Railway
Brinscall
Buckshaw Village
Wheelton
Textiles Museum
Euxton
Chatterton
Edenfield
Stubbins
R Yarrow
Chorley
Ramsbottom
Shuttleworth
Eccleston
Cowling
Edgworth
Charnock Richard
Turton Tower
Turton Bottoms
Belmont
Chapeltown
Yarrow Valley
456
WINTER HILL
Egerton
Nuttall
Rivington
Jumbles
Summerseat
Greenmount
M61
Coppull
Grimeford Village
Mossy Lea
Adlington
Horwich
Eagley
Bromley Cross
Tottington
Chesham
Astley Bridge
Smithills Hall
BURY
Parbold
Blackrod
Ainsworth
Appley Bridge
Halliwell
Breightmet
Standish
BOLTON
Shevington
Aspull
Haigh Hall
Moses Gate
Marylebone
Deane
Little Lever
Radcliffe
Whitefield
112
113
Up Holland
Scholes
Newtown
Kearsley
Ince-in-Makerfield
Hindley
M60

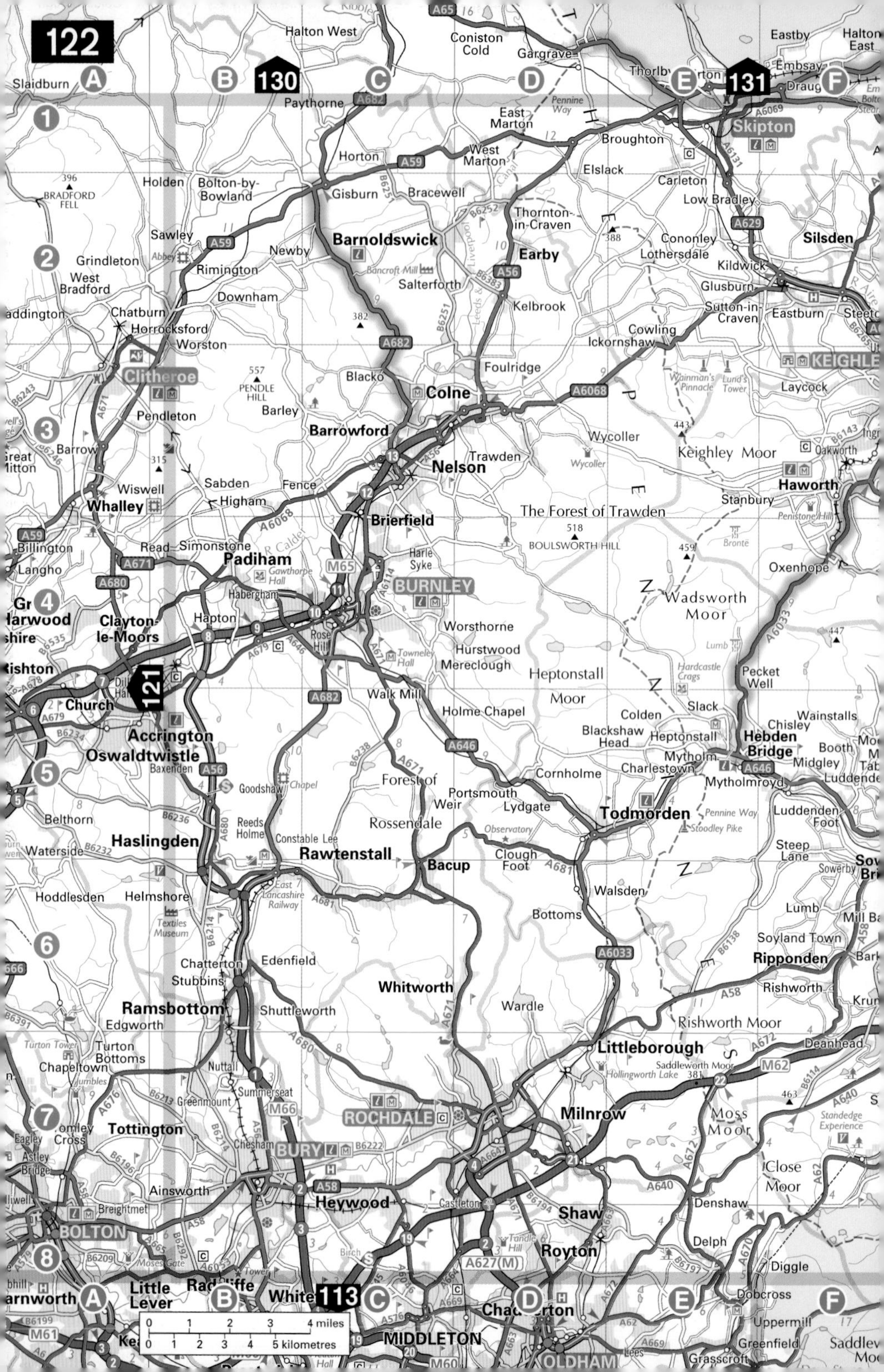
130
131
121
113
Slaidburn
Halton West
Coniston Cold
Gargrave
Eastby
Halton East
Embsay
Thorlby
Paythorne
East Marton
Pennine Way
Skipton
Broughton
Horton
West Marton
Elslack
Carleton
Holden
Bolton-by-Bowland
Gisburn
Bracewell
Low Bradley
396
BRADFORD FELL
Thornton-in-Craven
Sawley
Barnoldswick
Earby
388
Cononley
Silsden
Abbey
Newby
Lothersdale
Kildwick
Grindleton
Rimington
Bancroft Mill
Salterforth
Glusburn
West Bradford
Downham
Kelbrook
Sutton-in-Craven
Eastburn
Chatburn
Horrocksford
382
Cowling
Ickornshaw
Worston
Clitheroe
557
PENDLE HILL
Blacko
Foulridge
KEIGHLEY
Colne
Wainman's Pinnacle
Lund's Tower
Laycock
Barley
Pendleton
Barrowford
Wycoller
443
Keighley Moor
Oakworth
Barrow
315
Trawden
Nelson
Haworth
Sabden
Fence
Wiswell
Whalley
Higham
Stanbury
Brierfield
The Forest of Trawden
518
BOULSWORTH HILL
Penistone Hill
Bronte
Billington
Read
Simonstone
Padiham
R Calder
459
Langho
Harle Syke
Oxenhope
Gawthorpe Hall
BURNLEY
Wadsworth Moor
Clayton-le-Moors
Habergham
Hapton
Worsthorne
Rose Hill
447
Hurstwood
Towneley Hall
Mereclough
Lumb
Rishton
Heptonstall Moor
Hardcastle Crags
Pecket Well
Church
Accrington
Walk Mill
Slack
Colden
Wainstalls
Chisley
Holme Chapel
Oswaldtwistle
Blackshaw Head
Heptonstall
Hebden Bridge
Booth
Baxenden
Mytholm
Midgley
Charlestown
Cornholme
Mytholmroyd
Goodshaw
Chapel
Forest of Rossendale
Portsmouth
Weir
Lydgate
Belthorn
Reeds Holme
Todmorden
Luddenden Foot
Pennine Way
Stoodley Pike
Observatory
Waterside
Haslingden
Constable Lee
Rawtenstall
Bacup
Clough Foot
Steep Lane
Sowerby
Hoddlesden
Helmshore
East Lancashire Railway
Walsden
Textiles Museum
Lumb
Bottoms
Soyland Town
Chatterton
Edenfield
Ripponden
Stubbins
Whitworth
Rishworth
Ramsbottom
Shuttleworth
Wardle
Rishworth Moor
Edgworth
Turton Tower
Turton Bottoms
Littleborough
Deanhead
Chapeltown
Jumbles
Nuttall
Hollingworth Lake
Saddleworth Moor
381
Summerseat
463
Greenmount
Milnrow
Moss Moor
ROCHDALE
Standedge Experience
Tottington
Chesham
BURY
Close Moor
Eagley
Astley Bridge
Ainsworth
Heywood
Castleton
Denshaw
Breightmet
BOLTON
Shaw
Tandle Hill
Delph
Royton
Moses Gate
Tower
Birch
Diggle
Little Lever
Radcliffe
Whitefield
Chadderton
Dobcross
Farnworth
Uppermill
MIDDLETON
Greenfield
Lees
OLDHAM
Grasscroft
Saddleworth Moor
0 1 2 3 4 miles
0 1 2 3 4 5 kilometres

132
124
114
Ilkley
Otley
Guiseley
Yeadon
Bingley
Shipley
Horsforth
Pudsey
BRADFORD
LEEDS
Wetherby
Harewood
Bramhope
Morley
Rothwell
Batley
Dewsbury
Mirfield
Ossett
WAKEFIELD
Normanton
HUDDERSFIELD
Brighouse
Elland
Holmfirth
Meltham
Kirkburton
Cleckheaton
Heckmondwike
Liversedge
Queensbury
Wilsden
Horbury
Royston
Walton
Crofton
Kippax
Cudworth
BARNSLEY
Spofforth
Pannal
Follifoot
Scholes
Collingham
Shadwell
Scarcroft
Thorner
Swillington
Garforth
Moortown
Headingley
Armley
Beeston
Hunslet
Gildersome
Drighlington
Birkenshaw
Tong
Thornton
Clayton
Allerton
Saltaire
Baildon
Menston
Burley in Wharfedale
Weeton
Huby
Pool
Arthington
East Keswick
Bardsey
Wike
Lofthouse
Carlton
Ardsley
Woodkirk
Flockton
Emley
Lepton
Denby Dale
Darton
Mapplewell
Woolley
Notton
Cawthorne
Dodworth
Penistone
Honley
Netherton
Shelley
Skelmanthorpe
Clayton West
Scissett
Thurstonland
Brockholes
A59
A65
A660
A658
A61
A64
A58
A62
A638
A642
A635
A628
A629
A644
A650
A6120
M1
M62
M621
M606

124
132
133
123
115
A
B
C
D
E
F
1
2
3
4
5
6
7
8
YORK
LEEDS
WAKEFIELD
BARNSLEY
DONCASTER
Wetherby
Pontefract
Harrogate
Starbeck
Goldsborough
Plumpton Rocks
Little Ribston
Walshford
Hunsingore
Cattal
Kirk Hammerton
Overton
Nether Poppleton
Upper Poppleton
New Earswick
East Huntington
Rawcliffe
Clifton
Follifoot
Pannal
North Deighton
Cowthorpe
Tockwith
Hessay
Knapton
Acomb
Holgate
Osbaldwick
South Bank
Nunthorpe
Dringhouses
Fulford
Spofforth
Kirk Deighton
Bickerton
Long Marston
Rufforth
Hutton Wandesley
Kirkby Overblow
Stockfield Park
Sicklinghall
Bilton-in-Ainsty
Askham Bryan
Angram
Askham Richard
Healaugh
Walton
Dunkeswick
Linton
Boston Spa
Thorp Arch
Wighill
Bilbrough
Catterton
Bishopthorpe
Copmanthorpe
Netherby
Chapel Hill
Harewood
Collingham
R Wharfe
Newton Kyme
Acaster Malbis
Naburn
Harewood House
East Keswick
Clifford
Colton
Deighton
Wike
Bardsey
East Rigton
Tadcaster
Oxton
Escrick
Eccup Reservoir
Bramham
Bolton Percy
Appleton Roebuck
Bramham Park
Stutton
Kirkby Wharfe
Acaster Selby
Scarcroft
Thorner
Towton
Ulleskelf
Stillingfleet
Shadwell
Sand Hills
Ryther
Moor Allerton
Chapel Allerton
Tropical World
Roundhay
Aberford
R Cock
Cawood
Kelfield
Gledhow
Harehills
Barwick in Elmet
Saxton
Church Fenton
Riccall
Seacroft
Scholes
Barkston Ash
Wistow
R Ouse
Lotherton Hall
Woodhouse
Manston
Cross Gates
Little Fenton
Barlby
Sheepscar
Sherburn in Elmet
Halton
Whitkirk
Osmondthorpe
Colton
Garforth
Micklefield
Thorpe Willoughby
Cross Green
Temple Newsam
South Milford
Selby
Hunslet
Swillington
Steeton Hall Gateway
Hambleton
Brayton
Kippax
Lumby
Monk Fryston
Middleton Railway
Middleton
Great Preston
Ledsham
Rothwell
Ledston
Hillam
Gateforth
Bower's Row
Allerton Bywater
Fairburn
Burn
Carlton
Burton Salmon
Birkin
Selby Canal
Chapel Haddlesey
Ouzlewell Green
Mickletown
Camblesforth
Ardsley East
West Haddlesey
Temple Hirst
Lofthouse
Lofthouse Gate
Diggerland
Castleford
Brotherton
Beal
Carr Gate
Wakefield Europort
Sutton
Kellington
Hirst Courtney
Xscape
Knottingley
Hensall
Normanton
Ferrybridge
Eggborough
Snaith
Woodhouse
Ackton
Gowdall
Alverthorpe
Flanshaw
Kirkthorpe
Warmfield
Whitley
Heath
New Sharlston
Darrington
Great Heck
Featherstone
Sharlston
Belle Vue
Pollington
Horbury
Sandal Magna
High Ackworth
East Hardwick
Womersley
Nostell Priory
Crofton
Brockadale
Balne
Calder Grove
Hessle
Low Ackworth
Little Smeaton
Walden Stubbs
Aire and Calder
Wentbridge
R Went
Crigglestone
Walton
New Crofton
Wragby
Ackworth Moor Top
Kirk Smeaton
Sykehouse
Hill Top
Fenwick
Newmillerdam
Fitzwilliam
Thorpe Audlin
Norton
Ryhill
Kinsley
Badsworth
Moss
Woolley Edge
Havercroft
Upton
Askern
Notton
South Hiendley
Hemsworth
North Elmsall
Campsall
Woolley
Kirk Bramwith
Haywood
Staincross
Royston
Shafton
Skelbrooke
Stainforth
Brierley
South Elmsall
Burghwallis
Owston
South Bramwith
Darton
Carlton
Moorthorpe
Hampole
Skellow
Thorpe in Balne
Barnby Dun
Mapplewell
South Kirkby
Carcroft
New Lodge
Grimethorpe
Adwick le Street
Cudworth
Clayton
Hooton Pagnell
Kirk Sandall
Toll Bar
Woodlands
Pickburn
Highgate
Monk Bretton
Little Houghton
Great Houghton
Thurnscoe
Brodsworth
Arksey
Edenthorpe
Scawthorpe
Dodworth
Hickleton
Bentley
Billingley
Wheatley Hills
Armthorpe
Marr
Scawsby
Cusworth
Worsbrough
Bolton
Goldthorpe
A1(M)
A1
A19
A59
A61
A64
A63
A658
A661
A168
A1237
A1036
A659
A58
A6120
A642
A639
A656
A1246
A655
A650
A636
A638
A628
A6021
A6195
A645
A1238
A1041
A635
A630
A637
A633
A18
M1
M62
M621
B6164
B6163
B1224
B1222
B1223
B1217
B6137
B6136
B6134
B6378
B6428
B6273
B6132
B6474
B6422
B1220
B6411
B6449
P+R
0 1 2 3 4 miles
0 1 2 3 4 5 kilometres

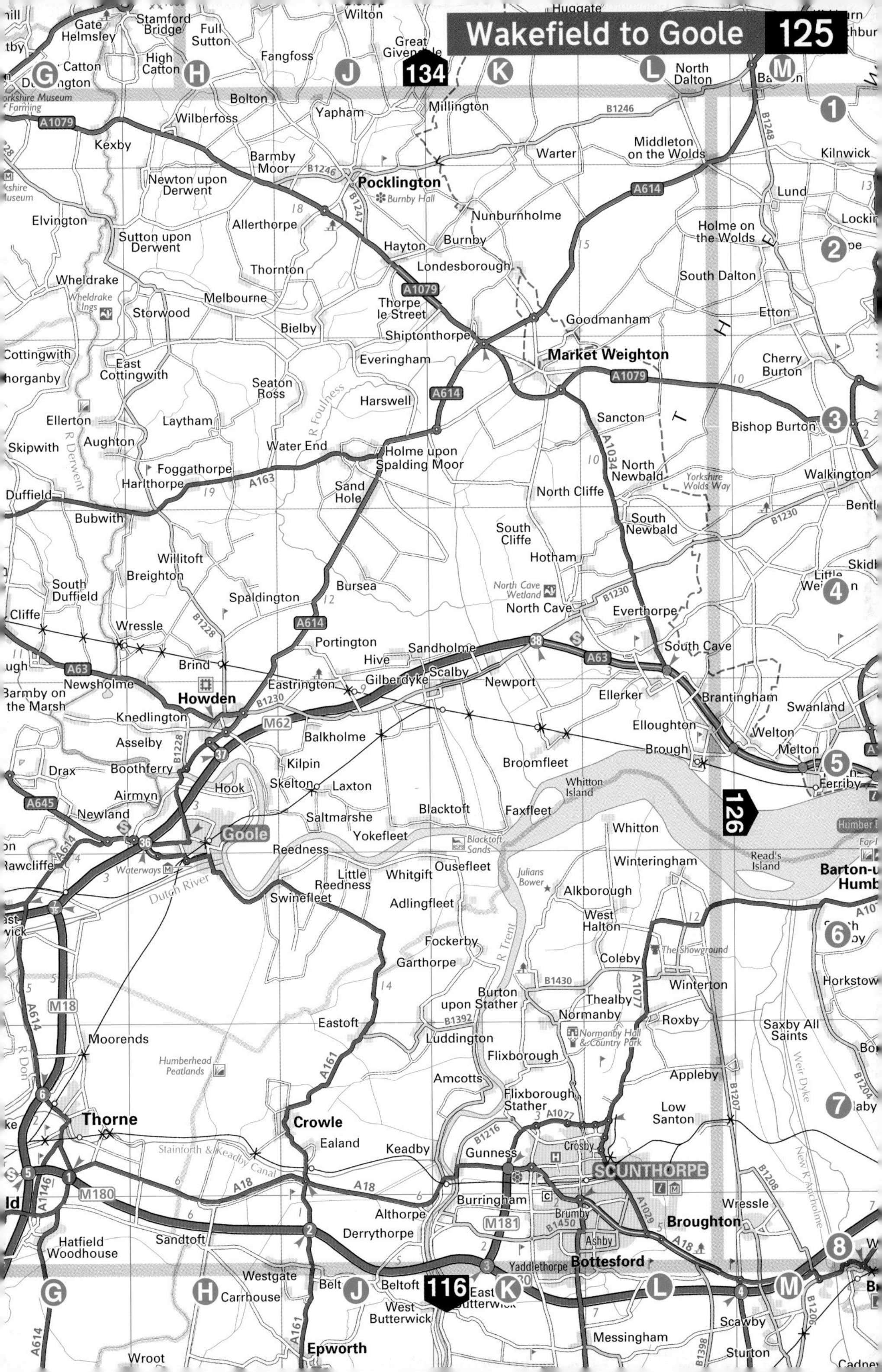
Stamford Bridge
Gate Helmsley
Full Sutton
Wilton
Huggate
Catton
High Catton
Fangfoss
Great Givendale
134
North Dalton
Yorkshire Museum of Farming
Bolton
Yapham
Millington
B1246
Wilberfoss
A1079
Kexby
Barmby Moor
Warter
Middleton on the Wolds
Kilnwick
Newton upon Derwent
Pocklington
Burnby Hall
A614
Lund
Elvington
Allerthorpe
Nunburnholme
Holme on the Wolds
Sutton upon Derwent
Hayton
Burnby
Thornton
Londesborough
South Dalton
Wheldrake
Wheldrake Ings
Melbourne
Thorpe le Street
Storwood
Bielby
Goodmanham
Etton
Shiptonthorpe
Cottingwith
East Cottingwith
Everingham
Market Weighton
Cherry Burton
Thorganby
Seaton Ross
Harswell
R Foulness
Sancton
Bishop Burton
Ellerton
Laytham
Aughton
Skipwith
Water End
Holme upon Spalding Moor
A1034
North Newbald
Yorkshire Wolds Way
Walkington
Foggathorpe
Harlthorpe
A163
R Derwent
Duffield
Sand Hole
North Cliffe
South Newbald
B1230
Bubwith
South Cliffe
Hotham
Willitoft
Breighton
South Duffield
Bursea
North Cave Wetland
North Cave
Everthorpe
Little Weighton
Spaldington
Cliffe
Wressle
B1228
Portington
Sandholme
South Cave
A63
Brind
Hive
Scalby
Newsholme
Gilberdyke
Newport
Ellerker
Brantingham
Barmby on the Marsh
Eastrington
Howden
Swanland
Knedlington
M62
Elloughton
Welton
Asselby
Balkholme
Brough
Melton
Drax
Boothferry
Kilpin
Broomfleet
Ferriby
Airmyn
Hook
Skelton
Laxton
Whitton Island
A645
Newland
Saltmarshe
Blacktoft
Faxfleet
126
Goole
Yokefleet
Blacktoft Sands
Whitton
Humber Bridge
Rawcliffe
Reedness
Ousefleet
Winteringham
Read's Island
Waterways Museum
Dutch River
Little Reedness
Whitgift
Julians Bower
Alkborough
Barton-upon-Humber
Swinefleet
Adlingfleet
West Halton
Fockerby
The Showground
Garthorpe
Coleby
R Trent
M18
A614
B1430
Winterton
Horkstow
Burton upon Stather
Thealby
A1077
Eastoft
B1392
Normanby
Roxby
Saxby All Saints
Moorends
Luddington
Normanby Hall & Country Park
Humberhead Peatlands
Flixborough
Weir Dyke
R Don
A161
Amcotts
Appleby
B1204
Flixborough Stather
Low Santon
B1207
Thorne
Crowle
Ealand
Keadby
B1216
Gunness
Crosby
Stainforth & Keadby Canal
SCUNTHORPE
A18
M180
A1146
Burringham
A1029
B1208
New R Ancholme
Wressle
Althorpe
Brumby
Broughton
Hatfield Woodhouse
Sandtoft
Derrythorpe
M181
B1450
Ashby
Yaddlethorpe
Bottesford
Westgate
Belt
Beltoft
116
East Butterwick
Carrhouse
West Butterwick
Scawby
B1206
Messingham
Epworth
B1398
Sturton
Wroot

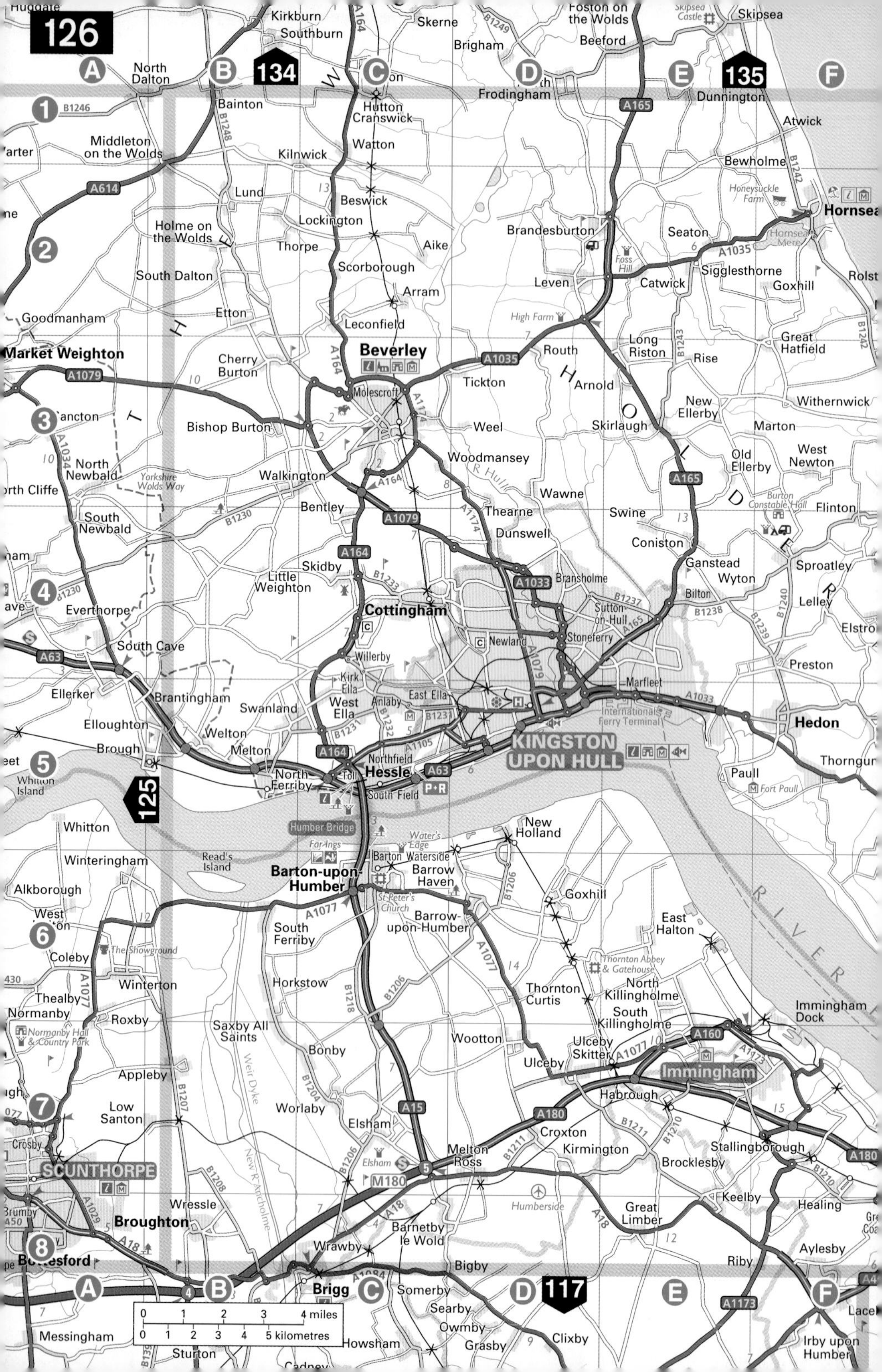

Kirkburn
Southburn
Skerne
Foston on the Wolds
Skipsea Castle
Skipsea
Brigham
Beeford
A
North Dalton
B
134
C
D
E
135
F
Frodingham
Dunnington
1
B1246
Bainton
Hutton Cranswick
A165
Atwick
Middleton on the Wolds
B1248
Watton
Kilnwick
Bewholme
A614
Lund
Beswick
Honeysuckle Farm
B1242
Hornsea
2
Holme on the Wolds
Lockington
Brandesburton
Seaton
Hornsea Mere
Thorpe
Aike
Foss Hill
A1035
Scorborough
Sigglesthorne
South Dalton
Leven
Catwick
Goxhill
Arram
Etton
High Farm
Goodmanham
Leconfield
Long Riston
B1243
Great Hatfield
Market Weighton
Beverley
A164
A1035
Routh
Rise
Cherry Burton
A1079
Tickton
Arnold
Molescroft
New Ellerby
Withernwick
3
Sancton
Bishop Burton
A1174
Weel
Skirlaugh
Marton
A1034
North Newbald
Woodmansey
Old Ellerby
West Newton
Walkington
Yorkshire Wolds Way
North Cliffe
A164
R Hull
A165
Wawne
Burton Constable Hall
Flinton
Thearne
Swine
B1230
South Newbald
Bentley
A1079
A1174
Dunswell
Coniston
A164
Ganstead
Sproatley
Skidby
Wyton
Little Weighton
A1033
Bransholme
B1233
4
B1230
Bilton
B1240
Lelley
Everthorpe
Cottingham
B1237
Sutton-on-Hull
B1238
B1239
A165
South Cave
Newland
Stoneferry
A63
Willerby
A1079
Preston
Kirk Ella
Marfleet
Ellerker
Brantingham
West Ella
Anlaby
East Ella
A1033
Swanland
International Ferry Terminal
Hedon
B1231
Elloughton
B1232
Welton
B1231
A1105
KINGSTON UPON HULL
Brough
Melton
A164
Northfield
Thorngumbald
5
Whitton Island
North Ferriby
Hessle
A63
Toll
Paull
125
South Field
P+R
Fort Paull
Humber Bridge
New Holland
Whitton
Far Ings
Water's Edge
Barton Waterside
Winteringham
Read's Island
Barrow Haven
Barton-upon-Humber
B1206
Alkborough
Goxhill
A1077
St Peter's Church
West Halton
Barrow-upon-Humber
East Halton
South Ferriby
6
The Showground
RIVER
Coleby
A1077
Thornton Abbey & Gatehouse
Winterton
Horkstow
B1218
B1206
Thealby
Thornton Curtis
North Killingholme
Normanby
Immingham Dock
Roxby
South Killingholme
Saxby All Saints
Normanby Hall & Country Park
Wootton
A160
Weir Dyke
Bonby
Ulceby Skitter
A1077
A1173
Ulceby
Immingham
Appleby
B1207
B1204
Habrough
7
Low Santon
Worlaby
A15
A180
Crosby
Elsham
Croxton
B1211
B1210
Kirmington
Stallingborough
A180
Elsham
New R Ancholme
Melton Ross
SCUNTHORPE
M180
Brocklesby
B1206
B1210
B1208
Humberside
A18
Keelby
Healing
Wressle
A1029
Barnetby le Wold
Great Limber
Brumby
Broughton
A18
8
Wrawby
Aylesby
Bottesford
Bigby
Riby
A
B
Brigg
C
A1084
Somerby
D
117
E
F
A1173
Searby
Laceby
Messingham
Ownby
0 1 2 3 4 miles
0 1 2 3 4 5 kilometres
Howsham
Grasby
Clixby
Irby upon Humber
Sturton
Cadney

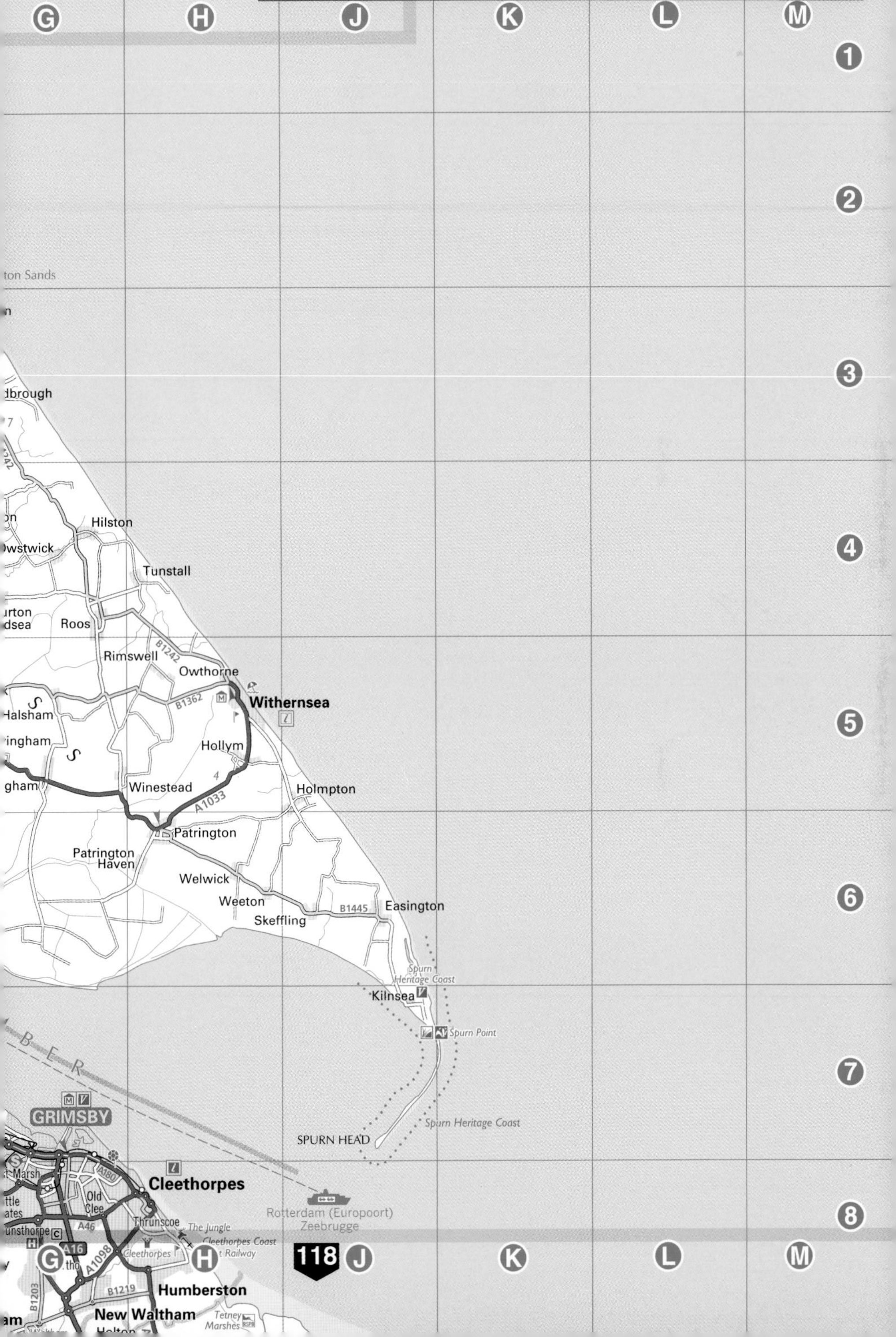
G
H
J
K
L
M
1
2
3
4
5
6
7
8
ton Sands
dbrough
Hilston
wstwick
Tunstall
urton
dsea
Roos
Rimswell
B1242
Owthorne
Withernsea
B1362
Halsham
ingham
Hollym
gham
Winestead
A1033
Holmpton
Patrington
Patrington Haven
Welwick
Weeton
Skeffling
B1445
Easington
Spurn Heritage Coast
Kilnsea
Spurn Point
Spurn Heritage Coast
SPURN HEAD
GRIMSBY
Cleethorpes
Old Clee
A180
A46
A16
A1098
Thrunscoe
The Jungle
Cleethorpes Coast Light Railway
Rotterdam (Europoort)
Zeebrugge
118
B1219
B1203
Humberston
New Waltham
Tetney Marshes

A B C D E F
1 2 3 4 5 6 7 8
Hallsenna Moor
Drigg
Holmrook
Eskdale
652
HARTER FELL
Muncaster Mill
Ravenglass & Eskdale Railway
River Esk
Devoke Water
Seathwaite Tarn
Ravenglass
Roman Bath House
Muncaster
A595
136
Hall Dunnerdale
137
Seathwaite
Waberthwaite
573
WHITFELL
Ulpha
LAKE DISTRICT NATIONAL PARK
Broughton Mills
A593
Hycemoor
Selker Bay
Bootle
Swinside Stone Circle
Broughton-in-F
Lady Hall
Foxfield
600
BLACK COMBE
Whitbeck
The Green
Gutterby Spa
Whicham
The Hill
Silecroft
Kirkby-in-
Beck S
Soutergate
Kirksanton
A5093
Millom
Haverigg
Haverigg Point
Ireleth
Askam in Furness
Lindal in Furness
Sandscale Haws
South Lakes Safari Zoo
North Walney
Dalton-in-Furness
BARROW-IN-FURNESS
Newton
Furness Abbey
Bow Bridge
Dendron
Vickerstown
Barrow Island
A590
A5087
ISLE OF WALNEY
Ramp
Sheep Island
Piel Castle
Piel Island
Piel Bar
Hilpsford Point
South Walney
0 1 2 3 4 miles
0 1 2 3 4 5 kilometres

Fells
Outgate
High Wray
Troutbeck Bridge
Far End
Hawkshead Hill
Hawkshead
Courthouse
Windermere Steamboats & Museum
Ings
Garth Row
Grayrigg
Bowness-on-Windermere
Hill Top
Far Sawrey
Near Sawrey
Esthwaite Water
Brantwood
Yacht 'Gondola'
Coniston Water
Grizedale
Grizedale Forest Park
137
138
B5284
Burneside
A591
A685
M6
Blackwell
Winster
Kendal
Firbank
Underbarrow
A684
Satterthwaite
Furness Fells
Graythwaite Hall
Crosthwaite
217
New Hutton
Killington Lake (southbound only)
A5084
High Nibthwaite
Thwaite Head
A592
Windermere
Brigsteer
Oxenholme
Natland
B6254
Middleshaw
Killington
Stott Park Bobbin Mill
321
GUMMERS HOW
Rusland
Cross
Finsthwaite
Row
A5074
A591
Sizergh Castle
A65
Old Hutton
Oxen Park
Colton
Whitbarrow
Fell Foot Park
Staveley
Lowick Green
Lakeside & Haverthwaite Railway
Newby Bridge
Levens
Sedgwick
Stainton
Lakeland Motor Museum
A5092
Bouth
Spark Bridge
Haverthwaite
Witherslack
Ayside
Levens Hall
Leasgill
Hincaster
A590
Westmorland
Crooklands
Endmoor
Preston Patrick
Old Town
Penny Bridge
Greenodd
High Newton
Heversham
Milnthorpe
284
Nook
Lupton
B5281
B5278
Arrad Foot
Meathop
B5282
River Kent
Whasset
B6385
Farleton
Kearstwick
Barrow Monument
222
HAMPSFELL
Lindale
Brown Robin
Storth
Beetham
B6384
A6070
Holme Park Fell
A65
Priory Gatehouse
Cartmel
Arnside
Holme
Hale
Hutton Roof
High Biggins
Low Biggins
Park Wood
Holker
Allithwaite
Grange-over-Sands
159
ARNSIDE KNOTT
Lakeland Wildlife Oasis
Burton-in-Kendal
Kirkby
Ulverston
Swarthmoor
Conishead Priory
Cark
B5278
Flookburgh
Silverdale
Yealand Redmayne
Leighton Hall
Burton-in-Kendal (northbound only)
Whittington
Great Urswick
Bardsea
Jack Scout
Priest Hutton
Yealand Conyers
130
Humphrey Head
Baycliff
Heald Brow
Warton
Old Rectory
Borwick
Arkholme
142
B6254
A683
Aldingham
MORECAMBE BAY
Carnforth
35A
35
Gressingham
Wennington
Over Kellet
A6
Hornby
Bolton-le-Sands
Nether Kellet
River Lune
Wray
Aughton
Claughton
A683
Farleton
Hest Bank
Morecambe
A5105
Slyne
Bare
Caton Green
Brookhouse
Halton
Caton
Torrisholme
34
A589
B5274
River Lune Millennium Park
Skerton
M6
P+R
Crossgill
Sandylands
B5273
A589
A683
Lancaster
R Roeburn
Lower Heysham
Higher Heysham
Heysham
Aldcliffe
Scotforth
560
WARD'S STONE
Douglas
Jubilee Tower
Overton
River Lune
Ellel
Sunderland
Glasson
Lancaster Canal
Galgate
A588
Forest of Bowland
R Wyre
Abbeystead
Cockersand
33
Dolphinholme
Cockerham
120
121
478
HAWTHORNTHWAITE FELL
Knott End-on-Sea
Pilling
COCKERHAM MOSS
B5272
Scorton
Calder Fell
Fleetwood

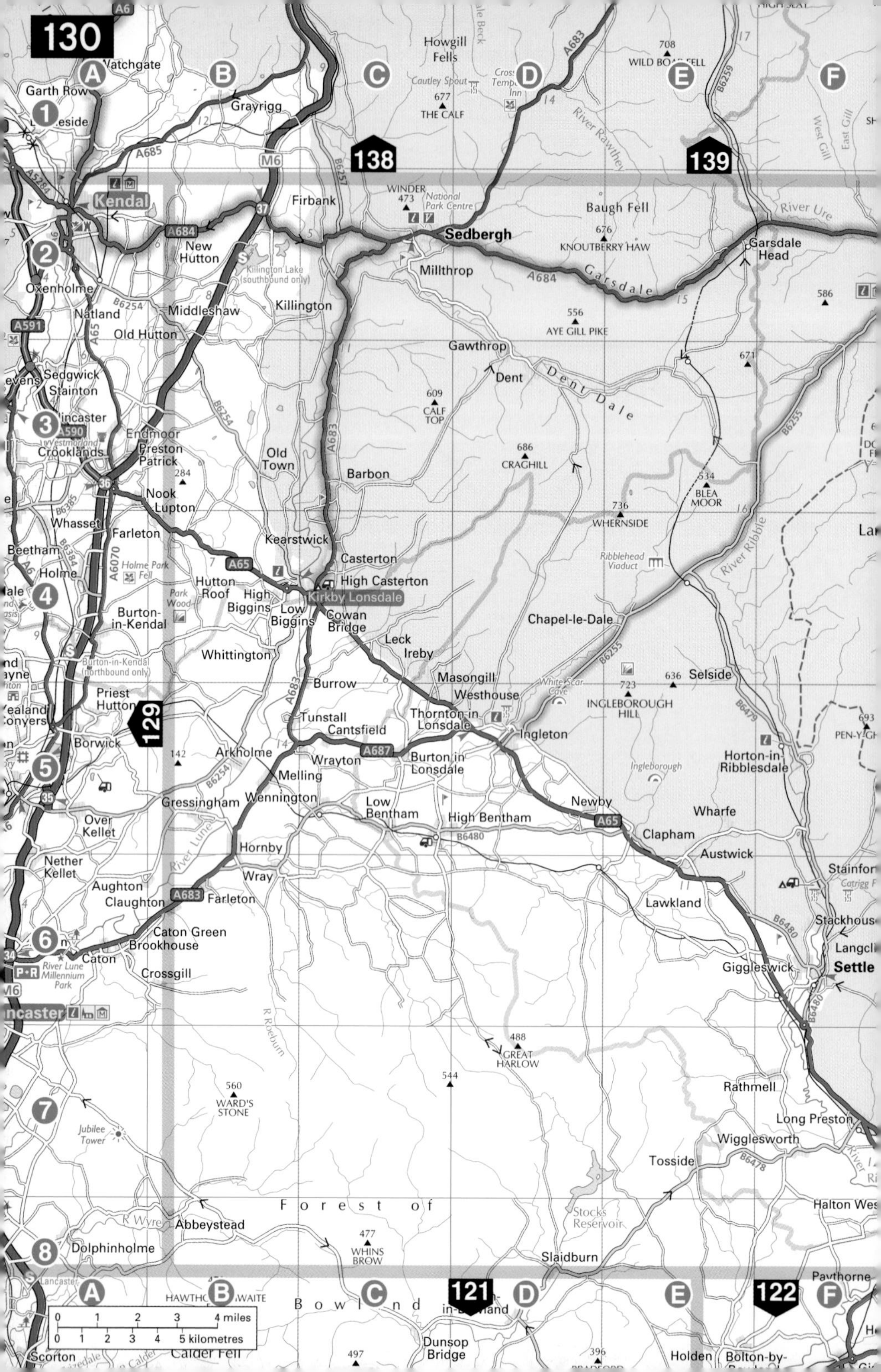
A6
Watchgate
Garth Row
Grayrigg
Howgill
Fells
Cautley Spout
677
THE CALF
A683
708
WILD BOAR FELL
B6259
River Rawthey
West Gill
East Gill
A685
M6
138
139
A5284
Kendal
B6257
WINDER
473
National
Park Centre
Firbank
Baugh Fell
River Ure
A684
New
Hutton
Sedbergh
676
KNOUTBERRY HAW
Garsdale
Head
Killington Lake
(southbound only)
Milllthrop
Garsdale
Oxenholme
586
B6254
Killington
Natland
Middleshaw
556
AYE GILL PIKE
A591
A65
Old Hutton
Gawthrop
671
Sedgwick
Stainton
Dent
Dent Dale
609
CALF
TOP
3
A590
Westmorland
Endmoor
Preston
Patrick
Crooklands
686
CRAGHILL
B6255
A683
Old
Town
284
Barbon
534
BLEA
MOOR
36
Nook
Lupton
B6385
736
WHERNSIDE
Whasset
Farleton
Kearstwick
River Ribble
Beetham
B6384
A6070
Holme Park
Fell
Ribblehead
Viaduct
Holme
A65
Casterton
Hutton
Roof
High Casterton
Park
Wood
High
Biggins
Kirkby Lonsdale
Low
Biggins
Cowan
Bridge
Chapel-le-Dale
Burton-
in-Kendal
Leck
Whittington
Ireby
B6255
Burton-in-Kendal
(northbound only)
Burrow
Masongill
723
INGLEBOROUGH
HILL
636
Selside
Priest
Hutton
White Scar
Cave
Westhouse
129
A683
Tunstall
Thornton-in-
Lonsdale
Ingleton
B6479
693
PEN-Y-GHENT
Borwick
Cantsfield
Arkholme
142
A687
Wrayton
Burton in
Lonsdale
Horton-in-
Ribblesdale
Ingleborough
5
B6254
Melling
Gressingham
Wennington
35
Low
Bentham
Newby
Over
Kellet
High Bentham
Wharfe
A65
B6480
Clapham
Hornby
River Lune
Nether
Kellet
Austwick
Wray
Stainforth
Catrigg Force
Aughton
Claughton
A683
Farleton
Lawkland
Stackhouse
B6480
6
Caton Green
Brookhouse
Langcliffe
Caton
River Lune
Millennium
Park
Giggleswick
Settle
P+R
M6
Crossgill
Lancaster
B6480
R Roeburn
488
GREAT
HARLOW
7
560
WARD'S
STONE
544
Rathmell
Jubilee
Tower
Long Preston
Wigglesworth
Tosside
B6478
River Ribble
Halton West
Forest of
R Wyre
Abbeystead
Stocks
Reservoir
477
WHINS
BROW
8
Dolphinholme
Slaidburn
Lancaster
Pawthorne
HAWTHORNTHWAITE
Bowland
121
122
0 1 2 3 4 miles
0 1 2 3 4 5 kilometres
Dunsop
Bridge
396
497
Calder Fell
Scorton
Holden
Bolton-by-

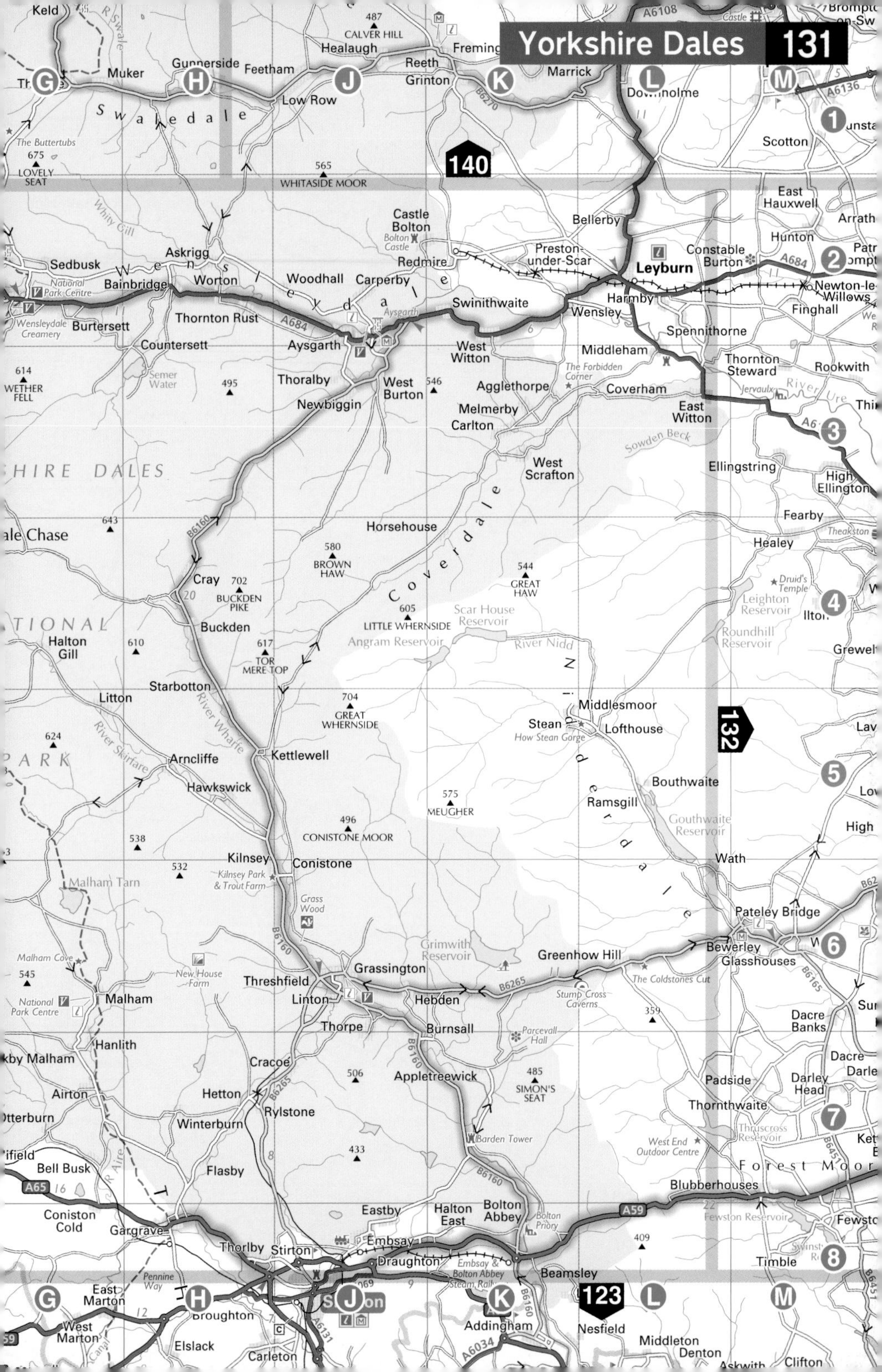
Keld
Muker
Gunnerside
Feetham
Healaugh
487 CALVER HILL
Reeth
Grinton
Fremington
Marrick
Downholme
Low Row
Swaledale
The Buttertubs
675 LOVELY SEAT
565 WHITASIDE MOOR
140
Scotton
East Hauxwell
Arrathorne
Hunton
Patrick Brompton
Constable Burton
Castle Bolton
Bolton Castle
Bellerby
Preston-under-Scar
Leyburn
Redmire
Askrigg
Sedbusk
Bainbridge
National Park Centre
Worton
Woodhall
Carperby
Wensleydale
Harmby
Newton-le-Willows
Finghall
Wensley
Swinithwaite
Aysgarth
Wensleydale Creamery
Burtersett
Thornton Rust
A684
Spennithorne
Countersett
West Witton
Middleham
Semer Water
614 WETHER FELL
495
Thoralby
West Burton
546
Agglethorpe
The Forbidden Corner
Coverham
Thornton Steward
Rookwith
Jervaulx
River Ure
Newbiggin
Melmerby
Carlton
East Witton
Sowden Beck
West Scrafton
Ellingstring
High Ellington
YORKSHIRE DALES
NATIONAL PARK
643
Langstrothdale Chase
B6160
Horsehouse
Fearby
Theakston
Healey
580 BROWN HAW
544 GREAT HAW
Druid's Temple
Cray
702 BUCKDEN PIKE
Coverdale
605 LITTLE WHERNSIDE
Scar House Reservoir
Leighton Reservoir
Ilton
Buckden
Halton Gill
610
617 TOR MERE TOP
Angram Reservoir
River Nidd
Roundhill Reservoir
Grewelthorpe
Starbotton
Litton
704 GREAT WHERNSIDE
Middlesmoor
Stean
Lofthouse
How Stean Gorge
132
River Wharfe
624
River Skirfare
Kettlewell
Arncliffe
Nidderdale
Hawkswick
Bouthwaite
Ramsgill
575 MEUGHER
Gouthwaite Reservoir
496 CONISTONE MOOR
538
High
Wath
Kilnsey
Conistone
532
Kilnsey Park & Trout Farm
Malham Tarn
Grass Wood
Pateley Bridge
Bewerley
Glasshouses
Grimwith Reservoir
Greenhow Hill
Malham Cove
Threshfield
Grassington
B6265
The Coldstones Cut
545
New House Farm
Stump Cross Caverns
National Park Centre
Malham
Linton
Hebden
359
Thorpe
Burnsall
Parcevall Hall
Dacre Banks
Hanlith
Kirkby Malham
Cracoe
Dacre
506
485 SIMON'S SEAT
Appletreewick
Padside
Darley Head
Airton
Hetton
Thornthwaite
Otterburn
Rylstone
Winterburn
Barden Tower
West End Outdoor Centre
Thruscross Reservoir
433
Forest Moor
Hellifield
Bell Busk
Flasby
River Aire
A65
Blubberhouses
Coniston Cold
Eastby
Halton East
Bolton Abbey
Bolton Priory
A59
Fewston Reservoir
Gargrave
Embsay
409
Thorlby
Stirton
Draughton
Embsay & Bolton Abbey Steam Railway
Beamsley
Timble
Pennine Way
East Marton
Broughton
Skipton
123
Addingham
Nesfield
West Marton
Elslack
Carleton
A6131
A6034
Middleton
Denton
Askwith
Clifton
Leeds & Liverpool Canal

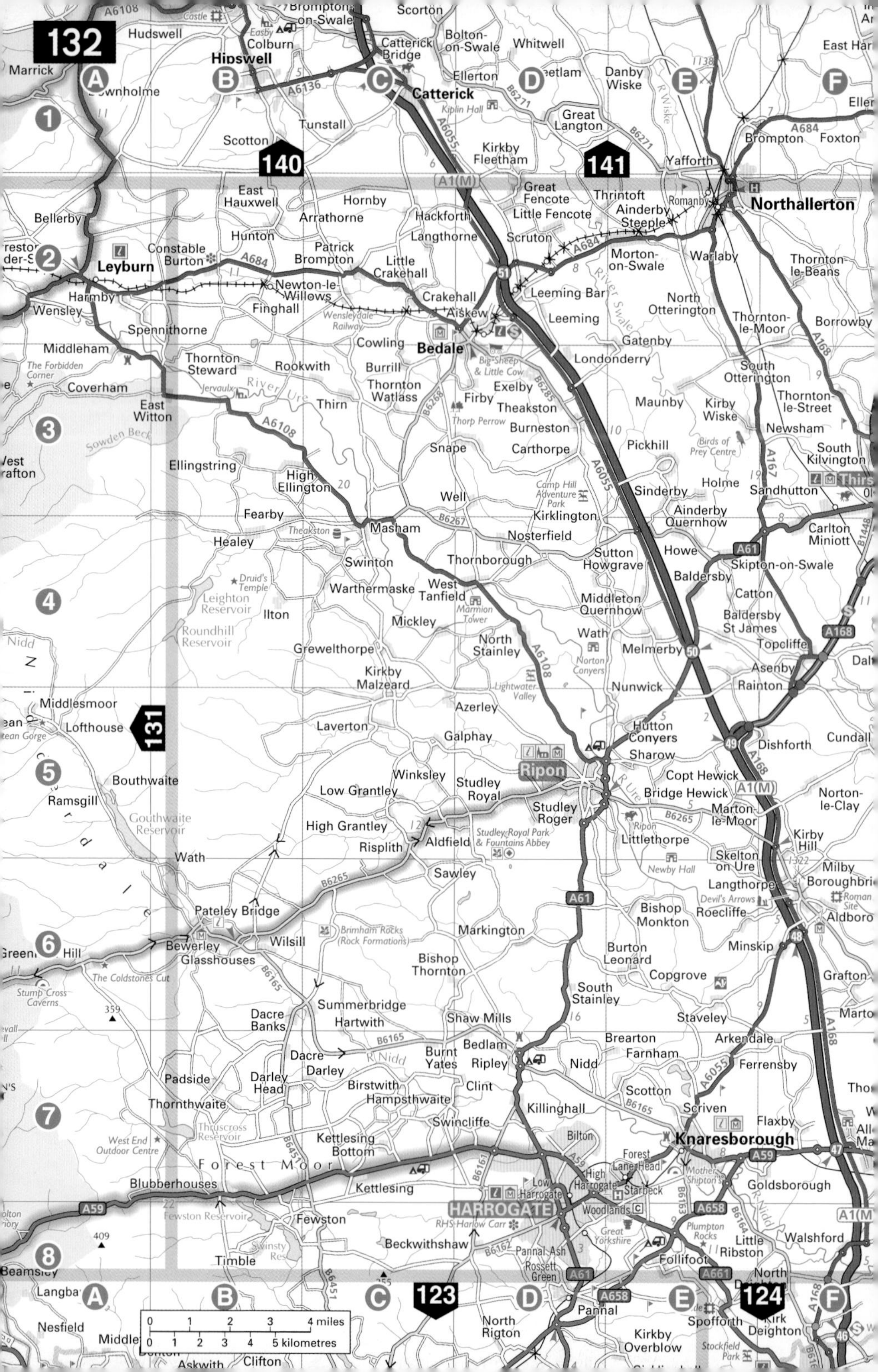
Hudswell
Hipswell
Colburn
Marrick
Downholme
Catterick Bridge
Catterick
Scorton
Bolton-on-Swale
Whitwell
Ellerton
Danby Wiske
Northallerton
Brompton
Foxton
Tunstall
Scotton
Kiplin Hall
Great Langton
Kirkby Fleetham
140
141
Yafforth
Romanby
Great Fencote
Little Fencote
Thrintoft
Ainderby Steeple
East Hauxwell
Hornby
Hackforth
Arrathorne
Langthorne
Scruton
Bellerby
Hunton
Constable Burton
Patrick Brompton
Leyburn
Little Crakehall
Morton-on-Swale
Warlaby
Thornton-le-Beans
Harmby
Wensley
Newton-le-Willows
Finghall
Crakehall
Leeming Bar
Leeming
North Otterington
Thornton-le-Moor
Borrowby
Spennithorne
Aiskew
Wensleydale Railway
Middleham
The Forbidden Corner
Coverham
Thornton Steward
Rookwith
Cowling
Bedale
Gatenby
Burrill
Big Sheep & Little Cow
Londonderry
South Otterington
Jervaulx
River Ure
Thornton Watlass
Exelby
Firby
East Witton
Thirn
Theakston
Maunby
Kirby Wiske
Thornton-le-Street
Thorp Perrow
Burneston
Newsham
Sowden Beck
West Tanfield
Snape
Carthorpe
Pickhill
Birds of Prey Centre
South Kilvington
Ellingstring
High Ellington
Camp Hill Adventure Park
Sinderby
Holme
Sandhutton
Thirsk
Well
Kirklington
Ainderby Quernhow
Fearby
Carlton Miniott
Healey
Theakston
Masham
Nosterfield
Howe
Swinton
Thornborough
Sutton Howgrave
Baldersby
Skipton-on-Swale
Druid's Temple
Warthermaske
Catton
Leighton Reservoir
Ilton
Marmion Tower
Middleton Quernhow
Baldersby St James
Roundhill Reservoir
Mickley
Wath
Topcliffe
Grewelthorpe
North Stainley
Melmerby
Norton Conyers
Asenby
Kirkby Malzeard
Rainton
Lightwater Valley
Nunwick
Middlesmoor
Azerley
Lofthouse
How Stean Gorge
131
Laverton
Hutton Conyers
Galphay
Dishforth
Cundall
Sharow
Ripon
Winksley
Copt Hewick
Bouthwaite
Studley Royal
Low Grantley
Bridge Hewick
Norton-le-Clay
Ramsgill
Studley Roger
Marton-le-Moor
Gouthwaite Reservoir
High Grantley
Studley Royal Park & Fountains Abbey
Aldfield
Littlethorpe
Kirby Hill
Risplith
Wath
Sawley
Newby Hall
Skelton on Ure
Milby
Boroughbridge
Langthorpe
Devil's Arrows
Roman Site
Nidderdale
Pateley Bridge
Bishop Monkton
Roecliffe
Aldborough
Brimham Rocks (Rock Formations)
Markington
Wilsill
Bewerley
Greenhow Hill
Glasshouses
Burton Leonard
Minskip
The Coldstones Cut
Bishop Thornton
Copgrove
Grafton
Stump Cross Caverns
South Stainley
Summerbridge
Dacre Banks
Hartwith
Shaw Mills
Staveley
Marton
Brearton
Arkendale
Bedlam
Burnt Yates
Farnham
Ferrensby
Dacre
Darley
Ripley
Nidd
Padside
Darley Head
Birstwith
Clint
Scotton
Hampsthwaite
Thornthwaite
Killinghall
Scriven
Flaxby
Thruscross Reservoir
Swincliffe
Bilton
West End Outdoor Centre
Kettlesing Bottom
Knaresborough
Forest Moor
Forest Lane Head
Mother Shipton's
High Harrogate
Goldsborough
Blubberhouses
Kettlesing
Low Harrogate
Starbeck
Fewston Reservoir
Fewston
HARROGATE
Woodlands
RHS Harlow Carr
Great Yorkshire
Plumpton Rocks
Walshford
Beckwithshaw
Pannal Ash
Little Ribston
Swinsty Res
Rossett Green
Follifoot
Timble
North Deighton
Beamsley
Langbar
123
124
Pannal
Spofforth
Nesfield
North Rigton
Kirk Deighton
Middleton
Kirkby Overblow
Stockfield Park
Askwith
Clifton
A6108
A6136
A6055
A684
B6271
A1(M)
A168
A167
A61
A6108
B6267
B6268
B6285
B6265
B6165
B6451
B6161
A59
B6162
B6163
B6164
A658
A661
A1(M)
0 1 2 3 4 miles
0 1 2 3 4 5 kilometres

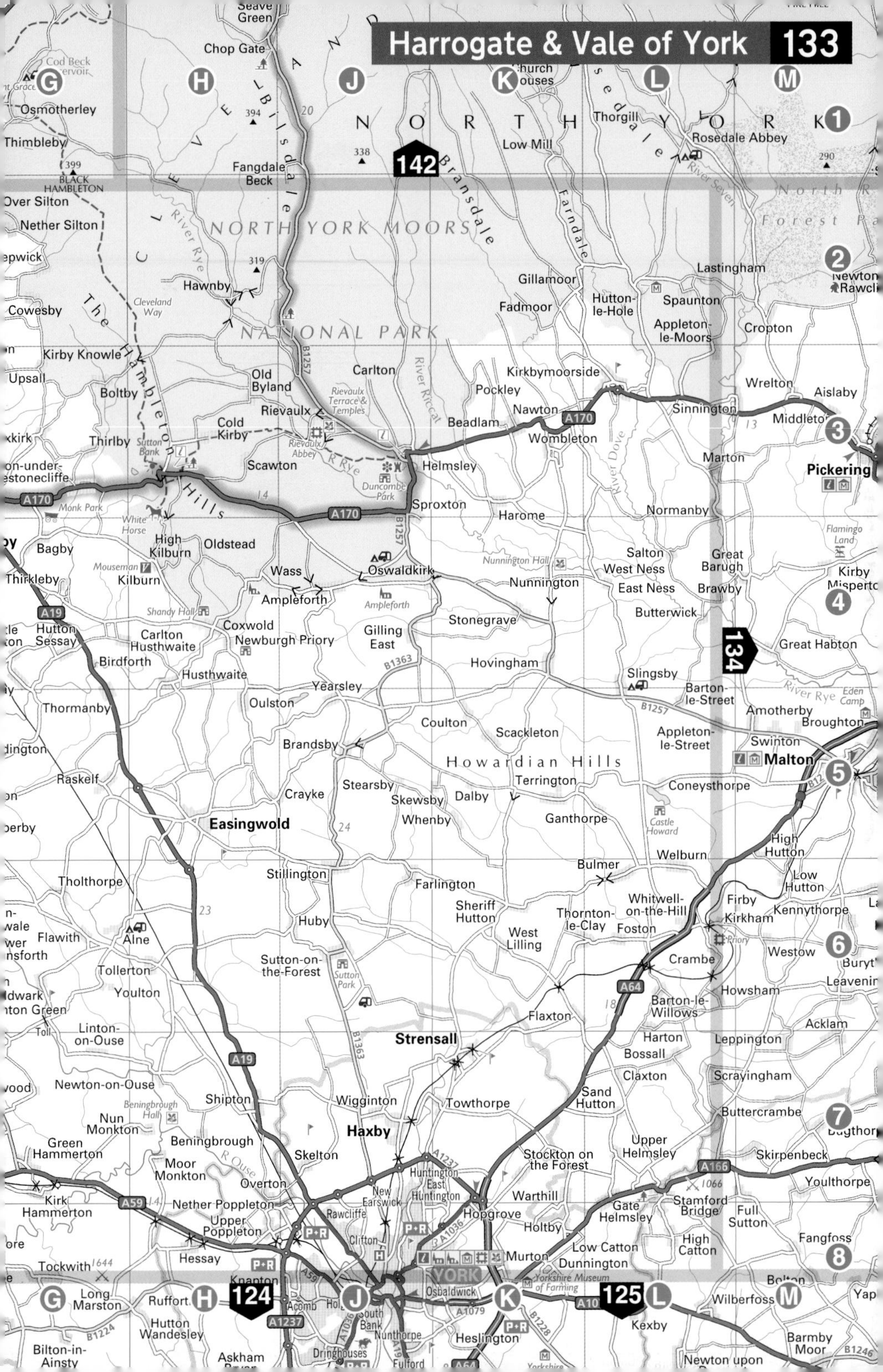

G
H
J
K
L
M
1
2
3
4
5
6
7
8
Seave Green
Chop Gate
Cod Beck Reservoir
Osmotherley
Thimbleby
399
BLACK HAMBLETON
Over Silton
Nether Silton
Cowesby
Kirby Knowle
Upsall
Boltby
Thirlby
Sutton Bank
CLEVELAND
Bilsdale
394
338
20
N O R T H Y O R K
142
Church Houses
Thorgill
Low Mill
Rosedale Abbey
Rosedale
River Seven
290
Fangdale Beck
River Rye
NORTH YORK MOORS
Bransdale
Farndale
North Riding Forest Park
319
Hawnby
Cleveland Way
The Hambleton Hills
NATIONAL PARK
B1257
Gillamoor
Fadmoor
Hutton-le-Hole
Lastingham
Spaunton
Appleton-le-Moors
Cropton
Newton Rawcliffe
Carlton
River Riccal
Kirkbymoorside
Pockley
Old Byland
Rievaulx Terrace & Temples
Rievaulx
Cold Kirby
Rievaulx Abbey
R Rye
Beadlam
Nawton
A170
Wombleton
Sinnington
Wrelton
Aislaby
Middleton
13
Marton
Pickering
Scawton
Helmsley
Duncombe Park
River Dove
14
A170
Monk Park
White Horse
Sproxton
Harome
Normanby
Flamingo Land
High Kilburn
Oldstead
Bagby
Thirkleby
Mouseman
Kilburn
Wass
Oswaldkirk
Nunnington Hall
Nunnington
Salton
West Ness
East Ness
Great Barugh
Brawby
Kirby Misperton
Ampleforth
Shandy Hall
A19
Hutton Sessay
Carlton Husthwaite
Coxwold
Newburgh Priory
Gilling East
Stonegrave
Butterwick
134
Great Habton
Birdforth
Husthwaite
B1363
Hovingham
Slingsby
Barton-le-Street
River Rye
Eden Camp
Thormanby
Yearsley
Oulston
B1257
Amotherby
Broughton
Coulton
Scackleton
Appleton-le-Street
Swinton
Malton
Brandsby
Howardian Hills
Terrington
Coneysthorpe
Raskelf
Stearsby
Crayke
Skewsby
Dalby
Whenby
Easingwold
24
Ganthorpe
Castle Howard
High Hutton
Welburn
Bulmer
Stillington
Farlington
Tholthorpe
Low Hutton
Whitwell-on-the-Hill
Firby
Kirkham
Kennythorpe
Sheriff Hutton
Thornton-le-Clay
Foston
Priory
23
Huby
West Lilling
Flawith
Alne
Westow
Sutton-on-the-Forest
Sutton Park
Crambe
Tollerton
Youlton
A64
Howsham
Leavening
18
Barton-le-Willows
Flaxton
Toll
Linton-on-Ouse
Acklam
B1363
Strensall
Harton
Leppington
Bossall
A19
Claxton
Scrayingham
Newton-on-Ouse
Sand Hutton
Shipton
Wigginton
Towthorpe
Beningbrough Hall
Nun Monkton
Buttercrambe
Green Hammerton
Haxby
Beningbrough
Upper Helmsley
Skirpenbeck
Moor Monkton
R Ouse
Skelton
Stockton on the Forest
A1237
Huntington
A166
Overton
East Huntington
1066
Youlthorpe
Kirk Hammerton
A59
14
Nether Poppleton
New Earswick
Warthill
Gate Helmsley
Stamford Bridge
Full Sutton
Rawcliffe
Hopgrove
Upper Poppleton
P+R
A1036
Holtby
High Catton
Clifton
Low Catton
Fangfoss
Hessay
Murton
Dunnington
Tockwith
1644
P+R
Knapton
YORK
Yorkshire Museum of Farming
Bolton
124
A59
Osbaldwick
125
Long Marston
Ruffort
Acomb
South Bank
A1079
A10
Wilberfoss
B1224
A1237
B1228
Kexby
Hutton Wandesley
A1036
Nunthorpe
A19
P+R
Heslington
Barmby Moor
Bilton-in-Ainsty
Askham
Dringhouses
Fulford
A64
Newton upon
B1246

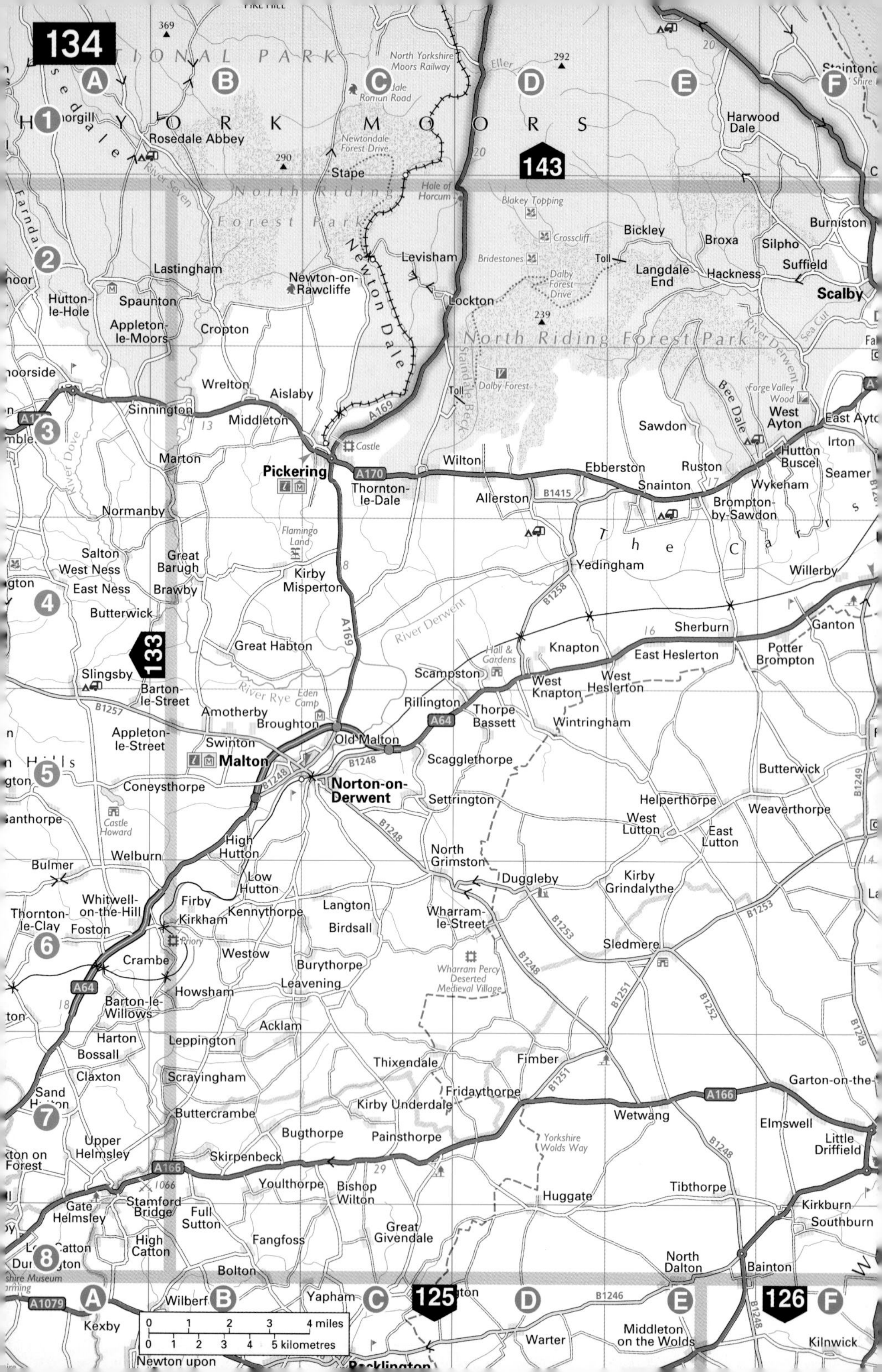
134
143
133
125
126
A
B
C
D
E
F
1
2
3
4
5
6
7
8
NATIONAL PARK
YORK MOORS
North Yorkshire Moors Railway
Rosedale Abbey
River Seven
Farndale
Newtondale Forest Drive
Stape
North Riding Forest Park
Hole of Horcum
Blakey Topping
Crosscliff
Bridestones
Dalby Forest Drive
Toll
Bickley
Langdale End
Broxa
Hackness
Harwood Dale
Burniston
Silpho
Suffield
Scalby
Sea Cut
River Derwent
Lastingham
Spaunton
Hutton-le-Hole
Appleton-le-Moors
Cropton
Newton-on-Rawcliffe
Levisham
Lockton
Newton Dale
Staindale Beck
Dalby Forest
Forge Valley Wood
Bee Dale
West Ayton
East Ayton
Irton
Seamer
Wrelton
Aislaby
Sinnington
Middleton
Pickering
Castle
A170
A169
Thornton-le-Dale
Wilton
Allerston
B1415
Ebberston
Snainton
Ruston
Hutton Buscel
Wykeham
Brompton-by-Sawdon
Sawdon
Marton
River Dove
Normanby
Salton
West Ness
East Ness
Great Barugh
Brawby
Butterwick
Flamingo Land
Kirby Misperton
The Carrs
Yedingham
Willerby
B1258
River Derwent
Great Habton
Hall & Gardens
Knapton
Sherburn
Ganton
East Heslerton
Potter Brompton
Slingsby
Barton-le-Street
B1257
River Rye
Eden Camp
Amotherby
Broughton
Scampston
Rillington
West Knapton
West Heslerton
Thorpe Bassett
Wintringham
A64
Appleton-le-Street
Swinton
Malton
Old Malton
B1248
Norton-on-Derwent
Scagglethorpe
Settrington
Coneysthorpe
Castle Howard
Helperthorpe
Butterwick
Weaverthorpe
West Lutton
East Lutton
B1249
Welburn
Bulmer
High Hutton
Low Hutton
North Grimston
Duggleby
Kirby Grindalythe
Whitwell-on-the-Hill
Thornton-le-Clay
Foston
Firby
Kirkham
Priory
Kennythorpe
Langton
Birdsall
Wharram-le-Street
B1253
Sledmere
Crambe
Westow
Burythorpe
Leavening
Wharram Percy Deserted Medieval Village
Howsham
Barton-le-Willows
Acklam
B1251
B1252
Harton
Bossall
Leppington
Claxton
Scrayingham
Thixendale
Fimber
Sand Hutton
Buttercrambe
Fridaythorpe
Kirby Underdale
Wetwang
A166
Garton-on-the-
Elmswell
Upper Helmsley
Bugthorpe
Painsthorpe
Yorkshire Wolds Way
Little Driffield
Skirpenbeck
1066
Youlthorpe
Bishop Wilton
Gate Helmsley
Stamford Bridge
Full Sutton
Huggate
Tibthorpe
Kirkburn
Southburn
Fangfoss
Great Givendale
High Catton
Low Catton
Dunnington
North Dalton
Bainton
Bolton
A1079
Wilberfoss
Yapham
B1246
Kexby
Warter
Middleton on the Wolds
Kilnwick
Newton upon
Pocklington
0 1 2 3 4 miles
0 1 2 3 4 5 kilometres

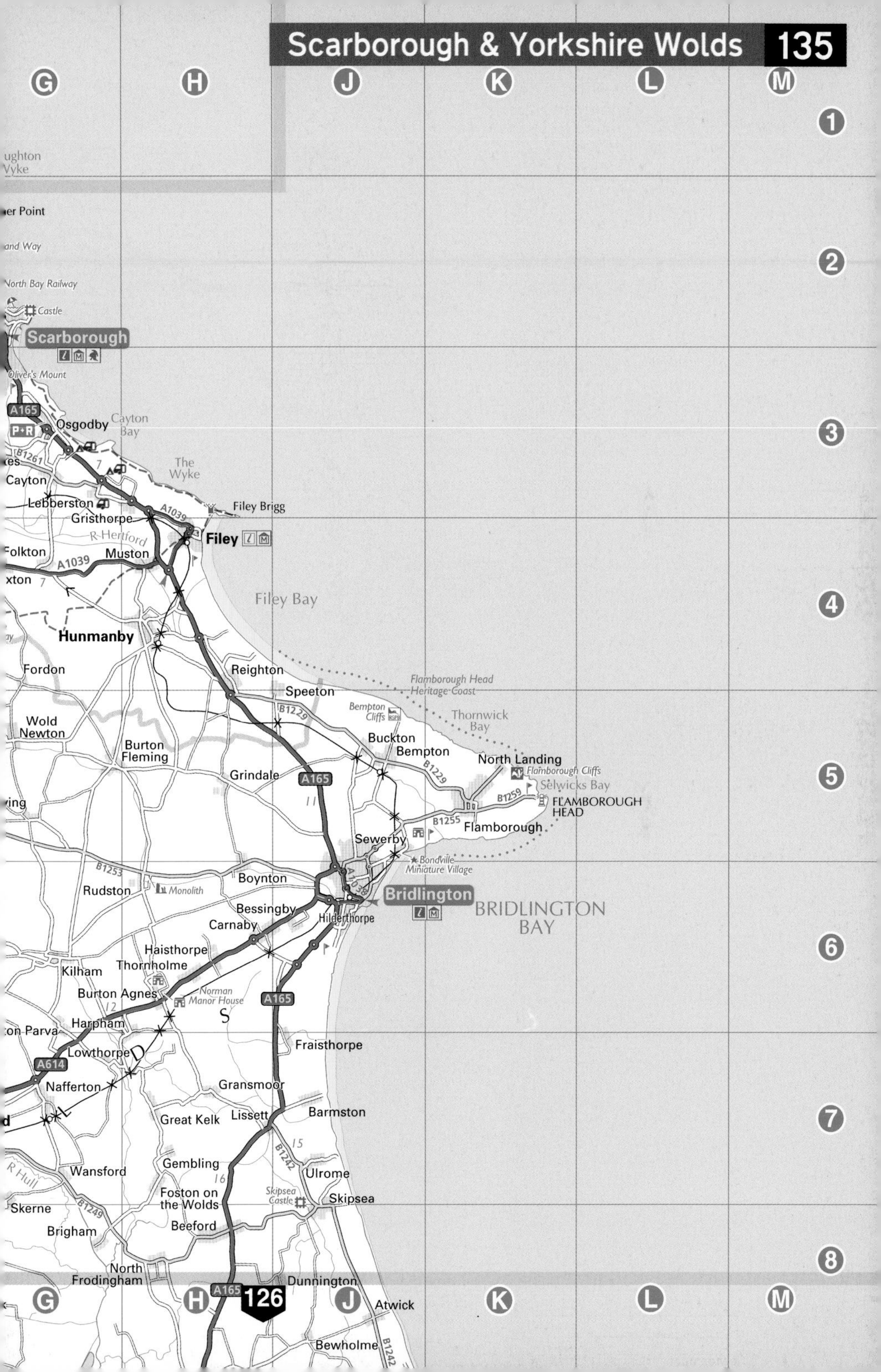
G
H
J
K
L
M
1
2
3
4
5
6
7
8
North Bay Railway
Castle
Scarborough
Oliver's Mount
A165
Osgodby
Cayton Bay
B1261
Cayton
The Wyke
Lebberston
Gristhorpe
Filey Brigg
A1039
R Hertford
Filey
Folkton
Muston
Filey Bay
Hunmanby
Fordon
Reighton
Speeton
Flamborough Head Heritage Coast
Bempton Cliffs
B1229
Thornwick Bay
Wold Newton
Burton Fleming
Buckton
Bempton
North Landing
Flamborough Cliffs
Selwicks Bay
B1259
FLAMBOROUGH HEAD
Grindale
B1255
Flamborough
Sewerby
Bondville Miniature Village
B1253
Boynton
A1038
Rudston
Monolith
Bridlington
BRIDLINGTON BAY
Bessingby
Carnaby
Hilderthorpe
Haisthorpe
Thornholme
Kilham
Burton Agnes
Norman Manor House
Harpham
Lowthorpe
A614
Nafferton
Fraisthorpe
Gransmoor
Great Kelk
Lissett
Barmston
B1242
Wansford
R Hull
Gembling
Ulrome
Foston on the Wolds
Skipsea Castle
Skipsea
Skerne
B1249
Brigham
Beeford
North Frodingham
Dunnington
126
Atwick
Bewholme

A
B
C
D
E
F
1
2
3
4
5
6
7
8
147
128
Crosscanonby
Crosby
Fort
River Ellen
Maryport
Dearham
A594
Tallen
Brideki
Flimby
Broughton Moor
Standingstone
Dovenby
Great Broughton
Camerton
Papcastle
A66
Seaton
Great Clifton
Brigham
Greysouthen
Stainburn
Little Clifton
Eaglesfield
Workington
Moss Bay
Mossbay
Westfield
Salterbeck
High Harrington
Harrington
A596
A595
A597
Deanscales
Branthwaite
Dean
Ullock
Pardshaw
Distington
Common End
B5306
Gilgarran
Mockerkin
Lowca
Parton
Howgate
Low Moresby
R. Keekle
A5086
Loweswater
Lamplugh
572
Asby
Arlecdon
Rowrah
Kirkland
Whitehaven
High Leys
Hensingham
Frizington
B5295
B5294
Saltom Bay
Cleator Moor
Mirehouse
Sandwith
Ennerdale Bridge
Ennerdale Water
River Ehen
B5345
Rottington
Bigrigg
Cleator
St Bees Head
St Bees Head Heritage Coast
River Calder
St Bees
Egremont
533
LANK RIGG
L A K
Worm Gill
Thornhill
Haile
River Bleng
Nethertown
Beckermet
Calder Bridge
R. Ehen
Cross
Wellington
Sellafield Station
Gosforth
B5343
Sant
Seascale
Hallsenna Moor
Drigg
Holmrook
Muncaster Mill
River
Ravenglass
Roman Bath House
Muncaster
Wabert
Hycemoor
Selker Bay
Bootl
0
1
2
3
4 miles
0
1
2
3
4
5 kilometres

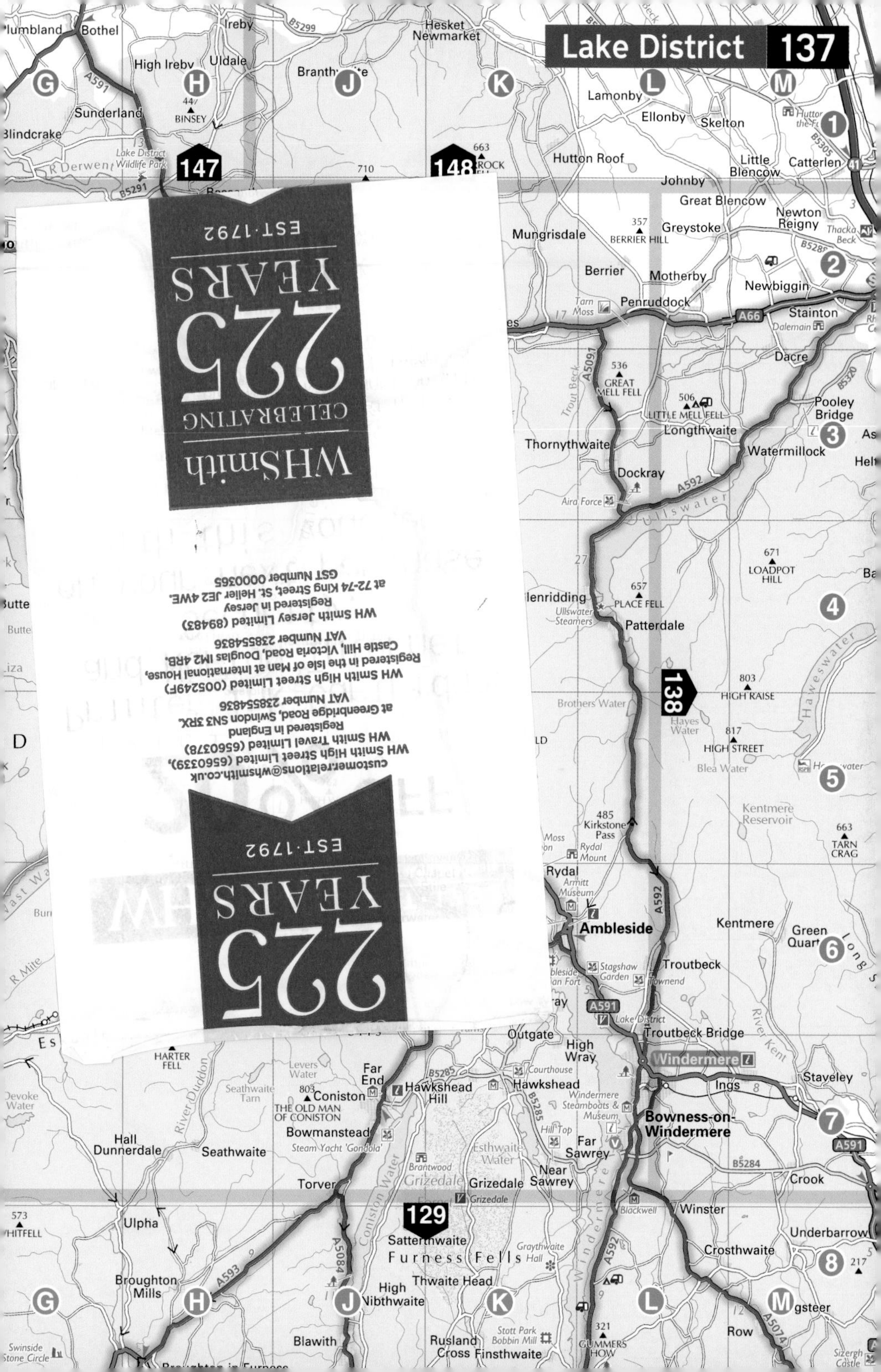
Plumbland
Bothel
Ireby
B5299
Hesket Newmarket
High Ireby
Uldale
Sunderland
447 BINSEY
Blindcrake
Lake District Wildlife Park
R Derwent
B5291
147
148
663
710
Lamonby
Ellonby
Skelton
Hutton Roof
Little Blencow
Catterlen
B5305
41
Johnby
Great Blencow
357 BERRIER HILL
Greystoke
Newton Reigny
Mungrisdale
Berrier
Motherby
Newbiggin
B5288
Tarn Moss
Penruddock
A66
Stainton
Dalemain
Dacre
A5091
536 GREAT MELL FELL
506 LITTLE MELL FELL
Longthwaite
Pooley Bridge
B5320
Trout Beck
Thornythwaite
Watermillock
Dockray
A592
Aira Force
Ullswater
671 LOADPOT HILL
657 PLACE FELL
Glenridding
Ullswater Steamers
Patterdale
Haweswater
803 HIGH RAISE
138
Brothers Water
Hayes Water
817 HIGH STREET
Blea Water
Kentmere Reservoir
485 Kirkstone Pass
663 TARN CRAG
Rydal Mount
Rydal
Armitt Museum
Ambleside
Kentmere
Green Quarter
Stagshaw Garden
Troutbeck
Townend
A591
Lake District
Troutbeck Bridge
River Kent
Outgate
High Wray
Windermere
Staveley
Ings
HARTER FELL
Levers Water
Seathwaite Tarn
Far End
B5285
Courthouse
Hawkshead
Hawkshead Hill
803 Coniston
THE OLD MAN OF CONISTON
Devoke Water
Windermere Steamboats & Museum
Bowness-on-Windermere
Bowmanstead
Steam Yacht 'Gondola'
River Duddon
Hall Dunnerdale
Seathwaite
Hill Top
Far Sawrey
Esthwaite Water
Brantwood
B5284
Grizedale
Near Sawrey
Crook
Torver
Coniston Water
Blackwell
Winster
573 WHITFELL
Ulpha
129
Satterthwaite
A5084
Furness Fells
Graythwaite Hall
Underbarrow
Crosthwaite
Broughton Mills
A593
Thwaite Head
High Nibthwaite
A592
217
Swinside Stone Circle
Blawith
Rusland
Stott Park Bobbin Mill
Finsthwaite
321 GUMMERS HOW
Row
A5074
Sizergh Castle
G
H
J
K
L
M

A
B
C
D
E
F
1
2
3
4
5
6
7
8
Hutton End
Lamonby
Ellonby
Skelton
Hutton Roof
663 CARROCK FELL
Hutton-in-the-Forest
Little Blencow
Catterlen
Johnby
Great Blencow
Newton Reigny
247 LAZONBY FELL
Plumpton
Salkeld Dykes
Glassonby
Gamblesby
Great Salkeld
Long Meg & her Daughters
Little Salkeld
Hunsonby
Melmerby
710 MELMERBY FELL
Winskill
Ousby
Langwathby
Skirwith
148
703 BOWSCALE FELL
Mungrisdale
357 BERRIER HILL
Greystoke
Thacka Beck
Penrith
Castle
Edenhall
Blencarn
R Eamont
Berrier
Motherby
Newbiggin
Brougham Castle
Culgaith
Penruddock
Tarn Moss
Stainton
Dalemain
Henge
Countess Pillar
Eamont Bridge
Oasis Whinfell Park
220
Acorn Bank Garden
Newbiggin
Temple Sowerby
Scales
Rheged Centre
Yanwath
Clifton Hall
Wetheriggs Animal Rescue Centre
CenterParcs
Kirkby Thore
Dacre
Tirril
Clifton
Cilburn Moss
Long Marton
536 GREAT MELL FELL
506 LITTLE MELL FELL
Pooley Bridge
Melkinthorpe
Cliburn
River Eden
Longthwaite
Lowther
Hackthorpe
Thornythwaite
Mosedale Beck
Trout Beck
Watermillock
Askham
Helton
Lakeland Bird of Prey Centre
Great Strickland
Morland
Bolton
Dockray
Newby
Kings Meaburn
856 GREAT DODD
Aira Force
Ullswater
Colby
Little Strickland
River Lyvennet
Appleby-in-Westmorland
840 STYBARROW DODD
671 LOADPOT HILL
Sleagill
Bampton
Bampton Grange
Reagill
657 PLACE FELL
Glenridding
Ullswater Steamers
Patterdale
Rosgill
Maulds Meaburn
950 HELVELLYN
Shap Abbey
Shap
Crosby Ravensworth
Haweswater
Keld Chapel
137
803 HIGH RAISE
Brothers Water
Grisdale Tarn
873 FAIRFIELD
Hayes Water
817 HIGH STREET
Swindale River
316 Shap Summit
Blea Water
Haweswater
Great Asby Scar
LAKE DISTRICT
NATIONAL
PARK
Kentmere Reservoir
663 TARN CRAG
412
Orton
485 Kirkstone Pass
Wordsworth
White Moss Common
Rydal Mount
Crookdale Beck
Borrow Beck
Tebay
R Lune
Rydal
Armitt Museum
Rydal Water
Bridge House
Ambleside
Kentmere
Green Quarter
Long Sleddale
Tebay
Troutbeck
Skelwith Bridge
Ambleside Roman Fort
Stagshaw Garden
Townend
Low Wray
Lake District
Troutbeck Bridge
River Kent
Low Borrowbridge
Langdale
The Tarns
Outgate
High Wray
Windermere
Courthouse
Hawkshead
Ings
Staveley
Watchgate
Windermere Steamboats & Museum
Bowness-on-Windermere
Garth Row
Hill Top
Grayrigg
Esthwaite Water
Far Sawrey
Burneside
Near Sawrey
Grizedale
Crook
Kendal
Blackwell
Winster
129
Underbarrow
130
Graythwaite Hall
Crosthwaite
New Hutton
217
Killington Lake (southbound only)
Oxenholme
Brigsteer
Killington
Stott Park Bobbin Mill
Rusland
Cross
Finsthwaite
Natland
Middleshaw
Old Hutton
Sizergh Castle
473 WINDER
0 1 2 3 4 miles
0 1 2 3 4 5 kilometres
M6
A6
A66
A686
A592
A591
A5091
A685
A684
A5284
A65
B5305
B6413
B6412
B5288
B5320
B6261
B6260
B6257
B6254
B5284
B5285

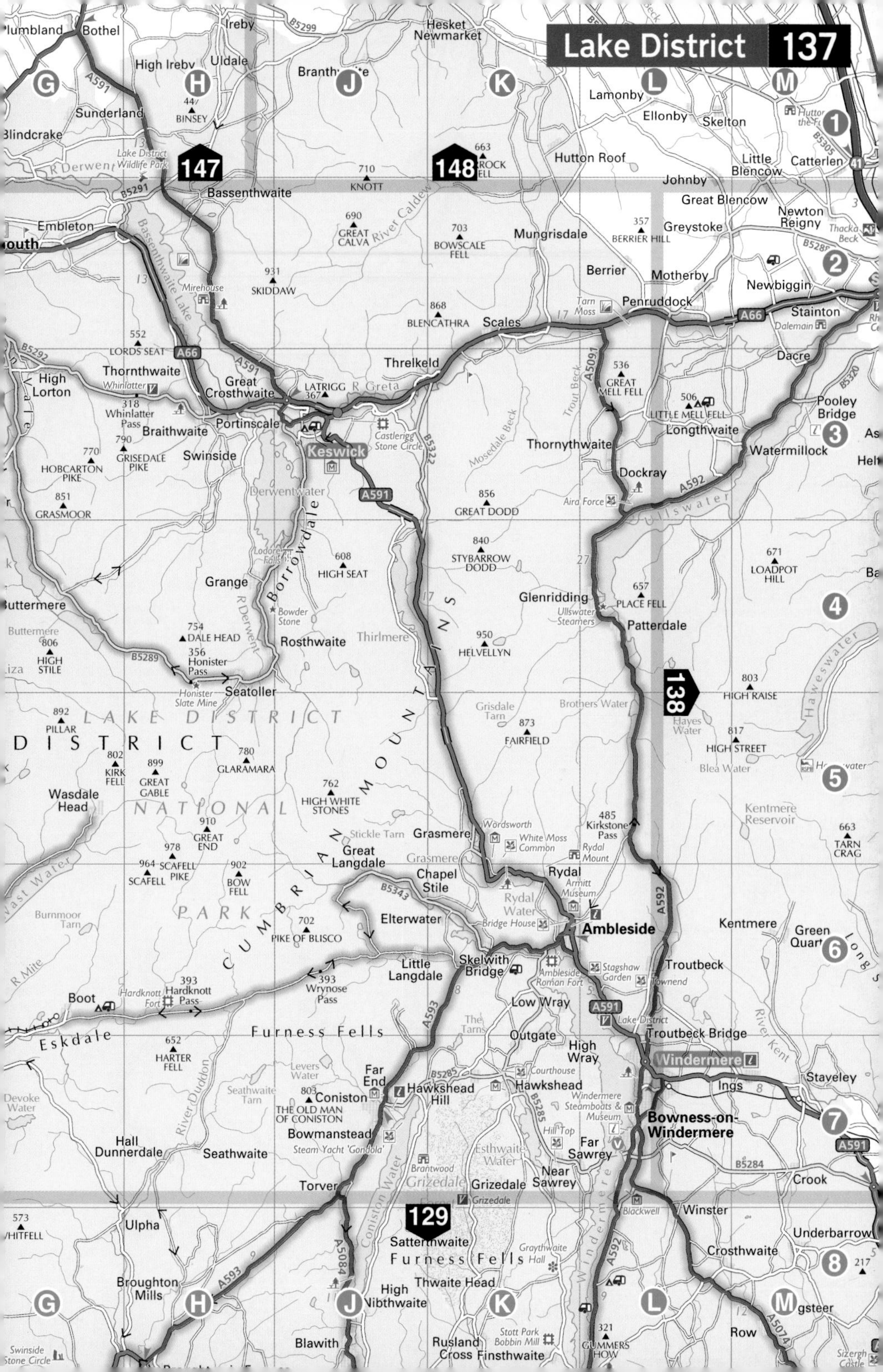
Plumbland
Bothel
Ireby
B5299
Hesket Newmarket
High Ireby
Uldale
Branthwaite
447 BINSEY
Sunderland
Blindcrake
Lamonby
Ellonby
Skelton
Hutton the Forest
Lake District Wildlife Park
R Derwent
147
148
663
710 KNOTT
Hutton Roof
Little Blencow
Catterlen
Johnby
B5291
Bassenthwaite
Great Blencow
Newton Reigny
Embleton
690 GREAT CALVA
River Caldew
703 BOWSCALE FELL
Mungrisdale
357 BERRIER HILL
Greystoke
Thacka Beck
Bassenthwaite Lake
B5288
Berrier
Motherby
Newbiggin
Mirehouse
931 SKIDDAW
Tarn Moss
Penruddock
868 BLENCATHRA
Scales
A66
Stainton
Dalemain
552 LORDS SEAT
B5292
Thornthwaite
Whinlatter
Great Crosthwaite
LATRIGG 367
R Greta
Threlkeld
A5091
536 GREAT MELL FELL
Dacre
B5320
High Lorton
318 Whinlatter Pass
Braithwaite
Portinscale
Castlerigg Stone Circle
Keswick
B5322
506 LITTLE MELL FELL
Longthwaite
Pooley Bridge
770 HOBCARTON PIKE
790 GRISEDALE PIKE
Swinside
Mosedale Beck
Trout Beck
Thornythwaite
Watermillock
851 GRASMOOR
Derwentwater
A591
856 GREAT DODD
Dockray
Aira Force
A592
Ullswater
Borrowdale
Lodore Falls
608 HIGH SEAT
840 STYBARROW DODD
671 LOADPOT HILL
Grange
R Derwent
Glenridding
657 PLACE FELL
Ullswater Steamers
Patterdale
Buttermere
Bowder Stone
754 DALE HEAD
Rosthwaite
Thirlmere
950 HELVELLYN
806 HIGH STILE
B5289
356 Honister Pass
Seatoller
Honister Slate Mine
138
803 HIGH RAISE
Haweswater
892 PILLAR
LAKE DISTRICT NATIONAL PARK
Grisdale Tarn
873 FAIRFIELD
Brothers Water
Hayes Water
817 HIGH STREET
802 KIRK FELL
899 GREAT GABLE
780 GLARAMARA
Blea Water
Wasdale Head
762 HIGH WHITE STONES
CUMBRIAN MOUNTAINS
485 Kirkstone Pass
Kentmere Reservoir
910 GREAT END
Stickle Tarn
Grasmere
Wordsworth
White Moss Common
663 TARN CRAG
978 SCAFELL PIKE
964 SCAFELL
902 BOW FELL
Great Langdale
Rydal Mount
Chapel Stile
Rydal
Armitt Museum
Wast Water
B5343
Rydal Water
A592
Burnmoor Tarn
702 PIKE OF BLISCO
Elterwater
Bridge House
Ambleside
Kentmere
Green Quarter
R Mite
393 Wrynose Pass
Little Langdale
Skelwith Bridge
Ambleside Roman Fort
Stagshaw Garden
Troutbeck
Townend
Boot
Hardknott Fort
393 Hardknott Pass
A593
Low Wray
A591
Lake District
Troutbeck Bridge
Eskdale
Furness Fells
The Tarns
Outgate
High Wray
River Kent
652 HARTER FELL
Levers Water
Far End
Windermere
Staveley
B5285
Courthouse
Ings
Devoke Water
Seathwaite Tarn
803 THE OLD MAN OF CONISTON
Coniston
Hawkshead Hill
Hawkshead
Windermere Steamboats & Museum
Bowness-on-Windermere
River Duddon
Bowmanstead
Hill Top
Far Sawrey
Steam Yacht 'Gondola'
Esthwaite Water
B5284
Hall Dunnerdale
Seathwaite
Brantwood
Grizedale
Near Sawrey
Crook
Coniston Water
Torver
Grizedale Forest
573 WHITFELL
129
Blackwell
Winster
Ulpha
A5084
Satterthwaite
Underbarrow
Furness Fells
Graythwaite Hall
A592
Crosthwaite
217
Broughton Mills
A593
Thwaite Head
High Nibthwaite
Brigsteer
Row
A5074
321 GUMMERS HOW
Swinside Stone Circle
Blawith
Rusland Cross
Stott Park Bobbin Mill
Finsthwaite
Sizergh Castle
G
H
J
K
L
M
1
2
3
4
5
6
7
8

148
137
129
130
A
B
C
D
E
F
1
2
3
4
5
6
7
8
Hutton End
Lamonby
Ellonby
Skelton
Hutton-in-the-Forest
Hutton Roof
663 CARROCK FELL
Little Blencow
Catterlen
Johnby
Great Blencow
Newton Reigny
Greystoke
357 BERRIER HILL
703 BOWSCALE FELL
Mungrisdale
Berrier
Motherby
Newbiggin
Penruddock
Tarn Moss
Scales
Stainton
Dalemain
Dacre
Rheged Centre
536 GREAT MELL FELL
506 LITTLE MELL FELL
Longthwaite
Thornythwaite
Mosedale Beck
Trout Beck
Dockray
Aira Force
Watermillock
Pooley Bridge
Ullswater
856 GREAT DODD
840 STYBARROW DODD
Glenridding
Ullswater Steamers
657 PLACE FELL
Patterdale
950 HELVELLYN
Grisdale Tarn
873 FAIRFIELD
Brothers Water
Hayes Water
803 HIGH RAISE
817 HIGH STREET
Blea Water
671 LOADPOT HILL
Haweswater
LAKE DISTRICT NATIONAL PARK
485 Kirkstone Pass
Kentmere Reservoir
663 TARN CRAG
Wordsworth
White Moss Common
Rydal Mount
Rydal
Rydal Water
Armitt Museum
Bridge House
Ambleside
Ambleside Roman Fort
Stagshaw Garden
Townend
Troutbeck
Low Wray
The Tarns
Outgate
Lake District
Troutbeck Bridge
High Wray
Windermere
Courthouse
Hawkshead
Windermere Steamboats & Museum
Bowness-on-Windermere
Hill Top
Far Sawrey
Esthwaite Water
Near Sawrey
Grizedale
Blackwell
Winster
Crosthwaite
Graythwaite Hall
Stott Park Bobbin Mill
Rusland
Cross
Finsthwaite
Ings
Staveley
Kentmere
Green Quarter
Long Sleddale
River Kent
Garth Row
Burneside
Crook
Underbarrow
217
Brigsteer
Sizergh Castle
Oxenholme
Natland
Old Hutton
Kendal
New Hutton
Killington Lake (southbound only)
Killington
Middleshaw
Watchgate
Grayrigg
Low Borrowbridge
Tebay
Orton
Shap Summit
316
Crookdale Beck
Borrow Beck
Swindale
Askham
Helton
Bampton
Bampton Grange
Rosgill
Shap Abbey
Shap
Keld Chapel
Lowther
Hackthorpe
Lakeland Bird of Prey Centre
Clifton
Clifton Hall
Tirril
Yanwath
Eamont Bridge
Henge
Countess Pillar
Brougham Castle
Wetheriggs Animal Rescue Centre
Oasis Whinfell 220 Park
Center Parcs
Cilburn Moss
Penrith
Castle
Thacka Beck
Plumpton
247 LAZONBY FELL
Lazonby
Salkeld Dykes
Glassonby
Great Salkeld
Little Salkeld
Long Meg & her Daughters
Gamblesby
710 MELMERBY FELL
Melmerby
Hunsonby
Ousby
Winskill
Langwathby
Skirwith
Edenhall
R Eamont
Blencarn
Culgaith
Acorn Bank Garden
Newbiggin
Temple Sowerby
Kirkby Thore
Long Marton
River Eden
Melkinthorpe
Cliburn
Great Strickland
Morland
Newby
Bolton
Kings Meaburn
Colby
Little Strickland
Sleagill
Reagill
Maulds Meaburn
Crosby Ravensworth
River Lyvennet
Great Asby Scar
412
R Lune
Langdale
Cautley
Winder 473
M6
A6
A66
A591
A592
A685
A684
A686
A5091
A65
B5305
B6413
B6412
B5288
B5320
B5284
B5285
B6260
B6261
B6254
B6257
0 1 2 3 4 miles
0 1 2 3 4 5 kilometres

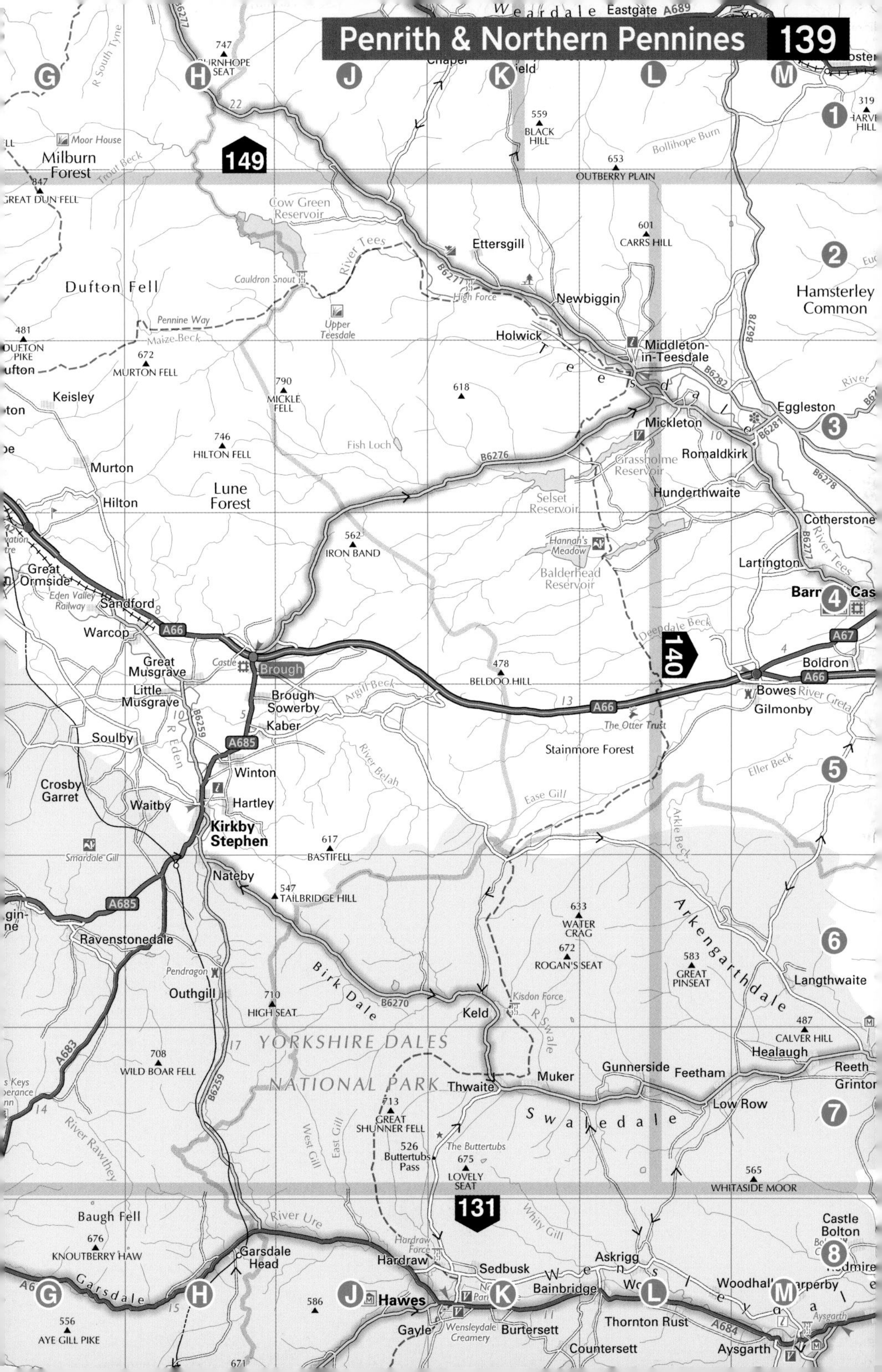
Weardale
Eastgate
A689
B6277
747
BURNHOPE SEAT
R South Tyne
G
H
J
K
L
M
1
2
3
4
5
6
7
8
22
Moor House
Milburn Forest
Trout Beck
149
559
BLACK HILL
Bollihope Burn
653
OUTBERRY PLAIN
319
847
GREAT DUN FELL
Cow Green Reservoir
601
CARRS HILL
Ettersgill
River Tees
Cauldron Snout
Dufton Fell
B6277
High Force
Newbiggin
Hamsterley Common
Pennine Way
Maize Beck
Upper Teesdale
Holwick
Middleton-in-Teesdale
B6278
481
DUFTON PIKE
672
MURTON FELL
B6282
790
MICKLE FELL
618
Teesdale
Keisley
Eggleston
Mickleton
B6281
10
746
HILTON FELL
Fish Loch
B6276
Grassholme Reservoir
Romaldkirk
Murton
B6278
Lune Forest
Hilton
Selset Reservoir
Hunderthwaite
Cotherstone
562
IRON BAND
Hannah's Meadow
Great Ormside
Balderhead Reservoir
Lartington
River Tees
Eden Valley Railway
Sandford
Warcop
A66
Deepdale Beck
140
A67
Boldron
Great Musgrave
Castle
Brough
478
BELDOO HILL
A66
Little Musgrave
Brough Sowerby
Argill Beck
13
Bowes
River Greta
Gilmonby
B6259
R Eden
Kaber
A66
The Otter Trust
Soulby
A685
River Belah
Stainmore Forest
Eller Beck
Winton
Crosby Garret
Waitby
Hartley
Ease Gill
Arkle Beck
Kirkby Stephen
Smardale Gill
617
BASTIFELL
Nateby
547
TAILBRIDGE HILL
A685
Arkengarthdale
633
WATER CRAG
Ravenstonedale
672
ROGAN'S SEAT
583
GREAT PINSEAT
Pendragon
Birk Dale
Langthwaite
Outhgill
710
HIGH SEAT
B6270
Kisdon Force
Keld
R Swale
487
CALVER HILL
A683
708
WILD BOAR FELL
17
YORKSHIRE DALES NATIONAL PARK
Healaugh
Reeth
Muker
Gunnerside
Feetham
Grinton
Thwaite
B6259
Low Row
14
713
GREAT SHUNNER FELL
Swaledale
River Rawthey
West Gill
East Gill
The Buttertubs
526
Buttertubs Pass
675
LOVELY SEAT
565
WHITASIDE MOOR
131
Baugh Fell
River Ure
Whitty Gill
Castle Bolton
676
KNOUTBERRY HAW
Hardraw Force
Garsdale Head
Hardraw
Askrigg
Sedbusk
Wensleydale
Redmire
Garsdale
Bainbridge
Woodhall
Carperby
586
Hawes
15
11
556
AYE GILL PIKE
Gayle
Wensleydale Creamery
Burtersett
Thornton Rust
A684
Aysgarth
Countersett
671

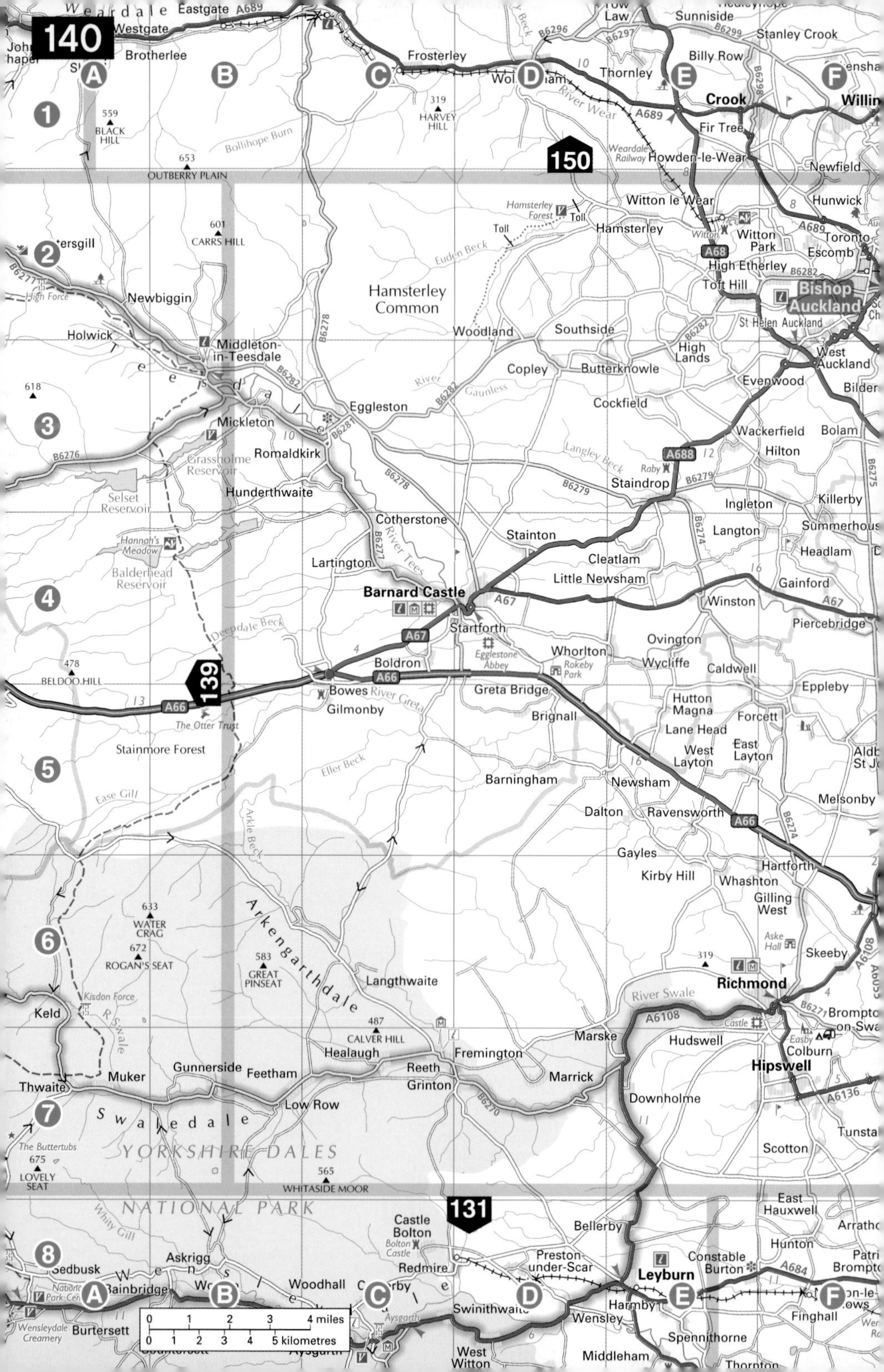

140
Weardale
Eastgate
Westgate
A689
Brotherlee
A
B
C
D
E
F
1
559
BLACK HILL
653
OUTBERRY PLAIN
Bollihope Burn
Frosterley
319
HARVEY HILL
Wolsingham
Thornley
B6296
B6297
Tow Law
Sunniside
B6299
Stanley Crook
Billy Row
B6298
Crook
Fir Tree
Willington
River Wear
A689
150
Weardale Railway
Howden-le-Wear
Newfield
Witton le Wear
Hunwick
Hamsterley Forest
Toll
Hamsterley
Witton
Witton Park
Toronto
Escomb
A68
High Etherley
B6282
Toft Hill
Bishop Auckland
St Helen Auckland
West Auckland
601
CARRS HILL
2
B6277
High Force
Newbiggin
Holwick
Middleton-in-Teesdale
Teesdale
Euden Beck
Hamsterley Common
Woodland
Southside
B6282
High Lands
Copley
Butterknowle
Evenwood
River Gaunless
Cockfield
Bilderdale
B6278
Eggleston
B6281
618
3
Mickleton
Romaldkirk
B6276
Grassholme Reservoir
Selset Reservoir
Hunderthwaite
10
Wackerfield
Bolam
Hilton
Langley Beck
Raby
A688
12
Staindrop
B6279
B6278
Ingleton
Killerby
B6275
Cotherstone
Stainton
B6274
Langton
Summerhouse
Headlam
Hannah's Meadow
Balderhead Reservoir
4
B6277
River Tees
Lartington
Cleatlam
Little Newsham
16
Gainford
Barnard Castle
A67
Startforth
Winston
A67
Piercebridge
Deepdale Beck
A67
Boldron
Egglestone Abbey
Whorlton
Ovington
Wycliffe
Rokeby Park
Caldwell
Eppleby
478
BELDOO HILL
139
13
A66
The Otter Trust
Bowes
River Greta
A66
Gilmonby
Greta Bridge
Brignall
Hutton Magna
Forcett
Lane Head
Stainmore Forest
5
Eller Beck
West Layton
East Layton
Aldbrough St John
Barningham
16
Newsham
Dalton
Ravensworth
Melsonby
Ease Gill
Arkle Beck
A66
B6274
Gayles
Kirby Hill
Hartforth
Whashton
Gilling West
Arkengarthdale
633
WATER CRAG
6
672
ROGAN'S SEAT
583
GREAT PINSEAT
Aske Hall
Skeeby
319
Richmond
A6108
A6055
Langthwaite
River Swale
A6108
Kisdon Force
Keld
R Swale
487
CALVER HILL
Castle
B6271
Brompton-on-Swale
Marske
Hudswell
Easby
Colburn
Healaugh
Fremington
Hipswell
Muker
Gunnerside
Feetham
Reeth
Grinton
Marrick
A6136
Thwaite
7
Low Row
B6270
Downholme
11
Swaledale
Tunstall
YORKSHIRE DALES
The Buttertubs
675
LOVELY SEAT
565
WHITASIDE MOOR
Scotton
NATIONAL PARK
Whity Gill
131
Castle Bolton
Bellerby
East Hauxwell
Arrathorne
Hunton
8
Sedbusk
Askrigg
Bolton Castle
Redmire
Preston-under-Scar
Constable Burton
Leyburn
A684
Patrick Brompton
Wensleydale
Nation Park Centre
Bainbridge
Woodhall
Carperby
Harmby
Newton-le-Willows
Swinithwaite
Wensley
Finghall
Wensleydale Creamery
Burtersett
Aysgarth
0 1 2 3 4 miles
0 1 2 3 4 5 kilometres
Spennithorne
West Witton
Middleham
Thornton

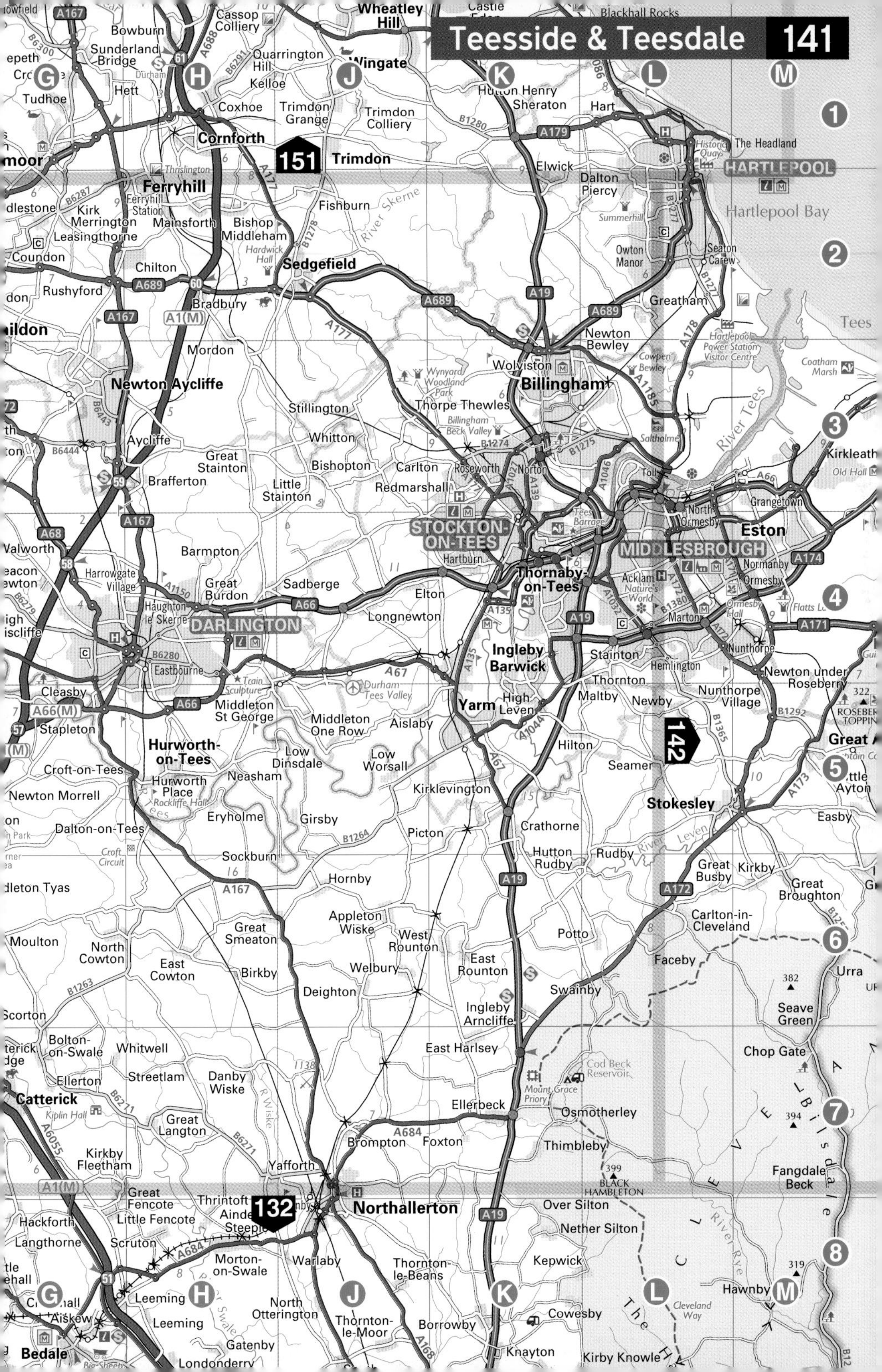
Wheatley Hill
Cassop Colliery
Castle Eden
Blackhall Rocks
Bowburn
Sunderland Bridge
Quarrington Hill
Wingate
Kelloe
Hett
Tudhoe
Coxhoe
Trimdon Grange
Trimdon Colliery
Hutton Henry
Sheraton
Hart
Cornforth
Trimdon
Elwick
The Headland
Historic Quay
HARTLEPOOL
Ferryhill
Ferryhill Station
Dalton Piercy
Hartlepool Bay
Fishburn
River Skerne
Kirk Merrington
Mainsforth
Bishop Middleham
Leasingthorne
Summerhill
Coundon
Hardwick Hall
Sedgefield
Owton Manor
Seaton Carew
Chilton
Rushyford
Bradbury
Greatham
Tees
Newton Bewley
Hartlepool Power Station Visitor Centre
Mordon
Wolviston
Cowpen Bewley
Coatham Marsh
Newton Aycliffe
Wynyard Woodland Park
Billingham
Thorpe Thewles
Stillington
Billingham Beck Valley
Saltholme
River Tees
Whitton
Aycliffe
Great Stainton
Bishopton
Carlton
Roseworth
Norton
Tolls
Kirkleatham
Old Hall
Brafferton
Little Stainton
Redmarshall
Grangetown
North Ormesby
Eston
STOCKTON-ON-TEES
Tees Barrage
MIDDLESBROUGH
Walworth
Barmpton
Hartburn
Normanby
Harrowgate Village
Great Burdon
Sadberge
Thornaby-on-Tees
Acklam
Nature's World
Ormesby
Haughton le Skerne
Elton
Ormesby Hall
Flatts Lane
DARLINGTON
Longnewton
Marton
Ingleby Barwick
Stainton
Nunthorpe
Eastbourne
Hemlington
Newton under Roseberry
Cleasby
Train Sculpture
Durham Tees Valley
Thornton
Maltby
Newby
Nunthorpe Village
Middleton St George
High Leven
Yarm
Roseberry Topping
Stapleton
Middleton One Row
Aislaby
Great Ayton
Hurworth-on-Tees
Low Dinsdale
Low Worsall
Hilton
Seamer
Croft-on-Tees
Neasham
Hurworth Place
Kirklevington
Little Ayton
Newton Morrell
Rockliffe Hall
Stokesley
Eryholme
Girsby
Crathorne
Easby
Dalton-on-Tees
Picton
Croft Circuit
Hutton Rudby
Rudby
River Leven
Sockburn
Great Busby
Kirkby
Great Broughton
Hornby
Appleton Wiske
Carlton-in-Cleveland
West Rounton
Potto
Moulton
North Cowton
Great Smeaton
East Cowton
East Rounton
Faceby
Urra
Welbury
Birkby
Deighton
Swainby
Ingleby Arncliffe
Seave Green
Scorton
Bolton-on-Swale
Whitwell
East Harlsey
Chop Gate
Cod Beck Reservoir
Streetlam
Danby Wiske
Ellerton
Mount Grace Priory
Catterick
Kiplin Hall
Ellerbeck
Osmotherley
Great Langton
Brompton
Foxton
Thimbleby
Kirkby Fleetham
Yafforth
BLACK HAMBLETON
Fangdale Beck
Great Fencote
Thrintoft
Northallerton
Over Silton
Little Fencote
Ainderby Steeple
Nether Silton
Hackforth
Langthorne
Scruton
Morton-on-Swale
Warlaby
Thornton-le-Beans
Kepwick
Leeming
North Otterington
Cowesby
Cleveland Way
Hawnby
Aiskew
Thornton-le-Moor
Borrowby
Gatenby
Bedale
Londonderry
Knayton
Kirby Knowle
CLEVELAND
Bilsdale
River Rye
River Wiske
River Swale
A167
A688
A177
A689
A179
A19
A1(M)
A1185
A178
A1027
A139
A1046
A66
A174
A1032
A135
A171
A172
A173
A67
A1044
A68
A1150
A66(M)
A6055
A684
A168
B6300
B6291
B6287
B1278
B1280
B1277
B1274
B1275
B6443
B6444
B6279
B6280
B1380
B1292
B1365
B1264
B1263
B6271
B1257
151
142
132
G
H
J
K
L
M
1
2
3
4
5
6
7
8
382
394
399
319
322

A
B
C
D
E
F
1
2
3
4
5
6
7
8
151
141
133
Blackhall Rocks
Hutton Henry
Sheraton
Hart
A179
A1086
The Headland
Historic Quay
HARTLEPOOL
Hartlepool Bay
Elwick
Dalton Piercy
Summerhill
B1277
Owton Manor
Seaton Carew
A19
A689
Greatham
A178
Tees Bay
Newton Bewley
Hartlepool Power Station Visitor Centre
Cowpen Bewley
Wolviston
Billingham
A1185
Coatham Marsh
Redcar
Marske-by-the-Sea
Saltburn-by-the-Sea
River Tees
Saltholme
Thorpe Thewles
B1274
B1275
Roseworth
Norton
A1027
A139
A1046
Tolls
Kirkleatham
Old Hall
A1042
B1269
A1085
A174
Saltburn Smugglers
STOCKTON-ON-TEES
Tees Barrage
North Ormesby
A66
Grangetown
Eston
New Marske
Upleatham
Brotton
Skelton
Loftus
Kilton
Wilton
Dunsdale
MIDDLESBROUGH
A174
A173
B1268
Hartburn
Thornaby-on-Tees
Acklam
Nature's World
Normanby
Ormesby
Ormesby Hall
Flatts Lane
A171
Boosbeck
Lingdale
Kilton Thorpe
Margrove Park
Woodhill
Liverton
Stanghow
A135
A1032
B1380
A172
Marton
A19
Ingleby Barwick
Stainton
Hemlington
Nunthorpe
Newton under Roseberry
Guisborough
Guisborough Forest
Hutton Lowcross
Cleveland Way
A171
Moorsholm
Scaling
Gerrick
B1366
Yarm
High Leven
Thornton
Maltby
Newby
Nunthorpe Village
322
ROSEBERRY TOPPING
A1044
B1292
B1365
Great Ayton
Captain Cook Monument
Commondale
Hilton
Seamer
A67
A173
Little Ayton
Kildale
The Moors National Park Centre
301
Danby
Castleton
Ainthorpe
River Esk
Kirklevington
Stokesley
Easby
Battersby
Crathorne
River Leven
Hutton Rudby
Rudby
Great Busby
Kirkby
Great Broughton
Ingleby Greenhow
Westerdale
A19
A172
Carlton-in-Cleveland
B1257
Potto
East Rounton
Faceby
382
454
Urra
URRA MOOR
NORTH YORK
CLEVELAND HILLS
Swainby
Seave Green
Ingleby Arncliffe
369
East Harlsey
Chop Gate
Cod Beck Reservoir
Mount Grace Priory
Church Houses
NATIONAL
Rosedale
Ellerbeck
Osmotherley
394
Bilsdale
20
NORTH YORK
Thorgill
Thimbleby
Low Mill
Rosedale Abbey
399
BLACK HAMBLETON
338
Bransdale
Fangdale Beck
River Seven
Farndale
A19
Over Silton
Nether Silton
River Rye
Kepwick
319
Lastingham
Hawnby
Gillamoor
Hutton-le-Hole
Spaunton
Fadmoor
Appleton-le-Moors
Cowesby
Knayton
Kirby Knowle
0 1 2 3 4 miles
0 1 2 3 4 5 kilometres

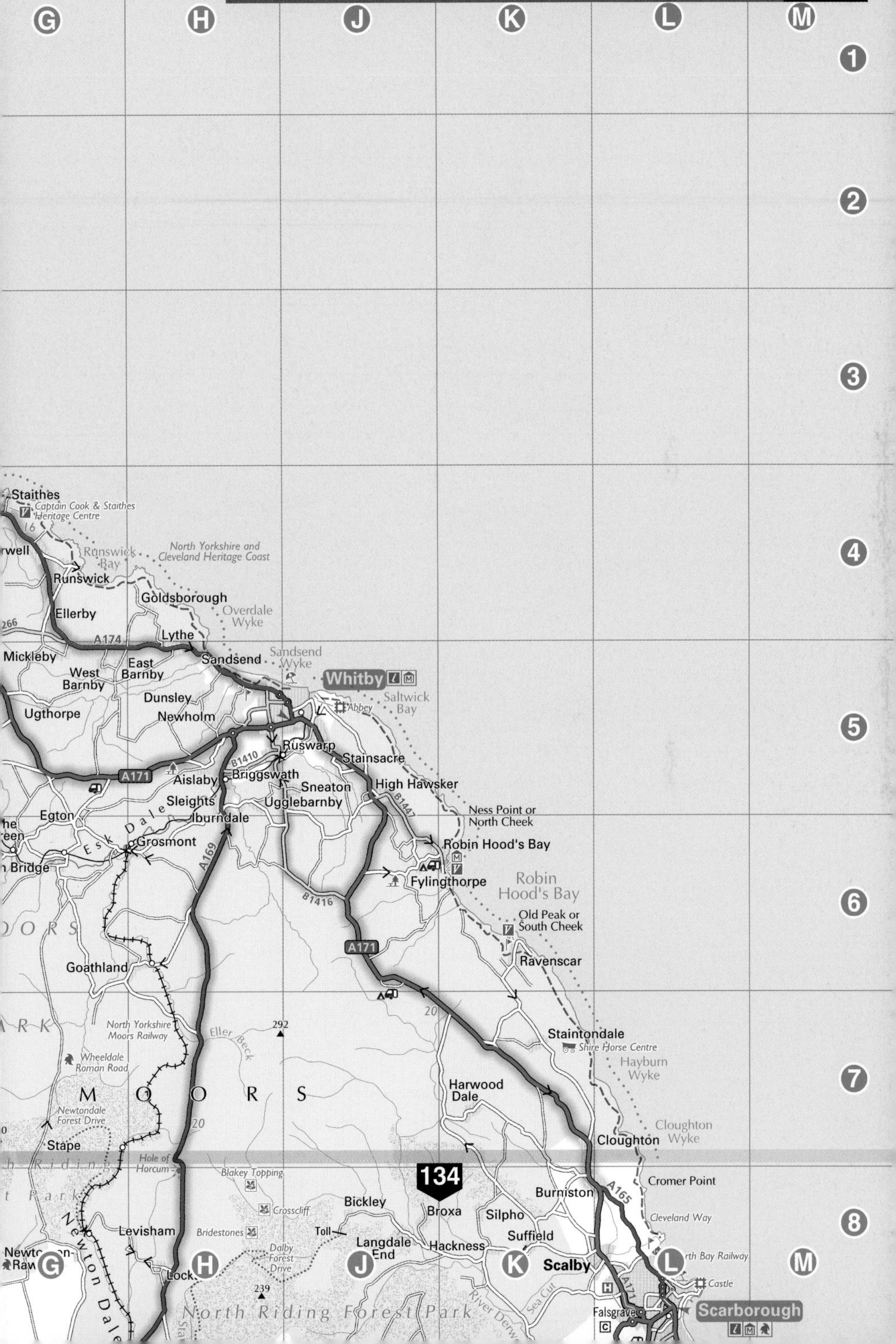
G
H
J
K
L
M
1
2
3
4
5
6
7
8
Staithes
Captain Cook & Staithes Heritage Centre
Runswick Bay
North Yorkshire and Cleveland Heritage Coast
Runswick
Goldsborough
Overdale Wyke
Ellerby
Lythe
A174
Mickleby
Sandsend
Sandsend Wyke
West Barnby
East Barnby
Whitby
Abbey
Saltwick Bay
Dunsley
Ugthorpe
Newholm
Ruswarp
B1410
Stainsacre
A171
Aislaby
Briggswath
Sneaton
High Hawsker
Sleights
Ugglebarnby
B1447
Egton
Iburndale
Esk Dale
Ness Point or North Cheek
Grosmont
Robin Hood's Bay
A169
Fylingthorpe
B1416
Robin Hood's Bay
Old Peak or South Cheek
A171
Ravenscar
Goathland
North Yorkshire Moors Railway
Eller Beck
292
20
Staintondale
Shire Horse Centre
Wheeldale Roman Road
Hayburn Wyke
M O O R S
Harwood Dale
Newtondale Forest Drive
20
Cloughton Wyke
Stape
Cloughton
Hole of Horcum
Blakey Topping
134
Cromer Point
Burniston
A165
Crosscliff
Bickley
Broxa
Silpho
Levisham
Bridestones
Toll
Cleveland Way
Suffield
Langdale End
Hackness
Dalby Forest Drive
Newton Dale
Scalby
North Bay Railway
Castle
239
A171
Falsgrave
Scarborough
North Riding Forest Park
River Derwent
Sea Cut

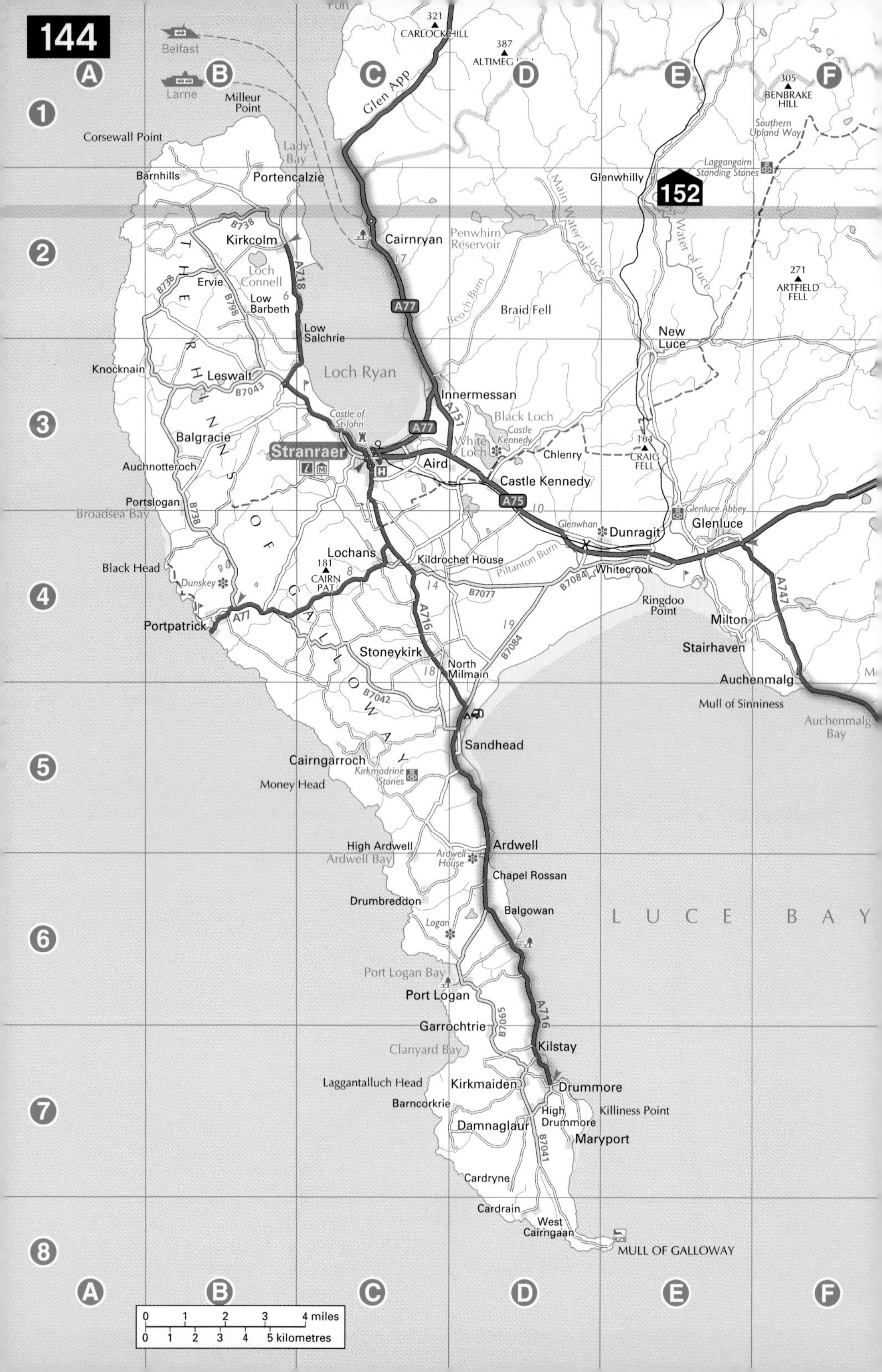
Belfast
Larne
Milleur Point
Corsewall Point
Lady Bay
Barnhills
Portencalzie
Kirkcolm
Loch Connell
Ervie
Low Barbeth
Low Salchrie
Knocknain
Leswalt
Loch Ryan
Balgracie
Castle of St John
Stranraer
Auchnotteroch
Portslogan
Broadsea Bay
Black Head
Dunskey
Portpatrick
THE RHINNS OF GALLOWAY
Lochans
181 CAIRN PAT
Stoneykirk
North Milmain
Sandhead
Cairngarroch
Kirkmadrine Stones
Money Head
High Ardwell
Ardwell Bay
Ardwell House
Ardwell
Chapel Rossan
Drumbreddon
Balgowan
Logan
Port Logan Bay
Port Logan
Garrochtrie
Clanyard Bay
Kilstay
Laggantalluch Head
Kirkmaiden
Drummore
Barncorkrie
High Drummore
Killiness Point
Damnaglaur
Maryport
Cardryne
Cardrain
West Cairngaan
MULL OF GALLOWAY
321 CARLOCK HILL
387 ALTIMEG HILL
Glen App
Cairnryan
Penwhirn Reservoir
Braid Fell
Beoch Burn
Innermessan
Black Loch
Castle Kennedy
White Loch
Aird
Chlenry
Castle Kennedy
Glenwhan
Dunragit
Kildrochet House
Piltanton Burn
Whitecrook
Ringdoo Point
Glenwhilly
Main Water of Luce
Water of Luce
New Luce
164 CRAIG FELL
Glenluce Abbey
Glenluce
Milton
Stairhaven
Auchenmalg
Mull of Sinniness
Auchenmalg Bay
LUCE BAY
305 BENBRAKE HILL
Southern Upland Way
Laggangairn Standing Stones
271 ARTFIELD FELL
152
A77
A718
A751
A75
A716
A747
B738
B798
B7043
B7077
B7084
B7042
B7065
B7041
A B C D E F
1 2 3 4 5 6 7 8
0 1 2 3 4 miles
0 1 2 3 4 5 kilometres

Creebank
Bargrennan
Glentrool
716
LAMACHAN HILL
675
654
Loch
Black Water of Dee
325
CAIRN EDWARD
Loch Ochiltree
Knowe
440
GARLICK HILL
Galloway Deer Range
Murray's Monument
402
ROUND FELL
471
FELL OF FLEET
Wood of Cree
153
River Bladnoch
184
GALLOWAY
Loch Grannoch
Loch Fleet
208
AUCHENCLOY HILL
Skerrow
Carseriggan
Penkill Burn
R Cree
Minnigaff
710
CAIRNSMORE OF FLEET
Challoch
Barfad
Newton Stewart
B7079
Creebridge
214
CULVENNAN FELL
Kirroughtree
Big Water of Fleet
Cairnsmore of Fleet
Little Water of Fleet
Shennanton
A714
Palnure
335
WHITE TOP OF CULREACH
B735
A75
Carstramon Wood
B733
Craighlaw
Kirkcowan
Baltersan
Upper Ruscoe
R Bladnoch
Causeway End
Gem Rock
B796
Fleet Valley
146
Creetown
Gatehouse of Fleet
Clugston
Torhouse Stone Circle
Kirkmabreck
455
CAIRNHARROW
Anwoth
Fell Loch
B7052
THE
B733
Wigtown
Cardoness Castle
Bladnoch
Carsluith
Cairnholy Chambered Cairns
B7005
Water of Malzie
MACHARS
Kirwaugh
Carsluith Castle
Girthon
Braehead
Ravenshall Point
Mossyard
Fleet Bay
Lennox Plunton
B7005
B7052
B7085
Kirkinner
Orchardton Bay
Culshabbin
Margrie
B7004
Barrachan
Whauphill
Islands of Fleet
Little Airies
Culscadden
A746
Kirkandrews
Elrig
Druchtag Motte
B7085
Sorbie
Wigtown Bay
B7052
Garlieston
Mochrum
Pouton
Borness
Drumtrodden Cup & Ring
Galloway House
Drumtrodden Standing Stones
Drummoddie
Broughton Mains
Cruggleton Bay
Ringdoo Point
Port William
Big Balcraig
B7004
B7063
B7021
'Wren's Egg' Standing Stones
Priory
Barsalloch Fort
Monreith
Whithorn Story
Barsalloch Point
Rispain Camp
Whithorn
Point of Leg
A747
A746
Portyerrock
St Ninian's Cave
B7004
Isle of Whithorn
Kidsdale
St Ninian's Chapel (ruin)
Cutcloy
BURROW HEAD
G
H
J
K
L
M
1
2
3
4
5
6
7
8

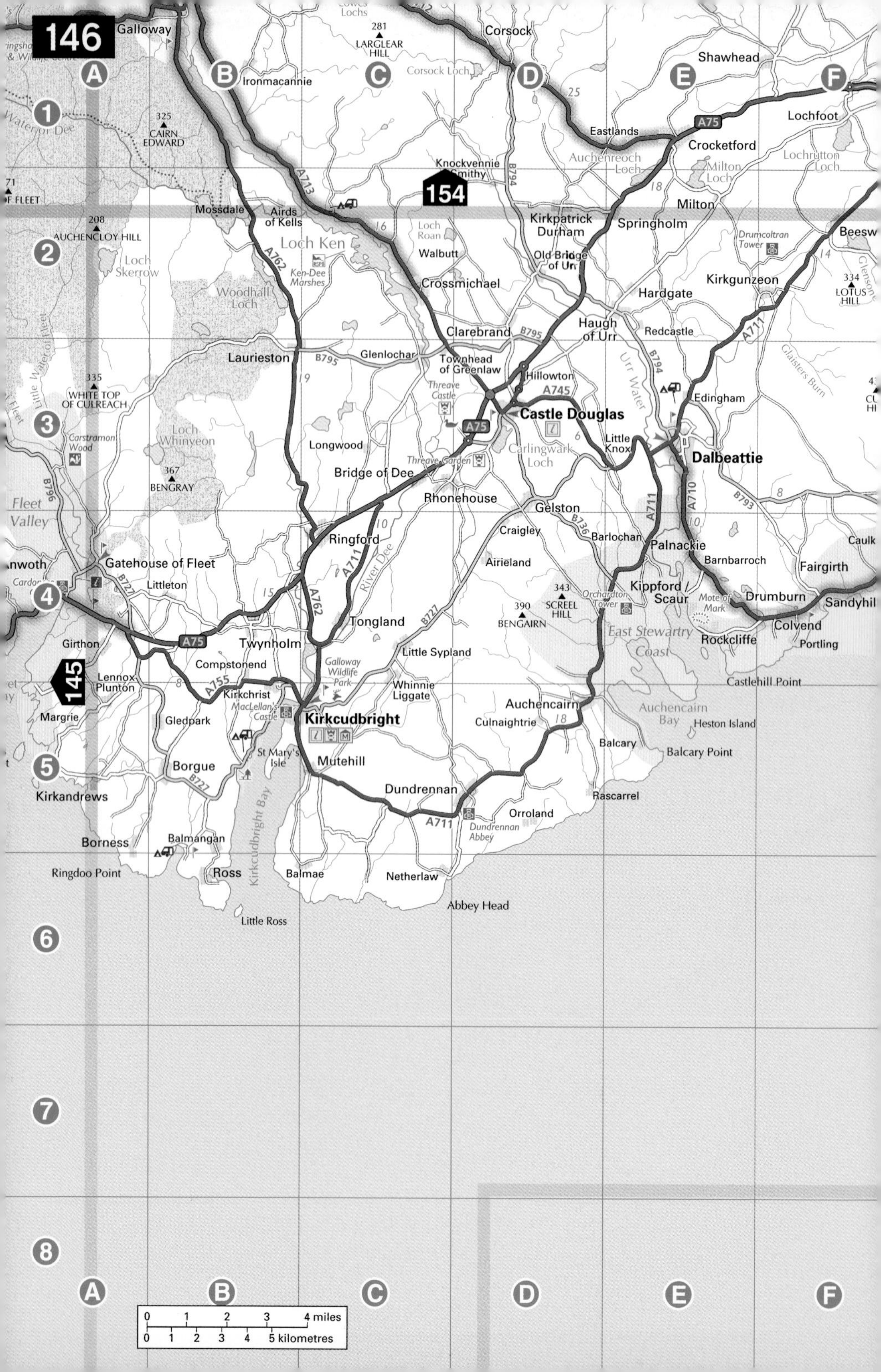
Galloway
Lowes Lochs
281 LARGLEAR HILL
Corsock
Corsock Loch
Ironmacannie
Shawhead
Lochfoot
325 CAIRN EDWARD
Water of Dee
Eastlands
Crocketford
A75
Knockvennie Smithy
154
Auchenreoch Loch
Milton Loch
Lochrutton Loch
B794
A713
OF FLEET
Mossdale
Airds of Kells
Milton
Springholm
Kirkpatrick Durham
208 AUCHENCLOY HILL
Loch Ken
Loch Roan
Walbutt
Drumcoltran Tower
Beeswing
Loch Skerrow
A762
Ken-Dee Marshes
Old Bridge of Urr
Crossmichael
Hardgate
Kirkgunzeon
334 LOTUS HILL
Woodhall Loch
Clarebrand
B795
Haugh of Urr
Redcastle
A711
Laurieston
Glenlochar
Townhead of Greenlaw
Hillowton
Urr Water
Glaisters Burn
335 WHITE TOP OF CULREACH
Little Water of Fleet
Threave Castle
A745
Edingham
Castle Douglas
Carstramon Wood
Loch Whinyeon
Longwood
Carlingwark Loch
Little Knox
Dalbeattie
367 BENGRAY
Threave Garden
Bridge of Dee
A710
B796
Fleet Valley
Rhonehouse
Gelston
B793
Craigley
B736
Barlochan
Palnackie
Caulk
Ringford
Barnbarroch
Airieland
Fairgirth
Anwoth
Gatehouse of Fleet
Cardoness
B727
Littleton
River Dee
343 SCREEL HILL
Orchardton Tower
Kippford / Scaur
Mote of Mark
Drumburn
Sandyhills
390 BENGAIRN
Tongland
Colvend
Girthon
A75
Twynholm
Little Sypland
East Stewartry Coast
Rockcliffe
Portling
145
Lennox Plunton
Compstonend
Galloway Wildlife Park
Castlehill Point
A755
Kirkchrist
Whinnie Liggate
Auchencairn
Auchencairn Bay
Heston Island
Margrie
Gledpark
MacLellan's Castle
Kirkcudbright
Culnaightrie
Balcary
Balcary Point
St Mary's Isle
Mutehill
Borgue
Kirkandrews
Dundrennan
Rascarrel
Kirkcudbright Bay
Orroland
A711
Dundrennan Abbey
Borness
Balmangan
Ringdoo Point
Ross
Balmae
Netherlaw
Abbey Head
Little Ross
A B C D E F
1 2 3 4 5 6 7 8
0 1 2 3 4 miles
0 1 2 3 4 5 kilometres

Lochside
Lincluden
Maxwell Town
A75
A709
Roucan
240
CARTHAT HILL
Kettleholm
Roman Camp
Waterbeck
G
H
J
K
L
M
Dumfries
A780
Collin
Greenlea
Racks
Dalton
River Annan
Ecclefechan
Hoddom Cross
A74(M)
B7076
Eaglesfield
1
Thomas Carlyle's Birthplace
Kirtlebridge
Merkland Cross
Bonshaw Tower
Robgill Tower
Islesteps
Kingholm Quay
Mouswald
B725
Carrutherstown
Hoddom Mains
Brydekirk
Lochar Water
B724
155
B7020
B723
B722
Kelton
Kirkconnell Flow
Conheath
Kelhead
Creca
Hollee
A710
Glencaple
Bankend
Clarencefield
Ruthwell Cross
24
Annan
2
Kirkconnell
Nith Estuary
Sweetheart Abbey
Corn Mill
New Abbey
Ruthwell
Savings Banks
Cummertrees
Howes
Powfoot
A75
Shearington
Caerlaverock Castle
Bowhouse
Ingleston
Blackshaw
Caerlaverock Wetlands Centre
Dornock
Eastriggs
Newbie
Loch Kindar
16
569
CRIFFELL
Torduff Point
Bowness-on-Solway
Port Carlisle
3
Glasson
Glasson Moss
Campfield Marsh
Hadrian's Wall Path
Carse Bay
Bowness Common
Drumburgh
Kirkbean
Carsethorn
Cardurnock
Drumburgh Moss
Borron Point
Grune Point
Anthorn
Arbigland
Skinburness
Moricambe Bay
Kirkbride
Mainsriddle
Loaningfoot
Gill Foot Bay
Southerness
Southerness Point
SOLWAY FIRTH
B5307
Newton Arlosh
4
Silloth
Seaville
South Solway Mosses
Biglands
B5302
Abbey Town
Holm Cultram
Kelsick
148
Oulton
Lessonhall
Beckfoot
Dundraw
R Waver
Waverbridge
5
Wigton
B5300
Newtown
Blencogo
Waverton
Holme St Cuthbert
B5301
Bromfield
Mawbray
Dubmill Point
Langrigg
A595
Bolton Low Houses
18
13
Westnewton
16
Allonby
Fletchertown
Allonby Bay
6
Hayton
Aspatria
B5299
Blennerhasset
A596
Prospect
Boltongate
Oughterside
Allerby
Torpenhow
Crosscanonby
Crosby
Plumbland
Bothel
Ireby
Fort
Gilcrux
A591
High Ireby
Uldale
River Ellen
Maryport
Dearham
447
BINSEY
7
A594
Tallentire
Sunderland
8
Blindcrake
Flimby
Broughton Moor
Bridekirk
Lake District Wildlife Park
R Derwent
Standingstone
Dovenby
A595
B5291
Bassenthwaite
136
Great Broughton
Papcastle
Jennings
137
Camerton
Embleton
Bassenthwaite Lake
Seaton
Great Clifton
A66
Brigham
Cockermouth
8
Greysouthen
931
SKIDDAW
Workington
Stainburn
Little Clifton
Eaglesfield
Mirehouse
A596
Mossbay
Westfield
Moss Bay
Salterbeck
A595
Deanscales
552
LORDS SEAT
A66
B5292

156
137
138
147
Longtown
Gretna
Gretna Green
Springfield
Kirkpatrick-Fleming
Canonbie
Rowanburn
Pentonbridge
Sleetbeck
Evertown
Milltown
Woodhouselees
Timpanheck
Solwaybank
Chapelknowe
Eaglesfield
Robgill Tower
Hollee
Creca
Rigg
Eastriggs
Redkirk Point
Torduff Point
Port Carlisle
Glasson
Drumburgh
Burgh by Sands
Beaumont
Rockcliffe
Westlinton
Smithfield
Scalebyhill
Scaleby
Kirklinton
Boltonfellend
Hethersgill
Walton
Newtown
Burtholme
Brampton
Irthington
Laversdale
Oldwall
Low Crosby
High Crosby
Newby East
Linstock
Warwick Bridge
Hayton
How Mill
Fenton
Heads Nook
Great Corby
Wetheral
Scotby
CARLISLE
Stanwix
Knowlefield
Harraby
Upperby
Morton
Belle Vue
Cummersdale
Blackwell
Newby West
Little Orton
Moorhouse
Kirkandrews upon Eden
Grinsdale
Cargo
Monkhill
Thurstonfield
Kirkbampton
Little Bampton
Great Orton
Aikton
Wiggonby
Biglands
Drumleaning
Thursby
Dalston
Buckabank
Cumwhinton
Cumwhitton
Cotehill
Wreay
Low Hesket
Southwaite
High Hesket
Aiketgate
Armathwaite
Ainstable
Castle Carrock
Wigton
West Curthwaite
Gaitsgill
Rosley
Westward
Welton
Ivegill
Sebergham
Boltongate
Caldbeck
Hesket Newmarket
Ireby
Uldale
Branthwaite
Bassenthwaite
Calthwaite
Staffield
Kirkoswald
Hutton End
Plumpton
Salkeld Dykes
Lamonby
Ellonby
Skelton
Hutton Roof
Little Blencow
Catterlen
Johnby
Great Blencow
Newton Reigny
Greystoke
Mungrisdale
Berrier
Penruddock
Motherby
Newbiggin
Stainton
Penrith
Eamont Bridge
Yanwath
Tirril
Langwathby
M6
A7
A75
A6071
A689
A69
A595
A596
A6
A66
A686
B6357
B7076
B721
B5307
B5302
B5305
B5299
B6263
B6413
B6412
B5288
FAULDS BROW 343
KNOTT 710
CARROCK FELL 663
GREAT CALVA 690
BOWSCALE FELL
BERRIER HILL 357
LAZONBY FELL 247
River Esk
River Lyne
R Eden
River Caldew
Hadrian's Wall Path
Solway Moss
Glasson Moss
Drumburgh Moss
Finglandrigg Woods
Todhills Rest Area
Solway Aviation
Carlisle
Wetheral Priory Gatehouse
Hutton-in-the-Forest
Dalemain
Rheged Centre
Brougham Castle
Clifton Hall
Tarn Moss
0 1 2 3 4 miles
0 1 2 3 4 5 kilometres

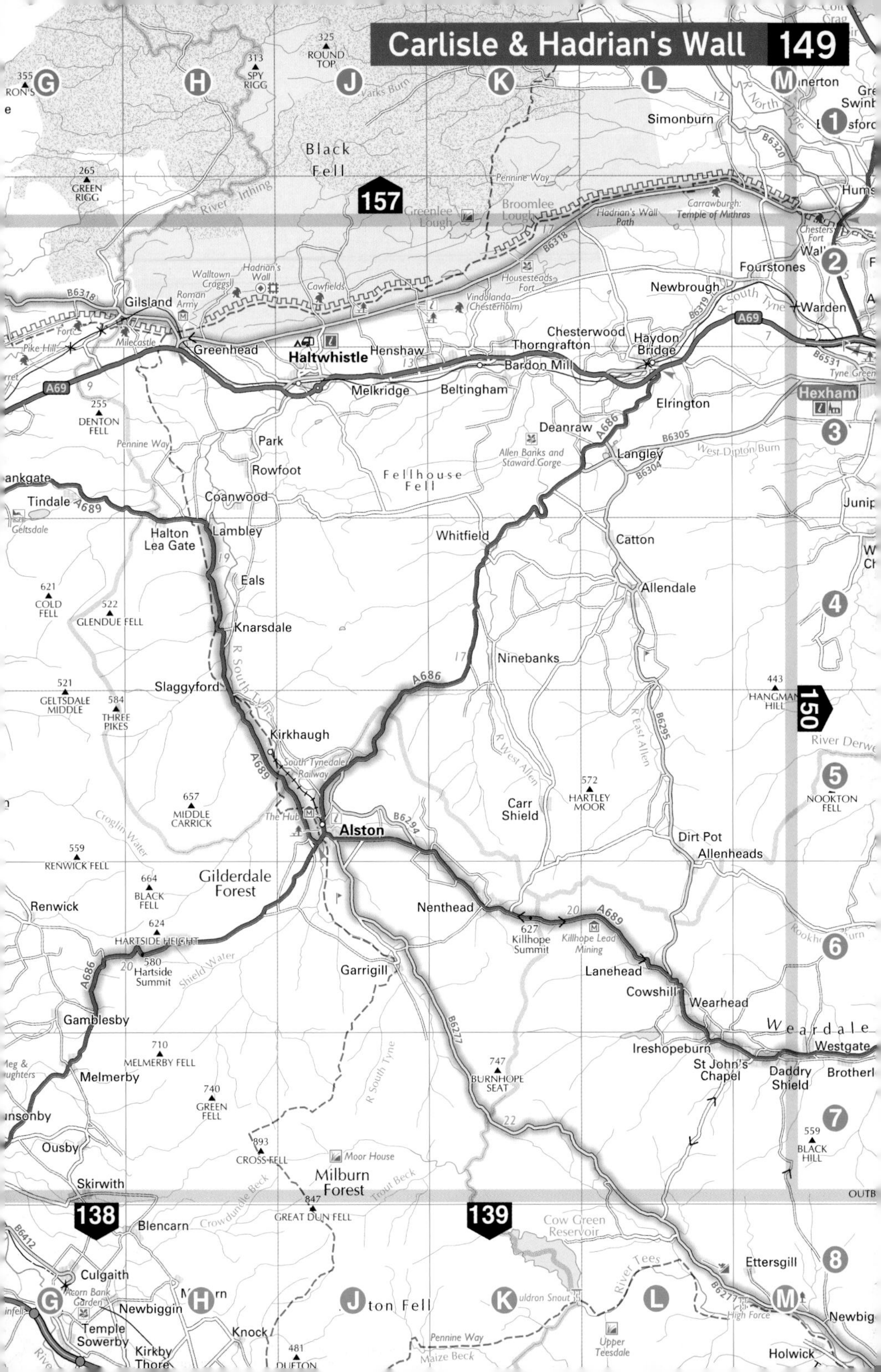
G
H
J
K
L
M
1
2
3
4
5
6
7
8
325 ROUND TOP
313 SPY RIGG
355
265 GREEN RIGG
Black Fell
River Irthing
157
Pennine Way
Greenlee Lough
Broomlee Lough
Hadrian's Wall Path
Carrawburgh: Temple of Mithras
Simonburn
R North Tyne
B6320
Chesters Fort
Fourstones
Newbrough
Warden
B6318
Walltown Crags
Hadrian's Wall
Roman Army
Cawfields
Housesteads Fort
Vindolanda (Chesterholm)
Gilsland
Fort
Pike Hill
Milecastle
Greenhead
Haltwhistle
Henshaw
Chesterwood
Thorngrafton
Haydon Bridge
R South Tyne
B6319
A69
Bardon Mill
Melkridge
Beltingham
Elrington
B6531
Tyne Green
Hexham
255 DENTON FELL
Pennine Way
Park
Rowfoot
Deanraw
A686
Allen Banks and Staward Gorge
Langley
B6305
B6304
West Dipton Burn
Fellhouse Fell
Coanwood
Tindale
A689
Geltsdale
Halton Lea Gate
Lambley
Whitfield
Catton
Eals
Allendale
621 COLD FELL
522 GLENDUE FELL
Knarsdale
Ninebanks
521 GELTSDALE MIDDLE
584 THREE PIKES
Slaggyford
443 HANGMAN HILL
150
River Derwent
B6295
R East Allen
R West Allen
Kirkhaugh
South Tynedale Railway
657 MIDDLE CARRICK
572 HARTLEY MOOR
NOOKTON FELL
Carr Shield
Croglin Water
The Hub
Alston
B6294
Dirt Pot
Allenheads
559 RENWICK FELL
664 BLACK FELL
Gilderdale Forest
Renwick
Nenthead
627 Killhope Summit
Killhope Lead Mining
624 HARTSIDE HEIGHT
580 Hartside Summit
Shield Water
Garrigill
Lanehead
Cowshill
Wearhead
Weardale
Westgate
Ireshopeburn
St John's Chapel
Daddry Shield
Gamblesby
710 MELMERBY FELL
Melmerby
B6277
747 BURNHOPE SEAT
740 GREEN FELL
R South Tyne
559 BLACK HILL
Ousby
893 CROSS FELL
Moor House
Milburn Forest
Trout Beck
Skirwith
847 GREAT DUN FELL
Crowdundle Beck
138
139
Blencarn
Cow Green Reservoir
B6412
Culgaith
Ettersgill
River Tees
Acorn Bank Garden
Newbiggin
Temple Sowerby
High Force
Knock
Pennine Way
481 DUFTON
Upper Teesdale
Maize Beck
Kirkby Thore
Holwick

Swinburne
Bavington
Belsay Hall, Castle & Gardens
A696
Hallington Reservoir
Kirkheaton
Hallington
River Blyth
Milbourne
Great Swinburne
Colwell
Ryal
Ingoe
Berwick Hill
Barrasford
B6342
B6309
Heugh
Ponteland
Dinnington
B6320
A6079
A68
Chollerton
Bingfield
Fenwick
Stamfordham
Dalton
Darras Hall
Newcastle
Humshaugh
Great Whittington
Matfen
158
River Pont
B6323
Great Kenton Bank
Hadrian's Wall
Chesters Fort
Harlow Hill
Black Callerton
B6918
Wall
Fallowfield
B6318
Hadrian's Wall Path
Rudchester
Halton
Halton Shields
B6318
B6324
Warden
Acomb
Sandhoe
Aydon Castle
B6321
Horsley
Heddon-on-the-Wall
B6528
Throckley
Westerhope
A69
South Tyne
Aydon
George Stephenson's Birthplace
Tyne Riverside
Newburn
NEW
B6531
Tyne Green
Corbridge
B6530
Newton
A69
Ovington
Ovingham
Wylam
Castle
Claravale
Ryton
A6085
Scotswood
Hexham
A695
Dilston
Cherryburn
Crawcrook
B6317
Eltringham
A695
Blaydon
Prudhoe
B6306
B6307
Riding Mill
Bywell
Mickley Square
Priestclose Wood
Winlaton
Greenside
Derwent Walk
Broomhaugh
Stockfield
High Mickley
Coalburns
B6315
Barlow
A694
Painshawfield
Hedley on the Hill
High Spen
Juniper
New Ridley
Highfield
Sunniside
Slaley
Chopwell
Rowlands Gill
Gibside
Whitley Chapel
A68
Blackhall Mill
Derwentcote Steel Furnace
Whittonstall
B6309
Hamsterley
Burnopfield
Newlands
B6310
Hobson
Causey Arch
Tanfield
357
DUKESFIELD FELL
B6306
Ebchester
Tantobie
A694
Medomsley
Tanfield Lea
A6076
Derwent Reservoir
Shotley Bridge
B6308
Dipton
Stanley
443
149
B6278
Benfieldside
B6309
B6168
A693
Bridgehill
Blackhill
Leadgate
South Moor
Blanchland
Pow Hill
Consett
Annfield Plain
River Derwent
B6278
Templetown
Iveston
Edmundbyers
A692
Delves
A6076
Holmside
Hunstanworth
Castleside
478
NOOKTON FELL
379
CROSS RIGG
Healeyfield
Rowley
Burnhope
Lanchester
18
A691
Pot
Allenheads
540
BOLT'S LAW
408
SKAYLOCK HILL
B6296
River Browney
Diggerland
Esh
Cornsay
Quebec
Satley
Cornsay Colliery
Esh Winning
Rookhope Burn
Rookhope
A68
B6278
516
COLLIER LAW
Hedleyhope Fell
B6301
Waskerley Beck
Stanhope
East Hedleyhope
Weardale
Eastgate
A689
Tow Law
Sunniside
B6299
Westgate
B6296
B6297
Stanley Crook
St John's Chapel
Daddry Shield
Brotherlee
Frosterley
Billy Row
Oakenshaw
B6298
Wolsingham
Thornley
River Wear
A689
Crook
Willington
559
BLACK HILL
319
HARVEY HILL
Fir Tree
Bollihope Burn
653
OUTBERRY PLAIN
Weardale Railway
Howden-le-Wear
Newfield
140
Hamsterley Forest
Witton le Wear
Hunwick
Toll
Hamsterley
Witton Park
A689
Toronto
601
CARRS HILL
Euden Beck
A68
High Etherley
Escomb
Ireshopeburn
B6277
High Force
Hamsterley Common
Toft Hill
B6282
Bishop Auckland
St Helen Auckland
0 1 2 3 4 miles
0 1 2 3 4 5 kilometres
Holwick
Middleton-
Woodland
Southside
High

Whitley Bay
Tynemouth
North Shields
Longbenton
Wallsend
Jarrow
Hebburn
Felling
GATESHEAD
SOUTH SHIELDS
Whitburn
SUNDERLAND
WASHINGTON
Birtley
Pelton
Chester-le-Street
Houghton-le-Spring
Hetton-le-Hole
Murton
Seaham
Easington Colliery
Easington
Peterlee
Durham
Shotton Colliery
Thornley
Wheatley Hill
Wingate
Cornforth
Ferryhill
Trimdon
Sedgefield
HARTLEPOOL
Amsterdam (IJmuiden)
Durham Heritage Coast
159
141
142

A
B
C
D
E
F
1
2
3
4
5
6
7
8
162
144
Culzean Bay
Culzean C
& Country Park
Maidenhead Bay
Maidens
A719
22
12
Kirkos
Souter Joh
Cottage
Turnberry
Turnberry
Turnberry Bay
Dipple
Wallac
Kilgrammie
A77
B741
Water of Gi
340
Ailsa Craig
Old Dailly
B7035
Penkill
B7035
B734
Girvan
Dounepark
Woodland
Pinminnoch
8
297
GREY HILL
Pinmore
13
Balligmorrie
Lendalfoot
A714
A77
Bennane Head
Pinwherry
Colmonell
9
B734
River Stinchar
Muck Water
B734
Duisk River
Heronsford
Ballantrae
Water of Tig
Barrhill
Belfast
Currarie Port
437
BENERAIRD
321
CARLOCK HILL
387
ALTIMEG HILL
Larne
Glen App
305
BENBRAKE HILL
Milleur Point
Southern Upland Way
Corsewall Point
Lady Bay
Laggangairn Standing Stones
Barnhills
Portencalzie
Glenwhilly
Main Water of Luce
Cross Water of Luce
B738
Kirkcolm
Cairnryan
17
271
ARTFIELD FELL
B738
Ervie
Loch Connell
6
A718
B798
Low Barbeth
A77
Beoch Burn
Braid Fell
Low Salchrie
New
Knockna
0 1 2 3 4 miles
0 1 2 3 4 5 kilometres
Innermessan
A751
Black Loch
Castle of St John

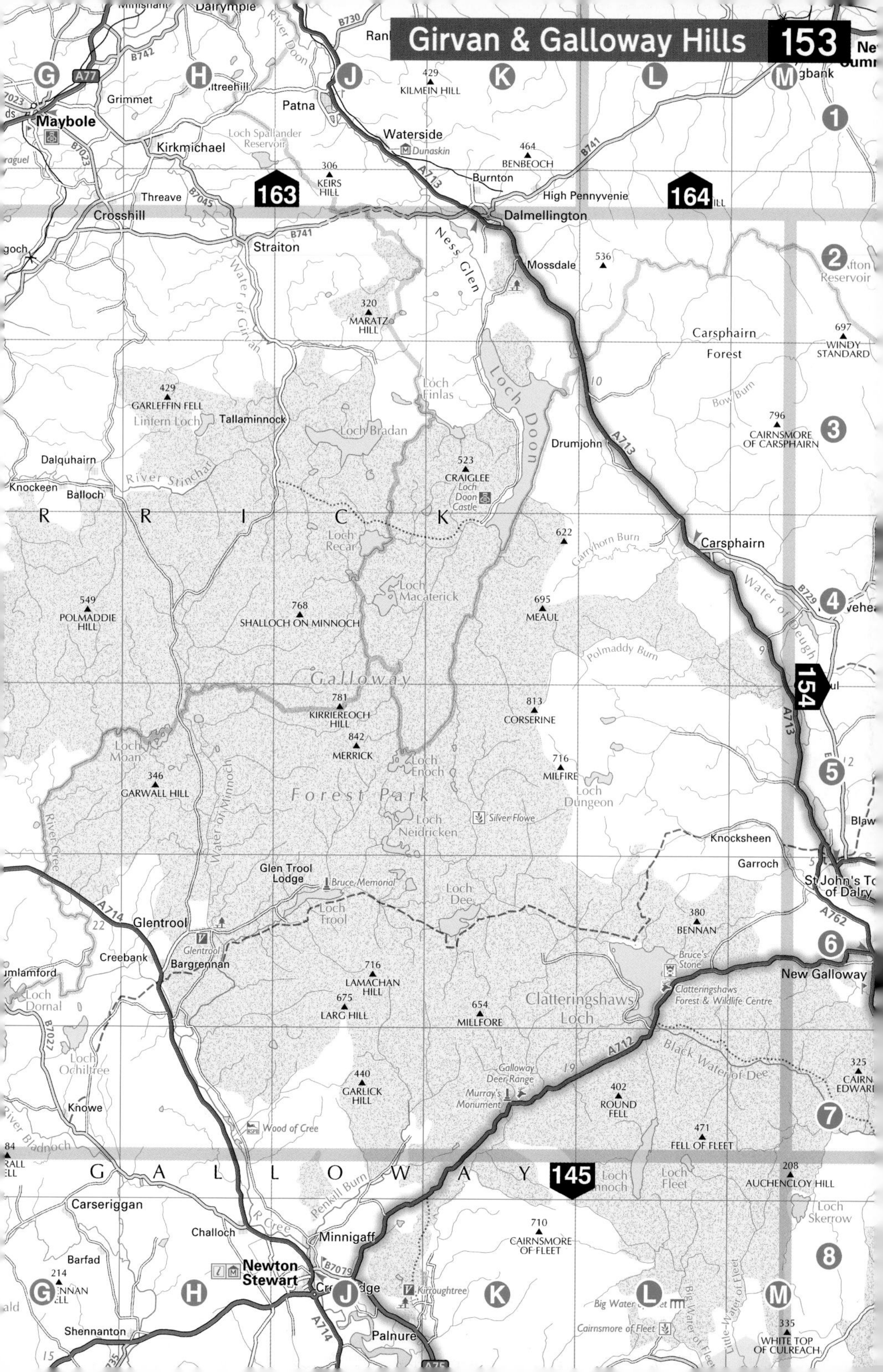

Dalrymple
Maybole
Grimmet
Kirkmichael
Crosshill
Threave
Straiton
Patna
Waterside
Dunaskin
Burnton
High Pennyvenie
Dalmellington
Mossdale
Ness Glen
Loch Spallander Reservoir
306 KEIRS HILL
429 KILMEIN HILL
464 BENBEOCH
163
164
536
320 MARATZ HILL
Water of Girvan
Carsphairn Forest
697 WINDY STANDARD
796 CAIRNSMORE OF CARSPHAIRN
Bow Burn
Loch Doon
Loch Finlas
Loch Bradan
429 GARLEFFIN FELL
Linfern Loch
Tallaminnock
Drumjohn
Dalquhairn
River Stinchar
Knockeen
Balloch
523 CRAIGLEE
Loch Doon Castle
R G I C K
Loch Recar
622
Carrick
Garryhorn Burn
Carsphairn
Water of Deugh
549 POLMADDIE HILL
768 SHALLOCH ON MINNOCH
Loch Macaterick
695 MEAUL
Polmaddy Burn
Galloway
Forest Park
781 KIRRIEREOCH HILL
842 MERRICK
813 CORSERINE
154
716 MILFIRE
Loch Moan
346 GARWALL HILL
Loch Enoch
Water of Minnoch
Loch Neidricken
Silver Flowe
Loch Dungeon
River Cree
Knocksheen
Garroch
St John's Town of Dalry
Glen Trool Lodge
Bruce Memorial
Loch Dee
Loch Trool
A714
Glentrool
Creebank
Bargrennan
380 BENNAN
Bruce's Stone
New Galloway
A762
716 LAMACHAN HILL
675 LARG HILL
654 MILLFORE
Clatteringshaws Loch
Clatteringshaws Forest & Wildlife Centre
Loch Dornal
Loch Ochiltree
B7027
A712
Black Water of Dee
325 CAIRN EDWARD
440 GARLICK HILL
Galloway Deer Range
Murray's Monument
402 ROUND FELL
471 FELL OF FLEET
Knowe
Wood of Cree
River Bladnoch
G A L L O W A Y
145
Loch Grannoch
Loch Fleet
208 AUCHENCLOY HILL
Loch Skerrow
Carseriggan
Challoch
Penkill Burn
R Cree
Minnigaff
710 CAIRNSMORE OF FLEET
Barfad
Newton Stewart
B7079
Kirroughtree
Big Water of Fleet
Little Water of Fleet
Cairnsmore of Fleet
Shennanton
A714
Palnure
335 WHITE TOP OF CULREACH
A77
A713
B741
B742
B7023
B7045
B730
B729
G H J K L M
1 2 3 4 5 6 7 8

154
164
153
146
A
B
C
D
E
F
1
2
3
4
5
6
7
8
New Cumnock
Kirkland
Kelloholm
Newtown
Sanquhar
Ulzieside
Mennock
Wanlockhead Beam Engine
Wanlockhead
Mining
732
LOWTHER HILL
Lowther Hills
594
HARE HILL
Blackcraig
Kello Water
700
BLACKCRAIG
Euchan Water
Enterkin Burn
River Nith
HILL
Afton Reservoir
450
CLOUD HILL
Polgown
478
Enterkinfoot
Durisdeermil
Gateslack
East Morton
475
COUNTAM
554
CAIRNKINNA HILL
Cleuch-head
A76
A702
Drumlanrig
Morton Castle
697
WINDY STANDARD
Forest
Bow Burn
796
CAIRNSMORE OF CARSPHAIRN
598
COLT HILL
Big Carlae
Old Auchenbrack
Auchenhessnane
Carronbridge
Tibbers
NITHSDALE
Benbuie
Shinnel Water
Scaur Water
Burnhead
Penpont
Thornhill
Southern Upland Way
532
CORNHARROW HILL
337
BENNAN
Water of Ken
Carsphairn
Stenhouse
Tynron
Keir Mill
Closeburn
Water of Deugh
B729
Knowehead
Moniaive
Kirkland
Kirkpatrick
Maxwelton
Keir Hills
Glenhoul
Black Water
Glencrosh
Craigneston
385
WETHER HILL
A713
A702
431
BOGRIE HILL
Skelston
Snade
Blackwood
Lag
B7000
Sundaywell
Dunscore
Throughgate
Loch Urr
Loch Howie
Blawquhairn
Knocksheen
Garroch
St John's Town of Dalry
Bogue
B7075
A762
Stepford
392
SKEOCH HILL
Drumpark
Balmaclellan
Lowes Lochs
A712
New Galloway
281
LARGLEAR HILL
Corsock
Shawhead
Ironmacannie
Corsock Loch
Water of Dee
325
CAIRN EDWARD
471
OF FLEET
Eastlands
A75
Lochfoot
Crocketford
Auchenreoch Loch
Lochrutton Loch
Milton Loch
Knockvennie Smithy
B794
Mossdale
Airds of Kells
Milton
Kirkpatrick Durham
Springholm
208
AUCHENCLOY HILL
Loch Roan
Loch Ken
Walbutt
Old Bridge of Urr
Drumcoltran Tower
Loch Skerrow
Ken-Dee Marshes
A762
Woodhall Loch
Crossmichael
Hardgate
Kirkgunzeon
334
LOTUS HILL
Clarebrand
B795
Haugh of Urr
Redcastle
A711
Laurieston
Townhead of Greenlaw
Hillowton
A745
Urr Water
Glaisters Burn
335
WHITE TOP OF CULREACH
Threave Castle
Edingham
Castle Douglas
Little Water of Fleet
0 1 2 3 4 miles
0 1 2 3 4 5 kilometres

Devil's Beef Tub
808
504
Nether Howcleugh
728
YOKE
560
WINTERCLEUCH FELL
550
BLACK KNOWE
474
GREYGILL FELL
B719
Blacklaw
Bridgend
Daer Reservoir
692
678
CAPEL FELL
165
A74(M)
166
Kirkhope
A701
Moffat
Moffat Water
554
WHITESIDE HILL
688
LOCH FELL
B7076
Southern Upland Way
15
Beattock
Kinnel Water
Kinnelhead
R. Annan
Davington
668
GANA HILL
476
CRAIG FELL
White Esk
Rae Burn
696
QUEENSBERRY
Johnstone
Samye Ling Monas
Fort
512
Eskdalemuir
399
Lochwood
Mitchellslacks
Newton Wamphray
Capel Water
Water of Ae
Sandyford
B723
St Ann's
B7020
Glenkill Burn
16
Johnstonebridge
Annandale Water
Castle O'er
353
Burnfoot
A701
Gillesbie
Dinwoodie
Boreland
Dryfe Water
Kirkland
A74(M)
Ae
Townhead
Greyrigg
331
HART FELL
Parkgate
156
Nethermill
Jardine Hall
Templand
Ae Bridgend
Corrie
Cumrue
Nethercleuch
Shieldhill
Millhousebridge
Auchencairn
Duncow
Marjoriebanks
Applegarth Town
River Nith
B723
Amisfield
Tinwald
Lochmaben
17
Lockerbie
319
GRANGE FELL
B7068
Kirkton
Bankshill
A709
Holywood Village
Locharbriggs
Lochmaben Castle
Tundergarth
Greenhill
18
Heath Hall
Lincluden Collegiate Church
Hightae
Roman Camp
Torthorwald
Waterbeck
Lochside
A75
A709
Roucan
240
CARTHAT HILL
B725
B7076
Lincluden
Kettleholm
Middlebie
Maxwell Town
A780
Collin
B722
Kirtle Water
Dumfries
Greenlea
River Annan
19
Ecclefechan
B7076
A74(M)
Eaglesfield
Dalton
Hoddom Cross
B725
20
Thomas Carlyle's Birthplace
Racks
Isleseps
Kingholm Quay
B725
Merkland Cross
A75
Mouswald
Carrutherstown
Hoddom Mains
Kirtlebridge
B724
Lochar Water
Bonshaw Tower
Robgill Tower
Kelton
Brydekirk
B7020
21
Kirkconnell Flow
B725
Conheath
147
Kelhead
Creca
Hollee
Glencaple
Bankend
Clarencefield
Ruthwell Cross
A710
B722
B6357
Kirkconnell
24
B723
Annan
Nith Estuary
Ruthwell
B724
Sweetheart Abbey
Shearington
Howes
A75
Corn Mill
Caerlaverock Castle
Savings Banks
Cummertrees
New Abbey
Ingleston
Bowhouse
Powfoot
Caerlaverock Wetland Centre
Blackshaw
Dornock
Eastriggs
Loch Kindar
Torduff Point
569
Bowness-on-Solway
G
H
J
K
L
M
1
2
3
4
5
6
7
8

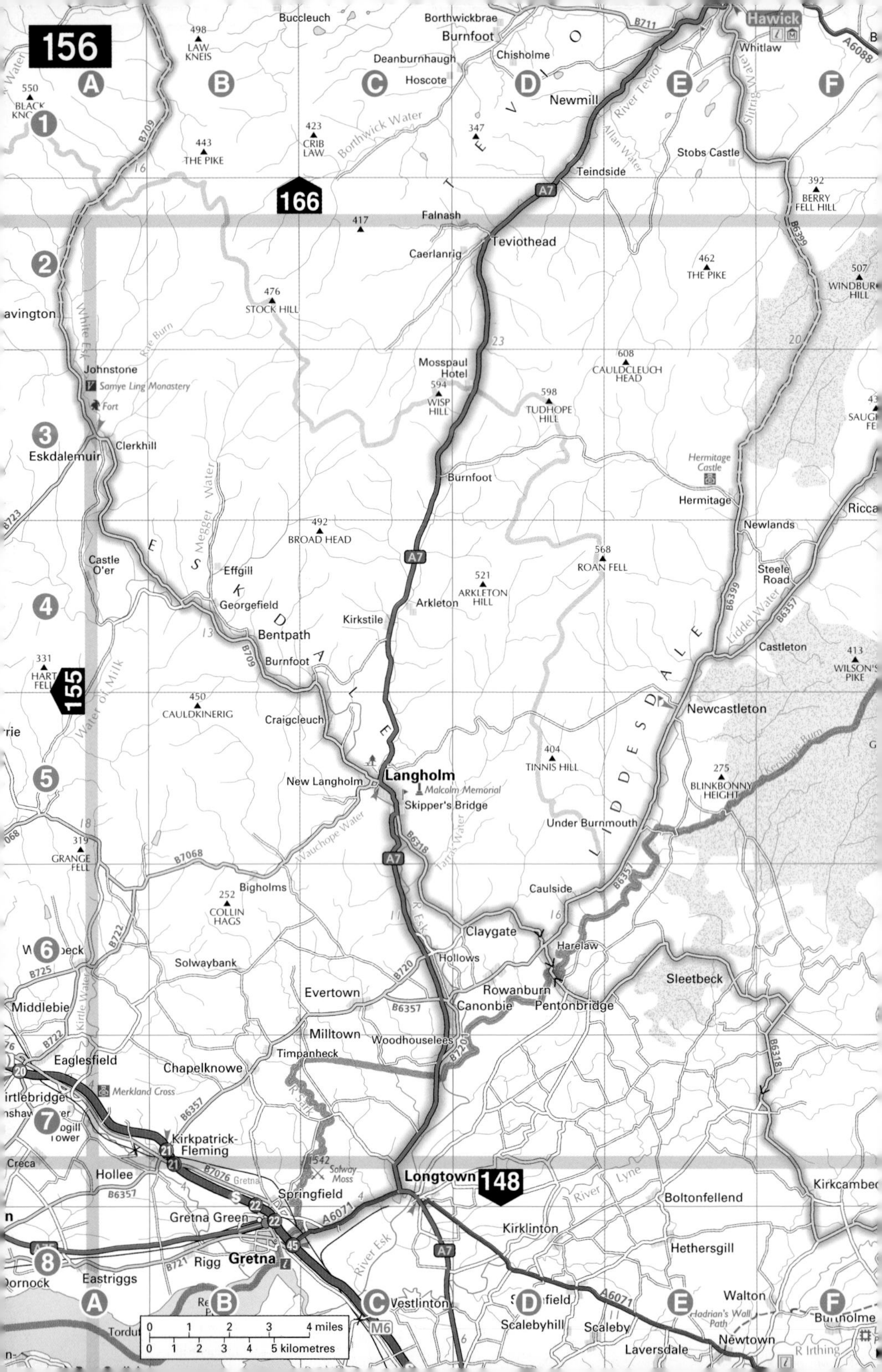

166
155
148
A
B
C
D
E
F
1
2
3
4
5
6
7
8
Buccleuch
Borthwickbrae
Burnfoot
Deanburnhaugh
Hoscote
Chisholme
Newmill
Hawick
Whitlaw
498 LAW KNEIS
550 BLACK KNO
443 THE PIKE
423 CRIB LAW
Borthwick Water
347
TEVIOT
River Teviot
Allan Water
Slitrig Water
Stobs Castle
Teindside
392 BERRY FELL HILL
417
Falnash
Teviothead
Caerlanrig
462 THE PIKE
507 WINDBURN HILL
476 STOCK HILL
avington
White Esk
Rae Burn
Johnstone
Samye Ling Monastery
Fort
Mosspaul Hotel
594 WISP HILL
608 CAULDCLEUCH HEAD
598 TUDHOPE HILL
Clerkhill
Eskdalemuir
Megget Water
Burnfoot
Hermitage Castle
Hermitage
Ricca
Newlands
492 BROAD HEAD
ESKDALE
Castle O'er
Effgill
Georgefield
568 ROAN FELL
521 ARKLETON HILL
Arkleton
Steele Road
Kirkstile
Bentpath
Burnfoot
Liddel Water
Castleton
413 WILSON'S PIKE
331 HART FELL
450 CAULDKINERIG
Craigcleuch
Newcastleton
Water of Milk
LIDDESDALE
404 TINNIS HILL
275 BLINKBONNY HEIGHT
Kershope Burn
New Langholm
Langholm
Malcolm Memorial
Skipper's Bridge
Under Burnmouth
Wauchope Water
Tarras Water
319 GRANGE FELL
Bigholms
252 COLLIN HAGS
Caulside
R Esk
Claygate
Harelaw
Solwaybank
Hollows
Sleetbeck
Evertown
Rowanburn
Canonbie
Pentonbridge
Middlebie
Kirtle Water
Milltown
Woodhouselees
Timpanheck
Eaglesfield
Chapelknowe
Merkland Cross
irtlebridge
R Sark
Kirkpatrick-Fleming
Creca
Hollee
Solway Moss
Longtown
Springfield
River Lyne
Boltonfellend
Kirkcambeck
Gretna Green
Kirklinton
Hethersgill
Rigg
Gretna
River Esk
Dornock
Eastriggs
Walton
Vestlinton
Scalebyhill
Scaleby
Hadrian's Wall Path
Burtholme
Newtown
R Irthing
Laversdale
Tordut
A7
A6088
A6071
A75
M6
B709
B711
B6399
B6357
B723
B7068
B6318
B722
B725
B720
B721
B7076
Kirkpatrick-Fleming
0 1 2 3 4 miles
0 1 2 3 4 5 kilometres

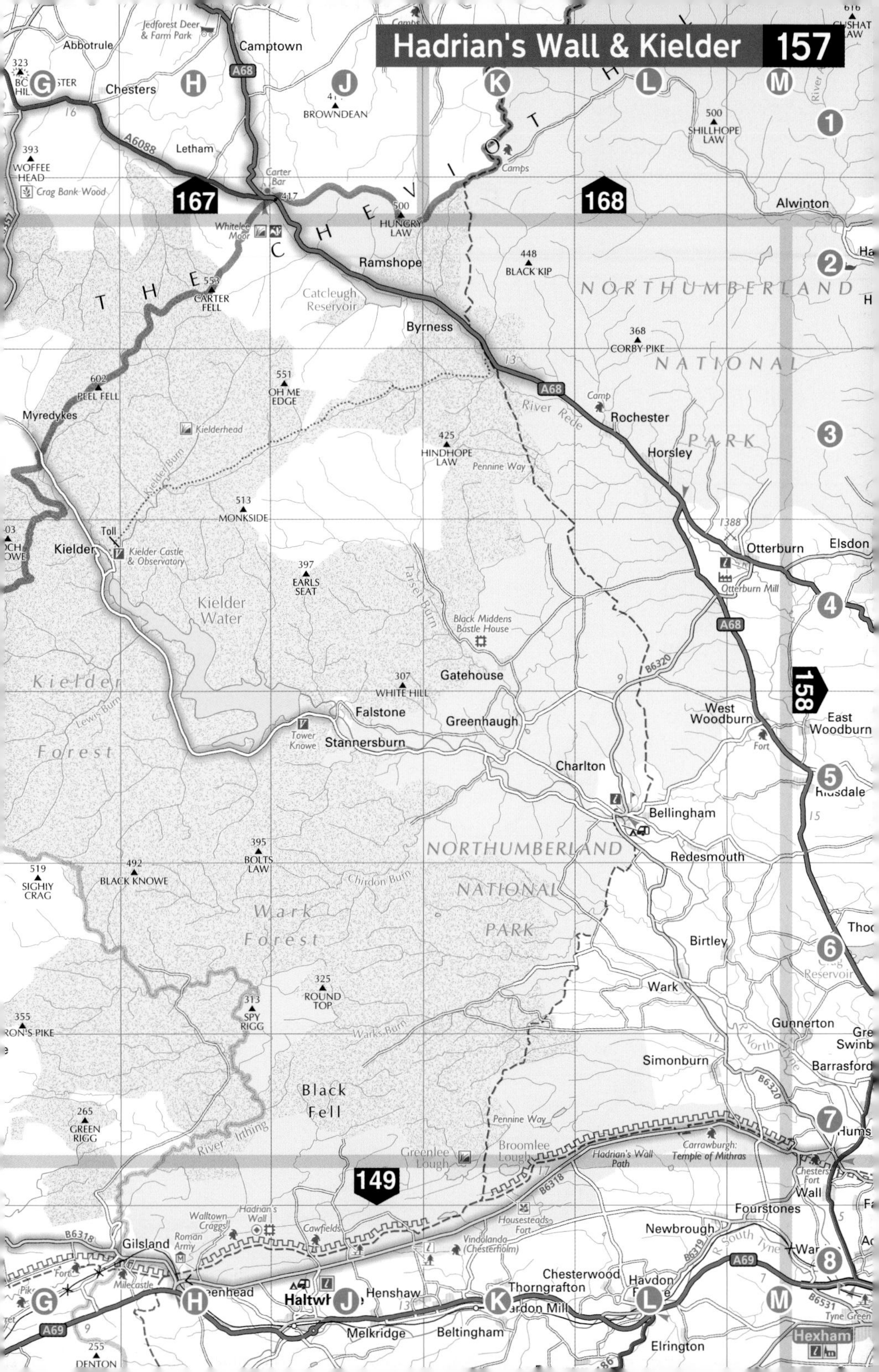
Abbotrule
Jedforest Deer & Farm Park
Camptown
Chesters
Letham
BROWNDEAN
393 WOFFEE HEAD
Crag Bank Wood
A6088
A68
Carter Bar
417
167
168
500 HUNGRY LAW
500 SHILLHOPE LAW
Camps
Alwinton
THE CHEVIOT
Whitelee Moor
Ramshope
553 CARTER FELL
Catcleugh Reservoir
448 BLACK KIP
NORTHUMBERLAND NATIONAL PARK
Byrness
368 CORBY PIKE
602 PEEL FELL
551 OH ME EDGE
Myredykes
Kielderhead
Kielder Burn
425 HINDHOPE LAW
Pennine Way
River Rede
Rochester
Horsley
Camp
513 MONKSIDE
Toll
Kielder
Kielder Castle & Observatory
397 EARLS SEAT
1388
Otterburn
Elsdon
Otterburn Mill
Kielder Water
Tarset Burn
Black Middens Bastle House
B6320
Kielder Forest
Lewis Burn
307 WHITE HILL
Gatehouse
158
Falstone
Greenhaugh
West Woodburn
East Woodburn
Tower Knowe
Stannersburn
Fort
Charlton
Risdale
Bellingham
Redesmouth
395 BOLTS LAW
519 SIGHTY CRAG
492 BLACK KNOWE
Chirdon Burn
Wark Forest
Birtley
325 ROUND TOP
Wark
313 SPY RIGG
355
Warks Burn
Gunnerton
R North Tyne
Simonburn
Barrasford
Black Fell
265 GREEN RIGG
River Irthing
Pennine Way
Greenlee Lough
Broomlee Lough
Hadrian's Wall Path
Carrawburgh: Temple of Mithras
Chesters Fort
Wall
149
B6318
Walltown Craggs
Hadrian's Wall
Cawfields
Housesteads Fort
Fourstones
Newbrough
Gilsland
Roman Army
Vindolanda (Chesterholm)
Fort
Milecastle
R South Tyne
B6319
A69
Chesterwood
Haydon
Thorngrafton
Henshaw
Melkridge
Beltingham
Elrington
B6531
Tyne Green
Hexham
255 DENTON
G H J K L M
1 2 3 4 5 6 7 8

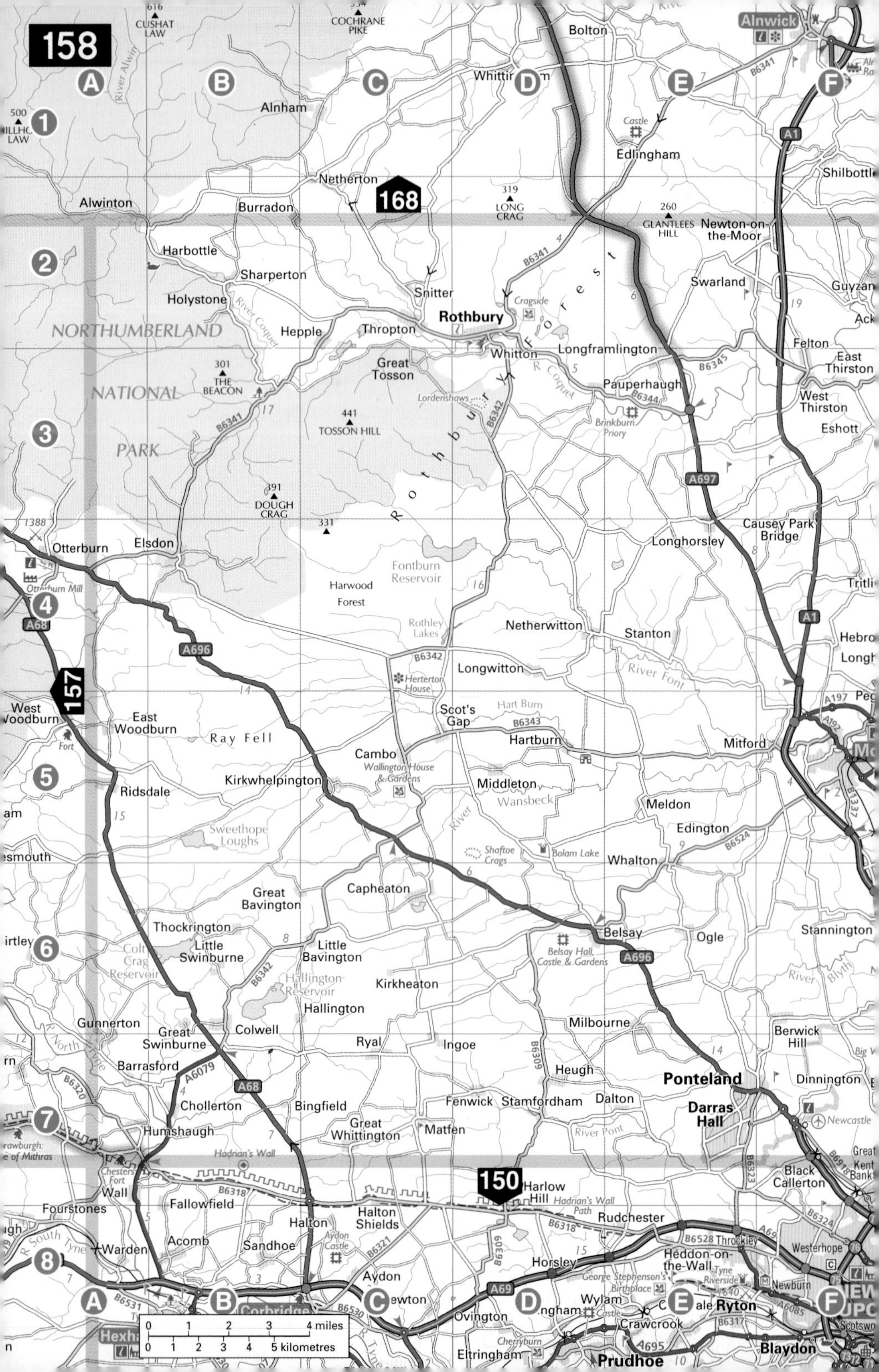

158
Alnwick
Bolton
Whittingham
Alnham
Castle
Edlingham
Netherton
168
Alwinton
Burradon
319 LONG CRAG
260 GLANTLEES HILL
Newton-on-the-Moor
Shilbottle
Harbottle
Sharperton
Holystone
Snitter
Swarland
Guyzance
Rothbury
Cragside
Thropton
Hepple
NORTHUMBERLAND
NATIONAL
PARK
Great Tosson
Whitton
Longframlington
Felton
East Thirston
West Thirston
Pauperhaugh
Brinkburn Priory
Lordenshaws
301 THE BEACON
441 TOSSON HILL
Eshott
Rothbury Forest
391 DOUGH CRAG
331
1388
Otterburn
Elsdon
Otterburn Mill
Causey Park Bridge
Longhorsley
Fontburn Reservoir
Harwood Forest
Rothley Lakes
Netherwitton
Stanton
157
Longwitton
Herterton House
River Font
West Woodburn
East Woodburn
Ray Fell
Scot's Gap
Hart Burn
Hartburn
Mitford
Cambo
Wallington House & Gardens
Kirkwhelpington
Middleton
Wansbeck
Ridsdale
Meldon
Edington
Sweethope Loughs
Shaftoe Crags
Bolam Lake
Whalton
Capheaton
Great Bavington
Thockrington
Little Swinburne
Little Bavington
Belsay
Ogle
Stannington
Belsay Hall, Castle & Gardens
Colt Crag Reservoir
Hallington Reservoir
Kirkheaton
Hallington
Gunnerton
Great Swinburne
Colwell
Ryal
Ingoe
Milbourne
Berwick Hill
Barrasford
Heugh
Ponteland
Dinnington
Chollerton
Bingfield
Fenwick
Stamfordham
Dalton
Darras Hall
Newcastle
Humshaugh
Great Whittington
Matfen
River Pont
Hadrian's Wall
Chesters Fort
Wall
150
Harlow Hill
Black Callerton
Fallowfield
Fourstones
Halton
Halton Shields
Rudchester
Acomb
Sandhoe
Aydon Castle
Warden
Horsley
Heddon-on-the-Wall
Throckley
Westerhope
Newburn
Aydon
George Stephenson's Birthplace
Tyne Riverside
Wylam
Ryton
Corbridge
Hexham
Ovington
Crawcrook
Blaydon
Scotswood
Cherryburn
Eltringham
Prudhoe
0 1 2 3 4 miles
0 1 2 3 4 5 kilometres
A1
A68
A69
A696
A697
A6079
B6341
B6342
B6343
B6344
B6345
B6318
B6320
B6321
B6309
B6323
B6324
B6524
B6528
B6530
B6531
B6317
A695

G
H
J
K
L
M
1
2
3
4
5
6
7
8
169
151
Lesbury
Seaton Point
Alnmouth
Alnmouth Bay
A1068
Warkworth
Amble
Coquet Island
High Hauxley
Togston
Broomhill
B1330
Druridge Bay
Druridge Bay
North Northumberland Heritage Coast
Widdrington
Widdrington Station
Cresswell
Ellington
Lynemouth
A189
Woodhorn
Beacon Point
QE2
Ashington
A197
Hirst
Newbiggin-by-the-Sea
B1334
Wansbeck Riverside
Bothal
A196
A1147
Bedlington
A193
Blyth
B1331
Cowpen
Newsham
B1505
A192
A1061
New Hartley
Seaton
Seaton Sluice
Seaton Hall
Cramlington
B1326
A190
Seaton Delaval
St Mary's
B1322
B1325
A1148
Dudley
Wide Open
Earsdon
Whitley Bay
Monkseaton
Cullercoats
A1056
Killingworth
Shiremoor
Murton
A191
Tynemouth
Forest Hall
New York
Tynemouth Priory & Castle
Amsterdam (IJmuiden)
Rising Sun
North Shields
Longbenton
South Gosforth
Willington
SOUTH SHIELDS
A1058
Jesmond
Wallsend
Int. Ferry Terminal
Tyne Tunnel
A187
A185
Heaton
Jarrow
Westoe
A183
Marsden Bay
Walker
Hebburn
Marsden
Souter Lighthouse & The Leas
Byker
B1313
River Tyne
A1300
Felling
Monkton
B1298
Souter Point
A184
Cleadon
Whitburn

346
BEINN SHOLUM
Eilean
a' Chuirn
171
Rudha Mòr
A
B
C
D
E
F
1
2
3
4
5
6
7
8
165
MAOL BUIDHE
Port
Ellen
A846
Ardbeg
Rudha na
Gainmhich
Lagavulin
Laphroaig
3
ISLAY
THE OA
Port Ellen-Kennacraig
Kilnaughton
Bay
Texa
Lower
Killeyan
Risabus
Kinnabus
Loch
Kinnabus
American
Monument
MULL
OF OA
Rudha nan Leacan
Earad
0 1 2 3 4 miles
0 1 2 3 4 5 kilometres

GIGHA
Ardminish
Achamore
Rhunahaorine Point
Rhunahaorine
CRUACH MHIC GOUGAIN
264 CNOC-AN SAMHLAI
172
Tayinloan
Sound of Gigha
Cara
Grogport
Barmollack
Pirnmill
Penrioch
North Arran
Loch Tanna
715 BEINN BHARRAIN
Whitefarland
Imachar
Balliekine
Glen Iorsa
Glen Catacol
354 CRUACH NAN GABHAR
A83
Muasdale
Glenacardoch Point
Belloch
Barr Water
Glenbarr
MacAlister Clan
Carradale Water
B842
B879
Carradale
Bridgend
Carradale House
Dippen
Waterfoot
Carradale Point
Carradale Bay
Iorsa Water
162
ARRAN
454 BEINN AN TUIRC
Torrisdale
319
Cleongart
408 BORD MOR
Saddell Water
Saddell
Saddell Bay
Auchagallon Stone Circle
Machrie
Machrie Bay
Machrie Moor Stone Circles
Tormore
Moss Farm Road Stone Circle
Balmichael
Bellochantuy Bay
Bellochantuy
Lussa Loch
396 SGREADAN HILL
Ugadale
Tangy Loch
Torbeg
Shiskine
Drumadoon Point
Blackwaterfoot
Drumadoon Bay
Kilpatrick
Kilpatrick Dun
Brown Head
Glen Lussa
Peninver
Ardnacross Bay
Kilkenzie
KINTYRE
KILBRANNAN SOUND
Kilmichael
Corriecravie
Torr a' Chaisteal Fort
Sliddery
Machrihanish Bay
Campbeltown
Machrihanish
Campbeltown Loch
Island Davaar
Campbeltown-Ardrossan (May-Sept)
Drumlemble
B843
Stewarton
Kilkerran
Kildalloig
352 BEINN GHUILEAN
Achinhoan
385 THE STATE
446 CNOC MOY
Dalsmeran
Conie Glen
Glen Kerran
Ru Stafnish
Glen Breakevie
Strone Glen
Cattadale
Polliwilline Bay
Macharioch
Southend
Carskey
Dunaverty
Carskey Bay
Sanda Sound
Sheep Island
Sanda Island
Borgadalemore Point
G H J K L M
1 2 3 4 5 6 7 8

Catacol
Isle of Arran
Glen Chalmadale
A841
Glen Catacol
North Arran
834
CAISTEAL ABHAIL
Loch Tanna
Penrioch
Pirnmill
715
BEINN BHARRAIN
Glen Iorsa
874
GOATFELL
792
BEINN NUIS
Glen Rosa
Sannox
Corrie
Merkland Point
Brodick Castle, Garden & Country Park
Brodick Bay
Iorsa Water
Balliekine
ARRAN
Auchagallon Stone Circle
Machrie
Machrie Bay
Brodick
Strathwhillan
Corriegills
512
A'CHRUACH
B880
Machrie Moor Stone Circles
Tormore
Moss Farm Road Stone Circle
Balmichael
503
BEINN BHREAC
Balmichael
Clauchlands Point
Margnaheglish
Lamlash
Lamlash Bay
Holy Island
Cordon
Torbeg
Shiskine
Drumadoon Point
Blackwaterfoot
Drumadoon Bay
Kilpatrick
Kilpatrick Dun
Glen Scorrodale
Auchencairn
Kingscross
Knockenkelly
Carn Ban
Whiting Bay
Brown Head
Glen Ashdale
Largymore
Corriecravie
Kilmory Water
Torr a' Chaisteal Fort
Sliddery
Largybeg
Dippen
Dippen Head
Kilmory
Lagg
Torrylin Cairn
Bennan
Kildonan
Bennan Head
Pladda
FIRTH OF CLYDE
Campbeltown · Brodick (May-Sept, Sat only)
Campbeltown · Ardrossan (May-Sept)
Portencross
Farland Head
B7048
Sea
Turnberry
Turnberry Bay
340
Ailsa Craig
0 1 2 3 4 miles
0 1 2 3 4 5 kilometres

173
161
152

Dalry
Burnhouse
Blackshaw
Munnoch
Dalgarven
Kilwinning
Stevenston
Saltcoats
Ardeer
Irvine
Fullarton
Irvine Bay
Gailes
Barassie
Troon
Royal Troon
Lady Isle
Monkton
Prestwick
New Prestwick
Ayr Bay
Wallacetown
Ayr
Doonfoot
Heads of Ayr
Alloway
Burns Cottage
Robert Burns Birthplace
Fisherton
Dunure
Culroy
Drumshang
Croy Brae (Electric Brae)
Knoweside
Culzean Bay
Culzean Castle & Country Park
Pennyglen
Whitefaulds
Maybole
Crossraguel Abbey
Kirkoswald
Souter Johnnie's Cottage
Crosshill
Roan of Craigoch
Wallacetown
Kilgrammie
Dailly
Water of Girvan
Penkill
Auchentiber
High Cross
Crossgates
Stewarton
Fergushill
Torranyard
Benslie
Eglinton
Cunninghamhead
Girdle Toll
Perceton
Kilmaurs
Springside
Knockentiber
Dreghorn
Crosshouse
Knockinlaw
Dean Castle
KILMARNOCK
Gatehead
Drybridge
Earlston
Riccarton
Shortlees
Dundonald
Castle
Symington
Bogend
Loans
Craigie
Helenton
Wallace Monument Tower
Tarbolton
Bachelors' Club
Mossblown
St Quivox
Whitletts
Annbank
Gadgirth
River Ayr
Belmont
Joppa
Coylton
Barbiestown
Martnaham Loch
Hollybush
Minishant
Dalrymple
River Doon
Rankinston
Grimmet
Guiltreehill
Patna
Kirkmichael
Threave
Straiton
Loch Spallander Reservoir
Waterside
Dunaskin
KILMEIN HILL
KEIRS HILL
BENBEOCH
Burnton
High Pennyvenie
Dalmellington
Ness Glen
Mossdale
MARATZO HILL
GARLEFFIN FELL
Tallaminnock
Loch Finlas
Fenwick
Waterside
Laigh Fenwick
Moscow
Polbaith Burn
Crookedholm
Hurlford
Galston
Newmilns
Greenholm
Middleyard
Carnell
Crosshands
Auchmillan
Mauchline
Failford
Haugh
Catrine
Ayr Gorge Woodlands
Stair
Trabboch
Trabbochburn
Lugar Water
Ochiltree
Auchinleck
Dumfries House
Palmerston
Drongan
Garrallan
Skares
Sinclairston
CARSGAILOCH HILL
Dalgig
ENOCH
BALLAGIOCH HILL
Laigh Clunch
Lochgoin Reservoir
CUNNINGHAM
174
153
164

175
163
153
154
Stonehouse
Strathaven
Kirkmuirhill
Lesmahagow
Galston
Auchinleck
Cumnock
New Cumnock
Glassford
Chapelton
Carnduff
Sandford
Caldermill
Drumclog
Darvel
Newmilns
Greenholm
Priestland
Dungavel
Muirkirk
Kames
Glenbuck
Carmacoup
Sorn
Catrine
Limmerhaugh
Cronberry
Lugar
Logan
Holmhead
Laigh Glenmuir
Dumfries House
Palmerston
Garrallan
Skares
Roadside
Sinclairston
Mansfield
Connel Park
Bankglen
Craigbank
Dalgig
Kirkconnel
Kelloholm
Newtown
Sanquhar
Ulzieside
Mennock
Blackcraig
Kirkland
Meikle Carco
Fingland
High Pennyvenie
Dalmellington
Mossdale
Polgown
Carsphairn Forest
Afton Reservoir
Whitelee Windfarm
Dunwan Dam
Lochgoin
Waterside
Middleyard
Auchmillan
Haugh
Boghead
New Trows
Auchlochan
Stockbriggs
Coalburn
Douglas W
Draffan
Blackwoo
Strutherhill
Ashgill
Spirit of Scotland
1679
1307
361 LAIRDS SEAT
335 MILL RIG
383 DISTINKHORN
408 MID HILL
466 MIDDLEFIELD LAW
461 AUCHINGILLOCH
522 NUTBERRY HILL
492 PRIESTHILL HEIGHT
593 CAIRN TABLE
440 DRYRIGS HILL
497 WARDLAW HILL
562
478 MOUNT STEWART
450 HALFMERK HILL
503 COCKER HILL
363 CARSGAILOCH HILL
594 HARE HILL
568 ENOCH HILL
700 BLACKCRAIG
450 CLOUD HILL
478
475 COUNTAM
554
598 COLT HILL
536
697
796
Avon Water
Glen Water
Polbaith Burn
Kype Water
Logan Water
River Nethan
River Ayr
Lugar Water
Gass Water
Glenmuir Water
Spango Water
River Nith
Kello Water
Euchan Water
Loch D
A71
A70
A76
A723
A77
A719
B743
B745
B7086
B7078
B7037
B744
B713
B705
B7036
B7083
B7046
B741
0 1 2 3 4 miles
0 1 2 3 4 5 kilometres

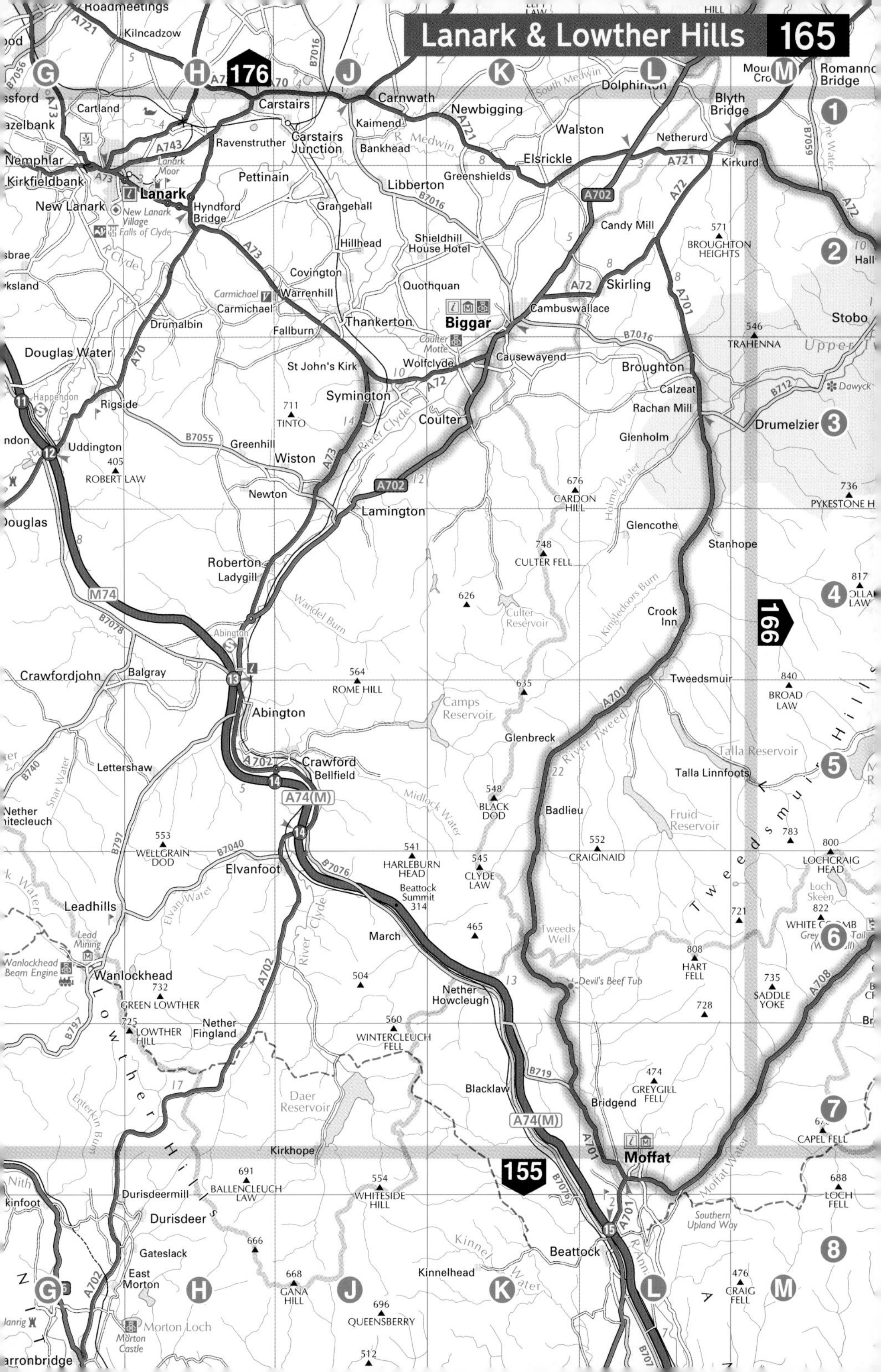
176
166
155
Roadmeetings
Kilncadzow
Carstairs
Carnwath
Cartland
Kaimend
Newbigging
Walston
Dolphinton
Blyth Bridge
Romanno Bridge
Netherurd
Kirkurd
Elsrickle
Ravenstruther
Carstairs Junction
Bankhead
Greenshields
Nemphlar
Kirkfieldbank
Lanark
Lanark Moor
Pettinain
Libberton
New Lanark
New Lanark Village
Falls of Clyde
Hyndford Bridge
Grangehall
Candy Mill
571 BROUGHTON HEIGHTS
Hillhead
Shieldhill House Hotel
Covington
Quothquan
Skirling
Carmichael
Warrenhill
Cambuswallace
Drumalbin
Thankerton
Biggar
Stobo
Fallburn
Coulter Motte
546 TRAHENNA
Douglas Water
St John's Kirk
Wolfclyde
Causewayend
Broughton
Happendon
Symington
Calzeat
Dawyck
Rigside
711 TINTO
Rachan Mill
Drumelzier
Coulter
Uddington
Greenhill
Glenholm
405 ROBERT LAW
Wiston
River Clyde
Newton
676 CARDON HILL
736 PYKESTONE H
Lamington
Douglas
Holms Water
Glencothe
Stanhope
748 CULTER FELL
Roberton
Ladygill
626
Culter Reservoir
Kingledoors Burn
817
Crook Inn
Wandel Burn
Abington
Crawfordjohn
Balgray
564 ROME HILL
635
Tweedsmuir
840 BROAD LAW
Camps Reservoir
Abington
Glenbreck
River Tweed
Talla Reservoir
Lettershaw
Crawford
Bellfield
Talla Linnfoots
548 BLACK DOD
Midlock Water
Badlieu
Fruid Reservoir
Snar Water
Nether Whitecleuch
783
553 WELLGRAIN DOD
541 HARLEBURN HEAD
552 CRAIGINAID
800 LOCHCRAIG HEAD
Elvanfoot
545 CLYDE LAW
Beattock Summit 314
Elvan Water
Leadhills
Loch Skeen
Lead Mining
465
Tweeds Well
721
822 WHITE COOMB
Grey Mare's Tail
March
808 HART FELL
Wanlockhead Beam Engine
Wanlockhead
504
Devil's Beef Tub
735 SADDLE YOKE
732 GREEN LOWTHER
Nether Howcleugh
River Clyde
725 LOWTHER HILL
Nether Fingland
560 WINTERCLEUCH FELL
728
Lowther Hills
Tweedsmuir Hills
474 GREYGILL FELL
Blacklaw
Bridgend
Daer Reservoir
Enterkin Burn
Moffat
CAPEL FELL
Kirkhope
691 BALLENCLEUCH LAW
554 WHITESIDE HILL
688 LOCH FELL
Nith
Kinfoot
Durisdeermill
Durisdeer
Moffat Water
Southern Upland Way
666
Gateslack
Beattock
Kinnelhead
Kinnel Water
R. Annan
East Morton
668 GANA HILL
476 CRAIG FELL
696 QUEENSBERRY
Morton Loch
Morton Castle
512
Carronbridge
A721
A73
A743
A70
A702
A72
A701
A708
M74
A74(M)
B7016
B7056
B7055
B7078
B7040
B7076
B797
B740
B719
B7059
B712
South Medwin
R. Medwin
R. Clyde

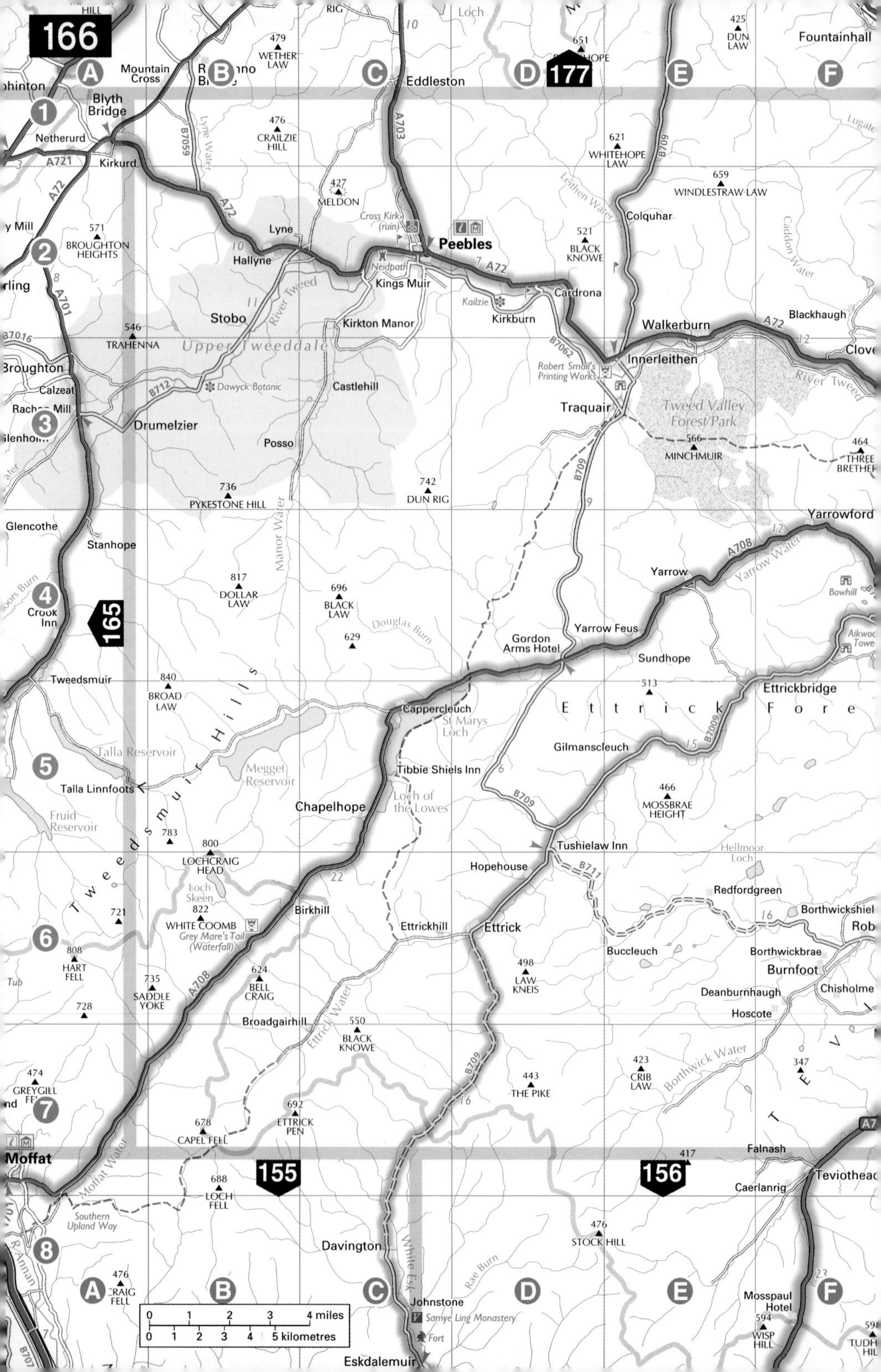
166
177
165
155
156
A B C D E F
1 2 3 4 5 6 7 8
Mountain Cross
Blyth Bridge
Netherurd
Kirkurd
Eddleston
Fountainhall
479 WETHER LAW
651
425 DUN LAW
476 CRAILZIE HILL
621 WHITEHOPE LAW
659 WINDLESTRAW LAW
427 MELDON
Cross Kirk (ruin)
Peebles
Lyne
Hallyne
Neidpath
Kings Muir
Kailzie
Kirkburn
Cardrona
Colquhar
521 BLACK KNOWE
571 BROUGHTON HEIGHTS
Stobo
River Tweed
Kirkton Manor
Walkerburn
Blackhaugh
Innerleithen
Robert Smail's Printing Works
546 TRAHENNA
Upper Tweeddale
Broughton
Calzeat
Dawyck Botanic
Castlehill
Drumelzier
Posso
Traquair
Tweed Valley Forest Park
566 MINCHMUIR
464 THREE BRETHER
Leithen Water
Caddon Water
Lyne Water
Manor Water
736 PYKESTONE HILL
742 DUN RIG
Glencothe
Stanhope
Yarrowford
Yarrow
Yarrow Water
Bowhill
817 DOLLAR LAW
696 BLACK LAW
629
Douglas Burn
Crook Inn
Gordon Arms Hotel
Yarrow Feus
Sundhope
Tweedsmuir
840 BROAD LAW
Cappercleuch
St Marys Loch
513
Ettrickbridge
Ettrick Forest
Talla Reservoir
Megget Reservoir
Tweedsmuir Hills
Gilmanscleuch
Talla Linnfoots
Tibbie Shiels Inn
Loch of the Lowes
Chapelhope
466 MOSSBRAE HEIGHT
Fruid Reservoir
783
800 LOCHCRAIG HEAD
Loch Skeen
822 WHITE COOMB
Grey Mare's Tail (Waterfall)
Tushielaw Inn
Hopehouse
Hellmoor Loch
Redfordgreen
Borthwickshiel
Birkhill
Ettrickhill
Ettrick
Buccleuch
Borthwickbrae
Burnfoot
Chisholme
721
808 HART FELL
735 SADDLE YOKE
624 BELL CRAIG
498 LAW KNEIS
Deanburnhaugh
Hoscote
728
Broadgairhill
550 BLACK KNOWE
Ettrick Water
Borthwick Water
474 GREYGILL FELL
443 THE PIKE
423 CRIB LAW
347
692 ETTRICK PEN
678 CAPEL FELL
Moffat
Moffat Water
417
Falnash
Teviothead
688 LOCH FELL
Southern Upland Way
Caerlanrig
476 STOCK HILL
Davington
White Esk
Rae Burn
R Annan
476 CRAIG FELL
Johnstone
Samye Ling Monastery
Fort
Mosspaul Hotel
594 WISP HILL
Eskdalemuir
A72
A721
A701
A703
A708
B7059
B709
B7062
B712
B7009
B711
B7016
0 1 2 3 4 miles
0 1 2 3 4 5 kilometres

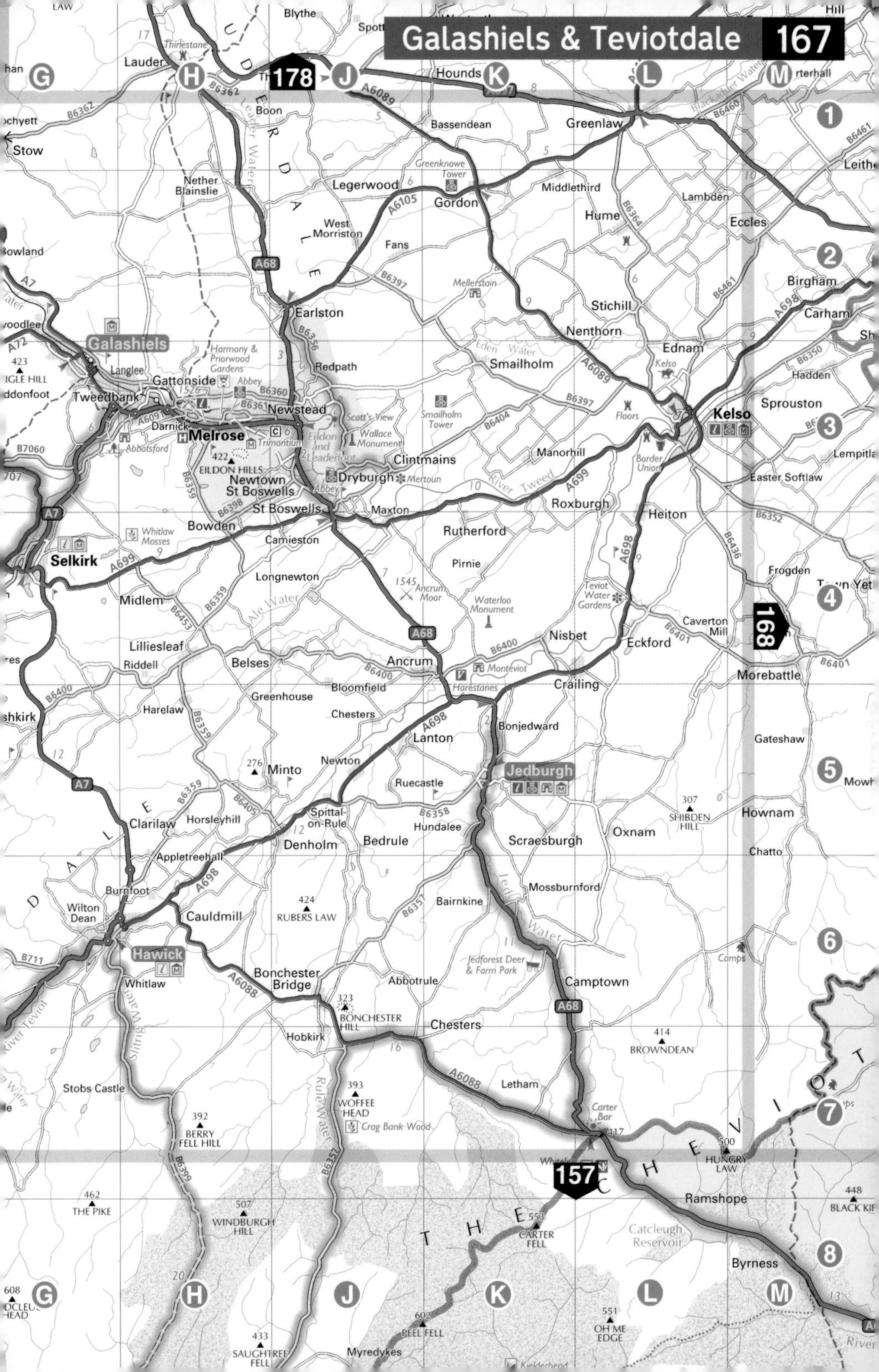

178
168
157
G
H
J
K
L
M
1
2
3
4
5
6
7
8
Blythe
Spott
Thirlestane
Lauder
Hounds
rterhall
Boon
Bassendean
Greenlaw
Blackadder Water
B6460
B6461
Leith
B6362
chyett
Stow
Nether Blainslie
Leader Water
Legerwood
Greenknowe Tower
Gordon
Middlethird
Lambden
Hume
Eccles
West Morriston
A6105
Fans
Bowland
A68
A7
B6397
Mellerstain
Stichill
Bingham
Carham
Earlston
Nenthorn
Ednam
A698
woodlee
Galashiels
Harmony & Priorwood Gardens
Redpath
Eden Water
Smailholm
A6089
Kelso
B6350
Hadden
423
Langlee
Gattonside
Abbey
B6360
B6397
Floors
Sprouston
ddonfoot
Tweedbank
B6361
Newstead
Scott's View
Smailholm Tower
B6404
Kelso
Darnick
Melrose
Trimontium
Wallace Monument
Eildon and Leaderfoot
Manorhill
Border Union
Lempitla
B7060
Abbotsford
422
EILDON HILLS
Clintmains
Newtown St Boswells
Dryburgh
Mertoun
Abbey
River Tweed
A699
Easter Softlaw
B6359
B6398
St Boswells
Maxton
Roxburgh
Heiton
B6352
Bowden
Whitlaw Mosses
Camieston
Rutherford
Selkirk
Pirnie
B6436
Frogden
Longnewton
1545 Ancrum Moor
Teviot Water Gardens
Town Yet
Midlem
Ale Water
Waterloo Monument
Caverton Mill
B6453
Nisbet
Eckford
B6401
Lilliesleaf
B6400
Riddell
Belses
Ancrum
Monteviot
Morebattle
Harestanes
Crailing
B6400
Greenhouse
Bloomfield
Chesters
Harelaw
Bonjedward
Lanton
Gateshaw
276
Minto
Newton
Jedburgh
12
Ruecastle
Mowh
B6359
B6405
Spittal-on-Rule
B6358
307 SHIBDEN HILL
Hownam
Clarilaw
Horsleyhill
Hundalee
Denholm
Bedrule
Scraesburgh
Oxnam
Appletreehall
Chatto
Burnfoot
Mossburnford
Wilton Dean
424 RUBERS LAW
Cauldmill
B6357
Bairnkine
Jed Water
B711
Hawick
Camps
Bonchester Bridge
A6088
Jedforest Deer & Farm Park
Whitlaw
Abbotrule
Camptown
323 BONCHESTER HILL
River Teviot
Slitrig Water
Hobkirk
Chesters
414 BROWNDEAN
393 WOFFEE HEAD
Stobs Castle
Letham
Rule Water
Carter Bar
417
Crag Bank Wood
392 BERRY FELL HILL
500 HUNGRY LAW
B6399
Whitelee
462 THE PIKE
507 WINDBURGH HILL
553 CARTER FELL
Ramshope
448 BLACK KIP
Catcleugh Reservoir
THE CHEVIOT
Byrness
608 DCLEUG HEAD
602 PEEL FELL
551 OH ME EDGE
433 SAUGHTREE FELL
Myredykes
Kielderhead
River

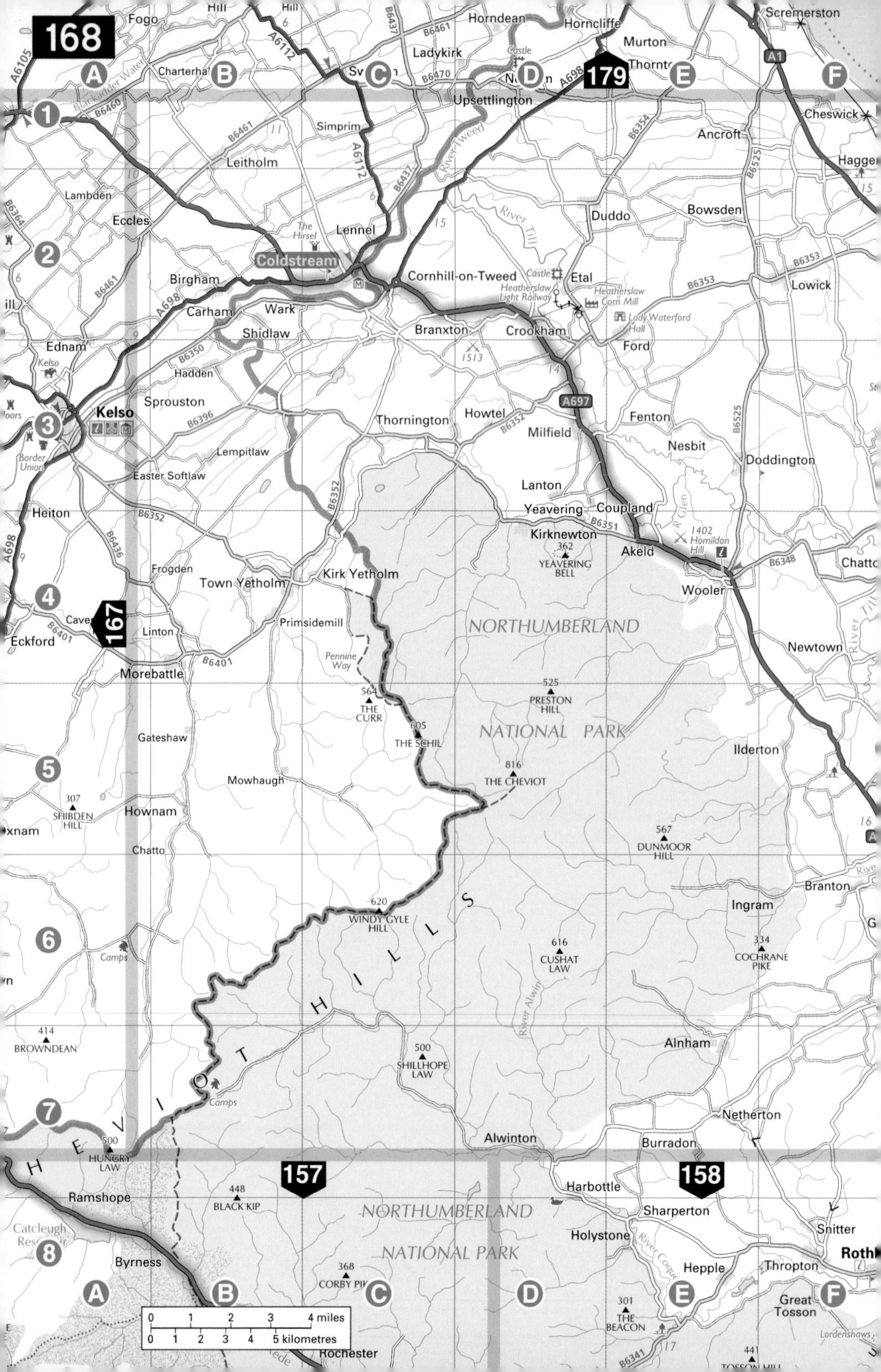
Fogo
Charterhall
Blackadder Water
Swinton
Ladykirk
Horndean
Horncliffe
Murton
Thornton
Norham
Castle
Scremerston
Upsettlington
Simprim
Leitholm
Lambden
Eccles
Ancroft
Cheswick
Haggerston
Bowsden
Duddo
River Till
River Tweed
The Hirsel
Lennel
Coldstream
Cornhill-on-Tweed
Castle
Etal
Heatherslaw Light Railway
Heatherslaw Corn Mill
Lady Waterford Hall
Lowick
Birgham
Carham
Wark
Shidlaw
Branxton
Crookham
Ford
1513
Ednam
Kelso
Hadden
Sprouston
Thornington
Howtel
Milfield
Fenton
Nesbit
Doddington
Border Union
Lempitlaw
Easter Softlaw
Lanton
Yeavering
Coupland
Heiton
Kirknewton
Akeld
R Glen
1402 Homildon Hill
362 YEAVERING BELL
Frogden
Town Yetholm
Kirk Yetholm
Wooler
Chatton
Eckford
Linton
Primsidemill
Pennine Way
NORTHUMBERLAND
Newtown
River Till
Morebattle
564 THE CURR
525 PRESTON HILL
605 THE SCHIL
NATIONAL PARK
Gateshaw
Ilderton
816 THE CHEVIOT
Mowhaugh
307 SHIBDEN HILL
Hownam
Oxnam
567 DUNMOOR HILL
Chatto
Branton
Ingram
620 WINDY GYLE HILL
Camps
616 CUSHAT LAW
334 COCHRANE PIKE
CHEVIOT HILLS
River Alwin
414 BROWNDEAN
500 SHILLHOPE LAW
Alnham
Camps
Netherton
500 HUNGRY LAW
Alwinton
Burradon
Harbottle
Ramshope
448 BLACK KIP
NORTHUMBERLAND
NATIONAL PARK
Sharperton
Snitter
Catcleugh Reservoir
Holystone
River Coquet
Byrness
368 CORBY PIKE
Hepple
Thropton
Rothbury
Great Tosson
301 THE BEACON
Lordenshaws
Rochester
441 TOSSON HILL
A6105
B6460
B6461
A6112
B6437
B6470
A698
A1
B6354
B6525
B6364
B6353
B6350
A697
B6396
B6352
B6351
B6436
B6348
B6401
B6341
179
167
157
158
A
B
C
D
E
F
1
2
3
4
5
6
7
8
0 1 2 3 4 miles
0 1 2 3 4 5 kilometres

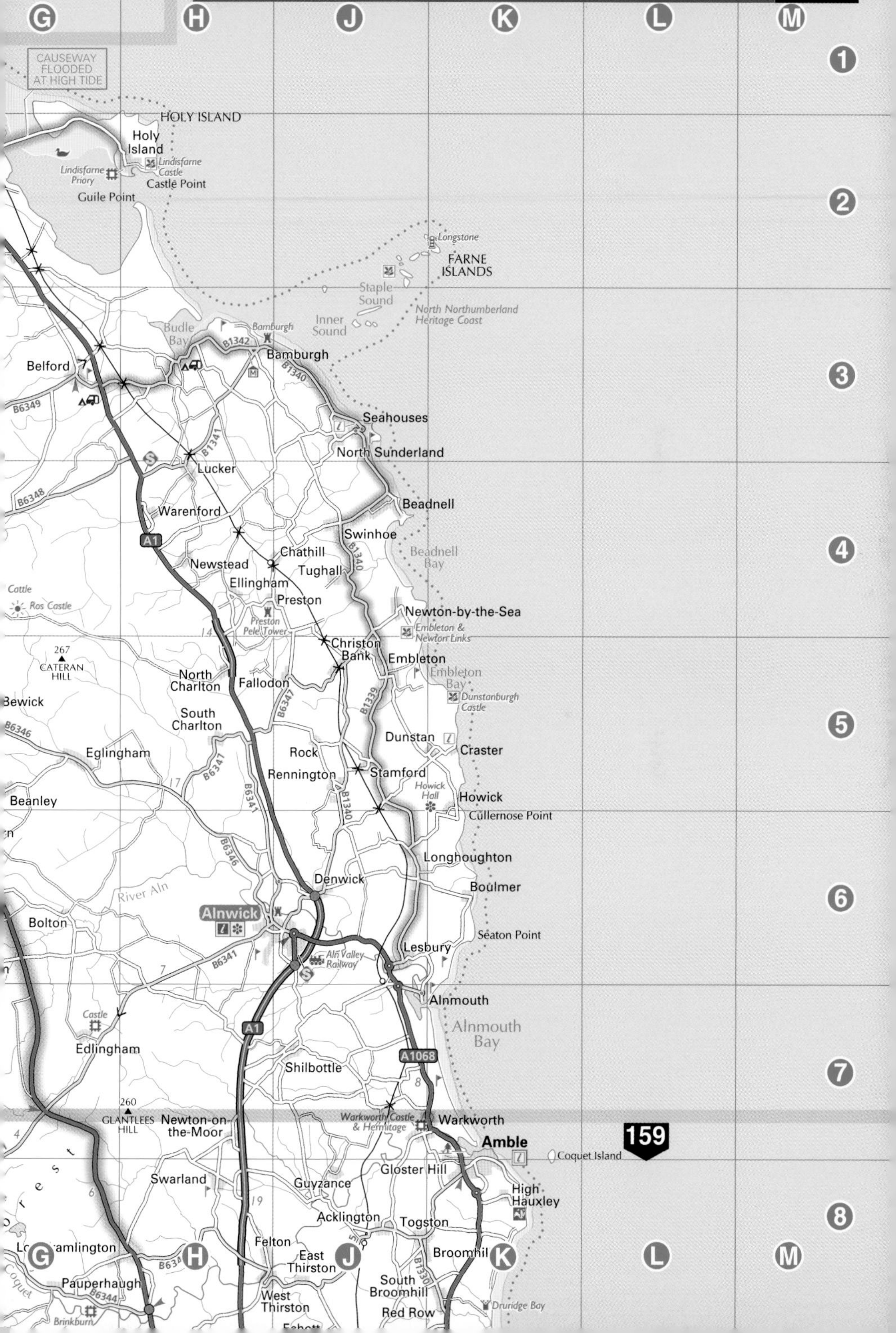
G
H
J
K
L
M
1
2
3
4
5
6
7
8
CAUSEWAY FLOODED AT HIGH TIDE
HOLY ISLAND
Holy Island
Lindisfarne Castle
Lindisfarne Priory
Castle Point
Guile Point
Longstone
FARNE ISLANDS
Staple Sound
Inner Sound
North Northumberland Heritage Coast
Budle Bay
Bamburgh
B1342
B1340
Belford
B6349
Seahouses
North Sunderland
B1341
Lucker
B6348
Warenford
Beadnell
Swinhoe
A1
Chathill
Beadnell Bay
Newstead
Tughall
Ellingham
Cattle
Ros Castle
Preston
Preston Pele Tower
Newton-by-the-Sea
Embleton & Newton Links
Christon Bank
Embleton
Embleton Bay
267
CATERAN HILL
North Charlton
Fallodon
B6347
B1339
Dunstanburgh Castle
Bewick
South Charlton
B6346
Dunstan
Craster
Eglingham
Rock
B6347
Rennington
Stamford
Howick Hall
Howick
Beanley
B6341
B1340
Cullernose Point
B6346
Longhoughton
Denwick
Boulmer
River Aln
Alnwick
Bolton
Seaton Point
Aln Valley Railway
Lesbury
B6341
Alnmouth
Castle
Alnmouth Bay
A1
Edlingham
A1068
Shilbottle
260
GLANTLEES HILL
Newton-on-the-Moor
Warkworth Castle & Hermitage
Warkworth
159
Amble
Coquet Island
Gloster Hill
Swarland
Guyzance
High Hauxley
Acklington
Togston
Felton
East Thirston
Broomhill
Pauperhaugh
B6344
Brinkburn
Coquet
West Thirston
South Broomhill
B1330
Red Row
Druridge Bay

A
B
C
D
E
F
18
1
2
3
4
5
6
7
8
Dubh
ISLA
Nave Island
Ardnave
Point
Gort
Ton Mhòr
Kilnave
Sanaigmore
Eilean Mòr
Loch Gruinart
Loch
Gorr
Rudha Lamanais
Lecht Gruinart
B8018
B8017
Saligo Bay
Gruinart
Gleann Mòr
Loch
Gorm
Coul Point
Sunderland
B8018
Kilchoman
Machir
Bay
A847
Loch
Indaal
Bruichladdich
Kilchiaran Bay
Bowmore
ISLAY
RHINNS OF
Port
Charlotte
231
BEINN TART A'MHILL
River
Lossit Bay
Laggan
Point
Nereabolls
Duich R
Rudha na
Faing
A847
Portnahaven
Port Wemyss
Laggan
Orsay
Bay
RHINNS
POINT
Rudha Mòr
Kintr
160
165
MAOL BU
THE
Lower
Killevan
Rise
0 1 2 3 4 miles
0 1 2 3 4 5 kilometres

181
Scalasaig
Machrins
Garvard
Rudha Bàn
ORONSAY
Eilean Ghurdmail
Colonsay-Port Askaig
JURA
Shian Bay
Corpach Bay
466
BEINN BHREAC
Glen Grundale
Lussa River
453
RAINBERG MÒR
Ardlussa
Lussa Point
Lussagiven
A846
Loch Righ Mòr
Rudh' ant-Sàilein
Loch Tarbert
Rudha a' Mhàil
Rudha Bholsa
363
SGARBH BREAC
506
SCRINADLE
398
BEINN TARSUINN
Jura Forest
784
BEINN AN OIR
734
Paps of Jura
Loch a Chnuic Bhric
Bunnahabhain
316
GUIR-BHEINN
Jura
Knockrome
Ardfernal
Port Askaig
Feolin Ferry
560
GLASS BHEINN
Finlaggan
Loch Finlaggan
Kiells
529
DUBHA BHEINN
Keils
Craighouse
Small Isles
Ballygrant
Loch Ballygrant
Loch Lossit
342
BRAT BHEINN
Rudha na Gaillich
A846
Cabrach
266
BEINNE DUBH
Am Fraoch Eilean
Rudha na Tràille
Brosdale Island
Gartachossan
429
SGÒRR NAM FAOILEANN
Kilennan Burn
471
McArthur's Head
490
BEINN BHEIGEIR
Port Askaig - Kennacraig
Rudha Liath
Ardtalla
454
BEINN URARAIDH
Loch Uraraidh
Claggain Bay
Kintour
Kildalton Cross
Ardmore Point
346
BEINN SHOLUM
Eilean a' Chuirn
Port Ellen - Kennacraig
Port Ellen
A846
Lagavulin
Laphroaig
Texa
Rudha na Gainne
160
Sound of Jura
Sound of Islay
Keills Chapel
Loch Cille
Danna Island
St Cormac's Chapel
Kilmory Knap Chapel
Kilmory Bay
Point of Knap
172
Kilberry Head
Keppoch Point
Kinerara
Tarbert
GIGHA
Rhunahaorine Point
Ardminish
Achamore
Sound of Gigha
Tayinloan
Cara
G H J K L M
1 2 3 4 5 6 7 8

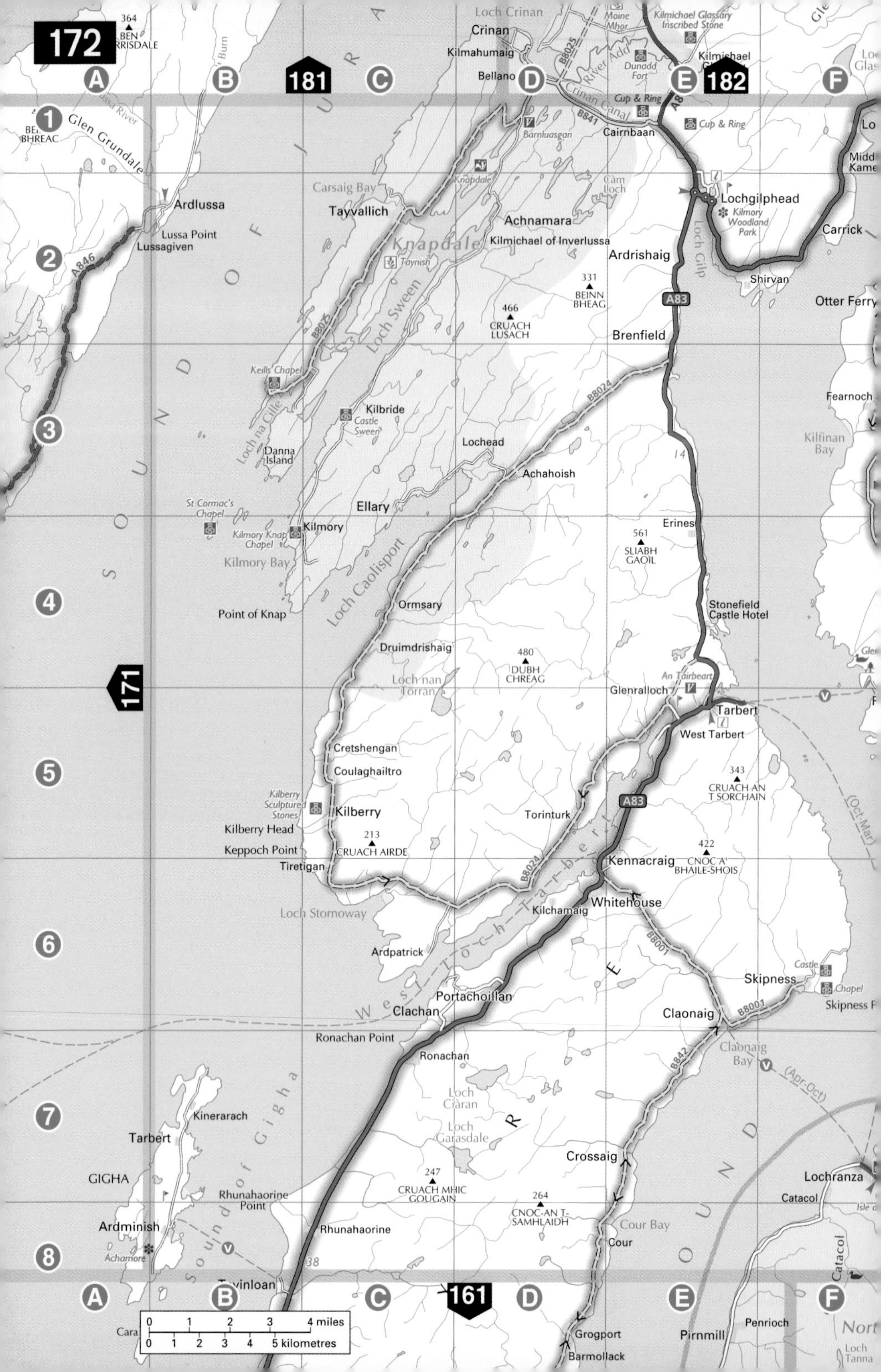

181
182
171
161
A
B
C
D
E
F
1
2
3
4
5
6
7
8
364
BEN GARRISDALE
BEN BHREAC
Glen Grundale
Lussa River
Burn
Loch Crinan
Crinan
Moine Mhor
Kilmichael Glassary Inscribed Stone
Kilmichael
Kilmahumaig
Bellano
Dunadd Fort
River Add
Crinan Canal
B8025
B841
Cup & Ring
Cairnbaan
Barnluasgan
Knapdale
Càm Loch
Lochgilphead
Kilmory Woodland Park
Middle Kames
Carrick
Ardlussa
Lussa Point
Lussagiven
A846
Carsaig Bay
Tayvallich
Achnamara
Kilmichael of Inverlussa
Knapdale
Taynish
Ardrishaig
Loch Gilp
Shirvan
Otter Ferry
331
BEINN BHEAG
A83
466
CRUACH LUSACH
Brenfield
Loch Sween
B8025
SOUND OF JURA
Keills Chapel
B8024
Loch na Cille
Kilbride
Castle Sween
Fearnoch
Kilfinan Bay
Lochead
Danna Island
Achahoish
14
St Cormac's Chapel
Ellary
Kilmory Knap Chapel
Kilmory
Erines
561
SLIABH GAOIL
Kilmory Bay
Loch Caolisport
Ormsary
Point of Knap
Stonefield Castle Hotel
Druimdrishaig
480
DUBH CHREAG
Loch nan Torran
An Tairbeart
Glenralloch
Tarbert
West Tarbert
Cretshengan
Coulaghailtro
343
CRUACH AN T SORCHAIN
Kilberry Sculptured Stones
Kilberry
Kilberry Head
Keppoch Point
213
CRUACH AIRDE
Torinturk
A83
(Oct-Mar)
Tiretigan
422
CNOC A' BHAILE-SHOIS
Kennacraig
B8024
West Loch Tarbert
Loch Stornoway
Kilchamaig
Whitehouse
B8001
Ardpatrick
Castle
Chapel
Skipness
Skipness Point
Portachoillan
Clachan
Claonaig
B8001
Ronachan Point
Ronachan
Claonaig Bay
(Apr-Oct)
B842
Loch Ciaran
Kinerarach
Tarbert
Loch Garasdale
Sound of Gigha
KINTYRE
Crossaig
GIGHA
247
CRUACH MHIC GOUGAIN
Lochranza
Catacol
Rhunahaorine Point
264
CNOC-AN T-SAMHLAIDH
Isle of Arran
Ardminish
Rhunahaorine
Cour Bay
Cour
Achamore
38
Tayinloan
Catacol
KILBRANNAN SOUND
Cara
Grogport
Barmollack
Pirnmill
Penrioch
North Glen Sannox
Loch Tanna
0
1
2
3
4 miles
0
1
2
3
4
5 kilometres

182
183
174
162
G
H
J
K
L
M
1
2
3
4
5
6
7
8
Barnacarry
505
CRUACH AN LOCHAIN
618
BEINN BHEAG
Loch Eck
Arddarroch
713
655
A886
B8000
A815
A814
Dunans Castle
643
742
BEINN MHOR
Argyll Forest Park
CREACHAN MOR
Sligrachan
Garelochhead
Rockville
Greenfield
Glen Fruin
B872
River Ruel
643
CLACH BHEINN
664
BEINN RUADH
Ardentinny
Glenmassen
Glen Massen
435
CRUACH CHUILCEACHAN
Coulport
Shandon
Gare Loch
B833
Benmore
548
STRONCHULLIN HILL
Loch Long
Kilmodan Sculptured Stones
432
CRUACH NAN CUILEAN
Loch Tarsan
601
SGORACH MOR
Clynder
Rhu
Hill House
Glendaruel
B836
Glen Lean
Rashfield
Ardbeg
Blairmore
Rosneath
Kilmun
Cove
606
Clachaig
A880
Stronafian
Holy Loch
Strone
A815
Glenkin
Sandbank
Kilcreggan
611
CRUACH NAN CAPULL
Ardnadam
Hunter's Quay
Firth
A885
Glenstriven
Kirn
Gourock
A8003
Loch Riddon
A886
454
BEINN BHREAC
503
BISHOP'S SEAT
Dunoon
Ashton
Lyle Hill
Cloch Point
A770
Larkfield
505
BEINN BHREAC
Kyles of Bute
Ardentraive
Braeside
Chrisswell
A78
Ardhallow
Lunderston Bay
Loch Thom
Port Driseach
Colintraive
Rhubodach
Altgaltraig
Loch Striven
Ardyne Burn
Ardgowan
Greenock Cut
391
KILMARNOCK HILL
Inverkip
Tighnabruaich
Kyles of Bute
322
BEINN RUADH
Dunan
Shielhill
Kames
Knockdow
Innellan
Garvock
Millhouse
BUTE
A886
267
KAMES HILL
Wemyss Bay
Blair's Ferry
Ardmaleish
A815
207
CNOC NA CARRAIGE
Kilbride
Ardyne Point
Toward
Upper Skelmorlie
St Colmac
Port Bannatyne
Toward Quay
Skelmorlie
CREUCH HILL
Kyles of Bute
Kildavanan
B875
Ardbeg
Ardlamont
Kildavaig
Ettrick Bay
Castle
Bogany Point
Ardlamont Bay
Rothesay
A844
Noddsdale Water
B878
A78
Ardlamont Point
St Mary's Chapel (ruin)
Ardencraig
Ascog
Knock Castle
522
HILL OF STAKE
Ballanlay
A844
Loch Ascog
Kerrycroy
Quarter
Routenburn
B881
Meikle Kilmory
Loch Fad
Skelmorlie Aisle
Midpark
Mount Stuart
Vikingar!
Inchmarnock
Largs
483
IRISH LAW
Bruchag
GREAT CUMBRAE ISLAND
A760
B896
B899
Ardscalpsie Bay
Kingarth
Kelburn Castle & Country Centre
Stravanan Bay
B881
Kilchattan Bay
Millport
Fairlie
Camphill Reservoir
Kilchattan
St Blane's Church
Sound of Bute
Fairlie Roads
371
COCK LAW
Sound of Arran
Garrochty
Hunterston Power Station
Garroch Head
Little Cumbrae Island
Drakemyre
Portencross
B7048
Blackshaw
Farland Head
West Kilbride
Munnoch
B781
B780
A737
Glen Chalmadale
A841
Seamill
B7047
B780
B714
Sannox
834
CAISTEAL ABHAIL
Corrie
Kilwinning
A78
A738

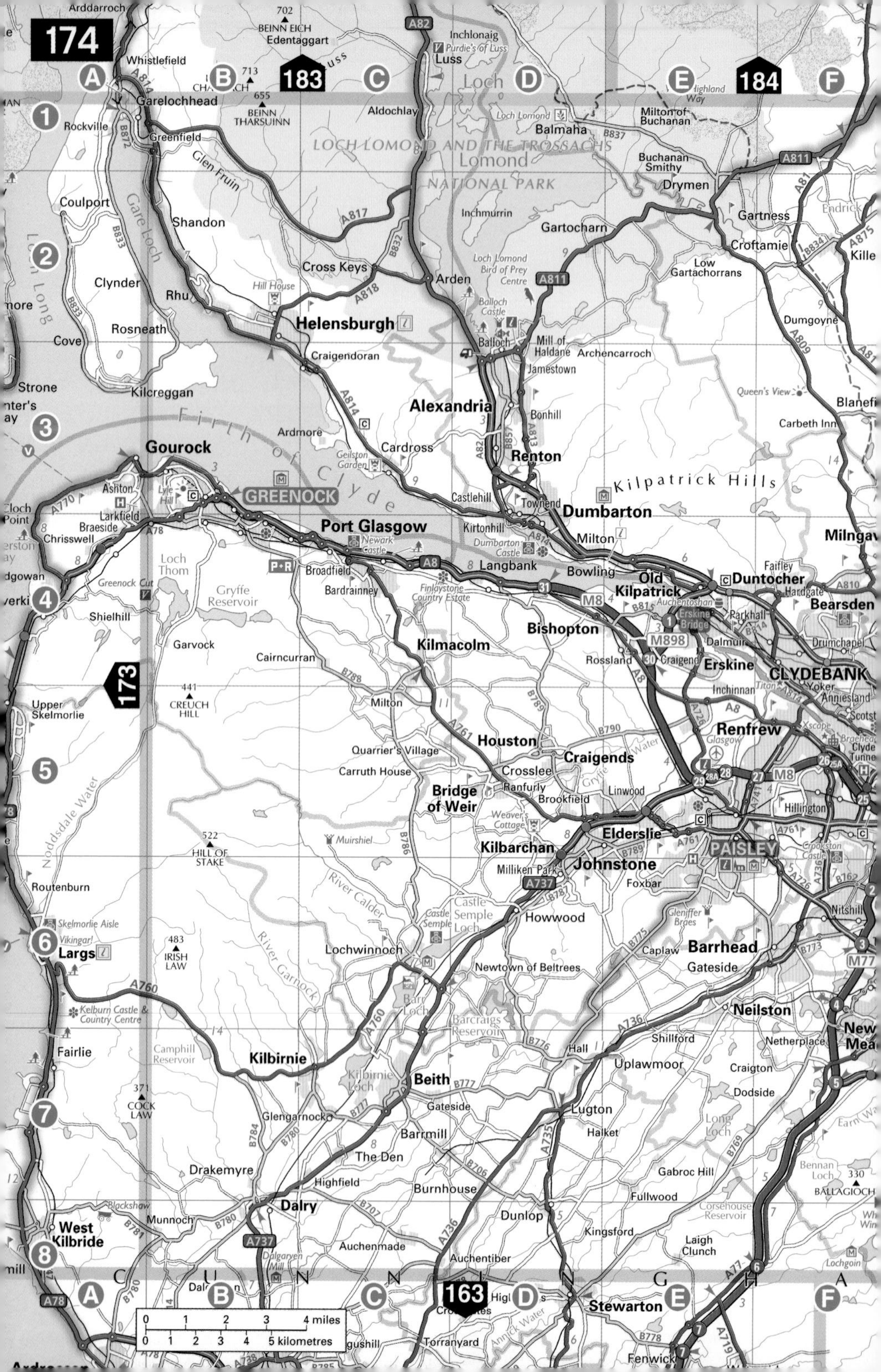
Arddarroch
702
BEINN EICH
Edentaggart
A82
Inchlonaig
Purdie's of Luss
Luss
Whistlefield
713
655
BEINN THARSUINN
183
184
173
163
Garelochhead
Aldochlay
Loch
Loch Lomond
Balmaha
Milton of Buchanan
West Highland Way
B837
Rockville
B872
Greenfield
LOCH LOMOND AND THE TROSSACHS NATIONAL PARK
Lomond
Buchanan Smithy
A811
Drymen
Glen Fruin
Gare Loch
Coulport
Shandon
A817
Inchmurrin
Gartocharn
Gartness
Endrick
Croftamie
A875
B834
Kille
Loch Long
B833
Clynder
Cross Keys
B832
Arden
Loch Lomond Bird of Prey Centre
Low Gartachorrans
Rhu
Hill House
A818
Balloch Castle
Dumgoyne
more
Cove
Rosneath
Helensburgh
Balloch
Mill of Haldane
Archencarroch
A809
Craigendoran
Jamestown
Strone
Kilcreggan
A814
Queen's View
Blanefi
Alexandria
Bonhill
A813
B857
A82
Carbeth Inn
Firth of Clyde
Ardmore
Renton
Gourock
Cardross
Geilston Garden
14
Kilpatrick Hills
Ashton
Lyle Hill
GREENOCK
Castlehill
Townend
Dumbarton
A770
Larkfield
Cloch Point
Braeside
Chrisswell
A78
Port Glasgow
Newark Castle
Kirtonhill
Dumbarton Castle
Milton
Milngav
P+R
Broadfield
A8
Langbank
Bowling
Old Kilpatrick
Duntocher
Faifley
Hardgate
A810
Loch Thom
Greenock Cut
Gryffe Reservoir
Bardrainney
Finlaystone Country Estate
31
M8
B815
Auchentoshan
Erskine Bridge
Parkhall
Bearsden
Shielhill
Garvock
Kilmacolm
Bishopton
M898
Dalmuir
B814
Drumchapel
Cairncurran
Rossland
30
Craigend
Erskine
CLYDEBANK
B788
Yoker
Anniesland
441
CREUCH HILL
Upper Skelmorlie
Milton
B789
A761
Inchinnan
Titan
A726
Renfrew
Scotst
Houston
B790
Glasgow
Xscape
Braehead
Clyde Tunnel
Quarrier's Village
Craigends
Gryffe Water
Carruth House
Crosslee
Ranfurly
Brookfield
Linwood
29
28A
28
27
26
25A
25
Bridge of Weir
Hillington
Noddsdale Water
Weaver's Cottage
Elderslie
522
HILL OF STAKE
Muirshiel
B786
Kilbarchan
Johnstone
Milliken Park
A737
B787
PAISLEY
Crookston Castle
Routenburn
River Calder
Foxbar
A736
B762
Castle Semple Loch
Skelmorlie Aisle
Vikingar!
Largs
483
IRISH LAW
River Garnock
Howwood
Lochwinnoch
Gleniffer Braes
Nitshill
B775
Caplaw
Barrhead
Gateside
B773
M77
Newtown of Beltrees
A760
Kelburn Castle & Country Centre
Barr Loch
Barcraigs Reservoir
Neilston
Fairlie
Camphill Reservoir
Kilbirnie
Shillford
Hall
B776
Netherplace
Uplawmoor
Craigton
Kilbirnie Loch
Beith
B777
371
COCK LAW
Gateside
Dodside
Glengarnock
B784
B780
Barrmill
Lugton
Halket
Long Loch
A735
Earn Water
The Den
B769
Drakemyre
Highfield
B706
Gabroc Hill
Bennan Loch
330
BALLAGIOCH
Burnhouse
Fullwood
Blackshaw
Munnoch
Dalry
Dunlop
Corsehouse Reservoir
West Kilbride
B781
B707
Kingsford
Laigh Clunch
Auchenmade
Auchentiber
Lochgoin
A77
A78
Dalgarven Mill
Stewarton
Torranyard
Annick Water
B778
Fenwick
A719
A738
B785
0 1 2 3 4 miles
0 1 2 3 4 5 kilometres
CUNNINGHAME

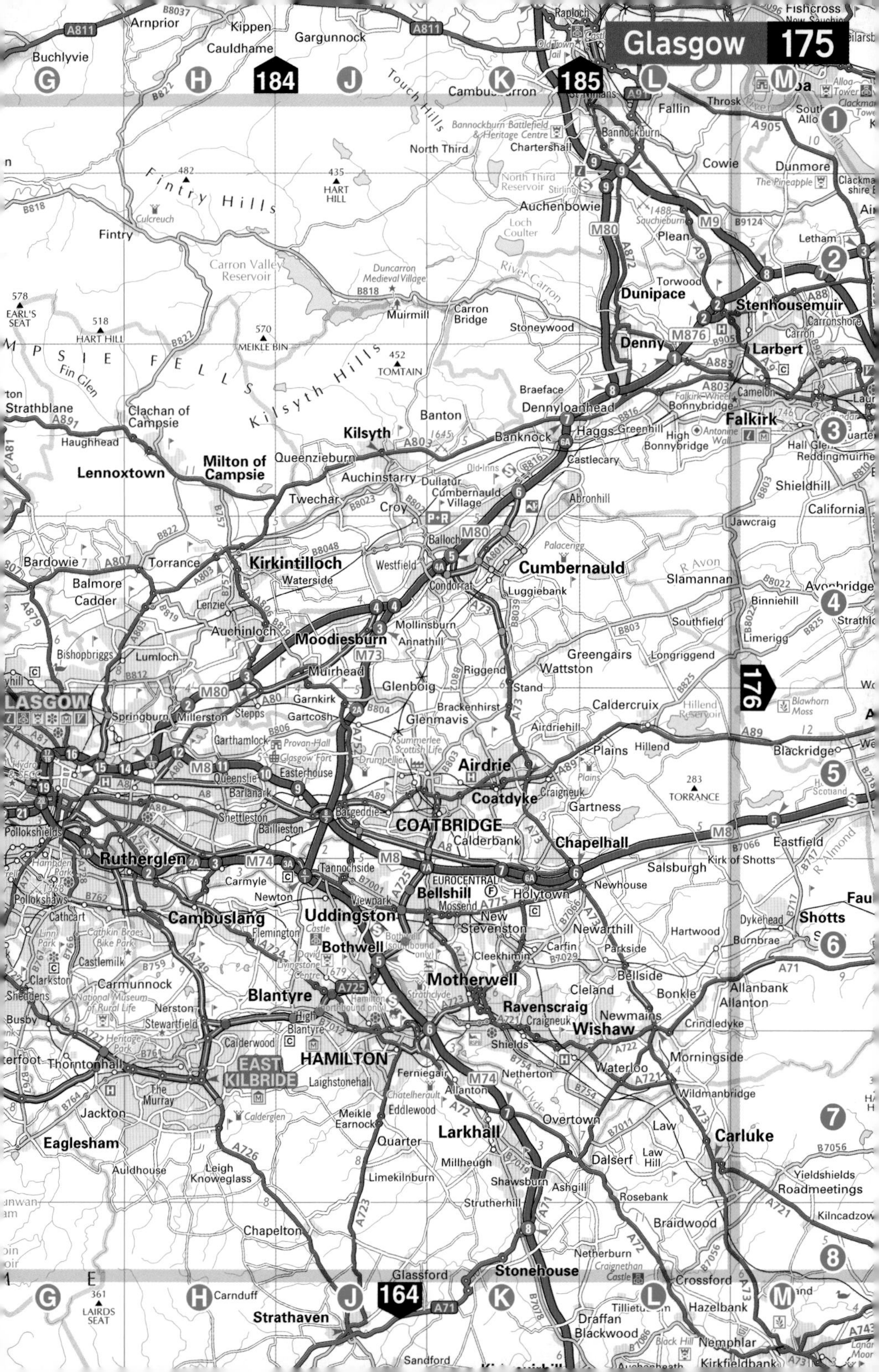
184
185
176
164
G
H
J
K
L
M
1
2
3
4
5
6
7
8
Arnprior
Kippen
Gargunnock
Cauldhame
Buchlyvie
Cambusbarron
Fallin
Throsk
Bannockburn
Bannockburn Battlefield & Heritage Centre
Chartershall
North Third
North Third Reservoir
Cowie
Dunmore
The Pineapple
Touch Hills
Fintry Hills
Culcreuch
Fintry
HART HILL
Auchenbowie
Loch Coulter
Plean
Letham
Carron Valley Reservoir
Duncarron Medieval Village
River Carron
Torwood
Dunipace
Stenhousemuir
Muirmill
Carron Bridge
Stoneywood
Denny
Larbert
Carronshore
EARL'S SEAT
MEIKLE BIN
TOMTAIN
Kilsyth Hills
Fin Glen
Strathblane
Clachan of Campsie
Braeface
Dennyloanhead
Banton
Bonnybridge
Falkirk
Falkirk Wheel
Camelon
Haughhead
Kilsyth
Banknock
Haggs
Greenhill
High Bonnybridge
Antonine Wall
Hall Glen
Reddingmuirhead
Lennoxtown
Milton of Campsie
Queenzieburn
Castlecary
Auchinstarry
Dullatur
Cumbernauld Village
Twechar
Croy
Abronhill
Shieldhill
California
Jawcraig
Balloch
Palacerigg
Bardowie
Torrance
Kirkintilloch
Westfield
Cumbernauld
Slamannan
Avonbridge
Balmore
Cadder
Waterside
Condorrat
Luggiebank
Lenzie
Binniehill
Auchinloch
Moodiesburn
Mollinsburn
Annathill
Southfield
Limerigg
Bishopbriggs
Lumloch
Muirhead
Riggend
Greengairs
Wattston
Longriggend
Glenboig
Stand
GLASGOW
Springburn
Millerston
Stepps
Garnkirk
Gartcosh
Brackenhirst
Glenmavis
Caldercruix
Hillend Reservoir
Blawhorn Moss
Garthamlock
Provan Hall
Glasgow Fort
Summerlee Scottish Life
Drumpellier
Airdriehill
Plains
Hillend
Blackridge
Queenslie
Easterhouse
Airdrie
Coatdyke
Craigneuk
Barlanark
TORRANCE
Shettleston
Baillieston
Bargeddie
COATBRIDGE
Gartness
Pollokshields
Rutherglen
Hampden Park
Calderbank
Chapelhall
Eastfield
Carmyle
Tannochside
EUROCENTRAL
Bellshill
Holytown
Salsburgh
Kirk of Shotts
Newhouse
Pollokshaws
Newton
Viewpark
Mossend
Cathcart
Cambuslang
Uddingston
New Stevenston
Newarthill
Hartwood
Dykehead
Shotts
Burnbrae
Cathkin Braes Bike Park
Linn Park
Flemington
Bothwell
Cleekhimin
Carfin
Parkside
Castlemilk
David Livingstone Centre
Bellside
Clarkston
Carmunnock
Motherwell
Cleland
Bonkle
Allanbank
Allanton
Sheddens
National Museum of Rural Life
Nerston
Blantyre
Strathclyde
Ravenscraig
Newmains
Crindledyke
Busby
Stewartfield
High Blantyre
Craigneuk
Wishaw
Calderwood
Shields
Thorntonhall
EAST KILBRIDE
HAMILTON
Netherton
Waterloo
Morningside
Laighstonehall
Ferniegair
Allanton
Wildmanbridge
The Murray
Chatelherault
Eddlewood
Jackton
Calderglen
Meikle Earnock
Larkhall
Overtown
Law
Carluke
Eaglesham
Quarter
Dalserf
Law Hill
Millheugh
Yieldshields
Roadmeetings
Auldhouse
Leigh Knoweglass
Limekilnburn
Shawsburn
Ashgill
Rosebank
Strutherhill
Kilncadzow
Chapelton
Braidwood
Netherburn
Craignethan Castle
Glassford
Stonehouse
Crossford
LAIRDS SEAT
Carnduff
Tillietudlem
Hazelbank
Strathaven
Draffan
Blackwood
Black Hill
Nemphlar
Kirkfieldbank
Sandford
M80
M9
M876
M73
M8
M74
A811
A91
A905
A872
A9
A88
A883
A803
A891
A81
A807
A879
A80
A73
A752
A8
A89
A725
A724
A749
A727
A726
A723
A71
A72
A721
A775
A722
A743
B8037
B822
B818
B9124
B905
B816
B8023
B802
B8048
B757
B819
B812
B806
B804
B803
B8039
B8022
B825
B7066
B717
B7001
B762
B759
B761
B764
B767
B766
B7012
B7029
B754
B7011
B7019
B7056
B7078
B7086
B7018
R Avon
R Almond
R Clyde

185
175
165
A
B
C
D
E
F
1
2
3
4
5
6
7
8
Fishcross
New Sauchie
Coalsnaughton
Gartmorn Dam & Visitor Centre
Forest Mill
Balgonar
Saline
Steelend
KNOCK HILL
Knockhill
Black Devon
Loch Glow
Cambus
Norwood
Keilarsbrae
Alloa
Alloa Tower
Clackmannan
Clackmannan Tower
Fallin
Throsk
South Alloa
Kennet
River Forth
Bannockburn
Cowie
Dunmore
The Pineapple
Clackmannanshire Bridge
Airth
Kincardine
Kincardine Bridge
Comrie
Oakley
Carnock
Blairhall
High Valleyfield
Culross Abbey
Culross Palace
Culross
Low Torry
Torry Bay
Newmills
Torryburn
Cairneyhill
Crossford
Crombie
Charlestown
Limekilns
Rosyth
Gowkhall
Milesmark
Townhill
Wellwood
Halbeath
Kingseat
Bowershall
CRAIGLUSCAR HILL
DUNFERMLINE
Sauchieburn
Plean
Letham
Torwood
Dunipace
Stenhousemuir
Carron
Carronshore
Skinflats
Grangemouth
Bo'ness
Bo'ness & Kinneil Railway
Grangepans
Carriden
Castle
Blackness
House of the Binns
Hopetoun
Queensferry Crossing
Denny
Larbert
Camelon
Falkirk Wheel
Bonnybridge
High Bonnybridge
Antonine Wall
Falkirk
Callendar Park
Laurieston
Dovecot
Westquarter
Hall Glen
Redding
Reddingmuirhead
Polmont
Rumford
Brightons
Whitecross
Kinneil House
Birkhill Claymine
Borrowstoun
Philpstoun
Newton
Shieldhill
California
Maddiston
Loan
Union Canal
Muiravonside
Linlithgow
Burnside
Bridgend
Three Miletown
Winchburgh
Kirkliston
Jawcraig
Standburn
Cockleroy
Beecraigs
Wester Ochiltree
Ecclesmachan
Broxburn
Newbridge
Uphall
Ratho
Ratho Viaduct
R Avon
Slamannan
Avonbridge
Binniehill
Southfield
Limerigg
Longriggend
Strathloanhead
Westfield
Preceptory
Torphichen
Cairnpapple Hill
Dechmont
Dechmont Road
Pumpherston
Almondell & Calderwood
Camps
Caldercruix
Hillend Reservoir
Blawhorn Moss
Woodend
Armadale
Bathville
Bathgate
Deans
Livingston
Boghall
Wilkieston
East Calder
Mid Calder
Kirknewton
Plains
Hillend
Blackridge
Westrigg
Polkemmet
Almond Valley
Livingston Village
Oakbank
TORRANCE
Heart of Scotland
East Whitburn
Seafield
Blackburn
Bellsquarry
Harthill
Whitburn
Stoneyburn
Polbeth
Ainville
Eastfield
Kirk of Shotts
Salsburgh
Longridge
Loganlea
Addiewell
West Calder
Linhouse Water
Water of Leith
Harperrig Reservoir
Newhouse
Fauldhouse
Greenburn
Breich
Dykehead
Shotts
Hartwood
Burnbrae
Stane
EAST CAIRN HILL
WEST CAIRN HILL
Cobbinshaw Loch
Bellside
Bonkle
Allanbank
Allanton
Headlesscross
Gladsmuir Hills
Crosswood Reservoir
Newmains
Crindledyke
WORM LAW
Woolfords
Tarbrax
Morningside
Waterloo
Wildmanbridge
HARE HILL
Forth
Wilsontown
Auchengray
South Tarbrax
HARROWS LAW
West Water
West Water Reservoir
Law
Carluke
Law Hill
Dalserf
Yieldshields
Roadmeetings
Braehead
LEFT LAW
MENDICK HILL
Rosebank
Kilncadzow
Braidwood
North Medwin
Dunsyre
Craignethan Castle
Crossford
Carnwath
South Medwin
Dolphinton
Tillietudlem
Hazelbank
Carstairs
Carstairs Junction
Newbigging
Walston
Netherurd
Kirkurd
Black Hill
Bankhead
R Medwin
Elsrickle
Pettinain
Kirkfieldbank
Greenshields
0 1 2 3 4 miles
0 1 2 3 4 5 kilometres
M9
M80
M876
M90
M8
A91
A905
A907
A876
A977
A985
A994
A88
A883
A803
A904
A993
A706
A801
A800
A89
A899
A779
A705
A71
A704
A70
A721
A722
A73
B9124
B905
B902
B816
B810
B803
B8022
B825
B8028
B8047
B8084
B792
B708
B7002
B718
B7066
B717
B7015
B7010
B7008
B7016
B7056
B9080
B9156
B8046
B7030
B7031
B913
B9037
B910
B914
B915
B916
B980

Cardenden
Gallatown
Chapel
Dysart
Kirkcaldy
Pathhead
Linktown
Cowdenbeath
Auchtertool
Donibristle
Balmule
Kinghorn
Aberdour
Pettycur
Pettycur Bay
Burntisland
St Bridget's Kirk
Silversands Bay
Inchcolm Abbey
Dalgety Bay
Inchkeith
FIRTH OF FORTH
Cramond Island
Dalmeny
Royal Yacht Britannia
EDINBURGH
Granton
Newhaven
Leith
Cramond
Lauriston Castle
Barnton
Davidson's Mains
Royal Botanic Garden
Warriston
St Triduana's Chapel
Blackhall
Murrayfield
Castle
Dynamic Earth
ARTHUR'S SEAT 251
Portobello
Joppa
Duddingston
Newcraighall
Craigmillar
Craigmillar Castle
Corstorphine
South Gyle
Craiglockhart
Morningside
Water of Leith
Blackford Hill
Royal Observatory
Liberton
Gilmerton
Juniper Green
Colinton
Currie
Bonaly
Malleny Garden
Kinleith
Malleny Mills
Hillend
Straiton
Loanhead
Bilston
Lasswade
Bonnyrigg
Polton
Roslin
Easter Howgate
Milton Bridge
Rosewell
Auchendinny
Penicuik
Pomathorn
Howgate
Silverburn
Carrington
ALLERMUIR HILL 493
Boghall
Woodhouselee
Castlelaw Hill Fort
Pentland Hills
Threipmuir Reservoir
CARNETHY HILL 576
SCALD LAW 579
Musselburgh
Fisherrow
Inveresk
Wallyford
Elphinstone
Whitecraig
Crossgatehall
Millerhill
Newton
Danderhall
Dalkeith
Dalkeith Park
Eskbank
Butterfly Farm
Newbattle
Mayfield
Chesterhill
Newtongrange
Dewarton
Vogrie
National Mining Museum
Newtonloan
Arniston
Gorebridge
Crichton Castle
Crichton
Newlandrig
Cousland
Pathhead
Prestonpans
Prestongrange Museum
Preston Market Cross
Cockenzie and Port Seton
Seton Collegiate Church
Seton Mains
Tranent
Macmerry
New Winton
Ormiston
Ormiston Market Cross
Longniddry
Elvingston
Huntington
Gladsmuir
Samuelston
Boggs Holdings
Pencaitland
East Saltoun
West Saltoun
Gilchriston
Humbie
Blegbie
Fala Dam
Fala
Soutra Summit 363
DUN LAW 394
TURF LAW 380
Gilston
Oxton
Carfrae
COLLIE LAW 383
Heriot
Fountainhall
Torquhan
Killochyett
Stow
Gosford Bay
Spittal
Aberlady
Aberlady Bay
Craigelaw Point
Luffness
Myreton Motor Museum
Ballencrieff
Gullane
Gullane Point
Gullane Bay
Muirfield
Dirleton
Eyebroughy
Yellowcraig
North Middleton
Temple
Mount Lothian
Rosebery Reservoir
Gladhouse Reservoir
Moorfoot Hills
Heriot Water
Leadburn
Craigburn
Waterheads
Portmore Loch
WHITE RIG 324
Linton
WETHER LAW 479
BLACKHOPE SCAR 651
DUN LAW 425
Eddleston
CRAILZIE HILL 476
WHITEHOPE LAW 621
R North Esk
A92
A921
A909
A720
A7
A68
A1
A199
A198
A6093
A6094
A6124
A701
A702
A703
A766
B6372
B6368
B7007
B709
186
166
178

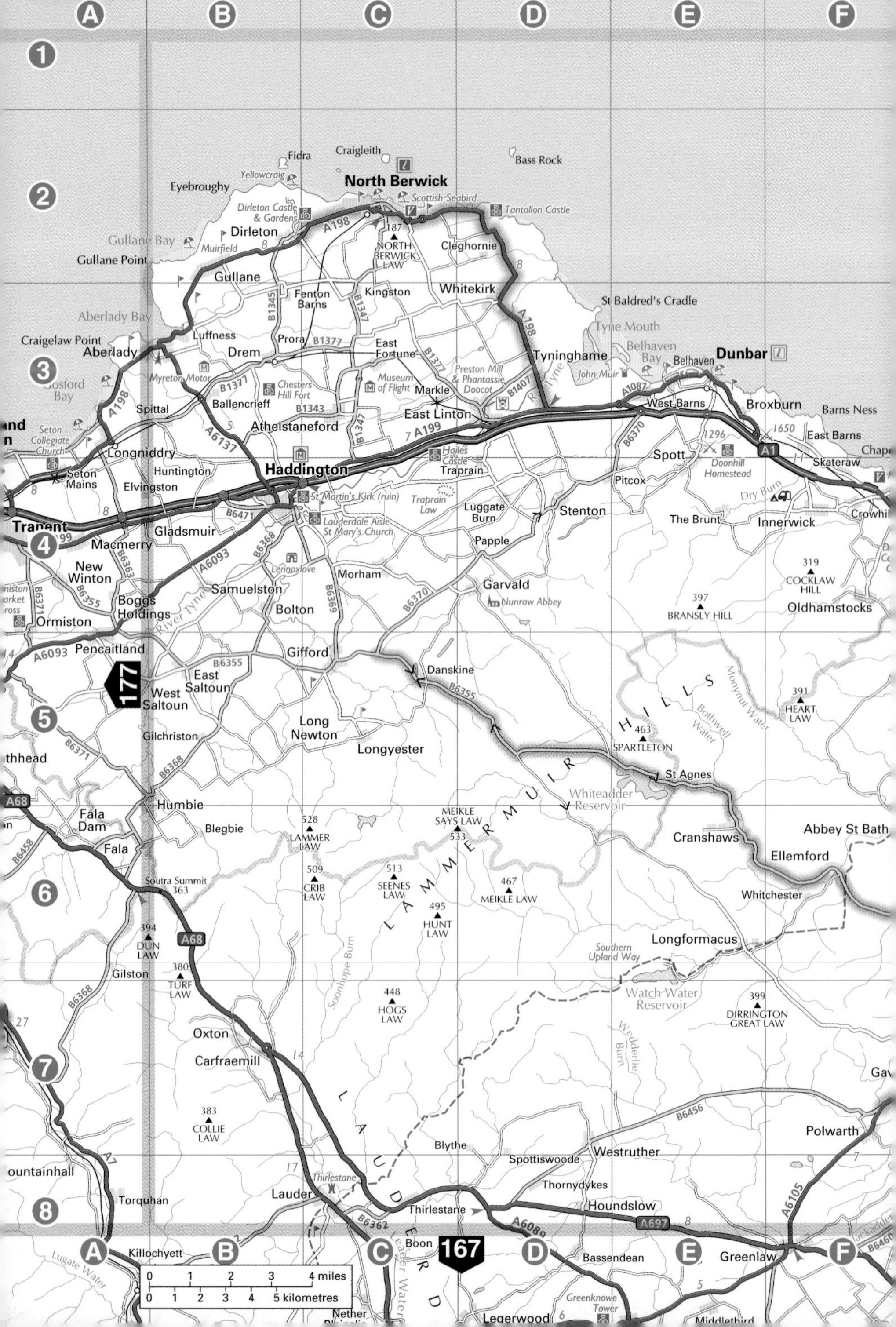
A
B
C
D
E
F
1
2
3
4
5
6
7
8
Fidra
Craigleith
Bass Rock
Yellowcraig
North Berwick
Eyebroughy
Scottish Seabird
Dirleton Castle & Gardens
Tantallon Castle
A198
187
NORTH BERWICK LAW
Dirleton
Cleghornie
Gullane Bay
Muirfield
Gullane Point
Gullane
Fenton Barns
Kingston
Whitekirk
B1345
B1347
St Baldred's Cradle
Aberlady Bay
Tyne Mouth
Craigelaw Point
Luffness
Prora
B1377
East Fortune
Belhaven Bay
Dunbar
Aberlady
Drem
Tyninghame
Belhaven
Myreton Motor
Museum of Flight
Preston Mill & Phantassie Doocot
John Muir
Gosford Bay
Spittal
Ballencrieff
Chesters Hill Fort
Markle
B1407
A1087
West Barns
Broxburn
Barns Ness
B1343
East Linton
Seton Collegiate Church
Athelstaneford
A6137
A199
B6370
1296
1650
East Barns
Longniddry
Hailes Castle
Spott
A1
Chape
Seton Mains
Huntington
Haddington
Traprain
Doonhill Homestead
Skateraw
Elvingston
Pitcox
St Martin's Kirk (ruin)
Traprain Law
Luggate Burn
Stenton
Dry Burn
Crowhi
B6471
The Brunt
Innerwick
Tranent
Gladsmuir
Lauderdale Aisle St Mary's Church
Macmerry
Papple
B6368
B6363
New Winton
A6093
Lennoxlove
Morham
319
COCKLAW HILL
Garvald
B6355
Samuelston
B6369
B6370
Nunraw Abbey
397
BRANSLY HILL
Oldhamstocks
Boggs Holdings
River Tyne
Bolton
B6371
Ormiston
Pencaitland
Gifford
177
Danskine
East Saltoun
West Saltoun
Monynut Water
391
HEART LAW
Bothwell Water
Long Newton
Gilchriston
Longyester
463
SPARTLETON
B6371
St Agnes
LAMMERMUIR HILLS
Whiteadder Reservoir
A68
Humbie
Fala Dam
Blegbie
528
LAMMER LAW
MEIKLE SAYS LAW
533
Abbey St Bathans
Cranshaws
B6458
Fala
Ellemford
509
CRIB LAW
513
SEENES LAW
467
MEIKLE LAW
Soutra Summit 363
Whitchester
495
HUNT LAW
394
DUN LAW
Longformacus
Southern Upland Way
Gilston
380
TURF LAW
Soonhope Burn
Watch Water Reservoir
399
DIRRINGTON GREAT LAW
448
HOGS LAW
Oxton
Carfraemill
Wedderlie Burn
LAUDERDALE
383
COLLIE LAW
B6456
Polwarth
Blythe
Westruther
Spottiswoode
Thornydykes
Thirlestane
Lauder
Houndslow
Torquhan
A7
A6105
A697
A6089
B6362
Killochyett
Boon
167
Bassendean
Greenlaw
Lugate Water
Leader Water
Greenknowe Tower
Legerwood
Nether
Middlethird
0 1 2 3 4 miles
0 1 2 3 4 5 kilometres

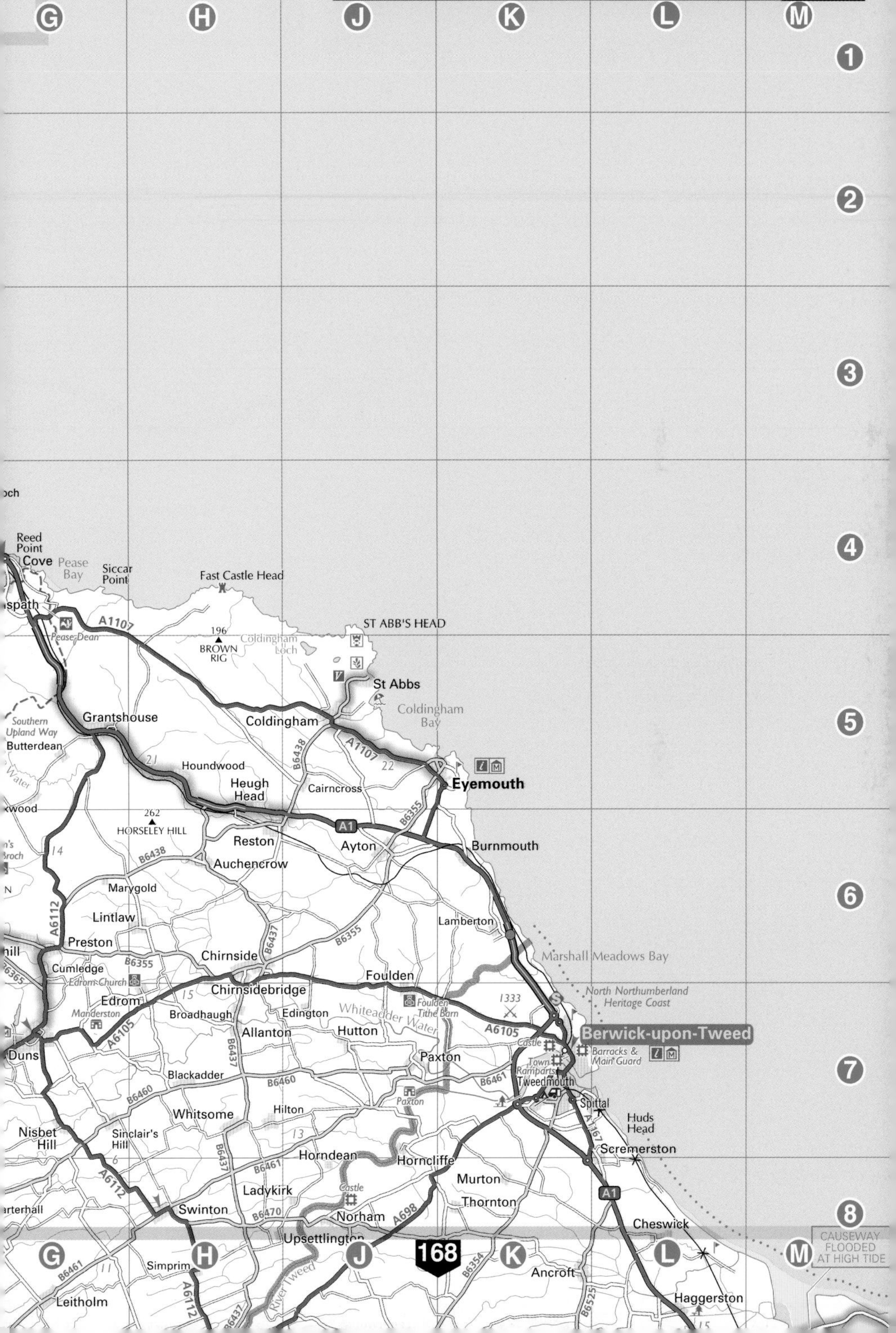
G
H
J
K
L
M
1
2
3
4
5
6
7
8
Reed Point
Cove
Pease Bay
Siccar Point
Fast Castle Head
ST ABB'S HEAD
196
BROWN RIG
Coldingham Loch
A1107
Pease Dean
St Abbs
Coldingham Bay
Grantshouse
Coldingham
Southern Upland Way
Butterdean
Houndwood
B6438
Heugh Head
Cairncross
A1107
22
21
Eyemouth
262
HORSELEY HILL
A1
B6355
Reston
Ayton
Burnmouth
B6438
Auchencrow
14
Marygold
A6112
Lintlaw
Lamberton
Preston
B6355
Chirnside
B6437
Marshall Meadows Bay
Cumledge
B6355
Edrom Church
Foulden
Edrom
15
Chirnsidebridge
North Northumberland Heritage Coast
Manderston
Broadhaugh
Edington
Whiteadder Water
Foulden Tithe Barn
1333
A6105
Allanton
Hutton
A6105
Berwick-upon-Tweed
Duns
Castle
Barracks & Main Guard
Paxton
Town Ramparts
B6437
Tweedmouth
Blackadder
B6460
B6461
B6460
Paxton
Spittal
Whitsome
Hilton
Huds Head
A1167
Nisbet Hill
Sinclair's Hill
13
B6437
Scremerston
Horndean
Horncliffe
A6112
B6461
Murton
Ladykirk
Castle
Thornton
A1
Swinton
B6470
Norham
A698
Cheswick
Upsettlington
168
CAUSEWAY FLOODED AT HIGH TIDE
Simprim
11
B6461
B6354
Ancroft
Leitholm
A6112
River Tweed
B6437
B6525
Haggerston
15

Bac Mòr or Dutchmans Cap
189
Little Colonsay
Staffa
Fingal's Cave
Loch na Keal, Isle of Mull
Inch Kenneth
Inchkenneth Chapel (ruin)
491
CREACH BHEINN
Fossil Tree
Burg
IONA
Iona Abbey & Nunnery
Baile Mór
MacLean's Cross
Sound of Iona
Rudha nan Cearc
Kintra
Fionnphort
Aridhglas
St Columba Exhibition Centre
Loch na Lathaich
A849
Bunessan
Loch Assapol
ROSS OF MULL
Soa Island
Erraid
Uisken
Ardchiavaig
Rudha Ardalanish
Torran Rocks
Eilean Dubh
Balnahard
Kiloran Bay
COLONSAY
Kiloran
Kilchattan
B8087
Scalasaig
B8086
Machrins
Colonsay
B8085
171
Oronsay
Rudha Bàn
Dubh Eilean
0 1 2 3 4 miles
0 1 2 3 4 5 kilometres

Macquarie Mausoleum
BEINN NAN LUS
ISLE OF MULL
190
Eorsa
Loch na Keal
BEINN MHEADHO
766 DUN DA GHAOITHE
Craignure
Duart Bay
Duart Point
Duart
Torosay
Lochdonhead
Lochdon
Gorten
Loch Don
Grass Point
966 BEN MORE
704 CRUACHAN DEARG
A849
B8035
Glen More
Strathcoil
247 CARN BAN
Aird of Kinloch
698 BEN CREACH
717 BEN BUIE
Loch Fuaran
Loch Spelve
Croggan
KERRERA
Pennycross
Pennyghael
503 BEINN NA CROISE
Leidle Water
Lochbuie
Loch Uisg
Rudha Seanach
337 MAOL BAN
Loch Buie
377 DRUIM FADA
376 BEINN CHREAGACH
Carsaig
Rudha Dubh
FIRTH OF LORNE
Malcolm's Point
Insh Island
Clachan
Clachan-Seil
SEIL
Ellenabeich
Easdale
Balvicar
B844
B8003
Colonsay - Oban
Cuan
Seil Sound
182
Garbh Eileach
Cullipool
Torsa
Degnish
Loch Melfort
Eilean Dubh Mòr
Arduaine
LUING
GARVELLACHS
Monastery & Beehive Cells
Eileach an Naoimh
LUNGA
Sound of Luing
Toberonochy
Shuna Sound
SHUNA
Scarba, Lunga and the Garvellachs
Craobh Haven
Shuna Point
Craigdhu
SCARBA
448 CRUACH SCARBA
Ardfern
B8002
Gulf of Corryvreckan
Aird
Loch Craignish
Craignish Point
Glengarrisdale Bay
295 CRUACH NA SEILCHEIG
Island Macaskin
Poltalloch
Ri Cruin
Glendebadel Bay
Loch Crinan
Crinan
364 BEN GARRISDALE
JURA
Kilmahumaig
B8025
Lealt Burn
Bellanoch
Corpach Bay
171
466 BEINN BHREAC
Glen Grundale
Lussa River
172
Barnluasgan
Knapdale
Carsaig Bay

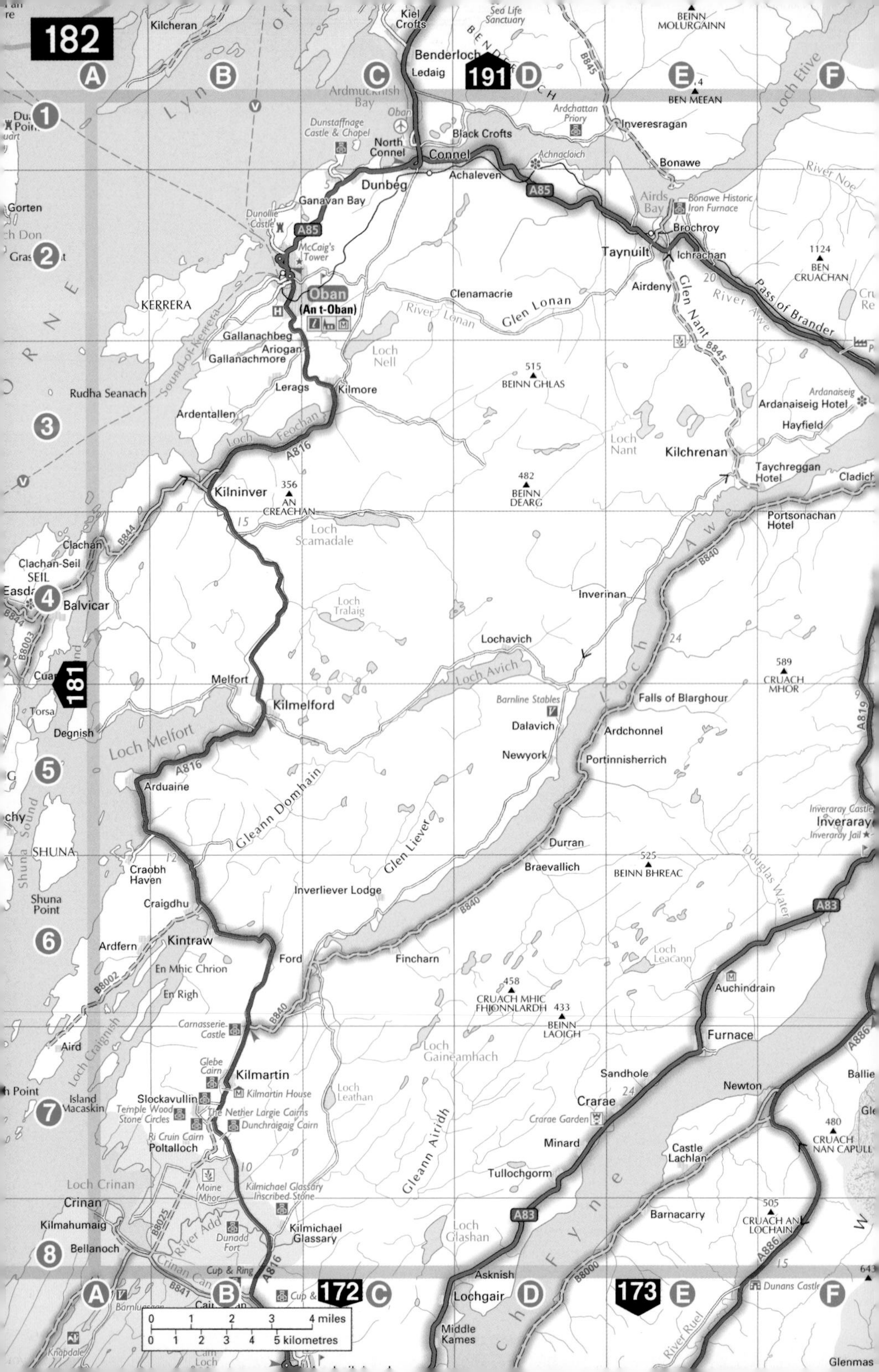
Kilcheran
Kiel Crofts
Sea Life Sanctuary
BEINN MOLURGAINN
Benderloch
Ledaig
191
BENDERLOCH
B845
BEN MEEAN
Loch Etive
Lynn of Lorn
Ardmucknish Bay
Oban
Dunstaffnage Castle & Chapel
Ardchattan Priory
Inveresragan
Black Crofts
North Connel
Connel
Achnacloich
Bonawe
Achaleven
A85
Dunbeg
River Noe
Airds Bay
Bonawe Historic Iron Furnace
Gorten
Ganavan Bay
Dunollie Castle
A85
Brochroy
Taynuilt
Ichrachan
1124
BEN CRUACHAN
McCaig's Tower
Airdeny
Glen Nant
River Awe
Pass of Brander
Clenamacrie
Glen Lonan
KERRERA
Oban
(An t-Oban)
River Lonan
Sound of Kerrera
Gallanachbeg
Ariogan
Gallanachmore
Loch Nell
B845
515
BEINN GHLAS
Lerags
Kilmore
Rudha Seanach
Ardanaiseig
Ardanaiseig Hotel
Ardentallen
Loch Feochan
Hayfield
Loch Nant
Kilchrenan
A816
Taychreggan Hotel
Cladich
356
AN CREACHAN
Kilninver
482
BEINN DEARG
Loch Scamadale
Portsonachan Hotel
Clachan
B844
Clachan-Seil
SEIL
Easdale
Balvicar
B844
B8003
Loch Tralaig
Inverinan
B840
Lochavich
Loch Avich
Loch Awe
589
CRUACH MHOR
Cuan
181
Melfort
Kilmelford
Barnline Stables
Falls of Blarghour
Torsa
Degnish
Loch Melfort
Dalavich
Ardchonnel
Newyork
Portinnisherrich
A819
A816
Arduaine
Gleann Domhain
Glen Liever
Inveraray Castle
Inveraray
Inveraray Jail
Shuna Sound
SHUNA
Durran
525
Craobh Haven
Braevallich
BEINN BHREAC
Douglas Water
Shuna Point
Craigdhu
Inverliever Lodge
B840
A83
Kintraw
Ardfern
En Mhic Chrion
Ford
Fincharn
Loch Leacann
B8002
En Righ
458
CRUACH MHIC FHIONNLARDH
433
BEINN LAOIGH
Auchindrain
Carnasserie Castle
B840
Furnace
Loch Craignish
Aird
Loch Gaineamhach
A886
Glebe Cairn
Kilmartin
Sandhole
Ballie
Island Macaskin
Slockavullin
Kilmartin House
Loch Leathan
Newton
Crarae
Temple Wood Stone Circles
The Nether Largie Cairns
Dunchraigaig Cairn
Crarae Garden
480
CRUACH NAN CAPULL
Ri Cruin Cairn
Poltalloch
Minard
Castle Lachlan
Gleann Airidh
Loch Crinan
Moine Mhor
Tullochgorm
Kilmichael Glassary Inscribed Stone
A83
505
CRUACH AN LOCHAIN
Crinan
B8025
River Add
Dunadd Fort
Kilmichael Glassary
Loch Glashan
Barnacarry
Kilmahumaig
Loch Fyne
A886
Bellanoch
A816
Crinan Canal
Cup & Ring
Asknish
B8000
643
B841
Cup &
172
173
Lochgair
Dunans Castle
Barnluasgan
River Ruel
Middle Kames
Knapdale
Glenmas
0 1 2 3 4 miles
0 1 2 3 4 5 kilometres

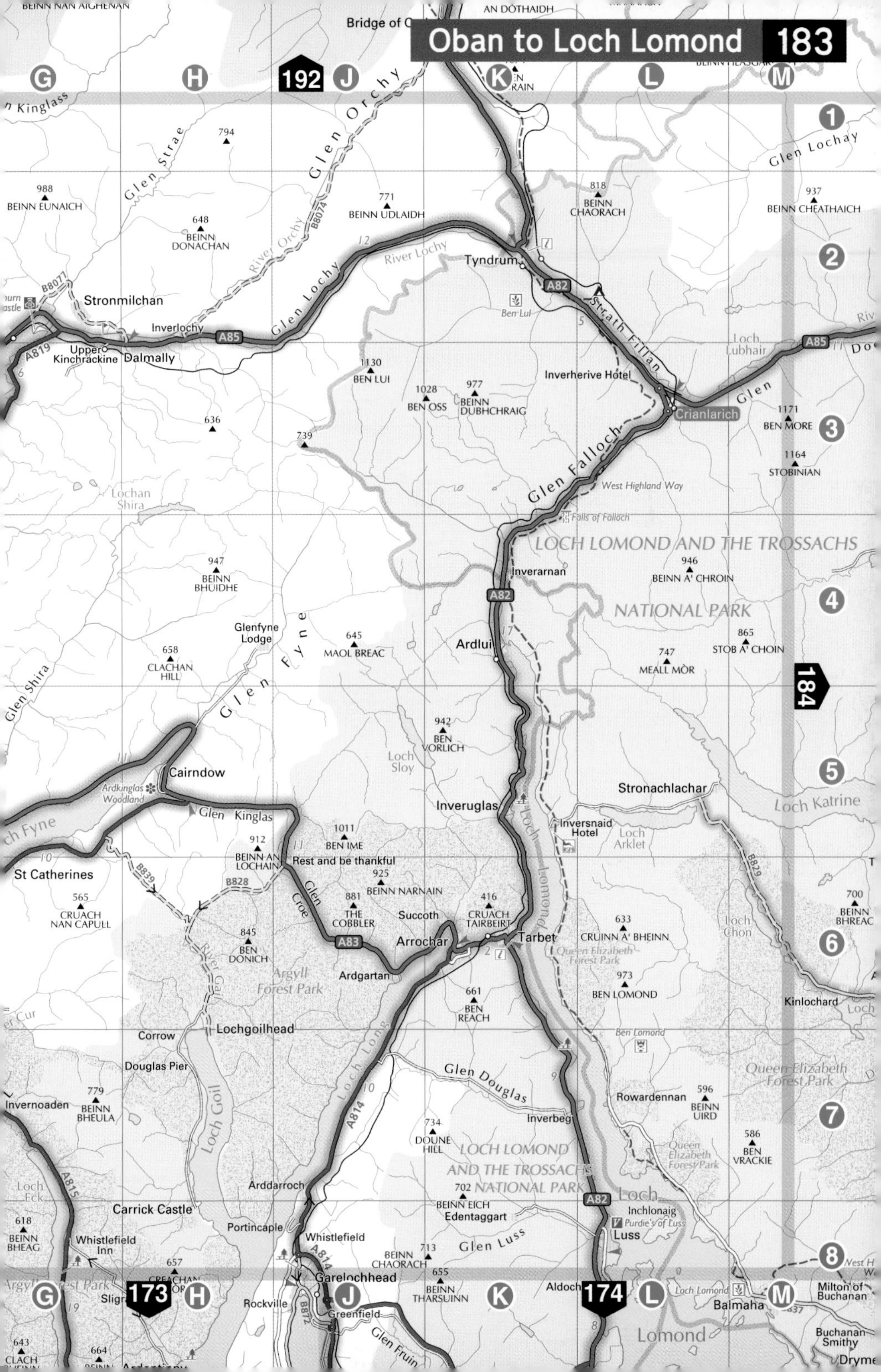
Tyndrum
Crianlarich
Dalmally
Stronmilchan
Inverlochy
Upper Kinchrackine
Inverherive Hotel
Falls of Falloch
Inverarnan
Ardlui
Inveruglas
Inversnaid Hotel
Stronachlachar
Glenfyne Lodge
Cairndow
Ardkinglas Woodland
Rest and be thankful
St Catherines
Succoth
Arrochar
Tarbet
Ardgartan
Lochgoilhead
Corrow
Douglas Pier
Invernoaden
Kinlochard
Rowardennan
Inverbeg
Arddarroch
Carrick Castle
Portincaple
Whistlefield
Whistlefield Inn
Edentaggart
Inchlonaig
Purdie's of Luss
Luss
Garelochhead
Rockville
Greenfield
Aldoch
Balmaha
Milton of Buchanan
Buchanan Smithy
LOCH LOMOND AND THE TROSSACHS NATIONAL PARK
Argyll Forest Park
Queen Elizabeth Forest Park
West Highland Way
Glen Orchy
Glen Strae
Glen Lochy
Glen Lochay
Strath Fillan
Glen Falloch
Glen Fyne
Glen Shira
Glen Kinglas
Glen Croe
Glen Douglas
Glen Luss
Glen Fruin
River Orchy
River Lochy
Loch Fyne
Loch Sloy
Loch Lomond
Loch Katrine
Loch Arklet
Loch Chon
Loch Long
Loch Goil
Loch Eck
Lochan Shira
Loch Lubhair
A82
A85
A83
A819
A814
A815
B8074
B8077
B828
B839
B829
B872
988 BEINN EUNAICH
794
648 BEINN DONACHAN
771 BEINN UDLAIDH
818 BEINN CHAORACH
937 BEINN CHEATHAICH
1130 BEN LUI
1028 BEN OSS
977 BEINN DUBHCHRAIG
1171 BEN MORE
1164 STOBINIAN
636
739
947 BEINN BHUIDHE
946 BEINN A' CHROIN
645 MAOL BREAC
658 CLACHAN HILL
865 STOB A' CHOIN
747 MEALL MÒR
942 BEN VORLICH
1011 BEN IME
912 BEINN AN LOCHAIN
925 BEINN NARNAIN
881 THE COBBLER
416 CRUACH TAIRBEIRT
565 CRUACH NAN CAPULL
845 BEN DONICH
633 CRUINN A' BHEINN
973 BEN LOMOND
700 BEINN BHREAC
661 BEN REACH
779 BEINN BHEULA
734 DOUNE HILL
596 BEINN UIRD
586 BEN VRACKIE
702 BEINN EICH
618 BEINN BHEAG
713 BEINN CHAORACH
655 BEINN THARSUINN
657
643
664
Ben Lui
Ben Lomond
192
173
174
184
G H J K L M
1 2 3 4 5 6 7 8

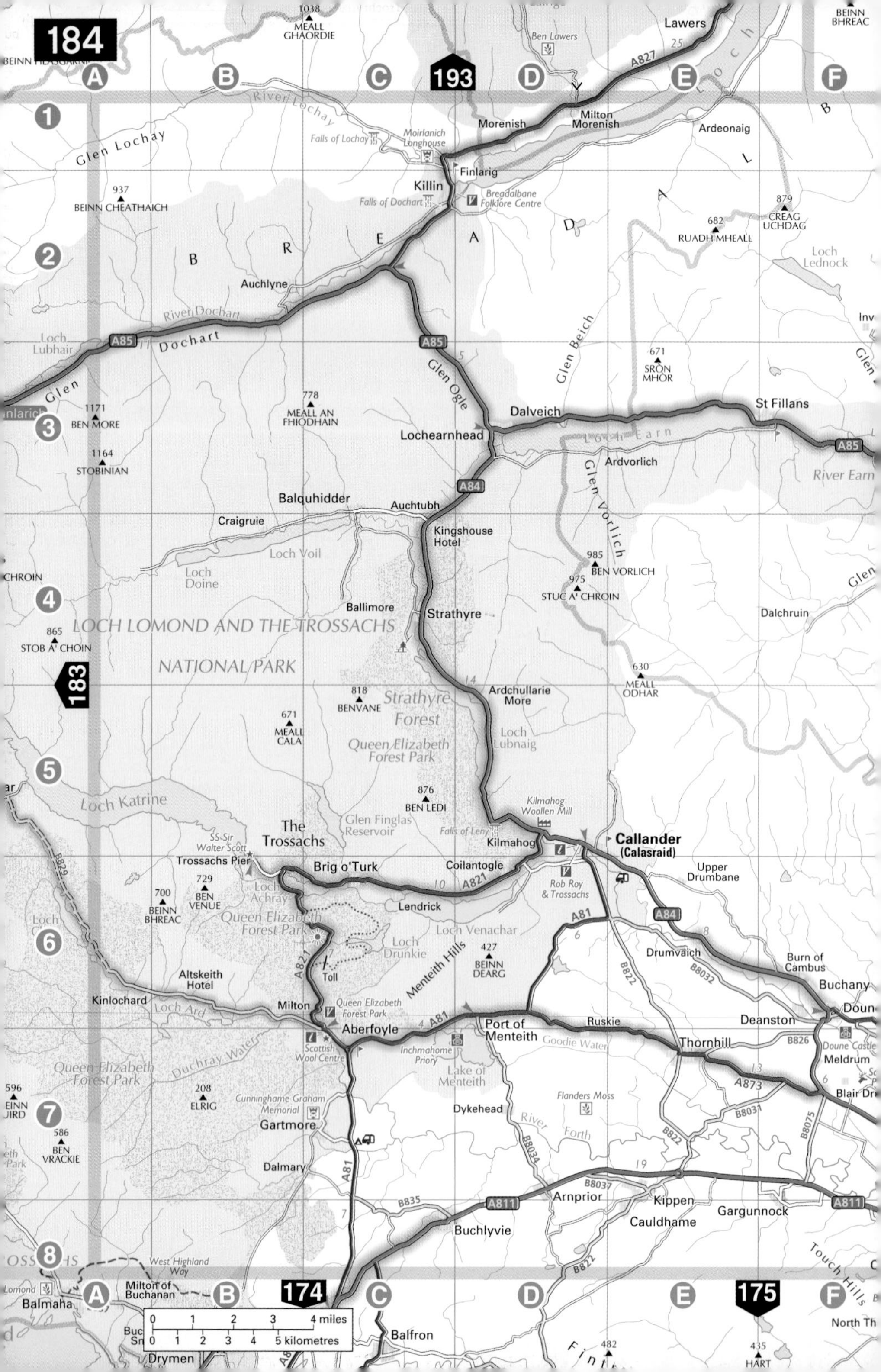
193
174
175
183
Lawers
Ben Lawers
Loch Tay
A827
Milton Morenish
Morenish
Ardeonaig
River Lochay
Glen Lochay
Falls of Lochay
Moirlanich Longhouse
Finlarig
Killin
Falls of Dochart
Breadalbane Folklore Centre
BREADALBANE
937 BEINN CHEATHAICH
1038 MEALL GHAORDIE
BEINN HEASGARNICH
BEINN BHREAC
879 CREAG UCHDAG
682 RUADH MHEALL
Loch Lednock
Auchlyne
River Dochart
Glen Dochart
Loch Lubhair
A85
Glen Beich
671 SRON MHOR
Glen Ogle
778 MEALL AN FHIODHAIN
1171 BEN MORE
1164 STOBINIAN
Dalveich
St Fillans
Lochearnhead
Loch Earn
Ardvorlich
River Earn
A84
Balquhidder
Auchtubh
Craigruie
Kingshouse Hotel
Loch Voil
Loch Doine
Glen Vorlich
985 BEN VORLICH
975 STUC A' CHROIN
Ballimore
Strathyre
Dalchruin
LOCH LOMOND AND THE TROSSACHS NATIONAL PARK
865 STOB A' CHOIN
630 MEALL ODHAR
818 BENVANE
Strathyre Forest
Ardchullarie More
671 MEALL CALA
Queen Elizabeth Forest Park
Loch Lubnaig
Loch Katrine
876 BEN LEDI
Kilmahog Woollen Mill
The Trossachs
Glen Finglas Reservoir
Falls of Leny
Kilmahog
Callander (Calasraid)
SS Sir Walter Scott
Trossachs Pier
Brig o'Turk
Coilantogle
Rob Roy & Trossachs
Upper Drumbane
B829
729 BEN VENUE
700 BEINN BHREAC
Loch Achray
A821
Lendrick
Loch Venachar
A81
Loch Drunkie
427 BEINN DEARG
Drumvaich
Burn of Cambus
B822
B8032
Toll
Menteith Hills
Altskeith Hotel
Kinlochard
Loch Ard
Milton
Queen Elizabeth Forest Park
Aberfoyle
Port of Menteith
Ruskie
Deanston
Buchany
Doune
Scottish Wool Centre
Inchmahome Priory
Goodie Water
Thornhill
B826
Doune Castle
Meldrum
Duchray Water
Lake of Menteith
A873
Blair Drummond
596
586 BEN VRACKIE
208 ELRIG
Cunninghame Graham Memorial
Flanders Moss
Dykehead
B8031
Gartmore
River Forth
B8034
B8075
Dalmary
B835
B8037
Arnprior
Kippen
Gargunnock
A811
Cauldhame
Buchlyvie
Touch Hills
West Highland Way
B822
Milton of Buchanan
Balmaha
Balfron
Drymen
North Third
482
435 HART
0 1 2 3 4 miles
0 1 2 3 4 5 kilometres

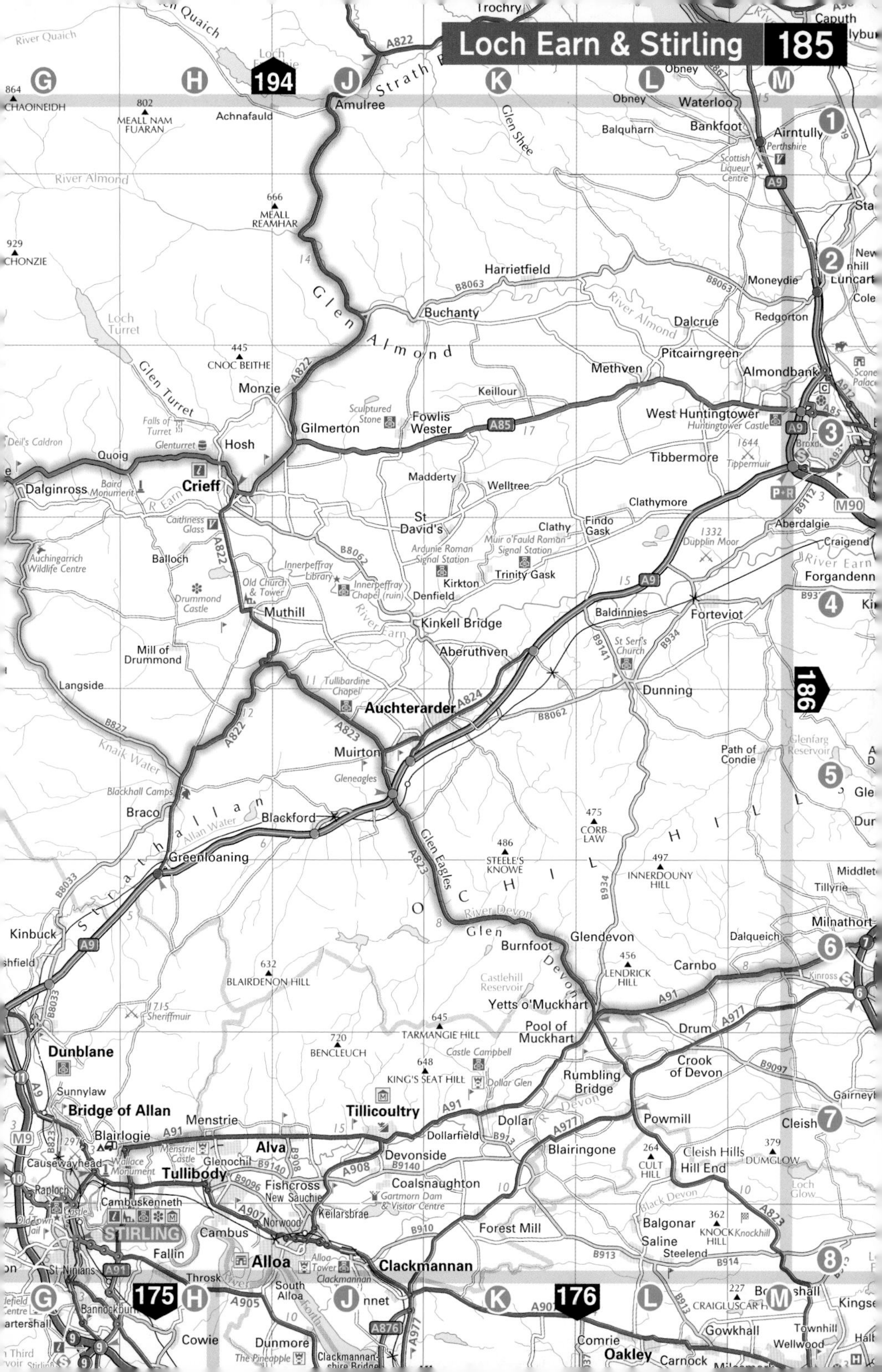

G
H
J
K
L
M
194
186
175
176
1
2
3
4
5
6
7
8
Loch Quaich
River Quaich
Trochry
Caputh
A822
Strath Braan
Loch Freuchie
Obney
Waterloo
Bankfoot
Balquharn
Airntully
864 CHAOINEIDH
802 MEALL NAM FUARAN
Achnafauld
Amulree
Glen Shee
Perthshire
Scottish Liqueur Centre
A9
River Almond
666 MEALL REAMHAR
929 CHONZIE
Harrietfield
B8063
Moneydie
Luncarty
Newmill
Stanley
Cole
Glen Almond
Buchanty
River Almond
Dalcrue
Redgorton
Loch Turret
445 CNOC BEITHE
Pitcairngreen
Methven
Almondbank
Scone Palace
A912
Glen Turret
Monzie
Keillour
Sculptured Stone
Fowlis Wester
West Huntingtower
Huntingtower Castle
Falls of Turret
Gilmerton
A85
Deil's Caldron
Glenturret
Hosh
1644 Tippermuir
Broxden
Quoig
Tibbermore
A93
Dalginross
Baird Monument
Crieff
R Earn
Madderty
Welltree
P+R
B9112
M90
Caithness Glass
Clathymore
St David's
Clathy
Findo Gask
Aberdalgie
Auchingarrich Wildlife Centre
Balloch
B8062
Ardunie Roman Signal Station
Muir o'Fauld Roman Signal Station
1332 Dupplin Moor
Craigend
River Earn
Forgandenny
Innerpeffray Library
Innerpeffray Chapel (ruin)
Kirkton
Trinity Gask
Old Church & Tower
Drummond Castle
Denfield
Muthill
River Earn
Kinkell Bridge
Baldinnies
Forteviot
B934
B9141
St Serf's Church
Mill of Drummond
Aberuthven
Dunning
Langside
Tullibardine Chapel
Auchterarder
A824
B8062
B827
A823
Glenfarg Reservoir
Path of Condie
Knaik Water
Muirton
Gleneagles
Blackhall Camps
Braco
Allan Water
Blackford
Strathallan
Glen Eagles
475 CORB LAW
486 STEELE'S KNOWE
497 INNERDOUNY HILL
Greenloaning
OCHIL HILLS
B8033
Middleton
Tillyrie
River Devon
Glen Devon
Milnathort
Kinbuck
Burnfoot
Glendevon
Dalqueich
632 BLAIRDENON HILL
456 LENDRICK HILL
Carnbo
Castlehill Reservoir
Kinross
A91
1715 Sheriffmuir
Yetts o'Muckhart
Pool of Muckhart
A977
Drum
645 TARMANGIE HILL
720 BENCLEUCH
Dunblane
Castle Campbell
648 KING'S SEAT HILL
Dollar Glen
Crook of Devon
B9097
Rumbling Bridge
Sunnylaw
Gairneybank
Bridge of Allan
Menstrie
Tillicoultry
Dollar
Powmill
Cleish
M9
Blairlogie
Dollarfield
B913
Blairingone
Alva
Menstrie Castle
264 CULT HILL
Cleish Hills
379 DUMGLOW
Causewayhead
Wallace Monument
Glenochil
B9140
B908
Devonside
A908
Hill End
Tullibody
B9096
Fishcross
New Sauchie
Coalsnaughton
Loch Glow
Raploch
Cambuskenneth
Gartmorn Dam & Visitor Centre
Black Devon
Castle
A907
Keilarsbrae
362 KNOCK HILL
Knockhill
Balgonar
Old Town Jail
STIRLING
Cambus
Norwood
B910
Forest Mill
Saline
Steelend
Fallin
Alloa
Alloa Tower
Clackmannan
B913
B914
St Ninians
Throsk
Clackmannan Tower
A905
South Alloa
Kennet
227 CRAIGLUSCAR HILL
Blairhall
Kingseat
Bannockburn
River Forth
A876
A977
Plean
Cowie
Dunmore
Gowkhall
Townhill
Wellwood
The Pineapple
Clackmannanshire Bridge
Comrie
Oakley
Carnock
Milesmark

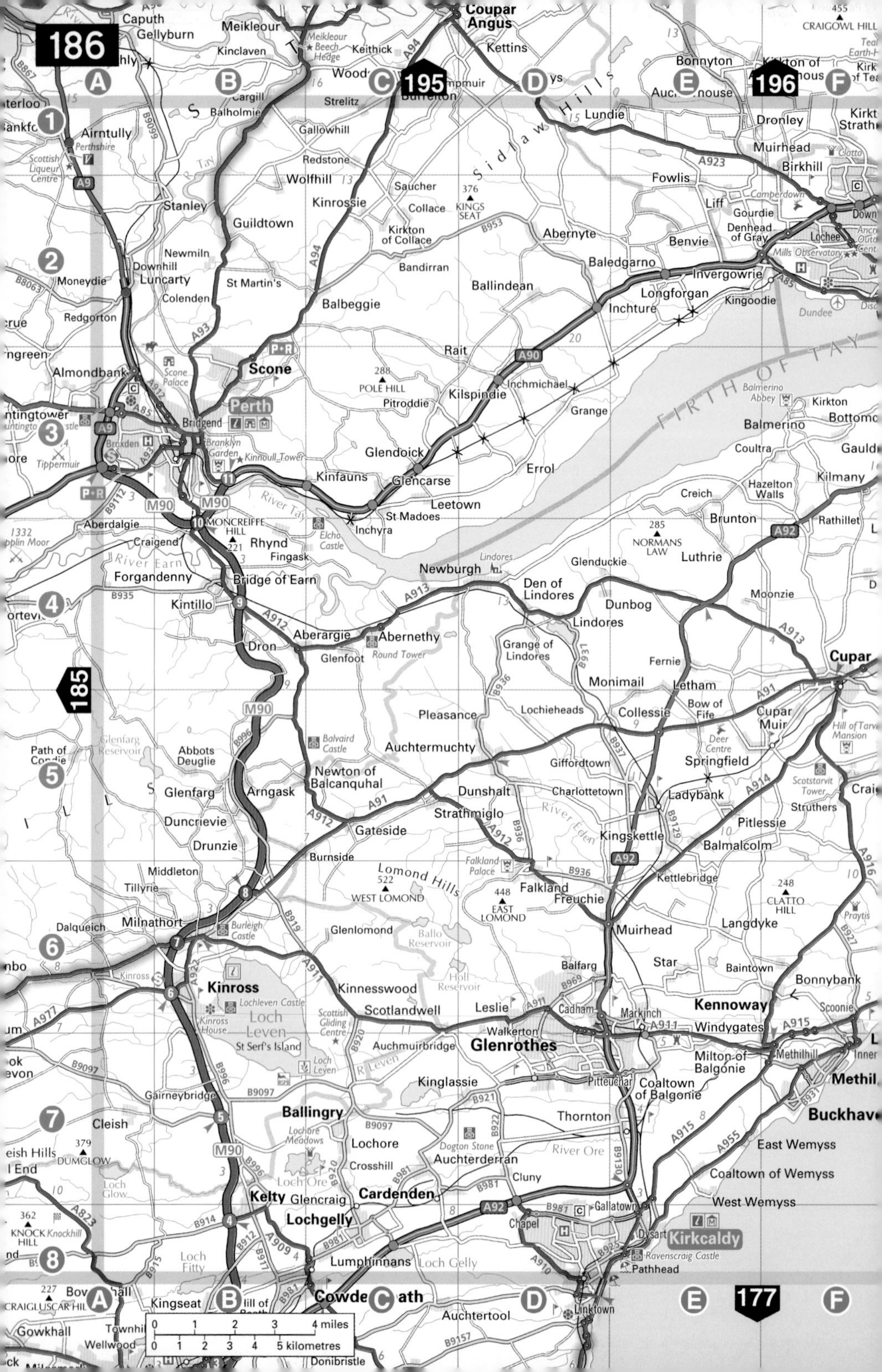
Coupar Angus
Caputh
Gellyburn
Meikleour
Kinclaven
Meikleour Beech Hedge
Keithick
Kettins
Woodside
Burrelton
Dys
Bonnyton
Kirkton of Auchterhouse
CRAIGOWL HILL
455
Cargill
Balholmie
Strelitz
Lundie
Dronley
Sidlaw Hills
Airntully
Perthshire
Scottish Liqueur Centre
Gallowhill
Redstone
Wolfhill
Saucher
376
KINGS SEAT
Collace
Kinrossie
Kirkton of Collace
Stanley
Guildtown
Fowlis
Muirhead
Birkhill
Camperdown
Liff
Gourdie
Denhead of Gray
Benvie
Lochee
Mills Observatory
Abernyte
Baledgarno
Invergowrie
Longforgan
Kingoodie
Inchture
Dundee
Newmiln
Downhill
Luncarty
Moneydie
St Martin's
Colenden
Redgorton
Bandirran
Ballindean
Balbeggie
Almondbank
Scone Palace
Scone
Rait
288
POLE HILL
Pitroddie
Kilspindie
Inchmichael
Grange
FIRTH OF TAY
Balmerino Abbey
Balmerino
Kirkton
Huntingtower
Huntingtower Castle
Tippermuir
Perth
Bridgend
Branklyn Garden
Kinnoull Tower
Broxden
Glendoick
Kinfauns
Glencarse
Errol
Coultra
Hazelton Walls
Kilmany
Creich
Leetown
St Madoes
Inchyra
River Tay
Elcho Castle
Brunton
Rathillet
1332
Aberdalgie
MONCREIFFE HILL
221
Rhynd
Fingask
285
NORMANS LAW
Luthrie
Craigend
River Earn
Forgandenny
Bridge of Earn
Newburgh
Lindores
Glenduckie
Den of Lindores
Kintillo
Dunbog
Moonzie
Aberargie
Abernethy
Round Tower
Dron
Glenfoot
Lindores
Grange of Lindores
Fernie
Cupar
Monimail
Letham
Bow of Fife
Pleasance
Lochieheads
Collessie
Cupar Muir
Hill of Tarvit Mansion
Glenfarg Reservoir
Path of Condie
Abbots Deuglie
Balvaird Castle
Auchtermuchty
Gifffordtown
Deer Centre
Springfield
Newton of Balcanquhal
Glenfarg
Arngask
Dunshalt
Charlottetown
Ladybank
Scotstarvit Tower
Struthers
Strathmiglo
River Eden
Pitlessie
Duncrievie
Gateside
Kingskettle
Balmalcolm
Drunzie
Burnside
Lomond Hills
522
WEST LOMOND
Falkland Palace
Kettlebridge
248
CLATTO HILL
Middleton
Tillyrie
448
EAST LOMOND
Falkland
Freuchie
Pratis
Milnathort
Burleigh Castle
Glenlomond
Dalqueich
Ballo Reservoir
Muirhead
Langdyke
Star
Baintown
Bonnybank
Balfarg
Kinross
Holl Reservoir
Kinnesswood
Cadham
Markinch
Kennoway
Windygates
Scoonie
Lochleven Castle
Kinross House
Loch Leven
St Serf's Island
Scottish Gliding Centre
Scotlandwell
Leslie
Walkerton
Glenrothes
Auchmuirbridge
Loch Leven
R Leven
Milton of Balgonie
Methilhill
Methil
Pitteuchar
Coaltown of Balgonie
Kinglassie
Gairneybridge
Ballingry
Buckhaven
Cleish
Lochore Meadows
Lochore
Dogton Stone
Thornton
379
DUMGLOW
Cleish Hills
Crosshill
Auchterderran
River Ore
East Wemyss
Loch Ore
Coaltown of Wemyss
Cluny
Loch Glow
Kelty
Glencraig
Cardenden
362
KNOCK HILL
Knockhill
West Wemyss
Lochgelly
Chapel
Gallatown
Dysart
Kirkcaldy
Ravenscraig Castle
Lumphinnans
Loch Gelly
Loch Fitty
Pathhead
227
CRAIGLUSCAR HILL
Kingseat
Hill of Beath
Cowdenbeath
Linktown
Auchtertool
Gowkhall
Townhill
Wellwood
Donibristle
0 1 2 3 4 miles
0 1 2 3 4 5 kilometres
A9
A93
A94
A90
A923
A85
A912
A913
A92
M90
A91
A914
A916
A977
A922
A911
A915
A955
A910
A909
A823
B9112
B935
B953
B996
B919
B920
B921
B922
B9097
B981
B914
B912
B915
B917
B936
B937
B9129
B927
B969
B9130
B9157
B8063
B9099
B867
185
195
196
177

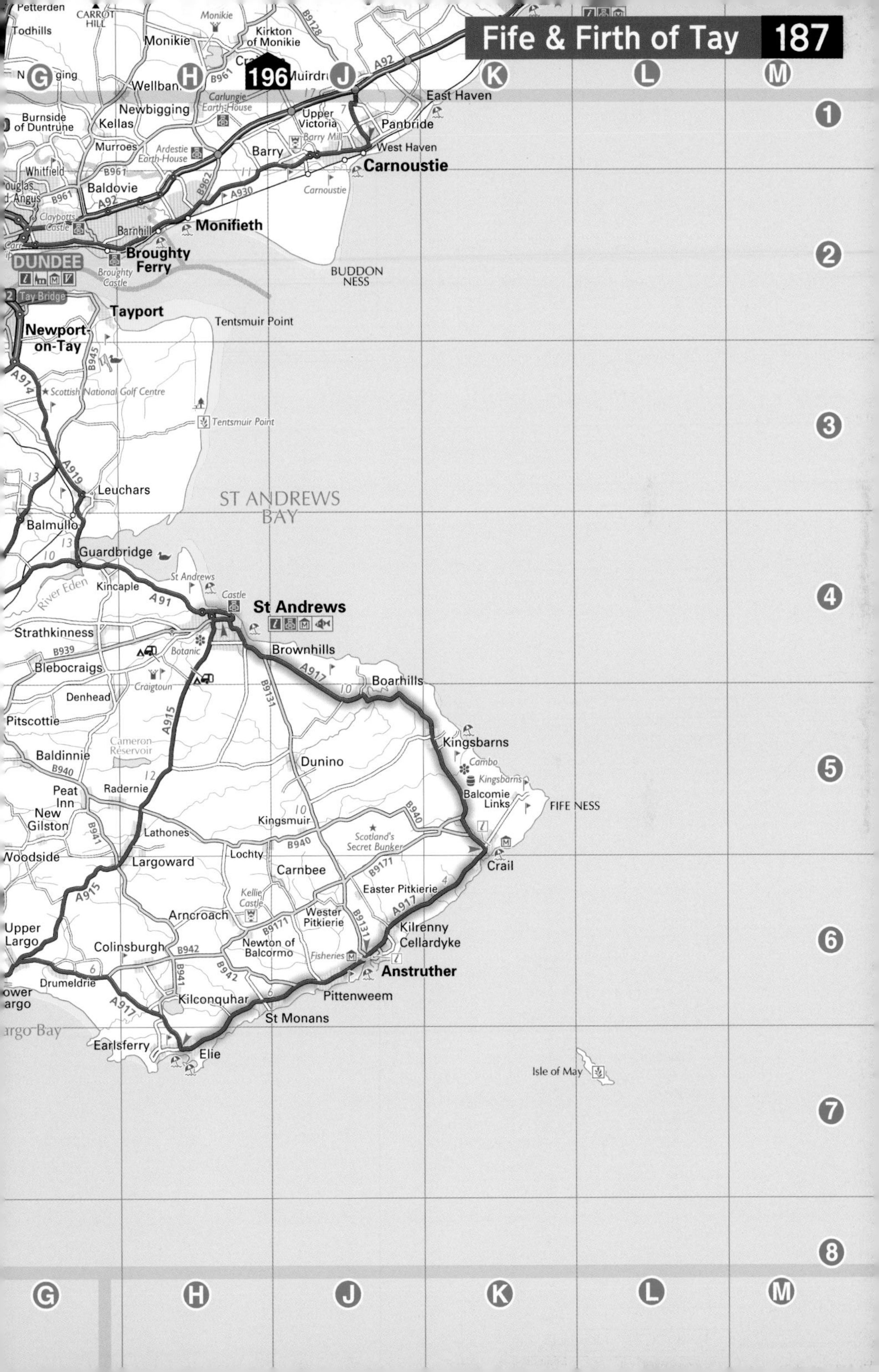

196
G
H
J
K
L
M
1
2
3
4
5
6
7
8
Petterden
CARROT HILL
Todhills
Monikie
Kirkton of Monikie
Wellbank
Newbigging
Burnside of Duntrune
Kellas
Carlungie Earth-House
Upper Victoria
Barry Mill
East Haven
Panbride
West Haven
Murroes
Ardestie Earth-House
Barry
Carnoustie
Whitfield
Baldovie
Claypotts Castle
Barnhill
Monifieth
Broughty Ferry
Broughty Castle
DUNDEE
BUDDON NESS
Tay Bridge
Tayport
Tentsmuir Point
Newport-on-Tay
Scottish National Golf Centre
Leuchars
ST ANDREWS BAY
Balmullo
Guardbridge
River Eden
Kincaple
St Andrews
Castle
Strathkinness
Botanic
Brownhills
Blebocraigs
Craigtoun
Boarhills
Denhead
Pitscottie
Cameron Reservoir
Kingsbarns
Cambo
Dunino
Baldinnie
Radernie
Balcomie Links
FIFE NESS
Peat Inn
New Gilston
Kingsmuir
Lathones
Scotland's Secret Bunker
Woodside
Largoward
Lochty
Crail
Carnbee
Easter Pitkierie
Kellie Castle
Wester Pitkierie
Arncroach
Kilrenny
Cellardyke
Upper Largo
Colinsburgh
Newton of Balcormo
Fisheries
Anstruther
Drumeldrie
Kilconquhar
Pittenweem
St Monans
Earlsferry
Elie
Isle of May
A92
A930
A914
A919
A91
A917
A915
B961
B962
B9128
B945
B939
B940
B941
B942
B9131
B9171

A
B
C
D
E
F
1
2
3
4
5
6
7
8
Arna
Grishipoll
Clabhach
Hogh Bay
Ballyhaugh
Totronald
Coll
Feall Bay
Arileod
Acha
Uig
Calgary Point
Crossapol Bay
Rudha Fasachd
Gunna
Loch Breachacha
Bagh a Chaisteil (Castlebay)
(Apr-Oct, Weds only)
Rudha Dubh
Caoles
Ruaig
B8069
Rudha Port Bhiosd
Clachan Mor
Balephetrish Bay
Loch Bhasapoll
Haugh Bay
Ballevullin
Cornoigmore
B8068
Kenovay
Gott Bay
Tiree
Kilkenneth
Moss
Heylipoll
B8065
Scarinish
Middleton
Crossapol
TIREE
Hynish Bay
Barrapoll
Loch a Phuill
B8067
Balemartine
Mannel
Rinn Thorbhais
Balephuil Bay
Hynish
0 1 2 3 4 miles
0 1 2 3 4 5 kilometres

198
Eilean nan Each
MUCK
Port Mor
Sanna Point
Sanna Bay
Sanna Bay
Portuairk
Achnaha
Kilmory
Ockle Point
Ockle
Branault
436
MEALL NAN CON
ARDNAMU
Ardnamurchan Point
Achosnich
B8007
Loch Mudle
342
BEINN NA SEILG
Kilchoan
Ormsaigmore
Mingary
527
BEN HIANT
Ardslignish
Bagh a Chaisteil (Castlebay)
Loch Baghasdail (Lochboisdale)
Eilean Mòr
Rudha Mòr
Rudha Sgor-innis
Bousd
Sorisdale
B8072
COLL
Coll - Oban
Eilean Ornsay
Ardmore Point
190
Auliston Point
Sorne Point
Glengorm Castle
Quinish Point
Tobermory
Calve Island
Caliach Point
292
'S AIRDE BEINN
Dervaig
Achnadrish House
B8073
Calgary
Calgary Bay
A848
444
SPEINNE MÒR
Loch Frisa
Treshnish Point
Ensay
342
CÀRN MÒR
ISLE OF MULL
Rudh' a' Chaoil
Burg
Glen Aros
390
Fanmore
CNOC AN DÀ CHINN
Glenaros House
Fladda
Ballygown
Loch Tuath
Eas Fors
333
BEINN NAN CÀRN
Killiechronan
B8035
Lunga
TRESHNISH ISLES
Gometra
ULVA
Oskamull
B8073
Gruline
Macquarie Mausoleum
Bac Mòr or Dutchmans Cap
Bac Beag
Loch na Keal, Isle of Mull
Eorsa
Loch na Keal
Little Colonsay
591
BEINN A' GH
180
Staffa
Fingal's Cave
Inchkenneth Chapel (ruin)
Balnahard
966
G H J K L M
1 2 3 4 5 6 7 8

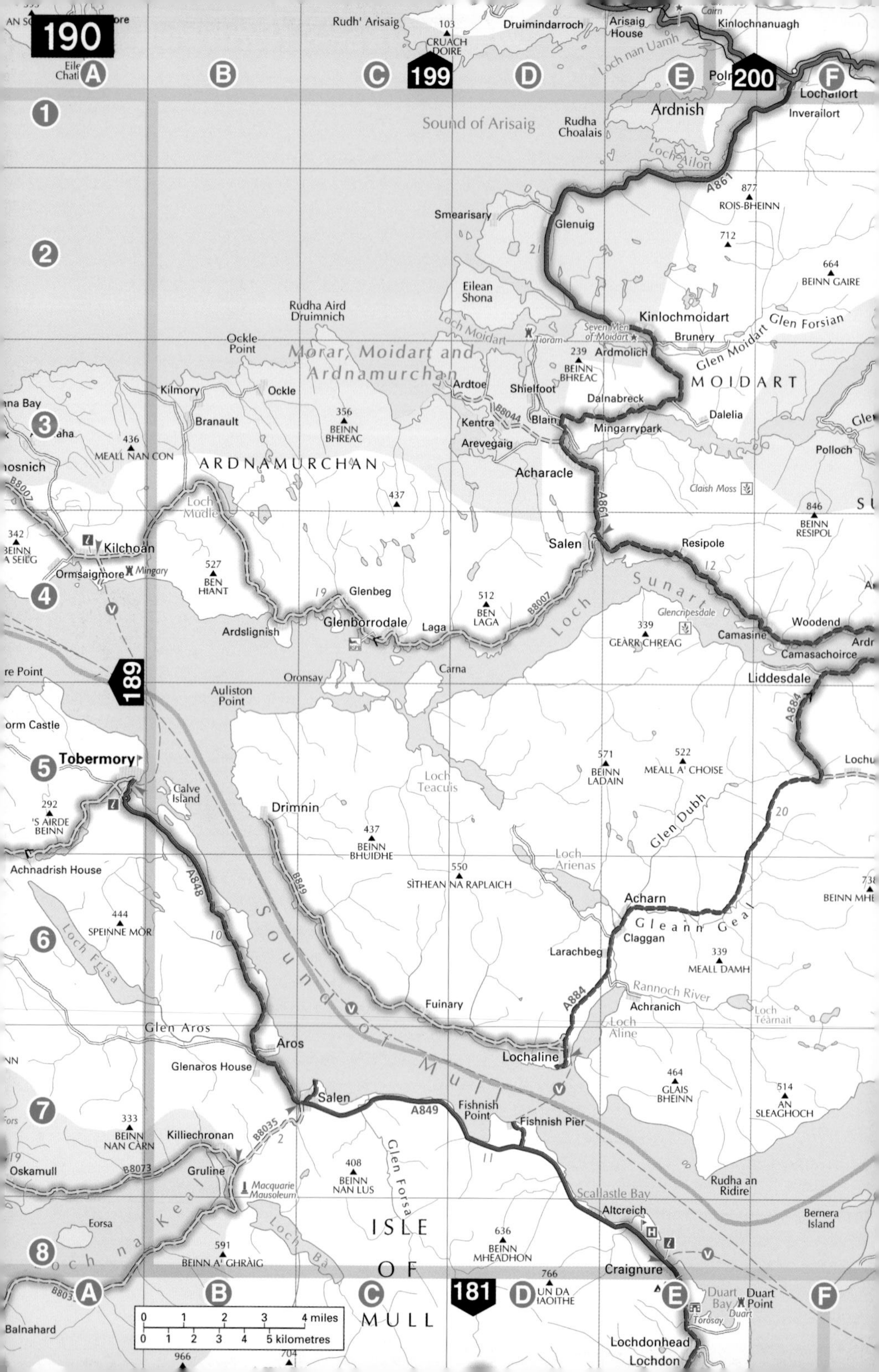

199
200
189
181
Rudh' Arisaig
103
CRUACH DOIRE
Druimindarroch
Arisaig House
Cairn
Kinlochnanuagh
Loch nan Uamh
Lochailort
Inverailort
Ardnish
Sound of Arisaig
Rudha Choalais
Loch Ailort
A861
877
ROIS-BHEINN
712
664
BEINN GAIRE
Smearisary
Glenuig
Eilean Shona
Kinlochmoidart
Glen Forsian
Seven Men of Moidart
Brunery
Glen Moidart
Rudha Aird Druimnich
Loch Moidart
Tioram
239
BEINN BHREAC
Ardmolich
MOIDART
Ockle Point
Morar, Moidart and Ardnamurchan
Ardtoe
Shielfoot
Dalnabreck
Kilmory
Ockle
356
BEINN BHREAC
B8044
Kentra
Blain
Mingarrypark
Dalelia
Branault
Arevegaig
Polloch
436
MEALL NAN CON
ARDNAMURCHAN
Acharacle
Claish Moss
B8007
Loch Mudle
437
846
BEINN RESIPOL
342
Kilchoan
Salen
Resipole
Ormsaigmore
Mingary
527
BEN HIANT
12
19
Glenbeg
512
BEN LAGA
Loch Sunart
Glencripesdale
Glenborrodale
Laga
339
GEÀRR CHREAG
Woodend
Ardslignish
Camasine
Camasachoirce
Carna
Oronsay
Liddesdale
Auliston Point
A884
Tobermory
571
BEINN LADAIN
522
MEALL A' CHOISE
Loch Teacuis
Calve Island
292
'S AIRDE BEINN
Drimnin
Glen Dubh
20
437
BEINN BHUIDHE
Loch Arienas
550
SÌTHEAN NA RAPLAICH
Achnadrish House
A848
B849
Acharn
444
SPEINNE MÒR
Gleann Geal
Claggan
Loch Frisa
10
Sound of Mull
Larachbeg
339
MEALL DAMH
Rannoch River
Achranich
Loch Tèarnait
Fuinary
A884
Loch Aline
Glen Aros
Aros
Lochaline
Glenaros House
464
GLAIS BHEINN
514
AN SLEAGHOCH
Salen
A849
Fishnish Point
Fishnish Pier
333
BEINN NAN CARN
Killiechronan
B8035
Glen Forsa
11
Oskamull
B8073
Gruline
408
BEINN NAN LUS
Macquarie Mausoleum
Rudha an Ridire
Scallastle Bay
Altcreich
Eorsa
Loch na Keal
Loch Bà
ISLE OF MULL
636
BEINN MHEADHON
Bernera Island
591
BEINN A' GHRÀIG
Craignure
766
Duart Bay
Duart Point
Torosay
B8035
Balnahard
0 1 2 3 4 miles
0 1 2 3 4 5 kilometres
Lochdonhead
Lochdon
966
704

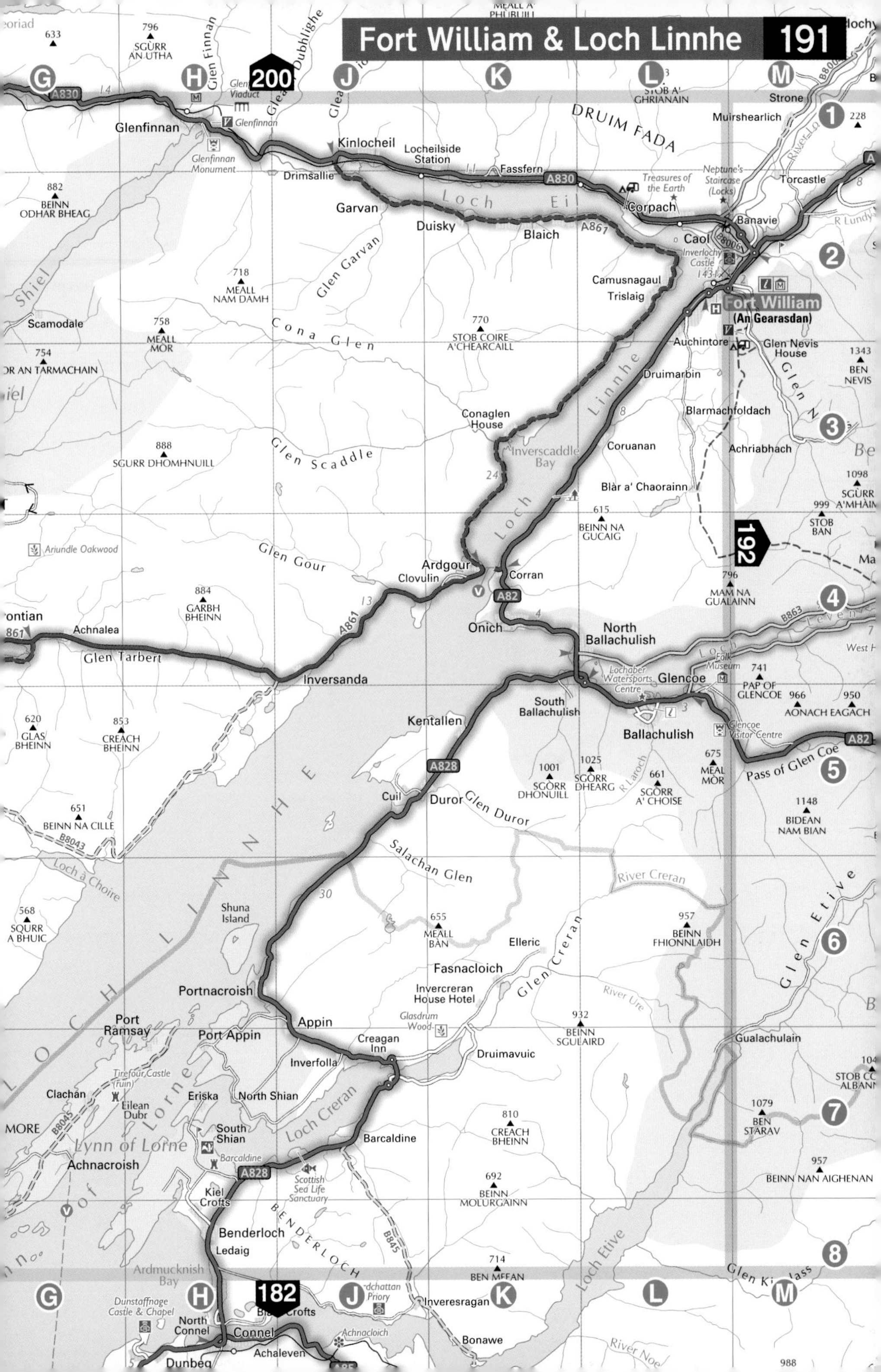
200
192
182
G H J K L M
1 2 3 4 5 6 7 8
Glenfinnan
Glenfinnan Viaduct
Glenfinnan Monument
Glen Finnan
A830
Kinlocheil
Locheilside Station
Fassfern
Drimsallie
DRUIM FADA
STOB A' GHRIANAIN
Strone
Muirshearlich
228
Treasures of the Earth
Neptune's Staircase (Locks)
Torcastle
Corpach
Banavie
Caol
Inverlochy Castle
B8006
Loch Eil
Garvan
Duisky
Blaich
A861
882 BEINN ODHAR BHEAG
Glen Garvan
718 MEALL NAM DAMH
Camusnagaul
Trislaig
Fort William (An Gearasdan)
Shiel
Scamodale
758 MEALL MÒR
754
Cona Glen
770 STOB COIRE A'CHEARCAILL
Auchintore
Glen Nevis House
1343 BEN NEVIS
Glen Nevis
Druimarbin
Blarmachfoldach
Conaglen House
Inverscaddle Bay
Loch Linnhe
Coruanan
Achriabhach
888 SGURR DHOMHNUILL
Glen Scaddle
Blàr a' Chaorainn
1098 SGÙRR A'MHÀIM
999 STOB BAN
615 BEINN NA GUCAIG
Ariundle Oakwood
Glen Gour
Ardgour
Clovulin
Corran
796 MAM NA GUALAINN
884 GARBH BHEINN
A82
Onich
North Ballachulish
B863
Achnalea
Glen Tarbert
Inversanda
Lochaber Watersports Centre
Folk Museum
Glencoe
741 PAP OF GLENCOE
966 AONACH EAGACH
950
South Ballachulish
Ballachulish
Glencoe Visitor Centre
620 GLAS BHEINN
853 CREACH BHEINN
Kentallen
A828
1001 SGÒRR DHONUILL
1025 SGÒRR DHEARG
661 SGÒRR A' CHOISE
675 MEALL MÒR
Pass of Glen Coe
Cuil
Duror
Glen Duror
1148 BIDEAN NAM BIAN
651 BEINN NA CILLE
B8043
Salachan Glen
River Creran
Loch a' Choire
568 SGURR A BHUIC
Shuna Island
655 MEALL BÀN
957 BEINN FHIONNLAIDH
Elleric
Glen Etive
Fasnacloich
Glen Creran
Portnacroish
Invercreran House Hotel
River Ure
Port Ramsay
Appin
Glasdrum Wood
932 BEINN SGULAIRD
Port Appin
Creagan Inn
Gualachulain
Druimavuic
Tirefour Castle (ruin)
Inverfolla
Clachan
Eriska
North Shian
Eilean Dubh
1079 BEN STARAV
810 CREACH BHEINN
South Shian
Loch Creran
Barcaldine
Lynn of Lorne
Achnacroish
Scottish Sea Life Sanctuary
692 BEINN MOLURGAINN
957 BEINN NAN AIGHENAN
B8045
LOCH LINNHE
Kiel Crofts
BENDERLOCH
B845
Benderloch
Ledaig
Loch Etive
714 BEN MEEAN
Ardmucknish Bay
Glen Kinglass
Dunstaffnage Castle & Chapel
Ardchattan Priory
Inveresragan
North Connel
Connel
Achnacloich
Bonawe
Dunbeg
Achaleven
River Noe
988

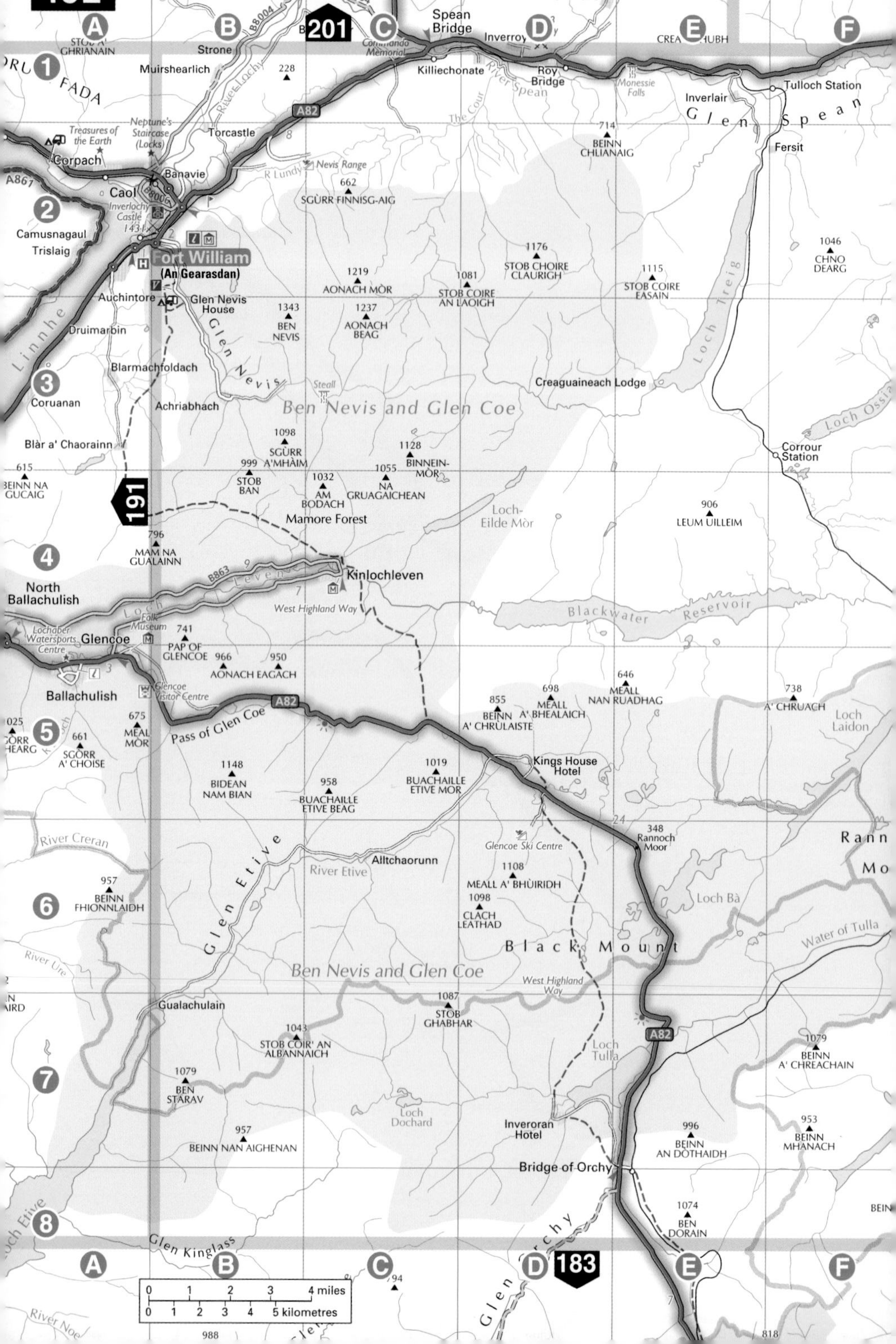

201
191
183
Gairlochy
Stronenaba
CEIRSLE
Bohuntine
1048
BEINN A' CHAORUNN
Spean Bridge
Inverroy
Roy Bridge
STOB A' GHRIANAIN
Strone
B8004
Commando Memorial
Killiechonate
River Spean
Monessie Falls
Inverlair
Tulloch Station
Glen Spean
Muirshearlich
228
River Lochy
A82
Treasures of the Earth
Neptune's Staircase (Locks)
Torcastle
8
The Cour
714
BEINN CHLIANAIG
Fersit
Corpach
Banavie
R Lundy
Nevis Range
A861
Caol
B8006
Inverlochy Castle 1431
662
SGÙRR FINNISG-AIG
Camusnagaul
Trislaig
Fort William
(An Gearasdan)
1176
STOB CHOIRE CLAURIGH
1046
CHNO DEARG
1219
AONACH MÒR
1081
STOB COIRE AN LAOIGH
1115
STOB COIRE EASAIN
Loch Treig
Auchintore
Glen Nevis House
1343
BEN NEVIS
1237
AONACH BEAG
Druimarbin
Loch Linnhe
Glen Nevis
Blarmachfoldach
Coruanan
Achriabhach
Steall
Creaguaineach Lodge
Ben Nevis and Glen Coe
Loch Ossian
Blàr a' Chaorainn
1098
SGÙRR A'MHÀIM
1128
BINNEIN MÒR
Corrour Station
615
BEINN NA GUCAIG
999
STOB BAN
1032
AM BODACH
1055
NA GRUAGAICHEAN
Mamore Forest
Loch Eilde Mòr
906
LEUM UILLEIM
796
MAM NA GUALAINN
North Ballachulish
B863
Loch Leven
Kinlochleven
West Highland Way
Blackwater Reservoir
Lochaber Watersports Centre
Glencoe
Folk Museum
741
PAP OF GLENCOE
966
AONACH EAGACH
950
Ballachulish
Glencoe Visitor Centre
Pass of Glen Coe
698
MEALL A' BHEALAICH
646
MEALL NAN RUADHAG
855
BEINN A' CHRÙLAISTE
738
A' CHRUACH
Loch Laidon
1025
SGORR DHEARG
675
MEALL MÒR
661
SGORR A' CHOISE
1148
BIDEAN NAM BIAN
958
BUACHAILLE ETIVE BEAG
1019
BUACHAILLE ETIVE MOR
Kings House Hotel
348
Rannoch Moor
24
River Creran
Glen Etive
Alltchaorunn
River Etive
Glencoe Ski Centre
957
BEINN FHIONNLAIDH
1108
MEALL A' BHÙIRIDH
1098
CLACH LEATHAD
Loch Bà
Black Mount
Water of Tulla
River Ure
Ben Nevis and Glen Coe
West Highland Way
Gualachulain
1087
STOB GHABHAR
1043
STOB COIR' AN ALBANNAICH
Loch Tulla
1079
BEINN A' CHREACHAIN
1079
BEN STARAV
Loch Dochard
Inveroran Hotel
957
BEINN NAN AIGHENAN
996
BEINN AN DOTHAIDH
953
BEINN MHANACH
Bridge of Orchy
Loch Etive
1074
BEN DORAIN
Glen Kinglass
Glen Orchy
River Noe
988
818
794
0 1 2 3 4 miles
0 1 2 3 4 5 kilometres

A86
G
H
J
K
L
M
202
194
184
747 BINNEIN SHUAS
1049 GEAL CHÀRN
896 MEALL CRUAIDH
769 CREAGAN MOR
94 CÀRN NA CAIM
Loch an Dùin
1
Loch Pattack
1088 BEINN A' CHLACHAIR
1034 CÀRN DEARG
975 A' MHARCONAICH
459 Drumochter Summit
926 GLAS MHEALL MOR
2
Loch Ericht
1101 BEINN EIBHINN
1008 BEINN UDLAMAIN
991 SGAIRNEACH MHOR
Dalnaspidal
1145 BEN ALDER
Loch Garry
20
Glen Garry
Dalnacardoch
3
844 MEALL A'BHEALAICH
952 SGÒR GAIBHRE
Loch Con
626 SRON A CHLAONAIDH
841 BEINN MHOLACH
Loch Errochty
864 BEINN PHARIAGAIN
Trinafour
B847
Glen Errochty
14
511 TORR DUBH
4
892 BEINN A' CHUALLAICH
Tay Forest Park
R Ericht
7
B846
Rannoch Station
Bridge of Ericht
Killichonan
Tay Forest Park
16
Kinloch Rannoch
Drumchastle
Dunalastair
R Tummel
Tummel Bridge
Dunan
B846
Finnart
Loch Rannoch
Inverhadden
Tempar
Dunalastair Water
Loch Eigheach
Bridge of Gaur
Carie
Camghouran
5
Tay Forest Park
1081 SCHIEHALLION
Glengoulandie Deer Park
Loch Rannoch and Glen Lyon
B846
1042 CÀRN MAIRG
745 MEALL A' MHUIC
1027 CÀRN GORM
931 MEALL BUIDHE
824 BEINN DEARG
860 CAM CHREAG
6
Fortingall
Tay Forest Park
Loch an Daimh
Glen Lyon
River Lyon
Bridge of Balgie
Kenmore
Fearnan
Acharn
924 MEALL A' CHOIRE LEITH
1116 MEALL GARBH
1000 MEALL GREIGH
780 MEALL LUAIDHE
7
908 BEINN NAN OIGHREAG
1214 BEN LAWERS
Lochan na Làirige
Leckbuie
713 BEINN BHREAC
1038 MEALL GHAORDIE
Ben Lawers
Lawers
25
A827
Loch Tay
8
SRÒN A' C
Milton Morenish
River Lochay
Falls of Lochay
Glen Lochay
Ardeonaig
Finlarig
Killin

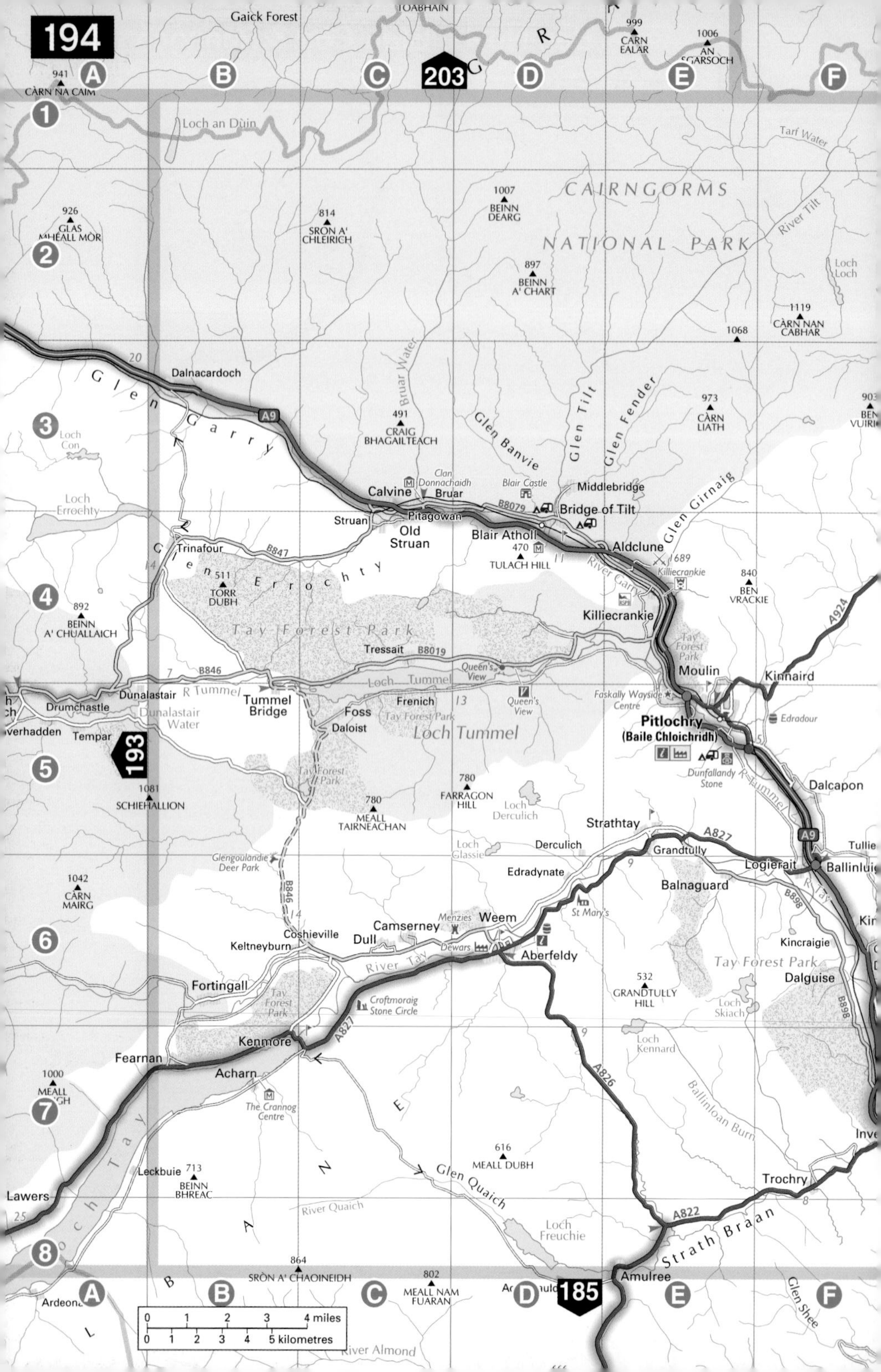
Gaick Forest
TOABHAIN
203
999 CARN EALAR
1006 AN SGARSOCH
941 CÀRN NA CAIM
Loch an Dùin
Tarf Water
CAIRNGORMS NATIONAL PARK
1007 BEINN DEARG
926 GLAS MHEALL MÒR
814 SRON A' CHLEIRICH
River Tilt
Loch Loch
897 BEINN A' CHART
1119 CÀRN NAN CABHAR
1068
20
Dalnacardoch
Glen Garry
A9
Bruar Water
491 CRAIG BHAGAILTEACH
Glen Banvie
Glen Tilt
Glen Fender
973 CÀRN LIATH
903 BEN VUIRICH
Loch Con
Loch Errochty
Clan Donnachaidh
Calvine
Bruar
Blair Castle
Middlebridge
B8079
Bridge of Tilt
Glen Girnaig
Struan
Pitagowan
Old Struan
Blair Atholl
Aldclune
Trinafour
B847
470 TULACH HILL
1689
Killiecrankie
840 BEN VRACKIE
Glen Errochty
14
511 TORR DUBH
River Garry
892 BEINN A' CHUALLAICH
Killiecrankie
A924
Tay Forest Park
Tressait
B8019
Tay Forest Park
Moulin
Kinnaird
B846
7
Queen's View
Loch Tummel
R Tummel
Dunalastair
Tummel Bridge
Frenich
13
Queen's View
Faskally Wayside Centre
Drumchastle
Dunalastair Water
Foss
Tay Forest Park
Pitlochry
(Baile Chloichridh)
Edradour
Kinloch Rannoch
Daloist
Loch Tummel
Tempar
193
5
Tay Forest Park
Dunfallandy Stone
R Tummel
Dalcapon
780 FARRAGON HILL
1081 SCHIEHALLION
780 MEALL TAIRNEACHAN
Loch Derculich
Strathtay
A827
A9
Tullie
Loch Glassie
Derculich
Grandtully
Logierait
Ballinluig
Glengoulandie Deer Park
Edradynate
9
Balnaguard
B898
R Tay
1042 CÀRN MAIRG
B846
St Mary's
14
Menzies
Weem
Camserney
Coshieville
Dull
Keltneyburn
Dewars
Aberfeldy
Kincraigie
River Tay
Tay Forest Park
Fortingall
532 GRANDTULLY HILL
Dalguise
Tay Forest Park
Croftmoraig Stone Circle
A827
Loch Skiach
B898
Kenmore
Loch Kennard
9
Fearnan
Acharn
A826
1000 MEALL
The Crannog Centre
Ballinloan Burn
Loch Tay
616 MEALL DUBH
Glen Quaich
713 BEINN BHREAC
Leckbuie
Trochry
Lawers
River Quaich
A822
8
25
Loch Freuchie
Strath Braan
864 SRÒN A' CHAOINEIDH
802 MEALL NAM FUARAN
Amulree
185
Glen Shee
Ardeonaig
BREADALBANE
0 1 2 3 4 miles
0 1 2 3 4 5 kilometres
River Almond
A B C D E F
1 2 3 4 5 6 7 8

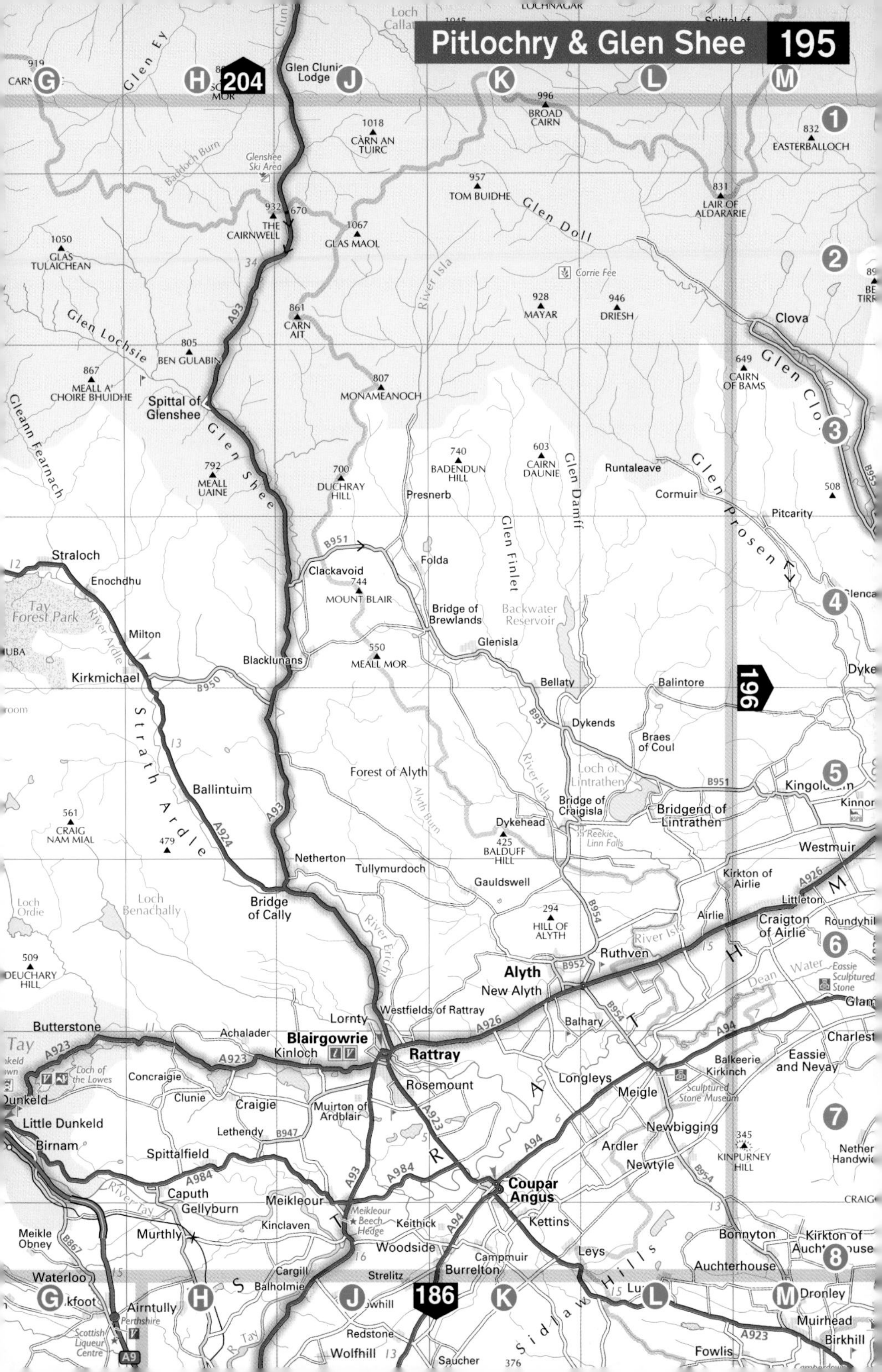

Glen Ey
Glen Clunie Lodge
204
BROAD CAIRN
EASTERBALLOCH
CÀRN AN TUIRC
Glenshee Ski Area
Baddoch Burn
TOM BUIDHE
Glen Doll
LAIR OF ALDARARIE
THE CAIRNWELL
GLAS MAOL
GLAS TULAICHEAN
Corrie Fee
River Isla
MAYAR
DRIESH
Clova
CARN AIT
Glen Lochsie
BEN GULABIN
MEALL A' CHOIRE BHUIDHE
Spittal of Glenshee
MONAMEANOCH
CAIRN OF BAMS
Glen Clova
Gleann Fearnach
Glen Shee
MEALL UAINE
DUCHRAY HILL
BADENDUN HILL
CAIRN DAUNIE
Glen Damff
Runtaleave
Cormuir
Glen Prosen
Presnerb
Pitcarity
Glen Finlet
Straloch
Folda
Enochdhu
Clackavoid
MOUNT BLAIR
Tay Forest Park
River Ardle
Bridge of Brewlands
Backwater Reservoir
Milton
Glenisla
MEALL MOR
Blacklunans
Kirkmichael
Bellaty
Balintore
196
Strath Ardle
Dykends
Braes of Coul
Forest of Alyth
Alyth Burn
Loch of Lintrathen
Kingoldrum
Ballintuim
Bridge of Craigisla
Bridgend of Lintrathen
CRAIG NAM MIAL
Dykehead
Reekie Linn Falls
BALDUFF HILL
Westmuir
Netherton
Tullymurdoch
Gauldswell
Kirkton of Airlie
Littleton
Loch Ordie
Loch Benachally
Bridge of Cally
River Ericht
HILL OF ALYTH
Airlie
Craigton of Airlie
Roundyhill
River Isla
DEUCHARY HILL
Ruthven
Alyth
New Alyth
Dean Water
Eassie Sculptured Stone
Westfields of Rattray
Lornty
Balhary
Butterstone
Achalader
Blairgowrie
Kinloch
Rattray
Charleston
Loch of the Lowes
Concraigie
Rosemount
Balkeerie
Kirkinch
Eassie and Nevay
Longleys
Meigle
Sculptured Stone Museum
Dunkeld
Clunie
Craigie
Muirton of Ardblair
Little Dunkeld
Lethendy
Newbigging
Birnam
Ardler
Spittalfield
KINPURNEY HILL
Nether Handwick
Newtyle
River Tay
Caputh
Gellyburn
Meikleour
Coupar Angus
Meikleour Beech Hedge
Keithick
Kettins
Meikle Obney
Kinclaven
Murthly
Woodside
Bonnyton
Kirkton of Auchterhouse
Campmuir
Leys
Cargill
Burrelton
Auchterhouse
Waterloo
Strelitz
Balholmie
186
Sidlaw Hills
Dronley
Airntully
Perthshire
Scottish Liqueur Centre
Redstone
Muirhead
Birkhill
Wolfhill
Saucher
Fowlis

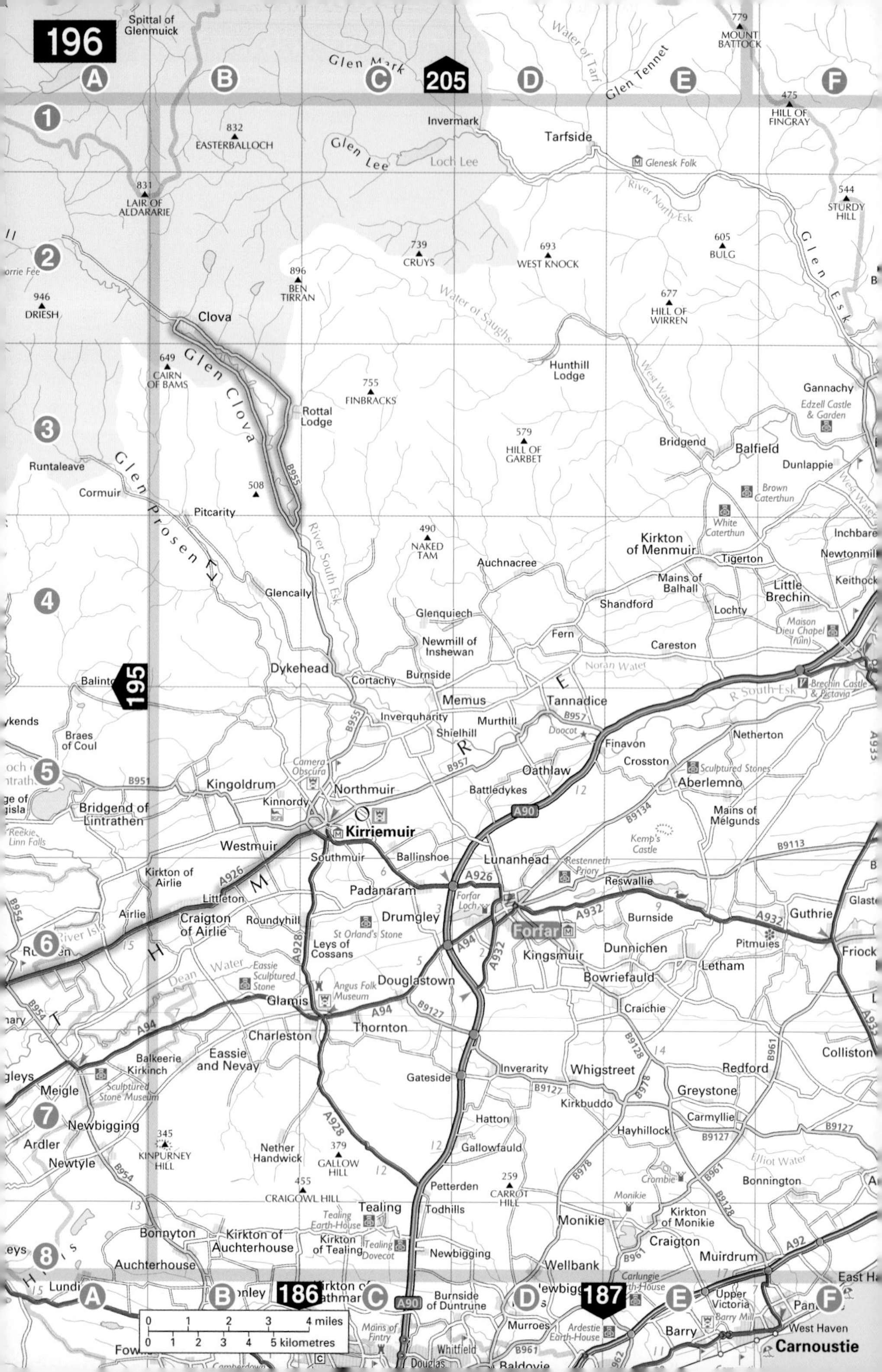

Spittal of Glenmuick
Glen Mark
205
779 MOUNT BATTOCK
Water of Tarf
Glen Tennet
A B C D E F
1
475 HILL OF FINGRAY
832 EASTERBALLOCH
Invermark
Tarfside
Glen Lee
Loch Lee
Glenesk Folk
831 LAIR OF ALDARARIE
River North Esk
544 STURDY HILL
2
Corrie Fee
739 CRUYS
693 WEST KNOCK
605 BULG
896 BEN TIRRAN
946 DRIESH
Water of Saughs
677 HILL OF WIRREN
Glen Esk
Clova
649 CAIRN OF BAMS
Glen Clova
755 FINBRACKS
Hunthill Lodge
West Water
Gannachy
Edzell Castle & Garden
Rottal Lodge
3
579 HILL OF GARBET
Bridgend
Balfield
Runtaleave
Glen Prosen
Dunlappie
Brown Caterthun
Cormuir
508
B955
Pitcarity
White Caterthun
River South Esk
490 NAKED TAM
Kirkton of Menmuir
Inchbare
Tigerton
Newtonmill
Auchnacree
Mains of Balhall
Keithock
Little Brechin
4
Glencally
Shandford
Glenquiech
Lochty
Maison Dieu Chapel (ruin)
Fern
Newmill of Inshewan
Careston
Dykehead
Noran Water
Burnside
Cortachy
Balintore
195
Brechin Castle & Pictavia
R South Esk
Memus
Tannadice
Inverquharity
Murthill
Kenny Kends
B957
Shielhill
Braes of Coul
Netherton
Doocot
Finavon
Crosston
5
Camera Obscura
B957
Sculptured Stones
Aberlemno
Loch of Lintrathen
B951
Oathlaw
Kingoldrum
Northmuir
Battledykes
Loch of Kinnordy
12
Mains of Melgunds
Bridgend of Lintrathen
A90
B9134
Kirriemuir
Reekie Linn Falls
Kemp's Castle
Westmuir
B9113
Southmuir
Ballinshoe
Lunanhead
Restenneth Priory
Kirkton of Airlie
A926
A926
Reswallie
Padanaram
Littleton
Forfar Loch
A932
Airlie
Drumgley
Burnside
Guthrie
Craigton of Airlie
Roundyhill
A932
B954
Forfar
St Orland's Stone
Pitmuies
6
River Isla
Ruthven
Leys of Cossans
Kingsmuir
Dunnichen
Friock
A94
A928
Letham
Dean Water
Eassie Sculptured Stone
A932
Bowriefauld
Douglastown
Angus Folk Museum
Glamis
Craichie
A94
B9127
B954
A94
Charleston
Thornton
Eassie and Nevay
B961
B9128
Colliston
Balkeerie Kirkinch
Inverarity
Whigstreet
Redford
Meigle
Gateside
Sculptured Stone Museum
B9127
Kirkbuddo
Greystone
B978
7
A928
Hatton
Carmyllie
Newbigging
Hayhillock
B9127
B9127
Ardler
345 KINPURNEY HILL
Nether Handwick
379 GALLOW HILL
Gallowfauld
Elliot Water
Newtyle
B954
Crombie
B961
Bonnington
Petterden
455 CRAIGOWL HILL
259 CARROT HILL
B978
Monikie
13
Tealing
Todhills
B9128
Kirkton of Monikie
Tealing Earth-House
Monikie
Bonnyton
Kirkton of Auchterhouse
Kirkton of Tealing
Tealing Dovecot
Craigton
A92
8
Newbigging
B961
Muirdrum
Auchterhouse
Wellbank
Carlungie Earth-House
East Haven
Lundie
186
187
Kirkton of Strathmartine
Burnside of Duntrune
Upper Victoria
Barry Mill
Panbride
A90
0 1 2 3 4 miles
0 1 2 3 4 5 kilometres
Mains of Fintry
Murroes
Ardestie Earth-House
Barry
West Haven
Carnoustie
Fowlis
Whitfield
B961
Douglas
Baldovie

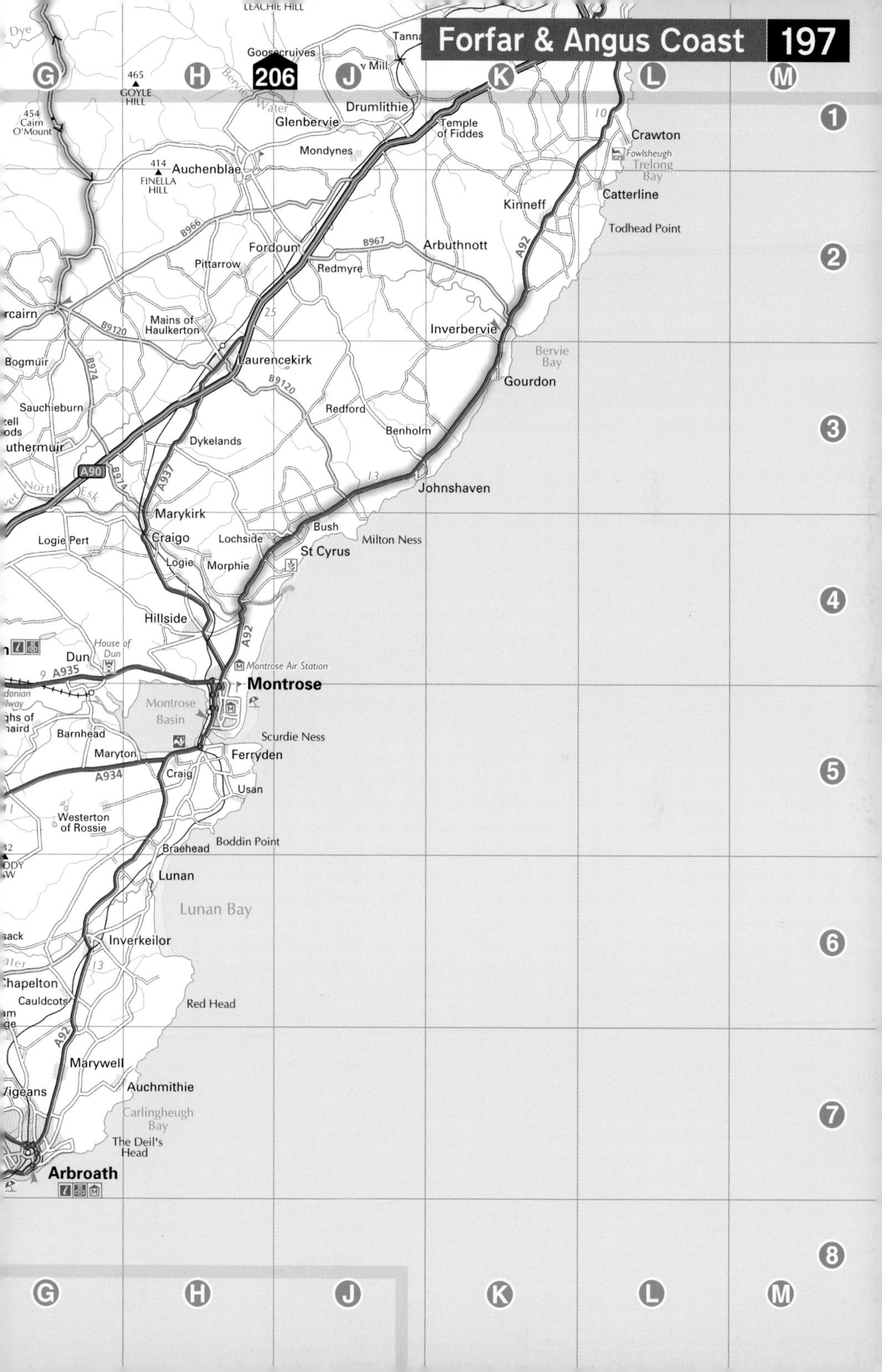
LEACHIE HILL
Dye
Goosecruives
206
Tanna
Mill
G
H
J
K
L
M
465
GOYLE HILL
454
Cairn O'Mount
Bervie Water
Drumlithie
Glenbervie
Temple of Fiddes
Crawton
Fowlsheugh
Trelong Bay
Mondynes
414
Auchenblae
FINELLA HILL
Catterline
Kinneff
Todhead Point
B966
Fordoun
B967
Arbuthnott
A92
Pittarrow
Redmyre
Mains of Haulkerton
B9120
Inverbervie
Bervie Bay
Bogmuir
B974
Laurencekirk
Gourdon
Sauchieburn
Redford
Benholm
Dykelands
A90
A937
Johnshaven
North Esk
Marykirk
Bush
Logie Pert
Craigo
Lochside
Milton Ness
St Cyrus
Logie
Morphie
Hillside
House of Dun
Dun
A935
Montrose Air Station
Montrose
Montrose Basin
Barnhead
Scurdie Ness
Maryton
Ferryden
A934
Craig
Usan
Westerton of Rossie
Braehead
Boddin Point
Lunan
Lunan Bay
Inverkeilor
Chapelton
Cauldcots
Red Head
Marywell
Auchmithie
Vigeans
Carlingheugh Bay
The Deil's Head
Arbroath
1
2
3
4
5
6
7
8

Talisker Bay
Talisker
Glen Eynort
Minginish
447
BEINN BHREAC
208
Loch Eynort
434
AN CRUACHIN
Glenbrittle House
Bualintur
Loch Brittle
Rudh' an Dùnain
Loch Baghasdail (Lochboisdale)
CANNA
210
CÀRN A' GHAILL
Garrisdale Point
A'Chill
Canna Harbour
Sanday
Sound of Canna
Kilmory Bay
Rudha Shamhnan Insir
302
MULLACH MÒR
A Bhrideanach
570
ORVAL
Kinlo
Oigh-sgeir
RÙM
Harris Bay
810
ASKIVAL
763
SGÙRR NAN GILLEAN
The Small Isles
Rudha nam Meirleach
Sound
Eilean nan Each
189
MU
A B C D E F
1 2 3 4 5 6 7 8
0 1 2 3 4 miles
0 1 2 3 4 5 kilometres

Sligachan
GLAMAIG
REAC
A87
Loch Ainort
Dunan
Luib
396
MULLACH NA CARN
209
G
H
J
K
L
M
ISLE OF SKYE
27
Pabay
(Caol Loch Aillse)
Skye Bridge
Kyleakin
1
A87
564
GLAS BHEIN MHÒRN
965
SGURR NAN GILLEAN
Scalpay
Corry
Broadford Bay
Waterloo
Lower Breakish
Upper Breakish
Broadford
Harrapool
Skulamus
974
SGURR ALASDAIR
The Cuillin Hills
Cuillin Hills
1009
SGÙRR ALASDAIR
708
BEINN DEORG MHÒR
732
BEINN NA CAILLICH
B8083
732
SGURR NA COINNICH
Otter Haven
927
BLAVEN
Loch na Crèitheach
Loch Coruisk
Torrin
14
A851
2
605
BEN ASLAK
894
GARS BHEINN
Kirkibost
B8083
Loch Slapin
300
BEINN NAN CARN
Heast
561
BEINN NA SEAMRAIG
344
BEN MEABOST
139
BEINN BHREAC
Loch Scavaig
Suisnish
Rudha Suisnish
Loch Eishort
Drumfearn
Loch na Dal
Sandaig Island
3
Elgol
Mol-chlach
Glasnakille
SOAY
298
SGORACH BREAC
Duisdalemore
Isleornsay
Ornsay
Tokavaig
Ord River
Strathaird Point
Rudha Buidhe
17
Tarskavaig
Tarskavaig Bay
Achnacloich
Loch nam Uamph
Teangue
Knock
Rudh' Ard Slisneach
SOUND OF SLEAT
Ferrindonald
Kilmore
Knock Bay
Inverguseran
4
Kilbeg
Armadale Castle
Clan Donald
A851
Airor
200
Glen Guseran
Ardvasar
Armadale
Calligarry
518
DRUIM NA CLUAIN-AIRIDHE
SOUND
Sandaig
Aird of Sleat
Sandaig Bay
5
Inverie
Roinne
Ard Thurinish
Point of Sleat
Inverie Bay
Rudha Raonuill
Courteachan
Mallaig
(Malaig)
Mallaigvaig
547
CÀRN A'GHOBHAIR
Glasnacardoch Bay
Loch an Nostaire
437
SGÙRR BHUIDHE
Loch Nevis
6
Beoraidbeg
Morar
Bracora
Bracorina
Tarbet
Swordland
B8008
Glenancross
Loch Morar
A830
503
CÀRN A' MHÀDAIDH-RUAIDH
Lettermorar
Bay of Laig
Cleadale
299
AN CRUACHAN
Laig
Eilean Ighe
Bunacaimb
7
Back of Keppoch
600
SIDHEAN MOR
EIGG
Luinga Mhòr
Arisaig
Loch nan Ceall
Prince Charlie's Cairn
Kildonnan
10
393
AN SGÙRR
Sandavore
Rudh' Arisaig
103
CRUACH DOIRE
Druimindarroch
Arisaig House
Kinlochnanuagh
Loch nan Uamh
Eilean Chathastail
Polnish
8
Lochailort
190
Arisaig
Rudha Choalais
Ardnish
Inveraliort
Loch Ailort
A861
877

Badicaul
Balmacara
Kyle of Lochalsh
(Caol Loch Aillse)
Pabay
Skye Bridge
Auchtertyre
Conchra
Loch Long
Camas Luinie
Glen Elchaig
River Elchaig
SGUMAN COINNTICH
Nostie
Bund
Carndu
210
Kirkton
Lochalsh Woodland Garden
Ardelve
Eilean Donan
Dornie
Kyleakin
A87
Loch Alsh
Lower Breakish
Upper Breakish
Keppoch
Letterfearn
Loch Duich
840
SGÙRR AN AIRGID
Inverinate
916
A'GHLAS-BHEINN
Morvich
732
SGURR NA COINNICH
Otter Haven
Kyle Rhea
603
BEINN A'CHUIRN
Bernera
Galltair
Carn-gorm
Ratagan
Ault a' chruinn
Invershiel
Shiel Bridge
A85
Kylerhea
(Apr-Oct)
Glenelg Bay
Glenelg
605
BEN ASLAK
408
BEINN A' CHAOINICH
350
Mam Ratagan
Moyle
Eilanreach
Kintail
FIVE SISTERS
1068
SGÙRR FHUARAN
561
BEINN NA SEAMRAIG
Glenelg Brochs
Glean Beag
Balvraid
Glen Shiel
Loch na Dal
Sandaig Island
1719
Isleornsay
Ornsay
974
BEINN SGRITHEAL
773
BEINN NAN CAORACH
1011
THE SADDLE
945
SGURR NA SGINE
SOUND OF SLEAT
Rudha Buidhe
Arnisdale
Loch Hourn
Glen Arnisdale
Rudh' Ard Slisneach
Corran
614
709
DRUM FADA
Knock
Kinloch Hourn
Inverguseran
784
BEINN NA CAILLICH
Barrisdale Bay
1026
SGURR A MHAORAICH
Glen Guseran
199
1019
LADHAR BHEINN
518
DRUIM NA CLUAIN-AIRIDHE
Knoydart
KNOYDART
Sandaig
940
LUINNE BHEINN
Loch
Sandaig Bay
Inverie
Loch an Dubh-Lochain
Inverie Bay
Rudha Raonuill
1003
SGURR MÒR
Mallaigvaig
547
CÀRN A'GHOBHAIR
854
BEINN BHUIDHE
1039
SGURR NA CICHE
Loch Nevis
Loch an Nostaire
437
SGURR BHUIDHE
879
SGURR MHURLAGAN
859
SGURR NAH-AIDE
Glen Dessarry
Morar
Bracorina
Bracora
Kylesmorar
Tarbet
723
SGURR BREAC
Murlaggan
Swordland
Loch Morar
Glen Pean
Lettermorar
716
AN STAC
503
CÀRN A' DAIDH-RUAIDH
Meoble
949
SGURR NAN COIREACHAN
964
SGÙRR THUILM
983
GULVAIN
710
MEITH BHEINN
960
600
SIDHEAN MÒR
River Meoble
Prince Charlie's Cairn
Loch Beoriad
Arisaig House
Kinlochnanuagh
633
796
SGÙRR AN UTHA
Glen Finnan
Gleann Dubhlighe
Gleann Fionnlighe
Polnish
Lochailort
A830
Glenfinnan Viaduct
Loch Eilt
Glenfinnan
190
191
Rudha Choalais
Kinlocheil
Locheilside Station
Glenfinnan Monument
Drimsallie
A861
877
882
0 1 2 3 4 miles
0 1 2 3 4 5 kilometres

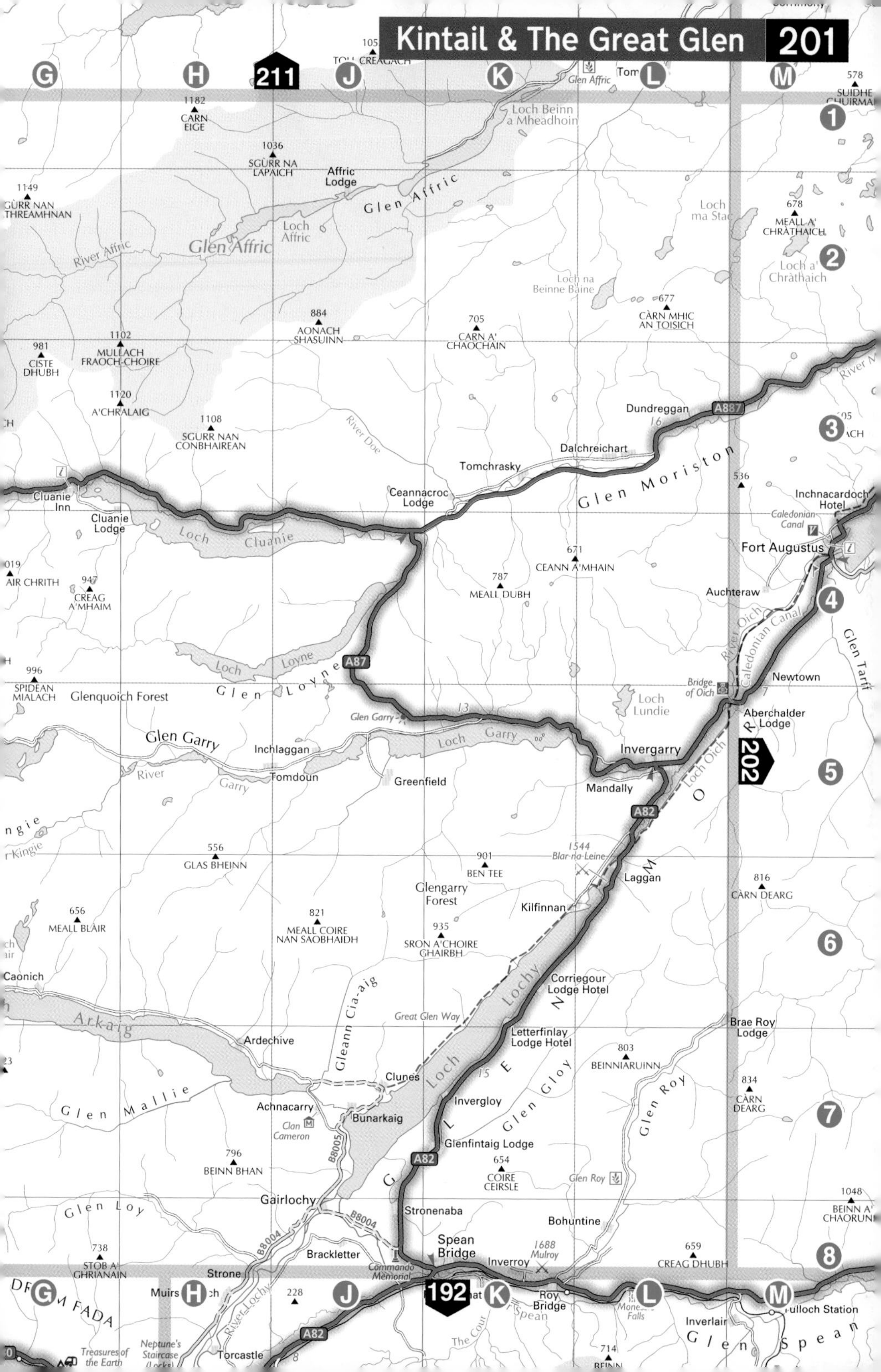
G
H
211
J
K
L
M
1
2
3
4
5
6
7
8
1182
CARN EIGE
1036
SGURR NA LAPAICH
Affric Lodge
Glen Affric
Loch Beinn a Mheadhoin
Tom
578
SUIDHE CHUIRMA
1149
GÙRR NAN THREAMHNAN
River Affric
Loch Affric
Glen Affric
Loch ma Stac
678
MEALL A' CHRÀTHAICH
Loch a' Chràthaich
Loch na Beinne Baine
677
CÀRN MHIC AN TOISICH
884
AONACH SHASUINN
705
CARN A' CHAOCHAIN
981
CISTE DHUBH
1102
MULLACH FRAOCH-CHOIRE
1120
A'CHRALAIG
1108
SGURR NAN CONBHAIREAN
River Doe
Dundreggan
A887
16
Dalchreichart
Tomchrasky
Glen Moriston
536
Inchnacardoch Hotel
Caledonian Canal
Fort Augustus
Cluanie Inn
Cluanie Lodge
Loch Cluanie
Ceannacroc Lodge
671
CEANN A'MHAIN
787
MEALL DUBH
Auchteraw
947
CREAG A'MHAIM
AIR CHRITH
Loch Loyne
A87
Glen Loyne
River Oich
Caledonian Canal
Glen Tarff
996
SPIDEAN MIALACH
Glenquoich Forest
Glen Garry
13
Bridge of Oich
Newtown
Loch Lundie
Aberchalder Lodge
Glen Garry
Inchlaggan
Loch Garry
Invergarry
Loch Oich
202
River Garry
Tomdoun
Greenfield
Mandally
A82
556
GLAS BHEINN
901
BEN TEE
1544
Blar-na-Leine
Laggan
816
CÀRN DEARG
Glengarry Forest
Kilfinnan
656
MEALL BLAIR
821
MEALL COIRE NAN SAOBHAIDH
935
SRON A'CHOIRE GHAIRBH
Caonich
Gleann Cia-aig
Corriegour Lodge Hotel
Loch Lochy
Arkaig
Great Glen Way
Brae Roy Lodge
Ardechive
Letterfinlay Lodge Hotel
803
BEINNIARUINN
Clunes
15
Glen Mallie
Achnacarry
Invergloy
Glen Gloy
Glen Roy
834
CÀRN DEARG
Clan Cameron
Bunarkaig
B8005
Glenfintaig Lodge
796
BEINN BHAN
A82
654
COIRE CEIRSLE
Glen Roy
1048
BEINN A' CHAORUNN
Gairlochy
Glen Loy
B8004
Stronenaba
Bohuntine
738
STOB A' GHRIANAIN
Brackletter
Spean Bridge
1688
Mulroy
Inverroy
659
CREAG DHUBH
Commando Memorial
Strone
Muirshearlich
228
192
Roy Bridge
Monessie Falls
Inverlair
Tulloch Station
River Lochy
River Spean
The Cour
A82
Neptune's Staircase (Locks)
Treasures of the Earth
Torcastle
714
Glen Spean
DRUIM FADA
GLEN MORE

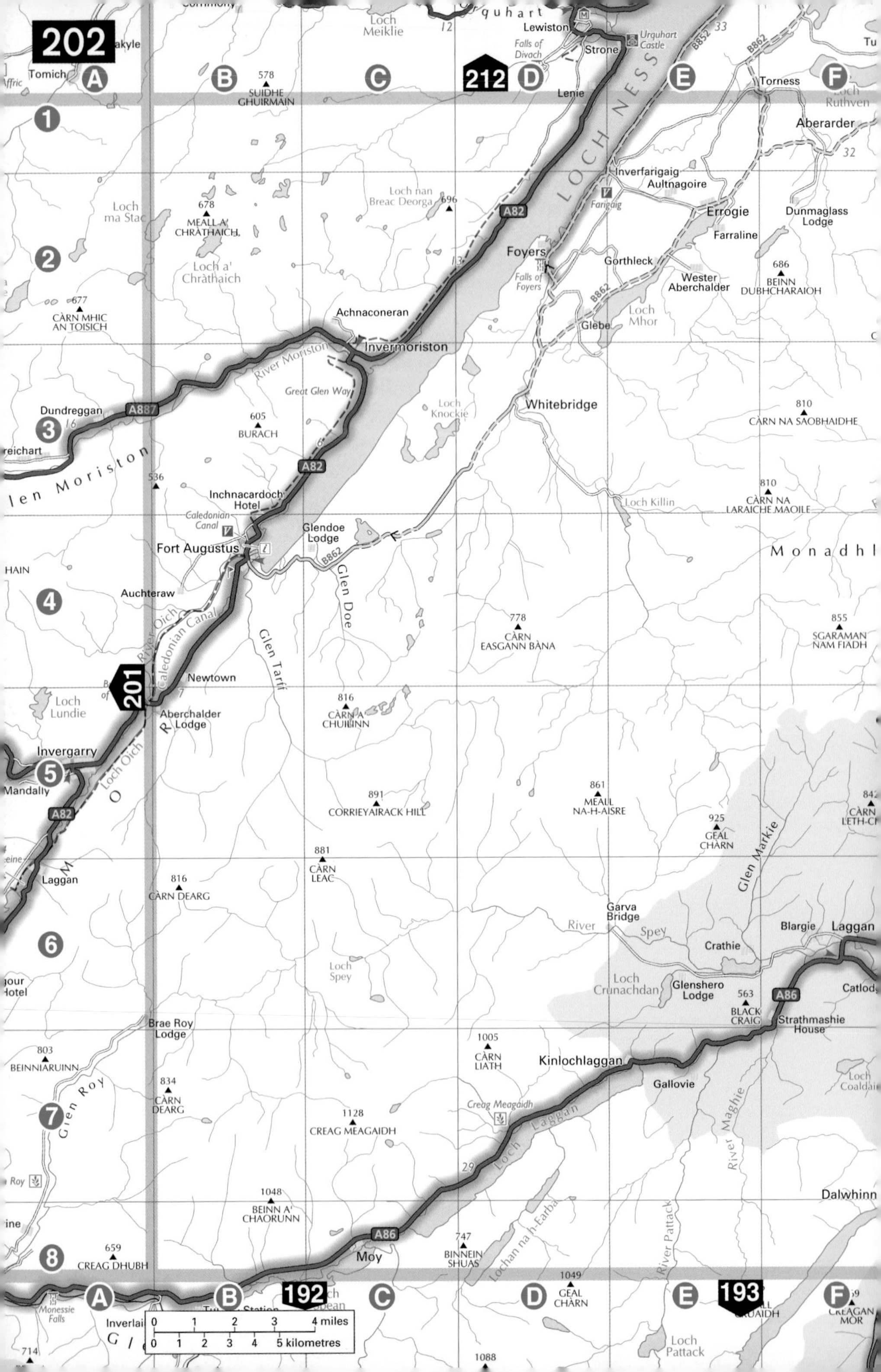
212
201
192
193
A
B
C
D
E
F
1
2
3
4
5
6
7
8
Tomich
Loch Meiklie
Urquhart
Lewiston
Falls of Divach
Strone
Urquhart Castle
Lenie
B852
B862
Torness
Loch Ruthven
Aberarder
578
SUIDHE GHUIRMAIN
LOCH NESS
Inverfarigaig
Aultnagoire
Farigaig
Errogie
Farraline
Dunmaglass Lodge
Loch ma Stac
678
MEALL A' CHRÀTHAICH
Loch a' Chràthaich
Loch nan Breac Deorga
696
A82
Foyers
Falls of Foyers
Gorthleck
Wester Aberchalder
686
BEINN DUBHCHARAIOH
677
CÀRN MHIC AN TOISICH
Achnaconeran
Invermoriston
Glebe
Loch Mhor
River Moriston
Great Glen Way
Loch Knockie
Whitebridge
810
CÀRN NA SAOBHAIDHE
Dundreggan
A887
605
BURACH
Glen Moriston
536
Inchnacardoch Hotel
Caledonian Canal
Loch Killin
CÀRN NA LARAICHE MAOILE
Fort Augustus
Glendoe Lodge
Monadhl
Glen Doe
Auchteraw
River Oich
Glen Tarff
778
CÀRN EASGANN BÀNA
855
SGARAMAN NAM FIADH
Newtown
Loch Lundie
816
CÀRN A' CHUILINN
Aberchalder Lodge
Invergarry
Mandally
Loch Oich
891
CORRIEYAIRACK HILL
861
MEALL NA-H-AISRE
925
GEAL CHARN
842
CÀRN LETH-C
Glen Markie
881
CÀRN LEAC
Laggan
CÀRN DEARG
Garva Bridge
River Spey
Blargie
Crathie
Loch Spey
Loch Crunachdan
Glenshero Lodge
563
BLACK CRAIG
A86
Catlod
Strathmashie House
Brae Roy Lodge
803
BEINNIARUINN
1005
CÀRN LIATH
Kinlochlaggan
Gallovie
Loch Coaldai
834
CÀRN DEARG
Glen Roy
Creag Meagaidh
1128
CREAG MEAGAIDH
Loch Laggan
River Maghie
Roy
1048
BEINN A' CHAORUNN
River Pattack
Dalwhinn
Lochan na h-Earba
747
BINNEIN SHUAS
659
CREAG DHUBH
Moy
1049
GEAL CHÀRN
Monessie Falls
Inverlai
CREAGAN MOR
Loch Pattack
714
1088
0
1
2
3
4 miles
0
1
2
3
4
5 kilometres

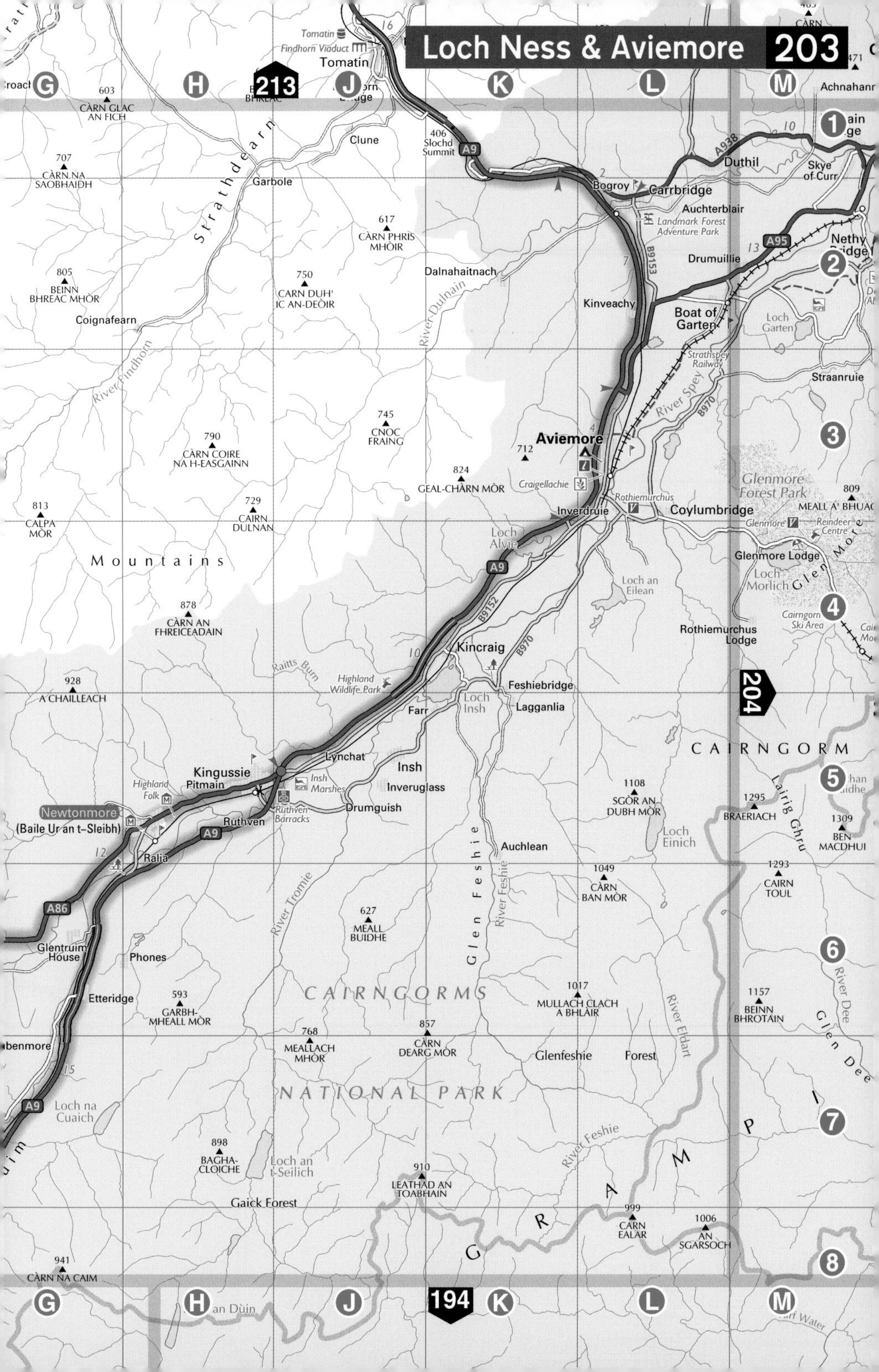
Tomatin
Findhorn Viaduct
Tomatin
213
406
Slochd
Summit
A9
603
CÀRN GLAC
AN FICH
707
CÀRN NA
SAOBHAIDH
Clune
Garbole
Strathdearn
617
CÀRN PHRIS
MHÒIR
805
BEINN
BHREAC MHÒR
750
CARN DUH'
IC AN-DEÒIR
Coignafearn
Dalnahaitnach
River Dulnain
River Findhorn
A938
Duthil
Skye
of Curr
Bogroy
Carrbridge
Auchterblair
Landmark Forest
Adventure Park
B9153
A95
Nethy
Bridge
Drumuillie
Kinveachy
Boat of
Garten
Loch
Garten
Strathspey
Railway
River Spey
B970
Straanruie
745
CNOC
FRAING
790
CÀRN COIRE
NA H-EASGAINN
Aviemore
712
824
GEAL-CHÀRN MÒR
Craigellachie
Glenmore
Forest Park
809
MEALL A' BHUAC
Rothiemurchus
Inverdruie
Coylumbridge
Glenmore
Reindeer
Centre
813
CALPA
MÒR
729
CAIRN
DULNAN
Loch
Alvie
Glenmore Lodge
Mountains
A9
Loch an
Eilean
Loch
Morlich
Glen More
878
CÀRN AN
FHREICEADAIN
B9152
Cairngorm
Ski Area
Rothiemurchus
Lodge
10
Kincraig
B970
928
A' CHAILLEACH
Raitts Burn
Highland
Wildlife Park
Feshiebridge
204
Farr
Loch
Insh
Lagganlia
CAIRNGORM
Lynchat
Insh
Kingussie
Pitmain
Highland
Folk
Insh
Marshes
Inveruglass
1108
SGÒR AN
DUBH MÒR
1295
BRAERIACH
Lairig Ghru
1309
BEN
MACDHUI
Newtonmore
(Baile Ur an t-Sleibh)
Ruthven
Ruthven
Barracks
Drumguish
A9
Loch
Einich
12
Ralia
Auchlean
1049
CÀRN
BAN MÒR
1293
CAIRN
TOUL
A86
River Tromie
Glen Feshie
River Feshie
627
MEALL
BUIDHE
Glentruim
House
Phones
River Dee
1017
MULLACH CLACH
A BHLÀIR
1157
BEINN
BHROTAIN
Etteridge
593
GARBH-
MHEALL MÒR
CAIRNGORMS
River Eidart
Glen Dee
768
MEALLACH
MHÒR
857
CÀRN
DEARG MÒR
Glenfeshie
Forest
NATIONAL PARK
15
A9
Loch na
Cuaich
River Feshie
898
BAGHA-
CLOICHE
Loch an
t-Seilich
910
LEATHAD AN
TOABHAIN
GRAMPI
Gaick Forest
999
CÀRN
EALAR
1006
AN
SGARSOCH
941
CÀRN NA CAIM
194
G
H
J
K
L
M
1
2
3
4
5
6
7
8

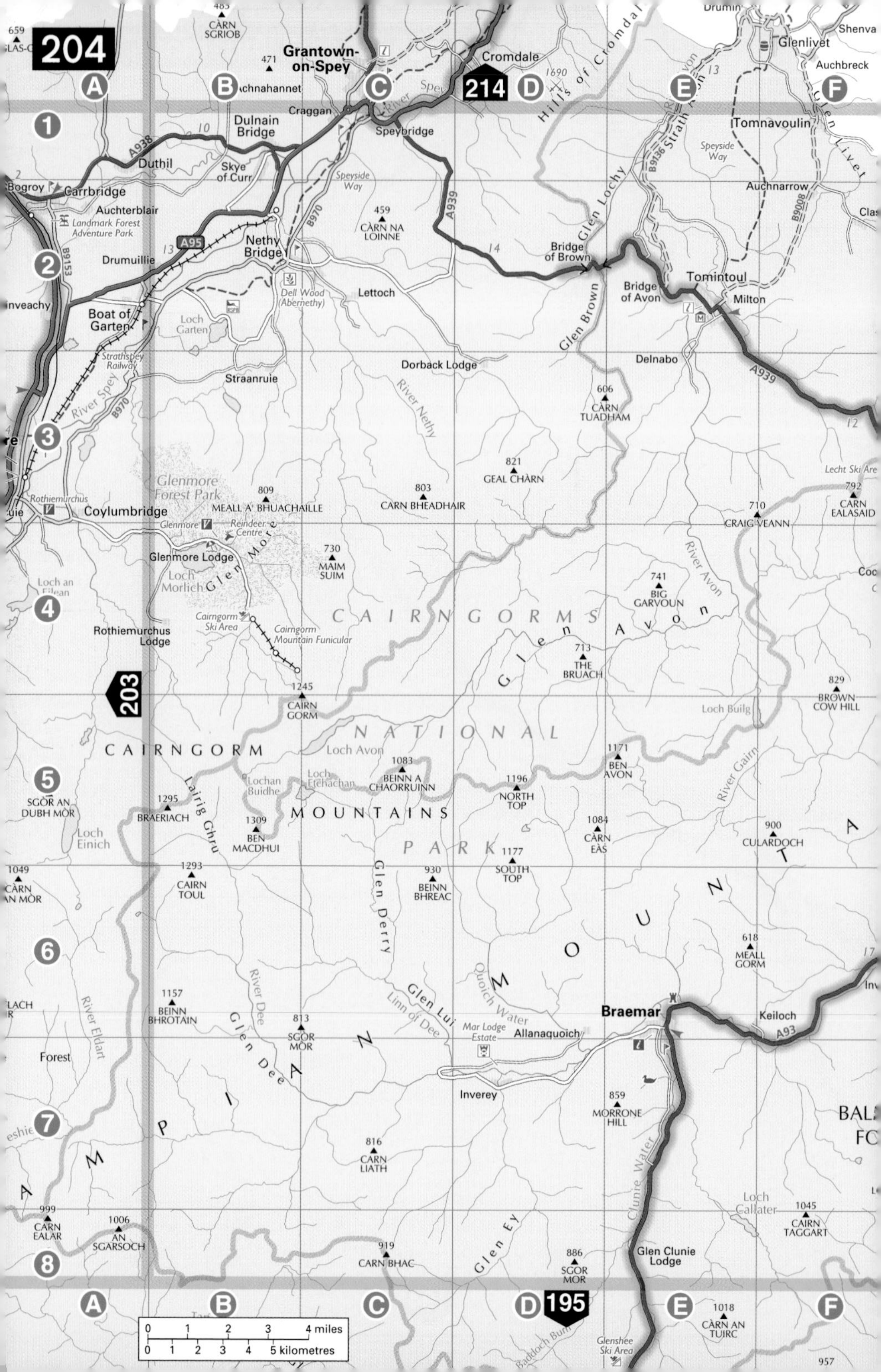

204
203
214
195
A B C D E F
1 2 3 4 5 6 7 8
Grantown-on-Spey
Cromdale
Hills of Cromdale
Achnahannet
CÀRN SGRIOB
Glenlivet
Auchbreck
Shenva
Drumin
Craggan
Dulnain Bridge
Speybridge
Tomnavoulin
Glen Livet
Duthil
Skye of Curr
Speyside Way
Strath Avon
Bogroy
Carrbridge
Auchterblair
Landmark Forest Adventure Park
Auchnarrow
CÀRN NA LOINNE
Nethy Bridge
Glen Lochy
Bridge of Brown
Drumuillie
Dell Wood (Abernethy)
Lettoch
Bridge of Avon
Tomintoul
Milton
Inveachy
Boat of Garten
Loch Garten
Glen Brown
Strathspey Railway
Dorback Lodge
Delnabo
Straanruie
River Nethy
River Spey
CÀRN TUADHAM
GEAL CHÀRN
Glenmore Forest Park
Rothiemurchus
Coylumbridge
MEALL A' BHUACHAILLE
CARN BHEADHAIR
Lecht Ski Area
CARN EALASAID
CRAIG VEANN
Glenmore
Reindeer Centre
Glenmore Lodge
MAIM SUIM
River Avon
Loch an Eilean
Loch Morlich
Glen More
BIG GARVOUN
CAIRNGORMS
Glen Avon
Cairngorm Ski Area
Cairngorm Mountain Funicular
Rothiemurchus Lodge
THE BRUACH
BROWN COW HILL
CAIRN GORM
Loch Builg
CAIRNGORM
NATIONAL
Loch Avon
BEN AVON
Lochan Buidhe
Loch Etchachan
BEINN A CHAORRUINN
NORTH TOP
River Gairn
SGÒR AN DUBH MÒR
BRAERIACH
Lairig Ghru
BEN MACDHUI
MOUNTAINS
CÀRN EAS
CULARDOCH
Loch Einich
PARK
SOUTH TOP
CÀRN AN MÒR
CAIRN TOUL
BEINN BHREAC
Glen Derry
MEALL GORM
BEINN BHROTAIN
River Dee
Glen Lui
Linn of Dee
Quoich Water
Braemar
Keiloch
River Eidart
Glen Dee
SGOR MOR
Mar Lodge Estate
Allanaquoich
Forest
Inverey
MORRONE HILL
GRAMPIAN
MOUNTAINS
CARN LIATH
Clunie Water
Loch Callater
CARN EALAR
AN SGARSOCH
CARN BHAC
Glen Ey
CAIRN TAGGART
Glen Clunie Lodge
SGOR MOR
CÀRN AN TUIRC
Baddoch Burn
Glenshee Ski Area
A938 A95 A939 A93 B9153 B970 B9136 B9008
0 1 2 3 4 miles
0 1 2 3 4 5 kilometres

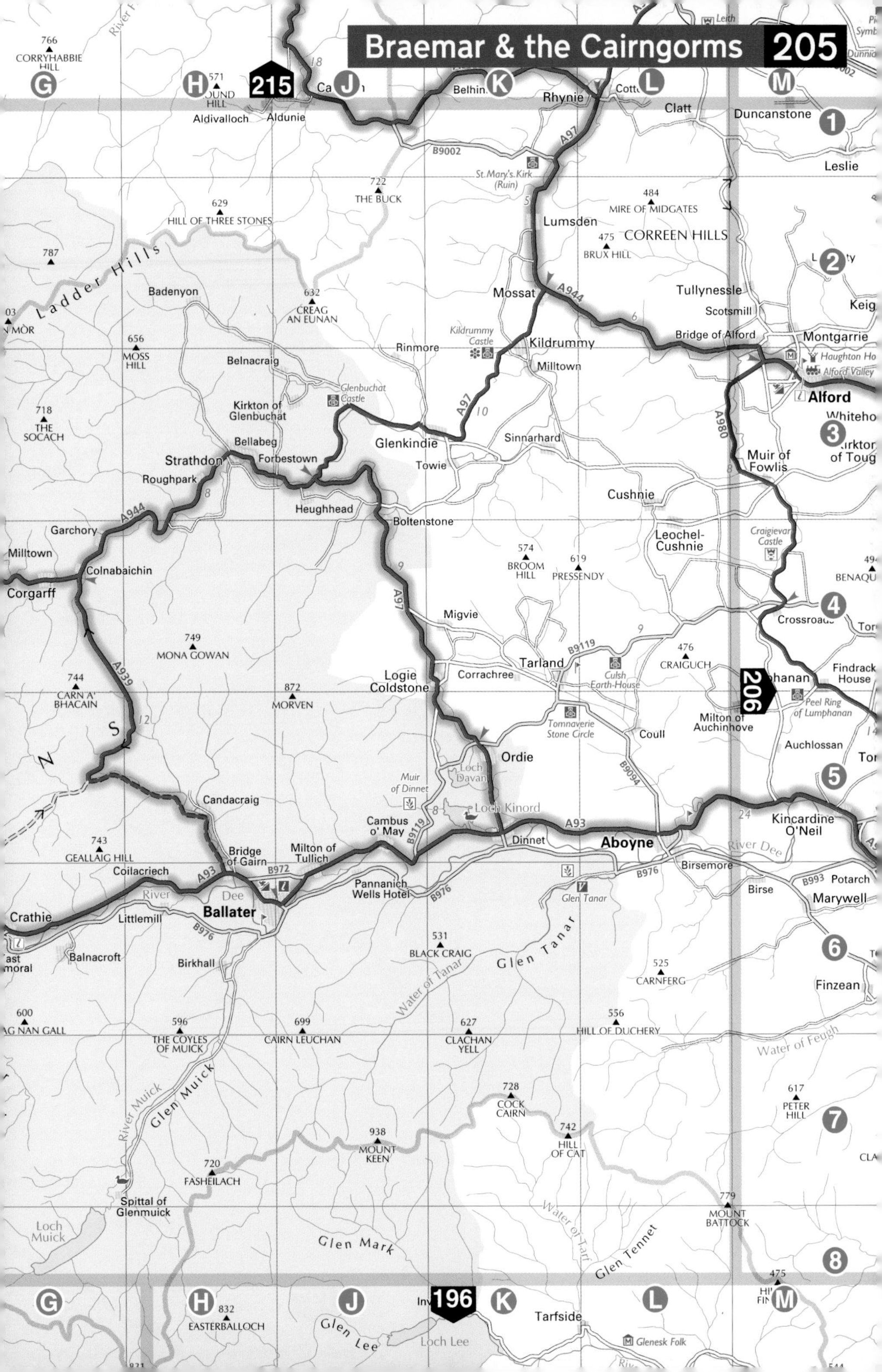
215
206
196
G
H
J
K
L
M
1
2
3
4
5
6
7
8
766 CORRYHABBIE HILL
571
Aldivalloch
Aldunie
Belhin
Rhynie
Clatt
Duncanstone
Leslie
B9002
St. Mary's Kirk (Ruin)
A97
722 THE BUCK
629 HILL OF THREE STONES
484 MIRE OF MIDGATES
Lumsden
475 BRUX HILL
CORREEN HILLS
787
Ladder Hills
Badenyon
632 CREAG AN EUNAN
Mossat
A944
Tullynessle
Scotsmill
Keig
656 MOSS HILL
Belnacraig
Rinmore
Kildrummy Castle
Kildrummy
Milltown
Bridge of Alford
Montgarrie
Haughton Ho
Alford Valley
718 THE SOCACH
Kirkton of Glenbuchat
Glenbuchat Castle
Alford
A980
Bellabeg
Strathdon
Forbestown
Glenkindie
Towie
Sinnarhard
Muir of Fowlis
Roughpark
Heughhead
Cushnie
Garchory
Boltenstone
Leochel-Cushnie
Craigievar Castle
Milltown
Colnabaichin
Corgarff
574 BROOM HILL
619 PRESSENDY
BENAQU
Migvie
Crossroads
749 MONA GOWAN
B9119
476 CRAIGUCH
744 CARN A' BHACAIN
A939
Logie Coldstone
Corrachree
Tarland
Culsh Earth-House
872 MORVEN
Findrack House
Peel Ring of Lumphanan
Milton of Auchinhove
Tomnaverie Stone Circle
Coull
Auchlossan
Ordie
Loch Davan
Muir of Dinnet
B9094
Candacraig
Loch Kinord
Cambus o' May
A93
Kincardine O'Neil
743 GEALLAIG HILL
Bridge of Gairn
Milton of Tullich
Dinnet
Aboyne
River Dee
Birsemore
Coilacriech
B972
Pannanich Wells Hotel
B976
Glen Tanar
B993
Potarch
Birse
Marywell
Crathie
Ballater
Littlemill
531 BLACK CRAIG
Balnacroft
Birkhall
Water of Tanar
525 CARNFERG
Finzean
600
596 THE COYLES OF MUICK
699 CAIRN LEUCHAN
627 CLACHAN YELL
556 HILL OF DUCHERY
Water of Feugh
Glen Muick
River Muick
728 COCK CAIRN
617 PETER HILL
938 MOUNT KEEN
742 HILL OF CAT
720 FASHEILACH
Spittal of Glenmuick
Water of Tarf
779 MOUNT BATTOCK
Loch Muick
Glen Mark
Glen Tennet
475
832 EASTERBALLOCH
Tarfside
Glen Lee
Loch Lee
Glenesk Folk

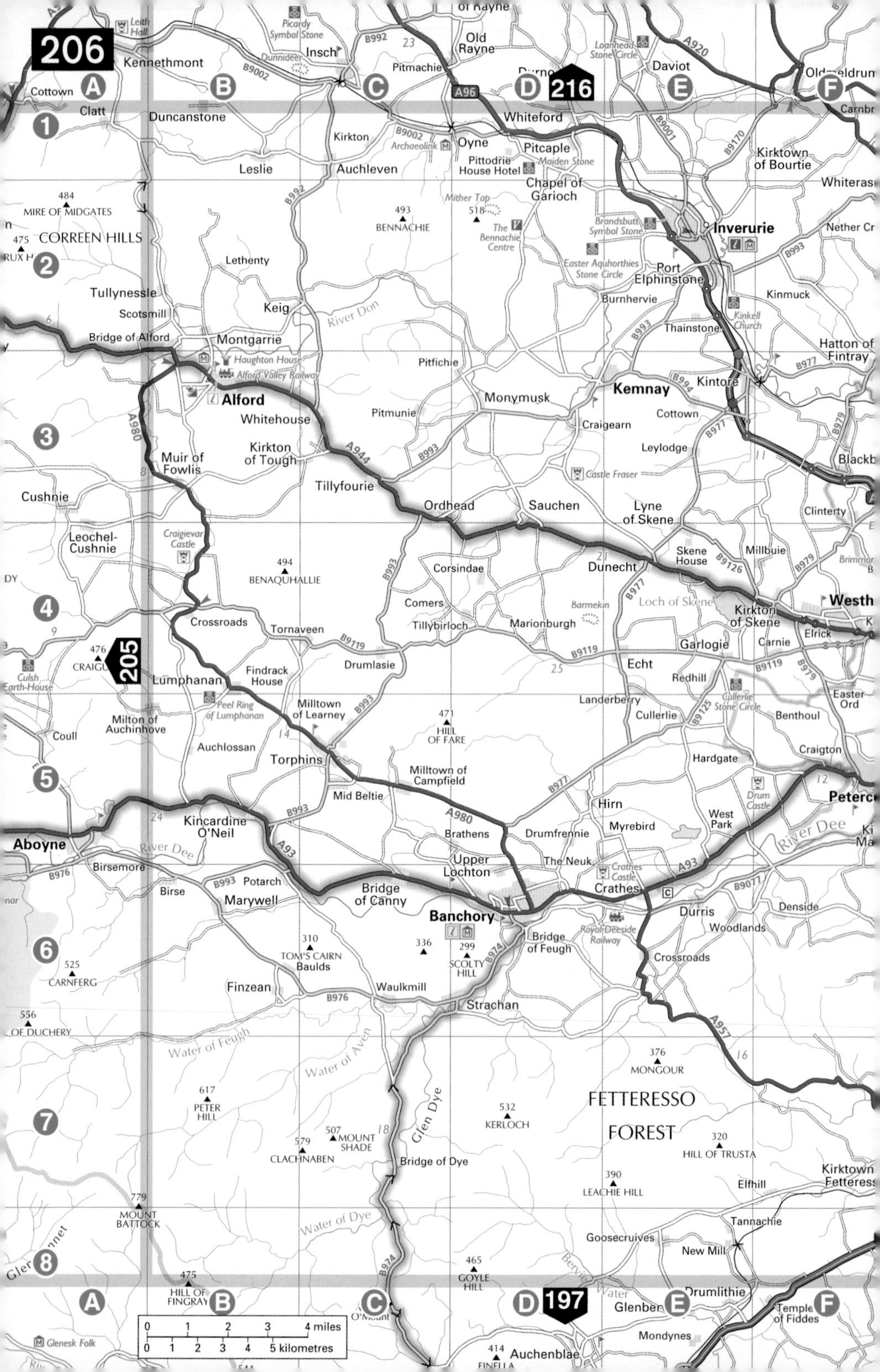

216
205
197
A
B
C
D
E
F
1
2
3
4
5
6
7
8
Leith Hall
Kennethmont
Cottown
Clatt
Duncanstone
B9002
Picardy Symbol Stone
Dunnideer
Insch
B992
23
Pitmachie
Old Rayne
A96
Durno
Loanhead Stone Circle
Daviot
A920
Oldmeldrum
Carnbr
Whiteford
B9001
B9170
Kirkton
Oyne
Archaeolink
Pittodrie House Hotel
Pitcaple
Maiden Stone
Kirktown of Bourtie
Leslie
Auchleven
Chapel of Garioch
Whiteras
484
MIRE OF MIDGATES
475
CORREEN HILLS
493
BENNACHIE
Mither Tap
518
The Bennachie Centre
Brandsbutt Symbol Stone
Inverurie
Nether Cr
B993
Lethenty
Easter Aquhorthies Stone Circle
Port Elphinstone
Tullynessle
Burnhervie
Kinmuck
Scotsmill
Keig
River Don
Kinkell Church
Thainstone
Bridge of Alford
Montgarrie
Hatton of Fintray
Haughton House
Alford Valley Railway
Pitfichie
B977
Kintore
B994
Kemnay
Monymusk
Alford
A980
Whitehouse
Pitmunie
Cottown
Craigearn
Kirkton of Tough
A944
B993
Leylodge
B979
Muir of Fowlis
Tillyfourie
Castle Fraser
Blackb
Cushnie
Ordhead
Sauchen
Lyne of Skene
Clinterty
Leochel-Cushnie
Craigievar Castle
494
BENAQUHALLIE
Corsindae
21
Dunecht
Skene House
Millbuie
B9126
Brimmor
B977
Loch of Skene
Barmekin
Westh
Comers
Tillybirloch
Marionburgh
Kirkton of Skene
Crossroads
Tornaveen
Elrick
476
CRAIGU
B9119
Drumlasie
Garlogie
Carnie
Culsh Earth-House
Lumphanan
Findrack House
25
Echt
B9119
Redhill
Peel Ring of Lumphanan
Landerberry
Cullerlie Stone Circle
Easter Ord
Milton of Auchinhove
Milltown of Learney
471
HILL OF FARE
B9125
Cullerlie
Benthoul
Coull
14
Auchlossan
Torphins
Hardgate
Craigton
Milltown of Campfield
12
Mid Beltie
Drum Castle
Peterc
B977
Hirn
24
Kincardine O'Neil
B993
A980
West Park
Brathens
Drumfrennie
Myrebird
River Dee
Aboyne
River Dee
A93
Upper Lochton
The Neuk
Crathes Castle
B976
Birsemore
Potarch
A93
B9077
Birse
B993
Marywell
Bridge of Canny
Crathes
Banchory
Durris
Denside
Royal Deeside Railway
Woodlands
310
TOM'S CAIRN
Baulds
336
299
SCOLTY HILL
Bridge of Feugh
B974
525
CARNFERG
Crossroads
Finzean
Waulkmill
B976
Strachan
556
OF DUCHERY
A957
Water of Feugh
Water of Aven
376
MONGOUR
16
617
PETER HILL
Glen Dye
532
KERLOCH
FETTERESSO
FOREST
507
MOUNT SHADE
18
579
CLACHNABEN
320
HILL OF TRUSTA
Bridge of Dye
Kirktown of Fetteresso
390
LEACHIE HILL
Elfhill
779
MOUNT BATTOCK
Water of Dye
Tannachie
Goosecruives
New Mill
465
GOYLE HILL
Bervie Water
475
HILL OF FINGRAY
B974
Drumlithie
Glenber
Temple of Fiddes
O'Mount
0 1 2 3 4 miles
0 1 2 3 4 5 kilometres
Glenesk Folk
Mondynes
414
FINELLA
Auchenblae

Ellon
Esslemont
Kirkton of Logie Buchan
Collieston
217
Pitmedden
Logierieve
Housieside
Udny Green
Udny Station
Newburgh
Pettymuk
Culterculen
Foveran
Tillygreig
Delfrigs
Causeyend
Balmedie
Whitecairns
Belhelvie
Kinmundy
Cothal
Potterton
Blackdog
Dyce
Middleton Park
Denmore
Kirkwall
Lerwick
Stoneywood
Bankhead
Bucksburn
Bridge of Don
Northfield
Old Aberdeen
Kittybrewster
ABERDEEN
Ruthrieston
Torry
Nigg Bay
Mannofield
Cults
Bieldside
Kincorth
Nigg
Altens Haven
Milton of Murtle
Banchory-Devenick
Cove Bay
Charlestown
Marywell
Hillside
Findon
Auchlee
Portlethen
Old Portlethen
Cammachmore Bay
Downies
Cammachmore
Newtonhill
Skateraw
Muchalls
Bridge of Muchalls
Doonie Point
Garron Point
Stonehaven Bay
Stonehaven
Dunnottar
Crawton
Fowlsheugh
Trelong Bay
A90
A92
A96
A956
A975
A920
B9000
B999
B979
B977
B997
B9119
B9077
B9005
G
H
J
K
L
M
1
2
3
4
5
6
7
8

A
B
C
D
E
F
1
2
3
4
5
6
7
8
Duntulm
A87
Tairbeart (Tarbert)
Lùb Score
Skye Museum of Island Life
Borneskitaig
Kilmuir
Heribusta
Kilvaxter
Balgown
218
Linicro
Totscore
River Rha
Idrigill
Uig (Uige)
Uig Bay
Loch nam Madadh (Lochmaddy)
Waternish Point
Ascrib Islands
283 BEN GEARY
Geary
Trumpan
Loch Snizort
Earlish
Ardmore Point
Gillen
Hallin
16
A87
River Hinnisdal
DUNVEGAN HEAD
Isay
Mingay
Stein
Lusta
Loch Bay
214 BEN DIUBAIG
Greshornish House Hotel
Loch Greshornish
Loch Snizort Beag
Kingsburgh
Claigan
Bay
Boreraig
Loch Dunvegan
327 BEINN BHREAC
B886
22
Treaslane
Uig
Flashader
A850
Loch Pooltiel
Upperglen
Feriniquarrie
Totaig
Edinbane
Bernisdale
Oisgill Bay
Milovaig
Glendale
Colbost
Dunvegan
A850
Waterstein
Lephin
B884
Colbost Croft
Toy
Dunvegan
Giant Angus MacAskill
Skeabost
Skinidin
Kilmuir
Caroy River
Neist Point
Lonmore
A864
265 BEN AKETIL
271 CRUACHAN BEINN A' CHEARCAILL
Moonen Bay
Duirnish
Roskhill
469 HEALAVAL MORE
Roag
Ramasaig
Orbost
Vatten
B885
Hoe Rape
488 HEALAVAL BHEAG
Glen Ose
ISLE OF
A863
Harlosh
Loch Caroy
Ose
Hoe Point
Harlosh Island
Colbost Point
368 BEINN NA BOINEID
Dun Beag
Bracadale
Loch Duagrich
Tarner Island
Loch Bracadale
Struan
Coillore
Ullinish Lodge Hotel
Wiay
23
Idrigill Point
Oronsay
Portnalong
Loch Harport
Fiskavaig
B8009
Rudha nan Clach
Fernilea
369 ARNAVAL
Carbost
Drynoch
Merkadale
Talisker Bay
Talisker
Glen Eynort
Minginish
447 BEINN BHREAC
Grula
198
0 1 2 3 4 miles
0 1 2 3 4 5 kilometres
Loch Eynort

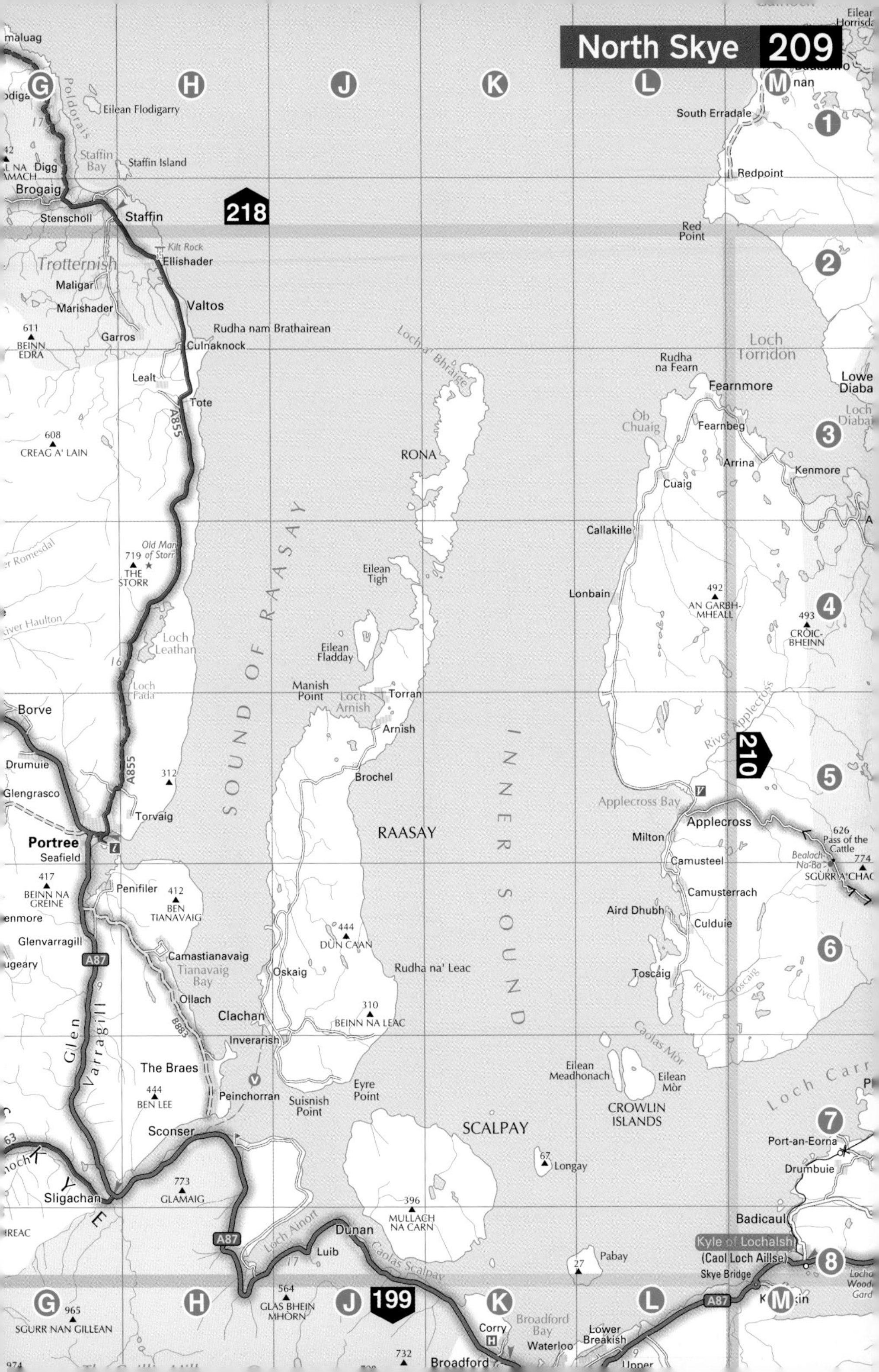
Eilean Flodigarry
Staffin Bay
Staffin Island
Digg
Brogaig
Stenscholl
Staffin
218
Kilt Rock
Trotternish
Ellishader
Maligar
Marishader
Valtos
611
BEINN EDRA
Garros
Rudha nam Brathairean
Culnaknock
Lealt
Tote
A855
608
CREAG A' LAIN
Old Man of Storr
719
THE STORR
River Haulton
Loch Leathan
Loch Fada
Borve
Drumuie
Glengrasco
312
Torvaig
Portree
Seafield
417
BEINN NA GREINE
Penifiler
412
BEN TIANAVAIG
Glenvarragill
A87
Camastianavaig
Tianavaig Bay
Ollach
B883
Glen Varragill
The Braes
444
BEN LEE
Peinchorran
Sconser
773
GLAMAIG
Sligachan
SKYE
965
SGURR NAN GILLEAN
SOUND OF RAASAY
Loch a' Bhràige
RONA
Eilean Tigh
Eilean Fladday
Manish Point
Loch Arnish
Torran
Arnish
Brochel
RAASAY
444
DÙN CAAN
Oskaig
Rudha na' Leac
310
BEINN NA LEAC
Clachan
Inverarish
Eyre Point
Suisnish Point
SCALPAY
396
MULLACH NA CARN
Loch Ainort
Dunan
Luib
Caolas Scalpay
564
GLAS BHEIN MHÒRN
199
Corry
Broadford Bay
Broadford
732
INNER SOUND
67
Longay
27
Pabay
Eilean Meadhonach
Eilean Mòr
Caolas Mòr
CROWLIN ISLANDS
Lower Breakish
Waterloo
South Erradale
Redpoint
Red Point
Loch Torridon
Rudha na Fearn
Fearnmore
Òb Chuaig
Fearnbeg
Arrina
Kenmore
Cuaig
Callakille
Lonbain
492
AN GARBH-MHEALL
493
CROIC-BHEINN
River Applecross
210
Applecross Bay
Applecross
Milton
626
Pass of the Cattle
Bealach-Na-Ba
774
Camusteel
Camusterrach
Aird Dhubh
Culduie
Toscaig
River Toscaig
Loch Carron
Port-an-Eorna
Drumbuie
Badicaul
Kyle of Lochalsh
(Caol Loch Aillse)
Skye Bridge
A87
G
H
J
K
L
M
1
2
3
4
5
6
7
8

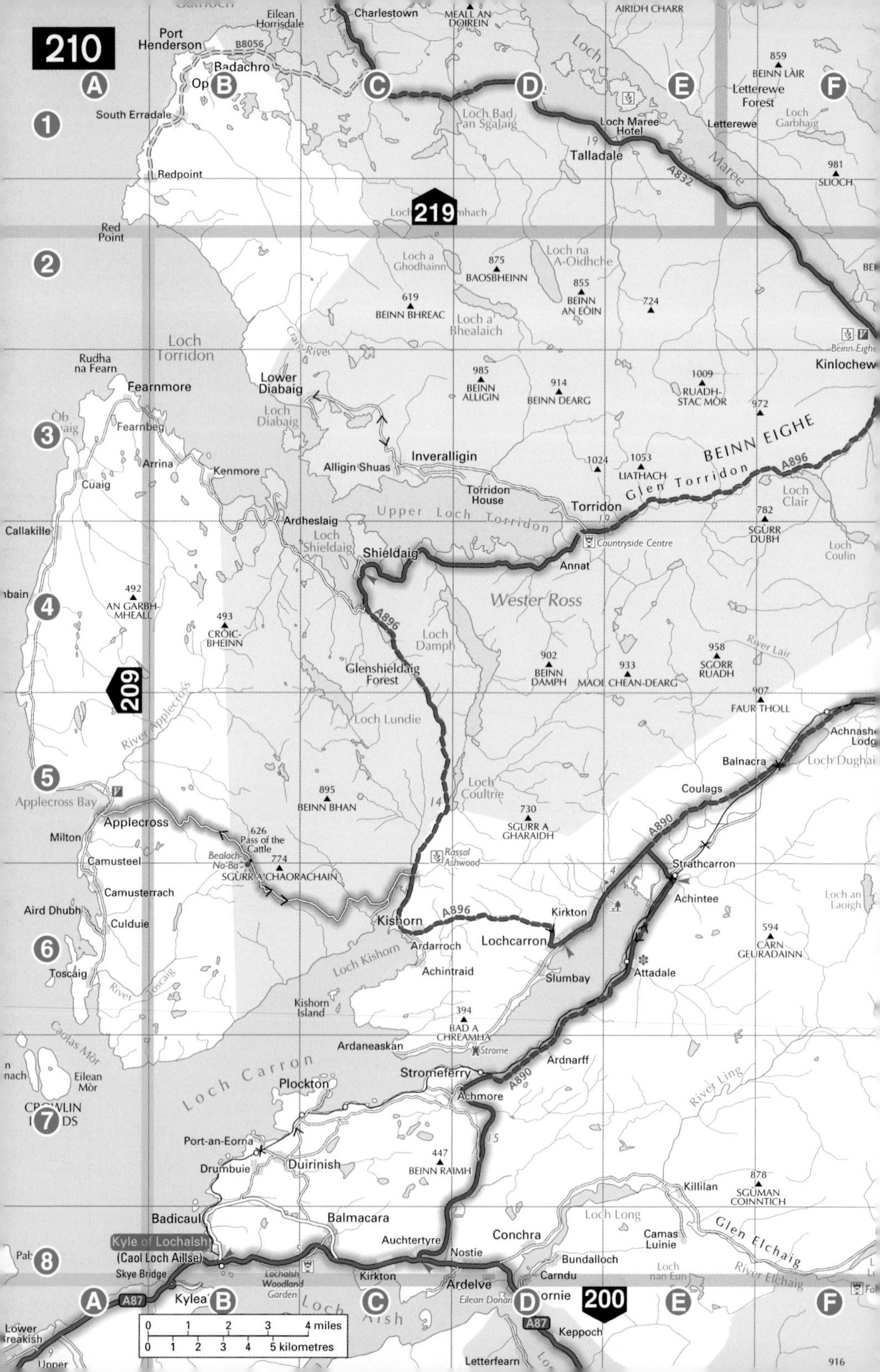
Eilean Horrisdale
Charlestown
MEALL AN DOIREIN
AIRIDH CHARR
Port Henderson
B8056
Badachro
Opinan
South Erradale
Loch Bad an Sgalaig
Loch Maree
Loch Maree Hotel
Talladale
19
A832
859
BEINN LÀIR
Letterewe Forest
Letterewe
Loch Garbhaig
981
SLIOCH
Redpoint
219
Red Point
Loch a Ghodhainn
875
BAOSBHEINN
Loch na h-Oidhche
855
BEINN AN EÒIN
619
BEINN BHREAC
Loch a' Bhealaich
724
Beinn Eighe
Kinlochewe
Loch Torridon
Rudha na Fearn
Fearnmore
Lower Diabaig
Loch Diabaig
Craig River
985
BEINN ALLIGIN
914
BEINN DEARG
1009
RUADH-STAC MÒR
972
BEINN EIGHE
Fearnbeg
Arrina
Cuaig
Kenmore
Alligin Shuas
Inveralligin
1024
1053
LIATHACH
Glen Torridon
A896
Torridon House
Torridon
Loch Clair
Callakille
Ardheslaig
Upper Loch Torridon
Loch Shieldaig
Shieldaig
Countryside Centre
Annat
782
SGÙRR DUBH
Loch Coulin
492
AN GARBH-MHEALL
493
CROIC-BHEINN
Wester Ross
Loch Damph
Glenshieldaig Forest
902
BEINN DAMPH
933
MAOL CHEAN-DEARG
958
SGORR RUADH
River Lair
907
FAUR THOLL
209
River Applecross
Loch Lundie
Achnashellach Lodge
Balnacra
Loch Dughaill
Applecross Bay
Loch Coultrie
895
BEINN BHAN
Coulags
14
Applecross
626
Pass of the Cattle
730
SGURR A GHARAIDH
A890
Milton
Bealach-Na-Ba
774
SGÙRR A' CHAORACHAIN
Rassal Ashwood
Camusteel
Strathcarron
Camusterrach
Achintee
Loch an Laoigh
Aird Dhubh
Culduie
Kishorn
A896
Kirkton
Lochcarron
594
CÀRN GEURADAINN
Ardarroch
Toscaig
Loch Kishorn
Achintraid
Slumbay
Attadale
River Toscaig
Kishorn Island
394
BAD A CHREAMHA
Caolas Mòr
Ardaneaskan
Strome
Eilean Mòr
Ardnarff
Loch Carron
Stromeferry
A890
River Ling
CROWLIN ISLANDS
Plockton
Achmore
15
Port-an-Eorna
Duirinish
447
BEINN RAIMH
Drumbuie
878
Killilan
SGUMAN COINNTICH
Badicaul
Balmacara
Loch Long
Kyle of Lochalsh
(Caol Loch Aillse)
Conchra
Camas Luinie
Glen Elchaig
Auchtertyre
Nostie
Bundalloch
Skye Bridge
Lochalsh Woodland Garden
Kirkton
Carndu
Loch nan Eun
River Elchaig
A87
Kyleakin
Ardelve
Eilean Donan
Dornie
200
Loch Alsh
Lower Breakish
A87
Keppoch
Upper
Letterfearn
916
0 1 2 3 4 miles
0 1 2 3 4 5 kilometres

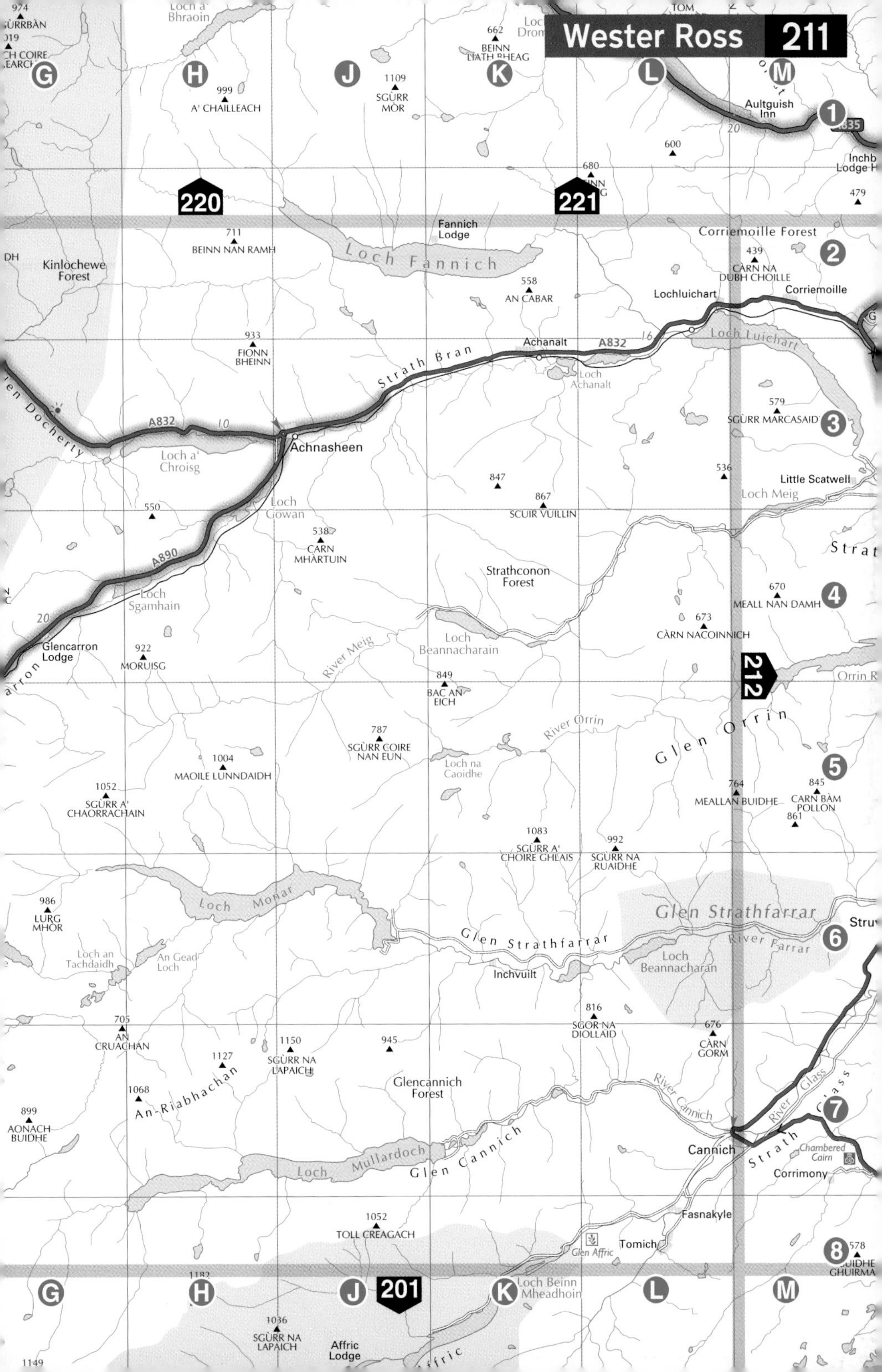

974
SGÙRRBÀN
Loch a' Bhraoin
662
BEINN LIATH BHEAG
TOM
G
H
J
K
L
M
999
A' CHAILLEACH
1109
SGÙRR MÒR
Aultguish Inn
1
A835
20
600
680
Inchb Lodge H
479
220
221
Fannich Lodge
711
BEINN NAN RAMH
Loch Fannich
Corriemoille Forest
439
CÀRN NA DUBH CHOILLE
2
Corriemoille
Kinlochewe Forest
558
AN CABAR
Lochluichart
933
FIONN BHEINN
Strath Bran
Achanalt
A832
16
Loch Luichart
Loch Achanalt
Glen Docherty
A832
10
Achnasheen
Loch a' Chroisg
579
SGÙRR MARCASAIDH
3
847
536
Little Scatwell
Loch Meig
867
SCUIR VUILLIN
550
Loch Gowan
538
CARN MHÀRTUIN
A890
Strathconon Forest
Strat
Loch Sgamhain
670
MEALL NAN DAMH
4
673
CÀRN NACOINNICH
20
Glencarron Lodge
922
MORUISG
Loch Beannacharain
River Meig
212
Orrin R
849
BAC AN EICH
River Orrin
Glen Orrin
787
SGÙRR COIRE NAN EUN
1004
MAOILE LUNNDAIDH
Loch na Caoidhe
5
1052
SGÙRR A' CHAORRACHAIN
764
MEALLAN BUIDHE
845
CARN BÀM POLLON
861
1083
SGÙRR A' CHOIRE GHLAIS
992
SGÙRR NA RUAIDHE
986
LURG MHOR
Loch Monar
Glen Strathfarrar
Stru
Glen Strathfarrar
River Farrar
6
Loch an Tachdaidh
An Gead Loch
Inchvuilt
Loch Beannacharan
816
SGOR NA DIOLLAID
705
AN CRUACHAN
1150
SGÙRR NA LAPAICH
945
676
CÀRN GORM
1127
River Glass
1068
An-Riabhachan
Glencannich Forest
River Cannich
7
899
AONACH BUIDHE
Loch Mullardoch
Glen Cannich
Cannich
Strath Glass
Chambered Cairn
Corrimony
1052
TOLL CREAGACH
Fasnakyle
Glen Affric
Tomich
8
578
GHUIRMA
G
H
J
201
K
Loch Beinn Mheadhoin
L
M
1036
SGÙRR NA LAPAICH
Affric Lodge
1149

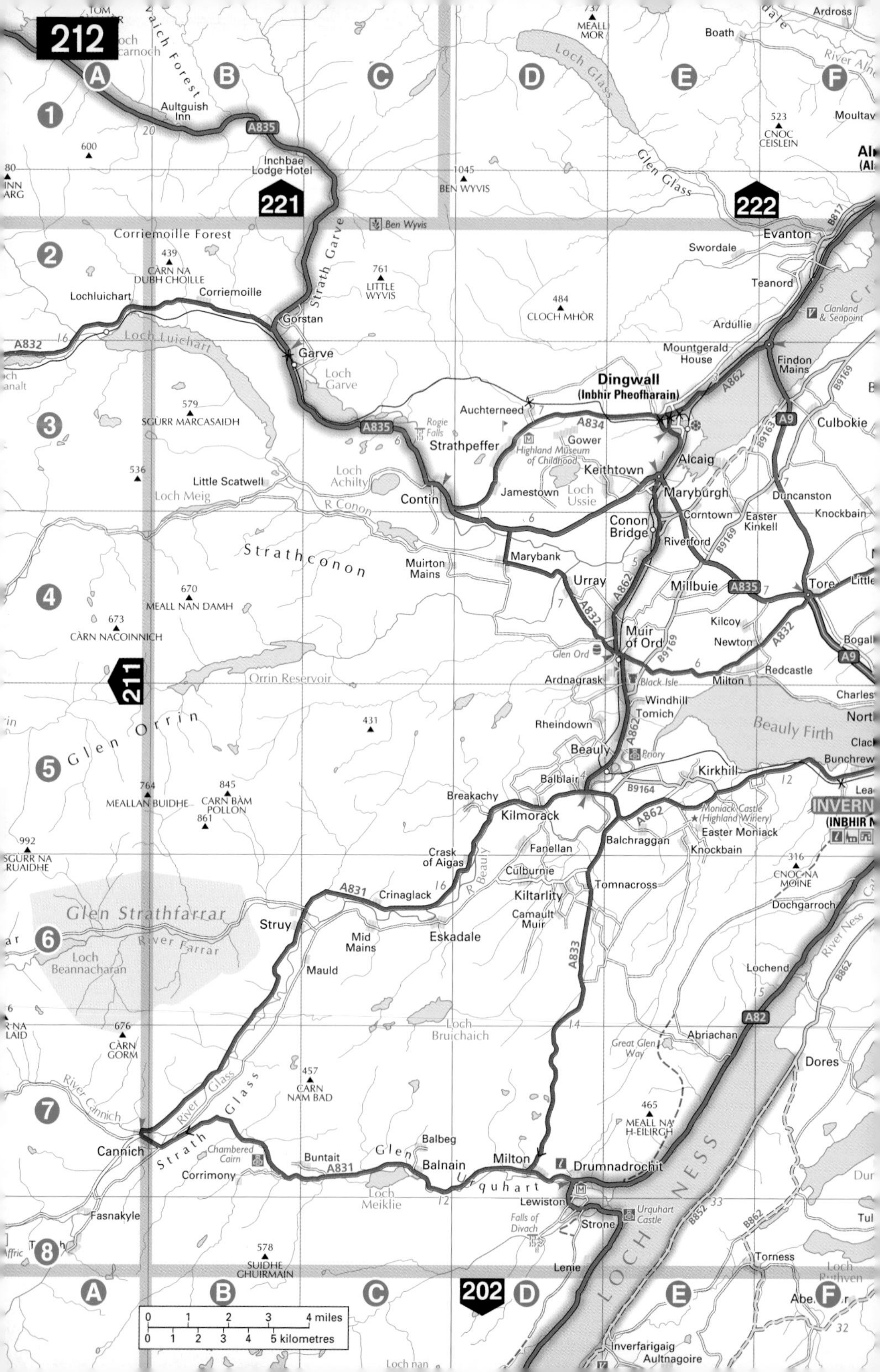

221
222
211
202
A835
A832
A834
A862
A831
A833
A82
A9
B817
B9169
B9163
B9164
B852
B862
Aultguish Inn
Inchbae Lodge Hotel
Ben Wyvis
1045
BEN WYVIS
Loch Glass
Glen Glass
Boath
Ardross
523
CNOC CEISLEIN
Moultav
Evanton
Swordale
Teanord
Clanland & Seapoint
Ardullie
Mountgerald House
Findon Mains
Culbokie
Corriemoille Forest
439
CÀRN NA DUBH CHOILLE
Corriemoille
Lochluichart
Loch Luichart
Strath Garve
761
LITTLE WYVIS
484
CLOCH MHÒR
Gorstan
Garve
Loch Garve
Dingwall
(Inbhir Pheofharain)
Auchterneed
Rogie Falls
Strathpeffer
Highland Museum of Childhood
Gower
Alcaig
Keithtown
Maryburgh
579
SGÙRR MARCASAIDH
600
536
Little Scatwell
Loch Meig
Loch Achilty
Contin
Jamestown
Loch Ussie
Duncanston
Knockbain
R Conon
Conon Bridge
Corntown
Easter Kinkell
Riverford
Strathconon
Muirton Mains
Marybank
Urray
Millbuie
Tore
670
MEALL NAN DAMH
673
CÀRN NACOINNICH
Muir of Ord
Kilcoy
Newton
Glen Ord
Orrin Reservoir
Ardnagrask
Black Isle
Milton
Redcastle
Windhill
Tomich
Rheindown
Beauly Firth
Beauly
Priory
Kirkhill
Glen Orrin
431
764
MEALLAN BUIDHE
845
CARN BÀM POLLON
861
Balblair
Breakachy
Kilmorack
Moniack Castle (Highland Winery)
Easter Moniack
Balchraggan
Knockbain
992
SGÙRR NA RUAIDHE
Crask of Aigas
Fanellan
Culburnie
Kiltarlity
Tomnacross
316
CNOC NA MOINE
Dochgarroch
Glen Strathfarrar
River Farrar
Loch Beannacharan
Crinaglack
Struy
Camault Muir
Eskadale
Mid Mains
Mauld
Lochend
River Ness
Loch Bruichaich
Abriachan
676
CÀRN GORM
Great Glen Way
Dores
457
CARN NAM BAD
465
MEALL NA H-EILIRGH
River Cannich
River Glass
Strath Glass
Cannich
Chambered Cairn
Corrimony
Buntait
Glen Urquhart
Balbeg
Balnain
Milton
Drumnadrochit
Loch Meiklie
Lewiston
Falls of Divach
Strone
Urquhart Castle
Fasnakyle
LOCH NESS
578
SUIDHE GHUIRMAIN
Lenie
Torness
Loch Ruthven
Inverfarigaig
Aultnagoire
0 1 2 3 4 miles
0 1 2 3 4 5 kilometres

Shandwick Bay
Kildary
Milton
Kilmuir
Barbaraville
Pitcalnie
Nigg
Nigg Bay
Nigg Ferry
Rhicullen
Millcraig
Tomich
Achnagarron
Balintraid
Saltburn
Dalmore
Invergordon
223
Cromarty
Hugh Miller's Cottage
Newton
Navity
Balblair
Resolis
Cromarty Bay
Udale Bay
Allerton
Jemimaville
Upper Eathie
Brae
Firth
MORAY FIRTH
Culbin Forest
Kintessack
Raddery
Fairy Glen
Killen
Rosemarkie
Groam House
Cathedral
Fortrose
Chanonry Point
Avoch
Fort-George & The Highlanders' Museum
Whiteness Head
Nairn
(Inbhir Nàrann)
Culbin Sands
Brodie Castle
Dyke
Brodie
Tradespark
Ardersier
Moss-side
Househill
Boath Doocot
Auldearn
1645
Whitemire
Foynesfield
Conicavel
Gollanfield
Lochside
Munlochy Bay
Fisherton
Inverness
MORAY FIRTH
Clephanton
Cawdor
Righoul
Piperhill
Culcharry
Fornighty
Littlemill
Logie Steading
Kilmuir
Castle Stuart
Easter Dalziel
Alturlie Point
Tornagrain
Croy
River Nairn
214
Relugas
Newton
Cantraywood
Balloch
Culloden
Smithton
Kirkton of Barevan
Clunas
Redburn
Ardclach Bell Tower
Ferness
Culcabock
Resaurie
Culloden Viaduct
Culloden Battlefield & Visitor Centre
Clava Cairns
323
CÀRN MAOL
401
CÀRN A' CHRASGIE
Knocknagael Boar Stone
Milton of Leys
Daviot House
Drummossie Muir
548
BEINN BHUIDHE MHOR
Bridge of Dulsie
Daviot
609
CÀRN NAN TRI-TIGHEARNAN
464
Lochindorb
Lochindorb Lodge
Balnafoich
Loch Moy
Moy
483
Farr
Ruthven
River Findhorn
633
CÀRN AN T-SEAN-LIATHANAICH
615
CÀRN NA H-EASGAINN
Strathnairn
Balvraid
485
CÀRN SGRIOB
Tomatin
Findhorn Viaduct
Raigbeg
617
659
CÀRN GLAS-CHOIRE
471
600
BEINN BHREAC
Croachy
603
CÀRN GLAC AN FICH
Findhorn Bridge
Dulnain Bridge
203
Clune
406
Slochd Summit
707
CÀRN NA SAOBHAIDH
Strathdearn
Garbole
Bogroy
Carrbridge
Duthil
Skye of Curr
A9
A96
A832
A939
A938
B817
B9163
B9160
B9092
B9006
B9039
B9091
B9090
B9101
B9177
B8082
B851
B861
B9154
B9007
B9175
G
H
J
K
L
M
1
2
3
4
5
6
7
8

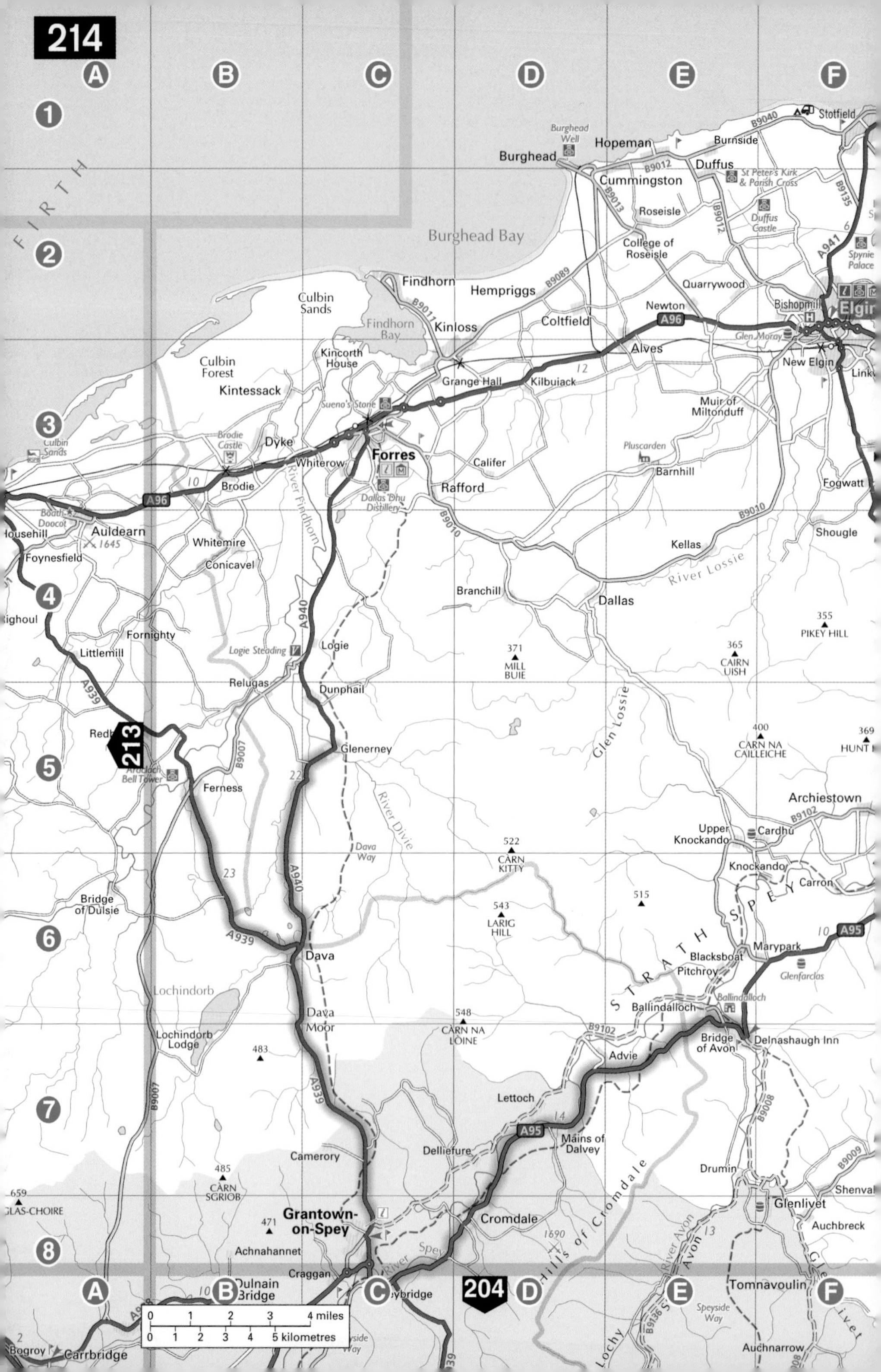
A
B
C
D
E
F
1
2
3
4
5
6
7
8
FIRTH
Burghead Well
Burghead
Hopeman
Stotfield
B9040
Burnside
Duffus
B9012
St Peter's Kirk & Parish Cross
Cummingston
B9013
B9135
Roseisle
B9012
Duffus Castle
Burghead Bay
College of Roseisle
A941
Spynie Palace
Findhorn
Hempriggs
B9089
Quarrywood
Culbin Sands
Newton
Bishopmill
Elgin
B9011
Findhorn Bay
Kinloss
Coltfield
A96
Glen Moray
Alves
Kincorth House
New Elgin
Culbin Forest
Grange Hall
Kilbuiack
12
Linkw
Kintessack
Sueno's Stone
Muir of Miltonduff
Culbin Sands
Brodie Castle
Dyke
Pluscarden
Whiterow
Forres
Califer
Barnhill
10
Brodie
River Findhorn
Rafford
Fogwatt
A96
Dallas Dhu Distillery
Boath Doocot
B9010
B9010
Househill
Auldearn
1645
Whitemire
Kellas
Shougle
Foynesfield
Conicavel
River Lossie
Branchill
Dallas
Righoul
A940
355
PIKEY HILL
Fornighty
Logie
371
MILL BUIE
365
CAIRN UISH
Littlemill
Logie Steading
Relugas
Dunphail
A939
Redb
213
Glen Lossie
400
CARN NA CAILLEICHE
369
HUNT
Glenerney
Ardclach Bell Tower
B9007
Ferness
22
River Divie
Archiestown
B9102
Upper Knockando
Cardhu
Dava Way
522
CARN KITTY
23
A940
Knockando
Carron
515
Bridge of Dulsie
543
LARIG HILL
STRATH SPEY
10
A95
A939
Dava
Marypark
Blacksboat
Pitchroy
Glenfarclas
Lochindorb
Dava Moor
548
CARN NA LOINE
Ballindalloch
Ballindalloch
Lochindorb Lodge
483
B9102
Bridge of Avon
Delnashaugh Inn
Advie
A939
Lettoch
B9007
B9008
14
A95
Mains of Dalvey
Camerory
Dellefure
485
CARN SGRIOB
Hills of Cromdale
B9009
Drumin
Shenval
659
GLAS-CHOIRE
Grantown-on-Spey
Glenlivet
471
Cromdale
1690
Auchbreck
River Avon
Avon
13
Achnahannet
River Spey
Craggan
Dulnain Bridge
Tomnavoulin
204
Speyside Way
Lochy
B9136
Livet
Bogroy
Carrbridge
Auchnarrow
0 1 2 3 4 miles
0 1 2 3 4 5 kilometres

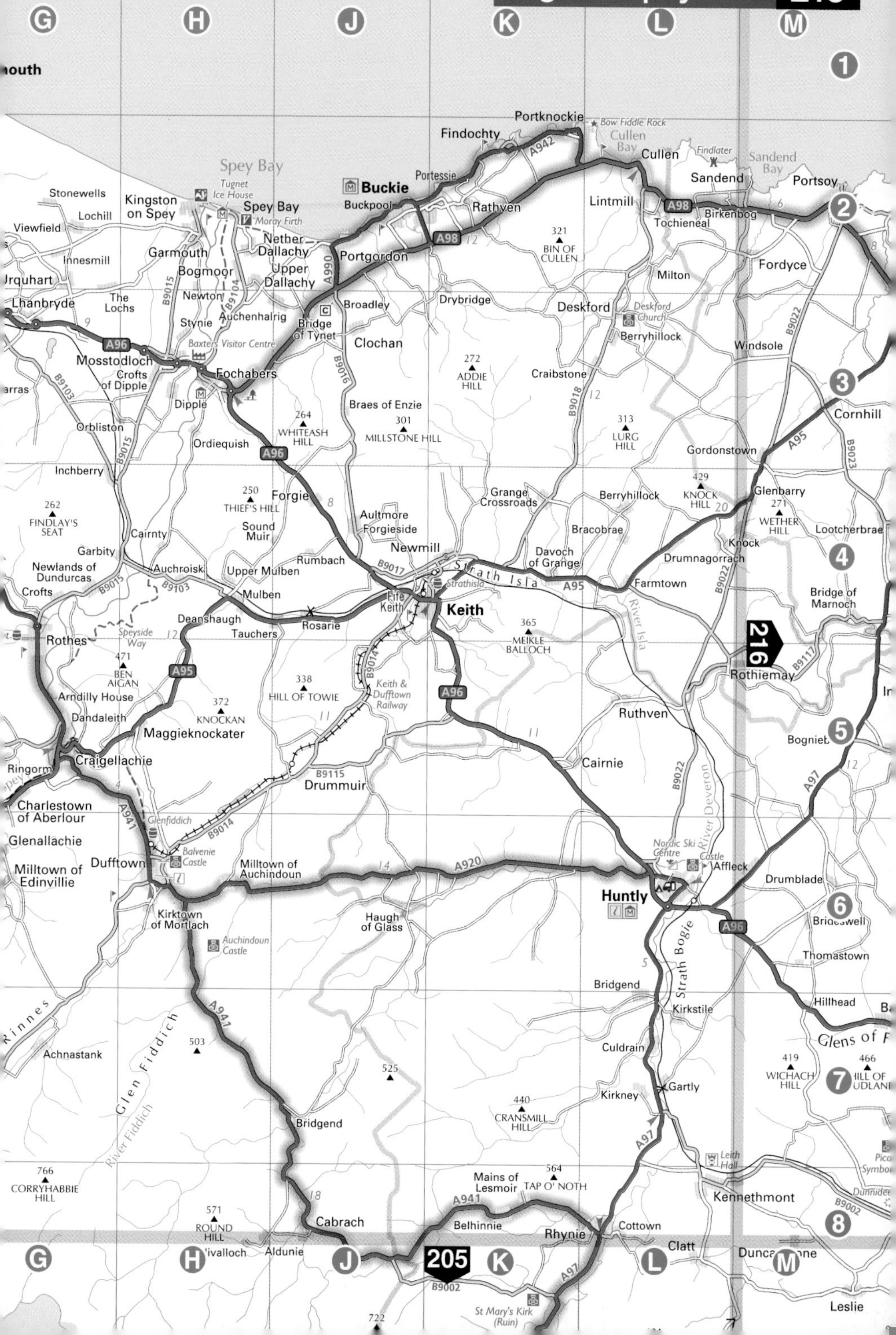
G
H
J
K
L
M
1
2
3
4
5
6
7
8
Portknockie
Bow Fiddle Rock
Findochty
Cullen Bay
Cullen
Findlater
Sandend Bay
Sandend
Portsoy
Spey Bay
Tugnet Ice House
Portessie
Buckie
Buckpool
Rathven
Lintmill
Birkenbog
Tochieneal
Stonewells
Kingston on Spey
Spey Bay
Moray Firth
Lochill
Viewfield
Innesmill
Garmouth
Nether Dallachy
Upper Dallachy
Portgordon
321 BIN OF CULLEN
Milton
Fordyce
Urquhart
Bogmoor
The Lochs
Newton
Broadley
Drybridge
Deskford
Deskford Church
Lhanbryde
Stynie
Auchenhalrig
Bridge of Tynet
Clochan
Berryhillock
Windsole
Baxters Visitor Centre
Mosstodloch
Crofts of Dipple
Fochabers
272 ADDIE HILL
Craibstone
Dipple
Braes of Enzie
Cornhill
Orbliston
264 WHITEASH HILL
301 MILLSTONE HILL
313 LURG HILL
Ordiequish
Gordonstown
Inchberry
429 KNOCK HILL
Glenbarry
250 THIEF'S HILL
Forgie
Grange Crossroads
Berryhillock
262 FINDLAY'S SEAT
Sound Muir
Aultmore
Forgieside
271 WETHER HILL
Lootcherbrae
Bracobrae
Cairnty
Newmill
Knock
Garbity
Davoch of Grange
Drumnagorrach
Newlands of Dundurcas
Auchroisk
Upper Mulben
Rumbach
Strath Isla
Strathisla
Farmtown
Crofts
Mulben
Fife Keith
Keith
River Isla
Bridge of Marnoch
Deanshaugh
Rosarie
Tauchers
365 MEIKLE BALLOCH
Rothes
Speyside Way
216
471 BEN AIGAN
Rothiemay
338 HILL OF TOWIE
Keith & Dufftown Railway
Arndilly House
372 KNOCKAN
Ruthven
Dandaleith
Maggieknockater
Bognieb
Craigellachie
Cairnie
Ringorm
B9115
Drummuir
Charlestown of Aberlour
River Deveron
Glenfiddich
Glenallachie
Nordic Ski Centre
Castle
Balvenie Castle
Affleck
Milltown of Edinvillie
Dufftown
Milltown of Auchindoun
Drumblade
Huntly
Kirktown of Mortlach
Haugh of Glass
Bridewell
Auchindoun Castle
Thomastown
Strath Bogie
Bridgend
Kirkstile
Hillhead
Glen Fiddich
Glens of F
Achnastank
503
Culdrain
419 WICHACH HILL
466 HILL OF UDLANE
525
Gartly
Kirkney
440 CRANSMILL HILL
Bridgend
River Fiddich
Leith Hall
766 CORRYHABBIE HILL
Mains of Lesmoir
564 TAP O' NOTH
Kennethmont
571 ROUND HILL
Cabrach
Belhinnie
Rhynie
Cottown
Clatt
Aldunie
205
St Mary's Kirk (Ruin)
Leslie
722
A96
A98
A942
A990
A95
A920
A941
A97
B9015
B9104
B9103
B9016
B9018
B9022
B9023
B9017
B9014
B9117
B9002

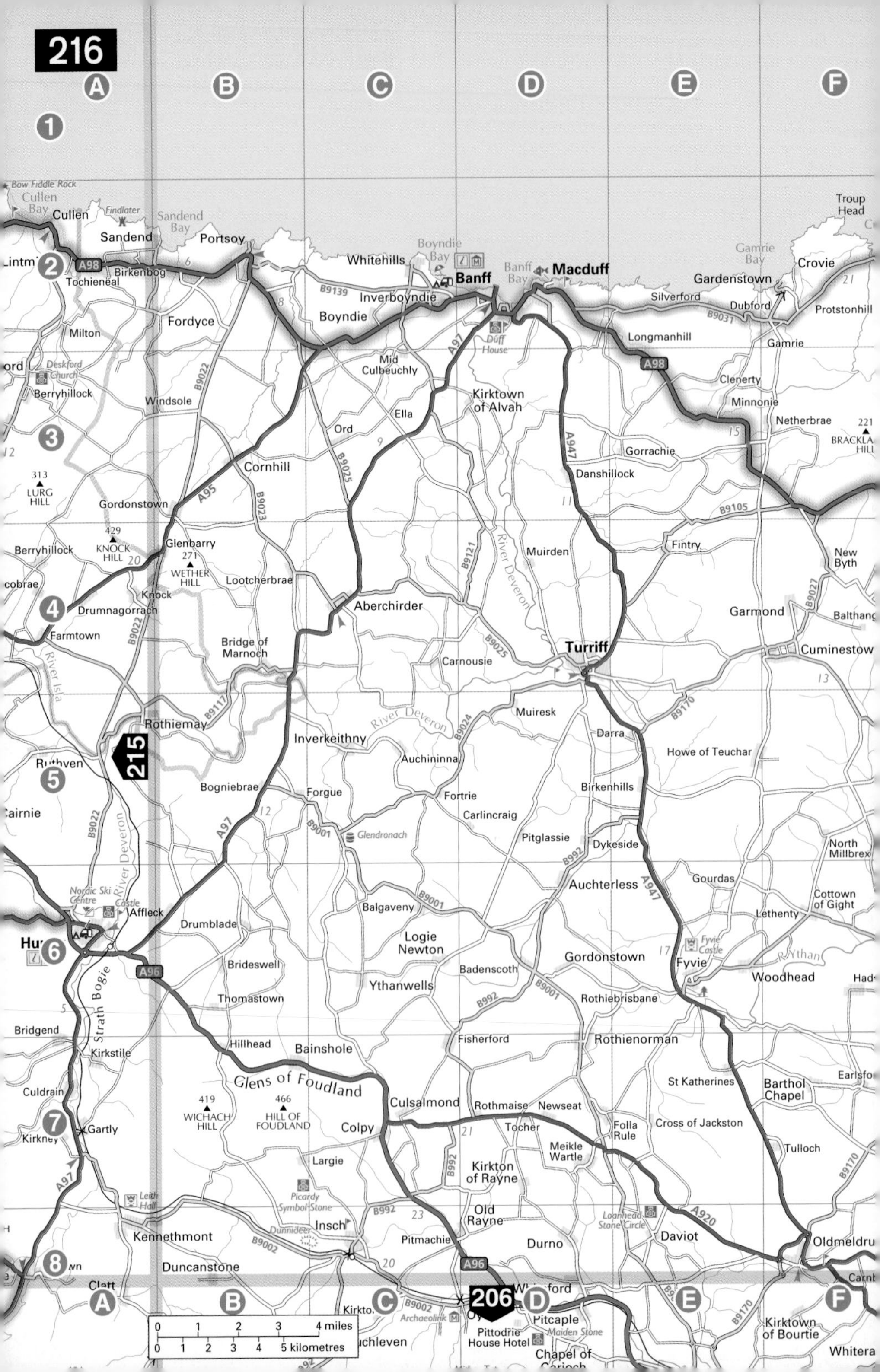
A
B
C
D
E
F
1
2
3
4
5
6
7
8
Bow Fiddle Rock
Cullen Bay
Cullen
Findlater
Sandend Bay
Sandend
Portsoy
Boyndie Bay
Whitehills
Banff Bay
Banff
Macduff
Gamrie Bay
Gardenstown
Crovie
Troup Head
Lintmill
A98
Birkenbog
Tochieneal
B9139
Inverboyndie
Boyndie
Silverford
Dubford
B9031
Protstonhill
Milton
Fordyce
Duff House
Longmanhill
Gamrie
Deskford Church
Deskford
Berryhillock
B9022
Windsole
Mid Culbeuchly
A97
Kirktown of Alvah
Clenerty
Minnonie
Netherbrae
221
BRACKLA HILL
Ella
Ord
A947
Gorrachie
313
LURG HILL
Cornhill
B9025
Danshillock
A95
B9023
Gordonstown
B9105
429
KNOCK HILL
Glenbarry
271
WETHER HILL
B9121
River Deveron
Muirden
Fintry
New Byth
Berryhillock
Lootcherbrae
Knock
Cornabrae
Drumnagorrach
Aberchirder
B9027
Garmond
Balthangie
Farmtown
Bridge of Marnoch
B9025
Turriff
Cuminestown
River Isla
Carnousie
B9117
Muiresk
B9170
Rothiemay
River Deveron
B9024
Inverkeithny
Darra
Howe of Teuchar
215
Ruthven
Auchininna
Bogniebrae
Forgue
Fortrie
Birkenhills
Cairnie
Carlincraig
B9001
Glendronach
Pitglassie
Dykeside
North Millbrex
B992
Auchterless
Nordic Ski Centre
Castle
Affleck
Balgaveny
Gourdas
Cottown of Gight
Drumblade
Lethenty
Huntly
Logie Newton
Fyvie Castle
Brideswell
Gordonstown
Fyvie
R. Ythan
Badenscoth
Woodhead
A96
Strath Bogie
Ythanwells
Thomastown
Rothiebrisbane
Bridgend
Fisherford
Rothienorman
Hillhead
Bainshole
Kirkstile
Glens of Foudland
St Katherines
Barthol Chapel
Earlsford
Culdrain
Culsalmond
419
WICHACH HILL
466
HILL OF FOUDLAND
Rothmaise
Newseat
Colpy
Folla Rule
Cross of Jackston
Gartly
Tocher
Kirkney
Meikle Wartle
Tulloch
Largie
Kirkton of Rayne
Leith Hall
Picardy Symbol Stone
Old Rayne
Loanhead Stone Circle
A920
Insch
Dunnideer
Pitmachie
Kennethmont
Durno
Daviot
Oldmeldrum
B9002
Duncanstone
Clatt
Whiteford
206
Kirkton
B9002
Archaeolink
Oyne
Pitcaple
Maiden Stone
Pittodrie House Hotel
Chapel of Garioch
Auchleven
Kirktown of Bourtie
Whiterashes
B9170
0 1 2 3 4 miles
0 1 2 3 4 5 kilometres

G
H
J
K
L
M
Castle Lighthouse & Museum
Kinnaird Head
Rosehearty
Sandhaven
Pittulie
Fraserburgh
Peathill
Fraserburgh Bay
Craigiefold
Kirktown
Cairnbulg
Aberdour Bay
Percyhorner
Inverallochy
Maggie's Hoosie
Whitelinks Bay
Coburby
Pitblae
Mid Ardlaw
A90
B9033
St Combs
Boyndlie
B9032
Memsie
A98
Memsie Cairn
Rathen
Crofts of Savoch
A981
Newburgh
Lonmay
Rattray Head
234
WAUGHTON HILL
Loch of Strathbeg
Crimond
Blackhill
B9093
Strichen
A952
New Leeds
B9093
Leys
Denhead
Backfolds
Kirktown
St Fergus
Fetterangus
Rora
A90
A981
A950
Deer Abbey
River Ugie
Dunshillock
B9106
Maud
Aden
Inverugie
B9029
B9029
Mintlaw
Longside
Old Deer
Aberdeenshire Farming
Buchanhaven
Peterhead
Blackhill of Clackriach
A950
Peterhead
B9028
Stuartfield
A948
Inverquhomery
Drymuir
Bulwark
A982
Peterhead Bay
Millbreck
Hillhead of Cocklaw
Nether Kinmundy
Burnhaven
Nethermuir
Knaven
Clola
Buchan Ness
B9030
Kinnadie
Blackhill
Stirling
Boddam
Auchnagatt
Lendrum Terrace
Kinknockie
Inkhorn
Longhaven
Coldwells
Ardallie
A90
A952
A948
Bullers of Buchan
Auchiries
Hatton
North Haven
Slains
Arthrath
Muirtack
Cruden Bay
Bogbrae
Chapel Hill
B9005
Ythanbank
A975
Bay of Cruden
Birness
Whinnyfold
The Skares
Auchedly
Altar Tomb of William Forbes
Artrochie
Kinharrachie
Ythsie
Ellon
P+R
Kirkton of Logie Buchan
Esslemont
B9005
Kirktown of Slains
B999
A920
Collieston
Pitmedden
Pitmedden Garden
Logierieve
Forvie
Housieside
B9000
207
Udny Station
A90
Newburgh
Pettymuk
Culterculle
Foveran

A
B
C
D
E
F
1
2
3
4
5
6
7
8
Loch Shell
Loch
Erisort
SOUND OF SHIANT
SHIANT
ISLANDS
Fladda-chùain
Eilean Trodday
Rudha Hunish
North
Duntulm
Duntulm
Kilmaluag
A855
Tairbeart
(Tarbert)
Lùb Score
Skye Museum
of Island Life
Flodigarry
Poldorais
Eilean Flodigarry
Borneskitaig
Heribusta
Kilmuir
Kilvaxter
542
MEAL NA
SUIREAMACH
Digg
Staffin
Bay
Staffin Island
Balgown
Brogaig
Stenscholl
Staffin
Linicro
Totscore
464
BIODA
BUIDHE
Kilt Rock
Ellishader
Loch nam Madadh
(Lochmaddy)
208
209
Trotternish
River Rha
Maligar
Idrigill
Marishader
Valtos
Uig
(Uige)
River Conon
611
BEINN
EDRA
Rudha nam Brathairean
Garros
Uig Bay
Culnaknock
Loch a' Bh
Loch Sgiport
Earl
Tote
A855
0 1 2 3 4 miles
0 1 2 3 4 5 kilometres
608
Pennich

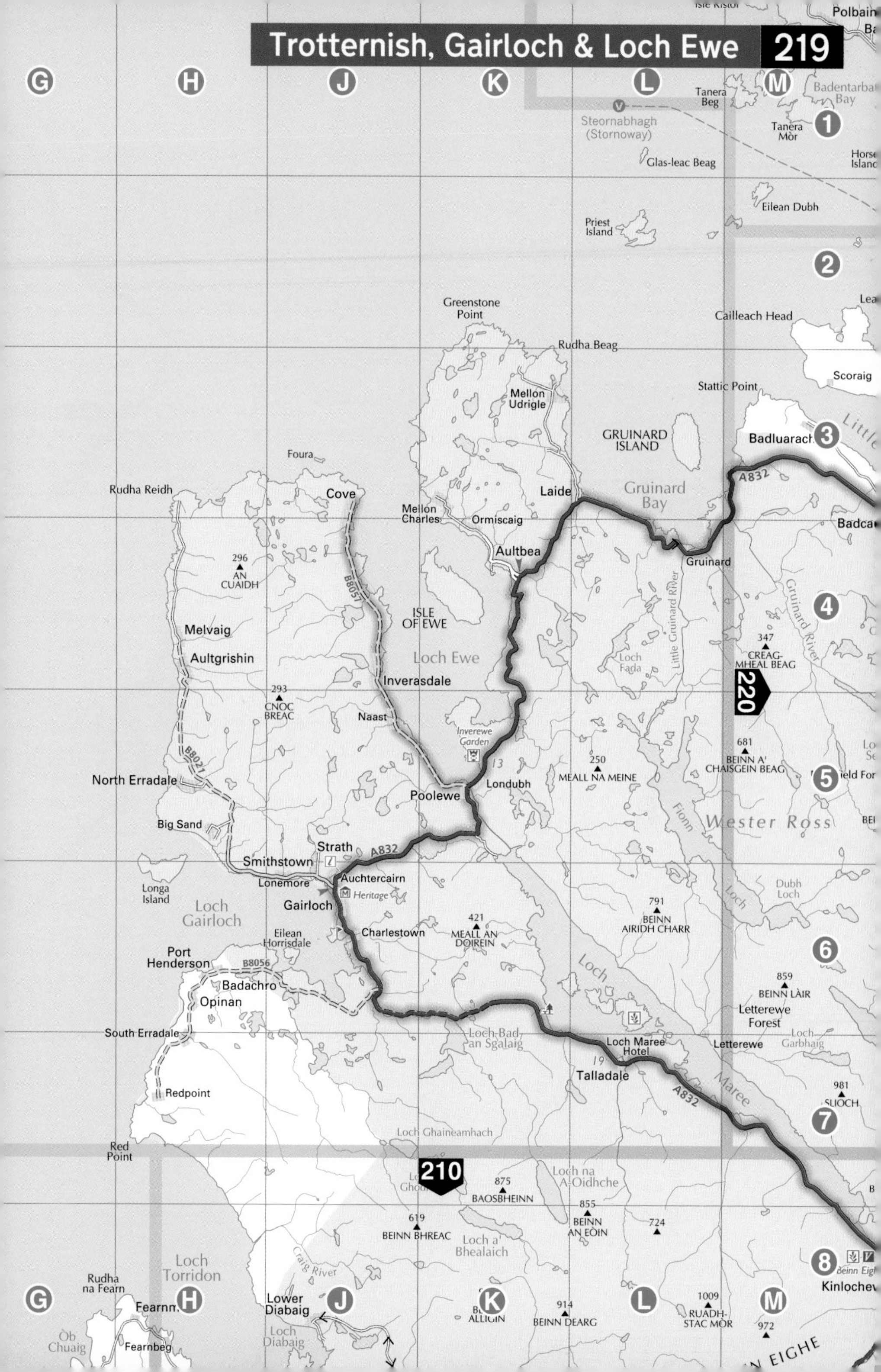
G
H
J
K
L
M
1
2
3
4
5
6
7
8
Tanera Beg
Badentarbat Bay
Steornabhagh (Stornoway)
Tanera Mòr
Glas-leac Beag
Eilean Dubh
Priest Island
Greenstone Point
Rudha Beag
Cailleach Head
Scoraig
Mellon Udrigle
Stattic Point
GRUINARD ISLAND
Badluarach
Foura
Rudha Reidh
Cove
Laide
Gruinard Bay
A832
Mellon Charles
Ormiscaig
Aultbea
Gruinard
296 AN CUAIDH
B8057
ISLE OF EWE
Little Gruinard River
Gruinard River
Melvaig
Aultgrishin
Loch Ewe
Loch Fada
347 CREAG-MHEAL BEAG
Inverasdale
293 CNOC BREAC
Naast
220
Inverewe Garden
B8021
250 MEALL NA MEINE
681 BEINN A' CHAISGEIN BEAG
North Erradale
Londubh
Poolewe
Big Sand
Fionn
Wester Ross
Strath
A832
Smithstown
Lonemore
Auchtercairn
Heritage
Longa Island
Gairloch
Dubh Loch
Loch Gairloch
421 MEALL AN DOIREIN
791 BEINN AIRIDH CHARR
Eilean Horrisdale
Charlestown
Port Henderson
B8056
Loch
Badachro
Opinan
859 BEINN LÀIR
Letterewe Forest
South Erradale
Loch Bad an Sgalaig
Loch Maree Hotel
Letterewe
Loch Garbhaig
Talladale
A832
Maree
981 SLIOCH
Redpoint
Loch Ghaineamhach
Red Point
210
Loch na A-Oidhche
875 BAOSBHEINN
855 BEINN AN EÒIN
619 BEINN BHREAC
724
Loch a' Bhealaich
Loch Torridon
Craig River
Rudha na Fearn
Lower Diabaig
Loch Diabaig
ALLIGIN
914 BEINN DEARG
1009 RUADH-STAC MÒR
972
Kinlochewe
Beinn Eighe
Òb Chuaig
Fearnbeg
EIGHE

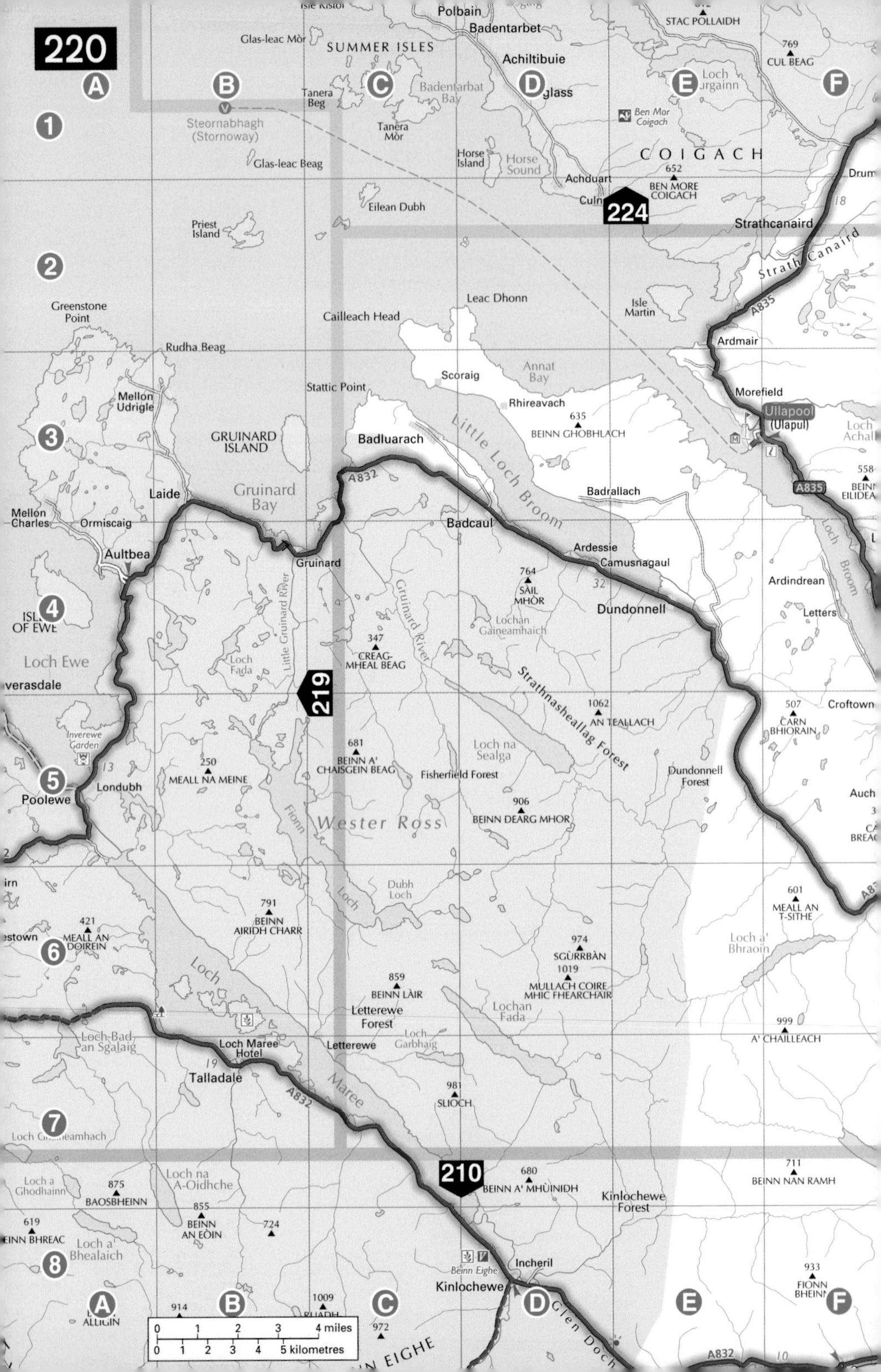

A
B
C
D
E
F
1
2
3
4
5
6
7
8
Isle Ristol
Polbain
Badentarbet
STAC POLLAIDH
Glas-leac Mòr
SUMMER ISLES
Achiltibuie
769
CUL BEAG
Tanera Beg
Badentarbat Bay
glass
Loch urgainn
Steornabhagh (Stornoway)
Ben Mor Coigach
Tanera Mòr
Horse Island
Horse Sound
COIGACH
Glas-leac Beag
652
BEN MORE COIGACH
Achduart
Culn
224
Drum
Eilean Dubh
18
Priest Island
Strathcanaird
Strath Canaird
Leac Dhonn
Isle Martin
Greenstone Point
Cailleach Head
A835
Ardmair
Rudha Beag
Scoraig
Annat Bay
Static Point
Morefield
Mellon Udrigle
Rhireavach
Ullapool (Ulapul)
635
BEINN GHOBHLACH
Loch Achall
GRUINARD ISLAND
Badluarach
Little Loch Broom
558
BEINN EILIDEA
A832
A835
Gruinard Bay
Badrallach
Laide
Mellon Charles
Ormiscaig
Badcaul
Loch Broom
Aultbea
Ardessie
Camusnagaul
Gruinard
764
SÀIL MHÒR
32
Ardindrean
ISLE OF EWE
Little Gruinard River
Gruinard River
Lochan Gaineamhaich
Dundonnell
Letters
347
CREAG-MHEAL BEAG
Loch Ewe
Loch Fada
Strathnasheallag Forest
verasdale
219
1062
AN TEALLACH
507
CARN BHIORAIN
Croftown
Inverewe Garden
681
BEINN A' CHAISGEIN BEAG
Loch na Sealga
Dundonnell Forest
13
250
MEALL NA MEINE
Fisherfield Forest
Poolewe
Londubh
906
BEINN DEARG MHOR
Auch
Fionn
Wester Ross
Dubh Loch
601
MEALL AN T-SITHE
791
BEINN AIRIDH CHARR
421
MEALL AN DOIREIN
estown
974
SGÙRRBÀN
Loch a' Bhraoin
1019
MULLACH COIRE MHIC FHEARCHAIR
859
BEINN LÀIR
Loch
Letterewe Forest
Lochan Fada
999
A' CHAILLEACH
Loch Bad an Sgalaig
Loch Maree Hotel
Letterewe
Loch Garbhaig
19
Talladale
Maree
981
SLIOCH
A832
Loch Gainneamhach
210
680
BEINN A' MHÙINIDH
711
BEINN NAN RAMH
Loch na A-Oidhche
Loch a Ghodhainn
875
BAOSBHEINN
Kinlochewe Forest
855
BEINN AN EÒIN
619
BEINN BHREAC
724
Loch a' Bhealaich
Beinn Eighe
Incheril
933
FIONN BHEIN
Kinlochewe
1009
914
ALLIGIN
RUADH
972
Glen Docherty
EIGHE
A832
10
0 1 2 3 4 miles
0 1 2 3 4 5 kilometres

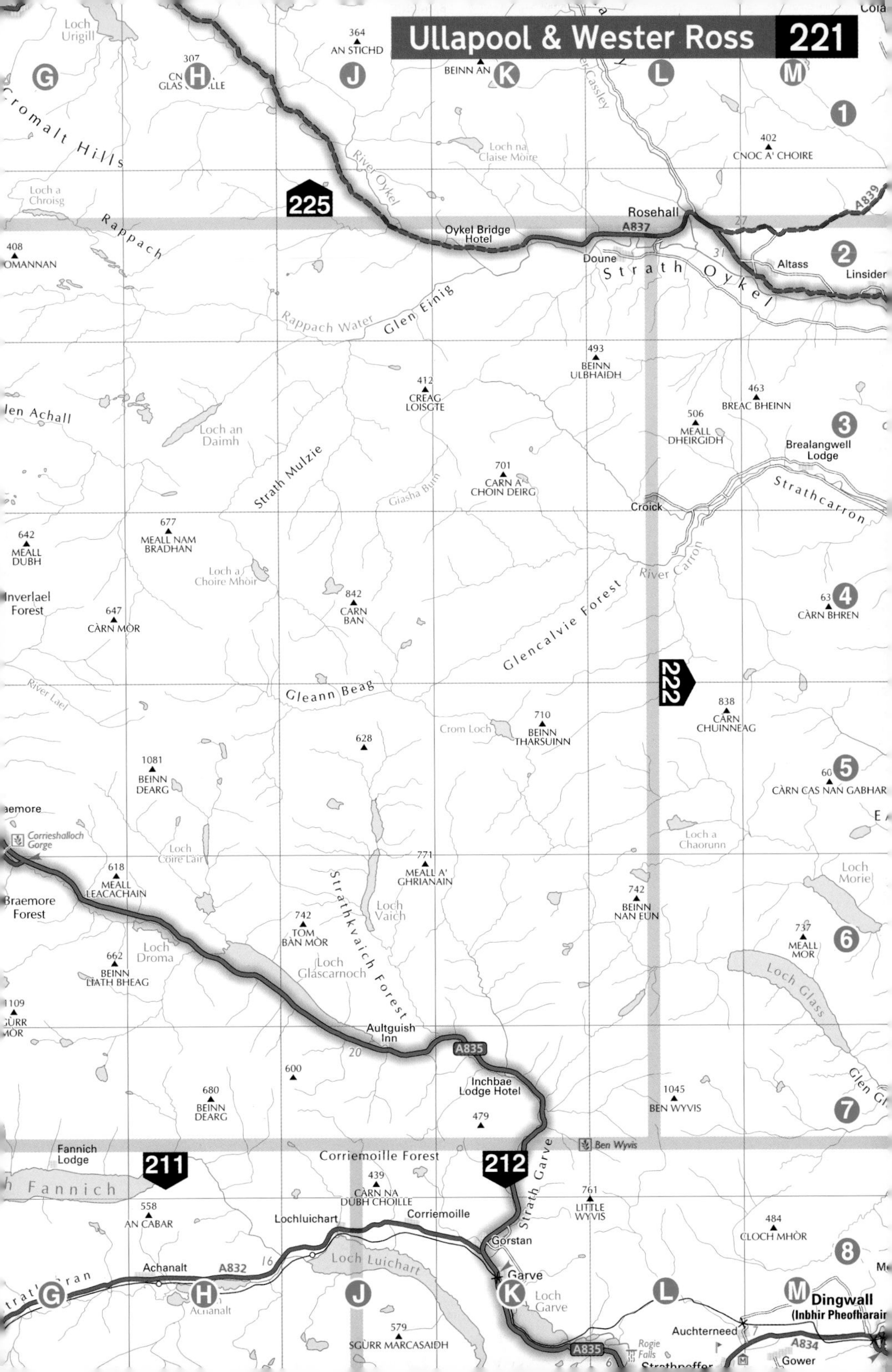
Loch Urigill
364
AN STICHD
BEINN AN
307
Cromalt Hills
Loch na Claise Mòire
402
CNOC A' CHOIRE
Loch a Chroisg
225
River Oykel
Rosehall
A837
A839
Rappach
Oykel Bridge Hotel
Doune
Strath Oykel
Altass
Linside
408
Rappach Water
Glen Einig
493
BEINN ULBHAIDH
412
CREAG LOISGTE
463
BREAC BHEINN
506
MEALL DHEIRGIDH
Glen Achall
Loch an Daimh
Brealangwell Lodge
Strath Mulzie
701
CARN A' CHOIN DEIRG
Giasha Burn
Croick
Strathcarron
677
MEALL NAM BRADHAN
642
MEALL DUBH
Loch a Choire Mhòir
River Carron
Glencalvie Forest
Inverlael Forest
842
CARN BAN
647
CÀRN MÒR
CÀRN BHREN
River Lael
Gleann Beag
222
838
CARN CHUINNEAG
710
BEINN THARSUINN
Crom Loch
628
1081
BEINN DEARG
CÀRN CAS NAN GABHAR
Corrieshalloch Gorge
Loch a Chaorunn
Loch Coire Lair
771
MEALL A' GHRIANAIN
Loch Morie
618
MEALL LEACACHAIN
Strathkvaich Forest
742
BEINN NAN EUN
Braemore Forest
Loch Vaich
742
TOM BÀN MÒR
737
MEALL MOR
Loch Droma
662
BEINN LIATH BHEAG
Loch Glascarnoch
Loch Glass
1109
Aultguish Inn
A835
600
Inchbae Lodge Hotel
1045
BEN WYVIS
680
BEINN DEARG
479
Fannich Lodge
Corriemoille Forest
Ben Wyvis
211
212
Loch Fannich
439
CÀRN NA DUBH CHOILLE
Strath Garve
761
LITTLE WYVIS
558
AN CABAR
Lochluichart
Corriemoille
484
CLOCH MHÒR
Gorstan
Achanalt
A832
Loch Luichart
Garve
Loch Garve
Dingwall
(Inbhir Pheofharain)
579
SGÙRR MARCASAIDH
Auchterneed
A835
Rogie Falls
A834
Gower

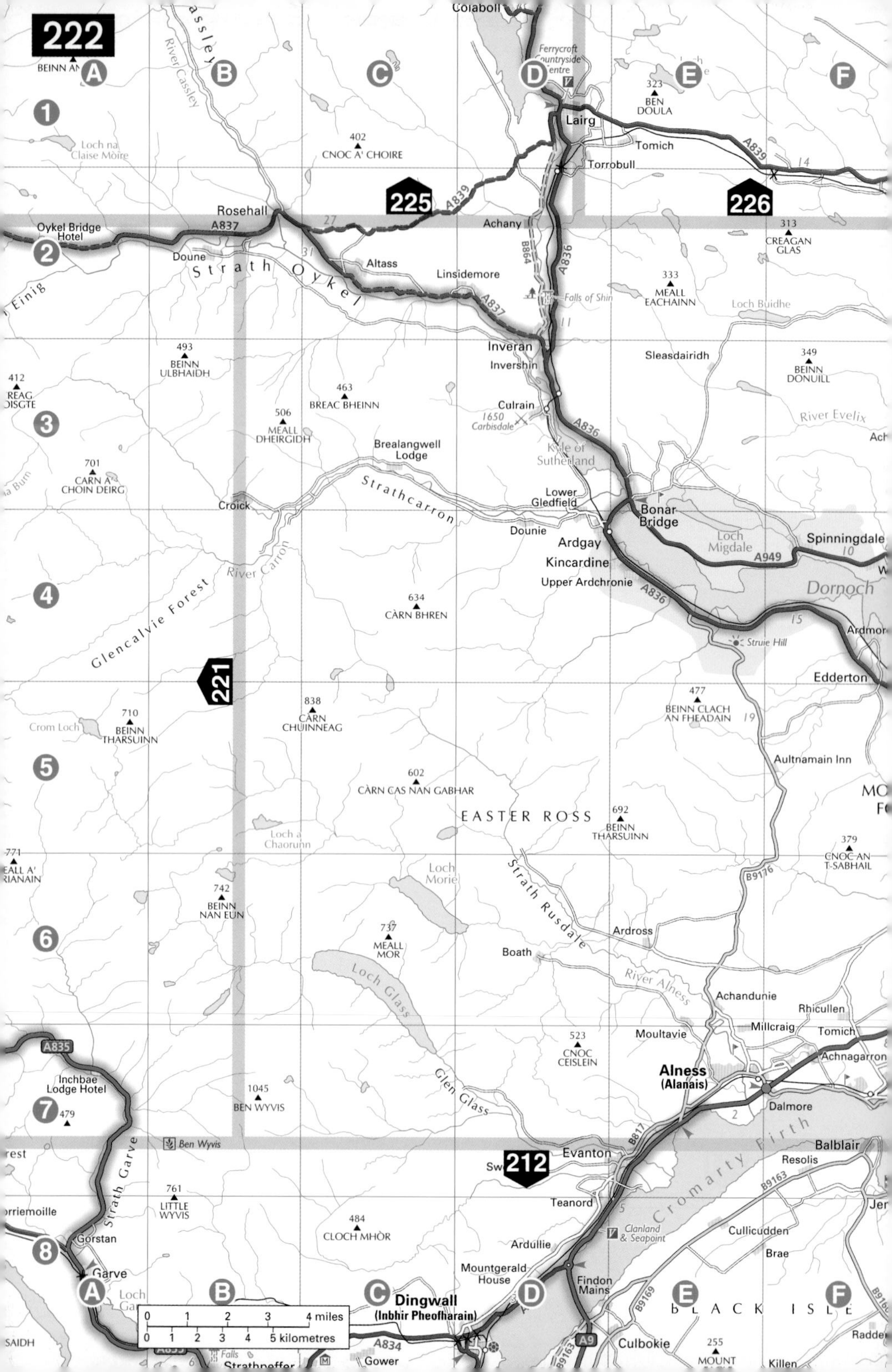
Colaboll
Ferrycroft Countryside Centre
Lairg
Tomich
Torrobull
A839
BEN DOULA
CNOC A' CHOIRE
Loch na Claise Mòire
River Cassley
Rosehall
Oykel Bridge Hotel
A837
Doune
Strath Oykel
Altass
Achany
Linsidemore
A836
B864
Falls of Shin
MEALL EACHAINN
Loch Buidhe
CREAGAN GLAS
225
226
Inveran
Invershin
Culrain
1650 Carbisdale
Sleasdairidh
BEINN DONUILL
River Evelix
BEINN ULBHAIDH
BREAC BHEINN
MEALL DHEIRGIDH
CARN A' CHOIN DEIRG
Brealangwell Lodge
Kyle of Sutherland
Strathcarron
Croick
Lower Gledfield
Dounie
Bonar Bridge
Ardgay
Kincardine
Upper Ardchronie
Loch Migdale
Spinningdale
A949
Dornoch
River Carron
Glencalvie Forest
CÀRN BHREN
Struie Hill
Edderton
Ardmore
221
CÀRN CHUINNEAG
BEINN THARSUINN
Crom Loch
BEINN CLACH AN FHEADAIN
Aultnamain Inn
CÀRN CAS NAN GABHAR
EASTER ROSS
Loch a' Chaorunn
CNOC AN T-SABHAIL
B9176
Loch Morie
Strath Rusdale
BEINN NAN EUN
MEALL MOR
Ardross
Boath
Loch Glass
River Alness
Achandunie
Rhicullen
Millcraig
Tomich
Moultavie
CNOC CEISLEIN
Alness (Alanais)
Achnagarron
Dalmore
A835
Inchbae Lodge Hotel
BEN WYVIS
Ben Wyvis
Glen Glass
Strath Garve
B817
Evanton
212
Cromarty Firth
Balblair
Resolis
B9163
Teanord
LITTLE WYVIS
CLOCH MHÒR
Clanland & Seapoint
Cullicudden
Brae
Gorstan
Garve
Ardullie
Mountgerald House
Findon Mains
Dingwall (Inbhir Pheofharain)
BLACK ISLE
B9169
A834
A9
Culbokie
MOUNT
Strathpeffer
Gower
Killen
0 1 2 3 4 miles
0 1 2 3 4 5 kilometres

River Brora
Dalreavoch Lodge
Loch Horn
520 BEN HORN
378 CAGAR FEOSAIG
Dalchalm
Brora
227
Doll
Carn Liath
A9
Backies
446 BEN LUNDIE
383 BEN BHRAGGIE
Rhives
Dunrobin Castle
Golspie
Golspie Burn
Torboll
Cambusavie Platform
Loch Fleet
Badninish
Skelbo
Skelbo Street
Fourpenny
Embo
Birichin
B9168
Embo Street
Pitgrudy
Evelix
A949
Royal Dornoch
Camore
Dornoch
Historylinks
Cuthill
Dornoch Point
Dornoch Firth
Dornoch Firth Bridge
Innis Mhor
Tarbat Ness
Wilkhaven
Brucefield
Portmahomack
Glenmorangie
Morangie
Inver
Rockfield
Arboll
B9165
284
Tain (Baile Dhubhthaich)
Toulvaddie
Lochslin
Loch Eye
Rhynie
Hill of Fearn
Balmuchy
Hilton of Cadboll Chapel (ruin)
Newfield
Fearn
Tullich
B9166
Hilton
Arabella
Balintore
Ballchraggan
Shandwick
Shandwick Bay
Kildary
Ankerville
Milton
B9175
Kilmuir
Pitcalnie
Barbaraville
Nigg
Balintraid
Nigg Bay
Nigg Ferry
Moray Firth
Cromarty
Cromarty Bay
Hugh Miller's Cottage
213
214
Burghead
Newton
B9163
Allerton
Navity
Findhorn
Culbin Sands
Findhorn Bay
B9011
Upper Eathie
Kincorth House
Culbin Forest
Kintessack
Grange Hall
Sueno's Stone
Whiteness Head
Nairn
Brodie
G H J K L M
1 2 3 4 5 6 7 8

224
A
B
C
D
E
F
1
2
3
4
5
6
7
8
Scourie Bay
A894
Scourie
Scourie More
Badcall
Badcall Bay
Loch a' Mhuilinn
386
BEN AUSKAIRD
228
Rudh' a' Mhucard
17
419
BEN STROME
OLDANY ISLAND
Eddrachillis Bay
Loch a' Chàirn Bhàin
Kylestrome
Kylesku
Unapool
Point of Stoer
Old Man of Stoer
Culkein Drumbeg
Culkein
Clashnessie Bay
Oldany
Drumbeg
Achnacarnin
Nedd
B869
Clashmore
Loch Poll
Glen Leirg
Loch an Leothaid
776
SAIL GHORM
809
QUINAG
Clashnessie
Stoer
A894
Clachtoll
Bay of Clachtoll
Loch Beannach
GLAS
Achmelvich Bay
Rhicarn
11
Loch Assynt
Achmelvich
A837
Ardvreck
Baddidarrach
539
BEINN GHARBH
Soyea Island
Loch Inver
Lochinver
Strathan
Assynt - Coigach
Inverkirkaig
Loch na Gainimh
847
CANISP
Stronchrubie
Loanan
River Kirkaig
Fionn Loch
732
SUILVEN
Rhu Coigach
Eilean Mòr
River
Enard Bay
Loch Awe
Rubha Mòr
Reiff
Achnahaird
Càm Loch
Altandhu
Loch Sionascaig
Loch Veyatie
Eilean Mullagrach
849
CUL MÒR
Ledmore Junction
Loch Osgaig
Knockan
Elphin
Isle Ristol
Polbain
612
STAC POLLAIDH
Badentarbet
Loch Urigill
Glas-leac Mòr
SUMMER ISLES
769
CUL BEAG
Achiltibuie
Knockan Crag
Tanera Beg
Badentarbat Bay
Loch Lurgainn
Polglass
Ben Mor Coigach
Cromalt Hills
Steornabhagh (Stornoway)
Tanera Mòr
Glas-leac Beag
Horse Island
Horse Sound
COIGACH
652
BEN MORE COIGACH
Achduart
Drumrunie Lodge
Culnacraig
18
Loch a Chroisg
Eilean Dubh
Priest Island
Strathcanaird
220
Strath Canaird
408
NA DROMANNAN
A835
Leac Dhonn
Cailleach Head
Isle Martin
Ardmair
Scoraig
Annat Bay
Stattic Point
Morefield
0 1 2 3 4 miles
0 1 2 3 4 5 kilometres
635
Ullapool (Ulapul)
Loch Achall
Glen Achall
GRUINARD ISLAND
Badluarach

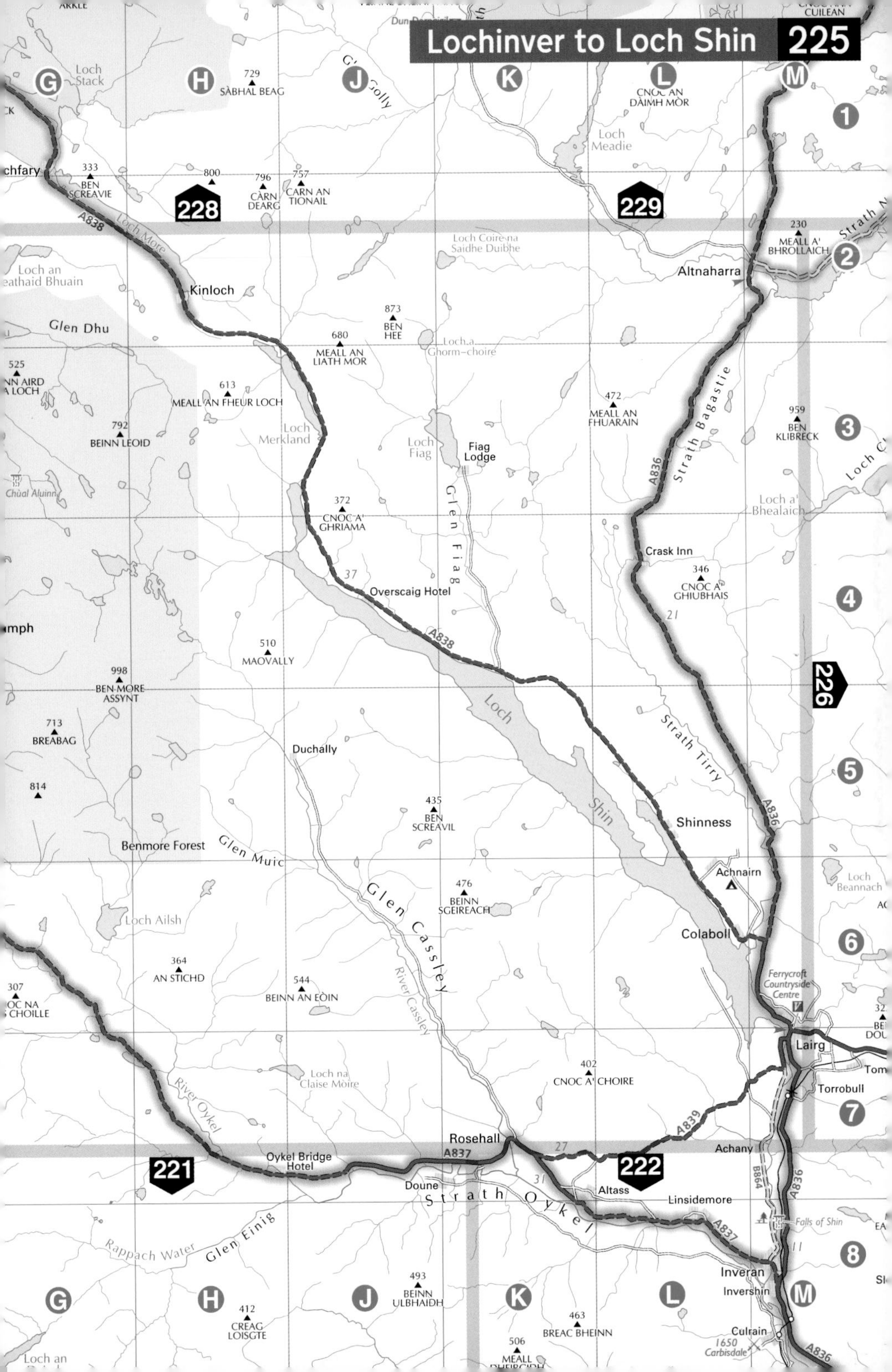
Loch Stack
729
SÀBHAL BEAG
Golly
CNOC AN DÀIMH MÒR
Loch Meadie
333
BEN SCREAVIE
800
796
CÀRN DEARG
757
CARN AN TIONAIL
228
229
A838
Loch More
230
MEALL A' BHROLLAICH
Strath
Loch Coire na Saidhe Duibhe
Altnaharra
Loch an Leathaid Bhuain
Kinloch
873
BEN HEE
Glen Dhu
680
MEALL AN LIATH MOR
Loch a Ghorm-choire
525
613
MEALL AN FHEUR LOCH
472
MEALL AN FHUARAIN
Strath Bagastie
959
BEN KLIBRECK
792
BEINN LEOID
Loch Merkland
Loch Fiag
Fiag Lodge
A836
Chùal Aluinn
Glen Fiag
372
CNOC A' GHRIAMA
Loch a' Bhealaich
Crask Inn
346
CNOC A' GHIUBHAIS
37
Overscaig Hotel
21
A838
510
MAOVALLY
226
998
BEN MORE ASSYNT
Loch Shin
713
BREABAG
Duchally
Strath Tirry
814
435
BEN SCREAVIL
Shinness
Benmore Forest
Glen Muic
Achnairn
Loch Beannach
476
BEINN SGEIREACH
Glen Cassley
Loch Ailsh
Colaboll
364
AN STICHD
307
544
BEINN AN EÒIN
River Cassley
Ferrycroft Countryside Centre
Lairg
Loch na Claise Mòire
402
CNOC A' CHOIRE
Torrobull
River Oykel
A839
Rosehall
27
Achany
221
Oykel Bridge Hotel
A837
222
Doune
31
Altass
Linsidemore
B864
Strath Oykel
A837
Falls of Shin
Rappach Water
Glen Einig
11
Inveran
493
BEINN ULBHAIDH
Invershin
412
CREAG LOISGTE
463
BREAC BHEINN
Culrain
1650 Carbisdale
506
A836

226
229
230
225
223
A
B
C
D
E
F
1
2
3
4
5
6
7
8
Loch Syre
Syre
River Naver
NA CUAICHE
217 CNOC A' BHREUN BHAID
345 CNOC NAM TRI-CHLACH
Loch Cròcach
294 POLE HILL
259 BEINN ROSAIL
B871
404 BEINN MHADADH
588 BEN GRIAM BEG
Loch Druim a-Chliabhain
590 BEN GRIAM MOR
337 MEAL A' BHEALAIDH
Halladale
Forsinard
Strath Naver
12
B873
16
Loch an Ruathair
A897
230 MEALL A' BHROLLAICH
270 BEADAIG
Loch Naver
River Mallart
Loch Rimsdale
Loch nan Clàr
Loch Badanloch
Loch Arichlinie
Loch an Altan Fhearna
Loch Truderscaig
River Helmsdale
Kinbrace
959 BEN KLIBRECK
Loch Choire Forest
694 CREAG N-IOLAIRE
434 CNOC AN LIATH-BHAID MHÒIR
202 CNOC DAIL-CHAIRN
713 CREAG MHÒR
Loch Choire
Loch a' Bhealaich
Borrobol Forest
Strath Free
Loch Ascaig
364 CNOC NA BREUN-CHOILLE
388 CREAG NAM FIADH
Learable Hill Cairns, Stone Row & Stone Circles
Gorm-loch Mòr
Ben Armine Forest
Strath Skinsdale
Strath
Glas-loch Mòr
337 CNOC NA H-INNSE MOIRE
462 MEALIAN LIATH MOR
421 CNOC NAN CRÙBAG MÒR
A836
Black Water
Loch Beannach
317 SITHEAN ACHADH NAN EUN
River Brora
293 CNOC LEAMHNACHD
Balnacoil Lodge
539 COL-BHEINN
Strath Brora
Loch Brora
Ferrycroft Countryside Centre
Loch Craggie
Dalreavoch Lodge
323 BEN DOULA
Loch Horn
520 BEN HORN
Lairg
Tomich
A839
14
Torrobull
Golspie Burn
378 CAGAR FEOSAIG
Rogart
Doll
Backies
Carn Liath
A9
313 CREAGAN GLAS
446 BEN LUNDIE
383 BEN BHRAGGIE
Dunrobin Castle
B864
333 MEALL EACHAINN
Rhives
Golspie
Falls of Shin
Torboll
Loch Buidhe
Sleasdairidh
349 BEINN DONUILL
Loch Fleet
Culrain
Badninish
Skelbo
Skelbo Street
Fourpenny
Achvaich
0 1 2 3 4 miles
0 1 2 3 4 5 kilometres

Altnabreac Station
CNOC NAN GALL
Rumsdale Water
Strathmore
Dalnawillan Lodge
Loch an Thulachan
Loch Sand
Achavanich
Loch Rangag
248 STEMSTER HILL
226 COIRE NA BEINN
Glutt Water
230
348 BEN ALISKY
231
287 BEN-A-CHIELT
Upper Lybster
Glutt Lodge
264 CNOCAN CONACHREAG
Swiney
Invershore
Lybster
Lybster Bay
Forse
40
KNOCKFIN HEIGHTS
Houstry
Land-hallow
Smerral
Latheron
Dunbeath Water
Latheronwheel
Janetstown
317 CNOC LOCH MHADADH
Berriedale Water
A9
Laidhay Croft
437
Braemore
Dunbeath
Dunbeath Bay
484 MAIDEN PAP
705 MORVEN
Knockally
518 CNOC AN EIREANNAICH
Ramscraigs
626 SCARABEN
Borgue
Langwell Forest
20
Newport
554 CREAG SCALABSDALE
Langwell House
Berriedale
Lodge
401 CNOC NA MAOILE
416 BEINN DUBHAIN
Badbea Historic Village
A897
Torrish
River Helmsdale
404 CREAG THORARAIDH
Ord of Caithness
Timespan
Navidale House Hotel
West Helmsdale
East Helmsdale
Helmsdale
591 BEINN NA MEILICH
Gartymore
Portgower
Glen Loth
Lothmore
Lothbeg
21
G
H
J
K
L
M
1
2
3
4
5
6
7
8

A
B
C
D
E
F
1
2
3
4
5
6
7
8
CAPE WRATH
Kearvaig Bay
Cléit Dhubh
Faraid Head
371
SGRIBHIS-BHEINN
297
CNOC A GHIUBHAIS
300
MAOVALLY
Balnakeil Bay
Balnakeil
Sango Bay
THE PARPH
Durness
457
FASHVEN
Sangomore
Smoo
Sangob
Keoldale
Loch Airigh na Beinne
Kyle of Durness
Sandwood Bay
Sandwood Loch
Loch Meadaidh
485
CREAG RIABACH
468
BEINN DEARG MHÒR
464
MEALL NA MÒINE
Rudh' an Fhir Leithe
Strath Shinary
423
MEALL MEADHONACH
A838
331
GHLAS-BHEINN
Sheigra
Balchreick
Blairmore
19
521
FARVEALL
489
MEALL NA CRÀ
Laid
Oldshoremore
355
AN SOCACH
773
BEINN SPIONNAIDH
Kinlochbervie
Loch Clash
Badcall
Loch Inchard
B801
801
CRANSTACKIE
Achriesgill
Strath Dionard
River Dionard
Strath Beag
31
A838
520
AN LEAN-CH
Rhiconich
Loch na Claise Càrnaich
Rudha Ruadh
908
FOINAVEN
Skerricha
Fanagmore
Loch Laxford
Tarbet
A838
Foindle
HANDA ISLAND
North-west Sutherland
Loch na Tuadh
7
Laxford Bridge
River Laxford
786
ARKLE
Scourie Bay
FEINN
A894
Scourie
Scourie More
Loch Stack
729
SÀBHAL BEAG
Glen Golly
721
BEN STACK
Badcall
Strath Stack
Badcall Bay
386
BEN AUSKAIRD
Loch a' Mhuilinn
Achfary
333
BEN SCREAVIE
800
796
CÀRN DEARG
757
CARN AN TIONAIL
Rudh' a' Mhucard
A838
Loch More
17
224
225
OLDANY ISLAND
Eddrachillis Bay
419
BEN STROME
Loch an Leathaid-Bhuain
Loch a' Chàirn Bhàin
Kylestrome
Kinloch
Culkein Drumbeg
Kylesku
Loch Glendhu
Glen Dhu
Olda
Drumbeg
B869
Unapool
680
MEALL AN LIATH MOR
Nedd
525
BEINN A DA LOCH
Loch Glencoul
613
MEALL AN FHEUR LOCH
Loch Poll
0 1 2 3 4 miles
0 1 2 3 4 5 kilometres
792
BEINN LEOID
Loch Merkland
QUINAG

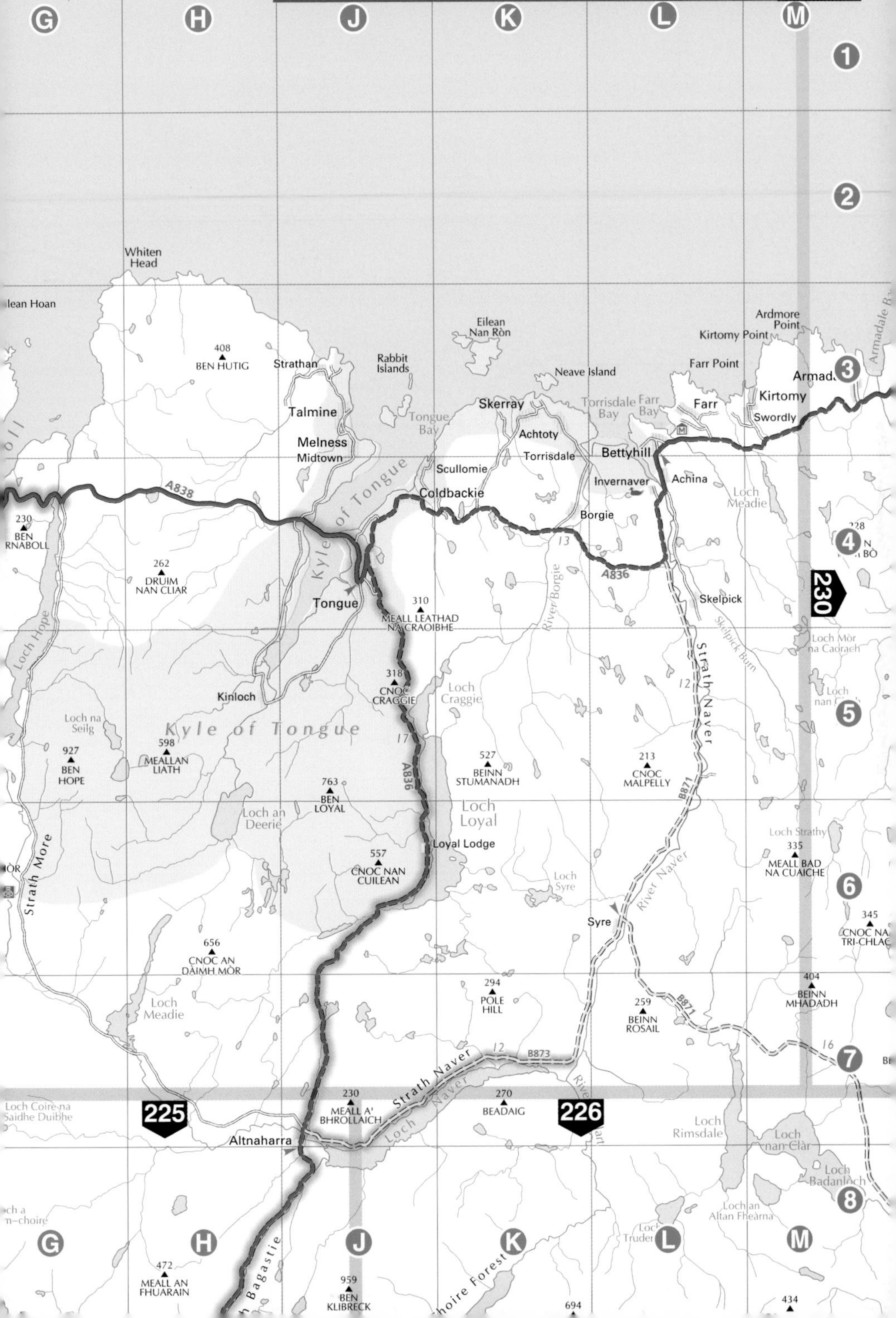
G
H
J
K
L
M
1
2
3
4
5
6
7
8
Whiten Head
Eilean Hoan
408 BEN HUTIG
Strathan
Rabbit Islands
Eilean Nan Ròn
Neave Island
Kirtomy Point
Ardmore Point
Farr Point
Armadale Bay
Armad
Talmine
Melness
Midtown
Tongue Bay
Skerray
Torrisdale Bay
Farr Bay
Farr
Kirtomy
Swordly
Achtoty
Torrisdale
Bettyhill
Scullomie
Invernaver
Achina
Coldbackie
Borgie
Loch Meadie
A838
Kyle of Tongue
230 BEN LOYAL
262 DRUIM NAN CLIAR
13
A836
River Borgie
Tongue
310 MEALL LEATHAD NA CRAOIBHE
Skelpick
Skelpick Burn
230
Loch Mòr na Caorach
Loch Hope
318 CNOC CRAGGIE
Loch Craggie
Kinloch
Strath Naver
12
Loch nan
Loch na Seilg
Kyle of Tongue
598 MEALLAN LIATH
927 BEN HOPE
17
527 BEINN STUMANADH
213 CNOC MALPELLY
763 BEN LOYAL
B871
Loch an Deerie
Loch Loyal
Loch Strathy
Strath More
Loyal Lodge
335 MEALL BAD NA CUAICHE
557 CNOC NAN CUILEAN
Loch Syre
River Naver
345 CNOC NA TRI-CHLAC
Syre
656 CNOC AN DÀIMH MÒR
404 BEINN MHADADH
294 POLE HILL
259 BEINN ROSAIL
Loch Meadie
B871
16
12
B873
Strath Naver
230 MEALL A' BHROLLAICH
270 BEADAIG
Loch Naver
Loch Coire na Saidhe Duibhe
225
226
Loch Rimsdale
Loch nan Clàr
Altnaharra
Loch Badanloch
Loch an Altan Fhearna
Loch Truder
472 MEALL AN FHUARAIN
959 BEN KLIBRECK
Bagastie
Choire Forest
694
434

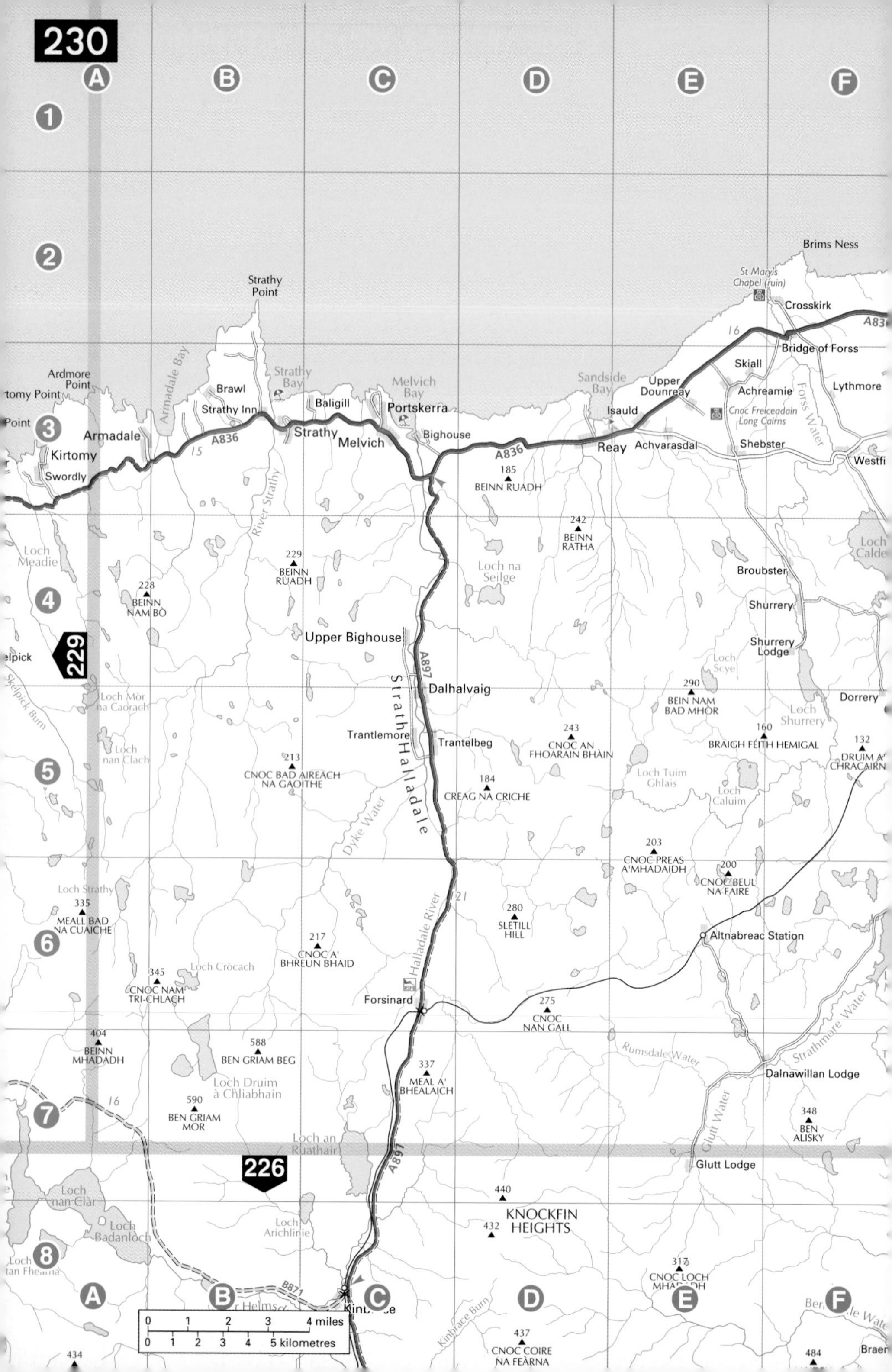
A
B
C
D
E
F
1
2
3
4
5
6
7
8
Brims Ness
St Mary's Chapel (ruin)
Crosskirk
A836
16
Bridge of Forss
Skiall
Lythmore
Strathy Point
Ardmore Point
Kirtomy Point
Point
Armadale Bay
Strathy Bay
Melvich Bay
Sandside Bay
Upper Dounreay
Achreamie
Forss Water
Brawl
Baligill
Portskerra
Isauld
Cnoc Freiceadain Long Cairns
Strathy Inn
Armadale
Strathy
Melvich
Bighouse
Reay
Achvarasdal
Shebster
Westfi
Kirtomy
Swordly
A836
15
185
BEINN RUADH
242
BEINN RATHA
Loch Meadie
River Strathy
229
BEINN RUADH
Loch na Seilge
Broubster
Loch Calde
228
BEINN NAM BÒ
Shurrery
Upper Bighouse
229
Skelpick
Shurrery Lodge
Loch Scye
A897
Strath Halladale
Dalhalvaig
290
BEIN NAM BAD MHOR
Dorrery
Skelpick Burn
Loch Mòr na Caorach
Loch Shurrery
Trantlemore
Trantelbeg
243
CNOC AN FHOARAIN BHÀIN
160
BRAIGH FÉITH HEMIGAL
132
DRUIM A' CHRACAIRN
Loch nan Clach
213
CNOC BAD AIREACH NA GAOITHE
Loch Tuim Ghlais
Loch Caluim
184
CREAG NA CRICHE
Dyke Water
203
CNOC PREAS A'MHADAIDH
200
CNOC BEUL NA FAIRE
Loch Strathy
335
MEALL BAD NA CUAICHE
Halladale River
21
280
SLETILL HILL
Altnabreac Station
217
CNOC A' BHREUN BHAID
Loch Cròcach
345
CNOC NAM TRI-CHLACH
Forsinard
275
CNOC NAN GALL
404
BEINN MHADADH
588
BEN GRIAM BEG
337
MEAL A' BHEALAICH
Rumsdale Water
Strathmore Water
Dalnawillan Lodge
Loch Druim à Chliabhain
16
590
BEN GRIAM MOR
Glutt Water
348
BEN ALISKY
Loch an Ruathair
226
A897
Glutt Lodge
Loch nan Clàr
440
KNOCKFIN HEIGHTS
Loch Badanloch
Loch Arichlinie
432
Loch nan Fhearna
317
CNOC LOCH MHADAIDH
B871
Kinbrace
Kinbrace Burn
0 1 2 3 4 miles
0 1 2 3 4 5 kilometres
437
CNOC COIRE NA FEÀRNA
434
484
Braen

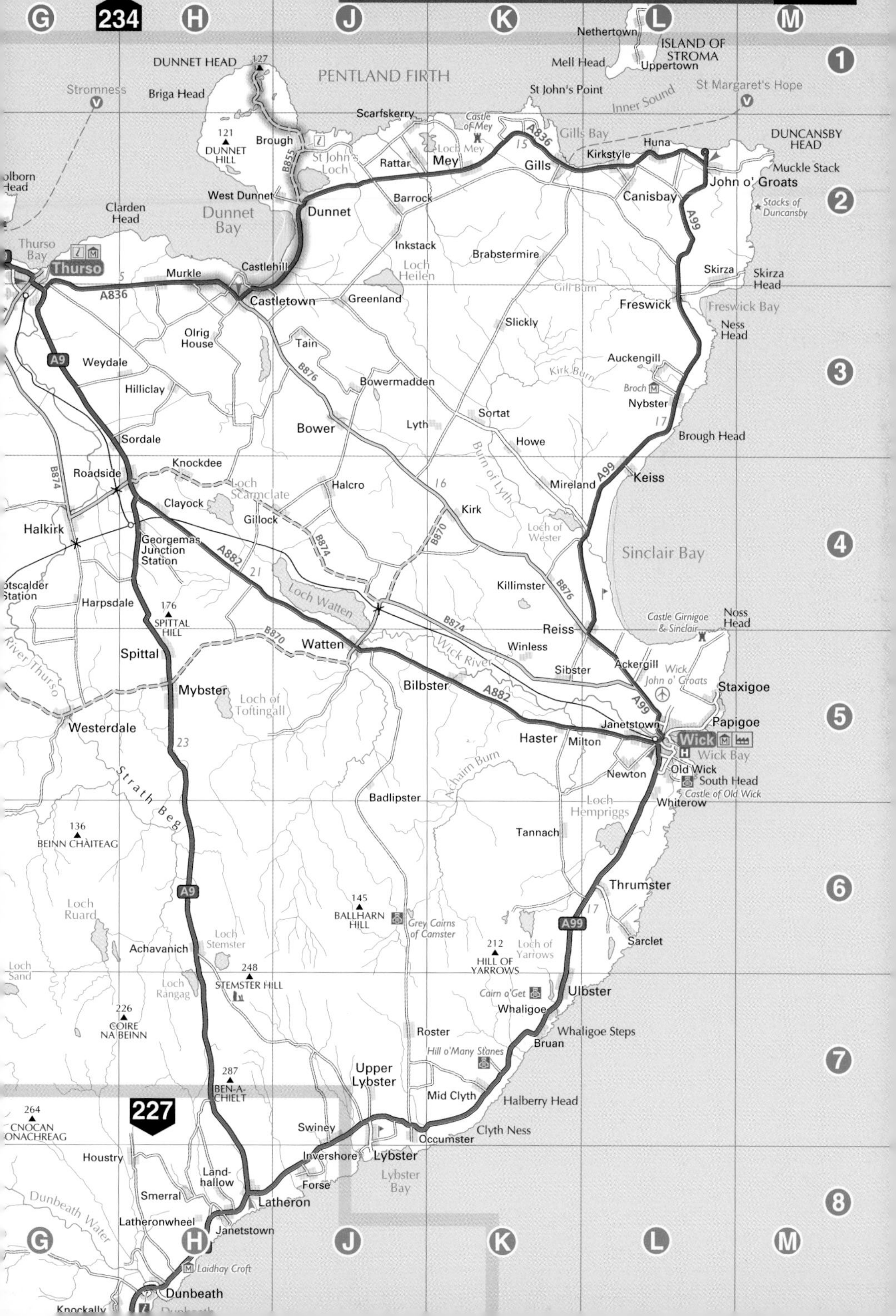

234
227
PENTLAND FIRTH
DUNNET HEAD
127
Stromness
Briga Head
121
DUNNET HILL
Brough
St John's Loch
West Dunnet
Dunnet
Dunnet Bay
Clarden Head
Thurso Bay
Thurso
Murkle
Castlehill
Castletown
A836
A9
B855
B874
B876
B870
A882
A99
Nethertown
ISLAND OF STROMA
Uppertown
Mell Head
St John's Point
Inner Sound
St Margaret's Hope
Gills Bay
Scarfskerry
Castle of Mey
Loch Mey
Rattar
Mey
Gills
Kirkstyle
Huna
DUNCANSBY HEAD
Muckle Stack
John o' Groats
Canisbay
Stacks of Duncansby
Barrock
Inkstack
Loch Heilen
Brabstermire
Greenland
Gill Burn
Skirza
Skirza Head
Freswick
Freswick Bay
Ness Head
Slickly
Olrig House
Tain
Weydale
Hilliclay
Bowermadden
Auckengill
Kirk Burn
Broch
Nybster
Sortat
Lyth
Bower
Brough Head
Howe
Sordale
Knockdee
Roadside
Loch Scarmclate
Halcro
Mireland
Keiss
Clayock
Gillock
Kirk
Burn of Lyth
Halkirk
Georgemas Junction Station
Loch of Wester
Sinclair Bay
Altnabreac Station
Loch Watten
Killimster
Harpsdale
176
SPITTAL HILL
Castle Girnigoe & Sinclair
Noss Head
Reiss
Spittal
Watten
Winless
Wick River
Ackergill
Wick John o' Groats
Staxigoe
Sibster
River Thurso
Mybster
Loch of Toftingall
Bilbster
Janetstown
Papigoe
Westerdale
Haster
Milton
Wick
Wick Bay
Old Wick
Newton
South Head
Castle of Old Wick
Strath Beg
Achairn Burn
Badlipster
Whiterow
Loch Hempriggs
136
BEINN CHÀITEAG
Tannach
Thrumster
Loch Ruard
145
BALLHARN HILL
Grey Cairns of Camster
Sarclet
212
HILL OF YARROWS
Loch of Yarrows
Loch Stemster
Achavanich
248
STEMSTER HILL
Loch Sand
Loch Rangag
Ulbster
Cairn o'Get
Whaligoe
226
COIRE NA BEINN
Whaligoe Steps
Roster
Bruan
Hill o'Many Stanes
287
BEN-A-CHIELT
Upper Lybster
Mid Clyth
Halberry Head
264
CNOCAN CONACHREAG
Swiney
Clyth Ness
Occumster
Houstry
Invershore
Lybster
Lybster Bay
Land-hallow
Forse
Smerral
Dunbeath Water
Latheron
Latheronwheel
Janetstown
Laidhay Croft
Dunbeath
Knockally

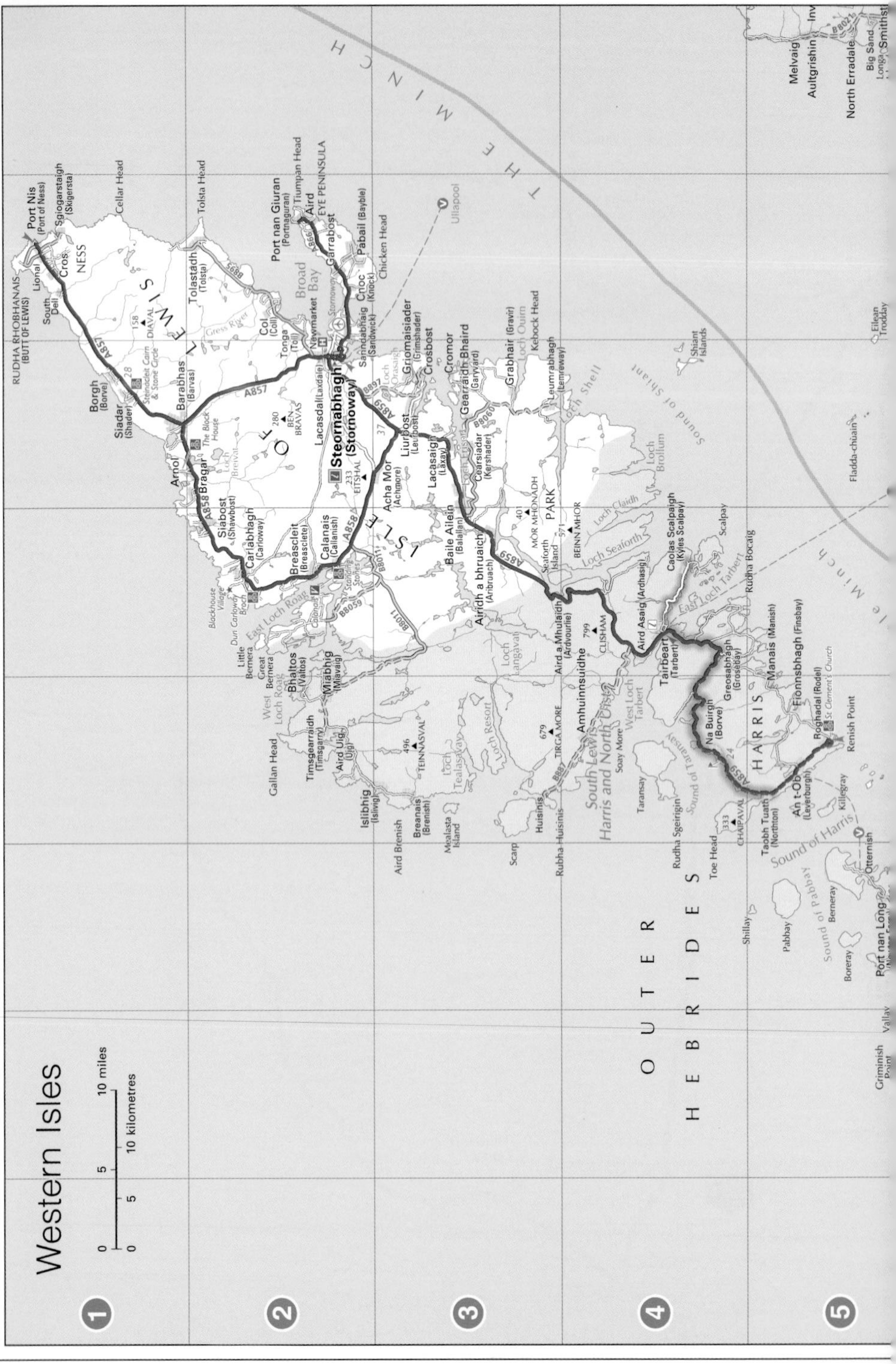
Western Isles
0 5 10 miles
0 5 10 kilometres
1
2
3
4
5
THE MINCH
ISLE OF LEWIS
OUTER HEBRIDES
HARRIS
PARK
NESS
EYE PENINSULA
RUDHA RHOBHANAIS (BUTT OF LEWIS)
Port Nis (Port of Ness)
Sgiogarstaigh (Skigersta)
Cellar Head
Tolsta Head
Tiumpan Head
Port nan Giuran (Portnaguran)
Aird
Garrabost
Pabail (Bayble)
Chicken Head
Cnoc (Knock)
Broad Bay
Lional
Cros
South Dell
Tolastadh (Tolsta)
Col (Coll)
Tonga (Toll)
Newmarket
Sanndabhaig (Sandwick)
Steòrnabhagh (Stornoway)
Lacasdal (Laxdale)
Borgh (Borve)
Siadar (Shader)
Barabhas (Barvas)
Arnol
Bragar
Siabost (Shawbost)
Càrlabhagh (Carloway)
Breascleit (Breasclete)
Calanais (Callanish)
Acha Mòr (Achmore)
Liurbost (Leurbost)
Lacasaigh (Laxay)
Baile Ailein (Balallan)
Airidh a bhruaich (Arnbruach)
Griomaisiader (Grimshader)
Crosbost
Cromor
Gearraidh Bhaird (Garyvard)
Cearsiadar (Kershader)
Grabhair (Gravir)
Kebock Head
Leumrabhagh (Lemreway)
Loch Shell
Sound of Shiant
Shiant Islands
Loch Brollum
Loch Claidh
Loch Seaforth
Seaforth Island
Caolas Scalpaigh (Kyles Scalpay)
Scalpay
East Loch Tarbert
Rudha Bocaig
Aird Asaig (Ardhasig)
Tairbeart (Tarbert)
Greosabhagh (Grosebay)
Manais (Manish)
Fionnsbhagh (Finsbay)
Roghadal (Rodel)
St Clement's Church
Renish Point
Na Buirgh (Borve)
An t-Ob (Leverburgh)
Taobh Tuath (Northton)
Killegray
Sound of Harris
Otternish
Berneray
Pabbay
Sound of Pabbay
Boreray
Shillay
Toe Head
CHAPAVAL
Rudha Sgeirigin
Taransay
Sound of Taransay
Soay More
West Loch Tarbert
Amhuinnsuidhe
Aird a Mhulaidh (Ardvourlie)
CLISHAM
Loch Langavat
Loch Resort
TIRGA MORE
Huisinis
Rubha Huisinis
Scarp
South Lewis, Harris and North Uist
Loch Tealasavay
TEINNASVAL
Breanais (Brenish)
Aird Brenish
Mealasta Island
Islibhig (Islivig)
Aird Uig (Uig)
Timsgearraidh (Timsgarry)
Gallan Head
Miabhig (Miavaig)
Bhaltos (Valtos)
West Loch Roag
Great Bernera
Little Bernera
Dun Carloway Broch
Blackhouse Village
East Loch Roag
Standing Stones
Loch Orasaigh
Steinacleit Cairn & Stone Circle
The Block House
Loch Breivat
Gress River
DIAVAL
BEN BRAVAS
EITSHAL
MÒR MHONADH
BEINN MHOR
Ullapool
Melvaig
Aultgrishin
North Erradale
Big Sand
Smithstown
Fladda-chùain
Eilean Trodday
Port nan Long
Griminish Point
Vallay
A857
A858
A859
B895
B897
B8060
B8011
B8059
B8021

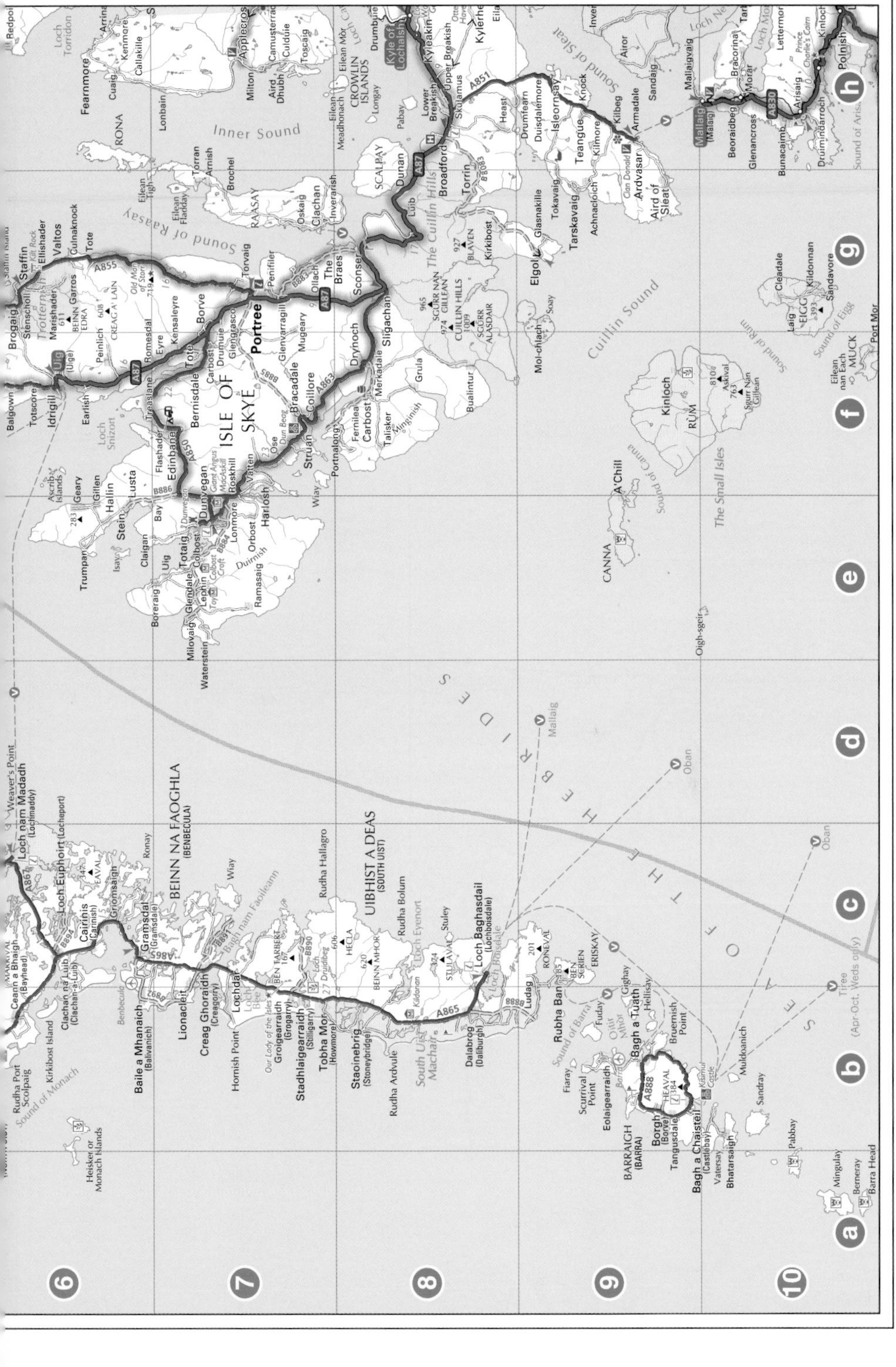
ISLE OF SKYE
Portree
Dunvegan
Uig
Staffin
Broadford
Kyleakin
Kyle of Lochalsh
RAASAY
SCALPAY
Sound of Raasay
Inner Sound
CROWLIN ISLANDS
RONA
Applecross
Sound of Sleat
Armadale
Mallaig
Arisaig
CANNA
RUM
EIGG
MUCK
Cuillin Sound
The Small Isles
Sound of Rum
Sound of Eigg
Sound of Canna
SEA OF THE HEBRIDES
BEINN NA FAOGHLA (BENBECULA)
UIBHIST A DEAS (SOUTH UIST)
Loch nam Madadh (Lochmaddy)
Loch Baghasdail (Lochboisdale)
BARRAIGH (BARRA)
ERISKAY
Bagh a Chaisteil (Castlebay)
Heisker or Monach Islands
Sound of Monach
Mingulay
Berneray
Barra Head
Pabbay
Sandray
Vatersay
Oban
Tiree (Apr-Oct, Weds only)
A87
A850
A855
A863
A851
A830
A865
A888
a
b
c
d
e
f
g
h
6
7
8
9
10

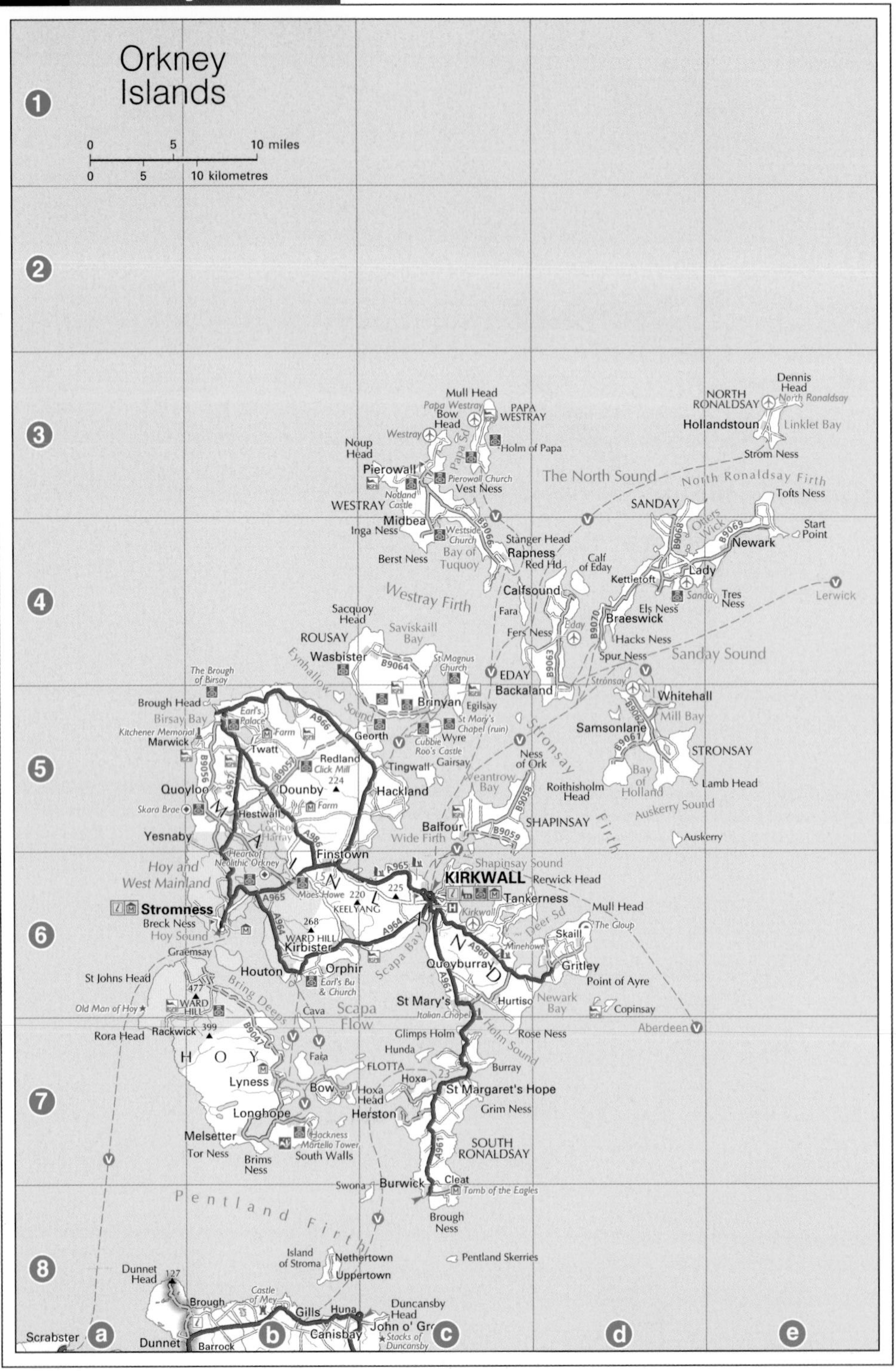
Orkney Islands
0 5 10 miles
0 5 10 kilometres
1
2
3
4
5
6
7
8
a
b
c
d
e
Mull Head
Papa Westray
PAPA WESTRAY
Bow Head
Westray
Holm of Papa
Noup Head
Papa Sd
Pierowall
Pierowall Church
Vest Ness
Notland Castle
WESTRAY
Midbea
Inga Ness
Westside Church
B9066
Stanger Head
Rapness
Red Hd
Berst Ness
Bay of Tuquoy
NORTH RONALDSAY
Dennis Head
North Ronaldsay
Hollandstoun
Linklet Bay
Strom Ness
The North Sound
North Ronaldsay Firth
SANDAY
Tofts Ness
B9068
Otters Wick
B9069
Start Point
Newark
Calf of Eday
Kettletoft
Lady
Sanday
Tres Ness
Lerwick
Westray Firth
Calfsound
Fara
Sacquoy Head
ROUSAY
Saviskaill Bay
B9070
Els Ness
Braeswick
Eday
Fers Ness
Hacks Ness
Wasbister
B9064
St Magnus Church
B9063
Spur Ness
Sanday Sound
Eynhallow Sound
EDAY
Backaland
Stronsay
The Brough of Birsay
Brough Head
Birsay Bay
Earl's Palace
Kitchener Memorial
Marwick
Farm
Twatt
A966
Brinyan
Egilsay
St Mary's Chapel (ruin)
Georth
Cubbie Roo's Castle
Wyre
Whitehall
Mill Bay
B9062
Samsonlane
B9061
Stronsay Firth
B9056
A967
B9057
Redland
Click Mill
224
Tingwall
Gairsay
Ness of Ork
STRONSAY
Quoyloo
Dounby
Hackland
Veantrow Bay
B9058
Roithisholm Head
Bay of Holland
Lamb Head
Skara Brae
Farm
Hestwall
Loch of Harray
MAINLAND
Auskerry Sound
Balfour
SHAPINSAY
Yesnaby
A986
Wide Firth
B9059
Auskerry
Finstown
Heart of Neolithic Orkney
A965
Shapinsay Sound
Hoy and West Mainland
KIRKWALL
Rerwick Head
Stromness
Moes Howe
220
KEELYLANG
225
Tankerness
Mull Head
Breck Ness
268
A965
Kirkwall
The Gloup
Hoy Sound
A964
WARD HILL
Kirbister
Deer Sd
Skaill
Graemsay
Minehowe
A960
Quoyburray
Gritley
Houton
Orphir
Scapa Bay
St Johns Head
Point of Ayre
477
Earl's Bu & Church
Bring Deeps
A961
WARD HILL
Old Man of Hoy
Cava
Scapa Flow
St Mary's
Hurtiso
Newark Bay
Copinsay
Italian Chapel
Rora Head
Rackwick
399
B9047
Glimps Holm
Holm Sound
Rose Ness
Aberdeen
Hunda
HOY
Fara
FLOTTA
Burray
Lyness
Hoxa
23
Bow
Hoxa Head
St Margaret's Hope
Longhope
Herston
Grim Ness
Melsetter
Hackness Martello Tower
South Walls
A961
SOUTH RONALDSAY
Tor Ness
Brims Ness
Swona
Burwick
Cleat
Tomb of the Eagles
Pentland Firth
Brough Ness
Island of Stroma
Nethertown
Pentland Skerries
Uppertown
Dunnet Head
127
Castle of Mey
Brough
Gills
Huna
Duncansby Head
Scrabster
Canisbay
John o' Gr
Stacks of Duncansby
Dunnet
Barrock

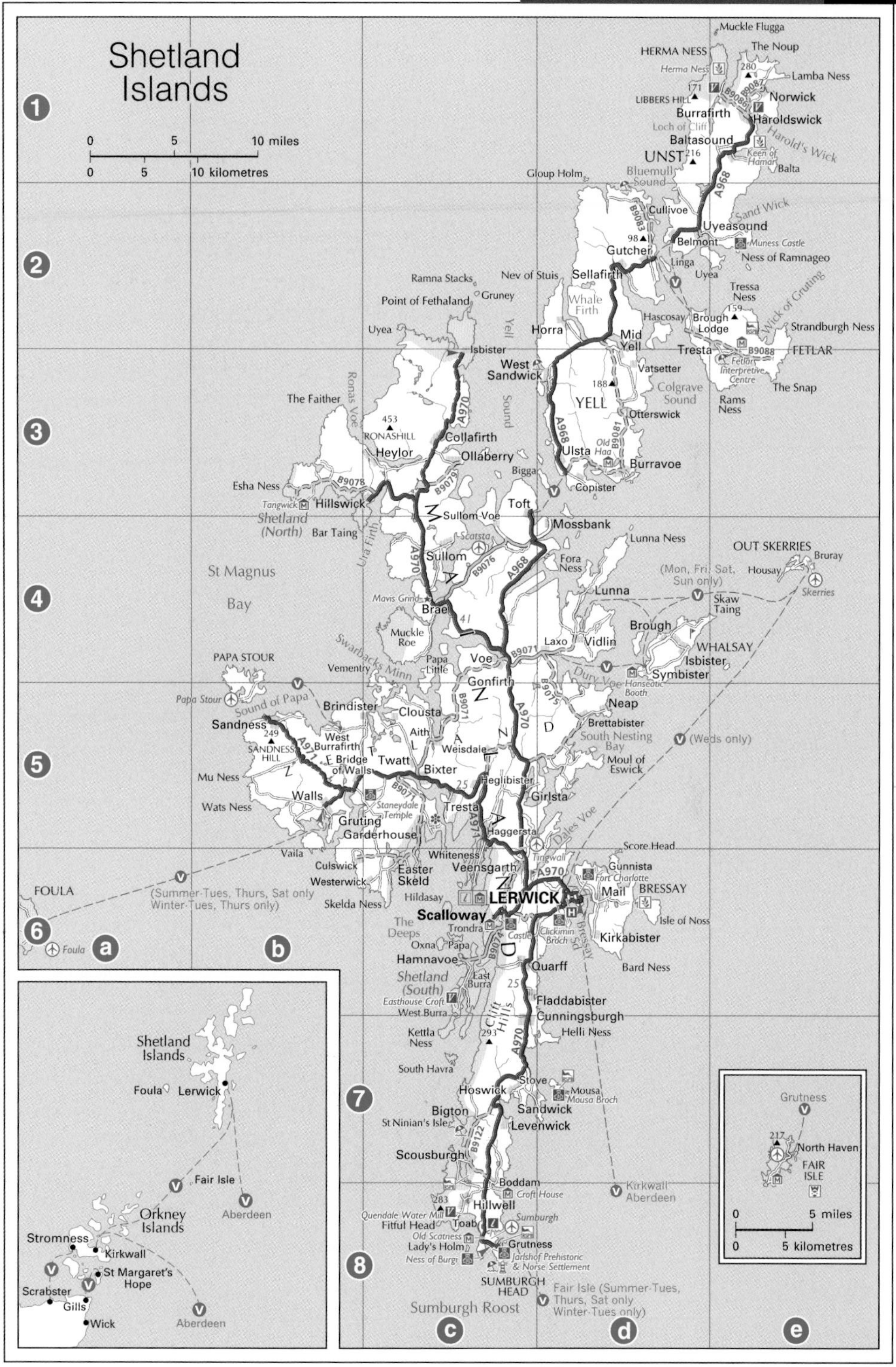

Shetland Islands
0 5 10 miles
0 5 10 kilometres
1
2
3
4
5
6
7
8
a
b
c
d
e
Muckle Flugga
HERMA NESS
Herma Ness
The Noup
280
Lamba Ness
171
LIBBERS HILL
Norwick
Burrafirth
Haroldswick
Loch of Cliff
Harold's Wick
Baltasound
UNST
216
Keen of Hamar
Balta
Gloup Holm
Bluemull Sound
B9083
Cullivoe
A968
Sand Wick
Uyeasound
98
Belmont
Muness Castle
Gutcher
Ness of Ramnageo
Linga
Uyea
Ramna Stacks
Nev of Stuis
Sellafirth
Tressa Ness
Gruney
Point of Fethaland
Whale Firth
Wick of Gruting
159
Hascosay
Brough Lodge
Strandburgh Ness
Uyea
Yell
Horra
Mid Yell
Isbister
Tresta
B9088
FETLAR
West Sandwick
Vatsetter
Fetlar Interpretive Centre
Ronas Voe
188
Colgrave Sound
The Snap
The Faither
Sound
YELL
Rams Ness
453
RONASHILL
A970
Otterswick
Collafirth
B9081
Heylor
Ollaberry
Ulsta
Old Haa
Burravoe
Bigga
Esha Ness
B9078
B9079
Copister
Tangwick
Hillswick
Toft
Shetland (North)
Sullom Voe
Mossbank
Bar Taing
Scatsta
Lunna Ness
OUT SKERRIES
Bruray
Ura Firth
Fora Ness
Housay
St Magnus
Sullom
B9076
(Mon, Fri, Sat, Sun only)
Skerries
Bay
Mavis Grind
Lunna
Skaw Taing
Brae
Muckle Roe
Laxo
Vidlin
Brough
WHALSAY
PAPA STOUR
Swarbacks Minn
Papa Little
Voe
B9071
Isbister
Vementry
Dury Voe
Symbister
Hanseatic Booth
Papa Stour
Sound of Papa
Gonfirth
B9075
Neap
Brindister
Clousta
Sandness
249
SANDNESS HILL
West Burrafirth
Aith
Brettabister
South Nesting Bay
(Weds only)
Bridge of Walls
Twatt
Weisdale
Moul of Eswick
Mu Ness
Bixter
Heglibister
Walls
Girlsta
Wats Ness
Staneydale Temple
Tresta
Gruting
Garderhouse
Haggersta
Dales Voe
Vaila
Whiteness
Tingwall
Score Head
Culswick
Veensgarth
Gunnista
FOULA
Westerwick
Easter Skeld
Fort Charlotte
Mail
BRESSAY
(Summer-Tues, Thurs, Sat only Winter-Tues, Thurs only)
Hildasay
LERWICK
Skelda Ness
Scalloway
Isle of Noss
The Deeps
Trondra
Castle
Clickimin Broch
Bressay Sd
Kirkabister
Foula
Oxna
Papa
Hamnavoe
Quarff
Bard Ness
Shetland (South)
East Burra
Easthouse Croft
Fladdabister
West Burra
Cunningsburgh
Clift Hills
Kettla Ness
293
Helli Ness
South Havra
Stove
Hoswick
Mousa
Mousa Broch
Sandwick
Bigton
St Ninian's Isle
Levenwick
B9122
Scousburgh
Boddam
Croft House
Kirkwall Aberdeen
283
Quendale Water Mill
Hillwell
Sumburgh
Fitful Head
Toab
Old Scatness
Grutness
Lady's Holm
Ness of Burgi
Jarlshof Prehistoric & Norse Settlement
SUMBURGH HEAD
Fair Isle (Summer-Tues, Thurs, Sat only Winter-Tues only)
Sumburgh Roost
Grutness
217
North Haven
FAIR ISLE
0 5 miles
0 5 kilometres
Shetland Islands
Foula
Lerwick
Fair Isle
Aberdeen
Orkney Islands
Stromness
Kirkwall
St Margaret's Hope
Scrabster
Gills
Wick
Aberdeen

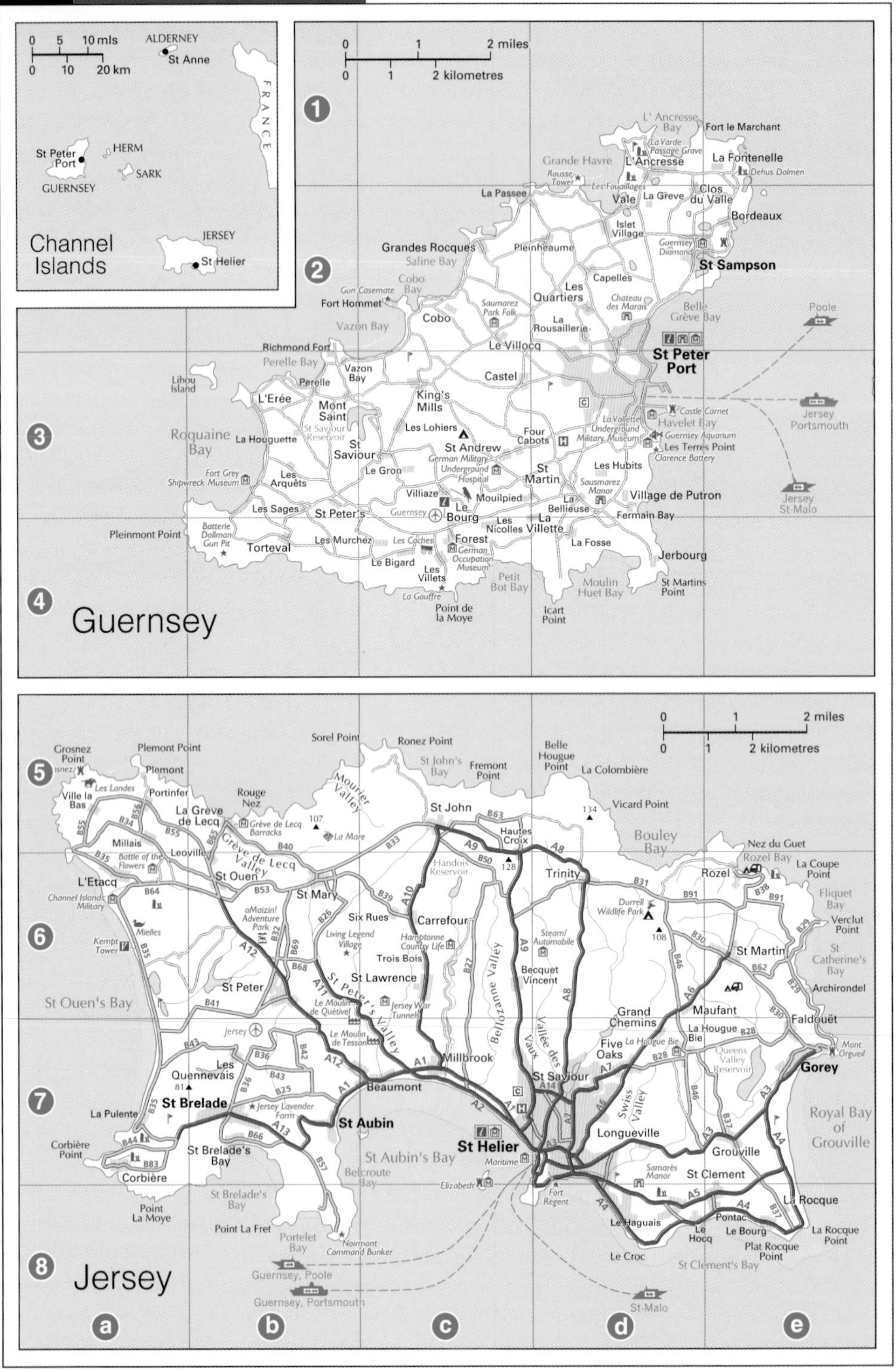

0 5 10 mls
0 10 20 km
ALDERNEY
St Anne
FRANCE
St Peter Port
HERM
SARK
GUERNSEY
JERSEY
St Helier
Channel Islands
0 1 2 miles
0 1 2 kilometres
L' Ancresse Bay
Fort le Marchant
La Varde Passage Grave
Grande Havre
L'Ancresse
La Fontenelle
Dehus Dolmen
Rousse Tower
Les Fouaillages
La Passee
Vale
La Greve
Clos du Valle
Islet Village
Bordeaux
Grandes Rocques
Saline Bay
Pleinheaume
Guernsey Diamond
St Sampson
Cobo Bay
Gun Casemate
Fort Hommet
Capelles
Les Quartiers
Chateau des Marais
Belle Grève Bay
Poole
Vazon Bay
Cobo
Saumarez Park Folk
La Rousaillerie
Le Villocq
St Peter Port
Richmond Fort
Perelle Bay
Lihou Island
Perelle
Vazon Bay
Castel
L'Erée
Mont Saint
King's Mills
Jersey Portsmouth
Castle Cornet
Havelet Bay
Roquaine Bay
La Houguette
St Saviour Reservoir
Les Lohiers
Four Cabots
La Valette Underground Military Museum
Guernsey Aquarium
Les Terres Point
Clarence Battery
St Saviour
St Andrew
German Military Underground Hospital
Les Hubits
Fort Grey Shipwreck Museum
Les Arquêts
Le Gron
St Martin
Sausmarez Manor
Villiaze
Mouilpied
La Bellieuse
Village de Putron
Jersey St-Malo
Les Sages
St Peter's
Guernsey
Le Bourg
Les Nicolles
La Villette
Fermain Bay
Pleinmont Point
Batterie Dollman Gun Pit
Torteval
Les Murchez
Les Caches
Forest
German Occupation Museum
La Fosse
Le Bigard
Les Villets
Petit Bot Bay
Moulin Huet Bay
Jerbourg
St Martins Point
La Gouffre
Point de la Moye
Icart Point
Guernsey
0 1 2 miles
0 1 2 kilometres
Grosnez Point
Plemont Point
Sorel Point
Ronez Point
Belle Hougue Point
La Colombière
Plemont
St John's Bay
Fremont Point
Les Landes
Ville la Bas
Portinfer
Rouge Nez
Mourier Valley
Vicard Point
La Grève de Lecq
Grève de Lecq Barracks
107
La Mare
St John
134
Millais
Leoville
Grève de Lecq Valley
Hautes Croix
Bouley Bay
Battle of the Flowers
Handois Reservoir
128
Nez du Guet
Rozel Bay
La Coupe Point
L'Etacq
St Ouen
Trinity
Rozel
Channel Islands Military
St Mary
Durrell Wildlife Park
Fliquet Bay
aMaizin! Adventure Park
Six Rues
Carrefour
Verclut Point
Mielles
108
Kempt Tower
Living Legend Village
Hamptonne Country Life
Steam/ Automobile
St Martin
St Catherine's Bay
Trois Bois
Bellozanne Valley
Becquet Vincent
St Peter
St Lawrence
St Peter's Valley
Archirondel
St Ouen's Bay
Le Moulin de Quétivel
Jersey War Tunnels
Grand Chemins
Maufant
Jersey
Le Moulin de Tesson
Vallée des Vaux
La Hougue Bie
Faldouët
Five Oaks
Mont Orgueil
Les Quennevais
Millbrook
Queens Valley Reservoir
Gorey
81
Beaumont
St Saviour
Swiss Valley
St Brelade
Jersey Lavender Farm
Royal Bay of Grouville
La Pulente
St Aubin
Longueville
St Helier
Grouville
Corbière Point
St Brelade's Bay
St Aubin's Bay
Maritime
Samarès Manor
St Clement
Corbière
Belcroute Bay
Elizabeth
Fort Regent
St Brelade's Bay
La Rocque
Point La Moye
Pontac
Point La Fret
Le Haguais
Le Hocq
Le Bourg
La Rocque Point
Portelet Bay
Noirmont Command Bunker
Plat Rocque Point
Le Croc
St Clement's Bay
Jersey
Guernsey, Poole
Guernsey, Portsmouth
St-Malo
A1 A2 A3 A4 A5 A6 A7 A8 A9 A10 A11 A12 A13 A14
B25 B26 B27 B28 B29 B30 B31 B32 B33 B34 B35 B36 B37 B38 B39 B40 B41 B42 B43 B44 B46 B50 B53 B55 B56 B57 B62 B63 B64 B65 B66 B68 B69 B83 B91
1 2 3 4 5 6 7 8
a b c d e

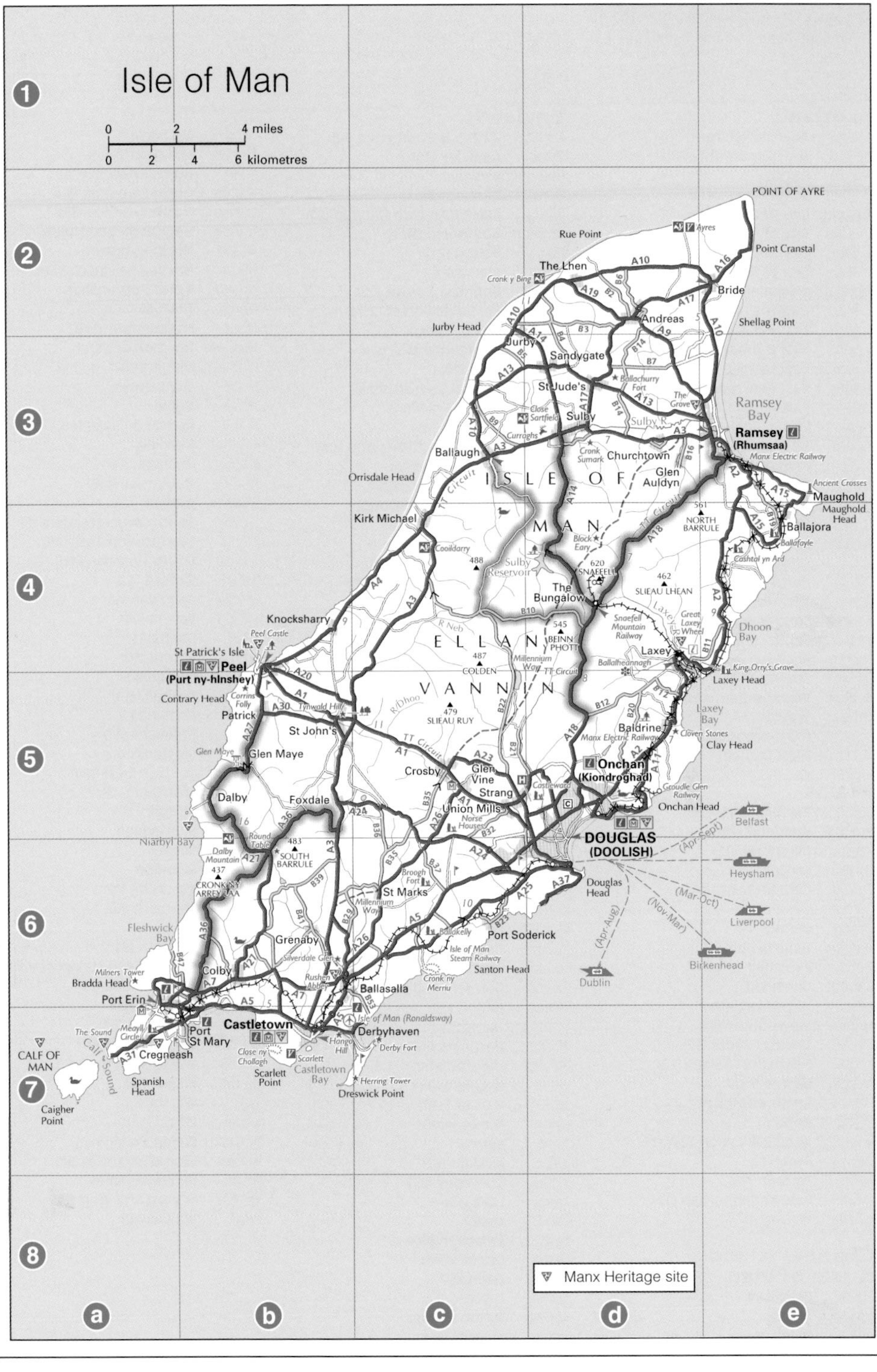
Isle of Man
0 2 4 miles
0 2 4 6 kilometres
POINT OF AYRE
Ayres
Rue Point
Point Cranstal
The Lhen
Cronk y Bing
Bride
Andreas
Shellag Point
Jurby Head
Jurby
Sandygate
Ballachurry Fort
St Jude's
The Grove
Ramsey Bay
Close Sartfield
Sulby
Sulby R.
Curraghs
Ramsey
(Rhumsaa)
Manx Electric Railway
Ballaugh
Cronk Sumark
Churchtown
Glen Auldyn
Orrisdale Head
TT Circuit
ISLE OF MAN
Ancient Crosses
Maughold
Maughold Head
561 NORTH BARRULE
Ballajora
Ballafayle
Kirk Michael
Block Eary
Cashtal yn Ard
Cooildarry
488
Sulby Reservoir
620 SNAEFELL
462 SLIEAU LHEAN
The Bungalow
Knocksharry
R Neb
545 BEINN PHOTT
Snaefell Mountain Railway
Great Laxey Wheel
Dhoon Bay
Peel Castle
St Patrick's Isle
Peel
(Purt ny-hInshey)
ELLAN VANNIN
487 COLDEN
Millennium Way
Laxey
Ballalheannagh
King Orry's Grave
Laxey Head
Contrary Head
Corrins Folly
Patrick
Tynwald Hill
R Dhoo
479 SLIEAU RUY
Laxey Bay
Baldrine
St John's
Cloven Stones
Clay Head
Glen Maye
Manx Electric Railway
Crosby
Glen Vine
Onchan
(Kiondroghad)
Strang
Castleward
Groudle Glen Railway
Dalby
Foxdale
Union Mills
Norse Houses
Onchan Head
Belfast
Niarbyl Bay
Round Table
483 SOUTH BARRULE
DOUGLAS
(DOOLISH)
(Apr-Sept)
Dalby Mountain
437 CRONK NY ARREY LAA
Broogh Fort
St Marks
Douglas Head
Heysham
(Mar-Oct)
(Nov-Mar)
Liverpool
Millennium Way
Fleshwick Bay
Grenaby
Ballakelly
Isle of Man Steam Railway
Port Soderick
Santon Head
(Apr-Aug)
Birkenhead
Dublin
Silverdale Glen
Rushen Abbey
Cronk ny Merriu
Milners Tower
Bradda Head
Colby
Ballasalla
Port Erin
Isle of Man (Ronaldsway)
Castletown
Derbyhaven
Port St Mary
The Sound
Meayll Circle
Hango Hill
Derby Fort
CALF OF MAN
Calf Sound
Cregneash
Close ny Chollagh
Scarlett
Scarlett Point
Castletown Bay
Spanish Head
Herring Tower
Dreswick Point
Caigher Point
Manx Heritage site
a b c d e
1 2 3 4 5 6 7 8

Index to place names

This index lists places appearing in the main-map section of the atlas in alphabetical order. The reference following each name gives the atlas page number and grid reference of the square in which the place appears. The map shows counties and administrative areas, together with a list of the abbreviated name forms used in the index. The top 100 places of tourist interest are indexed in **red**, World Heritage sites in **green**, motorway service areas in **blue**, airports in blue *italic* and National Parks in green *italic*.

Scotland

Abers	**Aberdeenshire**
Ag & B	**Argyll and Bute**
Angus	**Angus**
Border	**Scottish Borders**
C Aber	**City of Aberdeen**
C Dund	**City of Dundee**
C Edin	**City of Edinburgh**
C Glas	**City of Glasgow**
Clacks	**Clackmannanshire (1)**
D & G	**Dumfries & Galloway**
E Ayrs	**East Ayrshire**
E Duns	**East Dunbartonshire (2)**
E Loth	**East Lothian**
E Rens	**East Renfrewshire (3)**
Falk	**Falkirk**
Fife	**Fife**
Highld	**Highland**
Inver	**Inverclyde (4)**
Mdloth	**Midlothian (5)**
Moray	**Moray**
N Ayrs	**North Ayrshire**
N Lans	**North Lanarkshire (6)**
Ork	**Orkney Islands**
P & K	**Perth & Kinross**
Rens	**Renfrewshire (7)**
S Ayrs	**South Ayrshire**
S Lans	**South Lanarkshire**
Shet	**Shetland Islands**
Stirlg	**Stirling**
W Duns	**West Dunbartonshire (8)**
W Isls	**Western Isles (Na h-Eileanan an Iar)**
W Loth	**West Lothian**

Wales

Blae G	**Blaenau Gwent (9)**
Brdgnd	**Bridgend (10)**
Caerph	**Caerphilly (11)**
Cardif	**Cardiff**
Carmth	**Carmarthenshire**
Cerdgn	**Ceredigion**
Conwy	**Conwy**
Denbgs	**Denbighshire**
Flints	**Flintshire**
Gwynd	**Gwynedd**
IoA	**Isle of Anglesey**
Mons	**Monmouthshire**
Myr Td	**Merthyr Tydfil (12)**
Neath	**Neath Port Talbot (13)**
Newpt	**Newport (14)**
Pembks	**Pembrokeshire**
Powys	**Powys**
Rhondd	**Rhondda Cynon Taff (15)**
Swans	**Swansea**
Torfn	**Torfaen (16)**
V Glam	**Vale of Glamorgan (17)**
Wrexhm	**Wrexham**

Channel Islands & Isle of Man

Guern	**Guernsey**
Jersey	**Jersey**
IoM	**Isle of Man**

England

BaNES	**Bath & N E Somerset (18)**
Barns	**Barnsley (19)**
Bed	**Bedford**
Birm	**Birmingham**
Bl w D	**Blackburn with Darwen (20)**
Bmouth	**Bournemouth**
Bolton	**Bolton (21)**
Bpool	**Blackpool**
Br & H	**Brighton & Hove (22)**
Br For	**Bracknell Forest (23)**
Bristl	**City of Bristol**
Bucks	**Buckinghamshire**
Bury	**Bury (24)**
C Beds	**Central Bedfordshire**
C Brad	**City of Bradford**
C Derb	**City of Derby**
C KuH	**City of Kingston upon Hull**
C Leic	**City of Leicester**
C Nott	**City of Nottingham**
C Pete	**City of Peterborough**
C Plym	**City of Plymouth**
C Port	**City of Portsmouth**
C Sotn	**City of Southampton**
C Stke	**City of Stoke-on-Trent**
C York	**City of York**
Calder	**Calderdale (25)**
Cambs	**Cambridgeshire**
Ches E	**Cheshire East**
Ches W	**Cheshire West and Chester**
Cnwll	**Cornwall**
Covtry	**Coventry**
Cumb	**Cumbria**
Darltn	**Darlington (26)**
Derbys	**Derbyshire**
Devon	**Devon**
Donc	**Doncaster (27)**
Dorset	**Dorset**
Dudley	**Dudley (28)**
Dur	**Durham**
E R Yk	**East Riding of Yorkshire**
E Susx	**East Sussex**
Essex	**Essex**
Gatesd	**Gateshead (29)**
Gloucs	**Gloucestershire**
Gt Lon	**Greater London**
Halton	**Halton (30)**
Hants	**Hampshire**
Hartpl	**Hartlepool (31)**
Herefs	**Herefordshire**
Herts	**Hertfordshire**
IoS	**Isles of Scilly**
IoW	**Isle of Wight**
Kent	**Kent**
Kirk	**Kirklees (32)**
Knows	**Knowsley (33)**
Lancs	**Lancashire**
Leeds	**Leeds**
Leics	**Leicestershire**
Lincs	**Lincolnshire**
Lpool	**Liverpool**
Luton	**Luton**
M Keyn	**Milton Keynes**
Manch	**Manchester**
Medway	**Medway**
Middsb	**Middlesbrough**
N Linc	**North Lincolnshire**
N Som	**North Somerset (34)**
N Tyne	**North Tyneside (35)**
N u Ty	**Newcastle upon Tyne**
N York	**North Yorkshire**
NE Lin	**North East Lincolnshire**
Nhants	**Northamptonshire**
Norfk	**Norfolk**
Notts	**Nottinghamshire**
Nthumb	**Northumberland**
Oldham	**Oldham (36)**
Oxon	**Oxfordshire**
Poole	**Poole**
R & Cl	**Redcar & Cleveland**
Readg	**Reading**
Rochdl	**Rochdale (37)**
Rothm	**Rotherham (38)**
Rutlnd	**Rutland**
S Glos	**South Gloucestershire (39)**
S on T	**Stockton-on-Tees (40)**
S Tyne	**South Tyneside (41)**
Salfd	**Salford (42)**
Sandw	**Sandwell (43)**
Sefton	**Sefton (44)**
Sheff	**Sheffield**
Shrops	**Shropshire**
Slough	**Slough (45)**
Solhll	**Solihull (46)**
Somset	**Somerset**
St Hel	**St Helens (47)**
Staffs	**Staffordshire**
Sthend	**Southend-on-Sea**
Stockp	**Stockport (48)**
Suffk	**Suffolk**
Sundld	**Sunderland**
Surrey	**Surrey**
Swindn	**Swindon**
Tamesd	**Tameside (49)**
Thurr	**Thurrock (50)**
Torbay	**Torbay**
Traffd	**Trafford (51)**
W & M	**Windsor and Maidenhead (52)**
W Berk	**West Berkshire**
W Susx	**West Sussex**
Wakefd	**Wakefield (53)**
Warrtn	**Warrington (54)**
Warwks	**Warwickshire**
Wigan	**Wigan (55)**
Wilts	**Wiltshire**
Wirral	**Wirral (56)**
Wokham	**Wokingham (57)**
Wolves	**Wolverhampton (58)**
Worcs	**Worcestershire**
Wrekin	**Telford & Wrekin (59)**
Wsall	**Walsall (60)**

ORKNEY ISLANDS
SHETLAND ISLANDS
WESTERN ISLES (Na h-Eileanan an Iar)
HIGHLAND
MORAY
SCOTLAND
Aberdeen
ABERDEENSHIRE
ANGUS
PERTH & KINROSS
Dundee
ARGYLL AND BUTE
STIRLING
FIFE
1
FALK
Edinburgh
8
2
4
Glasgow
7
6
W LOTH
E LOTH
5
3
NORTH AYRSHIRE
S LANS
SCOTTISH BORDERS
E AYRS
S AYRS
DUMFRIES & GALLOWAY
NORTHUMBERLAND
Newcastle upon Tyne
35
41
29
Sunderland
CUMBRIA
DURHAM
31
26
40
R & CL
Middlesbrough
IoM
NORTH YORKSHIRE
York
EAST RIDING OF YORKSHIRE
Bradford
Leeds
Kingston upon Hull
Blackpool
LANCASHIRE
25
32
53
N LINC
NE LIN
20
21
24
37
36
19
27
44
55
42
49
47
Manchester
38
Liverpool
33
51
48
Sheffield
56
30
54
IoA
CONWY
FLINTS
CHES W
CHES E
DERBYS
NOTTS
LINCOLNSHIRE
DENBGS
Stoke-on-Trent
WREXHAM
Nottingham
GWYNEDD
Derby
STAFFS
59
LEICS
RUTLAND
NORFOLK
Leicester
Peterborough
SHROPSHIRE
58
60
43
Birmingham
28
Coventry
46
CAMBS
POWYS
CERDGN
WORCS
WARWKS
NHANTS
SUFFOLK
BED
Milton Keynes
HEREFS
WALES
ENGLAND
C
BEDS
Luton
PEMBKS
CARMTH
GLOUCS
OXON
HERTS
ESSEX
MONS
12
9
16
13
15
11
Swansea
14
BUCKS
Southend-on-Sea
10
Cardiff
Bristol
39
Swindon
Reading
52
45
GREATER LONDON
50
17
MEDWAY
34
W BERK
57
23
18
WILTSHIRE
SURREY
KENT
HAMPSHIRE
SOMERSET
W SUSX
E SUSX
Southampton
DEVON
DORSET
22
Portsmouth
Bournemouth
Poole
IoW
Guernsey
CHANNEL ISLANDS
CORNWALL
Torbay
Jersey
Plymouth
IoS

A

Abbas Combe Somset 27 G6
Abberley Worcs 70 D2
Abberley Common Worcs 70 D2
Abberton Essex 62 B4
Abberton Worcs 71 H4
Abbess Roding Essex 60 F5
Abbeydale Sheff 114 F5
Abbey Dore Herefs 54 B3
Abbey Green Staffs 99 L2
Abbey St Bathans Border 178 F6
Abbeystead Lancs 130 B8
Abbey Town Cumb 147 L5
Abbey Valley Crematorium Derbys 101 H2
Abbey Village Lancs 121 J6
Abbey Wood Gt Lon 45 J4
Abbotrule Border 167 J6
Abbots Bickington Devon 9 K3
Abbots Bromley Staffs 100 B7
Abbotsbury Dorset 14 B5
Abbots Deuglie P & K 186 B5
Abbotsham Devon 22 F6
Abbotskerswell Devon 7 K3
Abbots Langley Herts 59 H7
Abbots Leigh N Som 38 D5
Abbotsley Cambs 75 J3
Abbots Morton Worcs 71 H4
Abbots Ripton Cambs 89 J7
Abbot's Salford Warwks 71 J4
Abbots Worthy Hants 29 J5
Abbotts Ann Hants 29 G3
Abbott Street Dorset 15 J3
Abdon Shrops 83 L6
Aberaeron Cerdgn 66 B3
Aberaman Rhondd 52 F7
Aberangell Gwynd 81 J2
Aberarder Highld 202 F1
Aberargie P & K 186 B4
Aberarth Cerdgn 66 B2
Aberavon Neath 51 L7
Abercanaid Myr Td 53 G7
Abercarn Caerph 37 K2
Abercastle Pembks 64 B7
Abercegir Powys 81 H3
Aberchalder Lodge Highld 202 B5
Aberchirder Abers 216 C4
Abercraf Powys 52 C5
Abercregan Neath 36 D2
Abercwmboi Rhondd 52 F7
Abercych Pembks 65 H6
Abercynon Rhondd 37 G2
Aberdalgie P & K 185 M4
Aberdare Rhondd 52 F7
Aberdaron Gwynd 94 C7
Aberdeen C Aber 207 H4
Aberdeen Airport C Aber 207 G3
Aberdeen Crematorium C Aber 207 G4
Aberdour Fife 177 G2
Aberdulais Neath 52 B7
Aberdyfi Gwynd 80 E4
Aberedw Powys 68 C5
Abereiddy Pembks 48 D2
Abererch Gwynd 95 G5
Aberfan Myr Td 53 G7
Aberfeldy P & K 194 D6
Aberffraw IoA 108 D7
Aberford Leeds 124 C3
Aberfoyle Stirlg 184 C7
Abergavenny Mons 53 L5
Abergele Conwy 110 C6
Abergorlech Carmth 66 D7
Abergwesyn Powys 67 J4
Abergwili Carmth 50 F2
Abergwynfi Neath 36 D2
Abergwyngregyn Gwynd 109 J6
Abergynolwyn Gwynd 80 F3
Aberkenfig Brdgnd 36 D4
Aberlady E Loth 178 B3
Aberlemno Angus 196 E5
Aberllefenni Gwynd 81 G2
Aberllynfi Powys 68 D6
Aberlour, Charlestown of Moray 215 G5
Abermule Powys 82 D5
Abernant Carmth 50 D2
Aber-nant Rhondd 52 F7
Abernethy P & K 186 C4
Abernyte P & K 186 D2
Aberporth Cerdgn 65 J4
Abersoch Gwynd 94 E6
Abersychan Torfn 53 K7
Aberthin V Glam 36 F5
Abertillery Blae G 53 K7
Abertridwr Caerph 37 H3
Abertridwr Powys 97 G8
Aberuthven P & K 185 K4
Aberystwyth Cerdgn 80 D6
Aberystwyth Crematorium Cerdgn 80 E6
Abingdon-on-Thames Oxon 41 J2
Abinger Common Surrey 31 J3
Abinger Hammer Surrey 31 H2
Abington Nhants 73 L3
Abington S Lans 165 H5
Abington Pigotts Cambs 75 K5
Abington Services S Lans 165 H4
Abingworth W Susx 18 F3
Ab Kettleby Leics 102 B7
Ablington Gloucs 56 C6
Abney Derbys 114 D5
Aboyne Abers 205 L5
Abram Wigan 112 E2
Abriachan Highld 212 E7
Abridge Essex 45 J2
Abronhill N Lans 175 K3
Abson S Glos 39 G5
Abthorpe Nhants 73 J5
Aby Lincs 118 F5
Acaster Malbis C York 124 E2
Acaster Selby N York 124 E3
Accrington Lancs 121 L5
Accrington Crematorium Lancs 121 L5
Acha Ag & B 188 F5
Achahoish Ag & B 172 D3
Achalader P & K 195 H7
Achaleven Ag & B 182 D1
Acha Mor W Isls 232 f3
Achanalt Highld 211 K3
Achandunie Highld 222 E6
Achany Highld 222 D2
Acharacle Highld 190 D3
Acharn Highld 190 E6
Acharn P & K 194 B7
Achavanich Highld 231 H6
Achduart Highld 224 C7
Achfary Highld 228 D7
A'Chill Highld 198 D4
Achiltibuie Highld 224 C6
Achina Highld 229 L4
Achinhoan Ag & B 161 J6
Achintee Highld 210 E6
Achintraid Highld 210 C6
Achmelvich Highld 224 C4
Achmore Highld 210 D7
Achmore W Isls 232 f3
Achnacarnin Highld 224 C3
Achnacarry Highld 201 J7
Achnacloich Highld 199 J4
Achnaconeran Highld 202 C2
Achnacroish Ag & B 191 G7
Achnadrish House Ag & B 189 L6
Achnafauld P & K 185 J1
Achnagarron Highld 222 F7
Achnaha Highld 189 L3
Achnahaird Highld 224 B5
Achnahannet Highld 214 B8
Achnairn Highld 225 L6
Achnalea Highld 191 G4
Achnamara Ag & B 172 D2
Achnasheen Highld 211 J3
Achnashellach Lodge Highld 210 F5
Achnastank Moray 215 G7
Achosnich Highld 189 K3
Achranich Highld 190 E6
Achreamie Highld 230 E3
Achriabhach Highld 192 B3
Achriesgill Highld 228 C5
Achtoty Highld 229 K3
Achurch Nhants 88 E6
Achvaich Highld 222 F3
Achvarasdal Highld 230 E3
Ackergill Highld 231 L5
Acklam Middsb 141 L4
Acklam N York 134 B7
Ackleton Shrops 84 D4
Acklington Nthumb 159 G2
Ackton Wakefd 124 C6
Ackworth Moor Top Wakefd 124 C7
Acle Norfk 93 J2
Acock's Green Birm 85 K6
Acol Kent 35 J2
Acomb C York 124 E1
Acomb Nthumb 150 B2
Aconbury Herefs 54 D2
Acton Ches E 98 F2
Acton Gt Lon 44 D4
Acton Staffs 99 J4
Acton Suffk 77 K5
Acton Beauchamp Herefs 70 C4
Acton Bridge Ches W 112 E6
Acton Burnell Shrops 83 K3
Acton Green Herefs 70 C4
Acton Park Wrexhm 97 M3
Acton Round Shrops 84 B4
Acton Scott Shrops 83 J5
Acton Trussell Staffs 99 L8
Acton Turville S Glos 39 J4
Adbaston Staffs 99 H6
Adber Dorset 26 E7
Adbolton Notts 101 L5
Adderbury Oxon 72 F7
Adderley Shrops 98 F4
Addiewell W Loth 176 D5
Addingham C Brad 123 G1
Addington Bucks 58 C3
Addington Gt Lon 45 G7
Addington Kent 33 H2
Addiscombe Gt Lon 45 G6
Addlestone Surrey 43 H7
Addlethorpe Lincs 119 H7
Adeyfield Herts 59 H6
Adfa Powys 82 B4
Adforton Herefs 69 H1
Adisham Kent 35 G4
Adlestrop Gloucs 56 E3
Adlingfleet E R Yk 125 K6
Adlington Lancs 121 J7
Admaston Staffs 100 B7
Admaston Wrekin 84 B2
Adpar Cerdgn 65 J6
Adsborough Somset 25 L5
Adscombe Somset 25 J4
Adstock Bucks 58 C3
Adstone Nhants 73 H4
Adversane W Susx 31 H6
Advie Highld 214 D7
Adwick le Street Donc 124 E8
Adwick upon Dearne Donc 115 J2
Ae D & G 155 H4
Ae Bridgend D & G 155 H5
Afan Forest Park Neath 36 D2
Affleck Abers 216 B6
Affpuddle Dorset 14 F4
Affric Lodge Highld 201 J2
Afon-wen Flints 110 F6
Afton IoW 16 D5
Agecroft Crematorium Salfd 113 J2
Agglethorpe N York 131 K3
Aigburth Lpool 111 L4
Aike E R Yk 126 C2
Aiketgate Cumb 148 E5
Aikton Cumb 148 B4
Ailsworth C Pete 89 G4
Ainderby Quernhow N York 132 E4
Ainderby Steeple N York 132 E2
Aingers Green Essex 62 D4
Ainsdale Sefton 120 D7
Ainstable Cumb 148 F5
Ainsworth Bury 121 L8
Ainthorpe N York 142 E5
Aintree Sefton 111 L2
Ainville W Loth 176 F5
Aird Ag & B 181 M7
Aird D & G 144 D3
Aird W Isls 232 g2
Aird a Mhulaidh W Isls 232 e3
Aird Asaig W Isls 232 e4
Aird Dhubh Highld 209 L6
Airdeny Ag & B 182 E2
Aird of Kinloch Ag & B 181 H2
Aird of Sleat Highld 199 J5
Airdrie N Lans 175 K5
Airdriehill N Lans 175 K5
Airds of Kells D & G 154 B7
Aird Uig W Isls 232 d2
Airidh a bhruaich W Isls 232 e3
Airieland D & G 146 D4
Airlie Angus 195 L6
Airmyn E R Yk 125 H5
Airntully P & K 186 A1
Airor Highld 199 L4
Airth Falk 176 B2
Airton N York 131 G7
Aisby Lincs 103 G5
Aisby Lincs 116 E3
Aish Devon 7 G4
Aish Devon 7 J4
Aisholt Somset 25 J4
Aiskew N York 132 D2
Aislaby N York 134 B3
Aislaby N York 143 H5
Aislaby S on T 141 J5
Aisthorpe Lincs 116 F5
Aith Shet 235 c5
Akeld Nthumb 168 E4
Akeley Bucks 73 K6
Albaston Cnwll 6 B2
Alberbury Shrops 83 G1
Albourne W Susx 19 H3
Albrighton Shrops 84 E3
Albrighton Shrops 98 C8
Alburgh Norfk 92 F6
Albury Herts 60 C3
Albury Surrey 31 H2
Albury Heath Surrey 31 H3
Alcaig Highld 212 E3
Alcaston Shrops 83 J6
Alcester Warwks 71 K3
Alcester Lane End Birm 85 J7
Alciston E Susx 20 B5
Alcombe Somset 24 F3
Alconbury Cambs 89 H7
Alconbury Weston Cambs 89 H7
Aldborough N York 132 F6
Aldborough Norfk 106 E5
Aldbourne Wilts 40 E5
Aldbrough E R Yk 127 G3

Aldbrough St John N York 140 F5
Aldbury Herts 58 F5
Aldcliffe Lancs 129 K7
Aldclune P & K 194 E4
Aldeburgh Suffk 79 K3
Aldeby Norfk 93 J5
Aldenham Herts 43 J2
Alderbury Wilts 28 D6
Alderford Norfk 106 D8
Alderholt Dorset 28 C8
Alderley Gloucs 39 H3
Alderley Edge Ches E 113 J5
Aldermans Green Covtry 86 D6
Aldermaston W Berk 41 L7
Alderminster Warwks 72 B5
Aldershot Hants 30 E2
Alderton Gloucs 55 M2
Alderton Nhants 73 K5
Alderton Suffk 79 H6
Alderton Wilts 39 J4
Aldfield N York 132 D5
Aldford Ches W 98 B2
Aldgate Rutlnd 88 E3
Aldham Essex 61 L3
Aldham Suffk 78 C5
Aldingbourne W Susx 18 C5
Aldingham Cumb 129 G5
Aldington Kent 34 E7
Aldington Worcs 71 J5
Aldington Corner Kent 34 E7
Aldivalloch Moray 205 H1
Aldochlay Ag & B 174 C1
Aldreth Cambs 90 C8
Aldridge Wsall 85 J4
Aldringham Suffk 79 J3
Aldsworth Gloucs 56 D6
Aldunie Moray 215 H8
Aldwark Derbys 100 E2
Aldwark N York 133 G6
Aldwick W Susx 18 C6
Aldwincle Nhants 88 E6
Aldworth W Berk 41 K4
Alexandria W Duns 174 D3
Aley Somset 25 J4
Alfington Devon 12 E3
Alfold Surrey 31 H5
Alfold Crossways Surrey 31 H4
Alford Abers 206 B3
Alford Lincs 118 F6
Alford Somset 26 E5
Alford Crematorium Lincs 118 F6
Alfreton Derbys 101 H2
Alfrick Worcs 70 D4
Alfrick Pound Worcs 70 D4
Alfriston E Susx 20 B5
Algarkirk Lincs 103 M5
Alhampton Somset 26 F4
Alkborough N Linc 125 K6
Alkham Kent 35 H6
Alkmonton Derbys 100 D5
Allaleigh Devon 7 J5
Allanaquoich Abers 204 D6
Allanbank N Lans 175 L6
Allanton Border 179 H7
Allanton N Lans 175 L6
Allanton S Lans 175 K7
Allaston Gloucs 54 F6
Allbrook Hants 29 J7
All Cannings Wilts 40 B7
Allendale Nthumb 149 L4
Allen End Warwks 85 L4
Allenheads Nthumb 149 L6
Allen's Green Herts 60 D5
Allensmore Herefs 69 J7
Allenton C Derb 101 G6
Aller Devon 24 B6
Aller Somset 26 B5
Allerby Cumb 147 J6
Allercombe Devon 12 D4
Allerford Somset 24 D3
Allerston N York 134 D3
Allerthorpe E R Yk 125 J2
Allerton C Brad 123 G4
Allerton Highld 213 H2
Allerton Lpool 111 L4
Allerton Bywater Leeds 124 C5
Allerton Mauleverer N York 132 F7
Allesley Covtry 86 C7
Allestree C Derb 101 G5
Allexton Leics 88 B4
Allgreave Ches E 113 L7
Allhallows Medway 46 D4
Alligin Shuas Highld 210 C3
Allington Dorset 13 L4
Allington Lincs 102 E4
Allington Wilts 28 D4
Allington Wilts 39 K5
Allington Wilts 40 B7
Allithwaite Cumb 129 J4
Alloa Clacks 185 J8
Allonby Cumb 147 J6
Alloway S Ayrs 163 J5
Allowenshay Somset 26 B8
All Stretton Shrops 83 J4
Alltchaorunn Highld 192 C6
Alltwalis Carmth 66 B7
Alltwen Neath 51 K5
Alltyblaca Cerdgn 66 C5
Allweston Dorset 26 F8
Almeley Herefs 69 G4
Almington Staffs 99 G5
Almondbank P & K 185 M3
Almondbury Kirk 123 H7
Almondsbury S Glos 38 E4
Alne N York 133 G6
Alness Highld 222 E7
Alnham Nthumb 168 E7
Alnmouth Nthumb 169 J7
Alnwick Nthumb 169 J6
Alperton Gt Lon 44 D4
Alphamstone Essex 77 K7
Alpheton Suffk 77 K4
Alphington Devon 11 L6
Alport Derbys 114 E8
Alpraham Ches E 98 E1
Alresford Essex 62 C4
Alrewas Staffs 85 L1
Alsager Ches E 99 H2
Alsop en le Dale Derbys 100 D2
Alston Cumb 149 J5
Alston Devon 13 H2
Alstone Gloucs 55 M2
Alstonefield Staffs 100 C2
Alston Sutton Somset 26 B2
Alswear Devon 23 L6
Altandhu Highld 224 B6
Altarnun Cnwll 9 G8
Altass Highld 222 C2
Altcreich Ag & B 190 D8
Altgaltraig Ag & B 173 H4
Althorne Essex 61 L7
Althorpe N Linc 125 K8
Altnabreac Station Highld 230 E6
Altnaharra Highld 225 M2
Alton Derbys 115 G8
Alton Hants 30 B4
Alton Staffs 100 B4
Alton Barnes Wilts 40 C7
Alton Pancras Dorset 14 D3
Alton Priors Wilts 40 C7
Alton Towers Staffs 100 B4
Altrincham Traffd 113 H4
Altrincham Crematorium Traffd 113 G4
Altskeith Hotel Stirlg 184 B6
Alva Clacks 185 J7
Alvanley Ches W 112 D6
Alvaston C Derb 101 H5
Alvechurch Worcs 85 J8
Alvecote Warwks 86 B3
Alvediston Wilts 27 L6
Alveley Shrops 84 D6
Alverdiscott Devon 23 H6
Alverstoke Hants 17 H3
Alverstone IoW 17 H5
Alverthorpe Wakefd 123 L6
Alverton Notts 102 C4
Alves Moray 214 E3
Alvescot Oxon 56 F6
Alveston S Glos 38 F3
Alveston Warwks 72 B3
Alvingham Lincs 118 E4
Alvington Gloucs 54 E7
Alwalton C Pete 89 G4
Alwinton Nthumb 168 D7
Alwoodley Leeds 123 K3
Alyth P & K 195 K6
Ambergate Derbys 101 G3
Amberley Gloucs 55 J7
Amberley W Susx 18 D3
Amble Nthumb 159 G2
Amblecote Dudley 84 F6
Ambler Thorn C Brad 123 G5
Ambleside Cumb 137 K6
Ambleston Pembks 49 G3
Ambrosden Oxon 57 L4
Amcotts N Linc 125 K7
Amersham Bucks 42 F2
Amersham Common Bucks 42 F2
Amersham Old Town Bucks 42 F2
Amersham on the Hill Bucks 58 F7
Amesbury Wilts 28 D3
Amhuinnsuidhe W Isls 232 d4
Amington Staffs 86 B3
Amisfield D & G 155 H5
Amlwch IoA 108 F3
Ammanford Carmth 51 J3
Amotherby N York 134 B5
Ampfield Hants 29 H6
Ampleforth N York 133 J4
Ampney Crucis Gloucs 56 B7
Ampney St Mary Gloucs 56 C7
Ampney St Peter Gloucs 56 B7
Amport Hants 28 F3
Ampthill C Beds 74 F6
Ampton Suffk 77 J1
Amroth Pembks 49 K6
Amulree P & K 185 J1
Amwell Herts 59 K5
Anaheilt Highld 191 G4
Ancaster Lincs 103 G4
Ancroft Nthumb 168 E1
Ancrum Border 167 K4
Anderby Lincs 119 G6
Andover Hants 29 G3
Andoversford Gloucs 56 A4
Andreas IoM 237 d2
Anerley Gt Lon 45 G6
Anfield Lpool 111 K3
Anfield Crematorium Lpool 111 K3
Angarrack Cnwll 3 G4
Angelbank Shrops 83 L7
Angle Pembks 48 E6
Anglesey IoA 108 E5
Anglesey Abbey Cambs 76 D3
Angmering W Susx 18 E5
Angram N York 124 D2
Ankerville Highld 223 H6
Anlaby E R Yk 126 C5
Anmer Norfk 105 H6
Anmore Hants 17 J1
Annan D & G 147 L2
Annandale Water Services D & G 155 J4
Annat Highld 210 D4
Annathill N Lans 175 J4
Anna Valley Hants 29 G3
Annbank S Ayrs 163 K5
Anne Hathaway's Cottage Warwks 71 L4
Annfield Plain Dur 150 F5
Anniesland C Glas 174 F5
Ansdell Lancs 120 D5
Ansford Somset 26 F5
Ansley Warwks 86 C5
Anslow Staffs 100 E7
Anslow Gate Staffs 100 D7
Anstey Herts 60 C2
Anstey Leics 87 G2
Anstruther Fife 187 J6
Ansty W Susx 19 J2
Ansty Warwks 86 E6
Ansty Wilts 27 L6
Anthorn Cumb 147 L4
Antingham Norfk 106 F5
An t-Ob W Isls 232 d5
Antonine Wall 175 L3
Anton's Gowt Lincs 103 M3
Antony Cnwll 6 B5
Antrobus Ches W 112 F5
Anwick Lincs 103 J3
Anwoth D & G 145 M4
Aperfield Gt Lon 32 D2
Apethorpe Nhants 88 E4
Apley Lincs 117 J6
Apperknowle Derbys 115 G5
Apperley Gloucs 55 K3
Appin Ag & B 191 J6
Appleby N Linc 126 B7
Appleby-in-Westmorland Cumb 139 G3
Appleby Magna Leics 86 C2
Appleby Parva Leics 86 C2
Applecross Highld 209 L5
Appledore Devon 23 G5
Appledore Devon 25 G8
Appledore Kent 34 C8
Appleford Oxon 41 K2
Applegarth Town D & G 155 J5
Appleshaw Hants 28 F2
Appleton Halton 112 D4
Appleton Oxon 57 H7
Appleton Warrtn 112 F5
Appleton-le-Moors N York 133 L3
Appleton-le-Street N York 134 B5
Appleton Roebuck N York 124 E3
Appleton Thorn Warrtn 112 F5
Appleton Wiske N York 141 J6
Appletreehall Border 167 H6
Appletreewick N York 131 K7
Appley Somset 25 G6
Appley Bridge Lancs 121 G8
Apse Heath IoW 17 G5
Apsley End C Beds 59 J2
Apuldram W Susx 18 A5
Arabella Highld 223 H6
Arbirlot Angus 196 F7
Arboll Highld 223 J5
Arborfield Wokham 42 C6
Arborfield Cross Wokham 42 C6
Arbourthorne Sheff 115 G4
Arbroath Angus 197 G7
Arbuthnott Abers 197 K2
Archddu Carmth 50 F5
Archdeacon Newton Darltn 141 G4
Archencarroch W Duns 174 D3
Archiestown Moray 214 F5
Archirondel Jersey 236 e6
Arclid Green Ches E 99 H1
Ardallie Abers 217 J6
Ardanaiseig Hotel Ag & B 182 F3
Ardaneaskan Highld 210 C7
Ardarroch Highld 210 C6
Ardbeg Ag & B 160 D1
Ardbeg Ag & B 173 J5
Ardbeg Ag & B 173 K2
Ardcharnich Highld 220 F4
Ardchiavaig Ag & B 180 E4
Ardchonnel Ag & B 182 D5

Ardchullarie More Stirlg 184 D5
Arddarroch Ag & B 183 J7
Arddleen Powys 82 F1
Ardechive Highld 201 H7
Ardeer N Ayrs 163 H2
Ardeley Herts 60 A3
Ardelve Highld 210 D8
Arden Ag & B 174 C2
Ardens Grafton Warwks 71 K4
Ardentallen Ag & B 182 B3
Ardentinny Ag & B 173 L2
Ardentraive Ag & B 173 H4
Ardeonaig Stirlg 184 E1
Ardersier Highld 213 J4
Ardessie Highld 220 D4
Ardfern Ag & B 182 A6
Ardfernal Ag & B 171 K4
Ardgartan Ag & B 183 J6
Ardgay Highld 222 D4
Ardgour Highld 191 K4
Ardgowan Inver 173 L4
Ardhallow Ag & B 173 K4
Ardhasig W Isls 232 e4
Ardheslaig Highld 210 B3
Ardindrean Highld 220 F4
Ardingly W Susx 32 C7
Ardington Oxon 41 H3
Ardlamont Ag & B 173 G5
Ardleigh Essex 62 C3
Ardleigh Heath Essex 62 C2
Ardler P & K 195 L7
Ardley Oxon 57 K3
Ardlui Ag & B 183 K4
Ardlussa Ag & B 172 B2
Ardmair Highld 220 E2
Ardmaleish Ag & B 173 J5
Ardminish Ag & B 172 B8
Ardmolich Highld 190 E3
Ardmore Ag & B 174 C3
Ardmore Highld 222 F4
Ardnadam Ag & B 173 K3
Ardnagrask Highld 212 E4
Ardnamurchan Highld 190 B3
Ardnarff Highld 210 D7
Ardnastang Highld 190 F4
Ardpatrick Ag & B 172 C6
Ardrishaig Ag & B 172 E2
Ardross Highld 222 E6
Ardrossan N Ayrs 163 G2
Ardsley East Leeds 123 K5
Ardslignish Highld 190 B4
Ardtalla Ag & B 171 J7
Ardtoe Highld 190 C3
Arduaine Ag & B 182 A5
Ardullie Highld 212 E2
Ardvasar Highld 199 K5
Ardvorlich P & K 184 D3
Ardvourlie W Isls 232 e3
Ardwell D & G 144 D5
Ardwick Manch 113 J3
Areley Kings Worcs 70 E1
Arevegaig Highld 190 D3
Arford Hants 30 D4
Argoed Caerph 53 J7
Argyll Forest Park Ag & B 183 J6
Aribruach W Isls 232 e3
Aridhglas Ag & B 180 D3
Arileod Ag & B 188 F5
Arinagour Ag & B 189 G5
Ariogan Ag & B 182 C3
Arisaig Highld 199 K7
Arisaig House Highld 199 L7
Arkendale N York 132 F7
Arkesden Essex 76 C7
Arkholme Lancs 130 B5
Arkleton D & G 156 C4
Arkley Gt Lon 44 E2
Arksey Donc 115 L1
Arkwright Town Derbys 115 H7
Arle Gloucs 55 L4
Arlecdon Cumb 136 E4
Arlesey C Beds 75 H7
Arleston Wrekin 84 B2
Arley Ches E 112 F5
Arley Warwks 86 C5
Arlingham Gloucs 55 G6
Arlington Devon 23 K4
Arlington E Susx 20 B4
Armadale Highld 199 K5
Armadale Highld 230 A3
Armadale W Loth 176 C5
Armathwaite Cumb 148 E5
Arminghall Norfk 92 F3
Armitage Staffs 85 J1
Armley Leeds 123 K4
Armscote Warwks 72 B5
Armthorpe Donc 115 L1
Arnabost Ag & B 188 F4
Arncliffe N York 131 H5
Arncroach Fife 187 H6
Arndilly House Moray 215 G5
Arne Dorset 15 H5
Arnesby Leics 87 H5
Arngask P & K 186 B5
Arnisdale Highld 200 C3
Arnish Highld 209 J5
Arniston Mdloth 177 K6
Arnol W Isls 232 f1
Arnold E R Yk 126 E3
Arnold Notts 101 L4
Arnprior Stirlg 184 D7
Arnside Cumb 129 K4
Aros Ag & B 190 B7
Arrad Foot Cumb 129 G4
Arram E R Yk 126 C2
Arran N Ayrs 162 B3
Arrathorne N York 132 C2
Arreton IoW 17 G5
Arrina Highld 210 B3
Arrington Cambs 75 K4
Arrochar Ag & B 183 K6
Arrow Warwks 71 J3
Arscott Shrops 83 J2
Artafallie Highld 212 F4
Arthington Leeds 123 K2
Arthingworth Nhants 87 L7
Arthrath Abers 217 H6
Artrochie Abers 217 J7
Arundel W Susx 18 D4
Asby Cumb 136 E3
Ascog Ag & B 173 J5
Ascot W & M 42 F6
Ascott-under-Wychwood Oxon 56 F4
Asenby N York 132 F4
Asfordby Leics 102 B8
Asfordby Hill Leics 102 B8
Asgarby Lincs 103 J4
Ash Kent 35 H3
Ash Kent 45 L6
Ash Somset 26 C7
Ash Surrey 30 E2
Ashampstead W Berk 41 K5
Ashbocking Suffk 78 E4
Ashbourne Derbys 100 D3
Ashbrittle Somset 25 G6
Ashburton Devon 7 H2
Ashbury Devon 10 D5
Ashbury Oxon 40 E4
Ashby N Linc 125 L8
Ashby by Partney Lincs 118 F7
Ashby cum Fenby NE Lin 118 C2
Ashby de la Launde Lincs 103 H2
Ashby-de-la-Zouch Leics 86 D1
Ashby Folville Leics 87 K2
Ashby Magna Leics 87 H5
Ashby Parva Leics 87 G5
Ashby Puerorum Lincs 118 D7
Ashby St Ledgers Nhants 73 H2
Ashby St Mary Norfk 93 G3
Ashchurch Gloucs 55 L2
Ashcombe Devon 11 L8
Ashcombe N Som 37 M7
Ashcott Somset 26 C4
Ashdon Essex 76 E6
Ashdown Forest E Susx 32 E6
Ashe Hants 29 K2
Asheldham Essex 62 A7
Ashen Essex 77 H6
Ashendon Bucks 58 B5
Asheridge Bucks 58 F6
Ashfield Stirlg 185 G6
Ashfield cum Thorpe Suffk 78 E3
Ashfield Green Suffk 92 F8
Ashford Devon 7 G6
Ashford Devon 23 H4
Ashford Kent 34 D6
Ashford Surrey 43 H6
Ashford Bowdler Shrops 69 K1
Ashford Carbonell Shrops 69 K1
Ashford Hill Hants 41 K7
Ashford in the Water Derbys 114 D7
Ashgill S Lans 175 K7
Ash Green Surrey 30 E2
Ash Green Warwks 86 D6
Ashill Devon 12 E1
Ashill Norfk 91 K3
Ashill Somset 25 L7
Ashingdon Essex 46 E2
Ashington Nthumb 159 G5
Ashington Somset 26 E6
Ashington W Susx 18 F3
Ashkirk Border 167 G5
Ashleworth Gloucs 55 J3
Ashleworth Quay Gloucs 55 J3
Ashley Cambs 77 G3
Ashley Ches E 113 H5
Ashley Devon 10 F3
Ashley Gloucs 39 L2
Ashley Hants 16 B4
Ashley Hants 29 G5
Ashley Kent 35 J5
Ashley Nhants 87 L5
Ashley Staffs 99 H5
Ashley Wilts 39 J6
Ashley Green Bucks 58 F6
Ash Magna Shrops 98 E4
Ashmansworth Hants 41 H8
Ashmansworthy Devon 22 E7
Ash Mill Devon 24 C6
Ashmore Dorset 27 K7
Ashmore Green W Berk 41 J6
Ashorne Warwks 72 C3
Ashover Derbys 115 G8
Ashow Warwks 72 C1
Ashperton Herefs 70 B6
Ashprington Devon 7 J4
Ash Priors Somset 25 J5
Ashreigney Devon 10 F3
Ash Street Suffk 78 B5
Ashtead Surrey 44 D8
Ash Thomas Devon 12 C1
Ashton Ches W 112 D7
Ashton Cnwll 3 G5
Ashton Devon 11 K7
Ashton Herefs 69 K2
Ashton Inver 173 L3
Ashton Nhants 73 L5
Ashton Nhants 88 F5
Ashton Common Wilts 39 K8
Ashton-in-Makerfield Wigan 112 E2
Ashton Keynes Wilts 40 B2
Ashton under Hill Worcs 71 H6
Ashton-under-Lyne Tamesd 113 L2
Ashurst Hants 16 D1
Ashurst Kent 32 F5
Ashurst Lancs 121 G8
Ashurst W Susx 19 G3
Ashurstwood W Susx 32 D5
Ash Vale Surrey 30 E2
Ashwater Devon 9 K5
Ashwell Herts 75 J6
Ashwell Rutlnd 88 C2
Ashwell End Herts 75 J6
Ashwellthorpe Norfk 92 D4
Ashwick Somset 26 F2
Ashwicken Norfk 105 H8
Askam in Furness Cumb 128 F4
Askern Donc 124 E7
Askerswell Dorset 14 A4
Askett Bucks 58 D6
Askham Cumb 138 D3
Askham Notts 116 C6
Askham Bryan C York 124 E2
Askham Richard C York 124 E2
Asknish Ag & B 172 F1
Askrigg N York 131 H2
Askwith N York 123 H2
Aslackby Lincs 103 H6
Aslacton Norfk 92 D5
Aslockton Notts 102 C4
Aspatria Cumb 147 K6
Aspenden Herts 60 B3
Aspley Guise C Beds 74 D7
Aspley Heath C Beds 74 D7
Aspull Wigan 121 J8
Asselby E R Yk 125 H5
Assington Suffk 77 L6
Assington Green Suffk 77 H4
Astbury Ches E 99 J1
Astcote Nhants 73 J4
Asterby Lincs 118 C5
Asterley Shrops 83 H3
Asterton Shrops 83 H5
Asthall Oxon 56 F5
Asthall Leigh Oxon 56 F5
Astle Highld 223 G3
Astley Shrops 98 D8
Astley Warwks 86 C5
Astley Wigan 113 G2
Astley Worcs 70 D2
Astley Abbots Shrops 84 C4
Astley Bridge Bolton 121 K7
Astley Cross Worcs 70 E1
Aston Birm 85 J5
Aston Ches E 98 E3
Aston Ches W 112 E5
Aston Derbys 114 D5
Aston Flints 111 J7
Aston Herts 59 L4
Aston Oxon 57 G7
Aston Rothm 115 J4
Aston Shrops 84 E5
Aston Shrops 98 D6
Aston Staffs 99 H4
Aston Staffs 99 K7
Aston Wokham 42 C4
Aston Wrekin 84 B2
Aston Abbotts Bucks 58 D4
Aston Botterell Shrops 84 B6
Aston-by-Stone Staffs 99 K6
Aston Cantlow Warwks 71 K3
Aston Clinton Bucks 58 E5
Aston Crews Herefs 54 F4
Aston End Herts 59 L3
Aston Fields Worcs 71 G1
Aston Flamville Leics 86 F5
Aston Ingham Herefs 55 G4
Aston le Walls Nhants 72 F4
Aston Magna Gloucs 71 L7
Aston Munslow Shrops 83 K6
Aston on Clun Shrops 83 H6
Aston Pigott Shrops 83 G3
Aston Rogers Shrops 83 G3
Aston Rowant Oxon 58 B7
Aston Somerville Worcs 71 J6
Aston-sub-Edge Gloucs 71 K6

Aston Tirrold Oxon 41 K3
Aston-upon-Trent Derbys 101 H6
Aston Upthorpe Oxon 41 K3
Astwick C Beds 75 J6
Astwood M Keyn 74 D5
Astwood Worcs 71 G2
Astwood Bank Worcs 71 J3
Aswarby Lincs 103 H4
Aswardby Lincs 118 E7
Atcham Shrops 83 K2
Athelhampton Dorset 14 E4
Athelington Suffk 78 E1
Athelney Somset 25 M5
Athelstaneford E Loth 178 C3
Atherington Devon 23 J6
Atherstone Warwks 86 C4
Atherstone on Stour Warwks 72 B4
Atherton Wigan 113 G2
Atlow Derbys 100 E3
Attadale Highld 210 E6
Atterby Lincs 117 G3
Attercliffe Sheff 115 G4
Atterton Leics 86 D4
Attingham Park Shrops 83 K2
Attleborough Norfk 92 C4
Attleborough Warwks 86 D5
Attlebridge Norfk 92 D1
Attleton Green Suffk 77 G4
Atwick E R Yk 126 F1
Atworth Wilts 39 J7
Aubourn Lincs 116 F8
Auchbreck Moray 214 F8
Auchedly Abers 217 G7
Auchenblae Abers 197 H1
Auchenbowie Stirlg 175 L2
Auchencairn D & G 146 D5
Auchencairn D & G 155 G5
Auchencairn N Ayrs 162 D4
Auchencrow Border 179 H6
Auchendinny Mdloth 177 H6
Auchengray S Lans 176 D7
Auchenhalrig Moray 215 J3
Auchenheath S Lans 164 F2
Auchenhessnane D & G 154 E3
Auchenlochan Ag & B 173 G4
Auchenmade N Ayrs 174 C8
Auchenmalg D & G 144 F4
Auchentiber N Ayrs 174 C8
Auchindrain Ag & B 182 E6
Auchindrean Highld 221 G5
Auchininna Abers 216 C5
Auchinleck E Ayrs 164 B5
Auchinloch N Lans 175 H4
Auchinstarry N Lans 175 J3
Auchintore Highld 191 L2
Auchiries Abers 217 K6
Auchlean Highld 203 K5
Auchlee Abers 207 G6
Auchleven Abers 206 C1
Auchlochan S Lans 164 F3
Auchlossan Abers 206 B5
Auchlyne Stirlg 184 B2
Auchmillan E Ayrs 164 A4
Auchmithie Angus 197 G7
Auchmuirbridge Fife 186 C6
Auchnacree Angus 196 D4
Auchnagatt Abers 217 H6
Auchnarrow Moray 204 F2
Auchnotteroch D & G 144 B3
Auchroisk Moray 215 H4
Auchterarder P & K 185 K5
Auchteraw Highld 202 B4
Auchterblair Highld 203 L2
Auchtercairn Highld 219 J6
Auchterderran Fife 186 C7
Auchterhouse Angus 196 B8
Auchterless Abers 216 D6
Auchtermuchty Fife 186 D5
Auchterneed Highld 212 D3
Auchtertool Fife 177 H1
Auchtertyre Highld 210 C8
Auchtubh Stirlg 184 C4
Auckengill Highld 231 L3
Auckley Donc 115 M2
Audenshaw Tamesd 113 K3
Audlem Ches E 98 F4
Audley Staffs 99 J3
Audley End Essex 76 D6
Audley End House & Gardens Essex 76 D6
Audnam Dudley 84 F6
Aughton E R Yk 125 G3
Aughton Lancs 111 L1
Aughton Lancs 129 L6
Aughton Rothm 115 J4
Aughton Wilts 28 E1
Aughton Park Lancs 112 B1
Auldearn Highld 213 L4
Aulden Herefs 69 J4
Auldgirth D & G 154 F5
Auldhouse S Lans 175 H7
Ault a' chruinn Highld 200 E2
Aultbea Highld 219 K4
Aultgrishin Highld 219 H4
Aultguish Inn Highld 221 J7
Ault Hucknall Derbys 115 J7
Aultmore Moray 215 J4
Aultnagoire Highld 202 E2
Aultnamain Inn Highld 222 F5
Aunsby Lincs 103 H5
Aust S Glos 38 E3
Austerfield Donc 116 A3
Austrey Warwks 86 C3
Austwick N York 130 E5
Authorpe Lincs 118 E5
Avebury Wilts 40 C6
Avebury Wilts 40 C6
Aveley Thurr 45 L4
Avening Gloucs 39 K2
Averham Notts 102 C2
Aveton Gifford Devon 7 G6
Aviemore Highld 203 L3
Avington W Berk 41 G6
Avoch Highld 213 G4
Avon Hants 15 L3
Avonbridge Falk 176 B4
Avon Dassett Warwks 72 E4
Avonmouth Bristl 38 D5
Avonwick Devon 7 G4
Awbridge Hants 28 F6
Awliscombe Devon 12 E3
Awre Gloucs 55 G6
Awsworth Notts 101 J4
Axbridge Somset 26 B1
Axford Hants 29 L3
Axford Wilts 40 E6
Axminster Devon 13 H3
Axmouth Devon 13 G4
Aycliffe Dur 141 G3
Aydon Nthumb 150 C2
Aylburton Gloucs 54 E7
Aylesbeare Devon 12 D4
Aylesbury Bucks 58 D5
Aylesbury Crematorium Bucks 58 D5
Aylesby NE Lin 126 F8
Aylesford Kent 33 J2
Aylesham Kent 35 H4
Aylestone C Leic 87 H4
Aylestone Park C Leic 87 H4
Aylmerton Norfk 106 E5
Aylsham Norfk 106 E6
Aylton Herefs 70 B6
Aylworth Gloucs 56 C4
Aymestrey Herefs 69 H2
Aynho Nhants 57 K2
Ayot St Lawrence Herts 59 K5
Ayr S Ayrs 163 J5
Aysgarth N York 131 J2
Ayshford Devon 25 G7
Ayside Cumb 129 J3
Ayston Rutlnd 88 C4
Ayton Border 179 J6
Azerley N York 132 C5

B

Babbacombe Torbay 7 L3
Babbs Green Herts 60 C5
Babcary Somset 26 E5
Babraham Cambs 76 D4
Babworth Notts 116 B5
Backaland Ork 234 d4
Backfolds Abers 217 J4
Backford Ches W 111 L6
Backies Highld 223 H2
Back of Keppoch Highld 199 K7
Backwell N Som 38 C6
Baconsthorpe Norfk 106 D5
Bacton Herefs 54 A2
Bacton Norfk 107 H5
Bacton Suffk 78 C2
Bacup Lancs 122 C6
Badachro Highld 219 J6
Badbury Swindn 40 D4
Badby Nhants 73 H3
Badcall Highld 228 B7
Badcall Highld 228 C4
Badcaul Highld 220 D3
Baddeley Edge C Stke 99 K3
Baddeley Green C Stke 99 K3
Baddesley Clinton Warwks 86 B8
Baddesley Ensor Warwks 86 C4
Baddidarrach Highld 224 D4
Baddinsgill Border 176 F7
Badenscoth Abers 216 D6
Badentarbet Highld 224 B6
Badenyon Abers 205 H2
Badger Shrops 84 D4
Badgeworth Gloucs 55 K4
Badgworth Somset 26 B2
Badicaul Highld 210 B8
Badingham Suffk 79 G2
Badlesmere Kent 34 D4
Badlieu Border 165 K5
Badlipster Highld 231 J5
Badluarach Highld 220 C3
Badninish Highld 223 G3
Badrallach Highld 220 D3
Badsey Worcs 71 J5
Badshot Lea Surrey 30 E2
Badsworth Wakefd 124 C7
Badwell Ash Suffk 78 B2
Bagber Dorset 27 H8
Bagby N York 133 G4
Bag Enderby Lincs 118 E6
Bagendon Gloucs 56 A6
Bagh a Chaisteil W Isls 233 b9
Bagh a Tuath W Isls 233 b9
Bagillt Flints 111 H6
Baginton Warwks 86 D8
Baglan Neath 51 L6
Bagley Shrops 98 B6
Bagley Somset 26 C3
Bagnall Staffs 99 L3
Bagshot Surrey 42 E7
Bagstone S Glos 39 G3
Bagworth Leics 86 F2
Bagwy Llydiart Herefs 54 C3
Baildon C Brad 123 H3
Baildon Green C Brad 123 H3
Baile Ailein W Isls 232 f3
Baile a Mhanaich W Isls 233 b6
Baile Mór Ag & B 180 D3
Baillieston C Glas 175 J5
Bainbridge N York 131 H2
Bainshole Abers 216 B7
Bainton C Pete 89 G3
Bainton E R Yk 126 B1
Baintown Fife 186 F6
Bairnkine Border 167 K6
Bakewell Derbys 114 E7
Bala Gwynd 96 E5
Balallan W Isls 232 f3
Balbeg Highld 212 C7
Balbeggie P & K 186 C2
Balblair Highld 212 D5
Balblair Highld 213 G2
Balby Donc 115 K2
Balcary D & G 146 E5
Balchraggan Highld 212 E5
Balchreick Highld 228 B4
Balcombe W Susx 32 B6
Balcomie Links Fife 187 K5
Baldersby N York 132 E4
Baldersby St James N York 132 E4
Balderstone Lancs 121 J4
Balderton Notts 102 D3
Baldinnie Fife 187 G5
Baldinnies P & K 185 L4
Baldock Herts 75 J7
Baldock Services Herts 75 J6
Baldovie C Dund 187 G2
Baldrine IoM 237 d5
Baldslow E Susx 20 F3
Bale Norfk 106 B5
Baledgarno P & K 186 D2
Balemartine Ag & B 188 C7
Balerno C Edin 177 G5
Balfarg Fife 186 D6
Balfield Angus 196 E3
Balfour Ork 234 c5
Balfron Stirlg 174 F1
Balgaveny Abers 216 C6
Balgonar Fife 185 L8
Balgowan D & G 144 D6
Balgowan Highld 202 F6
Balgown Highld 218 B7
Balgracie D & G 144 B3
Balgray S Lans 165 H5
Balham Gt Lon 44 F5
Balhary P & K 195 L6
Balholmie P & K 186 B1
Baligill Highld 230 C3
Balintore Angus 195 L5
Balintore Highld 223 J6
Balintraid Highld 223 G7
Balivanich W Isls 233 b6
Balkeerie Angus 196 B7
Balkholme E R Yk 125 J5
Ballachulish Highld 191 L5
Ballajora IoM 237 e4
Ballanlay Ag & B 173 H6
Ballantrae S Ayrs 152 C5
Ballasalla IoM 237 b6
Ballater Abers 205 J6
Ballaugh IoM 237 c3
Ballchraggan Highld 223 G6
Ballencrieff E Loth 178 B3
Ballevullin Ag & B 188 B6
Ball Green C Stke 99 K3
Ballidon Derbys 100 D2
Balliekine N Ayrs 161 L2
Balliemore Ag & B 182 F7
Balligmorrie S Ayrs 152 F4
Ballimore Stirlg 184 C4
Ballindalloch Moray 214 E6
Ballindean P & K 186 D2
Ballinger Common Bucks 58 E7
Ballingham Herefs 54 E2
Ballingry Fife 186 C7
Ballinluig P & K 194 F6
Ballinshoe Angus 196 C5
Ballintuim P & K 195 H5
Balloch Highld 213 H5
Balloch N Lans 175 K4
Balloch P & K 185 H4
Balloch S Ayrs 153 G3
Balloch W Duns 174 D3
Balls Cross W Susx 31 G6
Balls Green E Susx 32 E6
Ballygown Ag & B 189 K7
Ballygrant Ag & B 171 G5
Ballyhaugh Ag & B 188 F5
Balmaclellan D & G 154 B6
Balmae D & G 146 C6
Balmaha Stirlg 174 D1
Balmalcolm Fife 186 E5

Balmangan D & G 146 B5
Balmedie Abers 207 H2
Balmerino Fife 186 F3
Balmichael N Ayrs 162 B3
Balmore E Duns 175 G4
Balmuchy Highld 223 J5
Balmule Fife 177 G2
Balmullo Fife 187 G4
Balnacoil Lodge Highld 226 E6
Balnacra Highld 210 F5
Balnacroft Abers 205 G6
Balnafoich Highld 213 G7
Balnaguard P & K 194 E6
Balnahard Ag & B 180 F1
Balnahard Ag & B 180 F7
Balnain Highld 212 C7
Balnakeil Highld 228 F2
Balne N York 124 F6
Balquharn P & K 185 L1
Balquhidder Stirlg 184 C3
Balsall Common Solhll 86 B7
Balsall Heath Birm 85 J6
Balscote Oxon 72 E6
Balsham Cambs 76 E4
Baltasound Shet 235 e1
Baltersan D & G 145 J3
Balthangie Abers 216 F4
Baltonsborough Somset 26 D4
Balvicar Ag & B 181 M4
Balvraid Highld 200 C3
Balvraid Highld 213 K7
Bamber Bridge Lancs 121 H5
Bamber's Green Essex 60 F4
Bamburgh Nthumb 169 H3
Bamburgh Castle Nthumb 169 H3
Bamford Derbys 114 E5
Bampton Cumb 138 D4
Bampton Devon 24 E6
Bampton Oxon 56 F7
Bampton Grange Cumb 138 D4
Banavie Highld 191 L2
Banbury Oxon 72 F6
Banbury Crematorium Oxon 72 F6
Bancffosfelen Carmth 50 F3
Banchory Abers 206 D6
Banchory-Devenick Abers 207 G5
Bancycapel Carmth 50 E3
Bancyfelin Carmth 50 D2
Bandirran P & K 186 C2
Banff Abers 216 D2
Bangor Gwynd 109 H6
Bangor Crematorium Gwynd 109 H6
Bangor-on-Dee Wrexhm 98 B4
Bangors Cnwll 9 G5
Banham Norfk 92 C6
Bank Hants 16 C2
Bankend D & G 147 H2
Bankfoot P & K 185 M1
Bankglen E Ayrs 164 C6
Bankhead C Aber 207 G4
Bankhead S Lans 165 J1
Banknock Falk 175 K3
Banks Lancs 120 E6
Bankshill D & G 155 L5
Banningham Norfk 106 F6
Bannister Green Essex 61 H4
Bannockburn Stirlg 175 L1
Banstead Surrey 44 E7
Bantham Devon 6 F6
Banton N Lans 175 K3
Banwell N Som 38 B8
Bapchild Kent 34 C3
Bapton Wilts 27 M4
Barabhas W Isls 232 f1
Barassie S Ayrs 163 J3
Barbaraville Highld 223 G6
Barbieston S Ayrs 163 K5
Barbon Cumb 130 C3
Barbrook Devon 23 L2
Barby Nhants 73 G1
Barcaldine Ag & B 191 J7
Barcombe E Susx 19 L3
Barcombe Cross E Susx 19 L3
Barden Park Kent 33 G4
Bardfield End Green Essex 61 G2
Bardfield Saling Essex 61 G3
Bardney Lincs 117 J7
Bardon Leics 86 F2
Bardon Mill Nthumb 149 K3
Bardowie E Duns 175 G4
Bardrainney Inver 174 C4
Bardsea Cumb 129 G5
Bardsey Leeds 124 B2
Bardsey Island Gwynd 94 B7
Bardwell Suffk 91 L8
Bare Lancs 129 K6
Barfad D & G 145 G2
Barford Norfk 92 D3
Barford Warwks 72 C3
Barford St John Oxon 57 H2
Barford St Martin Wilts 28 B5
Barford St Michael Oxon 57 H2
Barfrestone Kent 35 H5
Bargeddie N Lans 175 J5
Bargoed Caerph 53 J7
Bargrennan D & G 153 H6
Barham Cambs 89 G7
Barham Kent 35 G5
Barham Suffk 78 D4
Barham Crematorium Kent 35 G5
Bar Hill Cambs 75 L2
Barholm Lincs 88 F2
Barkby Leics 87 J2
Barkby Thorpe Leics 87 J2
Barkestone-le-Vale Leics 102 C5
Barkham Wokham 42 C6
Barking Gt Lon 45 H3
Barking Suffk 78 C4
Barkingside Gt Lon 45 H3
Barking Tye Suffk 78 C4
Barkisland Calder 122 F6
Barkla Shop Cnwll 3 J2
Barkston Lincs 102 F4
Barkston Ash N York 124 D4
Barkway Herts 75 L7
Barlanark C Glas 175 H5
Barlaston Staffs 99 K5
Barlavington W Susx 18 C3
Barlborough Derbys 115 J6
Barlby N York 124 F4
Barlestone Leics 86 E3
Barley Herts 76 B6
Barley Lancs 122 B3
Barleythorpe Rutlnd 88 B2
Barling Essex 46 F3
Barlings Lincs 117 H6
Barlochan D & G 146 E4
Barlow Derbys 115 G6
Barlow Gatesd 150 E3
Barlow N York 124 F5
Barmby Moor E R Yk 125 J2
Barmby on the Marsh E R Yk 125 G5
Barmollack Ag & B 161 K1
Barmouth Gwynd 80 E1
Barmpton Darltn 141 H4
Barmston E R Yk 135 J7
Barnacarry Ag & B 182 E8
Barnack C Pete 88 F3
Barnard Castle Dur 140 D4
Barnard Gate Oxon 57 H6
Barnardiston Suffk 77 G5
Barnbarroch D & G 146 E4
Barnburgh Donc 115 J2
Barnby Suffk 93 K5
Barnby Dun Donc 124 F8
Barnby in the Willows Notts 102 E3
Barnby Moor Notts 116 A5
Barncorkrie D & G 144 D7
Barnes Gt Lon 44 E5
Barnes Street Kent 33 H4
Barnet Gt Lon 44 E2
Barnetby le Wold N Linc 126 C8
Barney Norfk 106 B6
Barnham Suffk 91 K7
Barnham W Susx 18 C5
Barnham Broom Norfk 92 C3
Barnhead Angus 197 G5
Barnhill C Dund 187 H2
Barnhill Moray 214 E3
Barnhills D & G 152 B7
Barningham Dur 140 D5
Barningham Suffk 91 L7
Barnoldby le Beck NE Lin 118 C2
Barnoldswick Lancs 122 C2
Barns Green W Susx 31 J6
Barnsley Barns 115 G1
Barnsley Gloucs 56 B6
Barnsley Crematorium Barns 115 G1
Barnstaple Devon 23 J5
Barnston Essex 61 G4
Barnston Wirral 111 J5
Barnstone Notts 102 B5
Barnt Green Worcs 85 H8
Barnton C Edin 177 G4
Barnton Ches W 112 F6
Barnwell All Saints Nhants 88 F6
Barnwell St Andrew Nhants 88 F6
Barnwood Gloucs 55 K4
Barr S Ayrs 153 G4
Barra W Isls 233 b9
Barra Airport W Isls 233 b9
Barrachan D & G 145 H5
Barraigh W Isls 233 b9
Barrapoll Ag & B 188 B7
Barrasford Nthumb 158 A7
Barrhead E Rens 174 F6
Barrhill S Ayrs 152 F5
Barrington Cambs 76 B5
Barrington Somset 26 B7
Barripper Cnwll 3 H4
Barrmill N Ayrs 174 C7
Barrock Highld 231 J2
Barrow Gloucs 55 K3
Barrow Lancs 121 L3
Barrow Rutlnd 88 C1
Barrow Somset 27 G5
Barrow Suffk 77 H2
Barrowby Lincs 102 E5
Barrowden Rutlnd 88 D4
Barrowford Lancs 122 C3
Barrow Gurney N Som 38 D6
Barrow Haven N Linc 126 D6
Barrow-in-Furness Cumb 128 E5
Barrow Island Cumb 128 E5
Barrow-upon-Humber N Linc 126 D6
Barrow upon Soar Leics 101 L8
Barrow upon Trent Derbys 101 G6
Barry Angus 187 J1
Barry V Glam 37 H6
Barry Island V Glam 37 H6
Barsby Leics 87 K2
Barsham Suffk 93 H5
Barston Solhll 86 B7
Bartestree Herefs 69 L6
Barthol Chapel Abers 216 F7
Bartholomew Green Essex 61 H4
Barthomley Ches E 99 H3
Bartley Hants 28 F8
Bartley Green Birm 85 H6
Bartlow Cambs 76 E5
Barton Cambs 76 B4
Barton Ches W 98 C2
Barton Gloucs 56 C3
Barton Lancs 120 E8
Barton Lancs 121 G3
Barton N York 141 G5
Barton Oxon 57 K6
Barton Torbay 7 K3
Barton Bendish Norfk 91 G3
Barton End Gloucs 39 J2
Barton Hartshorn Bucks 57 M2
Barton in Fabis Notts 101 K6
Barton in the Beans Leics 86 E3
Barton-le-Clay C Beds 59 H2
Barton-le-Street N York 133 L5
Barton-le-Willows N York 133 L6
Barton Mills Suffk 91 G8
Barton-on-Sea Hants 16 B4
Barton-on-the-Heath Warwks 56 E2
Barton Park Services N York 140 F5
Barton St David Somset 26 D5
Barton Seagrave Nhants 88 C7
Barton Stacey Hants 29 H3
Barton Town Devon 23 L4
Barton Turf Norfk 107 H7
Barton-under-Needwood Staffs 100 D8
Barton-upon-Humber N Linc 126 C6
Barton Waterside N Linc 126 C6
Barvas W Isls 232 f1
Barway Cambs 90 D7
Barwell Leics 86 F4
Barwick Devon 10 E4
Barwick Somset 26 E8
Barwick in Elmet Leeds 124 B3
Baschurch Shrops 98 B7
Bascote Warwks 72 E2
Bashall Eaves Lancs 121 K2
Basildon Essex 46 B3
Basildon & District Crematorium Essex 46 C3
Basingstoke Hants 29 M2
Basingstoke Crematorium Hants 29 K3
Baslow Derbys 114 E6
Bason Bridge Somset 25 M3
Bassaleg Newpt 37 L3
Bassendean Border 167 K1
Bassenthwaite Cumb 137 H2
Bassett C Sotn 29 H7
Bassingbourn-cum-Kneesworth Cambs 75 L5
Bassingham Lincs 102 E1
Bassingthorpe Lincs 102 F6
Bassus Green Herts 60 A3
Baston Lincs 89 G2
Bastwick Norfk 107 J8
Batchworth Herts 43 H2
Batcombe Dorset 14 C2
Batcombe Somset 27 G4
Batford Herts 59 J5
Bath BaNES 39 H7
Bathampton BaNES 39 H7
Bath, City of BaNES 39 H7
Bathealton Somset 25 G6
Batheaston BaNES 39 H6
Bathford BaNES 39 H6
Bathgate W Loth 176 D5
Bathley Notts 102 C2
Bathpool Cnwll 5 L2

Bathpool Somset 25 K6
Bath Side Essex 62 F2
Bathville W Loth 176 C5
Bathway Somset 26 E2
Batley Kirk 123 J5
Batsford Gloucs 71 L7
Battersby N York 142 D5
Battersea Gt Lon 44 F5
Battisford Tye Suffk 78 B4
Battle E Susx 20 F3
Battle Powys 52 F2
Battledykes Angus 196 D5
Battlesbridge Essex 46 C2
Battleton Somset 24 E6
Baughton Worcs 70 F6
Baughurst Hants 41 L7
Baulds Abers 206 B6
Baulking Oxon 40 F3
Baumber Lincs 117 L6
Baunton Gloucs 56 A6
Baverstock Wilts 28 B5
Bawburgh Norfk 92 D2
Bawdeswell Norfk 106 C7
Bawdrip Somset 25 M4
Bawdsey Suffk 79 H6
Bawtry Donc 115 M3
Baxenden Lancs 122 B5
Baxterley Warwks 86 C4
Bay Highld 208 D4
Bayble W Isls 232 g2
Baybridge Hants 29 K6
Baycliff Cumb 129 G5
Baydon Wilts 40 F5
Bayford Herts 60 A6
Bayford Somset 27 G5
Bayhead W Isls 233 b6
Baylham Suffk 78 D4
Baysham Herefs 54 E3
Bayston Hill Shrops 83 J2
Baythorne End Essex 77 G6
Bayton Worcs 84 C8
Bayworth Oxon 57 J7
Beachampton Bucks 73 L6
Beachamwell Norfk 91 H3
Beachy Head E Susx 20 C6
Beacon Devon 12 F2
Beacon End Essex 62 A3
Beacon Hill Notts 102 D2
Beacon Hill Surrey 30 E4
Beacon's Bottom Bucks 42 C2
Beaconsfield Bucks 42 F3
Beaconsfield Services Bucks 42 F3
Beadlam N York 133 K3
Beadlow C Beds 75 G6
Beadnell Nthumb 169 J4
Beaford Devon 10 E2
Beal N York 124 E5
Beal Nthumb 169 G2
Bealsmill Cnwll 6 A1
Beaminster Dorset 13 L3
Beamish Dur 150 F4
Beamish Museum Dur 150 F4
Beamsley N York 131 K8
Beanacre Wilts 39 K7
Beanley Nthumb 169 G5
Beardon Devon 10 D7
Beare Green Surrey 31 K3
Bearley Warwks 71 L3
Bearpark Dur 151 G6
Bearsden E Duns 174 F4
Bearsted Kent 33 K3
Bearstone Shrops 99 G5
Bearwood Birm 85 H6
Bearwood Herefs 69 H4
Bearwood Poole 15 K3
Beattock D & G 155 J2
Beauchamp Roding Essex 60 F6
Beaufort Blae G 53 J5
Beaulieu Hants 16 E3
Beauly Highld 212 E5
Beaumaris IoA 109 H6
Beaumaris Castle IoA 109 J6
Beaumont Cumb 148 C3
Beaumont Essex 62 E3
Beaumont Jersey 236 c7
Beaumont Leys C Leic 87 H2
Beausale Warwks 72 B1
Beauworth Hants 29 L6
Beaworthy Devon 10 C5
Beazley End Essex 61 H3
Bebington Wirral 111 K5
Beccles Suffk 93 J5
Becconsall Lancs 120 F6
Beckbury Shrops 84 D3
Beckenham Gt Lon 45 G6
Beckenham Crematorium Gt Lon 45 G6
Beckermet Cumb 136 E6
Beckfoot Cumb 147 J5
Beckford Worcs 71 H7
Beckhampton Wilts 40 C6
Beckingham Lincs 102 E2
Beckingham Notts 116 C4
Beckington Somset 27 J2
Beckjay Shrops 83 H7
Beckley E Susx 21 G2
Beckley Oxon 57 K5
Beck Row Suffk 91 G7
Beck Side Cumb 128 F3
Beckton Gt Lon 45 H4
Beckwithshaw N York 132 D8
Becontree Gt Lon 45 J3
Becquet Vincent Jersey 236 c6
Bedale N York 132 D2
Bedchester Dorset 27 J7
Beddau Rhondd 37 G4
Beddgelert Gwynd 95 K3
Beddingham E Susx 19 L4
Beddington Gt Lon 44 F6
Beddington Corner Gt Lon 44 F6
Bedfield Suffk 78 F2
Bedford Bed 74 F5
Bedford Crematorium Bed 75 G4
Bedhampton Hants 17 K2
Bedingfield Suffk 78 E2
Bedlam N York 132 D7
Bedlington Nthumb 159 G5
Bedlinog Myr Td 53 H7
Bedminster Bristl 38 E6
Bedminster Down Bristl 38 E6
Bedmond Herts 59 J7
Bednall Staffs 99 L8
Bedrule Border 167 J5
Bedstone Shrops 83 G7
Bedwas Caerph 37 J3
Bedwellty Caerph 53 J7
Bedworth Warwks 86 D6
Beeby Leics 87 J2
Beech Hants 30 B4
Beech Staffs 99 J5
Beech Hill W Berk 42 B7
Beechingstoke Wilts 40 C8
Beedon W Berk 41 J5
Beeford E R Yk 135 H8
Beeley Derbys 114 E7
Beelsby NE Lin 117 K2
Beenham W Berk 41 L6
Beer Devon 13 G5
Beer Somset 26 B5
Beercrocombe Somset 25 L7
Beer Hackett Dorset 14 B1
Beesands Devon 7 J7
Beesby Lincs 118 F5
Beeson Devon 7 J7
Beeston C Beds 75 H5
Beeston Ches W 98 D2
Beeston Leeds 123 K4
Beeston Norfk 91 K1
Beeston Notts 101 K5
Beeston Regis Norfk 106 E4
Beeswing D & G 146 F2
Beetham Cumb 129 K4
Beetham Somset 25 L8
Beetley Norfk 106 A8
Begbroke Oxon 57 J5
Begelly Pembks 49 J6
Beguildy Powys 82 D7
Beighton Norfk 93 H2
Beighton Sheff 115 H5
Beinn Na Faoghla W Isls 233 c7
Beith N Ayrs 174 C7
Bekesbourne Kent 35 G4
Belaugh Norfk 107 G8
Belbroughton Worcs 85 G7
Belchalwell Dorset 14 E1
Belchamp Otten Essex 77 J6
Belchamp St Paul Essex 77 H6
Belchamp Walter Essex 77 J6
Belchford Lincs 118 D6
Belford Nthumb 169 G3
Belgrave C Leic 87 H3
Belhaven E Loth 178 E3
Belhelvie Abers 207 H2
Belhinnie Abers 215 K8
Bellabeg Abers 205 H3
Bellanoch Ag & B 182 A8
Bellaty Angus 195 K4
Bell Busk N York 131 G7
Belleau Lincs 118 E5
Bell End Worcs 85 G7
Bellerby N York 131 L2
Belle Vue Cumb 148 C4
Belle Vue Wakefd 123 L6
Bellfield S Lans 164 F3
Bellfield S Lans 165 J5
Bellingdon Bucks 58 F6
Bellingham Nthumb 157 L5
Belloch Ag & B 161 H2
Bellochantuy Ag & B 161 H3
Bell o' th' Hill Ches W 98 D4
Bellshill N Lans 175 J6
Bellside N Lans 175 L6
Bellsquarry W Loth 176 E5
Bells Yew Green E Susx 33 G6
Belluton BaNES 38 E7
Belmaduthy Highld 213 G3
Belmont Bl w D 121 K7
Belmont Gt Lon 44 E7
Belmont S Ayrs 163 J5
Belmont Shet 235 d2
Belnacraig Abers 205 J3
Belper Derbys 101 G3
Belsay Nthumb 158 D6
Belses Border 167 J4
Belsford Devon 7 H4
Belsize Herts 59 G7
Belstead Suffk 78 D6
Belstone Devon 10 F6
Belthorn Lancs 121 L5
Beltinge Kent 47 K6
Beltingham Nthumb 149 K3
Beltoft N Linc 116 D1
Belton Leics 101 H7
Belton Lincs 102 F4
Belton N Linc 116 C1
Belton Norfk 93 K3
Belton Rutlnd 88 B3
Belton House Lincs 102 F5
Belvedere Gt Lon 45 J4
Belvoir Leics 102 D5
Bembridge IoW 17 J5
Bemerton Wilts 28 C5
Bempton E R Yk 135 J5
Benacre Suffk 93 K6
Benbecula W Isls 233 c7
Benbecula Airport W Isls 233 c6
Benbuie D & G 154 C3
Benderloch Ag & B 191 H8
Benenden Kent 33 K6
Benfieldside Dur 150 D4
Bengeo Herts 60 A5
Bengeworth Worcs 71 J5
Benhall Green Suffk 79 H3
Benhall Street Suffk 79 H3
Benholm Abers 197 K3
Beningbrough N York 133 H7
Benington Herts 59 M4
Benington Lincs 104 C3
Benllech IoA 109 G5
Benmore Ag & B 173 K2
Bennan N Ayrs 162 C5
Ben Nevis Highld 192 B3
Benniworth Lincs 117 K5
Benover Kent 33 J4
Ben Rhydding C Brad 123 H2
Benslie N Ayrs 163 J2
Benson Oxon 41 L3
Benthoul C Aber 206 F5
Bentley Donc 115 K1
Bentley E R Yk 126 C4
Bentley Hants 30 C3
Bentley Suffk 78 D6
Bentley Warwks 86 C4
Bentley Crematorium Essex 45 L2
Bentpath D & G 156 B4
Bentwichen Devon 24 B5
Bentworth Hants 30 A4
Benvie Angus 186 E2
Benville Dorset 14 A2
Benwick Cambs 89 L5
Beoley Worcs 71 J1
Beoraidbeg Highld 199 L6
Bepton W Susx 18 B3
Berden Essex 60 D3
Berea Pembks 48 D2
Bere Alston Devon 6 C3
Bere Ferrers Devon 6 C3
Bere Regis Dorset 14 F4
Bergh Apton Norfk 93 G4
Berinsfield Oxon 41 L2
Berkeley Gloucs 55 G7
Berkhamsted Herts 59 G6
Berkley Somset 27 J2
Berkswell Solhll 86 B7
Bermondsey Gt Lon 45 G4
Bernera Highld 200 C2
Bernisdale Highld 208 F4
Berrick Prior Oxon 41 L2
Berrick Salome Oxon 41 L2
Berriedale Highld 227 K4
Berrier Cumb 137 L2
Berriew Powys 82 D4
Berrington Shrops 83 K3
Berrington Worcs 69 L2
Berrington Green Worcs 69 L2
Berrow Somset 25 L2
Berrow Green Worcs 70 D3
Berryfields Bucks 58 C5
Berryhillock Moray 215 L3
Berryhillock Moray 215 L4
Berrynarbor Devon 23 J3
Berry Pomeroy Devon 7 J4
Bersham Wrexhm 97 L3
Bersted W Susx 18 C5
Berwick E Susx 20 B5
Berwick Bassett Wilts 40 C5
Berwick Hill Nthumb 158 F6
Berwick St James Wilts 28 B4
Berwick St John Wilts 27 L6
Berwick St Leonard Wilts 27 L5
Berwick-upon-Tweed Nthumb 179 K7
Bescar Lancs 120 E7
Besford Worcs 71 G5
Bessacarr Donc 115 L2
Bessingby E R Yk 135 J6
Bessingham Norfk 106 E5
Besthorpe Norfk 92 C4
Besthorpe Notts 116 D8
Bestwood Village Notts 101 K3
Beswick E R Yk 126 C2
Betchworth Surrey 31 K2
Bethel Gwynd 109 G7
Bethel IoA 108 E7
Bethersden Kent 34 C6

Bethesda Gwynd 109 J7
Bethesda Pembks 49 J4
Bethlehem Carmth 51 K1
Bethnal Green Gt Lon 45 G4
Betley Staffs 99 H3
Betsham Kent 45 L5
Betteshanger Kent 35 J4
Bettiscombe Dorset 13 K3
Bettisfield Wrexhm 98 C5
Bettws Newpt 37 L3
Bettws Cedewain Powys 82 C4
Bettws Evan Cerdgn 65 J5
Bettws-Newydd Mons 54 A6
Bettyhill Highld 229 L3
Betws Brdgnd 36 D3
Betws Bledrws Cerdgn 66 D4
Betws Gwerfil Goch Denbgs 97 G3
Betws-y-Coed Conwy 96 C2
Betws-yn-Rhos Conwy 110 C6
Beulah Cerdgn 65 J5
Beulah Powys 67 K4
Bevercotes Notts 116 B6
Beverley E R Yk 126 C3
Beverston Gloucs 39 K2
Bewcastle Cumb 156 F7
Bewdley Worcs 84 D7
Bewerley N York 132 B6
Bewholme E R Yk 126 E1
Bexhill E Susx 20 E4
Bexley Gt Lon 45 J5
Bexleyheath Gt Lon 45 J5
Bexwell Norfk 90 F3
Beyton Suffk 77 L2
Beyton Green Suffk 77 L2
Bhaltos W Isls 232 d2
Bhatarsaigh W Isls 233 b10
Bibury Gloucs 56 C6
Bicester Oxon 57 L4
Bickenhill Solhll 85 L6
Bicker Lincs 103 L5
Bickerstaffe Lancs 112 C2
Bickerton N York 124 C1
Bickford Staffs 84 F2
Bickington Devon 7 J2
Bickington Devon 23 H5
Bickleigh Devon 6 D4
Bickleigh Devon 12 B2
Bickley Ches W 98 D3
Bickley Gt Lon 45 H6
Bickley N York 134 E2
Bicknacre Essex 61 J7
Bicknoller Somset 25 H4
Bicknor Kent 33 L2
Bicton Shrops 82 F6
Bicton Shrops 83 J1
Bidborough Kent 32 F5
Biddenden Kent 33 L5
Biddenham Bed 74 E4
Biddestone Wilts 39 K5
Biddisham Somset 26 B2
Biddlesden Bucks 73 J6
Biddulph Staffs 99 K2
Biddulph Moor Staffs 99 K2
Bideford Devon 23 G6
Bidford-on-Avon Warwks 71 K4
Bielby E R Yk 125 J2
Bieldside C Aber 207 G5
Bierley IoW 17 G6
Bierton Bucks 58 D5
Big Balcraig D & G 145 H6
Bigbury Devon 6 F6
Bigbury-on-Sea Devon 6 F6
Bigby Lincs 117 H1
Big Carlae D & G 154 B3
Biggar S Lans 165 K2
Biggin Derbys 100 D2
Biggin Hill Gt Lon 32 D2
Biggin Hill Airport Gt Lon 45 H7
Biggleswade C Beds 75 H5
Bigholms D & G 156 B6
Bighouse Highld 230 C3
Bighton Hants 29 L4
Biglands Cumb 148 A4
Bignor W Susx 18 D3
Bigrigg Cumb 136 D5
Big Sand Highld 219 H5
Bigton Shet 235 c7
Bilborough C Nott 101 K4
Bilbrook Somset 25 G3
Bilbrough N York 124 E2
Bilbster Highld 231 K5
Bildershaw Dur 140 F3
Bildeston Suffk 78 B5
Billericay Essex 46 B2
Billesdon Leics 87 K3
Billesley Warwks 71 K3
Billingborough Lincs 103 J5
Billinge St Hel 112 D2
Billingford Norfk 92 E7
Billingford Norfk 106 B7
Billingham S on T 141 K3
Billinghay Lincs 103 J2
Billingley Barns 115 H1
Billingshurst W Susx 31 H6
Billingsley Shrops 84 C6
Billington C Beds 58 F4
Billington Lancs 121 L4
Billockby Norfk 93 J2
Billy Row Dur 150 E7
Bilsborrow Lancs 121 G3
Bilsby Lincs 119 G6
Bilsham W Susx 18 D5
Bilsington Kent 34 D7
Bilsthorpe Notts 101 M1
Bilston Mdloth 177 H5
Bilston Wolves 85 G4
Bilstone Leics 86 D3
Bilton E R Yk 126 E4
Bilton N York 132 D7
Bilton Warwks 86 F8
Bilton-in-Ainsty N York 124 D1
Binbrook Lincs 117 K3
Bincombe Dorset 14 D5
Binegar Somset 26 E2
Binfield Br For 42 D6
Binfield Heath Oxon 42 C5
Bingfield Nthumb 158 B7
Bingham Notts 102 B4
Bingley C Brad 123 G3
Binham Norfk 106 B5
Binley Covtry 86 E7
Binley Hants 29 H2
Binley Woods Warwks 86 E7
Binnegar Dorset 15 G5
Binniehill Falk 176 B4
Binscombe Surrey 30 F3
Binstead IoW 17 H4
Binsted Hants 30 C3
Binsted W Susx 18 D4
Binton Warwks 71 K4
Bintree Norfk 106 B7
Birch Essex 61 M4
Bircham Newton Norfk 105 J5
Bircham Tofts Norfk 105 J6
Birchanger Essex 60 E4
Birchanger Green Services Essex 60 E4
Birch Cross Staffs 100 C6
Bircher Herefs 69 J2
Birchfield Birm 85 J5
Birch Green Essex 61 M4
Birchgrove Cardif 37 J4
Birchgrove Swans 51 K5
Birchgrove W Susx 32 D7
Birchington Kent 35 J2
Birchley Heath Warwks 86 C5
Birchover Derbys 100 E1
Birch Services Rochdl 122 C8
Birch Vale Derbys 114 A4
Birchwood Lincs 116 F7
Birch Wood Somset 25 K8
Birchwood Warrtn 112 F4
Bircotes Notts 115 M3
Birdbrook Essex 77 G6
Birdforth N York 133 G4
Birdham W Susx 17 M3
Birdingbury Warwks 72 E2
Birdlip Gloucs 55 L5
Birdsall N York 134 C6
Birds Edge Kirk 123 J8
Birds Green Essex 60 F6
Birdsgreen Shrops 84 D6
Birdsmoorgate Dorset 13 K3
Birdwell Barns 115 G2
Birgham Border 168 B2
Birichin Highld 223 G3
Birkby N York 141 H6
Birkdale Sefton 120 D7
Birkenbog Abers 215 L2
Birkenhead Wirral 111 K4
Birkenhead (Queensway) Tunnel Lpool 111 K4
Birkenhills Abers 216 E5
Birkenshaw Kirk 123 J5
Birkhall Abers 205 H6
Birkhill Angus 186 F1
Birkhill D & G 166 B6
Birkin N York 124 E5
Birley Herefs 69 J4
Birley Carr Sheff 115 G3
Birling Kent 46 B7
Birlingham Worcs 71 G5
Birmingham Birm 85 J6
Birmingham Airport Solhll 85 L6
Birnam P & K 195 G7
Birness Abers 217 J7
Birse Abers 206 B6
Birsemore Abers 205 L5
Birstall Kirk 123 J5
Birstall Leics 87 H2
Birstwith N York 132 C7
Birtley Gatesd 151 G4
Birtley Herefs 69 G2
Birtley Nthumb 157 L6
Birtley Crematorium Gatesd 151 G4
Birts Street Worcs 70 D7
Bisbrooke Rutlnd 88 C4
Biscathorpe Lincs 118 C5
Bisham W & M 42 D4
Bishampton Worcs 71 H4
Bish Mill Devon 24 B6
Bishop Auckland Dur 140 F2
Bishopbridge Lincs 117 G4
Bishopbriggs E Duns 175 G4
Bishop Burton E R Yk 126 B3
Bishop Middleham Dur 141 H2
Bishopmill Moray 214 F2
Bishop Monkton N York 132 E6
Bishop Norton Lincs 117 G3
Bishopsbourne Kent 35 G4
Bishops Cannings Wilts 40 B7
Bishop's Castle Shrops 83 G5
Bishop's Caundle Dorset 27 G8
Bishop's Cleeve Gloucs 55 L3
Bishop's Frome Herefs 70 B5
Bishop's Green Essex 61 G4
Bishop's Hull Somset 25 J6
Bishop's Itchington Warwks 72 E3
Bishops Lydeard Somset 25 J5
Bishop's Norton Gloucs 55 J3
Bishop's Nympton Devon 24 B6
Bishop's Offley Staffs 99 H6
Bishop's Stortford Herts 60 D4
Bishop's Sutton Hants 29 L5
Bishop's Tachbrook Warwks 72 C3
Bishop's Tawton Devon 23 J5
Bishopsteignton Devon 7 K2
Bishopstoke Hants 29 J7
Bishopston Swans 51 H7
Bishopstone Bucks 58 D6
Bishopstone E Susx 19 M5
Bishopstone Herefs 69 H5
Bishopstone Kent 47 K6
Bishopstone Swindn 40 E4
Bishopstone Wilts 28 B6
Bishopstrow Wilts 27 K3
Bishop Sutton BaNES 38 E7
Bishop's Waltham Hants 29 K7
Bishopswood Somset 25 K8
Bishop's Wood Staffs 84 E2
Bishopsworth Bristl 38 E6
Bishop Thornton N York 132 D6
Bishopthorpe C York 124 F2
Bishopton Darltn 141 J3
Bishopton Rens 174 E4
Bishop Wilton E R Yk 134 C7
Bishton Newpt 38 B3
Bishton Staffs 100 A7
Bisley Gloucs 55 K6
Bisley Surrey 42 F8
Bissoe Cnwll 3 K3
Bisterne Hants 15 L3
Bitchfield Lincs 103 G6
Bittadon Devon 23 J3
Bittaford Devon 6 F4
Bitterley Shrops 83 L7
Bitterne C Sotn 29 J8
Bitteswell Leics 87 G6
Bitton S Glos 39 G6
Bix Oxon 42 B4
Bixter Shet 235 c5
Blaby Leics 87 H4
Blackadder Border 179 H7
Blackawton Devon 7 J5
Blackborough Devon 12 E1
Blackborough End Norfk 90 F1
Black Bourton Oxon 56 F6
Blackboys E Susx 20 B2
Blackbrook Derbys 101 G3
Blackbrook St Hel 112 D3
Blackbrook Staffs 99 H5
Blackburn Abers 206 F3
Blackburn Bl w D 121 K5
Blackburn W Loth 176 D5
Blackburn with Darwen Services Bl w D 121 K5
Black Callerton N u Ty 150 F2
Blackcraig E Ayrs 164 C7
Black Crofts Ag & B 182 D1
Blackdog Abers 207 H3
Black Dog Devon 11 J3
Blackdown Dorset 13 K2
Blacker Hill Barns 115 G2
Blackfen Gt Lon 45 J5
Blackfield Hants 16 E3
Blackford P & K 185 J5
Blackford Somset 26 B2
Blackford Somset 26 F6
Blackfordby Leics 101 G8
Blackhall C Edin 177 G4
Blackhall Colliery Dur 151 K6
Blackhall Mill Gatesd 150 E4
Blackhaugh Border 166 F2
Blackheath Gt Lon 45 G5
Blackheath Sandw 85 H6
Blackheath Suffk 93 J8
Blackheath Surrey 31 G3
Blackhill Abers 217 K3
Blackhill Abers 217 K5
Blackhill Dur 150 D5
Blackhill of Clackriach Abers 217 H5

Blackhorse Devon 12 C4
Blacklaw D & G 165 K7
Blackley Manch 113 J2
Blackley Crematorium Manch 113 J2
Blacklunans P & K 195 J4
Blackmarstone Herefs 69 K6
Blackmill Brdgnd 36 E3
Blackmoor Hants 30 C5
Blackmoor N Som 38 C7
Blackmoorfoot Kirk 123 G7
Blackmore Essex 60 F7
Blackmore End Essex 61 H2
Black Mountains 53 K3
Blackness Falk 176 E3
Blacknest Hants 30 D3
Black Notley Essex 61 J4
Blacko Lancs 122 C3
Black Pill Swans 51 J7
Blackpool Bpool 120 D4
Blackpool Devon 7 K6
Blackpool Airport Lancs 120 D4
Blackpool Zoo Bpool 120 D4
Blackridge W Loth 176 B5
Blackrod Bolton 121 J7
Blacksboat Moray 214 E6
Blackshaw D & G 147 J2
Blackshaw Head Calder 122 E5
Blackstone W Susx 19 H3
Black Street Suffk 93 K6
Blackthorn Oxon 57 L4
Blackthorpe Suffk 77 K2
Blacktoft E R Yk 125 J5
Blacktop C Aber 207 G4
Black Torrington Devon 10 C4
Blackwall Derbys 100 E3
Blackwall Tunnel Gt Lon 45 H4
Blackwater Cnwll 3 J3
Blackwater Hants 42 D7
Blackwater IoW 17 G5
Blackwater Somset 25 K7
Blackwaterfoot N Ayrs 162 A4
Blackwell Cumb 148 D4
Blackwell Derbys 101 H2
Blackwell Derbys 114 C6
Blackwell Warwks 72 B5
Blackwell Worcs 71 H1
Blackwood Caerph 37 J2
Blackwood D & G 154 F5
Blackwood S Lans 164 F1
Blacon Ches W 111 L7
Bladnoch D & G 145 J4
Bladon Oxon 57 J5
Blaenannerch Cerdgn 65 H5
Blaenau Ffestiniog Gwynd 96 A4
Blaenavon Torfn 53 K6
Blaenavon Industrial Landscape Torfn 53 K6
Blaenffos Pembks 65 H6
Blaengarw Brdgnd 36 D2
Blaengwrach Neath 52 D6
Blaengwynfi Neath 36 D2
Blaenpennal Cerdgn 66 E2
Blaenplwyf Cerdgn 80 D7
Blaenporth Cerdgn 65 J5
Blaenrhondda Rhondd 52 E7
Blaenwaun Carmth 50 B1
Blaen-y-Coed Carmth 50 D1
Blaen-y-cwm Rhondd 52 E7
Blagdon N Som 38 D8
Blagdon Somset 25 K7
Blagdon Torbay 7 K4
Blagdon Hill Somset 25 K7
Blaich Highld 191 K2
Blain Highld 190 D3
Blaina Blae G 53 J6
Blair Atholl P & K 194 D4
Blair Drummond Stirlg 184 F7
Blairgowrie P & K 195 J7
Blairhall Fife 176 D2
Blairingone P & K 185 K7
Blairlogie Stirlg 185 H7
Blairmore Ag & B 173 L2
Blairmore Highld 228 C4
Blair's Ferry Ag & B 173 G4
Blaisdon Gloucs 55 G5
Blakebrook Worcs 84 E7
Blakedown Worcs 84 F7
Blake End Essex 61 H4
Blakemere Ches W 112 D7
Blakemere Herefs 69 G6
Blakenall Heath Wsall 85 H3
Blakeney Gloucs 54 F6
Blakeney Norfk 106 B4
Blakenhall Ches E 99 G3
Blakenhall Wolves 85 G4
Blakesley Nhants 73 J4
Blanchland Nthumb 150 B5
Blandford Forum Dorset 15 G2
Blandford St Mary Dorset 15 G2
Blanefield Stirlg 174 F3
Blankney Lincs 103 H1
Blantyre S Lans 175 J6
Blàr a' Chaorainn Highld 191 L3
Blargie Highld 202 F6
Blarmachfoldach Highld 191 L3
Blaston Leics 88 B4
Blatherwycke Nhants 88 D4
Blawith Cumb 129 G2
Blawquhairn D & G 154 B5
Blaxhall Suffk 79 H3
Blaxton Donc 116 A2
Blaydon Gatesd 150 F3
Bleadney Somset 26 C3
Bleadon N Som 25 M1
Blean Kent 34 F3
Bleasby Notts 102 B3
Blebocraigs Fife 187 G4
Bleddfa Powys 68 E2
Bledington Gloucs 56 E4
Bledlow Bucks 58 C7
Bledlow Ridge Bucks 42 D2
Blegbie E Loth 178 B6
Blencarn Cumb 138 F2
Blencogo Cumb 147 L5
Blendworth Hants 30 B8
Blenheim Palace Oxon 57 H5
Blennerhasset Cumb 147 L6
Bletchingdon Oxon 57 J4
Bletchingley Surrey 32 B3
Bletchley M Keyn 58 E2
Bletchley Shrops 98 F5
Bletchley Park Museum M Keyn 74 C7
Bletherston Pembks 49 H4
Bletsoe Bed 74 E3
Blewbury Oxon 41 K4
Blickling Norfk 106 E6
Blidworth Notts 101 L2
Blidworth Bottoms Notts 101 L2
Blindcrake Cumb 147 K7
Blindley Heath Surrey 32 C4
Blisland Cnwll 5 H2
Blissford Hants 28 D8
Bliss Gate Worcs 84 D8
Blisworth Nhants 73 K4
Blithbury Staffs 100 B8
Blockley Gloucs 71 L7
Blofield Norfk 93 G2
Blofield Heath Norfk 93 G2
Blo Norton Norfk 92 B7
Bloomfield Border 167 J4
Blore Staffs 100 C3
Bloxham Oxon 72 E7
Bloxholm Lincs 103 H2
Bloxwich Wsall 85 H3
Bloxworth Dorset 15 G4
Blubberhouses N York 132 B7
Blue Anchor Somset 24 F3
Blue Bell Hill Kent 46 C7
Blue John Cavern Derbys 114 C5
Blundellsands Sefton 111 J2
Blundeston Suffk 93 L4
Blunham C Beds 75 H4
Blunsdon St Andrew Swindn 40 C3
Bluntington Worcs 84 F8
Bluntisham Cambs 89 L8
Blurton C Stke 99 K4
Blyborough Lincs 116 F3
Blyford Suffk 93 J7
Blymhill Staffs 84 E2
Blyth Notts 115 L4
Blyth Nthumb 159 H5
Blyth Bridge Border 165 M1
Blythburgh Suffk 93 J7
Blyth Crematorium Nthumb 159 H5
Blythe Border 178 D7
Blyth Services Notts 115 L4
Blyton Lincs 116 D3
Boarhills Fife 187 J5
Boarhunt Hants 17 H2
Boarstall Bucks 57 L5
Boath Highld 222 D6
Boat of Garten Highld 203 L2
Bobbing Kent 46 E6
Bobbington Staffs 84 E5
Bocking Essex 61 J4
Bocking Churchstreet Essex 61 J3
Boddam Abers 217 L6
Boddam Shet 235 c7
Boddington Gloucs 55 K3
Bodedern IoA 108 D5
Bodelwyddan Denbgs 110 D6
Bodenham Herefs 69 K4
Bodenham Wilts 28 D6
Bodenham Moor Herefs 69 K4
Bodewryd IoA 108 E4
Bodfari Denbgs 110 F7
Bodffordd IoA 108 F6
Bodfuan Gwynd 94 F5
Bodham Norfk 106 D4
Bodiam E Susx 33 K7
Bodicote Oxon 72 F6
Bodinnick Cnwll 5 H5
Bodle Street Green E Susx 20 D3
Bodmin Cnwll 5 G3
Bodmin Moor Cnwll 5 J1
Bodsham Kent 34 E5
Bodwen Cnwll 5 G4
Bogallan Highld 212 F4
Bogbrae Abers 217 J7
Bogend S Ayrs 163 K3
Boggs Holdings E Loth 177 L4
Boghall Mdloth 177 H5
Boghall W Loth 176 D5
Boghead S Lans 164 F2
Bogmoor Moray 215 H2
Bogmuir Abers 197 G3
Bogniebrae Abers 216 B5
Bognor Regis W Susx 18 C6
Bogroy Highld 203 L2
Bogue D & G 154 B6
Bohortha Cnwll 3 L5
Bohuntine Highld 201 L8
Bolam Dur 140 F3
Bolberry Devon 7 G7
Boldmere Birm 85 K5
Boldre Hants 16 C3
Boldron Dur 140 C4
Bole Notts 116 C4
Bolehill Derbys 100 F2
Bolham Devon 24 E7
Bolham Water Devon 25 J8
Bolingey Cnwll 3 K1
Bollington Ches E 113 L6
Bolney W Susx 31 L6
Bolnhurst Bed 74 F3
Bolnore W Susx 19 J2
Bolshan Angus 197 G6
Bolsover Derbys 115 J7
Bolsterstone Sheff 114 F3
Boltby N York 133 G3
Boltenstone Abers 205 J3
Bolton Bolton 121 L8
Bolton Cumb 138 F3
Bolton E Loth 178 B4
Bolton E R Yk 125 J1
Bolton Nthumb 169 G6
Bolton Abbey N York 131 K8
Bolton-by-Bowland Lancs 122 B1
Boltonfellend Cumb 148 E2
Boltongate Cumb 147 M6
Bolton-le-Sands Lancs 129 K6
Bolton Low Houses Cumb 147 M6
Bolton-on-Swale N York 141 G7
Bolton Percy N York 124 E3
Bolton upon Dearne Barns 115 J2
Bolventor Cnwll 5 J1
Bomere Heath Shrops 98 C8
Bonar Bridge Highld 222 E3
Bonawe Ag & B 182 E2
Bonby N Linc 126 C7
Boncath Pembks 65 H6
Bonchester Bridge Border 167 J6
Bondleigh Devon 10 F4
Bonds Lancs 121 G2
Bo'ness Falk 176 D3
Boney Hay Staffs 85 J2
Bonhill W Duns 174 D3
Boningale Shrops 84 E3
Bonjedward Border 167 K5
Bonkle N Lans 175 L6
Bonnington Angus 196 F7
Bonnington Kent 34 E7
Bonnybank Fife 186 F6
Bonnybridge Falk 175 L3
Bonnykelly Abers 217 G4
Bonnyrigg Mdloth 177 J5
Bonnyton Angus 196 B8
Bonsall Derbys 100 F2
Bonshaw Tower D & G 155 M7
Bont-Dolgadfan Powys 81 J4
Bont-goch Cerdgn 80 F6
Bontnewydd Cerdgn 66 E2
Bontnewydd Gwynd 95 H1
Bontuchel Denbgs 97 G2
Bonvilston V Glam 37 G5
Boode Devon 23 H4
Booker Bucks 42 D3
Boon Border 167 J1
Boosbeck R & Cl 142 E4
Boose's Green Essex 61 K2
Boot Cumb 137 G6
Booth Calder 122 F5
Boothby Graffoe Lincs 103 G2
Boothby Pagnell Lincs 102 F6
Boothferry E R Yk 125 H5
Boothstown Salfd 113 G2
Bootle Cumb 128 D2
Bootle Sefton 111 K3
Boraston Shrops 70 B1
Bordeaux Guern 236 e2
Borden Kent 34 B3
Borders Crematorium Border 167 H3
Boreham Essex 61 J6
Boreham Wilts 27 K3
Boreham Street E Susx 20 D4
Borehamwood Herts 44 D2

Boreland D & G 155 L4
Boreraig Highld 208 C4
Borgh W Isls 232 f1
Borgh W Isls 233 b9
Borgie Highld 229 K4
Borgue D & G 146 B5
Borgue Highld 227 K4
Borley Essex 77 J6
Borneskitaig Highld 218 B7
Borness D & G 146 A5
Boroughbridge N York 132 F6
Borough Green Kent 33 G2
Borrowash Derbys 101 H5
Borrowby N York 132 F2
Borrowstoun Falk 176 D3
Borstal Medway 46 B6
Borth Cerdgn 80 E5
Borthwickbrae Border 166 F6
Borthwickshiels Border 166 F6
Borth-y-Gest Gwynd 95 K5
Borve Highld 209 G5
Borve W Isls 232 d4
Borve W Isls 232 f1
Borve W Isls 233 b9
Borwick Lancs 129 L5
Bosbury Herefs 70 C5
Boscastle Cnwll 8 E6
Boscombe Bmouth 15 L4
Boscombe Wilts 28 D4
Bosham W Susx 17 L2
Bosherston Pembks 49 G8
Bosley Ches E 113 K7
Bossall N York 133 L7
Bossiney Cnwll 8 E6
Bossingham Kent 34 F5
Bossington Somset 24 D2
Bostock Green Ches W 112 F7
Boston Lincs 104 B4
Boston Crematorium Lincs 104 A4
Boston Spa Leeds 124 C2
Boswinger Cnwll 4 F7
Botallack Cnwll 2 C5
Botany Bay Gt Lon 59 M7
Botesdale Suffk 92 C7
Bothal Nthumb 159 G5
Bothamsall Notts 116 A6
Bothel Cumb 147 L6
Bothenhampton Dorset 13 L4
Bothwell S Lans 175 J6
Bothwell Services S Lans 175 J6
Botley Bucks 59 G7
Botley Hants 29 K8
Botley Oxon 57 J6
Botolph Claydon Bucks 58 B3
Botolphs W Susx 19 G4
Bottesford Leics 102 D5
Bottesford N Linc 125 L8
Bottisham Cambs 76 D3
Bottomcraig Fife 186 F3
Bottoms Calder 122 D6
Botusfleming Cnwll 6 B4
Botwnnog Gwynd 94 E6
Bough Beech Kent 32 E4
Boughrood Powys 68 C6
Boughton Nhants 73 L2
Boughton Norfk 91 G3
Boughton Notts 116 B7
Boughton Aluph Kent 34 D5
Boughton Green Kent 33 K3
Boughton Monchelsea Kent 33 K3
Boughton Street Kent 34 E3
Bouldon Shrops 83 K6
Boulmer Nthumb 169 K6
Boultham Lincs 116 F7
Bourn Cambs 75 K3
Bourne Lincs 103 H7
Bournebridge Essex 45 J2
Bournebrook Birm 85 J6
Bourne End Bucks 42 E3
Bourne End C Beds 74 D5
Bourne End Herts 59 G6
Bournemouth Bmouth 15 K4
Bournemouth Airport Dorset 15 L3
Bournemouth Crematorium Bmouth 15 L4
Bournes Green Sthend 46 E3
Bournheath Worcs 85 G8
Bournmoor Dur 151 H5
Bournville Birm 85 J7
Bourton Dorset 27 H5
Bourton Oxon 40 E3
Bourton Shrops 83 L4
Bourton Wilts 40 B7
Bourton on Dunsmore Warwks 72 E1
Bourton-on-the-Hill Gloucs 56 D2
Bourton-on-the-Water Gloucs 56 D4
Bousd Ag & B 189 G4
Bouth Cumb 129 H3
Bouthwaite N York 131 L5
Boveridge Dorset 28 B7
Bovey Tracey Devon 7 J1
Bovingdon Herts 59 G7
Bow Devon 11 G4
Bow Gt Lon 45 G4
Bow Ork 234 b7
Bow Brickhill M Keyn 74 C7
Bowbridge Gloucs 55 J6
Bowburn Dur 151 H7
Bowcombe IoW 16 F5
Bowd Devon 12 E4
Bowden Border 167 H4
Bowden Hill Wilts 39 L6
Bowdon Traffd 113 H4
Bower Highld 231 J3
Bowerchalke Wilts 28 A6
Bowermadden Highld 231 J3
Bowers Staffs 99 J5
Bowers Gifford Essex 46 C3
Bowershall Fife 176 F1
Bower's Row Leeds 124 B5
Bowes Dur 140 C4
Bowgreave Lancs 121 G2
Bowhouse D & G 147 H2
Bowland Border 167 G2
Bowley Herefs 69 K4
Bowlhead Green Surrey 30 E4
Bowling C Brad 123 H4
Bowling W Duns 174 E4
Bowmanstead Cumb 137 J7
Bowmore Ag & B 170 F6
Bowness-on-Solway Cumb 147 L3
Bowness-on-Windermere Cumb 137 L7
Bow of Fife Fife 186 E5
Bowriefauld Angus 196 E6
Bowsden Nthumb 168 E2
Bow Street Cerdgn 80 E6
Bowthorpe Norfk 92 E2
Box Gloucs 55 K7
Box Wilts 39 J6
Boxford Suffk 77 L6
Boxford W Berk 41 H6
Boxgrove W Susx 18 B4
Boxley Kent 33 K2
Boxmoor Herts 59 H6
Boxted Essex 62 B2
Boxted Essex 62 B2
Boxted Suffk 77 J4
Boxted Cross Essex 62 B2
Boxworth Cambs 75 L2
Boyden Gate Kent 47 L6
Boylestone Derbys 100 D5
Boyndie Abers 216 C2
Boyndlie Abers 217 G2
Boynton E R Yk 135 H6
Boysack Angus 197 G6
Boyton Cnwll 9 J6
Boyton Suffk 79 H5
Boyton Wilts 27 L4
Boyton Cross Essex 61 G6
Boyton End Suffk 77 G5
Bozeat Nhants 74 C3
Brabourne Kent 34 E6
Brabourne Lees Kent 34 E6
Brabstermire Highld 231 K2
Bracadale Highld 208 E6
Braceborough Lincs 88 F2
Bracebridge Heath Lincs 117 G7
Bracebridge Low Fields Lincs 116 F7
Braceby Lincs 103 G5
Bracewell Lancs 122 C2
Brackenfield Derbys 101 G2
Brackenhirst N Lans 175 K5
Bracklesham W Susx 17 L3
Brackletter Highld 201 J8
Brackley Nhants 73 H6
Bracknell Br For 42 E6
Braco P & K 185 H5
Bracobrae Moray 215 L4
Bracon Ash Norfk 92 E4
Bracora Highld 199 L6
Bracorina Highld 199 L6
Bradbourne Derbys 100 D3
Bradbury Dur 141 H2
Bradden Nhants 73 J5
Bradeley C Stke 99 K3
Bradenham Bucks 42 D2
Bradenstoke Wilts 39 M4
Bradfield Devon 12 D1
Bradfield Essex 62 D2
Bradfield Norfk 106 F5
Bradfield Sheff 114 F3
Bradfield W Berk 41 L6
Bradfield Combust Suffk 77 K3
Bradfield Green Ches E 99 G2
Bradfield Heath Essex 62 D3
Bradfield St Clare Suffk 77 K3
Bradfield St George Suffk 77 K3
Bradford C Brad 123 H4
Bradford Devon 9 L4
Bradford Abbas Dorset 26 E8
Bradford Leigh Wilts 39 J7
Bradford-on-Avon Wilts 39 J7
Bradford-on-Tone Somset 25 J6
Bradford Peverell Dorset 14 C4
Bradiford Devon 23 J5
Brading IoW 17 H5
Bradley Derbys 100 E4
Bradley Hants 29 M3
Bradley NE Lin 118 C1
Bradley Staffs 99 K8
Bradley Wolves 85 G4
Bradley Worcs 71 H3
Bradley Green Worcs 71 H3
Bradley in the Moors Staffs 100 B4
Bradley Stoke S Glos 38 E4
Bradmore Notts 101 L6
Bradninch Devon 12 C2
Bradnop Staffs 100 A2
Bradpole Dorset 13 L4
Bradshaw Calder 123 G4
Bradstone Devon 9 K8
Bradwall Green Ches E 113 H8
Bradwell Derbys 114 D5
Bradwell Essex 61 J4
Bradwell M Keyn 74 B6
Bradwell Norfk 93 K3
Bradwell Crematorium Staffs 99 J3
Bradwell-on-Sea Essex 62 B6
Bradwell Waterside Essex 62 B6
Bradworthy Devon 9 J3
Brae Highld 213 G2
Brae Shet 235 c4
Braeface Falk 175 K3
Braehead Angus 197 H5
Braehead D & G 145 J4
Braehead S Lans 176 C7
Braemar Abers 204 E6
Braemore Highld 221 G5
Braemore Highld 227 J3
Brae Roy Lodge Highld 201 L6
Braeside Inver 173 L4
Braes of Coul Angus 195 L5
Braes of Enzie Moray 215 J3
Braeswick Ork 234 d4
Braevallich Ag & B 182 D6
Brafferton Darltn 141 H3
Brafferton N York 132 F5
Brafield-on-the-Green Nhants 74 B3
Bragar W Isls 232 f2
Bragbury End Herts 59 L4
Braidwood S Lans 175 L8
Brailsford Derbys 100 E4
Braintree Essex 61 J4
Braiseworth Suffk 78 D1
Braishfield Hants 29 G6
Braithwaite Cumb 137 H3
Braithwell Donc 115 K3
Bramber W Susx 19 G4
Bramcote Warwks 86 E5
Bramcote Crematorium Notts 101 J5
Bramdean Hants 29 L5
Bramerton Norfk 93 G3
Bramfield Herts 59 M5
Bramfield Suffk 93 H8
Bramford Suffk 78 D5
Bramhall Stockp 113 K5
Bramham Leeds 124 C2
Bramhope Leeds 123 K2
Bramley Hants 41 M8
Bramley Leeds 123 K4
Bramley Rothm 115 J3
Bramley Surrey 31 G3
Bramley Corner Hants 41 M8
Bramling Kent 35 G4
Brampford Speke Devon 11 L5
Brampton Cambs 75 J1
Brampton Cumb 138 F3
Brampton Cumb 148 F3
Brampton Lincs 116 D5
Brampton Norfk 106 F7
Brampton Rothm 115 H2
Brampton Suffk 93 J6
Brampton Abbotts Herefs 54 E3
Brampton Ash Nhants 87 L6
Brampton Bryan Herefs 83 G8
Brampton-en-le-Morthen Rothm 115 J4
Bramshall Staffs 100 B6
Bramshaw Hants 28 F7
Bramshott Hants 30 D5
Bramwell Somset 26 B5
Branault Highld 190 B3
Brancaster Norfk 105 J4
Brancaster Staithe Norfk 105 J4
Brancepeth Dur 150 F7
Branchill Moray 214 D4
Branderburgh Moray 214 F1
Brandesburton E R Yk 126 E2
Brandeston Suffk 78 F3

Brandiston Norfk 106 D7
Brandon Dur 151 G6
Brandon Lincs 102 E3
Brandon Suffk 91 H6
Brandon Warwks 86 E7
Brandon Parva Norfk 92 C2
Brandsby N York 133 J5
Brandy Wharf Lincs 117 G3
Bran End Essex 61 G3
Branksome Poole 15 K4
Branksome Park Poole 15 K4
Bransbury Hants 29 H3
Bransby Lincs 116 E5
Branscombe Devon 12 F5
Bransford Worcs 70 E4
Bransgore Hants 16 A3
Bransholme C KuH 126 D4
Bransley Shrops 84 B7
Branston Leics 102 D6
Branston Lincs 117 G7
Branston Staffs 100 E7
Branston Booths Lincs 117 H7
Branstone IoW 17 G5
Brant Broughton Lincs 102 E2
Brantham Suffk 78 D7
Branthwaite Cumb 136 E3
Branthwaite Cumb 148 B7
Brantingham E R Yk 125 L5
Branton Donc 115 M2
Branton Nthumb 168 F6
Branton Green N York 132 F6
Branxton Nthumb 168 D2
Brassington Derbys 100 E2
Brasted Kent 32 E3
Brasted Chart Kent 32 E3
Brathens Abers 206 D5
Bratoft Lincs 119 G8
Brattleby Lincs 116 F5
Bratton Wilts 27 K2
Bratton Wrekin 84 B2
Bratton Clovelly Devon 10 C6
Bratton Fleming Devon 23 K4
Bratton Seymour Somset 26 F5
Braughing Herts 60 C3
Braunston Nhants 73 G2
Braunston Rutlnd 88 B3
Braunton Devon 23 H4
Brawby N York 134 B4
Brawl Highld 230 B3
Bray W & M 42 E4
Braybrooke Nhants 87 L6
Brayford Devon 23 L4
Bray Shop Cnwll 5 M2
Brayton N York 124 F4
Braywick W & M 42 E4
Breachwood Green Herts 59 J4
Breadsall Derbys 101 G5
Breadstone Gloucs 55 G7
Breage Cnwll 3 G5
Breakachy Highld 212 D5
Breakspear Crematorium Gt Lon 43 H3
Brealangwell Lodge Highld 222 C3
Bream Gloucs 54 E6
Breamore Hants 28 D7
Brean Somset 25 L1
Breanais W Isls 232 d3
Brearton N York 132 E7
Breascleit W Isls 232 e2
Breasclete W Isls 232 e2
Breaston Derbys 101 J5
Brechfa Carmth 66 C7
Brechin Angus 196 F4
Breckles Norfk 91 L5
Brecon Powys 53 G3
Brecon Beacons National Park 52 F3
Bredbury Stockp 113 L3
Brede E Susx 21 G3
Bredenbury Herefs 69 L3
Bredfield Suffk 78 F4
Bredgar Kent 34 B3
Bredhurst Kent 46 D7
Bredon Worcs 71 G6
Bredon's Hardwick Worcs 71 G7
Bredon's Norton Worcs 71 G6
Bredwardine Herefs 69 G5
Breedon on the Hill Leics 101 H7
Breich W Loth 176 C6
Breightmet Bolton 121 L8
Breighton E R Yk 125 G4
Breinton Herefs 69 J6
Bremhill Wilts 39 L5
Brenchley Kent 33 H5
Brendon Devon 24 B2
Brenfield Ag & B 172 E2
Brenish W Isls 232 d3
Brent Cross Gt Lon 44 E3
Brent Eleigh Suffk 77 L5
Brentford Gt Lon 44 D5
Brentingby Leics 102 C8
Brent Knoll Somset 25 M2
Brent Mill Devon 7 G4
Brent Pelham Herts 60 C2
Brentwood Essex 45 L2
Brenzett Kent 21 K1
Brenzett Green Kent 34 D8
Brereton Staffs 85 J1
Brereton Green Ches E 113 H8
Bressay Shet 235 d6
Bressingham Norfk 92 C7
Bretby Derbys 100 F7
Bretby Crematorium Derbys 100 F7
Bretford Warwks 86 E7
Bretforton Worcs 71 K5
Bretherton Lancs 121 G6
Brettabister Shet 235 d5
Brettenham Norfk 91 L6
Brettenham Suffk 77 L4
Bretton Flints 111 K8
Brewood Staffs 84 F2
Briantspuddle Dorset 14 F4
Brickendon Herts 60 A6
Bricket Wood Herts 59 J7
Brick Houses Sheff 114 F5
Bricklehampton Worcs 71 H6
Bride IoM 237 e2
Bridekirk Cumb 147 K7
Bridestowe Devon 10 D6
Brideswell Abers 216 B6
Bridford Devon 11 J7
Bridge Kent 35 G4
Bridgehampton Somset 26 E6
Bridge Hewick N York 132 E5
Bridgehill Dur 150 D5
Bridgemary Hants 17 H2
Bridgend Abers 215 L7
Bridgend Ag & B 161 K2
Bridgend Ag & B 171 G6
Bridgend Angus 196 E3
Bridgend Brdgnd 36 E4
Bridgend D & G 165 L7
Bridgend Devon 6 E6
Bridgend Fife 186 F5
Bridgend Moray 215 J7
Bridgend P & K 186 B3
Bridgend W Loth 176 E3
Bridgend of Lintrathen Angus 195 L5
Bridge of Alford Abers 206 B2
Bridge of Allan Stirlg 185 G7
Bridge of Avon Moray 204 E2
Bridge of Avon Moray 214 E7
Bridge of Balgie P & K 193 J6
Bridge of Brewlands Angus 195 J4
Bridge of Brown Highld 204 D2
Bridge of Cally P & K 195 J6
Bridge of Canny Abers 206 C6
Bridge of Craigisla Angus 195 K5
Bridge of Dee D & G 146 C3
Bridge of Don C Aber 207 H4
Bridge of Dulsie Highld 213 L6
Bridge of Dye Abers 206 C7
Bridge of Earn P & K 186 B4
Bridge of Ericht P & K 193 H5
Bridge of Feugh Abers 206 D6
Bridge of Forss Highld 230 F2
Bridge of Gairn Abers 205 H6
Bridge of Gaur P & K 193 H5
Bridge of Marnoch Abers 216 B4
Bridge of Muchalls Abers 207 G6
Bridge of Orchy Ag & B 192 E7
Bridge of Tilt P & K 194 D4
Bridge of Tynet Moray 215 J3
Bridge of Walls Shet 235 b5
Bridge of Weir Rens 174 D5
Bridgerule Devon 9 H4
Bridge Sollers Herefs 69 H6
Bridge Street Suffk 77 K5
Bridgetown Somset 24 E5
Bridge Trafford Ches W 112 C7
Bridgham Norfk 91 L6
Bridgnorth Shrops 84 C5
Bridgwater Somset 25 L4
Bridgwater Services Somset 25 L4
Bridlington E R Yk 135 J6
Bridport Dorset 13 L4
Bridstow Herefs 54 E3
Brierfield Lancs 122 C3
Brierley Barns 124 C7
Brierley Gloucs 54 F5
Brierley Hill Dudley 85 G6
Brigg N Linc 117 G1
Briggate Norfk 107 G6
Briggswath N York 143 H5
Brigham Cumb 136 F2
Brigham E R Yk 135 G8
Brighouse Calder 123 H6
Brighstone IoW 16 E5
Brighthampton Oxon 57 G7
Brightley Devon 10 E5
Brightling E Susx 20 D2
Brightlingsea Essex 62 C5
Brighton Br & H 19 J5
Brighton le Sands Sefton 111 J2
Brightons Falk 176 C3
Brightwalton W Berk 41 H5
Brightwell Suffk 78 F5
Brightwell Baldwin Oxon 41 M2
Brightwell-cum-Sotwell Oxon 41 L3
Brightwell Upperton Oxon 42 A2
Brignall Dur 140 D5
Brig o'Turk Stirlg 184 C6
Brigsley NE Lin 118 C2
Brigsteer Cumb 129 K2
Brigstock Nhants 88 D6
Brill Bucks 58 A5
Brill Cnwll 3 J5
Brilley Herefs 68 F5
Brimfield Herefs 69 K2
Brimfield Cross Herefs 69 K2
Brimington Derbys 115 H6
Brimley Devon 7 J1
Brimpsfield Gloucs 55 L5
Brimpton W Berk 41 K7
Brimscombe Gloucs 55 K7
Brimstage Wirral 111 J5
Brincliffe Sheff 115 F4
Brind E R Yk 125 H4
Brindister Shet 235 c5
Brindle Lancs 121 J5
Brineton Staffs 84 E2
Bringhurst Leics 88 B5
Bringsty Common Herefs 70 C4
Brington Cambs 88 F7
Briningham Norfk 106 C5
Brinkhill Lincs 118 E6
Brinkley Cambs 76 F4
Brinklow Warwks 86 E7
Brinkworth Wilts 40 A4
Brinscall Lancs 121 J6
Brinsley Notts 101 J3
Brinsworth Rothm 115 H4
Brinton Norfk 106 C5
Brinyan Ork 234 c5
Brisley Norfk 105 M7
Brislington Bristl 38 F6
Brissenden Green Kent 34 C6
Bristol Bristl 38 E5
Bristol Airport N Som 38 D7
Bristol Zoo Gardens Bristl 38 E5
Briston Norfk 106 C6
Britford Wilts 28 D5
Brithdir Caerph 53 J7
Brithdir Gwynd 96 B8
British Legion Village Kent 33 J2
Briton Ferry Neath 51 L6
Britwell Salome Oxon 42 A2
Brixham Torbay 7 L5
Brixton Devon 6 E5
Brixton Gt Lon 44 F5
Brixton Deverill Wilts 27 K4
Brixworth Nhants 73 L1
Brize Norton Oxon 56 F6
Brize Norton Airport Oxon 56 F6
Broad Alley Worcs 70 F2
Broad Blunsdon Swindn 40 D3
Broadbottom Tamesd 113 M3
Broadbridge W Susx 17 M2
Broadbridge Heath W Susx 31 J5
Broad Campden Gloucs 71 L6
Broad Carr Calder 123 G6
Broad Chalke Wilts 28 B6
Broadclyst Devon 12 C3
Broadfield Inver 174 C4
Broadford Highld 199 K2
Broadford Bridge W Susx 31 H6
Broadgairhill Border 166 C7
Broad Green Worcs 70 D4
Broadhaugh Border 179 H7
Broad Haven Pembks 48 E5
Broadheath Traffd 113 H4
Broadhembury Devon 12 E2
Broadhempston Devon 7 J3
Broad Hinton Wilts 40 C5
Broadland Row E Susx 21 G2
Broad Layings Hants 41 H7
Broadley Moray 215 J3
Broad Marston Worcs 71 K5
Broadmayne Dorset 14 D5
Broad Meadow Staffs 99 J3
Broadmoor Pembks 49 J6
Broadoak Dorset 13 K3
Broad Oak E Susx 20 C2
Broad Oak E Susx 21 G2
Broad Oak Herefs 54 C4
Broad Oak Kent 35 G3
Broad Oak St Hel 112 D3
Broad's Green Essex 61 H5
Broadstairs Kent 35 K2

Broadstone Poole 15 J4
Broadstone Shrops 83 K5
Broad Street E Susx 21 H3
Broad Street Kent 33 L2
Broad Town Wilts 40 C5
Broadwas Worcs 70 D4
Broadwater Herts 59 L4
Broadwater W Susx 18 F5
Broadwaters Worcs 84 E7
Broadway Pembks 48 E5
Broadway Somset 25 L7
Broadway Worcs 71 K6
Broadwell Gloucs 54 E5
Broadwell Gloucs 56 D3
Broadwell Oxon 56 E6
Broadwell Warwks 72 F2
Broadwindsor Dorset 13 K2
Broadwood Kelly Devon 10 F4
Broadwoodwidger Devon 9 K6
Brochel Highld 209 J5
Brochroy Ag & B 182 E2
Brockamin Worcs 70 D4
Brockbridge Hants 29 L7
Brockdish Norfk 92 E7
Brockenhurst Hants 16 C3
Brocketsbrae S Lans 164 F2
Brockford Street Suffk 78 D2
Brockhall Nhants 73 J2
Brockham Surrey 31 K2
Brockhampton Gloucs 56 B4
Brockhampton Hants 17 K2
Brockhampton Herefs 54 E2
Brockholes Kirk 123 H7
Brocklesby Lincs 126 E7
Brockley N Som 38 C6
Brockley Suffk 77 J1
Brockley Green Suffk 77 G5
Brockley Green Suffk 77 J4
Brockmoor Dudley 84 F5
Brockton Shrops 83 G3
Brockton Shrops 83 G6
Brockton Shrops 83 L5
Brockweir Gloucs 54 D7
Brockworth Gloucs 55 K5
Brocton Staffs 99 L8
Brodick N Ayrs 162 C3
Brodie Moray 214 B3
Brodsworth Donc 115 J1
Brogaig Highld 218 C7
Brokenborough Wilts 39 K3
Broken Cross Ches E 113 K6
Brokerswood Wilts 27 J2
Bromborough Wirral 111 K5
Brome Suffk 92 D7
Brome Street Suffk 92 D7
Bromeswell Suffk 79 G4
Bromfield Cumb 147 L5
Bromfield Shrops 83 J7
Bromham Bed 74 E4
Bromham Wilts 39 L7
Bromley Dudley 85 G6
Bromley Gt Lon 45 H6
Bromley Shrops 84 D4
Bromley Cross Bolton 121 L7
Brompton Medway 46 C6
Brompton N York 141 J7
Brompton-by-Sawdon N York 134 E3
Brompton-on-Swale N York 140 F7
Brompton Ralph Somset 25 G5
Brompton Regis Somset 24 E5
Bromsberrow Gloucs 70 D7
Bromsberrow Heath Gloucs 55 G2
Bromsgrove Worcs 71 G1
Bromyard Herefs 70 B4
Bronant Cerdgn 66 E2
Brongest Cerdgn 65 K5
Bronington Wrexhm 98 C4
Bronllys Powys 68 D7
Bronwydd Carmth 50 E2
Bronygarth Shrops 97 K5
Brook Hants 28 F8
Brook IoW 16 E5
Brook Kent 34 E6
Brook Surrey 30 F4
Brooke Norfk 93 G4
Brooke Rutlnd 88 B3
Brookenby Lincs 117 K3
Brookfield Rens 174 D5
Brookhampton Somset 26 F5
Brook Hill Hants 28 F8
Brookhouse Lancs 129 L6
Brookhouse Rothm 115 K4
Brookhouse Green Ches E 99 J1
Brookhouses Derbys 114 B4
Brookland Kent 21 K1
Brooklands Traffd 113 H4
Brookmans Park Herts 59 L7
Brook Street Essex 45 L2
Brook Street Kent 34 C7
Brookthorpe Gloucs 55 J5
Brookwood Surrey 42 F8
Broom C Beds 75 H6
Broom Rothm 115 H3
Broom Warwks 71 K4
Broome Norfk 93 H5
Broome Shrops 83 H7
Broome Worcs 84 F7
Broomedge Warrtn 113 G4
Broomfield Essex 61 H5
Broomfield Kent 33 L3
Broomfield Kent 47 K6
Broomfield Somset 25 K5
Broomfleet E R Yk 125 K5
Broomhaugh Nthumb 150 C3
Broom Hill Barns 115 H2
Broom Hill Notts 101 K3
Broomhill Nthumb 159 G3
Broompark Dur 151 G6
Brora Highld 226 F7
Broseley Shrops 84 C3
Brotherlee Dur 150 A7
Brotherton N York 124 D5
Brotton R & Cl 142 E4
Broubster Highld 230 F4
Brough Cumb 139 H4
Brough E R Yk 125 L5
Brough Highld 231 J2
Brough Notts 102 D2
Brough Shet 235 d4
Broughall Shrops 98 E4
Brough Lodge Shet 235 d2
Brough Sowerby Cumb 139 H5
Broughton Border 165 L3
Broughton Cambs 89 K7
Broughton Flints 111 K8
Broughton Hants 28 F5
Broughton Lancs 121 G4
Broughton M Keyn 74 C6
Broughton N Linc 126 B8
Broughton N York 122 D1
Broughton N York 134 B5
Broughton Nhants 88 B7
Broughton Oxon 72 E6
Broughton Salfd 113 J2
Broughton V Glam 36 E6
Broughton Astley Leics 87 G5
Broughton Gifford Wilts 39 K7
Broughton Green Worcs 71 G3
Broughton Hackett Worcs 71 G4
Broughton-in-Furness Cumb 128 F3
Broughton Mains D & G 145 J6
Broughton Mills Cumb 128 F2
Broughton Moor Cumb 147 J7
Broughton Poggs Oxon 56 E7
Broughty Ferry C Dund 187 H2
Brown Candover Hants 29 L4
Brown Edge Staffs 99 K2
Brownhill Abers 217 G6
Brownhills Fife 187 H4
Brownhills Wsall 85 J3
Browninghill Green Hants 41 L7
Brown Lees Staffs 99 K2
Brownsea Island Dorset 15 J5
Brown's Green Birm 85 J5
Browns Hill Gloucs 55 K7
Brownston Devon 7 G5
Broxa N York 134 E2
Broxbourne Herts 60 B6
Broxburn E Loth 178 E3
Broxburn W Loth 176 E4
Broxted Essex 60 F3
Bruan Highld 231 K7
Bruar P & K 194 C3
Brucefield Highld 223 K4
Bruchag Ag & B 173 J6
Bruichladdich Ag & B 170 E6
Bruisyard Suffk 79 G2
Bruisyard Street Suffk 79 G2
Brumby N Linc 125 K8
Brund Staffs 100 C1
Brundall Norfk 93 G2
Brundish Suffk 78 F1
Brundish Street Suffk 78 F1
Brunery Highld 190 E3
Brunswick Village N u Ty 159 G7
Brunthwaite C Brad 122 F2
Bruntingthorpe Leics 87 H5
Brunton Fife 186 E3
Brunton Wilts 28 E1
Brushford Devon 11 G4
Brushford Somset 24 E6
Bruton Somset 27 G4
Bryan's Green Worcs 70 F2
Bryanston Dorset 15 G2
Brydekirk D & G 155 L7
Bryher IoS 2 a1
Brympton Somset 26 D7
Bryn Carmth 51 G5
Bryn Neath 36 C3
Brynamman Carmth 51 K3
Brynberian Pembks 64 F7
Bryncir Gwynd 95 H4
Bryn-côch Neath 51 L5
Bryncroes Gwynd 94 D6
Bryncrug Gwynd 80 E3
Bryneglwys Denbgs 97 H3
Brynford Flints 111 G6
Bryn Gates Wigan 112 E2
Bryngwran IoA 108 D6
Bryngwyn Mons 54 B6
Bryngwyn Powys 68 D5
Bryn-Henllan Pembks 64 E6
Brynhoffnant Cerdgn 65 K4
Brynmawr Blae G 53 J5
Bryn-mawr Gwynd 94 D5
Brynmenyn Brdgnd 36 D4
Brynmill Swans 51 J6
Brynna Rhondd 36 F4
Brynrefail Gwynd 109 H8
Brynsadler Rhondd 37 G4
Bryn Saith Marchog Denbgs 97 G3
Brynsiencyn IoA 108 F7
Brynteg IoA 109 G5
Bryn-y-Maen Conwy 110 B6
Bualintur Highld 198 F2
Bubbenhall Warwks 86 D8
Bubwith E R Yk 125 H4
Buccleuch Border 166 E6
Buchanan Smithy Stirlg 174 E1
Buchanhaven Abers 217 L5
Buchanty P & K 185 J2
Buchany Stirlg 184 F6
Buchlyvie Stirlg 184 C8
Buckabank Cumb 148 C5
Buckden Cambs 75 H2
Buckden N York 131 H4
Buckenham Norfk 93 H3
Buckerell Devon 12 E3
Buckfast Devon 7 H3
Buckfastleigh Devon 7 H3
Buckhaven Fife 186 F7
Buckholt Mons 54 D5
Buckhorn Weston Dorset 27 H6
Buckhurst Hill Essex 45 H2
Buckie Moray 215 J2
Buckingham Bucks 73 K7
Buckland Bucks 58 E5
Buckland Devon 7 G6
Buckland Gloucs 71 J7
Buckland Herts 75 L7
Buckland Kent 35 J6
Buckland Oxon 41 G2
Buckland Surrey 31 K2
Buckland Brewer Devon 22 F7
Buckland Common Bucks 58 F6
Buckland Dinham Somset 27 H2
Buckland Filleigh Devon 10 C3
Buckland in the Moor Devon 7 G2
Buckland Monachorum Devon 6 D3
Buckland Newton Dorset 14 D2
Buckland Ripers Dorset 14 C6
Buckland St Mary Somset 25 L8
Buckland-Tout-Saints Devon 7 H6
Bucklebury W Berk 41 K6
Bucklers Hard Hants 16 E3
Bucklesham Suffk 78 F6
Buckley Flints 111 J8
Bucklow Hill Ches E 113 G5
Buckminster Leics 102 E7
Bucknall C Stke 99 K3
Bucknall Lincs 117 K7
Bucknell Oxon 57 K3
Bucknell Shrops 83 G8
Buckpool Moray 215 J2
Bucksburn C Aber 207 G4
Buck's Cross Devon 22 E6
Bucks Green W Susx 31 H5
Buckshaw Village Lancs 121 H6
Bucks Horn Oak Hants 30 D3
Buck's Mills Devon 22 E6
Buckton E R Yk 135 J5
Buckton Nthumb 169 G2
Buckworth Cambs 89 G7
Budby Notts 115 L7
Bude Cnwll 9 G4
Budge's Shop Cnwll 5 M4
Budleigh Salterton Devon 12 D6
Budock Water Cnwll 3 K5
Buerton Ches E 99 G4
Bugbrooke Nhants 73 J3
Bugle Cnwll 4 F4
Bugley Dorset 27 H6
Bugthorpe E R Yk 134 B7
Buildwas Shrops 84 B3
Builth Wells Powys 68 B4
Bulbridge Wilts 28 C5
Bulford Wilts 28 D3
Bulkeley Ches E 98 D2
Bulkington Warwks 86 E6
Bulkington Wilts 39 L8
Bulkworthy Devon 9 K3

Bullbrook Br For 42 E6
Bullington Hants 29 J3
Bullington Lincs 117 H6
Bulmer Essex 77 J6
Bulmer N York 133 L6
Bulmer Tye Essex 77 J6
Bulphan Thurr 45 M3
Bulwark Abers 217 H5
Bulwell C Nott 101 K4
Bulwick Nhants 88 D5
Bumble's Green Essex 60 C6
Bunacaimb Highld 199 K7
Bunarkaig Highld 201 J7
Bunbury Ches E 98 E2
Bunchrew Highld 212 F5
Bundalloch Highld 210 D8
Bunessan Ag & B 180 E3
Bungay Suffk 93 G5
Bunnahabhain Ag & B 171 H4
Bunny Notts 101 L6
Buntait Highld 212 C7
Buntingford Herts 60 B3
Bunwell Norfk 92 D5
Burbage Leics 86 F5
Burbage Wilts 40 E7
Burchett's Green W & M 42 D4
Burcombe Wilts 28 B5
Burcott Bucks 58 E4
Bures Essex 77 K7
Burford Oxon 56 E5
Burford Shrops 69 L2
Burg Ag & B 189 J7
Burgates Hants 30 C5
Burgess Hill W Susx 19 J2
Burgh Suffk 78 F4
Burgh by Sands Cumb 148 B3
Burgh Castle Norfk 93 K3
Burghclere Hants 41 J7
Burghead Moray 214 D1
Burghfield W Berk 42 A6
Burghfield Common W Berk 42 A6
Burgh Heath Surrey 44 E7
Burghill Herefs 69 J5
Burgh Island Devon 6 F6
Burgh le Marsh Lincs 119 G7
Burgh next Aylsham Norfk 106 F7
Burgh on Bain Lincs 117 L4
Burgh St Margaret Norfk 93 J2
Burgh St Peter Norfk 93 K5
Burghwallis Donc 124 E7
Burham Kent 46 B7
Buriton Hants 30 C7
Burland Ches E 98 E2
Burlawn Cnwll 4 F2
Burleigh Gloucs 55 K7
Burlescombe Devon 25 G7
Burleston Dorset 14 E4
Burley Hants 16 B2
Burley Rutlnd 88 C2
Burleydam Ches E 98 E4
Burley Gate Herefs 69 L5
Burley in Wharfedale C Brad 123 H2
Burley Street Hants 16 B2
Burley Wood Head C Brad 123 H2
Burlton Shrops 98 C7
Burmarsh Kent 34 E7
Burmington Warwks 72 C6
Burn N York 124 F5
Burnage Manch 113 K3
Burnaston Derbys 100 F6
Burnbrae N Lans 176 B6
Burnby E R Yk 125 K2
Burneside Cumb 138 D7
Burneston N York 132 D3
Burnett BaNES 38 F7
Burnfoot Border 166 F6
Burnfoot Border 167 H6
Burnfoot D & G 155 G4
Burnfoot D & G 156 C3
Burnfoot D & G 156 C4
Burnfoot P & K 185 K6
Burnham Bucks 42 F4
Burnham Deepdale Norfk 105 J4
Burnham Market Norfk 105 K4
Burnham Norton Norfk 105 K4
Burnham-on-Crouch Essex 46 F2
Burnham-on-Sea Somset 25 L2
Burnham Overy Norfk 105 K4
Burnham Overy Staithe Norfk 105 K4
Burnham Thorpe Norfk 105 K4
Burnhaven Abers 217 L5
Burnhead D & G 154 E3
Burnhervie Abers 206 D2
Burnhill Green Staffs 84 E4
Burnhope Dur 150 F5
Burnhouse N Ayrs 174 D7
Burniston N York 134 F2
Burnley Lancs 122 C4
Burnley Crematorium Lancs 122 B4
Burnmouth Border 179 K6
Burn of Cambus Stirlg 184 F6
Burnopfield Dur 150 F4
Burnsall N York 131 J7
Burnside Angus 196 C4
Burnside Angus 196 E6
Burnside Fife 186 B5
Burnside Moray 214 E1
Burnside W Loth 176 E3
Burnside of Duntrune Angus 187 G1
Burntisland Fife 177 H2
Burnton E Ayrs 163 L7
Burntwood Staffs 85 J2
Burntwood Green Staffs 85 J2
Burnt Yates N York 132 C7
Burnworthy Somset 25 J7
Burpham Surrey 31 G2
Burpham W Susx 18 E4
Burradon Nthumb 168 E7
Burrafirth Shet 235 e1
Burravoe Shet 235 d3
Burrells Cumb 138 F4
Burrelton P & K 195 K8
Burridge Devon 13 H2
Burridge Hants 17 G1
Burrill N York 132 C3
Burringham N Linc 125 K8
Burrington Devon 10 F2
Burrington Herefs 69 J1
Burrington N Som 38 C8
Burrough Green Cambs 76 F4
Burrough on the Hill Leics 87 L2
Burrow Lancs 130 C4
Burrow Somset 24 E3
Burrow Bridge Somset 26 A5
Burrowhill Surrey 42 F7
Burry Green Swans 50 F7
Burry Port Carmth 50 F5
Burscough Lancs 120 F7
Burscough Bridge Lancs 120 F7
Bursea E R Yk 125 J4
Bursledon Hants 16 F1
Burstall Suffk 78 D5
Burstock Dorset 13 K2
Burston Norfk 92 D6
Burstow Surrey 32 B5
Burstwick E R Yk 126 F5
Burtersett N York 131 G2
Burtholme Cumb 148 F3
Burthorpe Green Suffk 77 H2
Burtoft Lincs 103 L5
Burton Ches W 111 K6
Burton Ches W 112 D8
Burton Dorset 15 M4
Burton Lincs 116 F6
Burton Pembks 49 G6
Burton Somset 25 J3
Burton Wilts 39 J4
Burton Agnes E R Yk 135 H6
Burton Bradstock Dorset 13 L4
Burton Coggles Lincs 103 G7
Burton End Essex 60 E4
Burton Fleming E R Yk 135 G5
Burton Hastings Warwks 86 E5
Burton-in-Kendal Cumb 129 L4
Burton-in-Kendal Services Cumb 129 L4
Burton in Lonsdale N York 130 C5
Burton Joyce Notts 101 M4
Burton Latimer Nhants 88 C8
Burton Lazars Leics 87 L1
Burton Leonard N York 132 E6
Burton on the Wolds Leics 101 L7
Burton Overy Leics 87 J4
Burton Pedwardine Lincs 103 J4
Burton Pidsea E R Yk 127 G4
Burton Salmon N York 124 D5
Burton's Green Essex 61 K3
Burton upon Stather N Linc 125 K6
Burton upon Trent Staffs 100 E7
Burton Waters Lincs 116 F6
Burtonwood Warrtn 112 E3
Burtonwood Services Warrtn 112 E4
Burwardsley Ches W 98 D2
Burwarton Shrops 84 B6
Burwash E Susx 33 H7
Burwash Common E Susx 20 D2
Burwash Weald E Susx 20 D2
Burwell Cambs 76 E2
Burwell Lincs 118 E5
Burwen IoA 108 E3
Burwick Ork 234 c8
Bury Bury 122 B7
Bury Cambs 89 K6
Bury Somset 24 E6
Bury W Susx 18 D3
Bury Green Herts 60 D4
Bury St Edmunds Suffk 77 J2
Burythorpe N York 134 C6
Busby E Rens 175 G6
Buscot Oxon 40 E2
Bush Abers 197 J4
Bush Bank Herefs 69 J4
Bushbury Wolves 85 G3
Bushbury Crematorium Wolves 85 G3
Bushey Herts 43 J2
Bushey Heath Herts 43 J2
Bush Hill Park Gt Lon 45 G2
Bushley Worcs 70 F7
Bushmoor Shrops 83 J6
Bushton Wilts 40 B5
Bussage Gloucs 55 K7
Bussex Somset 26 A4
Butcombe N Som 38 D7
Bute Ag & B 173 H4
Butleigh Somset 26 D5
Butleigh Wootton Somset 26 D4
Butlers Marston Warwks 72 D4
Butley Suffk 79 H4
Buttercrambe N York 133 L7
Butterdean Border 179 G5
Butterknowle Dur 140 E3
Butterleigh Devon 12 C2
Buttermere Cumb 137 G4
Buttershaw C Brad 123 H5
Butterstone P & K 195 G7
Butterton Staffs 99 J4
Butterton Staffs 100 B2
Butterwick Lincs 104 C4
Butterwick N York 133 L4
Butterwick N York 134 F5
Buttington Powys 82 E2
Buttonoak Shrops 84 D7
Buxhall Suffk 78 B3
Buxted E Susx 20 A2
Buxton Derbys 114 B6
Buxton Norfk 106 F7
Buxton Heath Norfk 106 E7
Bwlch Powys 53 J4
Bwlchgwyn Wrexhm 97 K2
Bwlchllan Cerdgn 66 D3
Bwlchtocyn Gwynd 94 E7
Bwlch-y-cibau Powys 97 J8
Bwlch-y-ffridd Powys 82 B4
Bwlch-y-groes Pembks 65 H7
Bwlch-y-sarnau Powys 82 B8
Byers Green Dur 150 F7
Byfield Nhants 73 G4
Byfleet Surrey 43 H7
Byford Herefs 69 H6
Byker N u Ty 151 G3
Bylchau Conwy 110 D8
Byley Ches W 113 G7
Byrness Nthumb 157 K2
Bystock Devon 12 D5
Bythorn Cambs 88 F7
Byton Herefs 69 G2
Bywell Nthumb 150 D3
Byworth W Susx 31 G7

C

Cabourne Lincs 117 J2
Cabrach Ag & B 171 J5
Cabrach Moray 215 J8
Cabus Lancs 121 G2
Cadbury Devon 11 L4
Cadbury World Birm 85 J7
Cadder E Duns 175 G4
Caddington C Beds 59 H4
Caddonfoot Border 167 G3
Cadeby Donc 115 K2
Cadeby Leics 86 E3
Cadeleigh Devon 11 L4
Cade Street E Susx 20 C2
Cadgwith Cnwll 3 J7
Cadham Fife 186 D6
Cadishead Salfd 113 G3
Cadle Swans 51 J6
Cadley Lancs 121 G4
Cadley Wilts 28 E2
Cadley Wilts 40 E6
Cadmore End Bucks 42 C3
Cadnam Hants 28 F8
Cadney N Linc 117 G2
Cadoxton V Glam 37 H6
Cadoxton Juxta-Neath Neath 51 L5
Caeathro Gwynd 95 J1
Caenby Lincs 117 G4
Caeo Carmth 66 F6
Caerau Brdgnd 36 D2
Caerau Cardif 37 H5
Caer Farchell Pembks 48 D3
Caergeiliog IoA 108 D5
Caergwrle Flints 97 L2
Caerlanrig Border 156 D2
Caerleon Newpt 37 M3
Caernarfon Gwynd 108 F8

Caernarfon Castle Gwynd 108 F8
Caerphilly Caerph 37 J3
Caersws Powys 82 B5
Caerwedros Cerdgn 65 L4
Caerwent Mons 38 C3
Caerwys Flints 110 F6
Cairinis W Isls 233 c6
Cairnbaan Ag & B 172 E1
Cairnbulg Abers 217 J2
Cairncross Border 179 J5
Cairncurran Inver 174 C4
Cairndow Ag & B 183 H5
Cairneyhill Fife 176 E2
Cairngarroch D & G 144 C5
Cairngorms National Park 204 C5
Cairnie Abers 215 K5
Cairnorrie Abers 217 G6
Cairnryan D & G 144 C2
Cairnty Moray 215 H4
Caister-on-Sea Norfk 93 L2
Caistor Lincs 117 J2
Caistor St Edmund Norfk 92 F3
Calanais W Isls 232 e2
Calbourne IoW 16 E5
Calcot Flints 111 G6
Calcot Gloucs 56 C6
Calcot Row W Berk 42 A6
Calcots Moray 215 G2
Caldbeck Cumb 148 B6
Caldecote Cambs 75 L3
Caldecote Cambs 89 G5
Caldecote Highfields Cambs 75 L3
Caldecott Nhants 74 E2
Caldecott Oxon 41 J2
Caldecott Rutlnd 88 C5
Calderbank N Lans 175 K5
Calder Bridge Cumb 136 E6
Caldercruix N Lans 175 L5
Calder Grove Wakefd 123 L6
Caldermill S Lans 164 D2
Calder Vale Lancs 121 G2
Calderwood S Lans 175 H7
Caldey Island Pembks 49 K7
Caldicot Mons 38 C3
Caldmore Wsall 85 H4
Caldwell N York 140 E5
Calf of Man IoM 237 a7
Calfsound Ork 234 d4
Calgary Ag & B 189 J6
Califer Moray 214 D3
California Falk 176 B3
California Norfk 93 K1
Calke Derbys 101 G7
Calke Abbey Derbys 101 G7
Callakille Highld 209 L4
Callander Stirlg 184 D5
Callanish W Isls 232 e2
Callestick Cnwll 3 K2
Calligarry Highld 199 K5
Callington Cnwll 6 A3
Callow Herefs 69 J7
Callow End Worcs 70 E4
Callow Hill Wilts 40 B4
Calmore Hants 29 G7
Calmsden Gloucs 56 B6
Calne Wilts 39 M6
Calshot Hants 16 F3
Calstock Cnwll 6 C3
Calstone Wellington Wilts 40 B6
Calthorpe Norfk 106 E6
Calthorpe Street Norfk 107 J7
Calthwaite Cumb 148 E6
Calton Staffs 100 C3
Calveley Ches E 98 E2
Calver Derbys 114 E6
Calverhall Shrops 98 E5
Calverleigh Devon 11 L3
Calverton M Keyn 73 L6
Calverton Notts 101 L3
Calvine P & K 194 C3
Calzeat Border 165 L3
Cam Gloucs 55 H7
Camasachoirce Highld 190 F4
Camasine Highld 190 F4
Camas Luinie Highld 210 E8
Camastianavaig Highld 209 H6
Camault Muir Highld 212 D6
Camber E Susx 21 J2
Camberley Surrey 42 E7
Camberwell Gt Lon 44 F5
Camblesforth N York 124 F5
Cambo Nthumb 158 C5
Camborne Cnwll 3 H4
Camborne & Redruth Mining District Cnwll 3 H4
Cambourne Cambs 75 K3
Cambridge Cambs 76 C3
Cambridge Gloucs 55 H7
Cambridge Airport Cambs 76 C3
Cambridge City Crematorium Cambs 76 B3
Cambrose Cnwll 3 H3
Cambus Clacks 185 H8
Cambusavie Platform Highld 223 G3
Cambusbarron Stirlg 185 G8
Cambuskenneth Stirlg 185 G8
Cambuslang S Lans 175 H6
Cambus o' May Abers 205 J5
Cambuswallace S Lans 165 K2
Camden Town Gt Lon 44 F4
Cameley BaNES 38 E8
Camelford Cnwll 8 E7
Camelon Falk 176 B3
Camerory Highld 214 C7
Camerton BaNES 39 G8
Camerton Cumb 136 E2
Camghouran P & K 193 J5
Camieston Border 167 J4
Cammachmore Abers 207 G6
Cammeringham Lincs 116 F5
Camore Highld 223 G4
Campbeltown Ag & B 161 J5
Campbeltown Airport Ag & B 161 H5
Cample D & G 154 F4
Campmuir P & K 195 K8
Camps W Loth 176 E5
Campsall Donc 124 E7
Campsea Ash Suffk 79 G4
Campton C Beds 75 G6
Camptown Border 167 K6
Camrose Pembks 48 F4
Camserney P & K 194 C6
Camusnagaul Highld 191 L2
Camusnagaul Highld 220 D4
Camusteel Highld 209 L6
Camusterrach Highld 209 L6
Canada Hants 28 F7
Candacraig Abers 205 H5
Candlesby Lincs 118 F7
Candy Mill Border 165 L2
Cane End Oxon 42 B4
Canewdon Essex 46 E2
Canford Cliffs Poole 15 K5
Canford Crematorium Bristl 38 E5
Canford Heath Poole 15 J4
Canisbay Highld 231 L2
Canley Covtry 86 C7
Canley Crematorium Covtry 86 C7
Cann Dorset 27 K7
Canna Highld 198 C4
Cann Common Dorset 27 K7
Cannich Highld 211 L7
Cannington Somset 25 K4
Canning Town Gt Lon 45 H4
Cannock Staffs 85 H2
Cannock Chase Staffs 99 M8
Cannon Bridge Herefs 69 H6
Canonbie D & G 156 C6
Canon Frome Herefs 70 B5
Canon Pyon Herefs 69 J5
Canons Ashby Nhants 73 H4
Canonstown Cnwll 2 F4
Canterbury Kent 34 F3
Canterbury Cathedral Kent 34 F3
Cantley Norfk 93 H3
Canton Cardif 37 J5
Cantraywood Highld 213 J5
Cantsfield Lancs 130 C5
Canvey Island Essex 46 D4
Canwick Lincs 117 G7
Canworthy Water Cnwll 9 G6
Caol Highld 191 L2
Caolas Scalpaigh W Isls 232 e4
Caoles Ag & B 188 D6
Caonich Highld 201 G6
Capel Kent 33 H4
Capel Surrey 31 K4
Capel Bangor Cerdgn 80 E7
Capel Coch IoA 108 F5
Capel Curig Conwy 96 A2
Capel Dewi Carmth 50 F2
Capel Dewi Cerdgn 66 B6
Capel-Dewi Cerdgn 80 E6
Capel Garmon Conwy 96 C2
Capel Hendre Carmth 51 H4
Capel Iwan Carmth 65 J7
Capel le Ferne Kent 35 H6
Capelles Guern 236 d2
Capel Parc IoA 108 F4
Capel St Andrew Suffk 79 H5
Capel St Mary Suffk 78 C6
Capel Seion Cerdgn 80 E7
Capelulo Conwy 109 L6
Capenhurst Ches W 111 K6
Cape Wrath Highld 228 D1
Capheaton Nthumb 158 C6
Caplaw E Rens 174 E6
Cappercleuch Border 166 C5
Capstone Medway 46 C6
Capton Devon 7 J5
Caputh P & K 195 H7
Caradon Mining District Cnwll 5 L2
Carbeth Inn Stirlg 174 F3
Carbis Bay Cnwll 2 F4
Carbost Highld 208 F5
Carbost Highld 208 F7
Carbrook Sheff 115 G4
Carbrooke Norfk 91 L3
Car Colston Notts 102 B4
Carcroft Donc 124 E8
Cardenden Fife 186 C7
Cardhu Moray 214 F5
Cardiff Cardif 37 J5
Cardiff Airport V Glam 37 G6
Cardiff & Glamorgan Crematorium Cardif 37 J4
Cardiff Gate Services Cardif 37 K4
Cardiff West Services Cardif 37 H4
Cardigan Cerdgn 65 G5
Cardington Bed 74 F5
Cardington Shrops 83 K4
Cardinham Cnwll 5 H3
Cardrain D & G 144 D8
Cardrona Border 166 D2
Cardross Ag & B 174 C3
Cardross Crematorium Ag & B 174 C3
Cardryne D & G 144 D7
Cardurnock Cumb 147 L3
Careby Lincs 88 E1
Careston Angus 196 E4
Carew Pembks 49 H6
Carew Cheriton Pembks 49 H6
Carew Newton Pembks 49 H6
Carey Herefs 54 E2
Carfin N Lans 175 K6
Carfraemill Border 178 B7
Cargate Green Norfk 93 H2
Cargenbridge D & G 155 G7
Cargill P & K 195 J8
Cargo Cumb 148 C3
Cargreen Cnwll 6 C4
Carham Nthumb 168 B2
Carhampton Somset 24 F3
Carharrack Cnwll 3 J3
Carie P & K 193 K5
Carinish W Isls 233 c6
Carisbrooke IoW 16 F5
Cark Cumb 129 H4
Carkeel Cnwll 6 B4
Carlabhagh W Isls 232 e2
Carlbury Darltn 140 F4
Carlby Lincs 88 F2
Carleen Cnwll 3 G5
Carleton N York 122 E1
Carleton Crematorium Bpool 120 D3
Carleton Forehoe Norfk 92 C3
Carleton Rode Norfk 92 D5
Carleton St Peter Norfk 93 H3
Carlincraig Abers 216 D5
Carlingcott BaNES 39 G8
Carlisle Cumb 148 D4
Carlisle Airport Cumb 148 E3
Carlisle Crematorium Cumb 148 C4
Carlops Border 177 G6
Carloway W Isls 232 e2
Carlton Barns 124 B7
Carlton Bed 74 D4
Carlton Cambs 76 F4
Carlton Leeds 123 L5
Carlton Leics 86 E3
Carlton N York 124 F5
Carlton N York 131 K3
Carlton N York 133 J3
Carlton Notts 101 L4
Carlton S on T 141 J3
Carlton Suffk 79 H2
Carlton Colville Suffk 93 K5
Carlton Curlieu Leics 87 K4
Carlton Green Cambs 76 F4
Carlton Husthwaite N York 133 G4
Carlton-in-Cleveland N York 142 B6
Carlton in Lindrick Notts 115 L5
Carlton-le-Moorland Lincs 102 E2
Carlton Miniott N York 132 F4
Carlton-on-Trent Notts 116 D8
Carlton Scroop Lincs 102 F4
Carluke S Lans 175 L7
Carmacoup S Lans 164 F4
Carmarthen Carmth 50 E2
Carmel Carmth 51 H3
Carmel Flints 111 G6
Carmel Gwynd 95 H2
Carmichael S Lans 165 H2
Carmountside Crematorium C Stke 99 K3
Carmunnock C Glas 175 G6
Carmyle C Glas 175 H6
Carmyllie Angus 196 E7
Carnaby E R Yk 135 H6
Carnbee Fife 187 J6
Carnbo P & K 185 L6
Carn Brea Cnwll 3 H3
Carnbrogie Abers 216 F8
Carndu Highld 210 D8
Carnduff S Lans 164 D1
Carnell E Ayrs 163 L3

Carnforth Lancs 129 K5
Carn-gorm Highld 200 E2
Carnhell Green Cnwll 3 G4
Carnie Abers 206 F4
Carnkie Cnwll 3 H4
Carnkie Cnwll 3 J4
Carno Powys 81 K4
Carnock Fife 176 E1
Carnon Downs Cnwll 4 C7
Carnousie Abers 216 C4
Carnoustie Angus 187 J1
Carnwath S Lans 165 J1
Carol Green Solhll 86 C7
Carperby N York 131 J2
Carradale Ag & B 161 K2
Carrbridge Highld 203 L2
Carrefour Jersey 236 c6
Carreglefn IoA 108 E4
Carr Gate Wakefd 123 L5
Carrhouse N Linc 116 C1
Carrick Ag & B 172 F2
Carrick Castle Ag & B 183 H8
Carriden Falk 176 D3
Carrington Mdloth 177 J6
Carrington Traffd 113 H3
Carrog Denbgs 97 H4
Carron Falk 176 B2
Carron Moray 214 F6
Carronbridge D & G 154 F3
Carron Bridge Stirlg 175 K2
Carronshore Falk 176 B2
Carr Shield Nthumb 149 K5
Carrutherstown D & G 155 J7
Carruth House Inver 174 C5
Carrville Dur 151 H6
Carsaig Ag & B 181 H3
Carseriggan D & G 145 G2
Carsethorn D & G 147 H3
Carshalton Gt Lon 44 F6
Carsington Derbys 100 E2
Carskey Ag & B 161 H7
Carsluith D & G 145 K4
Carsphairn D & G 153 L4
Carstairs S Lans 165 H1
Carstairs Junction S Lans 165 J1
Carterton Oxon 56 F6
Carthew Cnwll 4 F5
Carthorpe N York 132 D3
Cartland S Lans 165 G1
Cartmel Cumb 129 H4
Carway Carmth 50 F4
Cashe's Green Gloucs 55 J6
Cassington Oxon 57 J5
Cassop Colliery Dur 151 J7
Castel Guern 236 c3
Casterton Cumb 130 C4
Castle Acre Norfk 91 J1
Castle Ashby Nhants 74 C3
Castlebay W Isls 233 b9
Castle Bolton N York 131 J2
Castle Bromwich Solhll 85 K5
Castle Bytham Lincs 103 G8
Castlebythe Pembks 49 H2
Castle Caereinion Powys 82 D3
Castle Camps Cambs 76 F6
Castle Carrock Cumb 148 F4
Castlecary Falk 175 K3
Castle Cary Somset 26 F5
Castle Combe Wilts 39 J5
Castle Donington Leics 101 H6
Castle Douglas D & G 146 D3
Castle Eaton Swindn 40 C2
Castle Eden Dur 151 K7
Castleford Wakefd 124 C5
Castle Frome Herefs 70 C5
Castle Gresley Derbys 100 F8
Castle Hedingham Essex 77 H7
Castlehill Border 166 C3
Castlehill Highld 231 H2
Castle Hill Suffk 78 D5
Castlehill W Duns 174 D3
Castle Howard N York 133 L5
Castle Kennedy D & G 144 D3
Castle Lachlan Ag & B 182 E7
Castlemartin Pembks 48 F7
Castlemilk C Glas 175 G6
Castlemorton Worcs 70 E6
Castlemorton Common Worcs 70 E6
Castle O'er D & G 156 A4
Castle Rising Norfk 105 G7
Castleside Dur 150 D5
Castle Stuart Highld 213 H4
Castlethorpe M Keyn 74 B5
Castleton Border 156 E4
Castleton Derbys 114 D5
Castleton N York 142 E5
Castleton Newpt 37 K4
Castleton Rochdl 122 D7
Castletown Highld 231 H3
Castletown IoM 237 b7
Castletown Sundld 151 J4
Castley N York 123 K2
Caston Norfk 91 L4
Castor C Pete 89 G4
Catacol N Ayrs 172 F7
Catcliffe Rothm 115 H4
Catcomb Wilts 40 A5
Catcott Somset 26 B4
Catcott Burtle Somset 26 B3
Caterham Surrey 32 C3
Catfield Norfk 107 H7
Catford Gt Lon 45 G5
Catforth Lancs 121 G4
Cathcart C Glas 175 G6
Cathedine Powys 53 H3
Catherington Hants 30 B8
Catherston Leweston Dorset 13 J4
Catisfield Hants 17 G2
Catlodge Highld 202 F6
Catmere End Essex 76 C6
Catmore W Berk 41 J4
Caton Lancs 129 L6
Caton Green Lancs 129 L6
Catrine E Ayrs 164 B4
Catsfield E Susx 20 E3
Catsgore Somset 26 D6
Catshill Worcs 85 G8
Cattadale Ag & B 161 H7
Cattal N York 133 G8
Cattawade Suffk 62 D2
Catterall Lancs 121 G3
Catterick N York 141 G7
Catterick Bridge N York 141 G7
Catterlen Cumb 148 E7
Catterline Abers 197 L2
Catterton N York 124 D2
Catteshall Surrey 31 G3
Catthorpe Leics 87 G7
Cattistock Dorset 14 B3
Catton N York 132 E4
Catton Nthumb 149 L4
Catwick E R Yk 126 E2
Catworth Cambs 88 F8
Caudle Green Gloucs 55 L6
Caulcott Oxon 57 K3
Cauldcots Angus 197 G6
Cauldhame Stirlg 184 E8
Cauldmill Border 167 H6
Cauldon Staffs 100 B3
Cauldwell Derbys 86 B1
Caulkerbush D & G 147 G4
Caulside D & G 156 D6
Caundle Marsh Dorset 27 G8
Caunton Notts 102 C1
Causeway End D & G 145 J3
Causeway End Essex 61 G4
Causewayend S Lans 165 K3
Causewayhead Stirlg 185 G7
Causeyend Abers 207 H2
Causey Park Bridge Nthumb 158 F3
Cavendish Suffk 77 J5
Cavenham Suffk 77 H1
Caversfield Oxon 57 L3
Caversham Readg 42 B5
Caverswall Staffs 99 L4
Caverton Mill Border 167 M4
Cawdor Highld 213 K4
Cawood N York 124 E3
Cawsand Cnwll 6 C5
Cawston Norfk 106 D7
Cawthorne Barns 123 K8
Caxton Cambs 75 K3
Caynham Shrops 83 K8
Caythorpe Lincs 102 F3
Caythorpe Notts 102 B4
Cayton N York 135 G3
Ceann a Bhaigh W Isls 233 b6
Ceannacroc Lodge Highld 201 K3
Cearsiadar W Isls 232 f3
Cefn Newpt 37 L3
Cefn-brîth Conwy 96 E3
Cefn-bryn-brain Carmth 51 L3
Cefn Cribwr Brdgnd 36 D4
Cefneithin Carmth 51 G3
Cefngorwydd Powys 67 J5
Cefn-mawr Wrexhm 97 L4
Cefn-y-pant Carmth 49 K3
Cellardyke Fife 187 J6
Cellarhead Staffs 99 L3
Cemaes IoA 108 E3
Cemmaes Powys 81 H3
Cemmaes Road Powys 81 H3
Cenarth Cerdgn 65 J6
Ceres Fife 186 F5
Cerne Abbas Dorset 14 C3
Cerney Wick Gloucs 40 B2
Cerrigydrudion Conwy 96 E3
Ceunant Gwynd 95 J1
Chaceley Gloucs 55 J2
Chacewater Cnwll 3 K3
Chackmore Bucks 73 K7
Chacombe Nhants 72 F5
Chadbury Worcs 71 H5
Chadderton Oldham 113 K1
Chaddesden C Derb 101 G5
Chaddesley Corbett Worcs 84 F8
Chaddlehanger Devon 6 C1
Chaddleworth W Berk 41 H5
Chadlington Oxon 57 G4
Chadshunt Warwks 72 D4
Chadwell Leics 102 C7
Chadwell Heath Gt Lon 45 J3
Chadwell St Mary Thurr 45 M4
Chadwick Worcs 70 E2
Chadwick End Solhll 86 B8
Chaffcombe Somset 13 J1
Chafford Hundred Thurr 45 L4
Chagford Devon 11 G7
Chailey E Susx 19 K2
Chainhurst Kent 33 J4
Chaldon Surrey 32 B3
Chale IoW 16 F6
Chale Green IoW 16 F6
Chalfont Common Bucks 43 G3
Chalfont St Giles Bucks 43 G2
Chalfont St Peter Bucks 43 G3
Chalford Gloucs 55 K7
Chalford Wilts 27 K2
Chalgrove Oxon 41 M2
Chalk Kent 46 A5
Chalkwell Kent 34 B2
Challacombe Devon 23 L3
Challoch D & G 145 H2
Challock Kent 34 D5
Chalton C Beds 59 G3
Chalton Hants 30 B7
Chalvey Slough 42 F4
Chalvington E Susx 20 B4
Chandler's Cross Herts 43 H2
Chandler's Ford Hants 29 H7
Channel Tunnel Terminal Kent 35 G6
Chanterlands Crematorium C KuH 126 D4
Chantry Somset 27 G3
Chantry Suffk 78 D5
Chapel Fife 186 D8
Chapel Allerton Leeds 123 L3
Chapel Allerton Somset 26 B2
Chapel Amble Cnwll 4 F2
Chapel Brampton Nhants 73 K2
Chapel Chorlton Staffs 99 J5
Chapelend Way Essex 77 G6
Chapel-en-le-Frith Derbys 114 B5
Chapel Green Warwks 72 F3
Chapel Haddlesey N York 124 E5
Chapelhall N Lans 175 K5
Chapel Hill Abers 217 K7
Chapel Hill Lincs 103 K2
Chapel Hill Mons 54 D7
Chapel Hill N York 123 L2
Chapelhope Border 166 C5
Chapelknowe D & G 156 B7
Chapel Lawn Shrops 82 F7
Chapel-le-Dale N York 130 E4
Chapel Leigh Somset 25 H5
Chapel of Garioch Abers 206 D1
Chapel Rossan D & G 144 D6
Chapel Row W Berk 41 L6
Chapel St Leonards Lincs 119 H6
Chapel Stile Cumb 137 K6
Chapelton Angus 197 G6
Chapelton Devon 23 J6
Chapelton S Lans 175 J8
Chapeltown Bl w D 121 L7
Chapeltown Moray 204 F2
Chapeltown Sheff 115 G3
Chapmanslade Wilts 27 J2
Chapmans Well Devon 9 J6
Chapmore End Herts 60 B5
Chappel Essex 61 L3
Chard Somset 13 H2
Chard Junction Somset 13 J2
Chardleigh Green Somset 13 H1
Chardstock Devon 13 H2
Charfield S Glos 39 G3
Charing Kent 34 C5
Charing Crematorium Kent 34 C5
Charingworth Gloucs 71 L6
Charlbury Oxon 57 G4
Charlcombe BaNES 39 H6
Charlcutt Wilts 39 M5
Charlecote Warwks 72 C3
Charlemont Sandw 85 H5
Charles Devon 23 L5
Charleston Angus 196 C7
Charlestown C Aber 207 H5
Charlestown C Brad 123 H3
Charlestown Calder 122 E5
Charlestown Cnwll 5 G5
Charlestown Cnwll 5 G5
Charlestown Fife 176 E2
Charlestown Highld 213 G5
Charlestown Highld 219 J6
Charlestown Salfd 113 J2
Charlestown of Aberlour Moray 215 G5
Charles Tye Suffk 78 B4
Charlesworth Derbys 114 A3

Charlinch Somset 25 K4
Charlottetown Fife 186 E5
Charlton Gt Lon 45 H4
Charlton Nhants 73 G7
Charlton Nthumb 157 K5
Charlton Oxon 41 H3
Charlton Somset 25 L6
Charlton Somset 27 G2
Charlton W Susx 18 B3
Charlton Wilts 27 K6
Charlton Wilts 39 L3
Charlton Worcs 71 H5
Charlton Wrekin 83 L2
Charlton Abbots Gloucs 56 B3
Charlton Adam Somset 26 D5
Charlton All Saints Wilts 28 D6
Charlton Down Dorset 14 D4
Charlton Horethorne Somset 26 F6
Charlton Kings Gloucs 55 L4
Charlton Mackrell Somset 26 D5
Charlton Marshall Dorset 15 G2
Charlton Musgrove Somset 27 G5
Charlton-on-Otmoor Oxon 57 K5
Charlton on the Hill Dorset 15 G2
Charlton St Peter Wilts 28 C1
Charlwood Hants 30 A5
Charlwood Surrey 31 L3
Charminster Dorset 14 D4
Charmouth Dorset 13 J4
Charndon Bucks 58 A3
Charney Bassett Oxon 41 G2
Charnock Richard Lancs 121 H7
Charnock Richard Crematorium Lancs 121 H6
Charnock Richard Services Lancs 121 H7
Charsfield Suffk 78 F3
Charter Alley Hants 41 L8
Charterhall Border 179 G8
Charterhouse Somset 26 D1
Chartershall Stirlg 175 K1
Chartham Kent 34 E4
Chartham Hatch Kent 34 E4
Chartridge Bucks 58 F7
Chart Sutton Kent 33 K4
Charvil Wokham 42 C5
Charwelton Nhants 73 G4
Chase Terrace Staffs 85 J2
Chasetown Staffs 85 J2
Chastleton Oxon 56 E3
Chasty Devon 9 J4
Chatburn Lancs 121 L2
Chatcull Staffs 99 H5
Chatham Medway 46 C6
Chatham Green Essex 61 H5
Chathill Nthumb 169 J4
Chatsworth House Derbys 114 E7
Chattenden Medway 46 C5
Chatteris Cambs 90 B6
Chatterton Lancs 122 B6
Chattisham Suffk 78 C6
Chatto Border 168 B5
Chatton Nthumb 168 F4
Chawleigh Devon 11 G3
Chawton Hants 30 B4
Cheadle Staffs 100 A4
Cheadle Stockp 113 K4
Cheadle Hulme Stockp 113 K4
Cheam Gt Lon 44 E7
Chearsley Bucks 58 B6
Chebsey Staffs 99 J6
Checkendon Oxon 42 A4
Checkley Ches E 99 G4
Checkley Staffs 100 B5
Chedburgh Suffk 77 H3
Cheddar Somset 26 C2
Cheddington Bucks 58 F4
Cheddleton Staffs 99 L3
Cheddon Fitzpaine Somset 25 K6
Chedgrave Norfk 93 H4
Chedington Dorset 13 L2
Chediston Suffk 93 H7
Chedworth Gloucs 56 B5
Chedzoy Somset 25 M4
Cheetham Hill Manch 113 J2
Cheldon Devon 11 H3
Chelford Ches E 113 J6
Chellaston C Derb 101 G6
Chellington Bed 74 D4
Chelmarsh Shrops 84 C5
Chelmondiston Suffk 78 E6
Chelmorton Derbys 114 C7
Chelmsford Essex 61 H6
Chelmsford Crematorium Essex 61 H6
Chelmsley Wood Solhll 85 L6
Chelsea Gt Lon 44 F4
Chelsfield Gt Lon 45 J7
Chelsworth Suffk 77 L5
Cheltenham Gloucs 55 L4
Cheltenham Crematorium Gloucs 55 L4
Chelveston Nhants 74 E1
Chelvey N Som 38 C6
Chelwood BaNES 38 F7
Chelwood Gate E Susx 32 D6
Cheney Longville Shrops 83 H6
Chenies Bucks 43 G2
Chepstow Mons 38 D2
Cherhill Wilts 40 B6
Cherington Gloucs 55 K7
Cherington Warwks 72 C6
Cheriton Hants 29 L5
Cheriton Kent 35 G7
Cheriton Pembks 49 G7
Cheriton Swans 50 F6
Cheriton Bishop Devon 11 H6
Cheriton Fitzpaine Devon 11 K4
Cherrington Wrekin 98 F8
Cherry Burton E R Yk 126 B3
Cherry Hinton Cambs 76 C3
Cherry Orchard Worcs 70 F4
Cherry Willingham Lincs 117 G6
Chertsey Surrey 43 H6
Cherwell Valley Services Oxon 57 K3
Cheselbourne Dorset 14 E3
Chesham Bucks 58 F7
Chesham Bury 122 B7
Chesham Bois Bucks 58 F7
Cheshunt Herts 60 B7
Chesil Beach Dorset 14 B6
Cheslyn Hay Staffs 85 H3
Chessetts Wood Warwks 85 L8
Chessington Gt Lon 44 D7
Chessington World of Adventures Gt Lon 44 D7
Chester Ches W 112 B7
Chesterblade Somset 26 F3
Chester Crematorium Ches W 111 L7
Chesterfield Derbys 115 G7
Chesterfield Crematorium Derbys 115 H6
Chesterhill Mdloth 177 K5
Chester-le-Street Dur 151 G5
Chester Moor Dur 151 G5
Chesters Border 167 J5
Chesters Border 167 K7
Chester Services Ches W 112 C6
Chesterton Cambs 76 C3
Chesterton Cambs 89 G4
Chesterton Gloucs 56 A7
Chesterton Oxon 57 K4
Chesterton Shrops 84 D4
Chesterton Staffs 99 J3
Chesterton Green Warwks 72 D3
Chesterwood Nthumb 149 L2
Chester Zoo Ches W 112 B7
Chestfield Kent 47 J6
Cheston Devon 7 G4
Cheswardine Shrops 99 G6
Cheswick Nthumb 168 F1
Chetnole Dorset 14 B2
Chettisham Cambs 90 D6
Chettle Dorset 27 L8
Chetton Shrops 84 B5
Chetwynd Wrekin 99 G7
Chetwynd Aston Wrekin 99 H8
Cheveley Cambs 76 F3
Chevening Kent 32 E2
Chevington Suffk 77 H3
Cheviot Hills 168 A7
Chevithorne Devon 24 F7
Chew Magna BaNES 38 E7
Chew Stoke BaNES 38 E7
Chewton Keynsham BaNES 38 F6
Chewton Mendip Somset 26 E2
Chicheley M Keyn 74 C5
Chichester W Susx 18 B5
Chichester Crematorium W Susx 18 B4
Chickerell Dorset 14 C6
Chicklade Wilts 27 K4
Chidden Hants 30 A7
Chiddingfold Surrey 30 F4
Chiddingly E Susx 20 B3
Chiddingstone Kent 32 E4
Chiddingstone Causeway Kent 32 F4
Chideock Dorset 13 K4
Chidham W Susx 17 L2
Chidswell Kirk 123 K6
Chieveley W Berk 41 J5
Chieveley Services W Berk 41 J6
Chignall St James Essex 61 G6
Chignall Smealy Essex 61 G5
Chigwell Essex 45 H2
Chigwell Row Essex 45 J2
Chilbolton Hants 29 H4
Chilcomb Hants 29 J5
Chilcombe Dorset 13 M4
Chilcompton Somset 26 F2
Chilcote Leics 86 C2
Childer Thornton Ches W 111 K6
Child Okeford Dorset 27 J8
Childrey Oxon 41 G3
Child's Ercall Shrops 98 F7
Childswickham Worcs 71 J6
Childwall Lpool 112 B4
Chilfrome Dorset 14 B3
Chilgrove W Susx 18 A3
Chilham Kent 34 E4
Chillaton Devon 10 C8
Chillenden Kent 35 H4
Chillerton IoW 16 F5
Chillesford Suffk 79 H4
Chillington Devon 7 J7
Chillington Somset 13 K1
Chilmark Wilts 27 L5
Chilmington Green Kent 34 C6
Chilson Oxon 56 F4
Chilsworthy Cnwll 6 B2
Chilsworthy Devon 9 J4
Chiltern Hills 42 C2
Chilterns Crematorium Bucks 42 F2
Chilthorne Domer Somset 26 D7
Chilton Bucks 58 B5
Chilton Dur 141 H2
Chilton Oxon 41 J4
Chilton Candover Hants 29 L4
Chilton Cantelo Somset 26 E6
Chilton Foliat Wilts 40 F6
Chilton Polden Somset 26 B4
Chilton Street Suffk 77 H5
Chilton Trinity Somset 25 L4
Chilwell Notts 101 K5
Chilworth Hants 29 H7
Chilworth Surrey 31 G3
Chimney Oxon 57 G7
Chineham Hants 30 A1
Chingford Gt Lon 45 G2
Chinley Derbys 114 B5
Chinnor Oxon 58 C7
Chipnall Shrops 99 G6
Chippenham Cambs 76 F1
Chippenham Wilts 39 L5
Chipperfield Herts 59 H7
Chipping Herts 60 B2
Chipping Lancs 121 J2
Chipping Campden Gloucs 71 L6
Chipping Norton Oxon 56 F3
Chipping Ongar Essex 60 E7
Chipping Sodbury S Glos 39 G4
Chipping Warden Nhants 72 F5
Chipstable Somset 25 G6
Chipstead Kent 32 E3
Chipstead Surrey 32 B2
Chirbury Shrops 82 F4
Chirk Wrexhm 97 L5
Chirnside Border 179 H6
Chirnsidebridge Border 179 H7
Chirton Wilts 40 B8
Chisbury Wilts 40 F6
Chiselborough Somset 26 C8
Chiseldon Swindn 40 D4
Chiselhampton Oxon 57 L7
Chisholme Border 166 F6
Chislehurst Gt Lon 45 H6
Chislet Kent 47 L6
Chisley Calder 122 F5
Chiswell Green Herts 59 J6
Chiswick Gt Lon 44 E4
Chisworth Derbys 113 M3
Chithurst W Susx 30 D6
Chittering Cambs 76 C1
Chitterne Wilts 27 M3
Chittlehamholt Devon 23 K7
Chittlehampton Devon 23 K6
Chittoe Wilts 39 L6
Chivelstone Devon 7 H7
Chivenor Devon 23 H4
Chlenry D & G 144 D3
Chobham Surrey 42 F7
Cholderton Wilts 28 E3
Cholesbury Bucks 58 F6
Chollerton Nthumb 158 B7
Cholsey Oxon 41 L3
Cholstrey Herefs 69 J3
Chop Gate N York 142 C7

Choppington Nthumb 159 G5
Chopwell Gatesd 150 E4
Chorley Ches E 98 E3
Chorley Lancs 121 H6
Chorley Shrops 84 C6
Chorleywood Herts 43 H2
Chorleywood West Herts 43 G2
Chorlton Ches E 99 G3
Chorlton-cum-Hardy Manch 113 J3
Chorlton Lane Ches W 98 C3
Choulton Shrops 83 H5
Chrishall Essex 76 C6
Chrisswell Inver 173 L4
Christchurch Cambs 90 C4
Christchurch Dorset 15 M4
Christchurch Newpt 37 M3
Christian Malford Wilts 39 L5
Christon N Som 38 B8
Christon Bank Nthumb 169 J5
Christow Devon 11 J7
Chudleigh Devon 11 K8
Chudleigh Knighton Devon 7 J1
Chulmleigh Devon 11 G3
Church Lancs 121 L5
Churcham Gloucs 55 H4
Church Aston Wrekin 99 H8
Church Brampton Nhants 73 K2
Church Broughton Derbys 100 D5
Church Cove Cnwll 3 J8
Church Crookham Hants 30 D2
Churchdown Gloucs 55 K4
Church Eaton Staffs 99 J8
Church End C Beds 75 H6
Churchend Essex 47 G2
Church End Essex 61 H3
Church End Gt Lon 44 E3
Church Enstone Oxon 57 G3
Church Fenton N York 124 D3
Churchfield Sandw 85 H5
Church Green Devon 12 F3
Church Hanborough Oxon 57 H5
Church Houses N York 142 E7
Churchill Devon 13 H3
Churchill N Som 38 C7
Churchill Oxon 56 F3
Churchill Worcs 71 G4
Churchill Worcs 84 F7
Churchinford Somset 25 K8
Church Knowle Dorset 15 H6
Church Langton Leics 87 K5
Church Lawford Warwks 86 F7
Church Leigh Staffs 100 A5
Church Lench Worcs 71 H4
Church Mayfield Staffs 100 D4
Church Minshull Ches E 98 F1
Church Norton W Susx 18 B6
Churchover Warwks 87 G7
Church Preen Shrops 83 K4
Church Pulverbatch Shrops 83 H3
Churchstanton Somset 25 J8
Churchstoke Powys 82 F5
Churchstow Devon 7 G6
Church Stowe Nhants 73 J3
Church Street Kent 46 B5
Church Stretton Shrops 83 J5
Churchtown Cnwll 5 H1
Churchtown Derbys 114 E8
Churchtown IoM 237 d3
Churchtown Lancs 121 G2
Church Village Rhondd 37 G3
Church Warsop Notts 115 K7
Churston Ferrers Torbay 7 K5
Churt Surrey 30 D4
Churton Ches W 98 B2
Churwell Leeds 123 K5
Chwilog Gwynd 95 G5
Chyandour Cnwll 2 E5
Cilcain Flints 111 G7
Cilcennin Cerdgn 66 C3
Cilfrew Neath 52 B7
Cilfynydd Rhondd 37 G3
Cilgerran Pembks 65 H6
Cilmaengwyn Neath 51 L4
Cilmery Powys 67 L4
Cilsan Carmth 51 H2
Ciltalgarth Gwynd 96 D4
Cilycwm Carmth 67 G6
Cimla Neath 36 B2
Cinderford Gloucs 54 F5
Cinder Hill Wolves 85 G5
Cippenham Slough 42 F4
Cirencester Gloucs 56 A7
City Gt Lon 45 G4
City Airport Gt Lon 45 H4
City of London Crematorium Gt Lon 45 H3
Clabhach Ag & B 188 F5
Clachaig Ag & B 173 J3
Clachan Ag & B 172 C6
Clachan Ag & B 182 A4
Clachan Ag & B 191 G7
Clachan Highld 209 H6
Clachan-a-Luib W Isls 233 c6
Clachan Mor Ag & B 188 C6
Clachan na Luib W Isls 233 c6
Clachan of Campsie E Duns 175 G3
Clachan-Seil Ag & B 181 M4
Clachnaharry Highld 213 G5
Clachtoll Highld 224 C3
Clackavoid P & K 195 J4
Clacket Lane Services Surrey 32 D3
Clackmannan Clacks 185 J8
Clackmannanshire Bridge Fife 176 C2
Clackmarras Moray 214 F3
Clacton-on-Sea Essex 62 E5
Cladich Ag & B 182 F3
Cladswell Worcs 71 J3
Claggan Highld 190 E6
Claigan Highld 208 C4
Clanfield Hants 30 B7
Clanfield Oxon 56 F7
Clanville Hants 28 F2
Clanville Somset 26 F5
Claonaig Ag & B 172 E6
Clapgate Herts 60 C3
Clapham Bed 74 F4
Clapham Gt Lon 44 F5
Clapham N York 130 E5
Clapham W Susx 18 F4
Clapton Somset 13 K2
Clapton Somset 26 F2
Clapton-in-Gordano N Som 38 C5
Clapton-on-the-Hill Gloucs 56 D4
Claravale Gatesd 150 E3
Clarbeston Pembks 49 H3
Clarbeston Road Pembks 49 H4
Clarborough Notts 116 B5
Clare Suffk 77 H5
Clarebrand D & G 146 D2
Clarencefield D & G 147 J2
Clarilaw Border 167 H5
Clarkston E Rens 175 G6
Clashmore Highld 223 G4
Clashmore Highld 224 C3
Clashnessie Highld 224 C3
Clashnoir Moray 204 F2
Clathy P & K 185 K4
Clathymore P & K 185 L3
Clatt Abers 205 L1
Clatter Powys 81 L5
Clatworthy Somset 25 G5
Claughton Lancs 121 G3
Claughton Lancs 130 B6
Claughton Wirral 111 J4
Claverdon Warwks 71 L2
Claverham N Som 38 C6
Clavering Essex 60 D2
Claverley Shrops 84 E5
Claverton BaNES 39 H7
Clawdd-coch V Glam 37 G5
Clawdd-newydd Denbgs 97 G3
Clawton Devon 9 J5
Claxby Lincs 117 J3
Claxton N York 133 L7
Claxton Norfk 93 H3
Claybrooke Magna Leics 86 F5
Clay Coton Nhants 87 H7
Clay Cross Derbys 115 H8
Claydon Oxon 72 F4
Claydon Suffk 78 D5
Claygate D & G 156 D6
Claygate Kent 33 J4
Claygate Surrey 44 D7
Clayhall Gt Lon 45 H3
Clayhanger Devon 24 F6
Clayhidon Devon 25 J7
Clayhill E Susx 21 G2
Clayock Highld 231 H4
Claypits Gloucs 55 H6
Claypole Lincs 102 D3
Clayton C Brad 123 G4
Clayton Donc 124 C8
Clayton W Susx 19 J3
Clayton-le-Moors Lancs 121 L4
Clayton-le-Woods Lancs 121 H6
Clayton West Kirk 123 K7
Clayworth Notts 116 B4
Cleadale Highld 199 G7
Cleadon S Tyne 151 J3
Clearbrook Devon 6 D3
Clearwell Gloucs 54 E6
Cleasby N York 141 G5
Cleat Ork 234 c8
Cleatlam Dur 140 E4
Cleator Cumb 136 D4
Cleator Moor Cumb 136 E4
Cleckheaton Kirk 123 J5
Cleehill Shrops 83 L7
Cleekhimin N Lans 175 K6
Clee St Margaret Shrops 83 L6
Cleethorpes NE Lin 127 H8
Cleeton St Mary Shrops 84 B7
Cleeve N Som 38 C7
Cleeve Oxon 41 L4
Cleeve Hill Gloucs 55 M3
Cleeve Prior Worcs 71 J5
Cleghornie E Loth 178 D2
Clehonger Herefs 69 J6
Cleish P & K 186 A7
Cleland N Lans 175 L6
Clenamacrie Ag & B 182 C2
Clenchwarton Norfk 104 F7
Clenerty Abers 216 E3
Clent Worcs 85 G7
Cleobury Mortimer Shrops 84 C7
Cleobury North Shrops 84 B6
Cleongart Ag & B 161 H3
Clephanton Highld 213 J4
Clerkhill D & G 156 A3
Cleuch-head D & G 154 E3
Clevancy Wilts 40 B5
Clevedon N Som 38 B6
Cleveleys Lancs 120 D2
Cleverton Wilts 39 L4
Clewer Somset 26 C2
Cley next the Sea Norfk 106 C4
Cliburn Cumb 138 E3
Cliddesden Hants 29 M2
Cliffe Medway 46 C5
Cliffe N York 125 G4
Cliff End E Susx 21 H3
Cliffe Woods Medway 46 C5
Clifford Herefs 68 E5
Clifford Leeds 124 C2
Clifford Chambers Warwks 71 L4
Clifford's Mesne Gloucs 55 G4
Clifton Bristl 38 E5
Clifton C Beds 75 H6
Clifton C Nott 101 K5
Clifton C York 133 J8
Clifton Calder 123 H6
Clifton Cumb 138 D2
Clifton Derbys 100 D4
Clifton Devon 23 J3
Clifton Donc 115 K3
Clifton Lancs 120 F4
Clifton N York 123 J2
Clifton Oxon 57 J2
Clifton Worcs 70 F5
Clifton Campville Staffs 86 B2
Clifton Hampden Oxon 41 K2
Clifton Reynes M Keyn 74 C4
Clifton upon Dunsmore Warwks 87 G7
Clifton upon Teme Worcs 70 C3
Cliftonville Kent 35 K1
Climping W Susx 18 D5
Clink Somset 27 H2
Clint N York 132 D7
Clinterty C Aber 206 F3
Clint Green Norfk 92 B2
Clintmains Border 167 J3
Clippesby Norfk 93 J2
Clipsham Rutlnd 88 D1
Clipston Nhants 87 K7
Clipston Notts 101 M5
Clipstone C Beds 58 F3
Clipstone Notts 115 L8
Clitheroe Lancs 121 L3
Clive Shrops 98 D7
Cliveden Bucks 42 E4
Clixby Lincs 117 J2
Cloatley Wilts 39 M3
Clocaenog Denbgs 97 G2
Clochan Moray 215 J3
Clodock Herefs 53 L3
Clola Abers 217 J5
Clophill C Beds 74 F6
Clopton Nhants 88 F7
Clopton Suffk 78 F4
Clopton Corner Suffk 78 F4
Clos du Valle Guern 236 d2
Closeburn D & G 154 F4
Closeburnmill D & G 154 F3
Closworth Somset 14 B1
Clothall Herts 59 L2
Clotton Ches W 112 D8
Clough Foot Calder 122 D5
Clough Head Calder 123 G6
Cloughton N York 143 K7
Clousta Shet 235 c5
Clova Angus 196 B2
Clovelly Devon 22 E6
Clovenfords Border 167 G3
Clovulin Highld 191 K4
Clowne Derbys 115 J6
Clows Top Worcs 70 C1
Cluanie Inn Highld 201 G3
Cluanie Lodge Highld 201 G3
Clugston D & G 145 H4
Clun Shrops 82 F7
Clunas Highld 213 K5
Clunbury Shrops 83 G7
Clunderwen Carmth 49 J4

Clune Highld 203 J1
Clunes Highld 201 J7
Clungunford Shrops 83 H7
Clunie P & K 195 H7
Clunton Shrops 83 G7
Cluny Fife 186 D7
Clutton BaNES 38 F8
Clutton Ches W 98 C2
Clutton Hill BaNES 38 F8
Clydach Mons 53 K5
Clydach Swans 51 K5
Clydach Vale Rhondd 36 F2
Clydebank W Duns 174 F4
Clydebank Crematorium W Duns 174 E4
Clyffe Pypard Wilts 40 B5
Clynder Ag & B 174 A2
Clyne Neath 52 C7
Clynnog-fawr Gwynd 95 G3
Clyro Powys 68 E5
Clyst Honiton Devon 12 C4
Clyst Hydon Devon 12 D3
Clyst St George Devon 12 C5
Clyst St Lawrence Devon 12 D3
Clyst St Mary Devon 12 C4
Cnoc W Isls 232 g2
Cnwch Coch Cerdgn 80 F8
Coad's Green Cnwll 5 L1
Coalburn S Lans 164 F3
Coalburns Gatesd 150 E3
Coaley Gloucs 55 H7
Coalhill Essex 61 J7
Coalpit Heath S Glos 38 F4
Coal Pool Wsall 85 H4
Coalport Wrekin 84 C3
Coalsnaughton Clacks 185 J7
Coaltown of Balgonie Fife 186 E7
Coaltown of Wemyss Fife 186 E7
Coalville Leics 86 E2
Coanwood Nthumb 149 H3
Coat Somset 26 C7
Coatbridge N Lans 175 J5
Coatdyke N Lans 175 K5
Coate Swindn 40 D4
Coate Wilts 40 B7
Coates Cambs 89 K4
Coates Gloucs 55 L7
Coates Lincs 116 E5
Coates W Susx 18 D3
Cobbaton Devon 23 K6
Coberley Gloucs 55 L5
Cobham Kent 46 A6
Cobham Surrey 43 J7
Cobham Services Surrey 43 J8
Cobnash Herefs 69 J3
Cobo Guern 236 c2
Cobridge C Stke 99 K3
Coburby Abers 217 H2
Cockayne Hatley C Beds 75 J5
Cock Bridge Abers 205 G4
Cockburnspath Border 179 G4
Cock Clarks Essex 61 K7
Cockenzie and Port Seton E Loth 177 L4
Cockerham Lancs 120 F1
Cockermouth Cumb 136 F2
Cockernhoe Herts 59 J4
Cockett Swans 51 J6
Cockfield Dur 140 E3
Cockfield Suffk 77 K4
Cockfosters Gt Lon 44 F2
Cock Green Essex 61 H4
Cocking W Susx 18 B3
Cocking Causeway W Susx 18 B2
Cockington Torbay 7 K3
Cocklake Somset 26 C2
Cockley Cley Norfk 91 H3
Cock Marling E Susx 21 H2
Cockpole Green Wokham 42 D4
Cockshutt Shrops 98 B6
Cockthorpe Norfk 106 B4
Cockwood Devon 12 C6
Cockyard Derbys 114 B5
Coddenham Suffk 78 D4
Coddington Herefs 70 C6
Coddington Notts 102 D2
Codford St Mary Wilts 27 L4
Codford St Peter Wilts 27 L4
Codicote Herts 59 K4
Codmore Hill W Susx 31 H7
Codnor Derbys 101 H3
Codrington S Glos 39 G5
Codsall Staffs 84 F3
Codsall Wood Staffs 84 F3
Coedpoeth Wrexhm 97 L3
Coed Talon Flints 97 L2
Coed-y-paen Mons 53 M7
Coffinswell Devon 7 K3
Cofton Devon 12 C6
Cofton Hackett Worcs 85 H7
Cogan V Glam 37 J6
Cogenhoe Nhants 74 B3
Cogges Oxon 57 G6
Coggeshall Essex 61 K4
Coignafearn Highld 203 H2
Coilacriech Abers 205 H6
Coilantogle Stirlg 184 D6
Coillore Highld 208 E6
Coity Brdgnd 36 E4
Col W Isls 232 g2
Colaboll Highld 225 L6
Colan Cnwll 4 D4
Colaton Raleigh Devon 12 D5
Colbost Highld 208 C5
Colburn N York 140 F7
Colby Cumb 138 F3
Colby IoM 237 b6
Colchester Essex 62 B3
Colchester Crematorium Essex 62 B4
Colchester Zoo Essex 62 A4
Cold Ash W Berk 41 K6
Cold Ashby Nhants 87 J7
Cold Ashton S Glos 39 H6
Cold Aston Gloucs 56 C4
Coldbackie Highld 229 J4
Cold Brayfield M Keyn 74 D4
Coldean Br & H 19 J4
Coldeast Devon 7 J2
Colden Calder 122 E5
Colden Common Hants 29 J6
Cold Hanworth Lincs 117 G5
Coldharbour Surrey 31 J3
Cold Higham Nhants 73 J4
Coldingham Border 179 J5
Cold Kirby N York 133 H3
Coldmeece Staffs 99 J6
Cold Norton Essex 61 K7
Cold Overton Leics 88 B2
Coldred Kent 35 H5
Coldridge Devon 11 G4
Coldstream Border 168 C2
Coldwaltham W Susx 18 D3
Coldwell Herefs 69 H7
Coldwells Abers 217 H6
Cole Somset 26 F5
Colebatch Shrops 83 G6
Colebrook Devon 12 C2
Colebrooke Devon 11 H5
Coleby Lincs 102 F1
Coleby N Linc 125 L6
Coleford Devon 11 H5
Coleford Gloucs 54 E6
Coleford Somset 27 G2
Colegate End Norfk 92 E6
Colehill Dorset 15 J3
Coleman's Hatch E Susx 32 D6
Colemere Shrops 98 B6
Colemore Hants 30 B5
Colenden P & K 186 B2
Colerne Wilts 39 J6
Colesbourne Gloucs 56 A5
Coleshill Bucks 42 F2
Coleshill Oxon 40 E2
Coleshill Warwks 85 L5
Coley BaNES 26 E1
Colgate W Susx 31 L5
Colinsburgh Fife 187 H6
Colinton C Edin 177 H5
Colintraive Ag & B 173 H4
Colkirk Norfk 105 L7
Coll Ag & B 189 G5
Coll W Isls 232 g2
Collace P & K 186 C2
Collafirth Shet 235 c3
Coll Airport Ag & B 188 F5
Collaton Devon 7 G7
Collaton St Mary Torbay 7 K4
College of Roseisle Moray 214 E2
College Town Br For 42 D7
Collessie Fife 186 E5
Collier Row Gt Lon 45 J2
Collier's End Herts 60 B4
Collier Street Kent 33 J4
Collieston Abers 217 K8
Collin D & G 155 H6
Collingbourne Ducis Wilts 28 E2
Collingbourne Kingston Wilts 28 E1
Collingham Leeds 124 B2
Collingham Notts 102 D1
Collington Herefs 70 B3
Collingtree Nhants 73 L4
Collins Green Warrtn 112 E3
Colliston Angus 196 F7
Colliton Devon 12 E2
Collyweston Nhants 88 E3
Colmonell S Ayrs 152 D5
Colmworth Bed 75 G3
Colnabaichin Abers 205 G4
Colnbrook Slough 43 G5
Colne Cambs 89 L7
Colne Lancs 122 D3
Colne Engaine Essex 61 K3
Colney Norfk 92 E3
Colney Heath Herts 59 K6
Coln Rogers Gloucs 56 B6
Coln St Aldwyns Gloucs 56 C6
Coln St Dennis Gloucs 56 B5
Colonsay Ag & B 180 E7
Colonsay Airport Ag & B 180 E8
Colpy Abers 216 C7
Colquhar Border 166 E2
Colsterworth Lincs 102 F7
Colston Bassett Notts 102 B5
Coltfield Moray 214 D2
Coltishall Norfk 106 F8
Colton Cumb 129 G3
Colton Leeds 124 B4
Colton N York 124 E2
Colton Norfk 92 D2
Colton Staffs 100 B7
Colt's Hill Kent 33 H4
Colvend D & G 146 F4
Colwall Herefs 70 D6
Colwell Nthumb 158 B6
Colwich Staffs 100 A7
Colwinston V Glam 36 E5
Colworth W Susx 18 C5
Colwyn Bay Conwy 110 B5
Colwyn Bay Crematorium Conwy 110 A5
Colyford Devon 13 G4
Colyton Devon 13 G4
Combe Oxon 57 H5
Combe W Berk 41 G7
Combe Down BaNES 39 H7
Combe Fishacre Devon 7 J3
Combe Florey Somset 25 J5
Combe Hay BaNES 39 G7
Combeinteignhead Devon 7 K2
Combe Martin Devon 23 J3
Combe Raleigh Devon 12 F3
Comberbach Ches W 112 F6
Comberford Staffs 85 L3
Comberton Cambs 75 L4
Comberton Herefs 69 K2
Combe St Nicholas Somset 13 H1
Combrook Warwks 72 C4
Combs Derbys 114 B6
Combs Suffk 78 C3
Combs Ford Suffk 78 C3
Combwich Somset 25 K3
Comers Abers 206 D4
Comhampton Worcs 70 E2
Commins Coch Powys 81 J3
Commondale N York 142 E5
Common End Cumb 136 D3
Common Moor Cnwll 5 K2
Compstall Stockp 113 L4
Compstonend D & G 146 B4
Compton Devon 7 K3
Compton Hants 29 J6
Compton Staffs 84 E6
Compton Surrey 30 F3
Compton W Berk 41 K4
Compton W Susx 30 C7
Compton Wilts 28 C2
Compton Abbas Dorset 27 K7
Compton Abdale Gloucs 56 B5
Compton Bassett Wilts 40 B6
Compton Beauchamp Oxon 40 F3
Compton Bishop Somset 26 B1
Compton Chamberlayne Wilts 28 B5
Compton Dando BaNES 38 F7
Compton Dundon Somset 26 C5
Compton Durville Somset 26 B7
Compton Greenfield S Glos 38 E4
Compton Martin BaNES 38 D8
Compton Pauncefoot Somset 26 F6
Compton Valence Dorset 14 B4
Comrie Fife 176 D1
Comrie P & K 185 G3
Conaglen House Highld 191 K3
Conchra Highld 210 D8
Concraigie P & K 195 H7
Conderton Worcs 71 G6
Condicote Gloucs 56 D3
Condorrat N Lans 175 K4
Condover Shrops 83 J3
Coney Hill Gloucs 55 J4
Coneyhurst Common W Susx 31 J6
Coneysthorpe N York 133 L5
Coney Weston Suffk 91 L7
Congerstone Leics 86 D3
Congham Norfk 105 H7
Congleton Ches E 113 J8
Congresbury N Som 38 C7
Conheath D & G 147 H2
Conicavel Moray 214 B4
Coningsby Lincs 103 L2
Conington Cambs 75 K2
Conington Cambs 89 H6
Conisbrough Donc 115 K2
Conisholme Lincs 118 E3

Coniston Cumb 137 J7
Coniston E R Yk 126 E4
Coniston Cold N York 131 G8
Conistone N York 131 J6
Connah's Quay Flints 111 J7
Connel Ag & B 182 C1
Connel Park E Ayrs 164 C6
Connor Downs Cnwll 3 G4
Conon Bridge Highld 212 E4
Cononley N York 122 E2
Consall Staffs 99 M3
Consett Dur 150 E5
Constable Burton N York 132 B2
Constable Lee Lancs 122 B5
Constantine Cnwll 3 J5
Constantine Bay Cnwll 4 D2
Contin Highld 212 C3
Conwy Conwy 109 L6
Conwy Castle Conwy 109 L6
Conyer's Green Suffk 77 K2
Cooden E Susx 20 E4
Cookbury Devon 9 K4
Cookham W & M 42 E4
Cookham Dean W & M 42 E4
Cookham Rise W & M 42 E4
Cookhill Worcs 71 J3
Cookley Suffk 93 H7
Cookley Worcs 84 E7
Cookley Green Oxon 42 B3
Cookney Abers 207 G6
Cook's Green Essex 62 E4
Cooks Green Suffk 77 L4
Cooksmill Green Essex 61 G6
Coolham W Susx 31 J6
Cooling Medway 46 C5
Coombe Cnwll 4 E5
Coombe Devon 7 L2
Coombe Devon 12 E4
Coombe Gloucs 39 H2
Coombe Hants 30 A7
Coombe Abbey Warwks 86 E7
Coombe Bissett Wilts 28 C6
Coombe Cellars Devon 7 K2
Coombe Hill Gloucs 55 K3
Coombe Keynes Dorset 14 F5
Coombe Pafford Torbay 7 L3
Coombes W Susx 19 G4
Coombes-Moor Herefs 69 G2
Coombeswood Dudley 85 H6
Coopersale Common Essex 60 D7
Copdock Suffk 78 D6
Copford Green Essex 61 L4
Copgrove N York 132 E6
Copister Shet 235 d3
Cople Bed 75 G5
Copley Dur 140 D3
Copmanthorpe C York 124 E2
Copmere End Staffs 99 J6
Copp Lancs 120 F3
Coppenhall Staffs 99 K8
Copperhouse Cnwll 2 F4
Coppingford Cambs 89 H7
Copplestone Devon 11 H4
Coppull Lancs 121 H7
Copsale W Susx 31 K6
Copster Green Lancs 121 K4
Copston Magna Warwks 86 F5
Cop Street Kent 35 J3
Copt Hewick N York 132 E5
Copthorne W Susx 32 B5
Copt Oak Leics 86 F2
Copythorne Hants 28 F8
Corbets Tey Gt Lon 45 K3
Corbière Jersey 236 a7
Corbridge Nthumb 150 C3
Corby Nhants 88 C5
Corby Glen Lincs 103 G7
Cordon N Ayrs 162 D4
Coreley Shrops 84 B8
Corfe Somset 25 K7
Corfe Castle Dorset 15 H6
Corfton Shrops 83 J6
Corgarff Abers 205 G4
Corhampton Hants 29 L7
Corley Warwks 86 C6
Corley Services Warwks 86 C6
Cormuir Angus 195 L3
Cornard Tye Suffk 77 K6
Cornforth Dur 151 H7
Cornhill Abers 216 B3
Cornhill-on-Tweed Nthumb 168 C2
Cornholme Calder 122 D5
Cornoigmore Ag & B 188 C6
Cornsay Dur 150 E6
Cornsay Colliery Dur 150 F6
Corntown Highld 212 E3
Corntown V Glam 36 E5
Cornwall Airport Newquay Cnwll 4 D3
Cornwell Oxon 56 F3
Cornwood Devon 6 E4
Cornworthy Devon 7 J5
Corpach Highld 191 L2
Corpusty Norfk 106 D6
Corrachree Abers 205 K4
Corran Highld 191 K4
Corran Highld 200 C4
Corrie D & G 155 L5
Corrie N Ayrs 162 C2
Corriecravie N Ayrs 162 B5
Corriegills N Ayrs 162 D3
Corriegour Lodge Hotel Highld 201 K6
Corriemoille Highld 212 B2
Corrimony Highld 212 B7
Corringham Lincs 116 E4
Corringham Thurr 46 B4
Corris Gwynd 81 G2
Corris Uchaf Gwynd 81 G2
Corrow Ag & B 183 H7
Corry Highld 199 K1
Corscombe Devon 10 F5
Corscombe Dorset 13 M2
Corse Gloucs 55 H3
Corse Lawn Gloucs 55 J2
Corsham Wilts 39 K6
Corsindae Abers 206 D4
Corsley Wilts 27 J3
Corsley Heath Wilts 27 J3
Corsock D & G 154 D6
Corston BaNES 39 G7
Corston Wilts 39 L4
Corstorphine C Edin 177 G4
Cortachy Angus 196 C4
Corton Suffk 93 L4
Corton Wilts 27 L4
Corton Denham Somset 26 F6
Coruanan Highld 191 L3
Corwen Denbgs 97 G4
Coryton Devon 10 C7
Coryton Thurr 46 C4
Cosby Leics 87 G4
Coseley Dudley 85 G5
Cosgrove Nhants 73 L6
Cosham C Port 17 J2
Cosheston Pembks 49 G6
Coshieville P & K 194 C6
Cossall Notts 101 J4
Cossington Leics 87 H2
Cossington Somset 26 A4
Costessey Norfk 92 E2
Costock Notts 101 L7
Coston Leics 102 D7
Coston Norfk 92 C3
Cote Oxon 57 G7
Cotebrook Ches W 112 E7
Cotehill Cumb 148 E5
Cotes Leics 101 K7
Cotesbach Leics 87 G6
Cotford St Luke Somset 25 J6
Cotgrave Notts 101 M5
Cothal Abers 207 G3
Cotham Notts 102 C3
Cotherstone Dur 140 C4
Cothill Oxon 57 J7
Cotleigh Devon 13 G3
Cotmanhay Derbys 101 J4
Coton Cambs 76 B3
Coton Nhants 73 J1
Coton Staffs 99 J7
Coton Clanford Staffs 99 K7
Coton Hill Shrops 83 J2
Coton in the Elms Derbys 86 B1
Cotswolds 55 M6
Cotswold Wildlife Park & Gardens Oxon 56 E6
Cott Devon 7 H4
Cottam Lancs 121 G4
Cottam Notts 116 D5
Cottenham Cambs 76 C2
Cottered Herts 60 A3
Cotteridge Birm 85 J7
Cotterstock Nhants 88 F5
Cottesbrooke Nhants 87 K8
Cottesmore Rutlnd 88 C2
Cottingham E R Yk 126 C4
Cottingham Nhants 88 B5
Cottingley C Brad 123 G3
Cottingley Hall Crematorium Leeds 123 K4
Cottisford Oxon 57 L2
Cotton Suffk 78 C2
Cottown Abers 206 E3
Cottown Abers 215 L8
Cottown of Gight Abers 216 F6
Cotts Devon 6 C3
Coughton Warwks 71 J3
Coulaghailtro Ag & B 172 C5
Coulags Highld 210 E5
Coull Abers 205 L5
Coulport Ag & B 173 L2
Coulsdon Gt Lon 32 B2
Coulston Wilts 27 L2
Coulter S Lans 165 K3
Coulton N York 133 K5
Coultra Fife 186 F3
Cound Shrops 83 L3
Coundon Dur 141 G2
Countersett N York 131 H2
Countess Wear Devon 12 B4
Countesthorpe Leics 87 H4
Counties Crematorium Nhants 73 K3
Countisbury Devon 24 B2
Coupar Angus P & K 195 K7
Coupland Nthumb 168 D3
Cour Ag & B 172 D8
Courteachan Highld 199 L6
Courteenhall Nhants 73 L4
Court Henry Carmth 51 H2
Courtsend Essex 47 G2
Courtway Somset 25 J5
Cousland Mdloth 177 K5
Cousley Wood E Susx 33 H6
Cove Ag & B 173 L2
Cove Border 179 G4
Cove Devon 24 E7
Cove Hants 30 E1
Cove Highld 219 J3
Cove Bay C Aber 207 H5
Covehithe Suffk 93 L6
Coven Staffs 85 G3
Coveney Cambs 90 C6
Covenham St Bartholomew Lincs 118 D3
Covenham St Mary Lincs 118 D3
Coventry Covtry 86 D7
Coventry Airport Warwks 86 D8
Coverack Cnwll 3 K7
Coverack Bridges Cnwll 3 H5
Coverham N York 131 L3
Covington Cambs 74 F1
Covington S Lans 165 J2
Cowan Bridge Lancs 130 C4
Cowbeech E Susx 20 C3
Cowbit Lincs 103 L8
Cowbridge V Glam 36 F5
Cowden Kent 32 E5
Cowdenbeath Fife 177 G1
Cowers Lane Derbys 100 F3
Cowes IoW 16 F3
Cowesby N York 133 G2
Cowfold W Susx 31 K6
Cowhill S Glos 38 E3
Cowie Stirlg 175 L1
Cowley Devon 11 K5
Cowley Gloucs 55 L5
Cowley Gt Lon 43 H4
Cowley Oxon 57 K7
Cowling Lancs 121 H6
Cowling N York 122 E2
Cowling N York 132 C3
Cowlinge Suffk 77 G4
Cowpen Nthumb 159 H5
Cowplain Hants 17 K1
Cowshill Dur 149 L6
Cowslip Green N Som 38 C7
Cowthorpe N York 132 F8
Coxbank Ches E 98 F4
Coxbench Derbys 101 G4
Coxford Cnwll 8 F5
Coxford Norfk 105 K6
Coxheath Kent 33 J3
Coxhoe Dur 151 H7
Coxley Somset 26 D3
Coxley Wick Somset 26 D3
Coxtie Green Essex 45 K2
Coxwold N York 133 H4
Coychurch Brdgnd 36 E4
Coychurch Crematorium Brdgnd 36 E4
Coylton S Ayrs 163 K5
Coylumbridge Highld 203 L3
Coytrahen Brdgnd 36 D4
Crabbs Cross Worcs 71 J2
Crabtree W Susx 31 K6
Crackenthorpe Cumb 138 F3
Crackington Haven Cnwll 8 F5
Crackley Staffs 99 J3
Crackley Warwks 86 C8
Crackleybank Shrops 84 D2
Cracoe N York 131 J7
Craddock Devon 25 G8
Cradley Dudley 85 G6
Cradley Herefs 70 D5
Cradley Heath Sandw 85 G6
Cradoc Powys 52 F2
Crafthole Cnwll 6 B5
Craggan Highld 204 C1
Craghead Dur 150 F5
Cragside House & Garden Nthumb 158 D2
Crai Powys 52 D3
Craibstone Moray 215 L3
Craichie Angus 196 E6
Craig Angus 197 H5
Craig Highld 211 G4
Craigbank E Ayrs 164 C6
Craigburn Border 177 H7
Craigcleuch D & G 156 C5
Craigdam Abers 216 F7
Craigdhu Ag & B 182 B6
Craigearn Abers 206 D3
Craigellachie Moray 215 G5
Craigend P & K 186 B4
Craigend Rens 174 E4
Craigendoran Ag & B 174 C3
Craigends Rens 174 D5
Craighlaw D & G 145 G3

Craighouse Ag & B 171 K5
Craigie P & K 195 H7
Craigie S Ayrs 163 K3
Craigiefold Abers 217 H2
Craigley D & G 146 D4
Craig Llangiwg Neath 51 K4
Craiglockhart C Edin 177 H4
Craigmillar C Edin 177 J4
Craigneston D & G 154 D5
Craigneuk N Lans 175 K5
Craigneuk N Lans 175 K6
Craignure Ag & B 190 E8
Craigo Angus 197 H4
Craigrothie Fife 186 F5
Craigruie Stirlg 184 B4
Craigton Angus 196 E8
Craigton C Aber 206 F5
Craigton E Rens 174 F7
Craigton Crematorium C Glas 174 F5
Craigton of Airlie Angus 196 B6
Crail Fife 187 K5
Crailing Border 167 L4
Craiselound N Linc 116 C2
Crakehall N York 132 C2
Crambe N York 133 L6
Cramlington Nthumb 159 G6
Cramond C Edin 177 G3
Cramond Bridge C Edin 177 G4
Cranage Ches E 113 H7
Cranberry Staffs 99 J5
Cranborne Dorset 28 B8
Cranbourne Br For 42 F5
Cranbrook Devon 12 C4
Cranbrook Kent 33 K6
Cranfield C Beds 74 D6
Cranford Gt Lon 43 J5
Cranford St Andrew Nhants 88 D7
Cranford St John Nhants 88 D7
Cranham Gloucs 55 K5
Crank St Hel 112 D2
Cranleigh Surrey 31 H4
Cranmore Somset 26 F3
Cranoe Leics 87 L4
Cransford Suffk 79 G2
Cranshaws Border 178 E6
Crantock Cnwll 4 C4
Cranwell Lincs 103 G3
Cranwich Norfk 91 H4
Cranworth Norfk 92 B3
Craobh Haven Ag & B 182 A6
Crarae Ag & B 182 E7
Crask Inn Highld 225 L4
Crask of Aigas Highld 212 D6
Craster Nthumb 169 K5
Cratfield Suffk 93 G7
Crathes Abers 206 E6
Crathes Crematorium Abers 206 E6
Crathie Abers 205 G6
Crathie Highld 202 E6
Crathorne N York 141 K5
Craven Arms Shrops 83 H6
Crawcrook Gatesd 150 E3
Crawford S Lans 165 J5
Crawfordjohn S Lans 165 G5
Crawley Hants 29 H4
Crawley Oxon 57 G5
Crawley W Susx 31 L4
Crawley Down W Susx 32 C5
Crawton Abers 197 L1
Cray N York 131 H4
Crayford Gt Lon 45 K5
Crayke N York 133 H5
Crays Hill Essex 46 B2
Creacombe Devon 24 C7
Creagan Inn Ag & B 191 J7
Creag Ghoraidh W Isls 233 c7
Creagorry W Isls 233 c7
Creaguaineach Lodge Highld 192 E3
Creaton Nhants 73 K1
Creca D & G 155 M7
Credenhill Herefs 69 J5
Crediton Devon 11 J5
Creebank D & G 153 H6
Creebridge D & G 145 J2
Creech Heathfield Somset 25 L6
Creech St Michael Somset 25 L6
Creed Cnwll 4 E6
Creekmouth Gt Lon 45 J4
Creeting St Mary Suffk 78 D3
Creeton Lincs 103 G8
Creetown D & G 145 K3
Cregneash IoM 237 a7
Creich Fife 186 E3
Creigiau Cardif 37 G4
Cremyll Cnwll 6 C5
Cressage Shrops 83 L3
Cressbrook Derbys 114 D6
Cresselly Pembks 49 H6
Cressex Bucks 42 D3
Cressing Essex 61 J4
Cresswell Nthumb 159 H4
Cresswell Pembks 49 H6
Cresswell Staffs 99 L5
Creswell Derbys 115 K6
Cretingham Suffk 78 F3
Cretshengan Ag & B 172 C5
Crewe Ches E 99 G2
Crewe-by-Farndon Ches W 98 B2
Crewe Crematorium Ches E 99 G2
Crewe Green Ches E 99 G2
Crew Green Powys 83 G1
Crewkerne Somset 13 K1
Crewton C Derb 101 G5
Crianlarich Stirlg 183 L3
Cribyn Cerdgn 66 C4
Criccieth Gwynd 95 J5
Crich Derbys 101 G2
Crichton Mdloth 177 K6
Crick Nhants 87 H8
Crickadarn Powys 68 C6
Cricket St Thomas Somset 13 J2
Crickhowell Powys 53 K4
Cricklade Wilts 40 C2
Cricklewood Gt Lon 44 E3
Crieff P & K 185 H3
Criggion Powys 82 F1
Crigglestone Wakefd 123 L7
Crimond Abers 217 K3
Crimplesham Norfk 90 F3
Crimscote Warwks 72 B5
Crinaglack Highld 212 C6
Crinan Ag & B 182 A8
Crindledyke N Lans 175 L6
Cringleford Norfk 92 E3
Crinow Pembks 49 J5
Croachy Highld 213 G8
Crockenhill Kent 45 J6
Crocker End Oxon 42 B3
Crockernwell Devon 11 H6
Crockerton Wilts 27 K3
Crocketford D & G 154 E7
Crockham Hill Kent 32 D3
Croeserw Neath 36 D2
Croes-goch Pembks 48 D2
Croes-lan Cerdgn 65 L5
Croesor Gwynd 95 L4
Croesyceiliog Carmth 50 E3
Croesyceiliog Torfn 37 L2
Croft Leics 87 G4
Croft Lincs 104 E1
Croft Warrtn 112 F3
Croftamie Stirlg 174 E2
Crofton Wakefd 124 B6
Croft-on-Tees N York 141 H5
Croftown Highld 220 F5
Crofts Moray 215 G4
Crofts of Dipple Moray 215 H3
Crofts of Savoch Abers 217 K3
Crofty Swans 51 G6
Croggan Ag & B 181 L3
Croglin Cumb 148 F5
Croick Highld 222 B3
Cromarty Highld 223 H7
Crombie Fife 176 E2
Cromdale Highld 214 D8
Cromer Herts 59 M3
Cromer Norfk 106 F4
Cromford Derbys 100 F2
Cromhall S Glos 39 G3
Cromor W Isls 232 f3
Cromwell Notts 102 D1
Cronberry E Ayrs 164 C5
Crondall Hants 30 C2
Cronton Knows 112 C4
Crook Cumb 138 C7
Crook Dur 150 E7
Crookedholm E Ayrs 163 L3
Crookham Nthumb 168 D2
Crookham W Berk 41 K7
Crookham Village Hants 30 C2
Crook Inn Border 165 L4
Crooklands Cumb 129 L3
Crook of Devon P & K 185 L7
Cropredy Oxon 72 F5
Cropston Leics 87 G2
Cropthorne Worcs 71 H5
Cropton N York 134 B2
Cropwell Bishop Notts 102 B5
Cropwell Butler Notts 102 B5
Cros W Isls 232 g1
Crosbost W Isls 232 f3
Crosby Cumb 147 J7
Crosby IoM 237 c5
Crosby N Linc 125 K7
Crosby Sefton 111 J2
Crosby Garret Cumb 139 G5
Crosby Ravensworth Cumb 138 F4
Croscombe Somset 26 E3
Cross Somset 26 B1
Crossaig Ag & B 172 E7
Crossapol Ag & B 188 C7
Cross Ash Mons 54 B4
Cross-at-Hand Kent 33 K4
Crosscanonby Cumb 147 J6
Crossdale Street Norfk 106 F5
Cross Flatts C Brad 123 G3
Crossford Fife 176 E2
Crossford S Lans 175 L8
Crossgatehall E Loth 177 K5
Crossgates E Ayrs 163 J1
Crossgates Fife 176 F1
Cross Gates Leeds 124 B4
Crossgates N York 134 F3
Crossgill Lancs 129 L6
Cross Green Leeds 123 L4
Cross Green Suffk 77 K4
Cross Green Suffk 78 B4
Cross Hands Carmth 51 H3
Crosshands E Ayrs 163 L4
Crosshill Fife 186 C7
Crosshill S Ayrs 163 J7
Crosshouse E Ayrs 163 K2
Cross Houses Shrops 83 K3
Cross in Hand E Susx 20 B2
Cross Inn Cerdgn 65 L3
Cross Keys Ag & B 174 C2
Crosskeys Caerph 37 K3
Crosskirk Highld 230 F2
Cross Lane IoW 17 G4
Cross Lane Head Shrops 84 C4
Crosslee Rens 174 D5
Crossmichael D & G 146 C2
Cross of Jackston Abers 216 E7
Cross o' th' hands Derbys 100 F4
Crossroads Abers 206 B4
Crossroads Abers 206 E6
Cross Street Suffk 92 E7
Crosston Angus 196 E5
Cross Town Ches E 113 H5
Crossway Green Worcs 70 E2
Crossways Dorset 14 E5
Crosswell Pembks 64 F6
Crosthwaite Cumb 129 J2
Croston Lancs 121 G6
Crostwick Norfk 92 F1
Crouch End Gt Lon 44 F3
Croucheston Wilts 28 B6
Crouch Hill Dorset 14 D1
Croughton Nhants 73 G7
Crovie Abers 216 F2
Crowan Cnwll 3 H4
Crowborough E Susx 32 F6
Crowcombe Somset 25 H4
Crowdecote Derbys 114 C7
Crowden Derbys 114 B2
Crow Edge Barns 114 D2
Crowell Oxon 58 C7
Crowfield Suffk 78 D3
Crowhill E Loth 178 F4
Crow Hill Herefs 54 F3
Crowhurst E Susx 20 F3
Crowhurst Surrey 32 D4
Crowland Lincs 89 J2
Crowland Suffk 78 B1
Crowlas Cnwll 2 F5
Crowle N Linc 125 J7
Crowle Worcs 71 G4
Crowle Green Worcs 71 G3
Crowmarsh Gifford Oxon 41 L3
Crown Corner Suffk 78 F1
Crownhill C Plym 6 C4
Crownhill Crematorium M Keyn 74 B6
Crownthorpe Norfk 92 C3
Crowntown Cnwll 3 H5
Crows-an-Wra Cnwll 2 D5
Crowthorne Wokham 42 D7
Crowton Ches W 112 E6
Croxdale Dur 151 G7
Croxden Staffs 100 B5
Croxley Green Herts 43 H2
Croxteth Lpool 111 L3
Croxton Cambs 75 J3
Croxton N Linc 126 D7
Croxton Norfk 91 K6
Croxton Norfk 106 B6
Croxton Staffs 99 H6
Croxton Kerrial Leics 102 D6
Croy Highld 213 J4
Croy N Lans 175 J3
Croyde Devon 23 G4
Croydon Cambs 75 K5
Croydon Gt Lon 44 F6
Croydon Crematorium Gt Lon 44 F6
Crubenmore Highld 203 G7
Cruckmeole Shrops 83 H2
Cruckton Shrops 83 H2
Cruden Bay Abers 217 K6
Crudgington Wrekin 98 F8
Crudwell Wilts 39 L2
Crumlin Caerph 37 K2
Crumplehorn Cnwll 5 K5
Crumpsall Manch 113 J2
Crundale Kent 34 E5
Crunwear Pembks 49 K5
Crux Easton Hants 29 H1
Crwbin Carmth 50 F3
Cryers Hill Bucks 42 E2
Crymych Pembks 65 G7
Crynant Neath 52 C6
Crystal Palace Gt Lon 45 G5
Cuaig Highld 209 L3
Cuan Ag & B 181 L4
Cubert Cnwll 4 C4
Cublington Bucks 58 D4
Cublington Herefs 69 H6

Cuckfield W Susx 32 B7
Cucklington Somset 27 H6
Cuckney Notts 115 K7
Cuddesdon Oxon 57 L7
Cuddington Bucks 58 C5
Cuddington Ches W 112 E7
Cuddington Heath Ches W 98 C3
Cudham Gt Lon 32 D2
Cudliptown Devon 10 D8
Cudnell Bmouth 15 K3
Cudworth Barns 124 B8
Cudworth Somset 13 J1
Cuffley Herts 59 M7
Cuil Highld 191 J5
Culbokie Highld 212 F3
Culburnie Highld 212 D6
Culcabock Highld 213 G5
Culcharry Highld 213 K4
Culcheth Warrtn 112 F3
Culdrain Abers 215 L7
Culduie Highld 209 L6
Culford Suffk 77 J1
Culgaith Cumb 138 E2
Culham Oxon 41 J2
Culkein Highld 224 C2
Culkein Drumbeg Highld 224 D2
Culkerton Gloucs 39 L2
Cullen Moray 215 L2
Cullercoats N Tyne 159 J7
Cullerlie Abers 206 E5
Cullicudden Highld 213 G2
Cullingworth C Brad 123 G3
Cuillin Hills Highld 199 G2
Cullipool Ag & B 181 L5
Cullivoe Shet 235 d2
Culloden Highld 213 H5
Cullompton Devon 12 C2
Cullompton Services Devon 12 D2
Culm Davy Devon 25 H7
Culmington Shrops 83 J6
Culmstock Devon 25 H8
Culnacraig Highld 224 C7
Culnaightrie D & G 146 D5
Culnaknock Highld 209 H2
Culrain Highld 222 D3
Culross Fife 176 D2
Culroy S Ayrs 163 H6
Culsalmond Abers 216 C7
Culscadden D & G 145 K5
Culshabbin D & G 145 G5
Culswick Shet 235 b6
Cultercullen Abers 207 H1
Cults C Aber 207 G5
Culverstone Green Kent 45 M7
Culverthorpe Lincs 103 G4
Culworth Nhants 73 G5
Culzean Castle & Country Park S Ayrs 163 G7
Cumbernauld N Lans 175 K4
Cumbernauld Village N Lans 175 K3
Cumberworth Lincs 119 G6
Cuminestown Abers 216 F4
Cumledge Border 179 G6
Cummersdale Cumb 148 D4
Cummertrees D & G 147 K2
Cummingston Moray 214 E1
Cumnock E Ayrs 164 B5
Cumnor Oxon 57 J7
Cumrew Cumb 148 F5
Cumrue D & G 155 J5
Cumwhinton Cumb 148 D4
Cumwhitton Cumb 148 E4
Cundall N York 132 F5
Cunninghamhead N Ayrs 163 J2
Cunningsburgh Shet 235 c7
Cupar Fife 186 F4
Cupar Muir Fife 186 F5
Curbar Derbys 114 E6
Curbridge Hants 17 G1
Curbridge Oxon 57 G6
Curdridge Hants 29 K8
Curdworth Warwks 85 L5
Curland Somset 25 L7
Curridge W Berk 41 J6
Currie C Edin 177 G5
Curry Mallet Somset 25 L6
Curry Rivel Somset 26 B6
Curtisden Green Kent 33 J5
Curtisknowle Devon 7 H5
Cury Cnwll 3 H6
Cushnie Abers 205 L3
Cusworth Donc 115 K2
Cutcloy D & G 145 J7
Cutcombe Somset 24 E4
Cuthill Highld 223 G4
Cutnall Green Worcs 70 F2
Cutsdean Gloucs 56 C3
Cutthorpe Derbys 115 G6
Cuxham Oxon 42 A2
Cuxton Medway 46 B6
Cuxwold Lincs 117 K2
Cwm Denbgs 110 E6
Cwmafan Neath 36 B3
Cwmaman Rhondd 52 F7
Cwmbach Carmth 50 B1
Cwmbâch Powys 68 D6
Cwmbach Rhondd 52 F7
Cwmbach Llechrhyd Powys 68 B4
Cwmbran Torfn 37 L2
Cwmcarn Caerph 37 K2
Cwmcarvan Mons 54 C6
Cwm-cou Cerdgn 65 J6
Cwm Crawnon Powys 53 H4
Cwmdare Rhondd 52 F7
Cwmdu Powys 53 J4
Cwmdu Swans 51 J6
Cwmduad Carmth 65 L7
Cwmfelin Brdgnd 36 D3
Cwmfelin Myr Td 53 H7
Cwmfelin Boeth Carmth 49 K4
Cwmfelinfach Caerph 37 J3
Cwmffrwd Carmth 50 E3
Cwmgiedd Powys 52 C5
Cwmgorse Carmth 51 K4
Cwmgwili Carmth 51 H4
Cwmhiraeth Carmth 65 K6
Cwm Llinau Powys 81 J2
Cwmllynfell Neath 51 L3
Cwmmawr Carmth 51 G3
Cwmparc Rhondd 36 E2
Cwmpengraig Carmth 65 K6
Cwmtillery Blae G 53 K6
Cwm-twrch Isaf Powys 52 B6
Cwm-twrch Uchaf Powys 51 L4
Cwm-y-glo Gwynd 109 H8
Cwmystwyth Cerdgn 81 H8
Cwrt-newydd Cerdgn 66 C5
Cyfarthfa Castle Museum Myr Td 53 G6
Cylibebyll Neath 51 L5
Cymer Neath 36 D2
Cymmer Rhondd 36 F3
Cynghordy Carmth 67 H6
Cynonville Neath 36 C2
Cynwyd Denbgs 97 G4
Cynwyl Elfed Carmth 65 L8

D

Daccombe Devon 7 K3
Dacre Cumb 138 C2
Dacre N York 132 B7
Dacre Banks N York 132 B6
Daddry Shield Dur 149 M7
Dadford Bucks 73 J6
Dadlington Leics 86 E4
Dagenham Gt Lon 45 J3
Daglingworth Gloucs 55 M6
Dagnall Bucks 59 G5
Dailly S Ayrs 152 F2
Dairsie Fife 187 G4
Dalabrog W Isls 233 b8
Dalavich Ag & B 182 D5
Dalbeattie D & G 146 E3
Dalby IoM 237 b5
Dalby N York 133 K5
Dalcapon P & K 194 F5
Dalchalm Highld 226 F7
Dalchreichart Highld 201 L3
Dalchruin P & K 184 F4
Dalcrue P & K 185 L2
Dalditch Devon 12 D5
Daldowie Crematorium C Glas 175 J6
Dale Derbys 101 H5
Dale Pembks 48 D6
Dalelia Highld 190 E3
Dalgarven N Ayrs 163 H1
Dalgety Bay Fife 177 G2
Dalgig E Ayrs 164 B6
Dalginross P & K 185 G3
Dalguise P & K 194 F6
Dalhalvaig Highld 230 C5
Dalham Suffk 77 G3
Daliburgh W Isls 233 b8
Dalkeith Mdloth 177 K5
Dallas Moray 214 D4
Dallinghoo Suffk 78 F4
Dallington E Susx 20 D2
Dallington Nhants 73 K3
Dalmally Ag & B 183 H3
Dalmary Stirlg 184 C7
Dalmellington E Ayrs 153 K2
Dalmeny C Edin 176 F3
Dalmore Highld 222 F7
Dalmuir W Duns 174 E4
Dalnabreck Highld 190 E3
Dalnacardoch P & K 194 B3
Dalnahaitnach Highld 203 K2
Dalnaspidal P & K 193 K2
Dalnawillan Lodge Highld 230 F7
Daloist P & K 194 C5
Dalqueich P & K 186 A6
Dalquhairn S Ayrs 153 G3
Dalreavoch Lodge Highld 226 D6
Dalry N Ayrs 174 B7
Dalrymple E Ayrs 163 J6
Dalserf S Lans 175 L7
Dalsmeran Ag & B 161 G6
Dalston Cumb 148 C5
Dalston Gt Lon 45 G3
Dalswinton D & G 155 G5
Dalton D & G 155 K7
Dalton N York 132 F4
Dalton N York 140 E5
Dalton Nthumb 158 E7
Dalton-in-Furness Cumb 128 F5
Dalton-le-Dale Dur 151 K5
Dalton-on-Tees N York 141 H5
Dalton Piercy Hartpl 141 L2
Dalveich Stirlg 184 D3
Dalwhinnie Highld 202 F7
Dalwood Devon 13 G3
Damerham Hants 28 C7
Damgate Norfk 93 J2
Damnaglaur D & G 144 D7
Danbury Essex 61 J6
Danby N York 142 F5
Danby Wiske N York 141 H7
Dandaleith Moray 215 G5
Danderhall Mdloth 177 J4
Danebridge Ches E 113 L7
Dane End Herts 60 B4
Danehill E Susx 32 D7
Dane Hills C Leic 87 H3
Dane Street Kent 34 E4
Danshillock Abers 216 D3
Danskine E Loth 178 C5
Darenth Kent 45 K5
Daresbury Halton 112 E5
Darfield Barns 115 H1
Dargate Kent 34 E3
Darite Cnwll 5 K3
Darland Medway 46 C6
Darlaston Wsall 85 H4
Darlaston Green Wsall 85 H4
Darley N York 132 C7
Darley Abbey C Derb 101 G5
Darley Bridge Derbys 100 E1
Darley Dale Derbys 114 F8
Darley Green Solhll 85 L8
Darleyhall Herts 59 J4
Darley Head N York 132 B7
Darlingscott Warwks 72 B6
Darlington Darltn 141 H4
Darlington Crematorium Darltn 141 G4
Darlton Notts 116 C6
Darnick Border 167 H3
Darowen Powys 81 H3
Darra Abers 216 E5
Darracott Devon 9 G2
Darracott Devon 23 G4
Darras Hall Nthumb 158 E7
Darrington Wakefd 124 D6
Darsham Suffk 79 J1
Darshill Somset 26 E3
Dartford Kent 45 K5
Dartford Crossing Kent 45 K5
Dartington Devon 7 H4
Dartmoor National Park Devon 10 F7
Dartmouth Devon 7 K5
Darton Barns 123 L7
Darvel E Ayrs 164 B2
Darwen Bl w D 121 K6
Datchet W & M 43 G5
Datchworth Herts 59 L4
Daubhill Bolton 121 K8
Daugh of Kinermony Moray 214 F6
Dauntsey Wilts 39 M4
Dava Highld 214 C6
Davenham Ches W 112 F7
Daventry Nhants 73 H3
Davidson's Mains C Edin 177 G4
Davidstow Cnwll 8 F7
Davington D & G 155 M2
Davington Hill Kent 34 D3
Daviot Abers 216 E8
Daviot Highld 213 H6
Daviot House Highld 213 H6
Davoch of Grange Moray 215 K4
Daw End Wsall 85 J4
Dawesgreen Surrey 31 K3
Dawley Wrekin 84 C2
Dawlish Devon 12 B6
Dawlish Warren Devon 12 C6
Daybrook Notts 101 L4
Daylesford Gloucs 56 E3
Deal Kent 35 K4
Dean Cumb 136 E3
Dean Devon 7 H3
Dean Devon 23 L2
Dean Hants 29 K7
Dean Oxon 57 G4
Dean Somset 26 F3
Dean Bottom Kent 45 L6
Deanburnhaugh Border 166 F6
Deancombe Devon 7 G3
Dean Court Oxon 57 J6
Deane Bolton 121 K8
Deane Hants 29 K2
Deanhead Kirk 122 F7
Deanland Dorset 27 M7
Dean Prior Devon 7 H3
Deanraw Nthumb 149 L3
Deans W Loth 176 D5
Deanscales Cumb 136 F2
Deanshanger Nhants 73 L6
Deanshaugh Moray 215 H4
Deanston Stirlg 184 F6
Dearham Cumb 147 J7

Debach Suffk 78 F4
Debden Essex 45 H2
Debden Essex 60 E2
Debenham Suffk 78 E2
Deblin's Green Worcs 70 E5
Dechmont W Loth 176 E4
Dechmont Road W Loth 176 D4
Deddington Oxon 57 J2
Dedham Essex 62 C2
Dedworth W & M 42 F5
Deene Nhants 88 D5
Deenethorpe Nhants 88 D5
Deepcar Sheff 114 F3
Deeping Gate C Pete 89 G2
Deeping St James Lincs 89 H2
Deeping St Nicholas Lincs 89 J1
Deerhurst Gloucs 55 K3
Defford Worcs 71 G5
Defynnog Powys 52 E3
Deganwy Conwy 109 L5
Degnish Ag & B 182 A5
Deighton C York 124 F2
Deighton N York 141 J6
Deiniolen Gwynd 109 H8
Delabole Cnwll 8 E7
Delamere Ches W 112 E7
Delfrigs Abers 207 H2
Delliefure Highld 214 D7
Dell Quay W Susx 18 A5
Delnabo Moray 204 E3
Delnashaugh Inn Moray 214 E7
Delny Highld 223 G6
Delph Oldham 122 E8
Delves Dur 150 E5
Dembleby Lincs 103 H5
Denaby Donc 115 J2
Denbigh Denbgs 110 E7
Denbighshire Crematorium Denbgs 110 E6
Denbrae Fife 186 F4
Denbury Devon 7 J3
Denby Derbys 101 H4
Denby Dale Kirk 123 J8
Denchworth Oxon 41 G3
Dendron Cumb 128 F5
Denfield P & K 185 K4
Denford Nhants 88 E7
Dengie Essex 62 B7
Denham Bucks 43 H3
Denham Suffk 77 H3
Denham Suffk 92 E8
Denham Green Bucks 43 H3
Denhead Abers 217 J4
Denhead Fife 187 G5
Denhead of Gray C Dund 186 F2
Denholm Border 167 J5
Denholme C Brad 123 G4
Denmead Hants 30 A8
Denmore C Aber 207 H3
Dennington Suffk 79 G2
Denny Falk 175 L2
Dennyloanhead Falk 175 L3
Den of Lindores Fife 186 D4
Denshaw Oldham 122 E7
Denside Abers 206 F6
Densole Kent 35 G6
Denston Suffk 77 H4
Denstone Staffs 100 C4
Denstroude Kent 34 E3
Dent Cumb 130 D3
Denton Cambs 89 G6
Denton Darltn 140 F4
Denton E Susx 19 L5
Denton Kent 35 G5
Denton Lincs 102 E6
Denton N York 123 H2
Denton Nhants 74 B3
Denton Norfk 93 G5
Denton Tamesd 113 L3
Denver Norfk 90 E3
Denwick Nthumb 169 J6
Deopham Norfk 92 C4
Deopham Green Norfk 92 C4
Depden Suffk 77 H3
Deptford Gt Lon 45 G4
Deptford Wilts 28 A4
Derby C Derb 101 G5
Derby Devon 23 J5
Derbyhaven IoM 237 b7
Derculich P & K 194 D5
Dereham Norfk 92 B2
Deri Caerph 53 H7
Derringstone Kent 35 G5
Derrington Staffs 99 K7
Derry Hill Wilts 39 L6
Derrythorpe N Linc 125 J8
Dersingham Norfk 105 H6
Dervaig Ag & B 189 K6
Derwen Denbgs 97 G3
Derwenlas Powys 80 F4
Derwent Valley Mills Derbys 100 F2
Derwentwater Cumb 137 J3
Desborough Nhants 88 B6
Desford Leics 86 F3
Deskford Moray 215 L3
Detling Kent 33 K2
Devauden Mons 54 C7
Devil's Bridge Cerdgn 81 G7
Devizes Wilts 40 A7
Devonport C Plym 6 C5
Devonside Clacks 185 J7
Devoran Cnwll 4 C7
Devoran & Perran Cnwll 3 K4
Dewarton Mdloth 177 K5
Dewlish Dorset 14 E3
Dewsbury Kirk 123 K6
Dewsbury Moor Crematorium Kirk 123 J6
Deytheur Powys 97 K8
Dibden Hants 16 E2
Dibden Purlieu Hants 16 E2
Dickleburgh Norfk 92 E6
Didbrook Gloucs 56 B2
Didcot Oxon 41 K3
Diddington Cambs 75 H2
Diddlebury Shrops 83 K6
Didling W Susx 18 A3
Didmarton Gloucs 39 J3
Didsbury Manch 113 J3
Digby Lincs 103 H2
Digg Highld 218 C7
Diggle Oldham 122 F8
Digmoor Lancs 112 C1
Dihewyd Cerdgn 66 C4
Dilham Norfk 107 G7
Dilhorne Staffs 99 L4
Dill Hall Lancs 121 L4
Dillington Cambs 75 G2
Dilston Nthumb 150 B3
Dilton Wilts 27 K2
Dilton Marsh Wilts 27 J2
Dilwyn Herefs 69 H4
Dinas Gwynd 94 E5
Dinas Pembks 64 E6
Dinas-Mawddwy Gwynd 81 J1
Dinas Powys V Glam 37 J6
Dinder Somset 26 E3
Dinedor Herefs 69 K6
Dingestow Mons 54 C6
Dingle Lpool 111 K4
Dingley Nhants 87 L6
Dingwall Highld 212 E3
Dinnet Abers 205 K5
Dinnington N u Ty 158 F7
Dinnington Rothm 115 K4
Dinnington Somset 26 B8
Dinorwic Gwynd 95 K1
Dinton Bucks 58 C5
Dinton Wilts 28 A5
Dinwoodie D & G 155 K4
Dinworthy Devon 9 J2
Dipford Somset 25 J6
Dippen Ag & B 161 K2
Dippen N Ayrs 162 D5
Dippertown Devon 10 C7
Dipple Moray 215 H3
Dipple S Ayrs 152 E2
Diptford Devon 7 G4
Dipton Dur 150 E4
Dirleton E Loth 178 B2
Dirt Pot Nthumb 149 L5
Diseworth Leics 101 J7
Dishforth N York 132 F5
Disley Ches E 113 L5
Diss Norfk 92 D7
Distington Cumb 136 D3
Distington Hall Crematorium Cumb 136 E3
Ditchampton Wilts 28 C5
Ditcheat Somset 26 F4
Ditchingham Norfk 93 G5
Ditchling E Susx 19 J3
Ditherington Shrops 83 K2
Ditteridge Wilts 39 J6
Dittisham Devon 7 K5
Ditton Kent 33 J2
Ditton Green Cambs 76 F3
Ditton Priors Shrops 83 L5
Dixton Mons 54 D5
Dobcross Oldham 113 M1
Dobwalls Cnwll 5 K3
Doccombe Devon 11 H7
Dochgarroch Highld 212 F6
Docking Norfk 105 J5
Docklow Herefs 69 L3
Dockray Cumb 137 L3
Doddinghurst Essex 60 F7
Doddington Cambs 90 B5
Doddington Kent 34 C4
Doddington Lincs 116 E7
Doddington Nthumb 168 E3
Doddington Shrops 84 B7
Doddiscombsleigh Devon 11 K7
Dodd's Green Ches E 98 E4
Dodford Nhants 73 H3
Dodford Worcs 85 G8
Dodington S Glos 39 H4
Dodington Somset 25 J4
Dodleston Ches W 98 A1
Dodside E Rens 174 F7
Dod's Leigh Staffs 100 A5
Dodworth Barns 114 F1
Doe Bank Birm 85 K4
Dogdyke Lincs 103 K2
Dogmersfield Hants 30 C2
Dolanog Powys 82 B2
Dolbenmaen Gwynd 95 J4
Dolfach Powys 81 K3
Dolfor Powys 82 C6
Dolgarrog Conwy 109 L7
Dolgellau Gwynd 96 B8
Doll Highld 226 F7
Dollar Clacks 185 K7
Dollarfield Clacks 185 K7
Dolphin Flints 111 H6
Dolphinholme Lancs 129 L8
Dolphinton S Lans 176 F8
Dolton Devon 10 E3
Dolwen Conwy 110 B6
Dolwyddelan Conwy 96 B3
Domgay Powys 97 L8
Doncaster Donc 115 L2
Doncaster North Services Donc 125 G7
Donhead St Andrew Wilts 27 K6
Donhead St Mary Wilts 27 K6
Donibristle Fife 177 G2
Doniford Somset 25 G3
Donington Lincs 103 K5
Donington on Bain Lincs 118 C5
Donington Park Services Leics 101 J7
Donisthorpe Leics 86 C2
Donnington Gloucs 56 D3
Donnington Shrops 83 L2
Donnington W Berk 41 J6
Donnington W Susx 18 B5
Donnington Wrekin 84 C2
Donnington Wood Wrekin 84 C2
Donyatt Somset 25 M8
Doonfoot S Ayrs 163 H5
Dorback Lodge Highld 204 D3
Dorchester Dorset 14 D4
Dorchester-on-Thames Oxon 41 L2
Dordon Warwks 86 C4
Dore Sheff 114 F5
Dores Highld 212 F7
Dorking Surrey 31 K2
Dormansland Surrey 32 D5
Dormington Herefs 69 L6
Dormston Worcs 71 H3
Dorney Bucks 42 F5
Dornie Highld 200 D1
Dornoch Highld 223 H4
Dornock D & G 147 M2
Dorrery Highld 230 F5
Dorridge Solhll 85 L8
Dorrington Lincs 103 H2
Dorrington Shrops 83 J3
Dorrington Shrops 99 G4
Dorsington Warwks 71 K4
Dorstone Herefs 69 G6
Dorton Bucks 58 B5
Douglas IoM 237 d6
Douglas S Lans 165 G4
Douglas and Angus C Dund 187 G2
Douglas Crematorium IoM 237 d5
Douglas Pier Ag & B 183 H7
Douglastown Angus 196 C6
Douglas Water S Lans 165 G3
Douglas West S Lans 164 F3
Doulting Somset 26 F3
Dounby Ork 234 b5
Doune Highld 221 L2
Doune Stirlg 184 F6
Dounepark S Ayrs 152 E3
Dounie Highld 222 D4
Dousland Devon 6 D3
Dove Dale Derbys 100 D3
Dove Holes Derbys 114 B6
Dovenby Cumb 147 J7
Dover Kent 35 J6
Dover Castle Kent 35 J6
Dovercourt Essex 62 F2
Doverdale Worcs 70 F2
Doveridge Derbys 100 C5
Doversgreen Surrey 31 L2
Dowally P & K 194 F6
Dowdeswell Gloucs 55 M4
Dowlais Myr Td 53 G6
Dowland Devon 10 E3
Dowlish Wake Somset 26 A8
Down Ampney Gloucs 40 C2
Downderry Cnwll 5 L5
Downe Gt Lon 45 H7
Downend Gloucs 39 J2
Downend S Glos 38 F5
Downfield C Dund 186 F2
Downgate Cnwll 6 A2
Downham Essex 46 B2
Downham Gt Lon 45 H5
Downham Lancs 122 B2
Downham Market Norfk 90 E3
Down Hatherley Gloucs 55 K4
Downhead Somset 26 E6
Downhead Somset 27 G3
Downhill P & K 186 A2
Downholme N York 140 E7
Downies Abers 207 H6
Downley Bucks 42 D2
Down St Mary Devon 11 H4
Downs Crematorium Br & H 19 J4
Downside Surrey 43 J8
Down Thomas Devon 6 D6

Downton Wilts 28 D6
Dowsby Lincs 103 J6
Doynton S Glos 39 G5
Draethen Caerph 37 K3
Draffan S Lans 164 F1
Drakeholes Notts 116 B4
Drakemyre N Ayrs 174 B7
Drakes Broughton Worcs 71 G5
Draughton N York 131 K8
Draughton Nhants 87 L7
Drax N York 125 G5
Draycote Warwks 72 F1
Draycott Derbys 101 H6
Draycott Gloucs 71 L7
Draycott Somset 26 C2
Draycott in the Clay Staffs 100 D6
Draycott in the Moors Staffs 99 M4
Drayton C Port 17 J2
Drayton Leics 88 B5
Drayton Norfk 92 E2
Drayton Oxon 41 J2
Drayton Oxon 72 E6
Drayton Somset 26 B6
Drayton Worcs 85 G7
Drayton Bassett Staffs 85 L4
Drayton Beauchamp Bucks 58 E5
Drayton Manor Park Staffs 85 L4
Drayton Parslow Bucks 58 D3
Drayton St Leonard Oxon 41 L2
Dreen Hill Pembks 48 F5
Drefach Carmth 51 G3
Drefach Carmth 65 K6
Drefach Cerdgn 66 C5
Dreghorn N Ayrs 163 J2
Drellingore Kent 35 H6
Drem E Loth 178 B3
Dresden C Stke 99 K4
Drewsteignton Devon 11 H6
Driffield E R Yk 134 F7
Driffield Gloucs 56 B7
Drift Cnwll 2 D5
Drigg Cumb 136 E7
Drighlington Leeds 123 J5
Drimnin Highld 190 B5
Drimpton Dorset 13 K2
Drimsallie Highld 191 J1
Dringhouses C York 124 E2
Drinkstone Suffk 77 L3
Drinkstone Green Suffk 77 L3
Drointon Staffs 100 A6
Droitwich Spa Worcs 70 F2
Dron P & K 186 B4
Dronfield Derbys 115 G5
Drongan E Ayrs 163 K5
Dronley Angus 186 E1
Droop Dorset 14 E2
Droxford Hants 29 L7
Droylsden Tamesd 113 K2
Druid Denbgs 97 G4
Druidston Pembks 48 E4
Druimarbin Highld 191 L3
Druimavuic Ag & B 191 K7
Druimdrishaig Ag & B 172 C4
Druimindarroch Highld 199 L7
Drum Ag & B 172 F3
Drum P & K 185 L7
Drumalbin S Lans 165 H2
Drumbeg Highld 224 D3
Drumblade Abers 216 B6
Drumbreddon D & G 144 C6
Drumbuie Highld 210 B7
Drumburgh Cumb 148 A3
Drumburn D & G 146 F4
Drumchapel C Glas 174 F4
Drumchastle P & K 193 L5
Drumclog S Lans 164 C2
Drumeldrie Fife 187 G6
Drumelzier Border 165 M3
Drumfearn Highld 199 L3
Drumfrennie Abers 206 D5
Drumgley Angus 196 C6
Drumguish Highld 203 J5
Drumin Moray 214 E7
Drumjohn D & G 153 L3
Drumlamford S Ayrs 153 G6
Drumlasie Abers 206 C4
Drumleaning Cumb 148 A5
Drumlemble Ag & B 161 H5
Drumlithie Abers 197 J1
Drummoddie D & G 145 H6
Drummore D & G 144 D7
Drummuir Moray 215 J5
Drumnadrochit Highld 212 D7
Drumnagorrach Moray 215 L4
Drumpark D & G 154 F6
Drumrunie Lodge Highld 224 E7
Drumshang S Ayrs 163 G6
Drumuie Highld 209 G5
Drumuillie Highld 204 B2
Drumvaich Stirlg 184 E6
Drunzie P & K 186 B5
Drybeck Cumb 138 F4
Drybridge Moray 215 K2
Drybridge N Ayrs 163 J3
Drybrook Gloucs 54 F4
Dryburgh Border 167 J3
Dry Doddington Lincs 102 D3
Dry Drayton Cambs 75 L3
Drymen Stirlg 174 E2
Drymuir Abers 217 G5
Drynoch Highld 208 F7
Dubford Abers 216 F2
Duchally Highld 225 J5
Ducklington Oxon 57 G6
Duddenhoe End Essex 76 C7
Duddingston C Edin 177 J4
Duddington Nhants 88 E4
Duddlestone Somset 25 K7
Duddo Nthumb 168 D2
Duddon Ches W 112 D8
Dudleston Shrops 97 M5
Dudleston Heath Shrops 98 A5
Dudley Dudley 85 G5
Dudley N Tyne 159 G7
Dudley Port Sandw 85 G5
Dudsbury Dorset 15 K3
Duffield Derbys 101 G4
Duffryn Neath 36 C2
Dufftown Moray 215 H6
Duffus Moray 214 E2
Dufton Cumb 139 G3
Duggleby N York 134 D6
Duirinish Highld 210 B7
Duisdalemore Highld 199 L3
Duisky Highld 191 K2
Dukestown Blae G 53 H6
Duke Street Suffk 78 C6
Dukinfield Tamesd 113 L2
Dukinfield Crematorium Tamesd 113 L2
Dulcote Somset 26 E3
Dulford Devon 12 D2
Dull P & K 194 C6
Dullatur N Lans 175 K3
Dullingham Cambs 76 F3
Dulnain Bridge Highld 204 B1
Duloe Bed 75 H3
Duloe Cnwll 5 K4
Dulverton Somset 24 E5
Dulwich Gt Lon 45 G5
Dumbarton W Duns 174 D4
Dumbleton Gloucs 71 H7
Dumfries D & G 155 G6
Dumgoyne Stirlg 174 F2
Dummer Hants 29 L3
Dumpton Kent 35 K2
Dun Angus 197 G4
Dunalastair P & K 193 L5
Dunan Ag & B 173 K4
Dunan Highld 209 J8
Dunan P & K 193 G5
Dunaverty Ag & B 161 H7
Dunball Somset 25 L3
Dunbar E Loth 178 E3
Dunbeath Highld 227 L3
Dunbeg Ag & B 182 C2
Dunblane Stirlg 185 G6
Dunbog Fife 186 E4
Duncanston Highld 212 F3
Duncanstone Abers 216 B8
Dunchideock Devon 11 K7
Dunchurch Warwks 72 F1
Duncow D & G 155 G5
Duncrievie P & K 186 B5
Duncton W Susx 18 C3
Dundee C Dund 186 F2
Dundee Airport C Dund 186 F2
Dundee Crematorium C Dund 186 F2
Dundon Somset 26 C5
Dundonald S Ayrs 163 J3
Dundonnell Highld 220 E4
Dundraw Cumb 147 L5
Dundreggan Highld 201 L3
Dundrennan D & G 146 D5
Dundry N Som 38 E6
Dunecht Abers 206 E4
Dunfermline Fife 176 F2
Dunfermline Crematorium Fife 176 F2
Dunfield Gloucs 40 C2
Dungavel S Lans 164 D3
Dungeness Kent 21 L3
Dunham Massey Traffd 113 H4
Dunham-on-the-Hill Ches W 112 C6
Dunham-on-Trent Notts 116 D6
Dunhampton Worcs 70 F2
Dunham Town Traffd 113 H4
Dunham Woodhouses Traffd 113 G4
Dunholme Lincs 117 G5
Dunino Fife 187 J5
Dunipace Falk 175 L2
Dunkeld P & K 195 G7
Dunkerton BaNES 39 G8
Dunkeswell Devon 12 E2
Dunkeswick N York 123 L2
Dunkirk Kent 34 E3
Dunkirk S Glos 39 H4
Dunk's Green Kent 33 G3
Dunlappie Angus 196 F3
Dunley Worcs 70 E2
Dunlop E Ayrs 174 D8
Dunmaglass Highld 202 F2
Dunmore Falk 176 B1
Dunnet Highld 231 J2
Dunnichen Angus 196 E6
Dunning P & K 185 L4
Dunnington C York 133 K8
Dunnington E R Yk 126 E1
Dunnington Warwks 71 J4
Dunoon Ag & B 173 K3
Dunphail Moray 214 C5
Dunragit D & G 144 E4
Duns Border 179 G7
Dunsby Lincs 103 J6
Dunscore D & G 154 F5
Dunscroft Donc 124 F8
Dunsdale R & Cl 142 D4
Dunsden Green Oxon 42 C5
Dunsdon Devon 9 J3
Dunsfold Surrey 31 G4
Dunsford Devon 11 J6
Dunshalt Fife 186 D5
Dunshillock Abers 217 J5
Dunsill Notts 101 J1
Dunsley N York 143 H5
Dunsley Staffs 84 F6
Dunsmore Bucks 58 E6
Dunsop Bridge Lancs 121 K1
Dunstable C Beds 59 G4
Dunstall Staffs 100 D7
Dunstan Nthumb 169 K5
Dunster Somset 24 F3
Duns Tew Oxon 57 J3
Dunston Gatesd 151 G3
Dunston Lincs 117 H8
Dunston Norfk 92 F3
Dunston Staffs 99 L8
Dunstone Devon 6 E5
Dunstone Devon 7 G2
Dunsville Donc 124 F8
Dunswell E R Yk 126 D4
Dunsyre S Lans 176 E8
Dunterton Devon 6 B1
Duntisbourne Abbots Gloucs 55 L6
Duntisbourne Rouse Gloucs 55 M6
Duntish Dorset 14 D2
Duntocher W Duns 174 E4
Dunton Bucks 58 D3
Dunton C Beds 75 J5
Dunton Norfk 105 L6
Dunton Bassett Leics 87 G5
Dunton Green Kent 32 F2
Duntulm Highld 218 C6
Dunure S Ayrs 163 G6
Dunvant Swans 51 H6
Dunvegan Highld 208 D5
Dunwich Suffk 79 K1
Durgan Cnwll 3 K5
Durham Dur 151 G6
Durham Cathedral Dur 151 G6
Durham Crematorium Dur 151 G6
Durham Services Dur 151 H7
Durham Tees Valley Airport S on T 141 J5
Durisdeer D & G 154 F2
Durisdeermill D & G 154 F2
Durleigh Somset 25 L4
Durley Hants 29 K7
Durley Wilts 40 E7
Durley Street Hants 29 K7
Durlock Kent 35 H3
Durlock Kent 35 J2
Durness Highld 228 F3
Durno Abers 216 D8
Duror Highld 191 K5
Durran Ag & B 182 D5
Durrington W Susx 18 F5
Durrington Wilts 28 D3
Durris Abers 206 E6
Dursley Gloucs 39 H2
Dursley Cross Gloucs 55 G4
Durston Somset 25 L5
Durweston Dorset 15 G2
Duston Nhants 73 K3
Duthil Highld 203 L1
Dutton Ches W 112 E5
Duxford Cambs 76 C5
Duxford Oxon 57 G7
Duxford IWM Cambs 76 C5
Dwygyfylchi Conwy 109 L6
Dwyran IoA 108 F7
Dyce C Aber 207 G3
Dyffryn Ardudwy Gwynd 95 K7
Dyffryn Cellwen Neath 52 D6
Dyke Lincs 103 J7
Dyke Moray 214 B3
Dykehead Angus 195 K5
Dykehead Angus 196 C4
Dykehead N Lans 176 B6
Dykehead Stirlg 184 D7
Dykelands Abers 197 H3
Dykends Angus 195 K5
Dykeside Abers 216 D5
Dymchurch Kent 34 E8
Dymock Gloucs 55 G2
Dyrham S Glos 39 H5
Dysart Fife 186 E8
Dyserth Denbgs 110 E5

E

Eagland Hill Lancs 120 F2
Eagle Lincs 116 E7
Eaglesfield Cumb 136 F2
Eaglesfield D & G 155 M7
Eaglesham E Rens 175 G7
Eagley Bolton 121 L7
Eakring Notts 102 A1
Ealand N Linc 125 J7
Ealing Gt Lon 44 D4
Eals Nthumb 149 H4
Eamont Bridge Cumb 138 D2
Earby Lancs 122 D2
Eardington Shrops 84 C5
Eardisland Herefs 69 H3
Eardisley Herefs 68 F5
Eardiston Shrops 98 A7
Eardiston Worcs 70 C2
Earith Cambs 89 L8
Earlestown St Hel 112 E3
Earley Wokham 42 C6
Earlham Norfk 92 E2
Earlham Crematorium Norfk 92 E2
Earlish Highld 208 F3
Earls Barton Nhants 74 C2
Earls Colne Essex 61 K3
Earls Common Worcs 71 G3
Earl's Croome Worcs 70 F6
Earlsdon Covtry 86 D7
Earlsferry Fife 187 H7
Earlsfield Gt Lon 44 E5
Earlsford Abers 216 F7
Earlsheaton Kirk 123 K6
Earl Shilton Leics 86 F4
Earl Soham Suffk 78 F2
Earl Sterndale Derbys 114 C7
Earlston Border 167 J2
Earlston E Ayrs 163 K3
Earlswood Surrey 32 B4
Earlswood Warwks 85 K8
Earnley W Susx 17 M3
Earsdon N Tyne 159 H7
Earsham Norfk 93 G5
Eartham W Susx 18 C4
Easby N York 142 C5
Easdale Ag & B 181 L4
Easebourne W Susx 30 E6
Easenhall Warwks 86 F7
Eashing Surrey 30 F3
Easington Bucks 58 B6
Easington Dur 151 K6
Easington E R Yk 127 J6
Easington R & Cl 142 F4
Easington Colliery Dur 151 K6
Easington Lane Sundld 151 J5
Easingwold N York 133 H5
Eassie and Nevay Angus 196 B7
East Aberthaw V Glam 37 G6
East Allington Devon 7 H6
East Anstey Devon 24 D6
East Ashey IoW 17 H5
East Ashling W Susx 17 M2
East Ayton N York 134 F3
East Barkwith Lincs 117 K5
East Barming Kent 33 J3
East Barnby N York 143 G5
East Barnet Gt Lon 44 F2
East Barns E Loth 178 F3
East Barsham Norfk 105 L5
East Beckham Norfk 106 E4
East Bedfont Gt Lon 43 H5
East Bergholt Suffk 78 C7
East Bilney Norfk 106 A8
East Blatchington E Susx 20 A5
East Boldon S Tyne 151 J3
East Boldre Hants 16 D3
Eastbourne Darltn 141 H4
Eastbourne E Susx 20 C5
Eastbourne Crematorium E Susx 20 D5
East Bradenham Norfk 91 L2
East Brent Somset 25 M2
Eastbridge Suffk 79 J2
East Bridgford Notts 102 B4
East Buckland Devon 23 L5
East Budleigh Devon 12 D5
Eastburn C Brad 122 F2
Eastbury Herts 43 J2
Eastbury W Berk 41 G5
East Butterwick N Linc 116 D1
Eastby N York 131 J8
East Calder W Loth 176 E5
East Carleton Norfk 92 E3
East Carlton Leeds 123 J2
East Carlton Nhants 88 B5
East Chaldon (Chaldon Herring) Dorset 14 E5
East Challow Oxon 41 G3
East Charleton Devon 7 H7
East Chelborough Dorset 14 A2
East Chiltington E Susx 19 K3
East Chinnock Somset 26 C8
East Chisenbury Wilts 28 C2
Eastchurch Kent 47 G5
East Clandon Surrey 31 H2
East Claydon Bucks 58 C3
East Coker Somset 26 D8
Eastcombe Gloucs 55 K6
East Compton Somset 26 E3
East Cornworthy Devon 7 J5
Eastcote Gt Lon 43 J3
Eastcote Nhants 73 K4
Eastcote Solhll 85 L7
Eastcott Wilts 28 A1
East Cottingwith E R Yk 125 G3
Eastcourt Wilts 40 E7
East Cowes IoW 16 F4
East Cowick E R Yk 125 G6
East Cowton N York 141 H6
East Cranmore Somset 27 G3
East Dean E Susx 20 B6
East Dean Gloucs 54 F4
East Dean Hants 28 F6
East Dean W Susx 18 B3
East Devon Crematorium Devon 12 D4
East Drayton Notts 116 C6
East Dulwich Gt Lon 45 G5
East Dundry N Som 38 E7
East Ella C KuH 126 C5
Eastend Essex 46 F2
East End Hants 16 D3
East End Hants 41 H7
East End Kent 33 L6
East End Oxon 57 H5
East End Somset 26 F3
Easter Balmoral Abers 205 G6
Easter Compton S Glos 38 E4
Easter Dalziel Highld 213 H4
Eastergate W Susx 18 C5
Easterhouse C Glas 175 J5
Easter Howgate Mdloth 177 H5
Easter Kinkell Highld 212 E4
Easter Moniack Highld 212 E5
Eastern Green Covtry 86 C7
Easter Ord Abers 206 F4
Easter Pitkierie Fife 187 J6
Easter Skeld Shet 235 c6
Easter Softlaw Border 168 A3
Easterton Wilts 28 A1
East Everleigh Wilts 28 D2
East Farleigh Kent 33 J3
East Farndon Nhants 87 K6
East Ferry Lincs 116 D2
Eastfield N Lans 176 B5
Eastfield N York 135 G3
East Fortune E Loth 178 C3
East Garston W Berk 41 G5
Eastgate Dur 150 B7
Eastgate Norfk 106 D7
East Goscote Leics 87 J2
East Grafton Wilts 40 E7
East Grimstead Wilts 28 E5
East Grinstead W Susx 32 D5
East Guldeford E Susx 21 J2
East Haddon Nhants 73 J2
East Hagbourne Oxon 41 K3
East Halton N Linc 126 E6
East Ham Gt Lon 45 H4
Easthampstead Park Crematorium Br For 42 D6
Easthampton Herefs 69 H2
East Hanney Oxon 41 H2
East Hanningfield Essex 61 J7
East Hardwick Wakefd 124 C6
East Harling Norfk 92 B6
East Harlsey N York 141 K7
East Harnham Wilts 28 C5
East Harptree BaNES 26 E1
East Harting W Susx 30 D7
East Hatch Wilts 27 L5
East Hatley Cambs 75 K4
East Hauxwell N York 132 B2
East Haven Angus 187 J1
East Heckington Lincs 103 K4
East Hedleyhope Dur 150 E6
East Helmsdale Highld 227 H5
East Hendred Oxon 41 J3
East Heslerton N York 134 E4
East Hoathly E Susx 20 B3
East Holme Dorset 15 G5
Easthope Shrops 83 L4
Easthorpe Essex 61 L4
East Horrington Somset 26 E3
East Horsley Surrey 31 H2
East Howe Bmouth 15 K4
East Huntington C York 133 J7
East Huntspill Somset 25 M3
East Ilsley W Berk 41 J4
Eastington Devon 11 H3
Eastington Gloucs 55 H6
Eastington Gloucs 56 C5
East Keal Lincs 118 E8
East Kennett Wilts 40 C6
East Keswick Leeds 124 B2
East Kilbride S Lans 175 H7
East Kirkby Lincs 118 D8
East Knighton Dorset 14 F5
East Knoyle Wilts 27 K5
East Lambrook Somset 26 B7
East Lancashire Crematorium Bury 122 B8
Eastlands D & G 154 E7
East Langdon Kent 35 J5
East Langton Leics 87 K5
East Lavant W Susx 18 B4
East Lavington W Susx 18 C3
East Layton N York 140 E5
Eastleach Martin Gloucs 56 D6
Eastleach Turville Gloucs 56 D6
East Leake Notts 101 K7
Eastleigh Devon 23 H5
Eastleigh Hants 29 J7
East Lexham Norfk 105 K8
Eastling Kent 34 C4
East Linton E Loth 178 D3
East Lockinge Oxon 41 H3
East London Crematorium Gt Lon 45 H4
East Lound N Linc 116 C2
East Lulworth Dorset 15 G6
East Lutton N York 134 E5
East Lydford Somset 26 E5
East Malling Kent 33 J2
East Marden W Susx 30 D8
East Markham Notts 116 C6
East Martin Hants 28 B7
East Marton N York 122 D1
East Meon Hants 30 B6
East Mersea Essex 62 C5
East Midlands Airport Leics 101 J7
East Molesey Surrey 43 J6
East Morden Dorset 15 G4
East Morton C Brad 123 G3
East Morton D & G 154 F3
East Ness N York 133 L4
Eastney C Port 17 J3
Eastnor Herefs 70 D6
East Norton Leics 87 L4
Eastoft N Linc 125 J7
East Ogwell Devon 7 J2
Easton Cambs 75 G1
Easton Devon 11 G6
Easton Dorset 14 D7
Easton Hants 29 K5
Easton Lincs 102 F6
Easton Norfk 92 D2
Easton Somset 26 D3
Easton Suffk 79 G3
Easton Wilts 39 K6
Easton Grey Wilts 39 K3
Easton-in-Gordano N Som 38 D5
Easton Maudit Nhants 74 C3
Easton-on-the-Hill Nhants 88 E3
Easton Royal Wilts 40 D7
East Orchard Dorset 27 J7
East Peckham Kent 33 H4
East Pennar Pembks 49 G6
East Pennard Somset 26 E4
East Perry Cambs 75 G2
East Portlemouth Devon 7 H7
East Prawle Devon 7 H8
East Preston W Susx 18 E5
East Putford Devon 9 K2
East Quantoxhead Somset 25 H3
East Rainton Sundld 151 H5
East Ravendale NE Lin 118 C2
East Raynham Norfk 105 L7
Eastrea Cambs 89 K4
East Riding Crematorium E R Yk 134 F5
Eastriggs D & G 147 M2
East Rigton Leeds 124 B2
Eastrington E R Yk 125 J4
Eastrop Swindn 40 D2
East Rounton N York 141 K6
East Rudham Norfk 105 K6
East Runton Norfk 106 E4
East Ruston Norfk 107 H6
Eastry Kent 35 J4
East Saltoun E Loth 178 B5
East Sheen Gt Lon 44 D5
East Shefford W Berk 41 H5
East Stockwith Lincs 116 C3
East Stoke Dorset 15 G5
East Stoke Notts 102 C3
East Stour Dorset 27 J6

East Stourmouth Kent 35 H3
East Stowford Devon 23 K6
East Stratton Hants 29 K4
East Studdal Kent 35 J5
East Taphouse Cnwll 5 J3
East-the-Water Devon 23 G6
East Thirston Nthumb 158 F3
East Tilbury Thurr 46 B5
East Tisted Hants 30 B5
East Torrington Lincs 117 J5
East Tuddenham Norfk 92 C2
East Tytherley Hants 28 F5
East Tytherton Wilts 39 L5
East Village Devon 11 J4
Eastville Bristl 38 E5
Eastville Lincs 104 C2
East Walton Norfk 91 G1
East Week Devon 10 F6
Eastwell Leics 102 C6
East Wellow Hants 28 F7
East Wemyss Fife 186 E7
East Whitburn W Loth 176 C5
Eastwick Herts 60 C5
East Wickham Gt Lon 45 J5
East Williamston Pembks 49 J6
East Winch Norfk 91 G1
East Winterslow Wilts 28 E5
East Wittering W Susx 17 L3
East Witton N York 131 L3
Eastwood Notts 101 J3
Eastwood Sthend 46 D3
East Woodburn Nthumb 158 A5
East Woodhay Hants 41 H7
East Worldham Hants 30 C4
East Wretham Norfk 91 K5
East Youlstone Devon 9 H2
Eathorpe Warwks 72 E2
Eaton Ches E 113 K7
Eaton Ches W 112 E8
Eaton Leics 102 D6
Eaton Norfk 92 E3
Eaton Notts 116 B6
Eaton Oxon 57 H7
Eaton Shrops 83 K5
Eaton Bray C Beds 58 F4
Eaton Constantine Shrops 83 L3
Eaton Green C Beds 58 F4
Eaton Hastings Oxon 56 E7
Eaton Mascott Shrops 83 K3
Eaton Socon Cambs 75 H3
Eaton upon Tern Shrops 98 F7
Ebberston N York 134 D3
Ebbesborne Wake Wilts 27 M6
Ebbw Vale Blae G 53 J6
Ebchester Dur 150 D4
Ebford Devon 12 C5
Ebley Gloucs 55 J6
Ebnal Ches W 98 C3
Ebrington Gloucs 71 L6
Ecchinswell Hants 41 J8
Ecclaw Border 178 F5
Ecclefechan D & G 155 L7
Eccles Border 168 A2
Eccles Kent 46 B7
Eccles Salfd 113 H2
Ecclesall Sheff 114 F5
Ecclesfield Sheff 115 G3
Eccleshall Staffs 99 J6
Eccleshill C Brad 123 H4
Ecclesmachan W Loth 176 E4
Eccles Road Norfk 92 B5
Eccleston Ches W 112 B8
Eccleston Lancs 121 G6
Eccleston St Hel 112 C3
Echt Abers 206 E4
Eckford Border 167 L4
Eckington Derbys 115 H5
Eckington Worcs 71 G6
Ecton Nhants 74 B2
Edale Derbys 114 C4
Eday Ork 234 d4
Eday Airport Ork 234 d4
Edburton W Susx 19 H4
Edderton Highld 222 F4
Eddleston Border 177 H8
Eddlewood S Lans 175 J7
Edenbridge Kent 32 D4
Edenfield Lancs 122 B6
Edenhall Cumb 138 E2
Edenham Lincs 103 H7
Eden Park Gt Lon 45 G6
Eden Project Cnwll 5 G5
Edensor Derbys 114 E7
Edentaggart Ag & B 183 K8
Edenthorpe Donc 115 L1
Edern Gwynd 94 E5
Edgbaston Birm 85 J6
Edgcott Bucks 58 B4
Edgcott Somset 24 D4
Edge Gloucs 55 J6
Edgefield Norfk 106 C5
Edgefield Green Norfk 106 D5
Edgerton Kirk 123 H6
Edgeworth Gloucs 55 L6
Edgmond Wrekin 99 G8
Edgton Shrops 83 H6
Edgware Gt Lon 44 D2
Edgworth Bl w D 121 L6
Edinbane Highld 208 E4
Edinburgh C Edin 177 H4
Edinburgh Airport C Edin 176 F4
Edinburgh Castle C Edin 177 H4
Edinburgh Old & New Town C Edin 177 H4
Edinburgh Royal Botanic Gardens C Edin 177 H4
Edinburgh Zoo RZSS C Edin 177 G4
Edingale Staffs 86 B2
Edingham D & G 146 E3
Edingley Notts 102 A2
Edingthorpe Norfk 107 G6
Edingthorpe Green Norfk 107 G6
Edington Border 179 J7
Edington Nthumb 158 E5
Edington Somset 26 B4
Edington Wilts 27 L2
Edington Burtle Somset 26 B3
Edingworth Somset 26 A2
Edithmead Somset 25 L2
Edith Weston Rutlnd 88 D3
Edlesborough Bucks 58 F4
Edlingham Nthumb 169 G7
Edlington Lincs 118 C7
Edmondsham Dorset 15 K1
Edmondsley Dur 151 G5
Edmondthorpe Leics 102 E8
Edmonton Gt Lon 45 G2
Edmundbyers Dur 150 C5
Ednam Border 167 L2
Edradynate P & K 194 D6
Edrom Border 179 H7
Edstaston Shrops 98 D6
Edstone Warwks 71 L3
Edwalton Notts 101 L5
Edwinstowe Notts 115 L7
Edworth C Beds 75 J6
Edwyn Ralph Herefs 70 B3
Edzell Angus 196 F3
Edzell Woods Abers 197 G3
Efail-fach Neath 36 B2
Efail Isaf Rhondd 37 G4
Efailnewydd Gwynd 94 F5
Efailwen Carmth 49 K3
Efenechtyd Denbgs 97 H2
Effgill D & G 156 B4
Effingham Surrey 31 J2
Efford Crematorium C Plym 6 D4
Egerton Bolton 121 K7
Egerton Kent 34 B5
Eggborough N York 124 E5
Eggbuckland C Plym 6 D4
Eggesford Devon 11 G3
Eggington C Beds 58 F3
Egginton Derbys 100 E6
Eggleston Dur 140 C3
Egham Surrey 43 G6
Egleton Rutlnd 88 C3
Eglingham Nthumb 169 G5
Egloshayle Cnwll 4 F2
Egloskerry Cnwll 9 H7
Eglwysbach Conwy 109 M7
Eglwys Cross Wrexhm 98 C4
Eglwyswrw Pembks 65 G6
Egmanton Notts 116 B7
Egremont Cumb 136 D5
Egremont Wirral 111 K3
Egton N York 143 G6
Egton Bridge N York 143 G6
Egypt Bucks 42 F3
Eigg Highld 199 G7
Eight Ash Green Essex 61 M3
Eilanreach Highld 200 C2
Eilean Donan Castle Highld 200 D1
Elan Valley Powys 67 J2
Elan Village Powys 67 K2
Elberton S Glos 38 E3
Elburton C Plym 6 D5
Elcombe Swindn 40 C4
Eldersfield Worcs 55 H2
Elderslie Rens 174 E5
Eldon Dur 141 G2
Elerch Cerdgn 80 F6
Elfhill Abers 206 F7
Elford Staffs 85 L2
Elgin Moray 214 F2
Elgol Highld 199 H3
Elham Kent 35 G6
Elie Fife 187 H7
Elim IoA 108 D4
Eling Hants 29 G8
Elkesley Notts 116 B6
Elkstone Gloucs 55 L5
Ella Abers 216 C3
Ellacombe Torbay 7 L3
Elland Calder 123 G6
Ellary Ag & B 172 C3
Ellastone Staffs 100 C4
Ellel Lancs 129 K7
Ellemford Border 178 F6
Ellenabeich Ag & B 181 L4
Ellenhall Staffs 99 J7
Ellen's Green Surrey 31 H4
Ellerbeck N York 141 K7
Ellerby N York 143 G4
Ellerdine Heath Wrekin 98 F7
Elleric Ag & B 191 K6
Ellerker E R Yk 125 L5
Ellerton E R Yk 125 G3
Ellerton N York 141 G7
Ellesborough Bucks 58 D6
Ellesmere Shrops 98 B5
Ellesmere Port Ches W 111 L6
Ellingham Norfk 93 H5
Ellingham Nthumb 169 H4
Ellingstring N York 132 B3
Ellington Cambs 75 H1
Ellington Nthumb 159 G4
Elliots Green Somset 27 J3
Ellisfield Hants 29 M3
Ellishader Highld 209 H2
Ellistown Leics 86 E2
Ellon Abers 217 H7
Ellonby Cumb 148 D7
Elloughton E R Yk 126 B5
Ellwood Gloucs 54 E6
Elm Cambs 90 C3
Elmbridge Worcs 70 F2
Elmdon Essex 76 C6
Elmdon Solhll 85 L6
Elmers End Gt Lon 45 G6
Elmer's Green Lancs 112 D1
Elmesthorpe Leics 86 F4
Elmhurst Staffs 85 K2
Elmley Castle Worcs 71 H6
Elmley Lovett Worcs 70 F1
Elmore Gloucs 55 H5
Elmore Back Gloucs 55 H5
Elm Park Gt Lon 45 K3
Elmsett Suffk 78 C5
Elmstead Market Essex 62 C3
Elmsted Kent 34 F5
Elmstone Kent 35 H3
Elmstone Hardwicke Gloucs 55 K3
Elmswell E R Yk 134 F7
Elmswell Suffk 78 B2
Elmton Derbys 115 J6
Elphin Highld 224 F6
Elphinstone E Loth 177 K4
Elrick Abers 206 F4
Elrig D & G 145 G5
Elrington Nthumb 149 L3
Elsdon Nthumb 158 B4
Elsenham Essex 60 E3
Elsfield Oxon 57 K6
Elsham N Linc 126 C7
Elsing Norfk 92 C1
Elslack N York 122 D2
Elson Hants 17 H3
Elsrickle S Lans 165 K2
Elstead Surrey 30 E3
Elsted W Susx 30 D7
Elsthorpe Lincs 103 H7
Elston Notts 102 C3
Elstow Bed 74 F5
Elstree Herts 44 D2
Elstronwick E R Yk 126 F4
Elswick Lancs 120 F3
Elswick N u Ty 151 G3
Elsworth Cambs 75 K2
Elterwater Cumb 137 K6
Eltham Gt Lon 45 H5
Eltham Crematorium Gt Lon 45 J5
Eltisley Cambs 75 J3
Elton Cambs 88 F5
Elton Ches W 112 C6
Elton Derbys 100 E1
Elton Herefs 69 J1
Elton Notts 102 C5
Elton S on T 141 J4
Eltringham Nthumb 150 D3
Elvanfoot S Lans 165 J6
Elvaston Derbys 101 H6
Elveden Suffk 91 J7
Elvetham Heath Hants 30 D1
Elvingston E Loth 178 A4
Elvington C York 125 G2
Elvington Kent 35 H5
Elwick Hartpl 141 K2
Elworth Ches E 99 H1
Elworthy Somset 25 G4
Ely Cambs 90 D7
Ely Cardif 37 H5
Emberton M Keyn 74 C5
Embleton Cumb 137 G2
Embleton Nthumb 169 J5
Embo Highld 223 H3
Emborough Somset 26 E2
Embo Street Highld 223 H3
Embsay N York 131 J8
Emery Down Hants 16 C2
Emley Kirk 123 K7
Emmington Oxon 58 C7
Emneth Norfk 90 C3
Emneth Hungate Norfk 90 D3
Empingham Rutlnd 88 D2
Empshott Hants 30 C5
Emstrey Crematorium Shrops 83 K2
Emsworth Hants 17 K2

Enborne W Berk 41 H7
Enborne Row W Berk 41 H7
Enderby Leics 87 G4
Endmoor Cumb 129 L3
Endon Staffs 99 L2
Endon Bank Staffs 99 L2
Enfield Gt Lon 60 B7
Enfield Crematorium Gt Lon 60 B7
Enfield Lock Gt Lon 60 B7
Enfield Wash Gt Lon 60 B7
Enford Wilts 28 C2
Engine Common S Glos 39 G4
Englefield W Berk 41 L6
Englefield Green Surrey 43 G6
English Bicknor Gloucs 54 E5
Englishcombe BaNES 39 G7
English Frankton Shrops 98 C6
Enham-Alamein Hants 29 G2
Enmore Somset 25 K4
Enmore Green Dorset 27 J6
Ennerdale Bridge Cumb 136 E4
Enochdhu P & K 195 G4
Ensay Ag & B 189 J6
Ensbury Bmouth 15 K3
Ensdon Shrops 83 H1
Enstone Oxon 57 G3
Enterkinfoot D & G 154 E2
Enville Staffs 84 E6
Eolaigearraidh W Isls 233 b9
Epney Gloucs 55 H5
Epperstone Notts 101 M3
Epping Essex 60 D7
Epping Green Essex 60 C6
Epping Upland Essex 60 C6
Eppleby N York 140 F5
Epsom Surrey 44 E7
Epwell Oxon 72 D6
Epworth N Linc 116 C2
Erbistock Wrexhm 97 M4
Erdington Birm 85 K5
Eridge Green E Susx 32 F6
Erines Ag & B 172 E4
Eriska Ag & B 191 H7
Eriskay W Isls 233 c9
Eriswell Suffk 91 G7
Erith Gt Lon 45 K4
Erlestoke Wilts 27 L2
Ermington Devon 6 F5
Erpingham Norfk 106 E6
Errogie Highld 202 E2
Errol P & K 186 D3
Erskine Rens 174 E4
Erskine Bridge Rens 174 E4
Ervie D & G 144 B2
Erwarton Suffk 78 F7
Erwood Powys 68 C6
Eryholme N York 141 H5
Eryrys Denbgs 97 J2
Escomb Dur 140 F2
Escrick N York 124 F2
Esgairgeiliog Powys 81 G3
Esh Dur 150 F6
Esher Surrey 43 J7
Eshott Nthumb 158 F3
Esh Winning Dur 150 F6
Eskadale Highld 212 C6
Eskbank Mdloth 177 J5
Eskdale Green Cumb 137 G6
Eskdalemuir D & G 156 A3
Esprick Lancs 120 E3
Essendine Rutlnd 88 F2
Essendon Herts 59 L6
Essich Highld 213 G6
Essington Staffs 85 G3
Esslemont Abers 217 H7
Eston R & Cl 142 C4
Etal Nthumb 168 D2
Etchilhampton Wilts 40 B7
Etchingham E Susx 33 J7
Etchinghill Kent 34 F6
Etchinghill Staffs 100 B8
Eton W & M 42 F5
Eton Wick W & M 42 F5
Etruria C Stke 99 K3
Etteridge Highld 203 G6
Ettersgill Dur 139 K2
Ettiley Heath Ches E 99 G1
Ettingshall Wolves 85 G4
Ettington Warwks 72 C5
Etton C Pete 89 G3
Etton E R Yk 126 B2
Ettrick Border 166 D6
Ettrickbridge Border 166 F4
Ettrickhill Border 166 C6
Etwall Derbys 100 F6
Euston Suffk 91 K7
Euxton Lancs 121 H6
Evanton Highld 212 F2
Evedon Lincs 103 H3
Evelix Highld 223 G4
Evenjobb Powys 68 F3
Evenley Nhants 73 H7
Evenlode Gloucs 56 E3
Evenwood Dur 140 E3
Evercreech Somset 26 F4
Everingham E R Yk 125 J3
Everleigh Wilts 28 D2
Eversholt C Beds 59 G2
Evershot Dorset 14 B2
Eversley Hants 42 C7
Eversley Cross Hants 42 C7
Everthorpe E R Yk 125 L4
Everton C Beds 75 H4
Everton Hants 16 C4
Everton Lpool 111 K3
Everton Notts 116 B4
Evertown D & G 156 C6
Evesbatch Herefs 70 C5
Evesham Worcs 71 J5
Evington C Leic 87 J3
Ewden Village Sheff 114 F3
Ewell Surrey 44 E7
Ewell Minnis Kent 35 H6
Ewelme Oxon 41 M3
Ewen Gloucs 40 A2
Ewenny V Glam 36 D5
Ewerby Lincs 103 J3
Ewhurst Surrey 31 H4
Ewhurst Green E Susx 20 F2
Ewhurst Green Surrey 31 H4
Ewloe Flints 111 J7
Eworthy Devon 10 C6
Ewshot Hants 30 D2
Ewyas Harold Herefs 54 B3
Exbourne Devon 10 E4
Exbury Hants 16 E3
Exebridge Somset 24 E6
Exelby N York 132 D3
Exeter Devon 11 L6
Exeter Airport Devon 12 C4
Exeter & Devon Crematorium Devon 12 B4
Exeter Services Devon 12 C4
Exford Somset 24 D4
Exfordsgreen Shrops 83 J3
Exhall Warwks 71 K4
Exhall Warwks 86 D6
Exlade Street Oxon 42 A4
Exminster Devon 12 B5
Exmoor National Park 24 D4
Exmouth Devon 12 C6
Exning Suffk 76 E2
Exton Devon 12 C5
Exton Hants 29 L7
Exton Rutlnd 88 D2
Exton Somset 24 E5
Exwick Devon 11 K6
Eyam Derbys 114 E6
Eydon Nhants 73 G4
Eye C Pete 89 J3
Eye Herefs 69 J2
Eye Suffk 92 D8
Eyemouth Border 179 K5
Eyeworth C Beds 75 J5
Eyhorne Street Kent 33 L3
Eyke Suffk 79 G4
Eynesbury Cambs 75 H3
Eynsford Kent 45 K6
Eynsham Oxon 57 H6
Eype Dorset 13 L4
Eyre Highld 208 F4
Eythorne Kent 35 H5
Eyton Herefs 69 J3
Eyton Shrops 98 C7
Eyton on Severn Shrops 83 L3
Eyton upon the Weald Moors Wrekin 84 B1

F

Faccombe Hants 41 H8
Faceby N York 141 L6
Fachwen Powys 82 B1
Faddiley Ches E 98 E3
Fadmoor N York 133 K2
Faerdre Swans 51 K5
Faifley W Duns 174 F4
Failand N Som 38 D6
Failford S Ayrs 163 L4
Failsworth Oldham 113 K2
Fairbourne Gwynd 80 E2
Fairburn N York 124 D5
Fairfield Derbys 114 B6
Fairfield Worcs 85 G7
Fairford Gloucs 56 D7
Fairgirth D & G 146 F4
Fair Green Norfk 90 F1
Fairhaven Lancs 120 D5
Fair Isle Shet 235 e7
Fair Isle Airport Shet 235 e7
Fairlands Surrey 30 F2
Fairlie N Ayrs 173 L7
Fairlight E Susx 21 G4
Fairmile Devon 12 E3
Fairmile Surrey 43 J7
Fairnilee Border 167 G3
Fair Oak Hants 29 J7
Fairoak Staffs 99 H6
Fair Oak Green Hants 42 A7
Fairseat Kent 45 L7
Fairstead Essex 61 J5
Fairstead Norfk 105 G8
Fairwarp E Susx 32 E7
Fairwater Cardif 37 H5
Fairy Cross Devon 22 F6
Fakenham Norfk 105 L6
Fakenham Magna Suffk 91 K7
Fala Mdloth 177 L6
Fala Dam Mdloth 177 L6
Faldingworth Lincs 117 H5
Faldouët Jersey 236 e7
Falfield S Glos 39 G2
Falkenham Suffk 79 G6
Falkirk Falk 176 B3
Falkirk Crematorium Falk 176 B3
Falkirk Wheel Falk 176 A3
Falkland Fife 186 D6
Fallburn S Lans 165 J2
Fallin Stirlg 185 H8
Fallodon Nthumb 169 J5
Fallowfield Manch 113 J3
Fallowfield Nthumb 150 B2
Falls of Blarghour Ag & B 182 E5
Falmer E Susx 19 K4
Falmouth Cnwll 3 K5
Falnash Border 156 D2
Falsgrave N York 134 F2
Falstone Nthumb 157 J5
Fanagmore Highld 228 B5
Fancott C Beds 59 G3
Fanellan Highld 212 D5
Fangdale Beck N York 142 C7
Fangfoss E R Yk 134 B8
Fanmore Ag & B 189 K7
Fannich Lodge Highld 211 K2
Fans Border 167 J2
Far Bletchley M Keyn 74 C7
Farcet Cambs 89 H5
Far Cotton Nhants 73 L3
Fareham Hants 17 H2
Far End Cumb 137 J7
Farewell Staffs 85 J2
Faringdon Oxon 40 F2
Farington Lancs 121 H5
Farlam Cumb 148 F3
Farleigh N Som 38 D6
Farleigh Surrey 32 C2
Farleigh Hungerford Somset 39 J8
Farleigh Wallop Hants 29 L3
Farlesthorpe Lincs 119 G6
Farleton Cumb 129 L4
Farleton Lancs 130 B6
Farley Staffs 100 B4
Farley Wilts 28 E5
Farley Green Surrey 31 H3
Farley Hill Wokham 42 C7
Farleys End Gloucs 55 H5
Farlington C Port 17 J2
Farlington N York 133 J6
Farlow Shrops 84 B7
Farmborough BaNES 38 F7
Farmcote Gloucs 56 B3
Farmers Carmth 66 E5
Farmington Gloucs 56 C5
Farmoor Oxon 57 J6
Far Moor Wigan 112 D2
Farmtown Moray 215 L4
Farnborough Gt Lon 45 H7
Farnborough Hants 30 E2
Farnborough W Berk 41 H4
Farnborough Warwks 72 E5
Farnborough Park Hants 30 E1
Farncombe Surrey 31 G3
Farndish Bed 74 D2
Farndon Ches W 98 B2
Farndon Notts 102 C3
Farne Islands Nthumb 169 J2
Farnell Angus 197 G5
Farnham Dorset 27 L7
Farnham Essex 60 D3
Farnham N York 132 E7
Farnham Suffk 79 H3
Farnham Surrey 30 D3
Farnham Common Bucks 42 F4
Farnham Royal Bucks 42 F4
Farningham Kent 45 K6
Farnley Leeds 123 K4
Farnley N York 123 J2
Farnley Tyas Kirk 123 H7
Farnsfield Notts 101 M2
Farnworth Bolton 113 G1
Farnworth Halton 112 D4
Far Oakridge Gloucs 55 L7
Farr Highld 203 K5
Farr Highld 213 G7
Farr Highld 229 L3
Farraline Highld 202 E2
Farringdon Devon 12 C4
Farrington Gurney BaNES 26 F1
Far Sawrey Cumb 137 K7
Farthinghoe Nhants 73 G6
Farthingstone Nhants 73 H4
Fartown Kirk 123 H6
Fasnacloich Ag & B 191 K6
Fasnakyle Highld 211 L8
Fassfern Highld 191 K2
Fatfield Sundld 151 H4
Fauldhouse W Loth 176 C6
Faulkbourne Essex 61 J5
Faulkland Somset 27 H1
Fauls Shrops 98 E6
Faversham Kent 34 D3
Fawdington N York 132 F5
Fawdon N u Ty 151 G2

Fawkham Green Kent 45 L6
Fawler Oxon 57 G4
Fawley Bucks 42 C3
Fawley Hants 16 F2
Fawley W Berk 41 H4
Faxfleet E R Yk 125 K5
Faygate W Susx 31 K5
Fazakerley Lpool 111 K3
Fazeley Staffs 85 L3
Fearby N York 132 B4
Fearn Highld 223 H6
Fearnan P & K 194 B7
Fearnbeg Highld 210 B3
Fearnmore Highld 209 L3
Fearnoch Ag & B 172 F3
Featherstone Staffs 85 G3
Featherstone Wakefd 124 C6
Feckenham Worcs 71 H3
Feering Essex 61 L4
Feetham N York 140 C7
Felbridge Surrey 32 C5
Felbrigg Norfk 106 E5
Felcourt Surrey 32 C5
Felindre Carmth 51 G2
Felindre Carmth 65 K6
Felindre Powys 82 D7
Felindre Swans 51 J5
Felindre Farchog Pembks 64 F6
Felingwm Isaf Carmth 51 G2
Felingwm Uchaf Carmth 51 G1
Felixkirk N York 133 G3
Felixstowe Suffk 79 G7
Felling Gatesd 151 G3
Felmersham Bed 74 E3
Felmingham Norfk 106 F6
Felpham W Susx 18 C5
Felsham Suffk 77 L3
Felsted Essex 61 G4
Feltham Gt Lon 43 J5
Felthamhill Surrey 43 H6
Felthorpe Norfk 106 E8
Felton Herefs 69 L5
Felton N Som 38 D7
Felton Nthumb 158 F3
Felton Butler Shrops 98 B8
Feltwell Norfk 91 G5
Fence Lancs 122 C3
Fence Rothm 115 H4
Fencott Oxon 57 L5
Fendike Corner Lincs 104 D1
Fen Ditton Cambs 76 C3
Fen Drayton Cambs 75 L2
Feniscowles Bl w D 121 J5
Feniton Devon 12 E3
Fenland Crematorium Cambs 90 B5
Fenn Green Shrops 84 D6
Fenn Street Medway 46 D5
Fenny Bentley Derbys 100 D3
Fenny Bridges Devon 12 E3
Fenny Compton Warwks 72 E4
Fenny Drayton Leics 86 D4
Fenstanton Cambs 75 K2
Fen Street Norfk 92 B4
Fenton Cambs 89 K7
Fenton Cumb 148 E4
Fenton Lincs 102 E3
Fenton Lincs 116 D6
Fenton Notts 116 C5
Fenton Nthumb 168 E3
Fenton Barns E Loth 178 B3
Fenwick Donc 124 F7
Fenwick E Ayrs 163 L2
Fenwick Nthumb 158 D7
Fenwick Nthumb 169 G2
Feock Cnwll 4 C7
Feolin Ferry Ag & B 171 H4
Fergushill N Ayrs 163 J2
Feriniquarrie Highld 208 B4
Fermain Bay Guern 236 d3
Fern Angus 196 D4
Ferndale Rhondd 36 F2
Ferndown Dorset 15 K3
Ferness Highld 214 B5
Fernham Oxon 40 F3
Fernhill Heath Worcs 70 F3
Fernhurst W Susx 30 E5
Fernie Fife 186 E4
Ferniegair S Lans 175 K7
Fernilea Highld 208 F7
Fernilee Derbys 114 A5
Fernwood Notts 102 D3
Ferrensby N York 132 E7
Ferrindonald Highld 199 K4
Ferring W Susx 18 F5
Ferrybridge Services Wakefd 124 D6
Ferryden Angus 197 H5
Ferryhill Dur 141 H2
Ferryhill Station Dur 141 H2
Ferry Point Highld 223 G4
Ferryside Carmth 50 D4
Ferrytown Highld 223 G4
Fersfield Norfk 92 C6
Fersit Highld 192 F2
Feshiebridge Highld 203 K4
Fetcham Surrey 31 J1
Fetlar Shet 235 e2
Fetterangus Abers 217 J4
Fettercairn Abers 197 G2
Fewston N York 132 B8
Ffairfach Carmth 51 J2
Ffair Rhos Cerdgn 67 G2
Ffestiniog Gwynd 96 A4
Ffestiniog Railway Gwynd 95 L4
Fforest Carmth 51 H5
Fforest Fach Swans 51 J6
Ffostrasol Cerdgn 65 L5
Ffrith Flints 97 L2
Ffynnongroyw Flints 111 G5
Fiag Lodge Highld 225 K3
Fickleshole Surrey 32 C2
Fiddington Somset 25 K4
Fiddleford Dorset 27 J8
Fiddlers Green Cnwll 4 C5
Field Staffs 100 A5
Field Dalling Norfk 106 B5
Field Head Leics 86 F2
Fifehead Magdalen Dorset 27 H6
Fifehead Neville Dorset 14 E1
Fifehead St Quintin Dorset 14 E1
Fife Keith Moray 215 J4
Fifield Oxon 56 E4
Fifield W & M 42 E5
Figheldean Wilts 28 D3
Filby Norfk 93 K2
Filey N York 135 H4
Filgrave M Keyn 74 C5
Filkins Oxon 56 E6
Filleigh Devon 23 K5
Fillingham Lincs 116 F4
Fillongley Warwks 86 C6
Filton S Glos 38 E5
Fimber E R Yk 134 D7
Finavon Angus 196 D5
Fincham Norfk 91 G3
Finchampstead Wokham 42 D7
Fincharn Ag & B 182 C6
Finchdean Hants 30 C8
Finchingfield Essex 61 G2
Finchley Gt Lon 44 F2
Findern Derbys 100 F6
Findhorn Moray 214 C2
Findhorn Bridge Highld 213 J8
Findochty Moray 215 K2
Findo Gask P & K 185 L4
Findon Abers 207 H6
Findon W Susx 18 F4
Findon Mains Highld 212 F3
Findrack House Abers 206 B4
Finedon Nhants 74 D1
Fingask P & K 186 C4
Fingest Bucks 42 C3
Finghall N York 132 B2
Fingland D & G 164 E6
Finglesham Kent 35 J4
Fingringhoe Essex 62 B4
Finlarig Stirlg 184 C1
Finmere Oxon 57 M2
Finnart P & K 193 H5
Finningham Suffk 78 C1
Finningley Donc 116 A2
Finsbay W Isls 232 d5
Finstall Worcs 71 H1
Finsthwaite Cumb 129 H2
Finstock Oxon 57 G5
Finstown Ork 234 b6
Fintry Abers 216 E4
Fintry Stirlg 175 H2
Finzean Abers 206 B6
Fionnphort Ag & B 180 D3
Fionnsbhagh W Isls 232 d5
Firbank Cumb 130 C2
Firbeck Rothm 115 K4
Firby N York 132 D3
Firby N York 134 B6
Firle E Susx 19 M4
Firsby Lincs 118 F8
Fir Tree Dur 150 E7
Fishbourne IoW 17 G4
Fishbourne W Susx 18 A5
Fishbourne Roman Palace W Susx 18 A5
Fishburn Dur 141 J2
Fishcross Clacks 185 J7
Fisherford Abers 216 C7
Fisherrow E Loth 177 K4
Fisher's Pond Hants 29 J7
Fisherton Highld 213 H4
Fisherton S Ayrs 163 H6
Fisherton de la Mere Wilts 27 M4
Fishery Estate W & M 42 E4
Fishguard Pembks 64 D6
Fishlake Donc 125 G7
Fishnish Pier Ag & B 190 D7
Fishponds Bristl 38 F5
Fishtoft Lincs 104 B4
Fishtoft Drove Lincs 104 A3
Fiskavaig Highld 208 E7
Fiskerton Lincs 117 H6
Fiskerton Notts 102 C3
Fittleton Wilts 28 D2
Fittleworth W Susx 18 D2
Fitz Shrops 98 C8
Fitzhead Somset 25 H5
Fitzwilliam Wakefd 124 C7
Five Ash Down E Susx 19 M2
Five Ashes E Susx 32 F7
Fivehead Somset 26 A6
Fivelanes Cnwll 9 G8
Five Oak Green Kent 33 H4
Five Oaks Jersey 236 d7
Five Oaks W Susx 31 H5
Five Roads Carmth 50 F4
Flackwell Heath Bucks 42 E3
Fladbury Worcs 71 H5
Fladdabister Shet 235 c6
Flagg Derbys 114 C7
Flamborough E R Yk 135 K5
Flamborough Head E R Yk 135 K5
Flamingo Land Theme Park N York 134 B4
Flamstead Herts 59 H5
Flamstead End Herts 60 B7
Flansham W Susx 18 C5
Flanshaw Wakefd 123 L6
Flasby N York 131 H7
Flash Staffs 114 A7
Flashader Highld 208 E4
Flaunden Herts 59 G7
Flawborough Notts 102 C4
Flawith N York 133 G6
Flax Bourton N Som 38 D6
Flaxby N York 132 F7
Flaxley Gloucs 55 G5
Flaxpool Somset 25 H4
Flaxton N York 133 K6
Fleckney Leics 87 J5
Flecknoe Warwks 73 G2
Fledborough Notts 116 D6
Fleet Dorset 14 C6
Fleet Hants 30 D2
Fleet Lincs 104 C7
Fleet Hargate Lincs 104 C7
Fleet Services Hants 30 D1
Fleetwood Lancs 120 D2
Fleggburgh Norfk 93 J2
Flemingston V Glam 36 F6
Flemington S Lans 175 H6
Flempton Suffk 77 J1
Fletchertown Cumb 147 L6
Fletching E Susx 19 L2
Flexbury Cnwll 9 G4
Flexford Surrey 30 F2
Flimby Cumb 147 H7
Flimwell E Susx 33 J6
Flint Flints 111 H6
Flintham Notts 102 C4
Flinton E R Yk 126 F4
Flitcham Norfk 105 H6
Flitton C Beds 74 F7
Flitwick C Beds 74 F7
Flixborough N Linc 125 K7
Flixborough Stather N Linc 125 K7
Flixton N York 135 G4
Flixton Suffk 93 G6
Flixton Traffd 113 H3
Flockton Kirk 123 J7
Flockton Green Kirk 123 K7
Flodigarry Highld 218 C6
Flookburgh Cumb 129 H4
Flordon Norfk 92 E4
Flore Nhants 73 J3
Flowton Suffk 78 C5
Flushing Cnwll 3 L4
Fluxton Devon 12 E4
Flyford Flavell Worcs 71 H4
Fobbing Thurr 46 B4
Fochabers Moray 215 H3
Fochriw Caerph 53 H6
Fockerby N Linc 125 K6
Foddington Somset 26 E5
Foel Powys 81 L2
Foggathorpe E R Yk 125 H3
Fogo Border 179 G8
Fogwatt Moray 214 F3
Foindle Highld 228 B5
Folda Angus 195 J4
Fole Staffs 100 B5
Foleshill Covtry 86 D6
Folke Dorset 26 F8
Folkestone Kent 35 H7
Folkingham Lincs 103 H5
Folkington E Susx 20 B5
Folksworth Cambs 89 G5
Folkton N York 135 G4
Folla Rule Abers 216 D7
Follifoot N York 132 E8
Folly Gate Devon 10 E5
Fonthill Bishop Wilts 27 L5
Fonthill Gifford Wilts 27 L5
Fontmell Magna Dorset 27 K7
Fontmell Parva Dorset 27 J8
Fontwell W Susx 18 C4
Foolow Derbys 114 D6
Forbestown Abers 205 H3
Forcett N York 140 F5
Ford Ag & B 182 C6
Ford Bucks 58 C6
Ford Derbys 115 H5
Ford Devon 22 F6
Ford Gloucs 56 C3
Ford Nthumb 168 E2
Ford Somset 25 H5
Ford Staffs 100 B2
Ford W Susx 18 D5
Ford Wilts 39 J5
Fordcombe Kent 32 F5
Fordell Fife 177 G2
Forden Powys 82 E4

Ford End Essex 61 G5
Forder Green Devon 7 H3
Fordham Cambs 76 F1
Fordham Essex 61 L3
Fordham Norfk 90 E4
Fordingbridge Hants 28 D8
Fordon E R Yk 135 G4
Fordoun Abers 197 J2
Fordstreet Essex 61 L3
Ford Street Somset 25 J7
Fordwich Kent 35 G3
Fordyce Abers 216 B2
Forebridge Staffs 99 L7
Forest Guern 236 c4
Forest Chapel Ches E 113 L6
Forest Gate Gt Lon 45 H3
Forest Green Surrey 31 J3
Forest Hall N Tyne 151 G2
Forest Hill Gt Lon 45 G5
Forest Hill Oxon 57 L6
Forest Lane Head N York 132 E7
Forest Mill Clacks 185 K8
Forest of Bowland Lancs 130 C8
Forest of Dean Gloucs 54 F5
Forest of Dean Crematorium Gloucs 54 F5
Forest Park Crematorium Gt Lon 45 J2
Forest Row E Susx 32 D6
Forestside W Susx 30 C8
Forfar Angus 196 D6
Forgandenny P & K 186 A4
Forge Hammer Torfn 37 L2
Forgie Moray 215 J4
Forgieside Moray 215 J4
Forgue Abers 216 B5
Formby Sefton 111 J1
Forncett End Norfk 92 D5
Forncett St Mary Norfk 92 E5
Forncett St Peter Norfk 92 E5
Fornham All Saints Suffk 77 J2
Fornham St Martin Suffk 77 J2
Fornighty Highld 213 L4
Forres Moray 214 C3
Forsbrook Staffs 99 L4
Forse Highld 227 M2
Forsinard Highld 230 C6
Fort Augustus Highld 202 B4
Forteviot P & K 185 L4
Forth S Lans 176 C7
Forthampton Gloucs 55 K2
Fort Hommet Guern 236 c2
Forth Rail Bridge C Edin 176 F3
Forth Road Bridge Fife 176 F3
Fortingall P & K 194 B6
Fort le Marchant Guern 236 d1
Forton Hants 29 H3
Forton Lancs 121 G1
Forton Shrops 83 H1
Forton Somset 13 J2
Forton Staffs 99 H7
Fortrie Abers 216 C5
Fortrose Highld 213 H3
Fortuneswell Dorset 14 D7
Fort William Highld 191 L2
Forty Hill Gt Lon 60 B7
Fosbury Wilts 40 F8
Foscot Oxon 56 E4
Fosdyke Lincs 104 A5
Foss P & K 194 C5
Fossebridge Gloucs 56 B5
Foster Street Essex 60 D6
Foston Derbys 100 D6
Foston Leics 87 H4
Foston Lincs 102 E4
Foston N York 133 L6
Foston on the Wolds E R Yk 135 H7
Fotherby Lincs 118 D3
Fotheringhay Nhants 88 F5
Foula Shet 235 a6
Foula Airport Shet 235 a6
Foulden Border 179 J7
Foulden Norfk 91 H4
Foul End Warwks 86 B4
Foulness Island Essex 47 G2
Foulon Vale Crematorium Guern 236 d3
Foulridge Lancs 122 D3
Foulsham Norfk 106 B7
Fountainhall Border 177 L8
Four Ashes Suffk 78 B1
Four Cabots Guern 236 c3
Four Crosses Powys 97 K8
Four Elms Kent 32 E4
Four Forks Somset 25 K4
Four Gotes Cambs 90 C1
Four Lanes Cnwll 3 J4
Four Marks Hants 30 A4
Four Mile Bridge IoA 108 C5
Four Oaks Birm 85 K4
Four Oaks Solhll 86 B7
Fourpenny Highld 223 H3
Four Roads Carmth 50 F4
Fourstones Nthumb 149 M2
Four Throws Kent 33 K7
Fovant Wilts 28 A5
Foveran Abers 207 H2
Fowey Cnwll 5 H5
Fowlhall Kent 33 J4
Fowlis Angus 186 E2
Fowlis Wester P & K 185 J3
Fowlmere Cambs 76 B5
Fownhope Herefs 69 L7
Foxbar Rens 174 E6
Foxcote Somset 27 G1
Foxdale IoM 237 b5
Foxearth Essex 77 J5
Foxfield Cumb 128 F3
Foxhole Cnwll 4 F5
Foxholes N York 134 F5
Foxley Norfk 106 C7
Foxt Staffs 100 B3
Foxton Cambs 76 B5
Foxton Leics 87 K5
Foxton N York 141 K7
Foxwood Shrops 84 B7
Foy Herefs 54 E3
Foyers Highld 202 D2
Foynesfield Highld 213 L4
Fraddon Cnwll 4 E4
Fradley Staffs 85 L2
Fradswell Staffs 99 M6
Fraisthorpe E R Yk 135 J7
Framfield E Susx 20 A2
Framingham Earl Norfk 92 F3
Framingham Pigot Norfk 92 F3
Framlingham Suffk 79 G2
Frampton Dorset 14 C4
Frampton Lincs 104 B5
Frampton Cotterell S Glos 38 F4
Frampton Mansell Gloucs 55 L7
Frampton-on-Severn Gloucs 55 H6
Framsden Suffk 78 E3
Framwellgate Moor Dur 151 G6
Franche Worcs 84 E7
Frankby Wirral 111 H4
Frankley Worcs 85 H7
Frankley Services Worcs 85 H7
Frankton Warwks 72 E1
Frant E Susx 33 G6
Fraserburgh Abers 217 J2
Frating Essex 62 C4
Frating Green Essex 62 C4
Fratton C Port 17 J3
Freathy Cnwll 6 B5
Freckenham Suffk 76 F1
Freckleton Lancs 120 F5
Freeby Leics 102 D7
Freefolk Hants 29 J2
Freeland Oxon 57 H5
Freethorpe Norfk 93 J3
Freethorpe Common Norfk 93 J3
Freiston Lincs 104 B4
Fremington Devon 23 H5
Fremington N York 140 D7
Frenchay S Glos 38 F5
Frenich P & K 194 C5
Frensham Surrey 30 D3
Freshfield Sefton 120 C8
Freshford Wilts 39 H7
Freshwater IoW 16 D5
Fressingfield Suffk 92 F7
Freston Suffk 78 E6
Freswick Highld 231 L3
Fretherne Gloucs 55 G6
Frettenham Norfk 106 F8
Freuchie Fife 186 E6
Freystrop Pembks 49 G5
Friar Park Sandw 85 H4
Friday Bridge Cambs 90 C3
Friday Street Suffk 79 H3
Fridaythorpe E R Yk 134 D7
Friern Barnet Gt Lon 44 F2
Friesthorpe Lincs 117 H5
Frieston Lincs 102 F3
Frieth Bucks 42 D3
Frilford Oxon 41 H2
Frilsham W Berk 41 K5
Frimley Surrey 42 E8
Frindsbury Medway 46 C6
Fring Norfk 105 H5
Fringford Oxon 57 L3
Frinsted Kent 34 B4
Frinton-on-Sea Essex 62 F4
Friockheim Angus 196 F6
Frisby on the Wreake Leics 102 B8
Friskney Lincs 104 D2
Friston E Susx 20 B6
Friston Suffk 79 J3
Fritchley Derbys 101 G3
Fritham Hants 28 E8
Frithelstock Devon 23 G7
Frithelstock Stone Devon 23 G7
Frithville Lincs 104 A3
Frittenden Kent 33 K5
Frittiscombe Devon 7 J6
Fritton Norfk 92 F5
Fritton Norfk 93 K4
Fritwell Oxon 57 K3
Frizinghall C Brad 123 H4
Frizington Cumb 136 E4
Frocester Gloucs 55 H7
Frodesley Shrops 83 K3
Frodsham Ches W 112 D6
Frogden Border 168 B4
Frog End Cambs 76 B5
Froggatt Derbys 114 E6
Froghall Staffs 100 A3
Frogmore Devon 7 H7
Frognall Lincs 89 H2
Frog Pool Worcs 70 E2
Frogwell Cnwll 6 A3
Frolesworth Leics 87 G5
Frome Somset 27 H2
Frome St Quintin Dorset 14 B2
Fromes Hill Herefs 70 C5
Froncysyllte Denbgs 97 K4
Fron-goch Gwynd 96 D5
Fron Isaf Wrexhm 97 L4
Frosterley Dur 150 C7
Froxfield Wilts 40 F6
Froxfield Green Hants 30 B6
Fryern Hill Hants 29 H7
Fryerning Essex 61 G7
Fuinary Highld 190 C6
Fulbeck Lincs 102 F3
Fulbourn Cambs 76 D4
Fulbrook Oxon 56 E5
Fulflood Hants 29 J5
Fulford C York 124 F2
Fulford Somset 25 K5
Fulford Staffs 99 L5
Fulham Gt Lon 44 E5
Fulking W Susx 19 H4
Fullarton N Ayrs 163 H2
Fuller Street Essex 61 H5
Fullerton Hants 29 G4
Fulletby Lincs 118 D6
Fullready Warwks 72 C5
Full Sutton E R Yk 134 B7
Fullwood E Ayrs 174 E7
Fulmer Bucks 43 G4
Fulmodeston Norfk 106 B6
Fulnetby Lincs 117 H5
Fulney Lincs 103 L7
Fulstow Lincs 118 D3
Fulwell Sundld 151 J3
Fulwood Lancs 121 H4
Fulwood Sheff 114 F4
Fundenhall Norfk 92 D4
Funtington W Susx 17 L2
Funtullich P & K 184 F3
Furley Devon 13 H2
Furnace Ag & B 182 E7
Furnace Carmth 51 G5
Furness Vale Derbys 114 A5
Furneux Pelham Herts 60 C3
Furzley Hants 28 F7
Fyfield Essex 60 F6
Fyfield Hants 28 F3
Fyfield Oxon 57 H7
Fyfield Wilts 40 C6
Fyfield Wilts 40 D7
Fylingthorpe N York 143 J6
Fyning W Susx 30 D6
Fyvie Abers 216 E6

G

Gabroc Hill E Ayrs 174 E7
Gaddesby Leics 87 K2
Gaddesden Row Herts 59 H5
Gadgirth S Ayrs 163 K5
Gaerllwyd Mons 38 C2
Gaerwen IoA 108 F7
Gailes N Ayrs 163 H3
Gailey Staffs 85 G2
Gainford Dur 140 F4
Gainsborough Lincs 116 D4
Gainsford End Essex 77 G7
Gairloch Highld 219 J6
Gairlochy Highld 201 J8
Gairneybridge P & K 186 B7
Gaitsgill Cumb 148 C5
Galashiels Border 167 G3
Galgate Lancs 129 K7
Galhampton Somset 26 F5
Gallanachbeg Ag & B 182 B2
Gallanachmore Ag & B 182 B3
Gallatown Fife 186 E8
Galleywood Essex 61 H7
Gallovie Highld 202 E7
Galloway Forest Park 153 J5
Gallowfauld Angus 196 D7
Gallowhill P & K 186 B1
Galltair Highld 200 C2
Galmpton Devon 7 G7
Galmpton Torbay 7 K5
Galphay N York 132 C5
Galston E Ayrs 163 L3
Gamblesby Cumb 149 G6
Gamlingay Cambs 75 J4
Gamlingay Great Heath Cambs 75 J4
Gamrie Abers 216 F2
Gamston Notts 101 L5
Gamston Notts 116 B6

Ganavan Bay Ag & B 182 B2
Ganllwyd Gwynd 96 B7
Gannachy Angus 196 F3
Ganstead E R Yk 126 E4
Ganthorpe N York 133 L5
Ganton N York 134 F4
Garbity Moray 215 H4
Garboldisham Norfk 92 B7
Garbole Highld 203 H1
Garchory Abers 205 G4
Gardeners Green Wokham 42 D6
Garden of England Crematorium Kent 46 E6
Gardenstown Abers 216 F2
Garden Village Sheff 114 E2
Garderhouse Shet 235 c5
Gare Hill Somset 27 H4
Garelochhead Ag & B 173 L1
Garford Oxon 41 H2
Garforth Leeds 124 B4
Gargrave N York 131 H8
Gargunnock Stirlg 184 F8
Garlic Street Norfk 92 E6
Garlieston D & G 145 K5
Garlinge Kent 35 J2
Garlinge Green Kent 34 F4
Garlogie Abers 206 E4
Garmond Abers 216 F4
Garmouth Moray 215 H2
Garmston Shrops 83 L3
Garn-Dolbenmaen Gwynd 95 J4
Garnkirk N Lans 175 J5
Garrabost W Isls 232 g2
Garrallan E Ayrs 164 B5
Garras Cnwll 3 J6
Garreg Gwynd 95 K4
Garrigill Cumb 149 J6
Garroch D & G 153 M6
Garrochtrie D & G 144 D7
Garrochty Ag & B 173 J7
Garros Highld 209 H2
Garsdale Head Cumb 130 E2
Garsdon Wilts 39 L3
Garshall Green Staffs 99 L5
Garsington Oxon 57 L7
Garstang Lancs 121 G2
Garston Herts 59 J7
Garston Lpool 112 B5
Gartachossan Ag & B 171 G6
Gartcosh N Lans 175 J5
Garth Powys 67 K5
Garth Wrexhm 97 K4
Garthamlock C Glas 175 H5
Garthmyl Powys 82 E4
Garthorpe Leics 102 D7
Garthorpe N Linc 125 K6
Garth Row Cumb 138 D7
Gartly Abers 215 L7
Gartmore Stirlg 184 C7
Gartness N Lans 175 K5
Gartness Stirlg 174 F2
Gartocharn W Duns 174 D2
Garton-on-the-Wolds E R Yk 134 F7
Gartymore Highld 227 H5
Garva Bridge Highld 202 E6
Garvald E Loth 178 D4
Garvan Highld 191 J2
Garvard Ag & B 171 G1
Garve Highld 212 B3
Garvellachs Ag & B 181 K5
Garvestone Norfk 92 B3
Garvock Inver 174 B4
Garway Herefs 54 C4
Garyvard W Isls 232 f3
Gasper Wilts 27 H5
Gastard Wilts 39 K6
Gasthorpe Norfk 91 L7
Gaston Green Essex 60 D5
Gatcombe IoW 16 F5
Gate Burton Lincs 116 D5
Gateforth N York 124 E5
Gatehead E Ayrs 163 K3
Gate Helmsley N York 133 L7
Gatehouse Nthumb 157 K4
Gatehouse of Fleet D & G 145 M4
Gateley Norfk 106 A7
Gatenby N York 132 E3
Gateshaw Border 168 B5
Gateshead Gatesd 151 G3
Gateside Angus 196 D7
Gateside E Rens 174 E6
Gateside Fife 186 C5
Gateside N Ayrs 174 C7
Gateslack D & G 154 F2
Gatley Stockp 113 J4
Gattonside Border 167 H3
Gatwick Airport W Susx 32 B5
Gaulby Leics 87 K4
Gauldry Fife 186 F3
Gauldswell P & K 195 K6
Gautby Lincs 117 K6
Gavinton Border 179 G7
Gawcott Bucks 58 B2
Gawsworth Ches E 113 K7
Gawthrop Cumb 130 D3
Gawthwaite Cumb 129 G3
Gaydon Warwks 72 D4
Gayhurst M Keyn 74 B5
Gayle N York 131 G2
Gayles N York 140 E5
Gayton Nhants 73 K4
Gayton Norfk 105 H8
Gayton Staffs 99 M6
Gayton le Marsh Lincs 118 F5
Gayton Thorpe Norfk 105 H8
Gaywood Norfk 105 G7
Gazeley Suffk 77 G2
Gearraidh Bhaird W Isls 232 f3
Geary Highld 208 D3
Gedding Suffk 77 L3
Geddington Nhants 88 C6
Gedling Notts 101 L4
Gedney Lincs 104 C7
Gedney Broadgate Lincs 104 C7
Gedney Drove End Lincs 104 D6
Gedney Dyke Lincs 104 C7
Gedney Hill Lincs 89 L2
Geeston Rutlnd 88 E3
Geldeston Norfk 93 H5
Gellifor Denbgs 110 F8
Gelligaer Caerph 37 H2
Gellilydan Gwynd 95 M4
Gellinudd Neath 51 K5
Gellyburn P & K 195 H8
Gellywen Carmth 50 C2
Gelston D & G 146 D3
Gelston Lincs 102 E4
Gembling E R Yk 135 H7
Gentleshaw Staffs 85 J2
Georgefield D & G 156 B4
George Green Bucks 43 G4
Georgeham Devon 23 G4
Georgemas Junction Station Highld 231 H4
George Nympton Devon 23 L6
Georth Ork 234 b5
Germansweek Devon 10 C6
Gerrans Cnwll 4 D8
Gerrards Cross Bucks 43 G3
Gerrick R & Cl 142 E5
Gestingthorpe Essex 77 J6
Geuffordd Powys 82 E2
Gidea Park Gt Lon 45 K3
Giffnock E Rens 175 G6
Gifford E Loth 178 C5
Giffordtown Fife 186 E5
Giggleswick N York 130 F6
Gigha Ag & B 171 L7
Gilberdyke E R Yk 125 K5
Gilchriston E Loth 178 B5
Gilcrux Cumb 147 K7
Gildersome Leeds 123 K5
Gildingwells Rothm 115 K4
Gilesgate Moor Dur 151 H6
Gileston V Glam 36 F6
Gilfach Caerph 53 J7
Gilfach Goch Brdgnd 36 F3
Gilfachrheda Cerdgn 65 L3
Gilgarran Cumb 136 E3
Gillamoor N York 133 K2
Gillen Highld 208 D3
Gillesbie D & G 155 K4
Gilling East N York 133 J4
Gillingham Dorset 27 J6
Gillingham Medway 46 C6
Gillingham Norfk 93 J5
Gilling West N York 140 F6
Gillock Highld 231 J4
Gills Highld 231 K2
Gilmanscleuch Border 166 E5
Gilmerton C Edin 177 J5
Gilmerton P & K 185 J3
Gilmonby Dur 140 C5
Gilmorton Leics 87 H6
Gilroes Crematorium C Leic 87 H3
Gilsland Nthumb 149 G2
Gilston Border 177 L6
Gilston Herts 60 D5
Gilwern Mons 53 K5
Gimingham Norfk 107 G5
Gipping Suffk 78 C2
Gipsey Bridge Lincs 103 M3
Girdle Toll N Ayrs 163 J2
Girlsta Shet 235 c5
Girsby N York 141 J5
Girthon D & G 146 A4
Girton Cambs 76 B3
Girton Notts 116 D7
Girvan S Ayrs 152 E3
Gisburn Lancs 122 C2
Gisleham Suffk 93 K5
Gislingham Suffk 78 C1
Gissing Norfk 92 D6
Gittisham Devon 12 E3
Gladestry Powys 68 E4
Gladsmuir E Loth 177 M4
Glais Swans 51 K5
Glaisdale N York 143 G6
Glamis Angus 196 C6
Glanaman Carmth 51 J3
Glandford Norfk 106 C4
Glandwr Pembks 49 K2
Glandyfi Cerdgn 80 F4
Glanllynfi Brdgnd 36 D3
Glan-rhyd Powys 52 B6
Glanton Nthumb 169 G6
Glanvilles Wootton Dorset 14 D2
Glan-y-don Flints 111 G5
Glapthorn Nhants 88 E5
Glapwell Derbys 115 J7
Glasbury Powys 68 D6
Glascwm Powys 68 D4
Glasfryn Conwy 96 E3
Glasgow C Glas 175 G5
Glasgow Airport Rens 174 E5
Glasgow Science Centre C Glas 175 G5
Glasinfryn Gwynd 109 H7
Glasnacardoch Bay Highld 199 L6
Glasnakille Highld 199 H3
Glassford S Lans 175 J8
Glasshouse Gloucs 55 G4
Glasshouses N York 132 B6
Glasson Cumb 148 A3
Glasson Lancs 129 K7
Glassonby Cumb 149 G7
Glasterlaw Angus 196 F6
Glaston Rutlnd 88 C4
Glastonbury Somset 26 D4
Glatton Cambs 89 H6
Glazebrook Warrtn 113 G3
Glazebury Warrtn 112 F3
Glazeley Shrops 84 C5
Gleaston Cumb 128 F5
Glebe Highld 202 D2
Gledhow Leeds 123 L3
Gledpark D & G 146 B5
Gledrid Shrops 97 L5
Glemsford Suffk 77 J5
Glenallachie Moray 215 G6
Glenancross Highld 199 K6
Glenaros House Ag & B 190 B7
Glen Auldyn IoM 237 d3
Glenbarr Ag & B 161 H3
Glenbarry Abers 216 B4
Glenbeg Highld 190 C4
Glenbervie Abers 197 J1
Glenboig N Lans 175 J5
Glenborrodale Highld 190 C4
Glenbranter Ag & B 183 G7
Glenbreck Border 165 K5
Glenbrittle House Highld 198 F2
Glenbuck E Ayrs 164 E4
Glencally Angus 196 B4
Glencaple D & G 147 H2
Glencarron Lodge Highld 211 G4
Glencarse P & K 186 C3
Glen Clunie Lodge Abers 204 E8
Glencoe Highld 191 L5
Glencothe Border 165 L4
Glencraig Fife 186 C7
Glencrosh D & G 154 D4
Glendale Highld 208 B4
Glendaruel Ag & B 173 G2
Glendevon P & K 185 K6
Glendoe Lodge Highld 202 C4
Glendoick P & K 186 C3
Glenduckie Fife 186 D4
Glenegedale Ag & B 170 F7
Glenelg Highld 200 C2
Glenerney Moray 214 C5
Glenfarg P & K 186 B5
Glenfield Leics 87 G3
Glenfinnan Highld 191 H1
Glenfintaig Lodge Highld 201 K7
Glenfoot P & K 186 C4
Glenfyne Lodge Ag & B 183 H4
Glengarnock N Ayrs 174 C7
Glengolly Highld 231 G3
Glengorm Castle Ag & B 189 K5
Glengrasco Highld 209 G5
Glenholm Border 165 L3
Glenhoul D & G 154 A5
Glenisla Angus 195 K4
Glenkin Ag & B 173 K3
Glenkindie Abers 205 K3
Glenlivet Moray 214 F8
Glenlochar D & G 146 C3
Glenlomond P & K 186 C6
Glenluce D & G 144 E4
Glenmassen Ag & B 173 J2
Glenmavis N Lans 175 K5
Glen Maye IoM 237 b5
Glenmore Highld 209 G6
Glenmore Lodge Highld 204 B4
Glen Nevis House Highld 192 B3
Glenochil Clacks 185 H7
Glen Parva Leics 87 H4
Glenquiech Angus 196 C4
Glenralloch Ag & B 172 E5
Glenridding Cumb 137 L4
Glenrothes Fife 186 D7
Glenshero Lodge Highld 202 E6
Glenstriven Ag & B 173 J3
Glentham Lincs 117 G4
Glentrool D & G 153 H6
Glen Trool Lodge D & G 153 J6
Glentruim House Highld 203 G6
Glentworth Lincs 116 F4
Glenuig Highld 190 D2
Glenvarragill Highld 209 G6
Glen Vine IoM 237 c5
Glenwhilly D & G 152 E7

Glespin S Lans 164 F4
Glewstone Herefs 54 E4
Glinton C Pete 89 H3
Glooston Leics 87 L4
Glossop Derbys 114 B3
Gloster Hill Nthumb 159 G2
Gloucester Gloucs 55 J4
Gloucester Crematorium Gloucs 55 J5
Gloucester Services Gloucs 55 J5
Gloucestershire Airport Gloucs 55 K4
Glusburn N York 122 F2
Glutt Lodge Highld 227 H2
Glympton Oxon 57 H4
Glynarthen Cerdgn 65 K5
Glyn Ceiriog Wrexhm 97 J5
Glyncorrwg Neath 52 D7
Glynde E Susx 19 L4
Glyndyfrdwy Denbgs 97 J4
Glynneath Neath 52 D6
Glynn Valley Crematorium Cnwll 5 H3
Glyntaff Crematorium Rhondd 37 H3
Glyntawe Powys 52 D5
Glynteg Carmth 65 K6
Gnosall Staffs 99 J7
Gnosall Heath Staffs 99 J7
Goadby Leics 87 L4
Goadby Marwood Leics 102 C7
Goatacre Wilts 40 A5
Goathill Dorset 26 F7
Goathland N York 143 H6
Goathurst Somset 25 K5
Gobowen Shrops 97 L5
Godalming Surrey 30 F3
Goddard's Green Kent 33 L6
Godmanchester Cambs 75 J1
Godmanstone Dorset 14 C3
Godmersham Kent 34 E5
Godney Somset 26 C3
Godolphin Cross Cnwll 3 G5
Godre'r-graig Neath 51 L4
Godshill IoW 17 G6
Godstone Surrey 32 C3
Goetre Mons 53 L6
Goff's Oak Herts 60 B7
Gogar C Edin 177 G4
Goginan Cerdgn 80 F7
Golan Gwynd 95 J4
Golant Cnwll 5 H5
Golberdon Cnwll 5 M2
Golborne Wigan 112 E3
Golcar Kirk 123 G7
Goldcliff Newpt 38 A4
Golden Green Kent 33 H4
Goldenhill C Stke 99 J2
Golden Pot Hants 30 B3
Golders Green Gt Lon 44 E3
Golders Green Crematorium Gt Lon 44 E3
Goldhanger Essex 61 L6
Goldington Bed 74 F4
Goldsborough N York 132 F7
Goldsborough N York 143 H4
Golds Green Sandw 85 H5
Goldsithney Cnwll 2 F5
Goldsworth Park Surrey 43 G8
Goldthorpe Barns 115 J2
Goldworthy Devon 22 F6
Gollanfield Highld 213 J4
Golspie Highld 223 H2
Gomeldon Wilts 28 D4
Gomshall Surrey 31 H2
Gonalston Notts 102 B3
Gonerby Hill Foot Lincs 102 E5
Gonfirth Shet 235 c4
Good Easter Essex 60 F5
Gooderstone Norfk 91 H3
Goodleigh Devon 23 J5
Goodmanham E R Yk 125 K2
Goodmayes Gt Lon 45 J3
Goodnestone Kent 34 D3
Goodnestone Kent 35 H4
Goodrich Herefs 54 E4
Goodrington Torbay 7 K4
Goodshaw Lancs 122 B5
Goodwick Pembks 64 C6
Goodworth Clatford Hants 29 G3
Goole E R Yk 125 H5
Goom's Hill Worcs 71 H4
Goonbell Cnwll 3 J2
Goonhavern Cnwll 3 K1
Goonvrea Cnwll 3 J2
Goosecruives Abers 206 E8
Gooseford Devon 11 G6
Goose Green Essex 62 D3
Goose Green S Glos 38 F5
Gooseham Cnwll 9 G2
Goosey Oxon 41 G3
Goosnargh Lancs 121 H3
Goostrey Ches E 113 H7
Gordano Services N Som 38 D5
Gordon Border 167 K2
Gordon Arms Hotel Border 166 D4
Gordonstown Abers 216 B3
Gordonstown Abers 216 D6
Gorebridge Mdloth 177 K6
Gorefield Cambs 90 B2
Gores Wilts 40 C8
Gorey Jersey 236 e7
Goring Oxon 41 L4
Goring-by-Sea W Susx 18 F5
Gorleston on Sea Norfk 93 L3
Gornal Wood Crematorium Dudley 85 G5
Gorrachie Abers 216 E3
Gorran Churchtown Cnwll 4 F7
Gorran Haven Cnwll 4 F7
Gorsedd Flints 111 G6
Gorse Hill Swindn 40 D3
Gorseinon Swans 51 H5
Gorsgoch Cerdgn 66 C4
Gorslas Carmth 51 H3
Gorsley Gloucs 55 G3
Gorsley Common Herefs 54 F3
Gorstan Highld 212 B2
Gorsty Hill Staffs 100 C6
Gorten Ag & B 181 L2
Gorthleck Highld 202 E2
Gorton Manch 113 K3
Gosbeck Suffk 78 D4
Gosberton Lincs 103 L6
Gosfield Essex 61 J3
Gosforth Cumb 136 E6
Gosforth N u Ty 151 G2
Gospel End Staffs 84 F5
Gosport Hants 17 H3
Gossington Gloucs 55 H7
Gotham Notts 101 K6
Gotherington Gloucs 55 L3
Gotton Somset 25 K5
Goudhurst Kent 33 J5
Goulceby Lincs 118 C5
Gourdas Abers 216 E6
Gourdie C Dund 186 F2
Gourdon Abers 197 K3
Gourock Inver 173 L3
Govan C Glas 174 F5
Goveton Devon 7 H6
Govilon Mons 53 K5
Gowdall E R Yk 124 F6
Gower Highld 212 D3
Gower Swans 51 G7
Gowerton Swans 51 H6
Gowkhall Fife 176 E1
Goxhill E R Yk 126 F2
Goxhill N Linc 126 D6
Grabhair W Isls 232 f3
Graffham W Susx 18 C3
Grafham Cambs 75 H2
Grafham Surrey 31 G3
Grafton N York 132 F6
Grafton Oxon 56 F7
Grafton Shrops 98 B8
Grafton Worcs 71 H6
Grafton Flyford Worcs 71 G4
Grafton Regis Nhants 73 L5
Grafton Underwood Nhants 88 D7
Grafty Green Kent 34 B5
Graig Conwy 109 M6
Graigfechan Denbgs 97 J2
Grain Medway 46 E5
Grainsby Lincs 118 C2
Grainthorpe Lincs 118 E3
Grampound Cnwll 4 E6
Grampound Road Cnwll 4 E5
Gramsdal W Isls 233 c6
Gramsdale W Isls 233 c6
Granborough Bucks 58 C3
Granby Notts 102 C5
Grandborough Warwks 72 F2
Grand Chemins Jersey 236 d7
Grandes Rocques Guern 236 c2
Grandtully P & K 194 E5
Grange Cumb 137 H4
Grange Medway 46 D6
Grange P & K 186 D3
Grange Crossroads Moray 215 K4
Grange Hall Moray 214 C3
Grangehall S Lans 165 J2
Grange Hill Essex 45 H2
Grangemill Derbys 100 E2
Grange Moor Kirk 123 J7
Grangemouth Falk 176 C3
Grange of Lindores Fife 186 D4
Grange-over-Sands Cumb 129 J4
Grangepans Falk 176 D3
Grange Park Nhants 73 L4
Grangetown R & Cl 142 C3
Grangetown Sundld 151 K4
Grange Villa Dur 151 G4
Gransmoor E R Yk 135 H7
Granston Pembks 64 C7
Grantchester Cambs 76 B4
Grantham Lincs 102 E5
Grantham Crematorium Lincs 102 F5
Granton C Edin 177 H3
Grantown-on-Spey Highld 214 C8
Grantshouse Border 179 G5
Grasby Lincs 117 H1
Grasmere Cumb 137 K5
Grasscroft Oldham 113 L1
Grassendale Lpool 111 L4
Grassington N York 131 J6
Grassmoor Derbys 115 H7
Grassthorpe Notts 116 C7
Grateley Hants 28 F3
Graveley Cambs 75 J2
Graveley Herts 59 L3
Gravelly Hill Birm 85 K5
Graveney Kent 34 E3
Gravesend Kent 46 A5
Gravir W Isls 232 f3
Grayingham Lincs 116 F3
Grayrigg Cumb 138 E7
Grays Thurr 45 L4
Grayshott Hants 30 E4
Grayswood Surrey 30 E4
Greasbrough Rothm 115 H3
Greasby Wirral 111 H4
Great Abington Cambs 76 D5
Great Addington Nhants 88 D7
Great Alne Warwks 71 K3
Great Altcar Lancs 111 K1
Great Amwell Herts 60 B5
Great Asby Cumb 138 F5
Great Ashfield Suffk 78 B2
Great Ayton N York 142 C5
Great Baddow Essex 61 H6
Great Badminton S Glos 39 J4
Great Bardfield Essex 61 G2
Great Barford Bed 75 G4
Great Barr Sandw 85 J4
Great Barrington Gloucs 56 E5
Great Barrow Ches W 112 C7
Great Barton Suffk 77 K2
Great Barugh N York 134 B4
Great Bavington Nthumb 158 C6
Great Bealings Suffk 78 F5
Great Bedwyn Wilts 40 F7
Great Bentley Essex 62 D4
Great Billing Nhants 74 B3
Great Bircham Norfk 105 J6
Great Blakenham Suffk 78 D4
Great Blencow Cumb 138 C2
Great Bolas Wrekin 98 F7
Great Bookham Surrey 31 J1
Great Bourton Oxon 72 F5
Great Bowden Leics 87 L5
Great Bradley Suffk 76 F4
Great Braxted Essex 61 K5
Great Bricett Suffk 78 C4
Great Brickhill Bucks 58 E3
Great Bridgeford Staffs 99 K6
Great Brington Nhants 73 J2
Great Bromley Essex 62 C3
Great Broughton Cumb 136 E2
Great Broughton N York 142 C6
Great Budworth Ches W 112 F6
Great Burdon Darltn 141 H4
Great Burstead Essex 46 B2
Great Busby N York 142 B6
Great Carlton Lincs 118 E4
Great Casterton Rutlnd 88 E2
Great Chalfield Wilts 39 K7
Great Chart Kent 34 C6
Great Chatwell Staffs 84 E1
Great Chell C Stke 99 K3
Great Chesterford Essex 76 D6
Great Cheverell Wilts 27 M1
Great Chishill Cambs 76 B6
Great Clacton Essex 62 E5
Great Clifton Cumb 136 E2
Great Coates NE Lin 126 F8
Great Comberton Worcs 71 G6
Great Corby Cumb 148 E4
Great Cornard Suffk 77 K6
Great Cowden E R Yk 126 F3
Great Coxwell Oxon 40 F2
Great Cransley Nhants 88 B7
Great Cressingham Norfk 91 J3
Great Crosthwaite Cumb 137 J3
Great Cubley Derbys 100 D5
Great Cumbrae Island N Ayrs 173 K6
Great Dalby Leics 87 L2
Great Denham Bed 74 E5

Great Doddington Nhants 74 C2
Great Dunham Norfk 91 K1
Great Dunmow Essex 61 G4
Great Durnford Wilts 28 C4
Great Easton Essex 60 F3
Great Easton Leics 88 B5
Great Eccleston Lancs 120 F3
Great Ellingham Norfk 92 B4
Great Elm Somset 27 H2
Great Everdon Nhants 73 H3
Great Eversden Cambs 75 L4
Great Fencote N York 132 D2
Great Finborough Suffk 78 B3
Greatford Lincs 88 F2
Great Fransham Norfk 91 K2
Great Gaddesden Herts 59 G5
Greatgate Staffs 100 B4
Great Gidding Cambs 89 G6
Great Givendale E R Yk 134 C8
Great Glemham Suffk 79 H3
Great Glen Leics 87 J4
Great Gonerby Lincs 102 E5
Great Gransden Cambs 75 J4
Great Green Cambs 75 K5
Great Green Suffk 77 K4
Great Habton N York 134 B4
Great Hale Lincs 103 J4
Great Hallingbury Essex 60 E4
Greatham Hants 30 C5
Greatham Hartpl 141 L2
Greatham W Susx 18 E3
Great Hampden Bucks 58 D7
Great Harrowden Nhants 74 C1
Great Harwood Lancs 121 L4
Great Haseley Oxon 57 M7
Great Hatfield E R Yk 126 F3
Great Haywood Staffs 99 M7
Great Heck N York 124 E6
Great Henny Essex 77 K6
Great Hinton Wilts 39 K8
Great Hockham Norfk 91 L5
Great Holland Essex 62 E4
Great Hollands Br For 42 E6
Great Horkesley Essex 62 B2
Great Hormead Herts 60 C3
Great Horton C Brad 123 H4
Great Horwood Bucks 58 C2
Great Houghton Barns 115 H1
Great Houghton Nhants 73 L3
Great Hucklow Derbys 114 D6
Great Kelk E R Yk 135 H7
Great Kimble Bucks 58 D6
Great Kingshill Bucks 42 E2
Great Langdale Cumb 137 J6
Great Langton N York 141 H7
Great Leighs Essex 61 H4
Great Limber Lincs 126 E8
Great Linford M Keyn 74 C6
Great Livermere Suffk 77 K1
Great Longstone Derbys 114 D6
Great Lumley Dur 151 H5
Great Malvern Worcs 70 D5
Great Maplestead Essex 77 J7
Great Marton Bpool 120 D4
Great Massingham Norfk 105 J7
Great Milton Oxon 57 L7
Great Missenden Bucks 58 E7
Great Mitton Lancs 121 K3
Great Mongeham Kent 35 K4
Great Moulton Norfk 92 E5
Great Musgrave Cumb 139 H4
Great Ness Shrops 98 B8
Great Notley Essex 61 H4
Great Oak Mons 54 B6
Great Oakley Essex 62 E3
Great Oakley Nhants 88 C6
Great Offley Herts 59 J3
Great Ormside Cumb 139 G4
Great Orton Cumb 148 B4
Great Ouseburn N York 133 G6
Great Oxendon Nhants 87 K6
Great Park N u Ty 158 F7
Great Parndon Essex 60 C6
Great Paxton Cambs 75 H2
Great Plumpton Lancs 120 E4
Great Plumstead Norfk 93 G2
Great Ponton Lincs 102 F6
Great Preston Leeds 124 B5
Great Raveley Cambs 89 J7
Great Rissington Gloucs 56 D5
Great Rollright Oxon 56 F2
Great Ryburgh Norfk 106 A6
Great Ryton Shrops 83 J3
Great Saling Essex 61 H3
Great Salkeld Cumb 148 F7
Great Sampford Essex 76 F7
Great Saughall Ches W 111 K7
Great Shefford W Berk 41 G5
Great Shelford Cambs 76 C4
Great Smeaton N York 141 H6
Great Snoring Norfk 105 M5
Great Somerford Wilts 39 L4
Great Soudley Shrops 99 G6
Great Stainton Darltn 141 H3
Great Stambridge Essex 46 E2
Great Staughton Cambs 75 G2
Great Steeping Lincs 118 F8
Great Stoke S Glos 38 F4
Greatstone-on-Sea Kent 21 L2
Great Strickland Cumb 138 D3
Great Stukeley Cambs 89 J8
Great Sturton Lincs 117 K6
Great Swinburne Nthumb 158 B6
Great Tew Oxon 57 H3
Great Tey Essex 61 L3
Great Thurlow Suffk 76 F4
Great Torrington Devon 23 H7
Great Tosson Nthumb 158 C3
Great Totham Essex 61 K5
Great Totham Essex 61 L5
Great Urswick Cumb 129 G5
Great Wakering Essex 46 F3
Great Waldingfield Suffk 77 K5
Great Walsingham Norfk 105 M5
Great Waltham Essex 61 H5
Great Warley Essex 45 L2
Great Washbourne Gloucs 71 H7
Great Weeke Devon 11 G7
Great Wenham Suffk 78 C6
Great Whittington Nthumb 158 C7
Great Wigborough Essex 62 A5
Great Wilbraham Cambs 76 D3
Great Wishford Wilts 28 B4
Great Witcombe Gloucs 55 K5
Great Witley Worcs 70 D2
Great Wolford Warwks 72 B7
Greatworth Nhants 73 G6
Great Wratting Suffk 77 G5
Great Wymondley Herts 59 K3
Great Wyrley Staffs 85 H3
Great Yarmouth Norfk 93 L3
Great Yarmouth Crematorium Norfk 93 K3
Great Yeldham Essex 77 H6
Greenburn W Loth 176 C6
Green End Herts 60 B2
Green End Herts 60 B4
Greenfield Ag & B 173 M1
Greenfield C Beds 74 F7
Greenfield Flints 111 H6
Greenfield Highld 201 J5
Greenfield Oldham 113 M2
Greenford Gt Lon 43 J4
Greengairs N Lans 175 K4
Greengates C Brad 123 J3
Greenham Somset 25 G7
Green Hammerton N York 133 G7
Greenhaugh Nthumb 157 K5
Greenhead Nthumb 149 H3
Green Heath Staffs 85 H2
Greenhill D & G 155 J6
Greenhill Falk 175 L3
Greenhill Kent 47 K6
Greenhill S Lans 165 H3
Greenhithe Kent 45 L5
Greenholm E Ayrs 164 B3
Greenhouse Border 167 H5
Greenhow Hill N York 131 L6
Greenland Highld 231 J3
Greenland Sheff 115 H4
Greenlaw Border 167 L1
Greenlea D & G 155 H6
Greenloaning P & K 185 H6
Greenmount Bury 122 B7
Greenock Inver 174 B3
Greenodd Cumb 129 G3
Green Ore Somset 26 E2
Green Quarter Cumb 138 C6
Greenshields S Lans 165 K2
Greenside Gatesd 150 E3
Greenside Kirk 123 H7
Greens Norton Nhants 73 J4
Greenstead Green Essex 61 K3
Green Street Herts 59 K7
Green Street Herts 60 D4
Green Street Green Kent 45 L6
Green Tye Herts 60 C4
Greenway Somset 25 L6
Greenwich Gt Lon 45 G4
Greenwich Maritime Gt Lon 45 H4
Greet Gloucs 56 B3
Greete Shrops 69 L1
Greetham Lincs 118 D7
Greetham Rutlnd 88 D2
Greetland Calder 123 G6
Greinton Somset 26 B4
Grenaby IoM 237 b6
Grendon Nhants 74 C3
Grendon Warwks 86 C4
Grendon Underwood Bucks 58 B4
Grenoside Sheff 115 G3
Grenoside Crematorium Sheff 114 F3
Greosabhagh W Isls 232 e4
Gresford Wrexhm 97 M2
Gresham Norfk 106 E5
Greshornish House Hotel Highld 208 E4
Gressenhall Norfk 91 L1
Gressenhall Green Norfk 91 L1
Gressingham Lancs 130 B5
Greta Bridge Dur 140 D5
Gretna D & G 148 B2
Gretna Green D & G 148 B2
Gretna Services D & G 148 B2
Gretton Gloucs 56 A2
Gretton Nhants 88 C5
Gretton Shrops 83 K4
Grewelthorpe N York 132 C4
Greyrigg D & G 155 J4
Greys Green Oxon 42 B4
Greysouthen Cumb 136 E2
Greystoke Cumb 138 B2
Greystone Angus 196 E7
Greywell Hants 30 B2
Griff Warwks 86 D5
Griffithstown Torfn 53 L7
Grimeford Village Lancs 121 J7
Grimesthorpe Sheff 115 G4
Grimethorpe Barns 124 C8
Grimley Worcs 70 E3
Grimmet S Ayrs 163 H7
Grimoldby Lincs 118 E4
Grimpo Shrops 98 A7
Grimsargh Lancs 121 H4
Grimsby NE Lin 127 G7
Grimsby Crematorium NE Lin 118 C1
Grimscote Nhants 73 J4
Grimscott Cnwll 9 H4
Grimshader W Isls 232 f3
Grimsthorpe Lincs 103 H7
Grimston Leics 102 B7
Grimston Norfk 105 H7
Grimstone Dorset 14 C4
Grimstone End Suffk 77 L2
Grindale E R Yk 135 H5
Grindleford Derbys 114 E6
Grindleton Lancs 121 L2
Grindley Brook Shrops 98 D4
Grindlow Derbys 114 D6
Grindon Staffs 100 B2
Gringley on the Hill Notts 116 C4
Grinsdale Cumb 148 C4
Grinshill Shrops 98 D7
Grinton N York 140 D7
Griomaisiader W Isls 232 f3
Griomsaigh W Isls 233 c6
Grishipoll Ag & B 188 F4
Gristhorpe N York 135 H3
Griston Norfk 91 L4
Gritley Ork 234 d6
Grittenham Wilts 40 B4
Grittleton Wilts 39 K4
Grizebeck Cumb 128 F3
Grizedale Cumb 137 K7
Groby Leics 87 G3
Groes Conwy 110 D8
Groes-faen Rhondd 37 G4
Groeslon Gwynd 95 H2
Groes-Wen Caerph 37 H3
Grogarry W Isls 233 b7
Grogport Ag & B 161 K1
Groigearraidh W Isls 233 b7
Gronant Flints 110 F5
Groombridge E Susx 32 F5
Grosebay W Isls 232 e4
Grosmont Mons 54 B3
Grosmont N York 143 H6
Groton Suffk 77 L6
Grouville Jersey 236 e7
Grove Notts 116 C5
Grove Oxon 41 H3
Grove Green Kent 33 K3
Grove Park Gt Lon 45 H5

Grovesend Swans 51 H5
Gruinard Highld 219 L4
Gruinart Ag & B 170 F5
Grula Highld 208 F8
Gruline Ag & B 190 B7
Grundisburgh Suffk 78 F4
Gruting Shet 235 c5
Grutness Shet 235 c8
Gualachulain Highld 192 B7
Guardbridge Fife 187 G4
Guarlford Worcs 70 E5
Guay P & K 194 F6
Guernsey Guern 236 c3
Guernsey Airport Guern 236 c3
Guestling Green E Susx 21 G3
Guestling Thorn E Susx 21 G3
Guestwick Norfk 106 C6
Guide Bridge Tamesd 113 L3
Guilden Morden Cambs 75 K5
Guilden Sutton Ches W 112 C7
Guildford Surrey 31 G2
Guildford Crematorium Surrey 31 G3
Guildtown P & K 186 B2
Guilsborough Nhants 87 J8
Guilsfield Powys 82 E2
Guiltreehill S Ayrs 163 J7
Guineaford Devon 23 J4
Guisborough R & Cl 142 D4
Guiseley Leeds 123 J3
Guist Norfk 106 B7
Guiting Power Gloucs 56 C3
Gullane E Loth 178 B2
Gulval Cnwll 2 E5
Gulworthy Devon 6 C2
Gumfreston Pembks 49 J7
Gumley Leics 87 K5
Gunby Lincs 102 E7
Gunby Lincs 118 F7
Gundleton Hants 29 L5
Gun Hill E Susx 20 C3
Gunn Devon 23 K5
Gunnerside N York 139 L7
Gunnerton Nthumb 158 A7
Gunness N Linc 125 K7
Gunnislake Cnwll 6 C2
Gunnista Shet 235 d6
Gunthorpe N Linc 116 D3
Gunthorpe Norfk 106 B5
Gunthorpe Notts 102 B4
Gunwalloe Cnwll 3 H6
Gurnard IoW 16 F4
Gurney Slade Somset 26 F2
Gurnos Powys 52 B6
Gussage All Saints Dorset 15 J1
Gussage St Andrew Dorset 27 L8
Gussage St Michael Dorset 15 J1
Guston Kent 35 J5
Gutcher Shet 235 d2
Guthrie Angus 196 F6
Guyhirn Cambs 90 B3
Guyzance Nthumb 158 F2
Gwaenysgor Flints 110 F5
Gwalchmai IoA 108 E6
Gwaun-Cae-Gurwen Carmth 51 K3
Gweek Cnwll 3 J6
Gwenddwr Powys 68 B6
Gwennap Cnwll 3 J4
Gwennap Mining District Cnwll 3 K3
Gwent Crematorium Mons 37 L2
Gwernaffield Flints 111 H7
Gwernesney Mons 54 B7
Gwernogle Carmth 66 C7
Gwernymynydd Flints 111 H8
Gwespyr Flints 110 F5
Gwinear Cnwll 3 G4
Gwithian Cnwll 3 G3
Gwyddelwern Denbgs 97 G3
Gwyddgrug Carmth 66 B7
Gwytherin Conwy 96 D1

H

Habberley Shrops 83 H3
Habberley Worcs 84 E7
Habergham Lancs 122 B4
Habertoft Lincs 119 G7
Habrough NE Lin 126 E7
Hacconby Lincs 103 J7
Haceby Lincs 103 G5
Hacheston Suffk 79 G3
Hackbridge Gt Lon 44 F6
Hackenthorpe Sheff 115 H5
Hackford Norfk 92 C3
Hackforth N York 132 C2
Hackland Ork 234 c5
Hackleton Nhants 74 B4
Hacklinge Kent 35 J4
Hackness N York 134 F2
Hackney Gt Lon 45 G3
Hackthorn Lincs 117 G5
Hackthorpe Cumb 138 D3
Hadden Border 168 B3
Haddenham Bucks 58 C6
Haddenham Cambs 90 C7
Haddington E Loth 178 B4
Haddington Lincs 116 E8
Haddiscoe Norfk 93 J4
Haddo Abers 216 F6
Haddon Cambs 89 G5
Hadfield Derbys 114 A3
Hadham Ford Herts 60 C4
Hadleigh Essex 46 D3
Hadleigh Suffk 78 B6
Hadley Worcs 70 F2
Hadley Wrekin 84 C2
Hadley End Staffs 100 C7
Hadley Wood Gt Lon 44 E1
Hadlow Kent 33 H3
Hadlow Down E Susx 20 B2
Hadnall Shrops 98 D7
Hadrian's Wall 150 B2
Hadstock Essex 76 D5
Hadzor Worcs 71 G3
Haggersta Shet 235 c5
Haggerston Nthumb 168 F2
Haggs Falk 175 L3
Hagley Herefs 69 L6
Hagley Worcs 85 G7
Hagworthingham Lincs 118 D7
Haile Cumb 136 E5
Hailey Oxon 57 G5
Hailsham E Susx 20 C4
Hail Weston Cambs 75 H3
Hainault Gt Lon 45 J2
Hainford Norfk 106 F8
Hainton Lincs 117 K5
Haisthorpe E R Yk 135 H6
Hakin Pembks 48 F6
Halam Notts 102 B2
Halbeath Fife 176 F1
Halberton Devon 24 F8
Halcro Highld 231 J4
Hale Cumb 129 K4
Hale Halton 112 C5
Hale Hants 28 D7
Hale Surrey 30 D2
Hale Traffd 113 H4
Halebarns Traffd 113 H4
Hales Norfk 93 H4
Hales Staffs 99 G5
Halesowen Dudley 85 G6
Hales Place Kent 34 F3
Hale Street Kent 33 H4
Halesworth Suffk 93 H7
Halewood Knows 112 C4
Halford Devon 7 J2
Halford Warwks 72 C5
Halfpenny Green Staffs 84 E5
Halfway House Shrops 83 G2
Halfway Houses Kent 46 F5
Halifax Calder 123 G5
Halket E Ayrs 174 D7
Halkirk Highld 231 G4
Halkyn Flints 111 H7
Hall E Rens 174 D7
Halland E Susx 20 A3
Hallaton Leics 87 L4
Hallatrow BaNES 38 F8
Hallbankgate Cumb 149 G3
Hall Dunnerdale Cumb 137 H7
Hallen S Glos 38 D4
Hallgarth Dur 151 H6
Hall Glen Falk 176 B3
Hall Green Birm 85 K7
Hallin Highld 208 D3
Halling Medway 46 B7
Hallington Lincs 118 D4
Hallington Nthumb 158 C6
Halliwell Bolton 121 K7
Halloughton Notts 102 B3
Hallow Worcs 70 E3
Hall's Green Herts 59 L3
Hallyne Border 166 B2
Halmore Gloucs 55 G7
Halnaker W Susx 18 B4
Halsall Lancs 120 E7
Halse Nhants 73 H6
Halse Somset 25 H5
Halsetown Cnwll 2 E4
Halsham E R Yk 127 G5
Halstead Essex 61 K2
Halstead Kent 45 J7
Halstead Leics 87 L3
Halstock Dorset 14 A2
Haltemprice Crematorium E R Yk 126 C4
Haltham Lincs 118 C8
Halton Bucks 58 E6
Halton Halton 112 D5
Halton Lancs 129 K6
Halton Leeds 123 L4
Halton Nthumb 150 C2
Halton Wrexhm 97 L4
Halton East N York 131 K8
Halton Gill N York 131 G4
Halton Holegate Lincs 118 F7
Halton Lea Gate Nthumb 149 H4
Halton Shields Nthumb 150 C2
Halton West N York 130 F8
Haltwhistle Nthumb 149 J3
Halvergate Norfk 93 J3
Halwell Devon 7 H5
Halwill Devon 10 C5
Halwill Junction Devon 10 C5
Ham Devon 13 G3
Ham Gloucs 55 G7
Ham Gt Lon 44 D5
Ham Kent 35 J4
Ham Somset 25 L6
Ham Wilts 41 G7
Hambleden Bucks 42 C3
Hambledon Hants 29 M7
Hambledon Surrey 30 F4
Hamble-le-Rice Hants 16 F2
Hambleton Lancs 120 E3
Hambleton N York 124 E4
Hambridge Somset 26 B6
Hambrook W Susx 17 L2
Hameringham Lincs 118 D7
Hamerton Cambs 89 G7
Ham Green Worcs 71 H2
Hamilton S Lans 175 J7
Hamilton Services S Lans 175 J6
Hamlet Dorset 14 B2
Hammersmith Gt Lon 44 E4
Hammerwich Staffs 85 J3
Hammoon Dorset 27 J8
Hamnavoe Shet 235 c6
Hampden Park E Susx 20 C5
Hampnett Gloucs 56 C5
Hampole Donc 124 D7
Hampreston Dorset 15 K3
Hampstead Gt Lon 44 E3
Hampstead Norreys W Berk 41 K5
Hampsthwaite N York 132 C7
Hampton C Pete 89 H5
Hampton Gt Lon 43 J6
Hampton Kent 47 K6
Hampton Shrops 84 D6
Hampton Swindn 40 D3
Hampton Worcs 71 H5
Hampton Bishop Herefs 69 L6
Hampton Court Palace Gt Lon 44 D6
Hampton Heath Ches W 98 D3
Hampton-in-Arden Solhll 86 B7
Hampton Lovett Worcs 70 F2
Hampton Lucy Warwks 72 B3
Hampton Magna Warwks 72 C2
Hampton Poyle Oxon 57 J5
Hampton Wick Gt Lon 44 D6
Hamptworth Wilts 28 E7
Hamsey E Susx 19 L3
Hamstall Ridware Staffs 100 C8
Hamstead Birm 85 J5
Hamstead Marshall W Berk 41 H7
Hamsterley Dur 140 E2
Hamsterley Dur 150 E4
Hamstreet Kent 34 D7
Ham Street Somset 26 D4
Hamworthy Poole 15 J4
Hanbury Staffs 100 D6
Hanbury Worcs 71 G2
Hanchurch Staffs 99 J4
Handa Island Highld 228 A6
Hand and Pen Devon 12 D4
Handbridge Ches W 112 B7
Handcross W Susx 31 L5
Handforth Ches E 113 J5
Handley Ches W 98 C2
Handley Derbys 101 G1
Handsworth Birm 85 J5
Handsworth Sheff 115 H4
Hanford C Stke 99 K4
Hanging Heaton Kirk 123 K6
Hanging Houghton Nhants 87 L8
Hanging Langford Wilts 28 B4
Hangleton Br & H 19 H4
Hanham S Glos 38 F6
Hankelow Ches E 98 F4
Hankerton Wilts 39 L3
Hanley C Stke 99 K3
Hanley Castle Worcs 70 E6
Hanley Child Worcs 70 B2
Hanley Swan Worcs 70 E6
Hanley William Worcs 70 C2
Hanlith N York 131 G7
Hanmer Wrexhm 98 C4
Hannaford Devon 23 J5
Hannington Hants 29 K1
Hannington Nhants 74 B1
Hannington Swindn 40 D2
Hannington Wick Swindn 40 D2
Hanslope M Keyn 74 B5
Hanthorpe Lincs 103 H7
Hanwell Gt Lon 44 D4
Hanwell Oxon 72 E5
Hanwood Shrops 83 J2
Hanworth Gt Lon 43 J6
Hanworth Norfk 106 E5

Happendon S Lans 165 G3
Happendon Services S Lans 165 G3
Happisburgh Norfk 107 H6
Happisburgh Common Norfk 107 H6
Hapsford Ches W 112 C6
Hapton Lancs 122 B4
Hapton Norfk 92 E4
Harberton Devon 7 H4
Harbertonford Devon 7 H5
Harbledown Kent 34 F3
Harborne Birm 85 H6
Harborough Magna Warwks 86 F7
Harbottle Nthumb 158 B2
Harbourneford Devon 7 G4
Harbury Warwks 72 D3
Harby Leics 102 C6
Harby Notts 116 E7
Harcombe Devon 11 K8
Harcombe Devon 12 F4
Harcombe Bottom Devon 13 J4
Harden C Brad 123 G3
Harden Wsall 85 H4
Hardenhuish Wilts 39 K5
Hardgate Abers 206 E5
Hardgate D & G 146 E2
Hardgate W Duns 174 F4
Hardham W Susx 18 E3
Hardingham Norfk 92 C3
Hardingstone Nhants 73 L3
Hardington Somset 27 H2
Hardington Mandeville Somset 13 M1
Hardington Marsh Somset 13 M1
Hardington Moor Somset 26 D8
Hardisworthy Devon 22 C7
Hardley Hants 16 E2
Hardley Street Norfk 93 H4
Hardraw N York 131 G2
Hardstoft Derbys 115 H8
Hardway Hants 17 H3
Hardway Somset 27 G5
Hardwick Bucks 58 D4
Hardwick Cambs 75 L3
Hardwick Nhants 74 B1
Hardwick Norfk 92 F5
Hardwick Oxon 57 G6
Hardwick Oxon 57 L3
Hardwick Wsall 85 J4
Hardwicke Gloucs 55 H5
Hardwicke Gloucs 55 K3
Hardwick Hall Derbys 115 J8
Hardy's Green Essex 61 M4
Hare Croft C Brad 123 G4
Harefield Gt Lon 43 H3
Hare Green Essex 62 D3
Hare Hatch Wokham 42 D5
Harehill Derbys 100 D5
Harehills Leeds 123 L4
Harelaw Border 167 H5
Harelaw D & G 156 D6
Harescombe Gloucs 55 J6
Haresfield Gloucs 55 J6
Harestock Hants 29 J5
Hare Street Essex 60 C6
Hare Street Herts 60 C3
Harewood Leeds 123 L2
Harewood End Herefs 54 D3
Harford Devon 6 F4
Hargrave Ches W 98 C1
Hargrave Nhants 74 F1
Hargrave Suffk 77 H3
Harkstead Suffk 78 E7
Harlaston Staffs 86 B2
Harlaxton Lincs 102 E6
Harlech Gwynd 95 K6
Harlech Castle Gwynd 95 K6
Harlescott Shrops 83 K1
Harlesden Gt Lon 44 E4
Harlesthorpe Derbys 115 J6
Harleston Devon 7 J6
Harleston Norfk 92 F6
Harleston Suffk 78 B3
Harlestone Nhants 73 K2
Harle Syke Lancs 122 C4
Harley Rothm 115 G2
Harley Shrops 83 L3
Harlington C Beds 59 G2
Harlington Donc 115 J2
Harlington Gt Lon 43 H5
Harlosh Highld 208 D6
Harlow Essex 60 D6
Harlow Carr RHS N York 132 D8
Harlow Hill Nthumb 150 D2
Harlthorpe E R Yk 125 H3
Harlton Cambs 75 L4
Harlyn Cnwll 4 D2
Harman's Cross Dorset 15 J6
Harmby N York 131 L2
Harmer Green Herts 59 L5
Harmer Hill Shrops 98 C7
Harmston Lincs 116 F8
Harnage Shrops 83 L3
Harnhill Gloucs 56 B7
Harold Hill Gt Lon 45 K2
Haroldston West Pembks 48 E4
Haroldswick Shet 235 e1
Harold Wood Gt Lon 45 K3
Harome N York 133 K3
Harpenden Herts 59 J5
Harpford Devon 12 E4
Harpham E R Yk 135 H7
Harpley Norfk 105 J7
Harpley Worcs 70 C3
Harpole Nhants 73 K3
Harpsdale Highld 231 G4
Harpswell Lincs 116 F4
Harpurhey Manch 113 K2
Harraby Cumb 148 D4
Harracott Devon 23 J6
Harrapool Highld 199 K2
Harrietfield P & K 185 K2
Harrietsham Kent 33 L3
Harringay Gt Lon 44 F3
Harrington Cumb 136 D3
Harrington Lincs 118 E6
Harrington Nhants 87 L7
Harringworth Nhants 88 D4
Harris W Isls 232 d4
Harrogate N York 132 D7
Harrogate Crematorium N York 132 E8
Harrold Bed 74 D3
Harrow Gt Lon 44 D3
Harrowbarrow Cnwll 6 B2
Harrowgate Village Darltn 141 H4
Harrow Green Suffk 77 J4
Harrow on the Hill Gt Lon 44 D3
Harrow Weald Gt Lon 44 D2
Harston Cambs 76 B4
Harston Leics 102 D6
Harswell E R Yk 125 J3
Hart Hartpl 151 L7
Hartburn Nthumb 158 D5
Hartburn S on T 141 K4
Hartest Suffk 77 J4
Hartfield E Susx 32 E6
Hartford Cambs 89 J8
Hartford Ches W 112 F6
Hartfordbridge Hants 42 C8
Hartford End Essex 61 G4
Hartforth N York 140 F6
Hartgrove Dorset 27 J7
Harthill Ches W 98 D2
Harthill N Lans 176 B5
Harthill Rothm 115 J5
Hartington Derbys 100 C1
Hartland Devon 22 D6
Hartland Quay Devon 22 C6
Hartlebury Worcs 70 E1
Hartlepool Hartpl 151 L7
Hartlepool Crematorium Hartpl 142 B2
Hartley Cumb 139 H5
Hartley Kent 33 K6
Hartley Kent 45 L6
Hartley Wespall Hants 42 B8
Hartley Wintney Hants 30 C1
Hartlip Kent 46 D7
Harton N York 133 L6
Harton S Tyne 151 J2
Hartpury Gloucs 55 J3
Hartshead Kirk 123 J6
Hartshead Moor Services Calder 123 H5
Hartshill C Stke 99 K4
Hartshill Warwks 86 D5
Hartshorne Derbys 100 F7
Hartwell Nhants 73 L4
Hartwith N York 132 C6
Hartwood N Lans 175 L6
Hartwoodmyres Border 166 F4
Harvel Kent 46 A7
Harvington Worcs 71 J5
Harvington Worcs 84 F8
Harwell Notts 116 B3
Harwell Oxon 41 J3
Harwich Essex 62 F2
Harwood Dale N York 143 K7
Harwood Park Crematorium Herts 59 L4
Harworth Notts 115 L3
Hasbury Dudley 85 G6
Hascombe Surrey 31 G4
Haselbech Nhants 87 K7
Haselbury Plucknett Somset 13 L1
Haseley Warwks 72 B2
Haselor Warwks 71 K3
Hasfield Gloucs 55 J3
Haskayne Lancs 120 E8
Hasketon Suffk 78 F4
Haslemere Surrey 30 E5
Haslingden Lancs 122 B6
Haslingfield Cambs 76 B4
Haslington Ches E 99 G2
Hassingham Norfk 93 H3
Hassocks W Susx 19 J3
Hassop Derbys 114 E6
Haster Highld 231 K5
Hastingleigh Kent 34 E5
Hastings E Susx 21 G4
Hastings Crematorium E Susx 21 G3
Hastingwood Essex 60 D6
Hastoe Herts 58 F6
Haswell Dur 151 J6
Haswell Plough Dur 151 J6
Hatch Beauchamp Somset 25 L7
Hatch End Gt Lon 43 J3
Hatchmere Ches W 112 D6
Hatcliffe NE Lin 117 K2
Hatfield Donc 125 G8
Hatfield Herefs 69 L3
Hatfield Herts 59 L6
Hatfield Broad Oak Essex 60 E5
Hatfield Heath Essex 60 E5
Hatfield Peverel Essex 61 J5
Hatfield Woodhouse Donc 125 G8
Hatford Oxon 41 G2
Hatherden Hants 29 G2
Hatherleigh Devon 10 D4
Hathern Leics 101 J7
Hatherop Gloucs 56 D6
Hathersage Derbys 114 E5
Hathersage Booths Derbys 114 E5
Hatherton Ches E 99 G3
Hatherton Staffs 85 G2
Hatley St George Cambs 75 K4
Hatt Cnwll 6 B4
Hattersley Tamesd 113 M3
Hatton Abers 217 K6
Hatton Angus 196 D7
Hatton Derbys 100 E6
Hatton Gt Lon 43 J5
Hatton Lincs 117 K6
Hatton Shrops 83 J5
Hatton Warrtn 112 E5
Hatton Warwks 72 B2
Hatton of Fintray Abers 206 F3
Haugh E Ayrs 163 L4
Haugham Lincs 118 D5
Haughhead E Duns 175 G3
Haughley Suffk 78 B3
Haughley Green Suffk 78 B2
Haugh of Glass Moray 215 J6
Haugh of Urr D & G 146 E2
Haughs of Kinnaird Angus 197 G5
Haughton Ches E 98 E2
Haughton Shrops 98 B6
Haughton Staffs 99 K7
Haughton le Skerne Darltn 141 H4
Haultwick Herts 60 B4
Haunton Staffs 86 B2
Hautes Croix Jersey 236 c6
Hauxton Cambs 76 B4
Havant Hants 17 K2
Havant Crematorium Hants 17 K2
Havenstreet IoW 17 G4
Havercroft Wakefd 124 B7
Haverfordwest Pembks 48 F4
Haverhill Suffk 76 F5
Haverigg Cumb 128 E4
Havering-atte-Bower Gt Lon 45 K2
Haversham M Keyn 74 B6
Haverthwaite Cumb 129 H3
Havyat N Som 38 C7
Hawarden Flints 111 J7
Hawbush Green Essex 61 J4
Hawen Cerdgn 65 K5
Hawes N York 131 G2
Hawe's Green Norfk 92 F4
Hawford Worcs 70 E3
Hawick Border 167 G6
Hawkchurch Devon 13 J3
Hawkedon Suffk 77 H4
Hawkeridge Wilts 27 K2
Hawkesbury S Glos 39 H3
Hawkesbury Upton S Glos 39 H3
Hawkhurst Kent 33 K6
Hawkinge Kent 35 G6
Hawkinge Crematorium Kent 35 G6
Hawkley Hants 30 C5
Hawkridge Somset 24 D5
Hawkshead Cumb 137 K7
Hawkshead Hill Cumb 137 K7
Hawksland S Lans 165 G2
Hawkstone Shrops 98 E6
Hawkswick N York 131 H5
Hawksworth Leeds 123 H3
Hawksworth Notts 102 C4
Hawkwell Essex 46 E2
Hawley Hants 42 E8
Hawling Gloucs 56 B4
Hawnby N York 133 H2
Haworth C Brad 122 F3
Hawstead Suffk 77 J3
Hawthorn Dur 151 K5
Hawthorn Hill Lincs 103 K2
Hawton Notts 102 C3
Haxby C York 133 J7

Haxey N Linc 116 C2
Haycombe Crematorium BaNES 39 G7
Haydock St Hel 112 E3
Haydon Bridge Nthumb 149 L3
Haydon Wick Swindn 40 C3
Hayes Gt Lon 43 J4
Hayes Gt Lon 45 H6
Hayes End Gt Lon 43 H4
Hayfield Ag & B 182 F3
Hayfield Derbys 114 B4
Hayhillock Angus 196 E7
Hayle Cnwll 2 F4
Hayle Port Cnwll 2 F4
Hayley Green Dudley 85 G6
Hayling Island Hants 17 K3
Hayne Devon 11 H7
Haynes (Church End) C Beds 74 F6
Haynes (Northwood End) C Beds 75 G6
Haynes (Silver End) C Beds 75 G6
Haynes (West End) C Beds 74 F6
Hay-on-Wye Powys 68 E6
Hayscastle Pembks 48 F3
Hayscastle Cross Pembks 48 F3
Hay Street Herts 60 C3
Hayton Cumb 147 K6
Hayton Cumb 148 E4
Hayton E R Yk 125 J2
Hayton Notts 116 B5
Haytor Vale Devon 7 H1
Haytown Devon 9 K3
Haywards Heath W Susx 19 J2
Haywood Donc 124 E7
Hazelbank S Lans 165 G1
Hazelbury Bryan Dorset 14 E2
Hazeleigh Essex 61 K7
Hazel Grove Stockp 113 L4
Hazelton Walls Fife 186 E3
Hazelwood Derbys 101 G4
Hazlemere Bucks 42 E2
Hazlerigg N u Ty 159 G7
Hazleton Gloucs 56 B4
Heacham Norfk 105 G5
Headbourne Worthy Hants 29 J5
Headcorn Kent 33 L4
Headingley Leeds 123 K4
Headington Oxon 57 K6
Headlam Dur 140 F4
Headlesscross N Lans 176 B6
Headless Cross Worcs 71 J2
Headley Hants 30 D4
Headley Hants 41 K7
Headley Surrey 31 K1
Headley Down Hants 30 D4
Headon Notts 116 C6
Heads Nook Cumb 148 E4
Heage Derbys 101 G3
Healaugh N York 124 D2
Healaugh N York 140 C7
Heald Green Stockp 113 J4
Heale Somset 25 K7
Heale Somset 26 B6
Healey N York 132 B4
Healeyfield Dur 150 D5
Healing NE Lin 126 F7
Heamoor Cnwll 2 E5
Heanor Derbys 101 H3
Heanton Punchardon Devon 23 H4
Heapham Lincs 116 E4
Heart of England Crematorium Warwks 86 E5
Heart of Scotland Services N Lans 176 B5
Heasley Mill Devon 24 B5
Heast Highld 199 K2
Heath Derbys 115 J7
Heath Wakefd 123 L6
Heath and Reach C Beds 58 F3
Heathcote Derbys 100 D1
Heather Leics 86 E2
Heathfield E Susx 20 C2
Heathfield Somset 25 J6
Heath Green Worcs 71 J1
Heath Hall D & G 155 H6
Heath Hayes & Wimblebury Staffs 85 H2
Heath Hill Shrops 84 D2
Heathrow Airport Gt Lon 43 H5
Heathton Shrops 84 E5
Heath Town Wolves 85 G4
Heatley Warrtn 113 G4
Heaton C Brad 123 H4
Heaton N u Ty 151 G2
Heaton Staffs 113 L8
Heaton Chapel Stockp 113 K3
Heaton Mersey Stockp 113 K4
Heaton Norris Stockp 113 K4
Heaton's Bridge Lancs 120 E7
Heaverham Kent 33 G2
Heavitree Devon 12 B4
Hebburn S Tyne 151 H3
Hebden N York 131 J6
Hebden Bridge Calder 122 E5
Hebing End Herts 60 A4
Hebron Carmth 49 K3
Hebron Nthumb 158 F4
Heckfield Hants 42 B7
Heckfield Green Suffk 92 E7
Heckfordbridge Essex 61 M4
Heckington Lincs 103 J4
Heckmondwike Kirk 123 J5
Heddington Wilts 39 M6
Heddon-on-the-Wall Nthumb 150 E2
Hedenham Norfk 93 G5
Hedge End Hants 29 J8
Hedgerley Bucks 42 F3
Hedging Somset 25 L5
Hedley on the Hill Nthumb 150 D3
Hednesford Staffs 85 H2
Hedon E R Yk 126 F5
Hedsor Bucks 42 E3
Heeley Sheff 115 G5
Heglibister Shet 235 c5
Heighington Darltn 141 G3
Heighington Lincs 117 G7
Heightington Worcs 70 D1
Heiton Border 167 L4
Hele Devon 12 C2
Hele Devon 23 H3
Helensburgh Ag & B 174 B2
Helenton S Ayrs 163 K3
Helford Cnwll 3 K6
Helford Passage Cnwll 3 K6
Helhoughton Norfk 105 K7
Helions Bumpstead Essex 76 F6
Helland Cnwll 5 G2
Hellescott Cnwll 9 H6
Hellesdon Norfk 92 E2
Hellidon Nhants 73 G3
Hellifield N York 131 G7
Hellingly E Susx 20 C4
Helmdon Nhants 73 H5
Helme Kirk 123 G7
Helmingham Suffk 78 E3
Helmsdale Highld 227 H5
Helmshore Lancs 122 B6
Helmsley N York 133 J3
Helperby N York 133 G5
Helperthorpe N York 134 E5
Helpringham Lincs 103 J4
Helpston C Pete 89 G3
Helsby Ches W 112 C6
Helston Cnwll 3 H5
Helstone Cnwll 8 E8
Helton Cumb 138 D3
Hemel Hempstead Herts 59 H6
Hemerdon Devon 6 E4
Hemingbrough N York 125 G4
Hemingby Lincs 118 C6
Hemingford Abbots Cambs 75 K1
Hemingford Grey Cambs 75 K1
Hemingstone Suffk 78 D4
Hemington Leics 101 J6
Hemington Nhants 88 F6
Hemington Somset 27 G2
Hemley Suffk 79 G6
Hemlington Middsb 142 B4
Hempnall Norfk 92 F5
Hempnall Green Norfk 92 F5
Hempriggs Moray 214 D2
Hempstead Essex 76 F6
Hempstead Medway 46 C6
Hempstead Norfk 106 D5
Hempstead Norfk 107 J6
Hempton Norfk 105 L6
Hempton Oxon 57 H2
Hemsby Norfk 107 K8
Hemswell Lincs 116 F4
Hemswell Cliff Lincs 116 F4
Hemsworth Wakefd 124 C7
Hemyock Devon 25 H8
Henbury Bristl 38 E5
Hendon Gt Lon 44 E3
Hendon Sundld 151 K4
Hendon Crematorium Gt Lon 44 E2
Hendy Carmth 51 H5
Henfield W Susx 19 G3
Hengoed Caerph 37 J2
Hengoed Powys 68 E4
Hengrave Suffk 77 J2
Henham Essex 60 E3
Heniarth Powys 82 C2
Henlade Somset 25 L6
Henley Dorset 14 D2
Henley Somset 26 B5
Henley Suffk 78 E4
Henley W Susx 30 E6
Henley-in-Arden Warwks 71 L2
Henley-on-Thames Oxon 42 C4
Henley's Down E Susx 20 E3
Henllan Cerdgn 65 K6
Henllan Denbgs 110 E7
Henllys Torfn 37 K3
Henlow C Beds 75 H6
Hennock Devon 11 J8
Henny Street Essex 77 K6
Henryd Conwy 109 L6
Henry's Moat (Castell Hendre) Pembks 49 H3
Hensall N York 124 F5
Henshaw Nthumb 149 J3
Hensingham Cumb 136 D4
Henstead Suffk 93 K6
Hensting Hants 29 J6
Henstridge Somset 27 G7
Henstridge Ash Somset 27 G7
Henton Oxon 58 C7
Henton Somset 26 C3
Henwick Worcs 70 E4
Henwood Cnwll 5 L2
Heol-y-Cyw Brdgnd 36 E4
Hepple Nthumb 158 C2
Hepscott Nthumb 158 F5
Heptonstall Calder 122 E5
Hepworth Kirk 114 D1
Hepworth Suffk 92 B8
Herbrandston Pembks 48 E6
Hereford Herefs 69 K6
Hereford Crematorium Herefs 69 J6
Hereson Kent 35 K2
Heribusta Highld 218 B7
Heriot Border 177 L7
Hermiston C Edin 177 G4
Hermitage Border 156 E3
Hermitage Dorset 14 C2
Hermitage W Berk 41 J5
Hermon Carmth 65 K7
Hermon Pembks 49 L2
Herne Kent 47 K6
Herne Bay Kent 47 K6
Herne Hill Gt Lon 44 F5
Herne Pound Kent 33 H3
Hernhill Kent 34 E3
Herodsfoot Cnwll 5 K4
Heronsford S Ayrs 152 D5
Herriard Hants 30 A3
Herringfleet Suffk 93 K4
Herringswell Suffk 77 G1
Herringthorpe Rothm 115 J3
Herrington Sundld 151 J4
Hersden Kent 35 G3
Hersham Surrey 43 J7
Herstmonceux E Susx 20 D3
Herston Ork 234 c7
Hertford Herts 60 B5
Hertford Heath Herts 60 B5
Hertingfordbury Herts 60 A5
Hesketh Bank Lancs 120 F5
Hesketh Lane Lancs 121 J3
Hesket Newmarket Cumb 148 C7
Hesleden Dur 151 K7
Heslington C York 124 F1
Hessay C York 133 H8
Hessenford Cnwll 5 L4
Hessett Suffk 77 L3
Hessle E R Yk 126 C5
Hessle Wakefd 124 C6
Hest Bank Lancs 129 K6
Heston Gt Lon 43 J5
Heston Services Gt Lon 43 J5
Hestwall Ork 234 b5
Heswall Wirral 111 J5
Hethe Oxon 57 L3
Hethersett Norfk 92 D3
Hethersgill Cumb 148 E2
Hett Dur 151 G7
Hetton N York 131 H7
Hetton-le-Hole Sundld 151 J5
Heugh Nthumb 158 D7
Heughhead Abers 205 J3
Heugh Head Border 179 H6
Heveningham Suffk 93 G8
Hever Kent 32 E4
Heversham Cumb 129 K3
Hevingham Norfk 106 E7
Hewas Water Cnwll 4 F6
Hewelsfield Gloucs 54 E7
Hewish Somset 13 K2
Hewood Dorset 13 J2
Hexham Nthumb 150 B3
Hextable Kent 45 K6
Hexthorpe Donc 115 K2
Hexton Herts 59 J2
Hexworthy Cnwll 9 K8
Hexworthy Devon 6 F2
Heybridge Essex 61 G7
Heybridge Essex 61 K6
Heybrook Bay Devon 6 D6
Heydon Cambs 76 B6
Heydon Norfk 106 D6
Heydour Lincs 103 G5
Heylipoll Ag & B 188 C7
Heylor Shet 235 c3
Heysham Lancs 129 J7
Heyshott W Susx 18 B3
Heytesbury Wilts 27 L3
Heythrop Oxon 57 G3
Heywood Rochdl 122 C7

Heywood Wilts 27 K2
Hibaldstow N Linc 116 F2
Hickleton Donc 115 J1
Hickling Norfk 107 J7
Hickling Notts 102 B6
Hickling Green Norfk 107 J7
Hickstead W Susx 31 L7
Hidcote Bartrim Gloucs 71 L6
Hidcote Boyce Gloucs 71 L6
High Ackworth Wakefd 124 C6
Higham Barns 114 F1
Higham Derbys 101 H2
Higham Kent 33 G4
Higham Kent 46 B5
Higham Lancs 122 B3
Higham Suffk 77 H2
Higham Suffk 78 B7
Higham Ferrers Nhants 74 D2
Higham Gobion C Beds 59 J2
Higham Hill Gt Lon 45 G3
Higham on the Hill Leics 86 E4
Highampton Devon 10 C4
Highams Park Gt Lon 45 H2
High Ardwell D & G 144 C6
High Auldgirth D & G 154 F5
High Bankhill Cumb 148 F6
High Beach Essex 60 C7
High Bentham N York 130 C5
High Bickington Devon 23 J7
High Biggins Cumb 130 B4
High Blantyre S Lans 175 J6
High Bonnybridge Falk 175 L3
High Bray Devon 23 L5
Highbridge Somset 25 L3
Highbrook W Susx 32 C7
High Brooms Kent 33 G5
Highburton Kirk 123 J7
Highbury Gt Lon 44 F3
Highbury Somset 27 G2
High Casterton Cumb 130 C4
High Catton E R Yk 133 L8
Highclere Hants 41 H8
Highcliffe Dorset 16 B4
High Coniscliffe Darltn 141 G4
High Crosby Cumb 148 E3
High Cross E Ayrs 163 K1
High Cross Hants 30 B6
High Cross Herts 60 B4
High Cross Warwks 71 L2
High Drummore D & G 144 D7
High Easter Essex 60 F5
High Ellington N York 132 B3
Higher Ansty Dorset 14 E2
Higher Bartle Lancs 121 G4
Higher Bockhampton Dorset 14 D4
Higher Brixham Torbay 7 L5
High Ercall Wrekin 98 E8
Higher Chillington Somset 13 K1
Higher Folds Wigan 113 G2
Higher Gabwell Devon 7 L3
Higher Heysham Lancs 129 J7
Higher Irlam Salfd 113 G3
Higher Kinnerton Flints 97 L1
Higher Muddiford Devon 23 J4
Higher Penwortham Lancs 121 G5
Higher Prestacott Devon 9 K5
Higher Town Cnwll 4 C6
Higher Town Cnwll 4 F4
Higher Town IoS 2 b1
Higher Walton Lancs 121 H5
Higher Walton Warrtn 112 E4
Higher Wambrook Somset 13 H2
Higher Waterston Dorset 14 D4
Higher Wheelton Lancs 121 J6
Higher Whitley Ches W 112 F5
Higher Wincham Ches W 113 G6
Higher Wraxhall Dorset 14 B3
Higher Wych Ches W 98 C4
High Etherley Dur 140 F2
Highfield Gatesd 150 E3
Highfield N Ayrs 174 C7
High Garrett Essex 61 J3
Highgate Gt Lon 44 F3
High Grantley N York 132 C5
High Green Norfk 92 D3
High Green Norfk 92 E5
High Green Sheff 115 G3
High Halden Kent 34 B7
High Halstow Medway 46 C5
High Ham Somset 26 B5
High Harrington Cumb 136 D3
High Harrogate N York 132 D7
High Hatton Shrops 98 E7
High Hauxley Nthumb 159 G2
High Hawsker N York 143 J5
High Hesket Cumb 148 E6
High Hoyland Barns 123 K8
High Hurstwood E Susx 32 E7
High Hutton N York 134 B5
High Ireby Cumb 147 M7
High Kilburn N York 133 H4
High Lands Dur 140 E3
Highlane Derbys 115 H5
High Lane Stockp 113 L4
High Lanes Cnwll 3 G4
Highleadon Gloucs 55 H4
High Legh Ches E 113 G5
Highleigh W Susx 18 A6
High Leven S on T 141 K5
Highley Shrops 84 D6
High Littleton BaNES 38 F8
High Lorton Cumb 137 G3
High Marnham Notts 116 D7
High Melton Donc 115 K2
High Mickley Nthumb 150 D3
Highmoor Oxon 42 B4
Highmoor Cross Oxon 42 B4
Highnam Gloucs 55 H4
High Newport Sundld 151 J4
High Newton Cumb 129 J3
High Nibthwaite Cumb 129 G2
High Offley Staffs 99 H7
High Ongar Essex 60 E7
High Onn Staffs 84 E1
High Park Corner Essex 62 C4
High Pennyvenie E Ayrs 163 L7
High Roding Essex 60 F4
High Salvington W Susx 18 F4
High Spen Gatesd 150 E3
Highsted Kent 34 B3
High Street Cnwll 4 F5
Highstreet Kent 34 E3
Highstreet Green Surrey 31 G4
Hightae D & G 155 J6
Highter's Heath Birm 85 J7
Hightown Sefton 111 J2
Hightown Green Suffk 77 L4
High Toynton Lincs 118 C7
High Valleyfield Fife 176 D2
Highweek Devon 7 J2
Highwood Essex 61 G7
Highwood Hill Gt Lon 44 E2
Highworth Swindn 40 D2
High Wray Cumb 137 K7
High Wych Herts 60 D5
High Wycombe Bucks 42 E2
Hilborough Norfk 91 J4
Hilcott Wilts 40 C8
Hildenborough Kent 32 F4
Hilden Park Kent 33 G4
Hildersham Cambs 76 D5
Hilderstone Staffs 99 L5
Hilderthorpe E R Yk 135 J6
Hilgay Norfk 90 E4
Hill S Glos 38 F2
Hill Warwks 72 F2
Hillam N York 124 D5
Hill Brow Hants 30 C6
Hillbutts Dorset 15 J3
Hill Chorlton Staffs 99 H5
Hillcliffane Derbys 100 F3
Hill Common Somset 25 H6
Hilldyke Lincs 104 B3
Hillend Fife 176 F2
Hill End Fife 185 L7
Hill End Gloucs 70 F6
Hillend Mdloth 177 H5
Hillend N Lans 175 L5
Hillesden Bucks 58 B3
Hillesley Gloucs 39 H3
Hillfarrance Somset 25 J6
Hill Green Kent 46 D7
Hillhead Abers 216 B7
Hill Head Hants 17 G2
Hillhead S Lans 165 J2
Hillhead of Cocklaw Abers 217 K5
Hilliclay Highld 231 H3
Hillingdon Gt Lon 43 H4
Hillington C Glas 174 F5
Hillington Norfk 105 H7
Hillmorton Warwks 87 G8
Hill of Beath Fife 176 F1
Hill of Fearn Highld 223 H5
Hillowton D & G 146 D3
Hill Ridware Staffs 100 B8
Hillside Abers 207 H5
Hillside Angus 197 H4
Hill Side Kirk 123 H6
Hills Town Derbys 115 J7
Hillstreet Hants 29 G7
Hillswick Shet 235 c3
Hill Top Sandw 85 H5
Hill Top Wakefd 123 L7
Hillwell Shet 235 c8
Hilmarton Wilts 40 A5
Hilperton Wilts 39 K8
Hilsea C Port 17 J2
Hilston E R Yk 127 G4
Hilton Border 179 H7
Hilton Cambs 75 K2
Hilton Cumb 139 G3
Hilton Derbys 100 E6
Hilton Dorset 14 E2
Hilton Dur 140 F3
Hilton Highld 223 J6
Hilton S on T 141 K5
Hilton Shrops 84 D4
Hilton Park Services Staffs 85 G3
Himbleton Worcs 71 G3
Himley Staffs 84 F5
Hincaster Cumb 129 L3
Hinchley Wood Surrey 44 D6
Hinckley Leics 86 E5
Hinderclay Suffk 92 B7
Hinderwell N York 143 G4
Hindhead Surrey 30 E4
Hindhead Tunnel Surrey 30 E4
Hindley Wigan 112 F1
Hindlip Worcs 70 F3
Hindolveston Norfk 106 C6
Hindon Wilts 27 K5
Hindringham Norfk 106 B5
Hingham Norfk 92 B3
Hinstock Shrops 99 G7
Hintlesham Suffk 78 C5
Hinton Herefs 69 G6
Hinton S Glos 39 G5
Hinton Shrops 83 H2
Hinton Ampner Hants 29 L6
Hinton Blewett BaNES 26 E1
Hinton Charterhouse BaNES 39 H8
Hinton-in-the-Hedges Nhants 73 H6
Hinton Martell Dorset 15 J2
Hinton on the Green Worcs 71 H6
Hinton Parva Swindn 40 E4
Hinton St George Somset 26 B8
Hinton St Mary Dorset 27 H7
Hinton Waldrist Oxon 57 G7
Hints Staffs 85 L3
Hinwick Bed 74 D3
Hinxhill Kent 34 D6
Hinxton Cambs 76 C5
Hinxworth Herts 75 J6
Hipperholme Calder 123 H5
Hipswell N York 140 F7
Hirn Abers 206 D5
Hirnant Powys 97 G7
Hirst Nthumb 159 G5
Hirst Courtney N York 124 F5
Hirwaun Rhondd 52 E6
Hiscott Devon 23 J6
Histon Cambs 76 B2
Hitcham Suffk 78 B4
Hitcham Causeway Suffk 78 B4
Hitcham Street Suffk 78 B4
Hitchin Herts 59 K3
Hither Green Gt Lon 45 H5
Hittisleigh Devon 11 H5
Hive E R Yk 125 J4
Hixon Staffs 100 A7
Hoaden Kent 35 H3
Hoar Cross Staffs 100 C7
Hoarwithy Herefs 54 D3
Hoath Kent 47 K7
Hobarris Shrops 82 F7
Hobkirk Border 167 J7
Hobson Dur 150 F4
Hoby Leics 102 A8
Hockering Norfk 92 C2
Hockerton Notts 102 B2
Hockley Essex 46 D2
Hockley Heath Solhll 85 L8
Hockliffe C Beds 58 F3
Hockwold cum Wilton Norfk 91 G6
Hockworthy Devon 25 G7
Hoddesdon Herts 60 B6
Hoddlesden Bl w D 121 L6
Hoddom Cross D & G 155 L7
Hoddom Mains D & G 155 K7
Hodgeston Pembks 49 H7
Hodnet Shrops 98 E6
Hodsock Notts 115 L4
Hodsoll Street Kent 45 M7
Hodson Swindn 40 D4
Hodthorpe Derbys 115 K6
Hoe Norfk 92 B1
Hogben's Hill Kent 34 D4
Hoggeston Bucks 58 D3
Hoggrill's End Warwks 86 B5
Hoghton Lancs 121 J5
Hognaston Derbys 100 E3
Hogsthorpe Lincs 119 H6
Holbeach Lincs 104 B7
Holbeach Bank Lincs 104 B6
Holbeach Clough Lincs 104 B6
Holbeach Drove Lincs 89 K2
Holbeach Hurn Lincs 104 C6
Holbeach St Johns Lincs 104 B8

Holbeach St Mark's Lincs 104 B6
Holbeach St Matthew Lincs 104 C6
Holbeck Notts 115 K6
Holberrow Green Worcs 71 H3
Holbeton Devon 6 F5
Holborn Gt Lon 44 F4
Holbrook Derbys 101 G4
Holbrook Suffk 78 E6
Holbrooks Covtry 86 D6
Holbury Hants 16 E2
Holcombe Devon 12 B7
Holcombe Somset 26 F2
Holcombe Rogus Devon 25 G7
Holcot Nhants 73 L1
Holden Lancs 122 B1
Holdenby Nhants 73 K2
Holder's Green Essex 61 G3
Holdgate Shrops 83 L5
Holdingham Lincs 103 H3
Holditch Dorset 13 J2
Holemoor Devon 10 B4
Holford Somset 25 J3
Holgate C York 124 E1
Holker Cumb 129 H4
Holkham Norfk 105 L4
Hollacombe Devon 9 K4
Holland Fen Lincs 103 L3
Holland-on-Sea Essex 62 E5
Hollandstoun Ork 234 e3
Hollee D & G 148 A2
Hollesley Suffk 79 H5
Hollicombe Torbay 7 K4
Hollingbourne Kent 33 L3
Hollingbury Br & H 19 J4
Hollingdon Bucks 58 E3
Hollington Derbys 100 E5
Hollington Staffs 100 B5
Hollingworth Tamesd 114 A3
Hollinsclough Staffs 114 B7
Hollins End Sheff 115 G5
Hollins Green Warrtn 113 G4
Hollinswood Wrekin 84 C2
Hollocombe Devon 10 F3
Holloway Derbys 100 F2
Holloway Gt Lon 44 F3
Hollowell Nhants 73 K1
Hollowmoor Heath Ches W 112 C7
Hollows D & G 156 C6
Hollybush Caerph 53 J7
Hollybush E Ayrs 163 K6
Hollybush Herefs 70 D6
Hollym E R Yk 127 H5
Holmbridge Kirk 114 C1
Holmbury St Mary Surrey 31 J3
Holmbush Cnwll 5 G5
Holmcroft Staffs 99 K7
Holme Cambs 89 H6
Holme Cumb 129 L4
Holme Kirk 114 C1
Holme N York 132 E3
Holme Notts 102 D2
Holme Chapel Lancs 122 C5
Holme Hale Norfk 91 K3
Holme Lacy Herefs 69 L7
Holme Marsh Herefs 69 G4
Holme next the Sea Norfk 105 H4
Holme on the Wolds E R Yk 126 B2
Holme Pierrepont Notts 101 L5
Holmer Herefs 69 K6
Holmer Green Bucks 42 E2
Holme St Cuthbert Cumb 147 J5
Holmes Chapel Ches E 113 H7
Holmesfield Derbys 114 F6
Holmeswood Lancs 120 F6
Holmethorpe Surrey 32 B3
Holme upon Spalding Moor E R Yk 125 J3
Holmewood Derbys 115 H7
Holmfirth Kirk 123 H8
Holmhead E Ayrs 164 B5
Holmpton E R Yk 127 J5
Holmrook Cumb 136 E7
Holmsford Bridge Crematorium N Ayrs 163 J2
Holmside Dur 150 F5
Holne Devon 7 G3
Holnicote Somset 24 E3
Holsworthy Devon 9 J4
Holsworthy Beacon Devon 9 K3
Holt Dorset 15 J2
Holt Norfk 106 C5
Holt Wilts 39 K7
Holt Worcs 70 E3
Holt Wrexhm 98 B2
Holtby C York 133 K8
Holt End Worcs 71 J1
Holt Heath Worcs 70 E2
Holton Oxon 57 L6
Holton Somset 27 G6
Holton Suffk 93 J7
Holton cum Beckering Lincs 117 J5
Holton le Clay Lincs 118 C2
Holton le Moor Lincs 117 H3
Holton St Mary Suffk 78 C6
Holwell Dorset 14 D1
Holwell Herts 59 K2
Holwell Leics 102 B7
Holwell Oxon 56 E6
Holwick Dur 139 K2
Holybourne Hants 30 B4
Holyhead IoA 108 C5
Holy Island IoA 108 C5
Holy Island Nthumb 169 H2
Holy Island Nthumb 169 H2
Holymoorside Derbys 115 G7
Holyport W & M 42 E5
Holystone Nthumb 158 B2
Holytown N Lans 175 K6
Holytown Crematorium N Lans 175 K6
Holywell C Beds 59 G5
Holywell Cambs 75 L1
Holywell Cnwll 4 B4
Holywell Dorset 14 B2
Holywell Flints 111 G6
Holywell Green Calder 123 G6
Holywell Lake Somset 25 H7
Holywell Row Suffk 91 G7
Holywood D & G 155 G6
Holywood Village D & G 155 G6
Homer Shrops 84 B3
Homer Green Sefton 111 K2
Homersfield Suffk 93 G6
Homington Wilts 28 C6
Honeybourne Worcs 71 K5
Honeychurch Devon 10 F4
Honeystreet Wilts 40 C7
Honey Tye Suffk 77 L7
Honiley Warwks 86 B8
Honing Norfk 107 G6
Honingham Norfk 92 D2
Honington Lincs 102 F4
Honington Suffk 91 K8
Honington Warwks 72 C6
Honiton Devon 12 F3
Honley Kirk 123 H7
Honor Oak Crematorium Gt Lon 45 G5
Hooe C Plym 6 D5
Hooe E Susx 20 E4
Hoo Green Ches E 113 G5
Hoohill Bpool 120 D3
Hook E R Yk 125 H5
Hook Gt Lon 44 D7
Hook Hants 30 B1
Hook Pembks 49 G5
Hook Wilts 40 B4
Hooke Dorset 14 A3
Hook Green Kent 33 H6
Hook Norton Oxon 57 G2
Hookway Devon 11 K5
Hooley Surrey 32 B3
Hoo St Werburgh Medway 46 C5
Hooton Levitt Rothm 115 K3
Hooton Pagnell Donc 124 D8
Hooton Roberts Rothm 115 J3
Hope Derbys 114 D5
Hope Devon 7 G7
Hope Flints 97 L2
Hope Staffs 100 C2
Hope Bagot Shrops 83 L8
Hope Bowdler Shrops 83 J5
Hopehouse Border 166 D6
Hopeman Moray 214 E1
Hope Mansell Herefs 54 F4
Hopesay Shrops 83 H6
Hope under Dinmore Herefs 69 K4
Hopgrove C York 133 K8
Hopperton N York 132 F7
Hopstone Shrops 84 D5
Hopton Derbys 100 E2
Hopton Staffs 99 L7
Hopton Suffk 92 B7
Hopton Cangeford Shrops 83 K7
Hopton Castle Shrops 83 G7
Hoptonheath Shrops 83 H7
Hopton on Sea Norfk 93 L4
Hopton Wafers Shrops 84 B7
Hopwas Staffs 85 L3
Hopwood Worcs 85 J7
Hopwood Park Services Worcs 85 J8
Horam E Susx 20 C3
Horbling Lincs 103 J5
Horbury Wakefd 123 K6
Horden Dur 151 K6
Hordle Hants 16 C4
Hordley Shrops 98 B6
Horfield Bristl 38 E5
Horham Suffk 92 E8
Horkesley Heath Essex 62 B3
Horkstow N Linc 126 B6
Horley Oxon 72 E5
Horley Surrey 32 B5
Hornblotton Green Somset 26 E5
Hornby Lancs 130 B5
Hornby N York 132 C2
Hornby N York 141 J6
Horncastle Lincs 118 C7
Hornchurch Gt Lon 45 K3
Horncliffe Nthumb 179 J7
Horndean Border 179 J8
Horndean Hants 30 B8
Horndon Devon 10 D8
Horndon on the Hill Thurr 46 A4
Horne Surrey 32 C4
Horner Somset 24 D3
Horning Norfk 107 H8
Horninghold Leics 88 B4
Horninglow Staffs 100 E7
Horningsea Cambs 76 C3
Horningsham Wilts 27 J3
Horningtoft Norfk 105 M7
Horns Cross Devon 22 F6
Hornsea E R Yk 126 F2
Hornsey Gt Lon 44 F3
Hornton Oxon 72 E5
Horra Shet 235 d2
Horrabridge Devon 6 D2
Horringer Suffk 77 J3
Horrocksford Lancs 121 L2
Horsebridge Devon 6 B2
Horsebridge E Susx 20 C4
Horsebridge Hants 29 G5
Horsehay Wrekin 84 C3
Horseheath Cambs 76 E5
Horsehouse N York 131 K4
Horsell Surrey 43 G8
Horseman's Green Wrexhm 98 C4
Horsey Norfk 107 K7
Horsey Somset 25 L4
Horsford Norfk 92 E1
Horsforth Leeds 123 J3
Horsham W Susx 31 K5
Horsham Worcs 70 D3
Horsham St Faith Norfk 92 E1
Horsington Lincs 117 K7
Horsington Somset 27 G6
Horsley Derbys 101 G4
Horsley Gloucs 39 J2
Horsley Nthumb 150 D2
Horsley Nthumb 157 L3
Horsleycross Street Essex 62 D3
Horsleyhill Border 167 H5
Horsley Woodhouse Derbys 101 H4
Horsmonden Kent 33 J5
Horspath Oxon 57 L6
Horstead Norfk 106 F8
Horsted Keynes W Susx 32 C7
Horton Bucks 58 F4
Horton Dorset 15 J2
Horton Lancs 122 C1
Horton Nhants 74 B4
Horton S Glos 39 H4
Horton Somset 25 L7
Horton Staffs 99 L2
Horton Swans 50 F7
Horton W & M 43 G5
Horton Wilts 40 B7
Horton Wrekin 84 C1
Horton-cum-Studley Oxon 57 L5
Horton Green Ches W 98 C3
Horton-in-Ribblesdale N York 130 F5
Horton Kirby Kent 45 K6
Horwich Bolton 121 J7
Horwood Devon 23 H6
Hoscote Border 166 F6
Hose Leics 102 B6
Hosh P & K 185 H3
Hoswick Shet 235 c7
Hotham E R Yk 125 L4
Hothfield Kent 34 C5
Hoton Leics 101 L7
Hough Ches E 99 G3
Hougham Lincs 102 E4
Hough Green Halton 112 C4
Hough-on-the-Hill Lincs 102 F3
Houghton Cambs 75 K1
Houghton Hants 29 G5
Houghton Pembks 49 G6
Houghton W Susx 18 D4
Houghton Conquest C Beds 74 F6
Houghton Green E Susx 21 H2
Houghton-le-Spring Sundld 151 H5
Houghton on the Hill Leics 87 J3
Houghton Regis C Beds 59 G4
Houghton St Giles Norfk 105 L5
Hound Green Hants 42 B8
Houndslow Border 178 D8
Houndwood Border 179 H5
Hounslow Gt Lon 43 J5
Househill Highld 213 L4
Houses Hill Kirk 123 J6
Housieside Abers 207 G1
Houston Rens 174 D5

Houstry Highld 227 K2
Houton Ork 234 b6
Hove Br & H 19 J5
Hoveringham Notts 102 B3
Hoveton Norfk 107 G8
Hovingham N York 133 K4
How Caple Herefs 54 E3
Howden E R Yk 125 H5
Howden-le-Wear Dur 150 E7
Howe Highld 231 K3
Howe N York 132 E4
Howe Norfk 92 F4
Howe Bridge Crematorium Wigan 112 F2
Howe Green Essex 61 J7
Howegreen Essex 61 K7
Howell Lincs 103 J4
Howe of Teuchar Abers 216 E5
Howes D & G 147 L2
Howe Street Essex 61 H5
Howe Street Essex 77 G7
Howey Powys 68 B3
Howgate Cumb 136 D3
Howgate Mdloth 177 H6
Howick Nthumb 169 K5
Howlett End Essex 76 E7
Howley Somset 13 H1
How Mill Cumb 148 E4
Howmore W Isls 233 b7
Hownam Border 168 B5
Howsham N Linc 117 H2
Howsham N York 133 L6
Howtel Nthumb 168 D3
How Wood Herts 59 J7
Howwood Rens 174 D6
Hoxa Ork 234 c7
Hoxne Suffk 92 E7
Hoy Ork 234 b7
Hoylake Wirral 111 H4
Hoyland Nether Barns 115 G2
Hoyland Swaine Barns 114 E1
Hubberston Pembks 48 E6
Huby N York 123 K2
Huby N York 133 J6
Hucclecote Gloucs 55 K4
Hucking Kent 33 L2
Hucknall Notts 101 K3
Huddersfield Kirk 123 H7
Huddersfield Crematorium Kirk 123 H6
Huddington Worcs 71 G3
Hudswell N York 140 E7
Huggate E R Yk 134 D7
Hughenden Valley Bucks 42 E2
Hughley Shrops 83 L4
Hugh Town IoS 2 b2
Huish Devon 10 D3
Huish Wilts 40 C7
Huish Champflower Somset 25 G5
Huish Episcopi Somset 26 B6
Huisinis W Isls 232 d3
Hulcott Bucks 58 D5
Hulham Devon 12 C5
Hulland Derbys 100 E3
Hulland Ward Derbys 100 E3
Hullavington Wilts 39 K4
Hullbridge Essex 46 D2
Hull, Kingston upon C KuH 126 D5
Hulme Manch 113 J3
Hulme Staffs 99 L4
Hulme Warrtn 112 E4
Hulme End Staffs 100 C2
Hulme Walfield Ches E 113 J7
Hulverstone IoW 16 E5
Hulver Street Suffk 93 K6
Humber Bridge N Linc 126 C5
Humberside Airport N Linc 126 D7
Humberston NE Lin 118 D1
Humberstone C Leic 87 J3
Humbie E Loth 178 B5
Humbleton E R Yk 126 F4
Humby Lincs 103 G6
Hume Border 167 L2
Humshaugh Nthumb 158 A7
Huna Highld 231 L2
Huncote Leics 87 G4
Hundalee Border 167 K5
Hunderthwaite Dur 140 C3
Hundleby Lincs 118 E7
Hundleton Pembks 49 G7
Hundon Suffk 77 G5
Hundred House Powys 68 C4
Hungarton Leics 87 K3
Hungerford Somset 25 G4
Hungerford W Berk 41 G6
Hungerford Newtown W Berk 41 G6
Hungerstone Herefs 69 J7
Hunmanby N York 135 H4
Hunningham Warwks 72 D2
Hunsbury Hill Nhants 73 K3
Hunsdon Herts 60 C5
Hunsingore N York 132 F8
Hunslet Leeds 123 L4
Hunsonby Cumb 149 G7
Hunstanton Norfk 105 G4
Hunstanworth Dur 150 B5
Hunsterson Ches E 99 G4
Hunston Suffk 77 L2
Hunston W Susx 18 B5
Hunstrete BaNES 38 F7
Hunsworth Kirk 123 J5
Hunter's Quay Ag & B 173 K3
Huntham Somset 25 M6
Hunthill Lodge Angus 196 D3
Huntingdon Cambs 89 J8
Huntingfield Suffk 93 G8
Huntington C York 133 J7
Huntington Ches W 112 B8
Huntington E Loth 178 B4
Huntington Herefs 68 E4
Huntington Staffs 85 H2
Huntley Gloucs 55 G4
Huntly Abers 215 L6
Hunton Kent 33 J4
Hunton N York 132 B2
Huntscott Somset 24 E3
Huntsham Devon 24 F7
Huntshaw Devon 23 H6
Huntspill Somset 25 L3
Huntstile Somset 25 K5
Huntworth Somset 25 L4
Hunwick Dur 140 F2
Hunworth Norfk 106 C5
Hurdcott Wilts 28 D5
Hurdsfield Ches E 113 L6
Hurley W & M 42 D4
Hurley Warwks 86 B4
Hurley Common Warwks 86 B4
Hurlford E Ayrs 163 L3
Hurn Dorset 15 L3
Hursley Hants 29 H6
Hurst Wokham 42 C5
Hurstbourne Priors Hants 29 H3
Hurstbourne Tarrant Hants 29 G2
Hurst Green E Susx 33 J7
Hurst Green Essex 62 C5
Hurst Green Lancs 121 K3
Hurst Green Surrey 32 D3
Hurst Hill Dudley 85 G5
Hurstpierpoint W Susx 19 J3
Hurstwood Lancs 122 C4
Hurtiso Ork 234 c6
Hurworth-on-Tees Darltn 141 H5
Hurworth Place Darltn 141 H5
Husbands Bosworth Leics 87 J6
Husborne Crawley C Beds 74 D7
Husthwaite N York 133 H4
Hutcliffe Wood Crematorium Sheff 115 G5
Huthwaite Notts 101 J2
Huttoft Lincs 119 G6
Hutton Border 179 J7
Hutton E R Yk 134 F8
Hutton Essex 45 M2
Hutton Lancs 121 G5
Hutton N Som 37 M8
Hutton Buscel N York 134 F3
Hutton Conyers N York 132 E5
Hutton Cranswick E R Yk 126 C1
Hutton End Cumb 148 D7
Hutton Henry Dur 151 K7
Hutton-le-Hole N York 133 L2
Hutton Lowcross R & Cl 142 D4
Hutton Magna Dur 140 E5
Hutton Roof Cumb 130 B4
Hutton Roof Cumb 148 C7
Hutton Rudby N York 141 K6
Hutton Sessay N York 133 G4
Hutton Wandesley N York 124 D1
Huxham Devon 12 B3
Huxley Ches W 98 D1
Huyton Knows 112 C4
Hycemoor Cumb 128 D2
Hyde Tamesd 113 L3
Hyde Heath Bucks 58 F7
Hyde Lea Staffs 99 K8
Hylands House & Park Essex 61 G7
Hyndford Bridge S Lans 165 H2
Hynish Ag & B 188 C8
Hyssington Powys 82 F5
Hythe Essex 62 B3
Hythe Hants 16 E2
Hythe Kent 34 F7
Hythe End W & M 43 G6

I

Ibberton Dorset 14 E2
Ible Derbys 100 E2
Ibsley Hants 15 L1
Ibstock Leics 86 E2
Ibstone Bucks 42 C2
Ibthorpe Hants 29 G2
Iburndale N York 143 H5
Ibworth Hants 29 K1
Ichrachan Ag & B 182 E2
Ickburgh Norfk 91 J4
Ickenham Gt Lon 43 H3
Ickford Bucks 57 M6
Ickham Kent 35 G3
Ickleford Herts 59 K2
Icklesham E Susx 21 H3
Ickleton Cambs 76 C5
Icklingham Suffk 91 H8
Ickornshaw N York 122 E2
Ickwell Green C Beds 75 G5
Icomb Gloucs 56 E4
Idbury Oxon 56 E4
Iddesleigh Devon 10 E3
Ide Devon 11 K6
Ideford Devon 7 K1
Ide Hill Kent 32 E3
Iden E Susx 21 H2
Iden Green Kent 33 J5
Iden Green Kent 33 K6
Idle C Brad 123 H3
Idless Cnwll 4 C6
Idlicote Warwks 72 C5
Idmiston Wilts 28 D4
Idole Carmth 50 E3
Idridgehay Derbys 100 F3
Idrigill Highld 208 F2
Idstone Oxon 40 E4
Iffley Oxon 57 K7
Ifield W Susx 31 L4
Ifold W Susx 31 G5
Iford Bmouth 15 L4
Iford E Susx 19 L4
Ifton Mons 38 C3
Ightfield Shrops 98 E5
Ightham Kent 33 G2
Ilam Staffs 100 C3
Ilchester Somset 26 D6
Ilderton Nthumb 168 F5
Ilford Gt Lon 45 H3
Ilford Somset 26 A7
Ilfracombe Devon 23 H2
Ilkeston Derbys 101 J4
Ilketshall St Andrew Suffk 93 H6
Ilketshall St Margaret Suffk 93 H6
Ilkley C Brad 123 G2
Illand Cnwll 5 L1
Illey Dudley 85 H7
Illogan Cnwll 3 H3
Illston on the Hill Leics 87 K4
Ilmer Bucks 58 C6
Ilmington Warwks 72 B5
Ilminster Somset 26 A8
Ilsington Devon 7 H2
Ilston Swans 51 H7
Ilton N York 132 B4
Ilton Somset 25 M7
Imachar N Ayrs 161 L2
Immingham NE Lin 126 F7
Immingham Dock NE Lin 126 F7
Impington Cambs 76 C2
Ince Ches W 112 C6
Ince Blundell Sefton 111 K2
Ince-in-Makerfield Wigan 112 E1
Inchbae Lodge Hotel Highld 221 K7
Inchbare Angus 196 F4
Inchberry Moray 215 G4
Incheril Highld 211 G3
Inchinnan Rens 174 E5
Inchlaggan Highld 201 J5
Inchmichael P & K 186 D3
Inchnacardoch Hotel Highld 202 B3
Inchnadamph Highld 224 F4
Inchture P & K 186 D2
Inchvuilt Highld 211 K6
Inchyra P & K 186 C4
Indian Queens Cnwll 4 E4
Ingatestone Essex 61 G7
Ingbirchworth Barns 114 E1
Ingestre Staffs 99 L7
Ingham Lincs 116 F5
Ingham Norfk 107 H7
Ingham Suffk 77 J1
Ingham Corner Norfk 107 H6
Ingleby Derbys 101 G6
Ingleby Arncliffe N York 141 K6
Ingleby Barwick S on T 141 K4
Ingleby Greenhow N York 142 C6
Ingleigh Green Devon 10 E4
Inglesbatch BaNES 39 G7
Inglesham Swindn 56 D7
Ingleston D & G 147 G2
Ingleton Dur 140 F3
Ingleton N York 130 D5
Inglewhite Lancs 121 H3
Ingoe Nthumb 158 C7
Ingol Lancs 121 G4
Ingoldisthorpe Norfk 105 G6
Ingoldmells Lincs 119 H7
Ingoldsby Lincs 103 G6
Ingram Nthumb 168 F6
Ingrave Essex 45 M2
Ingrow C Brad 122 F3

Ings Cumb 138 C7
Ingst S Glos 38 E3
Ingthorpe Rutlnd 88 E2
Ingworth Norfk 106 E6
Inkberrow Worcs 71 H3
Inkhorn Abers 217 H6
Inkpen W Berk 41 G7
Inkstack Highld 231 J2
Innellan Ag & B 173 K4
Innerleithen Border 166 E3
Innerleven Fife 186 F7
Innermessan D & G 144 C3
Innerwick E Loth 178 F4
Innesmill Moray 215 G2
Insch Abers 216 C8
Insh Highld 203 J5
Inskip Lancs 120 F3
Instow Devon 23 G5
Intake Sheff 115 H5
Inver Abers 204 F6
Inver Highld 223 J5
Inver P & K 194 F7
Inverailort Highld 190 F1
Inveralligin Highld 210 C3
Inverallochy Abers 217 K2
Inveran Highld 222 D2
Inveraray Ag & B 182 F5
Inverarish Highld 209 J7
Inverarity Angus 196 D7
Inverarnan Stirlg 183 K4
Inverasdale Highld 219 J4
Inverbeg Ag & B 183 K7
Inverbervie Abers 197 K2
Inverboyndie Abers 216 C2
Invercreran House Hotel Ag & B 191 K6
Inverdruie Highld 203 L3
Inveresk E Loth 177 K4
Inveresragan Ag & B 182 E1
Inverey Abers 204 D7
Inverfarigaig Highld 202 D2
Inverfolla Ag & B 191 J7
Invergarry Highld 201 L5
Invergeldie P & K 184 F2
Invergloy Highld 201 K7
Invergordon Highld 222 F7
Invergowrie P & K 186 F2
Inverguseran Highld 200 B4
Inverhadden P & K 193 L5
Inverherive Hotel Stirlg 183 L3
Inverie Highld 200 B5
Inverinan Ag & B 182 E4
Inverinate Highld 200 E2
Inverkeilor Angus 197 G6
Inverkeithing Fife 176 F2
Inverkeithny Abers 216 C5
Inverkip Inver 173 L4
Inverkirkaig Highld 224 C4
Inverlael Highld 220 F4
Inverlair Highld 192 E1
Inverliever Lodge Ag & B 182 C6
Inverlochy Ag & B 183 H2
Invermark Angus 196 D1
Invermoriston Highld 202 C3
Invernaver Highld 229 L4
Inverness Highld 213 G5
Inverness Airport Highld 213 J4
Inverness Crematorium Highld 212 F5
Invernoaden Ag & B 183 G7
Inveroran Hotel Ag & B 192 D7
Inverquharity Angus 196 C5
Inverquhomery Abers 217 J5
Inverroy Highld 201 K8
Inversanda Highld 191 J4
Invershiel Highld 200 E2
Invershin Highld 222 D3
Invershore Highld 231 J8
Inversnaid Hotel Stirlg 183 K5
Inverugie Abers 217 L5
Inveruglas Ag & B 183 K5
Inveruglass Highld 203 J5
Inverurie Abers 206 E2
Inwardleigh Devon 10 E5
Inworth Essex 61 L4
Iona Ag & B 180 D3
Iping W Susx 30 D6
iPort Logistics Park Donc 115 L2
Ipplepen Devon 7 J3
Ipsden Oxon 41 M4
Ipstones Staffs 100 A3
Ipswich Suffk 78 E5
Ipswich Crematorium Suffk 78 E5
Irby Wirral 111 J5
Irby in the Marsh Lincs 118 F8
Irby upon Humber NE Lin 117 K1
Irchester Nhants 74 D2
Ireby Cumb 147 M7
Ireby Lancs 130 C4
Ireleth Cumb 128 F4
Ireshopeburn Dur 149 L7
Irlam Salfd 113 G3
Irnham Lincs 103 G7
Iron Acton S Glos 39 G4
Ironbridge Wrekin 84 C3
Ironbridge Gorge Wrekin 84 C3
Ironmacannie D & G 154 B6
Ironville Derbys 101 H3
Irstead Norfk 107 H7
Irthington Cumb 148 E3
Irthlingborough Nhants 74 D1
Irton N York 134 F3
Irvine N Ayrs 163 H2
Isauld Highld 230 E3
Isbister Shet 235 c2
Isbister Shet 235 d4
Isfield E Susx 19 L3
Isham Nhants 88 C8
Isington Hants 30 C3
Islay Ag & B 171 G4
Islay Airport Ag & B 170 F7
Isle Abbotts Somset 26 A7
Isle Brewers Somset 26 A7
Isleham Cambs 90 F8
Isle of Dogs Gt Lon 45 G4
Isle of Grain Medway 46 E5
Isle of Lewis W Isls 232 f2
Isle of Man IoM 237 c4
Isle of Man Ronaldsway Airport IoM 237 b7
Isle of Mull Ag & B 181 J1
Isle of Purbeck Dorset 15 J5
Isle of Sheppey Kent 46 F6
Isle of Skye Highld 208 F6
Isle of Thanet Kent 35 J2
Isle of Walney Cumb 128 E6
Isle of Whithorn D & G 145 K7
Isle of Wight IoW 17 G5
Isle of Wight Crematorium IoW 17 G4
Isleornsay Highld 199 L3
Isles of Scilly IoS 2 b1
Isles of Scilly St Mary's Airport IoS 2 b2
Islesteps D & G 155 G7
Islet Village Guern 236 d2
Isleworth Gt Lon 44 D5
Isley Walton Leics 101 H7
Islibhig W Isls 232 d3
Islington Gt Lon 44 F3
Islington Crematorium Gt Lon 44 F3
Islip Nhants 88 E7
Islip Oxon 57 K5
Islivig W Isls 232 d3
Isombridge Wrekin 83 L2
Itchen Abbas Hants 29 K5
Itchen Stoke Hants 29 K5
Itchingfield W Susx 31 J5
Itteringham Norfk 106 D6
Itton Mons 38 C2
Itton Common Mons 38 C2
Ivegill Cumb 148 D6
Iver Bucks 43 G4
Iver Heath Bucks 43 G4
Iveston Dur 150 E5
Ivinghoe Bucks 58 F5
Ivinghoe Aston Bucks 58 F4
Ivington Herefs 69 J3
Ivybridge Devon 6 F5
Ivychurch Kent 21 K1
Ivy Hatch Kent 33 G3
Iwade Kent 46 E6
Iwerne Courtney Dorset 27 K8
Iwerne Minster Dorset 27 K8
Ixworth Suffk 77 L1
Ixworth Thorpe Suffk 91 K8

J

Jack-in-the-Green Devon 12 C4
Jackton S Lans 175 G7
Jacobstow Cnwll 9 G5
Jacobstowe Devon 10 E4
Jameston Pembks 49 H7
Jamestown Highld 212 D3
Jamestown W Duns 174 D3
Janetstown Highld 227 L3
Janetstown Highld 231 L5
Jardine Hall D & G 155 J5
Jarrow S Tyne 151 H3
Jasper's Green Essex 61 H3
Jawcraig Falk 175 L4
Jaywick Essex 62 D5
Jedburgh Border 167 K5
Jeffreyston Pembks 49 J6
Jemimaville Highld 213 H2
Jerbourg Guern 236 d4
Jersey Jersey 236 c6
Jersey Airport Jersey 236 b7
Jersey Crematorium Jersey 236 c7
Jesmond N u Ty 151 G2
Jevington E Susx 20 B5
Jockey End Herts 59 H5
Johnby Cumb 148 D7
John Lennon Airport Lpool 112 B5
John o' Groats Highld 231 L2
Johnshaven Abers 197 J3
Johnston Pembks 48 F5
Johnstone D & G 155 M3
Johnstone Rens 174 D5
Johnstonebridge D & G 155 J4
Johnstown Carmth 50 E2
Johnstown Wrexhm 97 L4
Joppa C Edin 177 J4
Joppa Cerdgn 66 D2
Joppa S Ayrs 163 K5
Jordanston Pembks 64 C7
Joyden's Wood Kent 45 K5
Juniper Nthumb 150 B3
Juniper Green C Edin 177 G5
Jura Ag & B 171 J2
Jurassic Coast Devon 13 H4
Jurby IoM 237 c2

K

Kaber Cumb 139 H5
Kaimend S Lans 165 J1
Kames Ag & B 173 G4
Kames E Ayrs 164 D4
Kea Cnwll 4 C7
Keadby N Linc 125 K7
Keal Cotes Lincs 104 B1
Kearsley Bolton 113 H1
Kearsney Kent 35 H6
Kearstwick Cumb 130 B4
Kedington Suffk 77 G5
Kedleston Derbys 100 F4
Keelby Lincs 126 E8
Keele Staffs 99 J4
Keele Services Staffs 99 J4
Keelham C Brad 123 G4
Keeston Pembks 48 F4
Keevil Wilts 39 L8
Kegworth Leics 101 J7
Kehelland Cnwll 3 G3
Keig Abers 206 B2
Keighley C Brad 122 F3
Keighley Crematorium C Brad 122 F3
Keilarsbrae Clacks 185 J8
Keillour P & K 185 K3
Keiloch Abers 204 E6
Keils Ag & B 171 K5
Keinton Mandeville Somset 26 D5
Keir Mill D & G 154 E4
Keisley Cumb 139 G3
Keiss Highld 231 L4
Keith Moray 215 J4
Keithick P & K 195 K8
Keithock Angus 196 F4
Keithtown Highld 212 E3
Kelbrook Lancs 122 D2
Kelby Lincs 103 G4
Keld N York 139 K6
Kelfield N York 124 F3
Kelham Notts 102 C2
Kelhead D & G 147 K2
Kellamergh Lancs 120 E5
Kellas Angus 187 G1
Kellas Moray 214 E4
Kellaton Devon 7 J7
Kelling Norfk 106 C4
Kellington N York 124 E5
Kelloe Dur 151 J7
Kelloholm D & G 164 E6
Kelly Devon 9 K8
Kelmarsh Nhants 87 K7
Kelmscott Oxon 56 E7
Kelsale Suffk 79 H2
Kelsall Ches W 112 D7
Kelshall Herts 75 K7
Kelsick Cumb 147 L5
Kelso Border 167 L3
Kelstedge Derbys 115 G8
Kelstern Lincs 118 C4
Kelston BaNES 39 G6
Keltneyburn P & K 194 B6
Kelton D & G 155 H7
Kelty Fife 186 B8
Kelvedon Essex 61 K4
Kelvedon Hatch Essex 60 F7
Kelynack Cnwll 2 C5
Kemback Fife 187 G4
Kemberton Shrops 84 D3
Kemble Gloucs 39 M2
Kemerton Worcs 71 G6
Kemeys Commander Mons 53 M6
Kemnay Abers 206 E3
Kempley Gloucs 54 F3
Kempley Green Gloucs 55 G3
Kempsey Worcs 70 F5
Kempsford Gloucs 40 D2
Kempshott Hants 29 L2
Kempston Bed 74 F5
Kempton Shrops 83 G6
Kemp Town Br & H 19 J5
Kemsing Kent 32 F2
Kenardington Kent 34 C7
Kenchester Herefs 69 J6
Kencot Oxon 56 E6
Kendal Cumb 129 L2
Kenfig Brdgnd 36 C4
Kenilworth Warwks 72 C1

Kenley Gt Lon 32 B2
Kenley Shrops 83 L4
Kenmore Highld 210 B3
Kenmore P & K 194 B7
Kenn Devon 11 L7
Kenn N Som 38 B6
Kennacraig Ag & B 172 D5
Kennall Vale Cnwll 3 J4
Kennerleigh Devon 11 J4
Kennessee Green Sefton 111 L2
Kennet Clacks 176 C1
Kennethmont Abers 215 L8
Kennett Cambs 77 G2
Kennford Devon 11 L7
Kenninghall Norfk 92 C6
Kennington Kent 34 D5
Kennington Oxon 57 K7
Kennoway Fife 186 F6
Kenny Somset 25 L7
Kenny Hill Suffk 90 F7
Kennythorpe N York 134 C6
Kenovay Ag & B 188 C6
Kensaleyre Highld 208 F4
Kensington Gt Lon 44 E4
Kensington Palace Gt Lon 44 E4
Kensworth Common C Beds 59 G4
Kentallen Highld 191 K5
Kent and Sussex Crematorium Kent 33 G5
Kentchurch Herefs 54 B3
Kentford Suffk 77 G2
Kentisbeare Devon 12 D2
Kentisbury Devon 23 K3
Kentish Town Gt Lon 44 F3
Kentmere Cumb 138 C6
Kenton Devon 12 B5
Kenton Gt Lon 44 D3
Kenton N u Ty 150 F2
Kenton Suffk 78 E2
Kenton Bankfoot N u Ty 150 F2
Kentra Highld 190 D3
Kent's Green Gloucs 55 H4
Kent's Oak Hants 28 F6
Kenwyn Cnwll 4 C6
Keoldale Highld 228 F3
Keppoch Highld 200 D1
Kepwick N York 133 G2
Keresley Covtry 86 D6
Kerrera Ag & B 182 B2
Kerris Cnwll 2 D5
Kerry Powys 82 D5
Kerrycroy Ag & B 173 J6
Kersall Notts 116 B8
Kersbrook Devon 12 D5
Kersey Suffk 78 B5
Kershader W Isls 232 f3
Kerswell Devon 12 D2
Kerswell Green Worcs 70 F5
Kesgrave Suffk 78 F5
Kessingland Suffk 93 L6
Kestle Cnwll 4 F6
Kestle Mill Cnwll 4 D4
Keston Gt Lon 45 H7
Keswick Cumb 137 J3
Keswick Norfk 92 E3
Kettering Nhants 88 C7
Kettering Crematorium Nhants 88 C7
Ketteringham Norfk 92 E3
Kettins P & K 195 K8
Kettlebaston Suffk 77 L4
Kettlebridge Fife 186 E6
Kettlebrook Staffs 86 B3
Kettleburgh Suffk 78 F3
Kettleholm D & G 155 K6
Kettleshulme Ches E 113 M5
Kettlesing N York 132 C7
Kettlesing Bottom N York 132 C7
Kettlestone Norfk 106 A6
Kettlethorpe Lincs 116 D6
Kettletoft Ork 234 d4
Kettlewell N York 131 H5
Ketton Rutlnd 88 E3
Kew Gt Lon 44 D5
Kew Royal Botanic Gardens Gt Lon 44 D5
Kewstoke N Som 37 M7
Kexby C York 125 G1
Kexby Lincs 116 E4
Key Green Ches E 113 K8
Keyham Leics 87 J3
Keyhaven Hants 16 C4
Keyingham E R Yk 127 G5
Keymer W Susx 19 J3
Keynsham BaNES 38 F6
Keysoe Bed 74 F3
Keysoe Row Bed 74 F3
Keyston Cambs 88 F7
Keyworth Notts 101 L6
Kibblesworth Gatesd 151 G4
Kibworth Beauchamp Leics 87 K5
Kibworth Harcourt Leics 87 K5
Kidbrooke Gt Lon 45 H5
Kidderminster Worcs 84 E7
Kidlington Oxon 57 J5
Kidmore End Oxon 42 B5
Kidsdale D & G 145 J7
Kidsgrove Staffs 99 J2
Kidwelly Carmth 50 E4
Kiel Crofts Ag & B 191 H8
Kielder Nthumb 157 G4
Kielder Forest 157 G5
Kiells Ag & B 171 H5
Kilbarchan Rens 174 D5
Kilbeg Highld 199 K4
Kilberry Ag & B 172 C5
Kilbirnie N Ayrs 174 C7
Kilbride Ag & B 172 C3
Kilbride Ag & B 173 H5
Kilbuiack Moray 214 D3
Kilburn Derbys 101 G4
Kilburn Gt Lon 44 E4
Kilburn N York 133 H4
Kilby Leics 87 J4
Kilchamaig Ag & B 172 D6
Kilchattan Ag & B 173 J7
Kilchattan Ag & B 180 E7
Kilcheran Ag & B 191 G8
Kilchoan Highld 189 L4
Kilchoman Ag & B 170 D5
Kilchrenan Ag & B 182 E3
Kilconquhar Fife 187 H6
Kilcot Gloucs 55 G3
Kilcoy Highld 212 E4
Kilcreggan Ag & B 173 L3
Kildale N York 142 D5
Kildalloig Ag & B 161 J5
Kildary Highld 223 G6
Kildavaig Ag & B 173 G5
Kildavanan Ag & B 173 H5
Kildonan Highld 227 G4
Kildonan N Ayrs 162 D5
Kildonan Lodge Highld 226 F4
Kildonnan Highld 199 G7
Kildrochet House D & G 144 C4
Kildrummy Abers 205 K2
Kildwick N York 122 F2
Kilfinan Ag & B 172 F3
Kilfinnan Highld 201 K6
Kilgetty Pembks 49 J6
Kilgrammie S Ayrs 152 F2
Kilgwrrwg Common Mons 38 C2
Kilham E R Yk 135 G6
Kilkenneth Ag & B 188 B7
Kilkenzie Ag & B 161 H4
Kilkerran Ag & B 161 J5
Kilkhampton Cnwll 9 H3
Killamarsh Derbys 115 J5
Killay Swans 51 H6
Killearn Stirlg 174 F2
Killen Highld 213 G3
Killerby Darltn 140 F3
Killerton Devon 12 C3
Killichonan P & K 193 J5
Killiechonate Highld 192 D1
Killiechronan Ag & B 190 B7
Killiecrankie P & K 194 E4
Killilan Highld 210 E7
Killimster Highld 231 K4
Killin Stirlg 184 C2
Killinghall N York 132 D7
Killington Cumb 130 C2
Killington Lake Services Cumb 130 B2
Killingworth N Tyne 159 G7
Killochyett Border 167 G1
Kilmacolm Inver 174 C4
Kilmahog Stirlg 184 D5
Kilmahumaig Ag & B 182 A8
Kilmaluag Highld 218 C6
Kilmany Fife 186 F3
Kilmarnock E Ayrs 163 K2
Kilmartin Ag & B 182 B7
Kilmaurs E Ayrs 163 K2
Kilmelford Ag & B 182 B5
Kilmersdon Somset 27 G2
Kilmeston Hants 29 L6
Kilmichael Ag & B 161 H5
Kilmichael Glassary Ag & B 182 B8
Kilmichael of Inverlussa Ag & B 172 D2
Kilmington Devon 13 H3
Kilmington Wilts 27 H4
Kilmington Common Wilts 27 H4
Kilmington Street Wilts 27 H4
Kilmorack Highld 212 D5
Kilmore Ag & B 182 C3
Kilmore Highld 199 K4
Kilmory Ag & B 172 C4
Kilmory Highld 190 B3
Kilmory N Ayrs 162 B5
Kilmuir Highld 208 D5
Kilmuir Highld 213 G4
Kilmuir Highld 218 B7
Kilmuir Highld 223 G6
Kilmun Ag & B 173 K3
Kilnave Ag & B 170 F4
Kilncadzow S Lans 176 B8
Kilndown Kent 33 J6
Kilninver Ag & B 182 B3
Kilnsea E R Yk 127 J7
Kilnsey N York 131 H6
Kilnwick E R Yk 126 C1
Kiloran Ag & B 180 E7
Kilpatrick N Ayrs 162 A4
Kilpeck Herefs 54 C3
Kilpin E R Yk 125 J5
Kilrenny Fife 187 J6
Kilsby Nhants 73 H1
Kilspindie P & K 186 C3
Kilstay D & G 144 D7
Kilsyth N Lans 175 J3
Kiltarlity Highld 212 D6
Kilton R & Cl 142 E4
Kilton Thorpe R & Cl 142 E4
Kilvaxter Highld 218 B7
Kilve Somset 25 H3
Kilvington Notts 102 D4
Kilwinning N Ayrs 163 H2
Kimberley Norfk 92 C3
Kimberley Notts 101 J4
Kimberworth Rothm 115 H3
Kimblesworth Dur 151 G5
Kimbolton Cambs 75 G2
Kimbolton Herefs 69 K3
Kimcote Leics 87 H6
Kimmeridge Dorset 15 H6
Kimpton Hants 28 F3
Kimpton Herts 59 K4
Kinbrace Highld 226 F3
Kinbuck Stirlg 185 G6
Kincaple Fife 187 G4
Kincardine Fife 176 C2
Kincardine Highld 222 E4
Kincardine Bridge Fife 176 C2
Kincardine O'Neil Abers 206 B5
Kinclaven P & K 195 J8
Kincorth C Aber 207 H5
Kincorth House Moray 214 C3
Kincraig Highld 203 K4
Kincraigie P & K 194 F6
Kindallachan P & K 194 F6
Kinerarach Ag & B 172 B7
Kineton Gloucs 56 C3
Kineton Warwks 72 D4
Kinfauns P & K 186 C3
Kingarth Ag & B 173 J6
Kingcausie Abers 207 G5
Kingcoed Mons 54 B6
Kingerby Lincs 117 H3
Kingham Oxon 56 E3
Kingholm Quay D & G 155 G7
Kinghorn Fife 177 H2
Kinglassie Fife 186 D7
Kingoldrum Angus 196 B5
Kingoodie P & K 186 E2
Kingsand Cnwll 6 C5
Kingsbarns Fife 187 K5
Kingsbridge Devon 7 H6
Kingsbridge Somset 24 F4
King's Bromley Staffs 85 K1
Kingsburgh Highld 208 F4
Kingsbury Gt Lon 44 D3
Kingsbury Warwks 86 B4
Kingsbury Episcopi Somset 26 B7
King's Caple Herefs 54 E3
Kingsclere Hants 41 K8
King's Cliffe Nhants 88 E4
Kings Clipstone Notts 115 L8
Kingscote Gloucs 39 J2
Kingscott Devon 23 H7
King's Coughton Warwks 71 J3
Kingscross N Ayrs 162 D4
Kingsdon Somset 26 D6
Kingsdown Kent 35 K5
Kingsdown Swindn 40 D3
Kingsdown Wilts 39 J6
Kingsdown Crematorium Swindn 40 D3
Kingseat Fife 176 F1
Kingsey Bucks 58 C6
Kingsfold W Susx 31 K4
Kingsford C Aber 206 F4
Kingsford E Ayrs 174 E8
Kingsgate Kent 35 K1
Kingshall Street Suffk 77 K3
King's Heath Birm 85 J7
Kings Hill Kent 33 H3
King's Hill Wsall 85 H4
Kings House Hotel Highld 192 D5
Kingshouse Hotel Stirlg 184 C4
Kingshurst Solhll 85 L6
Kingskerswell Devon 7 K3
Kingskettle Fife 186 E5
Kingsland Herefs 69 J3
Kingsland IoA 108 C5
Kings Langley Herts 59 H7
Kingsley Ches W 112 D6
Kingsley Hants 30 C4
Kingsley Staffs 100 A3
Kingsley Green W Susx 30 E5
Kingsley Park Nhants 73 L3
King's Lynn Norfk 104 F8
Kings Meaburn Cumb 138 E3
King's Mills Guern 236 c3
Kingsmuir Angus 196 D6
Kings Muir Border 166 C2
Kingsmuir Fife 187 J5
Kingsnorth Kent 34 D6
King's Norton Birm 85 J7
King's Norton Leics 87 K4
Kings Nympton Devon 23 L7
King's Pyon Herefs 69 J4

Kings Ripton Cambs 89 J7
King's Somborne Hants 29 G5
King's Stag Dorset 14 D1
King's Stanley Gloucs 55 J7
King's Sutton Nhants 72 F7
Kingstanding Birm 85 J4
Kingsteignton Devon 7 K2
Kingsthorne Herefs 54 D2
Kingsthorpe Nhants 73 L2
Kingston Cambs 75 L4
Kingston Cnwll 6 A2
Kingston Devon 6 F6
Kingston Dorset 14 E1
Kingston Dorset 15 H6
Kingston E Loth 178 C3
Kingston IoW 16 F6
Kingston Kent 35 G4
Kingston Bagpuize Oxon 57 H7
Kingston Blount Oxon 58 C7
Kingston Deverill Wilts 27 J4
Kingstone Herefs 69 H7
Kingstone Somset 26 B8
Kingstone Staffs 100 B6
Kingston Lacy House & Gardens Dorset 15 J3
Kingston Lisle Oxon 40 F3
Kingston near Lewes E Susx 19 K4
Kingston on Soar Notts 101 J6
Kingston on Spey Moray 215 H2
Kingston Russell Dorset 14 B4
Kingston St Mary Somset 25 K5
Kingston Seymour N Som 38 B6
Kingston upon Hull C KuH 126 D5
Kingston upon Thames Gt Lon 44 D6
Kingston upon Thames Crematorium Gt Lon 44 D6
King's Walden Herts 59 K4
Kingswear Devon 7 K5
Kingswells C Aber 207 G4
Kings Weston Bristl 38 D5
Kingswinford Dudley 84 F5
Kingswood Bucks 58 B4
Kingswood Gloucs 39 H3
Kingswood S Glos 38 F5
Kingswood Somset 25 H4
Kingswood Surrey 31 L1
Kingswood Warwks 71 L1
Kingswood Common Staffs 84 E3
Kings Worthy Hants 29 J5
Kingthorpe Lincs 117 J6
Kington Herefs 68 F3
Kington S Glos 38 F3
Kington Worcs 71 H4
Kington Langley Wilts 39 L5
Kington Magna Dorset 27 H6
Kington St Michael Wilts 39 K5
Kingussie Highld 203 H5
Kingweston Somset 26 D5
Kinharrachie Abers 217 H7
Kinharvie D & G 147 G2
Kinkell Bridge P & K 185 J4
Kinknockie Abers 217 J6
Kinleith C Edin 177 G5
Kinlet Shrops 84 C7
Kinloch Highld 198 F5
Kinloch Highld 225 H2
Kinloch Highld 229 H5
Kinloch P & K 195 J7
Kinlochard Stirlg 184 B6
Kinlochbervie Highld 228 C4
Kinlocheil Highld 191 J1
Kinlochewe Highld 210 F3
Kinloch Hourn Highld 200 E4
Kinlochlaggan Highld 202 E7
Kinlochleven Highld 192 C4
Kinlochmoidart Highld 190 E2
Kinlochnanuagh Highld 200 B8
Kinloch Rannoch P & K 193 L5
Kinloss Moray 214 C3
Kinmel Bay Conwy 110 D5
Kinmuck Abers 206 F2
Kinmundy Abers 207 G2
Kinnabus Ag & B 160 B2
Kinnadie Abers 217 H5
Kinnaird P & K 194 F5
Kinneff Abers 197 K2
Kinnelhead D & G 155 H2
Kinnell Angus 196 F6
Kinnerley Shrops 97 M7
Kinnersley Herefs 69 G5
Kinnersley Worcs 70 F5
Kinnerton Powys 68 E2
Kinnesswood P & K 186 C6
Kinnordy Angus 196 B5
Kinoulton Notts 102 B6
Kinross P & K 186 B6
Kinrossie P & K 186 C2
Kinross Services P & K 186 B6
Kinsham Herefs 69 G2
Kinsham Worcs 71 G7
Kinsley Wakefd 124 C7
Kinson Bmouth 15 K3
Kintail Highld 200 F2
Kintbury W Berk 41 G6
Kintessack Moray 214 B3
Kintillo P & K 186 B4
Kinton Herefs 83 H8
Kinton Shrops 98 A8
Kintore Abers 206 E3
Kintour Ag & B 171 H7
Kintra Ag & B 170 F8
Kintra Ag & B 180 D3
Kintraw Ag & B 182 B6
Kintyre Ag & B 161 J2
Kinveachy Highld 203 L2
Kinver Staffs 84 E6
Kippax Leeds 124 C4
Kippen Stirlg 184 E7
Kippford D & G 146 E4
Kipping's Cross Kent 33 H5
Kirbister Ork 234 b6
Kirby Bedon Norfk 93 G3
Kirby Bellars Leics 102 B8
Kirby Cane Norfk 93 H5
Kirby Cross Essex 62 E4
Kirby Grindalythe N York 134 D6
Kirby Hill N York 132 F5
Kirby Hill N York 140 E6
Kirby Knowle N York 133 G3
Kirby-le-Soken Essex 62 F4
Kirby Misperton N York 134 B4
Kirby Muxloe Leics 87 G3
Kirby Underdale E R Yk 134 C7
Kirby Wiske N York 132 E3
Kirdford W Susx 31 G6
Kirk Highld 231 K4
Kirkabister Shet 235 d6
Kirkandrews D & G 146 A5
Kirkandrews upon Eden Cumb 148 C4
Kirkbampton Cumb 148 B4
Kirkbean D & G 147 G3
Kirk Bramwith Donc 124 F7
Kirkbride Cumb 147 M4
Kirkbuddo Angus 196 E7
Kirkburn Border 166 D2
Kirkburn E R Yk 134 F7
Kirkburton Kirk 123 J7
Kirkby Knows 111 L2
Kirkby Lincs 117 H3
Kirkby N York 142 C6
Kirkby Fleetham N York 141 G7
Kirkby Green Lincs 103 H2
Kirkby-in-Ashfield Notts 101 J2
Kirkby-in-Furness Cumb 128 F3
Kirkby la Thorpe Lincs 103 J4
Kirkby Lonsdale Cumb 130 B4
Kirkby Malham N York 131 G7
Kirkby Mallory Leics 86 F4
Kirkby Malzeard N York 132 C5
Kirkbymoorside N York 133 L3
Kirkby on Bain Lincs 118 C8
Kirkby Overblow N York 123 L2
Kirkby Stephen Cumb 139 H5
Kirkby Thore Cumb 138 F3
Kirkby Underwood Lincs 103 H6
Kirkby Wharf N York 124 D3
Kirkcaldy Fife 186 D8
Kirkcaldy Crematorium Fife 186 D8
Kirkcambeck Cumb 148 F2
Kirkchrist D & G 146 B5
Kirkcolm D & G 144 B2
Kirkconnel D & G 164 E6
Kirkconnell D & G 147 G2
Kirkcowan D & G 145 G3
Kirkcudbright D & G 146 B5
Kirkdale Lpool 111 K3
Kirk Deighton N York 124 B1
Kirk Ella E R Yk 126 C5
Kirkfieldbank S Lans 165 G2
Kirkgunzeon D & G 146 F2
Kirk Hallam Derbys 101 J4
Kirkham Lancs 120 F4
Kirkham N York 134 B6
Kirkhamgate Wakefd 123 K6
Kirk Hammerton N York 133 G7
Kirkhaugh Nthumb 149 H5
Kirkheaton Kirk 123 H6
Kirkheaton Nthumb 158 C6
Kirkhill Highld 212 E5
Kirkhope S Lans 165 J7
Kirkibost Highld 199 H2
Kirkinch P & K 195 L7
Kirkinner D & G 145 J5
Kirkintilloch E Duns 175 H4
Kirk Ireton Derbys 100 E3
Kirkland Cumb 136 E4
Kirkland D & G 154 E4
Kirkland D & G 155 H4
Kirkland D & G 164 E6
Kirk Langley Derbys 100 F5
Kirkleatham R & Cl 142 D3
Kirkleatham Crematorium R & Cl 142 D3
Kirklevington S on T 141 K5
Kirkley Suffk 93 L5
Kirklington N York 132 D4
Kirklington Notts 102 B2
Kirklinton Cumb 148 D2
Kirkliston C Edin 176 F4
Kirkmabreck D & G 145 K4
Kirkmaiden D & G 144 D7
Kirk Merrington Dur 141 G2
Kirk Michael IoM 237 c4
Kirkmichael P & K 195 H4
Kirkmichael S Ayrs 163 J7
Kirkmuirhill S Lans 164 F2
Kirknewton Nthumb 168 D4
Kirknewton W Loth 176 F5
Kirkney Abers 215 L7
Kirk of Shotts N Lans 175 L5
Kirkoswald Cumb 148 F6
Kirkoswald S Ayrs 163 G7
Kirkpatrick D & G 154 F4
Kirkpatrick Durham D & G 154 D7
Kirkpatrick-Fleming D & G 156 B7
Kirk Sandall Donc 124 F8
Kirksanton Cumb 128 D4
Kirk Smeaton N York 124 D7
Kirkstall Leeds 123 K4
Kirkstead Lincs 103 K1
Kirkstile Abers 215 L7
Kirkstile D & G 156 C4
Kirkstyle Highld 231 L2
Kirkthorpe Wakefd 124 B6
Kirkton Abers 206 C1
Kirkton D & G 155 G6
Kirkton Fife 186 F3
Kirkton Highld 210 C8
Kirkton Highld 210 D6
Kirkton P & K 185 K4
Kirkton Manor Border 166 C2
Kirkton of Airlie Angus 195 L6
Kirkton of Auchterhouse Angus 196 B8
Kirkton of Barevan Highld 213 K5
Kirkton of Collace P & K 186 C2
Kirkton of Glenbuchat Abers 205 J3
Kirkton of Logie Buchan Abers 217 J7
Kirkton of Maryculter Abers 207 G5
Kirkton of Menmuir Angus 196 E4
Kirkton of Monikie Angus 196 E8
Kirkton of Rayne Abers 216 D7
Kirkton of Skene Abers 206 F4
Kirkton of Strathmartine Angus 186 F1
Kirkton of Tealing Angus 196 C8
Kirkton of Tough Abers 206 C3
Kirktown Abers 217 J2
Kirktown Abers 217 K4
Kirktown of Alvah Abers 216 D3
Kirktown of Bourtie Abers 206 F1
Kirktown of Fetteresso Abers 206 F7
Kirktown of Mortlach Moray 215 H6
Kirktown of Slains Abers 217 K8
Kirkurd Border 165 M1
Kirkwall Ork 234 c6
Kirkwall Airport Ork 234 c6
Kirkwhelpington Nthumb 158 C5
Kirk Yetholm Border 168 C4
Kirmington N Linc 126 D7
Kirmond le Mire Lincs 117 K3
Kirn Ag & B 173 K3
Kirriemuir Angus 196 C5
Kirstead Green Norfk 93 G4
Kirtlebridge D & G 155 M7
Kirtling Cambs 77 G3
Kirtling Green Cambs 76 F4
Kirtlington Oxon 57 J4
Kirtomy Highld 229 M3
Kirton Lincs 104 A5
Kirton Notts 116 B7
Kirton Suffk 78 F6
Kirtonhill W Duns 174 D4
Kirton in Lindsey N Linc 116 F2
Kirwaugh D & G 145 J4
Kishorn Highld 210 C6

Kislingbury Nhants 73 K3
Kittisford Somset 25 G6
Kitt's Green Birm 85 L6
Kittybrewster C Aber 207 H4
Kivernoll Herefs 54 C2
Kiveton Park Rothm 115 J5
Knaith Lincs 116 D5
Knap Corner Dorset 27 J6
Knaphill Surrey 42 F8
Knapp Somset 25 L6
Knapton C York 124 E1
Knapton N York 134 D4
Knapton Norfk 107 G5
Knapwell Cambs 75 K2
Knaresborough N York 132 E7
Knarsdale Nthumb 149 H4
Knaven Abers 217 G5
Knayton N York 132 F2
Knebworth Herts 59 L4
Knedlington E R Yk 125 H5
Kneesall Notts 116 B8
Kneeton Notts 102 B4
Knelston Swans 50 F7
Knenhall Staffs 99 L5
Knightcote Warwks 72 E4
Knightley Staffs 99 J7
Knighton C Leic 87 H4
Knighton Dorset 14 C1
Knighton Powys 82 F8
Knighton Somset 25 J3
Knighton Staffs 99 G4
Knighton Staffs 99 H6
Knighton on Teme Worcs 70 B1
Knightwick Worcs 70 D4
Knill Herefs 68 F3
Knipton Leics 102 D6
Kniveton Derbys 100 E3
Knock Cumb 138 F2
Knock Highld 199 K4
Knock Moray 215 L4
Knock W Isls 232 g2
Knockally Highld 227 K3
Knockan Highld 224 F6
Knockando Moray 214 F6
Knockbain Highld 212 E5
Knockbain Highld 212 F3
Knock Castle N Ayrs 173 L5
Knockdee Highld 231 H4
Knockdow Ag & B 173 J4
Knockdown Wilts 39 J3
Knockeen S Ayrs 153 G3
Knockenkelly N Ayrs 162 D4
Knockentiber E Ayrs 163 K2
Knockholt Kent 32 E2
Knockholt Pound Kent 32 E2
Knockin Shrops 97 M7
Knockinlaw E Ayrs 163 K2
Knocknain D & G 144 B3
Knockrome Ag & B 171 K4
Knocksharry IoM 237 b4
Knocksheen D & G 153 M5
Knockvennie Smithy D & G 154 D7
Knodishall Suffk 79 J3
Knodishall Common Suffk 79 J3
Knole Somset 26 C6
Knolls Green Ches E 113 J5
Knolton Wrexhm 98 B5
Knook Wilts 27 L3
Knossington Leics 88 B2
Knott End-on-Sea Lancs 120 E2
Knotting Bed 74 E2
Knotting Green Bed 74 E3
Knottingley Wakefd 124 D5
Knotty Ash Lpool 112 B3
Knowbury Shrops 83 L7
Knowe D & G 153 G7
Knowehead D & G 154 A4
Knoweside S Ayrs 163 G6
Knowle Bristl 38 E6
Knowle Devon 11 H5
Knowle Devon 12 C2
Knowle Devon 12 D6
Knowle Devon 23 H4
Knowle Shrops 83 L8
Knowle Solhll 85 L7
Knowle Somset 24 E3
Knowlefield Cumb 148 D4
Knowle Green Lancs 121 J3
Knowle St Giles Somset 13 J1
Knowl Hill W & M 42 D4
Knowsley Knows 112 C3
Knowsley Safari Park Knows 112 C3
Knowstone Devon 24 C6
Knox Bridge Kent 33 K5
Knoydart Highld 200 C5
Knucklas Powys 82 F8
Knuston Nhants 74 D2
Knutsford Ches E 113 H5
Knutsford Services Ches E 113 G6
Krumlin Calder 122 F6
Kuggar Cnwll 3 J7
Kyleakin Highld 200 B1
Kyle of Lochalsh Highld 210 B8
Kylerhea Highld 200 B2
Kylesku Highld 224 F2
Kylesmorar Highld 200 C6
Kyles Scalpay W Isls 232 e4
Kylestrome Highld 224 F2
Kynnersley Wrekin 84 C1
Kyrewood Worcs 69 L2

L

La Bellieuse Guern 236 d3
Lacasaigh W Isls 232 f3
Lacasdal W Isls 232 f2
Laceby NE Lin 117 K1
Lacey Green Bucks 58 D7
Lach Dennis Ches W 113 G6
Lackford Suffk 77 H1
Lackford Green Suffk 77 H1
Lacock Wilts 39 K6
Ladbroke Warwks 72 E3
Laddingford Kent 33 J4
Ladock Cnwll 4 D5
Lady Ork 234 d4
Ladybank Fife 186 E5
Ladygill S Lans 165 H4
Lady Hall Cumb 128 E3
Ladykirk Border 179 J8
Ladywood Birm 85 J6
Ladywood Worcs 70 F3
La Fontenelle Guern 236 e1
La Fosse Guern 236 d4
Lag D & G 154 F5
Laga Highld 190 D4
Lagavulin Ag & B 160 C1
Lagg N Ayrs 162 B5
Laggan Highld 201 L6
Laggan Highld 202 F6
Lagganlia Highld 203 K5
La Greve Guern 236 d2
La Grève de Lecq Jersey 236 b5
La Hougue Bie Jersey 236 d7
La Houguette Guern 236 b3
Laid Highld 228 F4
Laide Highld 219 L3
Laig Highld 199 G7
Laigh Clunch E Ayrs 174 E8
Laigh Fenwick E Ayrs 163 L2
Laigh Glenmuir E Ayrs 164 C5
Laighstonehall S Lans 175 J7
Laindon Essex 46 B3
Lairg Highld 225 M7
Laisterdyke C Brad 123 J4
Lake IoW 17 H5
Lake Wilts 28 C4
Lake District National Park Cumb 137 H5
Lakenheath Suffk 91 G6
Lakesend Norfk 90 D4
Laleston Brdgnd 36 D4
Lamarsh Essex 77 K7
Lamas Norfk 106 F7
Lambden Border 167 L2
Lamberhurst Kent 33 H6
Lamberhurst Down Kent 33 H6
Lamberton Border 179 K6
Lambeth Gt Lon 44 F4
Lambeth Crematorium Gt Lon 44 F5
Lambfair Green Suffk 77 G4
Lambley Notts 101 M4
Lambley Nthumb 149 H4
Lambourn W Berk 40 F5
Lambourne End Essex 45 J2
Lambs Green W Susx 31 L4
Lamerton Devon 6 C1
Lamesley Gatesd 151 G4
Lamington S Lans 165 J3
Lamlash N Ayrs 162 C3
Lamonby Cumb 148 D7
Lamorna Cnwll 2 E6
Lamorran Cnwll 4 D7
Lampeter Cerdgn 66 D5
Lampeter Velfrey Pembks 49 K5
Lamphey Pembks 49 H7
Lamplugh Cumb 136 F3
Lamport Nhants 87 L8
Lamyatt Somset 26 F4
Lanark S Lans 165 G2
Lancaster Lancs 129 K7
Lancaster & Morecambe Crematorium Lancs 129 K6
Lancaster Services Lancs 121 G1
Lanchester Dur 150 F5
Lancing W Susx 19 G5
L'Ancresse Guern 236 d1
Landbeach Cambs 76 C2
Landcross Devon 23 G6
Landerberry Abers 206 E4
Landford Wilts 28 E7
Land-hallow Highld 227 L2
Landican Crematorium Wirral 111 J4
Landimore Swans 50 F6
Landkey Devon 23 J5
Landore Swans 51 J6
Landrake Cnwll 6 B4
Land's End Airport Cnwll 2 C5
Landulph Cnwll 6 C4
Lane Cnwll 4 C4
Laneast Cnwll 9 G7
Lane End Bucks 42 D3
Lane End Wilts 27 J3
Lane Ends Derbys 100 E5
Laneham Notts 116 D6
Lane Head Dur 140 E5
Lanehead Dur 149 L6
Lane Head Wsall 85 H4
Langaller Somset 25 K6
Langar Notts 102 B5
Langbank Rens 174 D4
Langbar N York 123 G1
Langcliffe N York 130 F6
Langdale End N York 134 E2
Langdown Hants 16 E2
Langdyke Fife 186 E6
Langenhoe Essex 62 B4
Langford C Beds 75 H6
Langford Devon 12 D2
Langford Essex 61 K6
Langford Notts 102 D2
Langford Oxon 56 E7
Langford Budville Somset 25 H6
Langham Essex 62 B2
Langham Norfk 106 B4
Langham Rutlnd 88 B2
Langham Suffk 77 L1
Langho Lancs 121 K4
Langholm D & G 156 C5
Langlee Border 167 H3
Langley Hants 16 F3
Langley Herts 59 K4
Langley Kent 33 K3
Langley Nthumb 149 L3
Langley Slough 43 G5
Langley Somset 25 G5
Langley W Susx 30 D5
Langley Warwks 71 L3
Langley Burrell Wilts 39 L5
Langley Green Essex 61 L4
Langley Marsh Somset 25 G5
Langley Park Dur 150 F6
Langley Street Norfk 93 H3
Langley Upper Green Essex 76 C7
Langney E Susx 20 D5
Langold Notts 115 L4
Langore Cnwll 9 J7
Langport Somset 26 B6
Langrick Lincs 103 L3
Langridge BaNES 39 H6
Langrigg Cumb 147 K5
Langrish Hants 30 B6
Langsett Barns 114 E2
Langside P & K 185 G5
Langstone Hants 17 K2
Langthorne N York 132 C2
Langthorpe N York 132 F6
Langthwaite N York 140 C6
Langtoft E R Yk 134 F6
Langtoft Lincs 89 G2
Langton Dur 140 F4
Langton Lincs 118 C7
Langton Lincs 118 E7
Langton N York 134 C6
Langton by Wragby Lincs 117 J6
Langton Green Kent 32 F5
Langton Herring Dorset 14 C6
Langton Matravers Dorset 15 J6
Langtree Devon 10 C2
Langwathby Cumb 148 F7
Langwell House Highld 227 K4
Langwith Derbys 115 K7
Langwith Junction Derbys 115 K7
Langworth Lincs 117 H6
Lanhydrock House & Gardens Cnwll 5 H3
Lanivet Cnwll 5 G3
Lanlivery Cnwll 5 G4
Lanner Cnwll 3 J4
Lanreath Cnwll 5 J4
Lansallos Cnwll 5 J5
Lanteglos Cnwll 8 E7
Lanteglos Highway Cnwll 5 J5
Lanton Border 167 J5
Lanton Nthumb 168 D3
La Passee Guern 236 d2
Lapford Devon 11 H3
Laphroaig Ag & B 160 C1
Lapley Staffs 84 F2
La Pulente Jersey 236 a7
Lapworth Warwks 71 L1
Larachbeg Highld 190 E6
Larbert Falk 176 B3
Largie Abers 216 B7
Largiemore Ag & B 172 F2
Largoward Fife 187 H5
Largs N Ayrs 173 L6
Largybeg N Ayrs 162 D5
Largymore N Ayrs 162 D4
Larkfield Inver 173 L4
Larkfield Kent 33 J2
Larkhall S Lans 175 K7
Larkhill Wilts 28 C3
Larling Norfk 92 B5
La Rocque Jersey 236 e8

La Rousaillerie Guern ... 236 d2
Lartington Dur ... 140 C4
Lasham Hants ... 30 A3
Lasswade Mdloth ... 177 J5
Lastingham N York ... 133 L2
Latchford Warrtn ... 112 F4
Latchingdon Essex ... 61 L7
Latchley Cnwll ... 6 B2
Lathbury M Keyn ... 74 C5
Latheron Highld ... 227 L2
Latheronwheel Highld ... 227 L3
Lathones Fife ... 187 H5
Latimer Bucks ... 59 G7
Latteridge S Glos ... 38 F4
Lattiford Somset ... 27 G6
Latton Wilts ... 40 C2
Lauder Border ... 178 C8
Laugharne Carmth ... 50 C4
Laughterton Lincs ... 116 D6
Laughton E Susx ... 20 A3
Laughton Leics ... 87 J5
Laughton Lincs ... 103 H6
Laughton Lincs ... 116 D3
Laughton-en-le-Morthen Rothm ... 115 K4
Launcells Cnwll ... 9 H4
Launceston Cnwll ... 9 J7
Launton Oxon ... 57 L4
Laurencekirk Abers ... 197 H3
Laurieston D & G ... 146 B3
Laurieston Falk ... 176 B3
Lavendon M Keyn ... 74 D4
Lavenham Suffk ... 77 K5
Lavernock V Glam ... 37 J6
Laversdale Cumb ... 148 E3
Laverstock Wilts ... 28 D5
Laverstoke Hants ... 29 J2
Laverton Gloucs ... 71 J7
Laverton N York ... 132 C5
Laverton Somset ... 27 H2
La Villette Guern ... 236 d4
Lavister Wrexhm ... 98 A2
Law S Lans ... 175 L7
Lawers P & K ... 193 L7
Lawford Essex ... 62 C2
Lawford Somset ... 25 H4
Law Hill S Lans ... 175 L7
Lawhitton Cnwll ... 9 J7
Lawkland N York ... 130 E6
Lawns Wood Crematorium Leeds ... 123 K3
Lawrenny Pembks ... 49 H6
Lawshall Suffk ... 77 K4
Laxay W Isls ... 232 f3
Laxdale W Isls ... 232 f2
Laxey IoM ... 237 d4
Laxfield Suffk ... 93 G8
Laxford Bridge Highld ... 228 C6
Laxo Shet ... 235 d4
Laxton E R Yk ... 125 J5
Laxton Nhants ... 88 D4
Laxton Notts ... 116 B7
Laycock C Brad ... 122 F3
Layer Breton Essex ... 61 M4
Layer-de-la-Haye Essex ... 62 A4
Layer Marney Essex ... 61 L4
Layham Suffk ... 78 B6
Laymore Dorset ... 13 K2
Laytham E R Yk ... 125 H3
Lazonby Cumb ... 148 F6
Lea Derbys ... 101 G2
Lea Herefs ... 54 F4
Lea Lincs ... 116 D4
Lea Shrops ... 83 G5
Lea Wilts ... 39 L3
Leachkin Highld ... 212 F5
Leadburn Border ... 177 H7
Leadenham Lincs ... 102 F3
Leaden Roding Essex ... 60 F5
Leadgate Dur ... 150 E5
Leadhills S Lans ... 165 G6
Leafield Oxon ... 56 F5
Leagrave Luton ... 59 H4
Leake Common Side Lincs ... 104 C3
Lealholm N York ... 142 F5
Lealt Highld ... 209 H3
Lea Marston Warwks ... 86 B5
Leamington Hastings Warwks ... 72 F2
Leamington Spa Warwks ... 72 D2
Leap Cross E Susx ... 20 C4
Leasgill Cumb ... 129 K3
Leasingham Lincs ... 103 H3
Leasingthorne Dur ... 141 G2
Leatherhead Surrey ... 31 K1
Leathley N York ... 123 J2
Leaton Shrops ... 98 C8
Leaveland Kent ... 34 D4
Leavenheath Suffk ... 77 L6
Leavening N York ... 134 C6
Leaves Green Gt Lon ... 45 H7
Lebberston N York ... 135 G3
Le Bigard Guern ... 236 c4
Le Bourg Guern ... 236 c4
Le Bourg Jersey ... 236 e8
Lechlade on Thames Gloucs ... 56 E7
Lecht Gruinart Ag & B ... 170 E5
Leck Lancs ... 130 C4
Leckbuie P & K ... 193 L7
Leckford Hants ... 29 G4
Leckhampstead Bucks ... 73 K6
Leckhampstead W Berk ... 41 H5
Leckhampstead Thicket W Berk ... 41 H5
Leckhampton Gloucs ... 55 L4
Leckmelm Highld ... 220 F4
Leconfield E R Yk ... 126 C2
Ledaig Ag & B ... 191 H8
Ledburn Bucks ... 58 E4
Ledbury Herefs ... 70 C6
Ledgemoor Herefs ... 69 H4
Ledmore Junction Highld ... 224 F6
Ledsham Leeds ... 124 C4
Ledston Leeds ... 124 C5
Ledwell Oxon ... 57 H3
Lee Devon ... 23 H3
Lee Gt Lon ... 45 H5
Leebotwood Shrops ... 83 J4
Lee Brockhurst Shrops ... 98 D6
Leece Cumb ... 128 F5
Lee Chapel Essex ... 46 B3
Lee Clump Bucks ... 58 E6
Leeds Kent ... 33 L3
Leeds Leeds ... 123 K4
Leeds Bradford Airport Leeds ... 123 J3
Leeds Castle Kent ... 33 L3
Leedstown Cnwll ... 3 G4
Leek Staffs ... 99 M2
Leek Wootton Warwks ... 72 C2
Lee Mill Devon ... 6 E5
Leeming N York ... 132 D2
Leeming Bar N York ... 132 D2
Lee-on-the-Solent Hants ... 17 G3
Lees Derbys ... 100 E5
Lees Oldham ... 113 L2
Lees Green Derbys ... 100 E5
Leesthorpe Leics ... 87 L2
Leeswood Flints ... 97 K1
Leetown P & K ... 186 C3
Leftwich Ches W ... 112 F6
Legbourne Lincs ... 118 E5
Legerwood Border ... 167 J2
Legoland W & M ... 42 F5
Le Gron Guern ... 236 c3
Legsby Lincs ... 117 J4
Le Haguais Jersey ... 236 d8
Le Hocq Jersey ... 236 d8
Leicester C Leic ... 87 H3
Leicester Forest East Services Leics ... 87 G3
Leigh Dorset ... 14 C2
Leigh Gloucs ... 55 K3
Leigh Kent ... 32 F4
Leigh Surrey ... 31 L3
Leigh Wigan ... 112 F2
Leigh Wilts ... 40 B3
Leigh Worcs ... 70 D4
Leigh Beck Essex ... 46 D4
Leigh Delamere Wilts ... 39 K5
Leigh Delamere Services Wilts ... 39 K5
Leigh Green Kent ... 34 B7
Leigh Knoweglass S Lans ... 175 H7
Leigh-on-Sea Sthend ... 46 D3
Leigh Park Dorset ... 15 J3
Leigh Park Hants ... 17 K2
Leigh Sinton Worcs ... 70 D4
Leighswood Wsall ... 85 J3
Leighterton Gloucs ... 39 J3
Leighton Powys ... 82 E3
Leighton Shrops ... 84 B3
Leighton Bromswold Cambs ... 89 G7
Leighton Buzzard C Beds ... 58 F3
Leigh upon Mendip Somset ... 27 G3
Leigh Woods N Som ... 38 E6
Leinthall Earls Herefs ... 69 J2
Leinthall Starkes Herefs ... 69 J1
Leintwardine Herefs ... 83 H8
Leire Leics ... 87 G5
Leiston Suffk ... 79 J3
Leith C Edin ... 177 H3
Leitholm Border ... 168 B1
Lelant Cnwll ... 2 F4
Lelley E R Yk ... 126 F4
Lempitlaw Border ... 168 B3
Lemreway W Isls ... 232 f3
Lemsford Herts ... 59 L5
Lenchwick Worcs ... 71 J5
Lendalfoot S Ayrs ... 152 D4
Lendrick Stirlg ... 184 C6
Lendrum Terrace Abers ... 217 L6
Lenham Kent ... 34 B4
Lenham Heath Kent ... 34 B5
Lenie Highld ... 202 D1
Lennel Border ... 168 C2
Lennox Plunton D & G ... 146 A5
Lennoxtown E Duns ... 175 H3
Lenton C Nott ... 101 K5
Lenton Lincs ... 103 G6
Lenwade Norfk ... 106 D8
Lenzie E Duns ... 175 H4
Leochel-Cushnie Abers ... 205 L4
Leominster Herefs ... 69 K3
Leonard Stanley Gloucs ... 55 J7
Leoville Jersey ... 236 b6
Lephin Highld ... 208 B4
Leppington N York ... 134 B7
Lepton Kirk ... 123 J7
Lerags Ag & B ... 182 B3
L'Erée Guern ... 236 b3
Lerryn Cnwll ... 5 J4
Lerwick Shet ... 235 d6
Les Arquets Guern ... 236 b3
Lesbury Nthumb ... 169 J6
Les Hubits Guern ... 236 d3
Leslie Abers ... 206 B1
Leslie Fife ... 186 D6
Les Lohiers Guern ... 236 c3
Lesmahagow S Lans ... 164 F2
Les Murchez Guern ... 236 c4
Lesnewth Cnwll ... 8 F6
Les Nicolles Guern ... 236 c4
Les Quartiers Guern ... 236 d2
Les Quennevais Jersey ... 236 b7
Les Sages Guern ... 236 b3
Lessingham Norfk ... 107 H6
Lessonhall Cumb ... 147 L5
Les Villets Guern ... 236 c4
Leswalt D & G ... 144 B3
L'Etacq Jersey ... 236 a6
Letchmore Heath Herts ... 43 J2
Letchworth Garden City Herts ... 59 L2
Letcombe Bassett Oxon ... 41 G4
Letcombe Regis Oxon ... 41 G3
Letham Angus ... 196 E6
Letham Border ... 167 K7
Letham Falk ... 176 B2
Letham Fife ... 186 E4
Letham Grange Angus ... 197 G7
Lethendy P & K ... 195 H7
Lethenty Abers ... 206 B2
Lethenty Abers ... 216 F6
Letheringham Suffk ... 78 F3
Letheringsett Norfk ... 106 C5
Letterewe Highld ... 219 L7
Letterfearn Highld ... 200 D2
Letterfinlay Lodge Hotel Highld ... 201 K6
Lettermorar Highld ... 199 M7
Letters Highld ... 220 F4
Lettershaw S Lans ... 165 H5
Letterston Pembks ... 48 F2
Lettoch Highld ... 204 C2
Lettoch Highld ... 214 D7
Letton Herefs ... 69 G5
Letty Green Herts ... 59 M5
Letwell Rothm ... 115 K4
Leuchars Fife ... 187 G3
Leumrabhagh W Isls ... 232 f3
Leurbost W Isls ... 232 f3
Levedale Staffs ... 84 F1
Leven E R Yk ... 126 D2
Leven Fife ... 186 F7
Levens Cumb ... 129 K3
Levens Green Herts ... 60 B4
Levenshulme Manch ... 113 K3
Levenwick Shet ... 235 c7
Leverburgh W Isls ... 232 d5
Leverington Cambs ... 90 C2
Leverstock Green Herts ... 59 H6
Leverton Lincs ... 104 C3
Le Villocq Guern ... 236 c2
Levington Suffk ... 78 F6
Levisham N York ... 134 C2
Lew Oxon ... 56 F6
Lewannick Cnwll ... 9 H8
Lewdown Devon ... 10 C7
Lewes E Susx ... 19 L4
Leweston Pembks ... 48 F3
Lewisham Gt Lon ... 45 G5
Lewisham Crematorium Gt Lon ... 45 H5
Lewiston Highld ... 212 D8
Lewistown Brdgnd ... 36 E3
Lewknor Oxon ... 42 B2
Lewson Street Kent ... 34 C3
Lewtrenchard Devon ... 10 C7
Lexden Essex ... 62 A3
Lexworthy Somset ... 25 K4
Leybourne Kent ... 33 H2
Leyburn N York ... 131 L2
Leygreen Herts ... 59 K3
Ley Hill Bucks ... 59 G7
Leyland Lancs ... 121 H6
Leylodge Abers ... 206 E3
Leys Abers ... 217 J4
Leys P & K ... 195 K8
Leysdown-on-Sea Kent ... 47 G6
Leysmill Angus ... 196 F6
Leys of Cossans Angus ... 196 C6
Leysters Herefs ... 69 L2
Leyton Gt Lon ... 45 G3
Leytonstone Gt Lon ... 45 H3
Lezant Cnwll ... 5 M1
Lhanbryde Moray ... 215 G3
Libanus Powys ... 52 F3

Libberton S Lans 165 J2
Liberton C Edin 177 J4
Lichfield Staffs 85 K2
Lichfield & District Crematorium Staffs 85 L2
Lickey Worcs 85 H7
Lickey End Worcs 85 H8
Lickfold W Susx 30 F6
Liddesdale Highld 190 F4
Liddington Swindn 40 E4
Lidgate Suffk 77 G3
Lidlington C Beds 74 E6
Liff Angus 186 E2
Lifford Birm 85 J7
Lifton Devon 9 K7
Liftondown Devon 9 K7
Lighthorne Warwks 72 D4
Lighthorne Heath Warwks 72 D4
Lightwater Surrey 42 F7
Lightwater Valley Theme Park N York 132 D4
Lightwood C Stke 99 L4
Lilbourne Nhants 87 H7
Lilleshall Wrekin 84 D1
Lilley Herts 59 J3
Lilliesleaf Border 167 H4
Lillingstone Dayrell Bucks 73 K6
Lillingstone Lovell Bucks 73 K6
Lillington Dorset 26 F8
Lilliput Poole 15 K4
Lilstock Somset 25 J3
Limbury Luton 59 H3
Limekilnburn S Lans 175 J7
Limekilns Fife 176 E2
Limerigg Falk 176 B4
Limerstone IoW 16 E6
Lime Street Worcs 55 J2
Limington Somset 26 D6
Limmerhaugh E Ayrs 164 C4
Limpenhoe Norfk 93 H3
Limpley Stoke Wilts 39 H7
Limpsfield Surrey 32 D3
Limpsfield Chart Surrey 32 D3
Linby Notts 101 K3
Linchmere W Susx 30 E5
Lincluden D & G 155 G6
Lincoln Lincs 116 F7
Lincoln Crematorium Lincs 117 G7
Lincomb Worcs 70 E2
Lindale Cumb 129 J4
Lindal in Furness Cumb 128 F4
Lindfield W Susx 32 C7
Lindford Hants 30 D4
Lindley Kirk 123 G6
Lindores Fife 186 D4
Lindridge Worcs 70 C2
Lindsell Essex 61 G3
Lindsey Suffk 77 L5
Lindsey Tye Suffk 78 B5
Lingdale R & Cl 142 E4
Lingen Herefs 69 G2
Lingfield Surrey 32 C4
Lingwood Norfk 93 H2
Linicro Highld 218 B7
Linkend Worcs 55 J2
Linkenholt Hants 41 G8
Linkinhorne Cnwll 5 L2
Linktown Fife 177 J1
Linkwood Moray 214 F3
Linley Shrops 83 G5
Linley Green Herefs 70 C4
Linlithgow W Loth 176 D3
Linn Crematorium E Rens 175 G6
Linsidemore Highld 222 D2
Linslade C Beds 58 E3
Linstead Parva Suffk 93 G7
Linstock Cumb 148 D4
Linthurst Worcs 85 H8
Linthwaite Kirk 123 G7
Lintlaw Border 179 H6
Lintmill Moray 215 L2
Linton Border 168 B4
Linton Cambs 76 E5
Linton Derbys 86 C1
Linton Herefs 54 F3
Linton Kent 33 K3
Linton Leeds 124 B2
Linton N York 131 J6
Linton Hill Herefs 54 F3
Linton-on-Ouse N York 133 G7
Linwood Lincs 117 J4
Linwood Rens 174 E5
Lionacleit W Isls 233 b7
Lional W Isls 232 g1
Liphook Hants 30 D5
Liscard Wirral 111 J3
Liscombe Somset 24 D5
Liskeard Cnwll 5 K3
Lismore Ag & B 191 G7
Liss Hants 30 C5
Lissett E R Yk 135 H7
Lissington Lincs 117 J5
Lisvane Cardif 37 J4
Liswerry Newpt 37 M3
Litcham Norfk 105 L8
Litchborough Nhants 73 J4
Litchfield Hants 29 J2
Litherland Sefton 111 K2
Litlington Cambs 75 K6
Litlington E Susx 20 B5
Little Abington Cambs 76 D5
Little Addington Nhants 88 D8
Little Airies D & G 145 J5
Little Alne Warwks 71 K3
Little Altcar Sefton 111 J1
Little Amwell Herts 60 B5
Little Aston Staffs 85 K4
Little Ayton N York 142 C5
Little Baddow Essex 61 J6
Little Badminton S Glos 39 J4
Little Bampton Cumb 148 A4
Little Bardfield Essex 61 G2
Little Barford Bed 75 H3
Little Barningham Norfk 106 D5
Little Barrington Gloucs 56 D5
Little Barrow Ches W 112 C7
Little Bavington Nthumb 158 C6
Little Bedwyn Wilts 40 F7
Little Bentley Essex 62 D3
Little Berkhamsted Herts 59 M6
Little Billing Nhants 74 B3
Little Billington C Beds 58 F4
Little Birch Herefs 54 D2
Little Blakenham Suffk 78 D5
Little Blencow Cumb 148 E7
Little Bognor W Susx 31 G7
Little Bollington Ches E 113 G4
Little Bookham Surrey 31 J1
Littleborough Notts 116 D5
Littleborough Rochdl 122 D7
Littlebourne Kent 35 G3
Little Bourton Oxon 72 F5
Little Braxted Essex 61 K5
Little Brechin Angus 196 F4
Littlebredy Dorset 14 B5
Little Brickhill M Keyn 58 E2
Little Brington Nhants 73 J2
Little Bromley Essex 62 C3
Little Budworth Ches W 112 E7
Littleburn Highld 212 F4
Little Burstead Essex 46 A2
Littlebury Essex 76 D6
Littlebury Green Essex 76 C6
Little Bytham Lincs 103 G8
Little Carlton Lincs 118 E4
Little Casterton Rutlnd 88 E2
Little Cawthorpe Lincs 118 E5
Little Chalfont Bucks 43 G2
Little Chart Kent 34 C5
Little Chesterford Essex 76 D6
Little Cheverell Wilts 27 M2
Little Chishill Cambs 76 B6
Little Clacton Essex 62 E4
Little Clifton Cumb 136 E2
Little Coates NE Lin 127 G8
Little Comberton Worcs 71 G5
Little Common E Susx 20 E4
Little Compton Warwks 56 E3
Little Cornard Suffk 77 K6
Little Cowarne Herefs 69 L4
Little Coxwell Oxon 40 F2
Little Crakehall N York 132 C2
Little Cressingham Norfk 91 K4
Little Crosby Sefton 111 K2
Little Cubley Derbys 100 D5
Little Dalby Leics 87 L2
Littledean Gloucs 54 F5
Little Dewchurch Herefs 54 D2
Little Ditton Cambs 76 F3
Little Downham Cambs 90 D6
Little Driffield E R Yk 134 F7
Little Dunham Norfk 91 K2
Little Dunkeld P & K 195 G7
Little Dunmow Essex 61 G4
Little Durnford Wilts 28 C5
Little Easton Essex 60 F3
Little Eaton Derbys 101 G4
Little Ellingham Norfk 92 B4
Little Everdon Nhants 73 H3
Little Eversden Cambs 75 L4
Little Faringdon Oxon 56 E7
Little Fencote N York 132 D2
Little Fenton N York 124 D4
Little Fransham Norfk 91 K2
Little Gaddesden Herts 59 G5
Little Glemham Suffk 79 H3
Little Gorsley Herefs 55 G3
Little Gransden Cambs 75 J4
Little Green Somset 27 G2
Little Hadham Herts 60 C4
Little Hale Lincs 103 J4
Little Hallam Derbys 101 J4
Little Hallingbury Essex 60 D4
Littleham Devon 12 D6
Littleham Devon 23 G6
Littlehampton W Susx 18 D5
Little Harrowden Nhants 74 C1
Little Haseley Oxon 57 M7
Little Haven Pembks 48 E5
Littlehaven W Susx 31 K5
Little Hay Staffs 85 K3
Little Haywood Staffs 100 A7
Littlehempston Devon 7 J4
Little Hereford Herefs 69 K2
Little Horkesley Essex 62 A2
Little Hormead Herts 60 C3
Little Horsted E Susx 19 M3
Little Horton C Brad 123 H4
Little Horwood Bucks 58 C2
Little Houghton Barns 115 H1
Little Houghton Nhants 74 B3
Little Hucklow Derbys 114 D5
Little Hutton N York 133 G4
Little Irchester Nhants 74 C2
Little Keyford Somset 27 H3
Little Kimble Bucks 58 D6
Little Kineton Warwks 72 D4
Little Kingshill Bucks 58 E7
Little Knox D & G 146 E3
Little Langdale Cumb 137 J6
Little Langford Wilts 28 B4
Little Leigh Ches W 112 F6
Little Leighs Essex 61 H5
Little Lever Bolton 121 L8
Little Linford M Keyn 74 B5
Little Load Somset 26 C6
Little London Cambs 90 B4
Little London E Susx 20 C2
Little London Hants 29 G2
Little London Hants 41 L8
Little Longstone Derbys 114 D6
Little Maplestead Essex 77 J7
Little Marcle Herefs 70 C7
Little Marlow Bucks 42 E3
Little Massingham Norfk 105 J7
Little Melton Norfk 92 E3
Littlemill Abers 205 H6
Littlemill Highld 213 L4
Little Mill Mons 53 L7
Little Milton Oxon 57 L7
Little Missenden Bucks 58 F7
Littlemore Oxon 57 K7
Little Musgrave Cumb 139 H5
Little Ness Shrops 98 B8
Little Newcastle Pembks 49 G2
Little Newsham Dur 140 E4
Little Norton Somset 26 C7
Little Oakley Essex 62 F3
Little Oakley Nhants 88 C6
Little Orton Cumb 148 C4
Littleover C Derb 101 G5
Little Packington Warwks 86 B6
Little Paxton Cambs 75 H3
Little Petherick Cnwll 4 E2
Little Plumstead Norfk 93 G2
Little Ponton Lincs 102 F6
Littleport Cambs 90 E6
Little Preston Nhants 73 H4
Little Raveley Cambs 89 J7
Little Reedness E R Yk 125 J6
Little Ribston N York 132 F8
Little Rissington Gloucs 56 D4
Little Rollright Oxon 56 F3
Little Ryburgh Norfk 106 A6
Little Salkeld Cumb 148 F7
Little Sampford Essex 76 F7
Little Saughall Ches W 111 K7
Little Saxham Suffk 77 H2
Little Scatwell Highld 212 B3
Little Shelford Cambs 76 C4
Little Singleton Lancs 120 E3
Little Skipwith N York 125 G3
Little Smeaton N York 124 D6
Little Snoring Norfk 106 A6
Little Sodbury S Glos 39 H4
Little Somborne Hants 29 G5
Little Somerford Wilts 39 L4
Little Soudley Shrops 99 G6
Little Stainton Darltn 141 J3
Little Stanney Ches W 112 B6
Little Staughton Bed 75 G3
Little Steeping Lincs 118 F8
Little Stoke Staffs 99 K6

Littlestone-on-Sea Kent 21 L2
Little Stonham Suffk 78 D3
Little Stretton Leics 87 J4
Little Stretton Shrops 83 J5
Little Strickland Cumb 138 E4
Little Stukeley Cambs 89 H7
Little Sugnall Staffs 99 J6
Little Swinburne Nthumb 158 B6
Little Sypland D & G 146 C4
Little Tew Oxon 57 G3
Little Tey Essex 61 L4
Little Thetford Cambs 90 D7
Little Thorpe Dur 151 K6
Littlethorpe Leics 87 G4
Littlethorpe N York 132 E5
Little Thurlow Suffk 76 F4
Little Thurrock Thurr 45 L4
Littleton Angus 196 B6
Littleton Ches W 112 C7
Littleton D & G 146 B4
Littleton Hants 29 J5
Littleton Somset 26 C5
Littleton Surrey 43 H6
Littleton Drew Wilts 39 J4
Littleton-on-Severn S Glos 38 E3
Littleton Pannell Wilts 27 M2
Little Torrington Devon 10 D2
Littletown Dur 151 H6
Little Town Lancs 121 K4
Little Urswick Cumb 128 F5
Little Wakering Essex 46 F3
Little Walden Essex 76 D6
Little Waldingfield Suffk 77 K5
Little Walsingham Norfk 105 M5
Little Waltham Essex 61 H5
Little Weighton E R Yk 126 B4
Little Wenlock Wrekin 84 B3
Little Weston Somset 26 F6
Little Whitefield IoW 17 H4
Littlewick Green W & M 42 D4
Little Wilbraham Cambs 76 D3
Little Witcombe Gloucs 55 K5
Little Witley Worcs 70 D2
Little Wittenham Oxon 41 K2
Little Wolford Warwks 72 C7
Little Woodcote Gt Lon 44 F7
Littleworth Oxon 40 F2
Littleworth Staffs 99 L7
Littleworth Worcs 70 F4
Little Wymington Bed 74 D2
Little Wymondley Herts 59 K3
Little Wyrley Staffs 85 H3
Little Yeldham Essex 77 H6
Littley Green Essex 61 H4
Litton Derbys 114 D6
Litton N York 131 G5
Litton Somset 26 E1
Litton Cheney Dorset 14 A4
Liurbost W Isls 232 f3
Liverpool Lpool 111 K4
Liverpool Maritime Mercantile City Lpool 111 K4
Liversedge Kirk 123 J5
Liverton Devon 7 J2
Liverton R & Cl 142 F4
Livingston W Loth 176 E5
Livingston Village W Loth 176 E5
Lixwm Flints 111 G7
Lizard Cnwll 3 J8
Llanaelhaearn Gwynd 95 G4
Llanafan Cerdgn 66 F1
Llanafan-Fawr Powys 67 L4
Llanallgo IoA 109 G4
Llanarmon Dyffryn Ceiriog Wrexhm 97 J6
Llanarmon-yn-Ial Denbgs 97 J2
Llanarth Cerdgn 65 L3
Llanarth Mons 54 B5
Llanarthne Carmth 51 G2
Llanasa Flints 110 F5
Llanbadarn Fawr Cerdgn 80 E7
Llanbadarn Fynydd Powys 82 C7
Llanbadoc Mons 54 B7
Llanbeder Newpt 38 B3
Llanbedr Gwynd 95 K7
Llanbedr Powys 53 K4
Llanbedr-Dyffryn-Clwyd Denbgs 97 H2
Llanbedrgoch IoA 109 G5
Llanbedrog Gwynd 94 F6
Llanbedr-y-Cennin Conwy 109 L7
Llanberis Gwynd 95 K1
Llanbethêry V Glam 37 G6
Llanbister Powys 82 C8
Llanblethian V Glam 36 F5
Llanboidy Carmth 49 L3
Llanbradach Caerph 37 J3
Llanbrynmair Powys 81 J3
Llancadle V Glam 37 G6
Llancarfan V Glam 37 G6
Llancloudy Herefs 54 D4
Llandaff Cardif 37 J5
Llandanwg Gwynd 95 K6
Llanddaniel Fab IoA 109 G7
Llanddarog Carmth 51 G3
Llanddeiniol Cerdgn 66 D1
Llanddeiniolen Gwynd 109 H7
Llandderfel Gwynd 96 F5
Llanddeusant IoA 108 D4
Llanddew Powys 53 G2
Llanddewi Swans 50 F7
Llanddewi Brefi Cerdgn 66 F4
Llanddewi Rhydderch Mons 53 M5
Llanddewi Velfrey Pembks 49 K4
Llanddewi Ystradenni Powys 68 C2
Llanddoget Conwy 109 M8
Llanddona IoA 109 H5
Llanddowror Carmth 50 B3
Llanddulas Conwy 110 C6
Llanddwywe Gwynd 95 K7
Llanddyfnan IoA 109 G5
Llandefaelog-Tre'r-Graig Powys 53 H3
Llandefalle Powys 68 C7
Llandegfan IoA 109 H6
Llandegla Denbgs 97 J3
Llandegley Powys 68 D2
Llandegveth Mons 37 M2
Llandeilo Carmth 51 J2
Llandeilo Graban Powys 68 C5
Llandeloy Pembks 48 E3
Llandenny Mons 54 B7
Llandevaud Newpt 38 B3
Llandevenny Mons 38 B3
Llandinam Powys 82 B5
Llandissilio Pembks 49 J3
Llandogo Mons 54 D7
Llandough V Glam 36 F6
Llandough V Glam 37 J5
Llandovery Carmth 67 G7
Llandow V Glam 36 E5
Llandre Carmth 66 F6
Llandre Cerdgn 80 E6
Llandre Isaf Pembks 49 J2
Llandrillo Denbgs 97 G5
Llandrillo-yn-Rhos Conwy 110 B5
Llandrindod Wells Powys 68 B3
Llandrinio Powys 97 L8
Llandudno Conwy 109 L5
Llandudno Junction Conwy 109 M6
Llandulas Powys 67 J6
Llandwrog Gwynd 95 H2
Llandybie Carmth 51 J3
Llandyfaelog Carmth 50 E3
Llandyfriog Cerdgn 65 K6
Llandygai Gwynd 109 H7
Llandygwydd Cerdgn 65 H5
Llandyrnog Denbgs 110 F8
Llandyssil Powys 82 E4
Llandysul Cerdgn 65 L6
Llanedeyrn Cardif 37 K4
Llaneglwys Powys 68 B6
Llanegryn Gwynd 80 D3
Llanegwad Carmth 51 G2
Llaneilian IoA 108 F3
Llanelian-yn-Rhôs Conwy 110 B6
Llanelidan Denbgs 97 H3
Llanelieu Powys 68 D7
Llanellen Mons 53 L5
Llanelli Carmth 51 G5
Llanelli Crematorium Carmth 51 G5
Llanelltyd Gwynd 96 A8
Llanelwedd Powys 68 B4
Llanenddwyn Gwynd 95 K7
Llanengan Gwynd 94 E6
Llanerchymedd IoA 108 E5
Llanerfyl Powys 82 B2
Llanfachraeth IoA 108 D5
Llanfachreth Gwynd 96 B7
Llanfaelog IoA 108 D6
Llanfaelrhys Gwynd 94 D6
Llanfaethlu IoA 108 D4
Llanfair Gwynd 95 K6
Llanfair Caereinion Powys 82 C3
Llanfair Clydogau Cerdgn 66 E4
Llanfair Dyffryn Clwyd Denbgs 97 H2
Llanfairfechan Conwy 109 K6
Llanfairpwllgwyngyll IoA 109 G6
Llanfair Talhaiarn Conwy 110 C7
Llanfair Waterdine Shrops 82 E7
Llanfairynghornwy IoA 108 D4
Llanfair-yn-Neubwll IoA 108 C6
Llanfallteg Carmth 49 K4
Llanfallteg West Carmth 49 K4
Llanfarian Cerdgn 80 D7
Llanfechain Powys 97 J7
Llanfechell IoA 108 E3
Llanferres Denbgs 97 J1
Llanfihangel-ar-arth Carmth 66 B6
Llanfihangel Glyn Myfyr Conwy 96 F3
Llanfihangel Nant Bran Powys 67 K7
Llanfihangel Rhydithon Powys 68 D2
Llanfihangel Rogiet Mons 38 C3
Llanfihangel-y-Creuddyn Cerdgn 80 F7
Llanfihangel-yng-Ngwynfa Powys 82 C1
Llanfihangel yn Nhowyn IoA 108 D6
Llanfihangel-y-traethau Gwynd 95 K5
Llanfilo Powys 53 H2
Llanfoist Mons 53 L5
Llanfor Gwynd 96 E5
Llanfrechfa Torfn 37 L2
Llanfrynach Powys 53 G3
Llanfwrog Denbgs 97 H2
Llanfwrog IoA 108 C5
Llanfyllin Powys 97 H8
Llanfynydd Carmth 66 D8
Llanfynydd Flints 97 L2
Llanfyrnach Pembks 49 L2
Llangadfan Powys 81 L2
Llangadog Carmth 66 F8
Llangadwaladr IoA 108 E7
Llangaffo IoA 108 F7
Llangammarch Wells Powys 67 K5
Llangan V Glam 36 E5
Llangarron Herefs 54 D4
Llangathen Carmth 51 H2
Llangattock Powys 53 K4
Llangattock Lingoed Mons 54 A4
Llangedwyn Powys 97 J7
Llangefni IoA 108 F6
Llangeinor Brdgnd 36 E3
Llangeitho Cerdgn 66 E3
Llangeler Carmth 65 L6
Llangelynin Gwynd 80 D3
Llangendeirne Carmth 50 F3
Llangennech Carmth 51 H5
Llangennith Swans 50 E7
Llangernyw Conwy 110 B7
Llangian Gwynd 94 E6
Llangloffan Pembks 64 C7
Llanglydwen Carmth 49 K3
Llangoed IoA 109 J5
Llangollen Denbgs 97 K4
Llangolman Pembks 49 J3
Llangors Powys 53 H3
Llangower Gwynd 96 D6
Llangrannog Cerdgn 65 K4
Llangristiolus IoA 108 F6
Llangrove Herefs 54 D4
Llangunllo Powys 68 E1
Llangunnor Carmth 50 E2
Llangurig Powys 81 K7
Llangwm Conwy 96 F4
Llangwm Mons 54 B7
Llangwm Pembks 49 G5
Llangwnnadl Gwynd 94 D6
Llangwyryfon Cerdgn 66 D1
Llangybi Cerdgn 66 E4
Llangybi Gwynd 95 G4
Llangybi Mons 38 A2
Llangynhafal Denbgs 110 F8
Llangynidr Powys 53 J4
Llangynin Carmth 50 B2
Llangynog Carmth 50 D3
Llangynog Powys 97 G7
Llangynwyd Brdgnd 36 D3
Llanhamlach Powys 53 H3
Llanharan Rhondd 36 F4
Llanharry Rhondd 36 F4
Llanhennock Mons 38 A2
Llanhilleth Blae G 53 K7
Llanidloes Powys 81 K6
Llaniestyn Gwynd 94 E5
Llanigon Powys 68 E6
Llanilar Cerdgn 80 E8
Llanilid Rhondd 36 F4
Llanina Cerdgn 65 L3
Llanishen Cardif 37 J4
Llanishen Mons 54 C7
Llanllechid Gwynd 109 J7
Llanllowell Mons 54 B7
Llanllugan Powys 82 B3
Llanllwch Carmth 50 E2
Llanllwchaiarn Powys 82 C5
Llanllwni Carmth 66 C6
Llanllyfni Gwynd 95 H3
Llanmadoc Swans 50 F6
Llanmaes V Glam 36 F6
Llanmartin Newpt 38 B3
Llanmiloe Carmth 50 B4
Llannefydd Conwy 110 D7
Llannon Carmth 51 G4
Llannor Gwynd 94 F5

Llanon Cerdgn 66 C2
Llanover Mons 53 L6
Llanpumsaint Carmth 65 L8
Llanrhaeadr-ym-Mochnant Powys 97 H7
Llanrhian Pembks 48 D2
Llanrhidian Swans 50 F6
Llanrhychwyn Conwy 96 B1
Llanrhyddlad IoA 108 D4
Llanrhystud Cerdgn 66 C1
Llanrug Gwynd 109 G8
Llanrumney Cardif 37 K4
Llanrwst Conwy 96 C1
Llansadurnen Carmth 50 C4
Llansadwrn Carmth 66 F7
Llansadwrn IoA 109 H6
Llansaint Carmth 50 E4
Llansamlet Swans 51 K6
Llansanffraid Glan Conwy Conwy 109 M6
Llansannan Conwy 110 C7
Llansantffraed Powys 53 H4
Llansantffraed-Cwmdeuddwr Powys 67 L2
Llansantffraed-in-Elvel Powys 68 C4
Llansantffraid Cerdgn 66 C2
Llansantffraid-ym-Mechain Powys 97 K7
Llansawel Carmth 66 E7
Llansilin Powys 97 K6
Llansoy Mons 54 C7
Llanspyddid Powys 52 F3
Llanstadwell Pembks 48 F6
Llansteffan Carmth 50 D4
Llantarnam Torfn 37 L2
Llanteg Pembks 49 K5
Llanthewy Skirrid Mons 53 M5
Llanthony Mons 53 L3
Llantilio-Crossenny Mons 54 B5
Llantilio Pertholey Mons 53 L5
Llantrisant Mons 38 B2
Llantrisant Rhondd 37 G4
Llantrithyd V Glam 37 G6
Llantwit Fardre Rhondd 37 G3
Llantwit Major V Glam 36 F6
Llanuwchllyn Gwynd 96 D6
Llanvaches Newpt 38 B3
Llanvair Discoed Mons 38 C3
Llanvapley Mons 54 A5
Llanvetherine Mons 54 A5
Llanvihangel Crucorney Mons 53 L4
Llanwddyn Powys 96 F8
Llanwenog Cerdgn 66 C5
Llanwern Newpt 38 A3
Llanwinio Carmth 50 C1
Llanwnda Gwynd 95 H2
Llanwnda Pembks 64 C6
Llanwnnen Cerdgn 66 C5
Llanwnog Powys 82 B5
Llanwrda Carmth 66 F7
Llanwrin Powys 81 H3
Llanwrthwl Powys 67 L2
Llanwrtyd Wells Powys 67 J5
Llanwyddelan Powys 82 C4
Llanyblodwel Shrops 97 K7
Llanybri Carmth 50 D3
Llanybydder Carmth 66 C5
Llanycefn Pembks 49 J3
Llanychaer Pembks 64 D7
Llanymawddwy Gwynd 96 D8
Llanymynech Powys 97 K7
Llanynghenedl IoA 108 D5
Llanynys Denbgs 110 F8
Llanyre Powys 68 B3
Llanystumdwy Gwynd 95 H5
Llanywern Powys 53 H3
Llawhaden Pembks 49 H4
Llawryglyn Powys 81 K5
Llay Wrexhm 97 M2
Llechrhyd Caerph 53 H6
Llechryd Cerdgn 65 H5
Lledrod Cerdgn 66 E1
Lleyn Peninsula Gwynd 94 E5
Llithfaen Gwynd 94 F4
Lloc Flints 111 G6
Llowes Powys 68 D6
Llwydcoed Rhondd 52 F6
Llwydcoed Crematorium Rhondd 52 F6
Llwydiarth Powys 82 B1
Llwyncelyn Cerdgn 66 B3
Llwyndafydd Cerdgn 65 L4
Llwyngwril Gwynd 80 D2
Llwynmawr Wrexhm 97 K5
Llwynypia Rhondd 36 F2
Llynclys Shrops 97 L7
Llynfaes IoA 108 E5
Llysfaen Conwy 110 B6
Llyswen Powys 68 C6
Llysworney V Glam 36 E5
Llys-y-frân Pembks 49 H3
Llywel Powys 52 D3
Loan Falk 176 C3
Loanhead Mdloth 177 J5
Loaningfoot D & G 147 G4
Loans S Ayrs 163 J3
Lobhillcross Devon 10 C7
Lochailort Highld 200 B8
Lochaline Highld 190 D7
Lochans D & G 144 C4
Locharbriggs D & G 155 H6
Lochavich Ag & B 182 D4
Lochawe Ag & B 183 G2
Loch Baghasdail W Isls 233 c8
Lochboisdale W Isls 233 c8
Lochbuie Ag & B 181 J3
Lochcarron Highld 210 D6
Lochdar W Isls 233 b7
Lochdon Ag & B 181 L2
Lochdonhead Ag & B 181 L2
Lochead Ag & B 172 D3
Lochearnhead Stirlg 184 D3
Lochee C Dund 186 F2
Locheilside Station Highld 191 K2
Lochend Highld 212 F6
Locheport W Isls 233 c6
Loch Euphoirt W Isls 233 c6
Lochfoot D & G 154 F7
Lochgair Ag & B 172 F1
Lochgelly Fife 186 C8
Lochgilphead Ag & B 172 E2
Lochgoilhead Ag & B 183 H6
Lochieheads Fife 186 D5
Lochill Moray 215 G2
Lochindorb Lodge Highld 214 B7
Lochinver Highld 224 D4
Loch Lomond and The Trossachs National Park 184 A5
Lochluichart Highld 211 L2
Lochmaben D & G 155 J5
Lochmaddy W Isls 233 c6
Loch Maree Hotel Highld 219 L7
Loch nam Madadh W Isls 233 c6
Loch Ness Highld 202 E1
Lochore Fife 186 C7
Lochranza N Ayrs 172 F7
Lochside Abers 197 H4
Lochside D & G 155 G6
Lochside Highld 213 J4
Lochslin Highld 223 J5
Lochton S Ayrs 152 F6
Lochty Angus 196 E4
Lochty Fife 187 H5
Lochuisge Highld 190 F5
Lochwinnoch Rens 174 C6
Lochwood D & G 155 J3
Lockengate Cnwll 5 G4
Lockerbie D & G 155 K5
Lockeridge Wilts 40 C6
Lockerley Hants 28 F6
Locking N Som 38 A8
Locking Stumps Warrtn 112 F3
Lockington E R Yk 126 B2
Lockleywood Shrops 99 G6
Locksbottom Gt Lon 45 H6
Locks Heath Hants 17 G2
Lockton N York 134 C2
Loddington Leics 87 L3
Loddington Nhants 88 B7
Loddiswell Devon 7 G6
Loddon Norfk 93 H4
Lode Cambs 76 D3
Lode Heath Solhll 85 L7
Loders Dorset 13 L4
Lodge Hill Crematorium Birm 85 H6
Lodsworth W Susx 30 F6
Lofthouse Leeds 123 L5
Lofthouse N York 131 L5
Lofthouse Gate Wakefd 123 L5
Loftus R & Cl 142 F4
Logan E Ayrs 164 C5
Loganlea W Loth 176 C6
Loggerheads Staffs 99 G5
Logie Angus 197 H4
Logie Fife 186 F4
Logie Moray 214 C4
Logie Coldstone Abers 205 K4
Logie Newton Abers 216 C6
Logie Pert Angus 197 G4
Logierait P & K 194 F6
Logierieve Abers 217 H8
Login Carmth 49 K3
Lolworth Cambs 75 L2
Lonbain Highld 209 L4
Londesborough E R Yk 125 K2
London Gt Lon 45 G4
London Apprentice Cnwll 4 F6
London Colney Herts 59 K7
Londonderry N York 132 D3
London Gateway Services Gt Lon 44 D2
Londonthorpe Lincs 102 F5
London Zoo ZSL Gt Lon 44 F4
Londubh Highld 219 K5
Lonemore Highld 219 J6
Long Ashton N Som 38 D6
Long Bank Worcs 84 D8
Long Bennington Lincs 102 D4
Longbenton N Tyne 151 G2
Longborough Gloucs 56 D3
Long Bredy Dorset 14 B4
Longbridge Birm 85 H7
Longbridge Deverill Wilts 27 K4
Long Buckby Nhants 73 J2
Longburton Dorset 26 F8
Long Clawson Leics 102 B6
Longcliffe Derbys 100 E2
Longcombe Devon 7 J4
Long Compton Staffs 99 J7
Long Compton Warwks 56 F2
Longcot Oxon 40 F3
Long Crendon Bucks 58 B6
Long Crichel Dorset 15 J1
Longden Shrops 83 J3
Long Ditton Surrey 44 D6
Longdon Staffs 85 J2
Longdon Worcs 70 E7
Longdon Green Staffs 85 J2
Longdon upon Tern Wrekin 84 B1
Longdown Devon 11 K6
Longdowns Cnwll 3 J4
Long Duckmanton Derbys 115 H7
Long Eaton Derbys 101 J5
Longfield Kent 45 L6
Longford Covtry 86 D6
Longford Derbys 100 E5
Longford Gloucs 55 J4
Longford Shrops 98 F5
Longford Wrekin 99 G8
Longforgan P & K 186 E2
Longformacus Border 178 E6
Longframlington Nthumb 158 E3
Long Green Ches W 112 C7
Longham Dorset 15 K3
Longham Norfk 91 L1
Long Hanborough Oxon 57 H5
Longhaven Abers 217 L6
Longhirst Nthumb 158 F4
Longhope Gloucs 55 G4
Longhope Ork 234 b7
Longhorsley Nthumb 158 E4
Longhoughton Nthumb 169 J6
Long Itchington Warwks 72 E2
Longlane Derbys 100 E5
Long Lawford Warwks 86 F7
Longleat Safari & Adventure Park Wilts 27 J3
Longlevens Gloucs 55 J4
Longleys P & K 195 L7
Long Load Somset 26 C6
Longmanhill Abers 216 E2
Long Marston Herts 58 E5
Long Marston N York 124 D1
Long Marston Warwks 71 L5
Long Marton Cumb 138 F3
Long Melford Suffk 77 J5
Longmoor Camp Hants 30 C5
Longmorn Moray 214 F3
Longmoss Ches E 113 K6
Long Newnton Gloucs 39 K3
Longnewton Border 167 J4
Long Newton E Loth 178 B5
Longnewton S on T 141 J4
Longney Gloucs 55 H5
Longniddry E Loth 177 L3
Longnor Shrops 83 J4
Longnor Staffs 114 C8
Longparish Hants 29 H3
Long Preston N York 130 F7
Longridge Lancs 121 J3
Longridge W Loth 176 C5
Longriggend N Lans 175 L4
Long Riston E R Yk 126 E3
Longrock Cnwll 2 E5
Longsdon Staffs 99 L2
Longside Abers 217 K5
Longstanton Cambs 76 B2
Longstock Hants 29 G4
Longstowe Cambs 75 K4
Long Stratton Norfk 92 E5
Long Street M Keyn 74 B5
Longstreet Wilts 28 C2
Long Sutton Hants 30 C3
Long Sutton Lincs 104 C7
Long Sutton Somset 26 C6
Longthorpe C Pete 89 H4
Long Thurlow Suffk 78 B2
Longthwaite Cumb 138 B3
Longton Lancs 121 G5
Longtown Cumb 148 C2
Longtown Herefs 53 L3
Longueville Jersey 236 d7
Longville in the Dale Shrops 83 K5
Long Waste Wrekin 84 B1
Long Whatton Leics 101 J7
Longwick Bucks 58 C6

Long Wittenham Oxon 41 K2
Longwitton Nthumb 158 D4
Longwood D & G 146 C3
Longworth Oxon 57 G7
Longyester E Loth 178 C5
Lonmay Abers 217 J3
Lonmore Highld 208 D5
Looe Cnwll 5 K5
Loose Kent 33 K3
Loosley Row Bucks 58 D7
Lootcherbrae Abers 216 B4
Lopen Somset 26 B8
Loppington Shrops 98 C6
Lordshill C Sotn 29 H7
Lords Wood Medway 46 C7
Lornty P & K 195 J6
Loscoe Derbys 101 H3
Lossiemouth Moray 214 F1
Lostock Gralam Ches W 113 G6
Lostock Green Ches W 113 G6
Lostwithiel Cnwll 5 H4
Lothbeg Highld 227 G6
Lothersdale N York 122 E2
Lothmore Highld 227 G6
Loudwater Bucks 42 E3
Loughborough Leics 101 K8
Loughborough Crematorium Leics 101 K8
Loughor Swans 51 H6
Loughton Essex 45 H2
Loughton M Keyn 74 B6
Lound Lincs 103 H8
Lound Notts 116 B4
Lound Suffk 93 K4
Lount Leics 101 G8
Louth Lincs 118 D4
Lover Wilts 28 E7
Loversall Donc 115 L2
Loveston Pembks 49 J5
Lovington Somset 26 E5
Low Ackworth Wakefd 124 C6
Low Barbeth D & G 144 B2
Low Bentham N York 130 C5
Low Biggins Cumb 130 B4
Low Borrowbridge Cumb 138 E6
Low Bradfield Sheff 114 E3
Low Bradley N York 122 F2
Low Burnham N Linc 116 C2
Lowca Cumb 136 D3
Low Catton E R Yk 133 L8
Low Crosby Cumb 148 D3
Lowdham Notts 102 A3
Low Dinsdale Darltn 141 J5
Lower Aisholt Somset 25 J4
Lower Ansty Dorset 14 E2
Lower Apperley Gloucs 55 J3
Lower Ashton Devon 11 J7
Lower Assendon Oxon 42 C4
Lower Bartle Lancs 121 G4
Lower Basildon W Berk 41 L5
Lower Beeding W Susx 31 L6
Lower Benefield Nhants 88 E5
Lower Bentley Worcs 71 H2
Lower Boddington Nhants 72 F4
Lower Bourne Surrey 30 D3
Lower Brailes Warwks 72 C6
Lower Breakish Highld 199 L2
Lower Broadheath Worcs 70 E3
Lower Broxwood Herefs 69 G4
Lower Bullingham Herefs 69 K6
Lower Burgate Hants 28 D7
Lower Caldecote C Beds 75 H5
Lower Chapel Powys 68 B7
Lower Chicksgrove Wilts 27 L5
Lower Chute Wilts 28 F2
Lower Clapton Gt Lon 45 G3
Lower Clent Worcs 85 G7
Lower Cumberworth Kirk 123 J8
Lower Dean Bed 74 F2
Lower Diabaig Highld 210 C3
Lower Dicker E Susx 20 B4
Lower Down Shrops 83 G6
Lower Dunsforth N York 133 G6
Lower Egleton Herefs 70 B5
Lower End M Keyn 74 D6
Lower Eythorne Kent 35 H5
Lower Failand N Som 38 D5
Lower Farringdon Hants 30 B4
Lower Feltham Gt Lon 43 H6
Lower Froyle Hants 30 C3
Lower Gabwell Devon 7 L2
Lower Gledfield Highld 222 D4
Lower Godney Somset 26 C3
Lower Gornal Dudley 85 G5
Lower Gravenhurst C Beds 75 G7
Lower Green Kent 32 F5
Lower Green Kent 33 G5
Lower Halliford Surrey 43 H6
Lower Halstow Kent 46 E6
Lower Hamworthy Poole 15 J4
Lower Hardres Kent 34 F4
Lower Hartwell Bucks 58 C5
Lower Hergest Herefs 68 F4
Lower Heyford Oxon 57 J3
Lower Heysham Lancs 129 J7
Lower Houses Kirk 123 H7
Lower Irlam Salfd 113 G3
Lower Killeyan Ag & B 160 A2
Lower Langford N Som 38 C7
Lower Largo Fife 187 G6
Lower Leigh Staffs 100 A5
Lower Loxhore Devon 23 K4
Lower Lydbrook Gloucs 54 E5
Lower Lye Herefs 69 H2
Lower Machen Newpt 37 K3
Lower Merridge Somset 25 J4
Lower Middleton Cheney Nhants 73 G6
Lower Moor Worcs 71 H5
Lower Morton S Glos 38 F3
Lower Nazeing Essex 60 C6
Lower Penarth V Glam 37 J6
Lower Penn Staffs 84 F4
Lower Peover Ches E 113 H6
Lower Quinton Warwks 71 L5
Lower Raydon Suffk 78 C6
Lower Roadwater Somset 25 G4
Lower Seagry Wilts 39 L4
Lower Shelton C Beds 74 E6
Lower Shiplake Oxon 42 C4
Lower Shuckburgh Warwks 72 F3
Lower Slaughter Gloucs 56 D4
Lower Standen Kent 35 H6
Lower Stanton St Quintin Wilts 39 L4
Lower Stoke Medway 46 D5
Lower Stone Gloucs 38 F2
Lower Stow Bedon Norfk 91 L5
Lower Street Norfk 106 F5
Lower Street Suffk 78 D4
Lower Swanwick Hants 16 F1
Lower Swell Gloucs 56 D3
Lower Tean Staffs 100 A5
Lower Town Devon 7 G2
Lower Town Pembks 64 D6
Lower Upcott Devon 11 K8
Lower Upham Hants 29 K7
Lower Weare Somset 26 B2
Lower Welson Herefs 68 F4
Lower Westmancote Worcs 71 G6
Lower Whatley Somset 27 H3
Lower Whitley Ches W 112 E5
Lower Wield Hants 29 M4
Lower Willingdon E Susx 20 C5
Lower Withington Ches E 113 J7
Lower Woodford Wilts 28 C4
Lower Wraxhall Dorset 14 B3
Lowesby Leics 87 K3
Lowestoft Suffk 93 L5
Loweswater Cumb 137 G3
Low Fell Gatesd 151 G3
Lowfield Heath W Susx 31 L4
Low Gartachorrans Stirlg 174 E2
Low Grantley N York 132 C5
Low Ham Somset 26 B5
Low Harrogate N York 132 D7
Low Hesket Cumb 148 E5
Low Hutton N York 134 B6
Lowick Nhants 88 E7
Lowick Nthumb 168 F2
Lowick Green Cumb 129 G3
Low Lorton Cumb 137 G3
Low Marnham Notts 116 D7
Low Mill N York 142 E7
Low Moorsley Sundld 151 H5
Low Moresby Cumb 136 D3
Low Newton Cumb 129 J3
Low Row Cumb 149 G3
Low Row N York 140 B7
Low Salchrie D & G 144 B2
Low Santon N Linc 125 L7
Lowsonford Warwks 71 L2
Low Tharston Norfk 92 E4
Lowther Cumb 138 D3
Lowthorpe E R Yk 135 G7
Lowton Somset 25 J7
Low Torry Fife 176 D2
Low Worsall N York 141 J5
Low Wray Cumb 137 K6
Loxbeare Devon 11 L2
Loxhill Surrey 31 G4
Loxhore Devon 23 K4
Loxley Warwks 72 C4
Loxton N Som 26 A1
Loxwood W Susx 31 H5
Loyal Lodge Highld 229 J6
Lubenham Leics 87 K6
Luccombe Somset 24 E3
Luccombe Village IoW 17 H6
Lucker Nthumb 169 H4
Luckett Cnwll 6 B2
Lucking Street Essex 77 J7
Luckington Wilts 39 J4
Lucklawhill Fife 187 G3
Luckwell Bridge Somset 24 E4
Lucton Herefs 69 J2
Ludag W Isls 233 b9
Ludborough Lincs 118 D3
Ludbrook Devon 6 F5
Ludchurch Pembks 49 K5
Luddenden Calder 122 F5
Luddenden Foot Calder 122 F5
Luddesdown Kent 46 A6
Luddington N Linc 125 J7
Luddington Warwks 71 L4
Luddington in the Brook Nhants 89 G6
Ludford Lincs 117 K4
Ludford Shrops 83 K8
Ludgershall Bucks 58 A4
Ludgershall Wilts 28 E2
Ludgvan Cnwll 2 E5
Ludham Norfk 107 H8
Ludlow Shrops 83 K7
Ludney Somset 26 B8
Ludwell Wilts 27 K6
Ludworth Dur 151 J6
Luffness E Loth 178 B3
Lugar E Ayrs 164 C5
Luggate Burn E Loth 178 D4
Luggiebank N Lans 175 K4
Lugton E Ayrs 174 D7
Lugwardine Herefs 69 K6
Luib Highld 209 J8
Luing Ag & B 181 L5
Lulham Herefs 69 H6
Lullington Derbys 86 B2
Lullington Somset 27 H2
Lulsgate Bottom N Som 38 D7
Lulsley Worcs 70 D4
Lumb Calder 122 F6
Lumby N York 124 D4
Lumloch E Duns 175 H4
Lumphanan Abers 206 B4
Lumphinnans Fife 186 C8
Lumsden Abers 205 K2
Lunan Angus 197 H6
Lunanhead Angus 196 D6
Luncarty P & K 186 A2
Lund E R Yk 126 B2
Lund N York 125 G4
Lundie Angus 186 E1
Lundin Links Fife 187 G6
Lundin Mill Fife 187 G6
Lundy Devon 22 B3
Lunga Ag & B 181 L5
Lunna Shet 235 d4
Lunsford Kent 33 J2
Lunsford's Cross E Susx 20 E4
Lunt Sefton 111 K2
Luppitt Devon 12 F2
Lupset Wakefd 123 L6
Lupton Cumb 129 L4
Lurgashall W Susx 30 F6
Lurley Devon 11 L2
Luscombe Devon 7 J4
Luss Ag & B 183 L8
Lussagiven Ag & B 171 L2
Lusta Highld 208 D3
Lustleigh Devon 11 H8
Luston Herefs 69 J2
Luthermuir Abers 197 G3
Luthrie Fife 186 E4
Luton Devon 7 K1
Luton Devon 12 D2
Luton Luton 59 H4
Luton Medway 46 C6
Luton Airport Luton 59 J4
Lutterworth Leics 87 G6
Lutton Devon 6 E4
Lutton Devon 7 G4
Lutton Lincs 104 C7
Lutton Nhants 89 G6
Luxborough Somset 24 F4
Luxulyan Cnwll 5 G4
Luxulyan Valley Cnwll 5 G4
Lybster Highld 231 J7
Lydbury North Shrops 83 G6
Lydd Kent 21 K2
Lydd Airport Kent 21 L2
Lydden Kent 35 H5
Lydden Kent 35 K2
Lyddington Rutlnd 88 C4

Lydeard St Lawrence Somset 25 H5
Lydford Devon 10 D7
Lydford on Fosse Somset 26 E5
Lydgate Calder 122 D5
Lydham Shrops 83 G5
Lydiard Millicent Wilts 40 C3
Lydiard Tregoze Swindn 40 C4
Lydiate Sefton 111 K2
Lydiate Ash Worcs 85 H7
Lydlinch Dorset 27 H8
Lydney Gloucs 54 F7
Lydstep Pembks 49 J7
Lye Dudley 85 G6
Lye Green E Susx 32 F6
Lye Green Warwks 71 L2
Lye's Green Wilts 27 J3
Lyford Oxon 41 H2
Lymbridge Green Kent 34 F6
Lyme Regis Dorset 13 J4
Lyminge Kent 34 F6
Lymington Hants 16 C4
Lyminster W Susx 18 D5
Lymm Warrtn 113 G4
Lymm Services Warrtn 112 F4
Lympne Kent 34 F7
Lympsham Somset 25 M1
Lympstone Devon 12 C5
Lynchat Highld 203 J5
Lynch Green Norfk 92 D3
Lyndhurst Hants 16 C2
Lyndon Rutlnd 88 C3
Lyndon Green Birm 85 K6
Lyne Border 166 B2
Lyne Surrey 43 G7
Lyneal Shrops 98 C6
Lyneham Oxon 56 F4
Lyneham Wilts 40 A5
Lynemouth Nthumb 159 H4
Lyne of Skene Abers 206 E4
Lyness Ork 234 b7
Lyng Norfk 106 C8
Lyng Somset 25 M5
Lynmouth Devon 23 L2
Lynsted Kent 34 C3
Lynton Devon 23 L2
Lyon's Gate Dorset 14 C2
Lyonshall Herefs 69 G4
Lytchett Matravers Dorset 15 H4
Lytchett Minster Dorset 15 H4
Lyth Highld 231 K3
Lytham Lancs 120 E5
Lytham St Anne's Lancs 120 D5
Lythe N York 143 H5
Lythmore Highld 230 F3

M

Mabe Burnthouse Cnwll 3 K4
Mablethorpe Lincs 119 G4
Macclesfield Ches E 113 K6
Macclesfield Crematorium Ches E 113 K6
Macduff Abers 216 D2
Macharioch Ag & B 161 J7
Machen Caerph 37 K3
Machrie N Ayrs 162 A3
Machrihanish Ag & B 161 G5
Machrins Ag & B 180 E8
Machynlleth Powys 81 G4
Machynys Carmth 51 G5
Mackworth Derbys 100 F5
Macmerry E Loth 177 L4
Madderty P & K 185 K3
Maddiston Falk 176 C3
Madeley Staffs 99 H4
Madeley Wrekin 84 C3
Madingley Cambs 76 B3
Madley Herefs 69 H6
Madresfield Worcs 70 E5
Madron Cnwll 2 E5
Maenclochog Pembks 49 J3
Maendy V Glam 36 F5
Maentwrog Gwynd 95 L4
Maen-y-groes Cerdgn 65 L3
Maer Staffs 99 H5
Maerdy Rhondd 36 F2
Maesbrook Shrops 97 L7
Maesbury Shrops 97 L7
Maesbury Marsh Shrops 97 L7
Maesllyn Cerdgn 65 K5
Maesteg Brdgnd 36 D3
Maesybont Carmth 51 H3
Maesycwmmer Caerph 37 J2
Maggieknockater Moray 215 H5
Magham Down E Susx 20 C4
Maghull Sefton 111 K2
Magna Park Leics 87 G6
Magor Mons 38 B3
Magor Services Mons 38 B3
Maidenbower W Susx 32 B6
Maiden Bradley Wilts 27 J4
Maidencombe Torbay 7 L3
Maidenhayne Devon 13 H4
Maiden Head N Som 38 E6
Maidenhead W & M 42 E4
Maiden Newton Dorset 14 B3
Maidens S Ayrs 163 G7
Maiden's Green Br For 42 E5
Maiden Wells Pembks 49 G7
Maidford Nhants 73 H4
Maids Moreton Bucks 73 K7
Maidstone Kent 33 K3
Maidstone Services Kent 33 L3
Maidwell Nhants 87 L7
Mail Shet 235 d6
Maindee Newpt 37 L3
Mainland Ork 234 c6
Mainland Shet 235 c5
Mainsforth Dur 141 H2
Mains of Balhall Angus 196 E4
Mains of Balnakettle Abers 197 G2
Mains of Dalvey Highld 214 D7
Mains of Haulkerton Abers 197 H2
Mains of Lesmoir Abers 215 K8
Mains of Melgunds Angus 196 E5
Mainsriddle D & G 147 G4
Mainstone Shrops 82 F6
Maisemore Gloucs 55 J4
Major's Green Worcs 85 K7
Malborough Devon 7 G7
Maldon Essex 61 K6
Malham N York 131 G6
Maligar Highld 209 G2
Mallaig Highld 199 L6
Mallaigvaig Highld 199 L5
Malleny Mills C Edin 177 G5
Malltraeth IoA 108 E7
Mallwyd Gwynd 81 J2
Malmesbury Wilts 39 L3
Malmsmead Devon 24 C2
Malpas Ches W 98 C3
Malpas Cnwll 4 D7
Malpas Newpt 37 L3
Maltby Rothm 115 K3
Maltby S on T 141 L5
Maltby le Marsh Lincs 118 F5
Maltman's Hill Kent 34 B6
Malton N York 134 C5
Malvern Worcs 70 D5
Malvern Hills 70 D5
Malvern Link Worcs 70 E5
Malvern Wells Worcs 70 D6
Mamble Worcs 70 C1
Mamhilad Mons 53 L7
Manaccan Cnwll 3 K6
Manafon Powys 82 C3
Manais W Isls 232 d5
Manaton Devon 11 H8
Manby Lincs 118 E4
Mancetter Warwks 86 D4
Manchester Manch 113 J3
Manchester Airport Manch 113 J5
Manchester Crematorium Manch 113 J3
Mancot Flints 111 K7
Mandally Highld 201 L5
Manea Cambs 90 C5
Maney Birm 85 K4
Manfield N York 140 F4
Mangotsfield S Glos 38 F5
Manish W Isls 232 d5
Manley Ches W 112 D7
Manmoel Caerph 53 J7
Mannel Ag & B 188 C7
Manningford Bohune Wilts 40 C8
Manningford Bruce Wilts 40 C8
Manningham C Brad 123 H4
Manning's Heath W Susx 31 K5
Mannington Dorset 15 K2
Manningtree Essex 62 D2
Mannofield C Aber 207 H4
Manorbier Pembks 49 H7
Manorbier Newton Pembks 49 H7
Manorhill Border 167 K3
Manorowen Pembks 64 C7
Manor Park Gt Lon 45 H3
Manor Park Crematorium Gt Lon 45 H3
Mansell Gamage Herefs 69 H5
Mansell Lacy Herefs 69 H5
Mansfield E Ayrs 164 C6
Mansfield Notts 101 K1
Mansfield & District Crematorium Notts 101 K2
Mansfield Woodhouse Notts 115 K8
Manston Dorset 27 J7
Manston Kent 35 J2
Manston Leeds 124 B4
Manswood Dorset 15 J2
Manthorpe Lincs 88 F1
Manton N Linc 116 F2
Manton Rutlnd 88 C3
Manton Wilts 40 D6
Manuden Essex 60 D3
Maperton Somset 26 F6
Maplebeck Notts 102 B1
Mapledurham Oxon 42 A5
Mapledurwell Hants 30 B2
Maplehurst W Susx 31 K6
Maplescombe Kent 45 K7
Mapleton Derbys 100 D3
Mapperley Derbys 101 H4
Mapperley Park C Nott 101 L4
Mapperton Dorset 13 L3
Mappleborough Green Warwks 71 J2
Mappleton E R Yk 126 F2
Mapplewell Barns 123 L7
Mappowder Dorset 14 E2
Marazanvose Cnwll 4 C5
Marazion Cnwll 2 F5
Marbury Ches E 98 E4
March Cambs 90 B4
March S Lans 165 J6
Marcham Oxon 41 J2
Marchamley Shrops 98 E6
Marchington Staffs 100 C6
Marchros Gwynd 94 F7
Marchwiel Wrexhm 98 A3
Marchwood Hants 16 D1
Marcross V Glam 36 E6
Marden Herefs 69 K5
Marden Kent 33 J4
Marden Wilts 40 C8
Marden Thorn Kent 33 K5
Mardy Mons 53 L5
Mareham le Fen Lincs 103 L1
Mareham on the Hill Lincs 118 C7
Marehill W Susx 18 E3
Maresfield E Susx 19 M2
Marfleet C KuH 126 E5
Marford Wrexhm 98 A2
Margam Neath 36 B3
Margam Crematorium Neath 36 C4
Margaret Marsh Dorset 27 J7
Margaretting Essex 61 G7
Margaretting Tye Essex 61 G7
Margate Kent 35 K1
Margnaheglish N Ayrs 162 D3
Margrie D & G 145 M5
Margrove Park R & Cl 142 E4
Marham Norfk 91 G2
Marhamchurch Cnwll 9 G4
Marholm C Pete 89 G3
Mariansleigh Devon 24 B6
Marine Town Kent 46 F5
Marionburgh Abers 206 D4
Marishader Highld 209 H2
Maristow Devon 6 C3
Marjoriebanks D & G 155 J5
Mark Somset 26 B2
Markbeech Kent 32 E5
Markby Lincs 119 G5
Mark Cross E Susx 33 G6
Markeaton Crematorium C Derb 100 F5
Market Bosworth Leics 86 E3
Market Deeping Lincs 89 G2
Market Drayton Shrops 98 F5
Market Harborough Leics 87 K6
Market Lavington Wilts 28 A1
Market Overton Rutlnd 88 C1
Market Rasen Lincs 117 J4
Market Stainton Lincs 118 C5
Market Warsop Notts 115 K7
Market Weighton E R Yk 125 K3
Market Weston Suffk 92 B7
Markfield Leics 86 F2
Markham Caerph 53 J7
Markham Moor Notts 116 B6
Markinch Fife 186 E6
Markington N York 132 D6
Markle E Loth 178 C3
Marksbury BaNES 38 F7
Marks Tey Essex 61 L4
Markyate Herts 59 H5
Marlborough Wilts 40 D6
Marlcliff Warwks 71 K4
Marldon Devon 7 K3
Marlesford Suffk 79 G3
Marlingford Norfk 92 D2
Marloes Pembks 48 D5
Marlow Bucks 42 D3
Marlow Bottom Bucks 42 D3
Marlpit Hill Kent 32 D4
Marnhull Dorset 27 H7
Marple Stockp 113 L4
Marr Donc 115 K1
Marrick N York 140 D7

Marsden Kirk 122 F7
Marsden S Tyne 151 J3
Marshalswick Herts 59 K6
Marsham Norfk 106 E7
Marsh Baldon Oxon 57 K7
Marshborough Kent 35 J3
Marshbrook Shrops 83 J5
Marshchapel Lincs 118 E2
Marsh Farm Luton 59 H3
Marshfield Newpt 37 K4
Marshfield S Glos 39 H5
Marshgate Cnwll 8 F6
Marsh Gibbon Bucks 57 M4
Marsh Green Devon 12 D4
Marsh Green Kent 32 D4
Marshland St James Norfk 90 D2
Marsh Lane Derbys 115 H5
Marsh Street Somset 24 F3
Marshwood Dorset 13 J3
Marske N York 140 D6
Marske-by-the-Sea R & Cl 142 D3
Marston Herefs 69 G3
Marston Lincs 102 E4
Marston Oxon 57 K6
Marston Staffs 99 L6
Marston Wilts 27 L1
Marston Green Solhll 85 L6
Marston Magna Somset 26 E6
Marston Meysey Wilts 40 C2
Marston Montgomery Derbys 100 C5
Marston Moretaine C Beds 74 E6
Marston on Dove Derbys 100 E6
Marston St Lawrence Nhants 73 G6
Marston Trussell Nhants 87 K6
Marstow Herefs 54 D4
Marsworth Bucks 58 F5
Marten Wilts 40 F7
Martham Norfk 107 J8
Martin Hants 28 B7
Martin Kent 35 J5
Martin Lincs 103 J1
Martinhoe Devon 23 L2
Martin Hussingtree Worcs 70 F3
Martinstown Dorset 14 C5
Martlesham Suffk 78 F5
Martlesham Heath Suffk 78 F5
Martletwy Pembks 49 H5
Martley Worcs 70 D3
Martock Somset 26 C7
Marton Ches E 113 J7
Marton E R Yk 126 F3
Marton Lincs 116 D5
Marton Middsb 142 B4
Marton N York 132 F6
Marton N York 134 B3
Marton Shrops 82 F3
Marton Warwks 72 E2
Marton-le-Moor N York 132 E5
Martyr Worthy Hants 29 K5
Marwell Wildlife Hants 29 J6
Marwick Ork 234 b5
Marwood Devon 23 H4
Marybank Highld 212 D4
Maryburgh Highld 212 E3
Marygold Border 179 G6
Maryhill C Glas 175 G4
Maryhill Crematorium C Glas 175 G4
Marykirk Abers 197 H3
Marylebone Gt Lon 44 F4
Marylebone Wigan 121 H8
Marypark Moray 214 F6
Maryport Cumb 147 H7
Maryport D & G 144 D7
Marystow Devon 10 C7
Mary Tavy Devon 6 D1
Maryton Angus 197 H5
Marywell Abers 206 B6
Marywell Abers 207 H5
Marywell Angus 197 G7
Masham N York 132 C4
Masongill N York 130 C4
Masonhill Crematorium S Ayrs 163 J5
Mastin Moor Derbys 115 J6
Matching Green Essex 60 E5
Matching Tye Essex 60 E5
Matfen Nthumb 158 C7
Matfield Kent 33 H5
Mathern Mons 38 D3
Mathon Herefs 70 D5
Mathry Pembks 48 E2
Matlask Norfk 106 D5
Matlock Derbys 100 F1
Matlock Bath Derbys 100 F2
Matson Gloucs 55 J5
Mattersey Notts 116 B4
Mattingley Hants 42 B8
Mattishall Norfk 92 C2
Mattishall Burgh Norfk 92 C2
Mauchline E Ayrs 163 L4
Maud Abers 217 H5
Maufant Jersey 236 d6
Maugersbury Gloucs 56 D3
Maughold IoM 237 e3
Mauld Highld 212 C6
Maulden C Beds 74 F6
Maulds Meaburn Cumb 138 F4
Maunby N York 132 E3
Maundown Somset 25 G5
Mautby Norfk 93 K2
Mavesyn Ridware Staffs 85 J1
Mavis Enderby Lincs 118 E7
Mawbray Cumb 147 J5
Mawdesley Lancs 121 G7
Mawdlam Brdgnd 36 C4
Mawgan Cnwll 3 J6
Mawgan Porth Cnwll 4 D3
Mawla Cnwll 3 J3
Mawnan Cnwll 3 K5
Mawnan Smith Cnwll 3 K5
Mawsley Nhants 88 B7
Maxey C Pete 89 G2
Maxstoke Warwks 86 B6
Maxton Border 167 J4
Maxton Kent 35 J6
Maxwell Town D & G 155 G6
Maxworthy Cnwll 9 H6
May Bank Staffs 99 J3
Maybole S Ayrs 163 H7
Maybury Surrey 43 G8
Mayfield E Susx 33 G7
Mayfield Mdloth 177 K5
Mayfield Staffs 100 D4
Mayford Surrey 31 G1
May Hill Gloucs 55 G4
Mayland Essex 61 L7
Maylandsea Essex 61 L7
Maynard's Green E Susx 20 C3
Maypole Birm 85 J7
Maypole Green Norfk 93 J4
Maypole Green Suffk 77 K3
Meadgate BaNES 39 G8
Meadle Bucks 58 D6
Meadowfield Dur 151 G6
Meadwell Devon 9 K8
Meanwood Leeds 123 K3
Meare Somset 26 C3
Meare Green Somset 25 L6
Meare Green Somset 25 M6
Mearns E Rens 174 F7
Mears Ashby Nhants 74 B2
Measham Leics 86 D2
Meathop Cumb 129 J4
Meavy Devon 6 D3
Medbourne Leics 88 B5
Meddon Devon 9 H2
Meden Vale Notts 115 L7
Medmenham Bucks 42 D4
Medomsley Dur 150 E4
Medstead Hants 30 A4
Medway Crematorium Kent 46 C7
Medway Services Medway 46 D7
Meerbrook Staffs 99 M1
Meesden Herts 60 C2
Meeth Devon 10 E3
Meeting House Hill Norfk 107 G6
Meidrim Carmth 50 C2
Meifod Powys 82 D2
Meigle P & K 195 L7
Meikle Carco D & G 164 F6
Meikle Earnock S Lans 175 J7
Meikle Kilmory Ag & B 173 H6
Meikle Obney P & K 195 G8
Meikleour P & K 195 J7
Meikle Wartle Abers 216 D7
Meinciau Carmth 50 F4
Meir C Stke 99 L4
Melbourn Cambs 75 L5
Melbourne Derbys 101 G7
Melbourne E R Yk 125 H2
Melbury Abbas Dorset 27 K7
Melbury Bubb Dorset 14 B2
Melbury Osmond Dorset 14 B2
Melchbourne Bed 74 E2
Melcombe Bingham Dorset 14 E2
Meldon Devon 10 E6
Meldon Nthumb 158 E5
Meldreth Cambs 75 L5
Meldrum Stirlg 184 F7
Melfort Ag & B 182 B5
Meliden Denbgs 110 E5
Melin-y-wig Denbgs 97 G3
Melkinthorpe Cumb 138 D3
Melkridge Nthumb 149 J3
Melksham Wilts 39 K7
Melling Lancs 130 B5
Melling Sefton 111 L2
Mellis Suffk 92 C8
Mellon Charles Highld 219 K3
Mellon Udrigle Highld 219 K3
Mellor Lancs 121 J4
Mellor Stockp 113 M4
Mellor Brook Lancs 121 J4
Mells Somset 27 G2
Melmerby Cumb 149 G7
Melmerby N York 131 K3
Melmerby N York 132 E4
Melness Highld 229 J3
Melplash Dorset 13 L3
Melrose Border 167 H3
Melsetter Ork 234 b7
Melsonby N York 140 F5
Meltham Kirk 123 G7
Melton E R Yk 126 B5
Melton Suffk 79 G4
Melton Constable Norfk 106 C6
Melton Mowbray Leics 102 C8
Melton Ross N Linc 126 D7
Melvaig Highld 219 H4
Melverley Shrops 83 G1
Melvich Highld 230 C3
Membury Devon 13 H2
Membury Services W Berk 40 F5
Memsie Abers 217 H2
Memus Angus 196 C5
Menai Bridge IoA 109 H6
Mendham Suffk 92 F6
Mendip Crematorium Somset 26 E3
Mendip Hills 26 D2
Mendlesham Suffk 78 D2
Mendlesham Green Suffk 78 D2
Menheniot Cnwll 5 L4
Mennock D & G 164 F7
Menston C Brad 123 H2
Menstrie Clacks 185 H7
Mentmore Bucks 58 E4
Meoble Highld 200 C7
Meole Brace Shrops 83 J2
Meonstoke Hants 29 L7
Meopham Kent 45 M6
Mepal Cambs 90 B7
Meppershall C Beds 75 G7
Mere Ches E 113 G5
Mere Wilts 27 J5
Mere Brow Lancs 120 F6
Mereclough Lancs 122 C4
Mere Green Birm 85 K4
Mereworth Kent 33 H3
Meriden Solhll 86 B6
Merkadale Highld 208 F7
Merley Poole 15 J3
Merrion Pembks 48 F7
Merriott Somset 26 C8
Merrow Surrey 31 G2
Merry Hill Herts 43 J2
Merryhill Wolves 84 F4
Merrymeet Cnwll 5 L3
Mersea Island Essex 62 B5
Mersey Crossing Halton 112 D5
Mersham Kent 34 E6
Merstham Surrey 32 B3
Merston W Susx 18 B5
Merstone IoW 17 G5
Merthyr Cynog Powys 67 L6
Merthyr Mawr Brdgnd 36 D5
Merthyr Tydfil Myr Td 53 G6
Merthyr Vale Myr Td 53 G7
Merton Devon 10 D3
Merton Gt Lon 44 E6
Merton Norfk 91 K4
Merton Oxon 57 L4
Meshaw Devon 24 B7
Messing Essex 61 L4
Messingham N Linc 116 E2
Metfield Suffk 93 G7
Metherell Cnwll 6 B3
Metheringham Lincs 103 H1
Methil Fife 186 F7
Methilhill Fife 186 F7
Methlick Abers 217 G6
Methven P & K 185 L3
Methwold Norfk 91 G4
Methwold Hythe Norfk 91 G4
Mettingham Suffk 93 H5
Metton Norfk 106 E5
Mevagissey Cnwll 4 F6
Mexborough Donc 115 J2
Mey Highld 231 K2
Meyllteyrn Gwynd 94 D6
Meysey Hampton Gloucs 56 C7
Miabhig W Isls 232 d2
Miavaig W Isls 232 d2
Michaelchurch Herefs 54 D3
Michaelchurch Escley Herefs 69 G7
Michaelstone-y-Fedw Newpt 37 K4
Michaelston-le-Pit V Glam 37 J5
Michaelstow Cnwll 5 G1
Michaelwood Services Gloucs 39 G2
Micheldever Hants 29 K4
Micheldever Station Hants 29 K3
Michelmersh Hants 29 G6
Mickfield Suffk 78 D3
Micklebring Donc 115 K3
Mickleby N York 143 G5

Micklefield Leeds 124 C4
Mickleham Surrey 31 K2
Mickleover C Derb 100 F5
Mickleton Dur 140 B3
Mickleton Gloucs 71 L5
Mickletown Leeds 124 B5
Mickle Trafford Ches W 112 C7
Mickley N York 132 C4
Mickley Square Nthumb 150 D3
Mid Ardlaw Abers 217 H2
Midbea Ork 234 c4
Mid Beltie Abers 206 C5
Mid Calder W Loth 176 E5
Mid Clyth Highld 231 K7
Mid Culbeuchly Abers 216 C3
Middle Aston Oxon 57 J3
Middle Barton Oxon 57 H3
Middlebie D & G 155 L6
Middlebridge P & K 194 D3
Middle Chinnock Somset 26 C8
Middle Claydon Bucks 58 B3
Middleham N York 131 L3
Middle Handley Derbys 115 H6
Middlehill Wilts 39 J6
Middlehope Shrops 83 K5
Middle Kames Ag & B 172 F1
Middle Littleton Worcs 71 J5
Middlemarsh Dorset 14 C2
Middle Mayfield Staffs 100 C4
Middle Rasen Lincs 117 H4
Middle Rocombe Devon 7 K2
Middlesbrough Middsb 141 L4
Middleshaw Cumb 129 L2
Middlesmoor N York 131 K5
Middle Stoke Medway 46 D5
Middlestone Dur 141 G2
Middlestown Wakefd 123 K6
Middlethird Border 167 K2
Middleton Ag & B 188 B7
Middleton Derbys 100 F2
Middleton Derbys 114 D8
Middleton Essex 77 K6
Middleton Hants 29 H3
Middleton Herefs 69 K1
Middleton Leeds 123 L5
Middleton N York 123 G2
Middleton N York 134 B3
Middleton Nhants 88 B5
Middleton Norfk 90 F1
Middleton Nthumb 158 D5
Middleton P & K 186 B6
Middleton Rochdl 113 K1
Middleton Shrops 83 K7
Middleton Suffk 79 J2
Middleton Swans 50 E7
Middleton Warwks 85 L4
Middleton Cheney Nhants 73 G6
Middleton Crematorium Rochdl 113 K1
Middleton-in-Teesdale Dur 139 L3
Middleton Moor Suffk 79 J2
Middleton One Row Darltn 141 J5
Middleton-on-Sea W Susx 18 C5
Middleton on the Hill Herefs 69 K2
Middleton on the Wolds E R Yk 125 L2
Middleton Park C Aber 207 H3
Middleton Quernhow N York 132 E4
Middleton St George Darltn 141 J5
Middleton Scriven Shrops 84 C6
Middleton Stoney Oxon 57 K4
Middleton Tyas N York 141 G6
Middle Town IoS 2 a2
Middletown Powys 82 F2
Middle Tysoe Warwks 72 D5
Middle Wallop Hants 28 F4
Middlewich Ches E 113 G7
Middle Winterslow Wilts 28 E5
Middlewood Cnwll 5 L2
Middle Woodford Wilts 28 C4
Middlewood Green Suffk 78 D3
Middleyard E Ayrs 163 M3
Middlezoy Somset 26 B5
Midford BaNES 39 H7
Midgham W Berk 41 K6
Midgley Calder 122 F5
Midgley Wakefd 123 K7
Midhopestones Sheff 114 E2
Midhurst W Susx 30 E6
Mid Lavant W Susx 18 B4
Midlem Border 167 H4
Mid Mains Highld 212 C6
Midpark Ag & B 173 H6
Midsomer Norton BaNES 26 F1
Midtown Highld 229 J4
Mid Warwickshire Crematorium Warwks 72 C3
Mid Yell Shet 235 d3
Migvie Abers 205 K4
Milborne Port Somset 26 F7
Milborne St Andrew Dorset 14 F3
Milborne Wick Somset 26 F7
Milbourne Nthumb 158 E6
Milbourne Wilts 39 L3
Milburn Cumb 138 F2
Milbury Heath S Glos 38 F3
Milby N York 132 F6
Milcombe Oxon 72 E7
Milden Suffk 77 L5
Mildenhall Suffk 91 G8
Mildenhall Wilts 40 E6
Mileham Norfk 105 L8
Mile Oak Br & H 19 H4
Milesmark Fife 176 E2
Miles Platting Manch 113 J2
Mile Town Kent 46 F5
Milfield Nthumb 168 D3
Milford Derbys 101 G4
Milford Devon 22 C6
Milford Staffs 99 L7
Milford Surrey 30 F3
Milford Haven Pembks 48 F6
Milford on Sea Hants 16 C4
Milkwall Gloucs 54 E6
Millais Jersey 236 a5
Milland W Susx 30 D5
Mill Bank Calder 122 F6
Millbreck Abers 217 J5
Millbridge Surrey 30 D3
Millbrook C Beds 74 E6
Millbrook C Sotn 29 G8
Millbrook Cnwll 6 B5
Millbrook Jersey 236 c7
Mill Brow Stockp 113 L4
Millbuie Abers 206 F4
Millbuie Highld 212 E4
Millcorner E Susx 21 G2
Millcraig Highld 222 E7
Milldale Staffs 100 C2
Mill End Bucks 42 C4
Mill End Herts 60 B2
Millerhill Mdloth 177 J4
Miller's Dale Derbys 114 C6
Millerston C Glas 175 H5
Mill Green Cambs 76 F5
Mill Green Essex 61 G7
Mill Green Lincs 103 L7
Mill Green Suffk 77 L6
Mill Green Suffk 78 B3
Mill Green Suffk 78 D3
Millhalf Herefs 68 F5
Millheugh S Lans 175 K7
Mill Hill Gt Lon 44 E2
Millhouse Ag & B 173 G4
Millhousebridge D & G 155 K5
Millhouse Green Barns 114 E2
Millhouses Sheff 115 G5
Milliken Park Rens 174 D6
Millington E R Yk 125 J1
Millmeece Staffs 99 J5
Mill of Drummond P & K 185 H4
Mill of Haldane W Duns 174 D2
Millom Cumb 128 E4
Millport N Ayrs 173 K7
Mill Street Suffk 78 C1
Millthrop Cumb 130 C2
Milltimber C Aber 207 G5
Milltown Abers 205 G4
Milltown Abers 205 K3
Milltown D & G 156 C6
Milltown Devon 23 J4
Milltown of Auchindoun Moray 215 H6
Milltown of Campfield Abers 206 C5
Milltown of Edinvillie Moray 215 G6
Milltown of Learney Abers 206 C5
Milnathort P & K 186 B6
Milngavie E Duns 175 G4
Milnrow Rochdl 122 D7
Milnthorpe Cumb 129 K3
Milovaig Highld 208 B4
Milson Shrops 84 B8
Milstead Kent 34 B3
Milston Wilts 28 D3
Milthorpe Nhants 73 H5
Milton C Stke 99 K3
Milton Cambs 76 C2
Milton Cumb 148 F3
Milton D & G 144 F4
Milton D & G 154 E7
Milton Derbys 100 F7
Milton Highld 209 L5
Milton Highld 212 D7
Milton Highld 212 E4
Milton Highld 223 G6
Milton Highld 231 L5
Milton Inver 174 C5
Milton Kent 46 A5
Milton Moray 204 E2
Milton Moray 215 L2
Milton N Som 37 M7
Milton Notts 116 B6
Milton Oxon 41 J3
Milton Oxon 72 F7
Milton P & K 195 G4
Milton Pembks 49 H6
Milton Somset 26 C6
Milton Stirlg 184 B6
Milton W Duns 174 D4
Milton Abbas Dorset 14 F3
Milton Abbot Devon 9 K8
Milton Bridge Mdloth 177 H5
Milton Bryan C Beds 58 F3
Milton Clevedon Somset 26 F4
Milton Combe Devon 6 D3
Milton Damerel Devon 9 K3
Milton Ernest Bed 74 E4
Milton Green Ches W 98 C2
Milton Hill Oxon 41 J3
Milton Keynes M Keyn 74 C6
Milton Lilbourne Wilts 40 D7
Milton Malsor Nhants 73 K4
Milton Morenish P & K 184 D1
Milton of Auchinhove Abers 206 B5
Milton of Balgonie Fife 186 E7
Milton of Buchanan Stirlg 174 E1
Milton of Campsie E Duns 175 H3
Milton of Leys Highld 213 G6
Milton of Murtle C Aber 207 G5
Milton of Tullich Abers 205 J6
Milton on Stour Dorset 27 J5
Milton Regis Kent 46 E6
Milton-under-Wychwood Oxon 56 E4
Milverton Somset 25 H6
Milverton Warwks 72 C2
Milwich Staffs 99 L6
Minard Ag & B 182 D7
Minchinhampton Gloucs 55 K7
Minehead Somset 24 F3
Minera Wrexhm 97 L3
Minety Wilts 40 A3
Minffordd Gwynd 95 K5
Mingarrypark Highld 190 D3
Miningsby Lincs 118 D8
Minions Cnwll 5 L2
Minishant S Ayrs 163 J6
Minllyn Gwynd 81 J2
Minnigaff D & G 145 J2
Minnonie Abers 216 E3
Minskip N York 132 F6
Minstead Hants 16 C1
Minsted W Susx 30 D7
Minster Kent 35 J2
Minster Kent 46 F5
Minsterley Shrops 83 G3
Minster Lovell Oxon 56 F5
Minsterworth Gloucs 55 H5
Minterne Magna Dorset 14 C2
Minting Lincs 117 K6
Mintlaw Abers 217 J5
Mintlyn Crematorium Norfk 105 G8
Minto Border 167 H5
Minton Shrops 83 H5
Mirehouse Cumb 136 D4
Mireland Highld 231 K4
Mirfield Kirk 123 J6
Miserden Gloucs 55 L6
Miskin Rhondd 37 G4
Misson Notts 116 B3
Misterton Leics 87 G6
Misterton Notts 116 C3
Misterton Somset 13 L2
Mistley Essex 62 D2
Mitcham Gt Lon 44 F6
Mitcheldean Gloucs 54 F4
Mitchell Cnwll 4 D5
Mitchellslacks D & G 155 G3
Mitchel Troy Mons 54 C6
Mitford Nthumb 158 F5
Mithian Cnwll 3 J2
Mixbury Oxon 73 H7
Mobberley Ches E 113 H5
Mobberley Staffs 100 A4
Mochdre Powys 82 B5
Mochrum D & G 145 H5
Mockbeggar Kent 33 J4
Mockerkin Cumb 136 F3
Modbury Devon 6 F5
Moddershall Staffs 99 L5
Moelfre IoA 109 G4
Moelfre Powys 97 J6
Moffat D & G 155 J2
Moggerhanger C Beds 75 G5
Moira Leics 86 C1
Molash Kent 34 D4

Mol-chlach Highld 199 G3
Mold Flints 111 H8
Moldgreen Kirk 123 H7
Molehill Green Essex 60 E3
Molescroft E R Yk 126 C3
Molesworth Cambs 88 F7
Molland Devon 24 C5
Mollington Ches W 111 L7
Mollington Oxon 72 F5
Mollinsburn N Lans 175 J4
Mondynes Abers 197 J1
Monewden Suffk 78 F3
Moneydie P & K 185 M2
Moniaive D & G 154 D4
Monifieth Angus 187 H2
Monikie Angus 196 E8
Monimail Fife 186 E5
Monken Hadley Gt Lon 44 E1
Monk Fryston N York 124 D5
Monkhide Herefs 70 B5
Monkhill Cumb 148 C3
Monkhopton Shrops 84 B5
Monkland Herefs 69 J3
Monkleigh Devon 23 G7
Monknash V Glam 36 E6
Monkokehampton Devon 10 E4
Monkseaton N Tyne 159 H7
Monks Eleigh Suffk 77 L5
Monk's Gate W Susx 31 K6
Monks Heath Ches E 113 J6
Monk Sherborne Hants 29 L1
Monksilver Somset 25 G4
Monks Kirby Warwks 86 F6
Monk Soham Suffk 78 E2
Monks Risborough Bucks 58 D6
Monksthorpe Lincs 118 F7
Monk Street Essex 60 F3
Monkswood Mons 53 M7
Monkton Devon 12 F2
Monkton Kent 47 M6
Monkton S Ayrs 163 J4
Monkton S Tyne 151 H3
Monkton Combe BaNES 39 H7
Monkton Deverill Wilts 27 J4
Monkton Farleigh Wilts 39 J7
Monkton Heathfield Somset 25 K6
Monkton Wyld Dorset 13 J3
Monkwearmouth Sundld 151 J4
Monkwood Hants 30 A5
Monmore Green Wolves 85 G4
Monmouth Mons 54 D5
Monnington on Wye Herefs 69 G5
Monreith D & G 145 H6
Montacute Somset 26 D7
Montford Shrops 83 H1
Montford Bridge Shrops 83 H1
Montgarrie Abers 206 B2
Montgomery Powys 82 E4
Montrose Angus 197 H5
Mont Saint Guern 236 b3
Monxton Hants 28 F3
Monyash Derbys 114 D7
Monymusk Abers 206 D3
Monzie P & K 185 H3
Moodiesburn N Lans 175 J4
Moonzie Fife 186 E4
Moor Allerton Leeds 123 L3
Moorby Lincs 118 D8
Moor Crichel Dorset 15 J2
Moordown Bmouth 15 K4
Moore Halton 112 E5
Moor End Calder 122 F5
Moorends Donc 125 G7
Moorhead C Brad 123 H3
Moorhouse Cumb 148 B4
Moorhouse Notts 116 C7
Moorhouse Bank Surrey 32 D3
Moorlinch Somset 26 B4
Moor Monkton N York 133 H7
Moorsholm R & Cl 142 E4
Moorside Dorset 27 H7
Moor Street Birm 85 H6
Moorswater Cnwll 5 K3
Moorthorpe Wakefd 124 C7
Moortown Leeds 123 K3
Moortown Lincs 117 H2
Morangie Highld 223 G5
Morar Highld 199 L6
Moray Crematorium Moray 215 J3
Morborne Cambs 89 G5
Morchard Bishop Devon 11 H4
Morcombelake Dorset 13 K4
Morcott Rutlnd 88 D4
Morda Shrops 97 L6
Morden Dorset 15 H4
Morden Gt Lon 44 E6
Mordiford Herefs 69 L6
Mordon Dur 141 H2
More Shrops 83 G5
Morebath Devon 24 E6
Morebattle Border 168 B4
Morecambe Lancs 129 J6
Moredon Swindn 40 C3
Morefield Highld 220 E3
Morehall Kent 35 G7
Moreleigh Devon 7 H5
Morenish P & K 184 D1
Morestead Hants 29 K6
Moreton Dorset 14 F4
Moreton Essex 60 E6
Moreton Herefs 69 K2
Moreton Oxon 58 B6
Moreton Wirral 111 J4
Moreton Corbet Shrops 98 E7
Moretonhampstead Devon 11 H7
Moreton-in-Marsh Gloucs 56 D2
Moreton Jeffries Herefs 69 L5
Moreton Morrell Warwks 72 C4
Moreton on Lugg Herefs 69 K5
Moreton Pinkney Nhants 73 H5
Moreton Say Shrops 98 F5
Moreton Valence Gloucs 55 H6
Morfa Nefyn Gwynd 94 E4
Morham E Loth 178 C4
Morland Cumb 138 E3
Morley Ches E 113 J5
Morley Derbys 101 H4
Morley Leeds 123 K5
Morley Green Ches E 113 J5
Morley St Botolph Norfk 92 C4
Morningside C Edin 177 H4
Morningside N Lans 175 L7
Morningthorpe Norfk 92 F5
Morpeth Nthumb 158 F5
Morphie Abers 197 H4
Morrey Staffs 100 C8
Morriston Swans 51 J6
Morston Norfk 106 B4
Mortehoe Devon 23 G3
Morthen Rothm 115 J4
Mortimer W Berk 41 M7
Mortimer West End Hants 41 M7
Mortlake Gt Lon 44 E5
Mortlake Crematorium Gt Lon 44 D5
Morton Cumb 148 C4
Morton Derbys 101 H1
Morton Lincs 103 H7
Morton Lincs 116 D3
Morton Notts 102 B3
Morton Shrops 97 L7
Mortonhall Crematorium C Edin 177 H5
Morton-on-Swale N York 132 E2
Morton on the Hill Norfk 92 D1
Morvah Cnwll 2 D4
Morvich Highld 200 E2
Morville Shrops 84 C5
Morwenstow Cnwll 9 G2
Mosborough Sheff 115 H5
Moscow E Ayrs 163 L2
Moseley Birm 85 J6
Moseley Wolves 85 G4
Moseley Worcs 70 E3
Moss Ag & B 188 B7
Moss Donc 124 F7
Mossat Abers 205 K2
Mossbank Shet 235 d4
Moss Bank St Hel 112 D3
Mossbay Cumb 136 D2
Mossblown S Ayrs 163 K4
Mossburnford Border 167 K6
Mossdale D & G 154 B7
Mossdale E Ayrs 153 K2
Moss Edge Lancs 120 F2
Mossend N Lans 175 K6
Mossley Tamesd 113 L2
Mosspaul Hotel Border 156 D3
Moss-side Highld 213 K4
Mosstodloch Moray 215 H3
Mossyard D & G 145 L5
Mossy Lea Lancs 121 H7
Mosterton Dorset 13 L2
Moston Manch 113 K2
Mostyn Flints 111 G5
Motcombe Dorset 27 J6
Mothecombe Devon 6 F6
Motherby Cumb 138 B2
Motherwell N Lans 175 K6
Motspur Park Gt Lon 44 E6
Mottingham Gt Lon 45 H5
Mottisfont Hants 28 F6
Mottisfont Hants 28 F6
Mottistone IoW 16 E5
Mottram in Longdendale Tamesd 113 M3
Mottram St Andrew Ches E 113 K5
Mouilpied Guern 236 c3
Mouldsworth Ches W 112 D7
Moulin P & K 194 E4
Moulsecoomb Br & H 19 J4
Moulsford Oxon 41 L4
Moulsoe M Keyn 74 C6
Moultavie Highld 222 E7
Moulton Ches W 112 F7
Moulton Lincs 104 A7
Moulton N York 141 G6
Moulton Nhants 73 L2
Moulton Suffk 77 G2
Moulton V Glam 37 G6
Moulton Chapel Lincs 103 M8
Moulton St Mary Norfk 93 H3
Moulton Seas End Lincs 104 A6
Mount Cnwll 5 J3
Mountain C Brad 123 G4
Mountain Ash Rhondd 53 G7
Mountain Cross Border 176 F8
Mount Ambrose Cnwll 3 J3
Mount Bures Essex 61 L2
Mountfield E Susx 20 E2
Mountgerald House Highld 212 E3
Mount Hawke Cnwll 3 J2
Mountjoy Cnwll 4 D4
Mount Lothian Mdloth 177 H6
Mountnessing Essex 60 F8
Mounton Mons 38 D2
Mount Pleasant Derbys 101 G3
Mount Pleasant Suffk 77 G5
Mountsett Crematorium Dur 150 E4
Mountsorrel Leics 87 H2
Mount Tabor Calder 122 F5
Mousehole Cnwll 2 E6
Mouswald D & G 155 J7
Mow Cop Ches E 99 J2
Mowhaugh Border 168 B5
Mowmacre Hill C Leic 87 H3
Mowsley Leics 87 J5
Moy Highld 202 C8
Moy Highld 213 J7
Moyle Highld 200 D2
Moylegrove Pembks 64 F5
Muasdale Ag & B 161 H2
Muchalls Abers 207 G6
Much Birch Herefs 54 D3
Much Cowarne Herefs 70 B5
Much Dewchurch Herefs 54 C2
Muchelney Somset 26 B6
Muchelney Ham Somset 26 C6
Much Hadham Herts 60 C4
Much Hoole Lancs 120 F6
Muchlarnick Cnwll 5 K5
Much Marcle Herefs 54 F2
Much Wenlock Shrops 84 B4
Muck Highld 189 K1
Muckleburgh Collection Norfk 106 D4
Mucklestone Staffs 99 G5
Muckton Lincs 118 E5
Muddiford Devon 23 J4
Muddles Green E Susx 20 B3
Mudeford Dorset 16 A4
Mudford Somset 26 E7
Mudford Sock Somset 26 E7
Mugdock Stirlg 175 G3
Mugeary Highld 209 G6
Mugginton Derbys 100 F4
Muirden Abers 216 D4
Muirdrum Angus 196 F8
Muiresk Abers 216 D5
Muirhead Angus 186 E1
Muirhead Fife 186 E6
Muirhead N Lans 175 J4
Muirkirk E Ayrs 164 D4
Muirmill Stirlg 175 J2
Muir of Fowlis Abers 206 B3
Muir of Miltonduff Moray 214 E3
Muir of Ord Highld 212 E4
Muirshearlich Highld 192 B1
Muirtack Abers 217 J6
Muirton P & K 185 J5
Muirton Mains Highld 212 C4
Muirton of Ardblair P & K 195 J7
Muker N York 139 K7
Mulbarton Norfk 92 E4
Mulben Moray 215 H4
Mull Ag & B 181 J1
Mullion Cnwll 3 H7
Mullion Cove Cnwll 3 H7
Mumby Lincs 119 G6
Munderfield Row Herefs 70 B4
Munderfield Stocks Herefs 70 B4
Mundesley Norfk 107 G5
Mundford Norfk 91 H5
Mundham Norfk 93 G4
Mundon Hill Essex 61 K7
Mungrisdale Cumb 137 K2

Munlochy Highld 213 G4
Munnoch N Ayrs 174 B8
Munsley Herefs 70 B6
Munslow Shrops 83 K6
Murchington Devon 11 G7
Murcott Oxon 57 L5
Murkle Highld 231 H2
Murlaggan Highld 200 F6
Murroes Angus 187 G1
Murrow Cambs 89 L3
Mursley Bucks 58 D3
Murthill Angus 196 D5
Murthly P & K 195 H8
Murton C York 133 K8
Murton Cumb 139 G3
Murton Dur 151 J5
Murton N Tyne 159 H7
Murton Nthumb 179 K8
Musbury Devon 13 H4
Musselburgh E Loth 177 K4
Muston Leics 102 D5
Muston N York 135 H4
Muswell Hill Gt Lon 44 F3
Mutehill D & G 146 C5
Mutford Suffk 93 K6
Muthill P & K 185 H4
Mybster Highld 231 H5
Myddfai Carmth 52 B3
Myddle Shrops 98 C7
Mydroilyn Cerdgn 66 B4
Mylor Cnwll 4 C8
Mylor Bridge Cnwll 4 C8
Mynachlog ddu Pembks 49 K2
Mynydd-bach Mons 38 C2
Mynydd-Bach Swans 51 J6
Mynyddgarreg Carmth 50 E4
Mynydd Isa Flints 111 J8
Myrebird Abers 206 E5
Myredykes Border 157 G3
Mytchett Surrey 30 E1
Mytholm Calder 122 E5
Mytholmroyd Calder 122 F5
Myton-on-Swale N York 132 F6

N

Naast Highld 219 J5
Na Buirgh W Isls 232 d4
Naburn C York 124 F2
Nab Wood Crematorium C Brad 123 H3
Nackington Kent 34 F4
Nacton Suffk 78 F6
Nafferton E R Yk 135 G7
Nailsbourne Somset 25 K5
Nailsea N Som 38 C6
Nailstone Leics 86 E3
Nailsworth Gloucs 55 J7
Nairn Highld 213 K3
Nannerch Flints 111 G7
Nanpantan Leics 87 G1
Nanpean Cnwll 4 F5
Nanstallon Cnwll 5 G3
Nanternis Cerdgn 65 L3
Nantgaredig Carmth 50 F2
Nantglyn Denbgs 96 F1
Nantmel Powys 68 B2
Nantmor Gwynd 95 K4
Nant Peris Gwynd 95 K2
Nantwich Ches E 98 F3
Nantyglo Blae G 53 J6
Nant-y-moel Brdgnd 36 E2
Naphill Bucks 42 D2
Napton on the Hill Warwks 72 F3
Narberth Pembks 49 J4
Narborough Leics 87 G4
Narborough Norfk 91 H2
Nasareth Gwynd 95 H3
Naseby Nhants 87 K7
Nash Bucks 73 L7
Nash Newpt 37 M4
Nash Shrops 69 L1
Nassington Nhants 88 F4
Nateby Cumb 139 H6
Nateby Lancs 120 F2
National Memorial Arboretum Staffs 85 L1
National Motor Museum (Beaulieu) Hants 16 E2
National Space Centre C Leic 87 H3
Natland Cumb 129 L2
Naughton Suffk 78 B5
Naunton Gloucs 56 C4
Naunton Worcs 70 F6
Naunton Beauchamp Worcs 71 G4
Navenby Lincs 103 G2
Navestock Essex 45 K1
Navestock Side Essex 60 E8
Navidale House Hotel Highld 227 J5
Navity Highld 213 J2
Nawton N York 133 K3
Nayland Suffk 77 L7
Nazeing Essex 60 C6
Neap Shet 235 d5
Near Cotton Staffs 100 B4
Near Sawrey Cumb 137 K7
Neasden Gt Lon 44 E3
Neasham Darltn 141 H5
Neath Neath 51 L6
Neatham Hants 30 C4
Neatishead Norfk 107 H7
Nebo Cerdgn 66 D2
Nebo Conwy 96 C2
Nebo Gwynd 95 H3
Nebo IoA 108 F4
Necton Norfk 91 K2
Nedd Highld 224 D3
Nedging Suffk 78 B5
Nedging Tye Suffk 78 B4
Needham Norfk 92 F6
Needham Market Suffk 78 C4
Needingworth Cambs 75 L1
Neen Savage Shrops 84 C7
Neen Sollars Shrops 84 B8
Neenton Shrops 84 B6
Nefyn Gwynd 94 E4
Neilston E Rens 174 E6
Nelson Caerph 37 H2
Nelson Lancs 122 C3
Nemphlar S Lans 165 G1
Nempnett Thrubwell BaNES 38 D7
Nenthead Cumb 149 K6
Nenthorn Border 167 K2
Nercwys Flints 97 K1
Nereabolls Ag & B 170 E7
Nerston S Lans 175 H6
Nesbit Nthumb 168 E3
Nesfield N York 123 G1
Nesscliffe Shrops 98 B8
Neston Ches W 111 J6
Neston Wilts 39 K6
Netchwood Shrops 84 B5
Nether Alderley Ches E 113 J6
Netheravon Wilts 28 D2
Nether Blainslie Border 167 H2
Netherbrae Abers 216 F3
Nether Broughton Leics 102 B7
Netherburn S Lans 175 L8
Netherbury Dorset 13 L3
Netherby N York 123 L2
Nether Cerne Dorset 14 C3
Nethercleuch D & G 155 K5
Nether Compton Dorset 26 E7
Nether Crimond Abers 206 F2
Nether Dallachy Moray 215 H2
Netherend Gloucs 54 E7
Netherfield E Susx 20 E2
Netherfield Notts 101 L4
Nether Fingland S Lans 165 H7
Netherhampton Wilts 28 C5
Nether Handwick Angus 196 B7
Nether Haugh Rothm 115 H3
Netherhay Dorset 13 K2
Nether Headon Notts 116 C6
Nether Heage Derbys 101 G3
Nether Heyford Nhants 73 J3
Nether Howcleugh S Lans 165 K6
Nether Kellet Lancs 129 K6
Nether Kinmundy Abers 217 K5
Nether Langwith Notts 115 K7
Netherlaw D & G 146 C6
Netherley Abers 207 G6
Nethermill D & G 155 H5
Nethermuir Abers 217 G5
Netherne-on-the-Hill Surrey 32 B3
Netheroyd Hill Kirk 123 H6
Nether Padley Derbys 114 E6
Netherplace E Rens 174 F7
Nether Poppleton C York 133 J8
Netherseal Derbys 86 C2
Nether Silton N York 133 G2
Nether Stowey Somset 25 J4
Netherthong Kirk 123 H8
Netherton Angus 196 E5
Netherton Devon 7 K2
Netherton Dudley 85 G6
Netherton Kirk 123 H7
Netherton N Lans 175 K7
Netherton Nthumb 168 E7
Netherton P & K 195 J6
Netherton Sefton 111 K2
Netherton Stirlg 175 G3
Netherton Wakefd 123 K6
Nethertown Cumb 136 D5
Nethertown Highld 231 L1
Nethertown Staffs 100 C8
Netherurd Border 165 L1
Nether Wallop Hants 28 F4
Nether Wasdale Cumb 136 F6
Nether Westcote Gloucs 56 E4
Nether Whitacre Warwks 86 B5
Nether Whitecleuch S Lans 165 G5
Nether Winchendon Bucks 58 B5
Netherwitton Nthumb 158 D4
Nethy Bridge Highld 204 B2
Netley Hants 16 F2
Netley Marsh Hants 29 G8
Nettlebed Oxon 42 B3
Nettlebridge Somset 26 F2
Nettlecombe Dorset 13 M4
Nettleden Herts 59 G6
Nettleham Lincs 117 G6
Nettlestead Kent 33 H3
Nettlestead Green Kent 33 H3
Nettlestone IoW 17 H4
Nettlesworth Dur 151 G5
Nettleton Lincs 117 J2
Nettleton Wilts 39 J5
Netton Wilts 28 C4
Nevern Pembks 64 F6
Nevill Holt Leics 88 B5
New Abbey D & G 147 G2
New Aberdour Abers 217 G2
New Addington Gt Lon 45 G7
Newall Leeds 123 J2
New Alresford Hants 29 L5
New Alyth P & K 195 K6
Newark Ork 234 e4
Newark-on-Trent Notts 102 D2
Newarthill N Lans 175 K6
New Ash Green Kent 45 L6
New Balderton Notts 102 D3
New Barn Kent 45 L6
New Barnet Gt Lon 44 F2
Newbattle Mdloth 177 J5
New Bewick Nthumb 169 G5
Newbie D & G 147 L3
Newbiggin Cumb 138 C2
Newbiggin Cumb 138 F2
Newbiggin Cumb 148 F5
Newbiggin Dur 139 K2
Newbiggin N York 131 J3
Newbiggin-by-the-Sea Nthumb 159 H5
Newbigging Angus 187 H1
Newbigging Angus 195 L7
Newbigging Angus 196 C8
Newbigging S Lans 165 K1
Newbiggin-on-Lune Cumb 139 G6
New Bilton Warwks 86 F7
Newbold Derbys 115 G6
Newbold on Avon Warwks 86 F7
Newbold on Stour Warwks 72 B5
Newbold Pacey Warwks 72 C3
Newbold Verdon Leics 86 F3
New Bolingbroke Lincs 104 A2
Newborough C Pete 89 H3
Newborough IoA 108 E7
Newborough Staffs 100 C7
New Boultham Lincs 116 F7
Newbourne Suffk 78 F6
New Bradwell M Keyn 74 B6
New Brampton Derbys 115 G7
New Brancepeth Dur 151 G6
Newbridge C Edin 176 F4
Newbridge Caerph 37 K2
Newbridge Cnwll 2 D5
Newbridge D & G 155 G6
Newbridge Hants 28 F7
Newbridge IoW 16 E5
Newbridge Green Worcs 70 E6
Newbridge-on-Wye Powys 67 L3
New Brighton Wirral 111 J3
Newbrough Nthumb 149 L2
New Buckenham Norfk 92 C5
Newbuildings Devon 11 J4
Newburgh Abers 207 J1
Newburgh Abers 217 H3
Newburgh Fife 186 D4
Newburgh Lancs 121 G7
Newburgh Priory N York 133 H4
Newburn N u Ty 150 F2
Newbury Somset 27 G2
Newbury W Berk 41 J6
Newbury Park Gt Lon 45 J3
Newby Cumb 138 E3
Newby Lancs 122 B2
Newby N York 130 D5
Newby N York 142 B5
Newby Bridge Cumb 129 H3
Newby East Cumb 148 E4
New Byth Abers 216 F4
Newby West Cumb 148 C4
Newcastle Mons 54 C5
Newcastle Shrops 82 E6
Newcastle Airport Nthumb 158 F7
Newcastle Emlyn Carmth 65 J6
Newcastleton Border 156 E5

Newcastle-under-Lyme Staffs 99 J4
Newcastle upon Tyne N u Ty 151 G3
Newchapel Pembks 65 H6
Newchapel Surrey 32 C5
Newchurch IoW 17 G5
Newchurch Kent 34 E7
Newchurch Mons 38 C2
Newchurch Powys 68 E4
Newchurch Staffs 100 D7
New Costessey Norfk 92 E2
Newcraighall C Edin 177 J4
New Crofton Wakefd 124 B6
New Cross Gt Lon 45 G5
New Cross Somset 26 B7
New Cumnock E Ayrs 164 C6
New Deer Abers 217 G5
New Denham Bucks 43 H4
Newdigate Surrey 31 K3
New Duston Nhants 73 K3
New Earswick C York 133 J7
New Edlington Donc 115 K2
New Elgin Moray 214 F3
New Ellerby E R Yk 126 E3
Newell Green Br For 42 E6
New Eltham Gt Lon 45 H5
New End Worcs 71 J3
Newenden Kent 33 L7
New England C Pete 89 H4
Newent Gloucs 55 G3
New Ferry Wirral 111 K4
Newfield Dur 150 F7
Newfield Highld 223 H6
New Fletton C Pete 89 H4
New Forest National Park 16 C2
Newgale Pembks 48 E3
New Galloway D & G 154 B6
Newgate Street Herts 59 M6
New Gilston Fife 187 G5
New Grimsby IoS 2 a1
Newhall Ches E 98 E4
New Hartley Nthumb 159 H6
Newhaven C Edin 177 H3
Newhaven E Susx 19 L5
New Haw Surrey 43 H7
New Hedges Pembks 49 J6
New Holland N Linc 126 D5
Newholm N York 143 H5
New Houghton Derbys 115 J7
New Houghton Norfk 105 J6
Newhouse N Lans 175 L6
New Hutton Cumb 130 B2
Newick E Susx 19 L2
Newington Kent 35 G6
Newington Kent 46 E6
Newington Oxon 41 L2
New Inn Carmth 66 B6
New Inn Torfn 53 L7
New Invention Shrops 82 F7
New Lakenham Norfk 92 F3
New Lanark S Lans 165 G2
New Lanark Village S Lans 165 G2
Newland C KuH 126 D4
Newland Gloucs 54 D6
Newland N York 125 G5
Newland Somset 24 C4
Newland Worcs 70 E5
Newlandrig Mdloth 177 K6
Newlands Border 156 E4
Newlands Nthumb 150 D4
Newlands of Dundurcas Moray 215 G4
New Langholm D & G 156 C5
New Leake Lincs 104 C2
New Leeds Abers 217 J4
New Lodge Barns 123 L8
New Longton Lancs 121 G5
New Luce D & G 144 E3
Newlyn Cnwll 2 E5
Newmachar Abers 207 G2
Newmains N Lans 175 L6
New Malden Gt Lon 44 E6
Newman's Green Suffk 77 K5
Newmarket Suffk 76 F2
Newmarket W Isls 232 f2
New Marske R & Cl 142 D3
New Marston Oxon 57 K6
New Mill Abers 206 E8
Newmill Border 167 G7
New Mill Cnwll 2 E4
New Mill Kirk 123 H8
Newmill Moray 215 K4
Newmillerdam Wakefd 123 L7
Newmill of Inshewan Angus 196 C4
Newmills C Edin 177 G5
New Mills Derbys 113 M4
Newmills Fife 176 D2
Newmills Mons 54 D6
New Mills Powys 82 C4
Newmiln P & K 186 B2
Newmilns E Ayrs 164 B2
New Milton Hants 16 B4
New Mistley Essex 62 D2
New Moat Pembks 49 H3
Newney Green Essex 61 G6
Newnham Hants 30 B2
Newnham Herts 75 J6
Newnham Kent 34 C3
Newnham Nhants 73 H3
Newnham Worcs 70 B2
Newnham on Severn Gloucs 55 G5
New Ollerton Notts 116 A7
New Oscott Birm 85 K5
New Pitsligo Abers 217 G3
Newport Cnwll 9 J7
Newport E R Yk 125 K4
Newport Essex 76 D7
Newport Gloucs 39 G2
Newport Highld 227 K4
Newport IoW 16 F5
Newport Newpt 37 L3
Newport Pembks 64 E6
Newport Wrekin 99 H8
Newport-on-Tay Fife 187 G2
Newport Pagnell M Keyn 74 C5
Newport Pagnell Services M Keyn 74 C5
New Prestwick S Ayrs 163 J4
New Quay Cerdgn 65 L3
Newquay Cnwll 4 C4
Newquay Zoo Cnwll 4 C4
New Rackheath Norfk 93 G2
New Radnor Powys 68 E3
New Ridley Nthumb 150 D3
New Romney Kent 21 L2
New Rossington Donc 115 L2
New Sauchie Clacks 185 J7
Newseat Abers 216 D7
Newsham Lancs 121 G4
Newsham N York 132 E3
Newsham N York 140 E5
Newsham Nthumb 159 H6
New Sharlston Wakefd 124 B6
Newsholme E R Yk 125 H5
New Silksworth Sundld 151 J4
Newsome Kirk 123 H7
New Somerby Lincs 102 F5
New Southgate Crematorium Gt Lon 44 F2
Newstead Border 167 H3
Newstead Notts 101 K3
Newstead Nthumb 169 H4
New Stevenston N Lans 175 K6
Newthorpe Notts 101 J4
New Thundersley Essex 46 C3
Newton Ag & B 182 F7
Newton Border 167 J5
Newton Brdgnd 36 C5
Newton C Beds 75 J5
Newton Cambs 76 B5
Newton Cambs 90 B1
Newton Ches W 98 D1
Newton Ches W 112 B7
Newton Cumb 128 F5
Newton Derbys 101 H2
Newton Herefs 53 M2
Newton Herefs 69 K4
Newton Highld 212 F4
Newton Highld 213 H5
Newton Highld 213 J2
Newton Highld 231 L5
Newton Lincs 103 H5
Newton Mdloth 177 J4
Newton Moray 214 E2
Newton Moray 215 H2
Newton Nhants 88 C6
Newton Norfk 91 J1
Newton Notts 102 B4
Newton Nthumb 150 C3
Newton S Lans 165 H3
Newton S Lans 175 H6
Newton Sandw 85 J5
Newton Staffs 100 B7
Newton Suffk 77 K6
Newton W Loth 176 E3
Newton Warwks 87 G7
Newton Abbot Devon 7 K2
Newton Arlosh Cumb 147 L4
Newton Aycliffe Dur 141 G3
Newton Bewley Hartpl 141 K2
Newton Blossomville M Keyn 74 D4
Newton Bromswold Nhants 74 E2
Newton Burgoland Leics 86 D2
Newton-by-the-Sea Nthumb 169 J4
Newton by Toft Lincs 117 H4
Newton Ferrers Devon 6 E6
Newton Ferry W Isls 232 c5
Newton Flotman Norfk 92 E4
Newtongrange Mdloth 177 J5
Newton Green Mons 38 D3
Newton Harcourt Leics 87 J4
Newton Heath Manch 113 K2
Newtonhill Abers 207 G6
Newton-in-Bowland Lancs 121 K1
Newton Kyme N York 124 C2
Newton-le-Willows N York 132 C2
Newton-le-Willows St Hel 112 E3
Newtonloan Mdloth 177 J5
Newton Longville Bucks 58 D2
Newton Mearns E Rens 174 F7
Newtonmill Angus 196 F4
Newtonmore Highld 203 H5
Newton Morrell N York 141 G5
Newton of Balcanquhal P & K 186 B5
Newton of Balcormo Fife 187 H6
Newton-on-Ouse N York 133 H7
Newton-on-Rawcliffe N York 134 C2
Newton-on-the-Moor Nthumb 158 F2
Newton on Trent Lincs 116 D6
Newton Poppleford Devon 12 E4
Newton Purcell Oxon 57 L3
Newton Regis Warwks 86 C3
Newton Reigny Cumb 138 C2
Newton St Cyres Devon 11 K5
Newton St Faith Norfk 92 F1
Newton St Loe BaNES 39 G7
Newton St Petrock Devon 9 K3
Newton Solney Derbys 100 F7
Newton Stacey Hants 29 H4
Newton Stewart D & G 145 J3
Newton Tony Wilts 28 E4
Newton Tracey Devon 23 H6
Newton under Roseberry R & Cl 142 C5
Newton upon Derwent E R Yk 125 H2
Newton Valence Hants 30 B5
Newton Wamphray D & G 155 K3
Newton with Scales Lancs 120 F4
Newtown Cumb 147 J5
Newtown Cumb 148 E3
Newtown D & G 164 F7
Newtown Devon 12 D3
Newtown Devon 24 B6
New Town Dorset 27 L7
New Town Dorset 27 M7
New Town E Susx 19 M2
Newtown Gloucs 54 F7
Newtown Hants 29 L8
Newtown Herefs 70 B5
Newtown Herefs 70 C6
Newtown Highld 202 B4
Newtown IoW 16 E4
Newtown Nthumb 168 F4
Newtown Poole 15 K4
Newtown Powys 82 C5
Newtown Shrops 98 C6
Newtown Somset 25 L8
Newtown Staffs 99 K1
Newtown Wigan 112 E1
Newtown Worcs 70 F4
Newtown Linford Leics 87 G2
Newtown of Beltrees Rens 174 D6
Newtown St Boswells Border 167 J3
New Tredegar Caerph 53 H7
New Trows S Lans 164 F2
Newtyle Angus 195 L7
New Walsoken Cambs 90 C2
New Waltham NE Lin 118 C1
New Winton E Loth 177 L4
Newyork Ag & B 182 D5
New York Lincs 103 L2
New York N Tyne 159 H7
Neyland Pembks 49 G6
Nicholashayne Devon 25 H7
Nicholaston Swans 51 G7
Nidd N York 132 D7
Nigg C Aber 207 H5
Nigg Highld 223 H6
Nigg Ferry Highld 223 H7
Ninebanks Nthumb 149 K4
Nine Elms Swindn 40 C3
Ninfield E Susx 20 E3
Ningwood IoW 16 E5
Nisbet Border 167 K4
Nisbet Hill Border 179 G7
Niton IoW 17 F6
Nitshill C Glas 174 F6
Nocton Lincs 117 H8
Noke Oxon 57 K5
Nolton Pembks 48 E4
Nolton Haven Pembks 48 E4

No Man's Heath Ches W 98 D3
No Man's Heath Warwks 86 C2
Nomansland Devon 11 J3
Nomansland Wilts 28 E7
Noneley Shrops 98 C6
Nonington Kent 35 H4
Nook Cumb 129 L3
Norbiton Gt Lon 44 D6
Norbury Ches E 98 E3
Norbury Derbys 100 C4
Norbury Gt Lon 44 F6
Norbury Shrops 83 G5
Norbury Staffs 99 H7
Norchard Worcs 70 F2
Nordelph Norfk 90 D4
Nordley Shrops 84 C4
Norfolk Broads Norfk 93 K2
Norham Nthumb 179 J8
Norley Ches W 112 E6
Norleywood Hants 16 D3
Normanby Lincs 117 G4
Normanby N Linc 125 K7
Normanby N York 134 B3
Normanby R & Cl 142 C4
Normanby le Wold Lincs 117 J3
Normandy Surrey 30 F2
Norman's Green Devon 12 D2
Normanton C Derb 101 G5
Normanton Leics 102 D4
Normanton Notts 102 B2
Normanton Wakefd 124 B6
Normanton le Heath Leics 86 D2
Normanton on Cliffe Lincs 102 F4
Normanton on Soar Notts 101 K7
Normanton on the Wolds Notts 101 L6
Normanton on Trent Notts 116 C7
Norris Green Lpool 111 L3
Norris Hill Leics 86 D1
Norristhorpe Kirk 123 J6
Northall Bucks 58 F4
Northallerton N York 141 J7
Northam C Sotn 29 H8
Northam Devon 23 G5
Northampton Nhants 73 L3
Northampton Worcs 70 E2
Northampton Services Nhants 73 K3
North Anston Rothm 115 K5
North Ascot Br For 42 E6
North Aston Oxon 57 J3
Northaw Herts 59 L7
Northay Somset 13 H1
North Baddesley Hants 29 H7
North Ballachulish Highld 191 L4
North Barrow Somset 26 E5
North Barsham Norfk 105 L5
North Benfleet Essex 46 C3
North Berwick E Loth 178 C2
North Boarhunt Hants 17 H1
Northborough C Pete 89 H3
Northbourne Kent 35 J4
North Bovey Devon 11 H7
North Bradley Wilts 27 J1
North Brentor Devon 10 C8
North Brewham Somset 27 G4
Northbrook Hants 29 K4
North Buckland Devon 23 G4
North Burlingham Norfk 93 H2
North Cadbury Somset 26 F6
North Carlton Lincs 116 F6
North Carlton Notts 115 L4
North Cave E R Yk 125 K4
North Cerney Gloucs 56 A6
North Chailey E Susx 19 K2
Northchapel W Susx 30 F5
North Charford Hants 28 D7
North Charlton Nthumb 169 H5
North Cheam Gt Lon 44 E6
North Cheriton Somset 27 G6
North Chideock Dorset 13 K4
Northchurch Herts 58 F6
North Cliffe E R Yk 125 K3
North Clifton Notts 116 D6
North Cockerington Lincs 118 E4
North Connel Ag & B 182 C1
North Cornelly Brdgnd 36 C4
North Cotes Lincs 118 E2
Northcott Devon 9 J6
Northcourt Oxon 57 J7
North Cove Suffk 93 K5
North Cowton N York 141 G6
North Crawley M Keyn 74 D5
North Creake Norfk 105 K5
North Curry Somset 25 L6
North Dalton E R Yk 125 L1
North Deighton N York 124 B1
North Devon Crematorium Devon 23 H5
Northdown Kent 35 K2
North Downs 34 B4
North Duffield N York 125 G3
North Duntulm Highld 218 C6
North East Surrey Crematorium Gt Lon 44 E6
North Elmham Norfk 106 B7
North Elmsall Wakefd 124 D7
North End C Port 17 J3
North End Essex 61 G4
North End Hants 28 C7
North End Nhants 74 D2
North End W Susx 18 D5
Northend Warwks 72 E4
Northenden Manch 113 J4
North Erradale Highld 219 H5
North Evington C Leic 87 J3
North Fambridge Essex 61 K7
North Ferriby E R Yk 126 B5
Northfield Birm 85 H7
Northfield C Aber 207 G4
Northfield E R Yk 126 C5
Northfields Lincs 88 E2
Northfleet Kent 45 M5
North Frodingham E R Yk 135 H8
North Gorley Hants 15 M1
North Green Suffk 79 G3
North Greetwell Lincs 117 G6
North Grimston N York 134 C6
North Haven Shet 235 e7
North Hayling Hants 17 K2
North Hertfordshire Memorial Park & Crematorium Herts 59 K2
North Hill Cnwll 5 L1
North Hillingdon Gt Lon 43 H4
North Hinksey Village Oxon 57 J6
North Holmwood Surrey 31 K3
North Huish Devon 7 G5
North Hykeham Lincs 116 F7
Northiam E Susx 21 G2
Northill C Beds 75 G5
Northington Hants 29 K4
North Kelsey Lincs 117 H2
North Kessock Highld 213 G5
North Killingholme N Linc 126 E6
North Kilvington N York 132 F3
North Kilworth Leics 87 H6
North Kyme Lincs 103 J3
North Landing E R Yk 135 K5
Northlands Lincs 104 B2
Northleach Gloucs 56 C5
North Lee Bucks 58 D6
Northleigh Devon 12 F3
North Leigh Oxon 57 H5
North Leverton with Habblesthorpe Notts 116 C5
Northlew Devon 10 D5
North Littleton Worcs 71 J5
North Lopham Norfk 92 C6
North Luffenham Rutlnd 88 D3
North Marden W Susx 30 D7
North Marston Bucks 58 C4
North Middleton Mdloth 177 K6
North Millbrex Abers 216 F5
North Milmain D & G 144 C4
North Molton Devon 24 B5
Northmoor Oxon 57 H7
North Moreton Oxon 41 K3
Northmuir Angus 196 C5
North Mundham W Susx 18 B5
North Muskham Notts 102 D2
North Newbald E R Yk 125 L3
North Newington Oxon 72 E6
North Newnton Wilts 40 C8
North Newton Somset 25 L5
Northney Hants 17 K2
North Nibley Gloucs 39 H2
Northolt Gt Lon 43 J4
Northop Flints 111 H7
Northop Hall Flints 111 J7
North Ormesby Middsb 142 B4
North Ormsby Lincs 118 C3
Northorpe Kirk 123 J6
Northorpe Lincs 103 K5
Northorpe Lincs 116 E3
North Otterington N York 132 E2
North Owersby Lincs 117 H3
Northowram Calder 123 G5
North Perrott Somset 13 L1
North Petherton Somset 25 L5
North Petherwin Cnwll 9 H6
North Pickenham Norfk 91 J3
North Piddle Worcs 71 G4
North Poorton Dorset 13 M3
Northport Dorset 15 H5
North Queensferry Fife 176 F3
North Rauceby Lincs 103 G3
Northrepps Norfk 106 F5
North Reston Lincs 118 E5
North Rigton N York 123 K1
North Rode Ches E 113 K7
North Ronaldsay Ork 234 e3
North Ronaldsay Airport Ork 234 e3
North Runcton Norfk 90 F1
North Scarle Lincs 116 D7
North Shian Ag & B 191 H7
North Shields N Tyne 151 J2
North Shoebury Sthend 46 F3
North Shore Bpool 120 D3
North Side C Pete 89 K4
North Somercotes Lincs 118 F3
North Stainley N York 132 D4
North Stifford Thurr 45 L4
North Stoke BaNES 39 G6
North Stoke Oxon 41 L3
North Stoke W Susx 18 D4
North Street Kent 34 D3
North Street W Berk 41 M6
North Sunderland Nthumb 169 J3
North Tamerton Cnwll 9 J5
North Tawton Devon 10 F4
North Third Stirlg 175 K1
North Thoresby Lincs 118 D2
Northton W Isls 232 d5
North Town Devon 10 D3
North Town Somset 26 E3
North Town W & M 42 E4
North Tuddenham Norfk 92 C2
North Uist W Isls 233 b6
Northumberland National Park Nthumb 157 L3
North Walsham Norfk 107 G6
North Waltham Hants 29 K3
North Warnborough Hants 30 B2
North Weald Bassett Essex 60 D7
North Wheatley Notts 116 C4
Northwich Ches W 112 F6
Northwick Worcs 70 E3
North Widcombe BaNES 38 E8
North Willingham Lincs 117 K4
North Wingfield Derbys 115 H8
North Witham Lincs 102 F7
Northwold Norfk 91 H4
Northwood C Stke 99 K3
Northwood Gt Lon 43 H3
Northwood IoW 16 F4
Northwood Shrops 98 C6
Northwood Green Gloucs 55 G5
North Wootton Dorset 26 F8
North Wootton Norfk 105 G7
North Wootton Somset 26 E3
North Wraxall Wilts 39 J5
North York Moors National Park 142 F6
Norton Donc 124 E7
Norton E Susx 19 M5
Norton Gloucs 55 J3
Norton Halton 112 D5
Norton Nhants 73 H2
Norton Notts 115 L6
Norton Powys 68 F2
Norton S on T 141 K3
Norton Shrops 84 D4
Norton Suffk 77 L2
Norton W Susx 18 C4
Norton Wilts 39 K4
Norton Worcs 70 F4
Norton Worcs 71 J5
Norton Bavant Wilts 27 K3
Norton Bridge Staffs 99 K6
Norton Canes Staffs 85 H2
Norton Canes Services Staffs 85 H3
Norton Canon Herefs 69 H5
Norton Disney Lincs 102 E2
Norton Fitzwarren Somset 25 J6
Norton Green IoW 16 D5
Norton Hawkfield BaNES 38 E7
Norton Heath Essex 60 F6
Norton in Hales Shrops 99 G5
Norton in the Moors C Stke 99 K3

Norton-Juxta-Twycross Leics 86 D3
Norton-le-Clay N York 132 F5
Norton Lindsey Warwks 72 B2
Norton Little Green Suffk 77 L2
Norton Malreward BaNES 38 E7
Norton-on-Derwent N York 134 C5
Norton St Philip Somset 27 H1
Norton Subcourse Norfk 93 J4
Norton sub Hamdon Somset 26 C7
Norwell Notts 102 C1
Norwell Woodhouse Notts 116 B8
Norwich Norfk 92 F2
Norwich Airport Norfk 92 E2
Norwich (St Faith) Crematorium Norfk 92 F1
Norwick Shet 235 e1
Norwood Clacks 185 J8
Norwood Green Gt Lon 43 J5
Norwood Hill Surrey 31 L3
Norwoodside Cambs 90 B4
Noss Mayo Devon 6 E6
Nosterfield N York 132 D4
Nostie Highld 210 D8
Notgrove Gloucs 56 C4
Nottage Brdgnd 36 C5
Nottingham C Nott 101 L5
Notton Wakefd 123 L7
Notton Wilts 39 K6
Noutard's Green Worcs 70 E2
Nuffield Oxon 42 A3
Nunburnholme E R Yk 125 K2
Nuneaton Warwks 86 D5
Nunhead Gt Lon 45 G5
Nun Monkton N York 133 H7
Nunney Somset 27 G3
Nunnington N York 133 K4
Nunsthorpe NE Lin 127 G8
Nunthorpe C York 124 F1
Nunthorpe Middsb 142 C4
Nunthorpe Village Middsb 142 C5
Nunton Wilts 28 D6
Nunwick N York 132 E5
Nursling Hants 29 G7
Nutbourne W Susx 17 L2
Nutbourne W Susx 18 E3
Nutfield Surrey 32 B3
Nuthall Notts 101 K4
Nuthampstead Herts 76 B7
Nuthurst W Susx 31 K6
Nutley E Susx 32 D7
Nuttall Bury 122 B7
Nybster Highld 231 L3
Nyetimber W Susx 18 B6
Nyewood W Susx 30 D6
Nymans W Susx 31 L5
Nymet Rowland Devon 11 G4
Nymet Tracey Devon 11 G5
Nympsfield Gloucs 55 J7
Nynehead Somset 25 H6
Nyton W Susx 18 C5

O

Oadby Leics 87 J4
Oad Street Kent 34 B3
Oakamoor Staffs 100 B4
Oakbank W Loth 176 E5
Oak Cross Devon 10 D5
Oakdale Caerph 37 J2
Oake Somset 25 J6
Oaken Staffs 84 F3
Oakenclough Lancs 121 H2
Oakengates Wrekin 84 C2
Oakenshaw Dur 150 F7
Oakenshaw Kirk 123 H5
Oakford Cerdgn 66 B3
Oakford Devon 24 E6
Oakham Rutlnd 88 C2
Oakhanger Hants 30 C4
Oakhill Somset 26 F3
Oakington Cambs 76 B2
Oakle Street Gloucs 55 H4
Oakley Bed 74 E4
Oakley Bucks 57 M5
Oakley Fife 176 D1
Oakley Hants 29 K2
Oakley Suffk 92 E7
Oakridge Lynch Gloucs 55 K7
Oaksey Wilts 39 M2
Oakthorpe Leics 86 D2
Oakwood C Derb 101 G5
Oakworth C Brad 122 F3
Oare Kent 34 D3
Oare Somset 24 C3
Oare Wilts 40 D7
Oasby Lincs 103 G5
Oath Somset 26 B6
Oathlaw Angus 196 D5
Oatlands Park Surrey 43 H7
Oban Ag & B 182 B2
Oban Airport Ag & B 182 C1
Obley Shrops 83 G7
Obney P & K 195 G8
Oborne Dorset 26 F7
Occold Suffk 78 D1
Occumster Highld 231 J7
Ochiltree E Ayrs 163 L5
Ockbrook Derbys 101 H5
Ocker Hill Sandw 85 H5
Ockham Surrey 31 H1
Ockle Highld 190 B3
Ockley Surrey 31 J4
Ocle Pychard Herefs 69 L5
Odcombe Somset 26 D7
Odd Down BaNES 39 H7
Oddingley Worcs 71 G3
Oddington Gloucs 56 E3
Oddington Oxon 57 K5
Odell Bed 74 D3
Odiham Hants 30 C2
Odsal C Brad 123 H5
Odsey Cambs 75 K6
Odstock Wilts 28 D6
Odstone Leics 86 E3
Offchurch Warwks 72 D2
Offenham Worcs 71 J5
Offerton Stockp 113 K4
Offham E Susx 19 L3
Offham Kent 33 H2
Offham W Susx 18 D4
Offord Cluny Cambs 75 J2
Offord D'Arcy Cambs 75 J2
Offton Suffk 78 C5
Offwell Devon 12 F3
Ogbourne Maizey Wilts 40 D6
Ogbourne St Andrew Wilts 40 D6
Ogbourne St George Wilts 40 D5
Ogle Nthumb 158 E6
Oglet Lpool 112 C5
Ogmore V Glam 36 D5
Ogmore-by-Sea V Glam 36 D5
Ogmore Vale Brdgnd 36 E3
Okeford Fitzpaine Dorset 14 F1
Okehampton Devon 10 E5
Oker Side Derbys 100 F1
Okewood Hill Surrey 31 J4
Old Nhants 87 L8
Old Aberdeen C Aber 207 H4
Old Alresford Hants 29 L5
Oldany Highld 224 D2
Old Auchenbrack D & G 154 D3
Old Basford C Nott 101 K4
Old Basing Hants 30 A2
Old Beetley Norfk 106 A8
Oldberrow Warwks 71 K2
Old Bewick Nthumb 169 G5
Old Bolingbroke Lincs 118 E8
Old Bramhope Leeds 123 J2
Old Brampton Derbys 115 G6
Old Bridge of Urr D & G 146 D2
Old Buckenham Norfk 92 C5
Old Burghclere Hants 41 J8
Oldbury Sandw 85 H5
Oldbury Shrops 84 C5
Oldbury Warwks 86 C5
Oldbury-on-Severn S Glos 38 E2
Oldbury on the Hill Gloucs 39 J3
Old Byland N York 133 H3
Old Cantley Donc 115 L2
Oldcastle Mons 53 L3
Old Catton Norfk 92 F2
Old Clee NE Lin 127 G8
Old Cleeve Somset 25 G3
Old Colwyn Conwy 110 B6
Oldcotes Notts 115 L4
Old Dailly S Ayrs 152 F3
Old Dalby Leics 102 A7
Old Deer Abers 217 J5
Old Edlington Donc 115 K3
Old Ellerby E R Yk 126 E3
Old Felixstowe Suffk 79 G7
Oldfield Worcs 70 E2
Old Fletton C Pete 89 H4
Oldford Somset 27 H2
Old Forge Herefs 54 E4
Old Grimsby IoS 2 a1
Old Hall Green Herts 60 B4
Oldham Oldham 113 L1
Oldham Crematorium Oldham 113 K2
Oldhamstocks E Loth 178 F4
Old Harlow Essex 60 D5
Old Hunstanton Norfk 105 G4
Old Hurst Cambs 89 K7
Old Hutton Cumb 130 B2
Old Inns Services N Lans 175 K3
Old Kilpatrick W Duns 174 E4
Old Knebworth Herts 59 L4
Old Lakenham Norfk 92 F3
Oldland S Glos 38 F6
Old Langho Lancs 121 K4
Old Leake Lincs 104 C3
Old Malton N York 134 C5
Oldmeldrum Abers 216 F8
Oldmill Cnwll 6 B2
Old Milverton Warwks 72 C2
Oldmixon N Som 37 M8
Old Newton Suffk 78 C3
Old Portlethen Abers 207 H6
Old Radford C Nott 101 K4
Old Radnor Powys 68 E3
Old Rayne Abers 216 D8
Old Romney Kent 21 K2
Old Shoreham W Susx 19 G4
Oldshoremore Highld 228 C4
Old Sodbury S Glos 39 H4
Old Somerby Lincs 102 F5
Oldstead N York 133 H4
Old Stratford Nhants 73 L6
Old Struan P & K 194 C4
Old Swinford Dudley 84 F6
Old Thirsk N York 132 F3
Old Town Cumb 130 B3
Old Town E Susx 20 C5
Old Town IoS 2 b2
Old Trafford Traffd 113 J3
Oldwall Cumb 148 E3
Oldwalls Swans 50 F6
Old Warden C Beds 75 G5
Old Weston Cambs 89 G7
Old Wick Highld 231 L5
Old Windsor W & M 43 G5
Old Wives Lees Kent 34 E4
Old Woking Surrey 43 G8
Olgrinmore Highld 231 G5
Olive Green Staffs 100 C8
Oliver's Battery Hants 29 J6
Ollaberry Shet 235 c3
Ollach Highld 209 H6
Ollerton Ches E 113 H6
Ollerton Notts 116 A7
Ollerton Shrops 98 F7
Olney M Keyn 74 C4
Olrig House Highld 231 H3
Olton Solhll 85 K6
Olveston S Glos 38 E3
Ombersley Worcs 70 E2
Ompton Notts 116 B7
Onchan IoM 237 d5
Onecote Staffs 100 B2
Onibury Shrops 83 J7
Onich Highld 191 K4
Onllwyn Neath 52 C6
Onneley Staffs 99 H4
Onslow Green Essex 61 G4
Onslow Village Surrey 31 G2
Onston Ches W 112 E6
Opinan Highld 219 H6
Orbliston Moray 215 G3
Orbost Highld 208 D5
Orby Lincs 119 G7
Orchard Portman Somset 25 K6
Orcheston Wilts 28 B3
Orcop Herefs 54 C3
Orcop Hill Herefs 54 C3
Ord Abers 216 C3
Ordhead Abers 206 C3
Ordie Abers 205 K5
Ordiequish Moray 215 H3
Ordsall Notts 116 B5
Ore E Susx 21 G4
Orford Suffk 79 J4
Orford Warrtn 112 E4
Organford Dorset 15 H4
Orkney Islands Ork 234 c6
Orkney Neolithic Ork 234 b6
Orlestone Kent 34 D7
Orleton Herefs 69 J2
Orleton Worcs 70 C2
Orlingbury Nhants 74 C1
Ormesby R & Cl 142 C4
Ormesby St Margaret Norfk 93 K1
Ormesby St Michael Norfk 93 K1
Ormiscaig Highld 219 K4
Ormiston E Loth 177 L4
Ormsaigmore Highld 189 L4
Ormsary Ag & B 172 C4
Ormskirk Lancs 120 F8
Oronsay Ag & B 171 G2
Orphir Ork 234 b6
Orpington Gt Lon 45 J6
Orrell Sefton 111 K3
Orrell Wigan 112 D2
Orroland D & G 146 D5
Orsett Thurr 45 M4
Orslow Staffs 84 E1
Orston Notts 102 C4
Orton Cumb 138 F5
Orton Nhants 88 B7
Orton Staffs 84 F4
Orton Longueville C Pete 89 H4
Orton-on-the-Hill Leics 86 C3
Orton Waterville C Pete 89 H4
Orwell Cambs 75 L4
Osbaldeston Lancs 121 J4
Osbaldwick C York 124 F1
Osbaston Leics 86 E3
Osbaston Shrops 97 L7
Osborne House IoW 17 G4
Osbournby Lincs 103 H5

Oscroft Ches W 112 D7
Ose Highld 208 E6
Osgathorpe Leics 101 H8
Osgodby Lincs 117 H3
Osgodby N York 124 F4
Osgodby N York 135 G3
Oskaig Highld 209 H6
Oskamull Ag & B 189 L7
Osmaston Derbys 100 D4
Osmington Dorset 14 D5
Osmington Mills Dorset 14 E6
Osmondthorpe Leeds 123 L4
Osmotherley N York 141 K7
Osney Oxon 57 J6
Ospringe Kent 34 D3
Ossett Wakefd 123 K6
Ossington Notts 116 C8
Osterley Gt Lon 44 D5
Oswaldkirk N York 133 K4
Oswaldtwistle Lancs 121 L5
Oswestry Shrops 97 L6
Otford Kent 32 F2
Otham Kent 33 K3
Othery Somset 26 B5
Otley Leeds 123 J2
Otley Suffk 78 E4
Otterbourne Hants 29 J6
Otterburn N York 131 G7
Otterburn Nthumb 157 M4
Otter Ferry Ag & B 172 F2
Otterham Cnwll 8 F6
Otterhampton Somset 25 K3
Otternish W Isls 232 c5
Ottershaw Surrey 43 G7
Otterswick Shet 235 d3
Otterton Devon 12 E5
Ottery St Mary Devon 12 E4
Ottinge Kent 34 F6
Ottringham E R Yk 127 G5
Oughterside Cumb 147 K6
Oughtibridge Sheff 114 F3
Oughtrington Warrtn 113 G4
Oulston N York 133 H5
Oulton Cumb 147 M5
Oulton Norfk 106 D6
Oulton Staffs 99 K5
Oulton Suffk 93 L5
Oulton Broad Suffk 93 L5
Oulton Street Norfk 106 D6
Oundle Nhants 88 F6
Ounsdale Staffs 84 F5
Our Dynamic Earth C Edin 177 H4
Ousby Cumb 149 G7
Ousden Suffk 77 G3
Ousefleet E R Yk 125 K6
Ouston Dur 151 G4
Outgate Cumb 137 K7
Outhgill Cumb 139 H6
Outhill Warwks 71 K2
Outlane Kirk 123 G6
Out Rawcliffe Lancs 120 E3
Outwell Norfk 90 D3
Outwood Surrey 32 B4
Outwoods Staffs 99 H8
Ouzlewell Green Leeds 123 L5
Over Cambs 75 L1
Overbury Worcs 71 G6
Overcombe Dorset 14 D6
Over Compton Dorset 26 E7
Overdale Crematorium Bolton 121 K8
Over Haddon Derbys 114 D7
Over Kellet Lancs 129 L5
Over Kiddington Oxon 57 H4
Overleigh Somset 26 C4
Over Norton Oxon 56 F3
Over Peover Ches E 113 H6
Overpool Ches W 111 L6
Overscaig Hotel Highld 225 J4
Overseal Derbys 86 C1
Over Silton N York 133 G2
Oversland Kent 34 E3
Overstone Nhants 74 B2
Over Stowey Somset 25 J4
Overstrand Norfk 106 F4
Over Stratton Somset 26 B7
Overthorpe Nhants 72 F6
Overton C Aber 207 G3
Overton Hants 29 K2
Overton Lancs 129 J7
Overton N York 133 H7
Overton Shrops 69 K1
Overton Swans 50 F7
Overton Wakefd 123 K7
Overton Wrexhm 98 A4
Overtown N Lans 175 L7
Over Wallop Hants 28 F4
Over Whitacre Warwks 86 B5
Over Worton Oxon 57 H3
Oving Bucks 58 C4
Oving W Susx 18 B5
Ovingdean Br & H 19 K5
Ovingham Nthumb 150 D3
Ovington Dur 140 E4
Ovington Essex 77 H6
Ovington Hants 29 K5
Ovington Norfk 91 K3
Ovington Nthumb 150 D3
Ower Hants 28 F7
Owermoigne Dorset 14 E5
Owlerton Sheff 115 G4
Owlsmoor Br For 42 D7
Owlswick Bucks 58 C6
Owmby Lincs 117 G4
Owmby Lincs 117 H1
Owslebury Hants 29 K6
Owston Donc 124 E7
Owston Leics 87 L3
Owston Ferry N Linc 116 D2
Owstwick E R Yk 127 G4
Owthorne E R Yk 127 H5
Owthorpe Notts 102 A5
Owton Manor Hartpl 141 L2
Oxborough Norfk 91 G3
Oxcombe Lincs 118 D6
Oxenholme Cumb 129 L2
Oxenhope C Brad 122 F4
Oxen Park Cumb 129 G3
Oxenpill Somset 26 C3
Oxenton Gloucs 55 L2
Oxenwood Wilts 40 F8
Oxford Oxon 57 K6
Oxford Airport Oxon 57 J5
Oxford Crematorium Oxon 57 K6
Oxford Services Oxon 57 L6
Oxhey Herts 43 J2
Oxhill Warwks 72 C5
Oxley Wolves 84 F3
Oxley Green Essex 61 L5
Oxlode Cambs 90 C6
Oxnam Border 167 L5
Oxnead Norfk 106 F7
Oxshott Surrey 43 J7
Oxspring Barns 114 F2
Oxted Surrey 32 D3
Oxton Border 178 B7
Oxton N York 124 D2
Oxton Notts 101 M3
Oxton Wirral 111 J4
Oxwich Swans 51 G7
Oxwich Green Swans 50 F7
Oykel Bridge Hotel Highld 221 K2
Oyne Abers 206 D1
Oystermouth Swans 51 H7

P

Pabail W Isls 232 g2
Packington Leics 86 D1
Packmoor C Stke 99 K2
Padanaram Angus 196 C6
Padbury Bucks 58 B2
Paddington Gt Lon 44 F4
Paddlesworth Kent 35 G6
Paddlesworth Kent 46 B7
Paddock Wood Kent 33 H4
Padiham Lancs 122 B4
Padside N York 132 B7
Padstow Cnwll 4 E2
Padworth W Berk 41 L7
Pagham W Susx 18 B6
Paglesham Essex 46 F2
Paignton Torbay 7 K4
Pailton Warwks 86 F6
Painscastle Powys 68 D5
Painshawfield Nthumb 150 D3
Painsthorpe E R Yk 134 C7
Painswick Gloucs 55 K6
Painter's Forstal Kent 34 D3
Paisley Rens 174 E5
Paisley Woodside Crematorium Rens 174 E5
Pakefield Suffk 93 L5
Pakenham Suffk 77 L2
Paley Street W & M 42 E5
Palfrey Wsall 85 H4
Palgrave Suffk 92 D7
Pallington Dorset 14 E4
Palmerston E Ayrs 163 L5
Palnackie D & G 146 E4
Palnure D & G 145 J3
Palterton Derbys 115 J7
Pamber End Hants 41 L8
Pamber Green Hants 41 L8
Pamber Heath Hants 41 L7
Pamington Gloucs 55 L2
Pamphill Dorset 15 J3
Pampisford Cambs 76 C5
Panbride Angus 187 J1
Pancrasweek Devon 9 H4
Pandy Mons 53 M4
Pandy Tudur Conwy 110 B8
Panfield Essex 61 H3
Pangbourne W Berk 41 M5
Pangdean W Susx 19 J4
Pannal N York 123 L1
Pannal Ash N York 132 D8
Pannanich Wells Hotel Abers 205 J6
Pant Shrops 97 L7
Pantasaph Flints 111 G6
Pant-ffrwyth Brdgnd 36 E4
Pant Glas Gwynd 95 H3
Pantglas Powys 81 G4
Panton Lincs 117 K5
Pant-y-dwr Powys 81 L8
Pant-y-mwyn Flints 111 H8
Panxworth Norfk 93 H2
Papa Stour Airport Shet 235 b5
Papa Westray Airport Ork 234 c3
Papcastle Cumb 136 F2
Papigoe Highld 231 L5
Papple E Loth 178 D4
Papplewick Notts 101 K3
Papworth Everard Cambs 75 K3
Papworth St Agnes Cambs 75 J2
Par Cnwll 5 G5
Parbold Lancs 121 G7
Parbrook Somset 26 E4
Parc Gwynd 96 D5
Parc Gwyn Crematorium Pembks 49 K5
Parc Seymour Newpt 38 B3
Pardshaw Cumb 136 F3
Parham Suffk 79 G3
Park D & G 154 F4
Park Nthumb 149 H3
Park Corner Oxon 42 B3
Park Crematorium Hants 30 E2
Park Crematorium Lancs 120 E5
Parkend Gloucs 54 E6
Parkers Green Kent 33 G4
Park Farm Kent 34 D6
Parkgate Ches W 111 J6
Parkgate D & G 155 H4
Park Gate Hants 17 G2
Park Gate Leeds 123 J3
Parkgate Surrey 31 K3
Parkgrove Crematorium Angus 196 F6
Parkhall W Duns 174 E4
Parkham Devon 22 F6
Parkmill Swans 51 G7
Park Royal Gt Lon 44 D4
Parkside Dur 151 K5
Parkside N Lans 175 L6
Parkstone Poole 15 J4
Park Street Herts 59 J6
Park Wood Crematorium Calder 123 G6
Parndon Wood Crematorium Essex 60 C6
Parracombe Devon 23 L3
Parson Drove Cambs 89 L2
Parson's Heath Essex 62 B3
Partick C Glas 174 F5
Partington Traffd 113 G3
Partney Lincs 118 F7
Parton Cumb 136 D3
Partridge Green W Susx 19 G2
Parwich Derbys 100 D2
Passenham Nhants 73 L6
Paston Norfk 107 G5
Patcham Br & H 19 J4
Patching W Susx 18 E4
Patchway S Glos 38 E4
Pateley Bridge N York 132 B6
Pathhead Fife 186 E8
Pathhead Mdloth 177 K5
Path of Condie P & K 185 M5
Patna E Ayrs 163 K7
Patney Wilts 40 B8
Patrick IoM 237 b5
Patrick Brompton N York 132 C2
Patricroft Salfd 113 H2
Patrington E R Yk 127 H6
Patrington Haven E R Yk 127 H6
Patrixbourne Kent 35 G4
Patterdale Cumb 137 L4
Pattingham Staffs 84 E4
Pattishall Nhants 73 J4
Pattiswick Green Essex 61 K3
Paul Cnwll 2 E5
Paulerspury Nhants 73 K5
Paull E R Yk 126 E5
Paul's Dene Wilts 28 C5
Paulton BaNES 26 F1
Pauperhaugh Nthumb 158 D3
Pavenham Bed 74 E4
Pawlett Somset 25 L3
Paxford Gloucs 71 L6
Paxton Border 179 J7
Payhembury Devon 12 E3
Paythorne Lancs 122 C1
Peacehaven E Susx 19 L5
Peak District National Park 114 D3
Peak Forest Derbys 114 C5
Peakirk C Pete 89 H3
Peasedown St John BaNES 39 G8
Peaseland Green Norfk 92 C1
Peasemore W Berk 41 J5
Peasenhall Suffk 79 H2
Pease Pottage W Susx 31 L5
Pease Pottage Services W Susx 31 L5

Peaslake Surrey 31 H3
Peasley Cross St Hel 112 D3
Peasmarsh E Susx 21 H2
Peathill Abers 217 H2
Peat Inn Fife 187 G5
Peatling Magna Leics 87 H5
Peatling Parva Leics 87 H5
Pebmarsh Essex 77 J7
Pebworth Worcs 71 K5
Pecket Well Calder 122 E5
Peckforton Ches E 98 D2
Peckham Gt Lon 45 G5
Peckleton Leics 86 F4
Pedlinge Kent 34 F7
Pedmore Dudley 85 G6
Pedwell Somset 26 B4
Peebles Border 166 C2
Peel IoM 237 b4
Peel Green Crematorium Salfd 113 H3
Peene Kent 35 G6
Pegsdon C Beds 59 J2
Pegswood Nthumb 159 G5
Pegwell Kent 35 K2
Peinchorran Highld 209 H7
Peinlich Highld 208 F3
Peldon Essex 62 B5
Pelsall Wsall 85 H3
Pelton Dur 151 G4
Pelynt Cnwll 5 K5
Pemberton Carmth 51 G5
Pemberton Wigan 112 D2
Pembrey Carmth 50 E5
Pembridge Herefs 69 H3
Pembroke Pembks 49 G7
Pembroke Dock Pembks 49 G6
Pembrokeshire Coast National Park Pembks 48 E4
Pembury Kent 33 G5
Pen-allt Herefs 54 E3
Penallt Mons 54 D6
Penally Pembks 49 J7
Penarth V Glam 37 J6
Pen-bont Rhydybeddau Cerdgn 80 F6
Penbryn Cerdgn 65 J4
Pencader Carmth 66 B7
Pencaitland E Loth 177 L5
Pencarnisiog IoA 108 D6
Pencarreg Carmth 66 C5
Pencelli Powys 53 H3
Penclawdd Swans 51 G6
Pencoed Brdgnd 36 E4
Pencombe Herefs 69 L4
Pencraig Herefs 54 E4
Pencraig Powys 97 G6
Pendeen Cnwll 2 C4
Penderyn Rhondd 52 E6
Pendine Carmth 50 B4
Pendlebury Salfd 113 H2
Pendleton Lancs 121 L3
Pendock Worcs 55 H2
Pendoggett Cnwll 8 D8
Pendomer Somset 13 M1
Pendoylan V Glam 37 G5
Penegoes Powys 81 G4
Pen-ffordd Pembks 49 J3
Pengam Caerph 37 J2
Pengam Cardif 37 K5
Penge Gt Lon 45 G6
Pengelly Cnwll 8 E7
Penhallow Cnwll 3 K2
Penhalvean Cnwll 3 J4
Penhill Swindn 40 D3
Penhow Newpt 38 B3
Penicuik Mdloth 177 H6
Penifiler Highld 209 G6
Peninver Ag & B 161 J4
Penistone Barns 114 E2
Penkill S Ayrs 152 F3
Penkridge Staffs 85 G2
Penley Wrexhm 98 B4
Penllyn V Glam 36 F5
Penmachno Conwy 96 C3
Penmaen Caerph 37 J2
Penmaen Swans 51 G7
Penmaenmawr Conwy 109 K6
Penmaenpool Gwynd 95 M8
Penmark V Glam 37 G6
Penmount Crematorium Cnwll 4 C6
Penmynydd IoA 109 G6
Pennal Gwynd 80 F4
Pennan Abers 216 F2
Pennant Powys 81 J4
Pennerley Shrops 83 G4
Pennines 122 E4
Pennington Cumb 128 F4
Pennorth Powys 53 H3
Penn Street Bucks 42 F2
Penny Bridge Cumb 129 G3
Pennycross Ag & B 181 G3
Pennyghael Ag & B 181 H3
Pennyglen S Ayrs 163 H7
Pennymoor Devon 11 K3
Pennywell Sundld 151 J4
Penparc Cerdgn 65 H5
Penperlleni Mons 53 L6
Penpoll Cnwll 5 J5
Penponds Cnwll 3 H4
Penpont D & G 154 E4
Pen-rhiw Pembks 65 H6
Penrhiwceiber Rhondd 37 G2
Pen Rhiwfawr Neath 51 L4
Penrhiwllan Cerdgn 65 K6
Penrhiw-pal Cerdgn 65 K5
Penrhos Gwynd 94 F5
Penrhos Mons 54 B5
Penrhyn Bay Conwy 110 A5
Penrhyn-coch Cerdgn 80 E6
Penrhyndeudraeth Gwynd 95 K5
Penrice Swans 50 F7
Penrioch N Ayrs 161 L1
Penrith Cumb 138 D2
Penrose Cnwll 4 D2
Penruddock Cumb 138 B2
Penryn Cnwll 3 K4
Pensarn Conwy 110 C5
Pensax Worcs 70 C2
Penselwood Somset 27 H5
Pensford BaNES 38 F7
Pensham Worcs 71 G5
Penshaw Sundld 151 H4
Penshurst Kent 32 F4
Pensilva Cnwll 5 L2
Pensnett Dudley 85 G5
Pentewan Cnwll 4 F6
Pentir Gwynd 109 H7
Pentire Cnwll 4 C4
Pentlow Essex 77 J5
Pentney Norfk 91 G2
Pentonbridge Cumb 156 D6
Penton Mewsey Hants 29 G3
Pentraeth IoA 109 G5
Pentre Mons 54 B7
Pentre Rhondd 36 F2
Pentre Shrops 98 A8
Pentrebach Myr Td 53 G7
Pentre-bach Powys 52 E2
Pentre Berw IoA 108 F6
Pentrebychan Crematorium Wrexhm 97 L3
Pentrecelyn Denbgs 97 J2
Pentre-celyn Powys 81 J3
Pentre-chwyth Swans 51 J6
Pentre-cwrt Carmth 65 L6
Pentredwr Denbgs 97 J3
Pentrefelin Gwynd 95 J5
Pentrefoelas Conwy 96 D3
Pentregat Cerdgn 65 K4
Pentre-Gwenlais Carmth 51 H3
Pentre Hodrey Shrops 83 G7
Pentre Llanrhaeadr Denbgs 110 F8
Pentre Meyrick V Glam 36 E5
Pentre-tafarn-y-fedw Conwy 96 C1
Pentrich Derbys 101 G3
Pentridge Dorset 28 B7
Pen-twyn Mons 54 D6
Pentwynmaur Caerph 37 J2
Pentyrch Cardif 37 H4
Penwithick Cnwll 5 G5
Penybanc Carmth 51 H2
Penybont Powys 68 C2
Pen-y-bont Powys 97 K7
Pen-y-bont-fawr Powys 97 G7
Pen-y-bryn Pembks 65 G6
Penycae Wrexhm 97 L4
Pen-y-clawdd Mons 54 C6
Pen-y-coedcae Rhondd 37 G3
Penycwn Pembks 48 E3
Pen-y-felin Flints 111 G7
Penyffordd Flints 97 L1
Pen-y-Garnedd Powys 97 H7
Pen-y-graig Gwynd 94 D5
Penygraig Rhondd 36 F3
Penygroes Carmth 51 H3
Penygroes Gwynd 95 H2
Pen-y-Mynydd Carmth 50 F5
Penymynydd Flints 97 L1
Penysarn IoA 108 F4
Pen-y-stryt Denbgs 97 J3
Penywaun Rhondd 52 F6
Penzance Cnwll 2 E5
Peopleton Worcs 71 G4
Peplow Shrops 98 F7
Perceton N Ayrs 163 J2
Percyhorner Abers 217 H2
Perelle Guern 236 b3
Perham Down Wilts 28 E2
Periton Somset 24 E3
Perivale Gt Lon 44 D4
Perkins Village Devon 12 D4
Perlethorpe Notts 115 M7
Perranarworthal Cnwll 3 K4
Perranporth Cnwll 3 K1
Perranuthnoe Cnwll 2 F5
Perranwell Cnwll 3 K4
Perranzabuloe Cnwll 3 K2
Perry Birm 85 J5
Perry Barr Birm 85 J5
Perry Barr Crematorium Birm 85 J5
Perry Green Wilts 39 L3
Pershall Staffs 99 J6
Pershore Worcs 71 G5
Pertenhall Bed 74 F2
Perth P & K 186 B3
Perth Crematorium P & K 186 A3
Perthy Shrops 98 A5
Perton Herefs 69 L6
Perton Staffs 84 F4
Peterborough C Pete 89 H4
Peterborough Crematorium C Pete 89 H3
Peterborough Services Cambs 89 G5
Peterchurch Herefs 69 G6
Peterculter C Aber 206 F5
Peterhead Abers 217 L5
Peterlee Dur 151 K6
Petersfield Hants 30 C6
Peter's Green Herts 59 J4
Petersham Gt Lon 44 D5
Peters Marland Devon 10 C3
Peterstone Wentlooge Newpt 37 K4
Peterston-super-Ely V Glam 37 G5
Peterstow Herefs 54 E3
Peter Tavy Devon 6 D1
Petham Kent 34 F4
Petherwin Gate Cnwll 9 H6
Petrockstow Devon 10 D3
Pett E Susx 21 H3
Pettaugh Suffk 78 E3
Petterden Angus 196 C7
Pettinain S Lans 165 J2
Pettistree Suffk 79 G4
Petton Devon 24 F6
Petts Wood Gt Lon 45 J6
Pettycur Fife 177 H2
Pettymuk Abers 207 G1
Petworth W Susx 31 G6
Pevensey E Susx 20 D5
Pevensey Bay E Susx 20 D5
Pewsey Wilts 40 D7
Phepson Worcs 71 G3
Philham Devon 22 D6
Philiphaugh Border 166 F4
Phillack Cnwll 2 F4
Philleigh Cnwll 4 D7
Philpstoun W Loth 176 E3
Phoenix Green Hants 30 C1
Phones Highld 203 G6
Pibsbury Somset 26 C6
Pickburn Donc 115 K1
Pickering N York 134 C3
Picket Twenty Hants 29 H3
Pickford Covtry 86 C6
Pickhill N York 132 E3
Picklescott Shrops 83 J4
Pickmere Ches E 113 G6
Pickney Somset 25 J5
Pickwell Leics 87 L2
Pickworth Lincs 103 H5
Pickworth Rutlnd 88 E2
Picton Ches W 112 B7
Picton N York 141 K5
Piddinghoe E Susx 19 L5
Piddington Nhants 74 B4
Piddington Oxon 57 M5
Piddlehinton Dorset 14 D3
Piddletrenthide Dorset 14 D3
Pidley Cambs 89 K7
Piercebridge Darltn 140 F4
Pierowall Ork 234 c3
Pilgrims Hatch Essex 45 L2
Pilham Lincs 116 E3
Pillaton Cnwll 6 A3
Pillerton Hersey Warwks 72 C5
Pillerton Priors Warwks 72 C5
Pilley Barns 115 G2
Pilley Hants 16 D3
Pilling Lancs 120 E2
Pilning S Glos 38 D4
Pilsbury Derbys 114 C8
Pilsdon Dorset 13 K3
Pilsley Derbys 101 H1
Pilsley Derbys 114 E7
Pilson Green Norfk 93 H2
Piltdown E Susx 19 L2
Pilton Devon 23 J5
Pilton Nhants 88 E6
Pilton Rutlnd 88 D3
Pilton Somset 26 E3
Pimlico Herts 59 H6
Pimperne Dorset 15 G1
Pinchbeck Lincs 103 L7
Pin Green Herts 59 L3
Pinhoe Devon 12 C4
Pinley Green Warwks 72 B2
Pinminnoch S Ayrs 152 E4
Pinmore S Ayrs 152 E4
Pinn Devon 12 E5
Pinner Gt Lon 43 J3
Pinner Green Gt Lon 43 J3
Pinvin Worcs 71 G5
Pinwherry S Ayrs 152 E5

Pinxton Derbys 101 J2
Pipe and Lyde Herefs 69 K5
Pipe Aston Herefs 69 J1
Pipe Gate Shrops 99 G4
Piperhill Highld 213 K4
Pipewell Nhants 88 B6
Pirbright Surrey 30 F1
Pirnie Border 167 K4
Pirnmill N Ayrs 161 L1
Pirton Herts 59 J2
Pishill Oxon 42 B3
Pistyll Gwynd 94 F4
Pitagowan P & K 194 C3
Pitblae Abers 217 J2
Pitcairngreen P & K 185 M3
Pitcalnie Highld 223 H6
Pitcaple Abers 206 D1
Pitcarity Angus 196 B4
Pitchcombe Gloucs 55 J6
Pitchcott Bucks 58 C4
Pitchford Shrops 83 K3
Pitch Green Bucks 58 C7
Pitchroy Moray 214 E6
Pitcombe Somset 26 F5
Pitcox E Loth 178 E4
Pitfichie Abers 206 D3
Pitglassie Abers 216 D5
Pitgrudy Highld 223 H3
Pitlessie Fife 186 E5
Pitlochry P & K 194 E5
Pitmachie Abers 216 C8
Pitmain Highld 203 H5
Pitmedden Abers 217 G8
Pitmedden Garden Abers 217 G8
Pitminster Somset 25 K7
Pitmuies Angus 196 F6
Pitmunie Abers 206 C3
Pitney Somset 26 C5
Pitroddie P & K 186 C3
Pitscottie Fife 187 G5
Pitsea Essex 46 C3
Pitsford Nhants 73 L2
Pitstone Bucks 58 F5
Pittarrow Abers 197 H2
Pittenweem Fife 187 J6
Pitteuchar Fife 186 D7
Pittington Dur 151 H6
Pittodrie House Hotel Abers 206 D1
Pitton Wilts 28 E5
Pittulie Abers 217 H2
Pity Me Dur 151 G5
Pixham Surrey 31 K2
Plains N Lans 175 L5
Plaish Shrops 83 K4
Plaistow Gt Lon 45 H4
Plaistow W Susx 31 G5
Plaitford Hants 28 F7
Plawsworth Dur 151 G5
Plaxtol Kent 33 G3
Playden E Susx 21 H2
Playford Suffk 78 F5
Play Hatch Oxon 42 C5
Playing Place Cnwll 4 C7
Playley Green Gloucs 55 H2
Plealey Shrops 83 H3
Plean Stirlg 175 L2
Pleasance Fife 186 D5
Pleasington Bl w D 121 J5
Pleasington Crematorium Bl w D 121 J5
Pleasley Derbys 115 J8
Pleasurewood Hills Suffk 93 L4
Pleinheaume Guern 236 d2
Plemont Jersey 236 a5
Plemstall Ches W 112 C7
Pleshey Essex 61 G5
Plockton Highld 210 C7
Plowden Shrops 83 H6
Pluckley Kent 34 B5
Pluckley Thorne Kent 34 B5
Plumbland Cumb 147 K6
Plumley Ches E 113 G6
Plumpton Cumb 148 E7
Plumpton E Susx 19 K3
Plumpton Nhants 73 H5
Plumpton Green E Susx 19 K3
Plumstead Gt Lon 45 J4
Plumstead Norfk 106 D5
Plumtree Notts 101 L6
Plungar Leics 102 C5
Plurenden Kent 34 C7
Plush Dorset 14 D3
Plwmp Cerdgn 65 K4
Plymouth C Plym 6 C5
Plymouth Airport C Plym 6 D4
Plympton C Plym 6 D5
Plymstock C Plym 6 D5
Plymtree Devon 12 D2
Pockley N York 133 K3
Pocklington E R Yk 125 J2
Podimore Somset 26 D6
Podington Bed 74 D3
Podmore Staffs 99 H5
Pointon Lincs 103 J6
Pokesdown Bmouth 15 L4
Polbain Highld 224 B6
Polbathic Cnwll 6 A4
Polbeth W Loth 176 D5
Poldark Mine Cnwll 3 H5
Polebrook Nhants 88 F6
Polegate E Susx 20 C5
Polesden Lacey Surrey 31 J2
Polesworth Warwks 86 C3
Polglass Highld 224 C6
Polgooth Cnwll 4 F5
Polgown D & G 154 C2
Poling W Susx 18 E5
Poling Corner W Susx 18 E5
Polkerris Cnwll 5 H5
Pollington E R Yk 124 F6
Polloch Highld 190 F3
Pollokshaws C Glas 175 G6
Pollokshields C Glas 175 G5
Polmassick Cnwll 4 F6
Polmont Falk 176 C3
Polnish Highld 200 B8
Polperro Cnwll 5 K5
Polruan Cnwll 5 H5
Polstead Suffk 78 B6
Poltalloch Ag & B 182 B7
Poltimore Devon 12 C3
Polton Mdloth 177 J5
Polwarth Border 178 F7
Polyphant Cnwll 9 H7
Polzeath Cnwll 4 E1
Pomathorn Mdloth 177 H6
Pondersbridge Cambs 89 J5
Ponders End Gt Lon 45 G2
Ponsanooth Cnwll 3 K4
Ponsworthy Devon 7 G2
Pont Abraham Services Carmth 51 H4
Pontac Jersey 236 e8
Pontantwn Carmth 50 F3
Pontardawe Neath 51 K5
Pontarddulais Swans 51 H5
Pont-ar-gothi Carmth 51 G2
Pontarsais Carmth 66 B8
Pontblyddyn Flints 97 L1
Pontcysyllte Aqueduct Wrexhm 97 L4
Pontefract Wakefd 124 C6
Pontefract Crematorium Wakefd 124 C6
Ponteland Nthumb 158 F7
Ponterwyd Cerdgn 81 G7
Pontesbury Shrops 83 H3
Pontesford Shrops 83 H3
Pontfadog Wrexhm 97 K5
Pontfaen Pembks 64 E7
Pont-faen Powys 67 L7
Pontgarreg Cerdgn 65 K4
Ponthenry Carmth 50 F4
Ponthir Torfn 37 M2
Ponthirwaun Cerdgn 65 J5
Pontllanfraith Caerph 37 J2
Pontlliw Swans 51 H5
Pontlottyn Caerph 53 H6
Pontlyfni Gwynd 95 G3
Pontnêddféchan Neath 52 D6
Pontnewydd Torfn 37 L2
Pontrhydfendigaid Cerdgn 67 G2
Pont-rhyd-y-fen Neath 36 C2
Pontrhydygroes Cerdgn 81 G8
Pontrilas Herefs 54 B3
Pont Robert Powys 82 C2
Pontshaen Cerdgn 66 B5
Pontsticill Myr Td 53 G5
Pontwelly Carmth 65 L6
Pontyates Carmth 50 F4
Pontyberem Carmth 51 G4
Pontybodkin Flints 97 L2
Pontyclun Rhondd 37 G4
Pontycymer Brdgnd 36 D3
Pont-y-pant Conwy 96 B2
Pontypool Torfn 53 L7
Pontypridd Rhondd 37 G3
Pontywaun Caerph 37 K2
Pool Cnwll 3 H3
Pool Leeds 123 J2
Poole Poole 15 J4
Poole Crematorium Poole 15 J3
Poole Keynes Gloucs 39 M2
Poolewe Highld 219 K5
Pooley Bridge Cumb 138 C3
Poolfold Staffs 99 K1
Poolhill Gloucs 55 G3
Pool of Muckhart Clacks 185 L7
Pool Street Essex 77 H6
Poplar Gt Lon 45 G4
Porchfield IoW 16 F4
Poringland Norfk 92 F3
Porkellis Cnwll 3 J5
Porlock Somset 24 D3
Porlock Weir Somset 24 D2
Portachoillan Ag & B 172 C6
Port-an-Eorna Highld 210 B7
Port Appin Ag & B 191 H7
Port Askaig Ag & B 171 H5
Portavadie Ag & B 172 F4
Port Bannatyne Ag & B 173 J5
Portbury N Som 38 D5
Port Carlisle Cumb 147 M3
Port Charlotte Ag & B 170 E6
Portchester Hants 17 H2
Portchester Crematorium Hants 17 H2
Port Driseach Ag & B 173 G4
Port Ellen Ag & B 160 C1
Port Elphinstone Abers 206 E2
Portencalzie D & G 152 B7
Portencross N Ayrs 173 K8
Port Erin IoM 237 a6
Portesham Dorset 14 B5
Portessie Moray 215 K2
Port Eynon Swans 50 F7
Portfield Gate Pembks 48 F4
Portgate Devon 10 B7
Port Gaverne Cnwll 8 D8
Port Glasgow Inver 174 C4
Portgordon Moray 215 J2
Portgower Highld 227 H5
Porth Cnwll 4 C4
Porth Rhondd 36 F3
Porthallow Cnwll 3 K6
Porthallow Cnwll 5 K5
Porthcawl Brdgnd 36 C5
Porthcothan Cnwll 4 D2
Porthcurno Cnwll 2 C6
Port Henderson Highld 219 H6
Porthgain Pembks 64 A7
Porthgwarra Cnwll 2 C6
Porthill Staffs 99 J3
Porthkerry V Glam 37 G6
Porthleven Cnwll 3 H6
Porthmadog Gwynd 95 K5
Porth Navas Cnwll 3 K5
Porthoustock Cnwll 3 K6
Porthpean Cnwll 5 G5
Porthtowan Cnwll 3 J2
Porthyrhyd Carmth 51 G3
Portincaple Ag & B 183 J8
Portinfer Jersey 236 a5
Portington E R Yk 125 J4
Portinnisherrich Ag & B 182 D5
Portinscale Cumb 137 H3
Port Isaac Cnwll 8 D8
Portishead N Som 38 C5
Portknockie Moray 215 K2
Portland Dorset 14 D7
Portlethen Abers 207 H6
Portling D & G 146 F4
Portloe Cnwll 4 E7
Port Logan D & G 144 D6
Portmahomack Highld 223 K5
Portmeirion Gwynd 95 K5
Portmellon Cnwll 4 F6
Port Mor Highld 189 K1
Portnacroish Ag & B 191 H6
Portnaguran W Isls 232 g2
Portnahaven Ag & B 170 D7
Portnalong Highld 208 E7
Port nan Giuran W Isls 232 g2
Port nan Long W Isls 232 c5
Port Nis W Isls 232 g1
Portobello C Edin 177 J4
Portobello Wolves 85 G4
Port of Menteith Stirlg 184 D6
Port of Ness W Isls 232 g1
Porton Wilts 28 D4
Portpatrick D & G 144 B4
Port Quin Cnwll 8 C8
Port Ramsay Ag & B 191 H7
Portreath Cnwll 3 H3
Portreath Harbour Cnwll 3 H3
Portree Highld 209 G5
Port St Mary IoM 237 b7
Portscatho Cnwll 4 D8
Portsea C Port 17 J3
Portskerra Highld 230 C3
Portskewett Mons 38 D3
Portslade Br & H 19 H4
Portslade-by-Sea Br & H 19 H5
Portslogan D & G 144 B3
Portsmouth C Port 17 J3
Portsmouth Calder 122 D5
Portsmouth Dockyard C Port 17 J3
Port Soderick IoM 237 c6
Portsonachan Hotel Ag & B 182 F3
Portsoy Abers 216 B2
Port Sunlight Wirral 111 K5
Portswood C Sotn 29 H8
Port Talbot Neath 36 B3
Portuairk Highld 189 K3
Portway Sandw 85 H6
Portway Worcs 85 J8
Port Wemyss Ag & B 170 D7
Port William D & G 145 H6
Portwrinkle Cnwll 6 A5
Portyerrock D & G 145 K7
Poslingford Suffk 77 H5
Posso Border 166 B3
Postbridge Devon 10 F8
Postcombe Oxon 58 B7
Postling Kent 34 F6
Postwick Norfk 93 G2
Potarch Abers 206 B6
Potten End Herts 59 G6

Potter Brompton N York 134 F4
Potterhanworth Lincs 117 H7
Potterhanworth Booths Lincs 117 H7
Potter Heigham Norfk 107 J8
Potterne Wilts 39 M8
Potterne Wick Wilts 39 M8
Potters Bar Herts 59 L7
Potters Crouch Herts 59 J6
Potters Green Covtry 86 D6
Potters Marston Leics 87 G4
Potterspury Nhants 73 L6
Potter Street Essex 60 D6
Potterton Abers 207 H3
Potto N York 141 L6
Potton C Beds 75 J5
Pott Shrigley Ches E 113 L5
Poughill Cnwll 9 G4
Poughill Devon 11 K3
Poulner Hants 15 M2
Poulshot Wilts 39 L7
Poulton Gloucs 56 C7
Poulton Wirral 111 J4
Poulton-le-Fylde Lancs 120 D3
Poundbury Dorset 14 D4
Poundffald Swans 51 H6
Pound Green E Susx 20 B2
Pound Green Suffk 77 G4
Pound Hill W Susx 32 B5
Poundon Bucks 57 M3
Poundsgate Devon 7 G2
Poundstock Cnwll 9 G5
Pouton D & G 145 K5
Povey Cross Surrey 31 L3
Powburn Nthumb 168 F6
Powderham Devon 12 C5
Powerstock Dorset 13 M3
Powfoot D & G 147 K2
Powick Worcs 70 E4
Powmill P & K 185 L7
Poxwell Dorset 14 E5
Poyle Slough 43 G5
Poynings W Susx 19 H4
Poyntington Dorset 26 F7
Poynton Ches E 113 L5
Poynton Green Wrekin 98 E8
Praa Sands Cnwll 3 G5
Praze-an-Beeble Cnwll 3 H4
Prees Shrops 98 D5
Preesall Lancs 120 E2
Prees Green Shrops 98 E6
Prees Heath Shrops 98 E5
Prees Higher Heath Shrops 98 E5
Pren-gwyn Cerdgn 65 L5
Prenteg Gwynd 95 K4
Prescot Knows 112 C3
Prescott Devon 25 H8
Presnerb Angus 195 J3
Prestatyn Denbgs 110 E5
Prestbury Ches E 113 K6
Prestbury Gloucs 55 L4
Presteigne Powys 69 G2
Prestleigh Somset 26 F4
Preston Border 179 G6
Preston Br & H 19 J4
Preston Devon 7 K2
Preston Dorset 14 D5
Preston E R Yk 126 F4
Preston Gloucs 56 B7
Preston Herts 59 K3
Preston Kent 34 D3
Preston Kent 35 H3
Preston Lancs 121 H4
Preston Nthumb 169 H4
Preston Rutlnd 88 C3
Preston Somset 25 H4
Preston Torbay 7 K4
Preston Wilts 40 B5
Preston Bagot Warwks 71 L2
Preston Bissett Bucks 58 A3
Preston Bowyer Somset 25 H6
Preston Brockhurst Shrops 98 D7
Preston Brook Halton 112 E5
Preston Candover Hants 29 L3
Preston Capes Nhants 73 H4
Preston Crematorium Lancs 121 H4
Preston Green Warwks 71 L2
Preston Gubbals Shrops 98 C8
Preston on Stour Warwks 72 B4
Preston on the Hill Halton 112 E5
Preston on Wye Herefs 69 H6
Prestonpans E Loth 177 K4
Preston Patrick Cumb 129 L3
Preston Plucknett Somset 26 D7
Preston St Mary Suffk 77 L4
Preston-under-Scar N York 131 K2
Preston upon the Weald Moors Wrekin 84 C1
Preston Wynne Herefs 69 L5
Prestwich Bury 113 J1
Prestwick S Ayrs 163 J4
Prestwick Airport S Ayrs 163 J4
Prestwood Bucks 58 E7
Prickwillow Cambs 90 E6
Priddy Somset 26 D2
Priest Hutton Lancs 129 L5
Priestland E Ayrs 164 B2
Priest Weston Shrops 82 F4
Primrosehill Border 179 G6
Primrose Hill Dudley 85 G6
Primsidemill Border 168 B4
Princes Risborough Bucks 58 D7
Princethorpe Warwks 72 E1
Princetown Devon 6 E2
Priors Hardwick Warwks 72 F4
Priorslee Wrekin 84 C2
Priors Marston Warwks 72 F3
Priors Norton Gloucs 55 K3
Priston BaNES 39 G7
Prittlewell Sthend 46 E3
Privett Hants 30 B6
Prixford Devon 23 J4
Probus Cnwll 4 E6
Prora E Loth 178 C3
Prospect Cumb 147 K6
Prospidnick Cnwll 3 H5
Protstonhill Abers 216 F2
Prudhoe Nthumb 150 D3
Publow BaNES 38 F7
Puckeridge Herts 60 C4
Puckington Somset 26 B7
Pucklechurch S Glos 39 G5
Puddington Ches W 111 K6
Puddington Devon 11 J3
Puddletown Dorset 14 E4
Pudsey Leeds 123 J4
Pulborough W Susx 18 E3
Pulford Ches W 98 A2
Pulham Dorset 14 D2
Pulham Market Norfk 92 E6
Pulham St Mary Norfk 92 E6
Pulloxhill C Beds 74 F7
Pulverbatch Shrops 83 H3
Pumpherston W Loth 176 E4
Pumsaint Carmth 66 E6
Puncheston Pembks 49 G2
Puncknowle Dorset 14 A5
Punnett's Town E Susx 20 C2
Purbrook Hants 17 J2
Purfleet Thurr 45 K4
Puriton Somset 25 L3
Purleigh Essex 61 K7
Purley Gt Lon 44 F7
Purley W Berk 42 A5
Purse Caundle Dorset 27 G7
Purtington Somset 13 K2
Purton Gloucs 54 F6
Purton Gloucs 55 G7
Purton Wilts 40 C3
Purton Stoke Wilts 40 C3
Pury End Nhants 73 K5
Pusey Oxon 41 G2
Putley Herefs 70 B6
Putley Green Herefs 70 B6
Putney Gt Lon 44 E5
Putney Vale Crematorium Gt Lon 44 E5
Puttenham Surrey 30 F2
Puxley Nhants 73 L6
Puxton N Som 38 B7
Pwll Carmth 50 F5
Pwll-glâs Denbgs 97 H2
Pwllgloyw Powys 68 B7
Pwllheli Gwynd 94 F5
Pwllmeyric Mons 38 D2
Pwll Trap Carmth 50 C3
Pwll-y-glaw Neath 36 C2
Pye Bridge Derbys 101 H3
Pyecombe W Susx 19 J3
Pyle Brdgnd 36 C4
Pyleigh Somset 25 H5
Pylle Somset 26 E4
Pymoor Cambs 90 C6
Pymore Dorset 13 L4
Pyrford Surrey 43 H8
Pyrton Oxon 42 B2
Pytchley Nhants 88 C8
Pyworthy Devon 9 J4

Q

Quadring Lincs 103 L6
Quadring Eaudike Lincs 103 L5
Quainton Bucks 58 C4
Quantock Hills Somset 25 J4
Quarff Shet 235 c6
Quarley Hants 28 F3
Quarndon Derbys 101 G4
Quarrier's Village Inver 174 C5
Quarrington Lincs 103 H4
Quarrington Hill Dur 151 H7
Quarry Bank Dudley 85 G6
Quarrywood Moray 214 E2
Quarter N Ayrs 173 L6
Quarter S Lans 175 J7
Quatford Shrops 84 D5
Quatt Shrops 84 D6
Quebec Dur 150 F6
Quedgeley Gloucs 55 J5
Queen Adelaide Cambs 90 E7
Queen Camel Somset 26 E6
Queen Charlton BaNES 38 F6
Queen Elizabeth Forest Park Stirlg 184 B6
Queenhill Worcs 70 F6
Queen Oak Dorset 27 H5
Queen's Bower IoW 17 H5
Queensbury C Brad 123 G4
Queensferry Flints 111 K7
Queensferry Crossing Fife 176 F3
Queenslie C Glas 175 H5
Queen's Park Bed 74 F4
Queenzieburn N Lans 175 J3
Quendon Essex 60 E3
Queniborough Leics 87 J2
Quenington Gloucs 56 C7
Queslett Birm 85 J4
Quethiock Cnwll 5 L3
Quidenham Norfk 92 B6
Quidhampton Wilts 28 C5
Quinton Nhants 73 L4
Quintrell Downs Cnwll 4 D4
Quixwood Border 179 G5
Quoig P & K 185 H3
Quorn Leics 87 H1
Quothquan S Lans 165 J2
Quoyburray Ork 234 c6
Quoyloo Ork 234 b5

R

Raasay Highld 209 J5
Rachan Mill Border 165 L3
Rachub Gwynd 109 J7
Rackenford Devon 24 D7
Rackham W Susx 18 E3
Rackheath Norfk 93 G1
Racks D & G 155 H7
Rackwick Ork 234 a7
Radbourne Derbys 100 F5
Radcliffe Bury 113 H1
Radcliffe on Trent Notts 101 M5
Radclive Bucks 73 J7
Raddery Highld 213 H3
Radernie Fife 187 G5
Radford Covtry 86 D7
Radford Semele Warwks 72 D2
Radlett Herts 59 K7
Radley Oxon 57 K7
Radley Green Essex 60 F6
Radnage Bucks 42 C2
Radstock BaNES 27 G1
Radstone Nhants 73 H6
Radway Warwks 72 D5
Radwell Bed 74 E3
Radwell Herts 75 J7
Radwinter Essex 76 E6
Radyr Cardif 37 H4
Rafford Moray 214 C3
RAF Museum Cosford Shrops 84 E3
RAF Museum Hendon Gt Lon 44 E3
Ragdale Leics 102 A8
Raglan Mons 54 B6
Ragnall Notts 116 D6
Raigbeg Highld 213 J8
Rainbow Hill Worcs 70 F4
Rainford St Hel 112 C2
Rainham Gt Lon 45 K4
Rainham Medway 46 D6
Rainhill St Hel 112 C4
Rainhill Stoops St Hel 112 D4
Rainow Ches E 113 L6
Rainsbrook Crematorium Warwks 87 G8
Rainton N York 132 E4
Rainworth Notts 101 L2
Rait P & K 186 D3
Raithby Lincs 118 D5
Raithby Lincs 118 E7
Rake Hants 30 D5
Ralia Highld 203 H5
Ramasaig Highld 208 B5
Rame Cnwll 3 J4
Rame Cnwll 6 B6
Rampisham Dorset 14 B3
Rampside Cumb 128 F6
Rampton Cambs 76 B2
Rampton Notts 116 D5
Ramsbottom Bury 122 B6
Ramsbury Wilts 40 F6
Ramscraigs Highld 227 K3

Ramsdean Hants 30 B6
Ramsdell Hants 41 L8
Ramsden Oxon 57 G5
Ramsden Bellhouse Essex 46 B2
Ramsey Cambs 89 K6
Ramsey Essex 62 E2
Ramsey IoM 237 e3
Ramsey Forty Foot Cambs 89 K6
Ramsey Heights Cambs 89 J6
Ramsey Island Essex 61 M6
Ramsey Island Pembks 48 B3
Ramsey Mereside Cambs 89 K5
Ramsey St Mary's Cambs 89 J6
Ramsgate Kent 35 K2
Ramsgill N York 131 L5
Ramshope Nthumb 157 J2
Ramshorn Staffs 100 B4
Ramsnest Common Surrey 30 F5
Ranby Lincs 118 B5
Ranby Notts 116 A5
Rand Lincs 117 J5
Randalls Park Crematorium Surrey 44 D8
Randwick Gloucs 55 J6
Ranfurly Rens 174 D5
Rangemore Staffs 100 D7
Rangeworthy S Glos 39 G3
Rankinston E Ayrs 163 L6
Rannoch Station P & K 193 G5
Ranscombe Somset 24 E3
Ranskill Notts 116 A4
Ranton Staffs 99 J7
Ranton Green Staffs 99 J7
Ranworth Norfk 93 H1
Raploch Stirlg 185 G7
Rapness Ork 234 c4
Rascarrel D & G 146 D5
Rashfield Ag & B 173 K2
Rashwood Worcs 71 G2
Raskelf N York 133 G5
Rastrick Calder 123 H6
Ratagan Highld 200 E2
Ratby Leics 87 G3
Ratcliffe Culey Leics 86 D4
Ratcliffe on Soar Notts 101 J6
Ratcliffe on the Wreake Leics 87 J1
Rathen Abers 217 J3
Rathillet Fife 186 F3
Rathmell N York 130 F7
Ratho C Edin 176 F4
Ratho Station C Edin 176 F4
Rathven Moray 215 K2
Ratley Warwks 72 E5
Ratling Kent 35 H4
Ratlinghope Shrops 83 H4
Rattar Highld 231 J2
Rattery Devon 7 H4
Rattlesden Suffk 77 L3
Ratton Village E Susx 20 C5
Rattray P & K 195 J7
Raunds Nhants 88 E8
Ravenfield Rothm 115 J3
Ravenglass Cumb 136 F7
Raveningham Norfk 93 H4
Ravenscar N York 143 K6
Ravenscraig N Lans 175 K6
Ravensden Bed 74 F4
Ravenshead Notts 101 K2
Ravensthorpe Kirk 123 J6
Ravensthorpe Nhants 73 J1
Ravenstone Leics 86 E2
Ravenstone M Keyn 74 B4
Ravenstonedale Cumb 139 G6
Ravenstruther S Lans 165 H1
Ravensworth N York 140 E5
Rawcliffe C York 133 J8
Rawcliffe E R Yk 125 G6
Rawdon Leeds 123 J3
Rawdon Crematorium Leeds 123 J3
Rawling Street Kent 34 B3
Rawmarsh Rothm 115 H3
Rawreth Essex 46 C2
Rawridge Devon 12 F2
Rawtenstall Lancs 122 B6
Raydon Suffk 78 C6
Rayleigh Essex 46 D2
Rayne Essex 61 H4
Raynes Park Gt Lon 44 E6
Reach Cambs 76 E2
Read Lancs 122 B4
Reading Readg 42 B5
Reading Crematorium Readg 42 B5
Reading Services W Berk 42 A6
Reading Street Kent 34 B8
Reading Street Kent 35 K2
Reagill Cumb 138 E4
Realwa Cnwll 3 G4
Rearquhar Highld 223 G3
Rearsby Leics 87 J2
Reay Highld 230 D3
Reculver Kent 47 L6
Red Ball Devon 25 H7
Redberth Pembks 49 J6
Redbourn Herts 59 J5
Redbourne N Linc 116 F2
Redbrook Gloucs 54 D6
Redbrook Wrexhm 98 D4
Redbrook Street Kent 34 C7
Redburn Highld 213 L5
Redcar R & Cl 142 D3
Redcastle D & G 146 E2
Redcastle Highld 212 E4
Redding Falk 176 C3
Reddingmuirhead Falk 176 C3
Reddish Stockp 113 K3
Redditch Worcs 71 J2
Redditch Crematorium Worcs 71 J2
Rede Suffk 77 J4
Redenhall Norfk 92 F6
Redesmouth Nthumb 157 L5
Redford Abers 197 J3
Redford Angus 196 F7
Redford W Susx 30 E6
Redfordgreen Border 166 E6
Redgorton P & K 186 A2
Redgrave Suffk 92 C7
Redhill Abers 206 E4
Red Hill Bmouth 15 K4
Redhill Herts 59 M2
Redhill N Som 38 D7
Redhill Surrey 32 B3
Redisham Suffk 93 J6
Redland Bristl 38 E5
Redland Ork 234 b5
Redlingfield Suffk 78 E1
Redlingfield Green Suffk 78 E1
Red Lodge Suffk 77 G1
Redlynch Somset 27 G5
Redlynch Wilts 28 D7
Redmarley Worcs 70 D2
Redmarley D'Abitot Gloucs 55 H2
Redmarshall S on T 141 J3
Redmile Leics 102 D5
Redmire N York 131 K2
Redmyre Abers 197 J2
Rednal Shrops 98 A6
Redpath Border 167 J3
Redpoint Highld 219 H7
Red Roses Carmth 49 L5
Red Row Nthumb 159 G3
Redruth Cnwll 3 J3
Redstone P & K 186 C1
Red Street Staffs 99 J3
Red Wharf Bay IoA 109 G5
Redwick Newpt 38 B4
Redwick S Glos 38 D3
Redworth Darltn 141 G3
Reed Herts 75 L7
Reedham Norfk 93 J3
Reedness E R Yk 125 J6
Reeds Holme Lancs 122 B5
Reepham Lincs 117 H6
Reepham Norfk 106 D7
Reeth N York 140 C7
Reeves Green Solhll 86 C7
Regil N Som 38 D7
Reiff Highld 224 B5
Reigate Surrey 31 L2
Reighton N York 135 H4
Reisque Abers 207 G2
Reiss Highld 231 L5
Relubbus Cnwll 2 F5
Relugas Moray 214 B5
Remenham Wokham 42 C4
Remenham Hill Wokham 42 C4
Rempstone Notts 101 L7
Rendcomb Gloucs 56 A6
Rendham Suffk 79 H2
Rendlesham Suffk 79 H4
Renfrew Rens 174 F5
Renhold Bed 74 F4
Renishaw Derbys 115 J6
Rennington Nthumb 169 J5
Renton W Duns 174 D3
Renwick Cumb 149 G6
Repps Norfk 93 J1
Repton Derbys 100 F6
Resaurie Highld 213 H5
Resipole Highld 190 E4
Reskadinnick Cnwll 3 H3
Resolis Highld 213 G2
Resolven Neath 52 C7
Rest and be thankful Ag & B 183 J6
Reston Border 179 H6
Reswallie Angus 196 E6
Retford Notts 116 B5
Rettendon Essex 61 J7
Revesby Lincs 103 M1
Rewe Devon 12 B3
Rew Street IoW 16 F4
Reymerston Norfk 92 B3
Reynalton Pembks 49 J5
Reynoldston Swans 50 F7
Rezare Cnwll 6 A1
Rhandirmwyn Carmth 67 H5
Rhayader Powys 67 L2
Rheindown Highld 212 D5
Rhes-y-cae Flints 111 G7
Rhewl Denbgs 97 H1
Rhewl Denbgs 97 J4
Rhicarn Highld 224 D4
Rhiconich Highld 228 C5
Rhicullen Highld 222 F6
Rhigos Rhondd 52 E6
Rhireavach Highld 220 D3
Rhives Highld 223 H2
Rhiwbina Cardif 37 J4
Rhiwderyn Newpt 37 K3
Rhiwlas Gwynd 109 H7
Rhoden Green Kent 33 H4
Rhodes Minnis Kent 34 F6
Rhodiad-y-brenin Pembks 48 C3
Rhonehouse D & G 146 C3
Rhoose V Glam 37 G6
Rhos Carmth 65 L7
Rhos Neath 51 L5
Rhoscolyn IoA 108 C6
Rhoscrowther Pembks 48 F6
Rhosesmor Flints 111 H7
Rhosgoch Powys 68 D5
Rhoshill Pembks 65 H6
Rhoshirwaun Gwynd 94 D6
Rhoslefain Gwynd 80 D3
Rhosllanerchrugog Wrexhm 97 L3
Rhosmeirch IoA 108 F6
Rhosneigr IoA 108 D6
Rhosnesni Wrexhm 97 M3
Rhôs-on-Sea Conwy 110 B5
Rhossili Swans 50 E7
Rhostryfan Gwynd 95 H2
Rhostyllen Wrexhm 97 L3
Rhosybol IoA 108 F4
Rhos-y-gwaliau Gwynd 96 E5
Rhosymedre Wrexhm 97 L4
Rhu Ag & B 174 B2
Rhuallt Denbgs 110 F6
Rhubodach Ag & B 173 H4
Rhuddlan Denbgs 110 E6
Rhunahaorine Ag & B 172 C8
Rhyd Gwynd 95 L4
Rhydargaeau Carmth 50 F1
Rhydcymerau Carmth 66 D6
Rhyd-Ddu Gwynd 95 K3
Rhydlewis Cerdgn 65 K5
Rhydowen Cerdgn 66 B5
Rhyd-uchaf Gwynd 96 D5
Rhyd-y-clafdy Gwynd 94 F5
Rhyd-y-foel Conwy 110 C6
Rhydyfro Neath 51 K4
Rhyd-y-groes Gwynd 109 H7
Rhyd-y-pennau Cerdgn 80 E6
Rhyl Denbgs 110 D5
Rhymney Caerph 53 H6
Rhynd P & K 186 B4
Rhynie Abers 215 L8
Rhynie Highld 223 J5
Ribbesford Worcs 84 D8
Ribbleton Lancs 121 H4
Ribchester Lancs 121 J4
Riby Lincs 126 F8
Riccall N York 124 F3
Riccarton Border 156 F3
Riccarton E Ayrs 163 K3
Richards Castle Herefs 69 J1
Richmond Gt Lon 44 D5
Richmond N York 140 F6
Richmond Sheff 115 H4
Richmond Fort Guern 236 b3
Rickerscote Staffs 99 L7
Rickford N Som 38 C8
Rickham Devon 7 H7
Rickinghall Suffk 92 C7
Rickling Green Essex 60 E3
Rickmansworth Herts 43 H2
Riddell Border 167 H4
Riddlecombe Devon 10 F3
Riddlesden C Brad 123 G3
Ridge Dorset 15 H5
Ridge Herts 59 K7
Ridge Wilts 27 L5
Ridge Lane Warwks 86 C4
Ridgeway Derbys 115 H5
Ridgewell Essex 77 G6
Ridgewood E Susx 19 M2
Ridgmont C Beds 74 E7
Riding Mill Nthumb 150 C3
Ridlington Norfk 107 H6
Ridlington Rutlnd 88 B3
Ridsdale Nthumb 158 A5
Rievaulx N York 133 J3
Rigg D & G 148 B2
Riggend N Lans 175 K4
Righoul Highld 213 K4
Rigsby Lincs 118 F6
Rigside S Lans 165 G3
Riley Green Lancs 121 J5
Rilla Mill Cnwll 5 L2
Rillington N York 134 D5
Rimington Lancs 122 B2
Rimpton Somset 26 E6
Rimswell E R Yk 127 H5
Rinaston Pembks 49 G3
Rindleford Shrops 84 D4
Ringford D & G 146 C4
Ringland Norfk 92 D2

Ringmer E Susx 19 L3
Ringmore Devon 6 F6
Ringmore Devon 7 L2
Ringorm Moray 215 G5
Ringsfield Suffk 93 J5
Ringsfield Corner Suffk 93 J6
Ringshall Herts 59 G5
Ringshall Suffk 78 C4
Ringshall Stocks Suffk 78 C4
Ringstead Nhants 88 E7
Ringstead Norfk 105 H4
Ringwood Hants 15 L2
Ringwould Kent 35 K5
Rinmore Abers 205 J3
Ripe E Susx 20 B4
Ripley Derbys 101 H3
Ripley Hants 15 M3
Ripley N York 132 D7
Ripley Surrey 31 H1
Riplington Hants 30 A6
Ripon N York 132 D5
Rippingale Lincs 103 H6
Ripple Kent 35 J5
Ripple Worcs 70 F6
Ripponden Calder 122 F6
Risabus Ag & B 160 B2
Risbury Herefs 69 K4
Risby Suffk 77 H2
Risca Caerph 37 K3
Rise E R Yk 126 E3
Risegate Lincs 103 K6
Riseley Bed 74 F3
Riseley Wokham 42 B7
Rishangles Suffk 78 E2
Rishton Lancs 121 L4
Rishworth Calder 122 F6
Risley Derbys 101 J5
Risley Warrtn 112 F3
Risplith N York 132 C5
River Kent 35 J6
River W Susx 30 F6
Riverford Highld 212 E4
Riverhead Kent 32 F3
Rivington Lancs 121 J7
Rivington Services Lancs 121 J7
Roade Nhants 73 L4
Roadmeetings S Lans 176 B7
Roadside E Ayrs 164 B5
Roadside Highld 231 H4
Roadwater Somset 25 G4
Roag Highld 208 D5
Roan of Craigoch S Ayrs 153 G2
Roath Cardif 37 J5
Roberton Border 166 F6
Roberton S Lans 165 H4
Robertsbridge E Susx 20 E2
Roberttown Kirk 123 J6
Robeston Wathen Pembks 49 J4
Robgill Tower D & G 155 M7
Robin Hood Crematorium Solhll 85 K7
Robin Hood Doncaster Sheffield Airport Donc 115 M2
Robin Hood's Bay N York 143 K6
Roborough Devon 6 D4
Roborough Devon 10 E2
Roby Knows 112 B4
Rocester Staffs 100 C5
Roch Pembks 48 E3
Rochdale Rochdl 122 D7
Rochdale Crematorium Rochdl 122 C7
Roche Cnwll 4 F4
Rochester Medway 46 C6
Rochester Nthumb 157 L3
Rochford Essex 46 E3
Rochford Worcs 70 B2
Rock Cnwll 4 E2
Rock Nthumb 169 J5
Rock Worcs 70 D1
Rockbeare Devon 12 C4
Rockbourne Hants 28 C7
Rockcliffe Cumb 148 C3
Rockcliffe D & G 146 E4
Rockend Torbay 7 L4
Rock Ferry Wirral 111 K4
Rockfield Highld 223 K5
Rockfield Mons 54 C5
Rockford Devon 24 B2
Rockhampton S Glos 38 F2
Rockhill Shrops 82 F7
Rockingham Nhants 88 C5
Rockland All Saints Norfk 92 B4
Rockland St Mary Norfk 93 G3
Rockland St Peter Norfk 92 B4
Rockley Notts 116 B6
Rockville Ag & B 173 L1
Rockwell End Bucks 42 D3
Rodborough Gloucs 55 J6
Rodbourne Swindn 40 C4
Rodbourne Wilts 39 L4
Rodden Dorset 14 B5
Rode Somset 27 J2
Rode Heath Ches E 99 J2
Rodel W Isls 232 d5
Roden Wrekin 83 L1
Rodhuish Somset 24 F4
Rodington Wrekin 83 L1
Rodington Heath Wrekin 83 L1
Rodley Gloucs 55 H5
Rodmarton Gloucs 39 L2
Rodmell E Susx 19 L4
Rodmersham Kent 34 B3
Rodmersham Green Kent 34 B3
Rodney Stoke Somset 26 C2
Rodsley Derbys 100 D4
Roecliffe N York 132 E6
Roe Green Herts 59 K6
Roe Green Herts 75 K7
Roehampton Gt Lon 44 E5
Roffey W Susx 31 K5
Rogart Highld 226 C7
Rogate W Susx 30 D6
Rogerstone Newpt 37 L3
Roghadal W Isls 232 d5
Rogiet Mons 38 C3
Roke Oxon 41 L2
Roker Sundld 151 J3
Rollesby Norfk 93 J1
Rolleston Leics 87 K4
Rolleston Notts 102 C3
Rolleston on Dove Staffs 100 E6
Rolston E R Yk 126 F2
Rolvenden Kent 33 L6
Rolvenden Layne Kent 33 L7
Romaldkirk Dur 140 C3
Romanby N York 132 E2
Romanno Bridge Border 177 G8
Romansleigh Devon 24 B7
Romesdal Highld 208 F4
Romford Dorset 15 K1
Romford Gt Lon 45 K3
Romiley Stockp 113 L4
Romsey Cambs 76 C3
Romsey Hants 29 G6
Romsley Shrops 84 D6
Romsley Worcs 85 G7
Rona Highld 209 K3
Ronachan Ag & B 172 C7
Rookhope Dur 150 B6
Rookley IoW 17 G5
Rooks Bridge Somset 26 A2
Rooks Nest Somset 25 H5
Rookwith N York 132 C3
Roos E R Yk 127 G4
Roothams Green Bed 75 G3
Ropley Hants 29 M5
Ropley Dean Hants 29 L5
Ropsley Lincs 103 G5
Rora Abers 217 K4
Rorrington Shrops 82 F4
Rosarie Moray 215 J4
Rose Cnwll 3 K1
Rose Ash Devon 24 C6
Rosebank S Lans 175 L7
Rosebush Pembks 49 J2
Rosedale Abbey N York 142 F7
Rose Green Essex 61 L3
Rose Green Suffk 77 L5
Rose Green Suffk 77 L6
Rose Green W Susx 18 B5
Rosehall Highld 225 K7
Rosehearty Abers 217 H2
Rose Hill Lancs 122 C4
Rose Hill Crematorium Donc 115 L2
Roseisle Moray 214 E2
Roselands E Susx 20 C5
Rosemarket Pembks 49 G5
Rosemarkie Highld 213 H3
Rosemary Lane Devon 25 J7
Rosemount P & K 195 J7
Rosenannon Cnwll 4 E3
Rosewell Mdloth 177 J6
Roseworth S on T 141 K3
Rosgill Cumb 138 D4
Roskhill Highld 208 D5
Rosley Cumb 148 B6
Roslin Mdloth 177 H5
Rosliston Derbys 86 B1
Rosneath Ag & B 174 B2
Ross D & G 146 B6
Rossett Wrexhm 98 A2
Rossett Green N York 132 D8
Rossington Donc 115 L2
Rossland Rens 174 E4
Ross-on-Wye Herefs 54 E4
Roster Highld 231 J7
Rostherne Ches E 113 H5
Rosthwaite Cumb 137 H4
Roston Derbys 100 C4
Rosyth Fife 176 F2
Rothbury Nthumb 158 D2
Rotherby Leics 87 J1
Rotherfield E Susx 32 F7
Rotherfield Greys Oxon 42 B4
Rotherfield Peppard Oxon 42 B4
Rotherham Rothm 115 H3
Rotherham Crematorium Rothm 115 J3
Rothersthorpe Nhants 73 K3
Rotherwick Hants 30 B1
Rothes Moray 215 G4
Rothesay Ag & B 173 J5
Rothiebrisbane Abers 216 E6
Rothiemay Moray 215 M5
Rothiemurchus Lodge Highld 204 B4
Rothienorman Abers 216 D7
Rothley Leics 87 H2
Rothmaise Abers 216 D7
Rothwell Leeds 123 L5
Rothwell Lincs 117 J2
Rothwell Nhants 88 B7
Rottal Lodge Angus 196 B3
Rottingdean Br & H 19 K5
Rottington Cumb 136 D5
Roucan D & G 155 H6
Roucan Loch Crematorium D & G 155 H6
Rougham Norfk 105 K7
Rougham Suffk 77 K3
Rough Common Kent 34 F3
Roughpark Abers 205 H3
Roughton Lincs 118 C8
Roughton Norfk 106 F5
Roughton Shrops 84 D5
Roundbush Green Essex 60 F5
Round Green Luton 59 J4
Roundham Somset 13 K1
Roundhay Leeds 123 L3
Rounds Green Sandw 85 H5
Roundswell Devon 23 H5
Roundway Wilts 40 A7
Roundyhill Angus 196 C6
Rousay Ork 234 c4
Rousdon Devon 13 H4
Rousham Oxon 57 J3
Rous Lench Worcs 71 H4
Routenburn N Ayrs 173 L6
Routh E R Yk 126 D3
Row Cumb 129 K2
Rowanburn D & G 156 D6
Rowardennan Stirlg 183 L7
Rowarth Derbys 114 A4
Rowberrow Somset 38 C8
Rowde Wilts 39 L7
Rowen Conwy 109 L6
Rowfoot Nthumb 149 H3
Rowhedge Essex 62 B4
Rowington Warwks 72 B2
Rowland Derbys 114 E6
Rowland's Castle Hants 17 K1
Rowlands Gill Gatesd 150 E4
Rowledge Surrey 30 D3
Rowley Dur 150 D5
Rowley Regis Sandw 85 H6
Rowley Regis Crematorium Sandw 85 G6
Rowlstone Herefs 54 A3
Rowly Surrey 31 H4
Rowner Hants 17 H3
Rowney Green Worcs 71 J1
Rownhams Hants 29 G7
Rownhams Services Hants 29 H7
Rowrah Cumb 136 E4
Rowsham Bucks 58 D4
Rowsley Derbys 114 E7
Rowston Lincs 103 H2
Rowton Ches W 112 C8
Rowton Wrekin 98 E8
Roxburgh Border 167 L4
Roxby N Linc 125 L6
Roxton Bed 75 G4
Roxwell Essex 61 G6
Royal Leamington Spa Warwks 72 D2
Royal Sutton Coldfield Birm 85 K4
Royal Tunbridge Wells Kent 33 G5
Royal Wootton Bassett Wilts 40 B4
Royal Yacht Britannia C Edin 177 H3
Roy Bridge Highld 192 D1
Roydon Essex 60 C6
Roydon Norfk 92 D7
Roydon Norfk 105 H7
Roydon Hamlet Essex 60 C6
Royston Barns 124 B7
Royston Herts 75 L6
Royton Oldham 122 D8
Rozel Jersey 236 e6
Ruabon Wrexhm 97 L4
Ruaig Ag & B 188 D6
Ruan Lanihorne Cnwll 4 D7
Ruan Major Cnwll 3 J7
Ruan Minor Cnwll 3 J7
Ruardean Gloucs 54 F4
Ruardean Hill Gloucs 54 F5
Ruardean Woodside Gloucs 54 F5
Rubery Birm 85 H7
Rubha Ban W Isls 233 c9
Ruckhall Herefs 69 J6
Ruckinge Kent 34 D7
Ruckley Shrops 83 K4

Rudby N York 141 L6
Rudchester Nthumb 150 E2
Ruddington Notts 101 L6
Rudge Somset 27 J2
Rudgeway S Glos 38 F3
Rudgwick W Susx 31 H5
Rudheath Ches W 112 F6
Rudley Green Essex 61 K7
Rudloe Wilts 39 J6
Rudry Caerph 37 J3
Rudston E R Yk 135 H6
Rudyard Staffs 99 L2
Ruecastle Border 167 J5
Rufford Lancs 120 F7
Rufford Abbey Notts 115 M8
Rufforth C York 124 D1
Rugby Warwks 87 G7
Rugeley Staffs 100 B8
Ruishton Somset 25 K6
Ruislip Gt Lon 43 H3
Rùm Highld 198 F5
Rumbach Moray 215 J4
Rumbling Bridge P & K 185 L7
Rumburgh Suffk 93 H7
Rumford Cnwll 4 D2
Rumford Falk 176 C3
Rumney Cardif 37 K5
Runcorn Halton 112 D5
Runcton W Susx 18 B5
Runcton Holme Norfk 90 E2
Runfold Surrey 30 E3
Runhall Norfk 92 C3
Runham Norfk 93 K2
Runnington Somset 25 H6
Runswick N York 143 G4
Runtaleave Angus 195 L3
Runwell Essex 46 C2
Ruscombe Wokham 42 D5
Rushall Herefs 70 B7
Rushall Norfk 92 E6
Rushall Wilts 28 C1
Rushall Wsall 85 H4
Rushbrooke Suffk 77 K3
Rushbury Shrops 83 K5
Rushden Herts 60 A2
Rushden Nhants 74 D2
Rushenden Kent 46 E5
Rushford Norfk 91 K7
Rush Green Essex 62 E5
Rush Green Gt Lon 45 K3
Rush Green Warrtn 113 G4
Rushlake Green E Susx 20 D3
Rushmere Suffk 93 K6
Rushmoor Surrey 30 E4
Rushock Worcs 70 F1
Rusholme Manch 113 J3
Rushton Nhants 88 B6
Rushton Spencer Staffs 113 L8
Rushwick Worcs 70 E4
Rushyford Dur 141 G2
Ruskie Stirlg 184 D7
Ruskington Lincs 103 H3
Rusland Cross Cumb 129 H2
Rusper W Susx 31 K4
Ruspidge Gloucs 54 F5
Russell's Water Oxon 42 B3
Russ Hill Surrey 31 L4
Rusthall Kent 32 F5
Rustington W Susx 18 E5
Ruston N York 134 E3
Ruston Parva E R Yk 135 G6
Ruswarp N York 143 H5
Rutherford Border 167 K4
Rutherglen S Lans 175 H6
Ruthernbridge Cnwll 4 F3
Ruthin Denbgs 97 H2
Ruthrieston C Aber 207 H4
Ruthven Abers 215 L5
Ruthven Angus 195 L6
Ruthven Highld 203 H5
Ruthven Highld 213 J7
Ruthvoes Cnwll 4 E4
Ruthwell D & G 147 J2
Ruyton-XI-Towns Shrops 98 B7
Ryal Nthumb 158 C7
Ryall Dorset 13 K4
Ryall Worcs 70 F6
Ryarsh Kent 33 H2
Rydal Cumb 137 K6
Ryde IoW 17 H4
Rye E Susx 21 H2
Rye Foreign E Susx 21 H2
Rye Street Worcs 70 D7
Ryhall Rutlnd 88 F2
Ryhill Wakefd 124 B7
Ryhope Sundld 151 K4
Ryland Lincs 117 G5
Rylands Notts 101 K5
Rylstone N York 131 H7
Ryme Intrinseca Dorset 14 B1
Ryther N York 124 E3
Ryton Gatesd 150 E3
Ryton Shrops 84 D3
Ryton-on-Dunsmore Warwks 86 E8
RZSS Edinburgh Zoo C Edin 177 G4

S

Sabden Lancs 122 B3
Sacombe Herts 60 B4
Sacriston Dur 151 G5
Sadberge Darltn 141 H4
Saddell Ag & B 161 K3
Saddington Leics 87 J5
Saddlebow Norfk 90 E1
Saddlescombe W Susx 19 H4
Saffron Walden Essex 76 D6
Sageston Pembks 49 H6
Saham Hills Norfk 91 K3
Saham Toney Norfk 91 K3
Saighton Ches W 98 C1
St Abbs Border 179 J5
St Agnes Border 178 E5
St Agnes Cnwll 3 J2
St Agnes IoS 2 a2
St Agnes Mining District Cnwll 3 J2
St Albans Herts 59 J6
St Allen Cnwll 4 C5
St Andrew Guern 236 c3
St Andrews Fife 187 H4
St Andrews Botanic Garden Fife 187 H4
St Andrew's Major V Glam 37 H6
St Andrews Well Dorset 13 L4
St Anne's Lancs 120 D5
St Ann's D & G 155 J4
St Ann's Chapel Cnwll 6 B2
St Ann's Chapel Devon 6 F6
St Anthony Cnwll 3 K6
St Anthony's Hill E Susx 20 D5
St Arvans Mons 38 D2
St Asaph Denbgs 110 E6
St Athan V Glam 36 F6
St Aubin Jersey 236 b7
St Austell Cnwll 4 F5
St Bees Cumb 136 D5
St Blazey Cnwll 5 G5
St Boswells Border 167 J3
St Brelade Jersey 236 b7
St Brelade's Bay Jersey 236 b7
St Breock Cnwll 4 F2
St Breward Cnwll 5 H1
St Briavels Gloucs 54 E6
St Bride's Major V Glam 36 D5
St Brides-super-Ely V Glam 37 H5
St Brides Wentlooge Newpt 37 L4
St Budeaux C Plym 6 C4
Saintbury Gloucs 71 K6
St Buryan Cnwll 2 D6
St Catherines Ag & B 183 G6
St Chloe Gloucs 55 J7
St Clears Carmth 50 C3
St Cleer Cnwll 5 K3
St Clement Cnwll 4 D6
St Clement Jersey 236 e8
St Clether Cnwll 9 G7
St Colmac Ag & B 173 H5
St Columb Major Cnwll 4 E3
St Columb Minor Cnwll 4 D4
St Columb Road Cnwll 4 E4
St Combs Abers 217 K2
St Cross South Elmham Suffk 93 G6
St Cyrus Abers 197 J4
St David's P & K 185 K4
St Davids Pembks 48 C3
St Davids Cathedral Pembks 48 C3
St Day Cnwll 3 J3
St Dennis Cnwll 4 E4
St Dogmaels Pembks 65 G5
St Dominick Cnwll 6 B3
St Donats V Glam 36 E6
St Endellion Cnwll 4 F1
St Enoder Cnwll 4 D4
St Erme Cnwll 4 D6
St Erney Cnwll 6 B4
St Erth Cnwll 2 F4
St Erth Praze Cnwll 3 G4
St Ervan Cnwll 4 D2
St Eval Cnwll 4 D3
St Ewe Cnwll 4 F6
St Fagans Cardif 37 H5
St Fagans: National History Museum Cardif 37 H5
St Fergus Abers 217 K4
St Fillans P & K 184 F3
St Florence Pembks 49 J7
St Gennys Cnwll 8 F5
St George Conwy 110 D6
St Georges N Som 38 B7
St George's V Glam 37 H5
St Germans Cnwll 6 A4
St Giles in the Wood Devon 23 H7
St Giles-on-the-Heath Devon 9 K6
St Harmon Powys 81 L8
St Helen Auckland Dur 140 F2
St Helen's E Susx 21 G4
St Helens IoW 17 J5
St Helens St Hel 112 D3
St Helens Crematorium St Hel 112 C3
St Helier Gt Lon 44 E6
St Helier Jersey 236 d7
St Hilary Cnwll 2 F5
St Hilary V Glam 36 F5
St Ippollitts Herts 59 K3
St Ishmael's Pembks 48 E6
St Issey Cnwll 4 E2
St Ive Cnwll 5 L3
St Ives Cambs 75 K1
St Ives Cnwll 2 F3
St James's End Nhants 73 L3
St James South Elmham Suffk 93 G7
St Jidgey Cnwll 4 E3
St John Cnwll 6 B5
St John Jersey 236 c5
St John's IoM 237 b5
St John's Kent 32 F3
St Johns Surrey 43 G8
St Johns Worcs 70 E4
St John's Chapel Devon 23 H5
St John's Chapel Dur 149 M7
St John's Fen End Norfk 90 D2
St John's Kirk S Lans 165 J3
St John's Town of Dalry D & G 154 B6
St John's Wood Gt Lon 44 F4
St Jude's IoM 237 d3
St Just Cnwll 2 C5
St Just-in-Roseland Cnwll 4 D8
St Just Mining District Cnwll 2 D5
St Katherines Abers 216 E7
St Keverne Cnwll 3 K6
St Kew Cnwll 5 G1
St Kew Highway Cnwll 5 G2
St Keyne Cnwll 5 K4
St Lawrence Essex 62 A6
St Lawrence IoW 17 G6
St Lawrence Jersey 236 c6
St Lawrence Kent 35 K2
St Leonards Bucks 58 E6
St Leonards Dorset 15 L2
St Leonards E Susx 20 F4
St Levan Cnwll 2 C6
St Lythans V Glam 37 H6
St Mabyn Cnwll 5 G2
St Madoes P & K 186 C3
St Margarets Herefs 69 G7
St Margarets Herts 60 B5
St Margaret's at Cliffe Kent 35 K5
St Margaret's Hope Ork 234 c7
St Margaret South Elmham Suffk 93 G6
St Marks IoM 237 c6
St Martin Cnwll 3 J6
St Martin Cnwll 5 K5
St Martin Guern 236 d3
St Martin Jersey 236 e6
St Martin's IoS 2 b1
St Martin's P & K 186 B2
St Martin's Shrops 97 L5
St Mary Jersey 236 b6
St Mary Bourne Hants 29 H2
St Marychurch Torbay 7 L3
St Mary Church V Glam 36 F6
St Mary Cray Gt Lon 45 J6
St Mary in the Marsh Kent 21 L1
St Marylebone Crematorium Gt Lon 44 E3
St Mary's IoS 2 b1
St Mary's Ork 234 c6
St Mary's Bay Kent 21 L1
St Mary's Hoo Medway 46 D5
St Mary's Platt Kent 33 G2
St Maughans Green Mons 54 C5
St Mawes Cnwll 3 L5
St Mawgan Cnwll 4 D3
St Mellion Cnwll 6 B3
St Mellons Cardif 37 K4
St Merryn Cnwll 4 D2
St Michael Caerhays Cnwll 4 F7
St Michael Church Somset 25 L5
St Michael Penkevil Cnwll 4 D7
St Michaels Kent 34 B7
St Michaels Worcs 69 L2
St Michael's Mount Cnwll 2 F5
St Michael's on Wyre Lancs 120 F3
St Minver Cnwll 4 F1
St Monans Fife 187 H6

St Neot Cnwll 5 J3
St Neots Cambs 75 H3
St Newlyn East Cnwll 4 C5
St Nicholas Pembks 64 C7
St Nicholas V Glam 37 H5
St Nicholas-at-Wade Kent 47 L6
St Ninians Stirlg 185 G8
St Olaves Norfk 93 J4
St Osyth Essex 62 D5
St Ouen Jersey 236 b6
St Owens Cross Herefs 54 D3
St Paul's Cray Gt Lon 45 J6
St Paul's Walden Herts 59 K4
St Peter Jersey 236 b6
St Peter Port Guern 236 d3
St Peter's Guern 236 b3
St Peter's Kent 35 K2
St Peter's Hill Cambs 89 J8
St Pinnock Cnwll 5 J3
St Quivox S Ayrs 163 J5
St Sampson Guern 236 d2
St Saviour Guern 236 c3
St Saviour Jersey 236 d7
St Stephen Cnwll 4 E5
St Stephens Cnwll 6 B4
St Stephens Cnwll 9 J7
St Teath Cnwll 8 E8
St Tudy Cnwll 5 G1
St Twynnells Pembks 48 F7
St Veep Cnwll 5 J5
St Vigeans Angus 197 G7
St Wenn Cnwll 4 F3
St Weonards Herefs 54 D3
Salcombe Devon 7 H7
Salcombe Regis Devon 12 F5
Salcott-cum-Virley Essex 61 M5
Sale Traffd 113 H3
Saleby Lincs 118 F5
Sale Green Worcs 71 G3
Salehurst E Susx 20 F2
Salem Cerdgn 80 F6
Salen Ag & B 190 C7
Salen Highld 190 D4
Salford C Beds 74 D6
Salford Oxon 56 F3
Salford Salfd 113 J3
Salford Priors Warwks 71 J4
Salfords Surrey 32 B4
Salhouse Norfk 93 G1
Saline Fife 185 L8
Salisbury Wilts 28 C5
Salisbury Crematorium Wilts 28 D5
Salisbury Plain Wilts 28 B3
Salkeld Dykes Cumb 148 F7
Salle Norfk 106 D7
Salmonby Lincs 118 D6
Salperton Gloucs 56 B4
Salsburgh N Lans 175 L5
Salt Staffs 99 L6
Saltaire C Brad 123 H3
Saltaire C Brad 123 H3
Saltash Cnwll 6 B4
Saltburn Highld 223 G7
Saltburn-by-the-Sea R & Cl 142 E3
Saltby Leics 102 D7
Saltcoats N Ayrs 163 G2
Saltdean Br & H 19 K5
Salterbeck Cumb 136 D3
Salterforth Lancs 122 D2
Salterton Wilts 28 C4
Saltfleet Lincs 118 F3
Saltfleetby All Saints Lincs 118 F4
Saltfleetby St Clement Lincs 118 F3
Saltfleetby St Peter Lincs 118 F4
Saltford BaNES 39 G6
Salthouse Norfk 106 C4
Saltley Birm 85 K6
Saltmarshe E R Yk 125 J5
Saltney Flints 111 L8
Salton N York 133 L4
Saltrens Devon 23 G6
Saltwell Crematorium Gatesd 151 G3
Saltwood Kent 34 F7
Salvington W Susx 18 F5
Salwarpe Worcs 70 F3
Salway Ash Dorset 13 L3
Sambourne Warwks 71 J3
Sambrook Wrekin 99 G7
Sampford Arundel Somset 25 H7
Sampford Brett Somset 25 H4
Sampford Courtenay Devon 10 F5
Sampford Moor Somset 25 H7
Sampford Peverell Devon 25 G8
Sampford Spiney Devon 6 D2
Samsonlane Ork 234 d5
Samuelston E Loth 178 B4
Sanaigmore Ag & B 170 E4
Sancreed Cnwll 2 D5
Sancton E R Yk 125 L3
Sandaig Highld 199 L5
Sandal Magna Wakefd 123 L6
Sandavore Highld 199 G7
Sanday Ork 234 d4
Sanday Airport Ork 234 d4
Sandbach Ches E 99 H1
Sandbach Services Ches E 99 H1
Sandbank Ag & B 173 K3
Sandbanks Poole 15 K5
Sandend Abers 216 B2
Sanderstead Gt Lon 45 G7
Sandford Cumb 139 G4
Sandford Devon 11 J4
Sandford Dorset 15 H5
Sandford Hants 15 M3
Sandford IoW 17 G6
Sandford N Som 38 B8
Sandford S Lans 164 E2
Sandford-on-Thames Oxon 57 K7
Sandford Orcas Dorset 26 F7
Sandford St Martin Oxon 57 H3
Sandgate Kent 35 G7
Sandhaven Abers 217 H2
Sandhead D & G 144 D5
Sand Hills Leeds 124 B3
Sandhills Oxon 57 K6
Sandhills Surrey 30 F4
Sandhoe Nthumb 150 B2
Sandhole Ag & B 182 E7
Sand Hole E R Yk 125 J3
Sandholme E R Yk 125 J4
Sandhurst Br For 42 D7
Sandhurst Gloucs 55 J4
Sandhurst Kent 33 K7
Sandhutton N York 132 F3
Sand Hutton N York 133 L7
Sandiacre Derbys 101 J5
Sandilands Lincs 119 G5
Sandleheath Hants 28 C7
Sandleigh Oxon 57 J7
Sandley Dorset 27 H6
Sandness Shet 235 b5
Sandon Essex 61 H6
Sandon Herts 75 K7
Sandon Staffs 99 L6
Sandon Bank Staffs 99 L6
Sandown IoW 17 H5
Sandplace Cnwll 5 K4
Sandridge Herts 59 K6
Sandringham Norfk 105 H6
Sandsend N York 143 H5
Sandtoft N Linc 125 H8
Sandway Kent 34 B5
Sandwell Valley Crematorium Sandw 85 H5
Sandwich Kent 35 J3
Sandwick Shet 235 c7
Sandwick W Isls 232 g2
Sandwith Cumb 136 D4
Sandy C Beds 75 H5
Sandyford D & G 155 L4
Sandygate Devon 7 K2
Sandygate IoM 237 d3
Sandyhills D & G 146 F4
Sandylands Lancs 129 J6
Sandy Lane Wilts 39 L6
Sandy Park Devon 11 G6
Sangobeg Highld 228 F3
Sangomore Highld 228 F3
Sankyn's Green Worcs 70 E2
Sanna Bay Highld 189 K3
Sanndabhaig W Isls 232 g2
Sannox N Ayrs 162 C1
Sanquhar D & G 164 F7
Santon Bridge Cumb 136 F6
Santon Downham Suffk 91 J6
Sapcote Leics 86 F5
Sapey Common Herefs 70 C2
Sapiston Suffk 91 K7
Sapperton Gloucs 55 L7
Sapperton Lincs 103 G5
Saracen's Head Lincs 104 B6
Sarclet Highld 231 L6
Sarisbury Hants 17 G2
Sarn Gwynd 94 D6
Sarn Powys 81 K4
Sarn Powys 82 E5
Sarnau Cerdgn 65 K4
Sarnau Powys 82 E1
Sarn Park Services Brdgnd 36 D4
Saron Carmth 51 H3
Saron Gwynd 109 G7
Sarratt Herts 59 H7
Sarre Kent 47 L6
Sarsden Oxon 56 F4
Satley Dur 150 E6
Satterleigh Devon 23 L6
Satterthwaite Cumb 129 H2
Sauchen Abers 206 D3
Saucher P & K 186 C2
Sauchieburn Abers 197 G3
Saul Gloucs 55 H6
Saundby Notts 116 C4
Saundersfoot Pembks 49 K6
Saunderton Bucks 58 C7
Saunton Devon 23 G4
Sausthorpe Lincs 118 E7
Savile Town Kirk 123 K6
Sawbridge Warwks 73 G2
Sawbridgeworth Herts 60 D5
Sawdon N York 134 E3
Sawley Lancs 122 B2
Sawley N York 132 C6
Sawston Cambs 76 C5
Sawtry Cambs 89 H6
Saxby Leics 102 D8
Saxby Lincs 117 G4
Saxby All Saints N Linc 126 B7
Saxelbye Leics 102 B7
Saxham Street Suffk 78 C3
Saxilby Lincs 116 E6
Saxlingham Norfk 106 B5
Saxlingham Green Norfk 92 F4
Saxlingham Nethergate Norfk 92 F4
Saxlingham Thorpe Norfk 92 E4
Saxmundham Suffk 79 H2
Saxondale Notts 102 B4
Saxon Street Cambs 76 F3
Saxtead Suffk 78 F2
Saxtead Green Suffk 78 F2
Saxtead Little Green Suffk 78 F2
Saxthorpe Norfk 106 D6
Saxton N York 124 D3
Sayers Common W Susx 19 H3
Scackleton N York 133 K5
Scafell Pike Cumb 137 H5
Scaftworth Notts 116 A3
Scagglethorpe N York 134 C5
Scalasaig Ag & B 180 E8
Scalby E R Yk 125 K5
Scalby N York 134 F2
Scaldwell Nhants 73 L1
Scaleby Cumb 148 D3
Scalebyhill Cumb 148 D3
Scales Cumb 129 G5
Scales Cumb 137 K2
Scalford Leics 102 C7
Scaling N York 142 F4
Scalloway Shet 235 c6
Scalpay Highld 209 J7
Scamblesby Lincs 118 C5
Scamodale Highld 191 G2
Scampston N York 134 D4
Scampton Lincs 116 F5
Scaniport Highld 212 F6
Scapegoat Hill Kirk 123 G7
Scarba Ag & B 181 K6
Scarborough N York 135 G2
Scarcewater Cnwll 4 E5
Scarcliffe Derbys 115 J7
Scarcroft Leeds 124 B3
Scarfskerry Highld 231 J2
Scarinish Ag & B 188 D7
Scarisbrick Lancs 120 E7
Scarning Norfk 91 L2
Scarrington Notts 102 B4
Scartho NE Lin 118 C1
Scatsta Airport Shet 235 c4
Scaur D & G 146 E4
Scawby N Linc 116 F1
Scawsby Donc 115 K1
Scawthorpe Donc 115 K1
Scawton N York 133 H3
Scayne's Hill W Susx 19 K2
Scethrog Powys 53 H3
Scholar Green Ches E 99 J2
Scholemoor Crematorium C Brad 123 H4
Scholes Kirk 123 H8
Scholes Leeds 124 B3
Scholes Rothm 115 H3
Scholes Wigan 112 E1
Scissett Kirk 123 K7
Scleddau Pembks 64 C7
Scofton Notts 115 M5
Scole Norfk 92 D7
Scone P & K 186 B3
Sconser Highld 209 H7
Scoonie Fife 186 F6
Scopwick Lincs 103 H2
Scoraig Highld 220 C3
Scorborough E R Yk 126 C2
Scorrier Cnwll 3 J3
Scorton Lancs 121 G2
Scorton N York 141 G7
Scotby Cumb 148 D4
Scotch Corner N York 140 F6
Scotch Corner Rest Area N York 140 F6
Scotforth Lancs 129 K7
Scothern Lincs 117 G6
Scotlandwell P & K 186 C6
Scotscalder Station Highld 231 G4
Scot's Gap Nthumb 158 C5
Scotsmill Abers 206 B2
Scotstoun C Glas 174 F5
Scotswood N u Ty 150 F3
Scotter Lincs 116 E2
Scotterthorpe Lincs 116 E2

Scottish Seabird Centre E Loth 178 C2
Scottish Wool Centre Stirlg 184 C7
Scotton Lincs 116 E2
Scotton N York 132 E7
Scotton N York 140 F7
Scoulton Norfk 92 B4
Scourie Highld 228 B6
Scourie More Highld 228 B6
Scousburgh Shet 235 c7
Scrabster Highld 231 G2
Scraesburgh Border 167 K5
Scrane End Lincs 104 C4
Scraptoft Leics 87 J3
Scratby Norfk 93 K1
Scrayingham N York 133 L7
Scredington Lincs 103 H4
Scremby Lincs 118 F7
Scremerston Nthumb 179 L8
Screveton Notts 102 B4
Scriven N York 132 E7
Scrooby Notts 115 M4
Scropton Derbys 100 D6
Scrub Hill Lincs 103 L2
Scruton N York 132 D2
Scullomie Highld 229 J4
Sculthorpe Norfk 105 L6
Scunthorpe N Linc 125 K7
Seaborough Dorset 13 K2
Seabridge Staffs 99 J4
Seabrook Kent 35 G7
Seaburn Sundld 151 J3
Seacombe Wirral 111 K4
Seacroft Leeds 123 L4
Seafield Highld 209 G5
Seafield W Loth 176 D5
Seafield Crematorium C Edin 177 J4
Seaford E Susx 20 A6
Seaforth Sefton 111 K3
Seagrave Leics 101 L8
Seaham Dur 151 K5
Seahouses Nthumb 169 J3
Seal Kent 32 F2
Sealand Flints 111 K7
Seale Surrey 30 E2
Seamer N York 134 F3
Seamer N York 142 B5
Seamill N Ayrs 173 L8
Sea Palling Norfk 107 J6
Searby Lincs 117 H1
Seasalter Kent 47 H6
Seascale Cumb 136 E6
Seathwaite Cumb 137 H7
Seatoller Cumb 137 H4
Seaton Cnwll 5 L5
Seaton Cumb 136 E2
Seaton Devon 13 G4
Seaton E R Yk 126 E2
Seaton Kent 35 G3
Seaton Nthumb 159 H6
Seaton Rutlnd 88 C4
Seaton Carew Hartpl 142 B2
Seaton Delaval Nthumb 159 H6
Seaton Ross E R Yk 125 J3
Seaton Sluice Nthumb 159 H6
Seatown Dorset 13 K4
Seave Green N York 142 C7
Seaview IoW 17 J4
Seaville Cumb 147 K4
Seavington St Mary Somset 26 B7
Seavington St Michael Somset 26 B7
Sebergham Cumb 148 C6
Seckington Warwks 86 C3
Second Severn Crossing Mons 38 D3
Sedbergh Cumb 130 C2
Sedbury Gloucs 38 D2
Sedbusk N York 131 G2
Sedgeberrow Worcs 71 H6
Sedgebrook Lincs 102 D5
Sedgefield Dur 141 J2
Sedgeford Norfk 105 H5
Sedgehill Wilts 27 K5
Sedgemoor Crematorium Somset 25 L3
Sedgemoor Services Somset 26 A2
Sedgley Dudley 85 G5
Sedgley Park Bury 113 J2
Sedgwick Cumb 129 L3
Sedlescombe E Susx 20 F3
Sedrup Bucks 58 D5
Seend Wilts 39 L7
Seend Cleeve Wilts 39 L7
Seer Green Bucks 42 F3
Seething Norfk 93 G4
Sefton Sefton 111 K2
Seighford Staffs 99 K7
Seion Gwynd 109 H7
Seisdon Staffs 84 E4
Selattyn Shrops 97 K5
Selborne Hants 30 C5
Selby N York 124 F4
Selham W Susx 30 F7
Selhurst Gt Lon 45 G6
Selkirk Border 167 G4
Sellack Herefs 54 E3
Sellafield Station Cumb 136 E6
Sellafirth Shet 235 d2
Sellindge Kent 34 E6
Selling Kent 34 D4
Sells Green Wilts 39 L7
Selly Oak Birm 85 J6
Selmeston E Susx 20 B4
Selsdon Gt Lon 45 G7
Selsey Gloucs 55 J7
Selsey W Susx 18 B6
Selside N York 130 E4
Selsted Kent 35 G5
Selston Notts 101 J2
Selworthy Somset 24 E3
Semer Suffk 78 B5
Semington Wilts 39 K7
Semley Wilts 27 K6
Send Surrey 31 G1
Senghenydd Caerph 37 H3
Sennen Cnwll 2 C6
Sennen Cove Cnwll 2 C6
Sennybridge Powys 52 E3
Sessay N York 133 G4
Setchey Norfk 90 F2
Seton Mains E Loth 177 L4
Settle N York 130 F6
Settrington N York 134 C5
Sevenhampton Gloucs 56 B4
Sevenhampton Swindn 40 E3
Seven Hills Crematorium Suffk 78 F6
Seven Kings Gt Lon 45 J3
Sevenoaks Kent 32 F3
Sevenoaks Weald Kent 32 F3
Seven Sisters Neath 52 C6
Seven Star Green Essex 61 M3
Severn Beach S Glos 38 D4
Severn Bridge S Glos 38 E3
Severn Stoke Worcs 70 F5
Severn View Services S Glos 38 E3
Sevington Kent 34 D6
Sewards End Essex 76 E6
Sewell C Beds 59 G4
Sewerby E R Yk 135 J5
Seworgan Cnwll 3 J5
Sewstern Leics 102 E7
Sgiogarstaigh W Isls 232 g1
Shabbington Bucks 58 A6
Shackerstone Leics 86 D3
Shackleford Surrey 30 F3
Shader W Isls 232 f1
Shadforth Dur 151 H6
Shadingfield Suffk 93 J6
Shadoxhurst Kent 34 C7
Shadwell Norfk 91 L6
Shaftenhoe End Herts 76 B6
Shaftesbury Dorset 27 K6
Shafton Barns 124 B7
Shakerley Wigan 113 G2
Shalbourne Wilts 40 F7
Shalden Hants 30 B3
Shaldon Devon 7 L2
Shalfleet IoW 16 E5
Shalford Essex 61 H3
Shalford Surrey 31 G3
Shalford Green Essex 61 H3
Shalmsford Street Kent 34 E4
Shalstone Bucks 73 J7
Shamley Green Surrey 31 G3
Shandford Angus 196 D4
Shandon Ag & B 174 B2
Shandwick Highld 223 J6
Shangton Leics 87 K4
Shanklin IoW 17 H6
Shap Cumb 138 E4
Shapinsay Ork 234 c5
Shapwick Dorset 15 H3
Shapwick Somset 26 B4
Shard End Birm 85 L5
Shardlow Derbys 101 H6
Shareshill Staffs 85 G3
Sharlston Wakefd 124 B6
Sharman's Cross Solhll 85 K7
Sharnbrook Bed 74 E3
Sharnford Leics 86 F5
Sharoe Green Lancs 121 G4
Sharow N York 132 E5
Sharpenhoe C Beds 59 H2
Sharperton Nthumb 158 B2
Sharpness Gloucs 54 F7
Sharrington Norfk 106 C5
Shatterford Worcs 84 E7
Shaugh Prior Devon 6 D3
Shavington Ches E 99 G3
Shaw Oldham 122 D8
Shaw Swindn 40 C4
Shaw W Berk 41 J6
Shaw Wilts 39 K7
Shawbirch Wrekin 84 B2
Shawbost W Isls 232 e2
Shawbury Shrops 98 E7
Shawell Leics 87 G7
Shawford Hants 29 J6
Shawhead D & G 154 F6
Shaw Mills N York 132 C6
Shawsburn S Lans 175 K7
Shearington D & G 147 H2
Shearsby Leics 87 J5
Shearston Somset 25 L5
Shebbear Devon 10 C3
Shebdon Staffs 99 H7
Shebster Highld 230 E3
Sheddens E Rens 175 G6
Shedfield Hants 29 K8
Sheen Staffs 100 C1
Sheepridge Kirk 123 H6
Sheepscar Leeds 123 L4
Sheepscombe Gloucs 55 K6
Sheepstor Devon 6 E3
Sheepwash Devon 10 C4
Sheepy Magna Leics 86 D3
Sheepy Parva Leics 86 D3
Sheering Essex 60 E5
Sheerness Kent 46 F5
Sheerwater Surrey 43 H7
Sheet Hants 30 C6
Sheffield Sheff 115 G4
Sheffield City Road Crematorium Sheff 115 G4
Sheffield Park E Susx 19 L2
Shefford C Beds 75 G6
Sheigra Highld 228 B4
Sheinton Shrops 83 L3
Shelderton Shrops 83 H7
Sheldon Birm 85 L6
Sheldon Derbys 114 D7
Sheldon Devon 12 E2
Sheldwich Kent 34 D4
Shelfanger Norfk 92 D6
Shelford Notts 102 A4
Shelley Kirk 123 J7
Shelley Suffk 78 B6
Shellingford Oxon 40 F2
Shellow Bowells Essex 60 F6
Shelsley Beauchamp Worcs 70 D2
Shelsley Walsh Worcs 70 C2
Shelton Bed 74 F2
Shelton Norfk 92 F5
Shelton Notts 102 C4
Shelton Lock C Derb 101 G6
Shelton Under Harley Staffs 99 J5
Shelve Shrops 83 G4
Shelwick Herefs 69 K6
Shenfield Essex 45 L2
Shenington Oxon 72 D6
Shenley Herts 59 K7
Shenley Brook End M Keyn 74 B7
Shenley Church End M Keyn 74 B7
Shenmore Herefs 69 H6
Shennanton D & G 145 H3
Shenstone Staffs 85 K3
Shenstone Worcs 84 F8
Shenton Leics 86 E4
Shenval Moray 214 F7
Shephall Herts 59 L4
Shepherd's Bush Gt Lon 44 E4
Shepherdswell Kent 35 H5
Shepley Kirk 123 J8
Shepperton Surrey 43 H6
Shepreth Cambs 76 B5
Shepshed Leics 101 J8
Shepton Beauchamp Somset 26 B7
Shepton Mallet Somset 26 F3
Shepton Montague Somset 27 G5
Shepway Kent 33 K3
Sheraton Dur 151 K7
Sherborne Dorset 26 F7
Sherborne Gloucs 56 D5
Sherborne Somset 26 E1
Sherborne St John Hants 29 L1
Sherbourne Warwks 72 C3
Sherburn Dur 151 H6
Sherburn N York 134 E4
Sherburn Hill Dur 151 H6
Sherburn in Elmet N York 124 D4
Shere Surrey 31 H2
Shereford Norfk 105 L6
Sherfield English Hants 28 F6
Sherfield on Loddon Hants 42 B8
Sherford Devon 7 H6
Sheriffhales Shrops 84 D2
Sheriff Hutton N York 133 K6
Sheringham Norfk 106 E4
Sherington M Keyn 74 C5
Shernborne Norfk 105 H6
Sherrington Wilts 27 L4
Sherston Wilts 39 J3
Sherwood C Nott 101 K4
Sherwood Forest Notts 101 L1
Sherwood Forest Crematorium Notts 116 A7
Shetland Islands Shet 235 c5
Shettleston C Glas 175 H5
Shevington Wigan 121 H8
Sheviock Cnwll 6 B5
Shibden Head C Brad 123 G5

Shide IoW 16 F5
Shidlaw Nthumb 168 B2
Shiel Bridge Highld 200 E2
Shieldaig Highld 210 C4
Shieldhill D & G 155 H5
Shieldhill Falk 176 B3
Shieldhill House Hotel S Lans 165 J2
Shields N Lans 175 K7
Shielfoot Highld 190 D3
Shielhill Angus 196 C5
Shielhill Inver 173 L4
Shifnal Shrops 84 D2
Shilbottle Nthumb 169 J7
Shildon Dur 141 G3
Shillford E Rens 174 E6
Shillingford Devon 24 F6
Shillingford Oxon 41 L2
Shillingford Abbot Devon 11 K6
Shillingford St George Devon 11 K7
Shillingstone Dorset 14 F1
Shillington C Beds 75 G7
Shilton Oxon 56 E6
Shilton Warwks 86 E6
Shimpling Norfk 92 D6
Shimpling Suffk 77 J4
Shimpling Street Suffk 77 K4
Shincliffe Dur 151 H6
Shiney Row Sundld 151 H4
Shinfield Wokham 42 B6
Shinness Highld 225 L5
Shipbourne Kent 33 G3
Shipdham Norfk 91 L3
Shipham Somset 38 C8
Shiphay Torbay 7 K3
Shiplake Oxon 42 C5
Shipley C Brad 123 H3
Shipley W Susx 31 J6
Shipley Bridge Surrey 32 B5
Shipmeadow Suffk 93 H5
Shippon Oxon 41 J2
Shipston-on-Stour Warwks 72 B6
Shipton Gloucs 56 B4
Shipton N York 133 H7
Shipton Shrops 83 L5
Shipton Bellinger Hants 28 E3
Shipton Gorge Dorset 13 L4
Shipton Green W Susx 17 L3
Shipton Moyne Gloucs 39 K3
Shipton-on-Cherwell Oxon 57 J5
Shiptonthorpe E R Yk 125 K2
Shipton-under-Wychwood Oxon 56 F4
Shirburn Oxon 42 B2
Shirdley Hill Lancs 120 E7
Shirebrook Derbys 115 K7
Shiregreen Sheff 115 G3
Shirehampton Bristl 38 D5
Shiremoor N Tyne 159 H7
Shirenewton Mons 38 C2
Shireoaks Notts 115 K5
Shirland Derbys 101 H2
Shirley C Sotn 29 H8
Shirley Derbys 100 E4
Shirley Gt Lon 45 G6
Shirley Solhll 85 K7
Shirrell Heath Hants 29 L8
Shirvan Ag & B 172 E2
Shirwell Devon 23 J4
Shiskine N Ayrs 162 B4
Shobdon Herefs 69 H3
Shobrooke Devon 11 K5
Shoby Leics 102 B7
Shocklach Ches W 98 C3
Shoeburyness Sthend 46 F3
Sholden Kent 35 K4
Sholing C Sotn 16 F1
Shop Cnwll 9 G2
Shoreditch Gt Lon 45 G4
Shoreditch Somset 25 K6
Shoreham Kent 45 K7
Shoreham Airport W Susx 19 G5
Shoreham-by-Sea W Susx 19 H5
Shorley Hants 29 L6
Shorne Kent 46 B6
Shortgate E Susx 20 A3
Short Heath Birm 85 K5
Short Heath Wsall 85 H4
Shortlanesend Cnwll 4 C6
Shortlees E Ayrs 163 K3
Shorwell IoW 16 F5
Shoscombe BaNES 27 G1
Shotesham Norfk 92 F4
Shotgate Essex 46 C2
Shotley Suffk 78 F7
Shotley Bridge Dur 150 D4
Shotley Gate Suffk 78 F7
Shotley Street Suffk 78 F7
Shottenden Kent 34 D4
Shottery Warwks 71 L4
Shotteswell Warwks 72 E5
Shottisham Suffk 79 G5
Shottlegate Derbys 100 F3
Shotton Dur 151 K6
Shotton Flints 111 J7
Shotton Colliery Dur 151 J6
Shotts N Lans 176 B6
Shotwick Ches W 111 K6
Shougle Moray 214 F4
Shouldham Norfk 90 F2
Shouldham Thorpe Norfk 90 F2
Shoulton Worcs 70 E3
Shrawardine Shrops 83 H1
Shrawley Worcs 70 E2
Shrewley Warwks 72 B2
Shrewsbury Shrops 83 J2
Shrewton Wilts 28 B3
Shripney W Susx 18 C5
Shrivenham Oxon 40 E3
Shropham Norfk 92 B5
Shroton Dorset 27 K8
Shucknall Herefs 69 L6
Shudy Camps Cambs 76 E5
Shuna Ag & B 181 M5
Shurdington Gloucs 55 L4
Shurlock Row W & M 42 D5
Shurrery Highld 230 F4
Shurrery Lodge Highld 230 F4
Shurton Somset 25 J3
Shustoke Warwks 86 B5
Shute Devon 11 K5
Shute Devon 13 G3
Shutford Oxon 72 E6
Shut Heath Staffs 99 K7
Shuthonger Gloucs 70 F7
Shutlanger Nhants 73 K4
Shuttington Warwks 86 B3
Shuttlewood Derbys 115 J6
Shuttleworth Bury 122 B6
Siabost W Isls 232 e2
Siadar W Isls 232 f1
Sibbertoft Nhants 87 K6
Sibford Ferris Oxon 72 D6
Sibford Gower Oxon 72 D6
Sible Hedingham Essex 77 H7
Sibley's Green Essex 60 F3
Sibsey Lincs 104 B3
Sibson Cambs 89 G4
Sibson Leics 86 D4
Sibster Highld 231 K5
Sibthorpe Notts 102 C4
Sibthorpe Notts 116 B6
Sibton Suffk 79 H1
Sicklesmere Suffk 77 K3
Sicklinghall N York 124 B2
Sidbury Devon 12 E4
Sidbury Shrops 84 C6
Sidcot N Som 38 B8
Sidcup Gt Lon 45 J5
Siddington Ches E 113 J7
Siddington Gloucs 56 B7
Sidestrand Norfk 106 F4
Sidford Devon 12 E4
Sidlesham W Susx 18 B6
Sidley E Susx 20 E4
Sidmouth Devon 12 E5
Sigglesthorne E R Yk 126 E2
Sigingstone V Glam 36 F6
Silchester Hants 41 L7
Sileby Leics 87 H1
Silecroft Cumb 128 D3
Silfield Norfk 92 D4
Silkstone Barns 114 F1
Silkstone Common Barns 114 F1
Silk Willoughby Lincs 103 H4
Silloth Cumb 147 K4
Silpho N York 134 E2
Silsden C Brad 122 F2
Silsoe C Beds 74 F7
Silton Dorset 27 H5
Silverburn Mdloth 177 G6
Silverdale Lancs 129 K4
Silverdale Staffs 99 J3
Silver End Essex 61 K4
Silverford Abers 216 E2
Silverstone Nhants 73 J5
Silverton Devon 12 B2
Silvington Shrops 84 B7
Simonburn Nthumb 157 L7
Simonsbath Somset 24 B4
Simonstone Lancs 122 B4
Simprim Border 168 C1
Simpson M Keyn 74 C7
Simpson Cross Pembks 48 F4
Sinclair's Hill Border 179 G7
Sinclairston E Ayrs 163 L6
Sinderby N York 132 E3
Sinderland Green Traffd 113 G4
Sindlesham Wokham 42 C6
Sinfin C Derb 101 G6
Singleton Kent 34 D6
Singleton Lancs 120 E3
Singleton W Susx 18 B3
Singlewell Kent 46 A6
Sinnarhard Abers 205 K3
Sinnington N York 134 B3
Sinton Worcs 70 E3
Sinton Worcs 70 F2
Sinton Green Worcs 70 E3
Sissinghurst Kent 33 K5
Siston S Glos 39 G5
Sithney Cnwll 3 H5
Sittingbourne Kent 34 B3
Six Ashes Shrops 84 E5
Sixhills Lincs 117 K4
Six Mile Bottom Cambs 76 E3
Sixpenny Handley Dorset 27 M7
Six Rues Jersey 236 c6
Skaill Ork 234 d6
Skara Brae Ork 234 b5
Skares E Ayrs 164 B6
Skateraw Abers 207 G6
Skateraw E Loth 178 F4
Skeabost Highld 208 F5
Skeeby N York 140 F6
Skeffington Leics 87 L3
Skeffling E R Yk 127 J6
Skegby Notts 101 J1
Skegby Notts 116 C7
Skegness Lincs 119 H8
Skelbo Highld 223 H3
Skelbo Street Highld 223 H3
Skelbrooke Donc 124 D7
Skeldyke Lincs 104 B5
Skellingthorpe Lincs 116 F6
Skellow Donc 124 E7
Skelmanthorpe Kirk 123 J7
Skelmersdale Lancs 112 C1
Skelmorlie N Ayrs 173 L5
Skelpick Highld 229 L4
Skelston D & G 154 E5
Skelton C York 133 J7
Skelton Cumb 148 D7
Skelton E R Yk 125 H5
Skelton R & Cl 142 E4
Skelton on Ure N York 132 E5
Skelwith Bridge Cumb 137 K6
Skendleby Lincs 118 F7
Skene House Abers 206 E4
Skenfrith Mons 54 C4
Skerne E R Yk 135 G7
Skerray Highld 229 K3
Skerricha Highld 228 C5
Skerries Airport Shet 235 e4
Skerton Lancs 129 K6
Sketchley Leics 86 E5
Sketty Swans 51 J6
Skewsby N York 133 K5
Skiall Highld 230 E3
Skidby E R Yk 126 C4
Skigersta W Isls 232 g1
Skilgate Somset 24 F6
Skillington Lincs 102 E7
Skinburness Cumb 147 K4
Skinflats Falk 176 B2
Skinidin Highld 208 C5
Skipness Ag & B 172 F6
Skipper's Bridge D & G 156 C5
Skipsea E R Yk 135 J8
Skipton N York 122 E1
Skipton-on-Swale N York 132 E4
Skipwith N York 125 G3
Skirlaugh E R Yk 126 E3
Skirling Border 165 L2
Skirmett Bucks 42 C3
Skirpenbeck E R Yk 134 B7
Skirwith Cumb 149 G7
Skirza Highld 231 L2
Skokholm Island Pembks 48 C6
Skomer Island Pembks 48 C5
Skulamus Highld 199 K2
Skye Green Essex 61 L4
Skye of Curr Highld 204 B1
Slack Calder 122 E5
Slacks of Cairnbanno Abers 216 F5
Slad Gloucs 55 K6
Slade Devon 23 H3
Slade Green Gt Lon 45 K5
Slade Hooton Rothm 115 K4
Slaggyford Nthumb 149 H4
Slaidburn Lancs 130 D8
Slaithwaite Kirk 123 G7
Slaley Nthumb 150 B4
Slamannan Falk 176 B4
Slapton Bucks 58 F4
Slapton Devon 7 J6
Slapton Nhants 73 J5
Slaugham W Susx 31 L5
Slaughterford Wilts 39 J5
Slawston Leics 87 L5
Sleaford Hants 30 D4
Sleaford Lincs 103 H4
Sleagill Cumb 138 E4
Sleapford Wrekin 84 B1
Sleasdairidh Highld 222 E3
Sledmere E R Yk 134 E6
Sleetbeck Cumb 156 E6
Sleights N York 143 H5
Slickly Highld 231 K3
Sliddery N Ayrs 162 B5
Sligachan Highld 209 G7
Sligrachan Ag & B 173 K1
Slimbridge Gloucs 55 H7
Slindon Staffs 99 J6
Slindon W Susx 18 C4
Slinfold W Susx 31 J5
Slingsby N York 133 L4
Slip End C Beds 59 H4
Slip End Herts 75 K6
Slipton Nhants 88 D7
Slitting Mill Staffs 100 B8
Slockavullin Ag & B 182 B7
Sloncombe Devon 11 H7
Sloothby Lincs 119 G7
Slough Slough 43 G4

Slough Crematorium Bucks 43 G4
Slough Green Somset 25 L7
Slumbay Highld 210 D6
Slyne Lancs 129 K6
Smailholm Border 167 K3
Smallburgh Norfk 107 G7
Small Dole W Susx 19 G3
Smalley Derbys 101 H4
Smallfield Surrey 32 B5
Small Heath Birm 85 K6
Small Hythe Kent 34 B8
Smallridge Devon 13 H3
Smallthorne C Stke 99 K3
Smallworth Norfk 92 B7
Smannell Hants 29 G2
Smarden Kent 34 B6
Smarden Bell Kent 34 B6
Smart's Hill Kent 32 F5
Smearisary Highld 190 D2
Smeatharpe Devon 12 F1
Smeeth Kent 34 E6
Smeeton Westerby Leics 87 K5
Smerral Highld 227 L2
Smestow Staffs 84 F5
Smethwick Sandw 85 H6
Smisby Derbys 101 G8
Smithfield Cumb 148 D2
Smith's Green Essex 76 F6
Smithstown Highld 219 J6
Smithton Highld 213 H5
Smoo Highld 228 F3
Smythe's Green Essex 61 L4
Snade D & G 154 E5
Snailbeach Shrops 83 G3
Snailwell Cambs 76 F2
Snainton N York 134 E3
Snaith E R Yk 124 F6
Snape N York 132 D3
Snape Suffk 79 H3
Snape Street Suffk 79 H3
Snaresbrook Gt Lon 45 H3
Snarestone Leics 86 D2
Snarford Lincs 117 H5
Snargate Kent 34 D8
Snave Kent 34 D8
Sneaton N York 143 J5
Snelland Lincs 117 H5
Snelston Derbys 100 D4
Snetterton Norfk 92 B5
Snettisham Norfk 105 G5
Snitter Nthumb 158 C2
Snitterby Lincs 117 G3
Snitterfield Warwks 72 B3
Snitton Shrops 83 L7
Snodland Kent 46 B7
Snowdon Gwynd 95 K2
Snowdonia National Park 96 C6
Snow End Herts 60 C2
Snowshill Gloucs 71 K7
Soake Hants 17 J1
Soay Highld 199 G3
Soberton Hants 29 L7
Soberton Heath Hants 29 L8
Sockburn Darltn 141 J6
Soham Cambs 90 E8
Solas W Isls 232 c5
Soldridge Hants 29 M4
Sole Street Kent 34 E5
Sole Street Kent 46 A6
Solihull Solhll 85 L7
Sollers Dilwyn Herefs 69 H4
Sollers Hope Herefs 54 E2
Solva Pembks 48 D3
Solwaybank D & G 156 B6
Somerby Leics 87 L2
Somerby Lincs 117 H1
Somercotes Derbys 101 H2
Somerford Dorset 15 M4
Somerford Keynes Gloucs 40 A2
Somerley W Susx 17 M3
Somerleyton Suffk 93 K4
Somersal Herbert Derbys 100 C5
Somersby Lincs 118 D6
Somersham Cambs 89 L7
Somersham Suffk 78 C5
Somerton Oxon 57 J3
Somerton Somset 26 C5
Somerton Suffk 77 J4
Sompting W Susx 19 G5
Sonning Wokham 42 C5
Sonning Common Oxon 42 B4
Sopley Hants 15 M3
Sopwell Herts 59 J6
Sopworth Wilts 39 J3
Sorbie D & G 145 J5
Sordale Highld 231 G3
Sorisdale Ag & B 189 H4
Sorn E Ayrs 164 B4
Sortat Highld 231 K3
Sotby Lincs 117 K5
Sotterley Suffk 93 J6
Soughton Flints 111 H7
Soulbury Bucks 58 E3
Soulby Cumb 139 H5
Souldern Oxon 57 K2
Souldrop Bed 74 E3
Sound Ches E 98 F3
Sound Muir Moray 215 H4
Soundwell S Glos 38 F5
Sourton Devon 10 D6
Soutergate Cumb 128 F3
South Acre Norfk 91 J2
South Alkham Kent 35 H6
Southall Gt Lon 43 J4
South Allington Devon 7 J7
South Alloa Falk 185 J8
Southam Gloucs 55 L3
Southam Warwks 72 E3
South Ambersham W Susx 30 E7
Southampton C Sotn 29 H8
Southampton Airport Hants 29 J7
Southampton Crematorium Hants 29 H7
South Anston Rothm 115 K5
South Ashford Kent 34 D6
South Baddesley Hants 16 D3
South Ballachulish Highld 191 K5
South Bank C York 124 F1
South Barrow Somset 26 E5
South Beddington Gt Lon 44 F7
South Benfleet Essex 46 C3
Southborough Gt Lon 45 H6
Southborough Kent 33 G5
Southbourne Bmouth 15 L4
Southbourne W Susx 17 L2
South Bramwith Donc 124 F7
South Brent Devon 7 G4
South Brewham Somset 27 G4
South Bristol Crematorium Bristl 38 E6
South Broomhill Nthumb 159 G3
Southburgh Norfk 92 B3
South Burlingham Norfk 93 H3
Southburn E R Yk 134 F8
South Cadbury Somset 26 F6
South Carlton Lincs 116 F6
South Carlton Notts 115 L5
South Cave E R Yk 125 L4
South Cerney Gloucs 40 B2
South Chailey E Susx 19 K3
South Charlton Nthumb 169 H5
South Cheriton Somset 27 G6
South Church Dur 140 F2
Southchurch Sthend 46 E3
South Cliffe E R Yk 125 K4
South Clifton Notts 116 D7
South Cockerington Lincs 118 E4
South Cornelly Brdgnd 36 C4
Southcott Cnwll 9 G5
Southcott Devon 11 H8
Southcourt Bucks 58 D5
South Cove Suffk 93 K7
South Creake Norfk 105 K5
South Croxton Leics 87 K2
South Dalton E R Yk 126 B2
South Darenth Kent 45 K6
South Dell W Isls 232 g1
South Downs National Park 19 K4
South Duffield N York 125 G4
South Earlswood Surrey 32 B4
Southease E Susx 19 L5
South Elkington Lincs 118 D4
South Elmsall Wakefd 124 D7
Southend Ag & B 161 H7
Southend Airport Essex 46 E3
Southend Crematorium Sthend 46 E3
Southend-on-Sea Sthend 46 E3
Southerndown V Glam 36 D5
Southerness D & G 147 G4
South Erradale Highld 219 H7
Southerton Devon 12 D4
Southery Norfk 90 E5
South Essex Crematorium Gt Lon 45 L3
South Fambridge Essex 46 E2
South Ferriby N Linc 126 B6
South Field E R Yk 126 C5
Southfield Falk 175 L4
Southfleet Kent 45 L5
Southgate Gt Lon 44 F2
Southgate Swans 51 G7
South Gorley Hants 15 M1
South Gosforth N u Ty 151 G2
South Green Essex 46 B2
South Green Kent 33 L2
South Green Norfk 92 C2
South Gyle C Edin 177 G4
South Hanningfield Essex 61 H8
South Harting W Susx 30 C7
South Hayling Hants 17 K3
South Heath Bucks 58 E7
South Heighton E Susx 19 L5
South Hetton Dur 151 J6
South Hiendley Wakefd 124 B7
South Hill Cnwll 5 M2
South Hinksey Oxon 57 K7
South Holmwood Surrey 31 K3
South Hornchurch Gt Lon 45 K4
South Huish Devon 7 G7
South Hykeham Lincs 116 F8
South Hylton Sundld 151 J4
Southill C Beds 75 H6
Southington Hants 29 J2
South Kelsey Lincs 117 H2
South Kessock Highld 213 G5
South Killingholme N Linc 126 E7
South Kilvington N York 132 F3
South Kilworth Leics 87 H6
South Kirkby Wakefd 124 C7
South Kyme Lincs 103 K3
South Lanarkshire Crematorium S Lans 175 J7
South Leicestershire Crematorium Leics 87 H4
Southleigh Devon 12 F4
South Leigh Oxon 57 H6
South Leverton Notts 116 C5
South Lincolnshire Crematorium Lincs 103 L6
South Littleton Worcs 71 J5
South London Crematorium Gt Lon 44 F6
South Lopham Norfk 92 C7
South Luffenham Rutlnd 88 D3
South Lynn Norfk 104 F8
South Malling E Susx 19 L4
South Marston Swindn 40 D3
South Merstham Surrey 32 B3
South Milford N York 124 D4
South Milton Devon 7 G7
South Mimms Herts 59 L7
South Mimms Services Herts 59 L7
Southminster Essex 62 A7
South Molton Devon 23 L6
South Moor Dur 150 F5
Southmoor Oxon 41 H2
South Moreton Oxon 41 K3
Southmuir Angus 196 C5
South Mundham W Susx 18 B5
South Newbald E R Yk 125 L4
South Newington Oxon 57 H2
South Newton Wilts 28 C4
South Normanton Derbys 101 H2
South Norwood Gt Lon 45 G6
South Ockendon Thurr 45 L4
Southoe Cambs 75 H2
Southolt Suffk 78 E2
South Ormsby Lincs 118 E6
Southorpe C Pete 88 F3
South Otterington N York 132 E3
Southover Dorset 14 C4
South Owersby Lincs 117 H3
Southowram Calder 123 G5
South Oxfordshire Crematorium Oxon 41 H2
South Park Surrey 31 L2
South Perrott Dorset 13 L2
South Petherton Somset 26 B7
South Petherwin Cnwll 9 J8
South Pickenham Norfk 91 J3
South Pill Cnwll 6 B4
South Pool Devon 7 H7
South Poorton Dorset 13 M3
Southport Sefton 120 D6
Southport Crematorium Lancs 120 E7
South Queensferry C Edin 176 F3
South Rauceby Lincs 103 G4
South Raynham Norfk 105 L7
South Reddish Stockp 113 K3
Southrepps Norfk 106 F5
South Reston Lincs 118 E5

Southrey Lincs 117 J7
South Ronaldsay Ork 234 c7
Southrop Gloucs 56 D7
Southrope Hants 30 A3
South Runcton Norfk 90 F2
South Scarle Notts 116 D8
Southsea C Port 17 J3
South Shian Ag & B 191 H7
South Shields S Tyne 151 J2
South Shields Crematorium S Tyne 151 J3
South Shore Bpool 120 D4
Southside Dur 140 E2
South Stainley N York 132 D6
South Stifford Thurr 45 L4
South Stoke BaNES 39 H7
South Stoke Oxon 41 L4
South Stoke W Susx 18 D4
South Street Kent 34 E3
South Street Kent 47 J6
South Tarbrax S Lans 176 D7
South Tawton Devon 10 F6
South Tehidy Cnwll 3 H3
South Thoresby Lincs 118 E6
Southtown Norfk 93 L3
South Uist W Isls 233 c8
Southwaite Cumb 148 D6
Southwaite Services Cumb 148 D6
South Walsham Norfk 93 H2
Southwark Gt Lon 44 F4
South Warnborough Hants 30 B3
Southwater W Susx 31 J6
South Weald Essex 45 L2
Southwell Notts 102 B2
South West Middlesex Crematorium Gt Lon 43 J5
South Weston Oxon 42 B2
South Wheatley Notts 116 C4
Southwick Hants 17 J2
Southwick Nhants 88 E5
Southwick Sundld 151 J4
Southwick W Susx 19 H5
Southwick Wilts 27 J1
South Widcombe BaNES 38 E8
South Wigston Leics 87 H4
South Willesborough Kent 34 D6
South Willingham Lincs 117 K5
South Wingfield Derbys 101 G2
South Witham Lincs 102 F8
Southwold Suffk 93 K7
South Woodham Ferrers Essex 61 J7
South Wootton Norfk 105 G7
South Wraxall Wilts 39 J7
South Zeal Devon 10 F6
Sovereign Harbour E Susx 20 D5
Sowerby Calder 122 F6
Sowerby N York 132 F4
Sowerby Bridge Calder 122 F5
Sowood Calder 123 G6
Sowton Devon 6 D3
Sowton Devon 12 C4
Soyland Town Calder 122 F6
Spain's End Essex 76 F6
Spalding Lincs 103 L7
Spaldington E R Yk 125 H4
Spaldwick Cambs 89 G8
Spalford Notts 116 D7
Spanby Lincs 103 H5
Sparham Norfk 106 C8
Spark Bridge Cumb 129 G3
Sparkford Somset 26 E6
Sparkhill Birm 85 K6
Sparkwell Devon 6 E4
Sparrowpit Derbys 114 C5
Sparrows Green E Susx 33 H6
Sparsholt Hants 29 H5
Sparsholt Oxon 41 G3
Spaunton N York 133 L2
Spaxton Somset 25 K4
Spean Bridge Highld 201 K8
Spearywell Hants 28 F6
Speen Bucks 58 D7
Speen W Berk 41 J6
Speeton N York 135 J5
Speke Lpool 112 C5
Speldhurst Kent 32 F5
Spellbrook Herts 60 D4
Spencers Wood Wokham 42 B6
Spen Green Ches E 99 J1
Spennithorne N York 131 L2
Spennymoor Dur 151 G7
Spetchley Worcs 70 F4
Spetisbury Dorset 15 G3
Spexhall Suffk 93 H7
Spey Bay Moray 215 H2
Speybridge Highld 204 C1
Speyview Moray 215 G6
Spilsby Lincs 118 E7
Spinkhill Derbys 115 J5
Spinningdale Highld 222 F4
Spital Wirral 111 K5
Spital Hill Donc 115 L3
Spittal E Loth 178 B3
Spittal Highld 231 H5
Spittal Nthumb 179 L7
Spittal Pembks 49 G3
Spittalfield P & K 195 H7
Spittal of Glenmuick Abers 205 G7
Spittal of Glenshee P & K 195 H3
Spittal-on-Rule Border 167 J5
Spixworth Norfk 92 F1
Splatt Devon 10 E4
Splayne's Green E Susx 19 L2
Splottlands Cardif 37 K5
Spofforth N York 124 B1
Spondon C Derb 101 H5
Spooner Row Norfk 92 D4
Sporle Norfk 91 J2
Spott E Loth 178 E4
Spottiswoode Border 178 D7
Spratton Nhants 73 K1
Spreakley Surrey 30 D3
Spreyton Devon 11 G5
Spriddlestone Devon 6 D5
Spridlington Lincs 117 G5
Springburn C Glas 175 G5
Springfield D & G 148 B2
Springfield Essex 61 H6
Springfield Fife 186 E5
Springholm D & G 154 E7
Springside N Ayrs 163 J2
Springthorpe Lincs 116 E4
Springwell Sundld 151 H4
Springwood Crematorium Lpool 112 B4
Sproatley E R Yk 126 F4
Sproston Green Ches W 113 G7
Sprotbrough Donc 115 K2
Sproughton Suffk 78 D5
Sprouston Border 168 A3
Sprowston Norfk 92 F2
Sproxton Leics 102 D7
Sproxton N York 133 J3
Spurstow Ches E 98 D2
Spyway Dorset 14 A4
Stableford Shrops 84 D4
Stacey Bank Sheff 114 F4
Stackhouse N York 130 F6
Stackpole Pembks 49 G7
Stackpole Elidor Pembks 49 G7
Staddiscombe C Plym 6 D5
Stadhampton Oxon 57 L7
Stadhlaigearraidh W Isls 233 b7
Staffield Cumb 148 F6
Staffin Highld 218 D7
Stafford Staffs 99 L7
Stafford Crematorium Staffs 99 L7
Stafford Services (northbound) Staffs 99 K6
Stafford Services (southbound) Staffs 99 K6
Stagsden Bed 74 E5
Stainburn Cumb 136 E2
Stainby Lincs 102 E7
Staincross Barns 123 L7
Staindrop Dur 140 E3
Staines-upon-Thames Surrey 43 G6
Stainforth Donc 124 F7
Stainforth N York 130 F6
Staining Lancs 120 D4
Stainland Calder 123 G6
Stainsacre N York 143 J5
Stainton Cumb 129 L3
Stainton Cumb 138 C2
Stainton Donc 115 K3
Stainton Dur 140 D4
Stainton Middsb 141 L4
Stainton by Langworth Lincs 117 H6
Staintondale N York 143 K7
Stainton le Vale Lincs 117 K3
Stainton with Adgarley Cumb 128 F5
Stair E Ayrs 163 K5
Stairhaven D & G 144 E4
Staithes N York 143 G4
Stakes Hants 17 K2
Stalbridge Dorset 27 G7
Stalbridge Weston Dorset 27 G7
Stalham Norfk 107 H7
Stalisfield Green Kent 34 C4
Stallen Dorset 26 E7
Stallingborough NE Lin 126 F7
Stalmine Lancs 120 E2
Stalybridge Tamesd 113 L2
Stambourne Essex 77 G6
Stambourne Green Essex 77 G6
Stamford Lincs 88 E3
Stamford Nthumb 169 J5
Stamford Bridge Ches W 112 C7
Stamford Bridge E R Yk 133 L7
Stamfordham Nthumb 158 D7
Stamford Hill Gt Lon 45 G3
Stanbridge C Beds 58 F3
Stanbury C Brad 122 F3
Stand N Lans 175 K5
Standburn Falk 176 C4
Standeford Staffs 85 G3
Standen Kent 33 L5
Standerwick Somset 27 J2
Standford Hants 30 D4
Standingstone Cumb 147 J7
Standish Wigan 121 H7
Standlake Oxon 57 H7
Standon Hants 29 H6
Standon Herts 60 C4
Standon Staffs 99 J5
Stane N Lans 176 B6
Stanfield Norfk 105 M7
Stanford C Beds 75 H6
Stanford Kent 34 F6
Stanford Bishop Herefs 70 C4
Stanford Bridge Worcs 70 C2
Stanford Dingley W Berk 41 L6
Stanford in the Vale Oxon 41 G2
Stanford le Hope Thurr 46 B4
Stanford on Avon Nhants 87 H7
Stanford on Soar Notts 101 K7
Stanford on Teme Worcs 70 C2
Stanfree Derbys 115 J6
Stanghow R & Cl 142 E4
Stanground C Pete 89 H4
Stanhoe Norfk 105 J5
Stanhope Border 165 L4
Stanhope Dur 150 C6
Stanhope Kent 34 D6
Stanion Nhants 88 D6
Stanley Derbys 101 H4
Stanley Dur 150 F4
Stanley P & K 186 B2
Stanley Staffs 99 L3
Stanley Crook Dur 150 E7
Stanley Pontlarge Gloucs 55 M3
Stanmer Br & H 19 K4
Stanmore Gt Lon 44 D2
Stanmore Hants 29 J5
Stannersburn Nthumb 157 J5
Stanningfield Suffk 77 K3
Stannington Nthumb 158 F6
Stannington Sheff 114 F4
Stannington Station Nthumb 158 F5
Stansbatch Herefs 69 G3
Stansfield Suffk 77 H4
Stanstead Suffk 77 J5
Stanstead Abbotts Herts 60 C5
Stansted Kent 45 L7
Stansted Airport Essex 60 E4
Stansted Mountfitchet Essex 60 E3
Stanton Gloucs 71 J7
Stanton Nthumb 158 E4
Stanton Staffs 100 C4
Stanton Suffk 91 L8
Stanton by Bridge Derbys 101 G6
Stanton by Dale Derbys 101 J5
Stanton Drew BaNES 38 E7
Stanton Fitzwarren Swindn 40 D3
Stanton Harcourt Oxon 57 H6
Stanton in Peak Derbys 114 E8
Stanton Lacy Shrops 83 K7
Stanton Lees Derbys 114 E8
Stanton Long Shrops 83 L5
Stanton-on-the-Wolds Notts 101 M6
Stanton Prior BaNES 39 G7
Stanton St Bernard Wilts 40 C7
Stanton St John Oxon 57 L6
Stanton St Quintin Wilts 39 K4
Stanton Street Suffk 77 L2
Stanton under Bardon Leics 86 F2
Stanton upon Hine Heath Shrops 98 E7
Stanton Wick BaNES 38 E7
Stanway Essex 61 M3
Stanway Gloucs 56 B2
Stanwell Surrey 43 H5
Stanwick Nhants 74 E1
Stanwix Cumb 148 D4
Staoinebrig W Isls 233 b8
Stape N York 143 G7

Stapeley Ches E 99 G3
Stapenhill Staffs 100 E7
Staple Kent 35 H4
Staple Cross Devon 25 G7
Staplecross E Susx 20 F2
Staplefield W Susx 32 B7
Staple Fitzpaine Somset 25 K7
Stapleford Cambs 76 C4
Stapleford Herts 60 A5
Stapleford Leics 102 D8
Stapleford Lincs 102 E2
Stapleford Notts 101 J5
Stapleford Wilts 28 B4
Stapleford Abbotts Essex 45 K2
Staplegrove Somset 25 K6
Staplehay Somset 25 K6
Staplehurst Kent 33 K5
Staplestreet Kent 34 E3
Stapleton Herefs 69 G2
Stapleton Leics 86 E4
Stapleton N York 141 G5
Stapleton Shrops 83 J3
Stapleton Somset 26 C7
Stapley Somset 25 J8
Staploe Bed 75 G3
Staplow Herefs 70 C6
Star Fife 186 E6
Star Pembks 65 H7
Star Somset 38 C8
Starbeck N York 132 E7
Starbotton N York 131 H5
Starcross Devon 12 C6
Stareton Warwks 72 D1
Starlings Green Essex 60 D2
Starston Norfk 92 F6
Startforth Dur 140 D4
Startley Wilts 39 L4
Statenborough Kent 35 J4
Statham Warrtn 112 F4
Stathe Somset 26 A5
Stathern Leics 102 C6
Staughton Green Cambs 75 G2
Staunton Gloucs 54 D5
Staunton Gloucs 55 H3
Staunton on Arrow Herefs 69 G3
Staunton on Wye Herefs 69 G5
Staveley Cumb 129 H3
Staveley Cumb 138 C7
Staveley Derbys 115 H6
Staveley N York 132 E6
Staverton Devon 7 J3
Staverton Gloucs 55 K4
Staverton Nhants 73 G3
Staverton Wilts 39 J7
Stawell Somset 26 A4
Stawley Somset 25 G6
Staxigoe Highld 231 L5
Staxton N York 134 F4
Staynall Lancs 120 E2
Stean N York 131 K5
Stearsby N York 133 J5
Steart Somset 25 L3
Stebbing Essex 61 G3
Stechford Birm 85 K6
Stedham W Susx 30 E6
Steelend Fife 185 L8
Steele Road Border 156 F4
Steen's Bridge Herefs 69 K3
Steep Hants 30 C6
Steep Lane Calder 122 F5
Steeple Essex 61 M7
Steeple Ashton Wilts 27 K1
Steeple Aston Oxon 57 J3
Steeple Bumpstead Essex 76 F6
Steeple Claydon Bucks 58 B3
Steeple Gidding Cambs 89 G7
Steeple Langford Wilts 28 B4
Steeple Morden Cambs 75 K6
Steeton C Brad 122 F2
Stein Highld 208 D3
Stelling Minnis Kent 34 F5
Stembridge Somset 26 B7
Stenalees Cnwll 4 F4
Stenhouse D & G 154 D4
Stenhousemuir Falk 176 B2
Stenscholl Highld 218 D7
Stenson Fields Derbys 101 G6
Stenton E Loth 178 D4
Steornabhagh W Isls 232 f2
Stepaside Pembks 49 K6
Stepford D & G 154 E5
Stepney Gt Lon 45 G4
Steppingley C Beds 74 E7
Stepps N Lans 175 H5
Sternfield Suffk 79 H3
Stert Wilts 40 B8
Stetchworth Cambs 76 F3
Stevenage Herts 59 L3
Stevenston N Ayrs 163 H2
Steventon Hants 29 K2
Steventon Oxon 41 J3
Steventon End Essex 76 E6
Stevington Bed 74 E4
Stewartby Bed 74 E6
Stewartfield S Lans 175 H7
Stewarton Ag & B 161 H5
Stewarton E Ayrs 163 K1
Stewkley Bucks 58 D3
Stewley Somset 25 L7
Steyning W Susx 19 G4
Steynton Pembks 48 F6
Stibb Cnwll 9 G3
Stibbard Norfk 106 B6
Stibb Cross Devon 10 C2
Stibb Green Wilts 40 E7
Stibbington Cambs 88 F4
Stichill Border 167 L2
Sticker Cnwll 4 F5
Stickford Lincs 104 B1
Sticklepath Devon 10 F6
Stickney Lincs 104 B2
Stiffkey Norfk 106 A4
Stifford Clays Thurr 45 L4
Stilligarry W Isls 233 b7
Stillingfleet N York 124 F3
Stillington N York 133 J6
Stillington S on T 141 J3
Stilton Cambs 89 H5
Stinchcombe Gloucs 55 G7
Stinsford Dorset 14 D4
Stiperstones Shrops 83 G4
Stirchley Wrekin 84 C3
Stirling Abers 217 L6
Stirling Stirlg 185 G8
Stirling Castle Stirlg 185 G8
Stirling Services Stirlg 175 L2
Stirtloe Cambs 75 H2
Stirton N York 131 H8
Stisted Essex 61 J3
Stithians Cnwll 3 J4
Stivichall Covtry 86 D7
Stixwould Lincs 117 K7
Stoak Ches W 112 B6
Stobo Border 166 B2
Stoborough Dorset 15 H5
Stobs Castle Border 167 G7
Stobswood Nthumb 158 F3
Stock Essex 61 H7
Stock N Som 38 C7
Stockbridge Hants 29 G4
Stockbriggs S Lans 164 F3
Stockbury Kent 46 D7
Stockcross W Berk 41 H6
Stockerston Leics 88 B4
Stock Green Worcs 71 H3
Stocking Herefs 54 F2
Stockingford Warwks 86 D5
Stocking Pelham Herts 60 D3
Stockland Devon 13 G2
Stockland Bristol Somset 25 K3
Stockleigh English Devon 11 K4
Stockleigh Pomeroy Devon 11 K4
Stockley Wilts 39 M6
Stocklinch Somset 26 B7
Stockport Stockp 113 K4
Stockport Crematorium Stockp 113 K4
Stocksbridge Sheff 114 E2
Stocksfield Nthumb 150 D3
Stockton Herefs 69 K3
Stockton Norfk 93 H5
Stockton Shrops 84 C4
Stockton Warwks 72 E2
Stockton Wilts 27 M4
Stockton Wrekin 84 D1
Stockton Brook Staffs 99 K3
Stockton Heath Warrtn 112 E4
Stockton-on-Tees S on T 141 K4
Stockton on Teme Worcs 70 C2
Stockton on the Forest C York 133 K7
Stockwell End Wolves 84 F4
Stockwood Bristl 38 F6
Stockwood Dorset 14 B2
Stock Wood Worcs 71 H3
Stodmarsh Kent 35 G3
Stody Norfk 106 C5
Stoer Highld 224 C3
Stoford Somset 26 E8
Stoford Wilts 28 B4
Stogumber Somset 25 H4
Stogursey Somset 25 J3
Stoke Covtry 86 D7
Stoke Devon 22 C6
Stoke Hants 17 K3
Stoke Hants 29 H2
Stoke Medway 46 D5
Stoke Abbott Dorset 13 L3
Stoke Albany Nhants 88 B5
Stoke Ash Suffk 78 D1
Stoke Bardolph Notts 101 M4
Stoke Bliss Worcs 70 B2
Stoke Bruerne Nhants 73 L4
Stoke-by-Clare Suffk 77 G5
Stoke-by-Nayland Suffk 78 B7
Stoke Canon Devon 12 B3
Stoke Charity Hants 29 J4
Stoke Climsland Cnwll 6 A2
Stoke Cross Herefs 70 B4
Stoke D'Abernon Surrey 43 J8
Stoke Doyle Nhants 88 E6
Stoke Dry Rutlnd 88 C4
Stoke Edith Herefs 69 L6
Stoke Farthing Wilts 28 B6
Stoke Ferry Norfk 91 G4
Stoke Fleming Devon 7 K6
Stokeford Dorset 15 G5
Stoke Gabriel Devon 7 J4
Stoke Gifford S Glos 38 F4
Stoke Golding Leics 86 E4
Stoke Goldington M Keyn 74 B5
Stokeham Notts 116 C6
Stoke Hammond Bucks 58 E3
Stoke Holy Cross Norfk 92 F3
Stokeinteignhead Devon 7 L2
Stoke Lacy Herefs 70 B5
Stoke Lyne Oxon 57 K3
Stoke Mandeville Bucks 58 D6
Stokenchurch Bucks 42 C2
Stoke Newington Gt Lon 45 G3
Stokenham Devon 7 J7
Stoke-on-Trent C Stke 99 K3
Stoke Orchard Gloucs 55 K3
Stoke Poges Bucks 42 F4
Stoke Prior Herefs 69 K3
Stoke Prior Worcs 71 G2
Stoke Rivers Devon 23 K4
Stoke Rochford Lincs 102 F6
Stoke Row Oxon 42 B4
Stoke St Gregory Somset 25 M6
Stoke St Mary Somset 25 K6
Stoke St Michael Somset 26 F3
Stoke St Milborough Shrops 83 L6
Stokesby Norfk 93 J2
Stokesley N York 142 B5
Stoke sub Hamdon Somset 26 C7
Stoke Talmage Oxon 58 B7
Stoke Trister Somset 27 H5
Stoke upon Tern Shrops 98 F6
Stolford Somset 25 K3
Stondon Massey Essex 60 F7
Stone Bucks 58 C5
Stone Gloucs 39 G2
Stone Rothm 115 K4
Stone Staffs 99 K5
Stone Worcs 84 F7
Stone Allerton Somset 26 B2
Ston Easton Somset 26 F2
Stonebridge N Som 38 B7
Stonebridge Warwks 86 B6
Stonebroom Derbys 101 H2
Stone Cross Kent 35 J4
Stonecrouch Kent 33 J6
Stoneferry C KuH 126 D4
Stonefield Castle Hotel Ag & B 172 E4
Stonegate E Susx 33 H7
Stonegrave N York 133 K4
Stonehaven Abers 207 G7
Stonehenge Wilts 28 C3
Stonehouse C Plym 6 C5
Stonehouse Gloucs 55 J6
Stonehouse S Lans 175 K8
Stone in Oxney Kent 21 J1
Stoneleigh Warwks 86 D8
Stonesby Leics 102 D7
Stonesfield Oxon 57 H4
Stones Green Essex 62 E3
Stone Street Kent 33 G3
Stone Street Suffk 93 H6
Stonewells Moray 215 G2
Stoneybridge W Isls 233 b8
Stoneyburn W Loth 176 D5
Stoneygate C Leic 87 H3
Stoneykirk D & G 144 C4
Stoney Middleton Derbys 114 E6
Stoney Stanton Leics 86 F4
Stoney Stoke Somset 27 G5
Stoney Stratton Somset 26 F4
Stoneywood C Aber 207 G3
Stoneywood Falk 175 L2
Stonham Aspal Suffk 78 D3
Stonnall Staffs 85 J3
Stonor Oxon 42 B3
Stonton Wyville Leics 87 K4
Stony Houghton Derbys 115 J7
Stony Stratford M Keyn 73 L6
Stoodleigh Devon 23 K5
Stoodleigh Devon 24 E7
Stop 24 Services Kent 34 F7
Stopham W Susx 18 D2
Stopsley Luton 59 J3
Stornoway W Isls 232 f2
Stornoway Airport W Isls 232 g2
Storrington W Susx 18 E3
Storth Cumb 129 K4
Storwood E R Yk 125 H2

Stotfield Moray 214 F1
Stotfold C Beds 75 J7
Stottesdon Shrops 84 C6
Stoughton Leics 87 J3
Stoughton Surrey 31 G2
Stoughton W Susx 17 L1
Stoulton Worcs 70 F4
Stourbridge Dudley 84 F6
Stourbridge Crematorium Dudley 84 F6
Stourhead Wilts 27 H5
Stourpaine Dorset 15 G1
Stourport-on-Severn Worcs 70 E1
Stour Provost Dorset 27 H6
Stour Row Dorset 27 J7
Stourton Staffs 84 F6
Stourton Warwks 72 C6
Stourton Wilts 27 H5
Stourton Caundle Dorset 27 G7
Stove Shet 235 c7
Stoven Suffk 93 J6
Stow Border 167 G1
Stow Lincs 116 E5
Stow Bardolph Norfk 90 F3
Stow Bedon Norfk 91 L4
Stowbridge Norfk 90 E3
Stow-cum-Quy Cambs 76 D3
Stowe Shrops 82 F8
Stowe by Chartley Staffs 100 A6
Stowell Somset 27 G6
Stowey BaNES 38 E7
Stowford Devon 10 C7
Stowlangtoft Suffk 77 L2
Stow Longa Cambs 75 G1
Stow Maries Essex 61 K7
Stowmarket Suffk 78 C3
Stow-on-the-Wold Gloucs 56 D3
Stowting Kent 34 F6
Stowting Common Kent 34 F6
Stowupland Suffk 78 C3
Straanruie Highld 204 B3
Strachan Abers 206 D6
Strachur Ag & B 182 F6
Stradbroke Suffk 92 F8
Stradishall Suffk 77 H4
Stradsett Norfk 90 F3
Stragglethorpe Lincs 102 E3
Straiton Mdloth 177 H5
Straiton S Ayrs 153 H2
Straloch Abers 207 G2
Straloch P & K 195 G4
Stramshall Staffs 100 B5
Strang IoM 237 c5
Strangeways Salfd 113 J2
Strangford Herefs 54 E3
Stranraer D & G 144 C3
Stratfield Mortimer W Berk 42 A7
Stratfield Saye Hants 42 B7
Stratfield Turgis Hants 42 B7
Stratford Gt Lon 45 H3
Stratford St Andrew Suffk 79 H3
Stratford St Mary Suffk 78 C7
Stratford sub Castle Wilts 28 C5
Stratford Tony Wilts 28 C6
Stratford-upon-Avon Warwks 72 B4
Strath Highld 219 J5
Strathan Highld 224 D4
Strathan Highld 229 J3
Strathaven S Lans 164 D1
Strathblane Stirlg 175 G3
Strathcanaird Highld 220 F2
Strathcarron Highld 210 E6
Strathcoil Ag & B 181 K2
Strathdon Abers 205 H3
Strathkinness Fife 187 G4
Strathloanhead W Loth 176 C4
Strathmashie House Highld 202 F6
Strathmiglo Fife 186 C5
Strathpeffer Highld 212 D3
Strathtay P & K 194 E5
Strathwhillan N Ayrs 162 D3
Strathy Highld 230 B3
Strathy Inn Highld 230 B3
Strathyre Stirlg 184 C4
Stratton Cnwll 9 G4
Stratton Dorset 14 C4
Stratton Gloucs 56 A7
Stratton Audley Oxon 57 L3
Stratton-on-the-Fosse Somset 26 F2
Stratton St Margaret Swindn 40 D3
Stratton St Michael Norfk 92 E5
Stratton Strawless Norfk 106 F7
Streat E Susx 19 K3
Streatham Gt Lon 44 F5
Streatley C Beds 59 H3
Streatley W Berk 41 L4
Street Devon 12 F5
Street Somset 26 C4
Street Ashton Warwks 86 F6
Street Dinas Shrops 97 M5
Street End Kent 34 F4
Street End W Susx 18 A5
Streethay Staffs 85 K2
Streetlam N York 141 H7
Streetly Crematorium Wsall 85 J4
Streetly End Cambs 76 E5
Street on the Fosse Somset 26 F4
Strelitz P & K 186 C1
Strelley Notts 101 K4
Strensall C York 133 K7
Strensham Services (northbound) Worcs 70 F6
Strensham Services (southbound) Worcs 70 F6
Stretcholt Somset 25 L3
Strete Devon 7 J6
Stretford Traffd 113 H3
Strethall Essex 76 C6
Stretham Cambs 90 D8
Strettington W Susx 18 B4
Stretton Derbys 101 H1
Stretton Rutlnd 88 D1
Stretton Staffs 84 F2
Stretton Staffs 100 E7
Stretton Warrtn 112 F5
Stretton Grandison Herefs 70 B5
Stretton-on-Dunsmore Warwks 86 E8
Stretton on Fosse Warwks 72 B6
Stretton Sugwas Herefs 69 J6
Stretton under Fosse Warwks 86 F7
Stretton Westwood Shrops 83 L4
Strichen Abers 217 H4
Stringston Somset 25 J3
Strixton Nhants 74 C3
Stroat Gloucs 38 E2
Stroma Highld 231 L1
Stromeferry Highld 210 D7
Stromness Ork 234 b6
Stronachlachar Stirlg 183 L5
Stronafian Ag & B 173 H3
Stronchrubie Highld 224 F5
Strone Ag & B 173 L3
Strone Highld 192 B1
Strone Highld 212 E8
Stronenaba Highld 201 J8
Stronmilchan Ag & B 183 G2
Stronsay Ork 234 d5
Stronsay Airport Ork 234 d5
Strontian Highld 191 G4
Strood Medway 46 B6
Stroud Gloucs 55 J6
Stroud Hants 30 B6
Stroud Green Gloucs 55 J6
Stroxton Lincs 102 E6
Struan Highld 208 E6
Struan P & K 194 C4
Strumpshaw Norfk 93 H3
Strutherhill S Lans 175 K7
Struthers Fife 186 F5
Struy Highld 212 B6
Stuartfield Abers 217 H5
Stubbers Green Wsall 85 J3
Stubbington Hants 17 G2
Stubbins Lancs 122 B6
Stubton Lincs 102 E3
Stuckton Hants 28 D8
Studham C Beds 59 G5
Studland Dorset 15 J6
Studley Warwks 71 J2
Studley Wilts 39 L6
Studley Roger N York 132 D5
Studley Royal N York 132 D5
Studley Royal Park & Fountains Abbey N York 132 D5
Stuntney Cambs 90 D7
Sturmer Essex 77 G5
Sturminster Common Dorset 27 H8
Sturminster Marshall Dorset 15 H3
Sturminster Newton Dorset 27 H8
Sturry Kent 35 G3
Sturton N Linc 116 F2
Sturton by Stow Lincs 116 E5
Sturton le Steeple Notts 116 C5
Stuston Suffk 92 D7
Stutton N York 124 D3
Stutton Suffk 78 D7
Styal Ches E 113 J5
Stynie Moray 215 H3
Styrrup Notts 115 L4
Succoth Ag & B 183 K6
Suckley Worcs 70 C4
Sudborough Nhants 88 D6
Sudbourne Suffk 79 J4
Sudbrook Lincs 102 F4
Sudbrook Mons 38 D3
Sudbrooke Lincs 117 G6
Sudbury Derbys 100 D6
Sudbury Gt Lon 44 D3
Sudbury Suffk 77 K6
Suffield N York 134 F2
Suffield Norfk 106 F6
Sugnall Staffs 99 H6
Sugwas Pool Herefs 69 J6
Suisnish Highld 199 J3
Sulby IoM 237 d3
Sulgrave Nhants 73 G5
Sulham W Berk 41 M5
Sulhamstead W Berk 41 M6
Sullom Shet 235 c4
Sullom Voe Shet 235 c4
Sully V Glam 37 J6
Sumburgh Airport Shet 235 c8
Summerbridge N York 132 C6
Summercourt Cnwll 4 D5
Summerfield Norfk 105 J5
Summerhill Pembks 49 K6
Summerhouse Darltn 140 F4
Summersdale W Susx 18 B4
Summerseat Bury 122 B7
Summertown Oxon 57 K6
Sunbury-on-Thames Surrey 43 J6
Sundaywell D & G 154 E5
Sunderland Ag & B 170 E5
Sunderland Cumb 147 L7
Sunderland Lancs 129 J7
Sunderland Sundld 151 J4
Sunderland Bridge Dur 151 G7
Sunderland Crematorium Sundld 151 J4
Sundhope Border 166 E4
Sundon Park Luton 59 H3
Sundridge Kent 32 E3
Sunningdale W & M 42 F6
Sunninghill W & M 42 F6
Sunningwell Oxon 57 J7
Sunniside Dur 150 E7
Sunniside Gatesd 150 F3
Sunnyhill C Derb 101 G6
Sunnyhurst Bl w D 121 K6
Sunnylaw Stirlg 185 G7
Sunnymead Oxon 57 J6
Surbiton Gt Lon 44 D6
Surfleet Lincs 103 L6
Surlingham Norfk 93 G3
Surrex Essex 61 L4
Surrey & Sussex Crematorium W Susx 32 B5
Sustead Norfk 106 E5
Susworth Lincs 116 D2
Sutcombe Devon 9 J3
Sutcombemill Devon 9 J3
Sutterby Lincs 118 E6
Sutterton Lincs 103 M5
Sutton C Beds 75 J5
Sutton C Pete 89 G4
Sutton Cambs 90 C7
Sutton Devon 7 G7
Sutton E Susx 20 A5
Sutton Gt Lon 44 E7
Sutton Kent 35 J5
Sutton N York 124 D5
Sutton Norfk 107 H7
Sutton Notts 102 C5
Sutton Oxon 57 H6
Sutton Shrops 83 K2
Sutton Shrops 84 D6
Sutton Staffs 99 H7
Sutton Suffk 79 G5
Sutton W Susx 18 D3
Sutton-at-Hone Kent 45 K6
Sutton Bassett Nhants 87 L5
Sutton Benger Wilts 39 L5
Sutton Bonington Notts 101 K7
Sutton Bridge Lincs 104 D7
Sutton Cheney Leics 86 E4
Sutton Coldfield Birm 85 K4
Sutton Coldfield Crematorium Birm 85 K4
Sutton Courtenay Oxon 41 J2
Sutton cum Lound Notts 116 B5
Sutton Green Surrey 31 G1
Sutton Howgrave N York 132 D4
Sutton-in-Ashfield Notts 101 J1
Sutton-in-Craven N York 122 F2
Sutton Maddock Shrops 84 C3
Sutton Mallet Somset 26 A4
Sutton Mandeville Wilts 27 M5
Sutton Montis Somset 26 F6
Sutton-on-Hull C KuH 126 E4
Sutton on Sea Lincs 119 G5
Sutton-on-the-Forest N York 133 J6
Sutton on the Hill Derbys 100 E5

Sutton on Trent Notts 116 D7
Sutton St Edmund Lincs 89 L2
Sutton St James Lincs 104 C8
Sutton St Nicholas Herefs 69 K5
Sutton Scotney Hants 29 J4
Sutton-under-Brailes Warwks 72 C6
Sutton-under-Whitestonecliffe N York 133 G3
Sutton upon Derwent E R Yk 125 G2
Sutton Valence Kent 33 L4
Sutton Veny Wilts 27 K3
Sutton Waldron Dorset 27 K7
Sutton Weaver Ches W 112 D5
Sutton Wick BaNES 38 E8
Sutton Wick Oxon 41 J2
Swaby Lincs 118 E6
Swadlincote Derbys 100 F8
Swaffham Norfk 91 J2
Swaffham Bulbeck Cambs 76 D3
Swaffham Prior Cambs 76 E2
Swafield Norfk 107 G6
Swainby N York 141 L6
Swainsthorpe Norfk 92 F4
Swainswick BaNES 39 H6
Swalcliffe Oxon 72 E6
Swalecliffe Kent 47 J6
Swallow Lincs 117 K2
Swallow Beck Lincs 116 F7
Swallowcliffe Wilts 27 L6
Swallowfield Wokham 42 B7
Swanage Dorset 15 J6
Swanbourne Bucks 58 D3
Swan Green Ches W 113 G6
Swanland E R Yk 126 B5
Swanley Kent 45 K6
Swanley Village Kent 45 K6
Swanmore Hants 29 L7
Swannington Leics 86 E1
Swannington Norfk 106 D8
Swanpool Lincs 116 F7
Swanscombe Kent 45 L5
Swansea Swans 51 J6
Swansea Airport Swans 51 H7
Swansea Crematorium Swans 51 J5
Swansea West Services Swans 51 J5
Swanton Abbot Norfk 106 F7
Swanton Morley Norfk 92 B1
Swanton Novers Norfk 106 B6
Swan Village Sandw 85 H5
Swanwick Derbys 101 H2
Swanwick Hants 17 G1
Swarby Lincs 103 H4
Swardeston Norfk 92 E3
Swarkestone Derbys 101 G6
Swarland Nthumb 158 F2
Swarraton Hants 29 K4
Swarthmoor Cumb 129 G4
Swaton Lincs 103 J5
Swavesey Cambs 75 L2
Sway Hants 16 C3
Swayfield Lincs 103 G7
Swaythling C Sotn 29 H7
Sweetham Devon 11 K5
Sweethaws E Susx 32 E7
Sweets Cnwll 8 F5
Sweetshouse Cnwll 5 H4
Swefling Suffk 79 H2
Swepstone Leics 86 D2
Swerford Oxon 57 G2
Swettenham Ches E 113 J7
Swilland Suffk 78 E4
Swillington Leeds 124 B4
Swimbridge Devon 23 K5
Swimbridge Newland Devon 23 J5
Swinbrook Oxon 56 F5
Swincliffe N York 132 C7
Swinderby Lincs 116 E8
Swindon Gloucs 55 L3
Swindon Staffs 84 F5
Swindon Swindn 40 D4
Swine E R Yk 126 E4
Swinefleet E R Yk 125 H6
Swineshead Bed 74 F2
Swineshead Lincs 103 L4
Swiney Highld 227 M2
Swinford Leics 87 H7
Swingfield Minnis Kent 35 G6
Swingfield Street Kent 35 H6
Swingleton Green Suffk 77 L5
Swinhoe Nthumb 169 J4
Swinithwaite N York 131 K2
Swinside Cumb 137 H3
Swinstead Lincs 103 G7
Swinton Border 179 H8
Swinton N York 132 C4
Swinton N York 134 B5
Swinton Rothm 115 J2
Swinton Salfd 113 H2
Swithland Leics 87 G2
Swordale Highld 212 E2
Swordland Highld 200 B6
Swordly Highld 229 M3
Swynnerton Staffs 99 J5
Swyre Dorset 13 M5
Sychtyn Powys 81 L3
Syde Gloucs 55 L5
Sydenham Gt Lon 45 G5
Sydenham Oxon 58 B7
Sydenham Damerel Devon 6 B2
Syderstone Norfk 105 K6
Sydling St Nicholas Dorset 14 C3
Sydmonton Hants 41 J8
Syerston Notts 102 C3
Sykehouse Donc 124 F6
Symbister Shet 235 d4
Symington S Ayrs 163 J3
Symington S Lans 165 J3
Symondsbury Dorset 13 K4
Symonds Yat (West) Herefs 54 E5
Syre Highld 229 L6
Syreford Gloucs 56 B4
Syresham Nhants 73 J6
Syston Leics 87 J2
Syston Lincs 102 F4
Sytchampton Worcs 70 E2
Sywell Nhants 74 B2

T

Tackley Oxon 57 J4
Tacolneston Norfk 92 D4
Tadcaster N York 124 D2
Taddington Derbys 114 C7
Tadley Hants 41 L7
Tadlow Cambs 75 K5
Tadmarton Oxon 72 E6
Tadworth Surrey 44 E8
Taff's Well Rhondd 37 H4
Taibach Neath 36 B3
Tain Highld 223 G5
Tain Highld 231 J3
Tairbeart W Isls 232 e4
Takeley Essex 60 F4
Takeley Street Essex 60 E4
Talaton Devon 12 D3
Talbenny Pembks 48 E5
Taleford Devon 12 E3
Talerddig Powys 81 K4
Talgarreg Cerdgn 65 L4
Talgarth Powys 68 D7
Talisker Highld 208 E7
Talke Staffs 99 J2
Talke Pits Staffs 99 J3
Talkin Cumb 148 F4
Talladale Highld 219 L7
Talla Linnfoots Border 165 M5
Tallaminnock S Ayrs 153 J3
Tallarn Green Wrexhm 98 C4
Tallentire Cumb 147 K7
Talley Carmth 66 E7
Tallington Lincs 88 F2
Talmine Highld 229 J3
Talog Carmth 50 D1
Talsarn Cerdgn 66 D4
Talsarnau Gwynd 95 K5
Talskiddy Cnwll 4 E3
Talwrn IoA 109 G6
Tal-y-bont Cerdgn 80 E5
Tal-y-Bont Conwy 109 L7
Tal-y-bont Gwynd 95 K7
Tal-y-bont Gwynd 109 J7
Talybont-on-Usk Powys 53 H4
Tal-y-Cafn Conwy 109 M7
Tal-y-coed Mons 54 B5
Talysarn Gwynd 95 H2
Tamar Valley Mining District Devon 6 C3
Tamerton Foliot C Plym 6 C4
Tamworth Staffs 86 B3
Tamworth Services Warwks 86 B4
Tandridge Surrey 32 C3
Tanfield Dur 150 F4
Tanfield Lea Dur 150 F4
Tangley Hants 28 F2
Tangmere W Susx 18 B4
Tangusdale W Isls 233 b9
Tankerness Ork 234 c6
Tankersley Barns 115 G2
Tankerton Kent 47 J6
Tannach Highld 231 K6
Tannachie Abers 206 E8
Tannadice Angus 196 D5
Tanner's Green Worcs 85 J8
Tannington Suffk 78 F2
Tannochside N Lans 175 J6
Tansley Derbys 100 F1
Tansor Nhants 88 F5
Tantobie Dur 150 F4
Tanworth in Arden Warwks 71 K1
Tan-y-groes Cerdgn 65 J5
Taobh Tuath W Isls 232 d5
Taplow Bucks 42 E4
Tarbert Ag & B 172 B7
Tarbert Ag & B 172 E5
Tarbert W Isls 232 e4
Tarbet Ag & B 183 K6
Tarbet Highld 200 B6
Tarbet Highld 228 B5
Tarbolton S Ayrs 163 K4
Tarbrax S Lans 176 D7
Tardebigge Worcs 71 H2
Tarfside Angus 196 D1
Tarland Abers 205 K4
Tarleton Lancs 120 F6
Tarlton Gloucs 55 L7
Tarnock Somset 26 B2
Tarporley Ches W 112 D8
Tarrant Crawford Dorset 15 H2
Tarrant Gunville Dorset 27 L8
Tarrant Hinton Dorset 15 H1
Tarrant Keyneston Dorset 15 H2
Tarrant Launceston Dorset 15 H1
Tarrant Monkton Dorset 15 H2
Tarrant Rawston Dorset 15 H2
Tarrant Rushton Dorset 15 H2
Tarring Neville E Susx 19 L5
Tarrington Herefs 70 B6
Tarskavaig Highld 199 J4
Tarves Abers 217 G7
Tarvin Ches W 112 C7
Tasburgh Norfk 92 E4
Tatenhill Staffs 100 D7
Tathwell Lincs 118 D5
Tatsfield Surrey 32 D2
Tattenhall Ches W 98 C2
Tatterford Norfk 105 K6
Tattersett Norfk 105 K6
Tattershall Lincs 103 K2
Tattershall Thorpe Lincs 103 L1
Tattingstone Suffk 78 D6
Tattingstone White Horse Suffk 78 D6
Tatton Park Ches E 113 H5
Tatworth Somset 13 J2
Tauchers Moray 215 J4
Taunton Somset 25 K6
Taunton Deane Crematorium Somset 25 J6
Taunton Deane Services Somset 25 J7
Taverham Norfk 92 E2
Tavernspite Pembks 49 K5
Tavistock Devon 6 C2
Tavistock Devon 6 C2
Taw Green Devon 10 F5
Tawstock Devon 23 J5
Taxal Derbys 114 A5
Tay Bridge C Dund 187 G2
Taychreggan Hotel Ag & B 182 F3
Tay Forest Park P & K 194 C4
Tayinloan Ag & B 161 H1
Taynton Gloucs 55 G4
Taynton Oxon 56 E5
Taynuilt Ag & B 182 E2
Tayport Fife 187 G2
Tayvallich Ag & B 172 C2
Tealby Lincs 117 J4
Tealing Angus 196 C8
Team Valley Gatesd 151 G3
Teangue Highld 199 K4
Teanord Highld 212 F2
Tebay Cumb 138 E6
Tebay Services Cumb 138 E6
Tebworth C Beds 59 G3
Tedburn St Mary Devon 11 J6
Teddington Gloucs 55 L2
Teddington Gt Lon 44 D6
Tedstone Delamere Herefs 70 C3
Tedstone Wafer Herefs 70 C3
Teesside Crematorium Middsb 141 L4
Teeton Nhants 73 K1
Teffont Evias Wilts 27 M5
Teffont Magna Wilts 27 M5
Tegryn Pembks 65 H7
Teigh Rutlnd 88 C1
Teigngrace Devon 7 K2
Teignmouth Devon 12 B7
Teindside Border 166 F7
Telford Wrekin 84 C2
Telford Crematorium Wrekin 84 D2
Telford Services Shrops 84 D2
Tellisford Somset 27 J1
Telscombe E Susx 19 L5
Tempar P & K 193 L5
Templand D & G 155 J5
Temple Cnwll 5 J2
Temple Mdloth 177 J6
Temple Bar Cerdgn 66 C4

Temple Cloud BaNES 38 F8
Templecombe Somset 27 G6
Temple Grafton Warwks 71 K4
Temple Guiting Gloucs 56 C3
Temple Hirst N York 124 F5
Temple Normanton Derbys 115 H7
Temple of Fiddes Abers 197 K1
Temple Sowerby Cumb 138 E2
Templeton Devon 11 K3
Templeton Pembks 49 J5
Templetown Dur 150 E5
Tempsford C Beds 75 H4
Tenbury Wells Worcs 69 L2
Tenby Pembks 49 J7
Tendring Essex 62 D3
Tendring Green Essex 62 D3
Tendring Heath Essex 62 D3
Ten Mile Bank Norfk 90 E4
Tenterden Kent 34 B7
Terling Essex 61 J5
Ternhill Shrops 98 F6
Terregles D & G 155 G6
Terrington N York 133 K5
Terrington St Clement Norfk 104 E7
Terrington St John Norfk 90 D2
Teston Kent 33 J3
Testwood Hants 29 G8
Tetbury Gloucs 39 K2
Tetchill Shrops 98 B6
Tetcott Devon 9 J5
Tetford Lincs 118 D6
Tetney Lincs 118 D2
Tetsworth Oxon 58 B7
Tettenhall Wolves 84 F4
Tettenhall Wood Wolves 84 F4
Teversal Notts 101 J1
Teversham Cambs 76 C3
Teviothead Border 156 D2
Tewin Herts 59 L5
Tewkesbury Gloucs 55 K2
Teynham Kent 34 C3
Thackley C Brad 123 H3
Thainstone Abers 206 E2
Thakeham W Susx 18 F3
Thame Oxon 58 B6
Thames Ditton Surrey 44 D6
Thamesmead Gt Lon 45 J4
Thamesport Medway 46 E5
Thanet Crematorium Kent 35 K2
Thanington Kent 34 F4
Thankerton S Lans 165 J2
Tharston Norfk 92 E5
Thatcham W Berk 41 K6
Thaxted Essex 60 F2
Theakston N York 132 D3
Thealby N Linc 125 K6
Theale Somset 26 C3
Theale W Berk 41 M6
Thearne E R Yk 126 D3
The Beeches Gloucs 56 B7
Theberton Suffk 79 J2
The Braes Highld 209 H7
The Broads 93 K2
The Brunt E Loth 178 E4
The Bungalow IoM 237 d4
The Burf Worcs 70 E2
The Butts Gloucs 55 K5
The City Bucks 42 C2
The Common Wilts 28 E5
Theddingworth Leics 87 J6
Theddlethorpe All Saints Lincs 118 F4
Theddlethorpe St Helen Lincs 119 G4
The Deep C KuH 126 D5
The Den N Ayrs 174 C7
The Forstal Kent 34 D6
The Green Cumb 128 E3
The Green Essex 61 J4
The Green N York 143 G6
The Green Wilts 27 K5
The Headland Hartpl 151 M7
The Hill Cumb 128 E3
The Lee Bucks 58 E6
The Lhen IoM 237 d2
Thelnetham Suffk 92 B7
The Lochs Moray 215 G2
Thelveton Norfk 92 E7
Thelwall Warrtn 112 F4
Themelthorpe Norfk 106 C7
The Middles Dur 150 F5
The Moor Kent 33 K7
The Mumbles Swans 51 J7
The Murray S Lans 175 H7
The Neuk Abers 206 D5
Thenford Nhants 73 G6
The Reddings Gloucs 55 K4
Therfield Herts 75 L6
The Ross P & K 185 G3
The Spring Warwks 86 C8
The Stocks Kent 21 H1
The Strand Wilts 39 L8
Thetford Norfk 91 K6
Thetford Forest Park 91 J5
Theydon Bois Essex 60 D7
Thickwood Wilts 39 J5
Thimbleby Lincs 118 C7
Thimbleby N York 141 K7
Thingwall Wirral 111 J5
Thirkleby N York 133 G4
Thirlby N York 133 G3
Thirlestane Border 178 C8
Thirn N York 132 C3
Thirsk N York 132 F3
Thistleton Lancs 120 E3
Thistleton Rutlnd 102 E8
Thistley Green Suffk 90 F7
Thixendale N York 134 C7
Thockrington Nthumb 158 B6
Tholomas Drove Cambs 90 B3
Tholthorpe N York 133 G6
Thomastown Abers 216 B6
Thompson Norfk 91 K4
Thongsbridge Kirk 123 H8
Thoralby N York 131 J3
Thoresway Lincs 117 K3
Thorganby Lincs 117 K3
Thorganby N York 125 G3
Thorgill N York 142 E7
Thorington Suffk 93 J8
Thorington Street Suffk 78 B7
Thorlby N York 131 H8
Thorley Herts 60 D4
Thorley Street IoW 16 D5
Thormanby N York 133 G5
Thornaby-on-Tees S on T 141 K4
Thornage Norfk 106 C5
Thornborough Bucks 73 L7
Thornborough N York 132 D4
Thornbury C Brad 123 J4
Thornbury Devon 9 K3
Thornbury Herefs 70 B3
Thornbury S Glos 38 F3
Thornby Nhants 87 J7
Thorncliff Staffs 100 A2
Thorncliffe Crematorium Cumb 128 E5
Thorncombe Dorset 13 J2
Thorndon Suffk 78 D1
Thorndon Cross Devon 10 D6
Thorne Donc 125 G7
Thorner Leeds 124 B3
Thorne St Margaret Somset 25 H7
Thorney C Pete 89 K3
Thorney Notts 116 E6
Thorney Somset 26 B6
Thorney Hill Hants 16 A3
Thorney Island W Susx 17 L2
Thornfalcon Somset 25 L6
Thornford Dorset 26 E8
Thorngrafton Nthumb 149 K2
Thorngumbald E R Yk 126 F5
Thornham Norfk 105 H4
Thornham Magna Suffk 78 D1
Thornham Parva Suffk 92 D8
Thornhaugh C Pete 88 F4
Thornhill C Sotn 29 J8
Thornhill Cumb 136 D5
Thornhill D & G 154 F3
Thornhill Derbys 114 D5
Thornhill Kirk 123 K6
Thornhill Stirlg 184 E7
Thornholme E R Yk 135 H6
Thornicombe Dorset 15 G2
Thornington Nthumb 168 D3
Thornley Dur 150 E7
Thornley Dur 151 J6
Thornliebank E Rens 174 F6
Thorns Suffk 77 G4
Thornsett Derbys 114 A4
Thornthwaite Cumb 137 H3
Thornthwaite N York 132 B7
Thornton Angus 196 C6
Thornton Bucks 73 L7
Thornton C Brad 123 G4
Thornton E R Yk 125 H2
Thornton Fife 186 E7
Thornton Lancs 120 D3
Thornton Leics 86 F3
Thornton Middsb 141 L4
Thornton Nthumb 179 K8
Thornton Curtis N Linc 126 D6
Thornton Garden of Rest Crematorium Sefton 111 K2
Thorntonhall S Lans 175 G7
Thornton Heath Gt Lon 44 F6
Thornton Hough Wirral 111 J5
Thornton-in-Craven N York 122 D2
Thornton in Lonsdale N York 130 D5
Thornton-le-Beans N York 132 F2
Thornton-le-Clay N York 133 L6
Thornton-le-Dale N York 134 C3
Thornton le Moor Lincs 117 H3
Thornton-le-Moor N York 132 F2
Thornton-le-Moors Ches W 112 C6
Thornton-le-Street N York 132 F3
Thorntonloch E Loth 178 F4
Thornton Rust N York 131 H2
Thornton Steward N York 132 B3
Thornton Watlass N York 132 C3
Thornydykes Border 178 D8
Thornythwaite Cumb 137 L3
Thoroton Notts 102 C4
Thorp Arch Leeds 124 C2
Thorpe Derbys 100 D3
Thorpe E R Yk 126 B2
Thorpe N York 131 J6
Thorpe Notts 102 C3
Thorpe Surrey 43 G6
Thorpe Abbotts Norfk 92 E7
Thorpe Arnold Leics 102 C7
Thorpe Audlin Wakefd 124 D7
Thorpe Bassett N York 134 D5
Thorpe Bay Sthend 46 E3
Thorpe by Water Rutlnd 88 C4
Thorpe Constantine Staffs 86 C2
Thorpe End Norfk 93 G2
Thorpe Green Essex 62 E4
Thorpe Green Suffk 77 L4
Thorpe Hesley Rothm 115 G3
Thorpe in Balne Donc 124 F7
Thorpe Langton Leics 87 L5
Thorpe Lea Surrey 43 G6
Thorpe-le-Soken Essex 62 E4
Thorpe le Street E R Yk 125 K2
Thorpe Malsor Nhants 88 B7
Thorpe Mandeville Nhants 73 G5
Thorpe Market Norfk 106 F5
Thorpe Marriot Norfk 92 E1
Thorpe Morieux Suffk 77 L4
Thorpeness Suffk 79 K3
Thorpe on the Hill Lincs 116 E7
Thorpe Park Surrey 43 G6
Thorpe St Andrew Norfk 92 F2
Thorpe St Peter Lincs 104 D1
Thorpe Salvin Rothm 115 K5
Thorpe Satchville Leics 87 K2
Thorpe Thewles S on T 141 J3
Thorpe Tilney Lincs 103 J2
Thorpe Underwood N York 133 G7
Thorpe Waterville Nhants 88 E7
Thorpe Willoughby N York 124 E4
Thorrington Essex 62 C4
Thorverton Devon 11 L4
Thrandeston Suffk 92 D7
Thrapston Nhants 88 E7
Threapwood Ches W 98 C4
Threapwood Staffs 100 B4
Threave S Ayrs 163 J7
Three Bridges W Susx 32 B5
Three Chimneys Kent 33 L5
Three Cocks Powys 68 D6
Three Counties Crematorium Essex 61 J3
Three Crosses Swans 51 H6
Three Cups Corner E Susx 20 D2
Threekingham Lincs 103 H5
Three Leg Cross E Susx 33 H6
Three Legged Cross Dorset 15 K2
Three Mile Cross Wokham 42 B6
Threemilestone Cnwll 3 K3
Three Miletown W Loth 176 E3
Three Oaks E Susx 21 G3
Threlkeld Cumb 137 J3
Threshers Bush Essex 60 D6
Threshfield N York 131 J6
Thrigby Norfk 93 K2
Thrintoft N York 132 D2
Thriplow Cambs 76 B5
Throcking Herts 60 B3
Throckley N u Ty 150 E2
Throckmorton Worcs 71 H4
Throop Bmouth 15 L4
Thropton Nthumb 158 C2
Throsk Stirlg 176 B1
Throughgate D & G 154 F5
Throwleigh Devon 11 G6

Throwley Forstal Kent 34 C4
Thrumpton Notts 101 J6
Thrumster Highld 231 L6
Thrunscoe NE Lin 127 H8
Thrupp Gloucs 55 K7
Thrussington Leics 87 J1
Thruxton Hants 28 F3
Thruxton Herefs 69 J7
Thrybergh Rothm 115 J3
Thulston Derbys 101 H6
Thundersley Essex 46 C3
Thurcaston Leics 87 H2
Thurcroft Rothm 115 J4
Thurgarton Norfk 106 E5
Thurgarton Notts 102 B3
Thurgoland Barns 114 F2
Thurlaston Leics 87 G4
Thurlaston Warwks 72 F1
Thurlbear Somset 25 K7
Thurlby Lincs 89 G1
Thurlby Lincs 102 E1
Thurlby Lincs 119 G6
Thurleigh Bed 74 F3
Thurlestone Devon 7 G7
Thurloxton Somset 25 L5
Thurlstone Barns 114 E2
Thurlton Norfk 93 J4
Thurmaston Leics 87 H2
Thurnby Leics 87 J3
Thurne Norfk 93 J1
Thurnham Kent 33 K2
Thurning Nhants 88 F6
Thurning Norfk 106 C6
Thurnscoe Barns 115 J1
Thurrock Services Thurr 45 L4
Thursby Cumb 148 B5
Thursford Norfk 106 B5
Thursley Surrey 30 E4
Thurso Highld 231 G2
Thurstaston Wirral 111 H5
Thurston Suffk 77 L2
Thurstonfield Cumb 148 B4
Thurstonland Kirk 123 H7
Thurton Norfk 93 G4
Thurvaston Derbys 100 E5
Thuxton Norfk 92 B3
Thwaite N York 139 K7
Thwaite Suffk 78 D2
Thwaite Head Cumb 129 H2
Thwaite St Mary Norfk 93 G4
Thwing E R Yk 135 G5
Tibbermore P & K 185 L3
Tibbers D & G 154 E3
Tibberton Gloucs 55 H4
Tibberton Worcs 70 F3
Tibberton Wrekin 99 G7
Tibbie Shiels Inn Border 166 C5
Tibenham Norfk 92 D5
Tibshelf Derbys 101 H1
Tibshelf Services Derbys 101 H1
Tibthorpe E R Yk 134 E7
Ticehurst E Susx 33 H7
Tichborne Hants 29 L5
Tickencote Rutlnd 88 E2
Tickenham N Som 38 C6
Tickhill Donc 115 L3
Ticklerton Shrops 83 J5
Ticknall Derbys 101 G7
Tickton E R Yk 126 D3
Tidcombe Wilts 40 F8
Tiddington Oxon 57 M6
Tiddington Warwks 72 B4
Tidebrook E Susx 33 G7
Tideford Cnwll 6 A4
Tidenham Gloucs 38 E2
Tideswell Derbys 114 D6
Tidmarsh W Berk 41 M5
Tidmington Warwks 72 C6
Tidworth Wilts 28 E2
Tiers Cross Pembks 48 F5
Tiffield Nhants 73 K4
Tigerton Angus 196 E4
Tigh a Ghearraidh W Isls 233 b6
Tigharry W Isls 233 b6
Tighnabruaich Ag & B 173 G4
Tigley Devon 7 H4
Tilbrook Cambs 74 F2
Tilbury Thurr 45 M5
Tile Cross Birm 85 L6
Tile Hill Covtry 86 C7
Tilehurst Readg 42 A5
Tilford Surrey 30 E3
Tilgate W Susx 31 L4
Tilham Street Somset 26 E4
Tillicoultry Clacks 185 J7
Tillietudlem S Lans 164 F1
Tillingham Essex 62 B7
Tillington Herefs 69 J5
Tillington W Susx 30 F6
Tillington Common Herefs 69 J5
Tillybirloch Abers 206 D4
Tillyfourie Abers 206 C3
Tillygreig Abers 207 G2
Tillyrie P & K 186 B6
Tilmanstone Kent 35 J4
Tilney All Saints Norfk 104 F8
Tilney High End Norfk 104 E8
Tilney St Lawrence Norfk 90 D2
Tilshead Wilts 28 B2
Tilstock Shrops 98 D5
Tilston Ches W 98 C3
Tilstone Fearnall Ches W 98 E1
Tilsworth C Beds 59 G3
Tilton on the Hill Leics 87 L3
Tiltups End Gloucs 39 J2
Timberland Lincs 103 J2
Timbersbrook Ches E 113 K8
Timberscombe Somset 24 E3
Timble N York 132 B8
Timpanheck D & G 156 B7
Timperley Traffd 113 H4
Timsbury BaNES 38 F8
Timsbury Hants 29 G6
Timsgarry W Isls 232 d2
Timsgearraidh W Isls 232 d2
Timworth Suffk 77 J2
Timworth Green Suffk 77 J2
Tincleton Dorset 14 E4
Tindale Cumb 149 G3
Tingewick Bucks 58 A2
Tingrith C Beds 59 G2
Tingwall Airport Shet 235 c6
Tingwell Ork 234 c5
Tinhay Devon 9 K7
Tinsley Sheff 115 H4
Tinsley Green W Susx 32 B5
Tintagel Cnwll 8 E7
Tintern Parva Mons 54 D7
Tintinhull Somset 26 D7
Tintwistle Derbys 114 A3
Tinwald D & G 155 H5
Tinwell Rutlnd 88 E3
Tipton Sandw 85 G5
Tipton Green Sandw 85 G5
Tipton St John Devon 12 E4
Tiptree Essex 61 L5
Tiptree Heath Essex 61 L5
Tirabad Powys 67 J6
Tiree Ag & B 188 D7
Tiree Airport Ag & B 188 C7
Tiretigan Ag & B 172 C6
Tirley Gloucs 55 J3
Tiroran Ag & B 181 G2
Tirphil Caerph 53 H7
Tirril Cumb 138 D2
Tisbury Wilts 27 L5
Tissington Derbys 100 D3
Titchberry Devon 22 C6
Titchfield Hants 17 G2
Titchmarsh Nhants 88 E7
Titchwell Norfk 105 J4
Tithby Notts 102 B5
Titley Herefs 69 G3
Titsey Surrey 32 D3
Titson Cnwll 9 H5
Tittensor Staffs 99 K5
Tittleshall Norfk 105 L7
Titton Worcs 70 E1
Tiverton Ches W 98 D1
Tiverton Devon 24 E8
Tivetshall St Margaret Norfk 92 E6
Tivetshall St Mary Norfk 92 E6
Tixall Staffs 99 L7
Tixover Rutlnd 88 E4
Toab Shet 235 c8
Tobermory Ag & B 189 L5
Toberonochy Ag & B 181 L5
Tobha Mor W Isls 233 b7
Tocher Abers 216 D7
Tochieneal Moray 215 L2
Tockenham Wilts 40 B4
Tockholes Bl w D 121 K6
Tockington S Glos 38 E3
Tockwith N York 133 G8
Todber Dorset 27 J7
Toddington C Beds 59 G3
Toddington Gloucs 56 B2
Toddington Services C Beds 59 G3
Todenham Gloucs 72 B7
Todhills Angus 196 C8
Todhills Rest Area Cumb 148 C3
Todmorden Calder 122 D5
Todwick Rothm 115 J5
Toft Cambs 75 L4
Toft Lincs 88 F1
Toft Shet 235 c3
Toft Hill Dur 140 E2
Toft Monks Norfk 93 J4
Toft next Newton Lincs 117 H4
Toftrees Norfk 105 L6
Togston Nthumb 159 G2
Tokavaig Highld 199 J3
Tokers Green Oxon 42 B5
Tolastadh W Isls 232 g2
Toll W Isls 232 g2
Tolland Somset 25 H5
Tollard Royal Wilts 27 L7
Toll Bar Donc 124 E8
Toller Fratrum Dorset 14 B3
Toller Porcorum Dorset 14 B3
Tollerton N York 133 H6
Tollerton Notts 101 L5
Tollesbury Essex 62 A6
Tolleshunt D'Arcy Essex 61 L5
Tolleshunt Knights Essex 61 L5
Tolleshunt Major Essex 61 L5
Tolpuddle Dorset 14 E4
Tolsta W Isls 232 g2
Tolworth Gt Lon 44 D6
Tomatin Highld 213 J8
Tomchrasky Highld 201 K3
Tomdoun Highld 201 H5
Tomich Highld 211 L8
Tomich Highld 212 E5
Tomich Highld 222 F7
Tomich Highld 226 A7
Tomintoul Moray 204 E2
Tomnacross Highld 212 D6
Tomnavoulin Moray 204 F1
Tonbridge Kent 33 G4
Tondu Brdgnd 36 D4
Tonedale Somset 25 H6
Tong C Brad 123 J4
Tong Kent 34 C4
Tong Shrops 84 E3
Tonga W Isls 232 g2
Tonge Leics 101 H7
Tongham Surrey 30 E2
Tongland D & G 146 C4
Tong Norton Shrops 84 E2
Tongue Highld 229 J4
Tongwynlais Cardif 37 H4
Tonmawr Neath 36 C2
Tonna Neath 52 B7
Tonwell Herts 60 B5
Tonypandy Rhondd 36 F3
Tonyrefail Rhondd 36 F3
Toot Baldon Oxon 57 K7
Toot Hill Essex 60 E7
Toothill Swindn 40 C4
Tooting Gt Lon 44 F5
Tooting Bec Gt Lon 44 F5
Topcliffe N York 132 F4
Topcroft Norfk 92 F5
Topcroft Street Norfk 92 F5
Toppesfield Essex 77 G6
Toprow Norfk 92 E4
Topsham Devon 12 C5
Torbeg N Ayrs 162 A4
Torboll Highld 223 G2
Torbreck Highld 213 G6
Torbryan Devon 7 J3
Torcastle Highld 192 B2
Torcross Devon 7 J7
Tore Highld 212 F4
Torinturk Ag & B 172 D5
Torksey Lincs 116 D5
Tormarton S Glos 39 H5
Tormore N Ayrs 161 M3
Tornagrain Highld 213 J4
Tornaveen Abers 206 C4
Torness Highld 212 E8
Toronto Dur 140 F2
Torpenhow Cumb 147 L6
Torphichen W Loth 176 C4
Torphins Abers 206 C5
Torpoint Cnwll 6 C5
Torquay Torbay 7 L3
Torquay Crematorium Torbay 7 K3
Torquhan Border 177 L8
Torran Highld 209 J5
Torrance E Duns 175 H4
Torranyard N Ayrs 163 J1
Torridon Highld 210 D3
Torridon House Highld 210 D3
Torrin Highld 199 J2
Torrisdale Ag & B 161 K3
Torrisdale Highld 229 K3
Torrish Highld 227 G5
Torrisholme Lancs 129 K6
Torrobull Highld 226 A7
Torry C Aber 207 H4
Torryburn Fife 176 D2
Torteval Guern 236 b4
Torthorwald D & G 155 H6
Tortington W Susx 18 D5
Torton Worcs 84 E8
Tortworth S Glos 39 G2
Torvaig Highld 209 H5
Torver Cumb 137 J7
Torwood Falk 175 L2
Torwoodlee Border 167 G2
Torworth Notts 116 A4
Toscaig Highld 209 L6
Toseland Cambs 75 J3
Tosside Lancs 130 E7
Tostock Suffk 77 L2
Totaig Highld 208 C4
Tote Highld 208 F5
Tote Highld 209 H3
Totland IoW 16 D5
Totley Sheff 114 F5
Totnes Devon 7 J4
Toton Notts 101 J5
Totronald Ag & B 188 F5
Totscore Highld 208 F2
Tottenham Gt Lon 45 G3
Tottenhill Norfk 90 F2
Totteridge Gt Lon 44 E2
Totternhoe C Beds 59 G4
Tottington Bury 122 B7
Totton Hants 29 G8
Toulton Somset 25 J5
Toulvaddie Highld 223 J5
Tovil Kent 33 K3

Toward Ag & B 173 K5
Toward Quay Ag & B 173 J5
Towcester Nhants 73 K5
Towednack Cnwll 2 E4
Tower of London Gt Lon 45 G4
Towersey Oxon 58 B6
Towie Abers 205 K3
Tow Law Dur 150 E6
Town End Cambs 90 B4
Townend W Duns 174 D3
Townhead Barns 114 D2
Townhead D & G 155 H4
Townhead of Greenlaw D & G 146 C3
Townhill Fife 176 F1
Town Littleworth E Susx 19 L3
Towns End Hants 41 K8
Townshend Cnwll 3 G5
Town Street Suffk 91 H6
Town Yetholm Border 168 B4
Towthorpe C York 133 K7
Towton N York 124 D3
Towyn Conwy 110 D5
Toxteth Lpool 111 K4
Toynton All Saints Lincs 118 E8
Toy's Hill Kent 32 E3
Trabboch E Ayrs 163 K5
Trabbochburn E Ayrs 163 L5
Tradespark Highld 213 K3
Trafford Park Traffd 113 H3
Trallong Powys 52 E3
Tranent E Loth 177 L4
Tranmere Wirral 111 J4
Trantelbeg Highld 230 C5
Trantlemore Highld 230 C5
Trap Carmth 51 J2
Traprain E Loth 178 D4
Traquair Border 166 E3
Trawden Lancs 122 D3
Trawsfynydd Gwynd 96 A5
Trealaw Rhondd 36 F3
Treales Lancs 120 F4
Trearddur Bay IoA 108 C5
Treaslane Highld 208 F4
Trebetherick Cnwll 4 E1
Treborough Somset 24 F4
Trebullett Cnwll 5 M1
Treburley Cnwll 6 A1
Trecastle Powys 52 D3
Trecwn Pembks 64 D7
Trecynon Rhondd 52 F7
Tredegar Blae G 53 H6
Tredington Gloucs 55 K3
Tredington Warwks 72 C5
Tredunnock Mons 38 B2
Treen Cnwll 2 D6
Treeton Rothm 115 H4
Trefasser Pembks 64 C6
Trefecca Powys 53 H2
Trefeglwys Powys 81 L5
Treffgarne Pembks 49 G3
Treffgarne Owen Pembks 48 E3
Trefforest Rhondd 37 G3
Trefilan Cerdgn 66 D3
Trefin Pembks 64 B7
Trefnant Denbgs 110 E7
Trefonen Shrops 97 K6
Trefor Gwynd 94 F4
Trefriw Conwy 109 L8
Tregadillett Cnwll 9 H7
Tregare Mons 54 B6
Tregaron Cerdgn 66 F3
Tregarth Gwynd 109 H7
Tregeare Cnwll 9 H7
Tregeiriog Wrexhm 97 J5
Tregele IoA 108 D3
Treglemais Pembks 48 D2
Tregonetha Cnwll 4 E3
Tregonning & Gwinear Mining District Cnwll 3 G5
Tregony Cnwll 4 E6
Tregorrick Cnwll 4 F5
Tregoyd Powys 68 E6
Tre-groes Cerdgn 65 L5
Tregynon Powys 82 C4
Tre-gynwr Carmth 50 E2
Trehafod Rhondd 37 G3
Trehan Cnwll 6 B4
Treharris Myr Td 37 H2
Treherbert Rhondd 52 E7
Trekenner Cnwll 6 A1
Treknow Cnwll 8 D7
Trelawnyd Flints 110 F5
Trelech Carmth 65 J7
Treleddyd-fawr Pembks 48 C2
Trelewis Myr Td 37 H2
Trelights Cnwll 8 C8
Trelill Cnwll 5 G1
Trellech Mons 54 D6
Trelogan Flints 110 F5
Tremadog Gwynd 95 K4
Tremail Cnwll 8 F7
Tremain Cerdgn 65 H5
Tremaine Cnwll 9 G6
Tremar Cnwll 5 K3
Trematon Cnwll 6 B4
Tremeirchion Denbgs 110 F6
Trenance Cnwll 4 D3
Trenance Cnwll 4 E2
Trench Wrekin 84 C2
Trenear Cnwll 3 H5
Treneglos Cnwll 9 G7
Trent Dorset 26 E7
Trentham C Stke 99 K4
Trentishoe Devon 23 K2
Trent Vale C Stke 99 K4
Treoes V Glam 36 E5
Treorchy Rhondd 36 E2
Trequite Cnwll 5 G1
Trerhyngyll V Glam 36 F5
Trerulefoot Cnwll 5 M4
Tresaith Cerdgn 65 J4
Tresco IoS 2 a1
Trescowe Cnwll 3 G5
Tresean Cnwll 4 C4
Tresham Gloucs 39 H3
Treshnish Isles Ag & B 189 G7
Tresillian Cnwll 4 D6
Treskinnick Cross Cnwll 9 G5
Tresmeer Cnwll 9 G7
Tresparrett Cnwll 8 F6
Tressait P & K 194 C4
Tresta Shet 235 c5
Tresta Shet 235 e3
Treswell Notts 116 C5
Treswithian Downs Crematorium Cnwll 3 H3
Tre Taliesin Cerdgn 80 E5
Trethevey Cnwll 8 E6
Trethewey Cnwll 2 C6
Trethurgy Cnwll 5 G5
Tretire Herefs 54 D4
Tretower Powys 53 J4
Treuddyn Flints 97 K2
Trevalga Cnwll 8 E6
Trevalyn Wrexhm 98 B2
Trevarrian Cnwll 4 D3
Treveal Cnwll 4 C4
Treveighan Cnwll 8 E8
Trevellas Downs Cnwll 3 J2
Trevelmond Cnwll 5 K3
Treverva Cnwll 3 K5
Trevescan Cnwll 2 C6
Treviscoe Cnwll 4 E5
Trevone Cnwll 4 D2
Trevor Wrexhm 97 L4
Trewalder Cnwll 8 E7
Trewarmett Cnwll 8 E7
Trewavas Mining District Cnwll 3 G6
Trewen Cnwll 9 H7
Trewint Cnwll 9 G8
Trewithian Cnwll 4 D7
Trewoon Cnwll 4 F5
Treyford W Susx 30 D7
Trimdon Dur 151 J7
Trimdon Colliery Dur 151 J7
Trimdon Grange Dur 151 J7
Trimingham Norfk 107 G5
Trimley St Martin Suffk 78 F6
Trimley St Mary Suffk 79 G7
Trimsaran Carmth 50 F5
Trimstone Devon 23 H3
Trinafour P & K 194 B4
Tring Herts 58 F5
Trinity Angus 196 F4
Trinity Jersey 236 d6
Trinity Gask P & K 185 K4
Triscombe Somset 25 J4
Trislaig Highld 191 L2
Trispen Cnwll 4 D5
Tritlington Nthumb 158 F4
Trochry P & K 194 F7
Troedyraur Cerdgn 65 K5
Troedyrhiw Myr Td 53 G7
Trois Bois Jersey 236 c6
Troon Cnwll 3 H4
Troon S Ayrs 163 H3
Tropical World Roundhay Park Leeds 123 L3
Trossachs Stirlg 184 B5
Trossachs Pier Stirlg 184 B6
Troston Suffk 91 K8
Trotshill Worcs 70 F4
Trottiscliffe Kent 33 H2
Trotton W Susx 30 D6
Troutbeck Cumb 137 L6
Troutbeck Bridge Cumb 137 L7
Troway Derbys 115 H5
Trowbridge Wilts 39 J8
Trowell Notts 101 J4
Trowell Services Notts 101 J4
Trowse Newton Norfk 92 F3
Trudoxhill Somset 27 H3
Trull Somset 25 K6
Trumpan Highld 208 C3
Trumpet Herefs 70 B6
Trumpington Cambs 76 C4
Trunch Norfk 107 G5
Truro Cnwll 4 C6
Trusham Devon 11 K7
Trusley Derbys 100 E5
Trusthorpe Lincs 119 G5
Trysull Staffs 84 F5
Tubney Oxon 57 H7
Tuckenhay Devon 7 J5
Tuckhill Shrops 84 E6
Tuckingmill Cnwll 3 H3
Tuckingmill Wilts 27 L5
Tuckton Bmouth 15 L4
Tuddenham Suffk 77 G1
Tuddenham Suffk 78 E5
Tudeley Kent 33 G4
Tudhoe Dur 151 G7
Tudweiliog Gwynd 94 D5
Tuffley Gloucs 55 J5
Tufton Hants 29 J3
Tufton Pembks 49 H2
Tugby Leics 87 L4
Tugford Shrops 83 L6
Tughall Nthumb 169 J4
Tullibody Clacks 185 H7
Tullich Highld 212 F8
Tullich Highld 223 J6
Tulliemet P & K 194 F5
Tulloch Abers 216 F7
Tullochgorm Ag & B 182 D7
Tulloch Station Highld 192 F1
Tullymurdoch P & K 195 J5
Tullynessle Abers 206 B2
Tulse Hill Gt Lon 44 F5
Tumble Carmth 51 G3
Tumby Lincs 103 L1
Tumby Woodside Lincs 103 L2
Tummel Bridge P & K 194 B5
Tunbridge Wells Kent 33 G5
Tundergarth D & G 155 L6
Tunley BaNES 39 G8
Tunstall E R Yk 127 H4
Tunstall Kent 34 B3
Tunstall Lancs 130 B5
Tunstall N York 140 F7
Tunstall Norfk 93 J2
Tunstall Staffs 99 H6
Tunstall Suffk 79 H4
Tunstall Sundld 151 J4
Tunstead Derbys 114 C6
Tunstead Norfk 107 G7
Tunstead Milton Derbys 114 B5
Turgis Green Hants 42 B8
Turkdean Gloucs 56 C4
Tur Langton Leics 87 K5
Turleigh Wilts 39 J7
Turnastone Herefs 69 G7
Turnberry S Ayrs 152 E2
Turnditch Derbys 100 F3
Turner's Hill W Susx 32 C6
Turnhouse C Edin 177 G4
Turnworth Dorset 14 F2
Turriff Abers 216 D4
Turton Bottoms Bl w D 121 L7
Turves Cambs 89 L4
Turvey Bed 74 D4
Turville Bucks 42 C3
Turweston Bucks 73 H6
Tushielaw Inn Border 166 D5
Tutbury Staffs 100 E6
Tutshill Gloucs 38 D2
Tuttington Norfk 106 F6
Tuxford Notts 116 C7
Twatt Ork 234 b5
Twatt Shet 235 c5
Twechar E Duns 175 J3
Tweedbank Border 167 H3
Tweedmouth Nthumb 179 K7
Tweedsmuir Border 165 L4
Twelveheads Cnwll 3 K3
Twemlow Green Ches E 113 H7
Twenty Lincs 103 J7
Twerton BaNES 39 G7
Twickenham Gt Lon 44 D5
Twigworth Gloucs 55 J4
Twineham W Susx 19 H2
Twinstead Essex 77 J6
Twitchen Devon 24 C5
Two Dales Derbys 114 F8
Two Gates Staffs 86 B4
Two Waters Herts 59 H6
Twycross Leics 86 D3
Twycross Zoo Leics 86 C3
Twyford Bucks 58 A3
Twyford Hants 29 J6
Twyford Leics 87 K2
Twyford Norfk 106 B7
Twyford Wokham 42 C5
Twynholm D & G 146 B4
Twyning Green Gloucs 70 F6
Twynllanan Carmth 51 L2
Twywell Nhants 88 D7
Tyberton Herefs 69 H6
Tyburn Birm 85 K5
Tycroes Carmth 51 H4
Tycrwyn Powys 97 H8
Tydd Gote Lincs 104 D8
Tydd St Giles Cambs 90 B1
Tydd St Mary Lincs 104 C8
Tye Green Essex 76 E7
Tyldesley Wigan 113 G2
Tyler Hill Kent 34 F3
Tylorstown Rhondd 36 F2
Ty-nant Conwy 96 F4
Tyndrum Stirlg 183 K2
Ty'n-dwr Denbgs 97 K4
Tynemouth N Tyne 151 J2
Tynemouth Crematorium N Tyne 151 J2

Tyne Tunnel S Tyne 151 H2
Tyninghame E Loth 178 D3
Tynron D & G 154 E4
Tynygraig Cerdgn 66 F1
Ty'n-y-Groes Conwy 109 L7
Tyn-y-nant Rhondd 37 G4
Tyringham M Keyn 74 C5
Tyseley Birm 85 K6
Tythegston Brdgnd 36 D5
Tytherington Ches E 113 K6
Tytherington S Glos 38 F3
Tytherington Wilts 27 K3
Tytherleigh Devon 13 H2
Tytherton Lucas Wilts 39 L5
Tywardreath Cnwll 5 H5
Tywyn Gwynd 80 D4

U

Ubbeston Green Suffk 79 G1
Ubley BaNES 38 D8
Uckfield E Susx 19 M2
Uckinghall Worcs 70 F6
Uckington Gloucs 55 K3
Uddingston S Lans 175 J6
Uddington S Lans 165 G3
Udimore E Susx 21 H2
Udny Green Abers 207 G1
Udny Station Abers 207 G1
Uffculme Devon 25 G8
Uffington Lincs 88 F3
Uffington Oxon 40 F3
Uffington Shrops 83 K2
Ufford C Pete 89 G3
Ufford Suffk 79 G4
Ufton Warwks 72 E3
Ufton Nervet W Berk 41 M6
Ugadale Ag & B 161 K4
Ugborough Devon 7 G5
Uggeshall Suffk 93 J7
Ugglebarnby N York 143 H5
Ughill Sheff 114 E4
Ugley Essex 60 E3
Ugley Green Essex 60 E3
Ugthorpe N York 143 G5
Uibhist A Deas W Isls 233 c8
Uibhist A Tuath W Isls 233 b6
Uig Ag & B 188 F5
Uig Highld 208 C4
Uig Highld 208 F2
Uig W Isls 232 d2
Uigshader Highld 209 G5
Uisken Ag & B 180 E4
Ulbster Highld 231 K7
Ulceby Lincs 118 F6
Ulceby N Linc 126 D7
Ulceby Skitter N Linc 126 E7
Ulcombe Kent 33 L4
Uldale Cumb 147 M7
Uley Gloucs 55 H7
Ulgham Nthumb 159 G4
Ullapool Highld 220 E3
Ullenhall Warwks 71 K2
Ulleskelf N York 124 D3
Ullesthorpe Leics 87 G6
Ulley Rothm 115 J4
Ullingswick Herefs 69 L4
Ullinish Lodge Hotel Highld 208 E6
Ullock Cumb 136 E3
Ullswater Cumb 138 B3
Ullswater Steamers Cumb 137 L4
Ulpha Cumb 128 E2
Ulrome E R Yk 135 J7
Ulsta Shet 235 d3
Ulva Ag & B 189 K7
Ulverley Green Solhll 85 K6
Ulverston Cumb 129 G4
Ulwell Dorset 15 J6
Ulzieside D & G 164 F7
Umberleigh Devon 23 J6
Unapool Highld 224 F2
Underbarrow Cumb 129 K2
Under Burnmouth Border 156 E5
Undercliffe C Brad 123 J4
Underdale Shrops 83 K2
Underriver Kent 32 F3
Underwood Notts 101 J3
Undy Mons 38 C3
Union Mills IoM 237 c5
Unst Shet 235 d1
Unstone Derbys 115 G6
Upavon Wilts 28 C1
Upchurch Kent 46 D6
Upcott Devon 24 B5
Up Exe Devon 12 B2
Upgate Norfk 106 D8
Uphall Dorset 14 B2
Uphall W Loth 176 E4
Upham Devon 11 K3
Upham Hants 29 K7
Uphampton Herefs 69 H2
Uphampton Worcs 70 E2
Uphill N Som 37 L8
Up Holland Lancs 112 D1
Uplawmoor E Rens 174 E7
Upleadon Gloucs 55 H3
Upleatham R & Cl 142 D4
Uploders Dorset 13 L4
Uplowman Devon 24 F7
Uplyme Devon 13 H4
Up Marden W Susx 30 D8
Upminster Gt Lon 45 K3
Up Mudford Somset 26 E7
Up Nately Hants 30 B2
Upottery Devon 12 F2
Upper Affcot Shrops 83 J6
Upper Ardchronie Highld 222 E4
Upper Arley Worcs 84 D7
Upper Basildon W Berk 41 L5
Upper Beeding W Susx 19 G4
Upper Benefield Nhants 88 E5
Upper Bentley Worcs 71 H2
Upper Bighouse Highld 230 C4
Upper Boddington Nhants 72 F4
Upper Brailes Warwks 72 C6
Upper Breakish Highld 199 L2
Upper Broadheath Worcs 70 E4
Upper Broughton Notts 102 B7
Upper Bucklebury W Berk 41 K6
Upper Burgate Hants 28 D7
Upperby Cumb 148 D4
Upper Caldecote C Beds 75 H5
Upper Chapel Powys 67 L6
Upper Chicksgrove Wilts 27 L5
Upper Chute Wilts 28 F2
Upper Clapton Gt Lon 45 G3
Upper Clatford Hants 29 G3
Upper Cound Shrops 83 K3
Upper Cumberworth Kirk 123 J8
Upper Dallachy Moray 215 H2
Upper Deal Kent 35 K4
Upper Dean Bed 74 F2
Upper Denby Kirk 114 E1
Upper Dicker E Susx 20 B4
Upper Dounreay Highld 230 E3
Upper Dovercourt Essex 62 F2
Upper Drumbane Stirlg 184 E6
Upper Dunsforth N York 133 G6
Upper Eashing Surrey 30 F3
Upper Eathie Highld 213 J2
Upper Egleton Herefs 70 B5
Upper Elkstone Staffs 100 B2
Upper Ellastone Staffs 100 C4
Upper Farringdon Hants 30 B4
Upper Framilode Gloucs 55 H6
Upper Froyle Hants 30 C3
Upperglen Highld 208 E4
Upper Godney Somset 26 C3
Upper Gravenhurst C Beds 75 G7
Upper Green W Berk 41 G7
Upper Grove Common Herefs 54 E3
Upper Hale Surrey 30 D2
Upper Halliford Surrey 43 H6
Upper Hambleton Rutlnd 88 C3
Upper Harbledown Kent 34 F3
Upper Hartfield E Susx 32 E6
Upper Hatherley Gloucs 55 L4
Upper Heaton Kirk 123 H6
Upper Helmsley N York 133 L7
Upper Hergest Herefs 68 F4
Upper Heyford Nhants 73 J3
Upper Heyford Oxon 57 J3
Upper Hill Herefs 69 J4
Upper Hopton Kirk 123 J6
Upper Hulme Staffs 100 A1
Upper Inglesham Swindn 40 D2
Upper Killay Swans 51 H6
Upper Kinchrackine Ag & B 183 G2
Upper Knockando Moray 214 E5
Upper Lambourn W Berk 40 F4
Upper Landywood Staffs 85 H3
Upper Langford N Som 38 C7
Upper Langwith Derbys 115 K7
Upper Largo Fife 187 G6
Upper Leigh Staffs 100 A5
Upper Lochton Abers 206 D6
Upper Longdon Staffs 85 J2
Upper & Lower Stondon C Beds 75 H7
Upper Lybster Highld 231 J7
Upper Lydbrook Gloucs 54 E5
Upper Lye Herefs 69 H2
Uppermill Oldham 113 M1
Upper Milton Worcs 84 E8
Upper Minety Wilts 40 A3
Upper Mulben Moray 215 H4
Upper Netchwood Shrops 83 L5
Upper Nobut Staffs 100 B5
Upper Norwood W Susx 18 C3
Upper Poppleton C York 133 H8
Upper Ratley Hants 28 F6
Upper Rissington Gloucs 56 D4
Upper Rochford Worcs 70 B2
Upper Ruscoe D & G 145 L3
Upper Sapey Herefs 70 C2
Upper Seagry Wilts 39 L4
Upper Shelton C Beds 74 E5
Upper Sheringham Norfk 106 D4
Upper Skelmorlie N Ayrs 173 L5
Upper Slaughter Gloucs 56 D4
Upper Soudley Gloucs 54 F6
Upper Standen Kent 35 H6
Upper Stoke Norfk 92 F3
Upper Stowe Nhants 73 J3
Upper Street Hants 28 D7
Upper Street Norfk 93 H1
Upper Street Norfk 107 G8
Upper Street Suffk 77 H4
Upper Street Suffk 78 D4
Upper Sundon C Beds 59 H3
Upper Swell Gloucs 56 D3
Upper Tasburgh Norfk 92 E4
Upper Tean Staffs 100 A5
Upperthong Kirk 123 H8
Upperton W Susx 30 F6
Upper Town Herefs 69 L5
Uppertown Highld 231 L1
Upper Town N Som 38 D7
Upper Town Suffk 77 K2
Upper Tumble Carmth 51 G3
Upper Tysoe Warwks 72 D5
Upper Victoria Angus 187 J1
Upper Wardington Oxon 72 F5
Upper Welland Worcs 70 D6
Upper Wellingham E Susx 19 L3
Upper Weybread Suffk 92 F7
Upper Wield Hants 29 L4
Upper Winchendon Bucks 58 C5
Upper Woodford Wilts 28 C4
Upper Wraxall Wilts 39 J5
Uppingham Rutlnd 88 C4
Uppington Shrops 83 L2
Upsall N York 133 G3
Upsettlington Border 168 C1
Upshire Essex 60 C7
Up Somborne Hants 29 H5
Upstreet Kent 35 G3
Upton Bucks 58 C5
Upton C Pete 89 G4
Upton Cambs 89 H7
Upton Ches W 112 B7
Upton Cnwll 5 L2
Upton Devon 7 G7
Upton Devon 12 E2
Upton Dorset 14 E5
Upton Dorset 15 J4
Upton Halton 112 C4
Upton Hants 29 G1
Upton Hants 29 G7
Upton Leics 86 D4
Upton Lincs 116 E4
Upton Norfk 93 H2
Upton Notts 102 B2
Upton Notts 116 C6
Upton Oxon 41 K3
Upton Slough 43 G5
Upton Somset 24 F5
Upton Somset 26 C6
Upton Wakefd 124 D7
Upton Wirral 111 J4
Upton Bishop Herefs 54 F3
Upton Cheyney S Glos 39 G6
Upton Cressett Shrops 84 B5
Upton Grey Hants 30 B2
Upton Hellions Devon 11 J4
Upton Lovell Wilts 27 L4
Upton Magna Shrops 83 K2
Upton Noble Somset 27 G4
Upton Pyne Devon 11 L5
Upton St Leonards Gloucs 55 K5
Upton Scudamore Wilts 27 K2
Upton Snodsbury Worcs 71 G4
Upton-upon-Severn Worcs 70 F6

Upton Warren Worcs 71 G2
Upwaltham W Susx 18 C3
Upwell Norfk 90 C3
Upwood Cambs 89 J6
Urchfont Wilts 40 B8
Urmston Traffd 113 H3
Urquhart Moray 215 G2
Urquhart Castle Highld 212 E8
Urra N York 142 C6
Urray Highld 212 D4
Usan Angus 197 H5
Ushaw Moor Dur 151 G6
Usk Mons 54 B7
Usselby Lincs 117 H3
Usworth Sundld 151 H4
Utkinton Ches W 112 D7
Utley C Brad 122 F3
Uton Devon 11 J5
Utterby Lincs 118 D3
Uttoxeter Staffs 100 C5
Uxbridge Gt Lon 43 H4
Uyeasound Shet 235 d2
Uzmaston Pembks 49 G5

V

Vale Guern 236 d2
Vale Crematorium Luton 59 J3
Vale of Glamorgan Crematorium V Glam 37 H6
Valley IoA 108 C5
Valtos Highld 209 H2
Valtos W Isls 232 d2
Vange Essex 46 B3
Vatsetter Shet 235 d3
Vatten Highld 208 D5
Vaynor Myr Td 53 G6
Veensgarth Shet 235 c6
Velindre Powys 68 D7
Venngreen Devon 9 K3
Venn Ottery Devon 12 D4
Ventnor IoW 17 G6
Venton Devon 6 E4
Vernham Dean Hants 29 G1
Vernham Street Hants 41 G8
Verwood Dorset 15 K2
Veryan Cnwll 4 E7
Vickerstown Cumb 128 E5
Victoria Cnwll 4 F4
Vidlin Shet 235 d4
Viewfield Moray 215 G2
Viewpark N Lans 175 J6
Vigo Kent 45 M7
Village de Putron Guern 236 d3
Ville la Bas Jersey 236 a5
Villiaze Guern 236 c3
Vines Cross E Susx 20 C3
Vinters Park Crematorium Kent 33 K2
Virginia Water Surrey 43 G6
Virginstow Devon 9 K6
Vobster Somset 27 G2
Voe Shet 235 c4
Vowchurch Herefs 69 G7

W

Waberthwaite Cumb 128 D2
Wackerfield Dur 140 E3
Wacton Norfk 92 E5
Wadborough Worcs 70 F5
Waddesdon Bucks 58 C5
Waddesdon Manor Bucks 58 B5
Waddeton Devon 7 K4
Waddingham Lincs 117 G3
Waddington Lancs 121 L2
Waddington Lincs 116 F8
Wadebridge Cnwll 4 F2
Wadeford Somset 13 H1
Wadenhoe Nhants 88 E6
Wadesmill Herts 60 B4
Wadhurst E Susx 33 H6
Wadshelf Derbys 114 F7
Wadworth Donc 115 K3
Wainfleet All Saints Lincs 104 D2
Wainfleet St Mary Lincs 104 D2
Wainhouse Corner Cnwll 9 G5
Wainscott Medway 46 C6
Wainstalls Calder 122 F5
Waitby Cumb 139 H5
Waithe Lincs 118 C2
Wakefield Wakefd 123 L6
Wakefield Crematorium Wakefd 123 L7
Wake Green Birm 85 K6
Wakehurst Place W Susx 32 C6
Wakerley Nhants 88 D4
Wakes Colne Essex 61 L3
Walberswick Suffk 93 K8
Walberton W Susx 18 C4
Walbutt D & G 146 D2
Walcombe Somset 26 D3
Walcot Lincs 103 H5
Walcot Shrops 83 L2
Walcot Swindn 40 D4
Walcote Leics 87 H6
Walcot Green Norfk 92 D7
Walcott Lincs 103 J2
Walcott Norfk 107 H6
Walden Stubbs N York 124 E6
Walderslade Medway 46 C7
Walderton W Susx 17 L1
Walditch Dorset 13 L4
Waldridge Dur 151 G5
Waldringfield Suffk 79 G5
Waldron E Susx 20 B2
Wales Rothm 115 J5
Wales Somset 26 E6
Walesby Lincs 117 J3
Walesby Notts 116 B7
Walford Herefs 54 E4
Walford Herefs 83 H8
Walford Heath Shrops 98 C8
Walgherton Ches E 99 G3
Walgrave Nhants 74 B1
Walkden Salfd 113 G2
Walker N u Ty 151 H3
Walkerburn Border 166 E3
Walkeringham Notts 116 C3
Walkerith Lincs 116 C3
Walkern Herts 59 M3
Walker's Heath Birm 85 J7
Walkerton Fife 186 D6
Walkford Dorset 16 B4
Walkhampton Devon 6 D2
Walkington E R Yk 126 B3
Walkley Sheff 115 G4
Walk Mill Lancs 122 C5
Walkwood Worcs 71 J2
Wall Nthumb 150 A2
Wall Staffs 85 K3
Wallacetown S Ayrs 153 G2
Wallacetown S Ayrs 163 J5
Wallands Park E Susx 19 L4
Wallasey Wirral 111 J3
Wallasey (Kingsway) Tunnel Wirral 111 K4
Wall Heath Dudley 84 F5
Wallingford Oxon 41 L3
Wallington Gt Lon 44 F6
Wallington Hants 17 H2
Wallington Herts 75 K7
Wallisdown Poole 15 K4
Walls Shet 235 b5
Wallsend N Tyne 151 H2
Wallyford E Loth 177 K4
Walmer Kent 35 K5
Walmer Bridge Lancs 121 G5
Walmley Birm 85 K5
Walmley Ash Birm 85 K5
Walpole Suffk 93 H8
Walpole Cross Keys Norfk 104 E8
Walpole Highway Norfk 90 D2
Walpole St Andrew Norfk 104 D8
Walpole St Peter Norfk 90 C1
Walsall Wsall 85 H4
Walsden Calder 122 D6
Walsgrave on Sowe Covtry 86 E7
Walsham le Willows Suffk 78 B1
Walshford N York 132 F8
Walsoken Norfk 90 C2
Walston S Lans 165 K1
Walsworth Herts 59 K3
Walter's Ash Bucks 42 D2
Waltham Kent 34 E5
Waltham NE Lin 118 C2
Waltham Abbey Essex 60 C7
Waltham Chase Hants 29 K7
Waltham Cross Herts 60 B7
Waltham on the Wolds Leics 102 D7
Waltham St Lawrence W & M 42 D5
Walthamstow Gt Lon 45 G3
Walton Cumb 148 F3
Walton Derbys 115 G7
Walton Leeds 124 C2
Walton Leics 87 H6
Walton M Keyn 74 C7
Walton Powys 68 F3
Walton Somset 26 C4
Walton Suffk 79 G7
Walton W Susx 17 M2
Walton Wakefd 123 L6
Walton Wrekin 98 E8
Walton Cardiff Gloucs 55 K2
Walton East Pembks 49 H3
Walton Highway Norfk 90 C2
Walton-in-Gordano N Som 38 B5
Walton Lea Crematorium Warrtn 112 E4
Walton-le-Dale Lancs 121 H5
Walton-on-Thames Surrey 43 J6
Walton-on-the-Hill Staffs 99 L7
Walton on the Hill Surrey 31 L1
Walton-on-the-Naze Essex 62 F4
Walton on the Wolds Leics 101 L8
Walton-on-Trent Derbys 100 E8
Walton Park N Som 38 B6
Walton West Pembks 48 E5
Waltonwrays Crematorium N York 122 E1
Walworth Darltn 141 G4
Walworth Gt Lon 45 G4
Walwyn's Castle Pembks 48 E5
Wambrook Somset 13 H2
Wanborough Surrey 30 F2
Wanborough Swindn 40 E4
Wandsworth Gt Lon 44 E5
Wangford Suffk 93 K7
Wanlip Leics 87 H2
Wanlockhead D & G 165 G6
Wannock E Susx 20 C5
Wansford C Pete 88 F4
Wansford E R Yk 135 G7
Wanshurst Green Kent 33 K4
Wanstead Gt Lon 45 H3
Wanstrow Somset 27 G3
Wanswell Gloucs 55 G7
Wantage Oxon 41 H3
Wappenbury Warwks 72 E2
Wappenham Nhants 73 J5
Warbleton E Susx 20 C3
Warborough Oxon 41 L2
Warboys Cambs 89 K7
Warbreck Bpool 120 D3
Warbstow Cnwll 9 G6
Warburton Traffd 113 G4
Warcop Cumb 139 H4
Warden Nthumb 150 A2
Ward End Birm 85 K5
Wardington Oxon 72 F5
Wardle Ches E 98 E2
Wardle Rochdl 122 D6
Wardley Gatesd 151 H3
Wardley Rutlnd 88 B4
Wardlow Derbys 114 D6
Wardy Hill Cambs 90 C6
Ware Herts 60 B5
Wareham Dorset 15 H5
Warehorne Kent 34 D7
Warenford Nthumb 169 H4
Wareside Herts 60 C5
Waresley Cambs 75 J4
Warfield Br For 42 E6
Warfleet Devon 7 K6
Wargrave Wokham 42 C5
Warham Norfk 105 M4
Wark Nthumb 157 L6
Wark Nthumb 168 C2
Warkleigh Devon 23 K6
Warkton Nhants 88 C7
Warkworth Nhants 72 F6
Warkworth Nthumb 159 G2
Warlaby N York 132 E2
Warleggan Cnwll 5 J3
Warley Town Calder 122 F5
Warlingham Surrey 32 C2
Warmfield Wakefd 124 B6
Warmingham Ches E 99 G1
Warmington Nhants 88 F5
Warmington Warwks 72 E5
Warminster Wilts 27 K3
Warmley S Glos 38 F5
Warmsworth Donc 115 K2
Warmwell Dorset 14 E5
Warner Bros Studio Tour Herts 59 H7
Warnford Hants 29 L6
Warnham W Susx 31 J5
Warningcamp W Susx 18 D4
Warninglid W Susx 31 L6
Warren Ches E 113 K7
Warren Pembks 48 F7
Warrenhill S Lans 165 J2
Warren Row W & M 42 D4
Warren Street Kent 34 C4
Warrington M Keyn 74 C4
Warrington Warrtn 112 E4
Warriston C Edin 177 H4
Warriston Crematorium C Edin 177 H3
Warsash Hants 16 F2
Warslow Staffs 100 C2
Warter E R Yk 125 K1
Warthermaske N York 132 C4
Warthill N York 133 K7
Wartling E Susx 20 D4
Wartnaby Leics 102 B7
Warton Lancs 120 E5
Warton Lancs 129 K5
Warton Warwks 86 C3
Warwick Warwks 72 C2
Warwick Bridge Cumb 148 E4
Warwick Castle Warwks 72 C2
Warwick Services Warwks 72 D3
Wasbister Ork 234 c4

Wasdale Head Cumb 137 G5
Washaway Cnwll 5 G2
Washbourne Devon 7 J5
Washbrook Suffk 78 D6
Washfield Devon 11 L2
Washford Somset 25 G3
Washford Pyne Devon 11 J3
Washingborough Lincs 117 G7
Washington Sundld 151 H4
Washington W Susx 18 F3
Washington Services Gatesd 151 G4
Washwood Heath Birm 85 K5
Wasperton Warwks 72 C3
Wass N York 133 H4
Wast Water Cumb 137 G6
Watchet Somset 25 G3
Watchfield Oxon 40 E3
Watchgate Cumb 138 D7
Water Devon 11 H8
Waterbeach Cambs 76 C2
Waterbeach W Susx 18 B4
Waterbeck D & G 155 M6
Water End E R Yk 125 J3
Waterfall Staffs 100 B3
Waterfoot Ag & B 161 K3
Waterfoot E Rens 175 G7
Waterford Herts 60 A5
Waterheads Border 177 H7
Waterhouses Staffs 100 B3
Wateringbury Kent 33 H3
Waterloo Highld 199 K2
Waterloo N Lans 175 L7
Waterloo P & K 195 G8
Waterloo Pembks 49 G6
Waterloo Sefton 111 K2
Waterlooville Hants 17 J1
Watermead Bucks 58 D5
Watermillock Cumb 138 C3
Water Newton Cambs 89 G4
Water Orton Warwks 85 L5
Waterperry Oxon 57 L6
Waterrow Somset 25 G6
Watersfield W Susx 18 D3
Waterside Bl w D 121 K5
Waterside E Ayrs 163 K7
Waterside E Ayrs 163 L2
Waterside E Duns 175 J4
Waterstein Highld 208 B5
Waterstock Oxon 57 M6
Waterston Pembks 48 F6
Water Stratford Bucks 73 J7
Waters Upton Wrekin 98 F8
Watford Herts 43 J2
Watford Nhants 73 H2
Watford Gap Services Nhants 73 H2
Wath N York 132 B6
Wath N York 132 E4
Wath upon Dearne Rothm 115 H2
Watlington Norfk 90 E2
Watlington Oxon 42 B2
Watten Highld 231 J5
Wattisfield Suffk 92 B8
Wattisham Suffk 78 B4
Watton Dorset 13 L4
Watton E R Yk 126 C1
Watton Norfk 91 K4
Watton-at-Stone Herts 60 A4
Wattston N Lans 175 K4
Wattsville Caerph 37 J3
Waulkmill Abers 206 C6
Waunarlwydd Swans 51 H6
Waunfawr Cerdgn 80 E6
Waunfawr Gwynd 95 J2
Wavendon M Keyn 74 C6
Waveney Crematorium Suffk 93 J6
Waverbridge Cumb 147 L5
Waverton Ches W 112 C8
Waverton Cumb 147 L5
Wawne E R Yk 126 D3
Waxham Norfk 107 J7
Wayford Somset 13 K2
Waytown Dorset 13 L3
Way Village Devon 11 K3
Weacombe Somset 25 H4
Weald Oxon 56 F7
Wealdstone Gt Lon 44 D3
Weardley Leeds 123 K2
Weare Somset 26 B2
Weare Giffard Devon 23 G6
Wearhead Dur 149 L6
Wearne Somset 26 B5
Wear Valley Crematorium Dur 141 G2
Weasenham All Saints Norfk 105 K7
Weasenham St Peter Norfk 105 K7
Weaste Salfd 113 J2
Weaverham Ches W 112 E6
Weaverthorpe N York 134 E5
Webheath Worcs 71 H2
Wedderlairs Abers 216 F7
Weddington Warwks 86 D5
Wedhampton Wilts 40 B8
Wedmore Somset 26 C2
Wednesbury Sandw 85 H4
Wednesfield Wolves 85 G4
Weedon Bucks 58 D4
Weedon Bec Nhants 73 J3
Weedon Lois Nhants 73 H5
Weeford Staffs 85 K3
Weeke Hants 29 J5
Weekley Nhants 88 C7
Week St Mary Cnwll 9 H5
Weel E R Yk 126 D3
Weeley Essex 62 D4
Weeley Crematorium Essex 62 D4
Weeley Heath Essex 62 D4
Weem P & K 194 D6
Weethley Warwks 71 J4
Weeting Norfk 91 H5
Weeton E R Yk 127 H6
Weeton Lancs 120 E4
Weeton N York 123 K2
Weetwood Leeds 123 K3
Weir Lancs 122 C5
Weir Quay Devon 6 C3
Weisdale Shet 235 c5
Welborne Norfk 92 C2
Welbourn Lincs 102 F2
Welburn N York 133 L6
Welbury N York 141 J6
Welby Lincs 102 F5
Welcombe Devon 22 C7
Weldon Nhants 88 D5
Welford Nhants 87 J7
Welford W Berk 41 H5
Welford-on-Avon Warwks 71 K4
Welham Leics 87 L5
Welham Notts 116 B5
Welham Green Herts 59 L6
Well Hants 30 C3
Well Lincs 118 F6
Well N York 132 D3
Welland Worcs 70 E6
Wellbank Angus 196 D8
Wellesbourne Warwks 72 C4
Well Head Herts 59 K3
Welling Gt Lon 45 J5
Wellingborough Nhants 74 C2
Wellingham Norfk 105 L7
Wellingore Lincs 103 G2
Wellington Cumb 136 F6
Wellington Herefs 69 K5
Wellington Somset 25 H7
Wellington Wrekin 84 B2
Wellington Heath Herefs 70 C6
Wellow BaNES 39 H8
Wellow IoW 16 E5
Wellow Notts 116 A7
Wells Somset 26 D3
Wells-next-the-Sea Norfk 105 L4
Wellstye Green Essex 61 G4
Welltree P & K 185 K3
Wellwood Fife 176 E2
Welney Norfk 90 D5
Welshampton Shrops 98 C5
Welsh Frankton Shrops 98 A6
Welsh Newton Herefs 54 D4
Welshpool Powys 82 E3
Welsh St Donats V Glam 36 F5
Welton Cumb 148 C6
Welton E R Yk 126 B5
Welton Lincs 117 G5
Welton Nhants 73 H2
Welton le Marsh Lincs 119 G7
Welton le Wold Lincs 118 C4
Welwick E R Yk 127 H6
Welwyn Herts 59 L5
Welwyn Garden City Herts 59 L5
Wem Shrops 98 D6
Wembdon Somset 25 L4
Wembley Gt Lon 44 D3
Wembury Devon 6 D6
Wembworthy Devon 10 F3
Wemyss Bay Inver 173 L4
Wendens Ambo Essex 76 D7
Wendlebury Oxon 57 K4
Wendling Norfk 91 L2
Wendover Bucks 58 E6
Wendron Cnwll 3 H5
Wendron Mining District Cnwll 3 J5
Wendy Cambs 75 K5
Wenhaston Suffk 93 J7
Wennington Cambs 89 J7
Wennington Gt Lon 45 K4
Wennington Lancs 130 C5
Wensley Derbys 100 E1
Wensley N York 131 K2
Wentbridge Wakefd 124 D6
Wentnor Shrops 83 H5
Wentworth Cambs 90 C7
Wentworth Rothm 115 G2
Wenvoe V Glam 37 H6
Weobley Herefs 69 H4
Wepham W Susx 18 E4
Wereham Norfk 90 F3
Werrington C Pete 89 H3
Werrington Cnwll 9 J7
Wervin Ches W 112 B6
Wesham Lancs 120 F4
Wessex Vale Crematorium Hants 29 J7
Wessington Derbys 101 G2
West Acre Norfk 91 H1
West Alvington Devon 7 G6
West Anstey Devon 24 D6
West Ashby Lincs 118 C6
West Ashling W Susx 17 M2
West Ashton Wilts 27 K1
West Auckland Dur 140 F3
West Ayton N York 134 F3
West Bagborough Somset 25 J5
West Bank Halton 112 D5
West Barkwith Lincs 117 K5
West Barnby N York 143 G5
West Barns E Loth 178 E3
West Barsham Norfk 105 L5
West Bay Dorset 13 L4
West Beckham Norfk 106 D5
West Bedfont Surrey 43 H5
Westbere Kent 35 G3
West Bergholt Essex 62 A3
West Berkshire Crematorium W Berk 41 K6
West Bexington Dorset 14 A5
West Bilney Norfk 91 G1
West Blatchington Br & H 19 J4
West Boldon S Tyne 151 J3
Westborough Lincs 102 D4
Westbourne Bmouth 15 K4
Westbourne W Susx 17 L2
West Bowling C Brad 123 H4
West Bradenham Norfk 91 K2
West Bradford Lancs 121 L2
West Bradley Somset 26 E4
West Bretton Wakefd 123 K7
West Bridgford Notts 101 L5
West Bromwich Sandw 85 H5
Westbrook Kent 35 J2
Westbrook W Berk 41 H6
West Buckland Devon 23 K5
West Buckland Somset 25 J7
West Burrafirth Shet 235 b5
West Burton N York 131 J3
Westbury Bucks 73 J7
Westbury Shrops 83 G2
Westbury Wilts 27 K2
Westbury Leigh Wilts 27 K2
Westbury on Severn Gloucs 55 G5
Westbury-on-Trym Bristl 38 E5
Westbury-sub-Mendip Somset 26 D2
West Butterwick N Linc 116 D1
Westby Lancs 120 E4
West Byfleet Surrey 43 H7
West Cairngaan D & G 144 D8
West Caister Norfk 93 K2
West Calder W Loth 176 D5
West Camel Somset 26 E6
West Chaldon Dorset 14 E5
West Challow Oxon 41 G3
West Charleton Devon 7 H7
West Chiltington W Susx 18 E3
West Chinnock Somset 26 C8
West Clandon Surrey 31 H2
West Cliffe Kent 35 J5
Westcliff-on-Sea Sthend 46 E3
West Coker Somset 26 D8
Westcombe Somset 27 G4
West Compton Somset 26 E3
West Compton Abbas Dorset 14 B4
Westcote Gloucs 56 E4
Westcote Barton Oxon 57 H3
Westcott Bucks 58 B5
Westcott Devon 12 C2
Westcott Surrey 31 J2
West Cottingwith N York 125 G3
Westcourt Wilts 40 E7
West Cowick E R Yk 124 F6
West Cross Swans 51 H7
West Curthwaite Cumb 148 B5
Westdean E Susx 20 B5
West Dean W Susx 18 B3
West Dean Wilts 28 E6
West Deeping Lincs 89 G2
West Derby Lpool 111 L3
West Dereham Norfk 90 F4
West Down Devon 23 H3
Westdowns Cnwll 8 E7
West Drayton Gt Lon 43 H4
West Drayton Notts 116 B6
West Dunnet Highld 231 J2
West Ella E R Yk 126 C5
West End Bed 74 E4
West End Hants 29 J8
West End N Som 38 C6

West End Norfk 93 K2
West End Surrey 42 F7
West End Surrey 43 J7
West End Wilts 27 M6
West End Green Hants 42 A7
Wester Aberchalder Highld 202 E2
Westerdale Highld 231 G5
Westerdale N York 142 E6
Westerfield Suffk 78 E5
Westergate W Susx 18 C5
Westerham Kent 32 D3
Westerhope N u Ty 150 F2
Westerland Devon 7 K4
Westerleigh S Glos 39 G4
Westerleigh Crematorium S Glos 39 G5
Western Isles W Isls 232 d5
Wester Ochiltree W Loth 176 D4
Wester Pitkierie Fife 187 J6
Wester Ross Highld 220 C5
Westerton of Rossie Angus 197 G5
Westerwick Shet 235 c6
West Farleigh Kent 33 J3
West Farndon Nhants 73 G4
West Felton Shrops 97 M7
Westfield BaNES 26 F2
Westfield Cumb 136 D2
Westfield E Susx 21 G3
Westfield Highld 230 F3
Westfield N Lans 175 J4
Westfield Norfk 92 B2
Westfield W Loth 176 C4
Westfields of Rattray P & K 195 J6
Westgate Dur 150 A7
Westgate N Linc 125 J8
Westgate-on-Sea Kent 35 J2
West Grafton Wilts 40 E7
West Green Hants 30 C1
West Grimstead Wilts 28 E6
West Grinstead W Susx 31 K6
West Haddlesey N York 124 E5
West Haddon Nhants 73 J1
West Hagbourne Oxon 41 K3
West Hagley Worcs 84 F7
Westhall Suffk 93 J7
West Hallam Derbys 101 H4
West Halton N Linc 125 L6
Westham Dorset 14 C6
Westham E Susx 20 D5
West Ham Gt Lon 45 H4
Westham Somset 26 B3
Westhampnett W Susx 18 B4
West Handley Derbys 115 H6
West Hanney Oxon 41 H2
West Hanningfield Essex 61 H7
West Harnham Wilts 28 C5
West Harptree BaNES 38 E8
West Harting W Susx 30 C7
West Hatch Somset 25 L7
West Hatch Wilts 27 L5
West Haven Angus 187 J1
Westhay Somset 26 C3
West Heath Birm 85 J7
West Helmsdale Highld 227 H5
West Hendred Oxon 41 H3
West Hertfordshire Crematorium Herts 59 J7
West Heslerton N York 134 E4
West Hewish N Som 38 B7
Westhide Herefs 69 L5
Westhill Abers 206 F4
West Hill Devon 12 D4
West Hoathly W Susx 32 C6
West Holme Dorset 15 G5
Westhope Herefs 69 J4
Westhope Shrops 83 J6
West Horndon Essex 45 M3
Westhorpe Lincs 103 L6
Westhorpe Suffk 78 C2
West Horrington Somset 26 E3
West Horsley Surrey 31 H2
West Hougham Kent 35 H6
Westhoughton Bolton 112 F1
Westhouse N York 130 D5
Westhouses Derbys 101 H2
West Howe Bmouth 15 K4
Westhumble Surrey 31 K2
West Huntingtower P & K 185 M3
West Huntspill Somset 25 L3
West Hythe Kent 34 F7
West Ilsley W Berk 41 J4
West Itchenor W Susx 17 L3
West Kennett Wilts 40 C6
West Kilbride N Ayrs 173 L8
West Kingsdown Kent 45 L7
West Kington Wilts 39 J5
West Kirby Wirral 111 H4
West Knapton N York 134 D4
West Knighton Dorset 14 D5
West Knoyle Wilts 27 K5
Westlake Devon 6 F5
West Lambrook Somset 26 B7
West Lancashire Crematorium Lancs 120 F7
West Langdon Kent 35 J5
West Lavington W Susx 30 E7
West Lavington Wilts 28 A2
West Layton N York 140 E5
West Leake Notts 101 K7
Westleigh Devon 23 G5
Westleigh Devon 25 G7
West Leigh Somset 25 H5
Westleton Suffk 79 J2
West Lexham Norfk 91 J1
Westley Suffk 77 J2
Westley Waterless Cambs 76 E3
West Lilling N York 133 K6
Westlington Bucks 58 C6
West Linton Border 176 F7
Westlinton Cumb 148 D3
West Littleton S Glos 39 H5
West Lockinge Oxon 41 H3
West London Crematorium Gt Lon 44 E4
West Lothian Crematorium W Loth 176 D5
West Lulworth Dorset 14 F6
West Lutton N York 134 E5
West Lydford Somset 26 E5
West Lyng Somset 25 L5
West Lynn Norfk 104 F7
West Malling Kent 33 H2
West Malvern Worcs 70 D5
West Marden W Susx 30 C8
West Markham Notts 116 B6
Westmarsh Kent 35 H3
West Marsh NE Lin 127 G8
West Marton N York 122 D1
West Melbury Dorset 27 K7
West Meon Hants 29 M6
West Mersea Essex 62 B5
Westmeston E Susx 19 K3
West Midland Safari Park Worcs 84 E7
Westmill Herts 60 B3
West Milton Dorset 13 L3
Westminster Gt Lon 44 F4
Westminster Abbey & Palace Gt Lon 44 F4
West Molesey Surrey 43 J6
West Monkton Somset 25 K5
West Moors Dorset 15 K2
West Morden Dorset 15 G4
West Morriston Border 167 J2
West Mudford Somset 26 E7
Westmuir Angus 196 B5
West Ness N York 133 L4
Westnewton Cumb 147 K6
West Newton E R Yk 126 F3
West Newton Norfk 105 H6
West Newton Somset 25 L5
West Norwood Gt Lon 44 F5
West Norwood Crematorium Gt Lon 44 F5
Westoe S Tyne 151 J2
West Ogwell Devon 7 J2
Weston BaNES 39 G6
Weston Ches E 99 G3
Weston Devon 12 E3
Weston Devon 12 F5
Weston Hants 30 B6
Weston Herts 59 L3
Weston Lincs 103 M7
Weston N York 123 H2
Weston Nhants 73 H5
Weston Notts 116 C7
Weston Shrops 83 L5
Weston Shrops 97 L6
Weston Staffs 99 L6
Weston W Berk 41 H5
Weston Beggard Herefs 69 L6
Westonbirt Gloucs 39 J3
Weston by Welland Nhants 87 L5
Weston Colville Cambs 76 E4
Weston Corbett Hants 30 B3
Weston Coyney C Stke 99 L4
Weston Favell Nhants 73 L3
Weston Green Cambs 76 F4
Weston Heath Shrops 84 D2
Westoning C Beds 59 G2
Weston-in-Gordano N Som 38 C5
Weston Jones Staffs 99 H7
Weston Longville Norfk 92 D1
Weston Lullingfields Shrops 98 B7
Weston Mill Crematorium C Plym 6 C4
Weston-on-the-Green Oxon 57 K4
Weston Park Staffs 84 E2
Weston Patrick Hants 30 B3
Weston Rhyn Shrops 97 L5
Weston-sub-Edge Gloucs 71 K6
Weston-super-Mare N Som 37 L7
Weston-super-Mare Crematorium N Som 38 A7
Weston Turville Bucks 58 D6
Weston-under-Lizard Staffs 84 E2
Weston under Penyard Herefs 54 F4
Weston-under-Redcastle Shrops 98 E6
Weston under Wetherley Warwks 72 D1
Weston Underwood Derbys 100 F4
Weston Underwood M Keyn 74 C4
Weston-upon-Trent Derbys 101 H6
Westonzoyland Somset 25 M4
West Orchard Dorset 27 J7
West Overton Wilts 40 C6
Westow N York 134 B6
West Park Abers 206 E5
West Parley Dorset 15 K3
West Peckham Kent 33 H3
West Pelton Dur 151 G4
West Pennard Somset 26 D4
West Pentire Cnwll 4 B4
West Perry Cambs 75 G2
West Porlock Somset 24 D3
Westport Somset 26 B7
West Putford Devon 9 K2
West Quantoxhead Somset 25 H3
Westquarter Falk 176 B3
West Rainton Dur 151 H5
West Rasen Lincs 117 H4
Westray Ork 234 c3
Westray Airport Ork 234 c3
West Raynham Norfk 105 L7
Westrigg W Loth 176 B5
West Road Crematorium N u Ty 150 F2
Westrop Swindn 40 D2
West Rounton N York 141 K6
West Row Suffk 90 F7
West Rudham Norfk 105 K6
West Runton Norfk 106 E4
Westruther Border 178 D7
Westry Cambs 90 B4
West Saltoun E Loth 178 B5
West Sandford Devon 11 J4
West Sandwick Shet 235 d3
West Scrafton N York 131 K3
West Stafford Dorset 14 D4
West Stockwith Notts 116 C3
West Stoke W Susx 17 M2
West Stour Dorset 27 H6
West Stourmouth Kent 35 H3
West Stow Suffk 77 J1
West Stowell Wilts 40 C7
West Street Suffk 78 B1
West Suffolk Crematorium Suffk 77 J2
West Tanfield N York 132 D4
West Taphouse Cnwll 5 J3
West Tarbert Ag & B 172 E5
West Tarring W Susx 18 F5
West Thirston Nthumb 158 F3
West Thorney W Susx 17 L3
West Thorpe Notts 101 L7
West Thurrock Thurr 45 L4
West Tilbury Thurr 46 A4
West Tisted Hants 29 M5
West Torrington Lincs 117 J5
West Town Hants 17 K3
West Town N Som 38 C6
West Tytherley Hants 28 F5
West Walton Norfk 90 C2
Westward Cumb 148 B6
Westward Ho! Devon 23 G5
Westwell Kent 34 D5
Westwell Oxon 56 E6
Westwell Leacon Kent 34 C5
West Wellow Hants 28 F7
West Wembury Devon 6 D6
West Wemyss Fife 186 E7
Westwick Cambs 76 B2
West Wickham Cambs 76 E5
West Wickham Gt Lon 45 G6

West Williamston Pembks 49 H6
West Wiltshire Crematorium Wilts 39 K7
West Winch Norfk 90 F1
West Winterslow Wilts 28 E5
West Wittering W Susx 17 L3
West Witton N York 131 K2
Westwood Devon 12 C3
Westwood Kent 35 K2
Westwood Wilts 39 J8
West Woodburn Nthumb 157 M5
West Woodhay W Berk 41 H7
Westwoodside N Linc 116 C2
West Worldham Hants 30 C4
West Worthing W Susx 18 F5
West Wratting Cambs 76 E4
Wetheral Cumb 148 E4
Wetherby Leeds 124 B2
Wetherby Services N York 124 C1
Wetherden Suffk 78 B3
Wetheringsett Suffk 78 D2
Wethersfield Essex 61 H2
Wetherup Street Suffk 78 D2
Wetley Rocks Staffs 99 L3
Wettenhall Ches E 98 F1
Wetton Staffs 100 C2
Wetwang E R Yk 134 E7
Wetwood Staffs 99 H5
Wexcombe Wilts 40 F8
Weybourne Norfk 106 D4
Weybourne Surrey 30 D2
Weybread Suffk 92 F7
Weybread Street Suffk 92 F7
Weybridge Surrey 43 H7
Weycroft Devon 13 H3
Weydale Highld 231 H3
Weyhill Hants 28 F3
Weymouth Dorset 14 D6
Weymouth Crematorium Dorset 14 C6
Whaddon Bucks 74 B7
Whaddon Cambs 75 L5
Whaddon Gloucs 55 J5
Whaddon Gt Lon 44 F7
Whaddon Wilts 28 D6
Whaddon Wilts 39 K7
Whaley Derbys 115 K7
Whaley Bridge Derbys 114 A5
Whaley Thorns Derbys 115 K7
Whaligoe Highld 231 K7
Whalley Lancs 121 L4
Whalsay Shet 235 d4
Whalton Nthumb 158 E6
Whaplode Lincs 104 A7
Whaplode Drove Lincs 89 K2
Wharf Warwks 72 E4
Wharfe N York 130 E5
Wharles Lancs 120 F4
Wharley End C Beds 74 D5
Wharncliffe Side Sheff 114 F3
Wharram-le-Street N York 134 D6
Wharton Herefs 69 K4
Whashton N York 140 E6
Whasset Cumb 129 L4
Whatcote Warwks 72 C5
Whateley Warwks 86 B4
Whatfield Suffk 78 B5
Whatley Somset 13 J2
Whatley Somset 27 G3
Whatlington E Susx 20 F3
Whatton Notts 102 C5
Whauphill D & G 145 J5
Wheal Peevor Cnwll 3 J3
Wheatacre Norfk 93 K5
Wheathampstead Herts 59 K5
Wheatley Hants 30 C4
Wheatley Oxon 57 L6
Wheatley Hill Dur 151 J6
Wheatley Hills Donc 115 L1
Wheaton Aston Staffs 84 F2
Wheddon Cross Somset 24 E4
Wheelock Ches E 99 H2
Wheelton Lancs 121 J6
Wheldrake C York 125 G2
Whelford Gloucs 56 D7
Whelpley Hill Bucks 59 G6
Whempstead Herts 60 A4
Whenby N York 133 K5
Whepstead Suffk 77 J3
Wherstead Suffk 78 E6
Wherwell Hants 29 H3
Wheston Derbys 114 C6
Whetsted Kent 33 H4
Whetstone Leics 87 G4
Whicham Cumb 128 D3
Whichford Warwks 72 C7
Whickham Gatesd 150 F3
Whiddon Down Devon 11 G6
Whigstreet Angus 196 D7
Whilton Nhants 73 J2
Whimple Devon 12 D3
Whimpwell Green Norfk 107 H6
Whinburgh Norfk 92 B2
Whinnie Liggate D & G 146 C4
Whinnyfold Abers 217 K7
Whippingham IoW 17 G4
Whipsnade C Beds 59 G4
Whipsnade Zoo ZSL C Beds 59 G4
Whipton Devon 12 B4
Whisby Lincs 116 E7
Whissendine Rutlnd 88 B2
Whissonsett Norfk 105 L7
Whistlefield Ag & B 183 J8
Whistlefield Inn Ag & B 183 G8
Whistley Green Wokham 42 C5
Whiston Knows 112 C3
Whiston Nhants 74 B3
Whiston Rothm 115 H4
Whiston Staffs 84 F2
Whiston Staffs 100 B3
Whitbeck Cumb 128 D3
Whitbourne Herefs 70 D3
Whitburn S Tyne 151 J3
Whitburn W Loth 176 C5
Whitby N York 143 J5
Whitchester Border 178 F6
Whitchurch BaNES 38 F6
Whitchurch Bucks 58 D4
Whitchurch Cardif 37 J4
Whitchurch Devon 6 D2
Whitchurch Hants 29 J2
Whitchurch Herefs 54 D4
Whitchurch Oxon 41 M5
Whitchurch Pembks 48 D3
Whitchurch Shrops 98 D4
Whitchurch Canonicorum Dorset 13 K4
Whitchurch Hill Oxon 41 M5
Whitcombe Dorset 14 D5
Whitcot Shrops 83 H5
Whitcott Keysett Shrops 82 F6
Whiteacre Heath Warwks 86 B5
White Ball Somset 25 H7
Whitebridge Highld 202 D3
Whitebrook Mons 54 D6
Whitebushes Surrey 32 B4
Whitecairns Abers 207 H2
Whitechapel Gt Lon 45 G4
White Chapel Lancs 121 H3
Whitecliffe Gloucs 54 E6
White Colne Essex 61 L3
Whitecraig E Loth 177 K4
Whitecrook D & G 144 E4
White Cross Cnwll 3 H6
Whitecross Falk 176 C3
Whiteface Highld 222 F4
Whitefarland N Ayrs 161 L2
Whitefaulds S Ayrs 163 H7
Whitefield Bury 113 J1
Whitefield Somset 25 G5
Whiteford Abers 206 D1
Whitegate Ches W 112 F7
Whitehall Ork 234 d5
Whitehaven Cumb 136 D4
Whitehill and Bordon Hants 30 C5
Whitehills Abers 216 C2
Whitehouse Abers 206 C3
Whitehouse Ag & B 172 D6
Whitehouse Common Birm 85 K4
Whitekirk E Loth 178 D3
White Lackington Dorset 14 D3
Whitelackington Somset 26 B7
White Ladies Aston Worcs 71 G4
Whiteleaf Bucks 58 D6
Whiteley Hants 17 G1
Whiteley Bank IoW 17 G6
Whitemire Moray 214 B4
Whitemoor C Nott 101 K4
Whitemoor Cnwll 4 F4
Whiteness Shet 235 c6
White Notley Essex 61 J4
Whiteparish Wilts 28 E6
White Pit Lincs 118 E6
Whiterashes Abers 206 F2
White Roding Essex 60 E5
Whiterow Highld 231 L5
Whiterow Moray 214 C3
Whiteshill Gloucs 55 J6
Whitesmith E Susx 20 B3
Whitestaunton Somset 13 H1
Whitestone Cross Devon 11 K6
White Waltham W & M 42 D5
Whitewell Lancs 121 K2
Whitfield C Dund 187 G2
Whitfield Kent 35 J5
Whitfield Nhants 73 H6
Whitfield Nthumb 149 K4
Whitfield S Glos 38 F3
Whitford Devon 13 G4
Whitford Flints 111 G5
Whitgift E R Yk 125 J6
Whitgreave Staffs 99 K6
Whithorn D & G 145 J6
Whiting Bay N Ayrs 162 D4
Whitkirk Leeds 124 B4
Whitland Carmth 49 L4
Whitlaw Border 167 G6
Whitletts S Ayrs 163 J5
Whitley N York 124 E6
Whitley Readg 42 B6
Whitley Sheff 115 G3
Whitley Wilts 39 K6
Whitley Bay N Tyne 159 J7
Whitley Bay Crematorium N Tyne 159 H7
Whitley Chapel Nthumb 150 B4
Whitley Lower Kirk 123 J6
Whitminster Gloucs 55 H6
Whitmore Staffs 99 J4
Whitnage Devon 25 G7
Whitnash Warwks 72 D2
Whitney-on-Wye Herefs 68 F5
Whitsbury Hants 28 C7
Whitsome Border 179 H7
Whitson Newpt 38 B4
Whitstable Kent 47 J6
Whitstone Cnwll 9 H5
Whittingham Nthumb 168 F6
Whittingslow Shrops 83 H5
Whittington Derbys 115 G6
Whittington Gloucs 56 A4
Whittington Lancs 130 B4
Whittington Norfk 91 G4
Whittington Shrops 97 L6
Whittington Staffs 84 F6
Whittington Staffs 85 L2
Whittington Warwks 86 C4
Whittington Worcs 70 F4
Whittlebury Nhants 73 K5
Whittle-le-Woods Lancs 121 H6
Whittlesey Cambs 89 J4
Whittlesford Cambs 76 C5
Whitton N Linc 125 L5
Whitton Nthumb 158 D3
Whitton Powys 68 F2
Whitton S on T 141 J3
Whitton Shrops 83 L8
Whittonstall Nthumb 150 D4
Whitway Hants 41 J8
Whitwell Derbys 115 K6
Whitwell Herts 59 K4
Whitwell IoW 17 G6
Whitwell N York 141 G7
Whitwell Rutlnd 88 D2
Whitwell-on-the-Hill N York 133 L6
Whitwell Street Norfk 106 D7
Whitwick Leics 86 E1
Whitworth Lancs 122 D6
Whixall Shrops 98 D5
Whixley N York 133 G7
Whorlton Dur 140 E4
Whyle Herefs 69 L3
Whyteleafe Surrey 32 C2
Wibsey C Brad 123 H4
Wibtoft Warwks 86 F6
Wichenford Worcs 70 D3
Wichling Kent 34 B4
Wick Bmouth 15 L4
Wick Highld 231 L5
Wick S Glos 39 G5
Wick V Glam 36 E6
Wick W Susx 18 D5
Wick Worcs 71 G5
Wicken Cambs 76 E1
Wicken Nhants 73 L6
Wicken Bonhunt Essex 60 D2
Wickenby Lincs 117 H5
Wicken Green Village Norfk 105 K6
Wickersley Rothm 115 J3
Wicker Street Green Suffk 77 L6
Wickford Essex 46 C2
Wickham Hants 17 H1
Wickham W Berk 41 H6
Wickham Bishops Essex 61 K5
Wickhambreaux Kent 35 G3
Wickhambrook Suffk 77 H4
Wickhamford Worcs 71 J6
Wickham Green Suffk 78 D2
Wickham Market Suffk 79 G4
Wickhampton Norfk 93 J3
Wickham St Paul Essex 77 J7
Wickham Skeith Suffk 78 C2
Wickham Street Suffk 78 C1
Wick John o' Groats Airport Highld 231 L5
Wicklewood Norfk 92 C3
Wickmere Norfk 106 E5
Wick St Lawrence N Som 38 A7

Wicksteed Park Nhants 88 C7
Wickwar S Glos 39 G3
Widdington Essex 60 E2
Widdrington Nthumb 159 G3
Widdrington Station Nthumb 159 G4
Widecombe in the Moor Devon 7 G1
Widegates Cnwll 5 L4
Widemouth Bay Cnwll 9 G4
Wide Open N Tyne 159 G7
Widford Essex 61 H6
Widford Herts 60 C5
Widmer End Bucks 42 E2
Widmerpool Notts 101 M6
Widmore Gt Lon 45 H6
Widnes Halton 112 D4
Widnes Crematorium Halton 112 D4
Widworthy Devon 13 G3
Wigan Wigan 112 E1
Wigan Crematorium Wigan 112 E2
Wigborough Somset 26 C7
Wiggaton Devon 12 E4
Wiggenhall St Germans Norfk 90 E2
Wiggenhall St Mary Magdalen Norfk 90 E2
Wiggenhall St Mary the Virgin Norfk 90 E2
Wigginton C York 133 J7
Wigginton Herts 58 F6
Wigginton Oxon 57 H2
Wigginton Staffs 86 B3
Wigglesworth N York 130 F7
Wiggonby Cumb 148 B4
Wighill N York 124 D2
Wighton Norfk 105 M4
Wightwick Wolves 84 F4
Wigley Hants 29 G7
Wigmore Herefs 69 H2
Wigmore Medway 46 D6
Wigsley Notts 116 E7
Wigsthorpe Nhants 88 F6
Wigston Leics 87 H4
Wigston Fields Leics 87 H4
Wigston Parva Leics 86 F5
Wigthorpe Notts 115 L5
Wigtoft Lincs 103 L5
Wigton Cumb 148 A5
Wigtown D & G 145 J4
Wike Leeds 123 L3
Wilbarston Nhants 88 B5
Wilberfoss E R Yk 125 H1
Wilburton Cambs 90 C7
Wilby Nhants 74 C2
Wilby Norfk 92 B5
Wilby Suffk 78 F1
Wilcot Wilts 40 C7
Wilcott Shrops 98 B8
Wildboarclough Ches E 113 M7
Wilden Bed 75 G4
Wilden Worcs 84 E8
Wildmanbridge S Lans 175 L7
Wildmoor Worcs 85 G7
Wildsworth Lincs 116 D3
Wilford C Nott 101 K5
Wilford Hill Crematorium Notts 101 L5
Wilkesley Ches E 98 F4
Wilkhaven Highld 223 K4
Wilkieston W Loth 176 F5
Willand Devon 12 D1
Willaston Ches E 99 G3
Willaston Ches W 111 K6
Willen M Keyn 74 C6
Willenhall Covtry 86 D7
Willenhall Wsall 85 H4
Willerby E R Yk 126 C4
Willerby N York 134 F4
Willersey Gloucs 71 K6
Willersley Herefs 68 F5
Willesborough Kent 34 D6
Willesborough Lees Kent 34 D6
Willesden Gt Lon 44 E3
Willesley Wilts 39 J3
Willett Somset 25 H5
Willey Shrops 84 C4
Willey Warwks 86 F6
Willey Green Surrey 30 F2
Williamscot Oxon 72 F5
Willian Herts 59 L2
Willingale Essex 60 F6
Willingdon E Susx 20 C5
Willingham Cambs 76 B1
Willingham by Stow Lincs 116 E5
Willington Bed 75 G4
Willington Derbys 100 F6
Willington Dur 150 F7
Willington Kent 33 K3
Willington N Tyne 151 H2
Willington Warwks 72 C6
Willitoft E R Yk 125 H4
Williton Somset 25 G3
Willoughby Lincs 119 G6
Willoughby Warwks 73 G2
Willoughby-on-the-Wolds Notts 101 M7
Willoughby Waterleys Leics 87 H5
Willoughton Lincs 116 F3
Willows Green Essex 61 H4
Willtown Somset 26 B6
Wilmcote Warwks 71 L3
Wilmington Devon 13 G3
Wilmington E Susx 20 B5
Wilmington Kent 45 K5
Wilmslow Ches E 113 J5
Wilpshire Lancs 121 K4
Wilsden C Brad 123 G3
Wilsford Lincs 103 G4
Wilsford Wilts 28 C4
Wilsford Wilts 40 C8
Wilshaw Kirk 123 G8
Wilsill N York 132 B6
Wilson Leics 101 H7
Wilsontown S Lans 176 C7
Wilstead Bed 74 F5
Wilsthorpe Lincs 88 F2
Wilstone Herts 58 E5
Wilton Herefs 54 E3
Wilton N York 134 D3
Wilton R & Cl 142 C4
Wilton Wilts 28 C5
Wilton Wilts 40 E7
Wilton Dean Border 167 G6
Wimbish Green Essex 76 E7
Wimbledon Gt Lon 44 E6
Wimblington Cambs 90 B5
Wimboldsley Ches W 113 G8
Wimborne Minster Dorset 15 J3
Wimborne St Giles Dorset 28 B8
Wimbotsham Norfk 90 E3
Wimpole Cambs 75 L4
Wimpstone Warwks 72 B5
Wincanton Somset 27 G5
Winchburgh W Loth 176 E4
Winchcombe Gloucs 56 A3
Winchelsea E Susx 21 H3
Winchester Hants 29 J5
Winchester Services Hants 29 K4
Winchet Hill Kent 33 J5
Winchfield Hants 30 C1
Winchmore Hill Bucks 42 F2
Winchmore Hill Gt Lon 44 F2
Wincle Ches E 113 L7
Wincobank Sheff 115 G3
Windermere Cumb 137 L7
Windermere Steamboats & Museum Cumb 137 L7
Winderton Warwks 72 D6
Windhill Highld 212 E5
Windlesham Surrey 42 F7
Windmill Cnwll 4 D2
Windmill Hill E Susx 20 D4
Windmill Hill Somset 25 L7
Windrush Gloucs 56 D5
Windsole Abers 216 B3
Windsor W & M 42 F5
Windsor Castle W & M 42 F5
Windsoredge Gloucs 55 J7
Windsor Green Suffk 77 K4
Windygates Fife 186 E7
Wineham W Susx 31 L7
Winestead E R Yk 127 G5
Winfarthing Norfk 92 D6
Winford IoW 17 G5
Winford N Som 38 D7
Winforton Herefs 68 F5
Winfrith Newburgh Dorset 14 F5
Wing Bucks 58 E4
Wing Rutlnd 88 C3
Wingate Dur 151 J7
Wingerworth Derbys 115 G7
Wingfield C Beds 59 G3
Wingfield Suffk 92 F7
Wingfield Wilts 27 J1
Wingham Kent 35 H3
Wingrave Bucks 58 E4
Winkburn Notts 102 B2
Winkfield Br For 42 E6
Winkfield Row Br For 42 E6
Winkhill Staffs 100 B3
Winkleigh Devon 10 F4
Winksley N York 132 C5
Winlaton Gatesd 150 F3
Winless Highld 231 K5
Winmarleigh Lancs 120 F2
Winnall Hants 29 J5
Winnersh Wokham 42 C6
Winnington Ches W 112 F6
Winscombe N Som 38 B8
Winsford Ches W 112 F7
Winsford Somset 24 E4
Winsham Somset 13 J2
Winshill Staffs 100 F7
Winshwen Swans 51 K6
Winskill Cumb 149 G7
Winsley Wilts 39 J7
Winslow Bucks 58 C3
Winson Gloucs 56 C6
Winsor Hants 28 F8
Winster Cumb 129 J2
Winster Derbys 100 E1
Winston Dur 140 E4
Winston Suffk 78 E3
Winstone Gloucs 55 L6
Winswell Devon 10 D3
Winterborne Came Dorset 14 D5
Winterborne Clenston Dorset 14 F2
Winterborne Houghton Dorset 14 F2
Winterborne Kingston Dorset 15 G3
Winterborne Monkton Dorset 14 D5
Winterborne Stickland Dorset 14 F2
Winterborne Whitechurch Dorset 14 F3
Winterborne Zelston Dorset 15 G3
Winterbourne S Glos 38 F4
Winterbourne W Berk 41 J6
Winterbourne Abbas Dorset 14 C4
Winterbourne Bassett Wilts 40 C5
Winterbourne Dauntsey Wilts 28 D4
Winterbourne Earls Wilts 28 D5
Winterbourne Gunner Wilts 28 D4
Winterbourne Monkton Wilts 40 C6
Winterbourne Steepleton Dorset 14 C4
Winterbourne Stoke Wilts 28 B3
Winterburn N York 131 H7
Winteringham N Linc 125 L6
Winterley Ches E 99 H2
Winterslow Wilts 28 E5
Winterton N Linc 125 L6
Winterton-on-Sea Norfk 107 K8
Winthorpe Notts 102 D2
Winton Bmouth 15 K4
Winton Cumb 139 H5
Wintringham N York 134 D5
Winwick Cambs 89 G7
Winwick Nhants 87 J8
Winwick Warrtn 112 E3
Wirksworth Derbys 100 F2
Wirral 111 J4
Wirswall Ches E 98 D4
Wisbech Cambs 90 C2
Wisbech St Mary Cambs 90 B2
Wisborough Green W Susx 31 H6
Wiseman's Bridge Pembks 49 K6
Wiseton Notts 116 B4
Wishaw N Lans 175 L7
Wishaw Warwks 85 L5
Wisley Garden RHS Surrey 43 H8
Wispington Lincs 117 K6
Wissett Suffk 93 H7
Wissington Suffk 62 A2
Wistanstow Shrops 83 H6
Wistanswick Shrops 98 F6
Wistaston Ches E 99 G2
Wistaston Green Ches E 99 G2
Wiston Pembks 49 H4
Wiston S Lans 165 J3
Wiston W Susx 18 F3
Wistow Cambs 89 K7
Wistow N York 124 F4
Wiswell Lancs 121 L3
Witcham Cambs 90 C7
Witchampton Dorset 15 J2
Witchford Cambs 90 C7
Witcombe Somset 26 C6
Witham Essex 61 K5
Witham Friary Somset 27 H3
Witham on the Hill Lincs 88 F1
Withcall Lincs 118 C5
Withdean Br & H 19 J4
Witherenden Hill E Susx 33 H7
Witheridge Devon 11 J3
Witherley Leics 86 D4
Withern Lincs 118 F5
Withernsea E R Yk 127 H5
Withernwick E R Yk 126 F3
Withersdale Street Suffk 92 F7
Withersfield Suffk 76 F5
Witherslack Cumb 129 J3
Withiel Cnwll 4 F3
Withiel Florey Somset 24 F5
Withington Gloucs 56 B5
Withington Herefs 69 L5
Withington Manch 113 J3
Withington Shrops 83 L2
Withington Staffs 100 B5
Withleigh Devon 11 K3
Withnell Lancs 121 J6
Withybed Green Worcs 85 H8
Withybrook Warwks 86 E6
Withycombe Somset 24 F3
Withyham E Susx 32 E6
Withypool Somset 24 D4
Withywood Bristl 38 E6

Witley Surrey 30 F4
Witnesham Suffk 78 E4
Witney Oxon 57 G6
Wittering C Pete 88 F3
Wittersham Kent 21 H1
Witton Birm 85 J5
Witton Norfk 93 G2
Witton Norfk 107 H6
Witton Gilbert Dur 151 G5
Witton le Wear Dur 140 E2
Witton Park Dur 140 F2
Wiveliscombe Somset 25 G5
Wivelrod Hants 30 A4
Wivelsfield E Susx 19 K2
Wivelsfield Green E Susx 19 K2
Wivenhoe Essex 62 C4
Wiveton Norfk 106 C4
Wix Essex 62 E3
Wixams Bed 74 F5
Wixford Warwks 71 K4
Wixoe Suffk 77 G6
Woburn C Beds 58 F2
Woburn Safari Park C Beds 74 D7
Woburn Sands M Keyn 74 D7
Woking Surrey 43 G8
Woking Crematorium Surrey 42 F8
Wokingham Wokham 42 D6
Woldingham Surrey 32 C3
Wold Newton E R Yk 135 G5
Wold Newton NE Lin 118 C3
Wolfclyde S Lans 165 K3
Wolferton Norfk 105 G6
Wolfhill P & K 186 B2
Wolf's Castle Pembks 49 G3
Wolfsdale Pembks 48 F3
Wollaston Dudley 84 F6
Wollaston Nhants 74 C2
Wollaston Shrops 83 G2
Wollaton C Nott 101 K4
Wollaton Hall & Park C Nott 101 K5
Wollerton Shrops 98 F6
Wollescote Dudley 85 G6
Wolseley Bridge Staffs 100 A7
Wolsingham Dur 150 D7
Wolstanton Staffs 99 J3
Wolston Warwks 86 E7
Wolvercote Oxon 57 J6
Wolverhampton Wolves 85 G4
Wolverhampton Halfpenny Green Airport Staffs 84 E5
Wolverley Worcs 84 E7
Wolverton Hants 41 K8
Wolverton M Keyn 74 B6
Wolverton Warwks 72 B3
Wolverton Wilts 27 H5
Wolvesnewton Mons 54 C7
Wolvey Warwks 86 E6
Wolvey Heath Warwks 86 E5
Wolviston S on T 141 K3
Wombleton N York 133 K3
Wombourne Staffs 84 F5
Wombwell Barns 115 H2
Womenswold Kent 35 G5
Womersley N York 124 E6
Wonersh Surrey 31 G3
Wonford Devon 12 B4
Wonston Dorset 14 E2
Wonston Hants 29 J4
Wooburn Bucks 42 E3
Wooburn Green Bucks 42 E3
Woodacott Devon 9 K4
Woodall Rothm 115 J5
Woodall Services Rothm 115 J5
Woodbastwick Norfk 93 G1
Wood Bevington Warwks 71 J4
Woodborough Notts 101 M3
Woodborough Wilts 40 C7
Woodbridge Suffk 78 F5
Woodbury Devon 12 C5
Woodbury Salterton Devon 12 C5
Woodchester Gloucs 55 J7
Woodchurch Kent 34 C7
Woodcombe Somset 24 E3
Woodcote Gt Lon 44 F7
Woodcote Oxon 41 M4
Woodcote Wrekin 84 D1
Woodcroft Gloucs 38 D2
Wood Dalling Norfk 106 C6
Woodditton Cambs 76 F3
Woodeaton Oxon 57 K5
Wood End Gt Lon 43 J4
Wood End Herts 60 B3
Woodend Highld 190 F4
Woodend Nhants 73 H5
Woodend W Loth 176 C4
Woodend W Susx 17 M2
Wood End Warwks 71 K1
Wood End Wolves 85 G4
Wood Enderby Lincs 118 C8
Woodfalls Wilts 28 D7
Woodford Cnwll 9 G3
Woodford Gloucs 39 G2
Woodford Gt Lon 45 H2
Woodford Nhants 88 D7
Woodford Stockp 113 K5
Woodford Bridge Gt Lon 45 H2
Woodford Green Gt Lon 45 H2
Woodford Halse Nhants 73 G4
Woodford Wells Gt Lon 45 H2
Woodgate Birm 85 H6
Woodgate Devon 25 H7
Woodgate W Susx 18 C5
Woodgate Worcs 71 H2
Wood Green Gt Lon 44 F2
Woodgreen Hants 28 D7
Woodhall N York 131 J2
Woodhall Spa Lincs 117 K8
Woodham Bucks 58 B4
Woodham Surrey 43 H7
Woodham Ferrers Essex 61 J7
Woodham Mortimer Essex 61 K6
Woodham Walter Essex 61 K6
Wood Hayes Wolves 85 G3
Woodhead Abers 216 E6
Woodhill Shrops 84 D6
Woodhill Somset 26 A6
Woodhorn Nthumb 159 H4
Woodhouse Leeds 123 K4
Woodhouse Leics 87 G1
Woodhouse Sheff 115 H4
Woodhouse Wakefd 124 B6
Woodhouse Eaves Leics 87 G2
Woodhouselee Mdloth 177 H5
Woodhouselees D & G 156 D6
Woodhouses Oldham 113 K2
Woodhouses Staffs 100 D8
Woodhurst Cambs 89 K7
Woodingdean Br & H 19 K5
Woodkirk Leeds 123 K5
Woodland Abers 207 G2
Woodland Devon 6 F5
Woodland Devon 7 J3
Woodland Dur 140 D2
Woodland S Ayrs 152 E3
Woodlands Abers 206 E6
Woodlands Donc 124 E8
Woodlands Dorset 15 K2
Woodlands Hants 16 C1
Woodlands N York 132 E8
Woodlands (Coleshill) Crematorium Warwks 85 L5
Woodlands Park W & M 42 E5
Woodlands (Scarborough) Crematorium N York 134 F3
Woodlands (Scunthorpe) Crematorium N Linc 125 K7
Woodleigh Devon 7 H6
Woodley Wokham 42 C5
Woodmancote Gloucs 39 H2
Woodmancote Gloucs 55 L3
Woodmancote Gloucs 56 A6
Woodmancote W Susx 17 L2
Woodmancote W Susx 19 H3
Woodmancott Hants 29 K3
Woodmansey E R Yk 126 C3
Woodmansgreen W Susx 30 E6
Woodmansterne Surrey 32 B2
Woodmanton Devon 12 C5
Woodnesborough Kent 35 J4
Woodnewton Nhants 88 F5
Wood Norton Norfk 106 B6
Woodplumpton Lancs 121 G4
Woodrising Norfk 92 B3
Wood's Corner E Susx 20 D2
Woodseaves Staffs 99 H7
Woodsetts Rothm 115 K5
Woodsford Dorset 14 E4
Wood's Green E Susx 33 H6
Woodside Br For 42 F6
Woodside Fife 187 G5
Woodside Gt Lon 45 G6
Woodside P & K 195 K8
Woodside Crematorium Inver 174 B3
Woodstock Oxon 57 H5
Woodston C Pete 89 H4
Wood Street Norfk 107 H7
Wood Street Village Surrey 30 F2
Woodton Norfk 93 G5
Woodtown Devon 22 F6
Woodvale Crematorium Br & H 19 J4
Wood Walton Cambs 89 J7
Woofferton Shrops 69 K2
Wookey Somset 26 D3
Wookey Hole Somset 26 D2
Wool Dorset 14 F5
Woolacombe Devon 23 G3
Woolage Green Kent 35 H5
Woolaston Gloucs 54 E7
Woolaston Common Gloucs 54 E7
Woolavington Somset 25 M3
Woolbeding W Susx 30 E6
Woolbrook Devon 12 E5
Wooler Nthumb 168 E4
Woolfardisworthy Devon 11 J3
Woolfardisworthy Devon 22 E7
Woolfords S Lans 176 D6
Woolhampton W Berk 41 L6
Woolhope Herefs 69 L7
Woolland Dorset 14 E2
Woolley BaNES 39 H6
Woolley Cambs 89 G8
Woolley Wakefd 123 L7
Woolley Edge Services Wakefd 123 K7
Woolmere Green Worcs 71 G2
Woolmer Green Herts 59 L4
Woolminstone Somset 13 K2
Woolpit Suffk 77 L3
Woolstaston Shrops 83 J4
Woolsthorpe Lincs 102 D5
Woolsthorpe-by-Colsterworth Lincs 102 F7
Woolston C Sotn 16 E1
Woolston Shrops 97 L7
Woolston Somset 25 H4
Woolston Somset 26 F5
Woolston Warrtn 112 F4
Woolstone Gloucs 55 L3
Woolstone M Keyn 74 C6
Woolstone Oxon 40 F3
Woolston Green Devon 7 H3
Woolton Lpool 112 B4
Woolton Hill Hants 41 H7
Woolverstone Suffk 78 E6
Woolverton Somset 27 H2
Woolwich Gt Lon 45 H4
Woonton Herefs 69 G4
Woore Shrops 99 G4
Wootten Green Suffk 92 F8
Wootton Bed 74 E5
Wootton Kent 35 G5
Wootton N Linc 126 D7
Wootton Nhants 73 L3
Wootton Oxon 57 H4
Wootton Oxon 57 J7
Wootton Staffs 100 C4
Wootton Bassett Wilts 40 B4
Wootton Bridge IoW 17 G4
Wootton Courtenay Somset 24 E3
Wootton Fitzpaine Dorset 13 J4
Wootton Rivers Wilts 40 D7
Wootton St Lawrence Hants 29 L2
Wootton Wawen Warwks 71 L2
Worcester Worcs 70 F4
Worcester Crematorium Worcs 70 F3
Worcester Park Gt Lon 44 E6
Wordsley Dudley 84 F6
Worfield Shrops 84 D4
Workington Cumb 136 D2
Worksop Notts 115 L5
Worlaby N Linc 126 C7
Worlds End Hants 29 M8
Worlds End W Susx 19 J2
Worle N Som 38 A7
Worleston Ches E 98 F2
Worlingham Suffk 93 J5
Worlington Devon 11 H3
Worlington Suffk 91 G8
Worlingworth Suffk 78 F2
Wormbridge Herefs 54 B2
Wormegay Norfk 90 F2
Wormelow Tump Herefs 54 C3
Wormhill Derbys 114 C6
Wormingford Essex 61 M2
Worminghall Bucks 57 M6
Wormington Gloucs 71 J7
Wormit Fife 186 F3
Wormleighton Warwks 72 F4
Wormley Herts 60 B6
Wormley Surrey 30 F4
Wormshill Kent 34 B3
Wormsley Herefs 69 H5
Worplesdon Surrey 30 F2
Worrall Sheff 114 F3

Worsbrough Barns 115 G2
Worsbrough Bridge Barns 115 G2
Worsbrough Dale Barns 115 G2
Worsley Salfd 113 H2
Worstead Norfk 107 G7
Worsthorne Lancs 122 C4
Worston Devon 6 E5
Worston Lancs 122 B3
Worth Kent 35 J4
Wortham Suffk 92 C7
Worthen Shrops 83 G3
Worthenbury Wrexhm 98 B4
Worthing Norfk 106 B8
Worthing W Susx 18 F5
Worthing Crematorium W Susx 18 F4
Worthington Leics 101 H7
Worth Matravers Dorset 15 H6
Wortley Barns 114 F2
Wortley Leeds 123 K4
Worton N York 131 H2
Worton Wilts 39 L8
Wortwell Norfk 92 F6
Wotton-under-Edge Gloucs 39 H2
Wotton Underwood Bucks 58 B5
Woughton on the Green M Keyn 74 C6
Wouldham Kent 46 B7
Wrabness Essex 62 E2
Wrafton Devon 23 H4
Wragby Lincs 117 J6
Wragby Wakefd 124 C6
Wrangaton Devon 7 G4
Wrangle Lincs 104 C3
Wrangway Somset 25 H7
Wrantage Somset 25 L6
Wrawby N Linc 126 C8
Wraxall N Som 38 C6
Wraxall Somset 26 E4
Wray Lancs 130 B6
Wraysbury W & M 43 G5
Wrayton Lancs 130 C5
Wrea Green Lancs 120 E4
Wreay Cumb 148 D5
Wrecclesham Surrey 30 D3
Wrekenton Gatesd 151 G3
Wrelton N York 134 B3
Wrenbury Ches E 98 E3
Wreningham Norfk 92 E4
Wrentham Suffk 93 K6
Wrentnall Shrops 83 H3
Wressle E R Yk 125 G4
Wressle N Linc 126 B8
Wrestlingworth C Beds 75 J5
Wretton Norfk 91 G4
Wrexham Wrexhm 97 M3
Wrexham Industrial Estate Wrexhm 98 B3
Wribbenhall Worcs 84 E7
Wrinehill Staffs 99 H3
Wrington N Som 38 C7
Writhlington BaNES 27 G1
Writtle Essex 61 G6
Wrockwardine Wrekin 84 B2
Wroot N Linc 116 B2
Wrose C Brad 123 H3
Wrotham Kent 33 G2
Wroughton Swindn 40 C4
Wroxall IoW 17 G6
Wroxall Warwks 72 B1
Wroxeter Shrops 83 L2
Wroxham Norfk 107 G8
Wroxton Oxon 72 E6
Wyaston Derbys 100 D4
Wyberton East Lincs 104 B4
Wyboston Bed 75 H3
Wybunbury Ches E 99 G3
Wychbold Worcs 71 G2
Wychnor Staffs 85 L1
Wyck Rissington Gloucs 56 D4
Wycliffe Dur 140 E4
Wycoller Lancs 122 D3
Wycomb Leics 102 C7
Wycombe Marsh Bucks 42 E3
Wyddial Herts 60 B2
Wye Kent 34 E5
Wyke C Brad 123 H5
Wyke Dorset 27 H6
Wyke Champflower Somset 26 F4
Wykeham N York 134 E3
Wyken Covtry 86 D7
Wyken Shrops 84 D4
Wyke Regis Dorset 14 C6
Wykey Shrops 98 B7
Wylam Nthumb 150 E3
Wylde Green Birm 85 K5
Wylye Wilts 28 A4
Wymeswold Leics 101 L7
Wymington Bed 74 D2
Wymondham Leics 102 D8
Wymondham Norfk 92 D3
Wynford Eagle Dorset 14 B3
Wyre Forest Crematorium Worcs 84 E8
Wyre Piddle Worcs 71 G5
Wysall Notts 101 L6
Wythall Worcs 85 J7
Wytham Oxon 57 J6
Wythenshawe Manch 113 J4
Wyton Cambs 89 K8
Wyton E R Yk 126 E4
Wyverstone Suffk 78 C2
Wyverstone Street Suffk 78 B2

Y

Yaddlethorpe N Linc 116 E1
Yafforth N York 141 H7
Yalberton Torbay 7 K4
Yalding Kent 33 J3
Yanwath Cumb 138 D2
Yanworth Gloucs 56 B5
Yapham E R Yk 125 J1
Yapton W Susx 18 D5
Yarborough N Som 38 B8
Yarburgh Lincs 118 E3
Yarcombe Devon 13 G2
Yard Devon 24 B6
Yardley Birm 85 K6
Yardley Crematorium Birm 85 K6
Yardley Gobion Nhants 73 L5
Yardley Hastings Nhants 74 C3
Yardley Wood Birm 85 K7
Yarkhill Herefs 69 L6
Yarley Somset 26 D3
Yarlington Somset 26 F5
Yarm S on T 141 K5
Yarmouth IoW 16 D4
Yarnbrook Wilts 27 K1
Yarnfield Staffs 99 K6
Yarnscombe Devon 23 J6
Yarnton Oxon 57 J5
Yarpole Herefs 69 J2
Yarrow Border 166 E4
Yarrow Feus Border 166 E4
Yarrowford Border 166 F4
Yarwell Nhants 88 F4
Yate S Glos 39 G4
Yateley Hants 42 D7
Yatesbury Wilts 40 B6
Yattendon W Berk 41 K5
Yatton Herefs 69 H2
Yatton N Som 38 B7
Yatton Keynell Wilts 39 K5
Yaverland IoW 17 H5
Yaxham Norfk 92 B2
Yaxley Cambs 89 H5
Yaxley Suffk 92 D8
Yazor Herefs 69 H5
Yeading Gt Lon 43 J4
Yeadon Leeds 123 J3
Yealand Conyers Lancs 129 K5
Yealand Redmayne Lancs 129 K4
Yealmpton Devon 6 E5
Yearsley N York 133 J5
Yeaton Shrops 98 B8
Yeaveley Derbys 100 D4
Yeavering Nthumb 168 D4
Yedingham N York 134 D4
Yelford Oxon 57 G6
Yell Shet 235 d3
Yelling Cambs 75 J3
Yelvertoft Nhants 87 H7
Yelverton Devon 6 D3
Yelverton Norfk 93 G3
Yenston Somset 27 G7
Yeoford Devon 11 H5
Yeolmbridge Cnwll 9 J7
Yeovil Somset 26 D7
Yeovil Crematorium Somset 26 D7
Yeovil Marsh Somset 26 D7
Yeovilton Somset 26 D6
Yesnaby Ork 234 b5
Yetminster Dorset 14 B1
Yettington Devon 12 D5
Yetts o'Muckhart Clacks 185 L6
Yew Tree Sandw 85 H4
Y Felinheli Gwynd 109 G7
Y Ferwig Cerdgn 65 G5
Y Ffor Gwynd 95 G5
Y Gyffylliog Denbgs 97 G2
Yielden Bed 74 E2
Yieldshields S Lans 176 B7
Yiewsley Gt Lon 43 H4
Y Maerdy Conwy 96 F4
Ynysboeth Rhondd 37 G2
Ynysddu Caerph 37 J2
Ynyshir Rhondd 36 F3
Ynystawe Swans 51 K5
Ynysybwl Rhondd 37 G2
Yockleton Shrops 83 H2
Yokefleet E R Yk 125 J5
Yoker C Glas 174 F5
York C York 124 F1
York City Crematorium C York 124 F2
Yorkletts Kent 34 E3
Yorkley Gloucs 54 F6
Yorkshire Dales National Park 131 G4
York Town Surrey 42 E7
Youlgreave Derbys 114 E8
Youlthorpe E R Yk 134 B7
Youlton N York 133 G6
Yoxall Staffs 100 C8
Yoxford Suffk 79 H2
Y Rhiw Gwynd 94 D6
Ysbyty Ifan Conwy 96 C3
Ysbyty Ystwyth Cerdgn 67 G1
Ysceifiog Flints 111 G7
Ystalyfera Neath 52 B6
Ystrad Rhondd 36 F2
Ystrad Aeron Cerdgn 66 C4
Ystradfellte Powys 52 E5
Ystradgynlais Powys 52 C6
Ystrad Meurig Cerdgn 66 F2
Ystrad Mynach Caerph 37 H2
Ystradowen V Glam 36 F5
Ythanbank Abers 217 G7
Ythanwells Abers 216 C6
Ythsie Abers 217 G7

Z

Zeal Monachorum Devon 11 G4
Zeals Wilts 27 H5
Zelah Cnwll 4 C5
Zennor Cnwll 2 E4
Zouch Notts 101 J7
ZSL London Zoo Gt Lon 44 F4
ZSL Whipsnade Zoo C Beds 59 G4

Ireland

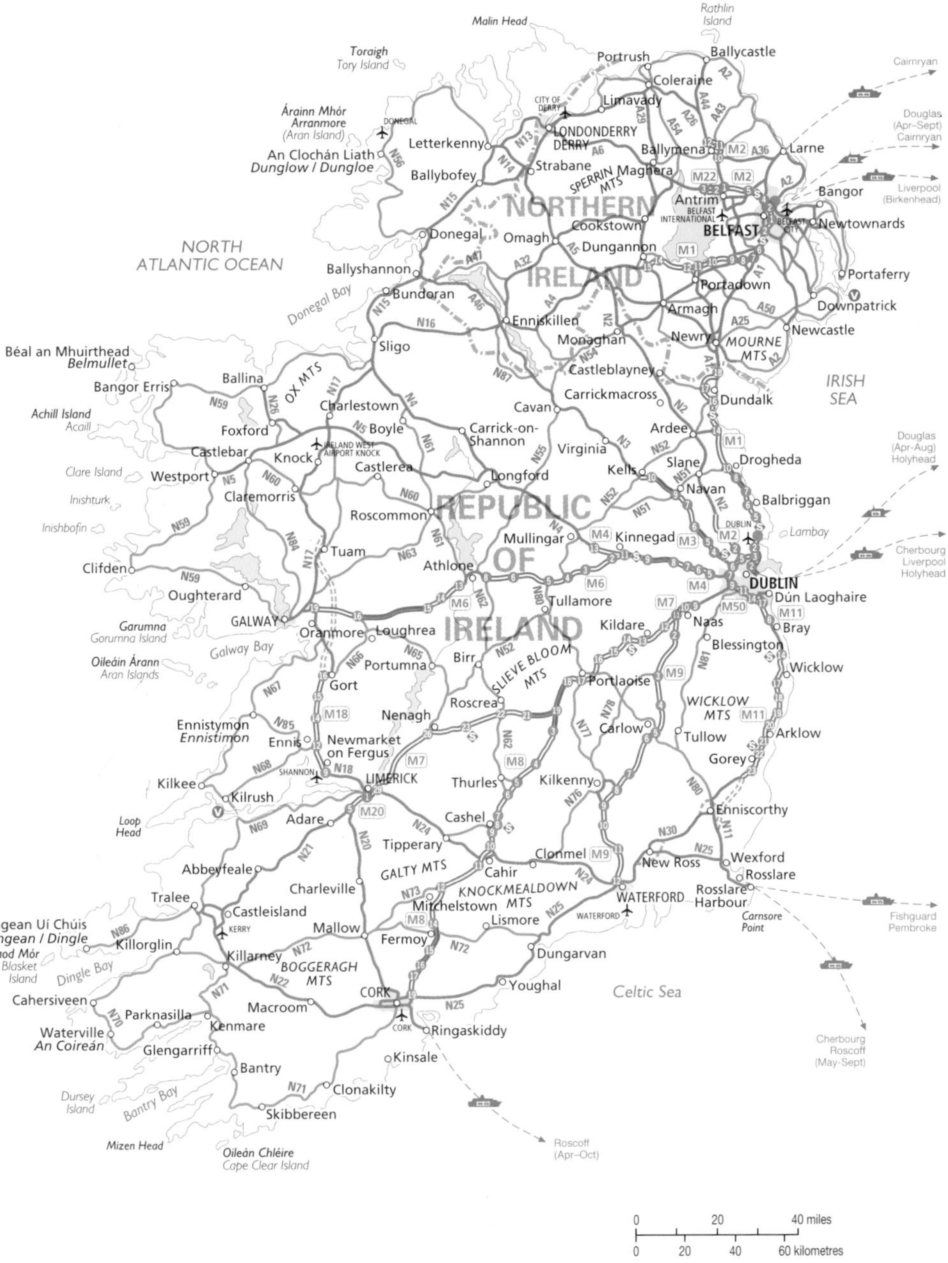
Malin Head
Rathlin Island
Toraigh
Tory Island
Portrush
Ballycastle
Coleraine
Cairnryan
Árainn Mhór
Arranmore
(Aran Island)
DONEGAL
CITY OF DERRY
Limavady
Douglas (Apr–Sept)
Cairnryan
LONDONDERRY
DERRY
Letterkenny
Ballymena
Larne
An Clochán Liath
Dunglow / Dungloe
Strabane
Maghera
SPERRIN MTS
Liverpool (Birkenhead)
Ballybofey
Antrim
Bangor
BELFAST INTERNATIONAL
NORTHERN IRELAND
BELFAST
BELFAST CITY
Newtownards
Cookstown
Donegal
Omagh
Dungannon
NORTH ATLANTIC OCEAN
Ballyshannon
Portaferry
Bundoran
Portadown
Donegal Bay
Armagh
Downpatrick
Enniskillen
Newcastle
Newry
Monaghan
MOURNE MTS
Béal an Mhuirthead
Belmullet
Sligo
Castleblayney
IRISH SEA
Ballina
OX MTS
Bangor Erris
Carrickmacross
Dundalk
Achill Island
Acaill
Charlestown
Cavan
Foxford
Boyle
Carrick-on-Shannon
Ardee
Douglas (Apr-Aug)
Holyhead
Castlebar
IRELAND WEST AIRPORT KNOCK
Virginia
Knock
Slane
Drogheda
Clare Island
Westport
Castlerea
Kells
Longford
Navan
Inishturk
Claremorris
REPUBLIC OF IRELAND
Balbriggan
Roscommon
Inishbofin
DUBLIN
Lambay
Mullingar
Kinnegad
Tuam
Cherbourg
Liverpool
Holyhead
Clifden
Athlone
DUBLIN
Oughterard
Tullamore
Dún Laoghaire
GALWAY
Kildare
Naas
Bray
Garumna
Gorumna Island
Oranmore
Loughrea
Blessington
Galway Bay
Birr
SLIEVE BLOOM MTS
Oileáin Árann
Aran Islands
Portumna
Wicklow
Gort
Portlaoise
Roscrea
WICKLOW MTS
Nenagh
Ennistymon
Ennistimon
Carlow
Tullow
Arklow
Ennis
Newmarket on Fergus
Gorey
SHANNON
LIMERICK
Thurles
Kilkenny
Kilkee
Kilrush
Loop Head
Adare
Cashel
Enniscorthy
Tipperary
Clonmel
New Ross
Wexford
Abbeyfeale
GALTY MTS
Cahir
Rosslare
KNOCKMEALDOWN MTS
Rosslare Harbour
Charleville
Tralee
WATERFORD
Fishguard
Pembroke
Castleisland
Mitchelstown
Carnsore Point
KERRY
WATERFORD
Daingean Uí Chúis
An Daingean / Dingle
Mallow
Lismore
Killorglin
Fermoy
An Blascaod Mór
Great Blasket Island
Killarney
Dungarvan
Dingle Bay
BOGGERAGH MTS
Cahersiveen
Youghal
Celtic Sea
Macroom
CORK
Parknasilla
Kenmare
CORK
Ringaskiddy
Cherbourg
Roscoff
(May-Sept)
Waterville
An Coireán
Glengarriff
Kinsale
Bantry
Clonakilty
Dursey Island
Bantry Bay
Skibbereen
Roscoff (Apr–Oct)
Mizen Head
Oileán Chléire
Cape Clear Island
0
20
40 miles
0
20
40
60 kilometres

Map pages north

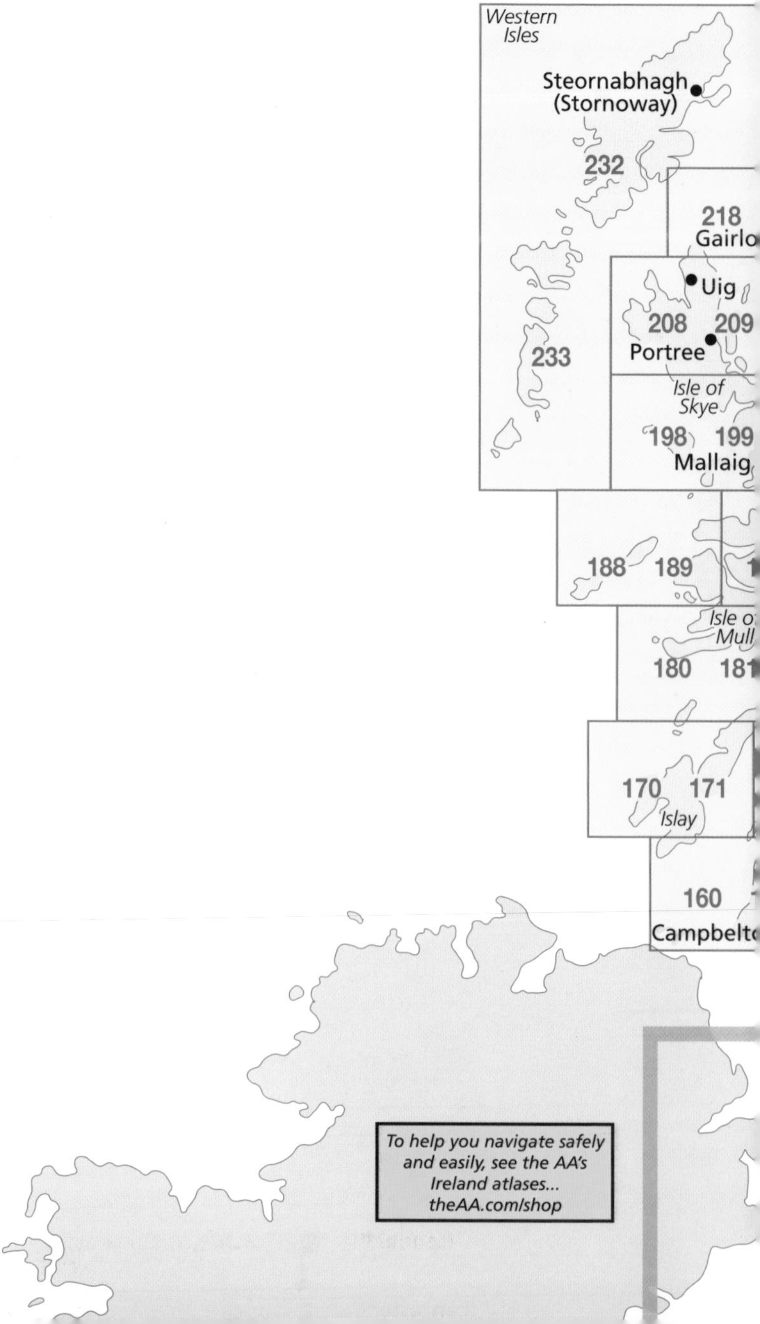

To help you navigate safely and easily, see the AA's Ireland atlases... theAA.com/shop